HN
273.

W. CUSHING · INITIALS AND PSEUDONYMS

WILLIAM CUSHING

INITIALS AND PSEUDONYMS
A DICTIONARY OF LITERARY DISGUISES

First Series

1969

GEORG OLMS VERLAG
HILDESHEIM · NEW YORK

Reprografischer Nachdruck der Ausgabe London 1886
Printed in Germany
Herstellung: Druckerei Lokay, 6101 Reinheim / Odw.
Best.-Nr. 5102 715

INITIALS AND PSEUDONYMS:

A

DICTIONARY OF LITERARY DISGUISES.

BY

WILLIAM CUSHING, B.A.,

FOR SOME YEARS ASSISTANT IN THE HARVARD UNIVERSITY LIBRARY; AND
COMPILER OF AN "INDEX TO THE NORTH AMERICAN REVIEW"
AND AN "INDEX TO THE CHRISTIAN EXAMINER."

———◦◦჻◦◦———

LONDON:

SAMPSON LOW, MARSTON, SEARLE & RIVINGTON,

Crown Buildings, 188, Fleet Street, E.C.

1886.

PREFACE.

THIS work is designed as a Dictionary of American and English Initials and Pseudonyms employed from the beginning of the 18th century to the present time; to which have been added some of the more recent and important Continental ones, and a few false-names, which, by a strict definition of words, would be called *soubriquets*.

A similar work by Mr. Albert R. Frey, of the Astor Library, New York City, was placed by the publishers at the writer's disposal, from which about two thousand titles were taken, and added to his own compilation, making an aggregate of twelve thousand initials and pseudonyms, and eight thousand real names of authors.

Attention is called to the very complete article, by Mr. Frey, on " Junius," to be found in the first part.

For the convenience of those using this dictionary, it may be well to state that the first part gives the initials and pseudonyms, followed by the real names, of the authors, together with some representative literary performance; and the method used in indexing, with some exceptions, is to treat the literary disguises as real names, and arrange them as is customary with the latter, *i.e.*, the last member of the initial or pseudonym is put first, and determines the alphabetical order. The second part contains the real names of authors, followed by the initials and pseudonyms, and short biographical notices.

The writer has endeavored to make this work both comprehensive and correct, and, in order to do this, has availed himself of the Harvard University Library, and every other source of information to which the kindness of those interested in the undertaking has given him access, and believes he has been enabled to produce a volume that will be useful to librarians and of interest to the general reader.

Notification of errors or omissions, or any information that would add to the value of the work, will be gladly received by the undersigned.

WILLIAM CUSHING.

Oct. 1, 1885.
    18 Wendell Street,
      Cambridge, Mass.

INITIALS AND PSEUDONYMS.

PART I.

*. *Henry Ward Beecher,* in the New York "Independent," author of "The Star Papers." N.Y. 1855.

*. *Rev. Benjamin Franklin De Costa,* in his letters to "The Advertiser" (Boston), during 1861–62.

*. *Charles Fenno Hoffman.* His signature in the New York "American," in which he published a series of brilliant articles.

***. *William Kelynack Dale.* Mammon; a poem. By . . . Penzance, 1856.

***. *Rev. Benjamin Franklin De Costa,* in his letters to "The Advertiser" (Boston), during 1861–62.

***, a Magistrate in the Countrey. *Sir Francis Grant, Lord Cullen.* A letter . . . giving a new historical account of designs, through the Christian world . . . Edinb. 1701.

***, Américain. *M. Paul Ulrich Dubuisson.* Abrégé de la Revolution de l'Amérique anglaise. Paris, 1778.

****. *Rev. Matthew Raine,* in Beloe's "Sexagenarian," Vol. I., chap. 40.

****. *Mrs. Amelia Opie,* in Beloe's "Sexagenarian," I., 411. 2d ed. L. 1818.

****. *Rev. John Lewis.* A dissertation on the antiquity and use of seals in England . . . L. 1740.

****, The Late Lord. *Henry Hyde, Lord Hyde and Cornbury.* The mistakes; . . . a comedy. L. 1758.

****, Priscilla. *Priscilla Wakefield.* Leisure hours; or, entertaining dialogues . . . By . . . L. 1794.

**** ******. *John Murray.* Letter to . . . on the Rev. W. L. Bowles's strictures on the life and writings of Pope. By the Right Hon. Lord Byron. L. 1821.

*****, ****. *Mrs. Anne Penny.* Poems, with a dramatic entertainment. L. 1772.

**** ******. *The Rev. James Pycroft.* The collegian's guide; or, recollections of college days . . . L. 1845.

******, Lady ——. *John Hall Stevenson.* Moral tales . . . 2d ed. L. 1783.

******, Sir ******. *Sir Robert Walpole.*

******g, ******s ***n, Esq. *Charles John Darling.* Scintillæ juris. L. 1877.

*******, M. A., Fellow of New College. *Thomas Le Mesurier.* Translations, chiefly from the Italian, of Petrarch and Metastasio. Oxf. 1795.

——. *John H. B. Latrobe.* Three great battles. Baltimore, 1863.

——, The Honourable Mr. *William Coombe.* The auction : a town eclogue. By . . . L. 1778.

—— ——, Esq., Member of Parliament for the County of ——. *Sir John Sinclair.* Lucubrations during a short recess . . . L. 1782.

—— ——, Lady. *Lady Wallace.* A letter to a friend, with a poem called "The ghost of Werter." By . . . L. 1788.

——s ——s, M. A. of the University of Oxford. *Charles Lucas.* Free thoughts on a general reform . . . Bath, 1796.

? ——. *Charles Wolcott Balestier.* A potent philter, contributed to "The Tribune" (N.Y.), 1884.

☞. *Joseph Addison,* in his contributions to "The Guardian."

☞. *J. Walker.* Miscellaneous observations upon authors ancient and modern. L. 1731–32.

☉. — See "Theta."

Miss Eliza Brown Chase. Over the border : Acadia, the home of Evangeline. B. 1884.

The above musical notes represent "E.B.C.," the initials of the author's name.

A (alpha). *Mr. Bowden.* Lyra apostolica. Derby and L. 1836.

The above work consists of a collection of poems reprinted from "The British Magazine," in which they had previously appeared over the following signatures:—

α (alpha). *Mr. Bowden* (as above).
β. *R. Hurrell Froude.*
γ. *John Keble.*
δ. *John Henry Newman.*
ε. *Isaac Williams.*
ζ. *Rev. Henry William Wilberforce.*

A. *Samuel Adams*, in the "Boston Gazette."

A. *William Henry Davenport Adams.* The desert world ... L. 1869.

A. *Wilkes Allen*, in "The Polyanthos" (Boston), 1806–07.

A. *Mrs. Allenby.* The starling of the spire; or, a bird's-eye view of the church as it was. [In verse.] ... L. 1866.

A. *Mr. Anthony.* Irwell, and other poems ... L. 1843.

A. *Matthew Arnold.* The strayed reveller. L. 1849. Empedocles on Etna. L. 1852.

A. *Benjamin Brierley.* Goin' to Cyprus. By A. Manchester, 1879.

A. *Rev. John Keble*, one of the contributors to "Tracts for the Times." L. 1840–48.

A. *Bishop Zachary Pearce.* Miscellaneous observations upon authors ancient and modern. L. 1731–32.

A. *Alexander Pope.* — See "Bavius."

A. *John Smith.* His signature to papers in the "Microcosm," published at Eton College. 1786 *et seq.*

A. *Joshua Smith.* Scandal [in verse]; by the biographer of Anacreon. Holt, Norfolk, 1827.

A. *Mrs. Caroline Anne Bowles Southey.* Chapters on churchyards, in "Blackwood's Magazine," commenced April, 1824.

These contributions to "Blackwood" were published separately in 1829, and 2d ed. in 1841.

A. *Ann Taylor.* The wedding among the flowers. [In verse.] ... L. 1808.

A., A. *Adam Anderson.* Jim Blake's tour from Clonave to London. Illustrated with sketches by E. N., A. R. A. [Erskine Nicol.] .. Preface and notes by A. A. Dublin, 1867.

A., A. *Mrs. Anna Atkins.* The colonel: a story of fashionable life, 1853. A page from the peerage, 1863. The perils of fashion, 1852.

A., A. A. *Hon. Alvey A. Adee.* Bacon's Promus. By .. In the "Republic," Washington, Feb., March, May, 1883.

A., A. H. *Andrew Hilliard Atteridge.* Islam. L. 1878.

A., A. S. *A. S. Atcheson.* The bread of life ... 1849.

A., B. *Benjamin Antrobus.* Buds and blossoms of piety ... 2d ed. L. 1691.

A. B. *Benjamin Franklin.* Proposed new version of the Bible; one of the bagatelles (written about 1778).

A. B. *Matthew Hole.* An antidote against the poison of some late pamphlets. Oxf. 1717.

A. B. A signature which has been attributed to *Junius* (*q.v.*). See Letter to the "Public Advertiser," Nov. 5, 1771, etc.

A. B. *Joseph Skidmore, Senior.* An essay on the Vth of Matthew, from verse 33rd to 37th ... L. 1713.

A. B. *Jonathan Swift.* See "A Person of Quality."

A., G. B. *Sir George Biddell Airy*, in his contributions to the "Athenæum." L.

A. B. Philologer. *Laurence Sterne.*

"I happened to be acquainted," says Sterne, "with a young man from Yorkshire, who rented a window in one of the paved alleys near Cornhill, for the sale of stationery. I hired one of the panes of glass from my friend, and stuck up the following advertisement with wafers:—

"Epigrams, anagrams, paragrams, chronograms, monograms, epitaphs, epithalamiums, prologues, epilogues, madrigals, interludes, advertisements, letters, petitions, memorials on every occasion, essays on all subjects, pamphlets for and against ministers, with sermons upon any text, or for any sect, to be written here on reasonable terms, by　　"A. B. Philologer."

"The uncommonness of the titles occasioned numerous applications, and at night I used privately to glide into the office to digest the notes or heads of the day, and receive the earnest, which was directed always to be left with the memorandums, the writing to be paid for on delivery, according to the subject." — *Percy Anecdotes.*

A., C. *Miss Charlotte Adams*, in contributions to "The Art Age." N.Y.

A., C. *Charlotte Anley.* Miriam; or, the power of truth, 1826. The prisoners of Australia, 1841.

A., C., Esq. *Christopher Anstey.* Britain's genius: a song ... Bath, 1797.

A., C. B. C. *C. B. C. Amicus.* Hints on life; and how to rise in society. By ... L. 1845.

A., C. E. *Clementine Edith Aiken.* The days we live in. B. 1876.

A., C. F. *Cecil Frances Alexander.* Hymns for little children ... L. 1862.

A. C. I. G. (A Cornishman in Gloucestershire.) *John White.* The humorous adventures of Tim Trevail, related in the pure, unadulterated vernacular. L. 1872.

A. D. C., The. *Francis Cowley Burnand.* Being personal reminiscences of the university "Amateur Dramatic Club," Cambridge. L. 1879.

A., D. J. B. de. *Don Juan Bautista de Arriaza.* Coleccion de algunos versos. Paris, 1805.

A., E. *Edward Aggas.* The defence of death ... L. 1576.

A., E. *Edwin Arnold.* The light of Asia; or, the great renunciation. ... L. 1879.

A. E. R. J. Lane. Marks and remarks for the catalogue of the exhibition of the Royal Academy. L. 1856.

A., E. *Edwin Arnold.* Political poems by Victor Hugo and Garibaldi. "Done into English by an Oxford graduate." 1868.

A., E. *Edward Atkinson.* Senator Sherman's fallacies; or, honesty the best policy. By ... B. 1868.

A., E. *Edward Archer* The small boy's mythological primer, in rhyme. L. 1858.

A., E. *Ezra Abbot.* A translation of the Gospels ... By A. Norton. [Edited by C. E. N., *i.e.*, C. E. Norton, and E. A.]

A., E. A. *Mrs. Elizabeth Allen Annable Needham.* Incidents in the lives of good men. By ... B. 186-.

A., E. C. *Mrs. Elizabeth Cary Agassiz.* Geological sketches. Edited ... 1866.

A., E. C. *Miss Emily C. Agnew.* Geraldine: a tale of conscience. L. 1837-39.

A., E. G. *E. G. Adams.* Battle at Fort Rice, July 28, 1865. Fort Rice, D. T., 1865.

A., E. M. *Ernst Moritz Arndt.* Wanderungen aus und um Godesberg. Bonn, 1844. Deutsche Lieder. Berlin, 1870.

A., E. S. *Ernest Silvanus Appleyard.* The sure hope of reconciliation. 1847.

A., E W. *Mrs. Eliza Winslow Allderdice.* Heart's delight. N.Y., 1879.

A., F. *Frederick Archer,* in his contributions to "The Keynote" (N.Y.).

A., F. *Rev. Frederick Arnold,* in "London Society," "Leisure Hour," 1867.

A. F. *James Otis.* Considerations on behalf of the colonists, etc. B. 1765.

A., F. C. *Frances Charlotte Armstrong.* Dick Ford and his father. L. 1875.

A., F. E. *Florence Emily Ashley.* Lagonells. [A tale.] ... L. 1872.

A. F. G. *John Lister.* Epigrams and jeux d'esprit. Edinb. 1870.

A. F. S. *Miss Sarah A. Flint.* Hope Douglass ... B. 1867.

A., G. *Grace Aguilar.* Home scenes and heart studies. L. 1852.

A., G. A. *G. A. Aynge.* Tecumseh; or, the death of the Shawnee chief ... Weymouth, 1830.

A., G. B. *George Biddell Airy.* Six lectures on astronomy. L. 1849.

A., G. F. *George French Angas.* Australia: a popular account ... L. 1865.

A. G. O. T. U O. C. *Owen Manning.* An inquiry into the grounds and nature of the several species of ratiocination ... 1754.

The above letters are the initials of "A gentleman of the University of Cambridge."

A, H. *Henry Attwell.* A book of thoughts. Selected ... L. 1865.

A, H. *Henry Alford,* Dean of Canterbury. Gurney's (J. H.) sermons on the Acts of the apostles. Edited by H. A. L. 1862.

A., H W. *Henry Wentworth Acland.* Prints for cottage walls ... Oxf. & L. 1862.

A., I. *Jasper Atkinson.* Catholic blinds for Protestant eyes ... L. 1829.

A., I. *John Atkinson.* The state of our circulation and currency considered .. L. 1826.

A., J. *John Aikin.* The arts of life ... L. 1802.

A., J. *John Ady.* An exordium to the reading of the sacred writings of the Old and New Testaments. L. 1807

A., J. *Jacob Abbot.* The little scholar learning to talk ... L. 1836.

A., J. *John Albee.* In memory of Gerald Fitz Gerald ... n.p. 1863.

A, J. *John Agg.* The ocean harp: a poem ... P. 1819.

A., J. *John Anstey.* The pleader's guide . . 1808.

A., J. *John Aikin, LL.D.* The woodland companion. L. 1802.

A., J., M.D. *John Arbuthnot, M.D* Examination of Dr. Woodward's account of the deluge ... By ... L. 1695.

A., J., and C., R. C. *John Adamson and R. C. C.* Ballads from the Portuguese translated and versified by ... Newcastle, 1846.

A., J L. *John Lavicount Anderdon.* The river Dove; with some quiet thoughts of the happy practice of angling ... L. 1845.

A., J. M. *Rev. John Marks Ashley.* The treatise of S. Catherine of Genoa on purgatory, newly translated ... 1878.

A., J. R., and J., M. C. *John Reed Appleton and Morris Charles Jones.* Evans. Newcastle-upon-Tyne, 1865.

A., J. S. *J. S. Attwood,* in his contributions to "Notes and Queries." L. 1876 *et seq.*

A., J. Y. *John Yonge Akerman.* Tales of other days ... L. 1830.

A., L. *Lombe Atthill.* The church of England recommended ... Halesworth, 1820.

A., L. *Louisa Anthony.* Traits of private life. Manchester, n.d.

A., L. L. *Mrs. G. R.* or *L. L. Adams.* A ride through the Holy Land. B. 1875.

A. L. O. E. (*i.e.,* A Lady of England.) *Miss Charlotte Maria Tucker,* in her numerous works for young people. L. 1875, etc.

A., L. S. *Louis Simon Auger.* Notice sur la vie et les ouvrages de Le Sage. Paris, 1813.

A., M. *Mrs. Maria Abdy.* Her signature in the "New Monthly." L about 1828.

A., M. *Matthew Arnold.* Christian life: its hopes, its fears, and its close. Edited by ... L. 1845.

A., M. *Mrs. M. Allen.* A history of Ford Abbey, Dorsetshire: late in the County of Devon. L. 1846.

A., M. *Thaddeus O'Mahony.* Questions on Locke's essay concerning human understanding. L. 1860.

A. M., Oxon. *W. S Moses.* Carpenterian Criticism. L. 1877.

A. M. B. A. *Marie Henri Beyle.* Histoire de la peinture en Italie Paris, 1817.

A., M. E. *M. E. Arnold.* The painted window: a poem. L. 1856.

A., N. *Nathaniel Ames.* Nautical reminiscences. Providence, 1832.

A., N. *Col. Nathan Appleton.* Sketch of the life of Albert Kintzing Post. By N. A. N.Y. 1873.

A., P., Minister of the Gospel. *Rev Peter Annet.* Judging for ourselves ... L. 1739.

A., P. G. *Prosper Gabriel Audran.* Grammaire Arabe en tableaux ... Paris, 1818.

. A., R. *Richard Alsop* (?) The enchanted lake of the Fairy Morgana. [Translated.] 1806.

A., R. *Robert Allsop.* Letters, conversations, and recollections of S. T. Coleridge ... Preface by ... L. 1858.

A., R. *Rev. Robert Aspland.* Sermons on various subjects, chiefly practical. L. 1847.

A. R. A. *James Cameron Lees, D.D.* A rollicking tour in Ireland. By Rag, Tag, and Bobtail; a rollicking tour in the land of the Gael. Paisley, 1878.

A., R. F. *Rachel Frances Antonina Dashwood Lee.* Memoirs of ... L. 1812.

A., S. *Samuel Ayscough.* Topographical description of Cudham, Kent, in "Gent. Mag." Sept. 1804., pp. 830–901.

A., S. A. *Samuel Austin Allibone.* An alphabetical index to the New Testament. ... P. 1868.

A., S. D. *S. D. Alexander.* Notes on New Testament literature. [By Joseph Addison Alexander.] Edited ... 1867.

A., S. M. *Stephen Merrill Allen.* Religion and science ... B. 1874.

A., T., Captain Light Dragoons. *Capt Thomas Ashe.* History of the Azores, or Western Islands ... L. 1813.

A., T., Gent. *Thomas Ashe.* Travels in America, performed in 1806 ... L. 1808.

A., T. B. *Thomas Bailey Aldrich.* The bells: a collection of chimes. N.Y. 1855.

A., T. K. *Thomas Kerchever Arnold.* A Latin Syntax and first reading book: ... L. 1836.

A. V. *Arthur Ashley Sykes.* A letter to the Rev. Dr. Sherlock ... L. 1717.

A., W. *William Allen.* The duty of abstaining from the use of West India produce. A speech ... L. 1792.

A., W. *W. Alexander.* Fruits of piety ... York, 1824.

A., W. *William Asplin.* — See "A presbyter of the Church of England."

A., W. B. *W. B. Anthony.* Essential memoranda of English grammar. Compiled ... 1881.

A., W. E. *William Edmonstoune Aytoun.* His signature in "Blackwood's Magazine."

A, W. E. A. *William Edward Armitage Axon.* Nixon's Cheshire prophecies ... With an ... essay on popular prophecies ... L. 1878.

A., W. H. D. *William Henry Davenport Adams.* Black's guide to the history, antiquities, and topography of the County of Surrey ... L. 1861.

A. Z. *Benjamin Gale.* The present state of the colony of Connecticut considered ... New L. 1755.

A***, Major.** *Charles Barwell Coles.* Short whist, its rise and progress, to which are prefixed precepts for tyros. By Mrs. B*****, with an essay ... by Prof. P. (*q.v.*). L. 1865.

By Mrs. B***** is meant Mrs. Battle, whose opinions on whist were contributed to "The Monthly Magazine." L. 1821. By "Elia" (*q.v.*).

A**d, Mr.** *William Arnold.* Mr. A—d's motives for renouncing the popish, and re-embracing the protestant religion in which he was educated, etc. L. 1758.

A**e, D*** of.** *John Campbell, 4th
Duke of Argyle.* Letter to the right honorable Sir ****** ******* [Robert Wal-
pole] upon ... expeditions. L. 1740.

A ****, P. C. *Philippe Charles Aubry.*
Lé Petrarque Français, Poésiés diverse
de ... Tours, 1801.

A——. *Arthur Cleveland Coxe.* St.
Jonathan; the lay of a Scald ... N.Y. 1838.

A. and L. *A. and L. Shore.* Fra
Dolcino, and other poems. L. 1870.

A—, the Rev. M. *Rev. George Fitzgerald Galaher, M.A.* Auricular confession proved to be contrary to Scripture.
L. 1875.

A—n, E—l of. *Willoughby Bertie,
Earl of Abingdon.* An adieu to the turf :
a poetical epistle from ... to his grace
the A—p [Archbishop] of Y—k [York].
L. 1778.

Ab. *Benjamin Brierley.* Ab-o'-th'-Yate
at the great show. [Signed "Ab."]
Reprinted from "Ben Brierley's Journal"
for August, 1869. Manchester, 1869.

Ab hissel. *Benjamin Brierley.* Ab-
o'-th'-Yate and the "Wreath." By ...
Manchester, 1879.

AB-o'-th'-Yate. *Benjamin Brierley.*
Ab-o'-th'-Yate and the cobbler of Alder-
burn on the great strike. By Ab. Manchester, 1878.

Abacrombi, Signor. *James Abercromby, Baron Dunfermline.* Thaumatur-
gics. Coal Hole, Pleasance ... Signor
A. (from Exchequer Land) formerly
Assistant-Juggler to Mr. Cunning ... [A
satire on J. A.'s candidature for the representation of Edinburgh.] Edinb. 1832.

Abafi, Lajos. *Lajos Aigner.* Mikes
Kelemen. [A biography.] Budapest, 1878.

Abati, Francesco. *William Winwood
Reade.* See-Saw: a novel ... L. 1865.

Abbie, Aunt. *Abby Skinner.* Carroll
Ashton ; or, the rewards of truthfulness ...
P. 1855.

Abbott, Alice Irving. *Miss H. H.
Burdick.*

Abbott, Rosa. *Rosa (Y.) Abbott
Parker.* Rosa Abbott Stories.

Abdallah. *Otway Curry,* who contributed to the press at Cincinnati under
this *nom de plume.*

Abdallah. *Augusto Pereira Soromenho.*

Abdallah, Khálid Eb'n. *Sir Henry
Taylor, K.C., D.C.L.* — See Khálid Eb'n
Abdallah.

Abdiel. *Samuel Hall.* — See Samuel
Hall, calling himself "Abdiel."

Abdiel. *Joshua William Brooks.* Abdiel's essays on the advent and kingdom
of Christ, and the events connected there-
with ... L. 1834.

Aberdeen. *Hugh D. McIntyre.*

Abolitionist, An. *Thomas Fisher,
Esq., F.S.A.* The negro's memorial ...
By ... L. 1825.

Abrabanel, Solomon. *William Ar-
nall.* The complaint of the children of
Israel ... By S. A. of the House of
David. L. 1736.

Abraham. *Abraham Norwood.* The
acts of the elders, commonly called the
book of Abraham. B. 1845.

Abraham, Brother. *Rev. Richard
King.* An answer to the letters of Peter
Plymley [Sydney Smith]. L. 1808.

Abraham, Father. *Benjamin Franklin.* Father Abraham's speech to a great
number of people, at a vendue ... B. 1807.

Abricht, Johann. *Jonathan Birch.*
Divine emblems embellished with etchings on copper ... designed and written
by J. A. L. 1838.

Absent Brother, An. *Daniel Wilson.*
Letters from ... 1823.

Absentee residing in Bath, An.
Rev. Edward Mangin. Utopia found ;
being an apology for Irish absentees.
By ... Bath, 1813.

Absented member, An. *Sir William Windham.* A letter ... upon the
present situation of the affairs of Great
Britain. L. 1739.

Academicus. — See "Antiquarius."

Academicus. *Rev. Aulay Macaulay,
M.A.* During his residence at the University of Glasgow he wrote many essays,
moral and literary, in "Ruddiman's
Weekly Magazine," under the signature
of "Academicus."

Academicus. *Charles Seager, M.A.*
Auricular confession ... Oxf. 1842.

Academicus. *William Pulteney Alison.*
Correspondence between A. and Con-
siliarius on the comparative merits of
phrenology, and the mental philosophy
of Reid and Stewart. Edinb. 1836.

Ace Clubs. *J. C. Loftin.* Friendship :
a poem ... Montgomery, Ala., 1871.

Acharius. *Fredrik Vilhelm Scholander.*
Luisella. 1867.

Acheta. *Miss L. M. Budgen.* March
winds and April showers ... By ...
L. 1854.

Acheta Domestica. *Miss L. M. Budgen.* Episodes of insect life. By A. D.
L. 1849–51.

Ackerlos, John. *John Stores Smith.*
Selections from the poetry of H. Heine,
trans. by J. A. L. 1854.

Ackermann, Gottlieb. *Franz Xaver
Mayer.* Volkspredigten und Homilien ...
Landshut, 1831.

Acorn. *James Oakes.*

Actæa. *Mrs. Elizabeth Cary Agassiz.* A first lesson in natural history. B. 1859.

Acton, Llewellin. *Wynne Edwin Baxter.* Perseverance ... L. 1863.

Actor, An. *Pierce Egan.* The life of ... L. 1825.

Actress, An. *Mrs. Anna Cora (Ogden Mowatt) Ritchie.* Autobiography of ...; or, eight years on the stage. B. 1854.

Actual Settler, An. *H. Y. Read.* Suggestions on ... colonization through the ... allotment system. By ... Montreal, 1865.

Adair, James. *Sir Richard Phillips.* Five hundred questions and exercises on Murray's ... English grammar. L. 1824.

"Adam." *Arthur Hugh Clough.*

In his Bothie of Tober-na-Vuolich, Hobbes was Ward Hunt; Adam, Clough himself; Lindsay, F. R. Johnson of Christ Church; Hewson, J. S. Winder of Oriel; Arthur, H. W. Fisher of Christ Church; Airlie, J. Deacon of Oriel; and Sir Hector ..., Mr. Farquharson.

Adam, Onkel. *Carl Anton Wetterbergh.* The fatal chain. From the Swedish of ... 1864.

Adam, Uncle. *George Mogridge.* The Chinese. By ... L. 1845.

Adam, Adam Fitz. *Edward Moore, R. O. Cambridge, Horace Walpole, Lord Chesterfield,* etc. The world. L. 1755-57.

Adam, Christian. *Carl Christian Thorvaldus Andersen.* Strid og Fred. Et Digt i sex sange. Copenhagen, 1858.

Adams, Moses. *Dr. George W. Bagby.* For Virginians only. What I did with my fifty millions. By ... P. 1874.

Adams, Stephen. *M. Maybrick.* A prominent English singer and writer of music. Among other songs he was the author of "Nancy Lee," of which more than 100,000 copies were sold.

Adams, Will. *John Neal.* Errata; or, the works of Will Adams: a novel. 1822.

Addie. *Adelaide J. Cooley.* Snowflake's pleasure-book; sunshine for dull days. N.Y. 1879.

Ad***gt*n, Dr. *Dr. A. Addington.* An appeal to the public; or, a review of the conduct of Dr. Ad——ng—n to Dr. Pigott. 1754.

Addison, D. C. *Charles Addison Daniell.* The street-singer: a poem. Chicago, 1880.

Addison, The American. *Joseph Dennie.* 1768-1812.

Addison of the North, The. *Henry Mackenzie.* 1754-1831.

Addums, Mozis. *Dr. George W. Bagby.* Letters to Billy Irvins in the "Southern Literary Messenger."

Adelaide. *Miss Elizabeth Bogart,* who, under this *nom de plume,* published her first poem in the "Long Island Star" (Brooklyn), in 1825.

Adeler, Max. *Charles Heber Clark.* Out of the hurly-burly; or, life in an odd corner. By ... P. 1874.

Adeline. *Mrs. E. F. A. Sergeant.* Ernald; or, the martyr of the Alps: and other poems ... With an introduction by A. L. 1843.

Adept, An. *Charles Johnston.* Chrysal; or, the adventures of a guinea ... By ... L. 1760.

Adhémar, Mme. la Csse D'. *Baron Étienne Léon Lamothe-Langon.* Souvenirs sur Marie-Antoinette ... et sur la cour de Versailles ... Paris, 1836.

Adina. *Rev. Joseph H. Ingraham.* The prince of the house of David; or, three years in the Holy City ... L. 1859.

Adirondack. *Lucius E. Chittenden.* Capture of Ticonderoga. Rutland, Vt. 1872.

Adjutor. *Rev. Joseph Bretland,* in the "Theological Repository." L.

Admiral. *Admiral Burney.* — See Lamb's "Elia": "The Wedding."

Admirer of Chivalry, An. *Edward Francis Head.* Poltroonius; a tragic farce in one act. B. 1856.

Admirer of the Fine Arts, An. *F. D. Astley.* Varnishando: a serio-comic poem. Manchester, 1809.

Admirer of a Great Genius, An. *Stephen Weston.* A short account of the late Mr. R. Porson ... L. 1808.

Admirer of Monarchy and Episcopacy, An. *Zachary Grey, LL.D.* English Presbyterian eloquence ... By ... L. 1736.

Admirer of Walter Scott, An. *John Roby.* The lay of the poor fiddler ... L. 1814.

Admonish Crime. *Rev. James Cook Richmond.* He published a pamphlet at Boston under the anagram of "Admonish Crime."

Adna, Aunt. *Mrs. Mary S. B. Dana.* Author of numerous tales for children, etc.

Adolf, L. *Adolf Lasson.* Herzenstille. Lieder und Sprüche. 1867.

Adrian. *James L. Cole.* He published some fugitive poetry in the "New York Statesman" and in the "Ontario Repository," under that signature.

Adrian. *Anne Kent.* Evelyn Stuart; or, Right versus Might. By A. L. 1846.

Adrienne. *Mrs. J. P. Creswell.*

Adrienne. *Miss Susan C. Hooper.* During the war one of the most prominent contributors to the "Magnolia Weekly," Richmond, Va.

Advena. *Evan Evans.* His bardic name.

Advena. *Digby Pilot Starkey,* who contributed to the "Dublin University Magazine," under this signature.

Adversum. *Edward Tuckerman.* — See "Notitia Literaria."

Advocate General, The. *Sir James Marriott, LL.D.* Plan of a code of laws for the Province of Quebec; reported ... L. 1774.

Advocate of the Cause of the People, An. *John Hope.* Letters on the impressing of seamen, in the "Public Advertiser."

Advocate of the Christian Revelation, An. *Caleb Fleming.* Remarks on ... [the] "True Gospel of Jesus Christ asserted" ... By ... L. 1738.

Ædituus. *John Smith.* Metrical remarks on modern castles and cottages ... L. 1813.

Aednr-nos, Seer l'Noh. *John Anderson.* The Chronicles of Reform of the Children of the Isles, in the days of Arthur [*i.e.*, A. Wellesley, Duke of Wellington], the chief ruler of the land, and his colleagues. Translated from the Chaldaic manuscript by the learned pundit S. I. A.—N. [A political satire in Biblical language.] Edinb. 1832.

Æmelia Julia. *Emily Julia Black.* Byron: Salathiel, or the martyrs; and other poems. By Æ. J. L. 1855.

Æneas. *James Francis Edward Stuart.* Æneas and his two sons: a true portrait. L. 1746.

Æschines. *Francis William Blagdon.* A few brief remarks on a pamphlet ... entitled Observations... By Æ. L. 1805.

Æsculapius. *Laurence H. Potts* (?), *M.D.* Oracular communications, addressed to students of the medical profession. By ... L. 1816.

Æsop. *Mrs. Lillie Devereux Blake.* In the New York "Telegram." Author of "Fettered for life" ... N.Y. 1874.

Æsop, George Washington. *George T. Lanigan,* in the New York "World."

Afflicted Husband, An. *Cuthbert Shaw.* Monody to the memory of a young lady who died in childbed. By ... L. 1768.

African Roscius, The. *Ira Aldridge.*

Afterwit, Anthony. *Benjamin Franklin,* in a letter contributed to the "Pennsylvania Gazette." P. July 10, 1732.

Afton, Effie. *Mrs. Frances Ellen Watkins Harper.* Eventide: a series of tales and poems. B. 1854.

Ag., A. *Alexander Agassiz.* Obituary. [A biographical notice of Count L. F. de

Pourtalès.] From the "Amer. Jour. of Science." Camb., Mass. 1880.

Agapida, Fray Antonio. *Washington Irving.* A chronicle of the conquest of Granada. By ... P. 1829.

Agate. *Whitelaw Reid.* After the war: a southern tour. 1865–66. Cin. 1866.

Agatha. *Bessie Lawrence* (?). Thanksgiving, and other poems. N.Y. 1880.

Agathon, Paul. *Elisabeth Schöjen.* Kamilla; Ragnvald; and Jane Gray. Copenhagen, 187–.

Aged Layman, An. *Dr. Richard Poole.* The grand contrast, God and man ... L. 1854.

Aged Minister, An. *Moses Dickinson.* An answer to a letter from an aged layman, to the clergy of the Colony of Connecticut ... New Haven, probably 1767.

Aged Native, An. *Thomas Sanderson.* An evening lay to the Vale of Sebergham. By ... in the "Carlisle Patriot."

Aged Parson, An. *Rev. Richard Warner.* The diary of ... Bath, 1848.

Agent for Barbados, The. *G. W. Jordan.* Copies of a letter containing queries respecting the state of the silver and copper coins in Barbados ... L. 1816.

Agent of the Corporation, The. *Caleb Eddy.* Historical sketch of the Middlesex canal ... B. 1843.

Ager. *R. M. Field,* in his account of the journey of the Prince of Wales through New England, contributed to "The Boston Post," etc.

Agg, John. *Frank Cahill,* in his contributions to "The Saturday Press." P.

Aghonne, Mme. d'. *Mme. Louise Lacroix.* Une amie de pension. P. 1870.

Aglaüs. *Henry Timrod,* who contributed poetry to the "Southern Literary Messenger," etc., and published a volume of poems. B. 1859.

Ago, Felix. *Samuel Stehman Haldeman.* Rhymes of the poets. P. 1868.

Agogos. *Charles William Day.* Maxims, experiences, and observations of Agogos. B. 1844.

Agrestis. *Gen. Joseph Alston* (?). Short review of the late proceedings at New Orleans, on suspending the writ of habeas corpus. Richmond, 1807.

Agricola. *James Anderson.* In 1790 he commenced the publication of "The Bee" (1790–94), consisting of essays philosophical and miscellaneous. Dr. A. wrote those marked "Senex," "Timothy

Hairbrain," "Alcibiades," and many others without signature.

Agricola. *William Elliott.* Author of Address before the St. Paul's Agricultural Society, Charleston, 1850; Fiesco, a tragedy, N.Y. 1850; and, Carolina sports by land and water, Charleston, 1856.

Agricola. *Rev. Percival Stockdale.* "In the summer of 1779, he wrote several political letters, with the signature of 'Agricola,' in the 'Public Advertiser.'"

Agricola. *W. F. Whitehouse.* Letters and essays on sugar farming in Jamaica. L. 1845.

Agricola. *John Young.* Letters of Agricola on the principles of vegetation and tillage... Halifax, N.S. 1822.

Agricola. *Rev. Charles Whitaker.* Letters on free trade. 1851.

Agricola. *James Anderson. LL.D.* Miscellaneous observations on planting and training timber-trees... Edinb. 1777.

Agrikler. *Joseph Edwards.* Rhymes in the West Country dialect... L. 1879.

Aguaverde, Antonio. *Alfred Trumble.* Contribution to "The Boys and Girls' Weekly" (N.Y.).

Aguecheek. *Charles Bullard Fairbanks,* who contributed sketches of foreign travel, and essays, to the Boston "Saturday Evening Gazette," under the signature of "Aguecheek." B. 1859.

Ahern, Anna. *Mrs. Frances West Atherton Pike.* Here and hereafter; or, the two altars. By... B. 1858.

Ahiezer. *William Brown.* A tender and affectionate address to, and expostulation with, the people of Israel, the Jews. Huntingdon, 1814.

Aikin, Berkeley. *Fanny Aikin Kortright.* The dean; or, the popular preacher. L. 1859; The old, old story, love, L. 1862.

Ailo, Thorny. *John Taylor,* the Water-poet. A full and compleat answer against the writer of the Tale of a tub in a tub, or a Tub lecture. By T. A.... L. 1642.

Aimwell, Walter. *William Simonds.* The Aimwell stories. B. 1863.

Ain [the Hebrew word for nobody]. *William Stevens.* A review of the Review of the new preface to the second edition of Mr. Jones's "Life of Bishop Horne." L. 1800.

Ainslie, Herbert, B.A. *Edward Maitland.* The pilgrim and the shrine; or, passages from the life and correspondence of... L. 1868.

Airy, Mr. *Robert Habersham,* in the "Harv. Univ. Collegian." Camb. 1830.

Ajax. *Mr. Ainley.* Social wastes and waste lands... L. 1862.

Akestes. *William Smith.* A few remarks on the expectant treatment of diseases... Bristol, 1847.

Akroates. *Josiah F. Polk.* A defence of the Protestant Bible... N.Y. 1844.

Alastor. *James Orton.* "Excelsior," or the realms of poesie, 1852; Poems, 1857; Caleb Redivivus, 1858. L.

Alaux, Gustave d'. *Maxime Raybaud.* L'empereur Soulouque et son empire. Paris, 1856.

Alazon. *Rev. Richard William Barnes.* Let well alone; or, removal of blemishes from church and state. L. 1860.

Alba. *Alexina B. White.* Little-folk songs. N.Y. 1871, and in her contributions to "The Riverside Magazine."

Albanés, A. d'. *Jean Alexandre Havard.* Notice sur La Fontaine... Paris, 1869.

Albanés Havard, d'. *Jean Alexandre Havard.* Voltaire et Mme. du Châtelet ... avec notes historiques par... Paris, 1863.

Albanicus. *The Right Hon. David Stewart Erskine, 11th Earl of Buchan and 6th Lord Cardross.*

"Lord Buchan was an occasional contributor to various periodical publications. His favorite signature was 'Albanicus,' under which, in a letter to his friend 'Hortus,' he describes his own delightful residence of Dryburgh Abbey in the fourth volume of 'The Bee.'"

There is also, in the "Gent. Mag." in 1784, a description of the grave of Ossian, with an epitaph in blank verse (vol. 54, p. 404), over the same signature.

Albano. *Count Karl August Adlersparre,* who published novels and lyrics under this name.

Albé. *George Gordon Noël, 6th Lord Byron.* The footprints of A. [*i.e.* Lord Byron]: a poem. Written by E. Brennan. Milan, 1874.

Alben, Rewk. *Benjamin Walker.* Rewk Alben the friar; his opinions on the ministry to the poor... Manchester, Eng. 1872.

Albert. *Rev. John Armstrong.* Sonnets from Shakespeare. By... L. 1791.

Albert. *Abbate Giovanni Battista Fortis.* Travels in Dalmatia. 1774.

Albin, Sébastien. *Mme. Hortense Lacroix Cornu.* Ballades et chants populaires (anciens et modernes) de l'Allemagne. Traduction nouvelle par S. A. Paris, 1841.

Albion. Four pleasant epistles written for the entertainment and gratification of four unpleasant characters; viz., a very exalted subject in his majesty's dominions [George, prince of Wales], the most unpatriotic man alive [C. J. Fox], the most artful man alive [R. B. Sheridan], and Second Childhood [E. Burke]. L. 1789.

Alcæus. *Samuel Boyse*, in the "Gent. Mag." 1741–43.

Alcæus. *James Montgomery*, in the "Poetical Register," 1801. Byron notices him in "English bards and Scotch reviewers": —

" With broken lyre and cheek serenely pale,
Lo! sad Alcæus wanders down the vale."

Alcibiades. *James Anderson.* — See "Agricola."

Alcibiades. *Alfred Tennyson*, in "Punch." Feb. and March, 1846.

Alcofribas, le magicien. *Jean Baptiste Alfred Assolant.* The fantastic history of the celebrated Du Pierrot ... L. 1875.

Alderani, Lorenzo. *Niccolò Ugo Foscolo.* Ultime lettere di Jacopo Ortis. Edited by L. A. L. 1814.

Alderman, The. *John Barber.* The city jilt; or, the A. turn'd beau, etc. L. 1740.

Aldiborontiphoscophornio. *James Ballantyne.* A nickname given him by Sir Walter Scott, in allusion to his pompous and dignified manner.

Aleph. *Humphry Fitzroy Woolrych.* Aleph v. Colenso. Maidstone, 1866.

Aleph. *William Harvey.* The old city, and its highways and byways ... L. 1865.

Alethes. *Thomas H. Baird*, in the Pittsburgh "Commercial Journal." 1851.

Alethes, Clerophilus. *John Constable* (?). A specimen of amendments candidly proposed to the compiler [Charles Dodd, *pseud.*, i.e., Hugh Tootell] of a work which he calls "The church history of England from the year 1500 to the year 1688." L. 1741.

Alethinos. *Rev. Hardinge Furenzo Ivers.* The audibleness of thought demonstrated, and its use explained. 1866.

Alethitheras. *L. Osborn.* Travels by sea and land. N.Y. 1868.

Alethphilos. *Mrs. Mary Anne Woolfrey.* Letters of ... Newport, Isle of Wight, 1839.

Aletor, Esq. *Robert E. Strahorn.*

Alex. *Eliza A. White.* As she would have it. P. 1873.

Alexander, Mrs. *Mrs. Annie F. Hector.* Her dearest foe, 1876; The wooing o't, 1873. L.

Alexander the Coppersmith. *W.* Boles. Milk for babes, meat for strong men, and wine for petitioners ... translated from the Arabic by ... Cork, 1731.

Alexander the Coppersmith, LL.D. *Thomas Erskine, Baron Erskine.* The speech of ... spoken at the meeting of the friends to the abuse of the freedom of the press. Jan. 10, 1793. [A satire upon T. Erskine, Baron Erskine.] L. 1793.

Alexander the Corrector. *Alexander Cruden.* The adventures of ... L. 1754. [He entitles himself corrector, from the nature of his office, which was to correct the press.]

Alexander, Sir Drawcansir. *Tobias George Smollett.* A faithful narrative of the base and inhuman arts that were lately practised upon the brain of Habbakkuk Hilding [i.e., Henry Fielding], justice, dealer, and chapman, who now lies at his house in Covent Garden, in a deplorable state of lunacy, a dreadful monument of false friendship and delusion. By D. A., fencing-master and philomath. L. 1752. — See "Brit. Mus. Cat."

Alexander, J. H., B.A. *Alexander II. Japp.* Lights on the way. Some tales within a tale, by the late J. H. A., B. A., with an explanatory note by H. A. Page [also a *pseud.* of the author]. L. 1878.

Alexander, John, a Joyner. *John Taylor*, the Water-poet. Love one another: a tub lecture preached at Watford in Hartfordshire, at a conventicle on the 25th of December last [1642]. L. 1642.

Alexandre. *Alexandre Davy Dumas.* La cour du roi Pétaud. Paris, 1829.

Alexis or the Worthy Unfortunate. *Rev. Humphrey Sydenham.* Being a true narrative of the affecting case of a young gentleman whose ruin was caused by the late rebellion. L. 1747.

Alexis, Willibald. *Georg Wilhelm Heinrich Haering.* Cabanis, 1832; Haus Dusterweg, 1836; die zwölf Nächte, 1838; Novellen, 1830–31; Neue Novellen, 1836.

Alfred. *Samuel Adams*, in the "Boston Gazette" (Oct. 2, 1769).

Alfred. *Dr. Girardin.* One of the writers, under this signature, of the essays in Wirt's "Old Bachelor" (1812).

Alfred. *Sir James Bland Burges Lamb, Bart, D.C.L.*, in "The Sun Newspaper." A series of letters under this signature, "in which he took a comprehensive view of the several states, political objects, and relative interests of all European governments. These letters he collected and published in 1792."

Alfred. *Grenville A. Sackett,* who under this signature wrote some of the best and most widely circulated poetry of the day in "The New York Mirror," "New York Times," and "Long Island Star."

Alfred. *Rev. Samuel Kydd.* China: its symbols, philosophy, antiquities. L. 1841.

Alfred. *Philip Withers.* Nemesis; or, a letter to Alfred [relating to the marriage of the Prince of Wales to Mrs. Fitzherbert] from ... L. 1789.

Alfred. *Rev. David Alfred Doudney.* Sympathy; or, words for the weak and weary. L. 1862.

Al Fresco. *Dr. Charles J. Kenworthy(?).*

Alfried, Johan. *Jean Jacques De Laet.* — See "Bogaerts, Felix."

Alguño, Señor. *Nathan Ames.* Childe Harvard: a romance of Cambridge ... B. 1848.

Ali Baba. *Aberigh Mackay,* contributor to "Vanity Fair," of many sketches of India life and society.

Ali Bey. *Samuel Lorenzo Knapp.* Extracts from a journal of travels in North America, consisting of an account of Boston and its vicinity. By ... B. 1818.

Ali Bey, El Abassi. *Domingo Badia-y-Leblich.* Voyages ... en Afrique et en Asie, pendant les années 1803, 1804, 1805, 1806, et 1807. Edited by B. [*i.e.,* J. B. Boniface de Roquefort]. Paris, 1814.

Alice, Cousin. *Mrs. Alice (Bradley Neal) Haven.* The Coopers; or, getting under way: a tale of real life. N.Y.

Alice, Cousin. *Miss Eliza Tabor.* St. Olave's: a novel. N.Y. 1870.

Alida. *Mrs. Catharine Stratton Ladd.* One of the *noms de plume* under which she has contributed tales, sketches, essays, and poems to various journals.

Alien, An. *Max Friedrich Mueller.* German love: from the papers of ... 1858.

Alient Baptist Dissenter, An. *Seth Brooks.* A plowman's complaint against a clergyman: being a letter to the Baptist Association at Philadelphia. By ... P. 1767.

Aligny. *Claude Félix Théodore Caruelle.* A French historical painter.

Aliqua. *Mrs. Eliza O. Peirson,* in the periodical press.

Aliquis. *Rev. Richard Marks,* who "communicated his religious history, in an anonymous form, to 'The Christian Guardian,' in several papers, bearing the signature of 'Aliquis,' which were afterwards published (still anonymously) in a volume entitled The retrospect; or, review of providential mercies." L. 1816.

Aliquis. *James Henry James.* Government as it is: a plea for parliamentary reform. By A. [In verse.] L. 1858.

Aliquis. *Rev. James Barr.* A letter to the Rev. George Harris, containing an examination of the arguments adduced in his lectures to prove the non-existence of the devil. Liverpool, 1820.

Alist. *Francis Barham.* Alist, an autobiography; or, an author's life in the nineteenth century. L. 1844.

Alister, R. *Alexander Robertson.* Extermination of the Scottish peasantry ... By ... Edinb. 1853.

All-Pride, Lord. *John Sheffield, Duke of Buckinghamshire.* A very heroical epistle from my Lord All-Pride to Dolcommon ... L. 1679.

Allan-Kardec. *Léon Hippolyte Denisart Rivail.* Le livre des esprits ... Paris, 1857.

Allde, Edward. *John Taylor,* the Water-poet. The pennyles pilgrimage, or the moneylesse perambulation of John Taylor, *alias* The King's Majestie's Water-poet. From London to Edenborough on foot. By E. A. L. 1618.

Alldred, Frederic. *Henry F. Reddall.*

Allen, Grahame. *George Arnold.*

Allen, John. *Oscar Clute.* The blessed bees. By ... N.Y. 1878.

Allen, Mrs. Josiah. *Marietta Holley.* My opinions and Betsey Bobbet's ... By J. A.'s wife. Hartford, 1875.

Allen, Paul. *John Neal* and *Tobias Watkins, M.D.* History of the American revolution. By P. A. P. 1821.

Paul Allen (1775–1826) was a journalist of Philadelphia and Baltimore. He had long promised this history, and obtained a large subscription for it; but Mr. Neal wrote the first volume, and Dr. Watkins the remainder.

Allendale, Alfred, Esq. *Theodore Edward Hook.* The man of sorrow. By ... L. 1809.

Allerdyce. *Robert Barclay.* Agricultural tour in the United States. L. 1842.

Allid. *George T. Lanigan.* National ballads of Canada ... Montreal, 1865.

Allin, Abby. *Mrs. A. A. Carter* (wife of Daniel S.). Home ballads: a book for New Englanders ... B. 1851.

Allison, Joy. *Mary A. Cragin.* Kate Jameson and her friends. B. 1872.

Allspice, Zekel. *John Cooper Vail.*

Allyn, Ellen. *Miss Christina Georgina Rossetti.* Her signature to poems published in "The Gem," London, of which only four numbers were published; written almost exclusively by the Rossettis, Holman Hunt, and Ford Madox Brown.

Allyne, Enylla. *Mrs. Spencer.*

Almaviva. *Harry St. Maur,* in his contributions to "The News-Letter" (Chicago, Ill.).

Alma Viva. *Clement Scott.* "The 'Smiff Papers' did much to extend the circulation of 'The Figaro,' as did also the dramatic criticism signed 'Alma Viva.' Mr. Doughty was the author of the first-mentioned feature; Mr. Clement Scott, of the second." — See "Journalistic London," p. 94.

Almaviva. *Clement Scott.* Drawing-room plays and parlor pantomimes. Collected ... L. 1870.

Almore, Caspar. *Frederick Williamson Beasley, D.D.* Papers from Overlook house. P. 1866.

Alof, V. *Nicholas V. Gogol.* Home life in Russia. By a Russian noble. L. 1854.

Alonzo. *John Wingfield,* in Byron's "Childish Recollections." Newark, 1807.

Alpha. *John Abraham,* in the "Ladies' Journal," of Liskeard, Cornwall. 1868–78.

Alpha. *George Walker, M.D.* Death's waiting-room; or, the Girondist's last supper. A dramatic sketch. By A. L. 1851.

Alpha. *Mrs. L. L. Phelps.* Grace Tilden; or, seven years' service for Christ. B. 1869.

Alpha. *Stephen M. Allen.* Religion and science; the letters of "Alpha" on the influence of spirit on imponderable actienic molecular substances, etc. By ... B. 1874.

Alphonso, S. G. *Alonzo G. Shears* of New Haven (Ct.), in his contributions to various periodicals.

Alpin. *William Wilson,* in his poems contributed to periodicals.

Alq, Mme. Louise d'. *Olga Ebhardt.* La science du monde ... Paris, 1876.

Alston, Edith. *Miss Mary Green Goodale* of New Orleans, whose poems have appeared in the journals of that city under this pen-name.

Altamont. *Rev. Charles Jenner.* Letters from ... in the capital, to his friends in the country. L. 1767.

Alter. *Rev. Joseph B. Owen.* Chess studies. L. 18–.

Alter Ego. *Robert E. Strahorn.* To the Rockies and beyond; or, a summer on the Union Pacific Railroad and branches. Omaha, 1879.

Altisonant, Lorenzo. *S. K. Hoshour.* Letters to 'Squire Pedant by ... Cin. 1850.

Alton. *A. L. Taveau.* The magic word. B. 1855.

Alumni of the University of Edinburgh. *John Lee, D.D., George Wilson, M.D., S. Brown, and others.* Edinburgh academic annual for 1840, consisting of contributions in literature and science. By ... Edinb. 1840.

Alumnus, An. *Rev. Daniel Oliver.* Address at Dartmouth College, May 19, 1825.

Alumnus, An. *John Gorham Palfrey.* A letter to the corporation ... of Harvard College ... B. 1835.

Alumnus Cantabrigiensis. *Thomas Ignatius Maria Forster.* Harmonia Musarum ... Bruges, 1843.
The preface is signed "T. F."

Alumnus Edinensis. *Alexander Peterkin.* A letter to the Right Honourable the Lord Provost of Edinburgh ... Edinb. 1836.

Alumnus of that College, An. *John Lowell, LL.D.* Further remarks on the memorial of the officers of Harvard College ... B. 1824.

Alun Glan. Bardic name of the Rev. *Thomas Jones.*

Alvarez, Espriella Manuel. *Robert Southey.* Letters from England. By ... L. 1807.

Amateur, An. *C. Badham.* Brief recollections, chiefly of Italy. By ... Glasgow, 1835.

Amateur, An. *Thomas Wilson.* Catalogue raisonné of the select collection of engravings of ... L. 1828.

Amateur, An. *Captain G. Boid.* A concise history and analysis of all the principal styles of architecture ... By ... L. 1828.

Amateur, An. *N. B. Engleheart.* A concise treatise on eccentric turning. By ... L. 1852.

Amateur, An. *William Cox.* Crayon sketches by ... N.Y. 1833.

Amateur, An. *Charles Clark.* A doctor's "Do"-ings; or, the entrapped heiress of Witham: a satirical poem. Totham, 1848. — See "Queerfellow, Quintin."

Amateur, An. *Col. George W. Hooper.* Down the river; or, practical lessons under the code duello. N.Y. 1874.

Amateur, An. *Archibald N Carmichael.* Genealogy of her majesty Queen Victoria ... Edin. 1845.

Amateur, An. *G. R. Walker.* Horses, their rational treatment . . . By . . . L. 1865.

Amateur, An. *Charles Winston.* An inquiry into the difference of style observable in ancient painted glass . . . By . . . Oxf. 1847.

Amateur, An. *James Hall.* The jotting book : a political and literary experiment. By . . . L. 1839.

Amateur, An. *James Kirke Paulding*(?). The new mirror for travellers ; and guide to the Springs. By . . . N.Y. 1828.

Amateur, An. *Bernard Barton.* Poems. By . . . L. 1818.

Amateur, An. *Charles Kirkpatrick Sharpe.* Portraits by . . . Edinb. 1832.

Amateur, An. *Pierce Egan, the Elder.* Real life in London; or, the rambles and adventures of Bob Tallyho, Esq., and his cousin the Hon. Tom Dashall through the metropolis . . . By . . . L. 1821.

Amateur, An. *Hon. E. S. Abbot,* afterwards *Baroness Colchester.* Views in London. [In verse.] By . . . Chiswick, 1833.

Amateur Casual, An. *James Greenwood,* in " The Pall Mall Gazette," who " gave it a good start by a graphic sketch of workhouse life, signed ' An Amateur Casual.' "

Amateur Farmer, An. *William Holt Beever.* Notes on fields and cattle, from the diary of . . . L. 1862.

Amateur Lambeth Casual. *James Greenwood.* The wilds of London . . . L. 1866; The true history of Little Ragamuffin, 1866.

Amateur of Fashion, An. *James K. Paulding.* Jokeby : a burlesque on Rokeby, a poem, in six cantos. L. 1813. [This parody has also been attributed to John Roby, Thomas Tegg, and to the brothers James and Horace Smith.]

Amateur Traveller, An. *James Watson Webb.* Altowan ; or, incidents of life and adventure in the Rocky Mountains. By . . . Edited by J. W. Webb. N.Y. 1846.

Ambassador, The. *Samuel Turner,* in Beloe's "Sexagenarian," Vol. II., 73. 2d ed. L. 1818.

Ambrose. *Rev. J. Ambrose Wight,* of Bay City, Mich., in his contributions to " The Evangelist."

Ambrose, Father. *Matthew Henry Barker,* who wrote a good deal under this designation and that of " The Wanderer," as well as that of " Old Sailor."

Ambrose, Paul. *John Pendleton Kennedy.* Mr. Ambrose's letters on the rebellion. N.Y. 1865.

Amelia. *Mrs. Amelia (Coppuck) Welby.* Poems. By A. N.Y. 1842.

A men der. *Benjamin F. Burnham.* A voice from the pews ; or, a tabernacle supplement. B. 1877.

American, An. *Freeman Hunt.* American anecdotes : original and select . . . B. 1830.

American, An. *Edward Habich.* The American Churches the bulwarks of American slavery By . . . Newburyport, Mass. 1842.

American, An. *William Cobbett.* Annals of blood . . . By . . . Camb. [Eng.] 1797.

American, An. *James F. Price.* Castle Crosier : a romance. By . . . Annapolis, Md. 1827.

American, An. *Noah Webster.* The revolution in France. N.Y. 1874.

American, An. *William Barton, A.M.* The constitutionalist : addressed to men of all parties in the United States . . . P. 1804.

American, An. *David Christy.* Cotton is king . . . Cin. 1855.

American, An. *Hezekiah Hartley Wright.* Desultory reminiscences of a tour through Germany, Switzerland, and France. B. 1838.

American, An. *Stephen Fiske.* English photographs . . . L. 1869.

American, An. *O. Prescott Hiller.* English and Scottish sketches. L. 1857.

American, An. *David Everett.* An essay on the rights and duties of nations, relative to fugitives from justice . . . B. 1807.

American, An. *Arthur Lee.* An essay in vindication of the continental colonies of America, from a censure of Adam Smith . . . L. 1764.

American, An. *Rev. Mathias Bruen.* Essays, descriptive and moral, on scenes in Italy, Switzerland, and France . . . Edinb. 1823.

American, An. *Lewis Cass.* An examination of the question now in discussion between the American and British governments, concerning the right of search. By . . . Baltimore, 1842.

American, An. *William Elliott.* Fiesco : a tragedy. N.Y. 1850.

American, An. *R. Davidson, Esq.* Geography epitomised . . . in verse . . . By . . . L. 1787.

American, An. *James Fenimore Cooper.* Gleanings in Europe : England. By . . . P. 1837.

American, An. *Theodore Sedgwick.*

Hints to my countrymen, by ... N.Y. 1826.

American, An. *Mrs. Lydia Maria Child.* Hobomok: a tale of early times ... B. 1824.

American, An. *Samuel Finley Breese Morse.* Imminent dangers to the free institutions of the United States through foreign immigration ... N.Y. 1835.

American, An. *Sidney Edwards Morse.* Letter on American slavery ... By ... N.Y. 1847.

American, An. *Henry M. Brackenridge.* Letter on South American affairs to Mr. Monroe. 1818.

American, An. *J. Pottinger.* Letters of ... mainly on Russia, etc. 1854.

American, An. *Alexander Hamilton.* Letters to "The Gazette of the United States." August 4–18, 1792.

American, An. *A. Robinson.* Life in California during a residence of several years in that territory ... N.Y. 1846.

American, An. *Benjamin Young Prime, M.D.* Muscipula sive Cambromyomachia. The mouse-trap: or, the battle of the Welsh and the mice, in Latin and English, with other poems in different languages. By ... N.Y. 1840.

American, An. *Henry Wadsworth Longfellow.* Outre-mer; or, a pilgrimage to the Old World. By ... L. 1835.

American, An. *Samuel Low.* The politician outwitted: a comedy ... N.Y. 1789.

American, An. *James Sloan.* Rambles in Italy in the years 1816–17. By ... Balt. 1818. [Also attributed to Theodore Lyman.]

American, An. *Alexander Hill Everett.* Remarks on Gov. C. Strong's speech ... B. 1814.

American, An. *Richard Biddle.* A review of Captain Basil Hall's travels in North America, in the years 1827 and 1828. L. 1830.

American, An. *George Henry Calvert.* Scenes and thoughts in Europe. N.Y. 1847.

American, An. *James E. DeKay.* Sketches of Turkey in 1831 and 1832. N.Y. 1833.

American, An. *Matthew Bennett Wynkoop.* Song leaves from the book of Life and Nature. By ... N.Y. 1852.

American, An. *Benjamin Church, M.D.* The times: a poem ... B. 1765.

American, An. *Rev. Charles Inglis.* True interest of America impartially stated. P. 1776.

American, An. *Duff Green.* The United States and England ... L. 1842.

American, An. *Joseph Hopkinson.* What is our situation? and what our prospects? ... P. 1799.

American, An, formerly a Member of Congress. *Fisher Ames.* The influences of democracy on liberty, property, and the happiness of society, considered. By ... L. 1835.

American in England, The. *Alexander Slidell Mackenzie.* The American in England. L. 1836.

American in London, An. *Rev. Calvin Colton.* The Americans. 1833.

American in Paris, The. *John Sanderson.* The American in Paris. L. 1838.

American in the Service of the Viceroy, An. *George Bethune English.* A narrative of the expedition to Dongola and Sennaar, under the command of His Excellence Ismael Pasha ... L. 1822.

American Long Resident at Constantinople, An. *Commodore David Porter.* Constantinople and its environs. ... N.Y. 1835.

American recently returned from Europe, An, *Robert Walsh.* A letter on the genius and dispositions of the French government ... P. 1810.

American Amateur in Europe, An. *James Jackson Jarves.* Art thoughts ... 1869.

American Angler, An. *John J. Brown.* American Angler's Guide ... By ... N.Y. 1845.

American Artist, An. *Laughton Osborn.* Handbook of young artists and amateurs in oil painting ... N.Y. 1845.

American Cato, The. *Samuel Adams,* so called by a newspaper writer. 1781.

American Citizen, An. *William Beach Lawrence,* as translator of Marbois' "History of Louisiana." P. 1830.

American Citizen, An. *Orville J. Victor.* The American rebellion ... By ... L. 1861.

American Citizen, An. *John Adams.* Discourses on Davila ... B. 1805.

American Citizen, An. *James Barr Walker, D.D.* The living questions of the age. By ... P. 1869.

American Citizen, An. *Linus Pierpont Brockett, M.D.* The philanthropic results of the war in America ... N.Y. 1864.

American Consul at London, The. *Freeman H. Morse.* ... American seamen. ... Letter from ... n. p. 1869.

American Englishman, An. *Samuel Mather,* of Boston. An attempt to show that America must be known to the Ancients ... B. 1773.

American Fabius, The. *George Washington*, so called in 1781.

American Farmer, An. *Hector St. John Crevecœur*. Letters. 1793.

American Farmer, An. *William Cobbett*. Notes on American gardening and fruit. P. 1803.

American Farmer, An. *Frederick Law Olmsted*. Walks and talks of . . . in England. N.Y. 1852.

American Gentleman, An. *Richard S. Coxe*.

American Gentleman, An. *William Cliffton*. Gifford's "The Baviad" and "Mæviad." [Also], A poetical epistle to the author, by an American gentleman. P. 1799.

American Gentleman, An. *Benjamin Young Prime, M.D.* The patriot muse . . . L. 1764.

American Gentleman, An. *John Sanderson*. Sketches of Paris: in familiar letters to his friends. P. 1838.

American Gentleman, An. *Richard Alsop*, as translator of The geographical, natural, and civil history of Chili. By Abbé don J. Ignatius Molina. Middletown, Ct. 1808.

American Gentleman, An. *Rev. Calvin Colton*. A voice from America to England. N.Y. 1837.

American Girl Abroad, An. *Miss Adeline Trafton*. An American girl abroad. B.

American Indian, An. *Henry Horne, Jr.* The citizen of nature: in a series of letters from . . . in London, to his friend at home. L. 1823.

American Lady, An. *Henry Wood*. Change for the "American Notes" . . . L. 1843.

American Lady, An. *M. Griffin*. Impressions of Germany . . . Dresden, 1866.

American Lady, An. *Mrs. Grant*. Memoirs . . . with sketches of manners and scenery in America . . . L. 1810.

American Navy Officer, An. *Nathaniel Fanning*. A narrative of the adventures of an American navy officer, who served during part of the American revolution under Paul Jones. N.Y. 1806.

American Novelist, The. *Mrs. H. B. Stowe*. Byron painted by his compeers . . . showing wherein the A. N. gives a truthful account, etc. L. 1869.

American Officer in the Service of France. *John Skey Eustace*. Letters on the crimes of George III. . . . Paris, 1794.

American Pastor, An. *Rev. Thomas Bacon*. Two sermons, preached to a congregation of black slaves . . . L. 1749.

American Physician, An. *Dr. Patrick Macaulay*. How the cholera is propagated . . . L. 1831.

American Spy, The. *Capt. Nathan Hale*. The A. S.; or, freedom's early sacrifice : a tale of the Revolution, founded on fact. Albany, 1857. [Written by Jeptha Root Simms.]

American Wanderer. *Arthur Lee*. American wanderer through Europe. L. 1783.

American Woman, An. *Mrs. L. B. Urbino*. An American woman in Europe . . .

American Woman, An. *Helen C. Smith*. Hints on dress . . . N.Y. 1872.

American Woman, An. *Mrs. H. C. Tracy Cutler*. Letter from . . . to . . . Lord Palmerston. 1862.

Americanus. *Caleb Evans*. A letter to the Rev. John Wesley . . . L. 1775.

Americus. *Francis Lieber*. Manual of political ethics. P.

Americus. *Oscar Montgomery Lieber*, in his contributions to "The Evening Post." N.Y. 1872.

Americus. *Vine Wright Kingsley*. Spain, Cuba, and the United States . . . N.Y. 1870.

Amerus. *Alexander Chalmers*. Character of Dr. Johnson as drawn by himself. "Gent. Mag.," April, 1788, p. 300; original letter of Dr. Johnson, June, 1788, p. 479.

Ames, Mrs. Nelly. *Eleanor Kirk*. Up Broadway, and its sequel. A life story. N.Y. 1870.

Amey. *Louis Xavier Eyma*. His signature to his translations and vaudevilles.

Ami, Un. *Rev. Thomas Hartley*. Autobiographie de Swedenborg. Sous ce titre : reponse à une lettre qu'un un ami m'a écrite. Saint-Amand, 1851.

Amica. *Miss Alice Pearce*. An acrostic on the Rev. R. H. Hitchins, in the "Cornish Magazine," 1828.

Amicus. *William A. Brewer*, in his contributions to various old New York periodicals.

Amicus. *Sir Thomas Fairbairn*, in the London "Times."

Amicus. *David Brown*. Defence of the British and foreign Bible society. Edinb. 1826.

Amicus. *James Gordon*. Eight letters on the subject of the Earl of Selkirk's pamphlet on Highland emigration . . . Edinb. 1806.

Amicus. *Joseph Lancaster*. Fruits of Christian love! a letter . . . on the religious instruction of their [the Quakers'] youth. L. 1808.

Amicus. *John Canton.* On the magnetic needle, in the " Gent. Mag.," December, 1761, p. 569.

Amicus. *William Alexander.* Quakerism unmasked: comprising a glance at J. Wilkinson's "Quakerism examined." By . . . York. 1839.

Amicus. *Rev. Benjamin Kent.* A sermon in Marlborough, July 9, 1734. Per . . . B. 1734.

Amicus Curiae. One of the pseudonyms attributed to Junius (*q.v.*). [The letter thus signed is dated June 10, 1769, and defends the letters of Junius.]

Amicus Curiæ. *John Payne Collier.* Criticisms on the bar. L. 1819.

Amicus Secundus. *William A. Thomson, D.D.* Brief statement of reasons for Bible societies in Scotland withdrawing their confidence in the British and foreign Bible society. Edinb. 1826.

Amigo. *Dr. Salmon Skinner,* in the N.Y. "Herald."

Amner. *George Steevens.* Rev. Richard Amner (1737–1803), a dissenting minister at Hampstead, near London, and afterwards at Coseley, in Staffordshire; still later, left off preaching and retired to his native town, Hinckley.

"Whilst a resident at Hampstead, he became the subject of malignant merriment to the learned commentator on Shakespeare, who, to his everlasting shame be it spoken, fathered on this harmless Divine many *ludicrous* notes of his own."

Amor Patriæ. *Thomas Crowley.* Dissertations on the grand dispute between Great Britain and America. By . . . L. 1774.

Amor Veritatis. *Rev. John Mortlock Daniell.* To F. Silver. [Letter, signed A. V., addressed to F. Silver, in reply to his pamphlet, entitled "Immanuel."] L. 1833.

Amyntor, Gerhard von. *Dagobert von Gerhard.* Ein priester, historie in sechs gesangen. Breslau, 1881.

Anacharsis. *Jean Jacques Barthélemy.* Voyage du jeune Anacharsis en Greece. Paris, 1788.

Anacreon, The French. *Pierre Laujon,* 1727–1811, perpetual president of the Caveau Moderne, a Paris club noted for its good dinners, but every member was obliged to be a poet.

Anacreon Moore. *Thomas Moore.* 1779–1852.

Anacreon of the Guillotine. *Barère de Vieuzac.* 1755–1841.

Anacreon, The Sicilian. *Giovanni Meli,* 1740–1815.

Analytical Teacher, An. *John U.*

Parsons. The analytical spelling-book . . . Portland, Me.

Anchor. *John Watts De Peyster.* Chancellorsville and its results . . . N.Y. 1865.

Ancien Curé du diocese de Quebec, Un. *Very Rev. Thomas Maguire.* Recueil de notes diverses sur le gouvernement d'une paroisse . . . Paris, 1830.

Ancien enfant de chœur, Un. *Émile Laurent.* Les abbés galants. P. 1882. Also ascribed to Émile Colombey.

Ancient Brahmin, An. *Robert Dodsley.* The Œconomy of human life . . . Written by . . . L. 1750.

Ancient, Oliver. *Robert W. McAlpine,* in his contributions to "Noah's Sunday Times" (N.Y.).

Andersson, Anna. *Anna Andersson Wästberg.* Styfmorsblommorna. 1857.

Anderson, Ralph. *Robert Heron.* A letter from R. A. Esq. to Sir J. Sinclair . . . Edinb. 1797.

Andolt, Ernst. *Bernhard Rudolf Abeken.* Studies on the Divine commedia of Dante. 1826.

Andrade. *João de Andrade Corvo de Camões.* Un conto ao serão, 1852.

André, W. J. *William Jerdan.*

In his autobiography he says: "I have not been a careful preserver of my productions, and have not (I now wish I had) a copy of my 'Eclogue,' which, if I remember rightly, appeared as the writing of W. J. André, an anagram of my name, which, like the signature of 'Teutha' (the ancient name of Tweed), used by me from the period of my earliest to my latest contributions to the press, may guide the curious (if such there may be) to many of the anonymous essays, in prose and verse, of William Jerdan."

Andrew of Mitchell Street. *John Andrews Jones.*

Andrew, James, A. M. *Andrew Mackay.* Astronomical and nautical tables . . . L. 1805.

Andrews, Joseph. *Henry Fielding.* The history of the adventures of . . . and of his friend Mr. Abraham Adams. L. 1742.

Ane of that ilk. *William Edmonstoune Aytoun.* Our Zion . . . By . . . 1840.

Ang, Phil. *John Pennyman.* A bright shining light, discovering the pretenders to it, to the . . . Quakers, etc. By . . . L. 1680.

Ange Bénigne. *Mme. la Comtesse Paul de Molènes,* in her contributions to "La Vie Parisienne."

Angelina. *Mrs. Angelina Levy Goetz,* in music to numerous songs, among others Sir Marmaduke; The stream of life. L. 1858.

Angelina. *Harriet Martineau.*

Angelina. *Thomas Prescott Prest.* Miser of Shoreditch: drama. N.Y. 1857.

Angeloni, Battista. *John Shebbeare, M.D.* Letters on the English nation. By B. A., a Jesuit . . . L. 1755.

Anglais Voyageur, Un. *Martin Sherlock.* Lettres d' . . . Geneva, 1779.

Angler, An. *Charles Lanman.* Adventures of . . . in Canada, Nova Scotia, and the United States. L. 1848.

Angler, An. *Thomas Tod Stoddart.* An angler's rambles and angling songs. L. 1866.

Angler, An. *John Henry Cliffe.* Notes and recollections of . . . rambles among the mountains of Wales. L. 1860.

Angler, An. *Sir Humphry Davy.* Salmonia ; or, days of fly-fishing. 1828.

Angler, A North Country. *Thomas Doubleday.* Coquet-dale fishing songs . . . Edinb. 1852.

Angler and Bibliopolist, An Old. *Thomas Boosey.* Piscatorial reminiscences and gleanings. L. 1835.

Anglicanæ Presbyter. *John Wesley.* C. Sallustii Crispi bellum Catiliniarum et Jugurthinum . . . edidit . . . L. 1749.

Anglicanus. *R. S. Ellis.* The traveller's handbook to Copenhagen and its environs. Copenhagen, 1853.

Anglicanus, L. T. *Arthur Penrhyn Stanley,* Dean of Westminster.

Anglicanus Presbyter. *Joseph Hemington Harris.* Auricular confession not the rule of the Church of England . . . L. 1852.

Anglo-American. *Sir Brenton Halliburton, Knt.,* who contributed frequently to the press, the most noteworthy of his writings being a series of letters, in 1813, on the American war, which appeared in the Halifax "Recorder," under this signature.

Anglo-Canadian, An. *Rev. Adam Townley, D.D.* Ten letters . . . on the Church and Church establishments . . . Toronto, 1839.

Angove, Grace. *Mrs. Grace Michell.* The gold fields of California, and struggles to win gold there and in England . . . 1868-69.

Anicetus. *William Adolphus Clark.* The cannonade. B. 1861.

Animal Painter, An. *James Wilson.* The rod and the gun ; and a voyage round the coasts of Scotland and the Isles.

Ann. *Mrs. Ann Thomas.* The dovecot. 1834.

Ann of Swansea. *Ann Kemble.* Cesario Rosalba ; or, the oath of vengeance : a romance. L. 1819.

Ann Jane. *Mrs. Ann Jane Morgan.* John Pottle, the farmer's man. L.

Anna Matilda. *Mrs. Hannah Park-*

house Cowley. She composed, besides other plays, two remarkably successful comedies called "The Runaway," and "The Belle's Stratagem." She also wrote "The Maid of Arragon," and other poems.

Anna Matilda. *Mrs. Hester (Lynch Thrale) Piozzi.* In 1785, during her residence at Florence, she contributed under the signature of "Anna Matilda" to the "Florence Miscellany." Florence, 1785.

Annibale. *Miss Anna Ballard.* Fifteen vocalises . . . B. 1870. Also in her contributions to "The Mail" (N.Y.).

Annotator. *John Calder.* Notes to Nichols's edition of "The Tatler." L.1786.

Annual Visitor, An. *Henry Huntt, M.D.* A visit to the Red Sulphur Spring of Virginia during the summer of 1837 . . . By . . . B. 1839.

Anonym, Walter, Residuary Legatee of the late. *Henry Jackson Sargent.* Feathers from a moulting muse. B. 1854.

Anonymous. *Benjamin Dawson.* Animadversions upon the conduct of the Rev. Dr. Rutherforth . . . L. 1768.

Anonymous, Londinensis. *Matthias Earbery, A.B.* A letter to Dr. Calamy . . . L. 1718. [Also ascribed to Thomas Lewis.]

Another considerable personage. *Sir William Drummond,* in Beloe's "Sexagenarian." Vol. II., p. 124, 2d ed. L. 1818.

Another Gentleman of Cambridge. *John Duncombe.* An evening contemplation in a college : being a parody on the Elegy in a country churchyard. By . . . L. 1753.

Another Gentleman of Lincoln's Inn. *Thomas Edwards.* A supplement to Mr. Warburton's edition of Shakespear . . . By . . . L. 1748.

Another Layman. *Warwick Palfray.* Remarks on the recent ordination at Beverly . . . Salem, 1824.

Another Member of Parliament. *Sir William Blackstone.* A letter to [Sir William Meredith] the author of "The Question Stated." L. 1769.

Anselmus. *Rev. Samuel W. Duffield,* of Bloomfield, N.J., in his contributions to "The Evangelist."

Anstey, F. *F. Anstey Guthrie.* Vice versa. L. 1882.

Anthony, Grey. *Henry Carl Schiller.* Christmas at the grange. Graham, 1845.

Anti-Abolitionist, An. *Russell Jarvis.* Facts and arguments against the election of General Cass . . . N.Y. 1848.

Anti-Belial. One of the pseudonyms attributed to *Junius* (*q.v.*).

The letters thus signed "are minor Philo-Juniuses, to explain, defend, and support the reputation of the principal."

Anti-Bureaucrat, An. *Adam Thom.* Remarks on the convention ... Montreal, 1835.

Anti-Cotton. *R. A. T. Gascoyne Cecil, Viscount Cranborne, Marquis of Salisbury,* in his contributions to "The Quarterly Review." L.

Anti-Draco. *John Disney.* Five letters to Sir Samuel Romilly ... L. 1810.

Anti-Fox. One of the pseudonyms attributed to *Junius* (*q.v.*).

Under this signature he replied to Mr. Fox, in a letter dated Oct. 16, 1771.

Anti-Harmonicus. *Alexander Peterkin.* A poetical epistle to J*** T*** [John Tait], Esq. Edinb. 1807.

Anti-Monopoly. *William Duane.* Observations on the principles and operation of banking ... Helmbold, 1804.

Anti-Quary. *William H. Tuthill.* His signature to a series of articles in the newspapers, consisting chiefly of incidents and anecdotes relative to early settlers of Cedar County, Iowa.

Anti-Scriblerus Histrionicus. *John Roberts.* — See "A Stroling Player."

Anti-Sejanus. *Rev. James Scott.* The author of political essays published under the signatures of "Anti-Sejanus" and "Old Slyboots."

Anti-Sejanus, Jr. One of the pseudonyms attributed to *Junius* (*q.v.*).

It is appended to a letter contributed to "The Public Advertiser," dated June 24, 1767, and which is principally devoted to attacks on Lords Bute and Chatham.

Anti-Socinus. *Anselm Bayly.* Remarks on David Levi's second letter to Dr. Priestley ... By ... L. 1787.

Anti Stuart. One of the pseudonyms attributed to *Junius* (*q.v.*).

This letter, contributed to "The Public Advertiser," and dated March 24, 1768, is a reply to a letter signed "Anti van Teague," the author of which had defended the grant to Sir James Lowther. That signature seems to indicate that "Junius" was supposed to be an Irishman, and Mr. Burke. "Junius" signs "Anti Stuart" in reference to John Stuart, Earl of Bute, whose daughter Sir James Lowther had married. He then attacks the *public* character of the Duke of Grafton, the Prime Minister, and says he had not meddled with his private character, which he left for the Duke to *earth* in, whenever he is hard run, "according to the laudable example" of Lord North. — WADE.

Anti-theatricus. *Thady Fitzpatrick.* — See "T. F."

Anti-Tindalian. *Robert Lyon.* A letter to the Rev. Mr. James Adams at Kinnaird ... Edinb. 1734.

Anticant, Dr. Pessimist. *Thomas Carlyle,* in Anthony Trollope's "Warden."

In the same, "Charles James (Grantly)" represents Bp. Blomfield of London; "Henry (Grantly)," Bp. Phillpotts of Exeter; and "Samuel (Grantly)," Bp. Wilberforce of Oxford, then of Winchester. In Trollope's political novels, "Mr. Gresham" is said to mean Mr. Gladstone; "Mr. Daubeny," Lord Beaconsfield; "Lord de Terrier," Lord Derby; and "Mr. Plantagenet Palisser," Lord Carlingford.

Anticipation. *John Dickinson.* An address on the past, present, and eventual relations of the United States to France. N.Y. 1803.

Antigallican, An. *John Free, D.D.* The monthly reviewers reviewed by ... L. 1755.

Antilore. *Daniel Dulany.* His signature in his newspaper controversy with Charles Carroll, before the American revolution.

Antipolemus. *Vicesimus Knox, D.D.* "At that time [1792] he translated and printed, under the title of 'Antipolemus,' the adage of Erasmus, 'Bellum dulce inexpertis.'" — See "Gent. Mag.," Sept. 1821.

Antiquarian, An. *Royal R. Hinman.* The blue laws of New Haven Colony ... Compiled ... Hartford, 1838.

Antiquarian, An. *Henry Phillips, Jr.* Historical sketches of the paper money issued by Pennsylvania ... P. 1862.

Antiquarian Doctor, An. *Thomas Amory.* An antiquarian doctor's sermon on an antiquated subject ... L. 1768.

Antiquarius. *John Loveday, D.C.L.* For many years a contributor to the "Gent. Mag.," under the signatures of "Antiquarius," "Academicus," "Vindex," "Scrutator," and others.

Antiquary, An. *Richard Thomson.* Chronicles of London Bridge. L. 1827, 1839.

Antiquary, An. *Alexander Maxwell Adams.* The Crawfurd peerage. Edinb. 1829.

Antiquary, An. *Samuel Pegge, LL.D.* Fitz-Stephen's description of the city of London, newly translated from the Latin original ... By ... : L. 1772.

Antiquary, An. *Col. Philip De la Motte.* The principal historical and allusive arms borne by families of the United Kingdom of Great Britain and Ireland. Collected by ... L. 1803.

Antiquary, An. *Thomas Wright.* Wanderings of ... L. 1861.

"Antiquary, The." *George Livermore.* The origin, history, and character of the New England Primer; being a series of articles contributed to the "Cambridge Chronicle" by ... Camb., Mass. 1849.

Antiquitatis Conservator. *Thomas Fisher, Esq., F.S.A.* The Crown Inn at Rochester, and its curious cellars, in the "Gent. Mag.," vol. 59, p. 1185.

Antonelli, Giuseppe. *Humphry Sandwith.* The hekim bashi; or, the adventures of ... a doctor in the Turkish service. L. 1864.

Antony. *Antoine Nicolas Béraud.* Guido Reni, 1833; Le Gars, 1834; Lélia, 1834; La Lescombat, 1841. Paris.

Anvil, Sir John. — *Crowley.* A manufacturer, the "Sir John Anvil" of Addison's "Spectator."

Ape. *Mons. Pellegrini,* in his contributions to "Vanity Fair" (L.).

Apex. *William A. Brewer,* in his contributions to "The Herald" (St. Joseph, Mo.).

Apostle of Temperance. *Rev. Theobald Mathew.*

Aptommas, Mr. *Mr. Thomas,* the harpist. A history of the harp. N.Y. 1864.

Aquila. *Samuel Alexander.* Serious thoughts on the fall and restoration of man ... By ... L. 1814.

Aquilius. *John Wilson.* Horæ Catullianæ, in "Blackwood's Magazine." Vol. 61, p. 374, etc.

Aq—s, Vive Valeque. *Rev. John Eagles.* — See "Blackwood's Magazine," vol. 78, p. 72. Also "Vive Valeque."

Aqvaticvs, Mercvrivs. *John Taylor,* the Water-poet. M. A.; or, the water-poet's answer to all that hath, or shall be writ by Mercvrivs Britanicvs. L. 1643.

Arachnophilus. *Adam White.* A contribution towards an argument for the plenary inspiration of Scripture ... L. 1851.

Arbitrator, An. *T. H. Williams.* Employers and employed. Manchester, 1856.

Arc, Gaston d'. *Maurice Champion.* Les inondations en France depuis le VIᵉ siècle jusqu'a nos jours ... Paris, 1858-64.

Archæologist, An. *Frederick William Fairholt, F.S.A.* Rambles of ... among old books and in old places ... L. 1871.

Archæologist, An. *Henry Noel Humphreys.* Stories by an archæologist and his friends. L. 1856.

Archæus. *Michael Aislabie Denham.* Antiquarian discoveries at Carleburg, County Palatine of Durham, A.D. 1856 ... Durham, 1856.

Archæus. *John Sterling.* Hymns of a hermit, in "Blackwood's Magazine,"

vol. 47, p. 80, etc. ["Archæus" was Sterling's signature in "Blackwood."]

Archard, Eliza. *Mrs. E. A. Conner,* in her contributions to "Truth" (N.Y.).

Archdeacon, The. *Rev. Edward Edwards.* Pity upon the poor. Preached ... in St. Mary's Church, Brecon ... By ... L. 1802.

Archdeacon of St. Alban's, The. *Samuel Horsley, D.C.L.* Letters from ... in reply to Dr. Priestley ... L. 1784.

Archer. *George A. Stockwell.*

Architect, An. *John Carter, F.A.S.* "In 1798, a series of communications was commenced in this miscellany [the 'Gent. Mag.'] under the title of 'Pursuits of architectural innovation' (1798-1817), with the signature of 'An Architect.'" These were universally ascribed to Mr. Carter.

Architect, An. *W. Bardwell.* Account of ancient and modern Westminster. By ... L. 1839.

Architect, An. *Arthur William Hakewill.* An apology for the architectural monstrosities of London ... By ... L. 1835.

Architect, An. *Christopher Davy.* Architectural precedents. L. 1840.

Architect, An. *Joseph Woods, Esq.* Letters of ... from France, Italy, and Greece. L. 1828.

Architect, An. *John Burley Waring.* Poems. By ... L. 1858.

Arco, Ciu D'. *Giuseppe Torelli.* C. de Cavour: commémoration ... Traduit de l'Italien. Paris, 1861.

Arcturus. *Mrs. Catharine Stratton Ladd,* one of the *noms de plume* under which she has contributed tales, sketches, essays, and poems to various journals.

Ardboe. *Gen. F. F. Millen,* in his contributions to various periodicals.

Arden, Henry T. *Henry Thomas Arnold.* Princess Charming; or, the bard, the baron, the beauty, the buffer, and the bogey. L. 1850.

Arden, Hope. *Mrs. R. A. Brennan.* Her heart belongs to me. Ballad. B. 1872.

· Ardesier-Macdonald, Charles. *Andrew K. H. Boyd,* who published in "Fraser's Magazine" a number of essays which appeared in 1860 under the title of "Recreations of a Country Parson."

Aretophilos. *Alexander Dalrymple.* Extracts from [G. Wither's] "Juvenilia," etc. Edited by A. L. 1785.

Argonaut. *Edwin D. Brickwood.* The arts of rowing and training ... By A. L. 1866.

Argonaut. *John Etches.* An authentic statement of all the facts relative to Nootka Sound ... L. 1790.

Argus. *Frederic James Prouting*, in his contributions to various English periodicals.

Argus. *Irwin Willes*, a sporting writer for "The Morning Post." L. He also signs "Argus the Exile."

Ariel. *Rev. Stephen Fiske*, in his contributions to "The New York Leader."

Ariel. *Buckner H. Payne.* The negro: what is his ethnological status ... Cin. 1867.

Ariosto of the North, The. *Sir Walter Scott.*

Aristarchus, Anti-Blomfieldianus. *Edmund Henry Barker.*

Aristénète. *François Félix Nogaret.* Les compères et les bambins. Paris, 1807.

Aristide. *Victor Marie Hugo.* Les Tu et les Vous, a political satire contributed to "Le Conservateur Littéraire" (Paris).

Aristides. *Francis William Blagdon.* In 1805, he suffered an imprisonment of six months in the King's Bench, as the author of a suppressed pamphlet, with the signature "Aristides," reflecting on the naval administration of Earl St. Vincent.

Aristides. *Noah Webster.* — See "A Federalist."

Aristides. *Alexander Contee Hanson.* Considerations on the proposed removal of the seat of government ... Annapolis, 1786.

Aristides. *Thomas L. McKenney.* Essays on the spirit of Jacksonism ... P. 1835.

Aristides. *William P. Van Ness.* An examination of the various charges exhibited against Aaron Burr, Esq. Wash., D.C. 1804.

Aristides. *Thomas Wilson Dorr.* Political frauds exposed ... Providence, R.I. 1838.

Aristippus. *John Gilbert Cooper.* Epistles to the great, from ... in retirement. L. 1757.

Aristobulus. *Rev. Thomas Woolston.* A letter to Dr. Bennet on the Quakers ... By ... L. 1720.

Aristobulus. *James Turner.* Thoughts on mixt communion ... Coventry, Eng. 1773.

Aristocles. *Samuel Johnson, D.D.* Ethices elementa; or, the first principles of moral philosophy ... B. 1746.

Aristocrat, An. *John Lettsom Elliot.* A letter to the electors of Westminster. L. 1850.

Aristocratic Tout. A name assumed by *T. Wood*, a sporting writer.

Aristogeiton. *Rev. P. Frazer.* An address to Baptists of all denominations, on the tenets of their religion. By ... L. 1837.

Aristophanes. *Arthur Boyrie.* Potter's field; or, the gentleman with the black humor. A tragedy. S. F. 1873.

Arkwright, Peleg. *David L. Proudfit.* Love among the gamins, in the "Daily Graphic" (N.Y.).

Arley. *Miles Peter Andrews.* His signature to poetry in "The World." L. 1788.

Arlington. *Robert M. Baxter*, in the New York "Star."

Armand. *Friedrich Armand Strubberg.* Ralph Norwood. Hannover, Cassel, 1860.

Armateur, L. M. B. *Louis Marie Prudhomme.* Dictionnaire universel, geographique ... de la France. Paris, 1804–05.

Armenian in Ireland, An. *Edm. Sexton Pery.* Letters ... to his friends at Trebisond ... L. 1757.

Army Chaplain, An. *Rev. Joseph Cross.* Camp and field: papers of ... 1863. Macon, 1864.

Army Surgeon, An. *Thomas T. Ellis.* Leaves from the diary of ... 1861–62. N.Y. 1863.

Armytage, Dudley. *William E. A. Axon.* Shakespeare's house. Glasgow, 1868.

Arnett, John Andrews. *John Hannett.* Bibliopegia; or, the art of bookbinding. L. 1835, 1837.

Arnold, A. *Alfred Salomons.* The Count of Talavera, from the Dutch of J. van Lennep. By A. A. L. 1880.

Arnold, Birch. *Mrs. J. M. D.* or *A. E. Bartlett.* Until the day break. P. 1877.

Arnold, Eric. *Henrietta Matson.* Acton; or, school and college days. 1882.

Arouet. *Joseph Brown Ladd*, the most of whose poems were addressed, under this signature, to "Amanda," a name by which he designated the young lady to whom he was attached.

Arp, Bill. *Charles H. Smith.* A side show of the Southern side of the war. N.Y. 1866.

Arpinas, Laurea. *Charles Kelsall.*

Arr, E. H. *Mrs. Ellen H. Rollins.* Old-time child-life. P. 1880.

Arrelsee. *Robert L. Cope.* The life, confessions, and adventures of Albert Teufel. Doylestown, P. 1867.

Arria. *Mrs. Eliza Lofton (Phillips) Pugh*, who published, under this *nom de plume*, short sketches, literary and political, in the New York "World," the New Orleans "Times," and other journals.

Arriala, Ramon de. *Mariano José de Larra.* Un desafio: drama... Madrid,1834.

Artist, An. *Lester A. Roberts* (?). Hugo Blanc, the artist: a tale of practical and ideal life. By... N.Y. 1867.

Artist, An. *George William Novice.* Lights in art: a review of ancient and modern pictures. By... Edinb. 1865.

Artist, An. *J. Beugo* (?). Poetry, miscellaneous and dramatic. By... Edinb. 1797.

Artist, An. *Mrs. Elizabeth Murray.* Sixteen years of an artist's life in Morocco, Spain, etc., 1842–58. L. 1859.

Artist, An. *Paul Kane.* Wanderings of... among the Indians of North America... L. 1859.

Artlove, Sir Andrew. *John Dennis.* A free consideration and confutation of Sir J. Edgar. By Sir A. A. L. 1791.

Arundell, Harris. *William Arundell Harris Arundell.* The fall of Sebastopol: a poem. By... L. 1855.

Ashe, Tom. *Jonathan Swift, D.D.* ... the dying speech of... whose brother, the Rev. Dillon Ashe, was nicknamed Dilly. 1711.

Ashton, Warren T. *William Taylor Adams.* Hatchie, the guardian slave; or, the heiress of Bellevue. A tale of the Mississippi and the South-west. B. 1853.

Asiaticus. *John Scott Waring.* Letters to the right honourable Henry Dundas on his inconsistency as the minister of India. L. 1792.

Asmodei, Count. *Count Vittorio Amadeo Alfieri.* The generous husband ... containing... the genuine memoirs of Count Asmodei. 1771.

Asmodeus. *Thomas Nichols* (?). Asmodeus in New York. N.Y. 1868.

Asmodeus. *Thaddeus W. Meighan* (?). The Jenny Lind mania in Boston; or, a sequel to Barnum's Parnassus... B. 1850.

Asmodeus Secundus. *Charles Sotheran.* Author of Percy Bysshe Shelley as a philosopher and reformer... N.Y. 1876.

Asmus. *Matthias Claudius.* Asmus omnia sua secum portans; oder, Werke des Wandsbecker Boten. Wandsbeck, 1774–1812.

Aspirant, An. *James Beresford.* Bibliosophia; or, book-wisdom. By... L. 1810.

Assistant Librarian, An. *Thomas Mason.* The free libraries of Scotland. By... Glasgow, 1880.

Assistant Secretary of State, The. *Pennock Pusey.* Statistics of Minnesota

for 1869: being the first annual report of... St. Paul, 1870.

Astarte. *Mrs. Ann Olivia Adams.* Poems. N.Y. 1865.

Astell, Hon. Edward. *Jane Timbury.* The male coquette; or, the history of the Hon. E. A. L. 1770.

Aston, Tony. *Anthony Aston.* A brief supplement to Colley Cibber, Esq., his lives of the late famous actors and actresses. By... L. 1747.

Astronomer Royal, The. *Sir George Biddell Airy.* Lunar motion. [By Jelinger Cookson Symons.] With letters from... L. 1856.

Asyncritus. *J. E. Howard.* The inward light. L. 1839.

Atall, Peter. *Robert Waln, Jr.* The Hermit on America... 1st and 2d series. P. 1819, 1821.

Atherton, Harper. *Frank Fowler.* Adrift; or, the rock in the South Atlantic... L. 1861.

Atom, Ann. *Miss Jeanette R. Haderman.* Against the world. B. 1873.

Attaché. *Mme. Frances Erskine (Inglis) Calderon de la Barca.* Attaché in Madrid, 1853–54. N.Y. 1856.

Attalus. *William Mudford.* The five nights of St. Albans. L. 1829.

Atticus. *Richard Heber,* in Dibdin's "Bibliomania."

Mr. Dibdin says of him, "Atticus unites all the activity of De Witt and Lomenie with the retentiveness of Magliabechi and the learning of Le Long... Yet Atticus doth sometimes sadly err. He has now and then an ungovernable passion to possess more copies of a book than there were ever parties to a deed, or stamina to a plant, and therefore I cannot call him a duplicate or a triplicate collector... But he atones for this by being liberal in the loan of his volumes. The learned and curious, whether rich or poor, have always free access to his library."

Atticus. *William Maccall.* He contributed to the London "Critic" [about 1845] many papers and reviews, generally employing the signature "Atticus."

Atticus. *Thomas Cooke.* The letters of... as printed in the "London Journal," in 1729 and 1730, on various subjects... L. 1731.

Atticus. *Richard Fitzwilliam, 7th Viscount Fitzwilliam.* Lettres d'Atticus... L. 1811.

Atticus. *De Witt Clinton.* Remarks on the proposed canal from Lake Erie to the Hudson River. N.Y. 1816.

Atticus. One of the pseudonyms adopted by *Junius* (*q.v.*).

The letters signed "Atticus" and "Brutus" relate chiefly to the growing disputes with the American colonies. — WADE, "Junius."

The first of these letters appeared in "The Public Advertiser," Aug. 19, 1768.

Atticus Secundus. *Joseph Bolles Manning.* Junius unmasked; or, Lord George Sackville proved to be Junius... B. 1828.

Atticus Secundus. *John MacDiarmid.* Letters of Junius, with preliminary dissertations and copious notes. By A. S. L. 1822.

Attorney, An. *Sir George Stephen.* — See "Caveat Emptor."

Attorney, An. *Samuel Warren.* Adventures of... in search of practice. L. 1839.

Attorney, An. *William Muir.* Letter to the law practitioners of Scotland on the attorney tax. Edinb. 1833.

Attorney-at-Law, An. *J. C. Wells.* My Uncle Toby: his table-talks and reflections. By... Cin. 1875.

Aubigny, D'. *Jean Marie Théodore Bauduin.* Washington; ou, l'Orpheline de la Pennsylvanie: melodrame en trois actes, etc. Paris, 1815.

Auctioneer, An. *G. Robins (?).* Professional excursions. By... L. 1843.

Audé, M. *Joseph Octave Delepierre.* Dissertation sur les idées morales des Grecs.

Audi Alteram Partem. *Lieut.-Gen. Thomas Perronet Thompson, F.R.S.*
"In 1848 he published a 'Catechism on the currency'; and in 1857–58–59 weekly letters to his constituents, under the title of 'Audi Alteram Partem,' mainly on the treatment of the native army and people of India."

Auer, Adelheid von. *Charlotte von Cosel.* Im Labyrinth der Welt. 1879.

Augspur. *Henry J. M. Sampson*, in "Fun's Prophet."

Augur. *William Blake.* America: a prophecy, 1793; Europe: a prophecy, 1794.

Augur. *Henry Mort Feist.* The racing prophet. L. 187–. Also in "London Life."

Augur. One of the pseudonyms attributed to *Junius* (*q.v.*).
The letter thus signed is dated Sept. 8, 1769, and reprobates the abusive language of the ministerial writers.

Auguste. *Kathinka Zitz.* — See "Zianitzka, K. Th."

Augustsohn, W. *Wilhelm von Kotzebue.* Zwei Sünderinnen. 18—.

Aunet, Léonie d', Madame. *Mme. Auguste François Biard.* Le voyage d'une femme au Spitzberg. Paris, 1854.

Aura. *William Gale*, in the London "Morning Advertiser."

Aura. *Mary Catharine Irvine.* Ashburn: a tale. L. 1857.

Aurelius. *John Gardner.* A brief consideration of the important services... which recommend Mr. Adams for the presidency... B. 1796.

Aurelius Prudentius, Americanus. *Samuel Mather*, of Boston. The sacred minister... B. 1773.

Austin, the late Arthur. *Prof. John Wilson.* Lights and shadows of Scottish life... Edinb. 1822.

Austin, Miss Betty. *Miss Eliza Howard Austin*, "better known as 'Miss Betsy Austin.' Amusing incidents are chronicled of her in the pages of Marryat's 'Peter Simple,' 'Tom Cringle's log,' and other naval authors."

Australie. *Mrs. Emily (Manning) Heron.* The balance of pain: and other poems. L. 1877.

Austro-Borealis. *Edward Josiah Stearns, D.D.* A platform for all parties. Balt. 1860.

Author, An. *William Warburton*, Bishop of Gloucester. A letter from... to a member of Parliament, concerning literary property. L. 1747.

Author, The. *Capt. — Clarke, R.M.* Angler's desideratum... with some new and valuable inventions by... from a practice of nearly half a century. Edinb. 1839.

Author, The. *Charles Edward Stewart.* Extracts from the regicide: an heroic poem... L. 1801.

Author, The. *William Edward Armitage Axon.* The tobacco question... considered... Revised by... 1871.

Author of "Modern Painters," The. *John Ruskin.* Modern painters.
To the editor of the "Weekly Chronicle," Letter signed... Sept. 23, 1843; also, Two letters from... in the "Artist and Amateur's Mag.," 1843–44; also, Danger to the National Gallery, in the "Times," Jan. 7, 1847; also, The Pre-Raphaelites. Letter to the editor of the "Times," May 13, 1851; also, The Pre-Raphaelite artists... "Times," May 30, 1851; also, The National Gallery, "Times," Dec. 29, 1852; all signed as above.

Author of "Susie L—'s Diary," The. *Miss Eliza Jane Cate.* She contributed many stories to "Peterson's Magazine," under the signature of "By the Author of Susie L—'s Diary."

Author of "The Life of Goethe," The. *George Henry Lewes.* Carlyle's Frederick the Great. By... In "Fraser's Magazine," December, 1858.

Authors of the "Dramatic Censor," The. *Francis Gentleman.* Bell's edition of Shakespeare's plays... By... L. 1774.

Autochthonos. *Edward Augustus Hopkins.*

Autocrat of the Breakfast Table. *Oliver Wendell Holmes*, who, under this *nom de plume*, contributed certain humorous papers to the "New England Magazine," in 1836, which he resumed some twenty years afterwards, in the "Atlantic Monthly."

Autograph. *Charles F. Coburn*, in the "Lowell Citizen."

Autolycus. *John Edwards*, in his contributions to the "Springfield Wheelmen's Gazette."

Autolycus. *Michael Aislabie Denham.* Odd names of places in the north of England. Durham, 1856.

Auton, C. *Augustus Hoppin.* Recollections of Auton house. B. 1881.

Avalanche, Sir Anthony. — *Blauvelt.* Fashion's analysis ; or, the winter in town : a satirical poem, by ... with notes, illustrations, etc. N.Y. 1807.

Avaline, Alfred d'. *André van Hasselt.* Essai sur l'histoire de la poesie française en Belgique. Bruxelles, 1838.

Avia. *Arthur S. Way(?).* The Odyssey of Homer done into English verse. By . : . L. 1880.

Avocat, Un. *Hon. Dominique Mondelet.* Traité sur la politique coloniale du Bas-Canada ... Montreal, 1835.

Avon, W. *William Kenrick.* A midsummer day's dream, and other poems. L. 1858.

Awkward Man, An. *F. L. Slous.* Leaves from the scrap-book of ... L. 1844.

Awl, Roby. *Robert Kirkwood.* — See "Jamie, Daft."

Axis. — See "Waverley."

Axtern, H. *Xavier Conté.* Mœurs et usages des Israélites, etc. Paris, 1858.

Aymar, Patterson. *Charles Knight*, in his contributions to "Knight's Quarterly Magazine."

Ayres, Alfred. *Dr. Thomas Embly Osmun.* The orthoëpist : a pronouncing manual, containing about 3,500 words. N.Y. 1880.

Azamat-Batuk. *Nicolas Léon Thieblin.* A little book about Great Britain. By ... L. 1870. Also in his contributions as war-correspondent of the "Pall Mall Gazette," 1870.

Azarias, Brother. *P. F. Mullany.* The development of English literature : the old English period. N.Y. 1879.

Azelée. *Mrs. Sarah C. (Smith) Yeiser*, whose contributions to the New Orleans "Crescent" were signed with this penname, and whose *nom de plume* of "Aunt Charity" is more familiar to Southern readers.

B.

B. *L. J. Bates*, ex-president of Detroit Bicycle Club ; an editorial writer of the "Detroit Post and Tribune."

B. *Rev. Robert Bland, B.A.*, in the "Greek Anthology."

"Those articles in the 'Greek Anthology' which were from his pen are distinguished by the signature B. Many of them had been published in a smaller previous work of his, entitled 'Translations chiefly from the Greek Anthology, with tales and miscellaneous poems.' L. 1806."

B. *Rev. William Copeland Borlase.* — See "Trinity Undergraduates."

B. *Braham, now a Christian.* — See Lamb's "Elia" : Imperfect Sympathies.

B. *Rt. Hon. George Canning, D.C.L.*, who "at Eton contributed to that celebrated display of rising talent entitled the 'Microcosm,' published in weekly numbers, from Nov. 6, 1786, to July 30, 1787. The essays signed 'B,' and a poem entitled 'The Slavery of Greece,' are the contributions of Mr. Canning."

B. *Bryan Waller Procter*, in the London "Literary Gazette."

B. *Rev. George Burden Bubier.* Hymns and sacred songs for Sunday-schools and social worship. Edited ... Manchester, 1855.

B. *Samuel Finley Breese Morse.* The present attempt to dissolve the American Union, a British aristocratic plot. By ... N.Y. 1862.

B. *William Black.* Readings by starlight, in the "Evening Star," signed "B."

B. *Oliver Bell Bunce.* Reconstruction of the Union. N.Y. 1862.

B. *A. Broderick.* Rhymes with a reason. By ... L. 1857.

B., Serjeant. *Robert Butler.* Narrative of the life and travels of ... Edinb. 1823.

B., A. *A. Bayne.* An introduction to the knowledge and practice of thoro' bass ... Edinb. 1717.

B., A. *Anne Beattie.* Songs in the desert. By ... Manchester, 1845.

B., A., Esquire. *Jonathan Swift, D.D.* A letter to the king at arms. 1721.

B., Don A. *Capt. Alexander Bruce.* A discourse of a cavalier gentleman . . . 1706.

B., A. B. *A. B. Braley.* Bosh about Bacon. By . . . In the "Sunday Telegraph" (Milwaukee, Wis.), May 20, 1883; also, The Bacon cranks . . . In the same paper, June 10, 1883.

B., A. C. *Amos C. Barstow.* Letters [from Europe]. 1873, n.p. n.d.

B., A. C. *Arthur Coke Burnell.* Specimens of S. Indian dialects. Collected . . . 1873.

B., A. G., Jr. *Albert Gallatin Browne, Jr.* In memoriam J. W. B. (*i.e.*, John W. Browne). B. 1860.

B., A. K. H. *Andrew Kennedy Hutchison Boyd.* The critical essays of a country parson. L. 1865.

B., A. L. *Mrs. Anna Letitia Barbauld.* Hymns in prose for children. By . . . L. 1781.

B., A. M. *A. M. Barkly.* Revised list of the ferns of South Africa. Cape Town, 1875.

B. B. *Caroline Oliphant*, the Baroness Nairn, in numerous fugitive poems contributed to Smith's "Scottish Minstrel," etc.

B. B. *Rev. William Stabback Johns* and *W. M. Rogers.* The fall of Alba. "Helston Gram. School Mag.," 1852.

B. B. *Benjamin Franklin.* A modest inquiry into the nature and necessity of a paper currency. P. 1729.

B., B. *Bernard Barton.* Triplets for the truth's sake. L. 1842.

B. B., The Hon. *Joseph Green, Esq.* Entertainment for a winter's evening . . . By me . . . the Hon. B. B., Esq. B. 1795.

B., Beatrice. *Miss Beatrice Biddle*, society editor of "The World" (N.Y.).

B., Betsy. *Mrs. Mary Therese Austin*, in her contributions to the "Argonaut" and the "Overland Monthly" (San Francisco, Cal.).

B., B. H. *Rev. Beaver Henry Blacker, M.A.* Gloucestershire notes and queries. Edited by . . . L. 1879.

B. B. M. A. C. [Black Balled Member of the Apollo Club, Son of Vermont]. *Henry Stevens.*

B., C. *C. Bullock.* Breaches in the family fireside. By the late Hugh Stowell . . . Edited . . . L. 1865.

B., C. *Mrs. C. (Bickersteth) Wheeler.* Dawn and sunrise . . . L. 1860.

B., C. *Charles Bucke.* The Italians; or, the fatal accusation : a tragedy. L. 1819.

B., C. *Christopher Batty.* The Kendal hymn book. Kendal, 1757. By J.

A., C. B., etc. Thirty of the hymns were by C. B.

B., C. *Charles Bathurst.* Remarks on the differences in Shakespeare's versification . . . L. 1857.

B., C. *Charles Butler.* Undivided allegiance of Roman Catholics to their sovereigns. By . . . L. 1825.

B., Mme. C—— de la. *Mme. Frances Erskine (Inglis) Calderon de la Barca.* Life in Mexico . . . L. 1843.

B., C. A. *Cyrus Augustus Bartol.* Influence of the Ministry at Large in the city of Boston. By a spectator. B. 1836.

B., C. B. *Charles Brockden Brown.* Wieland; or, the transformation. N.Y. 1798.

B., C. C. *Mrs. C. C. Benton.* France and her people. P. 1872.

B., C. C. *Rev. Charles Cardale Babington.* Index to the Baker manuscripts by four members of the "Cambridge Antiquarian Society" (J. J. S., C. C. B., etc.). 1848.

B., C. E. *C. E. Bowen.* Sybil and her live snowball . . . L. 1865.

B., C. F. *Charles F. Briggs.* Seaweeds from the shores of Nantucket. B. 1853.

B., C. J., Roman Catholic priest of Atherstone. *Rev. C. J. Bowen.* Hidden joy. Compiled . . . Derby, 1869.

B., C. T. *Rev. Charles Timothy Brooks, A.M.* Roman rhymes : . . . Newport, R.I., Aug. 27, 1869. Camb., Mass. 1869.

B., D. *Deodatus Bye*, in "Gent. Mag.," May, 1817, p. 445.

B., D. *Daniel Bagot.* Original hymns . . . Dublin, 1858.

B., D. *Daniel Benham.* Some account of the village of Tadley in Hampshire, 1862.

B., D. W. *D. W. Bartlett*, in the New York "Independent."

B., E. *Edward Burney*, in Lamb's "Elia"; Valentine's Day.

B., E. *Elias Brockett.* The advocate : a defence of the B. of Lichfield and Coventry . . . [Ironical.] L. 1732.

B., E. *Rev. Evelyn Bartow, M.A.* Bartow genealogy . . . [Balt 1878.]

B., E. *Edward Brooke.* A catalogue of modern law books . . . L. 1794.

B., E. *Rev. Edward Bentham.* A certain proposal of a certain little tutor . . . L. n.d.

B., E. *Rev. Edward Budge.* The city of God . . . L. 1850.

B., E. *Ezekiel Bacon, LL.D.* The gathered alumni of Yale to their Alma Mater, by a graduate of 1794. New Haven, 1846.

B., E. *Edward Bickersteth, D.D.* A

help to the study of the Scriptures. L.
1815.

B., E. *Miss Elizabeth Blower.* Maria:
a novel. L. 1785.

B., E. *Mrs. Ethel Lynn Beers.* The
picket guard; or, all quiet along the Potomac to-night, in "Harper's Weekly"
for November, 1861.

B., E. *Edward Brotherton.* The present state of popular education in Manchester and Salford ... Manchester, n.d.

B., E. *Mrs. E. Babington.* Selections
from the poems of C. Elliott. With a
memoir ... 1873.

B., E. *Elizabeth Bentley.* Stanzas on
Lord Nelson's death ... 1806.

B., E. *E. Bibby.* Thoughts in verse.
L. 1873.

B., E., D.D. *Edward Burton, D.D.*
The holy oblation ... By an Anglo-
Catholic priest. L. 1848.

B., E. C. *E. B. Christy.* G. Christy's
"Ethiopian Joke Book." Edited ...
1858.

B., E. C. C. *E. C. C. Baillie.* The
way of the wilderness, and other poems.
L. 1862.

B., E. E. *Miss Emma Elizabeth Brown,*
"author of the many charming sketches
and dainty little poems which have appeared over the signature of 'B., E. E.'"

B., E. F. *E. F. Bevan.* Songs of
Eternal Life. Trans. ... L. 1858.

B., E. G. *Edward George Ballard,
Esq.,* who "made many communications,
chiefly in verse, to a variety of periodicals, among which were the 'Literary
Chronicle' and the 'Imperial Magazine.' These were signed with his initials, 'E. G. B.'" He also wrote for the
"Gent. Mag." under the same signature.

B., E. H. *Rev. Edward Henry Bickersteth.* Poems and songs. L. 1848.

B., E. H. *E. H. Blackwell.* A practical treatise on the power to sell land
for taxes. Enlarged ... 1864.

B., E. J. *Miss Elise Justine Bayard,*
in "The Literary World," "The Knickerbocker."

B., E. J. *Mrs. E. J. Burbury.* The
trust. 1849.

B., E. L. *Edward Laman Blanchard.*
John [Hunt's] birthday ... Aug. 28,
1875. A birthday ode ... L. 1875.

B., E. L. *Sir Edward George Earle
Lytton Bulwer-Lytton,* Baron Lytton. The
lady of Lyons; or, love and pride: a play
... L. 1843.

B., E. M. *E. R. and E. M. Bliss.*
Three months in the Orient. Edited ...
1875.

B., E. O. *Mrs. E. O. Bull.* A sequel
to Mrs. Sherwood's questions for a little
child. By ... L. 1848.

B., E. S. *E. S. Burnaby.* John Bryant; or, the stag hunt: a true tale.
1868.

B., E. S. H. *Miss E. S. H. Bagnold.*
A handy book of English spelling ...
L. 1870.

B., E. V. *Hon. Mrs. Eleanor Vere
(Gordon) Boyle.* Child's play. Seventeen drawings, by ... L. 1852.

B., E. W. *E. W Baärnhielm.* Archibald Hamilton. B. 18-.

B., E. W. *Rev. Edward Waller Bar-
ker(?).* Vigilemus et oremus ... L.
1876.

B., F. *Francis Bourdillon.* Admission free. L. 1871.

B. F. *Edward Claudius Herrick,
A.M.* An answer to the Bible reader, No.
II., of Henry Jones, New York ... New
Haven, 1844.

B., F. *Francis Bowen, LL.D.* Berke-
ley and his philosophy. From the
"Christian Examiner" for July, 1838.
Camb., Mass. 1838.

B., F. *Sir Francis Beaufort.* Klint's
sailing directions for the Baltic. Edited ... 1854.

B., F. *F. Bayley.* The origin and
object of Roman Catholic doctrines ...
By a County Court Judge ... L.
1875.

B., F. N. *Frederick Napier Broome.*
Lady Barker's station life in New Zealand. Preface by ... L. 1869.

B., G. *George Brewer.* Maxims of
gallantry; or, the history of Count de
Verney ... 1793.

B. G. *Dr. Robinson.* Miscellaneous
observations upon authors ancient and
modern. L. 1731–32.

B., G. *George Burnett.* The Scottish
bar fifty years ago. Sketches of Scott
[Robert Scott Moncrieff] and his contemporaries, with biographical notices,
by ... Edinb. 1871.

B., G. C. *Rev. George Clement Boase.*
Thoughts and memories in verse. L.
1876.

B., G. E. *Rev. George Edward Biber.*
The kingdom and church of Hawaii ...
By a friend of the Hawaiian church mis-
sion. L. 1865.

B., G. F. *Sir George Ferguson Bowen,
G. C. M. G.* Handbook for travellers in
Greece ... L. 1854.

B., G. H. *G. H. Budd.* An offering
to the Muses, worthy of being "a burnt
offering." By ... L. 1836.

B., G. S. *G. S. Bryan, Esq.* Biographical sketch of Charles Fraser. Charleston, 1857.

Forms a supplement to the catalogue of his pictures, by S. G., *i.e.*, Samuel Gilman, D.D.

B., G. W. *George William Blunt*, in his contributions to the "Evening Post" (N.Y.).

B., H. *Hamilton Busbey*, in his contributions to the "Turf, Field, and Farm" (N.Y.).

B., H. *Henry Blundell*. An account of the statues, busts, bas-reliefs, cinerary urns, and other ancient marbles and paintings at Nice. Liverpool, 1803.

B., H. *H. Boaz*. The angler's progress: a poem . . . 1820.

B., H. *Henry Blackwell*. The gentleman's tutor for the small sword . . . L. 1730.

B., H. *Horace Binney*. The leaders of the old bar of Philadelphia. P. 1866.

B., H. *H. Blomfield*. The old ploughman again! . . . L. 1835.

B., H. *Henry Baldwin*. St. James's chronicle. The yearly chronicle for 1761. L. 1762.

B., H. *Rev. Henry Bailey*. A sermon . . . after the death of C. M. Betts. 1859.

B., H. *Harry Burke*. A story of the fifth commandment. L. 1866.

B., H. *Henry Bewley*. Thoughts and suggestions submitted to the consideration of the Society of Friends. By . . . Dublin, 1859.

B., H. *Henry Ballow*. A treatise of equity. L. 1737.

B., H., B. H. *Henry Beaufoy, Esq.*, of Hampton-wick. Journal kept by H. B. H. B. during an aerial voyage . . . from Hackney to East Thorpe, Essex, Aug. 29, 1811. L. 1811.

B., H. C. *Henry Clark Barlow, M.D.* God's temple-throne: a hymn. Roma, 1855.

B., H. E. *Sir Henry Edward Bunbury, Bart.* Narratives of some passages in the great war with France from 1799 to 1810. L. 1854.

B., H. N. W. *Harriet Newell Woods Baker*. Edith Withington: a book for girls . . . By . . . n.p. 1871.

B., H. R. F. *Henry Richard Fox Bourne*. J. S. Mill: notices of his life and works. Edited . . . L. 1873.

B., H. W. *Sir Henry Williams Baker*. A daily text book . . . L. 1854.

B., H. W. *Henry William Ball*. Notes on Mr. W. Fowler of Winterton, and his works. Hull, 1869.

B., I. *John Beale*. Herefordshire orchards . . . L. 1724.

B., I. L. *Mrs. Isabella L. (Bird) Bishop*. Notes on old Edinburgh. Edinb 1869.

B., J. *John Blanch.* — See "A Gentleman in Gloucestershire."

B., J. *John Charles Brooke.*

B., J. *Jeremy Bentham*. The ballot: a cure for the ballotophobia . . . Prescribed to H. Brougham. L. 1830.

B., J. *J. Bentley*. Banking: how to make it safe and profitable. L. 1858.

B., J. W. *Inglis*. Book-keeping . . . Manchester, 1871.

B., J. *John Blackburn*. The cat's pilgrimage . . . of J. N. Froude. With illustrations by . . . n.p. 1870.

B., J. *Rev. John Besly*. Chronicle of the family of Percy, by W. Peeris. Edited . . . Newcastle, 1847.

B., J. *Joseph Besse*. A cloud of witnesses, proving that the Bishop of Lichfield and Coventry . . . hath misrepresented the people called Quakers. L. 1732.

B., J. *John Bartlett*. A collection of familiar quotations . . . Camb., Mass. 1860.

B., J. *James Burgh*. The dignity of human nature . . . By . . . L. 1754.

B., J. *James Budd*. Directions for entrance into a religious life . . . L. 1701.

B., J. *John Brazer, D.D.* The efficacy of prayer, first published in the "Unitarian Advocate." B. 1832.

B., J. *J. Bragg*. Extracts on various subjects . . . L. 1862.

B., J. *Sir James Burrow*. A few thoughts upon pointing . . . L. 1768.

B., J. *Joseph Burton*. Gold and competition; or, the wailings of a commission man: a satire. Hull, 1863.

B., J. *James Beezley*. A letter to Dr. Formey, F.R.S. . . . L. 1776.

B., J. *Miss Jane Belknap*. Life of Jeremy Belknap, D.D. . . . N.Y. 1847.

B., J. *Rev. John Baylie*. Life, the day for work . . . L. 1854.

B., J. *James Buckridge*. The lives of the most eminent modern painters . . . L. 1754.

B., J. *J. Backhouse*. A memoir of Deborah Backhouse of York. York, 1828.

B., J. *John Budge*. Memoir of John Dunstone, who was blind forty-four years, till his death, in 1856. L. 1857.

B., J. *Rev. John Barrow*. Memoir of Sir J. Barrow, by Sir G. T. Staunton, Bart. Edited . . . 1852.

B., J. *Jane Bewick*. A memoir of Thomas Bewick. Edited . . . 1862.

B., J. *John Broughton.* Miscellanies in prose and verse . . . of Thomas Chatterton. Edited . .

B., J. *Jonathan Barrett.* Observations on endowments for charitable purposes. L. 1852.

B., J. *James Bateman.* The Oxford crisis . . . By a member of Magdalen College, Oxford. L. 1845.

B., J. *Joseph Bentley.* Politics made easy for Englishmen. L. 1859.

B., J. *John Bellows.* Ritualism or Quakerism? Being remarks on a pamphlet by J. W. C[udworth], entitled "Quakerism and the Church." L. 1870.

B., J. *Mrs. J. B. Blackburne.* Scenes of animal life and character . . . L. 1862.

B., J. *Joseph Barker.* Self-abasement and self-exaltation . . . Wortley, 1845.

B., J. *John Budge.* Some observations on important subjects . . . Camborne, 1846.

B., J. *Rev. John Badcock.* Thoughts on the building . . . of a . . . church at Summer-town, near Oxford . . . Oxf. 1832.

B., J., Nottingham. *John Burton,* in the "Evangelical Magazine" for 1805.

B., J., a Friend of the Aborigines Protection Society. *John Burtt.* The young patriot, and other poems . . . Manchester, 1846.

B., J., A Servant of Jesus Christ. *James' Bardwood.* Hearts-ease in heart-trouble . . . L. 1691.
Ascribed also to John Bunyan.

B., J. A. *John Alexander Baxter.* A selection of hymns and psalms . . . 1830.

B., J. B. E. *Jean Baptiste Émile Bailliere,* in the "Journal de la Librairie."

B., J. C. *John Coxe Boyce.* Poetical productions of my youth. Birmingham, 1842.

B., J. D. *J. D. Bayly.* Our homeless poor . . . L. 1860.

B., J. E. *J. E. Babron.* A day by the fire, and other papers . . . By Leigh Hunt. Edited . . . B. 1881.

B., J. E. *J. E. Brown.* The Dove on the Cross, and other thoughts in verse. L. 1849.

B., J. E. *J. E. Babron.* Lamb's "Elia." Edited . . . L. 1866.

B., J. G. *John George Bellett.* Short meditations . . . Dublin, 1866.

B., J. G. H. *John George Hamilton Bourne.* The exile of Idria: a German tale . . . L. 1833. The name is also given *John Gervase Hutchinson Bourne.*

B., J. H. *Joseph H. Buckingham,* in the "Boston Courier," 1840–48.

B., J. Harcourt. *J. Harcourt Bland.* An apology for war . . . 1854.

B., J. I. *John Ilderton Burn, Esq.* "For several years he acted on the committee of the Labourers' Friend Society, and contributed many valuable papers, under the signature of 'J. I. B.,' to the pages of the monthly publication 'The Labourers' Friend.'"

B., J. J., B.D. *Rev. James John Douglas.* The voice of prayer . . . Aberdeen, 1873.

B., J. K. *J. K. Bangs,* in his contributions to "Life" (N.Y.).

B., J. K. *J. K. Bloomfield.* Patient Susie; or, paying the mortgage . . . Cin. 1873.

B., J. M. *John Montgomerie Bell.* Bell's (A. M.) lectures on conveyancing . . . Edited . . . 1876.

B., J. P. *Joshua P. Blanchard.* Plan for terminating the war, by division of the U. S. . . . 1861.

B., J. R. *James R. Ballantyne.* The Tarka-Sangraha of Annam Bhatta. Edited . . . 1851.

B., J. T. *John Trotter Brockett.* Hints on . . a typographical society in Newcastle-upon-Tyne. Newcastle, 1818.

B., J. T. *Joseph Tinker Buckingham.* The rosary. B. 1834.

B., J. V. *Rev. James Vila Blake.* "The morning stars sang together" . . . B. 1869.

B., J. W. *John W. Bell.* An anti-Shakespearian plea. By . . . In the Madison (Wis.) "State Journal," July 22, 1882.

B., Lucinda. *Miss Lucinda Bowser.* Angel visitants. L. 18–.

B., L. H. *Lyman Hotchkiss Bagg.* His signature in the English "Stamp Collector's Magazine" (Bath), and "The Philatelist" (Brighton), and in similar American prints.

B., L. L. *Louis Lucien Bonaparte.* Orthographie applicable aux dialectes de la langue d'Oil . . . L. 1867.

B., M. *Mona (Drew) Bickersteth.* Poems. Wales, 1856.

B., M. *Mary Brook.* Reasons for the necessity of silent waiting, in order to the solemn worship of God . . . By . . . L. 1774.

B., M. E. *Mrs. Mary E. Bennett.* Queer people . . . By . . . N.Y. 1872.

B., M. H. *Mrs. Mary Hewins Burnham,* in her contributions to the "Republican" (St. Louis, Mo.).

B., M. I. *M. I. Bromley.* Poems. L. 1861.

B., M. I. *M. I. Booth.* The wooing of King Sigurd. Illustrated . . . 1864.

B. O. W. C. [Brethren of the White

Cross.] *James de Mille.* A book for boys. B. 1873.

B., R. *Nathaniel Crouch.* — See "Burton, Richard."

B., R. *Richard Barrett.* The Bible not a dangerous book . . . 2d ed. Dublin, 1821.

B., R. *Robert Brett.* Devotions for the sick-room. L. 1843. — Prayers in the time of cholera. By . . . L. 1849.

B., R. *Robert Bloomfield.* The history of little Davy's new hat. L. 1815.

B., R. *Richard Brown.* Hospitallaria . . . L. 1837.

B., R. *Rev. Robert Bolton.* The Lighted Valley; or, the closing scenes of a beloved sister . . . N.Y. 1850.

B., R. *Richard Brooke.* Remarks and conjectures on the voyage of the ships "Resolution" and "Discovery" in search of a northerly passage from Kampschatka to England after the death of Capt. Cook . . . By . . . L. 1780.

B., R. *Robert Browning.* A selection from the poetry of E. B. Browning. Edited . . . 1866.

B., R., Gent. *Robert Blackwell.* The corn-dealer's companion . . . L. 1726.

B., R., a Servant of the Church of Christ. *Robert Barclay.* A Catechism and Confession of Faith . . . L. 1726.

B., R. C. L. *Robert Casper Lee Bevan.* Accommodated texts; or, texts and contexts. By . . . L. 1854.

B., R. H. *R. H. Blades.* Who was Caxton? . . . a monograph. L. 1877.

B., R. J. *Robert Jefferson Breckinridge, D.D.* Jesus and the Coming Glory . . . Edited . . . B. 1865.

B., R. L. *Rev. Robert Lewis Bampfield.* Our fisheries: exhortation and prayers concerning them. (Chiefly from Bishop Wilson.) Great Yarmouth, 1858.

B., S. *Sylvester Baxter,* when Mexican correspondent of the "Boston Herald."

B., S. *Samuel Birch.* Italian mediæval coins . . . By . . . L. 1845.

B., S. *Samuel Brewster.* A letter to the parishioners of St. B[otolph] A[ldgate], recommending parochial communion . . . L. 1701.

B., S. *Samuel Barker.* Miscellaneous observations upon authors ancient and modern. L. 1731–32.

B., S. E. *Sir Samuel Egerton Brydges, Bart.* Arthur Fitz-Albini: a novel. By . . . L. 1810.

B., S. G. *Sarah G. Bagley.* Biography of self-taught men, continued . . . B. 1846–47.

B., S. L. M. *S. L. M. Barlow.* Let-

ter of C. Columbus describing his first voyage . . . Edited . . . L. 1875.

B., S. O. *S. O. Beeton.* The works of Lord Bacon . . . With a . . . memoir of the author by . . . L. 1877.

B., T. *Rev. Thomas Belsham.* The Book of Common Prayer reformed . . . Edited . . . L. 1813.

B., T. *Rev. Thomas Barker, M.A.* The canticles pointed for Anglican chants . . . By an English presbyter . . . L. 1863.

B., T. *Thomas Bates.* A few words on the temperance question . . . L. 1877.

B., T. *Thomas Brightwell.* Journal of a tour . . . 1825, through Belgium . . . Norwich, 1828.

B., T. *Rev. Thomas Brett.* A letter shewing why our English Bibles differ so much from the Septuagint . . . By . . . L. 1743.

B., T. *Thomas Burtt.* Ode . . . L. 1859.

B., T. *Thomas Boosey.* Piscatorial reminiscences and gleanings by an old angler and bibliopolist . . . L. 1835.

B., T. *Thomas Branch.* Principia legis or equitatis: being an alphabetical collection of 20,000 maxims, principles or rules, definitions, and memorable sayings in law and equity. By . . . L. 1753.

B., T. *Thomas Bowdler.* Twelve anniversary sermons preached before the Society for the Propagation of the Gospel in foreign parts. Edited . . . L. 1845.

B., T., Minister of the Gospel. *Thomas Bradbury.* A mug-house song. L. 1717.

B., T. B. *Thomas Bagnall Baker.* A doctrinal catechism of the Church of England . . . By . . . L. 1840.

B., T. C. *Thomas Christopher Banks.* A letter to . . . Lord Brougham . . . signed . . . L. 1831.

B., T. M. *T. M. Baker.* The slave lover; or, pride humbled: a tale. B. 1848.

B., T. S. *Thomas Squire Barrett.* An examination of . . . argument à priori for the existence of a Great First Cause. By . . . L. 1869.

B., T. S. *T. Seymour Burt.* Monody on the death of H. R. H., the Duchess of Kent. By . . . L. 1861.

B., V. *Vincent Brooks.* Chromo lithographs. L. 18–.

B., W. *William Bigg.* The art of swimming. L. 1832.

B., W. *Walter Bagehot.* Bocastle. "The Spectator," Sept. 22, 1866.

B., W. *William Burge.* The choral service of the Anglo-Catholic church. L. 1844.

B., W. *Rev. William Bright.* English Church defence tracts. Edited by H. P. L. [Henry Parry Liddon] and W. B. L. 1872.

B., W. *William Bromfield.* The faith of the true Christian, and the primitive Quaker's faith. By ... L. 1725.

B., W. *William Blake.* The gates of Paradise. L. 1793.

B., W. *William Bruce, D.D.* An introduction to the scanning of the Greek metres ... By ... Belfast, 1823.

B., W. *William Boyne.* A manual of Roman coins ... L. 1865.

B., W. *William Bennett.* My mother's meetings ... Edited ... L. 1863.

B., W. *William Blades.* The rules of the Candlewick Ward Club... L. 1876.

B., W. *William Brown.* Sketch of the life and character of the late Dr. William Brown ... Edinb. 1854.

B., W., Gent. *William Brown.* Impiety and superstition exposed: a poetical essay ... Edinb. 1710.

B., W., Gent. *William Breton.* Militia discipline. By ... L. 1717.

B., W., Fowey. *William Browne.* A geological puzzle; the beach at Ready-Money Cove, Fowey: "Hardwicke's Science Gossip," 1869.

B., W., and J. R. *Walter Besant* and *J. Rice.* This son of Vulcan: a novel. L. 1876.

B., W. A. *William A. Brewer,* in his contributions to the "Journal of Commerce " (N.Y.).

B., W. B. *W. B. Buchanan.* Baltimore; or, long, long time ago. Balt. 1853.

B., W. B. *William Balfour Baikie.* List of books and manuscripts relating to Orkney and Zetland ... By ... Kirkwall, 1847.

B., W. B. *William Binnington Boyce.* Sketches of Protestant missionary societies, 1872–73. Compiled ... L. 1874.

B., W. D. *William D. Bickham,* correspondent of the " Cincinnati Commercial," Rosecrans' campaign . . . Cin. 1863.

B., W. F. *W. F. Bateman.* Instructions given to the guild of St. John the Evangelist, Upper Norwood, in the course of the year 1876. By ... L. 1877.

B., W. H. *Rev. William Hiley Bathurst.* Metrical musings; or, thoughts on sacred subjects in verse. L. 1849.

B., W. J. *W. J. Battersby.* A complete Catholic directory ... compiled ... L. 1836.

B., W. J. *William John Butler, M.A.* School prayers for morning and evening. Compiled ... Oxf. 1848.

B., W. J. E. *Rev. William James. Early Bennett.* Advent readings from the Fathers ... By ... Oxf. 1852.

B., W. S. *Wilfrid Scawen Blunt.* Lady Blunt's Bedouin tribes of the Euphrates ... Edited ... L. 1879.

B., W. W. *W. W. Beldene.* A tribute to the memory of Gen. George B. Boomer ... About 1865.

B*, le baron.** *Charles Doris.* Amours secrètes de Napoléon Buonaparte . . Paris, 1817.

B*, Henri.** *Honoré de Balzac,* in his contributions to " La Caricature " (Paris).

B**, Bishop.** *Bishop Lewis Bagot,* in Beloe's " Sexagenarian," I., 422, 2d ed. L. 1818.

B**, Lieut. Col.** *Henry Charles Bunbury.* The whist-player: laws and practice of short whist. L. 1857.

B*****, Lord.** *Frederick Richard Chichester,* Earl of Belfast. The farce of life: a novel, 1852; Wealth and labour: a novel, 1853; The county magistrate; Naples, political, social, and religious, 1856; The fate of folly, 1859. L.

B*****, Lord.** *Henry Brougham,* Lord Brougham. The country magistrate: a novel. L. 1854.

B——, The Right Honourable the Earl of. *Colin Lindsay,* third Earl of Balcarres. An account of the affairs of Scotland relating to the revolution in 1688. L. 1714.

B——, Lord. *Henry St. John,* Lord Viscount Bolingbroke. Lord Bolingbroke's three letters on patriotism. L. 1749.

B——, Lord. *Frederick Richard Chichester,* Earl of Belfast. Masters and workmen: a tale ... L. 1851.

B——, Prof. *Mark H. Beecher* or *William W. Benedict.* — See " P., Z.," or " Pundison, Zachariah."

B——, Sergeant. *Robert Butler.* Narrative of the life and travels of . . . Edinb. 1823.

B——, E. *Edmund Burke.* Mr. E. B.'s answer to his own speech on the 11th of February, 1780. L. 1780.

B——, E., D.D. *Edward Bentham, D.D.* The honor of the University of Oxford defended ... L. 1781.

B——, F——. *Sir Francis Bernard.* The causes of the present distractions in America explained ... B. 1774.

B——, J——. *Joanna Baillie,* in Beloe's " Sexagenarian," I., 409, 2d ed. L. 1818.

B——, J——, M.D. *William Temple.* A vindication of commerce and the arts ... 1859.

B——, R——, Esq. *Richard Bentley.*
A letter to R— B—, Esq., author of the
new comedy called "The Wishes." L.
1761.

B—e, Dr. *Matthew Baillie, M.D.*, in
Beloe's "Sexagenarian," I., 314, 2d ed.
L. 1818.

B—e, Earl of. *John Stuart*, third Earl
of Bute. A man of abilities for the Earl
of B—e; or, Scotch politics defeated in
America . . . L. 1766.

B—e, the Right Hon. Lord. *Frederick Calvert*, Lord Baltimore. — See
"Young Gentleman of Sixteen, A."

B—n, Ch—. *Charles Bateman.* An
enquiry into a late very extraordinary
physical transaction at E[to]n . . . L.
1758.

B — — — — — — — ke, L — — d. *Henry
St. John*, Lord Viscount Bolingbroke.
Speech upon the convention. To the
tune of "A cobbler there was." L. 1739.

Bab. *William Schwenck Gilbert.* The
"Bab" ballads. L. 1869.

Babble, Nicholas, Esq. *Edward
Long.* The "Prater." L. 1757.

This imitation of the "Spectator" was published under the direction of J. Holcombe. Edward Long was a contributor.

Babbler. *Alfred Trumble*, in his contributions to "The Sunday News" (N.Y.).

Babbler, The. *Hugh Kelly*, in Owen's
"Weekly Chronicle," the "Public Ledger," the "Royal Chronicle," etc.

Baboon, Lewis. *France.* — See
"Strutt, Lord."

Bach, Jenny. *Jenny Fischer.*

Bachelor, A. *James Mac Grigor Allan.* The last days of . . . an autobiography. L. 1863.

Bachelor, A. *Donald Grant Mitchell.*
Reveries of . . . N.Y. 1869.

Bachelor of Arts, A. *A. J. P. Marshall.* The Oxford undergraduate of
twenty years ago. L. 1874.

Bachelor of Divinity, A. *William
Josiah Irons.* An answer to the Right
Rev. Dr. Wiseman's letter entitled "Conversion." L. 1847.

Bachelor, The Mysterious. *Dana
Boardman Clark.*

Bachelor, The Travelling. *James
Fenimore Cooper.* The travelling bachelor; or, notions of the Americans. N.Y.
1856.

Backwoodsman, A. *Hon. Thomas
D'Arcy McGee.* The Crown and the Confederation . . . Montreal, 1864.

Backwoodsman, A. *Dr. William
Dunlop.* Statistical sketches of Upper
Canada, for the use of emigrants. L.
1832.

Baconian. *William W. Ferrier.* Who
wrote Shakespeare? By . . . In the
Angola (Ind.) "Herald" for March and
February, 1881.

Bagatelle. *A. G. Bagot.* Sporting
sketches at home and abroad. By . . .
L. 1879.

Bailey. *Frederick Douglass.*

Bailey, Junior. *William Stevens Robinson*, in the "Carpet Bag," 1852.

Baker, Frank, D.O.N. *Richard Francis Burton.* Stone talk (Λιθοφωνημα):
being some of the marvellous sayings of
a petral portion of Fleet Street, London,
to one Doctor Polyglott, Ph.D. By . .
[In verse.] L. 1865.

Baker, The Literary. *Caleb Jeacocke*,
the celebrated baker, who disputed so
much at the Robin Hood Society, where
he presided, and was the author of A
vindication of the moral character of the
apostle Paul . . . L. 1765.

Baker Poet, The. *Jean Reboul*, author of "Poésies." Paris, 1836.

Baldwin, Rev. Edward. *William
Godwin.* The Pantheon . . . gods of
Greece, 1806; Fables, ancient and modern, 1821. L.

Balfour, Clara. *Mrs. Felicia Dorothea (Browne) Hemans.* Modern Greece:
a poem. L. 1817.

Balfour, Felix. *Watts Phillips*, in
the "London Journal."

Ballantyne, Colin, R.N. *William
Dunlop, M.D.*, who wrote sketches of Indian life, and other papers for "Blackwood," over this signature; a *nom de
guerre* under which, it is said, he figured
in India during his controversies with
Buckingham.

Ballinasloe. *Frederick Taylor.* Confessions of a horse-coper. L. 1861. He
also contributed to "The Field" (London), under this signature.

Balloonist. *Alfred Ford.*

Ball's Bluff Prisoner, A. *W. C.
Harris.* Prison-life in the tobacco warehouse at Richmond. By . . . P. 1862.

Balscopo, Giovanni Battista. *John
Trotter, Jr.* Travels in Phrenologasto . . .
L. 1829.

Baltimore Trader, A. *George Standish.* Adventures of . . . on the coast of
the Pacific. P. 187–.

Balwhidder, Rev. Micah. *John Galt.*
The annals of the parish . . . Edinb.
1821.

Bank Crash, Esq. *George Dutton.*
The present crisis; or, the currency . . .
Rochester, N.Y., 1857.

Banker Poet, The. *Charles Sprague.*

Bantley, Doctor R. *John Arbuthnot.*

Critical remarks on Capt. Gulliver's travels. By . . . Camb. 1735.

Bantry, Ign. L. — See "The Catholic Bishop of Bantry."

Baptist, A. *Rev. Henry Burgess, LL.D.* The Bible Translation Society of the Baptists shown to be uncalled for and injurious: . . . By . . . L. 1840.

Baptistet. *Alphonse Daudet.* Lettres sur Paris, in the "Petit Moniteur," 1865.

Baragwaneth, Robin. *John Jeffery.* The wooden horse for the rounder and the horse without a head . . . Penzance.

Baragweneth, Barzillai. *Mrs. Charlott Champion (Willyams) Pascoe.* Wan an' aell, a Cornish drawel, as zung, zold, an spauken . . . Penzance, 1861.

Barbadoes Planter, A. *John Ashley.* The sugar trade . . . By . . . L. 1734.

Barbarc, Une. *Marie Sophie Schmidt Colban.* Lettres de . . . Paris, 18–.

Barbarossa. *John Scott.* The lost principle; or, sectional equilibrium . . . Richmond, 1860.

Barber, A. *Joseph Moser.* The meal-tub plot; or, remarks on the powder tax. By . . . L. 1795.

Barber, George. *George Duckett Barber Beaumont,* in his legal works.

Barber Poet, The. *Jacques Jasmin.*

Barbican, Geoffrey. *Richard Thomson.* Chronicles of London Bridge. L. 1827. — See "Antiquary."

Barclay, Sydney. *Mrs. Lydia Minturn Post.* Grace Barclay's diary . . . N.Y. 1867.

Bard. *George Monck Berkeley.* His signature in the "World," 1788.

Bard, The. *Edward Jerningham.* The British album, containing the poems of Della Crusca . . . The bard, etc. L. 1790.

Bard of Ayrshire, The. *Robert Burns.*

Bard of Hope, The. *Thomas Campbell.*

Bard of Memory, The. *Samuel Rogers.*

Bard of Olney, The. *William Cowper.*

Bard of Rydal Mount, The. *William Wordsworth.*

Bard of the Forest, The. *William Wickenden.* Prose and poetry. By . . . L. 1852.

Bard, Samuel A. *Dr. Ephraim George Squier.* Waikna; or, adventures on the Mosquito shore. L. 1854.

Bards of Epworth, The. *S. Wesley, Sen., S. Wesley, Jun., C. Wesley, and M. Wesley.* The bards of Epworth; or, poetic gems from the Wesley cabinet. L. 1856.

Bareacres, Hon. Botibol. *John Burley Waring.* Poems inspired by certain pictures at the Art Treasures Exhibition, Manchester, by Tennyson Longfellow Smith, of Cripplegate Within . . . Illustrated . . . Manchester, 1857.

Barebone, Issachar. —— *Ralphs* (?). The Protester . . . By . . . L. 1753.

Barebones, Caustic. *Thomas Bridges.* The first volume of a new translation of Homer's Iliad, adapted to the capacity of honest English roast beef and pudding eaters. By . . . a broken apothecary . . . L. 1762.

Barnacle. *A. C. Barnes.*

Barnacle, Capt. *Charles M. Newell.* Leaves from an old log. Péhe Nú-e, the Tiger Whale of the Pacific. B. 1877.

Barnaval, Louis. *Charles De Kay.* Poems. [Edited (or probably written) by Charles De Kay.]

Barnes. *Greville Fennell.* The rail and the rod; or, the tourist-angler's guide to waters and quarters thirty miles around London . . . L. 1867.

Barnivelt, Esdras, Apoth. *Alexander Pope.* A key to the lock . . . By . . . L. 1718.

Barnwell. *Robert Barnwell Roosevelt.* Game fish of the northern states of American and British provinces. N.Y. 1862.

Barrett, Lawrence. *Larry Brannigan.* A nom de théâtre.

Barrett, Mary. *Mary O. Nutting.* The story of William the Silent and the Netherland war, etc. 1555–1584. By . . . B. 1869.

Barrett, Walter, Clerk. *Joseph A. Scoville.* The old merchants of New York city, N.Y. 1861–64.

Barrington, F. Clinton. *Julius Warren Lewis.*

Barrister, A. *Sir James Mackintosh,* in Beloe's "Sexagenarian," II., 106. 2d ed. L. 1818.

Barrister, A. *Henry Jeremy.* An analytical digest of the reports of cases decided in the courts of common law . . . L. 1818.

Barrister, A. *James Maitland Hog.* Brief view of British colonial slavery Edinb. 1827.

Barrister, A. *Richard Power.* A comparative state of the two rejected money bills in 1692 and 1769 . . . Dublin, 1770.

Barrister, A. *Frederick Lawrence.* Culverwell v. Sidebottom . . . By . . . L. 1857.

Barrister, A. *Sir James Fitzjames Stephen.* Essays. By . . . L. 1862.

Barrister, A. *Charles Clark, Esq.* A few words on the subject of Canada. By ... L. 1837.

Barrister, A. *Right Hon. Sir John Barnard Byles.* Free trade and its so-called sophisms ... examined by ... L. 1850.

Barrister, A. *Edward Reynolds.* A guide to the law : for general use. By ... L. 1865.

Barrister, A. *John Macgregor.* "Go out quickly" (Luke 14:21). By ... L. 1855.

Barrister, A. *Richard Harris.* Hints on Advocacy ... By ... L. 1879.

Barrister, A. *James Sedgwick, Esq.* Hints to the public and the legislature on the nature and effects of Evangelical preaching. By ... L. 1808.

Barrister, A. *Barron Field.* Hints to witnesses in courts of justice. By ... L. 1815.

Barrister, A. *Isaac Espinasse.* A letter from Catiline to the surviving members of the constitutional and other societies of the year 1794 ... L. 1810.

Barrister, A. *William Johnson.* Letter to Joshua Spencer, Esq., occasioned by his thoughts on an union [between Great Britain and Ireland]. By ... Dublin, 1798.

Barrister, A. *Henry H. Joy.* Letter to ... Lord Lyndhurst on the appointment of sheriffs in Ireland ... By ... L. 1838.

Barrister, A. *Sir John Taylor Coleridge.* Notes on the Reform Bill ... L. 1831.

Barrister, A. *Sir John Joseph Dillon.* The question as to the admission of Catholics to Parliament, considered ... L. 1801.

Barrister, A. *Richard Fenton.* A tour in quest of genealogy ... L. 1811.

Barrister, A. —— *Forbes.* A trip to Mexico; or, recollections of a ten-months' ramble in 1849–50 ... L. 1851.

Barrister, Another. *Reader Wainwright.* Letters to a Protestant divine in defence of Unitarianism. By ... etc. L. 1824.

Barrister at Law, A. *Sir John Eardley Eardley Wilmot.* An abridgment of Blackstone's commentaries on the laws of England ... L. 1822.

Barrister at Law, A. *Sir Benjamin Hobhouse.* A treatise on heresy ... By ... L. 1793.

Barrister-at-Law of the Inner-Temple, A. *Edmund Bott.* A collection of decisions of the Court of King's Bench upon the poor laws ... By ... L. 1771.

Barrister of Lincoln's Inn, A. *E. Boodle.* The Gospels collated ... L. 1843.

Barrister of the Inner Temple, A. *Leonard Mac-Nally.* Acts passed in Parliament. L. 1786.

Barrister of the Inner Temple, A. *George Spence, Esq., Q.C.* The Code Napoléon; or, the French civil code, literally translated, by ... L. 1827.

Barrister of the Inner Temple, A. *Thomas Edlyne Tomlins.* A familiar, plain, and easy explanation of the Law of Wills ... L. 1785.

Barrister, A Retired. *C. Ambler.* A review of the proceedings and arguments in a cause in Chancery between James Fox, Esq., and R. Mackreth, Esq. ... L. 1792.

Barrow, Rev. S. *Sir Richard Phillips.* The poor child's library. Questions on the New Testament. Sermons for schools. L. 1812.

Barrow-Knight, A. *Rev. Stuteville Isaacson.* Barrow-digging by a Barrowknight, in six fyttes. L. 1844–45.

Barrowcliffe, A. J. *Albert Julius Mott.* Amberhill. L. 1856.

Barteville, Alexis. *Edmond de Manne.* Chansons. Paris, 1835.

Bartholomew-Lane Man, A. *Alexander Chalmers.* Strictures on improvements proposed near the Bank, "Gent. Mag.," December, 1802. p. 1110.

Barton, Fanny M. *Mrs. M. F. Butts.* Three girls. B. 18–.

Barton, J. A. G. *Shoshee Chunder Dutt.* Historical Studies. L. 1879.

Bashful Irishman, A. *William Frederick Deacon.* The exile of Erin; or, the sorrows of ... L. 1835.

Bashibazouk. *William Harding,* in his contributions to the "Clipper" (N.Y.).

Bashi-Bazouk, Our own. *William Makepeace Thackeray.* Letters from the East by ... "Punch," 1854.

Basil. *Richard Walker.* The legend of Cosmo ... By ... L. 1860.

Basilicus. *Edmund Lenthal Swift.* The ecclesiastical supremacy of the Crown proved to be the common law of England ... L. 1814.

Basilicus. *Rev. Lewis Way.* Thoughts on the scriptural expectations of the Christian Church ... L. 181–.

Basté. *Pierre Eugène Grangé.* Les enfants d'Adam et d'Ève. Paris, 1840.

Bates, President. *L. J. Bates,* ex-president of Detroit Bicycle Club, an editorial writer of the "Detroit Post and Tribune."

Bathoniensis. *Jonas Dennis, B.C.L.* A challenge to the Pope ... Bath, 1830.

Batkins, Jefferson Scattering. *Joseph Stevens Jones.* Plays, N.Y. 1857; Life of Jefferson S. Batkins, member from Cranberry Centre, B. 1871.

Bavius. *Dr. John Martyn.* Memoirs of the Society of Grub-Street. L. 1737.

These memoirs commenced on Thursday, Jan. 8, 1730, were continued once a week, and attained their 138th (and last) number on Aug. 24, 1732. To this publication we owe the "Gentleman's Magazine"; for Cave projected an improvement on it to be published once a month. The signature of "Bavius" belongs to Dr. John Martyn, and that of "Mævius" to Dr. Richard Russell; and those papers signed." A" are by Alexander Pope. But in Carruthers' "Life of Pope" (1857) it is conjectured that Pope had free admission to the journal under any guise, and that some signed "M" and "B" are by him, and also that there were other contributors. — HALKETT AND LAING.

Bayard. *Franklin J. Ottarsen.* New York editor.

Bayard of India, The. *Sir Charles Napier.*

Bayard, The Polish. *Prince Joseph Poniatowski.*

Bayle, Mr. *Rev. Henry Penneck, M.A.* Apostolical Succession, everything else and a few things beside . . . Penzance, 1842.

Bayley, Alphabet. *Frederic W. N. Bayley.* The new tale of a tub: an adventure in verse. N.Y. 1869.

Beadle. *John Hanson Beadle.* Western wilds, and the men who redeem them. Cin. 1877.

Beakitorius. *Benjamin Disraeli,* Earl of Beaconsfield. — See "Gladiolus."

Beardless Yankee, The. *Dana Boardman Clark.*

Beaseley. *Samuel Beazley.* The roué, L. 1828; The Oxonians: a glance at society, L. 1830.

Beatrice. *Anne Manning.* An English girl's account of a Moravian settlement in the Black Forest. L. 1858.

Beauchamp, Philip. *Jeremy Bentham.* Analysis of the influence of natural religion on the temporal happiness of mankind . . . L. 1822.

Beauchamp, Shelsley. *T. Waldron Bradley.* Grantley Grange: benedicts and bachelors. L. 1874.

Beaufort, John, LL.D. *John Thelwall.* The daughter of adoption: a tale of modern times. L. 1801.

Beaujolais. *Hans Busk.* Maiden-hours and maiden-wiles. Designed by . . . L. 1869.

Beaumont, Averil. *Mrs. Margaret Hunt.* Magdalen Wynyard; or, the provocations of a Pre-Raphaelite . . . L. 1872.

Beaumont, George. *George Duckett Barber Beaumont,* in his legal works.

Beaumont, Sir Harry. *Rev. Joseph Spence.* Moralities . . . L. 1753, previously printed in the "Museum"; and Crito; or, a dialogue on beauty, L. 1752. — Under this *pseudonym* he also published a letter from F. Attiret, a French missionary, containing "A particular account of the Emperor of China's gardens." L. 1752.

Beautiful and Unfortunate Young Lady, A. *Rev. Thomas Sedgwick Whalley.* The fatal kiss: a poem . . . L. 1781.

Beauty, A. *Mrs. Edwin James.* Wanderings of . . . N.Y. 1873.

Beaver, Barrington, Esq. *William H. G. Kingston.* Adventures of Dick Onslow among the Redskins . . . L. 1863.

Beccaria Anglicus. *Rev. Richard Wright.* Letters on capital punishments . . . L. 1807.

Bede, Adam. *Robert Evans.*

"Adam Bede himself was the authoress' own father, Mr. Robert Evans . . . His brother Samuel [was] the Seth of the novel . . . Elizabeth Tomlinson [was] Dinah Morris. A poor girl, Mary Voce, was Hetty." "The [London] Sunday Magazine."

Bede, Cuthbert, B.A. *Rev. Edward Bradley.* The adventures of Mr. Verdant Green, an Oxford freshman. L. 1857.

Bede, Seth. *Samuel Evans.* Seth Bede "the Methody": his life and labours; chiefly written by himself. L. 1859.

Bedott, Widow Priscilla P. *Mrs. Frances Miriam (Berry) Whitcher.* Widow Bedott papers. N.Y. 1867.

Bee, Hookanit, Esq. *S. R. Wigram.* Flotsam and jetsam: a cargo of Christmas rhyme. L. 1853.

Bee, Jon. *John Badcock.* The dramatic works of Samuel Foote. With remarks on each play, and an essay on the life, genius, and writings of the author by . . . L. 1830.

Bee Hunter, The. *Col. Thomas Bangs Thorpe.* Mysteries of the backwoods . . . P. 1846.

Bee-master, "The Times." *John Cumming, D.D.* Bee-keeping. L. 1864.

Beef Eater, A. *George Vasey.* Illustrations of eating . . . L. 1847.

Beefeater, Domestic Chaplain to Fill Potts. *Rev. John Allan.* The Lentiad; or, Peter the Pope, and his pioneers the Puseymen pummelled and pounded with a Hudibrastic cudgel . . . L. 1853.

Beelzebub. *H. Newton Goodrich.* "I too" . . . L. 1856.

Beggar Boy, A. *James Dawson Burn.* The autobiography of . . . L. 1855.

Belani, H. E. R. *Karl Ludwig Häberlin.* Der Heimathlose. 1835.

Belarius of Cymbeline. *Estwick Evans.* The first of a series of a work in six numbers, in favor of the constitutionality of a national bank. W. 1862.

Belkine, Ivan. *Alexandre Sergeiévitch Pouchkine* [French spelling of his name]. Boris Godounow: a dramatic poem. St. Petersburg, 1831.

Bell, Acton. *Anne Brontë.* The tenant of Wildfell Hall. L. 1848.

Bell, Currer. *Mrs. Charlotte (Brontë) Nicholls.* Jane Eyre : an autobiography. L. 1847.

When the Brontë sisters published their volume of poetry in 1846, under their respective pseudonyms, numerous parties made the mistake of thinking that they were three brothers. Among others was Miss Martineau, who addressed a letter to Charlotte Brontë, — " Currer Bell, Esq."

" Averse to publicity, we veiled our own names under those of Currer, Ellis, and Acton Bell; the ambiguous choice being dictated by a sort of conscientious scruple of assuming Christian names positively masculine, while we did not declare ourselves women, because — without at the time suspecting that our mode of writing and thinking was not what is called ' feminine,' — we had a vague impression that authoresses are liable to be looked on with prejudice." — GASKELL, *Life of Brontë* (1858), p. 240.

Bell, Ellis. *Emily Jane Brontë.* Poems. L. 1846.

Bell, Mrs. Martin. *Mrs. Bell Martin.* Julia Howard. N.Y. 1850.

Bell, Solomon. *William Joseph Snelling.* Tales of travel in the north of Europe ; Tales of travel west of the Mississippi. B. 1830–31.

Belles of Mauchline, The.

" In Mauchline there dwells six proper young Belles.
  *   *   *   *   *   *
Miss Miller is fine, Miss Markland's divine,
Miss Smith she has wit, and Miss Betty is braw :
There's beauty and fortune to get wi' Miss Morton,
But Armour's the jewel for me o' them a'."
ROBERT BURNS.

Belphegor. *William Coombe.* The Diabo-lady ; or, a match in hell : a poem . . . L. 1777.

Belzebub. *Rev. Samuel Bourn.* A sure guide to hell . . . 1787.

Ben, Uncle. *Walter Cavendish Crofton.* Brief sketch of the life of Charles Baron Metcalfe . . . Kingston, 1846.

Ben, Uncle. *Mrs. Rhoda E. Waterman White.* Portraits of my married friends ; or, peeps into Hymen's kingdom. By . . . N.Y. 1858.

Benauly. A pseudonym adopted by the three brothers, *Austin, Benjamin Vaughan,* and *Lyman Abbott,* in two novels, "Conecut Corners" and "Matthew Carnaby."

The pseudonym is composed of the first syllable of the names of the three brothers.

Ben David. *John Jones, LL.D.* Three letters, addressed to the editor of the "Quarterly Review" . . . L. 1825.

Ben-Ezra, Juan Josafat. *Emanuel Lacunza.* The coming of Messiah in glory and majesty . . . L. 1827.

Ben-Saddi, Nathan. *Robert Dodsley.* The chronicle of the kings of England, from William the Conqueror to 1795 . . . Worcester, Mass. 1795.

Ben Uzäir, Salem. *Richard Hengist Horne.* Sithron, the Star-Stricken. Translated (Ala bereket Allah) from an ancient Arabic manuscript, by . . . L. 1883.

Ben Yamen. *Benjamin Peirce.* Ben Yamen's song of geometry . . . Cloverden, 1854.

Bendbow, Hesper. *George W. Archer.* More than she could bear : story of the Gachupin war in Texas. P. 1871.

Benedict. *Edward Walter Dawson.* Benedict's wanderings in Ireland, Scotland, Italy, and Sicily . . . New Haven, Ct. 1873.

Benedict. *Joseph Reed.* Letters [in defence of Mr. Garrick] printed originally in the "Morning Chronicle," and afterwards to Kenrick's "Love in the Suds." 5th ed. L. 177-.

Benedict, Mrs. Hester. *Mrs. T. P. Dickinson.* Vesta. P. 1872.

Beneficed Clergyman of the Established Church, A. *Rev. Harris Hamilton.* The doctrines of the Church of England neither Calvinistic nor Arminian . . . L. 1819.

Benengeli, Cid Hamet. *Thomas Babington Macaulay.* Fragments of an ancient romance. Leicester, 1826 ; L. 1861.

Benevolus. *William Duncombe.* — See "Philopropos."

Benevolus, Hilaris & Co. *John Britton.* The pleasures of human life ; in a dozen dissertations on male, female, and neuter pleasures . . . L. 1807.

Bengal Civilian, A. *William Edwards.* Reminiscences of . . . L. 1866.

Bengalensis. *Major John Scott Waring.*

Benjamin, Saint. *Richard Grant White.* The new gospel of peace. N.Y. 1863–66.

Benjamin the Florentine. *Benjamin Peirce.* Ben Yamen's song of geometry . . . Cloverden, 1854.

Benjamins, Mr. *Charles B. Hart.* Lothaw. 18-.

Bennet, H., M.A. *John Pinkerton, Esq.* The treasury of wit . . . L. 1787.

Bennet, Silvia. *Olivia Levison.*

Benning, Howe. *Mrs. Mary H. Henry.* Essie's journey and what she found in it. N.Y. 1871.

Benoni, Lorenzo. *Giovanni Domenico Ruffini.* Lorenzo Benoni; or, passages in the life of an Italian. Edinb. 1853.

Benson, Carl. *Charles Astor Bristed.* A letter to Dr. Henry Halford Jones [Josiah Gilbert Holland] (editor of the "Wintertown Democrat" ["Springfield Republican"]) concerning his habit of giving advice to everybody, and his qualifications for the task, by . . . N.Y. 1864.

Benson, Edgeworth. *John Scott.* Visit to Paris. Articles in the "London Magazine," of which he was editor, 1815.

Bentley, Walter. (A *nom de théâtre*.) *Begg,* fourth son of the Rev. Dr. Begg, of Edinborough.

Bentzon, Thérèse. *Marie Thérèse Blanc.* Georgette. Paris, 1880; also as a regular contributor to "Revue des Deux Mondes."

Bereaved Husband, A. *John Mockett Cramp.* A portraiture from life . . . Halifax, 1862.

Bérenger, Paul. *Jacques Albin Simon Collin de Plancy.* Voyage de . . . dans Paris, après quarante-cinq ans d'absence . . . Paris, 1818.

Berg, O. F. *Ottokar Franz Ebersberg.* Eine resolute Person. Berlin. 185-.

Berg, Wilhelm. *Lina (Weller) Schneider.* Geschichte der niederländischen Literatur. 1870-72.

Berger, Elizabeth. *Elizabeth S. Sheppard.* Charles Auchester. L. 187-.

"Elizabeth Sheppard (E. Berger) wrote three novels, viz., 'Charles Auchester,' 'Counterparts,' and 'Rumor.' Beethoven figures in 'Rumor' under the name of Rodomant, Porphyro represents Napoleon III., and Diamond Albany is intended for Disraeli. In 'Charles Auchester' Mendelssohn's sister Fanny is Cecilia. The other chief characters in the book were given correctly in 'Transcript' of April 28, 1884, the mistake being in not designating which belonged to 'Charles Auchester' and which to 'Rumor.' In the 'Atlantic Monthly,' June, 1862, will be found an article of some length upon Miss Sheppard and her works."

Berger, Ike L. *Thomas W. Eichelberger.*

Berintho. *Robert Roberthin,* in his poems contributed to H. Albert's "Arion."

Berkeley, Everard. *Tryon Edwards, S.T.D.* The world's laconics. 1852.

Berkeley Men. *Edwin Williams* and *Charles Edwards Lester.* Napoleon dynasty. N.Y. 1852.

Berkley, Mrs. Helen. *Mrs. Anna Cora (Ogden Mowatt) Ritchie.* The fortune hunter: a novel. P. 1854.

Berkshire Farmer, A. *John Osborne Sargent.* Chapters for the times. By . . . Lee, Berkshire Co., Mass. 1884.

Berliner. *Rev. Dr. Joseph Parrish Thompson,* from the time of his residence in Berlin, 1873.

Bernadille. *François Victor Fournel,* in "Le Français."

Bernard, Charles de. *Charles Bernard Du Grail de la Villette.* A fatal passion; or, Gerfaut. N.Y. 1874.

Bernard, H. H., Ph.D. *Rev. George Skinner.* Cambridge free thoughts and letters on bibliolatry. L. 1862.

Bernadino. *Thomas B. Chrystal,* in his contributions to the "Hackensack Republican."

Bernardo. *Joseph Haslewood,* in Dibdin's "Bibliomania."

Bernd von Guseck. *Karl Gustav von Berneck.* Der schlimmste Feind. 1870.

Bernhard, Karl. *Karl Saint-Aubin.* Œuvres complètes. Leipsic, 1840-47.

Bertall. *Charles Albert d'Arnoux.* La vigne: voyage autour des vins de France. Paris, 1878.

Bertaudière. *Louis Alexis Chamerovzow.* Chronicles of the Bastile. L. 1845.

Berthold, Ernst. *Mrs. Therese Albertina Louise (von Jakob) Robinson,* who, in 1822, translated Scott's "Old Mortality" and "Black Dwarf" into German under this *nom de plume.*

Berton, P. M. *Edgar Pemberton.* Charles Lysaght. L. 18-.

Bertram. *Walter Colton,* who, soon after graduating at Yale College, wrote a number of articles in prose and verse with this signature in various journals.

Berwick. *James Redpath,* correspondent and one of the editors of the "Tribune" (N.Y.).

Berwick, E. L. A., Esq. *James Reynolds.* The dwarf; or, mind and matter: a novel. L. 1855.

Berwick, Miss Mary. *Miss Adelaide Anne Procter.* Legends and Lyrics. L. 1858.

Beschter, Rev. John. *Rev. Anthony Kohlman, S. J.* The blessed reformation . . . P. 1818.

Besieged Resident. *Henry Du Pré Labouchere.* Diary of the besieged resident in Paris. L. 1872.

Besson, Charles. *Achille Étienne Fillias,* his signature in the "Science," etc., of Paris.

Beta. *Edward Barnard Bassett.* The model town . . . Camb. 1869.

Beta, H. *Heinrich Bettziech.* Die Bewirtschaftung des Wassers und die Ernten daraus ... Leipsic, 1808.

Betterton, Mr. Thomas. *William Oldys.* The history of the English stage. L. 1741.

Bettina. *Elisabeth (Brentano) von Arnim.* Correspondence of Goethe with a child. Berlin, 1835.

Betty. *Elizabeth O'Neil.* Opposition mornings, with Betty's remarks ... L. 1779.

Beulah. *Miss Fanny D. Bates.* My Sister Kitty. B. 1881.

Beverley. *Mrs. S. B. Hughes Cox,* who contributed to the papers of Vicksburg and Shreveport, Miss., among other articles, several appeals to the Southern people upon subjects pertaining to the Civil War, under this *nom de plume.*

Beverly, Elise. *Miss Eliza Spencer.* Mary Ashburton: a tale of Maryland life ... in "The Land we Love," 1867-68.

Biascioli. *Nicola Giuseppe Biagioli.* Trattato della poesia Italiana. Paris, 1819.

Bible Student, A. *Thomas Foster Barham.* Colonel Gardiner: a Christian drama ... L. 1823.

Bible Student, A. *Rev. John Hyde.* Our Eternal Homes ... L. 1864.

Biblicus. *Alexander Tilloch, LL.D.* Dissertations on the Sealed Book ... Arbroath, 1819. These letters originally appeared in the "Star" (L.) under the above signature.

Biblicus. *Rev. William Thorn.* The history of tithes, Patriarchal, Levitical, Catholic, and Protestant ... L. 1831.

Bibliomaniac, A. *Almon W. Griswold.* The library of ... N.Y. 1880.

Bibliophile. *Samuel Austin Allibone,* in his contributions to "Norton's Literary Gazette" (N.Y.).

Bibliophile, Un. *Pierre Deschamps.* Dictionnaire de géographie, ancienne et moderne ... Paris, 1870.

Bibliophile Jacob, Le. *Paul Lacroix,* in his "Bibliographie Molièresque" (2d ed., Paris, 1875), and many other works. The dedication of the above is signed "P. L. Jacob, Bibliophile."

Mons. Lacroix took his pseudonym from Jacob de Saint-Charles, a jesuitical *savant* of the reign of Louis XIII. and Louis XIV. This writer was called "Le Père Jacob," and was the author of "Traité des plus belles bibliothèques" (1644).

Bickerstaff, Isaac, Esq., Astrologer. *Sir Richard Steele,* as editor of the "Tatler," 1709-11. See "John Brightland."

Bickerstaff, Isaac, Esq., Student in Astrology, Commentator on the Occult Sciences, and one of the eighth order of poets of the cities of London and Westminster. *Jonathan Swift.* Bickerstaff's almanac ... L. 1710.

" Dr. Swift, when he had written these Predictions, being at a loss what name to prefix to them, observed a sign over a house where a locksmith dwelt, and found the name of Bickerstaff written under it, which being a name somewhat uncommon, he chose to call himself Isaac Bickerstaff. The name was afterward adopted by Mr. Steele, as author of the 'Tatler.' This humourous tract was seriously burnt by the Inquisition in Portugal, as the author was assured by Sir Paul Methuen, then ambassador at that court."—JOHN NICHOLS.

Bideford Rural Postman, The. *Edward Capern.* Poems, L. 1856; Ballads and songs, L. 1858.

Bienvenu, Louis. *Louis François Foucqueron.* L'ami de la famille : comédie en trois actes. Rennes, 1864.

Bifrons. One of the pseudonyms adopted by Junius (*q.v.*). The letter thus signed is dated April 23, 1768, and "charges the ministry with duplicity as their general characteristic."

Big-endians and Small-endians. *Catholics and Protestants.* — See "Flinnap the Lilliputian premier."

Bigex. *François Marie Arouët de Voltaire.* Trois lettres à l'abbé Foucher. Paris, 1769.

Biglow, Hosea. *James Russell Lowell.* Melibœus-Hipponax. The Biglow papers ... Camb. 1848; L. 1865.

Bigly, Cantell A. *George W. Peck.* Aurifodina; or, adventures in the gold region. N.Y. 1849.

Bigod, Ralph. *John Ralph Fenwick.* — See Lamb's "Elia." The Two Races of Men.

Billaber, She P. *Benjamin P. Shillaber.* His signature to lines in the "Boston Journal," December 22, 1880, addressed to Bismarck.

Billings, Josh. *Henry W. Shaw.* His book of sayings. 1866.

Binet, Satané. *Francisque Sarcey.*

Binney, Mrs. J. G. *Juliette Patterson Binney.* Twenty years in Burmah. P. 1880.

Biographer of Anacreon, The. *Joshua Smith.* — See "A."

Bion. *Robert Southey.* Poems by Bion and Moschus [*i.e.*, Robert Lovell]. Bristol, 1794.

Birch, Harry. *Charles Albert White.* Old Grimes's horse. Comic song. B. 1873.

Bird at Bromsgrove, A. *John Crane.* An address to bachelors, and the apron farmer. Birmingham, 1802.

Birkenbühl, Karl. *Hans Grasberger.* Singen und Sagen [poetry]. 1869.

Birmingham Clergyman, A. *John Cale Miller, D.D.* The bicentary controversy . . . L. 1862.

Birmingham Liberal, A. *J. Arthur Partridge.* Citizenship *versus* Secularists and Sacerdotalists in the matter of national teaching. L. 1873.

Bishop, The. *John Barrett Kerfoot, D.D.* The bishop's address and charge to the . . . Diocese of Pittsburgh . . . June 14th, 1870. Pittsburgh, 1870.

Bishop, The. *Daniel Wilson,* Bishop of Calcutta. Final report of St. Paul's cathedral, Calcutta . . . 1847.

Bishop of Capetown, The. *Rev. Robert Gray.* A statement relating to facts which have been misunderstood . . . in connexion with the consecration, trial, and excommunication of the Right Rev. Dr. Colenso. L. 1867.

Bishop of Cloyne, The. *Dr. George Berkeley.* A miscellany containing several tracts on various subjects. By . . . L. 1752.

Bishop of London, The. *Archibald Campbell Tait.* The dangers and safeguards of modern theology. L. 1861.

Bishop of Montreal, The. *George Jehoshaphat Mountain.* Journal of . . . during a visit to the Church Missionary Society's North-west American Mission [Red River] . . . L. 1845.

Bishop of Natal, The. *Rt. Rev. William Colenso, D.D.* The New Testament translated into Zulu-Kaffir. By . . . Ekukanyena. 18–.

Bishop of Oxford, The. *William Jackson.* Rise, progress, and present state of the dispute between the people of America and the Administration. L. 1776.

Bishop of the Church of England, A. *John Free, D.D.* Matrimony made easy . . . L. 1764.

Bitter, Arthur. *Samuel Haberstich.* Erzählungen, Novellen, und Gedichte. 1865–66.

Bizarre. *John Russell Young,* in his contributions to the "Chronicle" (Wash., D.C.).

Bishop, Thomas. *Mr. Hayes.* Koranzzo's feast; or, the unfair marriage: a tragedy. L. 1811.

"This most extraordinary production (doubtless the work of a madman) was written by one Hayes, a footman to Lord Belgrave. 150 copies were printed, of which more than 130 were burnt at Smeeton's fire. The 16 plates are quite as unique as the text."—*Ms. Note by* GEORGE DANIEL, *in his copy.*

Black Dwarf, The. *Thomas Jonathan Wooler.* A political lecture on heads. L. 1820.

Black, Ivory. *Thomas A. Janvier.* An effect in yellow, in the "Century" for August, 1884.

Blackburne, E. Owens. *Elizabeth Casey.* Illustrious Irishwomen . . . L. 1877.

Blackmantle, Bernard. *Charles Molloy Westmacott.* The English spy . . . comprising scenes and sketches in every rank of society . . . drawn from the life . . . L. 1826.

"In the pages of this extraordinary work figure all the notabilities of the day, either openly or under slight disguise; and Tom Best, Whiteheaded Bob, 'Pea-green' Hayne, Colonel Berkeley, Beau Brummell, Pierce Egan, the 'Golden' Ball, Dr. Kett (known as 'Horse Kett,' from his equine length of visage), Charles Mathews, Jemmy Gordon, and a host of others of equal notoriety, mingle, cheek by jowl, in the vivid and moving panorama." See "The Maclise Portrait-Gallery," p. 240.

In *Fitzalleyne* "'Samuel Pous' is Samuel Foote; 'Maria Pous,' his lovely daughter; 'Fitzalleyne of Berkeley' is the lady-killing colonel, 'William the Conqueror,' as he was termed by the buxom damsels of Cheltenham; 'Lord A—y' is the Regent's friend, Alvanley; 'Major H—r' is George Hanger, not so well known as Lord Coleraine; 'Mr. Optimus' is Tom Best, under whose fatal pistol poor Lord Camelford fell; 'Mary Carbon' is Mary Cole, the butcher's daughter of Gloucester, afterwards Countess of Berkeley; and the 'Pea-green Count' is the nincompoop, Hayne." See "The Maclise Portrait-Gallery," p. 239.

Blacksmith, A. *John Witherspoon, D.D.* A letter from . . . to the ministers and elders of the Church of Scotland . . . L. 1759.

Blacksmith, The Learned. *Elihu Burritt.* Walks in the Black Country and its green borderland. L. 1868.

Black-weil, James. *Jonathan Swift, D.D.* A friendly apology . . . by . . . Operator for the feet.

Blair, Rev. David. *Sir Richard Phillips.* A million of facts . . . L. 1835.

Blake, Mary. *Mrs. Mary N. Blakelee,* in her contributions to the "Century" on household matters.

Blanche. *Mrs. E. B. Field,* in her contributions to "Saturday Night" (P.).

Blank Etcetera, Sen. *Robert Charles Winthrop,* a member of the "Polyglot Club." See the "Harvard Register," December, 1827.

Blaze, Henri. *Ange Henri Blaze de Bury.* Études de Beethoven, Paris, 1833, in the "Revue des Deux Mondes"; Musique des drames de Shakspeare, Paris, 1835, in the same.

Blenkinsop, Vicesimus, LL.D.,

F.R.S., A.S.S., &c. *Theodore Edward Hook.* Tentamen; or, an essay towards the history of Whittington, sometime Lord Mayor of London. L. 1820.

Blind Preacher, The. *William Henry Milburn.* Ten years of a preacher's life. N.Y. 1859.

Blind Traveller. *James Emilius William Evelyn Gascoyne Cecil,* Viscount Cranbourne. He wrote many papers in "St. James's Medley," signed "The Blind Traveller."

Blind Traveller, The. *James Holman.* Travels in Madeira, Sierra Leone, Teneriffe . . . L. 1840.

Bloc. *Clarence F. Cobb.* The Vision of Judgment revived. Wash., D.C. 1870.

Blockade-Runner, A. *John Wilkinson.* Narrative of . . . N.Y. 1877.

Blockaded British Subject, A. *Miss Catherine C. Hopley* or *Miss Sarah L. Jones.* Life in the South from the commencement of the war, by . . . L. 1863.

Blodgett, Levi. *Theodore Parker.* The previous question between Andrews Norton and his alumni . . . B. 1840.

Blondel. *W. F. Williams,* in his contributions to the "New York Mail."

Bloodgood, Harry. *Carlo Moran.*

Bloomer, Ben. *Oscar C. Whittlesey.*

Bloomfield, Robert. *Elizabeth E. Flagg* (?) Little people whom the Lord loved. N.Y. 1871.

Blotter, Samuel. *Charles Henry Doe,* in the Boston "Galaxy."

Blount, Margaret. *Mrs. Mary O'Francis.* Clifford and the actress . . . P. 187–.

Blue, A. *Robert Huish.* Fitz-Allan . . . L. 1832.

Bluebell, Kingcups, Mignionette, and Thistle. Respectively, *Lady Hester G. Browne,* the *Misses Knatchbull, Miss Hume Middlemass,* and *R. Hume Middlemass, Senior,* in "The bouquet culled from Marylebone Gardens by Bluebell, Kingcups, and Mignionette, and arranged by Thistle." L. 1851–55.

Bluebell. *Lady Hester G. Browne.* The bouquet culled from Marylebone Gardens by Bluebell, etc., and arranged by Thistle. 1851–55.

Blue Bonnet. *Rev. Thomas Fenwick,* a Canadian clergyman who has contributed to the newspaper press, prose and verse, on subjects connected with temperance and religion, over this signature and " Hydrophilus."

Blue Jacket. *John Adolphus Berhard Dahlgren.* Essays on naval matters in the "National Gazette" of Philadelphia, 1834.

Bluenose, A. *George E. Fenety.* The lady and the dressmaker; or, a peep at fashionable folly . . . St. John, 1842.

Blue-Skin. *Joseph Blake.* Blue-Skin's ballad. 1724–25. By Jonathan Swift, D.D.

Bluff, Bachelor. *Oliver Bell Bunce.* Romance of the Revolution: stories of the days of '76. P. 1870.

Bluff, Harry. *Matthew Fontaine Maury.* Scraps from the lucky bag, by . . . in the "Southern Literary Messenger," 1839–40.

Blumtal, J. *James Blumtal Bellak.* Buds from the opera. B. 1854.

Blunt, Alexander. *Elias Bockett.* Geneva: a poem, address'd to the Right Hon. R— W— [Sir Robert Walpole]. By . . . Distiller. (In Miltonic verse.) L. 1729.

Bluster. *James Otis.* — See "Trowell, Adjutant."

Bob of Lyn. *Sir Robert Walpole.* The compleat history of Bob of Lyn. L. 1741.

Bobbin, Tim. *John Collier.* The Lancashire dialect . . . Manchester, 1859.

Bobbin, Tim, the Second. *Robert Walker.* Plebeian politics . . . Manchester, 1796.

Bodin, Camille. *Mme. Jenny (Dufourquet) Bastide.* El Allanico, 1833; Un remords, 1834. Paris.

Bogaerts, Felix. *Jean Jacques De Laet,* a Belgian journalist.

Boggs, Robert. *H. A. Clark.* After many days. N.Y. 1880.

Boggy, Tom. *William King, LL.D.* Two letters from honest . . . to Thomas Goddard, M.A., Canon of Windsor . . . L. 1710.

Bogor, Maria. *Annie Geiger.* Souvenirs de femme, 1875; Kousouma, 1877; also as a contributor to "Illustration" (Florence, Italy).

Bohemia, The Queen of. *Miss Ada Clare,* pseud. for *Mrs. Jane McElhinney.*

Bohemians, The King of the. *Henry Clapp, Jr.*

Boissy, M. de. *Baroness Elisabeth Guénard de Méré.* Trois moines. Paris, 182–.

Bolanden, Konrad von. *Joseph Eduard Konrad Bischoff.* Die Bartholomäusnacht. 1879.

Boleyn, Mrs. R. S. (A *nom de théâtre.*) *Fanny Whiteside Brough.*

Bolton Row. *Hon. Spencer Cecil Brabazon Ponsonby* (?). Peril. L. 18–. He was assisted by "Saville Row" (*q.v.*).

Bolton Rowe. *Clement Scott.*

Bolton Rowe. *B. C. Stephenson,* in

numerous contributions to periodicals, etc.

Bombet, L. Alexandre César. *Marie Henri Beyle.* Lives of Haydn and Mozart . . . L. 1818.

Bon Gaultier. *Theodore Martin* and *William Edmonstoune Aytoun.* The book of ballads. Edited . . . L. 1849. [Reprinted from "Blackwood's Magazine."]

Bon Vieux Temps, Le. The political letters over this signature contributed to the "Montreal Herald" (about 1815), have been ascribed both to a Mr. Viger and a Mr. Quesnel.

Boncœur, L. *Levina Buoncuore Urbino.* L'instructeur de l'enfance. B. 1864.

Bones, Brudder. *John F. Scott.* Brudder Bones's book of stump speeches and burlesque orations . . . N.Y. 1868.

Bonin, Blaise. *Mme. Amandine Lucile Aurore (Dupin) Dudevant* employed this signature occasionally in political pamphlets, etc.

Bonner, Sherwood. *Mrs. Kate Sherwood (Bonner) McDowall.* Dialect tales. N.Y. 1883.

Bookseller, A. *Charles Marsh.* The library: an epistle from . . . to a gentleman, his customer, desiring him to discharge his bill. L. 1766.

Bookseller, A. *John Dunton.* Religio Bibliopolæ; or, the religion of . . . L. 1728.

Bookworm. *Thomas F. Donnelly,* in his contributions to various periodicals.

Booth, Albert J. *Cecil Burleigh,* in contributions to various New York periodicals.

Booty, Bob. *Sir Robert Walpole.* Bob Booty's lost deal . . . L. 1742.

Bore, Dr. Helle. *Charles H. Smith.* — See "Bill Arp."

Bornnatural, A. *Henry Ellison.* Mad moments; or, first verse attempts . . . L. 1839.

Borys, Gontran. *Eugène Berthoud.* Les paresseux de Paris. Paris, 187–.

Bos. *George W. M. Reynolds.* Pickwick abroad. L. 1840.

Boscawen. *Nathaniel Greene,* successively editor of the "Concord Gazette," the "New Hampshire Gazette," at Portsmouth, the "Haverhill (Mass.) Gazette," the "Essex Patriot," and the "Boston Statesman."

Bossut, M. l'Abbé, Professor of Languages. *Sir Richard Phillips.* The first French Grammar. L.

Boston Amateur Poet, A. *John Patch.* The poet's offering. B. 1842.

Boston Bard, The. *Robert S. Coffin.*

The life of the Boston bard. Written by himself. Mount Pleasant, N.Y., 1825.

Boston Boy, A. *Andrew Eliot Belknap,* in the Boston newspapers.

Boston Merchant, A. *Silas Pinckney Holbrook.* Letters from, in the "Boston Courier," 183–.

Boston Rebel, The. *John Lowell* The author of many pamphlets and numerous papers in periodicals on politics, theology, agriculture, etc., under the signatures of "The Roxbury Farmer," "The Yankee Farmer," "The New England Farmer," "The Boston Rebel," etc

Boston Supernumerary, A. *Tom Ford.* Peep behind the curtain. By . . . B. 1850.

Bostonian, A. *Samuel Adams,* in the "Boston Gazette," April 24, 1769.

Bostonian, A. *John Lowell, LL.D.* The diplomatic policy of Mr. Madison unveiled . . . L. 1810.

Bostonian, A. *William Haliburton.* Effects of the stage on the manners of a people, and the propriety of encouraging and establishing a virtuous theatre. B. 1792.

Bostonian, A. *William Boott.* A fagot from the Coliseum. B. 1869.

Bostonian, A. *Edgar Allan Poe.* Tamerlane; and other poems. 1827.

Bostonian, A. *Benjamin Bussey Thatcher.* Traits of the Tea Party: memoir of G. R. T. Hewes. N.Y. 1835.

Boswell. *W. B. Johnson.*

Boswell Redivivus. *William Hazlitt,* in the "New Monthly Magazine," 1826–27.

Bouquet, Johnny. *George Alfred Townsend,* in his contributions to the "Tribune" (N.Y.).

Bourne, Margaret. *Mrs. Jennie A. (Abbott) Johnson.*

Bouverie, Bartholomew. *William Ewart Gladstone.* The Eton miscellany. By . . . 1827.

Bouverie, Lionel. *Rev. John Humphry St. Aubyn.* The elopement, or deadly struggle. By . . . L. 1838.

Bowline, Billy. *Henry S. Raymond.*

Boy, A. *Charles Nordhoff.* Man-of-war life: a boy's experience in the United States navy. N.Y. 1855.

Boy, A. *Samuel Smiles, Jr.* Round the world. By . . . L. 1872.

Boy, Tenpin. *Francis Shubael Smith.*

Boy Preacher, The. *Rev. Charles Haddon Spurgeon.*

Boyd, Belle. *Mrs. J. S. Hammond.*

Boyd, Belle. *Mrs. Belle Boyd Hardinge.* Belle Boyd in camp and prison. L. 1865.

Boyd, Walter, Esq., M.P. *William Coombe.* A letter to the Right Hon. William Pitt . . . L. 1811.

Boythorn. *William Stevens Robinson,* his signature in the " Worcester (Mass.) Transcript " in 1857–60.

Boz. *Charles Dickens.* The boarding house, No. II. In the "Monthly Magazine, or British Register of Politics, Literature, Art, Science, and Belles Lettres," London, for August, 1834.

This was the first paper to which the author appended the signature of " Boz."

Bozzy and Piozzi. *James Boswell* and *Mrs. Hester Lynch Piozzi.*

" Dr. Wolcot published a poem, in which he satirized Mr. Boswell and this literary lady [Mrs. Piozzi] under the titles of ' Bozzy and Piozzi.' "

Bracquemond. *Théodore Faullain de Banville.* Odes funambulesques. 1873.

Braddon, Paul. *J. Howard Van Arden.*

Bradley, John. *J. A. Lawson.* A narrative of travel and sport in Burmah, Siam, and the Malay Peninsula. L. 1876.

Bradshaw, Serjeant. *Sir James Bland Burges Lamb, Bart.* Heroic epistles from . . . in the Shades, to John Dunning, Esq. L. 1778.

Bradshaw, Wesley. *Charles Alexander.* Gertrude Morgan's adventures among the Indians of the far West. P. 18–.

Brag, Sir Jack. *Gen. John Burgoyne.*

Braganza. *H. A. Bragg.* Tekel; or, Cora Glencoe. P. 1870.

Bramble, Benjamin. *George Winter.* The farmer convinced; or, the reviewers of the "Monthly Review" anatomized . . . By . . . an old, experienced farmer. L. 1788.

Bramble, Matthew. *Andrew MacDonald.* Velina: a poetical fragment. Glasgow, 1782.

Brancassine, R. F. *Hughes R. P. Fraser Halle, LL.D.* Critical letters on scribbleomania. L. 1842.

Brandywine. *Alexander McGrew,* in the "Memphis Appeal."

Bras de Fer. *Comyns Cole,* in his contributions to "The World" (L.).

Breachan. *Rev. Robert Stephen Hawker, M.A.* Sir Beville: a poem; signed B. . . . 1861.

Brechin Poet, The. *Alexander Laing,* author of "Wayside flowers," "Archie Allan," etc.

Breitmann, Hans. *Charles Godfrey Leland.* Hans Breitmann's ballads. P. 187–.

Brenda. *Mrs. Castle Smith.* Little cousins; Especially those; Froggy's little brother; A Saturday's bairn. L. 18–.

Brennglas, Adolf. *Adolf Glassbrenner.* Berlin, wie es ist und — trinkt. 183–.

Brent, Linda. *Mrs. Harriet Jacobs.* Incidents in the life of a slave girl. B. 1861.

Brentford, Burke. *Nathan D. Urner,* in his contributions to the "New York Weekly."

Brevior, Thomas. *Thomas Shorter.* Poetry for school and home. Edited . . . L. 1861.

Brick, Jefferson. *Alexander Black,* in the "Brooklyn Times."

Brick, Titus. *Augustus Seaman.*

Brick, Titus A. *C. E. File,* in the New York " Star."

Brick, Titus A. *John Camden Hotten.* Awful crammers. L. 187–.

Bricktop. *George G. Small.* Trip of the "Porgie"; or, tacking up the Hudson . . . N. Y. 1874.

Bride of Fort Edward, The. *Miss Jane McCrie.* The bride of Fort Edward; founded on an incident of the Revolution. N.Y. 1839. By Miss Delia Bacon (?).

Briefless Barrister, A. *William Pitt Scargill.* Tales of . . . L. 1829.

Briggs, Jimuel. *Phillips Thompson.*

Bright Eyes. *Inshtatheamba.*

Brighte, John. *J. Duncan.* Witty sayings. L. 18–.

Brightland, John. *Sir Richard Steele.* A grammar of the English tongue . . . L. 1726.

The " Approbation " is signed " Isaac Bickerstaff, Censor."

Brindamour. *Jacques Albin Simon Collin de Plancy,* in his contributions to various French periodicals.

Brine, Barnaby, Esq., R.N. *William H. G. Kingston.* The cruise of the "Frolic"; or, yachting experiences of . . . L. 1860.

Brisk, Richard. *J. Duncan.* Railway book. L. 18–.

Bristol Bill. *Henry Hyde Parker.*

Bristol Junius, The. *John Matthew Gutch, Esq.*

Britannicus. *Thomas Gordon.* — See "An Englishman."

Britannicus. *Adam Thom,* a Canadian journalist, one of his signatures in the "Montreal Herald," 1837–38.

Britannicus. *Allan Ramsay, Jr.* Letters on the present disturbances in Great Britain and her American provinces. Rome, 1777.

Britannicus. *Niel Douglas.* A monitory address to Great Britain . . . 1792.

Britannicus. *Rev. George Clement Boase.* My native home: a song. "Cornish Magazine," 1828.

Britannicus. *Henry Boase.* An ode for the 25th October, 1809, on the celebration of George the Third's jubilee. "Poetical Mag.," 1809.

Britannicus. *John Stockdale Hardy, Esq., F.S.A.* A series of letters, addressed to a friend, upon the Roman Catholic question. By . . . 1820.

Britannicus. *Rt. Rev. Edward Copleston, D.D.* Two letters on Welsh bishops, signed . . . October, 1840.

Britannicus, Mela. *Charles Kelsall.* Remarks touching geography, especially that of the British Isles. L. 1825.

Britannicus, Probus. *Samuel Johnson, LL.D.* Marmor Norfolciense; or, an essay on an ancient prophetical inscription in Monkish rhyme, lately discovered near Lynn, in Norfolk. By . . . Reprinted, L. 1820.

British American, A. *Thomson Mason.* In 1774 he published a series of masterly papers on the duty of open resistance to the mother-country, of which the first was signed "A British American."

British American, A. *— Wetherby.* Dawn of a new empire . . . Halifax, 1864.

British Bostonian, A. *Rev. John Allen.* An oration upon the beauties of liberty; or, the essential rights of the Americans . . . New London, Conn., 1773. Also ascribed to Isaac Skillman.

British Canadian. *Edward Ermatinger,* in his letters to "The Spectator" (Hamilton, Can., about 1850).

British Commoner, A. *Edward Rupert Humphreys, LL.D.* Letters by . . . No. II., "The dangers of England and duties of Englishmen." L. 1855.

British Freeholder, A. *George Mason, Esq.* A. B. F.'s answer to Thomas Paine. L. 179–.

British Merchant, A. *Malachy Postlethwayt.* The African trade the great pillar and support of the British plantation trade in America. L. 1745.

British Merchant, A. *J. H. Renny.* Hints on wages, the corn-laws, high and low prices, paper money, and banking . . . L. 1832.

British Merchant, A. *Simon Cock.* Observations on the report . . . relative to the timber trade . . . L. 1821.

British Officer, A. *Colonel Leith Hay.* Memoirs of the late Lieutenant-General Sir James Leith, G.C.B. . . . L. 1818.

British Officer in the Service of the Czar, A. *Daniel Defoe.* An impartial history of the life and actions of Peter Alexovitz . . . L. 1723.

British Officer of Hussars, A. *— Owen.* The civil war in Portugal, and the siege of Oporto . . . L. 1836.

British Phidias, The. *Sir Francis Chantrey, R.A.*

British Resident, A. *John Scarth.* Twelve years in China. The people, the rebels, and the mandarins. Edinb. 1860.

British Resident of Twenty Years in the East, A. *James Henry Skene.* The frontier lands of the Christian and the Turk . . . L. 1853.

British Settler, A. *John Fleming.* The political annals of Lower Canada . . . Montreal, 1828.

British Soldier, A. *Michael Constable.* National lyrics, for the army and navy . . . Dublin, 1848.

British Spy, The. *William Wirt.* Letters . . . Richmond, 1803. Originally contributed to the "Argus" (Richmond, Va.).

British Subject, A. *Walter Millar Thorburn, B.A.* The great game: a plea for a British imperial policy . . . L. 1875.

British Subject, A. *Sir Francis Bond Head.* Three letters to Lord Brougham on the execution in Upper Canada of the traitors Lount and Matthews . . . L. 1838.

British Subject, A. *Mr. Beaufoy.* Tour through parts of the United States and Canada. L. 1828.

British Timon, The. *Charles Gosling.* — See "Gent. Mag.," LIV., 814.

Briton, A. *John Cleland,* who was the author of *long* letters given in the public press, from time to time, signed "A Briton," "Modestus," etc.

Briton, A. *W. P. Russell.* Animating hints for British statesmen . . . L. 1811.

Briton, A. *Morris Robinson,* 3d Lord Rokeby of Armagh, etc. An essay on bank-tokens, bullion, etc. Stockton, 1811.

Brittan, Belle. *Hiram Fuller.* Transformation scenes in the United States. N.Y. 187–.

Brittle, Gath. *Robert W. McAlpine,* in his contributions to periodical literature.

Britto-Batavus. *John Toland.* The description of Epsom. L. 1711.

Broadaxe. *Martin Knapp,* in his contributions to the "Rockland County Press" (N.Y.).

Broad Church. *Thomas Atcheson,* Louisville (Ky.), correspondent of "The Spirit of the Times" (N.Y.).

Broad Churchman, A. *E. A. Warriner.* Victor La Tourette. B. 1875.

Broadbent, Charles. *Charles G. Halpine,* as associate editor with B. P. Shillaber ("Mrs. Partington") of the "Carpet-bag." B. 1852.

Broadbrim. *J. H. Warwick.* Was Shakespeare a myth? In the Angola (Ind.) "Republican," May and June, 1881.

Broadluck, Cephas. *Allen W. Gazlay.* Races of mankind; with travels in Grubland. Cin. 1856.

Broadway Lounger, A. *George Alfred Townsend,* in his "Broadway Note-book," contributed to "The Tribune" (N.Y.).

Brock, Sallie A. *Mrs. Sarah A. (Brock) Putnam.* Kenneth my king. N.Y. 1872.

Broken-down Critic, A. *Charles Astor Bristed.* Pieces of . . . picked up by himself. Baden-Baden, 1858–59.

Bromley, Henry. *Anthony Wilson.* A catalogue of engraved English portraits. L. 1793.

Bronner, Benno. *Wilhelm Molitor.* Die Blume von Sizilien. 1880.

Bronson, Doctor. *W. A. Peters.*

Brook, A. *Johanne Antonie Broekel.* Licht und Schatten. 1880.

Brook, Babble. *John H. McNaughton,* of Caledonia (N.Y.), author of "Belle Mahone," and other popular lyrics.

Brook, Nelsie. *Mrs. Ellen Ross.* Little Mother Mattie. L. 18–.

Brook, Sarah. *Miss Caroline Emilia Stephen.* French history for English children.

Brooke, Arthur. *John Chalk Claris.* Durovernum; with other poems. L. 1818.

Brooke, Wesley. *George Lunt.* Eastford; or, household sketches, by . . . a novel. B. 1855.

Brooklyn. *Thomas Kinsella,* in the "Eagle" (Brooklyn).

Brooks, Chatty. *Miss Rosella Rice,* in her contributions to "Arthur's Magazine."

Broomstraw. *Alfred Duke,* in his contributions to the "State" (Richmond, Va.).

Brother, A. *William Biglow.* Commencement: a poem; or rather commencement of a poem. Recited before the Phi Beta Kappa Society . . . in Cambridge, Aug. 29, 1811. Salem, 1811.

Brother, A. *Rev. George Clement*

Boase. To husbands, fathers, and brothers . . . a word in season . . . L. 1848.

Brother Fish Dealer from the Far North, A. *Mr. Anderson.* A letter to the Duke of Richmond . . . L. 1844. The letter is signed, "The Originator of the Shetland Fishery Company."

Brother Methodist, A. *Rev. Benjamin Gough.* A few earnest words to British Methodists, from . . . Leeds, 1860.

Brother of the Apollo Lodge, 711, Oxford, A. *Bishop Walter Mant, M.A.* A Freemason's pocket companion . . . L. 1831.

Brother of the Birch, A. *William Cobbett.* A twig of birch for the butting calf . . . N.Y. 1795.

Brown, Mr. *William Makepeace Thackeray.* Mr. Brown's letters to a young man about town, in "Punch," 1849.

Brown, Isaac. *William Motherwell.* Renfrewshire characters and scenery. L. 1881.

Brown, James. *Joseph Robertson.* The new "Deeside Guide" . . . Aberdeen, 1834.

Brown, John. *James Edward Neild, M.D.* His signature to a letter to the editor of the "Melbourne (Victoria) Argus" in 1867, on "The Hamlet Controversy."

Brown, John, Esqre. *Thomas Jefferson Hogg.* Memoirs of Prince Alexy Haimatoff. Translated from the original Latin Mss. under the immediate inspection of the Prince. By . . . L. 1814.

Brown, The Late J. *Alexander Wheelock Thayer.* Signor Masoni, and other papers of the . . . Edited by . . . Berlin, 1862.

This is a collection of Mr. Thayer's contributions to American periodicals.

Brown, Pisistratus. *William Black.*

Brown, Polemophilus, Curate of P—n. *Alexander Geddes, LL.D.* A new year's gift to the good people of England . . . 1798.

Brown, Theomophilus. *Rev. Alexander Geddes.* A sermon preached on the day of the general fast, Feb. 27, 1799, by . . . L. 1799.

Brown, Thomas, redivivus. *Caroline Frances Cornwallis.* An exposition of the vulgar and common errors adapted to the year of grace MDCCCXLV. Edited . . . B. 1846.

Brown, Thomas, the Younger. *Thomas Moore.* Intercepted letters; or, the twopenny post bag. L. 1813.

Brown, Vandyke. *Frederic J. Prouting*, editor of the "Berkshire Bell and Counties' Review" (Reading).

Brown, Vandyke. *William Penn Brannan.* Harp of a thousand strings. 18-.

Browne, Dunn. *Rev. Samuel Fisk.* Letters from Europe, in the "Springfield Republican." 18-.

Browne, Junius Henri. *Albert Deane Richardson.* Four years in Secessia: adventures within and beyond the Union lines. N.Y. 1865.

Browne, Matthew. *William Brighty Rands.* The chain of lilies; and other poems. L. 1857.

Browning, Francis. *Francis Browning Owen.* Poems . . . Detroit, 1874.

Brownjohn, Bellamy. *Robert Carr Dunham.* No thoroughfare. B. 1868.

Brownjohn, John. *Charles Remington Talbot.* Miltiades Peterkin Paul: his adventures. B. 1877.

Brownlow, Parson. *William Gannaway Brownlow.*

Brownrig, Henry. *Douglas William Jerrold.* Black eyed Susan, L. 1826; The rent-day, L. 1830.

Brulart de Sillery, Stéphanie Félicité. *Mme. Stéphanie Félicité Ducrest de Saint-Aubin.* La botanique historique et littéraire. Paris, 1811.

Brummel, Beau. *George Bryan Brummel.*

Brumore. *N. Guyton de Morveau.* Traité curieux des charmes de l'amour conjugal dans ce monde et dans l'autre. Ouvrage [of Swedenborg] traduit du Latin . . . par . . . Brussels, 1881.

Bruno, G. *Alfred Jules Émile Fouillie.* Tour de la France par deux enfants. Paris, 187-.

Brunold, Friedrich. *August Friedrich Meyer.* Die Askanierburg Werbellin. Zurich, 1880.

Brunswick. *Miss Jeanette L. Gilder*, as correspondent in New York, for many years, of the "Boston Saturday Evening Gazette."

Brutus. *Fisher Ames*, in contributions to the newspapers of Boston (Mass.).

Brutus. *Henry Mackenzie, Esq.*

"In political literature he was the author of a 'Review of the Proceedings of the Parliament,' which met first in the year 1784, and of a series of letters under the signature of 'Brutus.'"

Brutus. *David Owen.*

Brutus. *Stephen Simpson*, who, under this signature, contributed to the Philadelphia "Aurora."

Brutus. *Robert James Turnbull.* The crisis; or, essays on the usurpations of the Federal Government. Charleston (S.C.), 1827.

Brutus. *Samuel Finley Breese Morse.* Foreign conspiracy against the liberties of the United States . . . N.Y. 1835.

Brutus. *Robert Coram.* Political inquiries . . . Wilmington (Del.), 1791.

Brutus. One of the signatures adopted by Junius (*q.v.*). He addressed a letter to Lord North under this name, dated Feb. 21, 1771. — See "Atticus."

Brutus, Lucius Junius. *William Cranch.* Examination of the President's reply to the N. Haven remonstrance. N.Y. 1801.

Bubb, Belle Z. *Samuel W. E. Beckner*, editor of the "Corner Stone" (N.Y.).

Buck, Ruth. *Mrs. Joseph Lamb.* How Charley helped his mother . . . L. 1861.

Buddle, Jasper. *Albert Smith*, who while a member of the London College of Surgeons, in 1838 *et seq.*, attracted attention by a series of papers in the "Medical Times," entitled "Jasper Buddle; or, Confessions of a Dissecting-room Porter."

Budlong, Pharaoh. *Frederic Beecher Perkins.* President Greeley, President Hoffman, and the resurrection of the Ring: a history . . . Budlington, 1872.

Budock, George. *Sydney Hodges.* A tale of the Western Counties.

Bürger, Hugo. *Hugo Lubliner.* Auf der Brautfahrt. 1880.

Bürger, W. *Theophile Étienne Joseph Thoré.* Histoire des peintres de toutes les écoles . . . Paris, 1863.

Buffalo Bill. *Hon. William F. Cody.*

Bull, John. *Great Britain and Ireland.* — See "Strutt, Lord."

Bull, Thomas. *William Jones.* A letter to John Bull, Esq. . . . L. 1793.

Bull, W. *Ann Jebb.* Two pennyworth of truth for a penny . . . L. 1793.

Bullcalf, Peter. *Joseph Storrs Fry.* The history of John Bull and his three sons . . . By . . . L. 1819.

Buller of Brasenose. *John Hughes, Esq.*, celebrated in "Christopher in the Tent," was a contributor to "Blackwood's Magazine," Edinb. 1819, etc.

Bullion, Thomas. *Joseph Langton* (?). Internal management of a country bank. L. 1850.

Bull-us, Hector. *James Kirke Paulding.* The diverting history of John Bull and Brother Jonathan. N.Y. 1812.

Bumpas, Azarias. *John Quincy Adams Griffin.* Reports of cases argued and decided in the Old Fogy Court, during Hilary and Michaelmas terms, before the Rt. Hon. Bepee Dicques, Baron Cucumbre, C.J., Hon. Danelle Needhame, B., and Hon. B. Roussiele, J., in the "Carpet-Bag," Boston, 1852.

Buncle, John, Esq. *Thomas Amory.* The life and opinions of John Buncle, Esq. L. 1756–66.

Bundelcund. *Edmund Burke,* in the "Washington Union," 1846.

Bunker Hill. *Rev. Benjamin Franklin De Costa,* in his letters to the "Advertiser" (Boston), during 1861–62.

Bunker Hill Boy, A. *John Quincy Adams Griffin.* Some fresh suggestions on the project of annexing Charlestown to Boston. By ... Charlestown, 1855.

Bunker, General. *C. Lorain Ruggles.* The great American scout and spy. N.Y. 1870.

Bunker, Timothy, Esq. *William Clift.* The Tim Bunker papers; or, Yankee farming. N.Y. 1868.

Bunsby, Jack. *Theodore H. Vandenburgh.*

Buntline, Ned. *Edward Z. C. Judson.* The king of the sea, N.Y. 1848; The ghouls of New York, N.Y. 1850.

Bunyan, John. *Rev. James Bardwood.* Heart's ease in heart-trouble ... By ... L. 1762.

Bunyan, John, Junior. *Rev. William Arnot.* The drunkard's progress ... Edinb. 1853.

Burghley, Feltham. *C. A. Ward.* England subsists by miracle. L. 1859.

Buritonensis, Johannes. *John Josias Arthur Boase.* Spicelegia, "Cornish Mag.," 1828.

Burleigh. *William Henry Burleigh.*

Burleigh. *Rev. Matthew Hale Smith.* Sunshine and shadow in New York, Hartford, 187–; also in his contributions to the "Boston Journal," etc.

Burlington. *Robert Sanders.* — See "Spencer, Nath."

Burlington, Charles, and others. *Robert Sanders, LL.D., and others.* The modern universal British traveller. L. 1779.

Burlington Hawkeye-man. *Robert J. Burdette.*

Burt, Caleb. *Cecil Burleigh.*

Burton, Junior. *Charles Lamb,* in his essay, On the melancholy of tailors, contributed to the "Reflector."

Burton, Alfred. *John Mitford, R.N.* The adventures of Johnny Newcome in the navy: a poem ... L. 1818.

Burton, H. A. *John Habberton.* Helen's babies: by their latest victim. B. 1876.

Burton, Richard. *Nathaniel Crouch.* Admirable curiosities, rarities, and wonders in Great Britain and Ireland. 10th ed. L. 1737.

Bury, Viscount, M.P. *William Coutts Keppel, Viscount Bury.* Exodus of the western nations. By ... L. 1865.

Busby, Scriblerus, LL.D. *Gulian Crommelin Verplanck.* "Prolegomena, notes, and other scholastic trimmings" to The epistles of Brevet Major Pindar Puff. N.Y. 1819.

Bushwhacker, Dr. *Frederic S. Cozzens.* Sayings of ... and other learned men. N.Y. 1867.

Buskin, Captain Sock. *W. J. Sorrel* (?). How to "get up" theatricals in a country house ... L. 1866.

Bust, Urastix. *Charles H. Fox.* Sable songster. Selected and arranged by ... P. 1859.

Busybody, The. *Benjamin Franklin.*

Benjamin Franklin "wrote a series of smart articles in his old, favourite style of the 'Spectator,' which he called 'The Busybody,' and which he published in Bradshaw's despised paper, throwing ridicule on Keimer and his 'Gazette.'" (Phila. 1728-). — ANDREWS's *History of Journalism.*

Busy Woman, A. *Mrs. Mary Bayard (Devereux) Clarke.* Mosses from a rolling stone; or, the idle moments of a busy woman. Winchester, Va. 186–.

Butcher, The. *William Fowler.*

Butler, Diana. *Mrs. Henrietta E. Tindal.* The heirs of Blackridge Manor: a tale of the past and the present ... L. 1856.

Butt, Boswell. *Charles H. Ross.* Hush Money: a life drama. L. 187–.

Butterfly, A. *Rev. J. A. Allan.* Day dreams by ... Kingston, Can. 1854.

Buttons. *T. J. C. Cowles.*

Byfield, T., M.D. *John Woodward, M.D.* The two Sosias ... [A satire on Dr. Mead.] L. 1719.

Byfielde, J. *John Freind, M.D.* A letter to the learned Dr. Woodward. L. 1719.

Byles. *Edmund Quincy,* in the "New York Tribune."

Byr, Robert. *Robert von Bayer.* Eine geheime Depesche. 1880.

Byrne, Janet. *Jane Besemeres.* Patsy's first glimpse of heaven. L. 1873.

Byro. *John Roby* (?). Compendium of county history. By ... in "Gent. Mag.," LXXXVI., Pt. 2, p. 313 *et seq.*

Byron, G. G. N., Baron. *Dr. Louis Eustache Polidori.* The Vampyre: a tale by the Right Honourable Lord B. L. 1819.

Byron, Lord. *Jacques Albin Simon Collin de Plancy.* La mort de Napoléon, dithryambe traduit de l'Anglais de Lord Byron: précédée d'une notice sur la vie et la mort de Napoléon Bonaparte, par Th. Moore (idem). Paris, 1821.

Bystander, A. *Patrick Fraser, LL.D.* Domestic economy, gymnastics, and music: an omitted clause in the education bill... Edinb. 1855.
Bystander, A. *Corbyn Morris.* A letter from... to a member of Parliament... L. 1741.

C.

ℭ. *Charles Clarke.* Twelve maxims on swimming. L. 1833.
C. The signature adopted by Junius (*q.v.*) in his private letters to Mr. Woodfall. Several letters to the "Public Advertiser" (*e.g.*, March 24, 1768, etc.) are also signed thus.
C. *Mrs. Francesca Anna (Pascalis) Canfield*, who made translations from the French and Italian, wrote original hymns in Italian, and was a frequent contributor, under various signatures, to literary journals.
C. *John Cogan*, in the "Times" (Brooklyn, N.Y.).
C. *Samuel Taylor Coleridge*, in Lamb's "Elia," *passim.*
C. *Rt. Hon. John Wilson Croker*, in "Notes and Queries," L. 1859.
C. *Rev. Edward Bouverie Pusey*, one of the contributors to "Tracts for the Times," L. 1840–48.
C. *Robert Smith.* His signature to papers in the "Microcosm," published at Eton College, 1787 *et seq.*
C. *Mrs. Caroline Anne (Bowles) Southey.* For more than twenty years her writings were published without her name, and many of them in "Blackwood's Magazine" under the signature of "C."
C. *Hon. Charles Yorke*, in his contributions to the "Athenian Letters"... L. 1741–43.
C. *Mathew Carey.* Advices and suggestions to increase the comforts of persons in humble circumstances. P. 1832.
C. *Rev. Arthur Cleveland Coxe.* Christian ballads. N.Y. 1840.
C. *Alexander Chalmers.* Dissenter's psalms, "Gent. Mag.," August, 1794, p. 696; Biographical anecdotes of the late Mr. Boswell, "Gent. Mag.," June, 1795, p. 469.
C. *Francis Kingston.* Essay on friendship, "Cornish Magazine," 1828.
C. *Edward Capper.* Miscellaneous observations upon authors, ancient and modern. L. 1731–32.
C., or Coadjutor. *Rev. Henry Meen, B.D.* Translator of "Coluthus Lyco-

polites," in Dr. Anderson's edition of "Translations," in which "C" stood for "Coadjutor," who was Mr. Meen.
C., Dr. *Samuel Cooper, D.D.*, in Beloe's "Sexagenarian," I., 39, 2d ed. L. 1818.
C., Lord. *Lord Camelford.* — See Lamb's "Elia." Distant correspondents.
C., Mrs. *Mrs. Maria Susanna Cooper*, in Beloe's "Sexagenarian," I., 40, 333, 2d ed. L. 1818.
C., A. *Antoine Caillot.* Abregé des voyages modernes... Paris, 1820.
C., A. *Alexander Cameron.* A letter to the Rev. John Smith, D.D.... on his Life of St. Columba. 1798.
C., A. *Alexander Chalmers.* Memoir of John Nichols, Esq., F.S.A.... L. 1826.
C., A., Esq. *Anthony Collins.* A dissertation on liberty and necessity... L. 1729.
C., Sir A. *Sir Astley Cooper.* — See Lamb's "Elia," Ellistoniana.
C., A. C. *Rev. Arthur Cleveland Coxe.* Saul: a mystery... N.Y. 1845.
C., A. N. *Archibald N. Carmichael.* Genealogy of her Majesty, Queen Victoria... Edinb. 1845.
C., B. *Benjamin Chandler.* The Apostles' Creed better than the Assembly's Catechism... L. 1720.
C., B. *Bracy Clark.* A new exposition of the horse's hoof. L. 1820.
C., B., Vestryman of Marylebone. *Bracy Clark.* An exposure of the corruption of the Saxon name Arm's Housen into Almshouses... L.
C., C. *Charles Coghlan.* Love and hate; or, the court of Charles I. A historical drama... L. 1857.
C., C. *Charles Clark.* Tiptree races: a comic punning poem, à la Hood's celebrated "Epping Hunt." L. 1834.
C., C. *Charles Chorley.* Translations, 1866; Verse, 1867; Horatian metres attempted in English, 1867; The episode of Hector and Andromache... 1867;

from the Italian of Tasso's sonnets, 1867 ; Truro.

C. C., *alias* **Chilly Charley.** *Charles Clark.* Bills, ills, and chills ; or, rhyme and fun about sixty-one. 1861.

C., Charles. *Charles Cousin.*

C. C. C. *William Ralston Balch*, in his contributions to various periodicals.

C., C. C. *Rev. C. C. Colton.* Remarks, critical and moral, on the talents of Lord Byron and the tendencies of Don Juan . . . L. 1819.

C., C. D. *Charles Dexter Cleveland.* First lessons in Greek . . . By . . . B. 1833.

C., C. M. *Charlotte Moon Clark.* How she came into her kingdom : a romance. Chicago, 1878.

C., C. P. *Charles Purton Cooper.* The case of Arnold *v.* Arnold . . . L. 1847.

C., C. S. *Charles Stuart Calverley.* Fly-leaves. N.Y. 1875.

C., D. *Dutton Cook,* in his contributions to the " World." L.

C. D. *S. De Morgan.* From matter to spirit . . . Ten years experience in spirit manifestations. With a preface by A. B. [*i.e.,* Augustus (?) De Morgan]. L. 1863.

C., E. *Elizabeth Cummings,* in her contributions to various periodicals on musical subjects.

C. E. *Mrs. Charlotte Elizabeth (Phelan) Tonna.* Maternal martyrdom, a fact illustrative of the improved spirit of popery in the 19th century. L. 1830.

C., E. *Edward Capell.* Notes and various readings to Shakespeare . . . L. 1783.

C., E. *Ebenezer Cornwall.* The unveiling of the everlasting Gospel . . . L. 1848.

C., E., Gent. *Ebenezer Cook.* Sotweed redivivus ; or, the planter's lookingglass. In burlesque verse. Calculated for the meridian of Maryland. By . . . Annapolis, 1730.

C., Mrs. E. *Mrs. Elizabeth Carter,* in Beloe's " Sexagenarian," I., 336. 2d ed. L. 1818.

C., E. B. *Miss Essie B. Cheesborough,* who, under these initials, wrote much for Southern periodicals.

C., E. B. *Eliza B. Chase.* Over the border. Acadia, the home of " Evangeline." By . . . B. 1884.

C., E. I. *Edward John Carlos.* His signature in the " Gent. Mag."

C., E. J. *Edward John Carlos.* Niche in St. Bartholomew's Church, London. L. 1841.

C., E. R. *Eustace R. Conder.* An

order for the solemnization of matrimony. L. 1854.

C., E. V. *E. V. Childe.* — See " A States'-man."

C., F. E. *Frederick E. Cushman.* History of the 28th regiment Massachusetts vols. . . . Wash., D.C. 1865.

C., F. M. *Frances Mary Cusack.* An illustrated history of Ireland . . . L. 1868.

C., F. S. *Francis Sewell Cole.* — See " Effessea."

C., G., Esq. *George Cartwright, Esq.* Labrador : a poetical epistle . . . Doncaster, 1785.

C., G. R. *George Richard Corner, Esq.* Grammar school of St. Olave's, Southwark, in " Gent. Mag.," 1836. Pt. I., pp. 15, 137.

C., H. *Howard Carroll,* in the New York " Times."

C., H. *Hugh Cleghorn, M.D.* Hortus Madraspatensis. Catalogue of plants . . . in the Agri-horticultural Society's gardens, Madras. Madras, 1853.

C., H. *Henry Chamberlain.* A new and complete history and survey of the cities of London and Westminster . . . L. 1770.

C., H. A. *Henry Acheson Crozier, M.R.C.S.* Parc-au-Chapel, Cape Cornwall. Exon. 1856.

C., H. F. *Henry F. Chorley.* Old love and new fortune : a play . . . L. 1850.

C., H. G., Esq. *H. G. Curran.* Confessions of a Whitefoot . . . L. 1884.

C., H. O. *Henry Octavius Coxe.* Forms of bidding prayer . . . Oxf. 1840.

C., H. S. *H. S. Cunningham.* Chronicles of Dustypore : a tale of modern Anglo-Indian society . . . L. 1875.

C., I. *Sir Ilay Campbell.* Hints upon the question of jury trial . . . L. 1809.

C., I., M.D. *Rev. James Clark.* Christ's impressions strong, sweet, and sensible on the hearts of believers . . . 1700.

C., I. E. B. *Irvine E. B. Cox.* The angler's diary . . . L. 1866–67.

C., J. *Rev. John Courtarey.* — See " A Clergyman."

C., J. *John Campbell.* The case of the publicans, both in town and country, laid open . . . L. 1752.

C., J. *John Corey.* A cure for jealousie : a comedy . . . L. 1701.

C., J. *Sir James Caldwell.* Debates relative to the affairs of Ireland . . . L. 1766.

C., J. *J. Clay.* The laws of short whist, edited by John Loraine Baldwin . . . and a treatise on the game by . . . L. 1864.

C., J. *J. Carrick* (?). Life of Sir William Wallace. 3d ed. L. and Glasgow, 1849.

C., J. *J. Clark.* Newcastle remembrancer, and freeman's pocket companion . . . • Newcastle, 1817.

C., J. *Rev. James Craig.* Spiritual life: poems on several divine subjects . . . Edinb. 1727.

C., J. *Joel Cook.* Summer rambles. P. n.d.

C., J. *John Canton.* On the thermometer and barometer, "Gent. Mag.," October and December, 1748, pp. 452 and 533.

C., J., Esq., a Volunteer. *John Calef.* The siege of the Penobscot by the rebels . . . L. 1781.

C., J., M.D. *Dr. J. Castro.* A dissertation on the method of inoculating the small-pox . . . L. 1721.

C., J., Med. D. *Rev. John Colbatch.* Memoirs of Denmark . . . L. 1700. Also ascribed to Jodocus Crull.

C., J., M.D. *John Cooke, M.D.* The new theory of generation . . . L. 1762.

C., J., M.D., Fellow of the Royal Society. *Jodocus Crull.* The antiquities of St. Peters . . . L. 1711.

C., J., one of the Ministers of the Gospel at Glasgow. *Rev. James Clark.* Just and sober remarks on some parts and passages of the overtures concerning kirk-sessions . . . 1720.

C., J. D. *John David Chambers.* A companion to Confession and Holy Communion . . . L. 1853. — See " A Layman."

C., J. F. *J. F. Coates,* in his contributions to the " Mail and Express " (N.Y.).

C., J. F. & L. *James Freeman,* and *Lilian, Clarke.* Exotics. B. 1875.

C., J. H. *James H. Connolly,* in his contributions to the " World " (N.Y.).

C., J. M. and C. *John Mill,* and *Charlotte, Chanter.* Jack Frost, and other tales. L. 1858.

C., J. P. *John Payne Collier.* A light Bondell of livly discourses called Churchyardes Charge, etc. Edited . . . L. 1870.

C., J. R. *Dr. John Rose Cormack.* Notice of the late Dr. Abercrombie. 1844.

C., L. *Rev. Lyman Coleman.* Guidebook of the Lehigh Valley Railroad . . . P. 1872.

C. L. I. O. *Joseph Addison.* In the " Tatler " his papers have no signature; in the " Spectator " they are either " C.," " L.," " I.," or " O. "; in the " Guardian " they are marked by a hand.

C., L. M. *Miss L. M. Cole.* Science of food. L. 1883.

C. L. M. *Alexander Chalmers.* Tribute to the memory of Dr. Andrew Kippis, " Gent. Mag.," October, 1795, p. 803, etc.

C., M. *Michael Constable.* — See " A British Soldier."

C., M. *Mathew Carey.* To Messrs. N. Goddard . . . the committee of the Boston merchants. P. 1828.

C., M. A. *Miss Mary Anne Cruse.* Cameron Hall . . . P. 1867.

C., C. M. *Charlotte Moon Clark.* How she came into her kingdom : a romance. Chic. 1878.

C., M. D. *Moncure D. Conway.* Shakespeare at home. Letter from . . . from Stratford-on-Avon, April 21, 1883. In the " Commercial Gazette," Cin., May 26, 1883.

C., M. J. *Mrs. M. J. Carrington.* Absa-ra-ka. Home of the crows . . . P. 1868.

C., M. J., Minister of the Gospel at Dirletown. *Rev. James Clark.* A discourse of the duties of people to their pastors . . . Edinb. 1701.

C., M. J., Minister of the Gospel in Glasgow. *James Clark.* Gospel cordials . . . Glasgow, 1722.

C., N. *Nicholas Carlisle.* — See " D., J.," *James Dallaway.*

C., P. P. *Rev. Philip Pearsall Carpenter.* On chanting. From the " Christian Reformer " for December, 1848. Warrington, Eng. 1848.

C., P. W. *Peleg Whitman Chandler.* The authenticity of the Gospels . . . from the " New Jerusalem Magazine," for June, 1866. B. n.d.

C., R. *Rev. Rowland Connor,* in his contributions to the " International Review."

C., R. *Rev. Robert Colvill.* The Caledonian heroine . . . Edinb. 1771.

C., R. *Richard Cattermole.* Gems of sacred literature. Edited . . . L. 1841.

C., R. *Robert Clark.* Golf: a royal and ancient game. Edinb. 1875.

C., R. *Robert Carruthers.* The history of Huntingdon. 1824.

C., R. *Robert Calder.* The lawfullness and necessitie of observing the anniversary fasts . . . 1710.

C., R. C. *Richard Charles Coxe.* The mercy at Marsden Rocks . . . Newcastle, 1844.

C., R. C. *Richard Colama Close.* Was Bacon Shakespeare? In the " Victorian Review," Melbourne, Australia, for November, 1880.

C., R. E. *Mrs. R. E. Cresswell.* Memories of her mother [Mrs. Fry], in a letter to her sisters . . . Lynn, 1845.

C., R. H. *Robert Henry Clive.* Documents connected with the history of Ludlow and the Lords Marchers. By ... L. 1841.

C., R. L. *Rev. Russell Lant Carpenter.* Free blacks and slaves. From the "Christian Reformer" for August, 1853. n.p., n.d.

C., S. *S. Courtauld.* Ferns of the British Isles described and photographed. L. 1877.

C., S. *Mrs. Croft.* A Gospel harmony of the events of Good Friday ... L. 1878.

C., S. *Samuel Colliber.* An impartial enquiry into the existence and nature of God ... L. 1718.

C., S. *Samuel Carter.* The law of executions. L. 1706.

C., S. *Stephen Crisp.* Short history of a long travel from Babylon to Bethel ... L. 1718.

C., S., Barrister at Law. *Samuel Carter.* Lex customaria; or, a treatise of copy-hold estates ... L. 1701.

C., S. S. *Samuel Stillman Conant* (?). The Circassian boy. Translated ... B. 1875.

C., S. T. *Samuel Taylor Coleridge*, in Lamb's "Elia": The two races of men.

C., T. *Thomas Carlyle.* His signature to some of the articles he contributed to "Brewster's Edinburgh Encyclopædia," in Vol. XIV., XV., and XVI.; also in "Macmillan's Magazine," July, 1862.

C., T. *Thomas Chatterton*, in the "Freeholder's Magazine."

C., T. *Thomas Crowley.* Account of a plan for civilizing the North American Indians. L. about 1766.

C., T. *Thomas Corbett.* An account of the expedition of the British fleet to Sicily, in the years 1718, 1719, and 1720 ... L. 1739.

C., T. *Thomas Church.* Entertaining passages relating to Philip's war. B. 1716.

C., T. *Thomas Crawfurd.* Notes and observations on Mr. George Buchanan's "History of Scotland." Edinb. 1708.

C., T. A. *Thomas Adolphus Cragoe.* The river Fal and Falmouth harbour, illustrated ... Truro, 1876.

C., Th. *Theodore Child*, in his contributions to the "Sun" (N.Y.).

C., T. G. *T. G. Carroll.* Clavis Pharmacopœia Collegii Dublinensis ... Dublin, 1825.

C., T. G. *Thomas Greaves Cary.* Destiny; Progress. 1848.

C. T. H. *Chauncy Hare Townshend.* Journal of a tour through part of the Western Highlands of Scotland in the summer of 1839, by ... Newcastle, 1839.

C. T. O. *Henry Headley*, who contributed to the "Gent. Mag.," under the signature of "C. T. O," "Poems, and other pieces," which were brought out in a separate volume, L. 1786.

C. V. S. *Sir Richard Davis Hanson.* Letters to and from Rome ... L. 1873.

C., W. *William Cheyne.*—See "A true Son of the Church of Scotland."

C., W. *William Cowley.* Don Juan reclaimed ... Sheffield, 1840.

C., W. *William Chambers.* Poems for young people. Edinb. 1851.

C., W., M.D., C.M., L.C. *William Coward.* The grand essay; or, a vindication of reason and religion ... L. 1704.

C., The Rev. W. *Rev. William Cole.* A key to the Psalms ... Camb. 1788.

C., W. and R. *William and Robert Chambers.* Shipwrecks, and tales of the sea. Edited ... L. 1860.

C., W. A. *William Andrew Chatto.* Views of ports and harbours ... Engraved by W. and E. Finden. With a descriptive letter-press by ... L. 1838.

C., W. A. *William A. Croffut*, in his contributions to various periodicals.

C., W. B. *William Butler Crittenden*, in several papers relative to reminiscences of American tragedians, contributed to the "Rochester (N.Y.) Union and Advertiser."

C., W. B. *William Bell Crafton.* A short sketch of the evidence for the abolition of the slave trade, delivered before a committee of the House of Commons ... L. 1792.

C., W. C. *William Charles Cotton.* Buzz a buzz; or, the bees [by Wilhelm Busch, a German artist]. Done freely into English by ... L. 1872.

C., W. C. *William C. Coward.* Victorianism; or, a re-organization of the people. L. 1843.

C., W. E., and T., S. C. *William Ellery Channing, D.D.*, and *Rev. Samuel Cooper Thacher, A.M.* Elements of religion and morality, in the form of a catechism. B. 1813.

C., W. W. *William Warland Clapp.* Joseph Dennie: editor of "The Portfolio," and author of "The Lay Preacher." Camb. Mass.

C***, Charles. *Charles Cousin.* Voyage dans un grenier. Paris, 1878.

C***, F. *Felix Carteaux.* Histoire des désastres de Saint Dominique ... Bordeaux, 1802.

C**, Hugh.** *Hugh Carew.* The life of Sir R. Carew. L. 1811.

C***, M.** *Charles Yves Cousin d'Avalon.* Gasconiana ... Paris, 1801.

C***, R*****.** *Richard Challoner, D.D.* The Catholick instructed in the sacraments, sacrifice, ceremonies, and observances of the Church. L. 1837.

C****, F********.** *Frederick Corfield.* The Mélange, containing the Lunarian: a tale ... Taunton, 1819.

C******, Mlle. V. de.** *Victorine Chastenay de Lanty.* Du génie des peuples anciens ... Paris, 1808.

C——, A——, Esq. *Anthony Collins.* A letter from the late A— C—, Esq., to the Reverend Dr. C— M— [Conyers Middleton] on his examination ... L. 1750.

C——, De La B——, Mme. *Mme. Frances Erskine (Inglis) Calderon de la Barca.* Life in Mexico ... B. 1843.

C——, E——. *Eliza Coltman.* Plain tales; or, the advantages of industry: adorned with copper plates ... L. about 1816.

C—s D—s, Bellamy Brownjohn, and Dombey. *Robert Carr Dunham.* No thoroughfare. B. 1868.

Caballero, Fernan. *Cecilia(Böhl de Faber) Arrom.* La familia di Alvareda. 1850.

Cabinet, Old. *Richard Watson Gilder,* successor of Dr. J. G. Holland as editor of the "Century."

Cadenus. *Jonathan Swift.* Cadenus and Vanessa [Miss Esther Vanhomrigh]: a poem. 1726.

Cadvan. *Hugh Williams.* His bardic name. He was editor of the "Cymro" (Bangor), and one of the translators of Mrs. Stowe's "Uncle Tom's Cabin" into Welsh.

Cadwallader. *William G. Hudson,* in his contributions to the "Daily Eagle," Brooklyn, N.Y.

Cæmeterius. *Richard Littlehales* (?), his signature to a letter in the "Microcosm," published at Eton College. 1787.

Cæsar. *Julius Bleyer,* of the "Evening Wisconsin" (Milwaukee), in letters to various newspapers.

Cæsariensis. *James Waddell Alexander,* in the "Newark Daily Advertiser" and the "Literary World."

Cagliostro, Alessandro, Conte di. *Giuseppe Balsamo.* Vie de ... connu sous le nom de ... Paris, 1791.

Caigh, Essay. *S. A. Kenner,* correspondent of the "Salt Lake City Herald" (Utah).

Caius. *Dr. James Currie,* in his contributions to the "Public Advertiser," L. 1780.

Caius. *Mathew Carey.* Address to the President of the United States. P. 1795.

Calder, Alma. *Mrs. Alma Calder Johnston.* Miriam's heritage: a tale of the Delaware. N.Y. 1878.

Caledfryn Gwilym. *Rev. William Williams,* author of the "Gawn Awen" (the Treasure of the Muse) and other volumes of poetry, and for forty years (1820–60) "one of the leaders of the poetical choir."

Caledonian Comet, The. *Sir Walter Scott.* The Caledonian comet, by J. Taylor. L. 1810.

Caledonian Fisher, A. *J. Rose.* An essay upon the British fisheries ... By ... Edinb. 1705.

Caledonius, Cincinnatus. *John Gordon Barbour.* Lights and shadows of Scottish character and scenery ... Edinb. 1824.

Caledonnicus. *Whitelaw Ainslie, M.D.* Fitz-Raymond; or, the rambler on the Rhine: a metrico-political sketch ... Edinb. & L. 1831.

Caliban. *Robert Buchanan,* in some poetical contributions to the "Spectator." L. 1867.

Caliban. *Hector A. Stuart.* Ben Nebo: a pilgrimage in the South Seas. San Fran. 1871.

Caliban. *Jules Arnaud Arsène Claretie,* in his contributions to "l'Illustration." Paris, 1865.

Caliban. *Louis Jean Emmanuel Gonzalès.* La servante du diable; and Les trois fiancées. Paris, 1877.

California Joe. *T. Head.*

Calisthenes. *Josiah Quincy, Jr.,* in the "Boston Gazette," Feb. 10, 177–.

Call-Boy, The. *Charles J. Smith,* in Noah's "Sunday Times."

Callender, Tom, Esq., Citizen of the World. *James Thomson Callender.* Letters to Alexander Hamilton, King of the Feds ... Being intended as a reply to a scandalous pamphlet lately published ... under the signature of "Junius Philænus." N.Y. 1802.

Caller Herrin'. *Caroline Symington.* Poems. L. 18–.

Calm Observer, A. *George Joy.* American question: a letter from ... to a Noble Lord ... L. 1812.

Calm Observer, A. *Sir David Brewster.* An examination of the letter addressed to Principal Hill, on the case of Mr. Leslie ... Edinb. 1808.

Calm Observer, A. *Vicesimus Knox, LL.D.,* or *Benjamin Vaughan.* Letters on the subject of the Concert of Princes.

and the dismemberment of Poland and France . . . L. 1793.

Calpe, Adadus. *Antonio D. de Pascual.* The two fathers . . . N.Y. 1852.

Calvinianus Presbyter. *Rev. Archibald Bruce.* Armus secularis . . . Edinb. 1788.

Calvinus. *James Grahame.* Another letter . . . to the Rev. Dr. Thomas M'Crie, and the Rev. Mr. Andrew Thomson, on the parody of Scripture, lately published in "Blackwood's Edinburgh Magazine." Edinb. 1817.

Calvinus Minor, Scoto Britannus. *Rev. Archibald Bruce.* Free thoughts on the toleration of Popery. 1780.

Cam. *Samuel Badcock.* The farmer and his ass, in the "Gent. Mag.," September, 1786, p. 790.

Cam. *Walter Lewis, M.D.* Whist: what to lead. L. 1866.

Cambridge Gentleman, A. *Mr. Rawson.* A letter to the Reverend Dr. Henry Sacheverell . . . L. 1710.

Cambridge Graduate, A. *Cornelius Neale Dalton.* Poems, original and translated. L. 1868.

Cambridge M.A., A. *Rev. Robert Rowe Knott.* The new aid to memory . . . L. 1839.

Cambridge Man, A. *Henry Arthur Bright.* Free blacks and slaves. L. 1853.

Camden of the Eighteenth Century, The. *Richard Gough.*

Cameron, Leila. *Mrs. Catherine A. (Richards) Du Bose.* The pastor's household. N.Y. 1858.

Cameroy. *James Woods Lane, S.T.D.,* in the "New York Observer," about 1851.

Camillus. *Fisher Ames,* in contributions to the newspapers of Boston.

Camillus. *Rufus King,* who advocated Jay's treaty in several eloquent speeches, 1795.

Camillus. *Adam Thom.* Anti-Gallic letters . . . Montreal, 1836.

Camillus. *Alexander Hamilton.* A defence of the treaty of amity . . . between the United States and Great Britain . . . N.Y. 1795.

Camillus. *J. Henry.* An enquiry into the evils of general suffrage and frequent elections in Lower Canada . . . Montreal, 1810.

Camillus. *William Duane.* The Mississippi question . . . P. 1803.

Camlan, Gorovna. *Rev. Rowland Williams.* Lays from the Cimbric lyre . . . L. 1846.

Campbell, Donald. *Stephen Cullen Carpenter.* A journey over land to India . . . L. 1796.

Campbell, Kate. *Mrs. Jane Elizabeth (Larcombe) Lincoln.* Under the name of "Kate Campbell," she was a large contributor to the periodicals published by Godey, Peterson, Sartain, Neal, etc., and to the annuals; afterwards she wrote for the Baptist religious publications.

Campbell, Mary. — See "M. E. B."

Canadian, A. *J. Bell Forsyth.* A few months in the East; or, a glimpse of the Red, the Dead, and the Black seas . . . Quebec, 1861.

Canadian, A. *Pierre de Salles La Terrière, M.D.* A political account of Lower Canada . . . L. 1830.

Canadian, A. *James Lynne Alexander.* Wonders of the West . . . Toronto, 1825.

Candid Enquirer. *James Anderson, LL.D.* The antiquity of the woollen manufacture, in the "Gent. Mag.," August, 1778, p. 348.

Candidate, An Illused. *J. C. Caley.* Indignant rhymes . . . L. 1859.

Candidate for Orders in the Church, A. *Joseph Salkeld.* Birds, blossoms, and fruit of the Church . . . N.Y. 1843.

Candide. *Jules Arnaud Arsène Claretie,* who, in 1868, published articles in the "Figaro" under this signature, which were marked by a bold denunciation of the double execution of Martin Bidauré, which took place in Var in 1851.

Candidus. *Thady Fitzpatrick.* — See "F., T."

Candidus. *Samuel Adams.* Address to the people of Pennsylvania, Feb. 3, 1775. He also contributed frequently, under this pseudonym, to the "Boston Gazette" and "Boston Evening Post," during the years 1768-1774.

Candidus. *Charles Inglis.* Plain truth. P. 1776.

Candor. *Noah Webster.* Articles in "Conn. Courant," July 29, 1793, On the French revolution, Trade with St. Domingo; Aug. 12, 1793, True republicanism.

Canne, John. *Samuel Butler,* the poet. The acts and monuments of our late Parliament. L. 1744.

Cannibal Jack. *Charles Beach.* The way to win. L. 1869.

Canon. *Henry William Pullen.* Modern Christianity, a civilized heathenism. Salisbury, 1872.

Canonicus. *Rev. William Shedd.* Letters to W. E. Channing on the existence and agency of fallen spirits. B. 1828.

Canonicus. *Charles Chauncy, D.D.* A second letter to the Rev. Mr. George

Whitefield, urging upon him the duty of repentance, and returning into the bosom of that church of which he professes himself a member. Designed as a supplement to the first letter. B. 1743.

Cantabar. *Josiah Harris.* A biographical notice of Thomas Stark, the Mevagissey Quaker. Bath.

Cantabrigiensis. *Richard Porson, M.A.* Letters on the Three Heavenly Witnesses, in the "Gent. Mag.," 1788, pp. 875, 1063; 1789, pp. 101, 297, 386, 512, 690; 1790, p. 128.

Cantabrigiensis. *Dr. Taylor.* Miscellaneous observations upon authors ancient and modern. L. 1731–32.

Cantabrigius. *Richard Owen Cambridge.*

Lord Chesterfield said of him : " *Cantabrigius* drinks nothing but water, and rides more miles in a year than the keenest sportsman."

Cantianus. *Rev. Edmund Marshall,* author, under this signature, of a series of articles in the "Kentish Gazette."

Canute, Judith. *Mrs. Juliet H. (Lewis) Campbell.* Eros and Anteros, the old love and the new. 18–.

Cap. *Paul Antoine Gratacap.* Recherches sur les lactates. Paris, 1838.

Cape Cod Bard, The. *Henry S. Ellenwood.* — See "Pindar, Peter, Jr."

Cape Colonist, A. *May Byrne.* Ingham Place . . . L. 1874.

Cape Correspondent, A. *G. W. Boyce.* The Zulu war. [In verse.] Wells, 1879.

Capelsay, John. *John Saunders Holt.* Life and opinions of Abraham Page. 1868.

Capo de Feuillide. *Jean Gabriel Cappot.* L'Histoire du peuple de Paris. Paris, 1844.

Capsadell, Louise. *Mrs. Hammond.* Her waiting heart. N.Y. 1875.

Capsicum. *Rev. George Charles Smith.* Tarbucket; or, the humble petition of the Bethel Union Society in the year 1820 . . . L. 1820.

Captain, The. *Rev. Edmund George Harvey, B.A.* Our cruise in the Undine. Journal of an English pair-oar expedition through France, Prussia . . . With etchings by one of ourselves. L. 1854.

Captain in the Navy, A. *Frederick Chamier.* The life of a sailor . . . L. 1832.

Captain of the "Cumberland," The. *Alfred Henry Alston.* Ready, O ready! or, these forty years . . . L. 1873.

Captive Missionaries, The. *Henry A. Stern, A. Rosenthal,* and *others.* Letters from . . . in Abyssinia. L. 1866.

Caqueteur. *Charles Hull Webb,* in his contributions to the "Boys and Girls' Weekly" (N.Y.).

Caractacus. *E. Sendall,* in the "Live Stock Journal" (L.).

Carboy, John. *John A. Harrington.* Between the crusts. N.Y. 1875.

Cardiganshire Landlord, A. *Col. Thomas Johnes.* A C. L.'s advice to his tenants. 180–.

Carey, Mathew, Jr. *Augustus R. Cazauran* (?). The Democratic speaker's hand-book . . . Cin. 1868.

Carl. *C. S. Newhall.* Joe and the Howards; or, armed with eyes. B. 187–.

Carl, and Cauty Carl. *Frederick William Sawyer.* Hits at American whims, and hints for home use. B. 1860. Originally published under the above signatures in the Boston "Evening Transcript," to which, from 1847, Mr. Sawyer was a regular contributor.

Carle. *Victorien Sardou.* Les femmes fortes. Paris, 1860.

Carleton. *Walter Churlton, M.D.*

Carleton. *Charles Carleton Coffin.* Caleb Krinkle. B. 187–.

Carleton, Carrie. *Mrs. Mary (Booth) Wright.* Inglenook: a story for children. N.Y. 1868.

Carleton, Capt. George. *Daniel Defoe.* The memoirs of an English officer . . . L. 1728. Also attributed to Jonathan Swift.

Carleton, Cousin May. *Mrs. M. A. (Early) Fleming.* Since the age of seventeen she has been on the staff of the New York "Mercury," writing under this pen-name.

Carlfried. *Charles F. Wingate.* Views and interviews on journalism. N.Y. 1875.

Carlin, Michel. *J. H. Bonnye.* Baldness: its cause and cure. Manchester, 1875.

Carlo Khan. *Charles James Fox.* "At the time when Fox was introducing his famous 'India Bill,' he got the title of 'Carlo Khan,' as supreme dictator of the East." — See "Northelia."

Carlone. *Charles Brown,* the friend of Keats. Les Charmettes and Rousseau, contributed to "The Liberal." Conf. "Notes and Queries," 6th Series, viii., p. 392.

Carlopago. *Karl Ziegler.* Vom Kothurn der Lyrik . . . 1869.

Carlos, Don. *Henry T. Cheever,* in his contributions to the "Sunday Mercury" (P.).

Carlton. *Joseph Caldwell, S.T.D.* Letters of . . . 1825.

Carlton, Admiral George. *King George IV.* of England. The voyage of . . . in search of loyalty: a poetic epistle. L. 1820.

Carlton, Jay. *Jay Carlton Goldsmith.*

Carlton, Robert, Esq. *Baynard Rust Hall, S.T.D.* The new purchase. N.Y. 1843.

Carluccio. *Charles Brown,* the friend of Keats. La Bella Tabaccaia, contributed to the "Examiner," 1823. Conf. "Notes and Queries," 6th Series, viii., p. 392.

Carlyle, Jupiter. *Alexander Carlyle,* whose friends remarked that his noble countenance bore a striking resemblance to the Jupiter Tonans of the Capitol.

Carmen Sylva. *Queen Elizabeth* of Roumania, who, under this pen-name, has just published four stories in verse. Stürme Bonn, 1882.

Carmichael. — *Vernon.* Grace Darling, the Maid of the Isles . . . Newcastle-upon-Tyne, 1839.

Carnes, Capt. *M. J. Cummings.* Uncle Anthony. B. 1873.

Carnhuanawe. *Thomas Price.* He contributed chiefly under the signature of "Carnhuanawe" [Man of the Sunny Mound], to fifteen Welsh periodicals.

Caro. *Mrs. Caroline Atherton (Briggs) Mason.* Her earlier poems were published in the Salem (Mass.) "Register," under the signature of "Caro."

Carolinian, A. *Edward J. Pringle.* Notes on Spain and the Spaniards. 1859 . . . Charleston, 1861.

Carolinian, A. *William Henry Drayton.* To their excellencies Richard Viscount Howe, Admiral; and William Howe, Esq., General . . . Charleston, S.C., 1776.

Caroll, Martha. *Martha Brooks.* How Marjory helped. B. 1874.

Carp. *Frank Carpenter,* Washington correspondent of the "Leader" (Cleveland, O.).

Carpus. *Samuel Cox.* Expository essays and discourses. L. 1877.

Carr, Gabrielle. *Mrs. Anne Steele.* Ephemera. L. 1865.

Poems written by Mrs. Steele, and illustrated by Lady Wood.

Carr, Helen. *Lady William Page Wood.* Ephemera. L. 1865.

The poems were written by Mrs. Steele, and illustrated by Lady Wood.

Carra, Emma. *Mrs. Avis S. Spenser.*

Carra, Emma. *Mrs. Agnes Jane Stibbes,* who, during the Civil War, con-

tributed novelettes and sketches to the "Field and Fireside" under this pen-name.

Carrie. *Miss Mary Caroline Griswold.* Zaidee: a tale of the early Christians; and other novelettes and poems, in the "Southern Field and Fireside." Charleston, S.C., 1864.

Carrie, Aunt. *Miss Caroline Tomlinson.*

Carrie, Aunt. *Caroline L. Smith* (?). Popular pastimes . . . or, amusements for old and young . . . Springfield, Mass., 1867.

Carrier Boy, and Carrier Mercury. *Rev. Charles Timothy Brooks.* Signatures to "addresses" which he wrote for the "carriers" of Newport (R.I.) papers.

Carroll, Lewis. *Rev. Charles Lutwidge Dodgson.* Alice's adventures in Wonderland. L. 1869.

Carry, Aunt. *Mrs. Caroline Elizabeth Sarah (Sheridan-Norton) Maxwell.* Aunt Carry's ballads for children. L. 1847.

Carson, Kit. *Christopher Carson.* Life and adventures of Kit Carson. N.Y. 1859.

Cartaphilus. *David Hoffman.* Chronicles selected from the originals of Cartaphilus, the Wandering Jew. L. 1858.

Carteromaco, Nicolò. *Nicolò Forteguerri.* Ricciardetto di . . . Milan, 1813.

Carthusian, A. *W. J. D. Ryder.* Chronicles of Charter-House. L. 1847.

Carton, R. C. *Richard Claude Critchett.* A nom de théâtre.

Carver, John, Esquire, Justice of the Peace and Quorum. *Nathaniel Shatswell Dodge.* Sketches of New England; or, memories of the country . . . N.Y. 1842.

Caryl, Arthur. *Laughton Osborn.* Arthur Caryl: a novel. 18–.

Casca. *John Thompson.* He published articles signed "Casca" and "Gracchus," before 1799, against the Federal administration in the Petersburg (Va.) "Gazette."

Caspar. *Mrs. Virginia Durant Covington.* — See "Fabian."

Caspipina, Tamoc. *Jacob Duché,* in "Caspipina's Letters" . . . Bath, 1777.

The word Caspipina is formed from the initial letters of "Curate at St. Peters, in Philadelphia in North America."

Cassander, J. *John Bruckner.* Criticisms on the diversions of Purley . . . L. 1790.

Cassio. *Edward S. Gould,* his signature in Mr. Charles King's "American."

Cassius. *Æedanus Burke.* Address

to the freemen of South Carolina. Charleston, 1783.

Castel Chuiso, Giorgione di. *Peter Bailey.* Sketches from St. George's Fields. L. 1820–21.

Ascribed by Lowndes to Sir John C. Hobhouse, Lord Broughton.

Castil-Blaze. *François Henri Joseph Blaze.* De l'opera en France. Paris, 1820.

Castlemon, Harry. *Charles A. Fosdick.* Frank and Archie series. P. 1865.

Catchpole, Margaret. *Rev. Richard Cobbold.* Adventures of . . . L. 1852.

Catholic, A. *Rev. John Lingard.* A new version of the four Gospels . . . L. 1836.

Catholic and Burkist, A. *Theobald MacKenna.* An argument against extermination . . . Dublin, 1800.

Catholic Bishop of Bantry, The. *T. Dicker*, of Lewes. An appeal for the erection of Catholic churches in the rural districts of England . . . L. 1852. On p. 22 he signs "Ign. L. Bantry" (*i.e.*, Ignatius Loyola, Bishop of Bantry).

Catholic Clergyman, A. *Most Rev. John Carroll.* An address to the Roman Catholics of the United States of America . . . Annapolis, 1784.

Catholic Clergyman of Baltimore, A. *J. B. David.* True piety; or, the day well spent . . . Baltimore, 1809.

Catholic, Irish. *James Warren Doyle.* An essay on education and the state of Ireland . . . Dublin, 1880.

Catholic Layman, A. *Mathew Carey.* Letters on religious persecution. 4th ed., P. 1827.

Catholic, A Protesting. *Alexander Geddes.* An answer to [Gibson] the Bishop of Comana's pastoral letter. L. 1790.

Catholick, A. *William Nokes.* Modest reflections on [Charles Trimnel] the Right Reverend the Bishop of Norwich, his late charge . . . 1710.

Catholicus. *Cardinal John Henry Newman*, in the London "Times."

Catholicus. *Rev. Joseph Mendham.* The Episcopal oath of allegiance to the Pope, in the Church of Rome . . . Birmingham, 1822.

Catholicus. *William Matthews.* A new and seasonable address to the disciplinarians of the people called Quakers, relative to tithes and taxes . . . Bath, 1798.

Catholicus. *Henry Cotton, D.C.L.* Notes on the Preface to the Rhemish Testament (printed in Dublin, 1813) . . . Dublin, 1817.

Catholicus, a peaceable member of the Society of Quakers. *Henry Portsmouth.* An essay on the simplicity of truth . . . L. 1779.

Catholicus, Johannes. *John Rutty, M.D.* An essay towards a contrast between Quakerism and Methodism . . . Bristol, 1771.

Catholicus, Presbyter. *Rev. William Harness.* Visiting societies and lay readers. L. 1844.

Catholicus verus. *Andrew Carmichael.* A letter to the Roman Catholic clergy of Ireland . . . L. 1824.

Catlyne, Mr., Q. C. *Martin Francis Mahony.* The adventures of . . . In "Fraser's Mag."

Cato. *Walter Ruding, Esq.*, of Westcotes, near Leicester. " His papers signed ' Cato,' ' Anglo-Saxon,' ' Millions,' etc., which appeared in the ' Leicester Chronicle,' manifested a praiseworthy regard for the constitutional rights of Englishmen."

Cato. *George Burges, Esq.* Cato to Lord Byron on the immorality of his writings. L. 1824.

Cato. *John Trenchard.* Cato's letters, in the "London Journal," 1720, and " British Journal," 1722.

These letters were published in book form in 1724, and several times afterwards.

Cato. *Ezekiel Webster.* Defence of the national administration . . . Concord, N.H., 1828.

Cato. *Thomas Gordon.* A discourse of standing armies . . . By . . . L. 1722.

Cato. *Alexander Hamilton.* Examination of the treaty of amity, commerce, and navigation, between the United States and Great Britain . . . N.Y. 1795.

Cato. *Stephen Higginson.* Examination of the treaty of amity, commerce, and navigation, between the United States and Great Britain . . . N.Y. 1795.

Cato. *Robert R. Livingston.* Observations on Mr. Jay's treaty, Nos. 1, 2, in the " American Remembrancer," 1795.

Cato, Marcus. *Earl of Bath.* — See "Florus, Julius."

Cato Parvus. *Richard Heber.* Bibliophobia . . . With notes by . . . L. 1832. By Mercurius Rusticus, *i.e.*, Thomas Frognall Dibdin. — See " Atticus."

Caudle, Mrs. Margaret. *Douglas William Jerrold*, Mrs. Caudle's curtain lectures. L. 1846.

Causeur. *William Alfred Hovey.* Causerie, in the " Evening Transcript." B. 1880.

Caustick, Christopher, M.D., A.S.S., Fellow of the Royal College of Physicians, Aberdeen. *Thomas Green Fessenden.* The modern philosopher; or, terrible tractoration . . . P. 1806.

Caustic, Cosmo, Gent. *Christopher Reid.* Killvillain: a catechetical ode, by the late Tyro Trimstave, M.D. With a preface and notes, by . . . Edinb. 1835.

Cauty Carl. *Frederick William Sawyer.* — See "Carl."

Cavalry Officer, A. *Capt. Maurice Hartland Mahon (?).* The handy horse book . . . Edinb. and L. 1865.

The preface is signed "Magenta," a sobriquet of the author.

Caveat Emptor, Gent. *Sir George Stephen.* The adventures of a gentleman in search of a horse. L. 1835.

Cavendish. *Henry Jones.* Card essays, Clay's decisions, and card-table talk. L. 1879.

Cavendish. *Capt. W. Johnson Neale.* Cavendish. L. 1841.

Cavendish. *Samuel Bevan.* To all who smoke: a few words in defence of tobacco; or, a plea for the pipe . . . L. 1857.

Caxton. *William Henry Rhodes.* Discovery of the Pacific Ocean: a sketch . . . in the "Hesperian," 1859.

Caxton, Laura. *Lizzie B. Comins.* Marion Berkley: a story for girls. B. 1870.

Caxton, Pisistratus. *Edward George Earle Lytton-Bulwer, Baron Lytton.* My novel. L. 1853.

Caxton, Tim. *John Close.* — See "Dowell, S."

Cayron, C. A. J. *C. A. Jules Noriac.* Ouvrages. Paris, 1863-70.

Cecil. *Charles James Apperley.*

Cecil. *Mrs. S. J. Battey.*

Cecil. *William Hone.* Cecil's sixty curious, interesting, and authentic narratives. L. 1824.

Cecil. *Charles Edward Fisher.* Kansas and the Constitution. B. 1856.

Cecil. *Cornelius Tongue.* Records of the chase, and memoirs of celebrated sportsmen . . . L. 1854.

Cecil, Arthur. *Arthur Cecil Blunt.* A *nom de théâtre.*

Cecil, Davenant. *Rev. Derwent Coleridge.* Under this *nom de plume* he became a contributor to "Knight's Quarterly Magazine."

Cecil, Dr. *Dabney Carr,* one of the writers, under this signature, of the essays in Wirt's (W.) "Old Bachelor," 1812.

Celatus. *Robert Owen.* The modern theme; or, education the people's right and nation's glory . . . L. 1847.

Celebrated Author of that Country, A. *Mrs. Eliza Haywood.* Memoirs of a certain island adjacent to the kingdom of Utopia . . . L. 1725.

Celebrated Commoner, A. *Rt. Hon. William Pitt, Earl of Chatham.* The celebrated speech of . . . L. 1766.

His speech in favor of the repeal of the American Stamp Act.

Celebrated Literary and Political Character, A. *Richard Glover.* Memoirs of . . . from 1742 to 1757 . . . L. 1813.

Celia. *Mrs. Celia M. (Kellum Burr) Burleigh,* who, under this pen-name, wrote prose and verse for the leading Western papers.

Cellarius. *Rev. Thomas Welbank Fowle.* A new analogy between revealed religion and the course and constitution of nature. L. 1881.

Celler, Ludovic. *Louis Leclerc.* Les décors, les costumes, et la mise en scène au XVIIe siècle, 1615-1680. Paris, 1869.

Celnart, Élisabeth Félicie. *Mme. Élisabeth Félicie Canard Bayle-Mouillard.* Bethsali; ou, la dispersion des Juifs. Paris, 1825.

Celt, The. *Thomas Davis,* in his contributions of lyrics and ballads to the "Dublin National," 1842 *et seq.*

Celtophile, A. *Rev. Francis Crawford, LL.D.* Ereuna; or, an investigation of the etymons of words and names, classical and Scriptural, through the medium of the Celtic . . . L. 1875.

Censor. *Oliver Bell Bunce.* Don't: a manual of mistakes and improprieties more or less prevalent in conduct and speech. N.Y. 1883.

Censor of the Age, The. *Thomas Carlyle.*

Centaur. *Charles Sass,* in his contributions to the "Mail and Express" (N.Y.).

Centz, P. C., barrister. *Bernard J. Sage.* Davis and Lee, L. 1865; The republic of letters, L. 1881.

Cerberus, The. *Nathan Haskell Dole,* as art, dramatic, and literary editor to the "Philadelphia Press."

Cerimon. *Dr. William Thomson.* The political purpose of the Renascence drama . . . Melbourne, 1878.

Certain Free Enquirer, A. *Peter Annet.* A collection of the tracts of . . . L. 1766.

Certain Northern Vicar, A. *Rev. John Ellison.* The will of . . . carefully copied . . . upon T—. [In verse.] 1765.

Also ascribed to Rev. W. Cooper.

Certain Traveller, A. *George Amory Bethune, M.D.* The uncertainties of travel. A plain statement by . . . B. 1880.

Certain Unknown Vicar, A. *Rev. W. Cooper.* Will of . . . L. 1765.

Cey, Arsène de. *François Arsène Chaise de Cahange.* La fille du curé. Paris, 1832.

Cezinski, Marie. *Miss H. A. Steinhauer.* Helen Egerton. P. 1873.

Chabreul, Mme. de. *Mme. Du Parquet.* Jeux et exercices des jeunes filles par . . . Paris, 1867.

Chaff, Gumbo. *Elias Howe, Jr.* Accordion songster. B. 1860.

Chairman of the Committee on the State of the Church, The. *Richard Sharp Mason, D.D.* A letter to the Bishop of North Carolina on . . . his late pastoral on the Salisbury convention . . . N.Y. 1850.

Chalière, Louis. *L. C. Norbert.* Ingenio. Paris, 186–.

Chalk, Old. *Henry Chadwick*, in the Brooklyn "Union."

Cham. *Amedeé de Noë*, the French caricaturist, who, from 1842, contributed numerous caricatures to albums and almanacs, and especially to the "Charivari," most of which were collected in albums, 1843–57.

Chamier, Capt. *William James.* Naval history of Great Britain; with additional notes and continuation. L. 1847.

Champ. *James Wells Champney.* All around a palette. By Lizzie W. Champney. Illustrated by . . . B. 1877.

Champfleury. *Jules François Félix Husson-Fleury.* Étude sur Balzac. Paris, 1851.

Champion Wing Shot of America, The. *A. H. Bogardus.* Field, cover, and trap shooting. By . . . N.Y. 187–.

Champlin. *George C. Mason*, the Newport (R.I.) correspondent of the New York "Evening Post."

Chancellor of the Exchequer, The. *William Ewart Gladstone.* Speech of . . . on the finance of the year and the treaty of commerce with France. Delivered in the House of Commons . . . February 10th, 1860. L. 1860.

Chandeneux, Claire de. *Mme. Emma Bérenger Bailly.* Secondes noces . . . Paris, 1881.

Chapel Minister, A. *Rev. John M'Gill.* The Biblical criticism of the Glasgow presbytery criticised. Glasgow, 1866.

Chaperon, A. *Mrs. Arabella Sullivan.* Recollections of . . . edited by Lady Dacre. L. 1833.

Chaplain, A. *Henry Norman Hudson.* Campaign with Gen. Butler. N.Y. 1865.

Chaplain, A. *Rev. John Luckey.* Prison sketches . . . N.Y. 1849.

Chaplain, The. *Bradford Kinney Peirce.* Stories from life which the chaplain told. B. 1866.

Chaplain in H. M. Indian Service, A. *Rev. James Mackay.* From London to Lucknow . . . L. 1860.

Chaplain of said Society, The. *Charles H. Wharton, D.D.* A letter to the Roman Catholics of the city of Worcester [England], from . . . stating the motives which induced him to relinquish their communion and become a member of the Protestant Church. P. 1784.

Chaplain of the U. S. Army, A. *Rev. Stephen A. Hodgman.* The nation's sin and punishment; or, the hand of God visible in the overthrow of slavery . . . N.Y. 1864.

Chaplain to the Mayorality, The. *Rev. Robert Crawford Dillon.* The Lord Mayor's visit to Oxford . . . L. 1826.

Charfy, Guiniad, Esq. *James Saunders* or *George Smeeton.* The fishwoman; or, the art of angling made easy . . . L. 1724.

Chariessa. *Mrs. Elizabeth Carter*, who contributed two papers to Dr. Johnson's "Rambler," No. 44, and No. 100, the latter on "Modish pleasures," and signed "Chariessa."

Charity, Aunt. *Mrs. Sarah C. Yeiser.* Her contributions to the New Orleans "Crescent" were signed "Azelée"; but her *nom de plume* of "Aunt Charity" was more familiar to Southern readers.

Charity-Organizationist, A. *J. Hornsby Wright.* Thoughts and experiences of . . . L. 1878.

Charles, Lord Hawkesbury. *Charles Jenkinson,* 1st Earl of Liverpool. A discourse on the conduct of the government of Great Britain, in respect to neutral nations, during the present war . . . L. 1758.

Charlet, Henri. *Pierre Giffard.* Procés de Racine. Paris, 1877.

Charley, Snarly. *Charles Clark.* The fashionable folly . . . 1860.

Charlie, Champaigne. *Charles Thorpe.*

Charlotte, Aunt. *Mary Charlotte Yonge.* Aunt C.'s evenings at home with the poets . . . L. 1881.

Charlotte Elizabeth. *Mrs. Charlotte*

Elizabeth (Browne Phelan) Tonna. Floral biography, 1860; Judah's lion, 1868. L.

Ch—rt—s, Fr—nc—s, Colonel. *Col. Francis Charteris.* Scotch gallantry display'd; or, the life and adventures of . . . L. 1730.

Chartist Parson. *Charles Kingsley,* who took part in the ragged school movement and in the various efforts to ameliorate the condition of the working classes, to such an extent as to earn this name, which was signed to magazine articles.

Chasuble, Archdeacon, D.D. *Thomas William Marshall.* The comedy of convocation in the English Church . . . N.Y. 1868.

Chatfield, the late Paul, M.D. *Horace Smith.* The tin trumpet; or, heads and tales for the wise and waggish . . . Edited by Jefferson Saunders, Esq. L. 1836.

Chatterbox, Charles, Esq. *William Biglow,* writer of the "Omnium Gatherum," in the "Federal Orrery." B. 1794 *et seq.*

Chatterer, A. *Samuel Adams,* in the "Boston Gazette," Aug. 20, 1770.

Chavette, Eugène. *Eugène Vachette.* Nous marions Virginie . . . 1879.

Chazel, Prosper. *Adolphe Le Reboullet.* Le chalet des sapins. Paris, 187-.

Cheakill, Sir Joseph, K.F., K.S. *Watson Taylor.* The Cross-Bath guide . . . L. 1815.

Cheeki, Tomo, the Creek Indian in Philadelphia. *Philip Freneau,* in his "Time-Piece," with this preliminary notice : —

"A number of eccentric writings under this title are in the hands of the editor of the "Time-Piece," said to be translated from one of the Indian languages of this country. They were transmitted to him more than two years ago, and a few numbers published in a gazette edited by him in a neighboring State, but discontinued with that paper."

Cheem, Aliph. *Walter S. Yeldham.* Lays of Ind. Calcutta, 1879.

Cheeryble Brothers. *William Grant and Brothers,* a well-known firm of Manchester, supposed to have been depicted by Mr. Dickens under this title.

Chelsea. *Charles Alexander Nelson,* as Boston correspondent of the "Bookseller and Stationer," Chic. 1883–84.

Cherith. *Miss Fannie Surtees.* Homespun stories, and Bric-à-brac stories. L. 1878.

Cheshire Weaver, The. *J. D. Latouche.* Anglia Restaurata . . . L. 1727.

Chesney, Esther. *Miss Clara V.*

Dargan. Under this signature, in 1860, she wrote several stories for the "Southern Guardian," published in Columbia, S.C., and in 1861 contributed to the "Southern Field and Fireside," Charleston.

Chester. *William Broome.* "Towards the close of his life he . . . amused himself with translating odes of Anacreon, which he published in the 'Gentleman's Magazine,' under the name of 'Chester.'" — CHALMERS, Vol. VII.

Chester, Elizabeth S. *Elizabeth A. Smith.*

Chester, John. *Rev. John Mitchell.* Derwent; or, recollections of young life in the country . . . N.Y. 1872.

Chevalier. *M. C. Hart,* in his contributions to the "Sunday Mercury" (P.).

Chicagoan, A. *James L. Batchelder.* Societyism and its evils . . . Chic. 1871.

Chickasaw, the Scout. *L. H. Naron.* Life and adventures of . . . Chic. 1865.

Chief Engineer of the Board of Sewerage Commissioners, The. *E. S. Chesbrough.* Chicago Sewerage Report . . . Chic. 1850.

Chief Incendiary of the House. *Samuel Adams.* So termed by Hutchinson in a letter to Richard Jackson, 1772.

Chierico, Dedimo. *Niccolò Ugo Foscolo.* Sterne's Sentimental Journey, translated . . . 1813.

Child of Candour, A. *Mrs. Mary Knowles (Molly Knowles).* Her signature to an interesting dialogue between Dr. Samuel Johnson and Mrs. Knowles, in the "Gent. Mag.," LXI., Pt. I., 500.

Chincapin. *W. R. Barber,* in his contributions to "Punchinello" (N.Y.).

Chinese Philosopher, A. *Oliver Goldsmith.* The citizen of the world; or, letters from . . . in London to his friend in the East. L. 1762.

Chip of the Young Block, A. *Maria Stewart Stewart.* Historical, political, and spiritual view of the history of Alexander Stewart . . . L. 1861.

Chiquita. *Eppie Bowdre Castlen.* Autumn dreams . . . N.Y. 1870.

Chirurgus. *John Dix.* "The great fact" examined and disproved; or, homœopathy unmasked . . . L. 1857.

Chislon. — *Nichols.* Memorial of A. B. Soule. Salem, 1866.

Chloroform. *William S. W. Ruschenberger, U.S.N.* Assimilated rank of the civil branch of the navy. P. 1848.

Chollet. *Louise E. Furniss,* in her contributions to "Harper's Magazine" (N.Y.).

Chor-Episcopus. *Rev. John Waugh.* Episcopacy examined ... Utica, N.Y., 1849.

Christabel. *Miss Mahoney,* of Kenmare. Poems on various occasions.

Christen, Ada. *Friderik Christine.* Aus dem Leben, 1876; Aus der Tiefe, 1878, etc.

Christian, A. *Gerard Legh.* A case of conscience resolved ... L. 1719.

Christian, A. *Andrew Henderson.* The case of the Jews considered, with regard to trade, commerce, manufactures, and religion ... L. 1753.

Christian, A. *William Hewetson.* A letter to the Clergy of England, in the County of Northumberland ... 1732.

Christian, A. *Gilbert Dalrymple.* A letter to ... Mr. Stebbing; being remarks upon his late book relating to sincerity ... L. 1718.

Christian Believer, A. *Alexander Dalrymple.* A letter to a friend on the Test Act. n.p. 1790.

Christian Poet. A. *John Holland.* The bazaar; or, money and the church: a rejected offering, in blank verse ... Sheffield, 1861.

Christian Whig, A. *Richard Watson, D.D.* A letter to the members of the House of Commons, respecting the petition for relief in the matter of subscription ... L. 1790.

Christian, Theophilus, Esq. *John Owen, M.A.* The fashionable world displayed ... L. 1804.

Christianus. *Joseph Cockfield,* of Upton, near Plaistow and West-Ham, Essex.

Christianus Phileleutherus. *Rev. Thomas Broughton.* Christianity distinct from the Religion of Nature ... L. 1732.

Christicola. *John Bevans, Jr.* Some tracts relating to the controversy between Hannah Barnard and the Society of Friends ... L. 1802.

Christlieb, Theophile. *Kathinka Zitz;* one of her pseudonyms.

Christodor. *Cornelius Peter Bock.*

Christophe, M., vigneron. *Jacques Boucher de Crève cœur de Perthes.* Opinions ... sur les prohibitions de la liberté du commerce. Paris, 1831–34.

Christrup, Jens. *Jens Christian Hostrup.* Den Tredie; Den gamle Elsker. 184–.

Christy, George. *George N. Harrington.*

Chroniqueuse. *Mrs. Olive Logan Sikes.* Photographs of Paris life ... L. 1861.

Chrononhotonthologos. *David Carey.* Ins and outs; or, the state of parties ... L. 1807.

Chrysal. *Sir William Scott, Lord Stowell.* Letters on the high price of bullion ... L. 1813.

Chrysanthea; Chrysantheus. *Mrs. Lilly C.,* and *Thomas Lake, Harris.* Hymns of the Two-in-one: for bridal worship of the New Life. Salem-on-Erie, 1876.

Chubb, Mr. *Thomas Johnson.* An essay on moral obligation ... L. 1731.

Church of England Divine, A. *Rev. Edward Synge.* Free-thinking in matters of Religion stated and recommended. L. 1727.

Church of England Man, A. *Jonathan Swift, D.D.* The sentiments of ... 1708.

Ch—ch—ll, Mr. C——. *Charles Churchill,* The Anti-Times. Addressed to ... L. 1764.

Churchill, Frank. *George Henry Lewes (?)* Taking by storm. L. 1850.

Churchman, A. *Rev. Arthur Philip Perceval, B.C.L.* An address to the members of the Church of England ... L. 1835.

Churchman, A. *R. B. N. Saumarez.* The Bible: Strictures on the imperfections of the present version ... Bath, 1848.

Churchman, A. *John Jay.* Caste and slavery in the United States. N.Y. 1843.

Churchman, A. *Alexander Chalmers.* Christening of ships, "Gent. Mag.," January, 1803, p. 40.

Churchman, A. *Rev. John Gordon Lorimer.* Church establishments defended ... 2d ed. Glasgow, 1833.

Churchman, A. *E. Bickersteth.* A help to the study of the Scriptures ... Norwich, 1815.

Churchman, A. *E. A. Humphrey.* Lessons on the liturgy of the Protestant Episcopal Church in America. B. 1861.

Churchman, A. *John Bowden, D.D.* Letter from ... to his friend in New Haven ... New Haven, 1808.

Churchman, A. *William Jay.* A letter to ... Bishop Hobart ... N.Y. 1823.

Churchman, A. *Rev. William Francis Wilkinson.* The Rector in search of a Curate ... L. 1843.

Churchman, A. *Brabazon Ellis.* Rejoinder to "A Dissenter's reply on the subject of Church rates, etc." ... Burslem, 1840.

Churchman, A. *Rev. Edward Smedley.* Religio Clerici. L. 1821.

Churchman, A. *Edward Berens, M.A.* Remarks on Lord Henley and Dr. Burton on Church reform. L. 1833.

Churchman, A. *Samuel Roffey Maitland, D.D.* The voluntary system ... Gloucester, Eng., 1834–35.

Churchman, A Broad. *Edward A. Warriner.* Victor La Tourette. B. 1875.

Churchman, An English. *Rev. Richard Sankey, M.A.* An English Churchman's reason for his hope. L. 1851.

Churchman, A Free. *Rev. Andrew Gray.* Dr. Struthers on the Free Church. Perth, 1845.

Churchman of the Diocese of New York, A. *William Jay.* A letter to the Right Rev. Bishop Hobart; occasioned by the strictures on Bible Societies, contained in his late charge to the Convention of New York. N.Y. 1823.— See "Corrector."

Churllow, R—t H—e E—d, L—d. *Edward Thurlow*, Baron Thurlow. An English green box; or, the green box of ... given by Mrs. Harvey to R. O'Tickle ... L. 1779.

Churne, William, of Staffordshire. *Rev. Francis Edward Paget.* The hope of the Katzekopfs: a fairy tale ... Rugeley, 1844.

Churton, Henry. *Albion Winegar Tourjée.* Toinette: a tale of transition. N.Y. 1875.

Cibber, Colley. *James Rees.* The life of Edwin Forrest. P. 1874. Mr. Rees has also, under this signature, published articles on "Shakespeare and Lord Bacon," June and July, 1874, in the "Sunday Mercury" (P.).

Cicely, Cousin. *L. Lermont.* Lewie; or, the bended twig. Auburn, N.Y., 1853.

Cicero. *Joseph Galloway.* Letter from ... to Catiline the Second [Charles James Fox] ... L. 1781.

Cicerone. *Rev. J. H. Bloom*, Vicar of Castleacre. Handbook to the ancient remains of Castleacre, Norfolk.

Cicestrensis, Presbyter. *Henry Latham.* Anthologia Davidica ... L. 1846.

Cigarette. *Willis H. Bocock*, in his contributions to the "Despatch" (Richmond, Va.).

Cincinnatus. *William Plumer.* For thirty years preceding his death, he contributed largely to the papers, under this pseudonym.

Cincinnatus. *Joseph Cawthorne.* The false alarm ... L. 1782.

Cincinnatus Caledonius. *John Gordon Barbour.* Lights and shadows of Scottish character and scenery. Edinb. 1824.

Cinna. *Robert Baldwin Sullivan*, who "was wont, in his younger days, to contribute papers of a humourous and playful character to the literary periodicals of the day. In Sibbald's 'Canadian Magazine,' published at York (Toronto) in 1833, are to be seen communications of his under the *nom de plume* of 'Cinna.'"

Cinna. *William Benjamin Wells*, who wrote for Wilkes' "Spirit of the Times" (N.Y.) with this signature. Author of "Canadiana" ... L. 1837.

Cirujano, M. M. C. *George Borlase Childs.* Barbadazulo Vanagloroso, the demon of the Castle Heights ... L. 1863.

Citizen, A. *James Hack, Jun.* An address to the inhabitants of Chichester, on the subject of the distribution of the Scriptures. Chichester, 1812.

Citizen, A. *Charles Christian.* A brief treatise on the police of the city of New York ... N.Y. 1812.

Citizen, A. *Hon. Timothy Fuller.* The election of President of the United States considered ... B. 1823.

Citizen, A. *Hugo Arnot.* A letter to the heritors, farmers, and inhabitants of the county of Edinburgh ... Edinb. 1775.

Citizen, A. *James Cleland.* Letter to the Honourable the Lord Provost, respecting the proposed Statute Labour Bill for Glasgow. Glasgow, 1819.

Citizen, A. *James B. Congdon.* Letter to the Representatives in the General Court, from the town of New Bedford ... New Bedford, 1847.

Citizen, A. *Francis Hare*, Bishop of Chichester. A letter to Sir. R. Brocas, Lord Mayor of London. L. 1730.

Citizen, A. *Hon. Henry Sherwood.* Letter ... on the Usury Laws ... Toronto, 1847.

Citizen, A. *Philip Livingston.* The other side of the question; or, a defence of the liberties of North America ... N.Y. 1774.

Also ascribed to Myles Cooper.

Citizen, A. *James Dunwoody Brownson De Bow.* The political annals of South Carolina ... Charleston, 1845.

The author also signs himself "J. D."

Citizen, A. *Edmund Kimball.* Reflections upon the Law of Libel ... B. 1823.

Citizen, A. *William Findley.* A review of the revenue system adopted by the first Congress under the Federal Constitution ... P. 1794.

Citizen, A. *Cyprian Rondeau Bunce.* A translation of the several charters, etc., granted . . to the citizens of Canterbury . . . 1791.

Citizen of Aberdeen, A. *William Gordon.* A letter to Mr. Francis Melvil . . . L. 1718.

Citizen of Albany. *Cuyler Staats.* Tribute to the memory of DeWitt Clinton . . . Albany, 1828.

Citizen of America, A. *Jonas Clopper.* — See "Thwackus, Herman."

Citizen of Baltimore, A. *John S. Tyson.* Life of Elisha Tyson, the philanthropist . . . Balt. 1825.

Citizen of Baltimore, A. *Richard II. Townsend.* Original poems.

Citizen of Boston, A. *George Richards.* The Declaration of Independence : a poem accompanied by odes, songs, etc., adapted to the day . . . B. 1793.

Citizen of Boston, A. *Alden Bradford.* A particular account of the battle of Bunker or Breed's Hill, on the 17th June, 1775. B. 1825.

Citizen of Boston, A. *Elias Hasket Derby.* Reality *vs.* Fiction . . . B. 1850. See "D., E. H."

Citizen of Boston, A. — *Ward.* Remarks upon an oration delivered [July 4, 1845] by Charles Sumner before the authorities of the city of Boston . . . B. 1845.

Citizen of Burlington, A. *Henry C. Carey.* Beauties of the monopoly system in New Jersey . . . P. 1848.

Citizen of Cambridgeport, A. *Daniel Nason.* A journal of a tour from Boston to Savannah, thence to Havana . . . Camb., Mass., 1849.

Citizen of Connecticut, A. *Henry Trumbull.* History of the discovery of America . . . Norwich, Conn., 1810.
Really by James Steward, D.D., and published as his own by II. T.

Citizen of London, A. *Francis Hawling.* The impertinent lovers . . . A comedy . . . L. 1723.

Citizen of Maine, A. *Edward Payson.* The Maine Law in the balance . . . Portland, Me., 1855.

Citizen of Maryland, A. *Rev. John Allen.* An essay on the policy of appropriations being made by the government of the United States, for purchasing, etc. the slaves thereof . . . Balt. 1826.

Citizen of Maryland, A. *Virgil Maxcy.* The Maryland Resolutions, and the objections to them considered . . . Balt. 1822.

Citizen of Maryland, A. *H. Mankin.* Thoughts on labor, capital, currency . . . Balt. 1864.

Citizen of Massachusetts, A. *Hermann Mann.* The Female Review . . . Dedham, Mass., 1797.

Citizen of Massachusetts, A. *Salma Hale.* History of the U. S. of America . . . Keene, 1832

Citizen of Massachusetts, A *John Lowell, LL.D.* The impartial inquirer . . . B. 1811.

Citizen of Massachusetts, A. *George Ticknor Curtis.* The merits of Thomas W. Dorr and George Bancroft, as they are politically connected . . . B. 1844.

Citizen of Massachusetts, A. *Alfred E. Giles.* The Mormon problem . . . B. 1882.
Also ascribed to James H. Hart.

Citizen of Massachusetts, A. *James Bowdoin.* Opinions respecting the commercial intercourse between the United States of America and the Dominions of Great Britain . . . B. 1797.

Citizen of Massachusetts, A. *James Sullivan.* The path to riches. An inquiry into the origin and use of money . . . B. 1792.

Citizen of Massachusetts, A. *James Trecothick Austin.* Remarks on Dr. Channing's "Slavery" . . . B. 1835.

Citizen of Massachusetts, A. *Oliver Holden.* Sacred dirges, hymns, and anthems, commemorative of the death of General George Washington . . . B. 1800.

Citizen of New England, A. *Isaac Hill.* Brief sketch of the life, character, and services of Major-General Andrew Jackson . . . Concord, N.H., 1828.

Citizen of New England, A. *Josiah Hooke (?).* The practical expositor and sententious reader . . . Gardiner, Me., 1829.

Citizen of New England, A. *Rev. Cyril Pearl.* Remarks on African Colonization and the abolition of slavery. Windsor, Vt., 1833.

Citizen of New York, A. *John H. Lathrop.* An address . . . on the . . . Anti-Masonic excitement . . . Albany, 1830.

Citizen of New York, A. *John Jay.* An address to the people of the State of New York . . . N.Y. 1787.

Citizen of New York, A. *Myron Holley.* An address to the people of the United States on the subject of the Anti-Masonic excitement, or new party . . . Albany, 1830.

Citizen of New York, A. *Russell Jarvis.* A biographical notice of Com. Jesse D. Elliott . . . P. 1835.

Citizen of New York, A. *Nicholas*

F. Beck. Considerations in favour of the construction of a great state road from Lake Erie to the Hudson River. Albany, 1827.

Citizen of New York, A. *Edmund Charles Genet.* Letter to the Electors of President and Vice-President of the United States. N.Y. 1808.

Citizen of New York, A. *Freeman Hunt.* Letters about the Hudson River and its vicinity. Written in 1835 and 1836 . . . N.Y. 1836.

Citizen of New York, A. *James Cheetham.* A narrative of the suppression by Col. Burr of the history of the Administration of John Adams . . . N.Y. 1812.

Citizen of New York, A. *James Hawkes.* A retrospect of the Boston Tea Party . . . N.Y. 1834.

Citizen of New York, A. *Rev. R. Fisher.* Seventeen Numbers, the signature of Neckar, upon the Causes of the present distress of the Country. N.Y. 1837.

Citizen of New York, A. *Clement Clarke Moore, LL.D.* A sketch of our political condition . . . N.Y. 1813.

Citizen of North Carolina, A. *H. K. Berguin.* Considerations relative to a Southern Confederacy. Raleigh, 1860.

Citizen of Pennsylvania, A. *Albert Gallatin.* An examination of the conduct of the Executive of the United States towards the French Republic . . . P. 1797.

Citizen of Pennsylvania, A. *Charles Ingersoll.* A letter to a friend in a Slave State . . . P. 1862.

Citizen of Pennsylvania, A. *Frederick Adolphus Packard, LL.D.* Thoughts on the condition and prospects of popular education in the United States . . . P. 1836.

Citizen of Pennsylvania, A. *William Bradford Reed.* Thoughts on Intervention, by . . . P. 1852.

Citizen of Philadelphia, A. *Mathew Carey.* Common sense addresses to the citizens of the Southern States . . . P. 1829.

Citizen of Philadelphia, A. *Benjamin Rush.* Letters on the Rebellion, to a citizen of Washington from . . . P. 1862.

Citizen of Philadelphia, A. *Paul Beck, Jr.* A proposal for altering the eastern front of the city of Philadelphia . . . P. 1820.

Citizen of the United States, A. *George Armroyd.* A connected view of the whole internal navigation of the United States . . . P. 1830.

Citizen of the United States, A. *Pelatiah Webster.* Essay on money as a medium of commerce . . . P. 1786.

Citizen of the United States, A. *Alexander Hill Everett.* Europe; or, a general survey of the principal Powers . . . L. 1822.

Citizen of the United States, A. *Joel R. Poinsett.* Notes on Mexico . . . P. 1824.

Citizen of the United States, A. *William Vans Murray.* Political sketches . . . L. 1787.

Citizen of the United States, A. *James McBride.* Symmes's theory of Concentric Spheres . . . Cin. 1826.

Citizen of the United States, A. *Silas Wood.* Thoughts on the state of the American Indians . . . N.Y. 1794.

Citizen of the United States, A. *Rev. John Cosens Ogden.* Tour through Upper and Lower Canada . . . Litchfield, 1799.

Citizen of the United States, A. *Charles Phelps.* Vermonters unmasked . . . N.Y. 1782.

Citizen of the United States, A. *Benjamin Lundy.* The war in Texas . . . P. 1837.

Citizen of Virginia, A. *John Taylor.* Arator: being a series of agricultural essays, practical and political, in sixty-one numbers . . . Georgetown, D.C., 1813.

Citizen of Virginia, A. *Rev. George Bourne.* The condensed anti-slavery Bible argument. N.Y. 1845.

Citizen of Virginia, A. *George Tucker.* Essays on various subjects of taste, morals, and national policy. Georgetown, D.C., 1822.

Citizen of the West, A. *Robert Dale Owen.* Pocahontas: a historical drama . . . N.Y. 1837.

Citizen of the World, A. *James Broadhead* or *James Boardman.* America and the American . . . L. 1833.

Citizen of the World, A. *Mathew Carey.* Fragment. Addressed to the sons and daughters of Humanity. P. 1796.

Citizen of the World, A. *J. Easby.* Manchester and the Manchester people . . . Manchester, 1843.

Citizen of the World, The. *Oliver Goldsmith.* — See " A Chinese Philosopher."

Citizen who continued all the while in London, A. *Daniel Defoe.* A journal of the plague year . . . L. 1722. Signed " H. F."

Citizen, The First. *Charles Carroll,* of Carrollton, in 1770–71.

Citoyen, Américain, Un. *William Lee.* Les États-Unis et l'Angleterre; ou, souvenirs et réflexions d' ... Bordeaux, 1814.

Citoyen des États-Unis, Un. *I. E. Bonnet.* Réponse aux principales questions, qui peuvent être faites sur les États-Unis de l'Amérique ... Lausanne, 1795.

Citoyen des États-Unis, Un. *George M. Gibbs.* Traité du 4 Juillet, 1831, entre la France et les États-Unis ... Paris, 1835.

Citrouillard, Joseph. *Joseph Jacques Commerson.* Les Binettes contemporaines ... Paris, 1854–59.

City Waiter, The. *John T. Bedford,* in his contributions to "Punch" (L.).

Ciudadano de los Estados Unidos, Un. *Alexander Hill Everett.* America; ó, examen general de la situacion politica ... Northampton, Mass., 1828.

Civilian. *Matthew James Higgins.*

Civilian, A. *William W. Stephens.* A review of the evidence before the second court-marshal on Lieutenant Perry, of the 46th regiment ... L. 1855.

Civilian, an Officer in the Bengal Establishment, A. *Sir Charles D'Oyly,* Bart. Tom Raw, the Griffin: a burlesque poem ... L. 1828.

Civis. *John Coles.* The Corporation Commission and the Municipal Companies of London ... L. 1834.

Civis. *Rev. Alexander Dunlop.* Emerson's orations to the modern Athenians; or, Pantheism. Edinb. 1848.

Civis. *Alexander Peterkin.* A letter to the Rt. Hon. E. Erskine ... Edinb. 1806, 1807.

Civis. *Sir Henry Russell.* Letters of "Civis" on India affairs, 1842–49; reprinted from the "Times" (L.).

Civis. *Rev. Charles Valentine Le Grice.* Letters on Church subjects in the West of Cornwall ... Truro, 1844.

Civis. *William Welfitt.* Minutes, collected from the ancient records and accounts in the Chamber of Canterbury, of transactions in that city from A.D. 1234, etc. Canterbury, 1801.

Civis. *Sir William Scott, Lord Stowell.* Some observations ... L. 1811.

Civis. *George Thomson.* Statement and review of a recent decision of the Judge of Police in Edinburgh ... Edinb. 1807.

Cladpole, Tim. *Richard Lower.* T. C.'s journey to Lunnun ... and written in pure Sussex doggerel by his uncle Tim. Brighton, 1831, '49, '50; J. C.'s trip to 'Merricur ... written ... by his father Tim ... Hailsham, 1844.

Clairville. *Louis François Nicolaie.* Les trois gamins. Paris, 1854.

Clara. *Mrs. Clara Coles.* Clara's poems. P. 1861.

Clara. *Miss Carrie Bell Sinclair.* Heart whispers; or, echoes of song. Her first appearance in print was in the "Georgia Gazette" (Augusta, Ga.), under this *nom de plume.*

Clara, Cousin. *Rev. Daniel Wise.* The Lindendale stories. N.Y. 18–.

Clara Augusta. *Mrs. S. Trask,* of Framingham, Mass.

Clara Belle. The letters in the "Enquirer" (Cin., O.) thus signed, are written by *Olive Logan, Mr. and Mrs. Junius Henri Browne,* and others.

Clare, Ida. *Mrs. Lelia J. (Robinson) Chute,* as correspondent of the "St. Louis Post-Dispatch," "Memphis (Tenn.) Avalanche," and other newspapers.

Clare, Mary Frances. *Mary Frances Cusack.* Her religious name.

Clare, Miss Ada. *Mrs. Jane McElhinney.* Only a woman's heart. N.Y. 1866. See "Bohemia, Queen of."

Clarence, Charles. *Barnard Rust Hall.*

Clarence, Fitzroy. *William Makepeace Thackeray.* Love songs made easy. "What makes my heart to thrill and grow?" Song. "Punch," March 6, 1847.

Claribel. *Mrs. Caroline Barnard.* Fireside thoughts, ballads ... L. 1865.

Claridge, John, Shepherd. *Dr. John Campbell,* known as "The Shepherd of Banbury," author of a Weather guide. 1744.

Clarinda. *Mrs. Agnes Craig Maclehose,* the "Clarinda" of Burns, the poet, who addressed her as a lover in a series of letters which have been often sought for publication, but in vain.

Clark, The Rev. T. *John Galt.* The Wandering Jew; or, the travels and observations of Harcach the Prolonged. L. 1820.

The initials of the concluding four sentences in the above work make the name of the author, thus:—G(reatuess), A(ll), L(iterally), T(o).

Clarke, Rev. C. C. *Sir Richard Phillips.* The hundred wonders of the world ... L. 1818.

Clarke, John. *Thomas Hartwell Horne, D.D.* Bibliotheca legum. L. 1810.

Clarke, N. H. Belden, Esq. *N. H. Belden.* O'Neal the Great. N.Y. 1857.

Clarke, R. S.—See "May, S."

Claudero, the Son of Nimrod. *James Wilson.* Poems on sundry occasions ... Edinb. 1758.

Claudia. *Miss Clara V. Dargan.* Under this *nom de plume* she published her first poem, "Forever Thine," in the "Courant," Charleston, S.C., 1859.

Claudia. *Mary P. Hack.* Consecrated women. By ... L. 1880.

Claudius. *Charles Ruelle.* La science populaire de Claudius. Paris, 1837.

Claudius, Martin. *Rosa Petzel.* The cottage by the lake ... Trans. ... P. 1869.

Clauren, H. *Karl Gottlob Samuel Heun.* Scherz und Ernst. Dresden, 1820-28.

Clavers, Mrs. Mary. *Mrs. Caroline Matilda (Stansbury) Kirkland.* Garland of poetry for the young. 1872.

Clay, Charles M. *Mrs. Charlotte Moon Clark.* Baby Rue. L. 1881.

Clayton, John. *John Alfred Clayton Calthrop.* A nom de théâtre.

Clayton, May. *Mrs. Mamie Wilson.*

Cleishbotham, Jedediah, Schoolmaster and Parish clerk of Ganderclough. *Sir Walter Scott.* Tales of My Landlord. Edinb. 1816.

Cleishbotham is supposed to be the editor, and his assistant, a certain Peter Pattieson, is credited with the authorship of the "Tales."

Clemens, Anglicanus. *Thomas Turton.* Remarks upon Mr. Evanson's preface to his translation of Knittel's new criticisms on 1 John, v. 7. Camb., Eng., 1829.

Clement. *Alonzo G. Shears,* in his contributions to various periodicals.

Cleon. *Edward Long,* in Byron's "Childish Recollections." Newark, 1807.

Clergyman, A. *Richard Valpy, D.D.* Address from ... to his parishioners. L. 1810.

Clergyman, A. *Jonathan Swift.* Advice to a son at the University design'd for Holy Orders. L. 1725.

Clergyman, A. *William Goode.* An answer to a letter addressed to the Lord Chancellor on the case of the Dissenters ... L. 1834.

Clergyman, A. *Samuel Horsley.* An apology for the liturgy and clergy of the Church of England ... L. 1790.

Clergyman, A. *Rev. John Morrison.* Australia as it is. L. 1867.

Clergyman, A. *Thomas Lewis.* Churches no charnel-houses ... L. 1726.

Clergyman, A. *Rev. William Sewell.* A clergyman's recreations; or, sacred thoughts in verse. L. 1831.

Clergyman, A. *Richard Tyrwhitt.* Concerning doubt. A letter to "A Layman." Oxf. and L. 1861.

Clergyman, A. *Rev. John Jackman.* The ... conduct of Mr. Peirce examined. Oxf. 1717.

Clergyman, A. *George Horne,* Bishop of Norwich. Considerations on the projected reformation of the Church of England ... L. 1772.

Clergyman, A. *Rev. Manton Robert Taylor.* Convocation. The new lay representation briefly considered ... L. 1852.

Clergyman, A. *Philip Morant.* The cruelties and persecutions of the Romish Church display'd ... L. 1728.

Clergyman, A. *Rev. Hugh Stowell.* The day of rest and other poems; by ... L. 183-.

Clergyman, A. *Henry Stebbing, D.D.* The doctrine of Justification by Faith in Jesus Christ ... L. 1757.

Clergyman, A. *Rev. John Balguy.* The foundation of moral goodness ... L. 1728.

Clergyman, A. *Rev. Benjamin Richings.* A general volume of epitaphs ... L. 1840.

Clergyman, A. *Rev. James Lupton, M.A.* Gulliver's travels. New edition, carefully edited ... L. 1867.

Clergyman, A. *Rev. James Murray.* A history of the churches in England and Scotland ... Newcastle-upon-Tyne, 1771.

Clergyman, A. *Rev. Beauchamp W. Stannus.* The inquiring parishioner ... L.

Clergyman, A. *Rev. William Robertson.* Journal of ... during a visit to the Peninsula. L. 1841.

Clergyman, A. *Rev. Mr. Parfect.* A letter ... giving his reasons for refusing to administer baptism in private, by the public form ... L. 1763.

Clergyman, A. *Rev. John Courtarey.* A letter ... to his parishioners ... on their breach of the Sabbath and neglect of all religion. About 1810. Signed "J. C."

Clergyman, A. *Rev. Skeffington Armstrong.* A letter to ... Lord Dufferin and Clandeboye, on the subject of the Irish branch of the United Church ... L. 1868.

Clergyman, A. *Rev. Peter Leopold Dyke Acland.* A letter to a physician on the domestic management of invalids in a mild winter climate ... Oxf. 1866.

Clergyman, A. *Nathaniel Paterson, D.D.* The Manse garden ... Glasgow. 1836.

Clergyman, A. *Rev. John Jackson.* Memoirs of the life and writings of Dr. Waterland ... L. 1736.

Clergyman, A. *Rev. James Franks, A.M.* Memoirs of pretended Prophets, who have appeared in different ages of the world, and especially in modern times . . . L. 1795.

Clergyman, A. *Rev. Charles Lyne, M.A.* Modern Methodism not in accordance with the principles and plans of the Rev. John Wesley during any period of his life. A dialogue between . . . and one of his Methodist parishioners . . . L. 1842.

Clergyman, A. *Rev. Edward Spooner.* Parson and people; or, incidents in the every-day life of . . . L. 1863.

Clergyman, A. *Rev. Henry John Dixon, M.A.* The sad experience of . . . of the Established Church. L. 1875.

Clergyman, A. *Rev. Arthur Ashley Sykes.* The safety of the Church . . . considered . . . L. 1715.

Clergyman, The. *Francis Hare, D.D.* The C.'s thanks to Phileleutherus for his remarks on the late discourse of free-thinking: in a letter to Dr. Bentley. L. 1713.

Clergyman, A Catholic. *Bishop John Carroll.* An address to Roman Catholics of the United States of America. Annapolis, 1784.

Clergyman in the Country, A. *Matthew Horbery.* Animadversions upon a late pamphlet (by John Jackson) entituled "Christian liberty asserted" . . . L. 1735.

Clergyman in the Country, A. *Rev. Isaac Madox.* The case of Dr. Rundle's promotion to the See of Glocester impartially considered . . . L. 1734.

Clergyman in the Country, A. *Rev. John Jackson.* A discourse shewing that the expositions which the Ante-Nicene Fathers have given of the texts alleged against the Reverend Dr. Clarke . . . are more agreeable, etc. L. 1714. Also ascribed to the Rev. Daniel Whitby.

Clergyman in the Country, A. *Rev. Samuel Bolde.* The duty of Christians . . . L. 1717.

Clergyman in the Country, A. *Rev. Arthur Ashley Sykes.* A modest plea for the baptismal and scripture-notion of the Trinity . . . L. 1720.

Clergyman in the Country, A. *Samuel Clarke, D.D., the son.* Reply to Dr. Waterland's defence of his queries . . . L. 1722.

Clergyman in the West, A. *Rev. Samuel Nicholson Kingdon, B.D.* Schism and its results . . . L. 1856.

Clergyman living in the Neighborhood of that famous Monument of Antiquity, A. *Rev. Stamford Wallis.* A dissertation in vindication of the antiquity of Stone Henge . . . Sarum, 1730.

Clergyman of the Church of England, A. *Rev. Moses Margoliouth.* The Anglo-Hebrews . . . L. 1856.

Clergyman of the Church of England, A. *Rev. Arthur Ashley Sykes.* An answer to the nonjurors' charge of schism upon the Church of England . . . L. 1716.

Clergyman of the Church of England, A. *Rev. J. Bradley Rhys.* An answer to some passages in a letter from the Bishop of Rochester to the Clergy upon the lawfulness of War . . . L. 1798.

Clergyman of the Church of England, A. *John Plumptre, D.D.* A concise view of the history of religious knowledge . . . Kidderminster, 1795.

Clergyman of the Church of England, A. *Rev. Legh Richmond.* The dairyman's daughter. L. 1822.

Clergyman of the Church of England, A. *Rev. Robert Shittler.* The domestic commentary on the whole Word of God. L. 1854.

Clergyman of the Church of England, A. *Rev. Benjamin Dawson, LL.D.* An examination of Dr. Rutherford's argument respecting the right of Protestant Churches to require the Clergy to subscribe to an established Confession of Faith and Doctrines . . . L. 1766.

Clergyman of the Church of England, A. *Rev. John Clowes.* The golden wedding ring. Manchester, 1813.

Clergyman of the Church of England, A. *Rev. Henry Walter.* A history of England . . . on Christian principles. L. 1828–39.

Clergyman of the Church of England, A. *Dr. Zachary Pearce.* A letter to the Clergy of the Church of England . . . L. 1722.

Clergyman of the Church of England, A. *Rev. John Firebrace.* A letter to the Rev. James Ibbetson . . . L. 1771.

Clergyman of the Church of England, A. *Rev. John Frederick Denison Maurice, M.A.* Letters to a member of the Society of Friends, by . . ., L. 1837–38; The kingdom of Christ, L.

Clergyman of the Church of England, A. *Rev. William Pace.* Lydia; or, conversion : a sacred drama . . . L. 1835.

Clergyman of the Church of England, A. *Rev. Thomas Stackhouse.* The miseries and great hardships of the inferiour Clergy ... L. 1722.

Clergyman of the Church of England, A. *Rev. Henry Comyn.* A parish lecture on Regeneration. L. 1850.

Clergyman of the Church of England, A. *Rev. Christian Lenny.* Shakspeare for schools ... L. 1847.

Clergyman of the Church of England, A. *Mathew Carey.* Vindiciae Hibernicae ... P. 1818.

Clergyman of the Church of Scotland, A. *Rev. William Peebles.* The crisis ... a poem. Edinb. 1803.

Clergyman of the Church of Scotland, A. *David Thorburn.* The Divine origin and perpetual and universal obligation of tithes. Edinb. 1841.

Clergyman of the Church of Scotland, A. *Charles John Brown, D.D.* Irish education ... Glasgow, 1832.

Clergyman of the Diocese of Durham, A. *Rev. Henry Phillpotts.* A letter to the author of " Remarks on a charge delivered by Shute [Barrington] " ... Newcastle-upon-Tyne, 1807.

Clergyman of the Diocese of Durham, A. *Thomas Le Mesurier.* A letter to the Right Honourable Earl Grey ... Durham, 1819.

Clergyman of the Established Church, A. *Rev. John Clowes,* of Manchester. An affectionate address to the Clergy ... on the theological writings of the Hon. Emanuel Swedenborg. Manchester, n.d.

Clergyman of the Established Church, A. *Rev. J. A. Wood.* A Biblical link; or, a connection of the Holy Scriptures ... L. 1849.

Clergyman of the Old School, A. *John Aiton, D.D.* Clerical economics ... Edinb. 1842.

Clergyman of the Protestant Episcopal Church, A. *Rev. G. W. Hyer.* How I became a Unitarian : explained ... B. 1852.

Clergyman thirteen years resident in the Interior of New South Wales, A. *John Morison.* Australia as it is ... L. 1867.

Clergyman, A Moderate, of the Synod of Aberdeen. *Rev. G. Skene Keith.* Address to the ministers of the Church of Scotland. 1797.

Clergyman's Daughter, A. *Selina Gaye.* Aunt Agnes; or, the why and the wherefore of life. An autobiography ... L. 1816.

Clergyman's Daughter, A. *Miss Eliza Smith.* The battles of the Bibles. Edinb. 1852.

Clergyman's Daughter, A. *Miss Maria Charlesworth.* The female visitor to the poor ... L. 1846.

Clergyman's Daughter, A. *Frances Lydia Bingham.* Hubert ; or, the orphans of St. Madelaine ... L. 1845.

Clergyman's Daughter, A. *Miss E. F. Lloyd.* Readings for the Sundays ... L. 1862.

Clergyman's Daughter, A. *Mrs. Helen Clacy.* Wonderful works ; or, the miracles of Christ. L. 1864.

Clergyman's Wife, A. *Mrs. Frances Elizabeth Georgina (Baynes) Carey-Brock.* Almost persuaded. L. about 1856.

Clergyman's Wife, A. *Mrs. Fanny (Wheeler) Hart.* Charade : armhole. Manchester, n.d.

Clergyman's Wife, A. *Mrs. S. E. Mapleton.* A letter to my class . . Leeds, 1852.

Clergyman's Wife, A. *Mrs. Fanny Alford.* Reminiscences by ... Edited by the Dean of Canterbury [Henry Alford]. L. 1860.

Clerical Friend, A. *Rev. George Huntington.* The autobiography of John Brown, the cord-wainer ... Edited ... Oxf. 1867.

Clerical Member of the Convocation, A. *Rev. Henry William Wilberforce.* The foundation of the Faith assailed in Oxford ... L. 1835.

Clerical Member of the Society for promoting Christian Knowledge, A. *Rev. Samuel Charles Wilks.* Strictures on the work entitled " Death-bed Scenes, etc.," in refutation of its doctrinal errors. L. 1833.

Clerical Recluse, A. *Rev. Francis Jacox.* Cues from all quarters; or, literary musings of ... L. 1871.

Clericus. *Rev. David Murray,* of Dysart. The Biblical student's assistant ... Edinb. 1844.

Clericus. *Rev. W. Cartwright.* Facts and fancies of salmon fishing ... L. Paris, and N.Y. 1874.

Clericus. *George Smith.* Facts designed to exhibit the real character and tendency of the American Colonization Society. Liverpool, 1833.

Clericus. *Rev. Augustus Clissold.* A letter to the Rev. the Vice-Chancellor of the University of Oxford on the present state of theology ... Oxf. 1856.

Clericus. *Rev. William Cartwright.* Rambles and recollections of a fly-fisher. L. 1854.

Clericus. *Rev. J. H. Pettingell.* The theological trilemma . . . N.Y. 1878.

Clericus Dorcestriensis. *Rev. J. L. Jackson, M.A.* Christ's Coming to Judgment . . . L. 1834.

Clericus Leicestriensis. *Rev. Aulay Macaulay.* Tour through South Holland and a part of the Austrian Netherlands, 1793. "Gent. Mag.," November, 1793, and the following volumes.

Clericus Surriensis. *Rev. Gilbert Buchanan, LL.D.*, in the "Gent. Mag."

Clerimont. *Mrs. Elizabeth Rowe.* Friendship in death . . . 4th ed. L. 1737.

Clerk of the "California," The. *Swaine Drake.* Account of a voyage for the discovery of a north-west passage by Hudson Streights to the western and southern ocean of America . . . L. 1748.

Clerke of Oxenforde, The. *John Pendleton Kennedy.* Blackwater chronicle: a narrative of an expedition . . . in Randolph county, Virginia. N.Y. 1853.

Cleveland, Kate. *Mrs. Rebecca S. (Reed) Nichols*, who contributed a series of sprightly papers to the "Cincinnati Herald" under this *nom de plume.*

Cliffe, Leigh. *George Jones.* The pilgrim of Avon. By . . . L. 1836.

Clifford, Charles. *Samuel William Henry Ireland.* The angler: a didactic poem. L. 1804.

Clifton, Tom. *Alfred Farthing Robbins.* In doubt. 1878.

Clifton, Zena. *Mrs. Lilian T. (Rozell) Messenger*, whose first writings appeared in the "Memphis Avalanche" under this *nom de plume.*

Climax, Christopher, Esq. *Josiah Thomas.* Riot [at Cambridge]: a mock heroic poem in three cantos, by . . . 1780.

Clinton, Walter. *William Henry Davenport Adams.* Sword and pen; or, English worthies in the reign of Elizabeth. Edinb. 1869.

CLIO. *Joseph Addison.* The letters in the "Spectator" composing the name of the Muse of History were written by Addison, and signed with each letter consecutively. It is also related that he only employed these letters to distinguish whether they had been written at Chelsea, London, Islington, or the office. — See also "C. L. I. O."

Clio. *Richard Gough.* Signature to his reply to "Euterpe," in the "St. James's Chronicle," 1787.

Clio. *Thomas Harwood*, the author of several letters in the "Gent. Mag.," under this *nom de plume.*

Clio. *Edwin J. Reilly.*

Clionas. *Sir Nicholas Harris Nicolas.* He was a frequent contributor to the "Gent. Mag." His signature, if not his own initials, was frequently "Clionas," an anagram of his surname.

Clothier, A. *John Blanch.* The beaux merchant: a comedy . . . L. 1714.

Clover, Sam. *Nugent Robinson,* in his contributions to the "Boys and Girls' Weekly" (N.Y.).

Clutterbuck, Capt. Cuthbert. *Sir Walter Scott.* The fortunes of Nigel. Edinb. 1822.

Clutterbuck, Cuthbert, of Kennaquhair, F.S.A., etc. *Alexander Hamilton, W.S.* Edith of Glammis . . . L. 1836.

Clyde, Alton. *Mrs. Arnold Jeffreys.* Tried and true, 187–; Underfoot, 187–.

Cobbler of Alsatia, The. *John Nichols, Esq., F.S.A.* "During his minority he produced some prose essays on the manners of the age . . . These were published in a periodical paper, written chiefly by Kelly, entitled the 'Babbler,' and in the 'Westminster Journal,' a newspaper, with the signature of 'The Cobbler of Alsatia.'"

Cobweb. *Joseph Tinker Buckingham.* Letters from Washington in the "Boston Courier," 1830 *et seq*

Cockloft, Pindar. *William Irving,* in "Salmagundi."

Cockney, A. *Mrs. S. Green.* Scotch novel reading; or, modern quackery . . . L. 1824.

Cocoa-tree, The. *Philip Francis.* Letter from . . . to the Country-gentleman. L. 1762.

Codex, Dr. *E. Gibson,* Bishop of London. A letter to . . . on the subject of his modest instruction to the Crown . . . L. 1734. By Gilbert Burnett, Bishop of Salisbury.

Cœlebs, M.A. *Major Thomas Tristem Spry Carlyon.* The laws and practice of whist . . . L. 1851. Also ascribed to Edward Augustus Carlyon.

Cœur, Pierre. *Mme. Anne Caroline Joséphine (Husson) de Voisons d'Ambre.* L'âme de Beethoven: a novel. P. 1876.

Coffin, Peter. *Theophilus Parsons.* Result of the convention of delegates holden at Ipswich . . . Newburyport, 1778.

Cogitans, John. *Charles Morey.* The spiritual mustard pot. Troy, N.Y., 1824.

Coit, Davida. *Vida D. Scudder.* How the rain-spirits were freed. 188–.

Colbert. *Mathew Carey.* Political economy. Examination of the treasurer's report. P. 1826.

Colcraft, Henry Rowe. *Henry Rowe Schoolcraft.* Alhalla; or, the Lord of Talladega: a tale of the Creek war . . . N.Y. 1843.

Colcroft, James. *John Webb Cole* (?), translator of M. Jules Simon's "Natural Religion." L. 1857.

Coles, Miriam. *Mrs. Sydney S. Harris.* Frank Warrington. N.Y. 1871.

Colet, Madame. *Louise Revoil.* Les fleurs du midi. Paris, 1836.

Collector, A. *Mr. Humphrey.* Conchology; or, natural history of shells . . . About 1780.

Collegian. A. *William Gilmore Simms* (?). Poems, by . . . Charlottesville, Va., 1833.

Collet, Stephen. *Thomas Byerley.* Relics of literature. L. 1823.

Collier, the late Joel, licentiate in music. *J. L. Bicknell.* Musical travels through England . . . L. 1785.

Ascribed also to Thomas Day and George Veal.

Colmolyn. *Charles Sotheran.* Percy Bysshe Shelley as a philosopher and reformer . . . N.Y. 1871.

Colombey, Émile. *Émile Laurent.* Ruelles, salons, et cabarets . . . P. 1858.

Colon & Spondee. *Royall Tyler,* who, under this pseudonym, furnished humorous articles to the "Farmer's Weekly Museum," Walpole, N.H., 1796–1800. Judge Tyler had previously written for the "Eagle," Hanover, N.H., under the same pseudonym, and later to the "Federal Orrery," Boston.

Colonist. *Mr. Sewell,* in his contributions to the "Montreal Herald" attacking the policy of Sir George Prevost.

Colonist, A. *Thomas Chandler Haliburton, M.A.* A reply to the report of the Earl of Durham . . . Halifax, 1839.

Colored Man, A. *Paul Jennings.* A C. M.'s reminiscences of James Madison. Brooklyn, N.Y., 1865.

Columbanus. *Charles O'Conor, D.D.* Columbanus ad Hibernos; or, seven letters . . . Buckingham, 1810–16.

Columella. *Clement Clarke Moore, LL.D.* An inquiry into the effects of our foreign carrying trade upon the agriculture, population, and morals of the country . . . N.Y. 1806.

Columella. *G. W. Pinney.* The new education . . . San Fran. 1874.

Colvil, Edward. *Mrs. Mary Lowell Putnam.* Fifteen days. An extract from Edward Colvil's journal. B. 1866.

Colvin, Cecil. *Francis Cowley Burnand.* My time, and what I have done with it . . . L. 1874.

Colwan, Robert Wringham. *James Hogg.* The private memoirs of a justified sinner. L. 1824. — See "A Justified Sinner."

Comet. *Mr. Walker,* in his contributions to the "Herald" (B., Mass.).

Comet Literary and Patriotic Club, The. *Thomas Browne.* Parson's horn-book. By . . . Dublin, 1831.

Comment, Cuthbert, Gent. *Abraham Tucker.* Man in quest of himself . . . L. 1763.

Committee, A. *G. W. Crawford* and *J. Applewhite.* Statistical address to the people of Austin and Washington counties, on the subject of railroads. Wash. D.C. 1852.

Committee appointed by the Passengers of the "Oceanus," A. *James Clark French* and *Edward Carey.* The trip of the "Oceanus" to Fort Sumter and Charleston, S.C. . . . Brooklyn, 1865.

Committee Man, A. *J. Nightingale.* The Scriptural Deacon . . . N.Y. 1845.

Common Sense. *Sir Richard Phillips,* in the "Monthly Magazine," London, of which he was editor and proprietor for about thirty years.

Commoner, A. *Rev. William Gould.* A letter to the commoners in Rockingham Forest . . . Stamford, 1744.

Communipaw. *Pliny Miles.* His letters from abroad, under this and less well-known pseudonyms, convey a graphic idea of foreign sight-seeing.

Companion Traveller, A. *Miss E. F. S. Harris.* From Oxford to Rome, and how it fared with some who lately made the journey. L. 1847.

The authoress subsequently became a Catholic, and publicly expressed her deep regret for many of the unauthorized statements, or false impressions concerning the Church of Rome, in the above work. — O. Hamst.

Compiler of "Anecdotes of distinguished Persons," The. *William Seward, Esq.* Biographiana. L. 1799.

Comprehensionist, A. *Frederick J. Wilson.* My rights! Your rights!! Our rights!!! My right to my tenancy as my freehold . . . L. 1876.

Comus. *Robert Michael Ballantyne.* The robber kitten. L. 1858.

Comyn, Alexandre de. *Charles Thomas Browne.* Irene. L. 1844.

Concivis. *G. H. Belden* (?). Letters to the people of the United States. N.Y. 1840.

Confederate Lady, The. *Mrs. Maud J. (Fuller) Young,* who, during the late civil war, wrote songs, etc., for the Confederates.

Congregational Minister, A. *Rev.*

William B. Orvis. The coming of Christ in his kingdom ... N.Y. 1869.

Connecticut Farmer's Boy, A. *Fitz-Greene Halleck,* whose first appearance in print was in "Holt's Columbian," New York, 1813, in a short poem bearing this signature.

Connecticut Pastor, A. *Rev. Enoch Fitch Burr.* Ecce Cœlum; or, parish astronomy. B. 1867.

Connecticut Pastor, A. *Rev. Joseph Darling Hull, A.M.* Plea for religious newspapers: a sermon preached to his own people on the Lord's Day, December 29, 1844, by ... Hartford, 1845.

Conover, Elizabeth. *Miss — Durgin.*

Conrad. *Alfred Bunn.* The stage, both before and behind the curtain ... L. 1840.

Conrad, Georg. *Prince George,* of Prussia. Dramatische Werke. 1870.

Conservative, A. *John Lettsom Elliot.* A letter to the Electors of Westminster. L. 1847.

Conservative, A. *James Dennistoun.* A letter to the Lord Advocate [Francis Jeffrey] on the Scottish Reform Bill. Edinb. 1832.

Consistent Loyalist, A. *John Parr.* Remarks on a late pamphlet entitled "A vindication of Governor Parr and his council" ... L. 1784.

Consistent Protestant, A. *Adam Calamy,* a writer in the "Gent. Mag." under this pseudonym, 1740 *et seq.*

Consistent Protestant, A. *Owen Manning.* Considerations on ... articles and liturgy of the Church of England ... L. 1774.

Consistent Protestant, A. *Richard Watson, D.D.* Considerations on the expediency of revising the liturgy ... L. 1790.

Consistent Whig, A. *Rt. Rev. Dr. Thomas Lewis O'Beirne.* Considerations on the late disturbances, by ... 1781.

Constance. *Mrs. Bessie W. (Johnson) Williams,* who, under this *nom de plume,* has published articles in "Scott's Magazine" and the "Mobile Sunday Times."

Constantia. *Mrs. Judith (Sargent) Murray.* The repository and gleaner. B. 1798. Mrs. Murray was also a contributor to the "Massachusetts Magazine" and the "Boston Weekly Magazine."

Constantin, L. A. *Léopold Auguste Constantin Hesse.* Bibliothekonomie ... Leipsic, 1840.

Constitution. *John Cartwright.* A letter to Edmund Burke, Esq., controverting the principles of the American government, laid down in his lately published speech on American taxation ... in the House of Commons, on the 19th of April, 1774. L. 1775.

Constitutional Reformer, A. *John Rutter.* History of the Shaftesbury Election, 1830 ... L. 1830.

Consul Abroad, A. *Luigi Monti.* Adventures of ... By Samuel Sampleton. B. 1878.

Consul's Daughter and Wife, A. *Mrs. John Elijah Blunt.* Twenty years' residence among the people of Turkey ... N.Y. 1878.

Consumptive, A. *Robert S. Coffin.* The eleventh hour ... B. 1827.

Contributor at Paris, The. *William Makepeace Thackeray.* The ballad of Bouillabaisse. "Punch," Feb. 17, 1849.

Contributor to "Bentley," A. *William Hollis.* Miscellaneous Latin poems, original and translations ... L. 1851.

Contributor to "Blackwood's Magazine," A. *William Pitt Scargill.* The usurer's daughter ... L. 1832.

Contributors to Tracts for the Times. By A. [*John Keble*], B. [*Isaac Williams*], C. [*Dr. Pusey*], D. [*J. H. Newman*], E. [*Thomas Keble*], F. [*Sir George Prevost, Bart.*], G. [*Rev. R. F. Wilson,* of Oriel]. Plain sermons. L. 1840–48.

Convert, A. *Rt. Rev. Richard Challoner.* The grounds of the old religion ... P. 1814.

Convert, A. *Rev. B. W. Whitcher.* The story of ... as told to his former parishioners after he became a Catholic. N.Y. 1875.

Convert from Anglicism, A. *George John Lloyd Crawley.* England, Greece, or Rome? A letter to a friend. York, 1853.

Conway, H. B. *H. B. Coulson.* A *nom de théâtre.*

Conway, H. Derwent. *Henry David Inglis.* Solitary walks through many lands. 3d ed. L. 1843.

Conway, Hugh. *Frederick John Fargus.* Called back. Bristol, 1883.

The work appeared originally in "Arrowsmith's Almanac," Bristol; was soon published in a separate form, and more than 80,000 copies were sold.

Conway, Mark. *Frank Cahill,* in his contributions to the "Saturday Press" (P.)

Conynghame, Kate. *Rev. Joseph Holt Ingraham.* The sunny South; or, the Southerner at home ... P. 1860.

Coodies. — See "Coody, Abimelech."

Coody, Abimelech. *Gulian Cromme-lin Verplanck.* An account of Abimelech Coody and other celebrated writers of New York . . . N.Y. 1815.

"In the year 1814, a writer appeared in a New York paper, assuming the name of Abimelech Coody, a mechanic of that place. He was a Federalist, and addressed himself principally to the party to which he belonged . . . The writer was soon ascertained to be Mr. Gulian C. Verplanck. Abimelech Coody was replied to by a writer over the signature of 'A Traveller' . . . who was said to be DeWitt Clinton, who said that he [Coody *alias* Verplanck] has become the head of a sect called the 'Coodies'" . . . See "The Croakers," N.Y. 1860; note, p. 152.

Cook, Hannah. *Mrs. Thomas Bradley.*

Coolidge, Susan. *Miss Sarah Chauncey Woolsey.* Mischief's Thanksgiving; and other stories. B. 1874.

Coombe, Count. *William Coombe, Esq.*

Coontie Attorney, A. *Charles Sandys.* Vindication of . . . L. 1847.

Cooper, Frank. *William Gilmore Simms.* Poems; Life of Capt. John Smith; Life of Chevalier Bayard. N.Y.

Cooper, Rev. Wm. U., B.A. *James G. Bertram.* Flagellation and the Flagellants . . . L. 1870.

Cope. *W. C. Copeland*, in the "Brooklyn Eagle."

Copper-Farthing Dean, The. *Jonathan Swift.* The most wonderful wonder that ever appear'd to the wonder of the British nation . . . L. 1726.

Copywell, James. *William Woty.* Shrubs of Parnassus, containing a variety of poetical essays, moral and comic . . . L. 1760.

Coquina. *G. O. Shields*, in several sporting works.

Cordelia. *Mme. Virginia Treves*, in "Nell' Azzurro."

Cordial Well-wisher to the cause of Universal Truth and Righteousness, A. *Miss Priscilla Hannah Gurney.* A comprehensive view of the nature of faith . . . L. 1816.

Cordier, Jules. *Eléonore Tenaille de Vaulabelle.*

Cordula. *Countess Irene de la Rocca.*

Coriat, Junior. *Samuel Paterson.* Another traveller; or, cursory remarks and critical observations made upon a journey through part of the Netherlands in the latter part of the year 1766. L. 1767.

Corinna. *Mrs. Elizabeth Thomas.* Pylades and Corinna; or, memoirs of the lives, amours, and writings of Richard Gwinnett, Esq., and Mrs. Elizabeth Thomas, Junr. L. 1731. — See "A Lady."

Coriolanus. *Col. W. Smith.* Remarks on the late infraction of the treaty at New Orleans. N.Y. 1803.

Corisande. *Mrs. Adolphe (Jerrold) Smith*, author of Sketches of society and scenery in the "London Graphic," the "Liverpool Courier," and a novel called "A Woman of Mind."

Corn-Law Rhymer, The. *Ebenezer Elliott.* More verse and prose . . . L. 1850.

Cornelius. *John Robison.* Extracts from Prof. Robison's "Proofs of a conspiracy." B. 1799.

Cornelius, Dr. *William Howitt.* The student life of Germany . . . L. 1842.

Cornet in the Hon. East India Company's Service, A. *Thomas L. Pettigrew.* Lucien Greville. L. 1833.

Cornish Chough, The. *Albert Charles Wildman*, in the "Western Daily Mercury" (English).

Cornish Curate, A. *Rev. Francis Edward Baston Cole.* The Methodistic tenet of conversion . . . Oxf. and L. 1854.

Cornish Lady, A. *Mrs. Emilie Earle (Steele) Hicks.* First lessons in useful things. Truro, 1868.

Cornish Vicar, A. *Rev. Robert Stephen Hawker, M.A.* A letter to a friend . . . L. 1857.

Cornishwoman, A. *Miss Ellen J. Pearce.* Peace or war? An appeal to the women of Great Britain and Ireland. Truro, 1876.

Cornubian, A. *Henry John Daniel.* The Anti-Newtonian Institute: a satire in two cantos. n.p., n.d.

Cornubian, A. *John Trenhaile.* Recreations in rhyme, by . . . L. 1834.

Cornwall. *C. H. Botsford*, in his letters entitled "Always Everywhere," contributed to the "Inter-Ocean" (Chic., Ill.).

Cornwall, Barry. *Bryan Waller Procter.* Memoir of Charles Lamb. L. 1866.

Cornwall, C. M. *Miss Mary Abigail Roe.* Free, yet forging their own chains. 187–.

Coroner's Clerk, A. *Rev. Erskine Neale.* The note-book of . . . reprinted from "Bentley's Miscellany."

Corporal. *Zenas T. Haines.* Letters from the 44th reg. M. V. M., 1862–63 . . . B. 1863.

Corporal of Riflemen, A. *Henry Beaufoy, Esq.* Scloppetaria; or, considerations on the nature and use of rifled barrel guns . . . L. 1808.

Corrector. *Bishop John Henry Ho-*

bart. A reply to a letter addressed to the Right Rev. Bishop Hobart, by William Jay, in a letter to that gentleman. N.Y. 1823.

Correggio. One of the pseudonyms attributed to Junius (*q.v.*). The letter thus signed bears the date Sept. 16, 1767, and caricatures the ministry.

Correspondant du Canadien, Le. *J. W. O'Brien.* Excursion aux provinces maritimes. Impressions de voyage . . . Quebec, 1864.

Corresponding Member of the Society for propagating Christian Knowledge, A. *Elisha Smith* The law of laws . . . L. 1719.

Corsair. *James Wood Davidson,* in his contributions to various Southern periodicals.

Corsincon. *Hugh Dalziel.* British dogs: their varieties, history, characteristics, breeding, management, and exhibition. L. 1880.

Corvinus. *Travers Twiss, D.C.H.* Hungary: its constitution and its catastrophe . . . L. 1850.

Corvinus, Jakob. *Wilhelm Raabe.* Chronik der Sperlingsgasse. 1857.

Cosmo. *John Mathew Gutch, Esq.* Letters of Cosmo. Bristol, Eng.

Cosmo. *John Hall-Stevenson.* Makarony fables . . . By . . . Mythogelastic Professor, and F.M.S. L. 1767.

Cosmopolitan, A. *Charles Henry Pullen.* Miss Columbia's public school; or, will it blow over? . . . L. 1871.

Cosmopolitan, A. *John Dix,* afterwards *Ross.* Pen and ink sketches of eminent English literary personages. L. 1850.

Cosmopolite. *Lorenzo Dow.* A cry from the wilderness . . . U.S. 1830.

Cosmopolite. *Alfred Tobias John Martin.* The Penzance library. A satire [in verse]. Penzance, 1842.

Cosmopolite. *James Lawson.* Tales and sketches. By . . . 1830.

Cosmopolite, A. *John Dix,* afterwards *Ross.* Sportsman in Ireland, with his summer route through the Highlands of Scotland . . . L. 1840.

Cotton, Robert Turner. *Mortimer Collins.* Mr. Carington. A tale . . . L. 1873.

Cotton Manufacturer, A. *Edward Atkinson.* Cheap cotton and free labor . . . B. 1861.

C(oulthurst), H. W., D.D., &c. *Rev. Alexander Geddes.* A sermon preached before the university of Cambridge, by . . . [in doggerel rhymes]. L. 1796.

Count, Noah. *Edwin H. Trafton,*

editor of the "Art Review" (N.Y. and Chic.), 1870–71.

Countreyman, A. *Rev. John Anderson, M.A.* A letter from . . . to a curat. Glasgow, 1711.

Country Bookseller, A. *George Miller.* Latter struggles in the journey of life . . . Edinb. 1833.

Country Clergyman, A. *Rev. Thomas Sikes. M.A.* An address to Lord Teignmouth . . . L. 1805.

Country Clergyman, A. *John Kinsman Tucker.* The catechism of the Church of England explained and illustrated. Ipswich, 1849

Country Clergyman, A. *Rev. Plumpton Wilson.* The connection between doctrine and duties . . . in a sermon by . . . L. 1826.

Country Clergyman, A. *Rev. W. Fletcher.* A C. C.'s humble and earnest appeal to the hearts and understandings of the Lords and Commons in Parliament assembled. L. 1833.

Country Clergyman, A. *Rev. Elisha Smith.* The cure of Deism; or, the mediatorial scheme by Jesus Christ the only true religion . . . L. 1737.

Country Clergyman, A. *Rev. Charles Dunster,* of Petworth, Sussex. Discursory considerations on St. Luke's preface . . . L. 1805.

Country Clergyman, A. *Rev. Robert Ingram.* An explanation of the Prophecy of the Seven Vials . . . L. 1780.

Country Clergyman, A. *Rev. John Butler.* The extent and limits of the subjection due to princes . . . L. 1747.

Country Clergyman, A. *Rev. William Dodwell.* Letter to the author of "Some considerations on the act to prevent clandestine marriages" . . . L. 1755.

Country Clergyman, A. *Rev. John Balguy.* Letter to a Deist, concerning the beauty . . . of moral virtue . . . L. 1726.

Country Clergyman, A. *Rev. John William Cunningham.* Morning thoughts . . . L. 1825.

Country Clergyman, A. *Rev. William Wake.* A letter . . . to his brother in the neighbourhood touching some reproaches cast upon the bishops. L. 1702.

Country Clergyman, A. *Samuel Wilberforce, D.D.* Note-book of . . . L. 1833.

Country Clergyman, A. *Rev. Edward Berens.* Pastoral advice to married persons. By . . . Oxf. 1821.

Country Clergyman, A. *Rev. C. G.*

Perceval. Plain sermons preached in a village church . . . L. 1851.

Country Clergyman, A. *Rev. Charles Dunster, M.A.* Psalms and hymns, selected . . . L. 1812.

Country Clergyman, A. *Rev. Edward Berens.* Tracts on the relative duties of married persons . . . Oxf. 1820.

Country Curate, A. *Rev. Zachary Grey.* A free and familiar letter to that great refiner of Pope and Shakespear, the Rev. Mr. William Warburton . . . With remarks upon the epistle of friend A. E. In which his unhandsome treatment of this celebrated writer is expos'd in the manner it deserves. L. 1750.

The "Epistle of friend A. E." is Grey's "Word or two of advice, etc." The letters "A. E." are the vowels in Zachary Grey.

Country Curate, A. *Rev. Erskine Neale.* The living and the dead . . . L. 1827.

Country Curate, A. *Rev. Charles Benjamin Tayler, M.A.* May you like it . . . L. 1823.

Country Curate, A. *Rev. James White.* Village poor-house. By . . . L. 1832.

Country Curate, The. *Rev. Alexander Robert Charles Dallas.* The C. C.'s offering to his parishioners . . . L. 1822.

Country-Divine, A. *Rev. William Binckes.* An expedient propos'd . . . L. 1701.

Country Divine, A. *Rev. Samuel Wesley.* A letter . . . concerning the education of the Dissenters . . . L. 1703.

Country Editor, A. *Johnson J. Hooper.* — See "Suggs, Simon."

Country Gentleman, A. *Sir Thomas Turton.* An address to the good sense and candour of the people of England, in behalf of the dealers in corn . . . L. 1800.

Country-Gentleman, A. *H. Halkerstoun,* of Rathillet, Fifeshire. Considerations on man, in his natural as well as moral state . . . Edinb. 1764.

Country Gentleman, A. *Sir Charles Bingham.* An essay on the use and necessity of establishing a militia in Ireland . . . Dub. 1767.

Country Gentleman, A. *Zachary Grey.* Examination of a late edition of Shakespeare . . . L. 1752.

Country Gentleman, A. *Rt. Hon. Edward Weston.* Family discourses . . . L. 1768.

Country Gentleman, A. *Rev. Richard Polwhele.* The family picture; or, domestic education: a poetic epistle

from . . . to his college friend the Bishop of *******. L. 1808.

Country Gentleman, A. *William Coombe, Esq.* A letter from . . . to a Member of Parliament. L. 1790.

Country Gentleman, A. *Sir Francis Grant, Lord Cullen.* A letter . . . to his friend in the city . . . n.p., n.d.

Country Gentleman, A. *William Kingsman,* of Petworth. A letter to the Right Honble. Sir John Sinclair, Bart. . . . L. 1811.

Country Gentleman, A. *William Fletcher.* Lights, shadows, and reflections of Whigs and Tories . . . L. 1841.

Country Gentleman, A. *Rt. Rev. Dr. Thomas Lewis O'Beirne.* Series of essays in a daily newspaper under the signature of . . . 1780.

Country Gentleman, The. *Rt. Hon. Edward Weston.* The C. G.'s advice to his neighbors. L. 1755.

Country Gentleman, The. *Abraham Tucker.* The C. G.'s advice to his son on the subject of party clubs. L. 1755.

Country Gentleman, formerly of the University of Cambridge, A. *Thomas James Mathias.* A letter to [John Mainwaring] the author of a pamphlet entitled "Remarks on the pursuits of literature" . . . L. 1798.

Country Magistrate, A. *Dr. Glasse.* The magistrate's assistant . . . Glocester, 1784.

Country Minister, A. *Caleb Wroe.* Four letters to a friend . . . L. 1725.

Also ascribed to Dr. Thomas Morgan.

Country Minister, A. *Rev. Alexander Dunlop.* The law of the Sabbath, of perpetual obligation . . . Edinb. 1847.

Country Parson, A. *Andrew Kennedy Hutchison Boyd, D.D.* Autumn holidays. L. 1864.

Country Parson, A. *Rev. Mr. Edwards* of Aldwinkle, Northamptonshire. A Christmas carol . . . L. 1715.

Country Parson, A. *Rev. W. Salisbury.* An epistle . . . to a residentiary of St. Paul's. Chelmsford, n.d.

Country Parson, A. *Rev. Henry Moule.* My kitchen garden . . . L. 1860.

Country Parson, A. *Rev. Francis Charles Hingeston-Randolph, M.A.* Records of a rocky shore; or, annals of our village . . . L. 1876.

Country Parson, A Retired. *Rev. Richard Warner.* Diary of . . . [in verse]. L. 1848.

Country Parson's Daughter, A. *Mrs. Elizabeth (Emra) Holmes.* Lawrence the martyr: scenes in our parish. 2d series. Bristol, 18–.

Country Pastor, A. *Rev. Richard Whately.* A letter to his parishioners on the disturbances which have lately occurred ... L. 1830.

Country Rector, A. *Rev. Spencer Cobbold.* The duty of acknowledging Jesus Christ in all we do: a sermon ... Ipswich, 1835.

Country School Master, A. *William Leggett.* Tales and sketches ... N.Y. 1829.

Country Vicar, A. *Rev. F. Mereweather.* A defence of moderation in religious practice, and opinion ... L. 1812.

Countryman, A. *Rev. Isaac Backus.* A letter ... concerning taxes to support religious worship ... L. 1771.

Countryman of Martin Luther, A. *Rev. Anthony Kohlman, S.J.* Centennial jubilee, to be celebrated ... throughout the United States ... in commemoration of the Reformation ... 1517 ... Balt. 1817.

County Court Judge, A. *F. Bayley.* The origin and object of Roman Catholic doctrines. L. 1875.

Cour, T. E. *W. G. T. Barter.* Two essays: life, law, and literature. L. 1863.

Courtenay, Peregrine. *William Mackworth Praed,* in "Knight's Quarterly Magazine," 1823–24.

Courtenay, Sir William Percy Honeywood, K.M. — See "Tom, J. N."

Couthouy, Marion. *Marion C. Smith,* in the "Philadelphia Bulletin."

Coventry. *Rev. Jonathan Evans,* in the "Gospel Magazine," 1777–78, and the "Christian Magazine," 1790–93.

Cowkeeper, The. *Samuel Wilberforce,* in the "John Bull," about 1827.

Coxe, Henry, Esq. *John Millard.* The gentleman's guide in his tour through France. L. 1817.

Crabtree, Culpepper, Esq. *Rev. Robert Jackson MacGeorge,* who edited the "Sederunts" in the "Anglo-American Magazine," Toronto. — See "Solomon of Streetsville."

Crackenthorpe, Mrs. The supposed editor of the "Female Tatler." L. 1709.

Craddock, Charles Egbert. *Miss Mary N. Murfree.* In the Tennessee mountains. B. 1884.

Craft, Zachary. *Charles Kelsall.* The first sitting of the committee on the proposed monument to Shakspeare, taken in shorthand ... Cheltenham, 1823.

Craig, J. H., of Douglas, Esquire. *James Hogg.* The hunting of Badlewe: a dramatic tale ... L. 1814.

Crambo, Cornelius. *William Barnes Rhodes, Esq.* Eccentric tales, in verse ... L. 1808.

Cramer, Julian. *Joseph Lemuel Chester.* He was a frequent contributor to the press, under various pseudonyms, of which the best known is "Julian Cramer."

Crassus, Lucius. *Alexander Hamilton.* Examination of the President's message ... N.Y. 1802.

Craven. *Capt. John William Carleton.* Hyde Marston; or, a sportsman's life ... L. 1844.

Crawley, junior. *Rt. Hon. John Wilson Croker,* in Lady Morgan's "Florence Macarthy."

Crawley, Capt. *George Frederick Pardon.* Guide to London and its suburbs. L.

Crawley, Captain Rawdon. *George Frederick Pardon.* Backgammon ... L. 1858.

Crayne, Ruth. *Mrs. Louisa Amelia (Pratt) M'Gaffey,* whose poems have been published in the "Ohio Cultivator," the "Odd Fellows' Casket and Review" (Cin.), and the "Ohio Farmer."

Crayon, Christopher. *James Ewing Ritchie,* in his contributions to the "Christian World," 1884.

Crayon, Geoffrey, Gent. *Washington Irving.* The sketch book. N.Y. 1820.

Crayon, Porte. *David Hunter Strother.* Virginia illustrated ... N.Y. 1857. Also in his contributions to "Harper's Magazine."

Crayon, Porte. *Bernard Isaac Durward.* Wild flowers of Wisconsin. 1872.

Credens. *Caleb Fleming.* An antidote for the rising age against scepticism and infidelity ... from ... to "Scepticus." L. 1765.

Crediton Poet, The. *C. Jones.*

Creole. *Mrs. A. M. C. Massena.* Marie's mistake. B. 1869.

Créole de la Louisiane, Un. *Eugène Musson.* Lettre à Napoléon III. sur l'esclavage aux États du Sud. Paris, 1862.

Cresinus. *Jedediah Hunt.* The cottage maid: a tale in rhyme. Cin. 1847. Also in his contributions to various periodicals.

Cress. *Mrs. Robert P. Porter,* in her contributions to the "Enquirer" (Cin.).

Creyton, Paul. *John Townsend Trowbridge.* Father Brighthopes; or, an old clergyman's vacation ... N.Y. 1853.

Crib, Tom. *Thomas Moore.* Tom Crib's memorial to Congress ... By one of the Fancy. [In verse.] L. 1819.

Crick, Susan. *Horace Mayhew* (?). Letters about missuses, by a maid of all-work . . . L. 1854.

Crimean Chaplain, A. *Henry Press Wright.* Recollections of . . . and the story of Prince Daniel and Montenegro. L. 1857.

Crine, George, M.D. *Sir John Hill.* The management of the gout . . . n.p. 1758.

Cringle, Tom. *Michael Scott.* The cruise of the "Midge." Edinb. 1836.

Crinkle, Nym. *Andrew C. Wheeler.* The chronicles of Milwaukee . . . Milwaukee, 1861. Also art critic of the N.Y. "World."

Crino. *Samuel J. Tilden.*

Crippled Fayette. *Thomas Fayette Jeffries.* "Crippled Fayette," of Rockingham . . . Mountain Valley, Va., 1857.

Crispin. *Dr. William Wagstaffe.* Crispin the cobler's confutation of Ben H—dly . . . L. 1711.

Crispinus. *John Westland Marston.* The patrician's daughter. L. 1841. He was one of the editors of the "National Magazine," and contributed to the "Athenæum" some stirring lyrics, of which the best known is his "Death ride at Balaclava."

Crispus. *Major C. C. Wheeler,* in the Brooklyn "Eagle."

Cristal, Maurice. *Maurice Germa.* Délassements du travail. Paris, 18–.

Crithannah, Job. *Jonathan Birch.* Fifty-one original fables, with morals and ethical index, written by . . . L. 1833.

Criticus. *Rev. William Orme.* Memoir of the controversy respecting the Three Heavenly Witnesses, I. John, v. 7 . . . L. 1830.

Critique. *Dennis B. Sheahan.*

Critique marié, Le. *Jules Gabriel Janin.* Le mariage du critique, in the "Journal des Débats." Paris, 1841.

Crito. Two letters bearing this signature have been attributed to Junius (q.v.). They appeared in the "Public Advertiser" for April 20 and 27, 1769, and are addressed to the Hon. Edward Weston.

Crito. *Samuel Brown,* in the London "Insurance Magazine."

Crito. *Rev. John Duncombe,* who, under this pseudonym and others, contributed to the "Gent. Mag." for twenty years, 1765–1785.

Crito. *Thomas Sanderson.* "As an author, Mr. Sanderson first became familiar to the public by various prose and poetical pieces, published under the signature of 'Crito' . . . in the 'Cumberland Pacquet.'"

Crito. *Charles Lamb.* On the danger of confounding moral with personal deformity, contributed to the "Reflector."

Crito. *John Millar.* Letters . . . on the causes, objects, and consequences of the present war. 2d ed. Edinb. 1796.

Crito. *Elijah Waring.* A poem on the death of that faithful and laborious minister of the Gospel, Benjamin Kidd. L. 1752.

Crito Cantabrigiensis. *Thomas Turton, D.D.* A vindication of the literary character of the late Professor Porson . . . L. 1827.

Croaker. *Joseph Rodman Drake.*

The first four of the once famous "Croaker Pieces" were written by him for the "New York Evening Post," in which they appeared between the 10th and 20th of March, 1819. Then Drake made Fitz-Greene Halleck a partner, and the remainder of the pieces were signed "Croaker and Co." The last one written by Drake was "The American Flag," and the last of the series, "Curtain Conversations," was contributed by Halleck.

Croaker and Co. *Joseph Rodman Drake* and *Fitz-Greene Halleck,* in the "New York Evening Post," 1819.

Crocus. *Charles C. Leonard.* History of Pithole . . . Pithole City, Pa., 1867.

Crœsus, Chippenham. *A. W. Cawston.* Fortunate youth; or . . . containing the commencement, action, and denouement of the Newmarket Hoax. 1818.

Croftangry, Chrystal. *Sir Walter Scott.* Chronicles of the Canongate. Edinb. 1826–28.

Croix, Blanche. *Charles Edward Long, Esq.* The crest of Howard, "Gent. Mag.," February, 1849.

Cromwell of New England, The. *Samuel Adams,* so termed in a London journal.

Croquelardon, Le R. P. Jean Gilles Loup Boniface. *Jacques Albin Simon Collin de Plancy.* Les trois animaux philosophes; ou, les voyages de l'ours de Saint-Corbinian . . . Paris, 1818.

Croquis, Alfred. *Daniel Maclise, R.A.* Portraits in "Fraser's Magazine."

Crosse, Launcelot. *M. Frank Carr.* Characteristics of Leigh Hunt. L. 1878.

C(rossman), C. O. *William Maginn,* in the "London Literary Gazette" in 182–.

Crossman, P. P. *William Maginn,* in the "London Literary Gazette" in 182–.

Crow, James. *George Stevenson Pine.*

Crowfield, Christopher. *Mrs. Harriet Beecher Stowe.* Home and home papers. B. 187–.

Crowquill, Alfred. *Alfred Henry Forrester.* The pictorial grammar. L. 187–.

Crowquill, Alfred. *Charles Robert Forrester,* as well as Alfred Henry, who used this pseudonym conjointly from 1826 to 1844.

Crucelli, F. *James A. Sidey.* Mistura curiosa: being a higgledy piggledy of Scotch English Irish Nigger golfing curling comic serious and sentimental odds . . . and fables . . . Edinb. 1869.

Cruiser, Benedict, M.M. (married man). *George Augustus Sala.* How I tamed Mrs. Cruiser . . . Edited . . . L. 1858.

Crusoe, Robinson. *Daniel Defoe.* The life and surprising adventures of . . . of York. Mariner. Written by himself. L. 1819.

Crust, Christie. *Eliza Freeman Denison.* Autumn leaves . . . Portland, Me., 1875.

Cryptonymus. *Joseph Gurney Bevan.* A brief reply to Catholicus's seasonable address to Disciplinarians . . . L. 1798.

Cryptonymus. *Kenneth Robert H. Mackenzie.* The royal Masonic cyclopædia of history, rites, symbolism, and biography. L. 1877.

Cub, The. *Charles James Fox.* The cub: a satire [on his dismissal from office]. L. 1774.

Cultivateur, Un Américain. *Hector St. John Crevecœur.* Lettres . . . écrites à Wm. S., Esq., 1770–1786. Paris, 1787.

Cultivateur de New Jersey, Un. *William Livingston.* Examen du gouvernement d'Angleterre . . . L. 1789.

Cumberland Landowner, A. *Sir James Robert George Graham.* Free trade in corn the real interest of the landlord . . . L. 1828.

Cumberland Poet, The. *William Wordsworth.*

Cumbermere, Lord Claudius Hastings. *Jean Baptiste Alfred Assolant.* Les aventures de K. Brunner . . . Paris, 1861.

Cuore, Lavinia Buon. *Mme. Lavinia Buoncuore Urbino.* Sunshine in the palace or cottage. B. 1854.

Curate of London, A. *Rev. Arthur Ashley Sykes.* A letter to . . . the Earl of Nottingham . . . L. 1721.

Curate of Wilts, A. *Rev. William Fleetwood.* A Letter to the Reverend Dr. Snape, wherein the authority of the Christian Priesthood is maintain'd . . . L. 1718. The letter is signed " S. T."

Curator of the Antiquities, The. *Rev. Charles Wellbeloved.* A descriptive

account of the antiquities in the grounds and in the museum of the Yorkshire Philosophical Society . . . York, 1852.

Curdle, Cream, *Irving Brown.* The character of the nurse's deceased husband in " Romeo and Juliet." By . . . Edited by W. Ord Hunter. n.p., n.d.

Curieux Septuagénaire, Un. *Baron Félix Sébastien Feuillet de Conches.* Souvenirs de jeunesse d' . . . Paris, 1877.

Curiosibhoy, Adersey. *Joseph S. Moore.* The " Parsee " letters, addressed to Horace Greeley, Sahib. N.Y., 1869.

Curioso, Il Parlante. *Don Ramon de Masonero y Romanos.* Panorama matritense. Madrid, 1835.

Curiosus. *George Oliver, D.D.* In 1828, in conjunction with the Rev. J. P. Jones of North Bovey, Dr. Oliver published the " Ecclesiastical Antiquities of Devon and Cornwall," a series of papers first contributed to the " Exeter and Plymouth Gazette," under the signatures of " Curiosus " and " Devoniensis." He also " contributed for many years a valuable series of letters, under the signature ' Curiosus,' to the columns of the ' Exeter Flying Post.' "

Curiosus. *John James Gibson Fuller.* Brasses formerly in Crowan Church. West Breton, 1868.

Curl-Pated. *John Hamilton Reynolds,* in the " London Magazine."

Curtiss, Percy. *Mrs. William N. Cox.* Richard Peters ; or, could he forgive him . . . B. 1872.

Curtius. *Dr. William Jackson,* author of letters in the " Public Ledger under this pseudonym.

Curtius. *Noah Webster.* His signature to a series of papers, in 1795, sustaining Jay's treaty.

Curtius. *John Taylor (?).* A defence of the measures of the Administration of Thomas Jefferson . . . Wash., D.C., 1804.

Curtius. *William J. Grayson.* Letters of Curtius. Charleston, S.C., 1851.

Curtius. *John Thompson.* Letters of Curtius. Richmond, 1804.

Cushman, Lilla N. *Anna M. S. Rossiter.*

Custos. *Thomas Bevan.* Lindley Murray Hoag and the Society of Friends. L. 1853.

Cutting, Pierce. *Charles Hull Webb,* in his contributions to the " Boys and Girls' Weekly " (N.Y.).

Cycla. *Mrs. Helen Clacy.* Aunt Dorothy's will: a novel. L. 1860.

Cyclos. *George E. Blackham, M.D.* An American bicycler.

Cyclos, a Member of the Glasgow Skating Club. *George Anderson.* The art of skating . . . Glasgow, 1852.

Cymon. *Frederick Thomas Somerby.*

Hits and dashes; or, a medley of sketches and scraps .·.. B. 1851.

Cypher, A. *H. Nutting.* A few plain remarks on decimal currency ... Luton, Beds., 1856.

Cypress, J., Jr. *William Post Hawes.* Sporting scenes and sundry sketches ... N.Y. 1842.

Cyrilla. *Baroness Tautphœus,* formerly *Miss Jemima Montgomery.* Cyrilla: a tale. L. 1853.

Cyrille. *Baron Adolphe d'Avril.* De Paris à l'Isle des Serpents à travers la Roumane la Hongrie, et les bouches du Danube. Paris, 1876.

D.

Δ. *David Macbeth Moir.* Biographical memoir of the late Mrs. Hemans. L. 1836.

Δ. *Francis Bàrham.* A loyal address to the Queen's Most Gracious Majesty ... L. 1840.

Δ. *Benjamin Disraeli.* Venetia. L. 1857.

δ. *John Henry Newman.* — See "a" (under alpha).

D. *Duke of Buccleugh.* To the D. of B.; animadverting upon his political conduct. Edinb. (?) 1776.

D. *Rev. Benjamin Franklin De Costa,* in his letters to the "Advertiser" (B.) during 1861–62.

D. *Rev. Charles Dyson.* "Four poems, contributed under the signature 'D,' to the volume entitled 'Days and seasons,' published in 1845, show ... the power and beauty with which he could write."

D. *John Frere.* His signature to papers in the "Microcosm," published at Eton College, 1787 *et seq.*

D. *Rev. John Henry Newman,* one of the contributors to "Tracts for the Times." L. 1840–48.

D. *Rev. David Malcolme.* An essay on the antiquities of Great Britain and Ireland [in letters signed "D."]. Edinb. 1838.

D. *Orville Dewey, D.D.* A letter on devotion at church. From the "Christian Examiner." Vol. IV., No. IV. B. 1827.

D. *John Dickinson.* Letters from a farmer in Pennsylvania to the inhabitants of the British Colonies. [The several letters signed "A Farmer," and the whole subscribed "D."] L. 1768.

D., Dr. *Dr. Nicholaus Delius.* Shakespeare. Edited ... L. 1854.

D., A. *Anne Dutton.* A discourse upon walking with God ... L. 1735.

D., A. *A. Darby.* An exhortation in Christian love to all who frequent horseracing, cock-fighting ... plays ... or any

other vain diversions ... By ... Shrewsbury, 1765.

D., A. *Mr. A. Dawson.* A guide to the musical tuition of very young children. By an old lady ... L. 1868.

D., A. *Mrs. A. Deane.* A tour through the upper provinces of Hindostan ... between the years 1804 and 1814 ... L. 1823.

D. A. Y. *David Elisha Dary.* His signature in the "Gent. Mag."

D., B. *Benjamin Dorr.* The history of a pocket prayer-book ... P. 1839.

D. B. *Charles M. Fleury, D.D.* Memoir. L. 1854.

D., B. F. *Benjamin Franklin De Costa.* Ticonderoga once more. N.Y. 1870.

D., C. *Mrs. Charles Dyson.* Memorials of a departed friend. L. 1833.

D., C. *Charles Deane.* New England's prospect ... By W. Wood. [With a "Preface to the present edition," signed "C. D."] B. 1865.

D., C. *Charles Dent.* Socialist excursion to Rosherville Gardens ... [Verses.] L. 1844.

D., C. A. *Mrs. C. A. De Wint.* Melzinga. N.Y. 1845.

D., C. B. *Rev. Charles Browne Dalton, M.A.* New Zealand. Letters from the Bishop to the Society for the propagation of the Gospel. Edited ... L. 1844.

D., C. C. *Charles Carroll Dawson.* Occasional thoughts and fancies. Des Moines, Iowa, 1860.

D., C. F. *Charles Force Deems,* author of "Triumph of peace and other poems," 185–, etc., editor of the "Southern Methodist Pulpit," and contributor to the London "Gent. Mag.," "Southern Methodist Quarterly," and other journals.

D. C. L. *Alexander James Beresford-Hope.* Letters on church matters. By ... From the "Morning Chronicle." L. 1851.

D. D., Cantab. *Richard Wilson.* The praises of T. Carlyle, the historian ...

(Praises of T. Wright, a learned historian ... Let the praises of other Chelsea worthies be added ...) L. 1873.

D., E. *Edward Denham*, in his contributions to the "State" (Richmond, Va.), etc.

D., E. *Edmond Douay.* Comme on devient un homme d'après les idées de B. Franklin. Edited ... Paris, 1865.

D., E. *Eliphalet Dyer.* Remarks on Dr. Gale's letter to J. W., Esq. n.p. 1769.

D., E. *Edward Dennant.* The sufferings of Christ, the glory of saints. By .. Ipswich, 1790.

D., E. *Rev. Edward Davison.* Tentamen theologicum; or, an attempt to assist the young clergyman ... in the choice of a subject for his sermon ... Durham, 1850.

D., E. *Emerson Dowson.* The youth's spelling, pronouncing, and explanatory theological dictionary ... L. 1818. — See " N. & Q.," 4th ser., xi., 402, 431.

D., E. A. *Mrs. E. A. Davenport.* Philip; or, content: a story. L. 1855.

D., E. F. *E. F. Dagley.* Fairy favours and other tales ... L. 1825.

D., E. H. *Elias Hasket Derby.* Reality *versus* fiction: a review ... B. 1850. — See " A Citizen of Boston."

D. F. *Daniel Defoe.* An enquiry into the occasional conformity of Dissenters ... L. 1701.

D., F. I. *Mrs. Florence I. Duncan.* Ye last sweet thing in corners ... P. 1880.

D., G. *George Dyer*, in Lamb's " Elia." Oxford in the Vacation.

D., — G. *George Daniel.* All's well that ends well ... with remarks ... L., about 1828.

D., G. *George Dodd.* Chambers' handy guide to the Kent and Sussex coast in six routes or districts. By ... L. 1863.

D., G. *G. Doughty.* Church-catechism ... L. 1703.

D., G. *George Daniel.* Democritus in London, with the mad pranks and comical conceits of Robin Goodfellow. By ... L. 1852.

D., G. *G. Dani.* England ... L. 1878.

D., G. *George Dunbar.* Herodotus, Græce et Latine ... Edited ... Edinb. 1806.

D., G. *George Darley.* The life of Virgil. Signed ... L. 1825.

D., G. *George Dyer.* The poetical works of J. Hammond and Lord Hervey, with biographical sketches of the authors. By ... L. 1818.

D., G., and B.; E. *George Daniel* and *Edwin Bentley.* Stanzas on Lord Nelson's death and victory. By ... L. 1806.

D., G. H. *Rev. George Henry Dashwood.* Sigilla antiqua. Engravings from ancient seals attached to deeds and charters [at] Stowe-Bardolph ... Stowe-Bardolph, 1847–62.

D., G. W. *George W. Driggs.* Opening of the Mississippi; or, two years' campaigning in the South-West ... Madison, Wis., 1864.

D. H. *Richard Gough*, his usual signature in the "Gent. Mag." His first communication to that periodical was an account of the village of Aldfriston in Sussex (Vol. XXXVII., p. 443) under this signature. "Antiquities at Aldfriston in Sussex."

D., H. *Henry Drummond.* A defence of the students of prophecy ... L. 1828.

D., H. *Harriet Dallaway.* Etchings of views in the vicarage of Letherhead, Surrey, by ... L. 1821.

D., H. *Hannah Doyle.* A few words on the third query ... L. 1860.

D., H. *Henry Davies.* Hours in the picture gallery of Thirlestone House, Cheltenham ... Cheltenham, 1846.

D., H. *Mrs. Harriet (Miller) Davidson.* Lines for little lips ... Edinb. 1856.

D., H. *Henry Dircks.* The Polytechnic College ... L. 1867.

D., H., Esq. *Hugh Doherty.* The discovery; or, the mysterious separation of ... and Ann his wife. By ... L. 1807.

D., H. *Ripensis. Heneage Dering.* Reliquæ Eboracenses. Per ... Eboraci, 1743.

D., H. A. *Miss Henriette Duff*, in "Temple Bar," "St. James's Magazine," the "Graphic," and the "Spectator."

D., H. B. *Henry Barton Dawson.* The colors of the United States first raised over the capitol of the Confederate States, April 3, 1865. Morrisania, 1866.

D., H. F. *Mrs. H. F. Delf.* "Safe in the arms of Jesus"; or, memorials of L. A. Delf. By her mother ... L. 1874.

D'I., I. *Isaac D'Israeli, Esq.* Remarks on the biographical accounts of the late Samuel Johnson, LL.D. ... in the "Gent. Mag.," December, 1786, p. 1123.

D., J. *James Dunwoody Brownson De Bow*, editor of the "Southern Quarterly Review," 1843–45, founder and editor of "De Bow's Monthly Review" at New Orleans, 1846–57 *et seq.*, author of "Industrial Resources and Statistics of the

Southern and Western **States**," 1853. — See "A Citizen."

D., J. *John Disturnell.* The Eastern tourist . . . N.Y. 1848.

D., J. *James Dafforne.* Fairholt's " Houses, haunts, and works of Rubens " . . . Edited . . . L. 1871.

D., J. *John Davidson.* The fall of the Pope, and the fate of the French President. L. 1852.

D., J. *John Dix,* afterwards *Ross.* Pen pictures of popular English preachers . . . L. 1851.

D., J. *Jane Dewhurst.* Poems . . . Kingston, 1858.

D., J. *John Davidson.* Remarks on some of the editions of the Acts of the Parliaments of Scotland. Edinb. 1792.

D., J. *John Davy.* Sir H. Davy's consolations in travel; or, the last days of a philosopher. Edited . . . L. 1851.

D., J. *James Dallaway.* Some account of the Cistertian Priory of Ripa Mola . . . In a letter . . . by . . . Edited by N. C., *i.e.,* Nicholas Carlisle. L. 1837.

D., J., Chirurgus. *John Dix.* — See " Chirurgus."

D., J. F. *J. F. Davis.* A vocabulary containing Chinese words and phrases peculiar to Canton and Macao . . . Macao, 1824.

D., J. H. *Rev. J. H. Davies.* The lady of the valley: an Essex legend. Colchester, 1875.

D., J. H. *J. Hamilton Dundas* (?). Scraps of a scribbler: being a few short poems . . . on various subjects. By . . . Edinb. 1834.

D., J. L. *J. L. Dowling.* Ye historie of Leadenhall [Market]. By . . . L. 1877.

D., J. M. *John Marriott Davenport.* Memorandum as to oaths . . . 1873.

D., J. N. *John Nelson Darby.* Notes on Scripture. Glasgow, 1866.

D., J. N. *Rev. John Neale Dalton, Jr.* Sermons to naval cadets. By . . . L. 1879.

D., J. R. *John Dix,* afterwards *Ross.* A hand-book of Newport and Rhode Island . . . Newport, 1852.

D., J. R. *James Reid Dill.* A sermon from the Grave. L. 1862.

D., J. W. *Rev. John William Donaldson.* A brief exposure of the Rev. J. S. Perowne. L. 1855.

D., J. W. *John William Dawson, LL.D.* Catalogue of Canadian plants in the Holmes Herbarium . . . Montreal, 1859.

D., J. W. *J. W. Duffy.* Julia Ingrand . . . From the Spanish. By . . . L. 1877.

D., L. *Leonard Digges.* Gerard, the unfortunate Spaniard. L. 1653.

D., M. *Matthew Dawes.* A letter to Lord Chatham, concerning the present war of Great Britain against America, etc. By a gentleman of the Inner Temple. L. 1776.

D., M. A. *Michael Aislabie Denham.* Folk lore; or, manners and customs of the North of England. By . . . Civ. Dunelm, 1850–52.

D., M. A. *Mrs. Mary Andrews Denison.* John Dane . . . B. 1874.

D., M. F. P. *Mary F. P. Dunbar.* The Shakespeare birthday book. [Mottoes selected by M. F. P. D.] L. 1875.

D., M. J. M. *Margaret Juliana Maria Dunbar.* Art and nature under an Italian sky. By . . . L. 1852.

D., M. M. *Mrs. Mary Mapes Dodge,* editor of " Saint Nicholas " (N.Y.).

D., N. B. *N. B. Dennys.* A short vocabulary of the Mongolian language, in the dialect chiefly used on the northern border of China . . . By the editor . . . Hong Kong, 1867.

D., N. H. *Nathan Haskell Dole,* as literary editor, and contributor, to the " Philadelphia Press."

D., P. *Philip Dodd.* No change for the worse, a mistaken notion. By . . . L. 1803.

D. P. (*i.e.,* Desiderius Pastor). *Rev. Gerard Moultree, M.A.,* who contributed thirty-five hymns to the " People's Hymnal " (1867), some of which are signed " D. P.," others " M," and one " The Primer."

D., R. *Richard Duppa.* Elements of the science of botany . . . L. 1809.

D., R. *Richard De Courcy.* Jehu's looking glass . . . Edinb. 1772.

D., R. H., Jr. *Richard Henry Dana, Jr.* Two years before the mast . . . N.Y. 1844.

D., S. — See " Dowell, Samuel."

D., S. *Selina Ditcher.* Life lost or saved . . . L. 1866.

D., S. A. *Samuel A. Drake* (?). Catalogue of the private library of S. G. Drake . . . (His life-work and his library, by S. A. D.) 1876.

D., S. G. *Samuel G. Drake.* Notice of W. T. Harris . . . [With a preface by S. G. D.] B. 1855.

D., S. M. *Mrs. Sarah Matilda Davis.* Life and times of Sir Philip Sidney. B. 1859.

D., S. R. *Rev. Spencer Rodney Drummond, M.A.* [A sermon preached after the funeral of C. Drummond. With a memoir by . . .] L. 1858.

D., T. *Thomas Delaune.* The image of the beast . . . L. 1712.

D., T. *Rev. Thomas Dale.* The widow . . . of Nain; and other poems. By . . . 1819.

D., T. F. *Thomas Frognall Dibdin.* Bibliography : a poem . . . L. 1812.

D., W. *William Drysdale,* correspondent of the " New York Times."

D., W. *W. Duncan.* Britain's glory; or, the downfall of the French Republic . . . L. 1794.

D., W. *W. Day.* A collection of psalms and hymns for public worship. Compiled . . . Evesham, 1795.

D., W. *Rev. William Dalton* (?). A course of sermons on the creed of Pope Pius IV. . . . Wolverhampton, 1841.

D., W. *William Douglass.* A dissertation concerning inoculation of the small pox. B. 1736.

D., W. *W. Davidson.* Letter to the Rev. John Cumming, D.D. . . . L. 1851.

D., W. *William Duane.* Remarks upon a speech delivered by Mrs. E. Cady Stanton! during the summer of 1870. P. 1870.

D., W. *Wedderburn Dundas.* St. Andrews. Lines by . . . 1838–39.

D., W., M.A. *William Derham.* The artificial clockmaker . . . L. 1700.

D., W. A. *William Augustus Davis.* Biographical notice of Charles Stearns Wheeler, A.M., who died at Leipzig, June 13, 1843, aged twenty-six years. By . . . B. 1843.

D., W. A. *Bishop William Abernethy Drummond.* The lawfullness of breaking faith with heretics . . . Edinb. 1778.

D., W. G. *William Giles Dix.* The deck of the " Crescent City " : a picture of American life. N.Y. 1853.

D., W. H. *William H. Dorman.* The close of twenty-eight years of association with J. N. D[arby] . . . L. 1866.

D., W. J. *William John Deane.* Lyra Sanctorum . . . Edited . . . L. 1850.

D., W. J. *W. J. Duncan.* Notes on the rate of discount in London . . . Edinb. 1877.

D., W. L. *W. L. Dickinson.* The little book of family prayer . . . With an introduction by . . . L. 1870.

D. Y. *Edmund Quincy,* in the " Anti-Slavery Standard."

D**.** *Henri Gabriel Duchesne.* Notice historique sur la vie et les ouvrages de J. B. Porta. Paris, 1801.

D**, Le duc de.** *Étienne Léon,* baron de Lamothe-Langon. Mémoires de Louis XVIII. . . . Paris, 1832.

D*, J. A.** *Jacques Antoine Dulaure.*

Pogonologia; or, a philosophical and historical essay on beards [the dedication signed " J. A. D*** "]. Translated from the French [by E. Drewe ?]. Exeter, 1786.

D*, J***.** *James Delacour.* Abelard to Eloisa : in answer to Mr. Pope's . . . Eloisa to Abelard. By . . . Dublin, 1730.

D***, S******.** *Susanna Dowson.* Poems, domestic and miscellaneous . . . Norwich, 1844.

D**n.** — *Dawson.* Observations on the conduct of Messrs. W*****cks and . . . towards Mr. R***d B**r [Brewer], their cashier. Dublin, 1755.

D*n, B**b.** *Bubb Dodington.* A dialogue between G[ile]s E[arl]e and . . . 1743.

D**n, J**n, D.D.** *John Duncan, D.D.* The plea for a private indulgence of grief. Addressed to the Hon. P**l*p B**v**ie [Philip Bouverie]. L. 1804.

D——. *Erasmus Darwin.* The botanic garden : a poem . . . L. 1791.

D——, Duke of. *William Cavendish,* 1st Duke of Devonshire. The charms of liberty : a poem by the late . . . L. 1709.

D——, D—— of. *Duke of Dorset.* The . . . letters to the L[or]d C[hance]ll[o]r of Ireland. L. 1753.

D——, His R. H., the. *Duke of Cumberland.* An attempt towards an apology for . . . [A satire by R. Bentley.] L. 1751.

D——, Benjamin. *Benjamin Disraeli.* Benjamin D——, his little dinner. Illustrated by " Whew." L. 1876.

A squib in prose and verse on the policy of B. Disraeli, Earl of Beaconsfield.

D——, G. *George Daniel.* Cumberland's British theatre . . . L. 1829–43.

D——, J. R. *Rev. James Reid Dill.* A sermon from the grave. Memoir of N. Sproule . . . L. 1862.

D—e, E. *Edward Dingle.* 'Tis a real good thing in a family. Signed . . . Plymouth, 18–.

D—k, S—n. *Stephen Duck.* The year of wonders : being a literal and poetical translation of an old Latin prophecy found near Merlin's Cave, by . . . L. 1738 (?).

D—n, Mr. *John Dryden.* A description of . . . funeral : a poem. L. 1700. By T. Brown (?).

D—n, Erasmus. *Erasmus Darwin.* The Golden Age : a poetical epistle from . . . to Thomas Beddoes, M.D. L. 1794.

D—n, J. *John Dean.* A genuine account of the ship S[usse]x . . . L. 1740.

D—s, C—s, Bellamy Brownjohn, and Dombey. *Robert Carr Dunham.* No thoroughfare. B. 1868.

D—st D—r, The. *Conyers Middleton, D.D.* The Deist Doctor detected; or, free remarks on Dr. M.'s examination. By Philotheos. L. 1750.

D–la–y, Rev. Dr. *Patrick Delany.* A letter of advice to the ... humbly propos'd to the consideration of a certain great Lord. [In verse.] Dublin, 1725.

D–ll–s, Revd. M–rm–d–ke. *Rev. Marmaduke Dallas.* A short and true state of the affair betwixt the Revd. J***m***t [Jemmet], Lord Bishop of C–rk [Cork] and R–ss [Ross], and ... Dublin, 1749.

D – – mm – – d, Mrs. *Mrs. Drummond.* The female speaker; or, the priests in the wrong: a poem ... L. 1735.

D'A., Anna. *Anna D'Almeida.* A lady's visit to Manilla and Japan ... L. 1873.

Dacre, Charlotte, better known by the name of "Rosa Matilda." *Mrs. Charlotte Dacre Byrne.* Hours of solitude. A collection of original poems ... L. 1805.

Dadd, B. *John H. Williams.*

Daddow, Daniel. *Charles Bennett.* Cornish comicalities in prose and verse. Truro, 1875.

Dagobert, Chrysostôme. *Jean Baptiste Alphonse Led'huy.* A bon chat bon rat, tit for tat ... L. 1855.

Dagonet. *George Robert Sims,* in his contributions to the "Referee." L. 1877 et seq.

"Daily News" special correspondent, The. *J. F. Maurice.* The Ashantee war [with England in 1873–74]. A popular narrative. By ... L. 1874.

Daisy, Winter. *Miss — Whiteway.* Ettie Knott; or, silver-lined clouds. By ... L. 1877.

Dakotah, Hal á. *General Henry Hastings Sibley,* in his contributions to "Porter's Spirit of the Times," etc.

Dale, Ellis. *G. A. McKenzie,* in his contributions to the "Canadian Monthly Magazine" (Toronto).

Dale, Salvia. *Mrs. Alice Dalsheimer.* "Her contributions to the 'New Orleans Times,' principally poetical, under this pen-name elicited encomiums and encouraging predictions of future success."

Dalgetty, Dugald. *Major-General Sir Alexander Murray Tulloch, K.C.B.,* who, under this signature, wrote in the Indian journals, calling attention to certain abuses practised on their soldiers by the Honorable East India Company.

Dalin, M. *Linda White Villari.*

Courtship and campaign: a Milanese tale of '66. 1873.

Dalmocand. *George Macdonald.* Poems and essays; or, a book for the times. By ... L. 1851.

Dalriada. *D. B. Knox,* of Armoy, Ireland, in his contributions to "Texas Siftings" (N.Y.).

Dalrymple, Gilbert, D.D. *Gerard Legh.* A letter from Edinburgh to Dr. Sherlock ... L. 1718.

Daly, Frederic. *Lewis Austin.* Henry Irving in England and America, 1838–84. L. 1884. — See "Lewis, Augustin."

Daly, John. *John Besemeres.* Old Salt: a serio-comic drama in two acts. L. 1868.

Damon. *Elias Brockett.* The yea and nay stock-jobbers; or, the 'Change-Alley Quakers anatomized. In a burlesque epistle to a friend at sea. L. 1720.

Danburian. *Charles E. A. Mac-Geachy.*

Danbury Newsman. *James Montgomery Bailey.* Life in Danbury. B. 1870.

Danforth, Harry. *C. J. Peterson.* A native and resident of Philadelphia; proprietor and co-editor of "Peterson's Ladies' National Magazine."

Dangerfield, John. *Oswald John Frederick Crawfurd.* Grace Tolmar: a novel .. L. 1872. Also in his contributions to the "New Quarterly Magazine" (L.).

Daniel. *Euarda Garcia.* Lucia Novela ... Buenos Aires, 1860.

Daniel, Bp. of Calcutta. *Daniel Wilson.* Expository lectures on St. Paul's epistle to the Colossians ... 1845.

Daniel, the Prophet. *Daniel Defoe.* D. the prophet no conjurer; or, his Scandal-Club's scandalous ballad, called the Tackers answered paragraph by paragraph. L. 1705.

Danmoniensis. *William Burt.* Desultory reflections on banks in general ... L. 1810.

D'Anvers, Caleb. *Nicholas Amhurst,* the name he assumed as editor of the "Craftsman" (L. 1726) in connection with *Pulteney* and *Bolingbroke.* He also wrote for the "Evening Post" under the name of "Philalethes."

D'Anvers, Caleb. *William Pulteney.* An argument against excises... L. 1733.

D'Anvers, Caleb, Esq. *Henry St. John, Viscount Bolingbroke.* The craftsman extraordinary ... L. 1729.

D'Anvers, N. *N. R. E. Bell.* Elementary history of art. L. 1874.

Dapiferus, Jacobus, Corcagiensis. *Jeremiah Daniel Murphy.* "Adventus in Hiberniam Regis vera atque perfecta historia," in "Blackwood's Mag.," October, 1821. He was also the author of "The Rising in the North," in "Blackwood," August, 1822.

Darby, John. *James Edmund Garretson, M.D.* Hours with ... P. 1877.

Darc, Daniel. *Maria Sidonia (Serrur) Regnier.* Revanche posthume. Paris, 1878.

Darcey, Daniel. *Maria Sidonia (Serrur) Regnier,* in contributions to the "Liberté," Paris, 1870, and other Parisian periodicals.

Dare, Shirley. *Mrs Susan C. (Dunning) Power.* Behaving ... N.Y. 1877.

Dare, Sydney. *Mrs. Martha J. Cochran,* in her contributions to "Harper's Young People" (N.Y.).

Darppil. *George Lippard.* Legends of the Revolution. 1847.

Daryl, Sidney. *Douglas Straight.* Harrow recollections ... L. 1867.

Dash, la comtesse. *Gabrielle Anne Cisterne de Courtiras, Vicomtesse de Saint-Mars.* Les aventures d'une jeune mariée. Paris, 1870.

Dashaway, Kate. *Mabella Ann Ward.*

Dashwood, Sylvanus. *George Stillman Hillard,* a member of the "Polyglot Club." — See the "Harvard Register," Camb., December, 1827.

Daubeny, Mr. *Benjamin Disraeli,* Lord Beaconsfield, in Trollope's novels.

Daugé, Henri. *Mrs. E. H. Hammond.* A fair philosopher. N.Y. 1882.

Daughter of the Church of England, A. *Mary Astell.* The Christian religion as professed by ... L. 1705.

Daughter of the Late Author of the "Cambrian Plutarch," A. *Mrs. A. E. (Parry) Nightingale.* Gleanings from the South, East, and West. L. 1843.

Daughter of the Late Serjeant [George] Wilson, A. *Miss Anne Wilson.* Lady Geraldine Beaufort, by ... L. 1802.

David, C. G. *David Goodman Croly.* A Positivist primer. By ... N.Y. 1871.

Davus. *Rev. John Cecil Tattersall, B.A.,* in Byron's "Childish Recollections." Newark, 1807.

Davy. The first two pieces of *Alexandre Dumas,* viz., "La chasse et l'amour" (1825) and "La noce et l'enterrement" were represented under this name.

Dawdle, Dolly. *Mrs. Mary C. (Painter) Lukens.*

Dawes, J. N. *Richard Porson, A.M.* His signature to a letter on some Greek constructions in the "Monthly Magazine," December, 1802.

Dawplucker, Jonathan, Esq. *John Barclay, M.D.* Remarks on Mr. John Bell's anatomy of the heart and arteries. L. 1799.

Daynell, V. *Wiltshire Starnton Austin, Jr.,* and another. Lives of the Poets-Laureate ... L. 1853.

Dayton, Captain Will. *Cecil Burleigh.* On the staff of the "New York Witness" in 1880 et seq., and has published poetry with this signature.

Deacon. *Hiram Calkins,* Albany correspondent of the "Spectator" (N.Y.).

Dead Beat. *Joseph Howard, Jr.,* in the "Brooklyn Eagle."

Dean. *Jonathan Swift, D.D.* Advice to a certain Dean. 17-.

Dean, The. *Jonathan Swift, D.D.* The Dean's provocation for writing The lady's dressing room. 1734.

Dean, The Copper-Farthing. *Jonathan Swift, D.D.* The most wonderful wonder that ever appear'd to the wonder of the British nation ... Written ... L. 1726.

Dean of Canterbury, The. *Henry Alford.* The Riviera: pen and pencil sketches from Cannes to Genoa. L. 1870.

Deane, Margery. *Mrs. Marie J. (Davis) Pitman.* European breezes. B. 1882.

Deans, Jennie. *Mrs. Jane Gray C. Swisshelm,* in her contributions to the "Saturday Gazette" (P.) et al.

De Bieville. *Edmond Desnoyers.* Les dévorants. Paris, 1843.

De Bury. *Ange Henri Blaze.* Le Faust de Gœthe. Paris, 1840.

De Camille. *Pauline Guyot Lebrun.* Une amitié de femme. Paris, 1843.

Decanus. *Very Rev. Edward Newenham Hoare.* English settlers' guide through Irish difficulties. L. 1850.

Decanver, H. C. *C. H. Cavender.* Catalogue of works ... in refutation of Methodism ... P. 1846.

Decayed Macaroni, A. *Christopher Anstey.* Liberality; or, memoirs of ... Bath, 1788.

Decimus. *Thomas Chatterton,* in the "Middlesex Journal."

Decius. *Samuel Jackson Gardner,* for some time editor of the Newark (N.J.) "Daily Advertiser"; wrote many essays for periodicals, under the signatures of "Decius," etc.

Decius. *John Nicholas.* D.'s letters on

the opposition to the Federal Constitution in Virginia. Richmond, 1789.

Also ascribed to Dr. Montgomery.

Decius. *Thomas Peregrine Courtenay.* Observations on the American treaty; in eleven letters . . . L. 1808.

Declan. *William Phelan, D.D.*

"A pamphlet which he published under the signature of 'Declan' (after an ancient worthy of the Irish church, who flourished before the dominion of the Pope was recognized in the 'holy isle') placed its author at the head of modern controversialists."

De Cordova. *R. J. De Cordova.* Mrs. Fizzlebury's new girl. N.Y. 1878.

De Courcy, Kate. *Miss Katherine Armstrong,* in her contributions to various periodicals.

Deen, Ethel. *Mrs. Augusta De Milly,* who, during the civil war, contributed to the literary journals of "Dixie"—principally the "Southern Field and Fireside" (Augusta), and "Magnolia Weekly" (Richmond)—under the signatures "E. D." and "Ethel Deen."

Deene, Kenner. *Mrs. Charlotte (Turner) Smith.* Christmas at the Cross Keys. L. 1863.

Defonz, Milo. *Milo Defonz Codding.* Defonz' phrenological chart . . . N.Y. 1863.

De Gleva, Mary. *Mary Roberts.* An account of Anne Jackson; with some particulars concerning the great plague and fire in London, written by herself. Edited by . . . L. 1832.

De Grasse, Will. *William Furniss.* Swallows on the wing . . . N.Y. 1866.

De Kay, Se. *Charles D. Kirke.* Wooing and warring in the wilderness. N.Y. 1860.

Also in his contributions to the "Courier-Journal," Louisville, Ky.

Delafield. *Mrs. Maria L. (Little) Child,* in her contributions to "Arthur's Magazine."

Delamothe, Émile. *Émile de Girardin.* His original name.

De Launay, Le Vicomte de. *Mme. Delphine (Gay) Girardin.* Lettres parisiennes. Paris, 1856.

Delaware Wagoner, A. *David Nelson.* Investigation of that . . . misrepresentation of truth set forth by Thomas Paine in his . . . "The Age of Reason" . . . Wilmington, Del., about 1800.

Delinquent Banker, A. *Sir John Dean Paul, Bart.* Rouge et noir, in six cantos. L. 1821.

Della Crusca. *Robert Merry.* Diversity: a poem . . . L. 1788.

Della Rosa, Signor. *Richard Coker.*

Delmar, Ide. *Miss Essie B. Cheesborough,* who, under this *nom de plume,* contributed to the "Southern Literary Gazette," etc.

Delorme, Charles, Esq. *Charles Rumball.* The marvellous and incredible adventures of Charles Thunderbolt, in the moon . . . L. 1851.

Delorme, Joseph. *Charles Augustin Sainte-Beuve.* Poésies de . . . Paris, 1829.

Delphine. *P. or Delphine P. Baker.* Solon; or, the Rebellion of '61. Chic. 1862.

Delta. *Edward Denham,* in his contributions to "Good Literature" (N.Y.).

Delta. *Henry W. Domett,* for eight years New York correspondent of the "Boston Transcript."

Delta. *Rev. Moses Harvey,* of St. Johns, Newfoundland, in his letters to the "Traveller" (B. 1870).

Delta. *Charles Deane.* Bibliographical reprints. B. 1865.

Delta. *David Macbeth Moir.* Poems. 1852.

Delta. *William Millett Boase, M.D.* Sketches of Cornwall in the "Selector Magazine," 1827.

Delver, A. *Alfred Alsop.* From dark to light; or, voices from the slums. By . . . Manchester, 1881.

Delver into Antiquity, A. *William Barclay David Donald Turnbull.* Fragmenta Scoto-monastica . . . Edinb. 1842.

Democritus. *George Daniel.* Democritus in London . . . with notes festivous . . . L. 1852.

Democritus. *Hugh Henry Brackenridge.* The standard of liberty: an occasional paper. P., about 1802.

Democritus, Doctor. *Charles Chauncy Emerson,* a member of the "Polyglot Club."—See the "Harvard Register," Camb., December, 1827.

Democritus, Junior. *Judah Lee Bliss.* — See "O. F. and A. K."

Democritus Junior. *Robert Burton.* The anatomy of melancholy . . . L. 1621.

Denarius. *Henry Cole, C.B.* Shall we keep the Crystal Palace? By . . . L. 1851.

Dennery (also D'Ennery). *Adolphe Philippe.* Le tribut de Zamora. Paris, 1881.

Densel, Mary. *Mrs. Mary Selden McCobb,* in her contributions to "Harper's Young People" (N.Y.).

Densyli. *L. Sidney* (?). A brief
statement of the Unitarian doctrine . . .
Rochester, Eng., 1844.

De Pembrcke, Morgan. *Morgan
Evans.* Poems. L. 1860.

De Pontaumont. *M. E. Lechanteur.*
La rosïère de Bricquebec. Liege, 1861.

The above work is translated word for word
from the "Pride of the Village" by Washington
Irving.

Deputy Governor, The. *Gilpin Gorst.*
A narrative of an excursion to Ireland
. . . L. 1825.

Derbyshire Working-Miner, A.
Anthony Tissington. A letter to a friend
on the mineral customs of Derbyshire
. . . L. 1768.

De Rosa, Ludovico. *Luisa (Emmanuel) Saredo.* Affare Zappoli, in the
"Corriere Italiano," Florence, 1860.

Derrick, Francis. *Mrs. Frances
Eliza Millett Notley.* Olive Varcoe . . .
L. 186–.

Descendant, A. *George Chambers,
LL.D.* A tribute to the principles, virtues, habits, and public usefulness of the
Irish and Scotch early settlers of Pennsylvania. By . . . Chambersburg, 1856.

**Descendant in the Fourth Genera-
tion, A.** *Dr. Charles Henry Parry.* A
memoir of Peregrine Bertie . . . L.
1838. The dedication is signed "C. H. P."

Descendant of the Plantagenet, A.
Mrs. Frances Mary English. The Tudors
and the Stuarts . . . L. 1858.

Désennuyée, A. *Mrs. Catherine Grace
Gore.* The diary of . . . L. 1836.

Desiré, Hazard. *Octave Feuillet.* He
made his first appearance in letters by
being one of the authors of the romance
"Le grand vieillard," which appeared in
"Le National," Paris, 1845.

Desormeaux, Joseph Ripault. *Antoine Dingé.* Discours sur l'histoire de
France. Paris, 1790.

Desprez, Ernest. *Eléonore Tenaille de
Vaulabelle.* Jours heureux. Paris, 1836.

De Stendhal. *Marie Henri Beyle.*
Histoire de la peinture en Italie . . .
Paris, 1817.

Desultory Reader, A. *Alexander
Graydon.* A number of his essays, very
popular at the time, will be found in the
Phila. "Portfolio," under the title of
"Notes of a desultory reader." 1813–14.

Detective, A. *Andrew Edmund Brae.*
Literary cookery, with reference to matter attributed [by J. P. Collier] to Coleridge and Shakespeare. A letter addressed to the "Athenæum." L. 1835.

Detective, A. *William Russell.* Strange
stories of . . . N.Y. 1864.

Detective, A. *J. Bennett.* Tom Fox;
or, the revelations of . . . L. 1860.

**Detective, The Female, The City
Detective, The Private Detective,** are
all for *Andrew Forrester.* L. 1863–68.

Detective Police Officer, A. *William Russell.* Diary of . . . By "Waters."
N.Y. 1864.

Detective's Daughter, A. *Mrs. Robert P. Porter,* in her contributions to the
"Press" (P.).

Detector. *Henry J. T. Drury,* of
King's College, Cambridge.

For an account of the hoax perpetrated by him
in 1810 upon Sir Walter Scott, under this pseudonym, see "Notes and Queries," 1st Ser., V.
438.

Detector. *Rev. Henry Gauntlett.* Letters to a stranger in Reading . . . L.
1810.

Determinatus. *Samuel Adams,* in
the "Boston Gazette," Aug. 8, 1768; Jan.
8, 1770.

De Terrier, Lord. *Edward Henry
Smith Stanley,* Earl of Derby, in Trollope's "The Prime Minister."

Detlef, Karl. *Klara Bauer.* Die
geheimnissvolle Sängerin; and Russische
Idyllen. 1878.

Detroit Free Press Man, The. *C. B.
Lewis.* "Quads odds": anecdote, humor, and pathos. Detroit, 187–.

Deutsch, Christian. *Johann Heinrich August Ebrard.* Stephan Klinger
1872.

Devon, H. T. *Thomas Hounsell Hodge,*
who wrote for the "Brit. Amer. Mag."
under this signature. Author of "A tale
of the Bay of Quinte," etc., in that journal.

Devoniensis. *Rev. J. P. Jones.* — See
"Curiosus."

Devonshire Dog-Trot, A. *John
Cooke.* Old England for ever, from . . .
1819.

Devonshire Poet, The. *Owen Jones.*
Poetic attempts. 1786. The author was
an uneducated wool-comber.

Dewall, Johannes van. *August
Kühne.* Die beiden Russinnen. 1880.

De Worfat, William. *Rev. Hutton
Beetham.* A bran new wark, containing
a true calendar of his thoughts concerning good nebberhood . . . Kendal, 1785.

D'Hele, Thomas. *Thomas Hales,* an
English dramatic writer, who produced
in French several successful comedies,
among which are "The judgment of
Midas" (1778), and "The jealous lover."

Dhu. *Robert W. McAlpine,* in his
contributions to the "Tribune" (N.Y.).

Dhu, Helen. *Charles Edwards Lester,*

Stanhope Burleigh: the Jesuits in our homes. A novel. By ... N.Y. 1855.

Diabolus. *Joseph Howard.* Corry O'Lanus, his views and experiences. N.Y. 1867.

Diana. *Mrs. Abigail (Smith) Adams.* The signature she used in correspondence with her young friends, before her marriage. She afterwards sometimes signed her letters " Portia."

Diarist, A. *Alexander Wheelock Thayer.* His signature to many articles published in " Dwight's Journal of Music."

Dicaióphilus Cantabrigiensis. *Rev. Roger Long, S.T.P.* The rights of churches and colleges defended ... L. 1731.

Didier, David. *Anatole Julien Chatelain.* Le jouer d'orgue: drame en un acte. Paris, 1866.

Digg, Dr. E. Goethe. *Benjamin Drew,* in the " Carpet-Bag " (B. 1852).

Dignify'd Clergy-man of the Church of England, A. *Rev. George Hickes.* The celebrated story of the Thebæan Legion no fable ... L. 1714.

Digress, Deloraine. *Robert Habersham.* His signature to a letter on " Digression " in the " Harvard Univ. Collegian," 1830.

Dilettante, A. *William Gardiner.* Music and friends; or, pleasant recollections of ... L. 1838.

Dinaux. *Jacques Félix Beudin* and *Prosper Parfait Goubaux.* Trente ans; ou, la vie d'un jouer. Paris, 1827.

D'Inc. *Margarita Ernesta Napollon,* in contributions to the " Sibero Pensiero."

Dinks. Not *H. W. Herbert,* but only edited by him. The sportsman's vade mecum ... N.Y. 1856.

Diodoros. *Johannes Henrik Tauber Fibiger.* Graabroderen (the Franciscans), 1880.

Diogenes, Jr. *John Brougham,* in the " Lantern," a humorous paper which he edited in New York City.

Diplomat, A. *Joseph Q. Nunes.* A diplomat on diplomacy ... P. 1863.

Diplomatic Servant, An old. *H. H. Parish.* British diplomacy illustrated in the affair of the " Vixen " ... Newcastle, 1838.

Diplomatist, A Rising. *Henry Wikoff.* The adventures of a rising diplomatist. N.Y. 1856.

Director, A. *Henry E. Pierrepont.* Historical sketch of the Fulton ferry ... Brooklyn, 1879.

Dirrill, Charles. *Richard Sill.* Re-

marks on Shakespeare's "Tempest" ... L. 1797.

Disbanded Volunteer, A. *Joseph Barber.* War letters of ... N.Y. 1864.

Disciple of Selden, A. *Henry Richard Vassall Fox,* 3d Lord Holland. Parliamentary talk ... L. 1836.

Disciple of the Prince of Peace, A. *Joseph Hemmings.* Mystic Babylon described ... L. 1843.

Dissenter. *Rev. Micaiah Towgood.* Dissenter's apology. L. 1739.

Dissenter, A. *Rev. John Ballantyne.* A comparison of Established and Dissenting Churches. Edinb. 1830.

Dissenter, A. *Rev. Daniel Neal.* A letter ... to the author of the " Craftsman " ... L. 1733.

Dissenter in the Country, A. *Rev. James Peirce.* An enquiry into the present duty of a low-church-man ... L. 1712.

Dissenting Gentleman, The. *Rev. Micaiah Towgood.* The dissenting gentleman's answer to the Rev. Mr. White's three letters. L. 1746.

Dissenting Minister, A. *Rev. Robert Christison.* Church defence, by ... L. 1874.

Dissenting Minister, A. *John R. Beard, D.D.* Government plan of education defended ... L. 1839.

Dissenting Minister, A. The work " Struggles for Life " (L. 1853) over this pseudonym has been variously attributed to the *Rev. William Leask,* of Kennington, *Rev. Thomas Binney,* and *Rev. Thomas T. Lynch.*—See "N. & Q.," 1st Ser., xii., 9, 52, 115.

Dissenting Minister, A. *Rev. Charles Lloyd.* Particulars of the life of ... 1812.

Distich, Dick. *Alexander Pope.* His signature to a paper contributed to the " Guardian."

Distinguished Living Character, A. *Sir Philip Francis.* The identity of Junius with ... established. By John Taylor. L. 1816.

Distinguished Southern Journalist, A. *Edward Alfred Pollard.* The early life, campaigns, and public services of Robert E. Lee ... N.Y. 1870.

D'Istria, Dora, Countess. *Helene Ghika, Princess Kolzow-Massalski.* Des femmes; par une femme. Paris, 1864.

Ditson, Dick. *M. L. Saley,* of Rockford (Ill.), in his contributions to various periodicals.

Ditto, Philo. *James Moore Smith,* in a communication to the " Daily Journal " (L., April 3, 1728), relative to Alexander Pope.

Diver, Jenny. *Mrs. Jane Jones.*

Diversity. *William B. Scott.* Essays on taxation and reconstruction. N.Y. 1866.

Divine of the Church of England, A. *James Macsparran, D.D.* America dissected; being a full and true account of all the American colonies ... In several letters, from ... Dublin, 1753.

Divine of the Church of England, A. *John King.* Animadversions on a pamphlet (by Increase Mather) intituled "A letter of advice to the churches of the Nonconformists in the English nation ... L. 1701.

Divine of the Church of England, A. *Thomas Burnet.* An appeal to common sense ... L. 1719.

Divine of the Church of England, A. *Rev. Mr. Scott.* An appeal to the understanding of the meanest capacities, for the truth of the Christian religion. L. 1728.

Dix, J. Ross. *George Spencer Phillips.*

Dix Quævidi. *Prof. Edward North, L.H.D.*, in his contributions to "North American Review," and "Knickerbocker Magazine"; and author of memorials of H. H. Curran and President Simeon North.

Dixie. *J. Dixie Doyle,* Washington correspondent of the "Spirit of the Times" (N.Y.).

Dixon. *Mme. Clémence (Harding) Masson,* author of numerous tales.

Dixon. *Sidney Andrews.* The South since the war; 14 weeks in Georgia and the Carolinas. B. 1866.

Dixon, Granby. *Henry Kingsley.* Oakshott Castle: the memoir of an eccentric nobleman. L. 1873.

Dobbins, Peter, Esq., R. C., U. S. A. *William Fessenden.* The political farrago ... Brattleboro, Vt., 1807.

Dobbs, Rev. Philetus, D.D. *Rev. Heman Lincoln Wayland.*

Doblado, Don Leucadio. *Joseph Blanco White, M.A.* Letters from Spain ... L. 1822.

Doctor, The. *George Henry Kingsley.* — See "Earl, The."

Doctor, The. *Robert Southey.* The Doctor ... L. 1853.

Doctor of Divinity, A, but not of Oxford. *Thomas Raffles, D.D.* (?). Hear the Church! A word for all. By ... L. 1839.

Doctor of Laws, A. *Hugh Baillie.* An appendix to a letter to Dr. Shebbeare ... 1775.

Doctor of Physic, A. *W. H. Taylor.* The book of travels of ... P. 1871.

Doctor of Physick, A. Probably *William Coward.* A discourse concerning the certainty of a future and immortal state. L. 1706.

Dodd, Charles. *Hugh Tootell.* An apology for the church history of England from 1500 to 1688 ... Being a reply to a ... libel, intitl'd "A specimen of amendments ... under the name of 'Clerophilus Alethes'" [John Constable]. L. 1742.

Dodd, Derrick. *Frank Gassaway.*

Dodd, Dr., and Chace Price. *William Coombe, Esqr.* A dialogue in the Shades between ... L. 1777.

Dodger. *Peter Thompson.*

Dods, Jeannie. *Miss Mackay,* in "Figaro" (L.).

Dods, Mrs. Margaret, of the Cleikum Inn, St. Ronans. *Mrs. Christina Jane Johnstone.* The cook and housewife's manual ... Edinb. 1826.

Dods, Meg. *Mrs. Christina Jane Johnstone.* — See "Mrs. Margaret Dods."

Doe, Dorothy. *Mrs. Galusha Anderson,* in the N.Y. "Examiner."

Doe, John. *George Cavendish Bentinck.* Barefaced imposters. A farce, in one act. By ... Richard Roe [i.e., the Hon. F. G. B. Ponsonby] and John Noakes [i.e., Tom Taylor]. L. 1854.

Doesticks, Q. K. Philander, P.B. [i.e., Perfect Brick]. *Mortimer M. Thompson.* Doesticks: what he says. N.Y. 1855.

Doggrel, Sir Iliad. *Sir Thomas Burnet,* and *George Ducket.* Homerides; or, a letter to Mr. Pope, occasioned by his intended translation of Homer. By ... L. 1715.

Dogood, Mrs. Silence. *Benjamin Franklin;* by whom the essays published in the "New England Courant" (B. 1722) under this signature are supposed to have been chiefly written.

Doherty, Sir Morgan O', Bart. — See "O'Doherty."

Dolent, Jean. *Antoine Fournier.* Le livre d'art des femmes : peinture, sculpture ... Paris, 1877.

Dolores. *Miss Dickson.* Music to numerous songs, — more than 50. 1854–68.

Dom Catalogus. *Pierre Gustave Brunet.* Curiosités bibliographiques et artistiques. Geneva, 1867.

Dom Jacobus. *Charles Potvin.* Les tablettes d'un libre-penseur. 1879.

Dom Liber. *Charles Potvin.* Le faux miracle du saint sacrement de Bruxelles. 1876.

Domal, C. *William Henry Simmons.*

His signature to "A Saturday Night" in the "Harvard Univ. Collegian," 1830.

Domestic Poet, The. *William Cowper.*

Domitian. One of the signatures of Junius (*q.v.*). The letters contributed to the "Public Advertiser" under this signature are recognized by Junius in his private letter to Mr. Woodfall, dated Feb. 22, 1772.

Don. *I. E. Diekenga.* Tom Chips. P. 1871. [Joint author with "Ouno," *i.e.*, T. M. Ashworth.]

Don Carlos. *Henry P. Cheever,* in the "Philadelphia Sunday Mercury."

Don Fuso. *Arnoldo Fusinato.* Gedichte. 1853–54.

Don Sacheverellio, Knight of the Firebrand. *Dr. Henry Sacheverell.* A character of . . . in a letter to Isaac Bickerstaff, Esq. Dublin, 1710. Subscribed John Distaff [*pseud.*].

Don Spavento. *Martin Cohn.* Typen und Silhouetten von Wiener Schriftstellern und Journalisten. 1874. — See "August Mels."

Donatello. *Francis Julius Le Moyne Burleigh,* who, in 1867, went into journalism, and has been on the staff of the "Chicago Evening Post," "Brooklyn Eagle," "Brooklyn Union," "New York World," "Times," "Tribune," and the "Witness," and was at one time editor and proprietor of the "Northampton (Mass.) Free Press."

Doncourt, Chevalier A. de. *Antoinette Joséphine Françoise Anne (Symon de Latreiche) Drohojowska.*

Doos, Gurreb. *John Prinsep.* Strictures and observations on the Mocurrery system of landed property in Brazil . . . L. 1794.

Dora, Sister. *Dorothy W. Pattison.*

Dorcastriensis. *Thaddeus Mason Harris, S.T.D.*

Dorset, St. John. *Rev. Hugo John Belfour.* Montezuma : a tragedy in five acts ; and other poems . . . L. 1822.

Doubtful Gentleman, A. *James Kirke Paulding.* Tales of a good woman. N.Y. 1829.

Doughty Champion in heavy armour, A. *Rev. Newcome Cappe.* Letters published in the "York Chronicle." L. 179–

In reply to the attack of Dr. Cooper, under the signature of "Erasmus," upon Mr. Lindsay on his resigning the living of Catterick.

Douglas, Edith. *Clara L. Burnham.* We Von Ardens. 188–.

Douglas, Marion. *Mrs. Annie Douglas (Greene) Robinson.* Picture-poems for young folks. B. 1871.

Doutney, Mrs. T. Narcisse. *Harriet G. Storer.* I told you so ; or, an autobiography . . . Camb., Mass.

Dow, Junior. *Elbridge Gerry Paige.* Short patent sermons. P. 187–.

Dowell, Samuel. *John Close.* A month in London ; or, the select adventures of S. D., the village bard, edited by A. M. Writewell. L. 1844.

In 1846 four numbers of a new edition were issued with the following title : "Adventures of an author ; or, the Westmoreland novelist." Edited by Tim Caxton.
All the above names are pseudonyms of Close.

Downing, Major Jack. *Charles Augustus Davis,* author of "Peter Scriber's Letters" and "Major Jack Downing's Letters," in the "New York Commercial Advertiser."

Downing, Major Jack. *Seba Smith.* The life and writings of . . . B. 1834.

Downright. One of the pseudonyms attributed to Junius (*q.v.*). The letter thus signed is dated Dec. 22, 1767, and contains an attack on Lord Chatham.

Doyle, Martin. *Ross Hickey.* Common things of every day life . . . Dublin, 1857.

Doyle, Thomas. *John J. More.* Five years in a lottery office . . . B. 1841.

Dragoon, A. *James Hadreth.* Dragoon campaigns to the Rocky Mountains . . . N.Y. 1836.

Drahlegne. *Frederick J. Englehardt,* in the "Turf, Field, and Farm" (N.Y.).

Drake, Francis, Esq. *Benjamin Humphrey Smart.* The metaphysicians . . . L. 1857.

Dralloc, N. *John Collard.* Praxis of logic for schools. L. 1799.

Dramatist, A. *B. Frere.* The adventures of . . . on a journey to the London managers. L. 1813.

Dranmor. *Ferdinand von Schmid.* Poetische Fragmente. Leipsic, 1865.

Draper, The. *William Webster, D.D.* The Draper's reply. L. 174–.

Draper of London, A. *Rev. W. Webster.* The consequences of trade, as to the wealth and strength of any nation . . . L. 1740.

Drapier, A. *James Atcherley.* A drapier's address to the good people of England . . . L. 1773.

Drapier, The. *Jonathan Swift.* The Hibernian patriot . . . Dublin and L. 1730.

Drawcansir, Sir Alexander, Knight. *Henry Fielding,* who in 1752 started the "Covent Garden Journal" under this name. See Andrews's "British Journalist."

Dreamer, A. *Major John André.*
This was his signature in "Rivington's Royal Gazette," in which he published the "Cow Chase," an heroic poem in three cantos, published in London in 1781. It was originally published on the morning of the day on which he was taken prisoner. The last stanza was:—
" And now I've closed my epic strain;
  I tremble as I show it,
Lest this same warrior-driver, Wayne,
  Should ever *catch the Poet.*"

Dreamer, A. *Henry Theodore Tuckerman.* Leaves from the diary of ... L. 1853.

Dreenan, Councillor. *James Russell Endean.* The political catechism for 1868; or, the verdict of facts. L. 1868.

Drekab, Maistre. *Leonard Baker.* Officiale handboke of ye Strivelin Fancye Fayre ... ye drawing-man. 1882.

Drille, Hearton, U.S.A. *Jeannie H. Grey.* Flirtation; or, Cupid's shoulder-strap tactics. N.Y. 1877.

Dropper, H. *Louis J. Jennings.* Eighty years of Republican government in the United States. L. 1868.

Drugger, Abel. *John Hardham.* The fortune tellers ... a medley. n.p., n.d.

Druid. *Henry M. Flint,* who wrote for the "New York World" over the signature "Druid."

Druid, The. *Henry Hall Dixon.* Saddle and sirloin; or, English farm and sporting worthies. L. 1870.

Druit, Henry. *William Flint.*

Drury, Karl. *Edgar Fawcett.* Chris, the car conductor; or, a brave man's fight with fate, in the "Family Star Paper." N.Y. 1884.

Dryasdust, The Rev. Dr. *Sir Walter Scott,* in the introduction to several of his novels.

Drydog, Doggrel. *Charles Clark.* September; or, sport and sporting. Colchester, 1856.

Du Baudrier, Sieur. *Jonathan Swift, D.D.* A new journey to Paris ... translated from the French. L. 1711.

Dubois, Alfred. *James Stuart Bowes,* who, under this pseudonym, "contributed a number of highly successful pieces to the London stage."

Dubourg, Antony. One of the pseudonyms of *Paul Lacroix.*

Ducaigne, R. E. *W. McKendree Heath.*

Du Camp, Jules. *Jules Lecomte.* Histoire de la Révolution de Février ... Paris, 1850.

Ducas, Theodore. *Charles Mills.* Travels of ... in Italy at the revival of letters and art. L. 1822.

Ducdame. *Henry Hooper.* Wash.

Boltor, M.D.; or, the life of an orator ... L. 1872.

Duchess, The. *Mrs. Maggie Argles.* Rossmoyne. P. 1883.

Duchillon. *Louis Dutens.* Memoirs of a traveller, now in retirement ... L. 1806.

Duckworth, Dr. Dodimus, A. N. Q. *Asa Greene.* The life and adventures of ... N.Y. 1833.

Dudley, Arthur. *Mme. Marie Pauline Rose (Stewart) Blaze de Bury,* who, from the age of 18 years, under the pseudonyms of "Arthur Dudley" and "Maurice Flassan," has published a considerable number of critical articles and novels in the "Revue de Paris" and in the "Revue des Deux-Mondes."

Dudley, Dorothy. *Mrs. Mary Williams (Greeley) Goodridge.*

Dudu. *Miss Julia Fletcher.* Kismet. B. 187–.

Duff, R. *Rev. Richard Gifford,* in the "Gent. Mag."

D'Uffey, Mr. *Thomas D'Urfey.* The Houbble Bubbles ... L. 1720.

Duffie, Thomas. *John Galt.* The steamboat. Edinb. 1822.

Dufour, Pierre. *Paul Lacroix.* L'histoire de la prostitution ... Brussels, 1861.

Dufourquet, Thalaris. *Mme. Jenny Dufourquet Bastide.* Un drame au palais des Tuileries. Paris, 1832.

Duggan, Dionysius. *William Maginn,* in the London "Literary Gazette." 182–.

Duke of Scampington. *E. C. G. Murray.* The member for Paris. L. 1871.

Dumpling-Eater, A. *Rev. Thomas Stona.* A letter to the Norfolk militia ... L. 1759.

Dunajew, Wanda von. *Aurora von Sacher-Masoch.* Roman einer tugendhaften Frau, und Echter Hermelin. 18–.

Dundreary, Lord. *Charles Kingsley.* Speech of Lord D. in section D. ... on the great Hippocampus Question. Camb. 1862.

Dunheved. *Alfred Farthing Robbins,* in his contributions to the "East Cornwall Times" (Launceston, Eng.).

Dunn, Aiken. *Thomas C. Latto,* in the Brooklyn "Times."

Dunn, Deborah. *Mrs. Frank R. Stockton,* in her contributions to various periodicals.

Dunshunner, Augustus Reginald, Esq., of St. Mirrens. *William Edmonstoune Aytoun.* Tales in "Blackwood," 1870.

D-nt-n, Mr. *Mr. Dunton.* Neck or nothing: a consolatory letter from . . . to Mr. C[u]rll, upon his being tost in a blanket . . . [In verse.] L. 1716. By Samuel Wesley (?).

Dupe, Johnny. *John Hancock,* in a letter from a loyalist in Boston to Dr. Church.

Duplessis, Armand. *Edmond Dennis de Manne and another.* Avant souper. Paris, 1864.

Dupré. *Edmond Dennis de Manne.*

Durand, Pierre. *Eugène Guinot,* who edited the "Siècle," Paris, till 1848, under this pseudonym, and at the same time produced *vaudevilles* under that of "Paul Vermond."

Durangelo, R. *Arnold Ruge.* Bianca della Rocca. 1869.

D'Urfey, Young. *Frederick Forrest.* A rattle for grown children . . . L. 1766.

Durocher, Léon. *Marie Roch Louis Reybaud,* who, under this pseudonym, contributed to the "National" (Paris).

Dusenbury, V. Hugo. *Henry C. Bunner,* editor of "Puck" (N.Y.).

Dustwich, Jonathan. *Tobias George Smollett.* The expedition of Humphrey Clinker . . . L. 1794.

Dusty. *Willard G. Nash.* A century of gossip; or, the real and the seeming New England life. Chic. 1876.

Dutiful Son, A. *Thomas George Fonnereau.* The diary of . . . L. 1849.

Duverney, Jacques. *L'Abbé Casimir Ulysse J. Chevalier.* Géologie contemporaine. Tours, 1867.

Dux, Lux. *Mrs. Anna Holyoke (Cutts) Howard,* in her contributions to the "Household" (Brattleboro, Vt.).

Dwight, Jasper. *William Duane.* Letter to George Washington . . . P. 1796.

Dy, W. H. *William H. Darby.* Baptism and the conflict of indwelling sin . . . L. 1859.

Dyce, Gilbert. *Percy Hetherington Fitzgerald.* Bella Donna; or, the cross before the name: a romance. By . . . L. 1864.

Dyson, Mr. *Rev. Sydney Smith.* Mr. D.'s speech to the freeholders on reform. 35th ed. L. 1831.

E.

ε. *Isaac Williams.* — See "**α**" (under "Alpha").

E. *Dr. William Heberden,* in his contributions to the "Athenian Letters" . . . L. 1741–43.

E. *Rev. Thomas Keble,* one of the contributors to "Tracts for the Times." L. 1840–48.

E. *Margarita Ernesta Napollon,* her signature in the "Sibero Pensiero."

E. *Thomas Erskine,* Lord Erskine. The farmer's vision. L. 1819.

E., Redruth. *Richard Edmonds, Jun.* Proposed reformation of the laws of England, in the "Cornish (Eng.) Magazine," 1828.

E. A. *Samuel Adams,* in the "Boston Gazette," Feb. 27, 1769.

E., A. *Rev. Arthur Ellis.* — See "A Layman."

E. C. *George Mackenzie,* Earl of Cromarty. An abstract of what was spoken in Parliament. n.p. 1705.

E., C. *Charlotte Elliot.* Hours of sorrow cheered and comforted . . . L. 1863.

E., C., M.D. *Charles Lamb* (?), in Hone's "Table Book."

E., D. *Sir David Erskine.* Annals and antiquities of Dryburgh and other places on the Tweed. By . . . Kelso, 1838.

E., D. *David Esdaile, D.D.* Contributions to natural history. Edinb. 1865.

E. G. *Rev. Edmond Hogan.* The history of the warr of Ireland from 1641 to 1653. Edited by . . . Dublin, 1873.

E., G. S. *George Samuel Emerson.* A sketch of the life of Francis William Greenwood. From the "Monthly Religious Magazine." B. 1847.

E., H. *Sir Henry Charles Englefield.* Description of a method of taking the differences of right ascension and declination . . . Bath, 1788.

E. H. C. M. *Rev. Nathan Davis.* Israel's true emancipation. L. 1852.

The letters E. H. C. M. stand for "Editor 'Hebrew Christians' Magazine.'"

E., J. *James Elia,* i.e., John Lamb, Charles's brother. — See Lamb's "Elia," "My relations."

E., J. *John Evelyn.* The charters of the city of London . . . L. 1738.

E., J. *Jonathan Ellis.* The justice of the present war against the French . . . Newport, R.I., 1755.

E., J., Esq. *John Elsum.* Epigrams upon the paintings of the most eminent masters . . . L. 1700.

E., J. C. *J. C. Erck.* The Irish Ecclesiastical Register ... Dublin, 1817.

E., L. *Louis Engel,* in his musical criticisms contributed to the "World" (L.).

E., L. *Mrs. L. Edwards.* Dial of meditation and prayer. L. 1858.

E., L. *Eleanor Eden.* Easton and its inhabitants ... L. 1858.

E. L. *Mrs. Lydia Lillybridge Simons.* Leisure hours; or, desultory pieces in prose and verse. Calcutta, 1846.

E., M. *Matthias Earbery.* Elements of policy, civil and ecclesiastical ... L. 1716.

E. M. E. *E. E. Millard.* Random casts; or, odds and ends from an angler's note-book. N.Y. 1878.

E. M. S. *Rev. James Dallaway, F.S.A.* "Mr. Dallaway was an occasional correspondent to the 'Gentleman's Magazine' under the signature 'E. M. S.' (Earl Marshal's Secretary), and he wrote several essays under the same signature in the 'General Chronicle and Literary Magazine,' published in 1811–12."

E., O. A. *Olaf A. Ericsson.* A cruise under six flags. By ... P. 1883.

E., P. G. *Sir Philip de Malpas Grey Egerton.* Grillion's Club, from its origin in 1812 to its fiftieth anniversary. By ... L. 1880.

E., R. W. *Ralph Waldo Emerson.* The wanderer: a colloquial poem. By William Ellery Channing. B. 1871. [The preface signed "R. W. E."].

E., T. *Thomas Edwards.* Free and candid thoughts on the Doctrine of Predestination. By ... Author of the "C[a]n[o]ns of Cr[i]t[i]c[i]sm." L. 1761.

E. T., Gent. *Simon Berington.* The memoirs of Sigr. Gaudentio di Lucca ... L. 1737.

E., W. *William Eaton.* Interesting detail of the operations of the American fleet in the Mediterranean [1804]. Springfield, Mass., 1805.

Earl, The. *George Robert Charles Herbert,* 13th Earl of Pembroke. South Sea bubbles, by ... and the Doctor [George Henry Kingsley]. L. 1872.

Early Settler, An. *Lt. Col. Samuel Strickland.* Twenty-seven years in Canada West; or, the experience of ... L. 1853.

Earnest, Elsie. *Mrs. M. V. Scruggs.* Sketches. Balt. 1874.

East Anglian, An. *Charles Feist.* Thoughts in rhyme. L. 1825.

Eastwood, Frances. *Mrs. D. C. Knevels.* Geoffrey the Lollard. N.Y. 1870.

Easy, James. *James Heywood,* in a letter to the "Spectator" (No. 268).

Eben-ezer. *Rev. Ebenezer Aldred.* The little book ... Derbyshire, 1811.

Ebn Osn. *Benjamin Stephenson.* Attempts at poetry. L. 1807.

Ebony. *William Blackwood,* a humorous appellation applied to him by James Hogg in the *jeu d'esprit* "The Chaldee Ms.," which appeared in "Blackwood's Magazine" for October, 1817.

Eboracus. *W. W. Broom.* Great and grave questions for American politicians ... B. 1866.

Eccletus. *Luke Howard.* A few notes on a letter to the Archbishops and Bishops of the Church of England ... L. 1806.

Echard, L. *Samuel Pegge.* On the promiscuous use of singulars and plurals among the Latin poets, "Gent. Mag.," 1790, p. 785. — See "Gent. Mag.," LXVI., p. 1083.

Echo, Oliver. *S. D. Forbes,* in his contributions to the "Evening Wisconsin."

Ecir. *Prof. Isaac L. Rice,* in the "Philadelphia Bulletin." Author of "What is Music?" N.Y. 187–.

Eclea-Nobj-moni. *Benjamin Coole.* A letter from a gentleman in the city to his kinsman in the country. L. 1705.

Ecneps, Phesoi. *Joseph Spence.* "In 1764 he was well portrayed by Mr. James Ridley, in his admirable 'Tales of the Genii,' under the name of 'Phesoi Ecneps (his own name read backwards) Dervish of the Groves, and a panegyrical letter from him to that ingenious moralist, under the same signature, is inserted in 'Letters of Eminent Persons,' Vol. III., p. 139."

Edax. *Charles Lamb,* in his essay on "Appetite," contributed to the "Reflector."

Edgar, Sir John. *Sir Richard Steele.* "In January, 1720, he began a paper under the name of Sir John Edgar called the 'Theatre,' which he continued every Tuesday and Saturday till the 5th of April following."

Edgerton, Wild. *Brock McVicker.*

Edianez, Anna. *Mlle. Zénaide Marie Anne Fleuriot,* who has written stories under the above pseudonym which have found great favor among French readers.

Edinburgh Burgess of 1786, An. *John Gladstone.* The justice and expediency of the plan contained in a report addressed ... to the Chancellor of the Exchequer ... Edinb. 1836.

Editor, An. *Lewis Gaylord Clark.* Knicknacks from an editor's table. N.Y. 1853.

Editor, The. *Ambrose Eccles.* The plays of King Lear and Cymbeline. By

William Shakspear. With notes and illustrations, selected ... by ... L. 1801.

Editor of "Bell's Life in London," The. *Frank L. Downing.* Fights for the championship. L. 1860.

Editor of "Chrysal," The. *Charles Johnston.* The history of Arsaces, Prince of Betlis. By ... Dublin, 1774–75.

Editor of "Columella," "Eugenius," The. *Rev. Richard Graves.* The reveries of solitude ... L. 1793.

Editor of "Dodsley's Collection of Old Plays," The. *Isaac Reed.* The plays of William Shakspeare ... The third edition, revised and augmented by ... L. 1785.

Editor of the "Examiner," The. (*James Henry*) *Leigh Hunt.* The "Reflector," a quarterly magazine, on subjects of philosophy, politics, and the liberal arts. Conducted by ... L. 1811.

Editor of the "Glossary of Architecture," The. *John Henry Parker.* Some account of domestic architecture in England, from Richard II. to Henry VIII. ... Oxford, 1859.

Editor of "Kind Words," The. *Benjamin Clarke.* The life of Jesus, for young people. By ... L. 1868.

Editor of "King Lear," The. *Charles Jennens.* The tragedy of King Lear, as lately published, vindicated ... L. 1772.

Editor of "Life in Normandy," The. *J. F. Campbell.* A short American tramp in the fall of 1854, by ... Edinb. 1865.

Editor of "Notes and Queries," The. *William John Thoms.* The E. of "Notes and Queries" and his friend, Mr. Singer; or, the questionable credit of that periodical. L. 1856. By William Robinson Arrowsmith.

Editor of "Once a Week," The. *Eneas Sweetland Dallas.* The Stowe-Byron controversy ... L. 1869.

Editor of "Salmagundi," The. *George Huddesford.* Les champignons du Diable; or, imperial mushrooms: a mock-heroic poem ... L. 1805.

Editor of a "Quarterly Review," The. *William Frederick Deacon.* Warreniana ... L. 1824.

Editor of that Edition, The. *Rev. William West.* A few words in reply to the "British Quarterly Review" on the new edition of Archbishop Leighton's works. By ... L. 1870.

Editor of that Journal, The. *Joseph Gurney Bevan* (?). A vindication of the American Colonization Society and the Colony of Liberia. Extracted from the "Herald of Peace." By ... L. 1832.

Editor of that Periodical, The. *Samuel Gardner Drake.* Review of Winthrop's Journal, as edited and published by the Hon. James Savage ... Prepared for ... the "New England Historical and Genealogical Register." By ... B. 1854.

Editor of the "Adventures of a Guinea," The. *Charles Johnston.* The history of John Juniper, Esq., *alias* Juniper Jack ... L. 1781.

Editor of the "Annals of Agriculture," The. *Arthur Young.* National danger, and the means of safety. By ... L. 1798.

Editor of the "Aurora." *Benjamin Franklin Bache.* Truth will out! The foul charges of the Tories against ... repelled ... P. 1798.

Editor of the "Boston Daily Advertiser," The. *Nathan Hale.* Remarks on ... a railroad ... from Boston to the Connecticut River ... B. 1827.

Editor of the "British Workman," The. *T. B. Smythies.* Stories about horses. Compiled ... L. 1876.

Editor of the "Canadian Freeman," The. *Francis Collins.* An abridged view of the Alien Question unmasked ... York, U.C., 1826.

Editor of the "Manchester Herald," The. *Joseph Aston.* Metrical records of Manchester ... L. 1822.

Editor of the "Monthly Repository," The. *Rev. Robert Aspland.* The Christian Reformer ... Hackney, 1815.

Editor of the "National," The. *George Jacob Holyoake.* The life of Thomas Paine ... L. 1847.

Editor of the "Newport Mercury," The. *George Champlin Mason.* Newport illustrated in a series of pen and pencil sketches. By ... N.Y. 1854.

Editor of the "Port Folio," The. *John E. Hall.* Memoirs of eminent persons, with portraits and facsimiles: written, and in part selected ... P. 1827.

Editor of the "Spiritual Quixote," The. *Rev. Richard Graves.* The coalition; or, the opera rehears'd: a comedy ... L. 1794.

Editor v. Publisher. *Edward Walford v. Elliot Stock.* A short narrative of his editorial connection with the "Antiquary," in 1879–80; by E. Walford. L. 1880.

Editors of the "Children's Friend," The. *Rev. William Wilson.* One hundred hieroglyphic Bible readings for the young. Compiled by ... L. 1869.

Edmund, The Right Rev., Bishop

of Chester. *Edmund Keene.* Sermon before the Society for Propagation of the Gospel in Foreign Parts, 1757. L. 1757.

Edwards, John H. *John Edward Haynes,* with Charles Haynes, author of "Star of hope," "Sabbath-school songs." N.Y. 187-. Also in his contributions to periodical literature.

Efendi, Murad. *Franz von Werner.* Balladen und Bilder. 1879.

Effessea. *Francis Sewell Cole.* Oceanica, etc. Southampton, 1871.

Effingham, C., Esq. *John Esten Cooke.* The Virginia comedians; or, old days in the Old Dominion . . . N.Y. 1855.

Egmont. *Ét. Michel Masse,* in his contributions to "Le Courrier du Bas-Rhin."

Eg—t, J., E—l of. *John, Earl of Egmont.* A letter from a person of distinction to the right hon. . . . L. 1749.

An answer to three pamphlets, of which Lord Egmont was the reputed author. The "Monthly Review." Vol. I., 1849, p. 238.

Ego. *Gabriel Norbert Billiart,* in his contributions to "La Monde Illustré" (Paris).

Egyptian Kafir, An. *Samuel Bailey.* Letters of . . . on a visit to England in search of a religion . . . L. 1839.

Egyptus. *Joseph Parrish Thompson, S.T.D.*

Eight Clergymen. *Rev. Hugh Stowell, Rev. John Cale,* etc. The Churchman armed. A course of lectures . . . L. 1864.

Eimi, C. Wilkins. *Charles Wilkins Webber.* Instinct, reason, and imagination, in the "Democratic Review." Vol. 15, p. 408.

ΕΛΑΧΙΣΤΟΣ. *Thomas Foster Barham.* Reliquiæ Seriæ; or, Christian musings . . . Short pieces in verse. By . . .

Elagnitin, J. *Joseph Nightingale.* Mock heroics, on snuff, tobacco, and gin, and a rhapsody on an inkstand. L. 1822.

El Atchby. *Lyman Hotchkiss Bagg.* His signature in the N.Y. "Graphic," April, 1873, and in the N.Y. "World," April, 1878.

Elberp. *George Henry Preble,* whose first article, composed in his 14th year, appeared in the "Experiment," Portland, Me., under this *nom de plume.*

Eld, George. *John Taylor,* the water-poet. Superbiæ flagellum; or, the whip of pride. L. 1621.

Elder of the Church of Scotland, An. *Hugh Barclay.* A plea for Christian union, by . . . Edinb. 185-.

Eldon, Dr. Abraham. *Thomas Wyse.*

The Continental traveller's oracle . . . L. 1828.

Elector, An. *Henry Romilly.* Public responsibility and vote by ballot. L. 1865.

Elector in 1771, An. *Samuel Adams,* in the "Boston Gazette," May 20, 1771.

Eleonora. *Eleanor Butler.* "Gay Eleonora's smile," in Anna Seward's "Llangollen Vale."

Eleven Sophomores. "Harry," by *C. F. Thwing;* "The bear," by *B. O. Peirce;* "Rose Bud's story," by *S. B. Stiles;* "Jamie's mice," by *C. H. Barrows;* "Santa Claus's deer," by *G. S. Pine;* "Maggie's walk," by *H. Hinkley;* "Chicken's mistake," by *C. A. Dickinson;* "About the stars," by *W. R. Page;* "Bertie's dream," by *F. A. Stimson;* "Bumble's first day at work," by *T. C. Williams;* "Bronco," by *A. A. Wheeler.* Stories for children. B. 1875.

Elfin. *Miss Georgiana Verrall.* A Cornish ghost story. A night's adventures at the Devil's Stile; or, Jacky Trevose and Mary Trevean. By "E." Truro, 1862.

Elfrida. *Mrs. Elizabeth (Simpson) Inchbald,* in Beloc's "Sexagenarian," II. 394. 2d ed. L. 1818.

Elhegos. *Elbridge Henry Goss,* in his contributions to the "Boston Advertiser," etc., from 1870.

Elia. *Charles Lamb,* in the celebrated "essays" contributed to the "London Magazine," 1820-25.

"The adoption of the signature was purely accidental. His first contribution was a description of the Old South Sea House, — where Lamb had passed a few months' novitiate as a clerk thirty years before, — and of its inmates, who had long passed away; and, remembering the name of a gay, light-hearted foreigner, who had fluttered there at that time, he subscribed his name to the essay."—T. N. TALFOURD.

Elia, Bridget. *Mary Lamb,* sister of Charles Lamb, was the author of "Mrs. Leicester's school . . . L. 1808.

Elia, James. *John Lamb,* brother of Charles Lamb.

Eliakim. *Count Modeste Gruau de la Barre.* Les visions d'Esaie et la nouvelle terre . . . Rotterdam, 1854.

Elias. *John Lingard, D.D.*

Perhaps his signature in the "Newcastle Courant," for which, in 1805, he wrote a series of letters, which were afterwards collected under the title of "Catholic loyalty vindicated"; or, more probably, of his anonymous pamphlets in his controversy with the Bishop of Durham and others, 1806-13.

Élie, Le Père. *Marie Maximilién Harel.* L'esprit du sacerdoce. Paris, 1818.

Eliot, George. *Mrs. Marian (Evans*

Lewes) Cross. Scenes of clerical life, 1858 ; Adam Bede, 1858. L. and Edinb.

" Nor can we omit, in concluding this notice of a most remarkable book, some notice of the disputes as to its authorship. The newspapers have been full of them. Mr. Anders, rector of Kirkby, writes early in April of this year to assure the world that ' the author of Adam Bede is Mr. Liggins, of Nuneaton, Warwickshire, and the characters whom he paints in Scenes of Clerical Life, are as familiar there as the twin spires of Coventry.' But just as we have satisfied our minds that this is the true state of the case, and are feeling greatly obliged to Mr. Anders, a wrathful letter from ' George Eliot' disturbs us; asking (not unreasonably) whether ' the act of publishing a book deprives a man of all claim to the courtesies usual amongst gentlemen?' . . . Then some gentleman is ' receiving subscriptions' as the ill-used author of Adam Bede. Finally, the Messrs. Blackwood, turning at last to throw a stone, declare that, ' those works are not written by Mr. Liggins, or by any one with a name like Liggins' . . . Now, upon all this we have only to remark, that we cordially agree in the dictum of Mr. Eliot, that ' the attempt to pry into what is obviously meant to be withheld, — his name, — is quite indefensible.'" — *Edinb. Rev.,* 1859.

Eliza. *Mrs. Elizabeth Carter.* The name under which she began to contribute verses to the " Gent. Mag.," at the age of seventeen.

Eliza. *Mrs. Eliza Jane (Poitevent) Nicholson,* in her contributions to the " Times-Democrat" (New Orleans, La.).

Eliza. *Anne Élisabeth (Petitpain) Voïart.* L'Algérien. Paris, 1816.

Eliza. *Mrs. Elizabeth Draper.* Letters from E. to Yorick [Laurence Sterne]. L. 1775.

Elizaphan of Parnach. *Benjamin Church, M.D.* Liberty and property vindicated, and the St—pm—n burnt . . . B. 1766.

Ellen. *Mrs. Rebecca S. (Reed) Nichols,* whose earliest poems were published in the Louisville " News Letter," under this *nom de plume.*

Ellen Louise. *Mrs. Ellen Louise (Chandler) Moulton,* who, in 1841, commenced furnishing prose contributions to the periodicals under this *nom de plume.*

Ellen of Exeter. *Mrs. Anne Maria Mackenzie.* The Neapolitan ; or, the test of integrity. L. 1796.

Ellersberg, Eduard. *Eduard Ziehen.* Gaston von Ronac. 186–.

Ellice, Lucy. *Miss Ellen Moriarty.* One of the *noms de plume* under which she wrote for Miles O'Reilly's " Citizen."

Elling, Franz von. *Karl Müller.*

Elliot, Edith. *Mrs. Anna Holyoke (Cutts) Howard,* in her contributions to the " Household " (Brattleboro, Vt.).

Elliot, Madge. *Margaret Eytinge.*

Elliott. *Samuel Elliott Coues.* Remarks on the Bunker Hill monument . . . Portsmouth, N.H., 1840.

Elliott, Elinor. *Ella S. Sargent.*

Elliott, Ruth. *Miss Lillie Peck.* A voice from the sea . . . L. 1876.

Elloie. *Miss Zoda Stith.* Poems. Nashville, Tenn., 1869.

Ellsworth. *Elmer E. Wadman,* in his contributions to various periodicals of Boston, Mass., etc.

Ellwood, Ella. *Ellen Shade.*

Elmar, Karl. *Karl Swiedack.* Die Wette um ein Herz. 1841.

Elmer Mitchell. Theophania ; or, a Scriptural view of the manifestation of the Logos, or pre-existent Messiah . . . L. 1857.

Elmwood. *James Russell Lowell.*

Elmwood, Elnathan, Esq. *Asa Greene.* A Yankee among the Nullifiers: autobiography. N.Y. 1833.

Elocution Walker. *John Walker.* A name given to him from his being a distinguished teacher of elocution.

Elohta Ttenrub. *Athole Burnett.*

Elon. *Dr. Linnaeus B. Anderson,* in his contributions to the " State " (Richmond, Va.).

The pseudonym is an anagram of Noel (Va.), his residence.

El Penseroso. *G. F. Lanigan,* a Canadian writer, who, under this signature, contributed to the " Western Journal."

Elvira. *Mrs. Perkins.* Harp of the willows. B. 1858.

Elysio, Filinto. *Francisco Manoel do Nascimento,* among whose works, published under this assumed name, are a number of odes and a translation of La Fontaine's " Fables."

Emanuel, Christian, Esq. *George Ensor.* Janus on Sion ; or, past and to come . . . L. 1816.

Embryo " Harvest Man," An. *Jeremiah Bigg.* Quakerieties, by . . . L. 1838.

Embryo M.P., An. — *North.* Anti-Coningsby ; or, the new generation grown old. L. 1844.

Emeff. *Mary Flagg,* in the " Home Journal."

Emendator. *Caleb Whitefoord.* Advice to editors of newspapers. L. 1799.

Emeritus. *Mr. Prower.* The Militiaman at home and abroad . . . L. 1857.

Emeritus Professor, An. *J. L. H. McCracken.* The art of making poetry by . . . in the 2d number of the " Knickerbocker."

Emerson, Sir James. *Sir James*

Emerson Tennent. Letters from the Ægean or Grecian Islands. L. 1829.
Assumed the name of "Tennent" in 1832.

Émery, Marie. *Mme. Vandenbussche.* Ivan ... N.Y. 1873.

Emigrant. *Samuel Sidney.* Emigrant's Journal. L. 1849–50.

Emigrant, An. *Adam Thom.* Letter to the Right Hon. E. G. Stanley ... Montreal, 1834.

Emigrant Farmer, An. *Rev. Joseph Abbott.* Memoranda of a settler in Lower Canada ... Montreal, 1842.

Emigrant Mechanic, An. *Alexander Harris.* Settlers and convicts; or, recollections of 16 years' labour in the Australian back-woods ... L. 1847.

Emilia. *Miss Pamelia S. Vinning,* a Canadian poet, who wrote for some time under this pen-name. She was afterwards a contributor to the "U. S. Mag.," which was merged in "Emerson's Mag.," then in "Emerson and Putnam's Mag.," and finally for several years in the "Great Republic Mag." Miss Vinning also wrote for the "Ladies' Repository," Cincinnati, and the "Canadian Illustrated News," Hamilton.

Emiliane, Gabriel d'. *Antonio Garin.* Ruses et fourberies des prêtres et des moines. Leipsic, 1845.

Emily. *Miss Emily Angove.* Clara May; or, bring your cares to Christ. Redruth, 1860.

Eminent Citizen of Virginia, An. *Benjamin Watkins Leigh.* Letters of Algernon Sydney in defence of civil liberty ... Richmond, 1830.

Eminent Collector in Edinburgh, An. *David Laing.* Catalogue of a portion of the rare and curious library of ... 1850.

Eminent Editor, An. *Hector Macneill.* Memoirs of the life and character of Gilbert Purring ... Edinb. 1805.

Eminent English Counsel, An. *John Longley.* Observations on the trial by jury ... Edinb. 1815.

Eminent Lawyer, An. *— Smith.* The opinion of ... concerning the right of appeal from the Vice-Chancellor of Cambridge to the Senate, etc. L. 1751.

Eminent Lawyer of Connecticut, An. *John Hooker.* New-England Loyal Publication Society ... Letter, written by ... n.p., n.d.

Eminent Lawyer of the Temple, An. *Dr. John Arbuthnot.* John Bull's Last Will and Testament ... 2d ed. L. 1713.
The preface is signed "Philonomus Eleutherus."

Eminent Literary Men. *Charles L Flint and others.* Eighty years' progress of the United States ... Hartford, 1868.

Eminent Tuner, An. *Thomas D'Almaine & Co.* D'Almaine & Co.'s new work upon the art of tuning the pianoforte and harmonium ... L. 1862.

Emma. *Miss M. L. Everist,* in her contributions to the "Globe-Democrat" (St. Louis, Mo.).

Emmeline. *Kathinka (Halein) Zitz.*

Emmeran, Eusebius. *Georg Friedrich Daumer.*

Emmet, Elizabeth. *Mrs. Elizabeth A. Comstock.*

Enemy to Peace, An. *Jonathan Swift, D.D.* A learned comment upon Dr. Hare's excellent sermon ... L. 1711.

Engelyom, Van. *Jules Lecomte.* Lettres sur les écrivains français. Bruxelles, 1837.

Engineer upon that Expedition, An. *Major Moncrief.* A short account of the expedition against Quebec, commanded by Major-General Wolfe, in the year 1759 ... L. n.d.

English-Catholic, of the Metropolitan Diocese, An. *Caleb Fleming.* A Catholic-epistle; or, pastoral letter ... L. n.d.

English Churchman, An. *T. H. Shaw.* The consumptive boy: a narrative by ... L. 1854.

English Civilian, An. *William Walton.* A reply to two pamphlets entitled "Illustrations of the Portuguese Question" ... and "The last days of the Portuguese Constitution" ... L. 1830.

English Connaught Ranger, An. *Edward Cooper.* The cure for Ireland. Dublin, 1850.

English Critic, An. *George Herbert Townsend.* William Shakespeare not an imposter. L. 1857.

English Detective, An. *William Russell.* Autobiography of ... By "Waters." L. 1863.

English Gentleman, An. *William Newnham Blane.* An excursion through the United States and Canada during the years 1822–23. L. 1824.

English Gentleman, An. *W. Windham.* A letter from ... giving an account of a journey to the glaciers ... in Savoy ... in 1741. L. 1744.

English Girl, An. *Anne Manning.* Account of a Moravian settlement in the Black Forest. L. 1858.

English, Goliah. *John Boyle,* Earl of Cork and Orrery. — See "G. K."

English Governess, The. *Mrs. Anna Harriette Leonowens.* The English governess at the Siamese Court, 1862–67. B. 1870.

English Grammar School Head Master, The. *Edward Rupert Humphreys, LL.D.* England's educational crisis . . . L. 1856.

English Journalist, An. *William Charles Mark Kent* [better known as *Charles Kent*]. What shall be done with Cardinal Wiseman? An inquiry. By . . . L. 1850.

English Lady, An. *Mrs. A. Phelps Bayman.* Notes and letters on the American war. L. 1864.

English Lady, An. *Mrs. A. Saint-George.* A sketch of the life of . . . Washington . . . N.Y. 1834.

English Landowner, An. *Sir Arthur Hallam Elton.* An inquiry into the alleged justice and necessity of the war with Russia . . . L. 1855.

English Merchant, An. *John Campbell.* The Spanish Empire in America . . . L. 1747.

English Officer, An. *Lieut. Col. Alexander Jardine.* Letters from Barbary, France, Spain, Portugal . . . L. 1788.

English Opium Eater, The. *Thomas De Quincey.* Confessions of an . . . L. 1845.

English Play-goer, An. *John Oxenford,* author of "Robin Hood": an opera . . . L. 1863.

English Priest, An. *Rev. S. B. Harper.* The catholicity of the Church's love and the humility of her ceremonial. L. 1850.

English Republican, An. *Algernon Charles Swinburne.* Notes of . . . on the Muscovite crusade. L. 1876.

English Resident, An. *T. M. Hughes.* Revelations of Spain in 1845 . . . L. 1845.

English Sappho, The. *Mrs. Mary Robinson.* The wild wreath. L. 1805.

English Sister of Mercy, An. *Miss Margaret Goodman.* Experiences of . . . L. 1861.

English Sportsman, The. *Hon. George Charles Grantley Fitz-Hardinge.* In the Western prairies. L. 1861.

English Terence, The. *Richard Cumberland,* to whom Goldsmith alludes in his "Retaliation" as "The Terence of England, the mender of hearts."

English Tory. *Sir Richard Steele.* The Guardian (No. 128, Aug. 7, 1713), etc.

English Traveller, An. *Orville*

Dewey. Letters of . . . on revivals of religion in America. B. 1828.

English Traveller, An. *Martin Sherlock.* New letters from . . . L. 1781.

English Traveller, An. *Rev. Joseph Hunter.* Notes . . . during a two days' sojourn at Ober-Wesel on the Rhine. L. 1847.

English Traveller at Rome, An. *William Godolphin,* Marquis of Blandford. A letter . . . to his father, of the 6th of May, 1721.

English Traveller in Spain, An. *John Talbot Dillon.* Letters . . . on the origin and progress of poetry in that kingdom . . . L. 1781.

Englishman. *William Sharp, Jr.* Englishman's remonstrance. L. 1771.

Englishman, An. — *Belton.* Angler in Ireland; or, an Englishman's rambles through Connaught and Munster, during the summer of 1833. L. 1834.

Englishman, An. *Thomas Paine.* Common sense; addressed to the inhabitants of America . . . P. 1776.

Englishman, An. *Samuel Phillips Day.* Down South; or, an Englishman's experience at the seat of war, 1861. L. 1862.

Englishman, An. *Thomas Gordon.* Francis, Lord Bacon . . . 5th ed. L. 1721.

The dedication is signed "Britannicus."

Englishman, An. *J. Dallinger.* The general use of machinery . . . Dallinghoo, 1821.

Englishman, An. *Dr. John Burton.* A genuine and true journal of the most miraculous escape of the Young Chevalier . . . L. 1749.

Englishman, An. *Philip Quarll.* The hermit; or, sufferings and other adventures of . . . L. 1727.

Englishman, An. *Henry Richard Vassall Fox,* 3d Baron Holland. Letter to a Neapolitan from . . . L. 1818.

Englishman, An. *Dr. John Jebb.* A letter to Sir William Meredith upon the subject of subscription to the liturgy . . . L. 1772.

Englishman, An. *John Cam Hobhouse,* Lord Broughton. Letters written by . . . resident at Paris . . . L. 1816.

Englishman, An. *John Horne Tooke.* The petition of . . . L. 1765.

Englishman, An. *James Bury.* Pickings up in Ireland . . . L. 1859.

Englishman, An. *Isaac Candler.* Summary view of America . . . L. 1824.

Englishman, An. *John Gough.* A

tour through Ireland in the years 1813 and 1814 ... By ... Dublin, 1817.

Englishman, An. *John Benwell.* Travels in America. L. 1853.

Englishman, An. *William Whittaker Barry.* A walking tour round Ireland in 1865. By ... L. 1867.

Englishman, An. *Edmund Wheeler.* What shall we do at Delphi? An E.'s letter to the Humanitarians. L. 1857.

Englishman Abroad, An. *Alexander Tighe Gregory.* Practical Paris guide. L. 1858.

Englishman, The. *Rev. Stephen Weston.* The Englishman abroad, 1824–25. L. 1825.

Englishman, The. *Thomas H. Gladstone.* The E. in Kansas ... N.Y. 1857.

Englishman, The Roving. *Eustace Clare Grenville Murray.* The roving Englishman ... L. 1854.

Englishman, A Young. *William Wirt.* The British spy; or, letters of ... Richmond, 1808.

Englishman in Switzerland, An. *Alexander Tighe Gregory.* A practical Swiss guide illustrated ... L. 1856.

Englishman resident at Paris, An. *John Cam Hobhouse, Lord Broughton.* Substance of letters from Paris in 1815. By ... L. 1816.

Englishwoman, An. *Miss Jane Porter.* Animated address to our fair countrywomen, in "Gent. Mag.," December, 1811, pp. 501–502.

Englishwoman, An. *Sarah Mytton Maury.* An E. in America. L. 1848.

Englishwoman, An. *Mrs. Barbara (Wreaks Hoole) Hofland.* A letter of ... L. 18–.

Englishwoman, An. *Mrs. M. Miller.* Letters from Italy ... L. 1776.

Englishwoman, An. *Mrs. Charlotte Ann (Waldie) Eaton.* Narrative of a residence in Belgium during the campaign of 1815 ... L. 1817.

Englishwoman, An. *Mme. Frances (Wright) D'Arusmont.* Views of society and manners in America. L. 1821.

Englishwoman, The. *Mrs. Sophia (Lane) Poole.* The E. in Egypt; letters from Cairo ... in 1842–44. L. 1844.

Englishwoman in America, The. *Mrs. Isabella (Bird) Mayo.* The aspects of religion in the United States of America. L. 1859.

Englishwoman in Utah, A. *Mrs. F. Stenhouse.* An Englishwoman in Utah ... 1880.

Englishwoman resident at Brussels in June, 1815, An. *Mrs. Charlotte Ann (Waldie) Eaton.* The days of the battle; or, Quatre Bras and Waterloo. L. 1853.

Ennuyée. *Mrs. Anna (Murphy) Jameson.* Diary of an Ennuyée. L. 1826.

Enoch. *Richard Laurence, LL.D.* The book of Enoch the Prophet ... Oxf. 1838.

Enos. *Cecil Percival Stone.* Aslané: a tale of the massacre of the Nestorian Christians. L. 1858.

Enquirer, An. *Judge George Tucker,* who, under this signature, contributed to Wirt's "British Spy."

Enquirer, The. *William Atkinson.* A letter in answer to one suspected to have been written by a stranger, assisted by the Jacobin priests of West-Riding. By ... L. 1801.

Enrique, Erratic. *Henry Clay Lukens,* of "New York Daily News," author of "Jets and Flashes." N.Y. 1883.

Ensanada. *Jacques Albin Simon Collin de Plancy.*

Epaminondas. *Gideon Granger.* Address of ... to citizens of the State of New York. Albany, 1819.

Epaminondas. *Augustus B. Woodward.* Considerations on the government of the Territory of Columbia. W. 1801.

Ephemera of "Bell's Life in London." *Edward Fitzgibbon.* A handbook of angling ... L. 1847.

Epicure, An. *Frederic Saunders.* Salad for the solitary and the social ... N.Y. 1871.

Epicurus Rotundus. *Shirley Brooks,* in London "Punch."

Epigram, Ephraim, Esq. *Ambrose Pitman, Esq.,* who, about the year 1788, resided in the Weald of Kent, occasionally figuring as a poetical correspondent of the "Maidstone Journal," under the above signature.

Episcopal Divine, An. *Dr. Hay.* Imparity among pastors ... n.p. 1703.

Episcopalian, An. *Rev. — Lake.* A letter respectfully addressed to the Lord Bishop of London... 2d ed. L. 1811.

Episcopalian, An. *Richard Whately.* Letters on the Church. By ... L. 1826.

Episcopalian of ... Maryland, An. *John Kewley.* An enquiry into the validity of Methodist Episcopacy ... Wilmington, 1807.

Epistleographos. *Gouverneur Carr.*

Epsilon. *Edward Denham,* in his contributions to the "Transcript" (B. Mass.).

Epsilon. *Richard Edmonds, Jun.* Mr. Peel's act. In the "Cornish (Eng.) Magazine." 1828.

Epsilon. *Rev. J. Baldwin Brown.* The moral government of God ... L. 1864.

Erasmus. *Miss Jeanette L. Gilder,* as regular literary correspondent in New York, of the "Philadelphia Press."

Erasmus. *Frederick May* (?). The Bible exposed by ... B. 1862.

Erasmus, W. J. *Erasmus Wilson.* Practical and surgical anatomy. L. 1838.

Erastus. *Rev. Joseph Jefferson,* of Basingbroke (Hants.), in his contributions to the "Gent. Mag." (L.).

Erceldoune. *Willis H. Bocock,* of the University of Virginia, in poems contributed to the "Central Presbyterian" (Richmond, Va.).

Erdan, Alexandre. *Alexandre André Jacob.*

Eremus. *John Wilson.* The snow storm, in "Blackwood's Magazine." Vol. 7, p. 37 *et seq.*

Erienensis. *Walter Cavendish Crofton.* Sketches of the Thirteenth Parliament of Upper Canada ... Toronto, 1840.

Eric-us. *Col. Adam Hood Burwell.* Talbot Road (1818), and other poems contributed to Canadian periodicals.

Erith, Lynn. *Edward Fox.* Poetical tentatives. L. 1854.

Ermite. *Rev. Patrick Eugene Moriarty.*

Ernst. *Mathias Jakob Schleiden.* Gedichte. 1858 and 1873.

Ernst, Julius. *Julius Stinde.*

Erodore. *Jacob Abbott.*

Erquar, Marie Jozon d'. *Joseph Marie Quérard.* Les supercheries littéraires dévoilées ... Paris, 1869.

Errynı, Malcolm J. *Malcolm J. Rymer.* Townsend the Runner. 18-.

Ervie. *Emily C. Pearson.* Echobank: a temperance tale ... N.Y. 1868.

Eskdale Tam. *Thomas Telford,* in "Ruddiman's Weekly Magazine." In early life he contributed several poetical pieces of merit to "R.'s W. M.," under the signature of "E. T." See Anderson's "The Scottish Nation," Vol. 3, p. 553.

Esmond, Henry, Esq. *William Makepeace Thackeray.* The history of Henry Esmond, Esq., a colonel in the service of Her Majesty Queen Anne; written by himself. L. 1852.

Espriella, Don Manuel Alvarez. *Robert Southey.* Letters from England ... L. 1807.

Essayist on the Passions, An. *Nicholas Michell.* The fatalist; or, the fortunes of Godolphin. L. 1840.

Essenus. *John Jones, LL.D.* A new version of the first three chapters of Genesis. L. 1819.

Essex Justice, An. *Andrew Johnston.* A pocket index to Oke and Stone. By ... Gloucester, 1877.

Estelle. *Miss Elizabeth Bogart,* who, under this signature, contributed many articles to the "New York Mirror" and other periodicals.

Estelle. *Mrs. Martha W. Frazer Brown,* whose poems were published in the "Southern Literary Messenger," etc.

Estelle. *Emily Marion Harris.*

Estelle. *Mrs. Piper.* Lucy Herbert ... B. 1863.

Esther, Aunt. *Mrs. John A. Smith.* Letters from Europe ... Chic. 1870.

Estoile, Pierre de l'. *Arsène Houssaye.* L'histoire en pantoufles, in "La Presse." Paris, 1861.

Etheridge, Kelsic. *W. B. Smith.* Egypt Ennis; or, prisons without walls. N.Y. 1876.

Ethophile, Un. *Docteur Imbert-Goorbeyre.* Un mot à M. le professeur Gonod, etc. 1845.

Etlar, Carit. *Karl Brosböll.* Salomon Baadsmand. 1880.

Etonian, An. *Charles Rowcroft.* Confessions of an Etonian. L. 1852.

Etonian, An. *Robert William Essington.* The legacy of ... Edited by Robert Nolands, sole executor. Camb. 1846.

Etonian, The Younger. *Rt. Hon. William Ewart Gladstone.* Ancient and modern genius compared, in the "Eton Miscellany." 1827.

Etoniensis. *Rt. Hon. William Ewart Gladstone,* in the London "Contemporary Review."

Ettrick Shepherd, The. *James Hogg.* The Altrive tales. The queer book: being a collection of poems. Edinb. 1832.

Eugène. *Édouard Roger de Bully Beauvoir.* Le cornet à piston. Paris, 1837.

Eugene. *Hugo Arnot.* A letter to the Lord Advocate of Scotland [Henry Dundas] ... Edinb. 1777.

Eugenie. *Kathinka (Halein) Zitz.*

Eugenius. *John Hall-Stevenson.* Crazy tales. L. 1762.

Eugenius Junior. *James Owen.* Church-pageantry display'd ... L. 1700.

Eugenius Philalethes. *Rev. Arthur Ashley Sykes.* The innocency of error, asserted and vindicated ... L. 1715.

Eulalie. *Mrs. Mary Eulalie Fee Shannon.* Buds, blossoms, and leaves: poems by ... Cin. 1854.

Eumenes. *William Griffith.* Eumenes: a collection of papers ... exhibiting some of the errors and omissions of the constitution of New Jersey ... Trenton, 1799.

Eunomus. *John James Park, LL.D.* Juridical letters: addressed to Right Hon. Robert Peel ... L. 1830.

Eupator. *Joseph Mendham.* Cardinal Allen's admonition to the nobility and people of England and Ireland ... A.D. 1558. Reprinted with a preface by ... L. 1842.

Euphranor. *James Bolivar Manson.* Contemporary Scottish art. A series of pen and ink pictures, drawn from the exhibition of 1864. By ... Edinb. 1864.

Euphrosyne. *Rev. Richard Graves,* who, under this name, published two volumes of poems which went through several editions.

Eureka. *Thomas N. Ralston, D.D.* Ecce unitas; or, a plea for Christian unity ... Cin. 1875.

European, An. *François Alexandre Frédéric,* Duc de la Rochefoucauld-Liancourt. On the prisons of Philadelphia ...

Européen, Un. *François Alexandre Frédéric,* Duc de la Rochefoucauld-Liancourt. Des prisons de Philadelphie ... P. 1796.

Euryalus. *George John,* 5th Earl of Delaware, in Byron's "Childish Recollections." Newark, 1807.

Εὐσεβεῖς. *Rev. R. Welton.* The clergy's tears; or, a cry against persecution ... n.p. 1715.

Eusebia. *Frances Thynne Somerset,* Countess of Hertford.

Eusebius. *Rev. Edward Dorr Griffin Prime,* who was for some years one of the editors of the N.Y. "Observer," in which his letters under this signature attracted considerable notice.

Eusebius. *Rev. Robert Boucher Nickolls, LL.D.* "On the growth of schism in the Church among the Methodistic clergy, and the means of checking it." In the "Anti-Jacobin" for May, 1809.

Eusebius. *Edmund Rack.* Reflections on the spirit and essence of Christianity. By ... L. 1771.

Eusebius Exoniensis. *Richard Polwhele.* An essay on the evidence from Scripture that the Soul immediately after the death of the body is ... in a state of happiness or misery ... L. 1819.

Euterpe. *Isaac D'Israeli, Esq.* "Verses addressed to Richard Gough, the 'Modern Camden,'" in the "St.

James's Chronicle" for Nov. 20, 1787.

Evangelical Preacher, An. *William Bengo Collyer, D.D.* An appeal to the legislature and to the public ... L. 1808.

Evangeline. *Miss Ellen A. Moriarty,* who, under this *nom de plume,* wrote for Miles O'Reilly's "Citizen."

Evangeline. *Mrs. A. E. Newman.* European leaflets, for young ladies ... N.Y. 1861.

Evans, Owen. *William Henry Anderdon.* The adventures of ... Edited by W. H. A. L. 1863.

Evelyn, Chetwood, Esq. *Robert Conger Pell.* The companion: after-dinner table-talk. N.Y. 1850.

Everett. *J. E. McAshan.* Houston (Tex.) correspondent of "Texas Siftings."

Everett, Paul. *Cornelia Lovejoy.*

Evergreen. *Washington Irving,* his signature in the "Salmagundi."

Everpoint. *Joseph M. Field.* The drama in Pokerville; and other stories. P. 1847.

Evolutionist, An. *John Fiske.* Excursions of ... B. 1883.

Ex-Barber to His Majesty the King of Great Britain, The. *Asa Greene.* Travels in America by ... N.Y. 1833. See "Fribbleton, George."

Ex-Colonel of the Adj.-Gen.'s Dept., An. *Charles Grahame Halpine.* Baked meats of the funeral. A collection of essays, poems ...

Ex-Consul, An. *Rev. Charles Wheeler Denison.* Antoine ... B. 1874.

Ex-Curate, An. *Rev. Edward John Watson.* An apology [for joining the R. C. Church] addressed to the clergy and congregations of Christ church and St. John's, St. Leonard's-on-the-Sea. By ... of the former church. L. 1877.

Ex-Dissenter, An. *George Rawston.* My life ... L. 1841.

Ex-Dissenting Minister, An. *Rev. Robert Christison.* The Liberationists unmasked, by ... Leeds, 1874.

Ex-Editor, An. *Col. Thomas Picton,* in his contributions to the "Spirit of the Times" (N.Y.).

Ex-Editor, An. *William Young.* Mathieu Ropars: et cetera. By ... N.Y. 1868.

Ex-M.P., An. *Henry Lambert.* Memoir of Ireland in 1850. L. 1851.

Ex-Member of the Society of Friends, An. *Edward Richardson, Jun.* Quakerism *versus* the Church. By ... L. 1860.

"**Ex-officio**" **Superintendent of the Department, The.** *John Hill Burton.* Memorandum on the collection and arrangement of the judicial statistics of Scotland. By . . . Edinb. 1868.

Ex-Orderly Sergeant, An. *John Mason* (?). Recollections of the early days of the national guard . . . the famous seventh regiment New York militia . . . N.Y. 1868.

Ex-Pension Agent, An. *Henry Morford.* Spur of Monmouth; or, Washington in arms. P. 1876.

Ex-Political, An. *E. B. Eastwick.* Dry leaves from young Egypt . . . L. 1849.

Ex-Surveyor General. *John Osborne Sargent.* Letter to General Hazen.

Excelsior. *Charles Fritts*, a technical writer on horology, in his contributions to periodical literature.

Exile, An. *Thomas Alexander Boswell.* The journal of . . . L. 1825.

Exilé, Un. *Yevgenii Obolenski.* Souvenirs d' . . . 1825–56, en Siberie. Leipsic, 1862.

Exile of Erin. *Rev. M. W. Newman*, in the "New York Tablet" and the "Irish American" (N.Y.).

Expatriated, An. *V. S. Zorawski.* A few words from . . . Cowes, 1844.

Experienced Carver, An. *George G. Foster.* New York in slices, by . . . being the original slices published in the "New York Tribune" . . . N.Y. 1849.

Experienced Clerk, An. *Henry Perkins.* Pounds, dims, cents, and mils; or, a real decimal coinage vindicated. Manchester, 1853.

Experienced Dyer, An. *Edward Andrew Parnell.* A practical treatise on dyeing and calico printing . . . N.Y. 1846.

Experienced Oculist, An. *G. H. Beer.* The art of preserving the sight . . . L. 1813.

Experienced Teacher, An. *A. Wrifford* (?). A brief development of the great secret of giving and receiving instruction . . . Concord, 1835.

Experienced Teacher, An. *— Borrenstein.* An easy method of acquiring the Hebrew . . . L. 1822.

Expertus. *Rev. Malcolm Maccoll.* Is Liberal policy a failure ? L. 1870.

Explorabilis. *Mrs. Eliza Haywood.* The invisible spy. By . . . L. 1759.

Expositor. *Aaron W. Leland.* A letter to the citizens of Charleston, embracing strictures . . . Charleston, S.C., 1818.

Extinguished Exile, An. *T. Wemys*

Reid, author of "Charlotte Brontë." N.Y. 1877.

Eyebright, Daisy. *Mrs. S. O. Johnson.* Every woman her own flower gardener. N.Y. 1871.

Eye Witness, An. *William E. S. Baker.* The battle of Coney Island ; or, free trade overthrown. P. 1883.

Eye-witness, An. *Rev. Thomas M'Lauchlan.* The depopulation system in the Highlands . . . Edinb. 1849.

Eye Witness, An. *Alexander Pope.* A full and true account of a horrid and barbarous revenge by poison, on the body of Mr. Edmund Curll, bookseller . . . L. 1716.

Eye-Witness, An. *Capt. John Murray Browne.* An historical view of the revolutions of Portugal, since the close of the Peninsular War. L. 1827.

Eye-Witness, An. *Edward Burk.* The hurricane : a poem . . . Bath, 1844.

Eye-Witness, An. *Henry Tanner.* The martyrdom of Lovejoy : an account of the life . . . Rev. Elijah P. Lovejoy . . . Chic. 1881.

Eye-Witness, An. *Lieut. Gordon Turnbull.* A narrative of the revolt and insurrection of the French inhabitants of the Island of Grenada. Edinb. 1795.

Eye Witness, An. *W. Walton.* Narrative of the political changes and events which have recently taken place in the Island of Terceira . . . L. 1829.

Eye-Witness, An. *Joseph Stock, D.D.* A narrative of what passed at Killala, in the county of Mayo . . . during the French invasion in the summer of 1798. By . . . Dublin, 1800.

Eye-Witness, An. *Charles Lamb.* Satan in search of a wife, with the whole process of his courtship and marriage, and who danced at the wedding; by . . . L. 1831.

Eyewitness, An. *Rev. George Robert Gleig.* The subaltern; or, sketches of the Peninsula War during the campaigns of 1813 and '14. By . . . L. 1825.

Eye Witness, An. *Thomas Savage.* A summary account of the marches, behaviour, and plunders of the rebels . . . L. 1746.

Eye-Witness to the Facts related. *Maj.-Gen. Andrew Burn.* A second address to the people of Great Britain ; containing a new and most powerful argument to abstain from the use of West India sugar. By . . . L. 1792.

Eyland, Major Seth, Late of the Mounted Rifles. *David E. Cronin.* The evolution of a life. N.Y. 1884.

Eyler, Emilié. *Mary Osten.* Grandmother's curiosity cabinet . . . B. 1869.

F.

F. *Nicholas Francis Flood Davin*, one of the authors of "Readings by Starlight," contributed to the "Evening Star," L. 1866.

F. — *Favell*, who left Cambridge because he was ashamed of his father, who was a house-painter there. — See Lamb's "Elia," "Christ's Hospital."

F. *Barron Field.* — See Lamb's "Elia," "My First Play."

F. *Sir George Prevost, Bart.*, one of the contributors to "Tracts for the Times," L. 1840–48.

F. *Thomas Ignatius Maria Forster.* Epistolarium; or, fasciculi of curious letters ... Bruges, 1845.

F. *William C. Folger.* Memoir of the late Hon. Walter Folger. New Bedford, 1874.

F. *Edward Fillebrown.* Richard Grant White and "The Bacon Shakespeare Craze." By ... In the "Commonwealth," Boston, March 31, 1883.

F. and F., J. F. *James Frederic Ferguson, Esq.*, in the "Gent. Mag.," March, 1853, p. 267, and August, 1855, p. 161.

F. A. C. T. *Osborne Howes,* Boston correspondent of the "Spectator" (N.Y.), etc.

F., A. P. *Alexander Penrose Forbes.* A memoir of the pious life and holy death of Helen Inglis ... L. 1854.

F., B. *Benjamin Furly* (?). The light upon the candlestick ... translated into English by ... L. 1811.

F., B., Esq. *Barron Field.* — See Lamb's "Elia," "Distant Correspondent," in a letter to B. F., Esq.

F., C. *Charles File*, in his contributions to the "Star" (N.Y.).

F., C. *Charles James Fox.* Epistle [in verse] from ... partridge-shooting, to the Honourable J. Townshend, cruising. By Richard Tickell. L. 1779.

F. C., The. *William Makepeace Thackeray.* Brighton in 1847. "Punch," 1847.

F., C. & E. C. *Catharine Foster* and *Elizabeth Colling.* A new metrical version of the Psalms of David. L. 1838.

F., Hon. C. J. *Hon. Charles James Fox.* The beauties of administration: a poem. With an heroic race to the palace between L[or]d Sh[e]lb[ur]ne and ... L. 1782.

F., E. *Edgar Fawcett*, in his contributions to the "Tribune" (N.Y.) etc.

F., E. *Edward Fillebrown* The biog-

raphy of William Shakespeare. By ... In the "Brooklyn Chronicle," May 27, 1882.

F., E. *Mrs. E. Fletcher.* Elidure and Edward ... L. 1825.

F., E. *E. Field.* A manual of devotions for sea-faring men. Oxf. 1854.

F., E. *Ebenezer Forsyth.* Shakespeare; some notes on his character and writings. L. 1867.

F., E., Jr. *Edward Fell, Jr.*, in the "Gent. Mag."

F., E. E. *Elizabeth E. Flagg.* Little people whom the Lord loved. N.Y. 1871.

F., E. T. *Edward Taylor Fletcher.* — See "Korah."

F., E. W. *Edwin Wilkins Field.* On Mr. Tagart's "Remarks on mathematical reasoning." From the "Christian Reformer," February, 1838. L. 1838.

F., F. *Francis Fauquier.* An essay on ways and means for raising money for the support of the present war ... L. 1756.

F., F. *Frederick Fysh.* Nature's voice in the Holy Catholic Church: a series of designs. L. & Derby, 1864.

F. F. of the Cedars. *Henry William Herbert.* Field sports in the United States ... L. 1849.

F., Greville, of Barnes. *Greville Fennell.* The rail and the rod; or, tourist angler's guide to waters and quarters thirty miles round London. L. 1867.

F., G. H. *Granville Hamilton Forbes.* No antecedent impossibility in miracles ... Oxf. 1861.

F., H. *Henry Foley.* — See "A Member of the Same Society."

F., H. L. *Henrietta Louisa Farrer.* The arrival at a new home. L. 1850.

F., H. R. *Henry Ralph Francis.* The fly-fisher and his library, by ... L. 1856. [A Cambridge (Eng.) essay.]

F., J. *John Fransham.* An exact account of the charge for supporting the poor of the city of Norwich ... L. 1720.

F., J. *John Fry.* The legend of Mary, Queen of Scots ... L. 1810.

F., J. *John Forster.* Memorials of John Hampden. By Lord Nugent. Fourth edition, with a memoir of the writer by ... L. 1860.

F., J. *James Freeman, S.T.D.* Remarks on the American universal geography. B. 1793.

F., J. F. *Hon. John F. Finerty,* of

Ohio, in his contributions to the "Tribune" (Chic. 1884).

F., J. G. A. *J. G. A. Forster.* A chronological abridgment of the Russian history . . . trans. by . . . L. 1767.

F., K. J. *K. J. Finlay.* By the loch and river side. Edinb. 1866.

F., M. F. E. *Mary Frances Elizabeth Boscawen,* Viscountess Falmouth. Bubbles of Spa water; or, six weeks in the Ardennes in 1876, by . . . Brighton, 1877.

F., M. H. *Mrs. M. H. Fiske,* in her contributions to the "Missouri Republican."

F., N. *Nicholas French.* — See "A Gentleman in the Country."

F., N. L. *Nathaniel Langdon Frothingham, D.D.* The home for destitute and incurable women. [A poem.] B. 18–.

F., O. *Oran Follett.* The Shakespeare plays; The theatre, etc. Who wrote Shakespeare? By . . . Sandusky, O., 1879.

F., O. L. *Mrs. Olive Leonard Foster,* who for 40 years responded to numberless solicitations for an original hymn or poem, and contributed to numerous newspapers and magazines under these initials.

F., P., Minister of the Church of England. *Rev. P. Fuller.* A letter to the Reverend Mr. Pyle . . . L. 1718.

F., R. *Richard Frankum.* The bee and the wasp: a fable in verse . . . L. 1861.

F., R. *Richard Finch.* Seasonable advice to a young clergyman . . . L. 1740.

F., R., Gent. *Robert Forbes.* Ajax: his speech to the Grecian knabbs; from Ovid's "Metam.," lib. XIII. . . . attempted in broad Buchans, by . . . 1755. 1869.

F. R. G. S., A. *Richard Francis Burton.* Wanderings in West Africa, from Liverpool to Fernando Po. By . . . L. 1863.

F., R. L. *R. L. Frere.* A few plain words on the sacrament of the Lord's Supper . . . Birmingham, 1831.

F., R. W. *R. W. Falconer.* Catalogue of Tenby plants. L. 1848.

F., S. A. *Miss Sarah A. Flint.* The conqueror. By . . . B. 1865.

F.S.A. *Rev. Latham Wainwright, F.S.A.* "Dr. Paley and Mr. Lytton Bulwer," in "Gent. Mag.," November, 1833.

F., S. H. *Sarah Hustler Fox.* Poems, original and translated. L. 1863.

F., S. M. *S. M. Fitton.* The four seasons. L. 1865.

F., T. *Thady Fitzpatrick.* An enquiry into the real merit of a certain popular performer . . . L. 1760.

The above work is directed against David Garrick. It consists of a series of letters, which originally appeared in the "Craftsman, or Gray's Inn Journal" over the following pseudonyms: "T. F."; "X. Y. Z."; "Theatricus"; "Anti-theatricus"; "Candidus"; "Philo-Tragicus"; "Ingenuus"; "W. W."; and "A Lover of Truth."

F., T. *Thomas Foxcroft.* A funeral sermon, occasion'd by several mournful deaths . . . B. 1722.

F. T. *Robert Fleming.* The history of hereditary-right . . . L. n.d.

F., T. *Thomas Ford.* Reminders in grammar and orthography . . . L. 1855.

F., T. *Thomas Flatman.* Virtus rediviva. [A collection of poems.] L. 1660.

F., T., Assistant-Curate at ——, and Joint-Lecturer of St. ——. *Rev. Thomas Francklin.* A letter to a bishop, concerning lectureships. L. 1768.

F., T. V. *Rev. Thomas Vincent Fosbery.* Hymns and poems . . . L. 1844.

F., W. *William Field.* An historical and descriptive account of the town and castle of Warwick, and of the neighbouring Spa of Leamington . . . Warwick, 1815.

F., W., Esq. *William Freke.* The fountain of monition and inter-communication divine . . . L. 1703.

F., W., Sir. *Sir W. Fownes.* Methods proposed for regulating the poor . . . Dublin, 1725.

F., W. A. *Lieut.-Col. William Augustus Fyers.* The Italian crisis . . . L. 1859.

F., W. D. *Wilhelm David Fuhrmann.* Leben . . . des Lucilio Vanini . . . Leipsic, 1810.

F., W. E. *W. E. Flaherty.* The annals of England. Oxford, 1876.

F., W. J. *William John Fitzpatrick.* Who wrote the Waverley novels? L. 1856.

F——, R——, Gent. *Robert Forbes.* Ajax: his speech to the Grecian knabbs. From Ovid's "Metam.," lib. XIII . . . Glasgow, 1755.

F——n, C. *C. Ferguson.* — See "F-r-n, Mr."

F-r-n, Mr. *C. Ferguson.* A letter address'd to every honest man in Britain . . . L. 1738. [The letter is signed "C. F——n."]

F——y, J——n. *John Fry.* Bibliographical memoranda . . . Bristol, 1816.

Fabian. *Mrs. Virginia Durant Covington,* who, during the late war, made her *début* as a writer in the "Southern

Field and Fireside," published at Augusta, Ga., as "Fabian," and since that time has been a frequent contributor to Southern periodicals under the assumed names of "Casper," "Popinack," and under her own name.

Fabius. *John Dickinson.* The letters of . . . in 1788, on the federal constitution, and in 1797 on the present situation of public affairs. Wilmington, Del., 1797.

Fabricius. *Joseph Galloway.* Fabricius; or, letters to the people of Great Britain. L. 1782.

Fac et Spera. *William Harding,* in his contributions to the "Clipper" (N.Y.).

Factory Hand of Waltham, A. *Josiah Bigelow.* Review of "An address to the workingmen of New England" . . . Camb., Mass., 1832.

Fadette. *Mrs. Minnie Reeves Rodney* or *Marian C. Legare Reeves.* Wearithorne; or, in the light of to-day . . . B. 1872.

The "Library of Congress" has the former name, the "Female Writers of the South," the latter.

Faed. — See "Waverley."

Fag, Frederick. *James Johnson.* The recess; or, autumnal relaxation in the Highlands and Lowlands . . . a serio-comic tour to the Hebrides. L. 1834.

Fair Inquirer, A. *Rev. John Hawkins.* A few remarks on an address to the Roman Catholics of the United States of America, occasioned by a letter addressed to the Catholics of Worcester by Mr. Wharton, their late chaplain. By the Right Rev. Dr. Carroll. By . . . Worcester, Eng., 1796.

Fairchild, Paul. *John A. Taylor.* Defense of insanity. N.Y. 1876.

Fairfax, Ruth. *Mrs. Agnes Jean Stibbes,* a favorite contributor of novelettes, poems, and sketches to Father Ryan's paper, the "Banner of the South," under this nom de plume.

Fairford, Alan. *John Kent,* editor of the "Canadian Literary Magazine," Toronto, 1834. "Under this signature in a widely-circulated periodical a series entitled "The English Layman."

Fairleigh, Frank. *Francis Edward Smedley,* who edited "Cruikshank's Magazine," etc., under this name.

Fairplay, Oliver. *Thomas Jefferson.* Proposals . . . for publishing the private and public life of the First Consul. P. 1804.

Faith Workless.— See "Methodist preacher in Cambridgeshire, A."

Faithful Monitor, A. One of the pseudonyms attributed to Junius (*q.v.*).

The letter bearing this signature is dated August 25, 1767, and censures the appointment of Lord Townshend as Lord Lieutenant of Ireland, and of his brother, the Hon. Charles Townshend, as Chancellor of the Exchequer.

Falconbridge. *Jonathan F. Kelly.* The memoirs of . . . a collection of humorous and every-day scenes. P. 1856.

Falcon Feather. *John Collier.* Lancashire dialect and poems. L. 1828.

Falconer, Edmund. *Edmund O'Rourke.* Extremes; or, men of the day : a comedy. L. 1859.

Falconer, Frank. *E. N. Carvalho,* in the "Turf, Field, and Farm" (N.Y.).

Fales, Fanny. *Mrs. Frances Elizabeth Smith.*

Falkland. *Fisher Ames.*

Falkland. *Nathaniel Chapman, M.D.,* in the "Philadelphia Portfolio."

Falkland. *Rev. John Robert Scott, D.D.* A review of the principal characters of the Irish House of Commons. Dublin, 1789.

Falkland. *Francis Perceval Eliot.* A series of letters . . . L. 1814.

Falkland, Frank. *G. L. Wilson.*

Falstaff, Sir John. For the supposed editor of the "Anti-Theatre." L. 1720.

Fanchon. *Mrs. Laura Brady Starr,* in her letters to the "Cleveland Leader" (O.).

Fanchon. *Mrs. Laura M. Sanford.* History of Erie County, Pennsylvania. P. 1862.

Fancy, One of the. *Frederick Taylor.* System of horse-taming . . . L. 1858.

Fancy, One of the. *Thomas Moore.* Tom Crib's memorial to Congress. L. 1819.

Fane, Florence. *Mrs. Frances Fuller Victor.* All over Oregon and Washington. San Fran. 1872.

Fane, Violet. *Mrs. Mary (Montgomerie Lamb) Singleton.* Collected verses . . . L. 1880.

Fan-Fan. *Mrs. Frances Irene (Burge) Smith.* Fan-fan stories. B. 1863.

Fanny, Aunt. *Mrs. Frances Dana (Barker) Gage,* who, under this signature, wrote many beautiful stories for children, besides stanzas and sketches.

Fanny, Aunt. *Mrs. Fanny Barrow.* All sorts of popguns. N.Y. 1869.

Fant, Eli. *Edward Bean Underhill.* Struggles and triumphs of religious liberty. N.Y. 1851; and his contributions to various periodicals.

Farbrick, Jonathan. *Silas Pinck-*

ney Holbrook. Letters from a mariner and travels of a tin peddler, contributed to the "Boston Courier." 183–.

Farmer. *Henry Brooke.* Farmer's letters. L. 1745.

Farmer, A. *Tristram Burges.* Address . . . to the honest men of all parties in the State of Rhode Island and Providence Plantations. n.p., n.d.

Farmer, A. *James Anderson, LL.D.* Essays relating to agriculture . . . Edinb. 1775.

Farmer, A. *Hon. Levi Lincoln, Jr.* A farmer's letters to the people. P. 1802.

Farmer, A. *Dr. Samuel Seabury.* Free thoughts on the proceedings of the Continental Congress held at Philadelphia, Sept. 5th, 1774. By . . . N.Y. 1774.
Also ascribed to Rev. Isaac Wilkins.

Farmer, A. — *Arbuthnot.* An inquiry into the connexion between the present price of provisions and the size of farms . . . L. 1773.

Farmer, A. *Dr. Laughan.* Letters addressed to the yeomanry of the United States. P. 1791.

Farmer, A. *Anthony Benezet (?).* A serious address to the rulers of America on the inconsistency of their conduct respecting slavery . . . Trenton, N.J., 1783.

Farmer, An American. *Hector St. John Crevecœur.* Letters from . . . P. 1794.

Farmer, An American. *Frederick Law Olmsted.* Walks and talks of . . . in England. N.Y. 1852.

Farmer, A Llanbrynmair. *S. Roberts(?).* Diosg Farm . . . Newtown, Eng., 1854.

Farmer, A Munster. *Thomas Moore.* Captain Rock detected. L. 1824.

Farmer, A New England. *John Lowell.* A dispassionate enquiry into the reasons alleged by Mr. Madison for declaring . . . war against Great Britain. L. 1808.

Farmer, A Pennsylvanian. *John Dickinson.* Letters to the inhabitants of the British colonies. P. 1767–68.

Farmer, The. *Arthur Young.* The F.'s letters to the people of England . . . L. 1767.

Farmer in Cheshire, A. *Benjamin Stillingfleet(?).* The honour and dishonour of agriculture . . . trans. by . . . n.p. 1760.

Farmer of New Jersey, A. *William Livingston.* Observations on government . . . N.Y. 1787.

Farmer, May. *Mrs. E. V. Wilson.*

Farmer's Boy, The. *Robert Bloomfield.*

Farningham, Marianne. *Mary Anne Hearne.* "Holiday sketches," in the "Christian World." 1868.

Farquharson, Martha. *Mrs. Martha Farquharson Finley.* Allan's fault. P. 187–.

Farthing Poet, The. *Richard Henqist Horne.* Orion: an epic poem. L. 1843.

Fast, Grip. *Frank Leslie Baker,* in his contributions to the "Morning Mail" (Lowell, Mass.).

Fat Contributor, Our. *William Makepeace Thackeray.* His signature (with others) to his articles in "Punch," from August 3, 1844, to October 23, 1847.

Fat Contributor, The. *A. Minor Griswold,* in the Cincinnati "Saturday Night," a humorous weekly, through the medium of which *Minor Griswold,* "The Fat Contributor," sportively derides care, for his fun-loving readers.

Father, A. *Rev. Hosea Hildreth.* A book for Massachusetts children, in familiar letters from a father . . . B. 1829.

Father, A. *Robert Ainslie.* A father's gift to his children. L. 183–.

Father, A. *John Gregory.* A father's legacy to his daughters. L. 1774.

Father, A. *Rev. James Paton.* Letters . . . to his son, a student of divinity. Edinb. 1796.

Father, A. *Benjamin Coole.* Miscellanies ; or, sundry discourses concerning trade, conversation, and religion. Being the advice of . . . to his children, on those subjects. L. 1712.

Father of America, The. *Samuel Adams.* So addressed by Stephen Sayre, a London banker, 1770.

Father of the American Revolution, The. *Samuel Adams.* So called in the "Independent Chronicle" (B.), 1803, in announcing his death.

Father of English Geology, The. *William Smith,* author of the first geological map of England.

Father of German Literature, The. *Gotthold Ephraim Lessing.*

Father of the late Thomas Rodd, The. *Thomas Rodd, Senior.* Manuscript catalogue of the late Mr. Malone's Shakesperian library. By . . . L. about 1818.

Father of the Society of Jesus, A. *F. J. Boudreaux.* The happiness of heaven. By . . . Balt. 1871.

Fawkes, Guy. *Edward James.*

Fax. *Augustine Barnum,* in his contributions to the "Mail and Express" (N.Y.).

Fay. *Mrs. Fayette Snead*, in her contributions to the "Courier-Journal" (Louisville, Ky.).

Fay, Frederick. *Dr. James Johnson.*

Fay, Gerda. *Caroline M. Gemmer.* Baby-land. L. 1877.

Feardana. *Robert Dwyer Joyce, M.D.* About twenty years ago the nom de plume "Feardana" was a household word among the reading portion of the Irish people. It was the veil behind which the young poet modestly hid his individuality. He was then a medical student at the Queen's University. The "Harp" and other periodicals published in Dublin and Cork at this time, and for several years, contained patriotic songs, short sketches, and historic ballads from his pen. "The Blacksmith of Limerick," which he wrote in the confused days succeeding '48, grew almost instantly into popular favor, and helped much to create and foster a new soul in Ireland. About that time, perhaps later, the "London Universal News," then edited by the lamented John F. O'Donnell ("Caviare"), a distinguished poet and literateur himself, in reviewing Joyce's "Ballads, Romances, and Songs"—published in book form by Duffy of Dublin—hailed Joyce as "The Scott of Ireland," a distinctive title most eminently deserved and deservedly bestowed. The book attained an extensive circulation, especially in the south of Ireland, where were located most of the stirring scenes, and incidents, and legendary and traditional reminiscences on which the "Ballads, Romances, and Songs" were founded. There is little doubt that Joyce's writings at that period had a powerful influence in developing the national spirit which, a few years later on, became so powerful and defiant under the name of "Fenianism," the spirit of physical resistance to foreign rule. The "Dublin Weekly Illustrated News," established less than 20 years ago, contained many a racy story, sketch, and poem from his pen. A little later the doctor, who was then Professor of English Literature in the Preparatory College of the Catholic University, Dublin, published "The Squire of Castleton," an historical novel, the scene of which was laid in the south of Ireland, as a serial in the "Dublin Irishman." It was subsequently republished in book form. When the "Dublin Irish People," the Fenian organ, was established in 1865, Dr. Joyce, under the nom de plume "Merulan" (the Wizard) became, by request of the leaders of the National party in Dublin, one of the regular contributors, and his fiery, patriotic, and able pen was recognized as a powerful aid in sustaining the grand spirit of patriotic resolve which was then rampant and defiant throughout the land.

Federal Farmer, The. *Richard Henry Lee.* Observations leading to a fair examination of the system of government proposed by the late convention ... 1787.

Federal Republican, A. *Henry William Desaussure.* Address to the citizens of South Carolina, on the approaching election of President and Vice-president. Charleston, 1800.

Federalist, A. *Noah Webster.* A letter to General Hamilton occasioned

by his letter to President Adams, about 1800. The letter is signed "Aristides."

Felicia. *Mrs. Mary Mitchell Collyer.* Letters from ... to Charlotte. L. 1750.

Felix. *Bon Louis Henri Martin.* Wolfthurm. Paris, 1830.

Felix, Marcus Minucius. *Sir David Dalrymple.* Octavius: a dialogue, by ... Edinb. 1781.

Felix, Minutius. *George Hardinge.* The essence of Malone. L. 1800-1.

Felix, N. *Nicholas Wanostrocht*, the younger. Felix ... on the use of a cricket bat: together with the history and use of the catapulta. L. 1845.

Fell, Archie. *Miss Mary J. Capron.* Apron strings, and which way they were pulled. N.Y. 1871.

Fell, J. *Richard Sterne.* The whole duty of man. By ... 1806.

Fellow of a College, A. *Capel Loft.* Self-formation; or, the history of an individual mind. L. 18–.

Fellow of the College, A. *Dr. Peter Shaw.* The juice of the grape ... L. 1724.

Fellow of *** College, Cambridge, A. *Gerard Francis Cobb.* The kiss of peace ... L. 1867.

Fellow of the Antiquarian Society, A. *Lieut.-Gen. George Robert Ainslie.* Illustrations of the Anglo-French coinage: from coins in the possession of the author, by ... L. 1830.

Fellow of the Antiquarian Society, A. *Foote Gower, M.D.* Sketch of the materials for a new history of Cheshire ... L. 1771.

Fellow of the Antiquarian Societies of London and Scotland, A. *Lieut.-Gen. George Robert Ainslie.* Illustrations of the Anglo-French coinage, from the cabinet of ... L. 1847.

Fellow of the Linnean Society, A. *John Murray.* The economy of vegetation. L. 1838.

Fellow of the Linnæan and Horticultural Societies, A. *J. W. Bennett.* A treatise on the coco-nut tree ... L. 1831.

Fellow of the Royal and Antiquarian Societies, A. *Josiah Forshall.* The apology of an Israelite for not becoming a Christian. Sidmouth, 1851.

Fellow of the Royal Society, A. *Cotton Mather.* The angel of Bethesda ... New-London, 1722.

Fellow of the Royal Society, A. *James Orchard Halliwell-Phillipps.* An introduction to the evidences of Christianity ... L. 1859.

Fellow of the Royal Society, A.

James William Gilbart, F.R.S. Logic for the million ... L. 1851.

Fellow of the Royal Society, A. *W. F. Stevenson.* Most important errors in chemistry, electricity, and magnetism pointed out and refuted ... L. 1846.

Fellow of the Society of Antiquaries of Scotland, A. *John Dick.* Here and there in England; including a pilgrimage to Stratford-upon-Avon ... L. 1871.

Fellow of the University College, Oxford. *Sir Edward West, M.A.* Essay on the application of capital to land ... L. 1815.

Fellow-Citizen, A. *Henry Cockburn, Lord Cockburn.* A letter to the inhabitants of Edinburgh, on the new police bill. Edinb. 1822.

Fellow Labourer, A. *John Maclaren.* The desk and the counter ... Edinb. 1844.

Fellow Sufferer, A. *John Park.* An address to the citizens of Massachusetts on the causes and remedy of our national distresses ... B. 1808.

Fellow-Townsman, A. *John Wickstead.* Address ... to the inhabitants of Shrewsbury. 1824.

Fellow-Townsman, A. *J. Bridge.* A letter intended for the "Manchester Guardian," now ... recommended to the ladies of the Anti-Corn-Law League. Manchester, 1843.

Female Friend, A. *Mrs. Moorhead.* Lines addressed to the Rev. James Davenport on his departure from Boston. By ... B. 1741.

Female Physician, A. *Jonathan Swift, D.D.* Receipt for cuckolding ... 1726.

Female Slave, A. *Mattie Griffiths.* Autobiography. N.Y. 1857.

Fenian Head Centre. *James Stephens.* Arrest and escape of James Stephens ... 186–.

Fenwood, Harry. *William W. Walsh.*

Ferishtah, Dervish-Seriosæ. *Robert Browning.* Divers fancies of ... L. 1884.

Fern. *Frank E. Hamilton.*

Fern, Fanny. *Mrs. Sara Payson (Willis Eldredge) Parton.* Fern leaves from Fanny's portfolio ... L. 1854.

Fernando, the Gothamite. *Fernando Wood.*

Ferney, Jules. *Étienne Arago,* who wrote for the "Siècle" under this signature.

Ferragus. *Louis Ulbach.* Lettres de Ferragus in "Le Figaro," Paris, 186–.

Ferrall, S. A. *Simon A. O'Ferrall.*

Ferret. *John Shebbeare, M.D.,* in Smollett's novel of "Sir Launcelot Greaves."

Ferry, Gabriel. *Eugène Louis Gabriel de Ferry de Bellemare.* Le dragon de la reine; ou, Costal, l'Indien. Roman historique. Paris, 1855. [Under the same pseud. M. L. de Bellemare has furnished numerous articles to the "Revue des Deux Mondes," 1846–52.]

Fiat Justitia. *Rev. Dr. Thomas Binney,* a celebrated independent divine.

Fiat Justitia. One of the pseudonyms adopted by Junius (*q.v.*).

The letter thus signed is dated May 19, 1768, and censures Lord Barrington.

Fidelia. *Mrs. Mary Lawrence.* — See "Una."

Fidelis. *Miss A. M. Machar,* in her contributions to various Canadian periodicals.

Fidelis. *William Brocklehurst Stonehouse, D.C.L.* The crusade of ... Derby, 1828.

Fidelis. *Dr. Power,* Bishop of Waterford. Letters on the royal veto ... Waterford, 1809. Reprinted from a newspaper called the "Shamrog," published at Waterford.

Fidget, Ferdinando. *Alexander Chalmers.* Lamentable decrease of rudeness, "Gent. Mag.," January, 1802, p. 26.

Field Officer, A. *Ross Lewin.* The life of a soldier: a narrative of twenty-seven years' service in various parts of the world ... L. 1834.

Field Officer of Cavalry, A. *Sir Digby Mackworth.* Diary of a tour through Southern India, Egypt, and Palestine, in the years 1821 and 1822. L. 1823.

Fielding, Fanny. *Miss Mary J. S. Upshur,* who, under this signature, has written for nearly every literary journal of the South, prose and poetry, from the "Southern Literary Messenger" to the "Richmond Pastime."

Fieldmouse, Timon. *William Brighty Rands.* The chain of lilies; and other poems. L. 1857.

Fifeshire Forester. *John Bethune.* Practical economy explained and enforced in a series of lectures by the brothers Alexander and John Bethune. Edinb. 1809.

On the title-page John Bethune designated himself a "Fifeshire Forester." Under the same title he contributed poems to the "Scottish Christian Herald."

Figaro. *Henry Clapp, Jr.,* in his contributions to various periodicals.

Figaro. *Mariano José de Larra.* Obras completas de Figaro. Paris, 1848.

Filia Ecclesiæ. *Sarah Anne (Ellis) Dorsey.* Agnes Graham. P. 1869.

Filter, Urbanus. Under this name *Benjamin Mecom*, a nephew of Franklin, published the "New England Magazine" (B. 1758).

Only three or four numbers were issued.

Fin-Bec. *William Blanchard Jerrold.* The Epicure's Year-book. L. 1867–68.

Finnegan, Terry. *James McCarroll.* Letters of . . . to the Hon. T. D. McGee. Toronto, 1864.

First Citizen, The. *Charles Carroll.* His signature in his newspaper controversy with Daniel Dulany in pre-Revolutionary times.

First Class Man of Balliol College, Oxford, A. *Thomas Nash.* The Medea of Euripides . . . literally translated . . . Oxf. 1869.

First Politician in the World, The. *Samuel Adams*, in a letter of Josiah Quincy, Jr., 1775, from London.

First of the Knickerbockers, The. *P. Hamilton Myers.* The First of the Knickerbockers. N.Y. 1848.

Fisher, Pay. *William Andrew Chatto.* The angler's souvenir. L. 1835, 1877.

Fisher in Small Streams, A. *William Linn Brown.* Scribblings and sketches, diplomatic, piscatory, and oceanic. P. 1844.

Fisherman, A. *George Rooper.* The autobiography of the late Salmo Salar, Esq. . . . Edited . . . L. 1867.

Fitzadam, Ismael. *John Macken.* The harp of the desert . . . By . . . formerly able seaman on board the —— frigate. L. 1818.

Fitzball, Edward. *Edward Ball.* Plays. N.Y. 1857.

Fitzboodle, George. *William Makepeace Thackeray*, who, under this pseudonym, contributed to "Fraser's Magazine" in 1842–44, "Confessions"; "Professions"; and "Men's Wives."

Fitz-Boodle, George Savage, Esq. *William Makepeace Thackeray.* Barmecide banquets with Joseph Bregion and Anne Miller, in "Fraser's Magazine," November, 1845.

Fitz Eustace, Father, a Mendicant Friar. *W. Fraser (?).* Essays. L. 1822.

Fitz Eustace, Randolph. *W. Fraser (?).* The brides of Florence: a play . . . L. 1824.

Fitzgibbons, Patrick. *John W. McDonnell*, in his contributions to the "Daily News" (N.Y.).

Fitz-Harding. *Dr. James Hook*, in

the London "John Bull," who, during his brother's charge of this journal, wrote a series of letters to various statesmen, under this signature.

Fitzhugh, Francis. *Francis Alexander Mackay.* The curse of Schamyl; and other poems. Edinb. 1857.

Fitzjersey, Horace. *Rev. Theodore William Alois Buckley*, editor of a large number of books for the London booksellers.

Fitznoodle, Francis. *B. B. Vallentine*, in his contributions to "Puck" (N.Y.).

Fitzosborne, Sir Thomas. *William Melmoth, Jr.* Letters on several subjects, by . . . L. 1742.

Fitzvictor, John. *Percy Bysshe Shelley.* Posthumous fragments of Margaret Nicholson. Oxf. 1810.

Fitzworm, Reginald. *John Boyle*, Earl of Cork and Orrery. — See "G. K."

Flaccus. *John Waters.*

Flaccus. *Thomas Ward.* Passaic: a group of poems touching that river; with other musings . . . N.Y. 1842.

Flag Officer, A. *Rear-Admiral Hawker.* Letter to His Grace, the Duke of Wellington, upon the state of the English navy . . . L. 1840.

Flag Officer, A. *Vice-Admiral Sir Charles Vinicombe Penrose.* Remarks on the conduct of the naval administration of Great Britain since 1815. By . . . L. 1830.

Flag Officer of Her Majesty's Fleet, A. *Admiral Sir Charles Napier.* The navy . . . L. 1838.

Flagellum. *Samuel William Henry Ireland.* All the blocks! or, an antidote to "All the Talents" . . . L. 1807.

Flambeau. *Floyd Vail*, in his contributions to the "Mail and Express" (N.Y.).

Flaneur. *Park Benjamin.*

Flaneur. *Col. Charles G. Greene*, in his contributions to the "Post" (Boston).

Flaneur. *Blakely Hall*, in his contributions to the "Argonaut" (San Francisco, Cal.), etc.

Flaneur. *Kenward Philip*, in the "Brooklyn Eagle."

Flaneur. *General Eber.* Ten years of Imperialism in France: impressions of a "Flaneur." 1862. — See "Flaneur, Un."

Flaneur, The. *Edmund Hodgson Yates.* Letters in the "Morning Star" (L. 1867). Also in his contributions to "Tinsley's Magazine" (L.).

Flaneur, Un. *George William Henry*

Villiers, 4th Earl of Clarendon. Dix ans d'impérialisme en France . . . Paris, 1863.

This work first appeared in English; it was corrected by the secretary of Lord Clarendon, the Hungarian General Eber, and was translated by M. Bernard Derosne.

Flassan, Maurice. *Mme. Marie Pauline Rose (Stewart) Blaze de Bury*, in the "Revue de Paris" and the "Revue des Deux Mondes."

Flather, John. *John Flather Archbold.* The law and practice in bankruptcy . . . L. 1842.

Fleetwood, Everard, Esq. *Samuel Burroughs, Esq.* An enquiry into the customary-estates and tenant-rights of those who hold lands of Church and other foundations . . . L. 1730.

Fleming, George. *Miss Julia Constance Fletcher.* The head of Medusa. B. 1880.

Flemming, Harford. *Mrs. Harriet (Hare) McClellan.* Cupid and the Sphinx. N.Y. 1878.

Fleta. *Miss Kate W. Hamilton (?).* The brave heart . . . P. 1868.

Flimnap, the Lilliputian Premier. *Sir Robert Walpole.*

In Swift's "Voyage to Lilliput," "Sir Robert Walpole suffered in the person of ' Flimnap, the Lilliputian Premier,' Tories and Whigs in the 'High-Heels and Low-Heels,' Catholics and Protestants in the ' Big-endians and Small-endians.'" — See TUCKERMAN's "History of English Prose Fiction," p. 174.

Flirt, A. *Lady Charlotte Maria (Campbell) Bury.* The history of a flirt, related by herself. L. 1840.

Florence. *Mrs. Frances Sargent (Locke) Osgood*, in early life a contributor to the "Juvenile Miscellany" under this signature.

Florence. *Miss Florence Tyng*, in sketches, etc., contributed to various periodicals.

Flori, C. de. *Mrs. Floride Clemson Lea.* Poet skies, and other experiments in versification. N.Y. 186-.

Florida, Aunt. *Phebe Travers.*

Florida, Charles. *Dr. J. B. F. Walker.*

Florio. *James Gordon Brooks*, who was for some time a contributor to periodicals under this signature.

Florio. *Dr. William (?) King.* An epistle [in verse] to . . . at Oxford. L. 1749; reprinted in the "Retrospective Review," 1835. By Thomas Tyrwhitt.

Florrie, Cousin. *Florence Bliss (?).* Christ or the world? which? . . . Balt. 1870.

Florus, Julius. *William Pitt.*

Before reporters were authorized to publish the proceedings of Parliament, Mr. Pitt was reported as "Julius Florus," Mr. Fox as "Cnœus Fulvius," the Earl of Winchelsea as "Caius Claudius Nero," and the Earl of Bath as "Marcus Cato."

Flower of Strathearn, The. *Lady Carolina Oliphant Nairn.*

Fluviatulis piscator. *Rev. Joseph Seccombe.* Business and diversion inoffensive to God, and necessary for the comfort and support of human society . . . B. 1743.

Fly-fisher, A. *Rev. W. Cartwright.* Rambles and recollections of . . . L. 1874.

Foa, Mme. Eugénie. *Mme. Eugénie Rebecca (Rodrigues) Gradis.* Le petit Robinson de Paris. Paris, 1840.

Foe to Ignorance, A. *Henry Mudge.* A letter to the ratepayers of Bodmin on the use to be made of the (old) poorhouse . . . 1840.

Fogle, Francis, Sen., Esq. *George Payson.* Romance of California; or, golden dreams and leaden realities, N.Y. 1854.

Folio, Felix. *John Page.*

Folio, Tom. *Joseph E. Babson*, who wrote frequent book-notices for the Boston "Transcript" under the signature of "Tom Folio."

Folio, Tom. *Thomas Rawlinson*, "for whom Mr. Addison is said to have intended his character of 'Tom Folio,' in the 'Tatler,' No. 158." — See "Chalmers," Vol. 26.

Follower of Locke, A. *Benjamin Humphrey Smart.* A letter to Dr. Whateley . . . L. 1851.

Foote, S., Junior. *Rev. Francis Wrangham.* Reform: a farce, modernized from Aristophanes . . . L. 1792.

Forbes, Glacier. *James David Forbes*, author of several works on the glaciers of the Alps.

Foreigner, A. *Robert S. Sturgis.* A F.'s evidence on the Chinese question. L. 1859.

Foreigner, A. *George Watterston.* Letters from Washington on the constitution and laws; with sketches of prominent characters . . . Wash., D.C., 1818.

Foremast Man, A. *Edward Hampden Rose*, author of several pieces which have appeared in the newspapers under this signature.

Forest Warbler. *M. R. McCormick.* The duke's chase; or, the diamond ring vs. the gold ring . . . Cin. 1871.

Forester, Frank. *Henry William Herbert.* Frank Forester's sporting scenes and characters. P. 18–.

Forester, Sherwood. *Spencer T. Hall.* The Forester's Offering. L. 1841.

Forestier, Paul. *Josephus Albertus Alberdingk-Thym,* a Dutch writer.

Forfarian, A. *W. Gray.* The martyred queen . . . Forfar, 1858.

Forfex. *Alonzo G. Shears,* of New Haven (Ct.), in his contributions to various periodicals.

The pseudonym is probably intended for the Latin equivalent of shears.

Forlorn Hope. *Mrs. Matilda A. Bailey,* a regular contributor to the "New Orleans Times." "A series of sketches [of hers] entitled 'Heart histories,' by . . . have been very popular." She has also written comic articles under the name of "Sam Waggle."

Former Curate of Hunslet, A. *Rev. James Akroyd Beaumont, M.A.* Poems : chiefly relating to children . . . Leeds, 1849.

Former Resident of Slave States, A. *Mrs. L. J. Barker.* Influence of slavery on the white population. N.Y. 1880.

Former Resident of the South, A. *Darius Lyman, Jr.* Leaven for Doughfaces ; or, three score and ten parables touching slavery . . . Cin. 1856.

Forrest, George, Esq., M.A. *Rev. John George Wood.* An account of the history and antiquities of St. Leonard's, Edinburgh : its chapel and hospital. Edinb. 1865.

Forrest, Mary. *Julia Deane Freeman.* The women of the South, N.Y. 1860 ; also in her contributions to the "Brooklyn Times" (N.Y.).

Forrest, Neil. *Mrs. Cornelia Floyd.* Fiddling Freddy. N.Y. 1871.

Forrester, Fanny. *Mrs. Emily C. (Chubbuck) Judson.* Trippings in Authorland ; and many other works.

She complained to N. P. Willis of the meagre remuneration she received for her literary productions, and the poet replied :—
"How can you expect any thing better? Your genius is not of a kind to affiliate with your name. Who will read a poem signed 'Chubbuck'? Sign yourself 'Fanny Forrester,' and you will see the change."
Miss Chubbuck adopted the above pseudonym thenceforth.

Forrester, Francis, Esq. *Daniel Wise.* Glen Morris stories. N.Y. 1874.

Forrester, Gilbert. *Mr. Henry Braddon,* who contributed to the old "Sporting Magazine," under this *nom*

de plume, and "A Member of the Burton Hunt."

Forrestier, Auber. *Miss Annie Aubertine Woodward.* Echoes from Mistland . . . Chic. 1877.

Forreyner, A. *John Dayman.* Letter by . . . in Blundell's school. Tiverton, 1819.

Forsch, Hermann. *Heinrich Albert Oppermann.* Studentenbilder ; oder, Deutschlands Arminen und Germanen. 1835.

Forsith, Nat. *Frank Stainforth.* Everybody's Christmas Annual. Hell upon earth . . . L. 1878.

Fortunio, Paulin M. *Jean Alexandre Paulin Niboyet.* La Dame de Spa . . . Paris, 1874.

Foster, Frank. *Daniel Puseley.* The Belgian volunteer's visit to England in 1867 . . . L. 1867.

Fountain, Lucy. *Kate Hilliard.*

Four of Us. *Henry James Finn, James W. Miller, Moses Whitney, Jr.,* and *Oliver C. Wyman.* Whim-Whams. B. 1828. The work is illustrated by Finn, and published by Peter Parley *(q.v.).* The title-page bears the following lines : —
" So prolyficke is oure penne
Ye'll thinke therre be a score of us ;
But, on ye wordes of Gentilmenne,
Therre be onely Four of Us.
We'll make ye smyle, or make ye sighe,
Thenne what can ye want more of us ;
Ye can't doe better than toe buye
This littell Boke, by Four of Us."

Fox, The. *Charles James Fox.* The book of the wars of Westminster : from the fall of the Fox, at the close of 1783, to the 20th day of the third month, 1784 . . . L. 1800. By "Nergalsharezerneborabmagshamgar" *(pseud.).*

Foxcar, Niclas. *Rev. Francis Jacox.* Shakespeare diversions ; a medley of motley wear. L. 1875.

Foxhunter Rough and Ready, The. *Paul Ourry Treby, Esq.* "He was for many years a contributor to the old 'Sporting Magazine,' under the name of 'The Foxhunter Rough and Ready.' "

Foxton, E. *Miss Sarah Hammond Palfrey.* Herman ; or, young knighthood . . . B. 1866.

Fr—. — *Franklin,* Grammar Master at Hertford. — See Lamb's "Elia," "Christ's hospital."

Frame, Robert. *Sir James Denham Stewart.* Considerations on the interests of the county of Lanark. L. 1769.

Frampton, Josiah. *William Gilpin.* Three dialogues on the amusements of clergymen. L. 1796.

France, A. de. *Ernest Alby.* La captivité du trompette escoffier. Paris, 1848.

Frances. *Mrs. Elizabeth Griffith.* The letters of Henry and Frances. 175–.

Written in conjunction with her husband, Richard Griffith, and said to contain the genuine correspondence between them. Their next publication, written also in conjunction, was "Two novels, in letters," 4 vols.; the first and second entitled "Delicate Distress," by "Frances," the third and fourth entitled the "Gordian knot," by "Henry." 1769.

Francesca. *Miss Francesca Alexander.* The story of Ida, edited with preface by John Ruskin, D.C.L. B. 1883.

"Let it be noted with thankful reverence that this is the story of a Catholic girl by a Protestant one, yet the two of them so united in the truth of the Christian faith and in the joy of its love, that they are absolutely unconscious of any difference in the forms or letter of their religion." — J. RUSKIN.

Franchi, Ausonio. *Cristoforo Bonavino.* Saggi di critica e polemica. 1871.

Francis, Virginia. *Virginia Francis Bateman.* A nom de théâtre.

Franco, Harry. *Charles F. Briggs.* The adventures of Harry Franco: a tale. N.Y. 1839.

"Harry Franco ... He has common sense in a way that's uncommon, Hates humbug and cant, and loves like a woman, Builds his dislikes with cards and his friendships of oak."

Frank, Parson. *Rev. Francis Jacox,* in "People's" and "Howitt's Magazines."

Frank, Uncle. *Francis Channing Woodworth.* Uncle Frank's pleasant pages for the fireside. L. 1857.

Franke, F. F. *Ferdinand Hauthal.* Gebete, Lieder und Gedichte; von ... Leipzig, 1838.

Franklin. *William Foster,* in the "Boston Courier," "Transcript," and other papers.

Franz, Arnold. *Dr. Francis Lieber.* Wein und Wonnelieder. Berlin, 1825.

Frater. *William George.* — See "Member of the Worcester Anglers' Society, A."

Frater. *Francis Lister Hawks.* Qualifications of lay delegates. N.Y. about 1848.

Frazer, Lawrence. *Lawrence Frazer Abbott.*

Fredair, Anna. *Miss Walker,* of Tuscaloosa. Minor Place. N.Y. 1869.

Frédéric, M. *Frédéric Dupetit-Méré.* Le fils banni: melodrame. Paris, 1815.

Frédol. *Horace Bénédict Alfred Moquin-Tandon.* Le monde de la mer. Paris, 1863.

Fredrika. *Miss H. F. D. Lyon.*

Free, Harry B. *Harry Free Boynton,* in the "Turf, Field, and Farm."

Free Church Elder, A. *William Mitchell.* National homage to Christ not disestablishment ... Glasgow, 1875.

Free Church Minister, A. *Rev. David C. A. Agnew.* An eye upon the Scottish Established Church ... Edinb. 1853.

Free Churchman, A. *Rev. Andrew Gray.* Dr. Struthers on the Free Church. Perth, 1845.

Free Inquirer, A. *Peter Annet.* A collection of tracts of a certain ... noted for his sufferings for his opinions. L. 1739.

Free Lance. *J. T. Denny,* in his contributions to various English periodicals.

Free Lance. *Alexander Richardson.* The future Church of Scotland ... By ... sometime President of the University Dialectic Society. Edinb. and L. 1870.

Free Man, A. *William Joseph Snelling.* Brief and impartial history of the life and actions of Andrew Jackson. By ... B. 1831.

Free Merchant in Bengal, A. *Capt. Joseph Price.* Five letters ... to Warren Hastings ... L. 1777.

Free-soiler from the Start. *John Gorham Palfrey.* Remarks on the proposed State constitution. B. 1853.

Free Thinker, A. *John Armstrong, M.D.* Conjectures upon the mortality of the human soul ... L. 1778.

Free Thinker, A. *Rev. A. B. Crocker.* Random sketches upon witches, dreams, love, and romance ... Albany, N.Y., about 1855.

Free-Thinker and a Christian, A. *John Mawer.* A layman's faith ... Newcastle-upon-Tyne, 1732.

Freeholder, A. *Henry Boase.* A brief exposition of the agricultural question ... L. 1823.

Freeholder, A. *William Pulteney,* Earl of Bath. An humble address to the knights, citizens, and burgesses elected to represent the Commons of Great Britain in the ensuing Parliament. L. 1734.

Freeholder, A. *John Erskine.* Reflections on the rise, progress, and probable consequences of the present contentions with the colonies. Edinb. 1776.

Freeholder and Landholder of Scotland, A. *John Campbell Colquhoun.* The constitutional principles of parliamentary reform. Edinb. 1831.

Freeholder, An Independent. *Thomas Thirlwall.* A calm ... address to Sir Francis Burdett, Bart. ... L. 1804.

Freeholder, A Yorkshire. *Samuel Bailey.* A discussion of parliamentary reform. L. 1831.

Freeholder of Surrey, A. *John Horne Tooke,* in the London "Public Advertiser," 1769.

Freeman. *William Henry Drayton.* He issued, under this signature, on the eve of the meeting of the Continental Congress, in 1774, a pamphlet in which he marked out the course to be pursued, and submitted a "bill of American rights." This publication cost him his place in the colonial judiciary, but made him president of the Provincial Congress, and soon after chief justice of the colony of South Carolina.

Freeman. *William Henry Drayton, Christopher Gadsden, John Mackenzie, and others.* A letter from . . . of South Carolina to the deputies of North-America . . . Charles Town, S.C., 1784.

Freeman, A. *George Allen.* Address to the freemen of Massachusetts. Worcester, 1832.

Freeman, A. *Jean Joseph Louis Blanc.* French correspondence, in the London "Spectator," 1867.

Freeman, A. *Jacob Bailey Moore.* The principles and acts of Mr. Adams' administration vindicated . . . Concord, N.H. 1828.

Freeman of Massachusetts, A. *John Daggett.* Remarks . . . concerning the location of the Boston and Providence R.R. through the burying ground in East Attleborough . . . B. 1834.

Freeman, Jonathan. *Morris Birkbeck,* the signature under which he contributed articles, in 1823, to the "Illinois Gazette" and the "Shawneetown Gazette" in opposition to the establishment of slavery.

Freeman, O. S. *Edward Coit Rogers.* Letters on slavery. B. 1855.

Freeman, Theophilus. *William Matthews.* A general epistle of brotherly admonition and counsel to the people called Quakers . . . L. 1803.

French Clergyman, A. *Rev. Stephen Theodore Badin.* The real principles of the Roman Catholics in reference to God and the country . . . Bardstown, Ky., 1805.

French Detective. *M. Canler.* Autobiography of . . . from 1818 to 1858 . . . L. 1862.

French Detective, A. *William Russell.* The experiences of . . . By "Waters." N.Y. 1864.

French Politician, The. *Edmond Scherer,* one of the editors of the Paris "Temps," and a senator, whose letters in the London "Daily News" (1877–78) gave a striking picture of the situation in France.

French Traveller, A. *Louis Simond.* Journal of a tour and residence in Great Britain during the years 1810 and 1811 by . . . Edinb. 1815.

Frenchman, Jack. *Jonathan Swift, D.D.* J. F.'s lamentation. An excellent song. 1708.

Frere, Alice M. *Mrs. Godfrey Clerk.*

Friar, The. *Phanuel Bacon, D.D.,* who was the author of "The Snipe," one of the best ballads in the English language, and founded on a fact; for the "Friar" denoted the author himself, and "Peter" his fellow collegian, *Peter Zinzan, M.D.* This ballad and "A Song of Similies," by Dr. Bacon, are preserved in the "Oxford Sausage."

Fribble, T. *Jonathan Swift, D.D.* Tittle-tattle, etc. [Consisting of extracts from Swift's "Polite Conversation."] 1749.

Fribbleton, Ex-Barber. *Asa Greene.* The travels of . . . in America. N.Y. 1835.

Fridolin, le Major. *A. de Valbezene.* La retraite des dix mille, etc., in the "Revue des Deux Mondes." Paris, 1851.

Friend, A [or Quaker]. *Elias Bockett.* Aminadab's courtship; or, the Quaker's wedding: a poem . . . L. 1717.

Friend, A. *Miss Mary Elizabeth Lee,* who, under this modest signature, contributed her earliest productions to the "Southern Rose," Charleston, S.C.

Friend, A. *Capt. J. A. Gilbert.* The change; or, a memoir of Lieut.-Col. Holcombe, C.B. L. 1847.

Friend, A. *Dr. William Kenrick.* A defence of Mr. Kenrick's review of Mr. Johnson's "Shakespeare" . . . L. 1766.

Friend, A. *John Oldmixon.* A defence of Mr. Maccartney. L. 1712.

Friend, A. *Sir Richard Hill.* Five letters to the Rev. Mr. F—r [Fletcher] relative to his vindication of the minutes of the Rev. Mr. John Wesley . . . L. 1771.

Friend, A. *Thomas Linning.* A letter . . . to Mr. John Mackmillan . . . n.p., n.d. but 1708.

Friend, A. *Robert Lundin Brown.* A letter to the Moderate Brethren. Edinb., n.p. but 1842.

Friend, A. *Giovanni Domenico Ruffini.* Lorenzo Benoni . . . Edinb. 1853.

Friend, A. *Zachary Grey, LL.D.* A word or two of advice to William Warburton, a dealer in many words; by . . . L. 1746.

Friend, A. *Luke Howard, F.R.S.* The Yorkshireman: a religious and literary journal. By . . . Pontefract, L., Leeds, and York, 1833–37.

Friend in the City, A. *George Meldrum.* A letter . . . to a member of Parliament anent patronages. Edinb. 1703.

Friend in the Country, A. *Rev. John Erskine.* Meditations and letters of a pious youth . . . Edinb. 1746.

Friend in the Country, A. *William Gibson.* A second letter from . . . to his friend in London [Elias Bockett]. L. 1717.

Friend of his Age, A. *Mr. Dawson.* A humble tribute to the memory of Mr. Abram Rumney . . . Alnwick, 1794.

Friend of Industry, A. *— Dearborn,* who, in 1784, under this signature, published in the "New Hampshire Gazette" an article suggesting the employment of convicts in prisons, a plan soon after generally adopted.

Friend of Mr. St[ee]le. *Jonathan Swift, D.D.* The importance of the Guardian considered . . . L. 1713.

Friend of Religious Liberty, A. *William Paley,* Arch-deacon of Carlisle. A defence of the considerations on the propriety of requiring a subscription to articles of faith . . . L. 1774.

Friend of Seamen, A. *William Allen, D.D.* Accounts of shipwreck and of other disasters at sea . . . Compiled . . . Brunswick, Me., 1823.

Friend of the Author, A. *John Barlow Seale.* An elegy on a family tomb [by J. J. Brundish] translated into Italian verse. Camb. 1783.

Friend of the Author, A. *Jonathan Swift, D.D.* Mr. C—ns's [Collins's] discourse of free-thinking put into plain English, by way of abstract, for the use of the poor . . . L. 1713.

Friend of the Family, A. *William Ayrton.* The adventures of a salmon in the River Dee. By . . . L. 1853.

Friend of the Negro, A. *Wilson Armistead.* The garland of freedom: a collection of poems, chiefly anti-slavery. Selected . . . L. 1853.

Friend of the People, A. *Richard Ronaldson.* Banks and a paper currency. P. 1857.

Friend of the People, A. *Rev. William Chalmers, A.M.* The Church question. Ayr, 1843.

Friend of the People, A. *Miss Sarah Jane Mayne.* Jane Rutherford; or, the miners' strike . . . L. 1854.

Friend of the People, A. *Rev. George Tod.* Letter to James Moncrieff, Esq. . . . Edinb. 1820.

Friend of the People, A Sincere. *Maurice Lothian.* The expediency of a secure provision for the ministers of the Gospel . . . Edinb. 1834.

Friend of the Road, A. *Elizur Wright.* The Northern Pacific Railroad, by . . . B. 1874.

Friend of the Secession, A. *Mr. Boston,* of Falkirk. An antidote against a new heresy . . . Dundee, 1779.

Friend of the South. *M. Pratt* (?). In answer to "Remarks on Channing's 'Slavery.'" B. 1836.

Friend of Truth, A. *John Cleaveland.* The Chebacco narrative rescu'd from the charge of falshood and partiality . . . B. 1738.

Friend of Truth, A. *George Scott.* A concise illustration of the doctrine of justification by faith . . . Edinb. 1832.

Friend of Truth and Peace, A. *William Walton.* The true interests of the European powers and the Emperor of Brazil . . . L. 1829.

Friend of Truth and Sound Policy, A. *Henry M. Brackenridge.* Strictures on a voyage to South America . . . Balt. 1820.

Friend of Youth, A. *Mary Clark.* Conversations on the history of Massachusetts from its first settlement to the present period. By . . . B. 1831.

Friend of Youth, A. *Samuel Willard, D.D.* The Franklin family primer . . . B. 1811.

Friend of Youth and Children, A. *Frederick White Evans.* Brief and moral instructions for the young . . . Worcester, Mass., 1858.

Friend to Accuracy, A. *Thomas Bland,* during many years a contributor to the "Gent. Mag." under this and other signatures.

Friend to American Enterprise, A. *George W. Simmons.* Oak Hall pictorial . . . B. 1854.

Friend to Both, A. *Thomas Bowdler.* Liberty, civil and religious . . . L. 1815.

Friend to Britain, A. *Dr. Chamberlayn.* The great advantages to both kingdoms of Scotland and England by an union. n.p. 1702.

Friend to Candour and Truth, A. *Stephen Jones.* Hypercriticism exposed . . . L. 1812.

Friend to Civil and Religious Liberty, A. *Henry Peckwell, D.D.* The account of an appeal from a summary conviction on the statute 22 Car. ii., c. i., to the Hon. C—rt of K. B. . . . L. n.d.

Friend to Education and Moral Improvement of the Labouring Poor, A. *Thomas Pole, M.D.* On the irreverent use of the sacred names. By ... Bristol, about 1823.

Friend to Emancipation, A. *John Clutton.* The Emancipation Bill examined. Hereford, 1825.

Friend to his Country, A. *Robert French.* The constitution of Ireland ... Dublin, 1770.

Friend to Liberty and Property, A. *Rev. John Lewis.* Advice to posterity concerning a point of the last importance. Written ... L. 1755.

Friend to Peace and Good Order, A. *Harrison Gray.* A few remarks upon some of the votes and resolutions of the Continental Congress ... n.p., probably P. 1775.

Friend to Religious Liberty, A. *Rev. John Palmer.* Free remarks on a sermon entitled "The requisition of subscription to the 39 articles and liturgy of the Church of England not inconsistent with Christian liberty" ... L. 1772.

Friend to the Church of England, A. *Francis Maseres.* The moderate reformer ... L. 1791.

Friend to the Churches, A. *Increase Mather.* A plea for the ministers of the Gospel ... B. 1706.

Friend to the Established Church, A. *Rev. Frederick Toll.* A plain and proper answer to this question: "Why does not the Bishop of Clogher, supposing him to be the author of the 'Essay on Spirit,' resign his preferments" ... L. 1753.

Friend to the Government, A. *Rev. W. Webster.* The draper confuted ... L. 1740.

Friend to the Liberty of his Country, A. *Benjamin Church, M.D.* — See "Elizaphan of Parnach."

Friend to the Natural and Religious Rights of Mankind, A. *Rev. William Graham,* of Whitehaven. An attempt to prove that every species of patronage is foreign to the nature of the Church ... Edinb. 1768.

Friend to the Peace of the Church of Scotland, A. *George M'Lelland.* An enquiry adapted to the present crisis ... Edinb. 1842.

Friend to the Sex, A. — *Adams.* Woman: sketches of the history, genius ... of the fair sex in all parts of the world ... L. 1790.

Friend to the Sisterhood, A. *William Hayley.* A philosophical, historical, and moral essay on old maids. By ... L. 1785.

Friend to the South, A. *Miss Belle Hardinge.* Belle Boyd, in camp and prison. L. 1865.

Friend to the West India Colonies and their Inhabitants, A. *James Tobin.* Cursory remarks upon the Reverend Mr. Ramsay's essay on the treatment and conversion of African slaves in the sugar colonies. L. 1785.

Friend to True Liberty, A. *Edmund Rack.* England's true interest in the choice of a new Parliament briefly considered ... L. 1774.

Friend to Truth, A. *Tyler Parsons.* Candid enquiries ... relative to the difficulties which existed in the town of Manchester, Mass. ... n.p. about 1820.

Friend to Youth, A. *Miss Sarah Hoare.* A poem on the pleasures and advantages of botanical pursuits, with notes; and other poems. By ... Bristol, n.d.

Friend, A Mutual. *Mrs. George Grote* (?). The case of the poor against the rich. L. 1850.

Friendly, Aunt. *Mrs. Sarah S. (Tuthill) Baker.* Meggie of "The Pines." N.Y. 18–.

Frog, Nicholas. The Netherlands. — See "Strutt, Lord."

Frohberg, Paul. *Friedrich Adami.* Dramatische Genrebilder aus der vaterländischen Geschichte. 1870.

Froissart, Jean. *Alphonse Daudet,* who has contributed to a large number of journals, and notably to the "Monde Illustré" and to the "Figaro," where his "Chroniques rimées," signed "Jean Froissart," have been much noticed.

Frost, S. Annie. *Mrs. S. A. Shields.*

Fru, F. *Emilie (Schmidt Flygare Dalin) Carlén.* Valdemar Klein. 1838.

Fuller, Violet. *Mrs. Eleanor Fullerton.* In 1871 she published a volume of her poems through Sampson Low & Son, London.

Fulvius, Cnœus. *Charles James Fox.* — See "Florus, Julius."

Fume, Joseph. *William Andrew Chatto.* A pipe of tobacco ... L. 1839.

Fungus, Barnaby, Esq. *Arthur Benoni Evans, D.D.* Fungusiana; or, the opinions and table-talk of the late ... L. 1809.

Fungus, Sir Ferdinando, Gent. — *Williams,* of Wadham College. New facts; or, the whitewasher ... 1790. Also ascribed to Mr. Simmonds of Blandford, Dorsetshire.

Funnidos, Rigdum, Gent. *John Ballantyne* (?). American broad grins. Edited ... L. 1838.

Funnidus, Rigdum. *Horace May-hew, Henry Mayhew,* and *Robert B. Brough,* editors of Cruikshank's "Comic Almanac."

Funny Man, A. *Ossian E. Dodge.* Comical doings of . . . N.Y. 187-.
Fusina, Fra. *Arnoldo Fusinato.* Gedichte. 1853–54.

G.

Γ. *Edward George Ballard, Esq.,* who wrote for the "Literary Magnet" and "World of Fashion" under this signature.

γ. *John Keble.* — See "a" (under alpha).

G. *Dr. John Green,* Bishop of Lincoln, in his contributions to the "Athenian Letters" . . . L. 1741–43.

G. *Rev. R. F. Wilson,* one of the contributors to "Tracts for the Times." L. 1840–48.

G. — See "The Lord and Lady There."

G. *L. C. Gent.* Familiar English quotations. L. 1877.

G., A. *Alfred Gatty, D.D.* The bell: its origin, history, and uses. L. 1847.

G., A. *Alexander Gardner.* A defence of infant baptism . . . Paisley, 1851.

G., A. *Agnes Giberne.* Mignonette . . . L. 1869.

G., A. *Asa Gray, M.D.* Review of Darwin's theory of the origin of species by means of natural selection. From the "Amer. Jour. of Science and Arts," March, 1860.

G., A., Gent. *John Humphreys Parry.* The maskers of Moorfields: a vision, by the late . . . Edited by W. Griffinhoof. L. 1815. — See "Griffinhoof, Anthony, Esq."

G., A. F. *Acton Frederick Griffith.* Bibliotheca Anglo-poetica . . . L. 1815.

G. A. F. *John Lister.* Epigrams and jeux d'esprit . . . Edinb. 1870.

G., A. F. *Mrs. A. F. Gaston.* Our maid-servants . . . L. 1866.

G., A. F. *Atkinson F. Gibson.* A tribute to the memory of William Grover, of Stanstead, by . . . Warwick, 1826.

G., A. H. *Alexander H. Grant.* Contributions to "London Society," chiefly poetical.

G., A. S. *A. S. Grenville.* Poetic effusions. B. 1822.

G., C. *Rev. Charles Gibbon,* of Lonmay. A letter by a delegate to the General Assembly . . . Aberdeen, 1840,

G., C. F. *Mrs. Catherine Frances (Grace) Gore.* Quid pro quo; or, the day of dupes: the prize comedy. L. 1844.

G. C. H., Esq., Barrister-at-law.

H. G. Curran. Confessions of a Whitefoot. Edited by . . . L. 1844.

G. C. J. *Mrs. Carrie J. Freeland.* Ansdale Hall; or, stand to your colors. B. 187-.

G., C. V. *Charles Vaughan Grinfield.* A century of acrostics . . . L. 1855.

G., D. *David Garrick.* An ode upon dedicating a building, and erecting a statue to Shakespeare, at Stratford-upon-Avon. By . . . L. 1769.

G., E. B. *Edward Burnaby Greene.* Hero and Leander: a poem. Tr. . . . L. 1773.

G., F. *Frederick Gale.* The public school matches . . . L. 1867.

G., F. *François Gaume.* Rome et ses papes. Paris, 1824.

G., F. T. *Hippolyte Adolphe Taine,* in his contributions to "La Vie Parisienne."

The above letters are the initials of "Frédéric Thomas Graindorge," another pseudonym of this author.

G., F. W., of the Middle Temple. *F. W. Guidickins.* An answer to Mr. Horace Walpole's late work entitled "Historic doubts on the reign and life of King Richard the Third . . . L. 1768.

G., G. *George Grenville.* A letter to . . . "Stiff in opinions, always in the wrong." L. 1767.

G., G. *G. Green.* The Shunamite. N.Y. 1810.

G., H. *Horace Greeley,* in his contributions to the "Tribune" (N.Y.).

G., H. *Rev. Harry Grey.* Brief sketches of the early history, conversion, and closing period of the life of Mary, second daughter of the Hon. John Grey . . . L. 1855.

G., H. *Hudson Gurney.* Cupid and Psyche . . . Trans. by . . . L. 1800.

G., H. B. *Mrs. H. B. (Goodwin) Talcott.* Dr. Howell's family. B. 1869.

G., H. B. *Mrs. H. B. Gerry.* Roger Deane's work. By . . . B. 1863.

G., H. M. *Miss H. Maria George,* in art and biographical sketches contributed to various periodicals.

G., H. M. *Henry Mayo Gunn.* History of Nonconformity in Warminster. L. 1853.

G., J. *John Goldicutt.* Heriot's Hospital, Edinburgh: the design of the celebrated architect, Inigo Jones. By ... L. 1836.

G., J. *John Green.* A journey from Aleppo to Damascus ... L. 1736.

G., J. *James Glassford.* Miscellanea ... Edinb. 1818.

G., J., late Serrishtehdar of Bengal. *James Grant.* An inquiry into the nature of Zemindary tenures ... L. 1810.

G., J. C. *Julia C. Grimani.* Sacred lyrics. L. 1849.

G., J. H. *Rev. John Hampden Gurney.* The pastor's last words ... L. 1862.

G., J. H. *Joseph H. Gibbs and others.* The Quadrilateral. 1865.

G., J. T. *Judith Towers Grant.* "Looking unto Jesus" ... Bath, 1852.

G. K. *John Boyle,* 4th Earl of Cork and Orrery.
"About 1753 Mr. Moore undertook the periodical publication called the 'World,' to which our noble author contributed three papers, viz., Nos. 47, 68, and 161 ... The Earl of Cork was a contributor likewise to the 'Connoisseur,' carried on by Mr. Thornton and Mr. Colman. In the last number of this publication G. K., which was his lordship's signature, is distinguished by the ingenious authors as their 'earliest and most frequent correspondent' ... His communications to the 'Connoisseur' were the most part of Nos. 14 and 17, the letter signed 'Goliah English' in No. 19, great part of Nos. 33 and 40, and the letters signed 'Reginald Fitzworm,' 'Michael Krawbridge,' 'Moses Orthodox,' and 'Thomas Vainall,' in Nos. 102, 107, 113, and 129."— CHALMERS, Vol. 6.

G., L. E. *Lucy Ellen Guernsey.* Irish Amy. P. 1854.

G. M. *Mrs. Stanley Leathes.* Soi-même. L. 1869.

G. P. *Samuel Pegge.* A defence of the propriety of the words "which art in heaven" in the Lord's prayer. "Gent. Mag.," 1754, p. 310. G. P., the initials of Paul Gemsege reversed, used one other time. — See "Gent. Mag.," LXVI., p. 979.

G., P. S. *Rev. Peter Southmead Glubb, B.D.* A libretto, containg The armoury, The holier rood, and The London season. By ... 1875.

G., R. *Rupert Green(?).* A brief history of Worcester; or, "Worcester Guide" improved ... By ... Worcester, 1806.

G., R. *Robert Graham, M.D.* (?). Characters of genera, extracted from the British flora of W. J. Hooker. Edinb. 1830.

G., R. *Richard Gough.* A comparative view of the antient monuments of India ... as described by different writers. By ... L. 1785.

G., R. *Richard Gilbert.* Liber scholasticus ... L. 1829.

G., R., a Clerk of the Court of Common-Pleas. *R. Gardiner.* Instructor clericalis ... In the Savoy, 1721–24.

G., R., junior. *Richard Gough.* The history of the Bible, translated from the French, by ... L. 1747.
This volume, consisting of 160 sheets in folio, was completed by him when he was twelve and a half years old, and was followed three years later by a translation of the "Customs of the Israelites," translated from the French of the abbot Fleury, by ... 1750.

G. R. G. *Rev. George Robert Gleig.* The light dragoon. L. 1844.

G., R. S. *Roscellus S. Guernsey,* in Shakespeare contributions to various periodicals.

G., S. *Samuel Gilman, D.D.* Catalogue of miniature portraits, landscapes, and other pieces, executed by Charles Fraser, Esq. ... Charleston, S.C., 1857.

G., S. *Samuel Grascome.* Certamen religiosum ... Oxf. 1704. — See also "A Presbyter of the Church of England."

G., S. *Simon Greenleaf.* Remarks on the exclusion of atheists as witnesses. B. 1839.

G., S. B. *S. B. Goslin.* [William Banister's] The art and science of change ringing ... Second edition, with corrections and additions. [By H. Haley and others. Edited ..] L. 1879.

G., T. *T. Gib.* Remarks on the Rev. Mr. Whitefield's journal ... L. 1738.

G., T. *Thomas Gwin.* Some memoirs of our dear deceased friend Josiah Ceane ... Plymouth, Eng., 1718.

G., T. M. *T. M. Gorman.* On the white horse mentioned in the "Revelation" [by Swedenborg]. Edited ... L. 1871.

G., W. — See Gifford, William.

G., W. *William Gardner.* The lawyers investigated ... Brentford, 1771.

G., W. *William Gauntley.* Remarks on a certain publication entitled "Macaulay's portrait of the founder of Quakerism." Sheffield, 1856.

G., W. *Sir William Gell.* Views in Barbary, and a picture of the Dey of Algiers, taken in 1813, by ... L. 1815.

G. W. One of the pseudonyms attributed to Junius (*q.v.*).
The two letters thus signed are dated March 29 and April 8, 1771, and are addressed to the Lord Mayor.

G., W. D. *William D. Gallagher.* Selections from the poetical literature of the West ... Cin. 1841.

G., W. R. *William Rathbone Greg*, in the London "Pall Mall Gazette."

G********, A. B., M.D. *Augustus Bozzi Granville.* Critical observations on Mr. Kemble's performances at the Theatre Royal, Liverpool. Liverpool, 1811.

G***, Ph. *Philippe Grouvelle.* Mémoires historiques sur les Templiers . . . Paris, 1805.

G——, Percival. *Peter Irving.* A Venetian tale (from the French). N.Y. 1820.

Gabble, Gridiron, Gent., Godson to Mother Goose. *Joseph Haslewood.* Green-room gossip; or, Gravity Gallinipt. A gallimaufry . . . got up to guile gymnastical and gynecocratic governments. Gathered and garnished by . . . L. 1809.

Gabriel, Virginia. *Mrs. Constance (Crane) Marsh.* Wolfe of the knoll; and other poems. N.Y. 1860.

Gaines, Garry. *Virginia S. Patterson.*

Gale, Ethel. *Helen E. Smith*, in the New York "Independent."

Galen. *Richard E. Parker*, in Wirt's (W.) "Old Bachelor" (Balt. 1812).

Galen, Philipp. *Ernst Philipp Karl Lange.* Der Alte vom Berge. Roman. Berlin, 1873.

Galloway Poet, The. *William Nicholson.* Tales in verse. 1814; 2d ed., Dumfries, about 1834.

Galoot. *Edward P. Kendall.*

Gambado, Geoffrey, Esq., Riding-Master. *Henry Bunbury.* Academy for grown horsemen . . . L. 1787.

Game Chicken, The. *Henry Pearce*, a celebrated pugilist, and once the champion of England.

Gamma. *Dr. John D. Osborne*, in his contributions to the "Picayune" (New Orleans, La.).

Gander, Sir Gregory, Knt. *George Ellis.* Poetry and tales. Bath, 1779.

Gaol Chaplain, A. *Rev. Erskine Neale.* Recollections of a gaol chaplain. Reprinted from "Bentley's Miscellany."

Gaolg, Ekal. *J. A. Lake Gloag.* The Jesuit; or, the man of the Morgue . . . Glasgow and L. 1876.

Gar. *J. Garczynski*, in the New York "Times."

Garon. *Rev. Joseph Bretland*, in the "Monthly Repository" (Hackney).

Garrard, Kenner. *Lewis Edward Nolan.* System of training cavalry horses . . . L. 1853.

Garrett, Edward and Ruth. *Mrs. Isabella (Fyvie) Mayo.* By still waters. L. 1874.

Garrulous, George. *George Arnold.* — See "Grahame, Allen."

Gastine, Civique de. *E. L. J. Toulotte.* Histoire de la république d'Haiti . . Paris, 1819.

Gaston, Marie. *Alphonse Daudet.*

Gath. *George Alfred Townsend.* Bohemian days. Three American tales. N.Y. 1880. Also in his contributions to numerous American periodicals.

Gathercoal, Rev. Rabshakeh, late Vicar of Tuddington. *Robert Mackenzie Beverley.* The posthumous letters of . . . L. 1835.

Gauden, Dr. *Charles Henry Wharton, D.D.*, in Horace Binney Wallace's "Literary criticisms," pp. 259–307. P. 1856.

Gavarni, Paul. *Sulpice Guillaume Chevalier.* Œuvres choisiés . . . Paris, 1845.

Gay, Delphine. *Mme. Émile de Girardin.* La croix de Berney. Paris, 1874.

Gay, Getty. *Mrs. William Bennett.*

Gay, Joseph. *John Durant de Breval.* The confederates. L. 1717.

This play, though published under the name of Gay, was written by Breval.

Gay, Mr. Joseph. *Alexander Pope.* Compleat key to the Non-Juror . . . L. 1720.

Gaylord, Glance. *Warren Ives Bradley.* The boy at Dr. Murray's . . . B. 1871.

Gazul, Clara. *Prosper Mérimée.* Théâtre de . . . Paris, 1825.

Gemsege, Paul. *Samuel Pegge.* A letter on poaching, in the "Gent. Mag." for the year 1751, p. 111 (and 75 other articles for the 11 years from 1746 to 1757).

This signature is the anagram of his name. See "Gent. Mag.," LXVI., pp. 979 et seq.

Genealogist, A. *Alexander Deuchar.* Concise view of the present state of the Succession . . . Edinb. 1839.

General Officer, A. *Hon. Henry Seymour Conway.* An address to the public on the late dismission of . . . By William Guthrie. L. 1764.

General Officer, A. — *Ford*, 5th Earl Cavan. A new system of military discipline, founded upon principle. By . . . 1773.

Genesee. *Prof. J. H. Gilmore*, in the New York "Examiner."

Genesee. *E. M. Crawford.* Cricket notes.

Genevese Traveller, A. *Matthew L. Davis*, in the London "Times."

Gent, A. *Alexander Anderson.* Joseph

the book-man: a heroi-comic poem . . .
Edin. 1821.

Gent, A. *Samuel Forster.* Mr. Benjamin Bennet's Presbyterian prejudice further display'd . . . Newcastle-upon-Tyne, 1726.

Gentile, A. *Dyer Daniel Lum.* Utah and its people; by . . . N.Y. 1882.

Gentleman, A. *Rev. Charles Audley Assheton Craven, M.A.* The adventures of . . . in search of the Church of England. L. 1853.

Gentleman, A. *Sir George Stephen.* Adventures of . . . in search of a horse. By Caveat Emptor, Gent. L. 1835.

Gentleman, A. *Elias Bockett.* A congratulatory letter to the Reverend Mr. Patrick Smith, M.A., Vicar of Great Paxton, Huntingdonshire, upon the publication of . . . "A Preservative against Quakerism." By . . . L. 1731.

Gentleman, A. *Sir John Leslie.* The connoisseur; or, modern fashions: a comedy in three acts. By . . . Inverness, 1818.

Gentleman, A. *Thomas Skinner Surr.* Consequences; or, adventures at Braxall Castle: a novel. L. 1796.

Gentleman, A. *Thomas Salmon.* A critical essay concerning marriage . . . L. 1724.

Gentleman, A. *Paul Dudley.* An essay on the merchandise of slaves and souls of men . . . B. 1731.

Gentleman, A. *John Esten Cooke.* Estcourt. Memoirs of . . . in " Bussell's Magazine," South Carolina.

Gentleman, A. *Priscilla Wakefield.* Excursions in America described in letters from . . . and his young companion to their friends in England. L. 1806.

Gentleman, A. *Francis Eyre, Esq.* A few remarks on The history of the decline and fall of the Roman empire, relative chiefly to the two last chapters. By . . . L. 1778.

Gentleman, A. *John Hippisley.* Flora: an opera . . . L. 1729.

Gentleman, A. *Rev. John White, B.D.* Free and impartial considerations upon the free and candid disquisitions relating to the Church of England. Addressed to the authors [John Jones] of the Disquisitions. By . . . L. 1751.

Gentleman, A. *Henry Penruddock Wyndham.* A G.'s tour through Monmouthshire and Wales . . . in 1774. L. 1775.

Gentleman, A. *Thomas Hull.* Genuine letters from . . . to a young lady, his pupil. L. 1772.

Gentleman, A. *Rev. George Harbin.*

The hereditary right of the crown of England asserted . . . L. 1713.

Gentleman, A. *Sir Henry Bate Dudley (?).* History of Essex. L. 1769–1772.

Gentleman, A. *Leonard Welsted.* Hymn to the Creator, written by . . . in "Gent. Mag.," October, 1790, p. 936.

Gentleman, A. *Andrew Wilson, M.D.* Human nature surveyed by philosophy and revelation . . . L. 1758.

Gentleman, A. *Mr. Robinson, of Kendal.* The intriguing milliners and attornies clerks . . . L. 1740.

Gentleman, A. *James Ramsay.* A letter . . . concerning toleration. Edinb. 1703.

Gentleman, A. *William Beckford.* Letters and observations written in a short tour through France and Italy. By . . . L. 1786.

Gentleman, A. *Anthony Hammond.* A modest apology, occasion'd by the late unhappy turn of affairs . . . L. 1721.

Gentleman, A. *John Hatfield.* A new Scarborough guide, containing customs, amusements, lodging-houses . . . L. 1797.

Gentleman, A. *Thomas Baker.* Reflections upon learning . . . L. 1708.

Gentleman, A. *William Bromley.* Several years' travels through Portugal, Spain, Italy . . . Performed . . . L. 1702.

Gentleman, A. *Edmond Hoyle.* A short treatise on the game of whist. L. 1742.

Gentleman, A. *John Adams.* Thoughts on government . . . B. 1788.

Gentleman (A), a Descendant of Dame Quickly. *James White.* Original letters . . . of Sir John Falstaff and his friends; now first made public by . . . L. 1796.

Gentleman and no Knight, A. *Zachary Grey, LL.D.* The Knight of Dumbleton foiled at his own weapons, etc. In a letter to Sir Richard "Cocks," knt. By . . . L. 1723.

Gentleman at Halifax, A. *Chief Justice Martin Howard, of North Carolina.* A letter . . . to his friend in Rhode Island . . . Newport, 1765.

Gentleman educated at Yale College, A. *William Livingston, Esq.* Philosophic solitude; or, the choice of a rural life: a poem . . . N.Y. 1847.

Gentleman formerly of Boston, A. *Edward Church, Jr.* The Dangerous Vice . . . Columbia, 1789.

The "Dangerous Vice" was John Adams, Also ascribed to Silvanus Bourne.

Gentleman formerly of Brazen-nose College, Oxford, A. Probably *Charles Manfield.* Interesting collection of curious anecdotes . . . L. 1790.

Gentleman formerly of Gray's Inn, A. *John Holt.* An attempte to rescue that aunciente English poet and playwrighte, Maister Williaume Shakespere, from the maney errours faulsely charged on him . . . L. 1749.

Gentleman in America, A. *Thomas Cooper, M.D.* Extract of a letter from . . . to a friend in England, on the subject of emigration. 1794.

Gentleman in Boston, A. *Charles Chauncy, D.D.* A letter from . . . to Mr. George Wishart, one of the ministers of Edinburgh, concerning the state of Religion in New England. Edinb. 1742.

Gentleman in Boston, A. *Lewis Tappan.* Letter from . . . to a Unitarian clergyman in that city. B. 1828.

Gentleman in Gloucestershire, A. *John Blanch.* Hoops into spinning-wheels: a tragi-comedy. Gloucester, 1725.

The epistle dedicatory is signed " J. B."

Gentleman in London, A. *William Knox.* The claim of the colonies to an exemption from internal taxes, imposed by authority of Parliament, examined. In a letter from . . . to his friend in America. L. 1765.

Gentleman in London, A. *Resta Paching.* Four topographical letters, written in July, 1755, upon a journey thro' Bedfordshire . . . from . . . Newcastle-upon-Tyne, 1757.

Gentleman in London, A. *William Smith.* A letter from . . . to his friend in Pennsylvania; with a satire . . . L. 1756.

Gentleman in Philadelphia, A. *John Dickinson.* The late regulations respecting the British colonies on the continent of America considered. In a letter from . . . to his friend in London. L. 1766.

Gentleman in Scotland, A. *Charles Leslie.* A letter . . . to his friend in England, against the sacramental test. 2d ed. L. 1708.

Gentleman in the City, A. *Benjamin Coole.* A letter . . . concerning the Quakers. L. 1705.

The letter is signed "Eclea-Nobj-moni," an anagram of the author's name.

Gentleman in the City, A. *Charles Leslie.* A letter . . . concerning the threaten'd prosecution of the Rehearsal . . . n.p. 1708.

Gentleman in the City, A. *Rev. Robert Wylie,* of Hamilton. A letter . . . to a minister in the country. Edinb. 1703.

Gentleman in the English House of Commons, A. *Edmund Burke.* A letter from . . . in vindication of his conduct, with regard to the affairs of Ireland . . . L. 1780.

Gentleman in the North, A. *Rev. Alexander M'Laggan,* of Little-Dunkeld. A letter . . . to a minister who has not intimated the act of parliament . . . n.p. 1737.

Gentleman in the North of Scotland, A. *Captain Edward Burt.* Letters from . . . to his friend in London, giving an account of the Highlands . . . L. 1754.

Gentleman in the Service of the East India Company, A. *Major Henry D. Robertson.* Examination of the principles and policy of the government of British India. L. 1829.

Gentleman in Town, A. *W. H. Logan.* Letter . . . regarding Keeley, the theatre, and other matters . . . Edinb. 1834.

" Signed "H. M."

Gentleman, Late an Officer in the Service of the Honourable East-India Company, A. *Mr. Evers.* A journal kept on a journey from Bassora to Bagdad . . . Horsham, 1784.

Gentleman, late of Bath, A. *Dr. Edward Harington.* An excursion from Paris to Fontainebleau. L. 1786.

Gentleman, late of the Inner Temple, A. *Henry Baker.* Essays, pastoral and elegiac . . . L. 1856.

Gentleman lately Resident on a Plantation, A. *Peter Marsden.* An account of the island of Jamaica . . . Newcastle, 1788.

Gentleman lately returned from America, A. *Mr. Hodgkinson.* Letters on emigration. L. 1794.

Gentleman, Native thereof, A. *John Blundell.* Memoirs and antiquities of the town and parish of Tiverton . . . Exeter, 1712.

Gentleman of Boston, A. *Nathan Hale.* Notes made during an excursion to the Highlands of New Hampshire and Lake Winnipiseogee. Andover, 1833.

Gentleman of Brazen-Nose College, Oxford, A. *Rev. John Ellis.* The knowledge of divine things from revelation . . . L. 1743.

Gentleman of Bristol, A. *S. Butler.* An essay upon education . . . With a plan of a new method. By . . . L. 1750 (?).

Gentleman of Cambridge, A. *Philip Bennet.* The beau philosopher: a poem. L. 1736.

Gentleman of Cambridge, A. *Corbyn Morris, F.R.S.* A letter to the Reverend Mr. Thomas Carte ... L. 1743.

Gentleman of Cambridge, A. *Thomas Hearne.* A letter to the Reverend the Prolocutor ... L. 1718.

Gentleman of Cambridge, A. *William Mason.* Mirth: a poem ... L. and Camb. 1774.

Gentleman of Cambridge, A. *Francis Fawkes.* The works of Anacreon, Sappho, Bion, Moschus, and Musæus. Translated into English by ... L. 1789.

Gentleman of Cambridge, Another. *Rev. John Duncombe.* An evening contemplation in a college: being a parody on the "Elegy in a country churchyard." L. 1753.

Gentleman of Christ-Church College, Oxon., A. Probably *Dr. Zachary Pearce,* Bishop of Rochester. A friendly letter to Dr. Bentley, occasioned by his new edition of "Paradise lost." L. 1732.

Gentleman of Connecticut, A. *William Cobbett.* The Democratiad: a poem. P. 1795.

Gentleman of Connecticut, A. *Joseph Huntington, D.D.* A plea before the ecclesiastical council at Stockbridge, in the cause of Mrs. Fisk ... 1779 ... Norwich, 1780.

Gentleman of Croydon, A. *T. Read.* The British harmonist. Croydon, 1795.

Gentleman of Foreign Extraction, A. *Jacob Duché.* Observations on a variety of subjects, literary, moral, and religious; in a series of original letters, written by ... who resided some time in Philadelphia ... P. 1774.

Gentleman of Gloucestershire, A. *Charles Shuckburgh.* Antiochus: a new tragedy. L. 1740.

Gentleman of Gray's Inn, A. *J. Crisp.* The conveyancer's guide ... L. 1821.

Gentleman of Halifax. *John Parr.* Vindication of Governor Parr and his council ... L. 1784.

Gentleman of Lincoln's Inn, A. *D. Douglas.* The biographical history of Sir William Blackstone ... L. 1782.

Gentleman of Lincoln's-Inn, A. *Henry Anderson.* An enquiry into the natural right of mankind to debate freely concerning religion ... L. 1737.

Gentleman of Lincoln's Inn, A. *Philip Carteret Webb.* A letter to ...

W. Warburton occasioned by some passages in ... "The divine legation of Moses demonstrated." By ... L. 1744.

Gentleman of Maryland, A. *Hugh Henry Brackenridge.* The battle of Bunkers Hill. A dramatic piece ... P. 1776. Ascribed also to John Burk.

Gentleman of Massachusetts, A. *Gamaliel Bradford.* The Writer: a series of original essays, moral and amusing. By ... B. 1822.

Gentleman of Middlesex, A. *James Johnston.* More essays of panegyricks ... L. 1731.

Gentleman of New York, A. *William Irving.* The poetical works of Thomas Campbell ... Balt. 1811.

Gentleman of one of the Inns of Court, A. *William Dodd, LL.D.* A new book of the Dunciad. By ... L. 1750.

Gentleman of Oxford, A. *George Smith Green.* A new version of "Paradise lost"; or, Milton paraphrased ... L. 1756.

Gentleman of Philadelphia, A. *Benjamin Franklin French.* Biographia Americana ... N.Y. 1825.

Gentleman of Portsmouth, N.H., A. *Jonathan Mitchell Sewall.* A versification of President Washington's excellent farewell address to the citizens of the United States. By ... Portsmouth, N.H., 1798.

Gentleman of Seventeen, A Young. *Ambrose Pitman.* Eugenio; or, the man of sorrow. L. 1780.

Gentleman of South Carolina, A. *C. B. Northrup.* Southern odes, by the Outcast ... Charleston, 1861.

Gentleman of Suffolk, A. — *Symonds.* A treatise on field diversions. By ... L. 1776.

Gentleman of the Army, A. *Col. David Humphreys.* A poem, addressed to the armies of the United States of America ... New Haven, 1780.

Gentleman of the Bar, A. *I. Daniel Rupp.* Early history of Western Pennsylvania, and of the West, and of western expeditions and campaigns from 1754 to 1833. By ... Pittsburg, Pa., 1846.

Gentleman of the Commission, A. *Ralph Heathcote, D.D.* Irenarch; or, justice of the peace's manual ... L. 1774.

Gentleman of the Committee, A. *Major William Brooke* (?). Plans of the Sunday-schools and School of Industry established in the city of Bath ... Bath, 1789.

Gentleman of the Faculty, A. *Hall Jackson.* Observations and remarks on the putrid malignant sore throat . . . Portsmouth, N.H., 1786.

Gentleman of the Faculty, A. *P. Hayes.* A serious and friendly address to the public on the consequences of neglecting coughs and colds . . . L. 1783.

Gentleman of the Force, A. (Signed "Policeman X. 54.") *William Makepeace Thackeray.* A Bow Street ballad. "Punch," Nov. 25, 1848.

Gentleman of the Inner Temple, A. *Robert Richardson.* The attorney's practice in the Court of King's Bench . . . L. 1739.

Gentleman of the Inner Temple, A. *John Campbell.* The case of the opposition impartially stated. L. 1742.

Gentleman of the Inner Temple, A. *W. Gardiner.* Conversations on the plurality of worlds . . . New trans. by . . . L. 1762.

Gentleman of the Inner Temple, A. *George Monck Berkeley.* An elegy on the death of Miss M—s . . . L. 1786.

Gentleman of the Inner Temple, A. *John Mottley.* The history and survey of the cities of London and Westminster . . . By . . . L. 1753.

Gentleman of the Inner Temple, A. *Matthew Dawes.* A letter to Lord Chatham concerning the present war of Great Britain against America . . . L. 1776.

Gentleman of the Inner Temple, A. *John Mallory.* Modern entries, in English . . . In the Savoy, 1734.

Gentleman of the Inns of Court, A. *Myles Davies.* ΕΙΚΩΝ ΜΙΚΡΟ-ΒΙΒΛΙΚΗ sive Icon libellorum; or, a critical history of pamphlets . . . L. 1715.

Gentleman of the Law, A. *Rev. Andrew Moir.* The indictment, trial, and sentence of Mess. T—s K—r, A—w B—n, and R—t M—n, before the Associate Synod, at the instance of the Rev. Adam Gib. By . . . Edinb. 1768.

Gentleman of the Medical Faculty, A. *Edward Bancroft.* An essay on the natural history of Guiana, in South America. L. 1769.

Gentleman of the Middle Temple, A. *James Ralph.* A critical history of the administration of Sir Robert Walpole . . . L. 1743.

Gentleman of the Middle Temple, A. *Robert Lucas* (?). A critical review of the liberties of British subjects . . . L. 1750.

Gentleman of the Middle Temple, A. *Counsellor King.* The frequented village: a poem. By . . . L. 1771.

Gentleman of the Middle Temple,

A. — *Pooley* (?). A general abridgement of cases in equity . . . L. 1757.

Also ascribed to *R. Foley, Sir G. Gilbert,* and *Mathew Bacon.*

Gentleman of the Middle Temple, A. *Timothy Cunningham.* The merchant's lawyer; or, the law of trade in general . . . L. 1761.

Gentleman of the Partie, A. *Jonas Hanway.* A journal of eight days' journey from Portsmouth to Kingston upon Thames . . . L. 1756.

Gentleman of the Province, A. *Samuel Andrew Peters, LL.D.* A general history of Connecticut . . . L. 1781.

Gentleman of the Temple, A. *John Kelly.* The married philosopher . . . L. 1732.

Gentleman of the University of Cambridge, A. *Owen Manning.* — See "A.G.O.T.U.O.C."

Gentleman of the University of Cambridge, A. *Zachary Grey.* A chronological and historical account of the most memorable earthquakes . . . Camb. 1750.

Gentleman of the University of Cambridge, A. *Richard Bulkeley.* Letters to Dr. Clarke, concerning liberty and necessity. L. 1717.

Gentleman of the University of Oxford, A. *Sir Richard Hill, Bart.* An address to persons of fashion, containing some particulars relating to balls . . . L. 1761.

Gentleman of the University of Oxford, A. *Percy Bysshe Shelley.* St. Irvyne; or, the Rosicrucian: a romance by . . . L. 1811.

Gentleman of Trinity College, Cambridge, A. *Thomas Dover.* Encomium argenti vivi . . . L. 1733.

Gentleman of Trinity College, Oxford, A. *William Loveling.* Latin and English poems. L. 1741.

Gentleman of Wadham College, A. *Rev. James Miller.* The humours of Oxford: a comedy . . . L. 1730.

Gentleman of Wadham College, Oxford, A. *John Swinton.* A critical dissertation concerning the words δαίμων and δαιμόνιον . . . L. 1738.

Gentleman of Wilkesbarre, A. *Isaac A. Chapman.* Sketch of the history of Wyoming. By . . . Wilkesbarre, Penn., 1830.

Gentleman on his Travels, A. *Mrs. Sarah Scott.* A description of Millenium Hall and the country adjacent, together with the characters of the inhabitants . . . L. 1762.

"Millenium Hall" is the name given to the rural

and elegant abode of a happy society of ladies, which the author professes to have met with in the west of England.

Gentleman resident in the Neighborhood, A. *Charles Snart.* Practical observations on angling in the river Trent; by ... who has made the amusement his study for upwards of twenty years. Newark, 1801.

Gentleman residing in this City, A. *Samuel Latham Mitchill, M.D.* The picture of New York ... N.Y. 1807.

Gentleman who has left his Lodgings, A. *Lord John Russell.* Essays and sketches of life and character. L. 1820.

The preface (dedicated to Thomas Moore, and omitted in the second edition) is signed " Joseph Skillet, the lodging-house keeper," who is supposed to publish these letters to pay the rent due to him by his absconded tenant.

Gentleman who has resided many years in Pennsylvania, A. *William Smith, D.D.* A brief state of the province of Pennsylvania ... L. 1755.

Gentleman who is particularly addressed in the Postscript of the Vindication of some Passages in the Fifteenth and Sixteenth Chapters of the Decline and Fall of the Roman Empire, The. *Francis Eyre, Esq.* A short appeal to the publick. L. 1799.

Gentleman, who resided five years on the Island, A. *John Campbell.* An exact and authentic account of the greatest white-herring fishery in Scotland ... L. 1750.

Gentleman, who resided some time in Philadelphia, A. *Rev. Jacob Duché.* Caspipina's letters ... Bath, 1777.

Gentleman who was an Officer under that general, A. *James Biggs.* History of Miranda ... L. 1809.

Gentleman who was a Swede, A. *George Sthalberg.* An history of the late revolution in Sweden ... Edinb. 1776.

Gentleman who was in the Town, A. *John Michelborne.* Ireland preserv'd; or, the siege of London-derry ... Dublin, 1739.

Gentleman, Walking, A. *Thomas Colley Grattan.* Highways and byeways. L. 1823.

Gentleman-Commoner of Oxford, A. *Rev. Samuel Croxall.* The fair Circassian: a dramatic performance. L. 1720.

Gentleman Farmer, A. *Henry Utrick Reay, Esq.* A short treatise on that useful invention called the "sportsman's friend; or, the farmer's footman." By ... of Northumberland ... Newcastle, 1801.

Geologist, A. *Hugh Miller.* Rambles of a geologist. B. 1858.

Geologist, A. *William Pengelly.* Scraps from my note-book. By ... in "Once a Week." 1871.

George, Farmer. *George III.,* of England.

"It is well known that the King's speech, on the opening of the session of 1770, spoke of the disease among the *horned cattle,* instead of attending to the violent agitation, and the more important topics of the time. Hence he obtained the name of "Farmer George."

George, Uncle. *Rev. Increase Niles Tarbox.* Uncle George's stories. B. 1868.

George, Amara. *Mathilde (Binder) Kaufmann.* Dissonanzen und Akkorde. Mainz, 1879.

George, Quiet. *George Frederick Pardon.* The juvenile museum ... L. 1849.

Georgia Lawyer, A. *Robert M. Charlton.* Leaves from the portfolio of ... in the N.Y. " Knickerbocker Magazine."

Geraint. *Frank McHale.*

Gérald, Louise. *Mlle. Mathilde de Lacoste.* Pseudonym used by her in several novels.

Gérard, Max. *Charles de Courcy.* Entre hommes, vaudeville ... 1858.

German Barber, The. *Julian E. Ralph,* in his contributions to various periodicals.

German Countess, A. *Ida Maria Louisa Gustava,* Gräfinn Hahn-Hahn. Letters of ... 1843–44. L. 1845.

German Milton, The. *Friedrich Gottlieb Klopstock.*

German Nobleman, A. *Francis J. Grund.* Aristocracy in America; from the sketch-book of ... L. 1839.

German Prince, A. *Hermann Ludwig Heinrich von Pückler-Muskau.* Tour in Germany, Holland, and England, 1826–27 ... L. 1832.

German Voltaire, The. *Christoph Martin Wieland.*

Gershom. *Maj.-Gen. Julius Edmund Goodwyn.* Antitypical parallels ... L. 1866.

Gertrude. *Mrs. Jane Cross (Bell) Simpson.* The piety of daily life. Illustrated by tales, by ... L. 1836. She also contributed to the "Edinburgh Literary Journal" of Feb. 26, 1831, under this pseudonym, the well-known hymn "Go when the morning shineth."

Gerundio, Fray. *Modesto Lafuente.* Teatro social del siglo XIX. Madrid, 184–.

Ghost of Harry the Eighth's Fool, The. *Alfred Henry Forrester.* A missile for Papists! A few remarks on Papacy. By . . . L. 1850.

Ghost of Vandegrab, The. *Sir James Mackintosh,* who wrote a series of letters for the London "Morning Chronicle," under this signature, 179–.

Ghost, of Willy Shakespeare, The. *G. M. Woodward.* Familiar verses from . . . to Sammy Ireland . . . L. 1796.

Gibbon, Edwarda. *C. J. Stone.* History of the decline and fall of the British Empire. Auckland, 2884, *i.e.,* 1884. — See "Notes and Queries," 6th Ser., IX., p. 199.

Gibbons, Lee, student of law. *Thomas Roscoe, Jr.* The cavalier : a romance. L. 1821.

Gifford, John. *Edward Foss.* An abridgment of Blackstone's commentaries. L. 1821.

Gifford, John. *John Richards Green.* A history of the political life of . . . Pitt. L. 1809.

Gifford, John, Esq. *Alexander Whellier.* The English Lawyer. L. 1827.

Gifford, William. *William Frederick Deacon.* Warreniana : with notes, critical and explanatory. By the editor of a "Quarterly Review." L. 1824.

Gift, Theo. *Miss Dora Havers.* A matter-of-fact girl . . . L. 1881.

Gilbert. *William Stevens Robinson.* His signature in the "New York Tribune," in 1857–60.

Gilderoy, Roland. *Charles Rowley, Jr.* The pictures of the year. Notes on the Academy . . . Manchester, 1878.

Gill, André. *Louis Alexandre Gosset de Guines,* who, besides caricatures which have rendered him celebrated, has published in the Paris "Rue" and "Peuple" remarkable articles.

Gilman, Mrs. Maria. *Charles Francis Barnard.* Bach and Beethoven. B. 1871.

Gilmore, Ernest. *Mrs. Helen H. Farley.*

Gimel. *Rev. Elisha Andrews,* who contributed many articles to the Boston "Christian Watchman" under this signature.

Girard, Just. *Just Jean Étienne Roy.* Priest of Auvrigny . . . N.Y. 1875.

Girard, Kate. *Mrs. George F. Rowe.*

Girl of the Period. *Mrs. Eliza Lynn Linton.* Girl of the period. L. 1869. Also in her contributions to the "Saturday Review" (L.).

Gladiolus. *William Ewart Gladstone.*

The battle of the genii ; or, Gladiolus and Beakitorius [*i.e.,* B. Disraeli, Earl of Beaconsfield]. A story of the general election . . . L. 1880.

Glananville. *Jacques Albin Simon Collin de Plancy.* Un million d'anecdotes Suisses . . . par le Baron de Glananville. Paris, 1861.

Glasgow Unfortunate, The. *George Donald.* Autobiography of . . . 185–.

Glasse, Mrs. *Dr. John Hill.* — See "A Lady."

Gleaner. *Nathaniel Ingersoll Bowditch,* in the "Boston Transcript," 1855, to which he contributed many articles of historical interest and value.

Gleaner. *Abbé Angel Denis M'Quin,* in the London "Literary Gazette," April, 1823.

Glenarvon, Lord. *George Gordon Nöel,* 6th Lord Byron.

Lady Caroline Lamb's novel, "Glenarvon," "is a curious medley as regards plot . . . but there are, nevertheless, some good things in it. Almost all the characters are portraits, and the following may be taken as a key to the work : 'Lord Glenarvon' is *Lord Byron* ; 'Lord Avondale,' *Mr. Lamb* ; 'Lady Calantha,' *Lady Caroline* ; 'The Great Nabob,' *Lord Holland* ; 'The Princess of Madagascar,' *Lady Holland* ; 'The Duke of Myrtleove,' *the Duke of Devonshire* ; 'Sir R. and Lady Mowbray,' *Lord and Lady Melbourne* ; 'Lady Mandeville,' *Lady Oxford* ; 'Lady Margaret Buchanan,' *the Duchess of Devon* ; 'Lady Sophia,' *Lady Morpeth* ; 'Lord Trelawny,' *Lord Granville* ; 'Miss Monmouth,' *Lady Byron* : 'The yellow hyena ; or, the pale poet,' *Samuel Rogers* ; 'Hoiouskim,' *Mr. Allen* ; 'Lord Dallas,' *Mr. Ward* ; and 'Sir E. St. Clare,' *Sir W. Farquhar."* — See "Gent. Mag.," October, 1883, p. 344.

Glenmore. *Donald Shaw.* Highland legends and fugitive pieces of original poetry, with translations from the Gaelic, and *vice versa* . . . Edinb. 1859.

Glenmore, Addie. *Mrs. Alice (McClure) Griffin,* who contributed verses to various papers and magazines under the signatures of "Muni Tell" and "Addie Glenmore," which afterwards appeared in a volume entitled "Poems." Cin. 1864.

Glenn, Gertrude. *Mrs. Mary (Harris) Ware,* in the "Home Circle," Nashville, and other Southern journals, and also in "Godey's Lady's Book."

Gloan. *Thomas A. Logan.* Breechloaders . . . N.Y. 1873.

Gloucestershire County Gentleman, A. *Chandos Leigh,* Baron Leigh. Three tracts, by . . . with other works, chiefly poetical, by the same author. L. 182–.

Glover, Augustus. *Sidney de Fivas.* A *nom de théâtre.*

Glowworm, A. *John Loraine Baldwin.* A glimpse at whist . . . 1866.

Glubbins, Mrs. *Clara I. N. Robinson.* Babbleton's baby ... L. 1877.
Glyndon, Howard. *Mrs. Laura C.* (*Redden*) *Searing.* Sounds from secret chambers. B. 1873.
Gnatho. *Alexander Pope*, in a letter contributed to the "Guardian." (No. 11, March 24, 1713.)
Godfather, An Absent. *Rev. Joseph Esmond Riddle, M.A.* Letters from ... L. 1837.
Godfrey. *Sylvester C. Gould*, his signature to poetical contributions between 1860 and 1870.
Godfrey, George. *Thomas Gaspey.* History of ... written by himself ... L. 1828.
Godin, Amélie. *Amélie* (*Speyer*) *Linz.* Sturm und Frieden. 1878.
Godolphin, Mary. *Lucy Aikin.* Evenings at home in words of one syllable ... L. 1869.
Goff, Elijer. *William Dawes.* Elijer Goff's trubbles, travels, and other amoozements (L. 1872); and other humorous works.
Goggle, Mungo Coulter. *Robert Douglas Hamilton, M.D.* Dr. Shaddow, of Goslington ...
Gold Digger, A. *J. Sherer.* Adventures of ... L. 1856.
Gold-Seeker, A. *William Shaw.* Golden dreams and waking realities ; being the adventures of ... in California and the Pacific. L. 1851.
Goldie. *James Carleton Goldsmith*, in his contributions to various periodicals.
Golding, Godfrey. *Alexander Hislop.* Book of good devices. Edinb. 186–.
Goldlace. *Lieut. E. P. Banning, U.S.N.*, in his contributions to various periodicals.
Goldsmith, Christabel. *Miss Fannie N. Smith.* Peace Pelican, spinster ... N.Y. 1881.
Goldsmith, Rev. J. *Sir Richard Phillips.* Biographical class-book. 18–.
Goldsworthy, Ralph. *Joseph Tonkin Rodda.* The best mining machinery. An essay by ... Falmouth, 1873.
Good Conscience, A. *Benjamin Franklin.* The art of procuring pleasant dreams, one of the bagatelles (written about 1778).
Good Gray Poet, The. *Walt Whitman.*
Good Hand, A. *Humphrey Wanley.* The grounds and principles of the Christian religion ... 5th ed. Edinb. 1732.
Good Vicar, The. *Rev. Richard DeCourcy.* The Salopian zealot ; or, ...

in a bad mood, by John the Dipper. 1778.
Goodman, David. *David Goodman Croly.* Name under which he edited the "Modern Thinker" (N.Y. 1870–73).
Gooft, Oofty. *Gus Phillips.*
Goose, Mother. *Rebecca* (*Wildgoose Hedges*) *Howse.* 1737–1818. Known in Oxford, Eng., by that name.
Goosequill, Benjamin, and Paragraph, Peter. *James Makittrick Adair.* Anecdotes of the life, adventures, and vindication of a medical Character, metaphorically defunct ... L. 1790.
Gopher. *Jacob Pentz.*
Gordon, Sir Cosmo. *Sir Samuel Egerton Brydges.* Letters on Lord Byron. L. 1824.
Gordon, Hewes. *E. G. H. Clarke.*
Gordon, Janet. *Mrs.* (*Janet Gordon*) *Hardy* (?). The Connells of Castle Connell. L. 1868.
Gordox. *Noah W. Pike.*
Gore, Mary. *William F. G. Shanks*, in his contributions to "Harper's Magazine" (N.Y.).
Gorham, Elsie. *Mrs. Carter.* Rainy day in the nursery. B. 187–.
Gorilla, A Learned. *Richard Grant White.* The fall of man ; or, the loves of the gorillas ... N.Y. 1871.
Gosebet, Paul. *Charles James Lever.* Confessions of .. L. 184–.
Gossip, John. *E. R. Champlin.*
Gothamite. *Col. Thomas Picton.*
Gotthelf, Jeremias. *Albert Bitzius.* Le miroir des paysans. 1836.
Gouraud, Julie. *Louise d'Aulnay.* A little boy's story. Trans. ... N.Y. 1869.
Governor, A. *W. H. Burgess.* Bethlem Hospital ... L. 1819.
Governor, The. *John Wentworth.* The memorial of P. Livius, one of His Majesty's council for the province of New Hampshire : with the Governor's answer ... 1773.
Governor, The. *Henry Morford.* Shoulder straps : a novel of New York and the army in 1862. P. 1863. Also in his contributions to the "N.Y. Atlas."
Governor of White Cross Street Prison, The. *T. Burdon.* Truth v. Fiction. An answer to a pamphlet by the ... styled "The double doom of the poor debtor," by an attorney-at-law. L. 1858.
Gowrie. *W. Anderson Smith.* "Off the chain." Notes and essays from the West Highlands. L. 1868.
Gracchus. *John Thompson*, who published articles signed "Casca" and

"Gracchus," against the Federal administration in the "Petersburg (Va.) Gazette." He also, in 1798, addressed letters signed "Curtius" to Chief-Justice Marshall, which were published in a volume in 1804.

Gracchus Americanus. *John G. Wells.* The Grange: a study in the science of history . . . N.Y. 1874. Also attributed to Thomas Shepard Goodwin.

Gracchus, Caius. *François Noel Babeuf*, who, near the end of 1794, founded at Paris "Le Tribun du Peuple" . . . in which, under this signature, he developed the doctrines of communism, the abolition of property, and the equality of goods.

Graduate, A. *Rev. Dr. John McCaul.* The university question considered. Montreal, 1845.

Graduate of Dame Europa's School, A. *Rev. John Edward Field.* The ladies' school across the water; or, how came John to be neutral? . . . Edited by . . . L.

Graduate of Medicine, A. *Rev. William Dansey.* Arrian on coursing . . . L. 1831.

Graduate of Oxford, A. *George Hughes.* Emmanuel: a poem . . . L. 1817.

Graduate of Oxford, A. *John Ruskin.* Modern painters . . . L. 1844.

Graduate of '69, A. *Lyman Hotchkiss Bagg.* Four years at Yale . . . New Haven, 1871.

Graduate of a University, A. *— Russell.* A catechism of the Christian religion . . . Oxf. 1828.

Graduate of the University of Oxford, A. *Mr. Townsend.* The dawn of freedom: a political satire . . . L. 1832.

Graduate of Yale of the Class of 1821. *Rev. John Mitchell.* Reminiscences of characters and scenes in college . . . New Haven, 1847.

Græculus. *Anthony Barclay, Esq.* For his own amusement, and to amuse and mystify a few of his friends, Mr. Barclay wrote under this signature a Greek version of Richard Henry Wilde's "My Life is like the Summer Rose; or, the Lament of the Captive," with a Latin translation, and ascribed the Greek to Alcæus. It found its way into print in the "North American Magazine," P. 1834, was decided by Greek scholars to be good Greek, and for a time seemed to show that Mr. Wilde had been guilty of gross plagiarism.

Graham, Grace. *Mrs. S. B. Titterington.* Mabel Livingstone; or, Christward led. B. 1872.

Graham, Rosa. *Sarah L. Post*, in the "New York Independent."

Grahame, Allen. *George Arnold.* As a writer of comic verse and humorous sketches, he had many pen-names, — "McArone," "Allen Grahame," "George Garrulous," etc.

Grahame, Nellie. *Mrs. A. K. Dunning.* First glass of wine. B. 1876.

Graindorge, Frédéric Thomas. *Hippolyte Adolphe Taine.* Notes on Paris; life and opinions of M. F. T. G. Trans. . . . N.Y. 1876.

Grandfather, A. *Sergius St. John.* First impressions; or, tales of . . . 18–.

Grandmother, A. *Mrs. C. J. Hambro.* Edda; or, the tales of a grandmother. L. 1847.

Grand-Nephew of Napoleon the Great, A. *William Charles Bonaparte Wyse.* In memoriam of the Prince Imperial of France. Four sonnets by . . . L. 1879.

Grandson of R. Aiken, The. *Peter Freeland Aiken.* Memorials of Robert Burns and some of his contemporaries and their descendants. By . . . L. 1876.

Grandville, J. J. *Jean Ignace Isidore Gérard.* Les fleures animées. Paris, 185–.

Granella, Victor. *Wilhelm Tangermann.* Herz und Welt [Dichtungen]. 1876.

Grangé. *Eugène Pierre Basté.* Le fils du portier. Paris, 1837.

Grant, Allan. *William Wilson*, for twenty years a contributor of poems to the periodicals under the *nom de plume* of "Allan Grant" and "Alpin."

Grant, Allan. *James Grant Wilson.* Mr. Secretary Pepys, with extracts from his diary . . . N.Y. 1867, etc.

Grant, Gerald. *Gertrude Grant.* The Old Cross Quarry. 1883.

Gratianus, Aurelius. *John M. Neale.* The exiles of Cebenna . . . 18–.

Graue Author of Middle and Unparty Principles, A. *John Humfrey.* Free thoughts continu'd upon several points . . . L. 1712.

Graves, Helen Forest. *Miss Lucy A. Randall.*

Gravière, Caroline. *Mme. Estelle Marie Louise (Crèveccœur) Ruelens*, who wrote for the "Étoile Belge" and the "Revue de Belgique" under this pseudonym.

Graviora Manent. *James R. Manley, M.D.* Letters on the College of Physicians and Surgeons. N.Y. 1841.

Gray, Barry. *Robert Barry Coffin.* Cakes and ale at Woodbiney from Twelfth Night to New Year's Day. N.Y. 1868.

Gray, Barton. *George H. Sass*, in the "New York Independent."

Gray, Ellis. *Mrs. Louisa T. Cragin.* Long ago: a year of child life ... B. 1878.

Gray, Iron. *Abel C. Thomas.* The gospel of slavery. A primer of freedom ... N.Y. 1864.

Gray, Robertson. *Rossiter Worthington Raymond.* Brave hearts: a novel. N.Y. 1873.

Gray, Simon. *Sir Alexander Boswell, Bart.* Edinburgh; or, the ancient Royalty ... Edinb. 1810.

Gray, Widett. *Dewitt Grinnell Ray.*

Gray Eagle. *Frederick J. Englehardt,* in his contributions to the "Turf, Field, and Farm" (N.Y.).

Graybeard. *John Franklin Graff.* "G.'s" Colorado. A trip to Denver in 1881–82. N.Y. 188–.

Grayson, Eldred, Esq. *Robert Hare.* Standish the Puritan: a tale of the American revolution ... N.Y. 1850.

Great Cham of Literature, The. *Dr. Samuel Johnson.*

Great Magician, The. *Sir Walter Scott.*

Great Man, The. *William Pitt.* An address to the Great Man ... L. 1758.

Great Moralist, The. *Dr. Samuel Johnson.*

Great Unknown, The. *Sir Walter Scott.*

Green, Invisible, Esq. *William G. Crippen.* Green peas, picked from the patch of ... Cin. 1856.

Green, John. *George H. Townsend.* Evans's music and supper rooms ... L. 1866.

Green, Paddy. *George H. Townsend.* Glees and madrigals. L. 18–.

Greendrake, Gregory, Esq. *Joseph Coad.* The angling excursions of ... in the counties of Wicklow, Meath, Westmeath, Longford, and Cavan. With additions by Geoffrey Greydrake, Esq. [*i.e.*, Thomas Ettingsall]. Dublin, 1832.

Greene, Gooseberry. *Miss J. Collins,* of Mt. Liberty, O., in her contributions, to various periodicals, on household economy, etc.

Greene, Hiram. *William A. Wilkins.*

Greenhorn, Joseph. *John T. Bedford,* member of the corporation of the city of London, in his contributions to "Punch" (L.)

Greenough, A. J. *Jane G. Avery.* The boys and girls of Beech Hill. B. 1871.

Greenwood, Grace. *Mrs. Sara Jane (Clarke) Lippincott.* Greenwood leaves:

a collection of sketches and letters. N.Y. 1849.

Gregg, George Gregory. *Robert W. McAlpine,* in his contributions to various Southern papers.

Greif, Martin. *Friedrich Hermann Frey.* Deutsche Gedenkblätter. 1875.

Gresham, Mr. *William Ewart Gladstone,* in Trollope's "The Prime Minister."

Greville, or **Greville, H.** *John Hawkesworth.* "In 1746, he wrote in that publication [the "Gent. Mag."], under the name of "Greville" [or "H. Greville"] "The Devil painter: a tale"; etc. In 1747, he contributed "The accident"; etc. In 1748, "The midsummer wish"; etc. In 1749, "Poverty insulted"; etc.

Gréville, Henri. *Alice Marie Céleste Henry Durand.* Louis Breuil. Paris, 1883; also as a contributor to the "Revue des Deux Mondes," etc.

Grey, Fannie. *Mrs. E. D. Huntley.*

Grey, Heraclitus. *Charles Marshall.* Playing trades. N.Y. 1879.

Greybeard, Gaffer. *Robert Sanders.* Lucubrations of ... L. 1773.

Greydrake, Geoffrey, Esq. *Thomas Ettingsall.* — See "Greendrake, Gregory, Esq."

Greye, Armar. *Mrs. Maria Greer.* Kimbolton Castle and Lady Jane Grey ... L. 1871.

Greylock, Godfrey. *Joseph Edward Adams Smith.* Taghconic; or, letters and legends about our summer home. B. 1852.

Greyson, R. E. H. *Henry Rogers.* Selections from the correspondence of ... L. 1857.

Grievous, Peter, Esq., A.B.C.D.E. *Francis Hopkinson, Esq.* A pretty story. Written in the year of our Lord 1774 ... P. 1774.

Griffin, Gregory. *George Canning, John Smith, Robert Smith,* and *John Frere.* The Microcosm: a periodical, by G. G., of the College of Eton. Windsor, 1809.

Griffinhoof, Anthony, Gent. *John Humphreys Parry.* The maskers of Moorfields: a vision. By the late Anthony Griffinhoof, Gent., edited by W. Griffinhoof. L. 1815.

The author and editor are the same person. The work is also attributed to George Colman, the Younger.

Griffinhoof, Arthur. *George Colman,* the Younger. Songs ... in the "Gay Deceivers" ... Turnham Green, 1804.

Griffinhoof, W. — See "Anthony Griffinhoof, Gent."

Grildrig, Solomon. *Dr. Thomas Rennell, Mr. Knight, the Rt. Hon. George Canning, and the sons of the Marquis of Wellesley,* as editors of and contributors to the "Miniature." Windsor, 1805.

The word "Grildrig" is taken from Gulliver's "Voyage to Brobdingnag." "Stratford Canning (now Lord Stratford de Redcliffe) was the working editor." The magazine was pecuniarily a failure, but its owners were relieved... through the purchase of the unsold copies by Mr. John Murray. This circumstance is said... to have introduced that publisher to George Canning... With Canning's [George] assistance, Murray took a fresh start in business, and by the aid of Canning's friends, many of whom were writers in the "Miniature," he was enabled to set on foot the "Quarterly Review."—W. P. COURTNEY. See "Notes and Queries," 5th Ser., IX., Feb. 16, '78.

Grile, Dod. — *Bierce, M.A.* Cobwebs from an empty skull. L. 1873.

Grimbosh, Herman. *Dr. Charles Mackay.* The Whirligig papers. L. 185-.

Grimes, Old. *Albert Gorton Greene.* The author of the lines "Old Grimes is dead, that good old man."

Grimes, Jeremiah, Jun., Gent. *Edward Holyoke Hedge,* a member of the "Polyglot Club," composed of the nine editors of the "Harvard (Univ.) Register," 1827–28.

Grimm. *Louis Amédée Eugène Achard.* Lettres parisiennes de...in "L'Epoque" 1846–47. Paris.

Grimm, Thomas. *Marie Henri Amédée Escoffier and others,* in "Le Petit Journal." Paris, 1873–80 et seq.

Grin. *Leo C. Evans,* in his contributions to the "Metropolis."

Grinagain, Giles. *William Hogarth.*

Grinder. *Harry H. Marks,* in the New York "Sunday Times."

Grinder, Miss Charity. *Mary Kyle Dallas.* The Grinder papers. Being the adventures of... N.Y. 1877.

Gringo, Harry. *Henry Augustus Wise.* Tales for the marines... B. 1855.

Grins and Gripes. *Ebenezer Bailey,* who wrote the articles under this head for the "New England Galaxy" (B.).

Grip. *J. D. Bengough,* of Toronto (Can.), in his contributions to various periodicals.

Gronovius. *Charles Valentine Le Grice, M.A.* General theorem for a ****** college declamation (in verse), with copious notes. By... Camb.

Grotius. *De Witt Clinton.* Vindication of Thomas Jefferson... N.Y. 1800.

Growler, The. *Spencer Wallace Coon.*

Grumbler, Anthony, Esq., of Grumbleton Hall. *David Hoffman.* Miscellaneous thoughts on men, manners, and things... P. 1837.

Grün, Anastasius. *Anton Alexander, Graf von Auersperg.* Gesammelte Werke. 1877.

Grundy, Miss. *Miss M. A. Sneed,* in her contributions to the "Post" (Wash. D.C.).

Guardian, A Retired. *William Bradley.* Sketches of the poor.

Guare, June. *Mrs. Harriet Adelia Ann (Burleigh) Cole.*

Guatimozin. *Frederick Jebb and others.* Guatimozin's letters on the present state of Ireland... L. 1779.

Guest, A. *Edward Jenkins.* The blot on the Queen's head... L. 1876.

Guildhelm. *William A. Brewer,* in his contributions to the "Shrine." Amherst, Mass., 1832.

Gulliver, Lemuel. *John Arbuthnot.* An account of the state of learning in the empire of Lilliput; together with the history and character of Bullum [i.e., Richard Bentley], the Emperor's library keeper... L. 1728.

Gulliver, Captain Lemuel. *Jonathan Swift.* Travels into several remote nations of the world. By... L. 1728.

Gum Leaf. *Mrs. Dexter.* Colonial gems; or, "The Ninety" foundation stones of our Parliament Houses... Melbourne, 1860.

Gurth. *G. Gilbert,* in several works on domestic animals.

Guseck, Bernd von. *Karl Gustav von Berneck.* Deutschland's Ehre. Leipsic, 1837.

Gushington, Angelina. *C. W. R. Cooke.* Thoughts on men and things... L. 1867.

Gushington, The Hon. Impulsia. *Helen Selina (Sheridan),* Baroness Dufferin, afterwards Countess of Gifford. Lispings from low latitudes... L. 1863.

Gussie. *Augusta Chambers.*

Gypsy. *Mrs. Grace Courtland.* A marked life; or, the autobiography of a clairvoyant... L. 1879.

H.

H. *E. Chibborn,* in his contributions on antiquarian subjects to "Saunders' News Letter" (Dublin, 1849–50).

H. *Mr. Hamel,* in his contributions, on musical subjects, to the "Reform" (Hamburg).

H. *Rev. Henry* (or *John) Heaton,* in his contributions to the "Athenian Letters" (L. 1741–43).

H. *Charles Grahame Halpine.* Lyrics by the letter H. N.Y. 1854.

H. *Rowland Gibson Hazard.* Our resources. N.Y. 1864.

H. *Luke Howard.* "Swear not at all" (Matt. **v.** 24). L. n.d.

H. *Henry Hutchinson.* An answer to observations (by "G. P." *i.e.,* G. Peacock) on the plans for the new library (at Cambridge); being a defence of the design presented by Messrs. Rickman (Thomas) and Hutchinson. By "H." Birmingham, 1831.

H., A. *Abraham Hayward.* Faust: a dramatic poem, by Goethe. Trans. by ... L. 1833.

H., A. B. *A. B. Hassan.* Contributions to the rhymes of the war. Balt. 1865.

H., A. C. *A. C. Haeselbairth,* in the New York "Mail."

H., A. H. *Anna Holyoke (Cutts) Howard,* in her contributions to various periodicals.

H., A. J. *Andrew Jackson Hamilton.* Federal Monthly. A party of the future. 186–.

H., A. S. *Arthur Sherburne Hardy.* Francesca of Rimini. P. 1878.

HB. *John Doyle,* a gentleman of Irish descent, and the reputed author of the celebrated "HB." sketches.

H. B. *Bishop James Doyle.* Political sketches of ... L. 1829–43.

H., B. F. *B. F. Hartshorne.* The Danes: a prize poem. 1864.

H., B. R. *Benjamin Robert Haydon.* Description of the drawings from the cartoons and Elgin marbles, by Mr. Haydon's pupils ... L. 1819.

H. B. T. *James Deacon Hume.* Letters on the corn laws, etc. ... L. 1835.

H., C. *Catherine Hughes.* The history of the township of Meltham ... By the late Joseph Hughes. Edited ... by ... Huddersfield, 1866.

H., C. *Chambers Hall.* The picture: a nosegay for amateurs, painters, etc. ... by ... L. 1837.

H. C., Esq. *Samuel William Henry Ireland.* The fisher boy: a poem ... L. 1808.

H., C. E. *Mrs. Caroline E. (I'Ans) Hawker.* Follow me; or, lost and found. A morality, from the German. By ... L. 1844.

H., C. F. *Cecil Frederick Holmes.* A vocabulary to Bland's Latin Hexameters and Pentameters ... L. 1863.

H., C. G. *Charles G. Hamilton.* The exiles of Italy. L. 1857.

H., C. M. *Miss C. M. Hewins,* librarian of the Hartford Library Association, in her letters to the "Literary News" (N.Y.).

H., C. W. *Chandos Wren Hoskyns.* Talpa; or, the chronicles of a clay farm ... L. 1852.

H. D. B. *William Hamper, Esq., F.S.A.*

"His earlier productions were poetical pieces, which were generally communicated to the pages of this ('Gent. Mag.') miscellany. The first of these we believe to have been the lines entitled 'The Beggar Boy,' in our number for September, 1798. In the following number is a more lively and spirited production, an anti-revolutionary song, beginning, 'To learn Johnny Bull *à la mode de Paris';* and, as a clever piece written with the same loyal and constitutional feelings, may be mentioned a ' Pindaric Address,' in January, 1801. These and many others are signed ' H. D. B.,'— the initials of Hamper, Deritend, Birmingham. He also uses the signature 'M.R.' (the final letters of his name) in ' Gent. Mag.,' March, 1811, September, 1816, and April, 1817."

H., E. *Sir Everard Home, Bart.,* in Beloe's "Sexagenarian," Vol. I., p. 320, 2d ed. L. 1818.

H., E. *Rev. Edward Hawarden.* An answer to Dr. Clark and Mr. Whiston concerning the Divinity of the Son and of the Holy Spirit ... L. 1729.

H., E. *Edward Hincks, D.D.* The Enchorial language of Egypt. Dublin, 1833.

H., E. *Ebenezer Henderson, D.D.* The geysers ... as seen in the years 1814 and 1815 ... Edinb. 1818.

H., E. *Emily Huntington.* Little lessons for little housekeepers. N.Y. 1875.

H., E. A. *Ethan Allen Hitchcock.* Remarks on the sonnets of Shakespeare; with the sonnets. By ... N.Y. 1865.

H., E. D. *Edward Dykes Hayward.* Reasons against martial law, courts martial, etc. L. 1866.

H., E. F. S. *Miss E. F. S. Harris.* Via dolorosa ... L. 1848.

H., E. L. *Edward Law Hussey.* Extracts from various authors, and fragments of table talk . . . Oxf. 1873.

H., E. M. *Emily Marion Harris.* Four messengers . . . L. 1870.

H., E. M. *Ellen Marvin Heaton.* The Octagon Club: a character study. N.Y. 1880.

H. E. O. *Thomas George Fonnereau.* Diary of a dutiful son. L. 1849.

H., F. *Mrs. F. (Howe) Hall,* in humorous sketches, etc., contributed to various periodicals.

H., F. *F. Hutchinson.* A compassionate address to those Papists who will be prevail'd with to examine the cause for which they suffer . . . L. 1716.

H., F. D. *Rt. Rev. Frederic Dan Huntington.* Helps to a holy Lent . . . N.Y. 1872.

H., F. E. *Fitzedward Hall.* M. de Tassy's history of Hindi literature. From the "Benares Magazine" for February, 1851.

H., F. E. H. *F. E. H. Haines.* Jonas King: missionary to Syria and Greece. N.Y. 1879.

H., F. L. *Florence Leslie Henderson.* Sketches in verse. By F. L. H. Truro, 1878.

H., F. S. *F. S. Hill.* The harvest festival. B. 1826.

H., F. W. *F. W. Halfpenny.* Catalogue of books on foreign law . . . L. 1849.

H., G. *George Hall.* An excursion from Jericho to the ruins of the ancient cities of Geraza and Amman, in the country east of the River Jordan. By . . . L. 1852.

H., G. *Gavin Hamilton.* Gray's elegy translated into Latin elegiacs . . . Edinb. 1877.

H. H. *Mrs. Helen Maria (Fiske Hunt) Jackson.* A century of dishonour; a sketch of the United States' government's dealings with some of the Indian tribes, etc. N.Y. 1881.

H., H. *Herbert Haines.* A manual for the study of monumental brasses . . . Oxf. 1848.

H., Sir H., Bart. *Sir Henry Halford.* Nugæ metricæ . . . 1839.

H., Hd. *Howard Hinton.* My comrades. N.Y. 1874.

H., H. L. *H. L. Henry.* Little Ada; or, the three new years. P. 1871.

H., H. N. *Henry Noel Humphreys.* The coins of England. L. 1846.

H., H. S. *Henry Scrine Hill.* Princetown, its history and its prison. By H. S. H. Plymouth, 1869.

H., I. *John Hewitt.* Description of the figures in the chart of ancient armour. L. 1847.

H., I. J. *Rev. James John Holroyd.* Gisela: a tragedy . . . L. 1839.

H., J. *John Humfrey.* — See "A lover of Peace and the Publick Good."

H., J. *James Handley.* — See "One of her Majesty's Surgeons."

H., J. *James Horsburgh.* — See "An Old Inhabitant."

H., J. *Rev. Joseph Hunter.* Antiquarian notices of Lupset, the Heath, and Sharlston, in the county of York. By . . . L. 1848.

H., J. *Joseph Hambleton.* Appendix to a letter . . . containing the replies of Mrs. C. and her family to "their friend" J. H. L. 1850.

H., J. *John Hawkins.* Essay on honesty, in "Gent. Mag.," 1739, pp. 117, 232.

H., J. *Joseph Highmore.* Essays, moral, religious, and miscellaneous . . . L. 1766.

H., J. *John Hutchinson.* Glory or gravity essential and mechanical . . . L. 1733.

H., J. *James Hogg.* Hints on the culture of character . . . Edited by . . . Edinb. 1855–56.

H., J. *John Hughes.* Lays of past days . . . L. 1850.

H., J. *J. Hayden.* A letter on family worship . . . L. 1853.

H., J. *John Harrison.* Letter on "Hai Ebn Yokdan," by J. H. Manchester, 1835.

H., J. *John Hallet.* The life of the Rev. Mr. Geo. Trosse . . . Exon, 1714.

H., Mrs. J. *Mrs. John Hunter,* in Beloe's "Sexagenarian," I., 415, 2d ed. L. 1818.

H., J. E. *John Eliot Hodgkin.* Fifty pen-and-ink sketches in exact facsimile by . . . from a copy of Polydore Vergil's "History of England . . . L. 1860.

H., J. O. *James Orchard Halliwell-Phillipps.* A newel which may turn out to be anything but a jewel. L. 1865. Also in his contributions to the "Athenæum" and other periodicals.

H., J. R. *James Ridgway Hakewell and another.* Athletica . . . Maidstone, 1871.

H., J. R. G. *John R. G. Hassard,* in his contributions to the "Tribune" (N.Y.).

H., J. T. *Rev. Joel Tyler Headley.* — See "Seatsfield."

H., L. *Miss Lucy Hooper.* "Most of her poems were contributed to the 'Long Island Star,' where they appeared under her initials."

H., L. C. *Laura Carter Holloway*, in her contributions to various periodicals.

H., L. C. *L. C. Hill*. Laure: the history of a blighted life. P. 1872.

H. M. *W. H. Logan.*— See "A Gentleman in Town."

H., M. *Murat Halstead*, in his letters to the "Cincinnati Commercial."

H., M. *Mrs. M. Hullah*. A few words about music ... L. 1851.

H., M. *Matilda Horsburgh*. Henry Morgan; or, the sower and the seed ... Edinb. 1863.

H., M. *Maria Hack*. A popular account of St. Paul's cathedral, etc. By :.. L. 1816.

H., M. H. *Mayo H. Haseltine*, in the "New York Sun."

H. M'K. *Rev. H. M. Mackenzie*. The lay of the Turings. L. 1849.

H., M. R. *Mrs. Mary R. Higham*. Athol. N.Y. 1873.

H., M. W. *M. W. Hazeltine*, in his criticisms in the "Sun" (N.Y.).

H., N. *N. Herrick*. History of the five wise philosophers ... L. 1711.

H., N. *Nathaniel Holmes*. "The Shakespearean myth" ... by ... In the St. Louis "Globe Democrat," November 17, 1881.

H. N. *Miss Griggs*. Songs for the Sorrowing ... N.Y. 1861.

H., P., M.D. *Paul Hiffernan, M.D.* Remarks on an ode on the death of his royal highness, Frederick, Prince of Wales. L. 1752.

H., R. *Robert Hobson*. The guide to Dovedale, Ilam, and scenes adjacent. By ... Ashbourn, 1841.

H., R. *Rev. Richard Harvey*. Hymns for young persons. L. 1834.

H., R. *Robert Hawker*. The plant of renown ... L. 1805.

H., R., Esq., near forty years a Practitioner in this Art. *Robert Howlett*. The angler's sure guide; or, angling improved, and methodically digested ... L. 1706.

H., R. C. *Sir Richard Colt Hoare, Bart.* Hints to travellers in Italy. By ... L. 1815.

"Among his communications to the 'Gent. Mag.' were, February, 1823, p. 113, an account of a Roman bath found at Farley; in August, 1827, p. 113, an account of a Roman villa at Littleton, Somerset; and in January, 1830, p. 17, an account of a Roman villa at Pitney, Somerset."

H., R. S. *Rev. Robert Stephen Hawker, M.A.* Mawgan of Melluach, the Cornish wrecker. Verses signed ... With a woodcut. "Once a Week," viii., 601–602. 1862–63.

H., R. S. *Robert S. Hunt.* Musings on Psalm cxix. Oxf. 1878.

H., R. S. *Robert S. Howland*. The pastoral relation. From the "Church Journal" (N.Y. 1856).

H., S. *Sophia Hume*. A caution to such as observe days and times ... By ... L. 1754.

H. S. *Ralph Thomas*. Going to the bar. Contributed to "Cobbett's Magazine," 1832.

H., S. *Spencer Hall*. Suggestions for the classification of the library now collecting at the Athenæum [club]. L. 1858.

H., S. J., Esquire. *St. John Honeywood, Esq.* Poem on reading President Washington's address declining a re-election to the presidency ... Albany, 1796.

H., T. *Thornton Hunt*, in Lamb's "Elia." Witches and other night-fears.

H., T. *Thomas Hewerdine*. The country-curate to the country-people ... L. 1701.

H., T. *Captain Thomas Hamilton*. Men and manners in America. Edinb. 1833.

H., T., Pharmacop. Rustican. *T. Hickes*. A compleat treatise of urines ... L. 1703.

H., T. B., R.A. *T. B. Hogarth, R.A.* The griffinage of the Hon. Newman Strange ... L. 1862.

H., T. R. *T. R. Higham*. A dialogue between Tim Thomas and Bill Bilkey, two Cornish miners ... Truro, 1866.

H., T. S. *Thulia Susannah Henderson*. Olga; or, Russia in the 10th century. L. 1855.

H., W. *William Hazlitt*, in Lamb's "Elia." Some sonnets of Sir Philip Sidney.

H., W. *William Horsnell*. The ice-bound ship and the dream ... Montreal, 1860.

H., W., Gent. *William Hunt*. The fall of Tarquin: a tragedy. York, 1713.

H., W., Junr. *William Hodgson*. The life and travels of John Pemberton ... L. 1844.

H., W. B. *William Beadon Heathcote, B.C.L.* The Psalter ... Oxf. 1845.

H., W. E. *Rev. William Edward Heygate*. The death of King Gerennius. Truro, 1848.

H., W. H. *William Henry Herbert*, in the New York "World."

H., W H. *William Henry Harvey, M.D.* Charles and Josiah; or, friendly conversations between a Churchman and a Quaker. L. 1862.

H., W. H. H. *W. H. H. Haseltine,* in the New York "Sun."

H., W. M. *Rev. Wyndham Madden Hutton.* Poems. By a member of the university of Oxford. Oxf. 1851.

H., W. R. *W. R. Hawkes.* The midnight intruder; or, Old Nick at C—lt—n H—se. A poem . . . L. 1816.

H. X. *Mrs. Brewster Macpherson.* "Gifts for men." Edinb. 1870.

H**, the Right Honourable Lady.** *Lady Annabella Eliza Cassandra Hawke.* Julia de Gramont . . . L. 1788.

H***, Mr.** *Jonas Hanway.* A journal of eight days' journey from Portsmouth to Kingston upon Thames, through Southampton, Wiltshire . . . By . . . L. 1756.

H . . . ., J . . . ., C.A.D.S. *J. Hornihold.* The grounds of the Christian's belief . . . Birmingham, 1771.

H——, M——. *Mrs. Mary Hays,* in Beloe's "Sexagenarian" I., 360. 2d ed. L. 1818.

H—k, Rt. Hon. P—p, E—l of. *Rt. Hon. Philip, Earl of Hardwick.* The humble petition of the Freethinkers to the . . . Lord High Chancellor of Great Britain . . . L. 1756.

Habitual Criminal, An. *Charles John Darling.* The criminal code bill . . . L. 1878.

Hacendado, Un. *Cristobal Madan.* Llamamiento de la Isla de Cuba a la Nacion Española . . . N.Y. 1854.

Hackle, Palmer, Esq. *Robert Blakey.* Hints on angling. L. 1846.

Hadermann, Jeanette R. *Mrs. Walworth.* Nobody's business. N.Y. 1878.

Hadgi Abd-el Hamid Bey. *Louis Du Couret.* L'Arabie heureuse. Souvenirs de voyages en Afrique et en Asie. Paris, 1860.

Hafiz. *Robert Stott,* who, under this signature, was inflicting the highest flown of odes upon the readers of the "Morning Post," and of whom Byron has said, "What would be the sentiments of the Persian Anacreon, Hafiz, could he rise from his splendid sepulchre at Sheeraz . . . and behold his name assumed by one Stott of Dromore."

Hail-fair, Lord. *Enos Cobb* (?). Fame and fancy; or, Voltaire improved . . . By . . . B. 1826.

Haines, Henry Harrison. *Harry Enton.*

Hairbrain, Timothy. *James Anderson.* In 1790 he commenced the publication of the "Bee" (1790–94), consisting of essays, philosophical and miscellaneous. *Dr. Anderson* wrote those marked

"Senex," "Timothy Hairbrain," "Alcibiades," and many others without signature.

Halcro, Claud. *John Breakenridge,* in his contributions to various Canadian periodicals (1843).

Halcyon. *Miss Maud Howe,* in her letters to Boston journals from New Orleans, La.

Haldane, Harry. *R. O. Heslop.* Geordy's last; Newcastle Folk-speech . . . Newcastle, 187–.

Halein, Tina. *Kathinka (Halein) Zitz.*

Half-Pay Officer, A. *Henry Robert Addison.* "All at sea"; or, recollections of . . . L. 1864.

Hall, Elfin. *Mrs. E. C. Perry.* 'Tween thou and me. 1879.

Hall, Motte. *Miss Essie B. Cheesborough,* who commenced her literary career at an early age, writing under the *noms de plume* of "Motte Hall," "Elma South," "Ide Delmar," and her own initials, "E. B. C."

Haller, Gustave. *Mme. Wilhelmine Joséphine (Simonin) Pould.* Renee and Franz. N.Y. 1878.

Haller, Joseph. *Henry Nelson Coleridge.* In Knight's "Quarterly Magazine." L. 1823–24.

Halliday, Andrew. *Andrew Halliday Duff.* The adventures of Mr. Wilderspin on his journey through life. L. 1860.

Hallowell, Florence B. *Miss Florence B. Getchell,* in her contributions to various periodicals.

Halm, Friedrich. *Eligius Franz Josef,* Freiherr von Münch-Bellinghausen. Der Sohn der Wildnis. Vienna, 1842.

Halter-maker, A. *Joseph Reed.* A rope's end for hempen monopolists . . . By . . . L. 1786.

Hamden. *Isaac Orr,* who published many papers in the New York "Commercial Advertiser," the "Boston Courier," etc.

Hamet the Moor. *Mr. Fielding,* a son of Henry Fielding. Heroick epistle . . . to the emperor of Morocco . . . L. 1780.

Hamilton. *Mathew Carey.* The Boston report and mercantile memorials. P. 1828.

Hamilton. *George Henry Whitman.* Essay on a congress of nations. B. 1840.

Hamilton. *William Hamilton, Esq.* A soliloquy. In imitation of Hamlet . . . By . . . L. 1794.

Hamilton. *W. R. Watson, Esq.* (?). The Whig party; its objects, its principles, its candidates, its duties, and its prospects. An address to the people of Rhode Island . . . Providence, 1844.

Hamilton, Gail. *Miss Mary Abigail Dodge.* Gala days. B. 1863.

Hamilton, John. *John Hamilton Reynolds.* The garden of Florence; and other poems . . . L. 1821.

Hamilton, May. *Miss Julia Tilt.* May Hamilton: an autobiography. L. 1857.

Hamlin, P., Tinman. *John Wolcot.* The horrors of bribery. Edited [or rather written] by P. Pindar. L. 1802.

Hampden. *Ebenezer Smith Thomas,* in the Charleston (S.C.) "City Gazette," 1810–14.

Hampden. *Noah Webster.* Article in the "Hampshire Gazette."

Hampden. *John B. Jervis.* Letters addressed to the friends of freedom and the Union . . . N.Y. 1856.

Hampden. *Thomas Lister, LL.D.* A mirror for princes . . . 1797.

Hampden. *Charles Hammond.* Reviews of the opinion of the Supreme Court of the United States . . . Steubenville, 1821.

Hampden, John. *Lord George Nugent Temple Grenville.* True and faithful relation of a worthy discourse between Colonel John Hampden and Colonel Oliver Cromwell. L. about 1830.

Hampshire Fisherman, A. *Richard Clarke Sewell, Esq., D.C.L.,* "a contributor to periodical literature, the papers of 'A Hampshire Fisherman,' in the 'Field' newspaper being by him."

Hamst, Olphar. *Ralph Thomas.* Aggravating ladies. L. 1880.

Hancock. *Franklin Dexter.* A letter to the Hon. Samuel A. Eliot . . . B. 1851.

Handloom Weaver, A. *William Thom.* Rhymes and recollections of . . . L. 1844.

Hannibal. *George Joseph L. W. Silliman.*

Hannibal, Julius Cæsar. *William H. Lewison.* Scientific discourses. N.Y. 1852.

Hanoum, Leila. *Mme. Piazzi.* Un drame à Constantinople. 188–.

Hanoverian, An. *Rev. Augustus Montague Toplady.* An old fox tarred and feather'd. Occasioned by what is called Mr. John Wesley's calm address to our American colonys . . . By . . . L. 1775.

Hanson. *John Hanson Beadle,* as correspondent of the "Cincinnati Gazette."

Haöle, A. *G. W. Bates.* Sandwich Island notes. 1854.

Happy, John. *J. P. Roberts.*

Harcourt, Vernon. *Thomas D. Suplée,* of Gambier (O.), in his contributions to various periodicals.

Hardcastle, Daniel. *Richard Page.*

Letter . . . on . . . the bank of England . . . L. 1826.

Hardcastle, Ephraim. *William Henry Pyne.* Wine and walnuts; or, after-dinner chit-chat. L. 1823.

Hardlines, Sir Gregory. *Sir Charles Trevelyan,* in Trollope's "The three clerks."

Hardy, John, Mariner. *Isaac Israel Hayes.*

Hardy, Uncle. *William Senior.* Notable shipwrecks. L. 18–.

Hare, John. *John Fairs.* A *nom de théâtre.*

Hargrave, Jasper. *George Hardinge.* — See "Owen, Junior."

Hari Kari. *Elias F. Carr.*

Harkaway. *Charles Marshall.* Sporting notes. L. 18–.

Harkaway, Jack. *Bracebridge Hemynge,* in numerous tales for juveniles.

Harland, Marion. *Mrs. Mary Virginia (Hawes) Terhune.* Alone, 1854; The hidden path, 1855.

Mrs. Tardy gives the *pseud.* as "Marian Harland."

Harold. *George Gordon Noël,* 6th Lord Byron. Lines to . . . [*i.e.,* author of "Childe Harold"], etc. 1841.

Haroun Alraschid. *Thomas Carlisle,* joint author. The unprofessional vagabond, with sketches from the life, by John Carlisle. L. 1873.

Harriet. *Miss Harriet White.* Verses, sacred and miscellaneous. 1853.

Harriet Annie. *Miss Harriet Annie Wilkins,* a Canadian poet, better known by her Christian names, they being generally appended to her contributions to the press. Author of the "Holly Branch," 1851, and the "Acacia," 1860. Hamilton, Can.

Harrington, The Earl of. *Rt. Hon. Leicester Fitzgerald Charles Stanhope.* The E. of H. on the Maine law . . . Derby, 1858.

Harrington, George F. *Rev. William M. Baker.* Inside: a chronicle of secession. N.Y. 1866.

Harrington, Ralph. *Ralph Thomas.* A few words on swimming . . . L. 1861.

Harris, Maria. *Maria Elizabeth Glossop.* A *nom de théâtre.*

Harro. *Paul Harring.* Dolores: a historical novel of South America . . . N.Y. 1847.

Harrovian, An Old. *Douglas Straight.* — See "Daryl, Sidney."

Harrow Tutor, A. *Cecil Frederick Holmes.* A vocabulary to Bland's "Latin Hexameters and Pentameters." L. 1863.

Harry, Uncle. *John Habberton.* Helen's babies ... By their latest victim ... Glasgow, 1877.

Hart, Gerald. *Thomas J. Irving.* In the rapids: a romance. P. 187–.

Hart, Senator Bob. *Rev. J. M. Sutherland,* once an American negro minstrel; in 1883 a revival preacher in Boston and elsewhere.

Harte, Bret. *Francis Bret Harte,* the celebrated novelist.

Hartwell, Mary. *Mrs. Mary Hartwell Catherwood.* A woman in armor. N.Y. 1875.

Harvard, Senior. *Henry Dana Ward.* The Bible: its testimony and its promises ... P. 1867.

Harwood, John. *Charles Miner,* in the "Village Record," West Chester, Pa., author of the "History of Wyoming." P. 1845.

Haselfoot, Edward. *William Sidney Walker,* in Knight's "Quarterly Magazine" (?).

Hastatus. *John Thomas Barber Beaumont, Esq.* Arcanum (The) of national defence. L. 1808.

Hatfield, S. E. *Mrs. Sibella Elizabeth (Hatfield) Miles.* The wanderer of Scandinavia; or, Sweden delivered, in five cantos; and other poems. L. 1826.

Hathaway, Anne. *Mrs. W. A. Ingham,* in her contributions to the "Herald" (Cleveland, O.).

Hattie, Aunt. *Mrs. Harriet Newell (Woods) Baker.* Art and artlessness. B. 1868.

Hautboy. *John Harper.*

Haven, Marion. *Mary P. Hazen.* Joanna; or, learning to follow Jesus. N.Y. 1871.

Havens, Cordelia. *Josephine Walcott.*

Hawkins, Tom, Esq. *Theodore William Alois Buckley.* The adventures of Sydenham Greenfinch. L. 185–.

Hawthorne, Alice. *Septimus Winner.* Hawthorne ballads. P. 1850.

Hawthorne, Emily. *Emily Thornton Charles.* Hawthorne blossoms. P. 1876.

Hawthorne, Helen. *Mrs. Helen Jane Woods,* of Montreal, in her contributions to various periodicals.

Hay, Elzey. *Fanny Andrews.* A mere adventurer. P. 1879.

Hayden, Sarah Marshall. *Mary Frazaer.* Early engagements. Cin. 1858.

Haywarde, Richard. *Frederic Swartwout Cozzens,* the writer of pleasant magazine papers under this signature.

He wrote for the "Knickerbocker Magazine" for several years, and afterwards for "Putnam's Monthly," and for his own periodical, the "Wine Press."

Hazard, Désiré. *Octave Feuillet,* who commenced his literary career in 1844 by contributing, in conjunction with MM. P. Bocage and Albert Aubert, to a romance called the "Grand Vieillard," which appeared in the "Paris National."

Hazard, Winning. *Albert De Vere.* Billiards made easy. L. 18–.

Hazel, Harry. *Justin Jones.* The flying Yankee. P. 187–.

Hazelton, Mabel. *C. H. Rand.* Aunt Matty. B. 1869.

Head, Archibald. *John M. Turner.*

Head of a Family, in Communion with the Church of Scotland, The. *Charles Cowan.* The analogy which subsists between the British constitution in its three estates of Queen, Lords, and Commons ... Edinb. 1840.

Head Master of an English Grammar School, The. *Edward Rupert Humphreys,* of the Cheltenham Grammar school. England's educational crisis ... L. 1856.

Head Master under the London School Board, A. *J. T. Amner.* Notes of lessons, and how to write them. By ... L. 1878.

Heard, I. *Mrs. J. H. Cutter,* in her contributions to various periodicals, etc.

Heartless Woman, A. *Mrs. Sue (Petigru) King.* The heart history of ... first published in the "Knickerbocker Magazine," and afterwards as "Sylvia's Lovers." N.Y. 1860.

Heath, Bushey. *William Jerdan.*

The little band of literary co-workers who seek or communicate information in the pleasant pages of "Notes and Queries" may like to be reminded that under the pseudonym of "Bushey Heath" was concealed the familiar name of *William Jerdan.* — See BATES's "Maclise Portrait Gallery," p. 3. L. 1883.

Heatherbell. *Eleanor Smith,* in "Good Words."

Hebrew Wood Chopper, The. *J. L. Stone.* Reply to Bishop Colenso's attack on the Pentateuch. By ... San Francisco, 1863.

Hedgehog, Humphrey. *John Gifford,* or rather for "Green, John Richards," who in 1788 *seq.,* supported the administration in various pamphlets and, under this pseud., féll foul of William Cobbett (*Peter Porcupine*).

Hefferman, Mr. Michael. *Samuel Ferguson.* Father Tom and the Pope; or, a night at the Vatican. As related by ... Master of the National School at

Tallymactaggart, in the county of Leitrim . . . N.Y. 1868.

This piece was first published in "Blackwood's Magazine," commencing in May, 1838.

Hegelingen, Absolutus von. *Otto Friedrich Gruppe.* Die Winde, oder: Ganz absolute Konstruktion der neuern Weltgeschichte durch Oberons Horn: gedichtet von . . . 1829.

Heilly, Georges d'. *Edmond Antoine Poinsot.* Dictionnaire des pseudonymes. Paris, 1868.

Heimburg, W. *Bertha Behrens.* Lottie of the mill. P. 1882.

Heinfetter, Herman. *Frederick Parker.* Letter . . . on Transubstantiation. L. 1848.

Heinrich, Karl. *Heinrich Keck.* Anna. Ein Idyll aus der Zeit der schleswig-holsteinischen Erhebung. 1880.

Heiter, Amalie. *Amalia,* Herzogin von Sachsen. Der Krönungstag. 1829.

Helen. *Mrs. Sarah Helen (Power) Whitman,* whose poetry appeared in annuals and periodicals under this signature.

Helene. *Countess Helene Häseler Hülsen,* who made her début as an author under this pseudonym, but in her later works uses her own name.

Helfenstein, Ernest. *Mrs. Elizabeth Oakes (Prince) Smith.* The salamander: a legend for Christmas. N.Y. 1853.

Helicon, Harry, Esq. *Joshua West.* London's glory . . . L. 1789.

Heliondé. *Sidney Whiting.*

Helios. *E. J. Muybridge.*

Heliostropolis, Secretary to the Emperor of the Moon. *Daniel Defoe.* The comical history of the life and death of Mumper, Generalissimo of King Charles the Second's dogs. L. 1704.

Hell, Theodor. *Karl Gottfried Theodor Winkler.* Notes de la lyre, Dresden, 1821; Nouvelles notes de la lyre, Brunswick, 1830.

Helmar, Eduard. *Ernst Koch.* Prinz Rosa-Stramin.

Helmina. *Wilhelmine Christine von Chézy,* who made herself known in Germany by the publication of some esteemed romances, and the composition of different librettos of operas, among others that of "Euryante," set to music by Weber.

Helvidius. *James Madison,* who, under this signature, replied to the "Letters of Pacificus" (Mr. Hamilton) in five "Essays."

Henderson, Harry. *Mrs. Harriet Elizabeth (Beecher) Stowe.* My wife and I; or, Harry Henderson's history. L. 1871.

Henderson, Marc Anthony. *Rev. George A. Strong.* The song of Milgenwatha . . . Cin. 1856.

Hengiston, J. W., Esq. *Cyrus Redding.* A Yankee steamer on the Atlantic, etc. By . . . in the "New Monthly Magazine." 1852–53.

Henricus. One of the pseudonyms attributed to Junius (*q.v.*).

The two letters thus signed are dated April 15 and May 21, 1771, and are addressed to the Earl of Suffolk.

Henry. *Richard Griffith.* — See "Frances."

Henry, Camille. *Countess Irene de la Rocca.* Une nouvelle Madeline. Paris, 1862.

Henry, Louis. *Albert Henry Lewis.* The Boston Boy. B. 1871.

Hensel, Octavia. *Hon. Mrs. Mary Alice Ives Seymour.* Life and letters of Louis Moreau Gottschalk. B. 1870.

Her Daughter. *Miss G. F. S. Daniell.* Aldershot: a record of Mrs. Daniell's work among the soldiers, and its sequel. By . . . L. 1879.

Her Daughter. *Elizabeth T. Spring.* Memorial of Eliza Butler Thompson . . . N.Y. 1879.

Her Father. *Nehemiah Adams, D.D.* Agnes, and the key of her little coffin. By . . . B. 1857.

Her Father. *Edward William Hooker, D.D.* A discourse, on the Sabbath following the funeral of Miss Elizabeth P. Hooker. By . . . Hartford, 1850.

Her Granddaughter. *Mrs. Flora Frances Wylde.* The autobiography of Flora M'Donald. Ed. by . . . L. 1870.

Her Husband. *Rev. John Keep.* Sketches of the religious life and faith of Mrs. Lydia Hale Keep of Oberlin. By . . . Oberlin, Ohio, 1866.

Her Mother. *Mrs. William Gardiner.* Brief memoir of Harriet [M. Gardiner], with some of her essays in prose and verse. By . . . Oberlin, 1855.

Her Mother. *Judith Towers Grant.* "Looking unto Jesus": a narrative of the brief race of a young disciple. L. 1854.

Her Mother. *Mrs. Joel Hawes.* Memoir of Mrs. Mary E. Van Lennep . . . Hartford, 1848.

Her Niece. *Charlotte Barrett.* Diary and letters of Madame D'Arblay. Edited by . . . L. 1842–46.

Her Sister. *Miss — Keary.* Memoir of Annie Keary. By . . . L. 1883.

Her Sister. *H. H. Lindesay.* Memorials of Charlotte Williams Wynn. Edited by . . . L. 1877.

Heraclides. *Edward Daniel Clarke.* The tomb of Alexander reviewed, in eight letters to a friend. By . . . L. 1806.

Herald Correspondent, A. *Charles O'Kelly.* The Mambi Land; or, the adventures of . . . in Cuba. L. 1874.

Herbert, Uncle. *Timothy Shay Arthur.* The budget . . . P. 1877.

Herbert, Edward. *John Hamilton Reynolds*, in the "London Magazine."

Herbert, Francis, Esq. It was under this name that *Bryant, Sands*, and *Verplanck*, in 1827–29, published the "Talisman" (N.Y.).

Herbert, T. *Rev. Herbert Todd, M.A.* Sketches by the wayside. By . . . L. 1867.

Herbert, William. A *nom de théâtre.* — *Eden*, son of Col. W. F. Eden, of the Madras army.

Hermann, Emily. *Mrs. Catharine Luders*, whose poems appeared from time to time, under this pen-name, in the magazines and the "Literary World."

Hermann, Theodor. *Theodor Hermann Pantenius.* Wilhelm Wolfschild. 1872.

Hermes. *B. Lumley.* Parliamentary practice . . . L. 1838.

Hermes. *Henry Miles, Jr.* The one hundred prize questions in Canadian history . . . 1880.

Hermine. *Mrs. Susan (Blanchard) Elder*, who, from the age of sixteen, has contributed much to the press under this signature.

Hermit. *Rev. Washington Frothingham*, in the Troy (N.Y.) "Times."

Hermit, The. *Robert Waln, Jr.* The hermit in America on a visit to Philadelphia. Ed. by Peter Atall. P. 1819.

Hermit, The. *Felix M'Donough.* The hermit in the country. L. 1820.

Hermit of Marlow, The. *Percy Bysshe Shelley.* We pity the plumage, but forget the dying bird . . . n.p., 1817.

"This is one of Shelley's most interesting tracts, and was printed and circulated for political purposes. The death of the Princess happened just at the time of the execution of Brandreth, Turner, and Ludlam, and afforded Shelley an opportunity of drawing a comparison between the two events, in which he displays such an amount of feeling as is seldom exhibited by one fellow-creature towards another, and in which some bitter attacks on the Government are not sparingly put forth. It is probable that the tract was suppressed on account of these remarks, which occasions its great rarity. Thos. Rodd, the eminent bookseller, soon after issued a reprint, consisting of a very limited number of copies."

Hermit of New York, The. *Rev. Washington Frothingham*, of Fonda, N.Y., in his contributions to the "Times" (Troy, N.Y.).

Heron, Robert, Esq. *John Pinkerton, Esq.* Letters of literature. L. 1785.

Hertfordshire Incumbent, A. *Rev. Joseph Williams Blakesley*, while Vicar of Ware, in a series of letters to the "Times" (L.) during the Crimean War, etc.

Hervé. *Florimond Ronger.*

Heteroscian. *Rowland G. Hazard.* Language: its connexion with the present constitution and future prospects of man . . . Providence, 1836.

Hewletts. *Alfred Duke*, in his contributions to the "State" (Richmond, Va.).

Hibernia. *Jonathan Swift, D.D.* A letter from a lady of quality, upon the general outcry against Wood's half-pence. Dublin, 1724.

Hibernicus. *William Bullen.* Contrasts between the Chancery and Superior Courts in Ireland and the same Courts in England. By . . . Dublin, 1861.

Hibernicus. *De Witt Clinton.* Letters on the natural history . . . of the state of New York. N.Y. 1822.

Hibernicus. *James Arbuckle.* Letters; or, a philosophical miscellany. 2d ed. L. 1734.

Hiberno-Anglus. *Sir John Joseph Dillon.* Letters of . . . L. 1812.

Hickory. *Thomas W. Jackson*, in his contributions to "Truth" (N.Y.).

Hid-Allan. *Allan Cunningham*, who wrote for the London "Star," and other papers, adopting in many instances this pseudonym.

Hieover, Harry. *Charles Bindley.* Practical horsemanship. L. 1856.

Hierophilos. *Rev. Patrick Eugene Moriarty.*

Hierophilus. *The most Rev. John McHale, D.D.*,

Roman Catholic Archbishop of Tuam, who in earlier life, while professor at Maynooth, published under this signature a series of controversial letters on Bible Societies, the Protestant Church in Ireland, and Roman Catholic Emancipation; and, in 1827, a work on the "Evidences and doctrines of the Catholic Church" since translated into the French and German languages.

Hierophilus. *John Toland.* A word to the honest priests. L. about 1710.

Hierro. *Victor Marie Hugo.* The first editions of "Hernani" and "Marion Delorme" (Paris, 1830) bore this signature.

Higgins, Zoraster. *Rev. Edward Eggleston,* in political ballads and satires upon the N.Y. city government under Wm. M. Tweed.

High Constable, The. *William Lee.* The constable's guide ... L. 1826.

High-Heels and Low-Heels. *Tories* and *Whigs.* — See "Flimnap, the Lilliputian Premier."

High Private, A. *Samuel Miller Quincy.* The man who was not a colonel. B. 1877.

Hilarius. *W. Feistkorn,* in his contributions to the German edition of "Puck" (N.Y).

Hilda. *Miss Hilda Siller,* daughter of Frank Siller of Milwaukee, and a writer of short stories.

Hildebrand. *Nikolaus Beets.* Camera obscura. Haarlem, 1839.

Hildebrand, Hall. *A. F. Birdsall.*

Hildegarde. *Mrs. Josephine R. Hoskins,* who wrote for the "South," a literary journal of New Orleans, under this pen-name.

Hilding, Habbakkuk, Justice, Dealer and Chapman. *Henry Fielding.* — See "Alexander, Drawcansir."

Hilton, David. *David Hilton Wheeler.* Brigandage in South Italy ... L. 1864.

Hilton, Maud. *Mrs. Frank Whicher.*

Him who should best understand it. *C. Sharpe, Esq.* A short address to ... [Signed "A Warning Voice."] Ipswich (?), 1832.

Hindoo Rajah, A. *Mrs. Elizabeth Hamilton.* Letters of ... L. 1796.

Hinds, John. *J. Bell.* Farriery taught on a new and easy plan ... P. 1848.

Hirsutus, Julius. *Julius Charles Hare.*

Sir William Gell notices Mr. Hare's translation of Niebuhr's "History of Rome" as being somewhat defective in style and idiom, and calls him, in allusion to his name, "Julius Hirsutus" (Hair-Hare). See "Gent. Mag.," April 1855, p. 424, note.

His Brother. *John P. Seddon.* Memoir and letters of T. Seddon, artist. By ... L. 1858.

His Brother. *John P. Foote.* Memoirs of the life of Samuel E. Foote, by ... Cin. 1860.

His Daughter. *Miss Josephine Brown.* Biography of an American bondman [William Wells Brown] ... B. 1856.

His Daughter. *Miss C. Marsh.* The life of the Rev. William Marsh ... N.Y. 1867.

His Daughter. *Miss L. J. Shaw.* Memoir of elder Elijah Shaw. By ... B. 1852.

His Daughter. *Mrs. Elizabeth Mary Odling.* Memoir of the late Alfred Smee ... L. 1878.

His Daughter. *Mme. Henriette de Witt.* Monsieur Guizot in private life. 1787–1874 ... L. 1880.

His Daughter. *Mrs. S. F. Ludomilla (Schetky) Rapallo.* Ninety years of work and play. Sketches from the public and private career of J. C. Schetky, late marine painter in ordinary to her Majesty. By ... Edinb. 1877.

His Eldest Son. *Jacob Halls Drew.* Samuel Drew, M.A., the self-taught Cornish man. A life lesson. By ... L. 1861.

His Eminence. *Cardinal N. P. S. Wiseman.* The new glories of the Catholic Church ... With a preface by ... L. 1855.

His Father. *Rev. Harry Croswell, D.D.* A memoir of the late Rev. Wm. Croswell, D.D. ...

His Father. *John Ballance.* Memoirs of Mr. J. des Carrières Ballance, late of Queen's College, Cambridge. Compiled by ... L. 1829.

His Father. *Walter Lowrie.* Memoirs of the Rev. Walter M. Lowrie, missionary to China. Edited by ... N.Y. 1849.

His Father. *Charles Thurber.* Our Charlie: a memorial. By ... Cambridge, 1863.

His Grace John Duke of ... *John Dunton.* Neck or nothing ... L. 1713.

His Grandson. *George Harrison.* Memoir of William Cookworthy, formerly of Plymouth. By ... L. 1854.

His Intimate Friend. *John Lowell.* Notice of the late Hon. Dudley Atkins Tyng, Jr. B. 1829.

His Majesty Himself. *Charles Hoyt,* in his letters to the "Boston Post."

His Mother. *Mrs. M. M. Rolls.* Excelsior: a truthful sketch of a lovely youth, B. G. L. R. [Bernard Glanville Lyndon Rolls]. By his mother. L. 1855.

His Mother. *Mrs. Marianne C. (Howe) Johnston.* The young chaplain. N.Y. 1876.

His Nephew. *John Treat Irving, Jr.* Life and letters of Washington Irving. By ... N.Y. 1862.

His Niece. *Miss Frances Dorothy Cartwright.* The life and correspondence of Major John Cartwright. By ... L. 1826.

His Respectful Neighbour, J. H. *Rev. John Humphrey,* of Frome. A letter to George Keith concerning the salvability of the heathen ... L. 1700.

His Sister. *Mrs. Sophia Lane Poole.* Life of Edward William Lane. By . . . L. 1877.

His Sister. *Miss Jessie Aitken Wilson.* Memoir of George Wilson. By . . . Edinb. 1860.

His Sister. *Mrs. Ann Bromfield Tracy.* Reminiscences of John Bromfield. By . . . Salem, Mass., 1852.

His Sister-in-Law and his Eldest Daughter. *Georgina Hogarth* and *Mamie Dickens.* The letters of Charles Dickens. Edited by . . . L. 1880.

His Son. *Robert Burns, Jr.* The Caledonian musical museum . . . Embellished with a portrait and fac-simile of the handwriting of Burns, and containing upwards of two hundred songs by that . . . bard. The whole edited by . . . L. 1809.

His Son. *Jelinger Cookson Symons.* Letters of consolation and advice from a father to his daughter on the death of her sister. By Jelinger Symons, B.D., rector of Whitburn, Durham. Fifth edition, with an explanatory preface by his son. L. 1818.

His Son. *John Church Hamilton.* The life of Alexander Hamilton. By . . . N.Y. 1834, 1840.

His Son. *Edward Robert Bulwer-Lytton,* Earl Lytton. Literary remains of Edward Bulwer, Lord Lytton. By . . . L. 1883.

His Son. *William A. McVickar, D.D.* The life of the Reverend John McVickar, S.T.D. By . . . N.Y. 1872.

His Son. *William Croswell Doane.* A memoir of the life of George Washington Doane, D.D., LL.D., Bishop of New Jersey. By . . . N.Y. 1860.

His Son. *Rev. George J. C. Duncan.* Memoirs of the Rev. Henry Duncan, D.D., Minister of Ruthwell. By . . . Edinb. 1848.

His Son. *John Addington Symonds.* Miscellanies . . . [by John Addington Symonds, the elder]. Edited by . . . L. 1872.

His Stepmother. *Mrs. Charles Churchill.* The praying school-boy: a brief memoir of R. E. H. Churchill. By . . . L. 1869.

His Three Daughters. *Katharine Prescott Wormeley, Mrs. Elizabeth (Wormeley) Latimer,* and *Mrs. Ariana Randolph (Wormeley) Curtis.* Recollections of Ralph Randolph Wormeley, Rear-Admiral, R.N. Written down by . . . N.Y. 1879.

His Twin Brother. *Oliver William Bourne Peabody.* Sermons by . . . W. B.

O. Peabody, with a memoir by . . . B. 1849.

His Widow. *Mrs. Fanny Byrne.* Memoirs of Miles Byrne [an Irish exile of 1798] . . . Edited by . . . Paris, 1863.

His Widow. *Mrs. Eliza Boaz.* The mission pastor . . . Rev. Thomas Boaz, LL.D., for 24 years missionary in Calcutta. L. 1862.

His Widow. *Elizabeth Davies.* Walks through the city of York. By Robert Davies. Edited by . . . L. 1880.

His Wife. *Mrs. Fanny E. (Grenfell) Kingsley.* Charles Kingsley. Portsmouth, 1877.

His Wife. *Mrs. Mary (Peabody) Mann.* Life of Horace Mann. B. 1865.

His Wife. *Mrs. Martha A. (Perry) Lowe.* Memoir of Charles Lowe. B. 1883.

His Wife. *Mrs. Alexandrine Macomb Cummins.* Memoir of George David Cummins, D.D. . . . N.Y. 1878.

Historian of Manchester, The. *John Whitaker.* A supplement to the first and second books of the history of Cornwall [by R. Polwhele] . . . By . . . Exeter, 1804.

Historicus. *Benjamin Franklin,* in his essay entitled "On the slave-trade," contributed to the "Federal Gazette." P. 1790.

Historicus. *Sir William George Granville Vernon-Harcourt.* American Neutrality. L. 1865.

Historicus. *Charles Cowley.* Letter to E. B. Bigelow, printed in the Lowell and other newspapers, July, 1858.

Hock, Mr. Francis. *John Osborne Sargent.* His signature to an "Extravaganza" in the Harvard Univ. "Collegian," 1830.

Hogg, Cervantes, F.S.M. (Fellow of the Swinish Multitude.) *Eaton Stannard Barrett.* The rising sun: a serio-comic, satiric romance . . . 1807–9.

Hogg, Nathan. *Henry Baird.* Letters in the Devonshire dialect. [In verse.] Exeter, 1847.

Hogo-Hunt, J. W., & Sunavill, J. F., Messrs. *John William Houghton and James Frank Sullivan.* The last daze of Pompeii. An antiquarian muddle . . .

Hoinos. *Rev. James Gilmour.* Among the Mongols. L. 1883.

Holbeach, Henry. *William Brightly Rands.* Student in life and philosophy. L. 1865.

Holding, Ephraim. *George Mogridge.* Homely hints to Sunday-school teachers. L. 1843.

Holm, Saxe. *Mrs. Helen Maria (Fiske Hunt) Jackson (?).* Stories. N.Y. 1874.

Holme, Daryl. *David Herbert.* The lost father; or, Cecilia's triumph . . . Edinb. 1870.

Holmes, Charles. *Charles Nordhoff,* in his contributions to "Harper's Magazine" (N.Y.).

Holmes, Margaret. *Mrs. M. V. Bates.*

Holmes, Sidney E. *Mrs. Sarah E. Henshaw.* Delia Bacon, in the "Advance," Dec. 26, 1867.

Holt, Harry, and Holt, Polly. *Miss Clara LeClerc,* who, in 1865, wrote a series of "Reveries" for the "Southern Literary Companion," by "Harry Holt," and replies, "Old Maid Reveries," by "Polly Holt."

Holyoke, Anna. *Mrs. Anna Holyoke (Cutts) Howard,* in her contributions to the "Household" (Brattleboro, Vt.).

Holyoke, Hetty. *Mrs. Caroline Snowden (Whitmarsh) Guild.* Never mind the face. N.Y. 1856.

Home, Cecil. *Mrs. Augusta (Davies) Webster.* The Brisons. By . . . in "Macmillan's Magazine," 1861.

Home, J. F. *Rev. John Reade,* the author of many fugitive and other poems, in Latin and English, of considerable merit, which appeared after 1856 in the "Gazette," "Transcript," and "Witness" (Montreal), under this signature, and the initials "R. J. C." and "J. R."

Homer. *Samuel H. Homan.*

Homespun, Sophia. *Mrs. Elizabeth H. Monmouth.* Much fruit . . . B. 1871.

Homme grave, Un. *Octave Delepierre, LL.D.* Nouvelles plaisantes recherches d' . . . sur quelques farceurs. L. 1860.

Homme de Rien, Un. *Louis Leonard de Loménie.* Galerie des contemporains illustres. Paris, 1846–47.

Homo. *Wilson MacDonald,* the sculptor, in his contributions to various periodicals.

Honest Man, An. *Charles Lloyd.* An honest man's reasons for declining to take any part in the new administration, in a letter to the Marquis of —— [Rockingham]. L. 1765.

Honest Man, An. *John Douglas, D.D.* Seasonable hints of . . . L. 1761.

Honest Sailor, An. *Admiral Edward Vernon.* Some seasonable advice from . . . [Being letters to the Admiralty, dated Aug.–Dec., 1745.] L. 1746.

Honestus. *Edward Norton.* The bank charter act of 1844 truthfully considered . . . L. 1857.

Honestus. *Benjamin Austin.* Observations on the pernicious practice of law. B. 1786.

Honey Bee. *Eliza A. E. Smith.*

Honeycomb, Will. *George Gordon.*

Honeycomb, William, Esq. *Richard Gardiner.* The history of Pudica [*Miss Sotherton*], a lady of N—rf—k. With an account of her five lovers; viz., Dick Merryfellow, Count Antiquary [*Mr. Earle*], Young Squire Fox [*Mr. Hare, Jun.*], of Dumplin-Hall, Jack Shadwell of the Lodge [*Mr. Buxton*], and Miles Dinglebob, of Popgun-hall, Esq. [*Mr. Branthwait*]. Together with Miss Pudica's sense of the word "*eclaircissement,*" and an epithalamium on her nuptials, by Tom Tenor, clerk of the parish. To the tune of "Green grow the rushes o'." By . . . L. 1754.

Honeycombe, Henry. *James Henry Leigh Hunt.* The Wishing Cap papers.

The author is a pretended descendant of the celebrated Will Honeycombe in the "Spectator."

Honorary Secretary, The. *J. Hopkinson.* Transactions of the Watford Natural History Society. Edited by . . . Watford, 1875.

Hon. Foreign Secretary to the Animals' Friend Society, The. *Thomas Forster, F.L.S.* An apology for the doctrine of Pythagoras, as compatible with that of Christianity . . . By . . . Boulogne sur Mer, 1858.

Honorary Secretary of the "Leander Club." *Sir Patrick Mac Chambaich de Colquhoun.* A companion to the "Oarsman's Guide." L. 1857.

Hon. Secretary of the Royal Eastern Yacht Club, The. *Archibald Young.* Yachting and rowing. By . . . L. 1866.

Honora, Lady. — See "A Lounger."

Honoria. *Marguerite A. Power.* The letters of a betrothed. L. 1858.

Honorius. *Noah Webster, LL.D.,* who, in 1783, published in the "Connecticut Courant" a series of papers signed "Honorius," in vindication of the Congressional Soldiers' Pay-bill.

Honourable Mr. ——, The. *William Coombe.* The auction: a town eclogue. L. 1778.

Hood, Eu. *Joseph Haslewood.* Of the London theatres, in "Gent. Mag.," August, 1813 *et seq.*

Hood, Thomas, the Younger. *Charles Clark, Esq.* Epsom races: a poem, comic, punning, and racy, by . . . 1836.

Hooker, Richard, Esq., of the Inner Temple. *William Webster, D.D.* The Weekly Miscellany. L. 1733.

Hoosier. *Samuel V. Morris,* who has been a contributor to the "Knickerbocker Magazine," to the Indiana "State Journal," and other "Hoosier" papers.

Hoosier, A. *Adolphus M. Hart.* Life in the far West; or, the adventures of ... N.Y.

Hope, Ansted. *Miss Burdett,* in the English "Family Herald."

Hope, Ascott R. *Robert Hope Moncrieff.* A book about boys. Edinb. 1868.

Hope, Ethel. *Mrs. Ina M. (Porter) Henry,* who was a contributor to "Land we Love" and other Southern magazines under her maiden name of "Ina M. Porter" and the pen-name of "Ethel Hope."

Hope, F. T. L. *Frederic William Farrar* (?). The three homes. L. 18–.

Hope, Grandmother. *Mrs. H. D. Knight.* Lottie Wilde's picnic ... N.Y. 1867.

Hope, Thomas, Esq. *Jonathan Swift, D.D.* The Swearer's Bank ... wherein the medical use of oaths is considered ... Dublin, 1721.

Hopeful, Gregory. *William Millett Boase, M.D.* Confessions of, in the "Selector; or, Cornish Magazine." Falmouth, 1828.

Hophthalmos, Friedrich. *Johann Christoph Friedrich Haug,* who began his literary career as an author by publishing "Sinngedichte von Friedrich Hophthalmos." Frankfort, 1791.

The pseudonym "Hophthalmos" is a jocular Greek equivalent of his own name (*Aug,* the eye, equal to Ophthalmos, and therefore Haug equal to "Hophthalmos").

Hopkins, John. *Mrs. Jane Marcet.* Notions on political economy. L. 1833.

Horam, the Son of Asmar. *Rev. James Ridley.* The tales of the Genii ... L. 1764.

Horatio. *John Pickens,* who wrote a number of poetical articles in prose and verse for the "New England Galaxy," some of them imitations of Horace, and signed "Horatio."

Horatius. *Horace Twiss, Esq., Q.C.* (?). St. Stephen's chapel: a satirical poem, by ... L. 1807.

Hormisdas-Peath, Sir. *Jacques Albin Simon Collin de Plancy.* Voyage au centre de la Terre ... Paris, 1821.

Horn, Otto. *Adolf Bauerle.* Therese Krones, 1854–55; and Ferdinand Raimund, 1855. Vienna.

Horn, W. O. v. *P. F. W. Oertel.* Erzählungen. Paris, 187–.

Hornbook, Adam. *Thomas Cooper.* Alderman Ralph. L. 1850.

Horne, Saxe. *Mrs. Helen Jane Woods,* of Montreal, in sketches, etc., contributed to various periodicals.

Hornem, Horace, Esq. *George Gordon Noël,* Lord Byron. The waltz: an apostrophic hymn. L. 1813.

A satire against dancing, which Byron was very anxious to suppress.

"I fear that a certain malicious publication on waltzing is attributed to me. This report, I suppose, you will take care to contradict, as the author, I am sure, would not like that I should wear his cap and bells."—Note in "Works" (ed. 1850), p. 456.

Horrible, Sir Hildebrand, The — of the English novelists. *William Godwin.*

Horse-Dealer, A. *Frederick Taylor.* Recollections of ... L. 1861.

Horst, Ben. *Edward G. Fast.* The gentleman of the color ... Balt. 1870.

Hortensius. *Sir William Bolland,* in Dr. Dibdin's "Bibliomania."

Hortensius. *D. Ramsay.*

Hortensius. *William Livingston.*

In 1776 *et seq.,* he published several essays, under this signature, in the "New Jersey Gazette," a paper established to oppose Rivington's "Royal Gazette," which was especially virulent against the "Don Quixote of the Jerseys," as it unceremoniously termed Gov. Livingston. In 1779, he also wrote under the same signature, in the "United States Magazine."

Hortensius. *Judge George Hay.* An essay on the liberty of the press ... P. 1799.

Horus. *G. C. Fisher.*

Hosmot, Hyton. *William Deal Baker, A.M.* The Saturniad: being a full and true account of the rise, progress, and downfall of the University of Quilsylvania [Pennsylvania]. By ... Translated by A. Lecutt, Esq. ... P. 1836.

Hospita. *Charles Lamb,* in his essay "On the immoderate indulgence of the pleasures of the palate," contributed to the "Reflector."

Hotspur. *Henry Buck,* in the London "Morning Advertiser" and the "Daily Telegraph."

Hotspur. *Henry Mort Feist,* in the "Daily Telegraph" and "Sporting Life" (L.).

Hotspur. *M. T. Walworth.* Twenty questions ... N.Y. 1882.

House Holder, A. *Samuel Miles Hopkins.* Letters concerning the general health ... N.Y. 1805.

Housekeeper, A. *Mrs. John Smith.* Confessions of ... P. 18–.

Housset, Arsène. *Arsène Houssaye.* Life in Paris. B. 1875.

Hovey, Wayne. *William Johnston.*

Howadji. *George William Curtis.* The Nile notes of . . . N.Y. 1867.

Howard. *Roland F. Coffin.*

Howard. *Joseph Dewey Fay* (the father of Theodore S. Fay), who was an earnest advocate of the abolition of imprisonment for debt, in numerous contributions to the public journals, under this signature.

Howard. *Mordecai Manuel Noah.* Essays on domestic economy. Originally published in the "National Advocate."

Howard, Caroline. *Mrs. Caroline Howard (Gilman Glover) Jervey.* A strange family. L. 1870.

Howard, Daisy. *Myra Daisy Mc-Crum.*

Howard, George, Esq. *Lieut. Francis C. Laird, R.N.* Lady Jane Grey and her times . . . L. 1822.

Howard, Harvey. *Will S. Faris.*

Howard, H. L. *Charles Jeremiah Wells.* Joseph and his brethren: a scriptural drama . . . L. 1824. — See "Fortnightly Rev.," Vol. XVII., pp. 217, 232.

Howard of "The Times." *Joseph Howard, Jr.,* in his contributions to the "Press" (P.), etc.

Howe, Henry. *Henry Howe Hutchinson.* A nom de théâtre.

Howe, Mary. *Jonathan Swift, D.D.* A letter to Miss Susannah Neville. 1732.

Hubbell, Myron. *William E. McElroy.*

Hudson, Frank. *George Kimball.*

Hughson, David, LL.D. *Edward Pugh.* An epitome of the privileges of London . . . L. 1816.

Hugomont, Edmond. *Hugh E. Montgomerie,* author of the novels and translations which appeared in the "Literary Garland," Montreal, under this signature.

Hull, Mr. *Tom Hill.* The "Mr. Hull" of Theodore Hook's "Gilbert Gurney," and the "Paul Pry" of John Poole.

Hum, O., & Co. *Frederic Saunders.* Life in New York. Edited [or rather written] by . . . N.Y. 1839.

Humble Expectant of the Promise, An. *Rev. William Burgh.* The coming of the Day of God . . . Dublin, 1826.

Humbug, Dr. *Joseph Reed.* Madrigal and Trulletta. A mock tragedy . . . With notes by the author . . . critic and censor-general. L. 1758.

Humm, Sir Henry. *George Alexander Stevens.* Distress upon distress; or, tragedy in true taste. A heroi-comi-parodi-tragedi-farci-cal burlesque. In two acts [and in verse] . . . With anno-

tations . . . by Sir H. H. and notes . . . by Paulus Purgantius Pedasculus . . . L. 1752.

Humphries, Jack. *Jonathan F. Kelly,* better known by his signatures of "Falconbridge," "Jack Humphries," and "Stampede."

Hunnibee, Kate. *Mrs. Laura E. Lyman,* joint author of "Philosophy of housekeeping." Hartford, 1869.

Hunter. *Parker Gillmore.* Hunter's adventures in the great West. L. 1871.

Hunter, A. *Capt. Flack.* A hunter's experiences in the Southern States. L. 1866.

Hunter, Harry. *Cyrus West Field.*

Hunter, Harry. *Henry Gibson.*

Hunter, Harry. *James L. Gould.*

Hunter, W. Ord. *Irving Brown.* — See "Curdle, Cream."

Huntington. *A. H. Clapp, D.D.*

Huntington, Faye. *Mrs. I. H. Foster.* Mrs. Deane's way. B. 1875.

Huntsman, A. *Thomas Assheton Smith.* Extracts from the diary of . . . L. 1838.

Huntsman, A. *Hon. George Charles Grantley-Fitz-Hardinge Berkeley.* Reminiscences of . . . L. 186–.

Hurlbut, Loammi N., M.D. *James Hammond Trumbull,* used in a series of papers in the "Independent" entitled "Limbus librorum."

Hurlothrumbo. *Thomas Simpson,* who "proposed and resolved many questions in the 'Ladies' Diaries,' sometimes under his own name and sometimes under fictitious names, such as 'Hurlothrumbo,' 'Kubernetes,' 'Patrick O'Cavenah,' 'Marmaduke Hodgson,' 'Anthony Shallow, Esq.,' and probably others. — See 'Diaries' for 1735–60." — CHALMERS, Vol. 28.

Hush, Bob. *Sir Robert Walpole.* Cameronian Whigs no patriots ; or, some remarkable exploits of Bob Hush. L. 1713.

Hyacinthe, Le père. *Le Père Charles Jean Marie Loyson.* Discours prononcé au congrès de Malines.

Hydrant Chuck. *J. F. Martin,* in his contributions to the "Fireman's Journal" (N.Y.).

Hydrophilus. *Rev. Thomas Fenwick.* — See "Blue Bonnet."

Hygeist, The. *James Morison, Esq.,* the vender of the "Vegetable Universal Medicines" commonly known as Morison's pills.

Hyperion. *Josiah Quincy, Jr.,* in the "Boston Gazette and Country Journal," Sept. 28 and Oct. 5, 1767, and Nov. 25, 1771.

I.

I., C. *Cosmo Innes.* Concerning some Scotch surnames. Edinb. 1860.

I., D. *Duncan Innes.* — See " A Layman."

I., G. *George Iliff.* Chronology in verse without numbers. L. 1855.

I., J. *James Ingram, D.D.* The church in the middle centuries ... Oxf. 1842.

I., W. *Rev. William Iago, B.A.* Infringing the bye-laws: a railway misadventure. Illustrated by "Phiz," and signed "W. I." in "London Society" (holiday number), 1869. Also in contributions to other periodicals.

Iago. *Sir Robert Walpole.* Iago display'd. The contents. Chap. I., How Cassio accused Iago of corruption, etc. L. 1731 (?).

Ianthe. *Lady Jane Elizabeth (Digby) Ellenborough,* in M. About's "La Grèce contemporaine." P. 1855.

Ianthe. *Mrs. Emma Catherine (Manley) Embury.* Guido; and other poems. N.Y. 182–.

Iater. *Dr. John Davis,* of Bath. An essay concerning pestilential contagion ... L. 1748.

Ἰατρος. *G. D. Yeats, M.D.* A biographical sketch of the life and writings of Patrick Colquhoun. L. 1818.

Iconoclast. *Charles Bradlaugh.* New life of David ... L.

Idamore. *Miss Mary Cutts.* Grondalla: a romance in verse. N.Y. 1866.

Idle Scholar, The. *Miss Julia Hatfield.* Bryant homestead-book. N.Y. 1870.

Idle Woman, An. *Mrs. Sue (Petigru) King.* Busy moments of ... Charleston, 185–.

Idle Woman, An. *Mrs. Frances (Minto) Elliot.* The diary of ... in Italy. L. 1872.

Idler. *Marguerite (Power) Gardiner,* Countess of Blessington. Idler in Italy, 1822-28. L. 1839-40.

Idler, An. *George Stillman Hillard,* who wrote for Buckingham's "New England Magazine" a series of "Literary Portraits," the articles "Selections from the papers of an Idler," etc.

Idler, An. *Chevalier Henry Wikoff.* Reminiscences of ... 1823-40. N.Y. 1880.

Idstone. *Rev. Thomas Pearce.* The Idstone papers. L. 1872.

Ignatius, Brother, Monk of the Order of Saint Benedict. *Joseph Ley-*

cester Lyne. The Catholic Church of England ... L. 1864.

Ignatius, Deacon of the Church of England. *Joseph Leycester Lyne.* May a monk serve God in the Church of England, or not? ... Oxf. n.d.

Ignatius, Father, Passionist. *Hon. and Rev. George Spencer.* The life of Blessed Paul of the Cross, translated. L. 1860.

Ignatius, O. S. B. *Joseph Leycester Lyne.* The Holy Isle: a legend of Bardsey Abbey. L. 1870.

Ignoto. *Richard Barnfield.*

Ignoto Secondo. *James Beresford,* in the London "Literary Gazette," 182–.

Ignotus. *James Franklin Fuller.* Culmshire folk. L. 1875.

Ignotus. *Ven. Arthur Blennerhasset Rowan, D.D., M.R.I.A.* Letters from Oxford, with notes by ... Dublin, 1843.

Ignotus. *Félix Platel.* Portraits d' Ignotus. Paris, 1878. These notices first appeared in "Figaro," under this signature.

Ignotus, Pictor. *William Blake.*

Il Musannif. *C. F. Mackenzie.* The romantic Land of Hind. By ... L. 1882.

Il Penseroso. *George Denison Prentice.*

Ill-used Candidate, An. *J. C. Caley.* Indignant rhymes. L. 1859.

Immortal Molly. *Mrs. Mary Fowle,* of Cambridge, England.

> "Being in her younger years long a celebrated toast, she was distinguished in the University by the name of the 'Immortal Molly,' which occasioned the following epigram by the Rev. Hans De Veil:
>
> 'Is Molly Fowle immortal? No.
> Yes but she is. I'll prove her so.
> She's fifteen now, and was, I know,
> Fifteen full years ago.'"

Impartial Bystander, An. *John Speed, M.D.* An I. B.'s review of the controversy concerning the wardenship of Winchester College. L. 1759.

Impartial Frenchman, An. *Thomas Pichon.* Genuine letters and memoirs relating to ... the islands of Cape Breton ... L. 1760.

Impartial Hand, An. *John Towne.* The argument of the Divine Legation fairly stated ... L. 1751.

Impartial Hand, An. *Samuel Johnson.* A compleat vindication of the licensers of the stage ... L. 1739.

Impartial Hand, An. *Rev. John*

Hildrop. The contempt of the clergy considered . . . L. 1739.

Impartial Hand, An. *Dr. John Mitchell.* The contest in America, between Great Britain and France . . . By . . . L. 1757.

Impartial Hand, An. *Sir Richard Steele.* The D—n of W—r (*i.e.*, Francis Hare, Dean of Worcester) still the same . . . L. 1720.
Also attributed to *Rev. Benjamin Hoadly.*

Impartial Hand, An. *Richard Rawlinson, LL.D.* The English topographer . . . By . . . L. 1720.

Impartial Hand, An. *Peter King,* Lord King. An enquiry into the constitution . . . of the primitive Church . . . L. 1691.

Impartial Hand, An. *Daniel Turner.* The fashionable daughter . . . By . . . L. 1774.

Impartial Hand, An. *Isaac Kimber.* The history of England, from the earliest accounts to . . . George II. . . . L. 1746.

Impartial Hand, An. *Richard Rowlands.* History of the lives and reigns of the kings of Scotland . . . Dublin, 1722.

Impartial Hand, An. *Rev. James Murray.* The history of religion. By . . . L. 1764.

Impartial Hand, An. *Sir John Hill, M.D.* The history of a woman of quality; or, the adventures of Lady Frail [*i.e.*, Anne, Viscountess Vane]. By . . . L. 1751.

Impartial Hand, An. *George Coad, Jr.,* of Exeter. A letter to the Honourable the Lords Commissioners of Trade and Plantations . . . L. 1747.

Impartial Hand, An. *Andrew Henderson.* The life of John [Dalrymple, 2d] Earl of Stair . . . By . . . L. 1743.

Impartial Hand, An. *Rev. Thomas Cox,* of Broomfield, Essex. Magna Britannia et Hibernia . . . In the "Savoy," 1720.

Impartial Hand, An. *Rev. Francis Hare.* A new defence of [Hoadly] the Lord Bishop of Bangor's sermon . . . L. 1720.

Impartial Hand, An. *William Duff.* A new and full critical, biographical, and geographical history of Scotland . . . L. 1749.

Impartial Hand, An. *Rev. Thomas Allen.* A proposal for a free and unexpensive election of Parliament . . . By . . . L. 1753.

Impartial Hand, An. *Dorothea Wentworth.* Remarks on the second volume of the memoirs of Mrs. Pilkington . . . By . . . Dublin, 1749.

Impartial Hand, An. *Thomas Foxcroft.* The ruling and ordaining power of Congregational bishops . . . B. 1724.

Impartial Hand, Who was an Eye-Witness to most of the Facts, An. *Andrew Henderson.* The history of the Rebellion, 1745 and 1746 . . . Edinb. 1748.

Impartial Inquirer, An. *R. Casway.* A miscellaneous metaphysical essay. L. 1748.
Also ascribed to *James Ralph.*

Impartial Reviewer, An. *Thomas O'Connor.* The Inquisition examined . . . N.Y. 1825.

Impartialist, An. *Samuel Adams,* on Robinson's assault on James Otis, in the "Boston Gazette," Sept. 25, 1769.

Impressed New Yorker, An. *William G. Stevenson.* Thirteen months in the rebel army . . . 1861–62. N.Y. 1862.

Inchiquin. *Robert Southey,* in his contributions to the "Quarterly Review" (L. 1814), etc.

Inchiquin, the Jesuit. *Charles Jared Ingersoll.* Inchiquin's letters. P. 1809.

Incognitus, Richardus. *Richard Brash.* An address to the people of the British Dominions . . . L. 1825.

Inconnue, L'. *Mrs. L. Virginia (Smith) French.* Kernwood; or, after many days . . . Louisville, Ky., 1868.

Incumbent of the English Church, Nairn, An. *Rev. William West.* The position of the English Church in Scotland . . . By . . . Edinb. 1866.

Indagator. *John Canton.* On the magnetic needle, in the "Gent. Mag.," September, 1761, p. 397; and November, 1761, p. 497.

Indagator. *Charles Clarke, Esq.* Remarkable particulars in our ancient parochial churches. "Gent. Mag.," August, 1787, p. 661.

Indagator Roffensis. *Charles Clarke, Esq.* His signature to a description of Woldham Church, in the "Gent. Mag." for July, 1789, p. 589.

Independent, An. *Josiah Quincy, Jr.,* in the "Boston Gazette," Feb. 12 and 26, 1770.

Independent Freeholder, An. *Thomas Thirlwall.* A calm and dispassionate address to Sir Francis Burdett, Bart. . . . n.p. 1804.

Independent Observer, An. *A. Redfoord.* Union necessary to security . . . By . . . Dublin, 1800.

Independent Voter, An. *Rowland Hunt.* Free thoughts on the late contested election for the borough of Shrewsbury. Shrewsbury, 1806.

Independent Whig, An. *John Almon*, in the London " Gazette," 1760 *et seq.*

Index, Q. P. *William McCrillis Griswold*. Indexes to the " International Review," etc. Bangor, 1880.

Indian Agent, An. *Henry W. De Puy*. Mishaps of an Indian agent convicted of not plundering the Indians. Albany, 1863.

Indian Journalist, An. *William Knighton, LL.D.* Tropical sketches; or, reminiscences of ... L. 1855.

Indian Official, An. *R. H. Hollingbery*. A handbook on gold and silver. L. 1878.

Indian Official, An. *Maj.-Gen. Sir William Henry Sleeman, K.C.B.* Rambles and recollections of ... L. 1844.

Indian Official, An. *Gen. Sir Orfeur Cavenagh.* Reminiscences ... L. 1884.

Indianian, An. *James Whitcomb.* The other side of " Facts for the People," in relation to a " Protective Tariff," by ... 1843.

Indicus. *Major Evans Bell.* The rajah and principality of Mysore. L. 1865.

Indigina. *Mrs. Adelaide McCord.*

Indigina. *Mrs. Dolores A. (Fuertos Menken Heenen) Newell.*

Indignatio. *Rev. Henry Taylor.* Confusion worse confounded ; rout on rout ; or, the Bishop of G—r's [Gloucester] commentary on Rice Evans's " Echo from Heaven," examined and exposed. By ... L. 1772.

Indophilus. *Sir Charles Edward Trevelyan and another.* Correspondence relating to the establishment of an Oriental college in London ... L. 1858.

Infidel Mathematician, An. *Dr. Halley.* The analyst; or, a discourse addressed to ... By the author of " The Minute philosopher " [G. Berkeley, Bishop of Cloyne]. L. 1734.

Ingenuus. *Thady Fitzpatrick.* — See " T. F."

Ingham, Col. Frederic. *Edward Everett Hale.* The Ingham papers. B. 1869.

Ingoldsby. *James Hildyard, B.D.* The Ingoldsby letters, in reply to the bishops in convocation and to the House of Lords, on the revision of the Book of Common Prayer. L. 1862–63.

Ingoldsby, Thomas, Esquire. *Richard Harris Barham, B.A.* The Ingoldsby legends ; or, mirth and marvels ... L. 1847.

Inhabitant, An. *F. K. Robinson.* A glossary of Yorkshire words and phrases ... L. 1855.

Inhabitant, An. *Thomas Thaxter.* A narrative of the proceedings in the north parish of Hingham from the time of Dr. Ware's leaving it to the ordination of Rev. Joseph Richardson and Mr. Henry Coleman. By ... Salem, 1807.

Inhabitant, An. *Henry Pownall.* Some particulars relating to the history of Epsom ... Epsom, 1825.

Inhabitant of Boston, An. *Andrew Newell (²).* Darkness at noon; or, the great solar eclipse of the 16th of June, 1806 ... B. 1806.

Inhabitant of Florida, An. *Z. Kingsley.* A treatise on the patriarchal system of society ... in America ... 1833.

Inhabitant of New England, An. *Timothy Dwight, D.D.* Remarks on the review of Inchiquin's letters published in the " Quarterly Review " ... B. 1815. Also ascribed to Jedidiah Morse, D.D.

Inhabitant of the Province, An. *Calvin Hatheway.* Sketches of New Brunswick ... St. John, 1825.

Inhabitant of the State of Maryland, An. *Rev. Charles Henry Wharton, D.D.* A poetical epistle to his excellency George Washington ... from ... L. 1780.

Inigo. *Charles Henry Webb.*

Injured Lady, The. *Jonathan Swift, D.D.* The story of ... Being a true picture of Scotch perfidy, Irish poverty, and English partiality. L. 1746.

Inkle, Mr. *Christopher Anstey.* An election ball, in poetical letters from ... at Bath to his wife at Gloucester ... Bath, 176–.

Innsly, Owen. *Miss Lucy W. Jennison.* Love poems and sonnets. By ... B. 1881.

Inquirer. *A. P. Happer.* A letter to Prof. Friedrich Max Mueller on the sacred books of China. By ... 1880.

Inquirer, An. *James Jackson Jarves.* The confessions of ... B. 1857.

Inquirer, The. *William Atkinson.* The guilt of Democratic scheming fully proved against the Dissenters ... By ... L. 1802.

Inspector, The. *Sir John Hill,* who wrote " The Inspector " for two years in the " Daily Advertiser," 1751–53.

Inspector, The. *Sir John Hill, M.D.* Letters from ... to a lady, with the genuine answers ... L. 1752. (Letters signed " J. H." and the answers " D.")

Instar omnium. *Samuel Adams.* So

termed by Gov. Hutchinson in a letter to Pownall. 1771.

Intimate Friend of his, An. *Rev. Richard Graves.* Recollection of some particulars in the life of the late William Shenstone, Esq., in a series of letters from . . . L. 1788.

Invalid, An. *Henry Matthews, Esq.* The diary of . . . in 1817–19. L. 1820.

Invalid, An. *Harriet Martineau.* Life in the sick-room, essays. L. 1844.

Invalid, An. *Frederic Townsend* (?). Musings of . . . N.Y. 185–.

Invalid, An. *Hon. Robert Fulke Greville.* Outlines selected from the blotting book of . . . 1825.

Invalid, An. *W. B. Aspinall.* San Remo as a winter residence. By . . . 1862–65. L. 1865.

Invalid, An. *John Strang, Esq., LL.D.* Travelling notes of . . . in search of health, first published in the "Glasgow Herald," but separately in 1863.

Investigator. *Jacob Barker.* The Rebellion; its consequences . . . By . . . New Orleans, 1866.

Investigator. *Daniel Oliver.* Remarks on a pamphlet entitled "Prof. Hale and Dartmouth College." 1846.

Investigator. *Samuel Wheeler.* The triangle . . . N.Y. 1832.

Iolo Fardd Glas. *Edward Williams,* the well-known Welsh bard and writer.

Ion. *Eugene Kingman,* in his contributions to the "Baltimore Sun."

Ione. *Mrs. Mary Elizabeth (Moore Hewitt) Stebbins.* Her earlier poems appeared in the "Knickerbocker Magazine" and other periodicals under this pen-name, and in Boston, in 1845, she published a volume entitled "Songs of our Land, and other Poems." Her name was originally Jane L. Moore.

Iota. *Rev. Joseph Jefferson,* of Basingbroke (Hants.), in his contributions to the "Gent. Mag." (L.), etc.

Iota. *Dr. John Francis Waller* (?). Adventures of a Protestant in search of a religion. Dublin, 186–.

Iota. *John Harland.* Stray leaves collected for the "Athenæum Bazaar." Manchester, 1843.

Ipolperroc. *Jonathan Couch,* in the "Imperial Magazine" and the "Pamphleteer," 1819 *et seq.*

Iredale, John. *B. B. Vallentine,* in his contributions to "Puck" (N.Y.).

Irenæus. *Rev. Samuel Irenæus Prime,* author of "The old white meeting-house; or, reminiscences of a country congregation," N.Y. 1845; also in his contributions to the "N.Y. Observer," etc.

Irenicus. *Joseph Besse.* The doctrine of the people called Quakers, in relation to bearing arms and fighting . . . L. 1746.

Irish Adopted Citizen, An. *George C. Collins.* Fifty reasons why the Honorable Henry Clay should be elected President of the United States. Balt. 1844.

Irish Archivist, An. *John T. Gilbert.* On the history, position, and treatment of the public records of Ireland. L. 1864.

Irish Bachelor, An. *— Abbot.* The freaks of Cupid : a novel . . . L. 1845.

Irish Catholic, An. *William James MacNeven.* An argument for independence, in opposition to an union . . . By . . . Dublin, 1799.

Irish Catholic, An. *James Warren Doyle.* Essay on education and the state of Ireland. Dublin, 1880.

Irish Catholic, An. *William Bullen.* A memoir of the Union. By . . . Dublin, 1843.

Irish Catholic Whig, An. *Charles O. Gorman.* An I. C. W. to his fellow-countrymen in the United States. Prov. 1852.

Irish Charles Dickens, The. *Mrs. May Laffan Hartley.*

Irish Country Gentleman, An. *William Parnell.* An inquiry into the causes of popular discontents in Ireland . . . L. 1804.

Irish Dignitary, An. *Rev. Thomas Lewis O'Beirne.* A letter . . . on the subject of tithes in Ireland. L. 1807.

Irish Gentleman, An. *Thomas Walford.* The scientific tourist through Ireland . . . By . . . L. 1818.

Irish Gentleman, An. *Thomas Moore.* Travels of . . . in search of a religion. L. 1833.

Irish Lady, An. *Mrs. J. R. Greer.* Vindication of friends . . . P. 1852.

Irish Land Owner, An. *Thomas Martin.* A plan for the settlement of the question of the sale and transfer, mortgage and registration of land. 2d ed. Dublin, 1862.

Irish National Journalist, An. *Richard Pigott.* Personal recollections of . . . Dublin, 1882.

Irish Peasant Poet, The. *C. P. O'Conor.*

Irish Police Magistrate, An. *Henry Robert Addison.* Recollections of . . . L. 1862.

Irish Sennachy, An. *Edward Smyth Mercer.* The Mercer chronicle . . . L. 1866.

Irish Traveller, An. *Richard Twiss,* in Beloe's "Sexagenarian." Vol. II., p. 52. 2d ed. L. 1818.

Irish Traveller, An. *Mr. Synge.* A biographical sketch of the struggles of Pestalozzi... Dublin, 1815.

Irish Whiskey-Drinker. *John Sheehan.* The Irish Whiskey-Drinker papers. L. 1868. Also his contributions to "Temple Bar," etc.

Irishman, An. *Thomas Moore.* Corruption and intolerance: two poems... L. 1808–9.

Irishwoman, An. *Miss Anna Perrier.* The Irishman. L. 1866. Republished from the "Englishwoman's Domestic Magazine."

Irner. *Bon Louis Henri Martin and another.* Wolfthurm. Paris, 1830.

Ironculus. *Lord H. Spencer.* His signature to letter and poem in the "Microcosm," published at Eton College, 1787.

Irondequoit. *Francis Trevelyan Buckland,* in his contributions to the "Examiner" (N.Y.).

Ironside, Nestor. *Sir Richard Steele,* as one of the editors of the "Guardian." L. 1713.

Ironside, Nestor, Esq. *Dr. Samuel Croscall.* Another original canto of Spencer... L. 1714.

Irraghticonnor. *John C. Hennessy,* in the "Celtic Monthly."

Irritable Man, An. *Robert Barry Coffin.* Matrimonial infelicities. N.Y. 1865.

Irving, Helen W. *Miss Anna H. Phillips.* Her first poem, "Love and fame," appeared in the N.Y. "Home Journal," 1847.

Irving, Henry. *John Henry Brodribb Irving.* Nom de théâtre.

Isa. *Mrs. Isa (Craig) Knox,* whose poems in the "Scotsman," signed "Isa," attracted attention, and led to her being placed on the staff of that journal.

Isaac, Lord Bishop of Worcester. *Isaac Madox, D.D.* A sermon... before... the... governors of the hospital for the small-pox and for inoculation... March 5, 1752. By... L. 1752.

Isabel. *Mrs. Anna Cora (Ogden Mowatt) Ritchie,* who gained some literary celebrity under the assumed titles of "Isabel" and "Helen Berkley," and a still wider reputation by her works under her own name.

Isabel. *William Gilmore Simms.* Pelayo; or, the cavern of Covadonga: a romance [in verse]. N.Y. 1836.

Isaline. *Janet De La Touche.* Jeannie; or, the flower of Glenburnie. L. 1879.

Ishmael. *Josiah Harris.* The pulpit of Cornwall: its preachers, and their teachings. Penzance, 1859.

Isidore. *Isidore G. Ascher, B.C.L.,* a Canadian poet. "For some years he had been known as the author of many poetical pieces; among which were some beautiful and tender lyrics, which had appeared in the provincial press, under his Christian name 'Isidore.'"

Iskander. *Alexander Herzen,* a Russian littérateur and politician, who, while writing under the censorship of the Czar until his fiftieth year, published his works under this pseudonym, — the Turkish translation of his Christian name, Alexander.

Israelite, An. *George Houston.* Israel vindicated... N.Y. 1820. Signed "Nathan Joseph."

It matters Not Who. *Rev. Edward Nares, B.D.* Heraldic anomalies. By... L. 1823.

Italian, An. *Charles Barinetti.* Voyage to Mexico and Havanna... By... N.Y. 1841.

Italian Nun, An. *William Coombe, Esq.* Letters of... L. 1789.

Ithuriel. *Clarence Hopper,* in his contributions to "Notes and Queries" (L.), etc.

Itinerant, An. *Abel Stevens, D.D., LL.D.* Sketches and incidents: a budget from the saddle-bags of... 18–.

Its Present Owner. *Colonel Thomas Wildman.* Newstead Abbey: its present owner, with reminiscences of Lord Byron. L. 1857.

Ixion. *Llewelyn H. Johnson,* the earliest "champion" amateur bicycle racer in America.

Ixion. *Leon N. Salmon.*

Izak. *John Isaac Ira Adams,* in the Boston "Republican," in 1857.

Izax, Ikabod. *G. S. Stebbins.* My satchel and I; or, literature on foot. Springfield, Mass., 187–.

J.

J., A. *Alexander Justice.* A general treatise of monies and exchanges . . . 1707. — See "A Well-wisher to Trade."

J., A., and R. A. *Absalom Jones* and *Richard Allen.* A narrative of the proceedings of the black people during the late awful calamity in Philadelphia, in the year 1793. P. 1794.

J., C. *C. Jacob.* An epitome of Mr. Gunton's History of Peterborough Cathedral. By . . . 11th ed. Peterborough, 1807.

J., C. *Rev. Charles Jenner.* The man of family . . . L. 1771.

J., C. A. *C. A. Jones.* S. John the Evangelist's day; or, the martyrdom of the will . . . L. 1859.

J., D. *David Jones.* The history of the house of Brunswick Lunenburgh . . . 1716.

J., D. W. *Douglas William Jerrold,* in the London "Belle Assemblée," 1824, and other periodicals.

J., E. *Edward Jarvis, M.D.* "Law of physical life," in the "Christian Examiner" for September, 1843.

J., E. *Miss E. Jolly.* The life and letters of Sydney Dobell. Ed. by . . . L. 1878.

J., E. A. *E. A. Jackson.* Christine Thornton; or, who is my neighbor? N.Y. 1870.

J. E. S. *James Carnegie,* Earl of Southesk. Herminius: a romance . . . Edinb. 1862.

J., G. *Giles Jacob.* An historical account of the lives and writings of our most considerable English poets . . . L. 1724.

J. G. J. — See "A Member of the Philadelphia Bar."

J., G. W. *G. W. Jordan.* New observations concerning the colours of thin transparent bodies . . . L. 1800.

J. H. *Denis Florence M'Carthy.* Justina: a play . . . Trans. by . . . L. 1848.

J., J. *Rev. Joseph Jefferson,* of Basingbroke (Hants.), in his contributions to the "Gent. Mag." (L.), etc.

J. K. L. *James Warren Doyle, R.C.,* Bishop of Kildare and Leighlin. Letters on the state of education in Ireland, and on Bible societies . . . Dublin, 1824.

J., L. J. *Louis J. Jennings,* formerly London correspondent of the "World" (N.Y.).

J., M. *Mary Jenkins.* A guide to star-gazing . . . L. 1861.

J., M. E. M. *Margaret Elizabeth Mary Jones.* Ismael and Cassander; or, the Jew and the Greek . . . L.

J., M. J. *Maria Jane Jewsbury.* Phantasmagoria . . . L. 1825.

J. O. *Matthew James Higgins.* The story of the Mhow court-martial (L. 1864); reprinted from the "Cornbill Magazine."

J. O. Y. *Mrs. S. S. Black.* Rambling chats and chatty ramblings . . . N.Y. 1873.

J., R. *Richard Jefferies.* The gamekeeper at home. L. 1878.

J., R. B. *Robert Baker Jones.* The vision of Mary; or, a dream of joy . . . 1856.

J., S. *Samuel Johnson.* Ad Urbanum. A copy of Latin verses, in March, 1738, addressed to Sylvanus Urban [Edward Cave], the editor "Gent. Mag.," March, 1738.

J., S. *Stephen Jones.* The history of Poland from its origin as a nation to the commencement of the year 1795 . . . L. 1795.

J., S. *Mrs. Sarah (Jackson Davis) Tappan.* Letters to a young Christian. By . . . N.Y. 1851.

J. S. of Dale. *Frederick Jesup Stimson.* Guerndale. N.Y. 1882.

J., S. L. *Sarah L. Jones.* Life in the South . . . L. 1863.

J. T., Esq. *John Wilson Croker.* An intercepted letter from Canton . . . Dublin, 1804.

J. V. Z. *Joseph Veazie.* Asphalt. Its preparation and application. B. 1875.

J., W. *W. Jordan.* Extracts from a journal kept during a voyage from Philadelphia to Calcutta . . . Serampore, 1812.

J., W. S. *W. S. Jordan,* of San Francisco, Cal., in his contributions to various periodicals.

J***, M. *Thomas Jefferson.* Observations sur la Virginie. Par . . . Paris, 1786.

J—M—N, E. *E. Jarmain.* An invalid's pastime . . . L.

J—ll. *Joseph Jekyll.* See Lamb's "Elia." — "The Old Bencher of the Inner Temple."

J—n, M. J. *Mrs. Mary J. Jourdan.* Mind's mirror: poetical sketches . . . Edinb. 1856.

J—ph—n, R—ph, of the Inner Temple. *Ralph Jephson.* The expounder expounded . . . L. 1740.

J—'s, H—d, Esq. *Hildebrand Jacob, Esq.* The curious maid. L. 17–.

Jabez. *Clement Mansfield Ingleby, M.A., LL.D.,* in "Notes and Queries" (L.), January, 1877.

Jablonsky, Boleslaw. *Karl Eugen Tupy.* Liebeslieder. 1841.

Jacla. *John Crane.* Remarks on coinage. L. 1859.

Jack, Cannibal. *Charles Beach.* Way to win. L. 18–.

Jackson, Josephine. *Mrs. C. B. Whitehead.*

Jackson, Stephen, Esq., of The Flatts, Malham Moor. *James Henry Dixon, LL.D.* Chronicles and stories of the Craven Dales. L. 1881.

First contributed to the pages of a small monthly publication issued at Skipton, 1853–57; afterward published in book form with the author's name.

Jackson, "Stonewall." *Thomas J. Jackson.*

"There is General Bee who, in addressing his own men at Bull Run, likened Thomas Jonathan Jackson to a 'stone wall'; and Wordsworth, who in his lines on Chatterton seems to have hit the popular view with his 'marvellous boy' better than Byron with his 'mad genius'; and Douglas Jerrold, who transmuted Charles into 'Good' Knight; and Hogg, the 'Ettrick Shepherd,' who found a synonym in 'Ebony' for Mr. Blackwood . . . and Scott, the originator of the phrase 'The Crafty,' in application to Archibald Constable; and he who gave to his school-fellows, James and James Ballantyne, the redoubtable names of two characters in Carey's 'Chrononhotonthologos,' 'Aldiborontiphoscophornio' and 'Rigdum Funnidos.'"—See "Gent. Mag." for January, 1883, p. 39.

Jacob, Lord Bishop of Quebec. *Jacob Mountain.* A sermon . . . at Quebec . . . January 10th, 1799 . . . By . . . Quebec, 1799.

Jacob Omnium's Hoss. *William Makepeace Thackeray.* Bow Street ballads, No. II. "Punch," Dec. 9, 1848.

Jacob, P. L., bibliophile. *Paul Lacroix.* Curiosités de histoire de France. Paris, 1858.

Jacobstaff. *George B. Eaton.*

Jacqueline. *Mrs. Josephine R. Hoskins.* Love's stratagem, in the "Southern Monthly," Memphis, 1861.

Jacques. *Jacques Claude Demogeot,* in "Contes et Causeries" (Paris, 1862).

Jacques, Cousin. *Louis Abel Beffroy de Reigny.* La petite Nanette. Paris, 1796.

Jahnsenykes, The Late Rev. Williamson, LL.D. *William Jenks, D.D.* Memoir of the Northern Kingdom, A.D. 1872 . . . Quebeck, 1901 [B. 1808].

Jake, Uncle. *Robert W. McAlpine.*

Jamaica Proprietor, A. *Charles*

Edward Long. Negro emancipation no philanthropy . . . L. 1830.

Jambon, Jean. *John Hay Atholl Macdonald.* Our trip to Blunderland. L. 1877.

James, Uncle. *James Rodwell.* The rat; its history . . . L. 1858.

James, S. T. *Horace E. Scudder.* Stories from my attic. N.Y. 1869.

Jamie, Daft. *James Wilson.* A laconic narrative of the life and death of . . . known by the name of Daft Jamie. [With] . . . anecdotes relative to him and his old friend, Roby Awl [R. Kirkwood]. Edina [Edinb.], 1829.

Jamie the Poeter. *James Hogg.*

Jamot, R. E. *Joseph Thomayer.* Natur und Menschen. 1880.

Jane. *Mrs. Mary E. (Moore) Hewitt,* who contributed many of her "Songs of our Lord and other Poems" to various periodicals under this pen-name.

Jane, Paul. *Adolphe van Soust de Borkenfeldt.* L'année sanglante. 1871.

Janetta. *Mrs. Janetta (Scott) Norweb.* The memoirs of Janetta: a tale, alas, too true. L. 181–.

Janus. *Dr. Johann Joseph Ignaz von Döllinger,* in numerous works upon religious topics.

Janus. *Johann Nepomuk Huber.* Das Papstthum und der Staat. Munich, 1870.

Janus Junius Eoganesius. *John Toland,* his signature to the preface of one of his works. His Christian name was Janus Junius; but the boys making a jest of it, the master ordered him to be called John, which name he retained ever after. "Eoganesius" was the name of his country, Inis-Eogan being the place of his birth.

Japanese Traveller, A. *Laurence Oliphant.* Moral reflections by . . . in the "North American Review." N.Y. 1877.

Signed "Sionara."

Japheth. *Theodore Dehon.* Cause and cure . . . Charleston, S.C., 1868.

Jaques. *J. Hain Friswell,* in his contributions to the "Evening Star" (L. 1867).

Jarvie, Nichol. *William McDonald Wood,* in the "Brooklyn Times."

Jarvis, Geoffry. *Elizabeth Hamilton.* Memoirs of modern philosophers. Bath, 1800.

Jasper. *E. P. Robinson.*

Jaunt, Jeremy. *George (?) Mogridge,* who, under this signature, contributed papers to the "Birmingham and Lichfield Chronicle."

Jay, W. M. L. *Miss Julia Louisa Matilda Woodruff.* Holden with cords . . . N.Y. 1874.

Jayhawker. *Col. J. H. Woodard*, in his contributions to the "Cincinnati Enquirer."

Jeames. *William Makepeace Thackeray.* The diary of C. Jeames de la Pluche, Esq., contributed to "Punch."

Jeames, Mr. *William Makepeace Thackeray.* Sentiments on the Cambridge election. "Punch," March 6, 1847.

Jeames of Buckley Square. *William Makepeace Thackeray.* A lucky speculator, etc., in "Punch," 1845.

Jeames, G. P. R., Esq. *William Makepeace Thackeray.* Barbazure. "Punch," July, 1847.

Jean, Father. *James Beal*, in his contributions to the "Echo" (L.).

Jean, J. de. *John Frazer.* Poems by ... Dublin, 18–.

Jean Jacques. *Jean Jacques Rousseau.*

Jean Paul. *Jean Paul Friedrich Richter*, in his earlier publications.

"But I return to our history and place myself amongst the dead, for all are out of the world who saw me come into it. My father was called John Christian Christopher Richter, and was Tertius (master of the third class at a gymnasium) and organist in Wunsiedel. My mother, who was the daughter of the cloth-weaver, John Paul Kuhn, in Hof, was named Sophia Rosina. The day after my birth I was baptized by the senior Apel. One godfather was the abovementioned John Paul, and the other John Frederic Theime, a book-binder, who did not know at that time to what quantities of his own handicraft he lent his name. From these two sponsors was the name of Jean Paul Frederic shot together. The grandfatherly half I translated into Jean Paul, and have thereby gained a name, the reasons for which shall be fully made known in future lectures."—*Autobiography.*

I call him frequently Jean Paul, without adding his surname, both because all Germany gives him that appellation, as an expression of affection for his person, and because he has himself sometimes assumed it in the title-pages to his works.—DeQuincey.

Jean Pierre. *S. W. Cooper*, in his contributions to the "Evening Bulletin" (P.), etc.

Jean-sans-peur. *Hippolyte Babou.* L'homme à la lanterne. Paris, 1868.

Jeanne Marie. *Jeanne Marie von Gayette-Georgens.* Sich selbst erobert. Ein Mädchenroman. 1873.

Jefferson. *Mathew Carey.* Examination of the Charleston (S.C.) Memorial. P. 1827.

Jefferson. *J. S. Richardson.* Speech in opposition to disunion, convention, and nullification. Charleston, 1830.

Jehan, Dr., of the Hall Ryal. *John Jamieson, D.D.* A new Bannatyne garland: compylit be ... Imprentit at Sanct Paulis Wark, at Zule, in the present zeir. MDCCCXXVIII.

Jehu, Junior. *T. Gibson Bowles*, editor of "Vanity Fair" (L.), in his weekly biographies contributed to that sheet.

Jenkins, S. Joshua. *E. D. Taylor.*

Jenks, Jacquetta Agneta Mariana, of Belgrove Priory in Wales. *William Beckford.* Azemia ... a novel ... L. 1797.

Jenny Maria. *Céline Renard.* Monde et solitude. Paris, 1878.

Jepphi, Recos. *Joseph Price.* Ministerial almanack ... L. 1783.

Jepson, Ring. *Henry Jepson Latham.* Among the Mormons. San Fran. 188–.

Jermyn, Dud. *Walter R. Benjamin.*

Jerry, Uncle. *Mrs. Anne (Emerson) Porter.* Letters to young mothers. B. 1854.

Jessamine, James. *Bryan Waller Procter*, in the London "Literary Gazette."

Jesse, Uncle. *C. E. Babb.* Talks about the war. Cin. 187–.

Jeune moraliste, Le. *Émile Deschamps.* Le jeune moraliste. Paris, 1826.

Jinks, Joshua Jedidiah. *W. B. Dick.* Uncle Josh's trunk-full of fun. N.Y. 187–.

Joannes, Count. *George Jones.* History of ancient America. N.Y. 1843.

Jobber, A. *Daniel Defoe.* The anatomy of Exchange Alley; or, a system of stock-jobbing ... L. 1719.

Jobbry, Archibald. *John Galt.* The member: an autobiography ... L. 1832.

Johannes Catholicus. *John Rutty.* An essay towards a contrast between Quakerism and Methodism ... Bristol, 1771.

John. *John Wesley Beach*, in numerous letters contributed to the "Sun" (N.Y.).

John. *Sampson Sandys.* John's letter to Dame Europa, expostulating against being called a coward. L. 1871.

John, Archbishop of Tuam. *John McHale, D.D.*, in several letters on the questions of the Church Establishment and Education.

John, Corporal. *Charles P. O'Conor.* Songs for soldiers. L. 1884. First published in William Fieldson's journal week after week.

John, Don. *Jean Ingelow.* Off the Skelligs. L. 1873.

John Earl of Stair. *John Dalrymple*, 5th Earl of Stair. The state of the national debt, the national income, and the national expenditure ... By ... Edinb. 1777.

John, Junior. *Thomas Gibson Bowles*, editor of the "London Vanity Fair."

John, Uncle. *Elisha Noyce.* The boy's book of industrial information. N.Y. 1858.

John, Uncle. *John Aikin.* Children's album of pretty pictures, with stories. N.Y. 18–.

John, Uncle. *J. J. Fuller.* Uncle John's flower-gatherers ... N.Y. 1869.

John, Uncle. *Edwin O. Chapman,* in " Our Boys' Own Stories." N.Y. 1879.

John ʹAt Stiles. *John Dowdall.* Traditionary anecdotes of Shakespeare. Collected in Warwickshire in the year 1693 ... L. 1838.

John of Enon. *David Benedict, D.D.* The watery war: a poetical description of the existing controversy between the Pedobaptists and Baptists ... B. 1808.

John, of Manchester. *John Bosworth,* as editor of the "Sailor, the Sinner, and the Saint: the eventful life of George Viney, late of Manchester" (L. 1853).

John of York. *John H. Tobin,* in the "Old New York Spirit."

John, Gabriel. *Thomas D'Urfey.* Essay towards the theory of the intelligible world intuitively considered. n.p., n.d.

Johnson, Abraham. *Dr. John Hill.* Lucina sine concubitu ... L. 1750.

Also attributed to Rev. H. Coventry.

Johnson, Benjamin F. *James Whitcomb Riley.* The Old Swimmin' Hole. Indianapolis, 1883.

Jonah. *John P. Wetmore.* An American bicycler.

Jonathan, Brother. *Octavius Blewitt.*

Jonathan, Uncle. *Jonathan Badgley.* English Grammar, taught in plain, familiar conversations, by ... Utica, N.Y., 1867.

Jones, Cupid. *Frank S. Saltus,* in his contributions to the "Clipper" (N.Y.).

Jones, Ignatius. *Graham A. Worth.*

Jones, Mrs. Jane. *Jenny Diver.*

Jones, Major Joseph. *William Theodore Thompson.* Major Jones's courtship. P. 1844.

Jones, T. Percy. *William Edmonstoune Aytoun.* Firmilian; or, the student of Badajoz: a spasmodic tragedy ... Edinb. 1854.

Jones, Thomas. *Charles Bright and others.* The Hamlet controversy ? ... L. 1867.

Jones, Trinity, or, Jones of Nayland. *William Jones,* of Nayland. The Catholic doctrine of the Trinity proved ... 1756.

Jonquil. *J. L. Collins.* Was she engaged ... P. 1875.

Jorrocks, Mr. John. *Robert Smith Surtees.* Jorrock's jaunts and jollities. L. 1859.

Joseph, Uncle. *Joseph Banks.* The trip to the Great Exhibition of Barnabas Blandydash and family. By ... L. 1851.

Joseph, Nathan. *George Houston.* — See " An Israelite."

Josephus, Jr. *Joseph Barry.* The annals of Harper's Ferry, from ... 1794 to ... 1869 ... Hagerstown, Md., 1869.

Josh, Uncle. *Otis Whitcomb,* of Swansea, N.H., in the original play entitled " Joshua Whitcomb."

Joslyn, Major Jep. *J. E. P. Doyle.*

Josslyn, Jeff. *J. E. Ferguson.* Washington correspondent of " Texas Siftings."

Journalist, A. *Samuel H. Hammond* and *Lewis W. Mansfield.* Country margins and summer rambles of ... N.Y. 1855.

Journalist, A. *Charles T. Congdon.* Reminiscences of ... B. 1880.

Journey-man, A. *Charles F. Blackburn.* A continental tour of eight days for forty-four shillings. L. 1879.

Journeyman Engineer, The. *Thomas Wright.* Johnny Robinson: the story of ... an "Intelligent Artisan." By ... L. 1868.

Journeyman Mason, A. *Hugh Miller.* Poems written in the leisure hours of ... Inverness, 1829.

Journeyman Printer, A. *Charles Manby Smith.* The working man's way in the world; or, the autobiography of a Journeyman Printer. L. 1853.

Journeyman Tailor, A. *P. D. Holthaus.* Wanderings of ... through Europe and the East, 1824–40. N.Y. 1842.

Joyeuse, Vyvian. *Winthrop Mackworth Praed,* in his contributions to " Knight's Quarterly Magazine " (L.).

Judy, Aunt. *Mrs. Margaret (Scott) Gatty.* The fairy godmothers, and other tales. L. 1851.

Jugg, M. T. *Joseph Howard, Jr.,* in the New York "Herald."

Jules. *Jean Joseph Garnier.* Traité du change. Paris, 1841.

Julia, Aunt. *Julia Colman.* Boys and girls' illustrated bird-book. N.Y. 1857.

Julian. *Karl Richard Waldemar Uschner.* Der letzte Minnesänger. 1875.

Julio. *Joseph Sykes, M.A.* Later poems ... L. 1871.

Julius. *Richard Rush.* Probably his signature in the Philadelphia "Portfolio" of 1803–4.

June, Jennie. *Mrs. Jennie (Cunningham) Croly.* Jennie Juneiana. Talks on women's topics. By ... B. 1864. Also in numerous works for juveniles.

June, Jessie. *Mrs. Simelde Forbes.*

Junia. *Caleb Whitefoord,* who wrote the letter in the "Public Advertiser" signed "Junia," which had the honor of being replied to by Junius himself.

Juniolus Canadensis. *Thomas Cary,* editor of the "Quebec Mercury," who, in 1813, published in that paper, under this pseud., an invective in the style of Junius, against Mr. Stuart, a member of the Lower Canadian House.

Junior Sophister, A. *Samuel Dexter.* The progress of science: a poem ... n.p. 1780.

Juniper. One of the pseudonyms attributed to Junius (*q.v.*).

The letter thus signed (Dec. 4, 1771), is designed, like those of Philo-Junius, "to explain, defend, and support the reputation of the principal."

Juniper, Julius, poet laureat to the Royal College of Physicians. *Thomas Foster, B.A.* The Brunoniad: an heroic poem ... L. 1789.

Junius. — See p. 145.

"At the time when the 'Letters' appeared, pamphlets abounded, fixing their authorship, to the perfect satisfaction of each pamphleteer, upon every public man; the 'Gent. Mag.' opened its columns to suggestions, and was filled with them; in 1824, the 'Monthly Magazine' renewed the subject; in 1837, pamphlets again appeared, with fresh lights, which flickered and went out; and lately, 'Notes and Queries' has worked like a mole on the subject; but they all have been gropings in the dark. We believe the 'Letters' have been fathered, with a greater or less degree of confidence, upon upwards of forty public characters. The most favoured were Sir Philip Francis, Lord Lyttelton, Colonel Barré, Burke, J. Dunning (afterwards Lord Ashburton), Chatham, Dr. Wilmott, Hugh Boyd, Wilkes, Horne Tooke, Lord George Sackville, Governor Pownall, Sir. G. Jackson, Maclean, and Dr. Sidney Swinney. The wildest conjectures have gained believers, and there have been madmen to lay them to George III., a Captain Allen, Suett the comedian, Combe (the author of 'Dr. Syntax'), Bickerton, an eccentric Oxonian, and an utterly unknown Mr. Jones. Who this famous writer was, will be a question asked by generations to follow us." — See ANDREWS's *British Journalism,* Vol. I., p. 185.

"Numerous were the disputants who, emulating the fame of Junius, now rushed into the lists with high-sounding Roman names. Marcus Antonius, Scipio, Brutus, Cato, Valerius, Virginius, played the buffoon in the 'Evening Post,' and thought they were dividing the laurels with the great gladiator of the 'Public Advertiser'; but they were Romans only in name. — Grubstreet claimed them for its own. Crabbe has had his laugh at them in his poem of 'The Newspaper':—

"'These Roman souls, like Rome's great sons, are known
To live in cells on labours of their own;

Thus Milo, could we see the noble chief,
Feeds, for his country's good, on legs of beef;
Camillus copies deeds for sordid pay.
Yet fights the public battles twice a day!
E'en now, the godlike Brutus views his score
Scroll'd on the bar board, swinging with the door,
Where, tippling punch, grave Cato's self you'll see,
And Amor Patriæ vending smuggled tea.'"

See ANDREWS's *British Journalism,* Vol. I., p. 187. See also DE QUINCEY's *Note-Book of an English Opium Eater.*

Junius. *Junius H. Browne.*

Junius. *Ebenezer Smith Thomas,* his signature in the "Charleston (S.C.) City Gazette," 1810–16.

Junius. *Rev. Calvin Colton.* The crisis of the country ... The credit system and the no credit system. N.Y. 1840.

Junius. *Thomas Rowe Edmonds, B.A.* On the reform of the income and property tax. A letter ... to Joseph Hume, Esq, M.P. "Daily News" (L.), 1853.

Junius, Jr. *George T. Denison.* A review of the militia policy of the present administration ... Hamilton, 1863.

Junius Americanus. *David Everett,* author of political essays in the "Boston Gazette" under this signature.

Junius Americanus. *Dr. Charles Lee,* a frequent contributor to the "Gazetteer" and "Public Advertiser" from 1769 to 1771. He is referred to by Junius in the latter's private correspondence with Mr. Woodfall.

Junius Americanus. *Arthur Lee.* The political detection ... L. 1770.

Junius Americanus. *George Osborne Stearns.* A review of "A Discourse occasioned by the death of Daniel Webster, preached ... October 31, by Theodore Parker" ... By ... B. 1853.

Junius Hibernicus. *John Egan,* in his letters to the "General Evening Post" (Dublin, 1781–82). — See "N. & Q.," 2d series, viii., 166.

Junius Secundus. *William Fletcher,* in his contributions to the "General Evening Post" (Dublin, 1781–82). — See "N. & Q.," 2d series, viii., 166.

Junius Secundus. *Charles Kelsall.* Constantine and Eugene ... By ... Brussels, 1818.

Jupiter of the Press, The. *The London Times.*

Juriscola. *Tench Coxe.* An examination of the conduct of Great Britain respecting Neutrals since the year 1791. B. 1808.

Jurisconsult. *S. S. Boyd.* Considerations on the appointment of a Justice of the Supreme Court of the United States ... Natchez (?), 1852.

Juris Consultus. *Rev. Alonzo Bowen Chapin*, contributor to the "Knickerbocker," etc., and author of a number of books and pamphlets.

Juryman, A. *William Creech.* An account of the trial of William Brodie and George Smith ... Edinb. 1788.

Juryman, A. *William Smellie.* An address to the people of Scotland on the nature, powers, and privileges of juries: by ... Edinb. 1784.

Justia, a Know-Nothing. *F. Colburn Adams.* Our world; or, the Democrats' rule ... L. 1855.

Justified Sinner, A. *James Hogg,* the Ettrick Shepherd. The private memoirs of A Justified Sinner, written by himself, with a detail of curious traditionary facts, etc. L. 1824.

The name of the "Sinner" is Robert Wringham Colwan.

Justinian. *Thomas Law.* Remarks on the report of the Secretary of the Treasury ... By ... Wilmington, Del., 1820.

Justinian, of South Carolina. *Lewis Cruger.* Sovereign Rights of the States ... W. 185–.

Justinophilus. *Samuel Badcock.* A letter addressed to Dr. Priestley. Exeter, 178–.

Justitia. *William A. Brewer,* in his contributions to various New York and Boston periodicals.

Justitia. *Bennett Lowe.* Photographic note book.

Justitia, M. *John Frearson.* The universal revival of religion ... L. 1858.

Justus. *C. Ebhardt.* La riforma delle biblioteche. Milan, 1876.

Juvenile, The. *Col. Thomas Picton,* in his contributions to the "Chronicle" (San Francisco, Cal.), etc.

Juvenis. *J. W. Stephenson.* Brent Knoll ... By ... L. 1837.

Juvenis. *R. G. Arrowsmith.* Doubts upon the reasoning of Dr. Paley ... L. 1811.

Juvenis Suffolciensis. *Robert Reeve,* in "Gent. Mag.," January, 1806, p. 17.

Juvinell, Uncle. *Morrison Heady.* The Farmer Boy [Washington], and how he became Commander-in-Chief ... B. 1864.

THE LETTERS OF "JUNIUS."

It is not my intention — and, even did I wish to do so, the limits of the present work forbid it — to give a complete history of these celebrated letters. The subject has been practically exhausted in the many excellent editions quoted hereafter, and I shall confine myself to the following statistics: —

I. The date of appearance of the letters signed "Junius," together with a list of the other signatures employed by this writer; to which latter pseudonyms, cross-references will be found scattered throughout this work.

II. A list of all the claimants to the authorship, with the respective merits of each.

III. A bibliography of the subject.

IV. Miscellaneous notes, etc.

I. The letters signed "Junius" appeared in the "Public Advertiser" of the following dates: —

Nov. 21, 1768.	Sept. 7, 1769.
Jan. 21, 1769.	Sept. 19, 1769.
Feb. 7, 1769.	Sept. 25, 1769.
Feb. 21, 1769.	Oct. 13, 1769.
Mar. 3, 1769.	Oct. 17, 1769.
Mar. 18, 1769.	Oct. 20, 1769.
Apr. 10, 1769.	Nov. 15, 1769.
Apr. 21, 1769.	(See "Modestus.")
Apr. 24, 1769.	Nov. 29, 1769.
May 30, 1769.	Dec. 12, 1769.
July 8, 1769.	Dec. 19, 1769.
July 19, 1769.	Feb. 14, 1770.
July 29, 1769.	Mar. 19, 1770.
Aug. 8, 1769.	Apr. 3, 1770.
Aug. 22, 1769.	May 28, 1770.

Aug. 22, 1770.	Sept. 28, 1771.
Nov. 14, 1770.	Sept. 30, 1771.
Jan. 30, 1771.	Oct. 5, 1771.
Apr. 22, 1771.	Nov. 2, 1771.
June 22, 1771.	Nov. 28, 1771.
July 9, 1771.	Jan. 21, 1772.
July 24, 1771.	(Two letters.)
Aug. 13, 1771.	

See also: — A. B. Amicus Curiae. Anti-Belial. Anti-Fox. Anti-Sejanus, Jun. Anti-Stuart. Atticus. Augur. Bifrons. Brutus. C. Correggio. Crito. Cumbriensis. Domitian. Downright. A Faithful Monitor. Fiat Justitia. G. W. Henricus. Juniper. L. L. A Labourer in the same Cause. Lucius. Mnemon. Moderator. Moderatus. Nemesis. Phalaris. Philo-Junius. Pomona. Poplicola. Q in the Corner. Scotus. Simplex. Temporum Felicitas. Testiculus. Testis. Valerius. Veteran. Vindex.

A Whig. Why? X. X. Y. Z. Your Real Friend.

See also "Notes and Queries," 1st Ser., vi. 239; xii. 299.

II. The following list of 51 names, embraces the personages to whom these celebrated letters have been attributed. The Roman numerals appended to the notes indicate the corresponding work in the bibliography (Part III.).

Adair, James, M.P., Serjeant at Law. d. 1798.

A Mr. Sergeant Adair was once produced, on the plea of certain ephemeral pamphlets, but the feebleness they evinced caused him to be quickly given up. — WADE, "Junius," ii. xv.

The reader should also consult the lengthy argument of Mr. Adair against granting a *nolle prosequi* in favor of the messengers of the House of Commons, and the reference to this case in Junius' letter of April 9, 1771.

Allen, Captain. — See "Notes and Queries," 1st Ser., xi. 302.

Barré, Lieut.-Col. Isaac, M.P.

In the works by Britton and Jaques (Nos. LXXXV. and LXXXVI.), I find the opinion expressed that Barré was aided by Lord Shelburne and Dunning (afterwards Lord Ashburton). The "Morning Herald," as early as 1813, stated that the Earl of Shelburne was probably Junius, and that Barré and Dunning assisted him.

For the claims advanced in favor of and against Barré, see Jaques' work, p. 141, Allibone, Britton, Wade, II. xxix. and No. LXXVI.

Bentinck, William Henry Cavendish.

His name is mentioned in Coventry's "Critical Enquiry" (see No. LXI.).

Bickerton, Mr.

In the "Oxford Spy" (Oxf.), 1818, p. 24, will be found a notice of this eccentric individual, who is said to have kept a horse in Hertford College, Oxford, which was sometimes seen looking out of a window on the second floor. For additional information, see "Notes and Queries," 1st Ser., xi. 370.

Boyd, Hugh M'Aulay. b. 1746; d. 1791.

Boyd's claims are summarily disposed of in Wade's work (No. LXXVII.). Almon, in the first volume of "Anecdotes," published in 1797, designates Boyd as the author of Junius. See also Wraxall, "Memoirs of his own Time," 1836, ii. 93–94, and Nos. XXX., XXXIII., XLIX., LI.

Boyd has been described as "an admirer of Junius, and vain enough to wish to be thought the author."

As to Macaulay Boyd's being the author of Junius's Letters, it is a *perfect joke;* no two characters can be more perfectly unlike than Boyd and Junius. — BUTLER, "Reminiscences," i. 84.

Burke, Rt. Hon. Edmund. b. 1728; d. 1797.

Bishop Markham, an early friend and patron of Burke, taxed the latter with the authorship of the "Letters," telling him that his house was a "nest of adders." Although Burke never made any positive denial to this imputation, he certainly disavowed any connection with Junius,

on three distinct occasions. Firstly, he said to Charles Townshend, "I give you my word and honour that I am not the author of Junius." — See Burke's "Correspondence," by Lord Fitzwilliam, i. 269–275. Secondly, he positively denied the imputed authorship, on being questioned by Sir William Draper; and lastly, he made a denial to Johnson, when he said, "I could not if I would, and I would not if I could." — See Boswell's "Johnson," iv., for the detailed circumstances.

It seems somewhat strange, however, that Burke should have been so generally suspected as the author. That such was the case, nevertheless, is obvious, not only from the opinion at first entertained by Sir William Draper, but from various public accusations conveyed in the periodicals of the day. The letter of Zeno in the "Public Advertiser," dated Oct. 15, 1771, is addressed "to Junius, *alias* Edmund the Jesuit of St. Omer's."

See also Wade's edition of Woodfall, II., xxvii. 138, and Nos. XXXVIII., LXII., LXIV., and LXXXVI.

Burke, William. — See No. LXXXVI.

Butler, John, Bishop of Hereford. d. 1802.

Butler was secretary to the Rt. Hon. Bilson Legge, Chancellor of the Exchequer, and Wilkes is said to have suspected him as the author. Butler, however, was a man of no political courage, and his works lack the fire which characterize the "Letters." His claims are discussed in Dr. Good's Essay, in the edition published in 1814.

Camden, Charles, Lord. b. 1713; d. 1794.

It appears almost ludicrous to note that the great Lord Camden was suspected, simply on the ground of his dislike to the law and politics of Chief Justice Mansfield. — WADE.

De Lolme, John Lewis. b. 1745 (?); d. 1807.

De Lolme's claims are advocated in Dr. Busby's work (see No. XLVI.), but it must be remembered that he only arrived in England in 1769. He is the author of an elegantly written "Essay on the English Constitution," which is quoted by Junius.

Dunning, John, afterwards **Lord Ashburton.** b. 1731; d. 1783.

The soul of Junius is, as we conjecture, commemorated in the picture exhibited in Sir Joshua Reynold's gallery, representing Lord Shelburne of Junius's day, Mr. Dunning, and Colonel Barré of parliamentary fame, in conference. — JAQUES, p. 141. (See Barré, *ante.*)

Heron espouses the claims of Dunning, and Britton includes him among his claimants; but a very strong point against him is the fact that he was appointed solicitor-general in December, 1767, and held that office until March, 1770. Hence, admitting that he was Junius, the famous letter "to the king," in December, 1769, must have proceeded from his Majesty's own solicitor-general! The Earl of Shelburne, who was intimately acquainted with Dunning, often declared that the latter did not "write a line of Junius."

Dyer, Samuel. b. 1725; d. 1772.

Dyer is referred to in Malone's "Life of Dryden," as "a man of excellent taste and profound erudition, whose principal literary work, *under a Roman signature,* when the veil with which for near thirty-six years it has been enveloped shall be removed, will place him in a high rank among English writers, and transmit a name now little known, with distinguished lustre to posterity."

Malone held the opinion that if Burke did not write the Letters, they were at least written by some one who had received considerable aid from Burke in composing them. It is said that upon Dyer's death, Burke obtained and destroyed all the papers which he had left behind him.

Malone strongly favored the claims of Dyer, but it must be remembered that this claimant was a very old man at the time when these letters appeared, a fact inconsistent with the vigor and fire they exhibit.

See also Dr. Good's Essay, and "Notes and Queries," 2d Ser., ix. 261.

Flood, Henry. b. 1732; d. 1791.

For extensive criticisms in favor of and against the claims of this Irish orator, the reader is referred to Dr. Good's Essay, Wade i. 79 (No. LXXVII.), and "Notes and Queries," 2d Ser., viii. 101, 189, 259.

Francis, Sir Philip. b. 1740; d. 1818.

The external evidence is, we think, such as would support a verdict in a civil, nay, in a criminal proceeding. The handwriting of Junius is the very peculiar handwriting of Francis, slightly disguised. As to the position, pursuits, and connections of Junius, the following are the most important facts which can be considered as clearly proved: First, that he was acquainted with the technical forms of the secretary of state's office; secondly, that he was intimately acquainted with the business of the War-office; thirdly, that he, during the year 1770, attended debates in the House of Lords, and took notes of speeches, particularly of the speeches of Lord Chatham; fourthly, that he bitterly resented the appointment of Mr. Chamier to the place of deputy-secretary of war; fifthly, that he was bound by some strong tie to the first Lord Holland. Now, Francis passed some years in the secretary of state's office. He was subsequently chief clerk of the War-office. He repeatedly mentioned that he had himself, in 1770, heard speeches of Lord Chatham; and some of these speeches were actually printed from his notes. He resigned his clerkship at the War-office from resentment at the appointment of Mr. Chamier. It was by Lord Holland that he was first introduced into the public service. Now, here are five marks, all of which ought to be found in Junius. They are all five found in Francis. We do not believe that more than two of them can be found in any other person whatever. If this argument does not settle the question, there is an end of all reasoning on circumstantial evidence. — MACAULAY.

My own impression is that the "Letters of Junius" were written by Sir Philip Francis. In a speech which I once heard him deliver at the Mansion House, concerning the partition of Poland, I had a striking proof that Francis possessed no ordinary powers of eloquence. — ROGERS, "Table Talk," p. 272.

I have inserted the foregoing quotations, to indicate what has been said in favor of Francis' claims; if the reader is curious enough to pursue the subject more extensively, he will find a chapter on the disputed question in the "Memoirs of Sir Philip Francis," by Parkes and Merivale, L. 1867, i. 223-303. See also Taylor's works, Nos. XL. and XLVIII.; Wade, ii. xxx.-xc., No. LXXVII.; "Notes and Queries," 1st Ser., xi. 117, and Nos. LIV., LVI., LVII., LXXVIII., XC.

The following letter, taken from the "Athenæum," March 16, 1861, may be of interest in this place : —

MY DEAR PARKES, —

I have often tried to guess the meaning of the motto to Junius, "*Stat nominis umbra*," " The shadow of the name stands." But in looking. the other day, at the title-page of the "Etymologicon Anglicanum," I thought that I could guess the meaning. The title is, —

Franciscii Junii
Francisci Filii
Etymologicon
Anglicanum.

And under the frontispiece are these words : —

Franciscus Junius,
Francisci Filius.

We know that Sir P. Francis often gave obscure hints as to his authorship of Junius. I think that by the words, "*Stat nominis umbra*," he meant to indicate that Junius was the son of Francis. This may seem far-fetched; but what other explanation of the motto can you give? My explanation is that he meant to establish a claim to the authorship, without being forced to make that claim; which, in fact, he never had the courage to do. N. W. SENIOR.

Taylor, in Woodfall's edition of 1812, was the first person who fixed upon Francis as the author; but he fell into one of the snares which Junius had adroitly laid for enquirers. Misled " by one of those well-contrived feints that were meant to mislead," Mr. Taylor inferred that Junius must be a person of advanced years, and fixed upon the Rev. Philip Francis, the father of Sir Philip, as the author. The elder Francis was a fine classical scholar, celebrated for his masterly translations of Horace and Demosthenes; but when Mr. Taylor discovered him to be ten years older than he had at first been led to believe, he devoted all his attention toward proving the claims of the younger man, and embodied his researches in a subsequent volume.

ADVERSE CRITICISMS UPON FRANCIS' CLAIMS.

Sir Nathaniel Wraxall is convinced that Sir Philip Francis was the author of Junius. I do not yet believe it. He was too vain a man to let the secret die with him. — SIR EGERTON BRYDGES' "Notes on Wraxall's Memoirs."

I persist in thinking that neither Mr. Burke nor Philip Francis was the author of the letters under the signature of Junius. I think the mind of the first so superior, and the mind of the latter so inferior, to that of Junius, as to put the supposition that either of them was Junius wholly out of the question. — MR. CHARLES BUTLER's Letter to Mr. E. H. Barker, June 14, 1828.

We must all grant that a strong case has been made out for Francis; but I could set up very stout objections to those claims. It was not in his nature to keep a secret. He would have told it from vanity, or from his courage, or from his patriotism. His bitterness, his vivacity, his acuteness, are stamped, in characters very peculiar, upon many publications that bear his name; and very faint indeed is their resemblance to the spirit, and, in an extended sense of the word, to the style, of Junius. — DR. PARR.

With reference to the claims of Sir Philip, I am inclined to use the form of argument called a "dilemma." Thus, if Sir Philip Francis was the author of the letters, he was a scurrilous libeller; if he was not, he was a *splendide mendax,— utrum horum mavis accipe.* — JOHN WILKINS, in 1865.

Francis' claims are also adversely discussed in Fellows' "The Posthumous Works of Junius," No. LXVII.; Jaques, p. 173, No. LXXV.; "Notes and Queries," 2d Ser., vi. 43; 3d Ser., viii. 183,

356, xi. 102; 4th Ser., xi. 130, 178, 202, 243, 387, 425, 465, 512, xii. 33, 69, 81; and Nos. LIV., LVIII., LXIV., LXXXVII.

George III., King of England.

" Ma'am Serres condemns all aspirers to pot
That prate of a Junius, since Uncle Wilmot
Ranks scribe of each letter she dares pledge her word,
As sure as not one came from King George the Third."

See Ireland's poem, " Scribbleomania," p. 308, for a curious note on this subject.

Gibbon, Edward. b. 1737; d. 1794.

This claimant, beyond holding a position, does not seem to have distinguished himself to any extent in the politics of his day, his mind being too absorbed in the great task which has made him famous. See Nos. LII., LIV.

Glover, Richard. b. 1712; d. 1785.

Johnston declares that he has no faith in the claim of Glover, although his advocates, as corroborative facts, assert that he " wore a bag, with his wig accurately dressed, and carried a small cocked hat under his arm, before the year 1776, and in this costume constantly walked, in fine weather, from his house in St. James Street, in Westminster, into the city"; this fact being brought forward in proof of his being identical with the " tall gentleman " who threw the letter into Mr. Woodfall's office in Ivy Lane.
Wraxall, in his "Memoirs of his own Time," 1836, ii. 97, states that Glover's son assured him that " he had not the least reason to suppose or to believe that his father composed the letters of Junius." See Nos. XLI., XLII.

Grattan, Henry. b. 1750; d. 1820.

Grattan's claims were advocated by R. Perry in 1851; in the 1806 edition of the " Letters," published by Almon, the compiler says that it was supposed by some that Grattan and Maclean were the joint authors. Mr. Almon addressed a letter of inquiry to the Irish patriot, which evoked the following reply : —

SIR, — I frankly assure you that I know nothing of Junius, except that I am *not* the author. When Junius began I was a boy, and knew nothing of politics, or the persons concerned in them.
I am, Sir, *not Junius*, but your very good wisher and obedient servant,

Dublin, Nov. 4, 1805.   H. GRATTAN.

Greatrakes, William. b. 1729; d. 1781.

This claimant is brought forward in the " Gent. Mag." for December, 1813, lxxxiii. 547; in Coventry's " Critical Enquiry," No. LXI.; and in Wraxall's " Memoirs."
Greatrakes, a native of Ireland, died suddenly at Hungerford, on his way from Bristol to London, and was buried there, with the words " *stat nominis umbra* " inscribed on his tombstone. As this motto figures on the " Junius " title-page, it is easy to imagine how he comes to be classed among the claimants. Britton undertakes to prove that Greatrakes was the amanuensis employed by Junius to copy his letters for the " Public Advertiser "; " but it ought first to be shown," says Wade, " that Junius employed an amanuensis. If he did, and Greatrakes was his penman, it could hardly give him a claim to the motto of his principal. That was a distinction, which, if it has any significance, could be applicable only to the shadow of a shade that wrote the letters, not the copyist of them."

Grenville, George. b. 1712; d. 1770.

The prime-minister died before the letters were discontinued, hence but little attention need be paid to his claims.

Grenville, James. d. 1783.

He was the brother of the preceding, and Lord of the Treasury. Although he has been accused of the authorship, he himself established no claims to the honor.

Hamilton, William Gerard. b. 1729; d. 1796.

This claimant is mentioned in Dr. Good's essay; and a letter in the " Public Advertiser " of Nov. 30, 1771, is addressed to William Junius Singlespeech, Esq. Fox said, that, although he would not back Hamilton against the field, he would back him against any single claimant; and Wraxall declares that, " throughout the various companies in which, from 1775 down to the present time, I have heard this mysterious question agitated, the great majority concurred in giving to Hamilton the merit of composing the ' Letters' under examination." Mrs. Piozzi and Samuel Johnson were both inclined to believe in his claims.
The only reason that appears for these letters ever having been attributed to Hamilton was that he happened to be aware of the context of a letter which did not make its appearance until the following day. (For a full account of this curious story, the reader is referred to " Notes and Queries," 2d Ser., vi. 44.)
The arguments against him are four in number, and very conclusive : —
1. He was Chancellor of the Exchequer in Ireland from September, 1769, to April, 1704, — the period when all the letters appeared.
2. When questioned on the subject, by Earl Temple, he positively denied the authorship. See Dr. Good's " Essay," p. 56.
3. Woodfall declared that neither Burke nor Hamilton were responsible for the Letters.
4. Hamilton again distinctly denied the authorship, just before his death, when questioned by a member of the House of Commons.

Hollis, James.

He is referred to, as a claimant, by Wade and Allibone.

Hollis, Thomas. b. 1720; d. 1774.

Alluded to in Coventry's " Critical Enquiry," No. LXI.

Jackson, Sir George, Secretary of the Admiralty.

For an account of the claims advanced in his favor, see " Notes and Queries," 1st Ser., i. 172, 276, 322.

Jones, Sir William. b. 1746; d. 1794.

Mentioned, as a claimant, by Coventry and Wade.

Kent, John. d. 1773.

Kent wished to pass for Junius; but, according to Almon, he was only a newspaper editor, at a small weekly salary. See the " Letter " dated July 21, 1769, in which Junius refers to this personage.

Lee, Maj.-Gen. Charles. b. 1731; d. 1782.

In 1803, Gen. Lee is said to have acknowledged himself the author. If the reader is desirous of seeing some curious evidence against the claimant, he is referred to Wade, i. 61–67.

While Girdlestone (Nos. xxxiii. and xxxvii.) as effectively espoused his claims.

Lloyd, Charles. d. 1773.

Lloyd was the private secretary to George Grenville, and among those who believed in his claims was Dr. Parr. It must not, however, be forgotten, that this claimant died, an old man, just after the letters had ceased, which fact is scarcely in harmony with the spirit they exhibit. See the interesting book by Mr. Barker, Nos. LXIII., LXIV.; also Jaques' work, 147–171, No. LXXV.

Lyttleton, Thomas, 2d Lord. b. 1744; d. 1779.

Mr. Dilke, in his "Papers of a Critic," vol. ii., and Mr. Thoms, in "Notes and Queries," 1st Ser., xi. 198, have shown that Lyttleton no longer deserves a place among the Junius claimants.

See also "Notes and Queries," 1st Ser., viii. 31; "Littell's Living Age," xlii. 223; and the "Quarterly Review," xc. 91.

Maclean, Laughlin. b. 1727; d. 1777.

This claimant had been under-secretary of state during Lord Shelburne's possession of the office for the southern department. (See Junius' "Letter," of date March 6, 1771.) During the years 1769 and 1770, when Junius was most active, Mr. Maclean "was absorbed in his own pecuniary difficulties consequent on gambling in India stock"; and in 1772 he was acting as collector in the city of Philadelphia in this country, while the "Letters" were still appearing in England. See Galt, "Life of West." Almon, in 1806, thought that he was a joint-author with Grattan. Twenty-two arguments have been published in favor of Maclean, in "Waldie's (P.) Library," edited by John Jay Smith. See also "Notes and Queries," 2d Ser., vii. 310.

Marshall, Rev. Edmund. d. 1797.

This gentleman, vicar of Charing, in Kent, occasionally wrote political letters in the "Kentish Gazette," over the pseudonym of "Cantianus." His claims are referred to in Nichols' "Literary Illustrations of the Eighteenth Century," viii. 680.

Paine, Thomas. b. 1737; d. 1809.

See No. LXXXIX. The audacity of the author of this work is my apology for its insertion.

Pitt, William, Earl of Chatham. b. 1708; d. 1778.

Chatham could not very well have been Junius, as the latter was very anxious to obtain duplicate proofs from the printer to forward to Pitt (see the "Chatham Papers," p. 52), and the celebrated letter to Lord Mansfield, it is well known, was sent to Chatham some days before it was printed. Moreover, Pitt, "though most effective in oratory, was careless in literary composition; inexact, loose, and repetitionary: very unlike Junius, who not only polished his public letters to the highest finish, but never let the most brief or trivial private note escape him unmarked by the hand of a master." See also "Notes and Queries," 3d Ser., viii. 356, 440, and Nos. xxxiv., LXX., LXXI., LXXIII., LXXXV.

Portland, William, Duke of. b. 1738; d. 1809.

See Mr. Johnston's work, No. xLVII., in which the author argues that the principal object of the "Letters" was the restoration of the estate of the Duke of Portland, part of which had been taken from him in 1767 and granted to Sir James Lowther, who had married Lord Bute's daughter.

Pownall, Thomas. b. 1722; d. 1805.
— See No. LXXXIV.

Rich, Lieut.-Col., Sir Robert. — See No. LXXXIII.

Roberts, John. d. 1772.

This gentleman was anonymously accused of having written the Letters in the "Public Advertiser," March 21, 1772, et passim. He died July 13, 1772, before the Junius Letters were discontinued.

Rosenhagen, Rev. Philip.

Upon the authority of Gerard Hamilton, it is related by Almon that Rosenhagen endeavored to obtain a pension from Lord North, by stipulating that Junius (he himself) should write no more. But there is no similarity in the handwriting of this claimant to that of Junius, and, moreover, Rosenhagen being of foreign extraction, could hardly be master of the idiomatic phraseology that Junius had at his command. See also "Notes and Queries," 3d Ser., v. 16.

Sackville, George, Viscount. b. 1716; d. 1785.

Dr. Good, in his preliminary essay to Woodfall's edition of 1812, states that "Sir William Draper divided his suspicions between this nobleman and Mr. Burke, and upon the personal and unequivocal denial of the latter, he transferred them entirely to the former: and that Sir William was not the only person who suspected his lordship even from the first, is evident from the private letter of Junius, which asserts that Swinney had actually called upon Lord Sackville and taxed him with being Junius, to his face. (See Private Letter, 5.)

Sackville on one occasion observed to a friend, "I should be proud to be capable of writing as Junius has done; but there are many passages in his letters I should be very sorry to have written." His lordship, moreover, was afterward created Lord George Germaine, a favorite of George III., and unlikely to be his accuser. See also Chalmers, "Appendix to the Supplemental Apology," p. 7 (No. xxx); Wraxall, "Memoirs of his own Time," ii. 90; and Nos. LXI., LXVI., LXXV.

Shelburne, Earl of, Marquis of Lansdowne. d. 1804.

He disclaimed the distinction, only a week before his death, on being personally applied to on the subject of Junius by the late Sir Richard Phillips. — WADE.
See also Barré and Dunning, ante.

Stanhope, Philip Dormer, Earl of Chesterfield. b. 1695; d. 1772.

Chesterfield was over seventy years of age when the Letters appeared, and Mr. Dilke, in the "Papers of a Critic," ii., states that he wrote to the Bishop of Waterford, — "I am prodigiously old, and every month of the calendar adds at least a year to my age. My hand trembles to that degree that I can hardly hold my pen. My understanding stutters and my memory fumbles."
See Nos. LV., LXXXIX., LXXX.

Suett, Richard. d. 1805.

See No. LIII. A work described as "a clumsy display of wit and learning; the former consisting of stale anecdotes and ill-put jokes; the latter of looked-for quotations. To justify his

catchpenny-title, about a dozen pages at the end
are given to the author's interview with a dying
stranger, who confessed himself to be Suett the
comedian, and the author of Junius.

Temple, Richard, Earl. b. 1711;
d. 1779.

The third volume of the " Grenville Papers,"
edited by William J. Smith (L. 1852), contains a
discussion on the authenticity of the Junius Letters, with specimens of the handwriting of Richard Grenville, Lord Temple, *et al.*, assuming the
latter to be Junius, and his wife the amanuensis.
Mr. Wade very justly observes that " Earl
Temple was not reputed by a discerning judge
to be a writer of competent power to wing the
shafts of Junius . . . Temple was an active politician, a Peer of Parliament, and brother-in-law
of Lord Chatham, and had no need of the ' Public Advertiser ' to circulate his opinions." See
No. LXIX.

Tooke, John Horne. b. 1736; d.
1812.

In the "Memoirs of John Horne Tooke," ii.
358, I find it stated that he always appeared
much perturbed when the subject of Junius was
introduced. He was once asked if he knew the
author, and crossing his knife and fork on his
plate and assuming a stern look, he answered,
"I do." "After this," says Mr. Stephen, " his
manner, tone, and attitude were all too formida-
ble to admit of any further interrogatories."
See Nos. VIII., XXVIII., XLIII., XLIV., LXV.,
LXVII.

Walpole, Horatio, Earl of Orford.
b. 1717; d. 1797.

Coventry has thoroughly exploded any claims
which this personage may have been invested
with. See Wilke's " Papers of a Critic," ii. 158.

Wedderburn, Alexander. Lord
Loughborough. b. 1733; d. 1805.

Lord Holland, in his " Memoirs of the Whig
Party," remarks that George III. always regarded Lord Loughborough as Junius. I believe that Lord Holland adds that King William
IV. was his informant.
Lord Campbell repudiates the notion of Wedderburn being Junius. Sir Nathaniel Wraxall,
in his " Memoirs of his own Time " (ii. 97),
states that " during many years of my life, notwithstanding the severity with which Wedderburn is treated by ' Junius,' I nourished a strong
belief, approaching to conviction, that the late
Earl of Rosslyn, then Mr. Wedderburn, was
himself the author of these Letters, and that
persons of credit had recognized the handwriting to be that of Mrs. Wedderburn, his first
wife."

Wilkes, John. b. 1727; d. 1797.

It is said that a wag first propagated the report that Wilkes was Junius, in the columns of
the " Gazetteer." He asserted that, while going
over St. George's Fields, he picked up a piece of
blotted MS., containing a portion of the last
Junius Letter, which had been thrown out with
the sweepings from King's Bench prison, where
Wilkes was then a prisoner. A correspondent
of the " Gent. Mag." (lix. 786) renewed the
statement, but nothing in support of the hypothesis has been produced.
John Mason Good, in his preliminary essay,
remarks, " that Wilkes is not the author must
be clear to every one who will merely give a
glance at either the public or the private letters.
Wilkes could not have abused himself in the
manner he is occasionally abused in the former;

nor would he have said in the latter (since there
was no necessity for his so saying), ' I have been
out of town for three weeks,' at a time when he
was closely confined in the King's Bench."
See Nos. VIII., XI.

Wilmot, James, D.D. b. 1726; d.
1807.

Wm. Beckford, the author of "Vathek," is
said in a conversation in the "New Monthly
Magazine," to have expressed his opinion that
Wilmot was Junius, but he adduced no facts to
prove his statement.
Probably the only other personage who believed in the claims of Wilmot was his niece, the
celebrated Olivia Wilmot Serres, *ci-devant*
Princess of Cumberland, and she was an impostor herself. See Nos. XXXIX., L.; the " Gent.
Mag." for 1813 and 1814; and " Notes and Queries," 4th Ser., ii. 113.

Wray, Daniel. b. 1701; d. 1783.

Wray was Deputy Teller of the Exchequer
by favor of the Hardwicke family. See Nichols'
" Illustrations of Literary History " ; " Notes
and Queries," 2d Ser., ii. 164; and No. LXVIII.

III. The Bibliography of Junius.

When a title is preceded by an asterisk (*), it
is to indicate that the work in question has been
personally examined by me. Subsequent editions
of the same work are omitted.

I. *Fearne, Charles.—An Impartial
answer to the Doctrine delivered in a
Letter which appeared in the Public
Advertiser under the signature of "Junius." L. 1769. 8vo.

II. *The Political Contest, containing
a Series of Letters between Junius and
Sir Will. Draper : also the whole of Junius's Letters to his Grace the D*** of
G****** [*i.e.,* the Duke of Grafton],
brought into one point of view. L.,
Newbery, *s. a.* but Aug. 1769. 8vo.

See also "Notes and Queries," 1st Ser., vi.
224, 239, 261, 285, 383.

III. The Political Contest, Part II. ;
being a Continuation of Junius' Letters
from the 6th of July to the present
Time. L., Newbery, *s. a.* but Sept. 1769.
8vo.

IV. The Political Contest, containing
all the Letters between Junius and Sir
William Draper. Also the whole of Junius's Letters to the D*k*s of G*****n
and B*****d [*i.e.,* Bedford]. And his
last Letter on the Rescue of a General
Officer. Dublin, 1769. 8vo.

Lowndes states that this is called the third
edition, and that it is probably a reprint of the
second London edition.

V. *A Collection of the Letters of
Atticus, Lucius, Junius, and others.
With observations and notes. L., Al-
mon, 1769. 8vo.

VI. [Same title.] New Edition, continued to the end of October, 1769. L.,
Almon, 1769. 8vo.

vii. [Same title.] New Edition, continued to the end of November, 1769. L., Almon, 1769. 8vo.

viii. *Interesting Letters selected from the Correspondence of Messrs. Wilkes, Horne [Tooke], Beckford, and Junius. With anecdotes never before published. L., Nicholl, 1769. 8vo.

This is a small pamphlet of 64 pages, and a parody on the subject.

ix. A Vindication of the D—— of G—— [i.e. the Duke of Grafton], in Answer to a Letter signed "Junius" inserted in the "Public Advertiser" of Saturday, the 18th of March. L., Nicholl, 1769. 8vo.

x. Two Letters from Junius to the D—— of G——, on the Sale of a Patent Place in the Customs at Exeter. To which is added, a Letter from Junius, containing an Address supposed to have been made to a Great Personage. Taken from the "Public Advertiser." L. [no publisher's name], December, 1769. 8vo.

xi. *An Address to Junius on his Letter in the "Public Advertiser," Dec. 19, 1769. L. [no publisher's name] 1769. 8vo.

A pamphlet, in which the letters are attributed to Wilkes. A second edition appeared in 1770.

xii. The Twelve Letters of Canana: on the impropriety of petitioning the King to dissolve the Parliament. L. [? a publisher's name] 1770. 8vo.

A pamphlet of 44 pages, and exceedingly scarce. See also "Notes and Queries," 2d Ser., vi. 44.

xiii. Two Remarkable Letters of Junius and the Freeholder, addressed to the K—— [i.e. the King], with Answers and Strictures. L. [no publisher's name] 1770. 8vo.

A pamphlet entitled "The King's Answer to Junius" appeared in Philadelphia the following year.

xiv. Letters of Junius. Dublin [? a publisher's name], 1770. 8vo.

A volume of 108 pages, and evidently a reprint of Almon's collection of the early letters. See v., vi., and vii., ante.

xv. A complete Collection of Junius's Letters, with those of Sir William Draper. L., A. Thomson, 1770. 8vo.

This publisher issued a second edition with the same title in March or April, 1770, which contained the letter of March 19th; a third edition in June, 1770, with the letters of April 3d and May 28th; and a fourth edition in August, 1770, which contained the letter of August 22d, addressed to Lord North.

xvi. Junius's Political Axioms, addressed to twelve millions of People in Great Britain and Ireland. L., V. Griffith, s. a. [? 1770]. 8vo.

xvii. *The Letters of Junius. L. [no publisher's name] 1770. 12mo.

This is J. Wheble's original edition, but does not bear his name. There is a vignette Cap of Liberty on the title-page. This work served Junius as copy for his edition of 1772. It concludes with the Letter to Lord North, dated Aug. 22, 1770. The second edition appeared the same year, bore Wheble's name on page 247, and ended with the letter to Mansfield dated Nov. 14, 1770. The first portion of the second volume also appeared toward the end of 1770; and the second portion, the following year. Wheble published two editions dated 1771, which must have appeared after Woodfall's edition; as the first of them concludes with the note about Horne Tooke, and the second contains the Philo-Junius Letters, and a letter to Lord Apsley dated February, 1775!!! See also xxii. et seq.

xviii. Letters addressed to the King, the Duke of Grafton, the Earls of Chesterfield and Sandwich, Lord Barrington, Junius, and the Rev. Mr. Horne [Tooke], under the signature of "P. P. S." L. [? a publisher's name] 1771. 8vo.

xix. *An Answer to Junius, shewing his imaginary Ideas and false Principles, his wrong Positions and random Conclusions. L., Organ, 1771. 8vo.

xx. *The genuine Letters of Junius, to which are prefixed Anecdotes of the Author. Piccadilly [no publisher's name], 1771. 8vo.

This is called the "Piccadilly Edition," and contains 366 pages. Lowndes thinks, from internal evidence, that there was an earlier edition, dated 1770, and ending on page 255. The authorship is fathered on Burke.

xxi. *Junius. L., Woodfall, 1772. 2 vols. 12mo.

The first authorized edition, printed under the author's inspection; preceded by a dedication of 10 pages, a preface of 22, and illustrated with notes. It was published March 3, 1772, without table of contents or index, but was re-issued about March, 1773, with both. Many years afterwards, the remaining copies of either this edition or a verbatim reprint appear to have been sold off, and the date erased by the purchaser from the title-page; which accounts for a supposed edition without date.—Lowndes.

Ewing, a Dublin publisher, issued a reprint of Woodfall's edition this same year, and added fourteen new letters, either written by, or replied to by Junius.

See also "Notes and Queries," 1st Ser., vi. 224, for a supposed edition of 1771.

xxii. The Letters of Junius. L., Wheble, 1772. 2 vols. 12mo.

[See xvii. ante.] The title-page of vol. 2 is struck off from the same copperplate, and "vol. 2" is introduced in type; and the MDCCLXXI. is turned into MDCCLXXII. by the addition of I., also in type. This edition, or at least the second volume of it, could not have been published until after January 21, 1772, as it contains the letter to Lord Camden.—Lowndes.

Numerous editions of the Letters were published during the succeeding twenty years, none of which call for any special notice.

xxiii. The Rights of the Sailors vindicated. In answer to a letter of Junius. L. [? a publisher's name] 1772. 8vo.

xxiv. [Hughes, Benjamin.] An Epistle to Junius. L. [? a publisher's name] 1774. 8vo.

xxv. * A serious Letter to the Public, on the late Transaction between Lord North and the Duke of Grafton. By Junius. L. [no publisher's name] 1778. 8vo.

A forgery, with which Junius had nothing to do.

xxvi. The Intrepid Magazine. L. 1784. 8vo.

Contains letters signed "Junius."

xxvii. Anecdotes of Junius: to which is prefixed the King's Reply. Southampton, Baker, 1788. 8vo.

These anecdotes are reprinted from the Piccadilly Edition of 1771.

xxviii. Junius discovered. By P. T., Esq. L., Fores, s. a. but 1789. 8vo.

Written by Philip Thicknesse, and in favor of Tooke.

xxix. * The Letters of Junius. A new edition with a copious index. L., Hamilton, 1792. 2 vols. 12mo.

The following editions also deserve passing mention : —
Bensley's, L. 1794, 2 vols., 12mo.
Campbell's, P. 1795, 16mo.
Mundell's, L. 1796, 8vo.
Bensley's, L. 1797, 2 vols., 8vo. [A few on L. P.]; L. 1798, 2 vols., 12mo and 8vo; L. 1799, 2 vols., 8vo.
Vernor & Hood's, L. 1800, 2 vols., 18mo; L. 1804, 1 vol., 18mo; L. 1806, 2 vols., 12mo.
Bensley's, L. 1801 and 1806, 2 vols., 8vo.

xxx. * Chalmers, George. — An Appendix to the Supplemental Apology . . . being the Documents for the Opinion that Hugh McAulay Boyd wrote Junius's Letters. L., 1800. 8vo.

xxxi. * The Letters of Junius, with Notes and Illustrations Historical, Political, Biographical, and Critical, by Robert Heron. L. 1802. 2 vols. 8vo.

An edition of this book was published in the same year, containing both volumes in one. A second edition, of two volumes, was published in 1804, containing 70 pages added to the preface of the first volume, and an appendix of 18 to the second. It was reprinted in Philadelphia and Boston the same year.

xxxii. * Almon, John. — The Letters of Junius Complete, with letters and articles to which he replied, and with notes biographical and explanatory; also a prefatory enquiry respecting the real author. L. 1806. 2 vols. 12mo.

The following editions appeared about this period : —
Ballantyne's, Edinb. 1807. 8vo.
Oddy's, L. 1811, 2 vols., 12mo.
Goodwin's, L. 1812, 2 vols., 12mo.

xxxiii. * [Girdlestone, Thomas.] — Reasons for rejecting the presumptive Evidence of Mr. Almon, that Mr. Hugh Boyd was the writer of Junius; with Passages selected to prove the real Author of the Letters of Junius. L. 1808. 8vo.

In favor of Major-General Charles Lee, of the American army.

xxxiv. [Fitzgerald, Mr.] — Another Guess at Junius, and a Dialogue in the Shades. L. 1809. 8vo.

In favor of William Pitt, Earl of Chatham.

xxxv. * Draper, Sir W. — Letters to Junius. L. 1812. 8vo.

A defence of the Earl of Granby and General Gansell.

xxxvi. * The Letters of Junius, including Letters by the same Writer, under other Signatures (now first collected). To which are added; his confidential Correspondence with Mr. Wilkes, and his private Letters addressed to H. S. Woodfall, with a preliminary Essay [by J. Mason Good, M.D.], Notes, etc. L., Woodfall, 1812. 3 vols. 8vo.

This edition was edited by George Woodfall; and copies are also found on Large Paper. It was reprinted in Philadelphia the following year, in two volumes, 8vo.

xxxvii. * Girdlestone, Dr. Thomas. — Facts tending to prove that General Lee was never absent from this Country for any length of time, during the years 1767, 1768, 1769, 1770, 1771, 1772, and that he was the Author of Junius. L. 1813. 8vo.

xxxviii. * Roche, John. — An Inquiry concerning the Author of the Letters of Junius; in which it is proved, by internal, as well as by direct and satisfactory Evidence, that they were written by the late Right Hon. Edmund Burke. L. 1813. 8vo.

xxxix. * Serres, Olivia Wilmot. — The Life of the Author of the Letters of Junius, the Rev. James Wilmot, D.D. By his niece. L. 1813. 8vo.

xl. * [Taylor, John.] — A Discovery of the Author of the Letters of Junius, founded on such Evidence and Illustrations as explain all the mysterious circumstances and apparent contradictions which have contributed to the concealment of this "most important secret of our times." L. 1813. 8vo.

In favor of Sir Philip Francis.

xli. * Duppa, Richard. — Memoirs of a celebrated literary and political Character, from 1742 to 1757, containing strictures of some of the most distinguished men of that time. L. 1813. 8vo.

In favor of Richard Glover.

XLII. * Duppa, Richard. — An Inquiry concerning the author of the Letters of Junius, with reference to the Memoirs by a celebrated Literary and Political Character. L. 1814. 8vo.

In favor of Richard Glover. A second edition, in which further extracts from curious Mss. memoirs were added, was published in the same year.

XLIII. * Blakeway, Rev. J. B. — An Attempt to ascertain the Authors of the Letters published under the signature of Junius. Shrewsbury, 1813. 8vo.

In favor of John Horne Tooke.

XLIV. Blakeway, Rev. J. B. — Sequel of an Attempt to discover Junius. L. 1815. 8vo.

In favor of John Horne Tooke.

XLV. * The Letters of Junius. L., Woodfall, 1814. 3 vols. 8vo.

This is Woodfall's second edition; containing several slight variations, and omitting the four pages of advertisement which occur in the edition of 1812.

XLVI. * Busby, Thomas. — Arguments and Facts demonstrating that the Letters of Junius were written by John Lewis De Lolme, author of the "History of the British Constitution," accompanied with Memoirs of that "most distinguished foreigner." L. 1816. 8vo.

XLVII. * [Johnston, A. G.] — Letters to a Nobleman, proving a late Prime Minister to have been Junius; and developing the secret motives which induced him to write under that and other signatures. With an Appendix, containing a celebrated case published by Almon in 1768. L. 1816. 8vo.

In favor of the Duke of Portland.

XLVIII. * [Taylor, John.] — The identity of Junius with a Distinguished Living Character established. With a Supplement, containing fac-similes of handwriting and other illustrations. L. 1816. 8vo.

In favor of Sir Philip Francis. A second and enlarged edition of this work appeared in 1818, and a third in 1828. The same author also published a supplement in 1817, consisting of fac-similes of handwriting, etc.; and a second edition of the latter appeared in the following year. See also "Notes and Queries," 1st Ser., i. 103, 258.

XLIX. * Chalmers, George. — The Author of Junius ascertained from a concatenation of circumstances amounting to Moral Demonstration. L. 1817. 8vo.

In favor of Hugh Boyd.

L. * [Serres, Olivia Wilmot.] — Junius. Sir Philip Francis denied: A Letter addressed to the British Nation. L. 1817. 8vo.

In favor of the Rev. James Wilmot, D.D.

LI. * Chalmers, George. — The Author of Junius ascertained from direct proofs ... with a Postscript evincing that Boyd wrote Junius, and not Francis. L. 1819. 8vo.

LII. Junius Unmasked. A well-known and most eminent literary character of the last century. L. 1819. 8vo.

In favor of Edward Gibbon, the historian.

LIII. * Junius with his Vizor up! ... by Aedipus Oronoko, Tobacconist and Snuffseller. Oxf. 1819. 8vo.

A burlesque in favor of Suett, the comedian.

LIV. * A Refutation of the Claims preferred for Sir Philip Francis and Mr. Gibbon to the Letters of Junius. L. 1819. 8vo.

LV. * [Cramp, William.] — The Author of Junius discovered in the Person of the celebrated Earl of Chesterfield. L. 1821. 8vo.

A second edition appeared in 1823, and a third in 1826.

LVI. * The Letters of Junius with preliminary Dissertations and copious Notes. By Atticus Secundus. Edinb. 1822. 8vo.

This edition was edited by John M'Diarmid, who claims that Sir Philip Francis was Junius.

LVII. * The Letters of Junius, with a Dissertation by I. W. Lake. Paris, 1822. 2 vols. 32mo.

Also in favor of Sir Philip Francis.

LVIII. * [Cramp, William.] — The Claims of Sir Philip Francis refuted; with a supplement to Junius discovered. L. 1822. 8vo.

LIX. Letters of Charles Butler, dated July, 1799, giving an account of the Inquiries of John Wilkes and Himself, relative to the Authorship of Junius. L. 1822. 8vo.

LX. * Lye, Francis. — The Beauties and Maxims of Junius and his correspondents. L. 1824. 12mo.

I have seen an edition dated 1823.

LXI. * Coventry, George. — A Critical Enquiry regarding the real Author of the Letters of Junius, proving them to have been written by Lord Viscount Sackville. L. 1825. 8vo.

LXII. * [Kelly, P.] — Junius proved to be Burke, with an Outline of his Biography. L. 1826. 8vo.

LXIII. Barker, Edward H. — The Claims of Sir Philip Francis to the Authorship of Junius disproved, in Letters to the Rev. M. Davy, M.D., Sir James

Mackintosh, Godfrey Higgins, and Uvedale Price. Privately Printed, Thetford,
1827. 8vo.

LXIV. * Barker, Edward H. — I. The
Claims of Sir Philip Francis, K.B., to
the Authorship of Junius's Letters, disproved: II. Some Enquiry into the
Claims of the late Charles Lloyd, Esq.,
to the composition of them: III. Observations on the Conduct, Character, and
Style of the Writings of the late Right
Hon. Edmund Burke: IV. Extracts
from the writings of several eminent
philologists, on the Laconic and Asiatic,
the Attic and Rhodian Styles of Eloquence. L. 1828. 12mo.

LXV. * Graham, John Andrew. — Memoirs of John Horne Tooke, together
with his valuable speeches and writings;
also containing proofs identifying him
as the author of the celebrated Letters
of Junius. New York, 1828. 8vo.

LXVI. * [Manning, Joseph Bolles.] —
Junius Unmasked; or, Lord George Sackville proved to be Junius. By Atticus
Secundus. With an Appendix, showing
that the author of the Letters of Junius
was also the author of the "History of
the Reign of George III.," and of "The
North Briton," ascribed to Mr. Wilkes.
B., Mass., 1828. 8vo.

The "History of the Reign of George III."
was published anonymously in 1770, at London.

LXVII. * [Fellows, John.] — The Posthumous Writings of Junius. To which
is prefixed an Inquiry respecting the
Author; also a sketch of the Life of
John Horne Tooke, and Correspondence
of Wilkes. N.Y. 1829. 8vo.

LXVIII. * Falconar, James. — The Secret Revealed; or, the Authorship of
Junius's Letters. L. 1830. 8vo.

In favor of Daniel Wray, deputy teller of the
exchequer, under Philip, second Earl of Hardwicke.

LXIX. * Newhall, Isaac. — Letters on
Junius, addressed to John Pickering,
Esq., showing that the author of that
celebrated work was Earl Temple. B.
1831. 12mo.

LXX. * Waterhouse, Benjamin. — An
Essay on Junius and his Letters, embracing a sketch of the life and character of William Pitt, Earl of Chatham,
and memoirs of certain other distinguished individuals, with Reflections,
historical, personal, and political, relating
to the affairs of Great Britain and
America from 1763 to 1785. B. 1831.
8vo.

LXXI. * Swinden, John. — Junius Lord
Chatham, and the "Miscellaneous Letters" proved to be spurious. L. 1833.
8vo.

LXXII. [West, William (?).] — Recollections of an Old Bookseller, relative to
the Junius Letters. Cork, 1835. 8vo.

LXXIII. Who was Junius? L. 1837.

In favor of Lord Chatham.

LXXIV. * Simons, N. W. (editor). —
"A Letter to an Honourable Brigadier-
General, Commander-in-Chief of his
Majesty's forces in Canada" (L. 1760).
Now first ascribed to Junius, etc. The
Refutation of the same, by an officer.
L. 1760.

Reprinted, with incidental notices of Lords
Townshend and Sackville, Sir Philip Francis,
and others. L. 1841. 12mo.

LXXV. * Jaques, John. — The History
of Junius and his Works; and a Review
of the Controversy respecting the identity of Junius. With an Appendix,
containing Portraits and Sketches by
Junius. L. 1843. 12mo.

In favor of Lord G. Sackville.

LXXVI. * Britton, John. — The Authorship of the Letters of Junius elucidated,
including a biographical memoir of Col.
Isaac Barrè, M.P. L. 1848. 8vo.

Some copies were printed on Large Paper.

LXXVII. * Wade, John. — Junius: including Letters by the same Writer
under other Signatures, to which are
added his confidential correspondence
with Mr. Wilkes and his private Letters
to Mr. H. S. Woodfall; A New and Enlarged Edition, with new evidence as to
the authorship, and an analysis by the
late Sir Harris Nicolas. L., Bohn, 1850.
2 vols. 12mo.

A second edition appeared in 1873.

LXXVIII. Some new facts, and a suggested new theory as to the Authorship
of the Letters of Junius. By Sir Fortu-
natus Dwarris, Knt. [pseud.]. *s.l. et a.*
privately printed [1850]. 8vo.

In favor of Sir Philip Francis. The author
claims that the "Letters" were not the work of
a single individual, but were probably written by
many of those to whom they have been attributed, under the supervision of Francis, who was
also the chief contributor.

LXXIX. * Cramp, William. — Junius
and his Works, compared with the character and Writings of Philip Dormer
Stanhope, Earl of Chesterfield. Lewes,
1850. 8vo.

A second edition appeared at London the following year.

LXXX. * Cramp, William. — Facsimile
Autograph Letters of Junius, Lord Chesterfield, and Mrs. C. Dayrolles. Showing that the wife of Mr. Solomon Day-

rolles was the amanuensis employed in copying the Letters of Junius for the Printer. With a postscript to the first Essay on Junius and his Works. L. 1851. 8vo.

LXXXI. Cramp, William. — Essay on the Authenticity of the four Letters of Atticus. L. 1851. 8vo.

See also " Notes and Queries," 1st Ser., i. 275, 322.

LXXXII. Parkes, J., and Merivale, H. — Memoirs of Sir Philip Francis, K.C.B., with Correspondence and Journals. L. 1852. 2 vols. 8vo.

A second edition appeared in 1867.

LXXXIII. * Ayerst, Francis. — The Ghost of Junius; or, the Authorship of the celebrated 'Letters' by this Anonymous Writer, deduced from a letter, etc., addressed, in 1775–76, by Lieutenant-General Sir Robert Rich, Bart., etc., to the Right Hon. Lord Viscount Barrington, etc. . . . L. 1853. 8vo.

In favor of Lieut.-Col. Sir Robert Rich.

LXXXIV. * Griffin, Frederick. — Junius discovered. B. 1854. 12mo.

In favor of Governor Pownall.

LXXXV. * Dowe, William. — Junius Lord Chatham: a biography setting forth the condition of English preceding and contemporary with the Revolutionary Junian period, and showing that the greatest Orator and Statesman was also the greatest Epistolary Writer of his age. L. 1857. 12mo.

The author had previously advocated the same theory, in the " Dublin University Magazine," xl. 20.

LXXXVI. Symons, J. C. — William Burke, the Author of Junius, an Essay on his Era. L. 1859. 12mo.

LXXXVII. * Hayward, A. — More about Junius. The Franciscan Theory unsound. L. 1868. 8vo.

Reprinted, with additions, from " Fraser's Magazine."

LXXXVIII. Chabot and Twistleton. — The Handwriting of Junius. L. 1871. 4to.

LXXXIX. * Junius Unmasked; or, Thomas Paine, the author of the Letters of Junius and the Declaration of Independence. Washington, D.C., 1872. 12mo.

XC. * The Handwriting of Junius professionally investigated by Mr. Charles Chabot (Expert). With Preface and Collateral Evidence by the Hon. Edward Twistleton. L. 1847. 4to.

An attempt to prove conclusively, by comparative handwriting, that Sir Philip Francis was the author of the letters.

IV. Some Miscellaneous Observations.

Here end my researches in the history of Junius, and in conclusion I shall place before the reader three quotations, from which he can choose as he wishes, and endeavor to settle this knotty question to his own satisfaction.

The first is from the introductory epistle to Scott's " Fortunes of Nigel," in which the author says: —

" A cause, however ingeniously pleaded, is not therefore gained. You may remember the neatly-wrought chain of circumstantial evidence so artificially brought forward to prove Sir Philip Francis's title to the Letters of Junius seemed at first irrefragible, yet the influence of the reasoning has passed away, and Junius, in the general opinion, is as much unknown as ever."

Lord Byron had evidently arrived at no very definite conclusion in respect to the authorship, for in his " Vision of Judgment " Junius appears among the shades, and is as inscrutable as he was on earth: —

" And several people swore from out the press,
They knew him perfectly; and one could swear
He was his father: upon which another
Was sure he was his mother's cousin's brother.

* * * * *

" I've an hypothesis — 'tis quite my own;
I never let it out till now, for fear
Of doing people harm about the throne,
And injuring some minister or peer
On whom the stigma might perhaps be blown;
It is — my gentle public, lend thine ear!
'Tis, that what Junius we were wont to call
Was really, truly, nobody at all."

Lastly, I cannot refrain from quoting the excellent view of the influence of Junius' labors as depicted by Messrs. Parkes and Merivale in their " Life of Sir Philip Francis," to wit: —

" That Junius can only be described with truth as a political adventurer there is no doubt. It is plain enough that his own personal success in life was involved in that of the party whose cause he adopted, or, to speak still more accurately, in the fall of the party which he attacked. And it is equally true that he was utterly unscrupulous in his use of means; that his sincerity, even when he was sincere, was apt to assume the form of the most ignoble rancor, and that no ties of friendship, or party, or connection, seem to have restrained his virulence. All this is but too deducible from the published anonymous writings only . . . But when all this has been said, there remains a residue of a higher order, which must in justice to him be fairly weighed in the balance. Notwithstanding all his sins against justice and truth, Junius was assuredly actuated at bottom by a strong and ardent public spirit. He was throughout a genuine lover of his country. He was earnest in behalf of her honor and of her liberties. He saw clearly that her road to the accomplishment of a higher destiny lay through the maintenance of that honor and the extension of those liberties. He hated with an honest hatred the meanness of principle and venality of conduct which characterized but too strongly the governments against which he fought, and tarnished the political genius of his time. And very remarkable was the success which attended his struggle against them. Great indeed were the practical victories achieved by the efforts of this nameless, obscure agitator. Freedom of the press and the personal freedom of the subject owe probably more to the writings of Junius than to the eloquence of Chatham or Burke, the law of Camden and Dunning. It is not too much to say that after the appearance of those writings, a new tone on these great subjects is found to prevail in our political literature. Doctrines which had previ-

ously met with almost general consent became exploded, truths which up to that time had been only timidly propounded were placed, in post-Junian times, on the order of the day. It is no doubt very true that he was only fighting in the van of an advancing cause, and that these public benefits would as certainly have been secured to us if Junius had never written. But it is just as certain that America would have been discovered had Columbus never existed; yet no one, therefore, contests the greatness of Columbus or the obligations under which mankind lies towards him."

And with this ends the history and bibliography of Junius.

ALBERT R. FREY.

K.

K. *John Collyer Knight.* Queried tracts, from Kitto's "Journal of Sacred Literature" (L. 1851).

K. *James Kenney.* Raising the wind: a farce. L. 1803. — See Lamb's "Elia," "The two races of men."

K., A. *Abner Kneeland,* in his contributions to periodical literature, etc.

K., A. *Annie Keary.* The heroes of Asgard and the giants of Jötunheim. L. 1857.

K., A. *A. Kennedy.* The high price of food. Edinb. 1860.

K., A. *Andrew Kippis.* "Dr. Watts's psalms," "Gent. Mag.," Sept. 1794, p. 794.

K., A. J. *Alfred John Kempe, Esq., F.S.A.* His signature in the "Gent. Mag."

Among his more valuable papers was a series under the title of "Londiniana"; another on ancient "English Battle-Fields"; one, in 1830, entitled, "Tavistock and its Abbey"; others, December, 1830, in 1831, 1832, and 1833.

K., C. *William Charles Mark Kent.* Dickens at Gadshill. Lines in the "Athenæum" of June 3, 1871.

K., C. *Rev. Charles Kingsley.* Hints to stammerers ... L. 1864.

K., C. E. *Mrs. Caroline E. (Kelly) Davis.* Little Apple-Blossom. B. 1863.

K., D. *David Ker,* in his letters to the "Times" (N.Y.).

K., E. D. *E. D. Kendall.* Master and pupil; or, school-life at Old Baldwin ... B. 1869.

K., H. *Herbert Kynaston.* Commemoration address in praise of Dean Colet. L. 1852.

K., H. St. A. *H. St. A. Kitching.* Moral plays ... L. 1832.

K., J. *John Kersey.* A new English dictionary ... L. 1702.

K., J., F.R.S. and S.A.Sc. *James*

Keir. The first part of a dictionary of chemistry, etc. Birmingham, 1789.

K., M. *Mary (Morris) Knowles.* Compendium of a controversy on water baptism. L. 1805.

K., M. A. *Mrs. Mary Anne Kelty.* Emma; or, recollections of a friend. L. 1850.

K., O. *Mme. O. K. Novikoff.* Skobeloff and the Slavonic cause. By ... L. 1883.

K., R. J. *Richard John King.* A handbook to Hereford Cathedral. By ... L. 1864.

K., R. M. *Robert Malcolm Kerr.* Nugae antiquae. By ... 1847.

K., T. *T. Knight,* of Papcastle. An examination of M. La Place's theory of capillary attraction. L. 1809.

K., T. *Thomas Keightley.* The fairy mythology. L. 1828.

K., W. *William Kingsford, C.E.* Impressions of the West and South ... Toronto, 1858.

K., W. *Bishop White Kennet.* A letter to the Lord Bishop of Carlisle concerning one of his predecessors, Bishop Merks ... 3d ed. L. 1713.

K., W. *William Kelly.* Notes on Ezekiel by ... L. 1876.

K., W., Esq. *William Kenrick.* An epistle to James Boswell, Esq. ... L. 1768.

K***, E., of M*** S***. *Edward King,* of Mansfield Street, London, in Beloe's "Sexagenarian," Vol. 2, p. 96. 2d ed. L. 1818.

K——, Rev. A——, A.M. *Rev. Alexander Keith.* Observations on the act for preventing clandestine marriages. By ... L. 1753.

Kaiser, Ernst. *Ewald August König.* Der Deserteur. 1866.

Kaloolah. *Mrs. Sarah Elizabeth (Hill-*

yer Ballard) Maynard, who published poems in various papers under this signature.

Kalula. *F. E. Ramsden,* in the "New York Dramatic News."

Kames, St. *S. Nugent Townshend.* Colorado; its agriculture, stock-feeding, scenery, and shooting (N.Y. 1879), originally contributed to the "Field" (L.).

Kaout 't 'Chouk, Tridace Nafé, Théobrôme de. *Henri Florent Delmotte.* Voyage pittoresque et industriel dans le Paraguay-roux et la Palingénésie Australe ... Mons, 1835.

Kapha, Belshazzar, the Jew. *Robert Dodsley.* The book of the chronicle of James the nephew ... L. 1743.

Karl, Henri. *Comte Jules de Carné.* Marguerite de Keradec. 1876.

Karl, Meister. *Charles Godfrey Leland.* Sketch book of Meister Karl. P. 1855.

Karlsten, Henry. *Charles Henry Lüders,* in his contributions to the "Evening Bulletin" (P.).

Kastus. *Charles Waddington.* De l'autorité d'Aristote au moyen-âge. 1877.

Kata Phusin. *John Ruskin.* The poetry of architecture, with illustrations by the author, and other papers, signed ... In Loudon's "Architectural Magazine," 1837–38. Also an article in the same journal, January, 1839.

Kate, Cousin. *Catherine Douglass Bell.* An autumn at Karnford ... Edinb. 1847.

Kathleen. *Mrs. Kate Ensworth,* in her contributions to the "Detroit Free Press."

Keeldar, Shirley. *Miss Ely.* The winding Wye: a song. The music by ... L. 1863.

Keen Hand, A. *Henry Farnie.* The Golfer's manual ... Cupar, 1857.

Keith, Leslie. *Miss Keith Johnston.* Nobody's lad ... L. 1882.

Keld. *Harry S. Hewitt,* in his contributions to the "Syracuse Herald" (N.Y.).

Kemperhausen. *Robert Pierce Gillies,* one of "Blackwood's" contributors and the "Kemperhausen" of the "Noctes Ambrosianæ."

Kendal, W. H. *William Hunter Grimston.* A nom de théâtre.

Kendal, Mrs. W. H. *Mrs. Margaret* ["Madge"] *(Robertson) Grimston.*

Kent, Alfred. *J. Dacres Devlin.* Two odes on occasion of the Cinque Ports festival at Dover, Aug. 30, 1839, in honour of the Duke of Wellington. L. 1839.

Kentuckian, A. *Asahel Langworthy* (?). A biographical sketch of Col. Richard M. Johnson. N.Y. 1843.

Kentuckian, A. *Samuel Smith Nicholas.* Martial law ... About 1842.

Kentucky Colonel, The. *Col. Maynard,* in his contributions to the "Sentinel" (Indianapolis, Ind.).

Kenwyn, Allen. *Rev. Samuel Pascoe.* On the Cornish coast: a series of thirteen excursions on Cornish shores. Truro, 1878. First appeared in the "Western Daily Mercury," under the above signature. He has been the author of verse and prose articles for the "Graphic," the Plymouth newspapers, and other periodicals.

Kerr, Orpheus C. *Robert Henry Newell.* Avery Glibun; or, between two fires: a romance. N.Y. 1867.

Kerr, Sherill. *Miss Julia Magruder,* in her contributions to various periodicals.

Ketch, Jack. *Thomas Kibble Hervey.* Australia, and other poems. L. 1824; also editor of the "Athenæum" (L.) 1846–1854.

Key-note. *Prof. Nathan Shepard,* in the "New York Examiner."

Khalid, Eb'n Abdallah. *Sir Henry Taylor, K.C., D.C.L.*

Khan, The. *Mr. Kernigan,* in his contributions to the "World" (Toronto, Can.).

Kilosa. *Harriet G. Hosmer.*

Kind, K. K. *Katherine C. Walker,* in her contributions to "Harper's Magazine" (N.Y.).

King, Alice. *Mrs. Alice King Hamilton,* in tales, etc., contributed to various periodicals.

King, Toler. *Mrs. Emily Fox.* Rose O'Connor ... Chic. 1880.

King, The. *Mr. Wasborough.* A letter from the king. L. 1820.

The letter is signed "Montague Williams."

King of Brobdignags, The. *George III. of Great Britain.*

"In other papers the conqueror of Europe [Bonaparte] was represented as a mere pigmy — as a man in miniature — when compared to King George and the Britons. In this spirit, Gillray in 1803 represented the King as the 'King of Brobdignags' eyeing his diminutive assailant through his opera-glass, as he held him in his hand."

King's Friend, A. *Thomas Pownall.* Considerations on the indignity suffered by the Crown ... L. 1772.

Kingcups. *The Misses Knatchbull.* The bouquet culled from Marylebone

Gardens. L. 1851–55. [See "Blue-bell."]

Kingsborough, Lord. *Edward King,* Viscount Kingsborough. Antiquities of Mexico . . . Ed. by . . . L. 1831.

Kingsford, Jane. *Charles Francis Barnard, Jr.* The soprano: a musical story. B. 1869.

Kingsman, A. *Rev. Robert William Essington, M.A.* Over volcanoes; or, through France and Spain in 1871. L. 1872.

Kinkel, Mme. *Elizabeth Sara Sheppard.* Almost a heroine. B. 1860.

Kirk, Eleanor. *Mrs. Eleanor Ames.* Up Broadway; and its sequel . . . N.Y. 1870.

Kirke, Edmund. *James Roberts Gilmore.* Life in Dixie's Land . . . N.Y. 1863.

Kirwan. *Rev. Nicholas Murray.* Romanism at home. N.Y. 1852.

Kit. *J. B. Adams,* in his contributions to the " Tribune " (Denver, Col.), etc.

Kit. *Prof. John Wilson (Christopher North).*

Kit. *Charles Asbury Stephens.* Camping out . . . B. 1872.

Kitcat, Dick. *Richard Doyle.* This name is given as that of the artist of the first five etchings of Maxwell's " Fortunes of Hector O'Halloran," published by Bentley (L.) in 1842.

Kitty, Aunt. *Maria Jane McIntosh.* Aunt Kitty's tales. N.Y. 1841–42.

Klausner, Chr. *Karl Richard Waldemar Uschner.*

Klikspaan. *Jan Kneppelhout.* Studententypen, 1841, and Studentenleven, 1844.

Klim, Niels. *Baron Ludwig von Holberg.* Voyage de Niels Klim. 18–.

Kn— Oxonian. *Rev. John Allan.* Fiddle-de-dee: a hurdy gurdy ode . . . by . . . corresponding member of the institute of common sense. Aberdeen, 1865.

Knickerbocker. *John S. Du Sollé,* in the " Philadelphia Sunday Despatch."

Knickerbocker. *John Austin Stevens, Jr.* Resumption of specie payment . . . N.Y. 1873.

Knickerbocker, Diedrich. *Washington Irving.* The history of New York. N.Y. 1809.

Knight, Charles D. *Mrs. R. L. Gilbert.* Thump's client. N.Y. 1880.

Knight, The. *Sir Robert Walpole.* A dialogue which lately pass'd between the Knight and his man John [a satirical poem]. L. 1740 (?).

Knight Errant, A. *Edward Du Bois, Esq.* My pocket book; or, hints for a ryght merrye and conceitede tour in quarto; to be called "The Stranger in Ireland in 1805." By . . . L. 1808.

Knight of Innishowen, The. *John Sheehan.*

Knight of Kerry. *Maurice Fitz-Gerald.* A letter to Sir Robert Peel on the endowment of the Roman Catholic Church in Ireland . . . L. 1845.

Knight of Morar, The. *Sir William Augustus Fraser., 4th Bart.* Coila's whispers . . . Edinb. 1869.

Knockdunder, Lieutenant Abel, H.P. *Andrew Shortrede.* Letter . . . on the proceedings of the Association for Promotion of the Fine Arts in Scotland. Edinb. 1840.

Knot, Maple. *Ebenezer Clemo.* The life and adventures of Simon Seek . . . Montreal, 1858.

Known Friend of Mr. Leslie, A. *Roger Laurence.* Mr. Leslie's defence from some erroneous and dangerous principles advanc'd . . . L. 1719.

Knutt, A. P. *Augustus M. D. Livandais.*

Korah. *Edward Taylor Fletcher,* who contributed articles to the "Literary Transcript" (Montreal), 1837–39, under this signature, " Tabitha," and his own initials.

Koran, M. *Valdemar Thisted.* Breve fra Helvede. 1871.

Krasnohorska, Eliska. *Henriette Pech.* Zum slawischen Süden. 1880.

Krawbridge, Michael. *John Boyle,* Earl of Cork and Orrery.

Kremlin. *William Stevens Robinson.* His signature in the " Hartford (Conn.) Press," in 1865.

Krik. *Henry G. Crickmore.* Guide to the turf (N.Y. 187–); and N.Y. " World."

Krinelbol. *Claude Prosper Jolyot de Crébillon.* — See " Zeokinizul."

Kroates. *Josiah F. Polk.*

Kron, Karl. *Lyman Hotchkiss Bagg.* Ten thousand miles on a bicycle. By . . . N.Y. 1885.

" Between '76 and '82 . . . I carried on a large correspondence, with the signature ' World's Coll. Chron.' (*i.e.* chronicler) ; though I never attached it to a published article, except advertisements or circulars. ' Kol Kron,' which I attached to many cycling sketches, '79 to '82 (including one article in ' Lippincott '), was simply a perversion of this signature. When I left the ' World,' I changed the ' Kol ' to ' Karl.' " — *Letter,* 1885.

Krone, Karl. *Tekla (Svensson) Juel,* with her two sisters, *Fanny Svensson* and *Alfhilda (Svensson) Mecklenburg.* Ei blot til Lyst. 1880.

Kruna. *Mrs. Julia P. Ballard.* The hole in the bag; and other stories. N.Y. 1877.

Krys. *Thomas B. Chrystal*, in his contributions to the "Morning Journal" (N.Y.).

Kuklos. *John Harris.* A review of Macaulay's teaching on the relationship of theology to the science of government. Montreal, 1874.

Kunst, Hermann, Philol. Professor. *Rev. Walter Chalmers Smith.* Olrig Grange. Glasgow, 1872.

Kwang Ching Ling. *Alexander Delmar.* Why should the Chinese go? San Francisco, 1878.

L.

Λ *or* λ. *Charles Edward Long, Esq.* "Memoir of Sir Henry Morgan, 'The Buccaneer,'" "Gent. Mag.," February and March, 1832, pp. 128, 231; "Monuments of the Long family," "Gent. Mag.," June, 1835, p. 588.

L. *Charles Edward Long, Esq.* "Gent. Mag.," August, 1849, p. 153.

L. *Rev. John Lawry*, Prebendary of Rochester, in his contributions to the "Athenian Letters" . . . L. 1741–43.

L. *George Frederick Beltz, Esq.* "Armorial decorations of Fonthill Abbey," in "Gent. Mag.," Vol. 92, Pt. 2, pp. 201, 317, 409.

L. *Catherine Swanwick.* Poems. L. 1858.

L. *Major Robert Lachlan.* Remarks on the state of education in the Province of Canada . . . Montreal, 1848.

L. *Israel Lombard.* Remarks on the tariff bill now before the United States senate. India Wharf [B.], January, 1861.

L. *James Lenox.* Shakespeare's plays in folio . . . "Hist. Mag." N.Y. 1861.

L., Lady. *Lady Lyons.* Olivia: a tale. L. 1847.

L., A. *Miss Abby Lee.* [Appendix to] Rhode Island tales. N.Y. 1839.

L., A. E. *A. E. Lancaster*, in his contributions to the "Evening Telegram" (N.Y.).

L., A. E. *Miss A. E. L. Lee.* The fruits of the valley. L. 1855.

L., C. E. *C. E. Lambert.* The barsinister . . . L. 1836.

L., C. H. *Charles Henry Lüders*, in his contributions to the "Evening Bulletin" (P.).

L., C. H. *Rev. Charles H. Leonard.* First steps in the open path. Prepared for the children and youth of the First (Universalist) Church of Christ, Chelsea, Mass. B. 1865.

L., D. *David Laing.* Notices regarding the metrical versions of the Psalms . . . Edinb. 1842.

L., E. *E. Lord.* Discursive remarks on modern education. L. 1841.

L. E. *Samuel Pegge.* "Observations on the Sunday clause in the militia bill," "Gent. Mag.," 1757, p. 58 (and forty other articles, from 1788 to 1795).

"L. E.,"—the final letters either of Samuel and Pegge, or of Paul Gemsege. See "Gent. Mag.," LXVI., pp. 981 and 1083.

L., E. *E. Lumb* (?). Scattered pearls strung together . . . L. 1860.

L., E. *Emma Lewis.* Treasures of darkness. By . . . P. 1854.

Preface signed "F. W."; *i.e. Francis Wharton.*

L., E. B. *Edward George Earle Lytton Bulwer-Lytton*, Baron Lytton. Harold, the last of the Saxon kings. L. 1848.

L., E. E. *E. Elizabeth Lay.* How to be a hero. B. 187–.

L., E. F. *E. F. Lloyd.* John Brown's trouble . . . 1863.

L., E. L. *Mrs. E. L. Lasselle.* Magdalen the enchantress . . . P. 1858.

L., E. M. *E. M. Lawson.* Records and traditions of Upton-on-Severn. By . . . L. 1869.

L., E. N. *Elizabeth N. Lockerby.* The wild brier; or, lays by an untaught minstrel. Charlottetown, 1866.

L., E. S. *Hon. Elizabeth Susan Law,* afterwards Lady Colchester. Giustina: a Spanish tale of real life. A poem . . . L. 1833.

L., F. G. *Frederick George Lee.* Lays of the Church . . . L. 1851. See "L. B."

L., G. *George Ludlam.* The mysterious murder; or, what's the clock? A melodrama . . . 1817.

L., H. A., the Old Shekarry. *Major Henry A. Leveson.* The camp fire. The forest and the field. L. 1865.

L. H. C. *Charles Henry Lüders*, in his contributions to the "Evening Bulletin" (P.).

L., H. E. S. *H. E. S. Leech.* Ferns which grow in New Zealand and the adjacent islands plainly described.

L., J. *Rev. James Lupton.* Gulliver's travels, new edition, carefully edited by a clergyman (J. L.). L. 1867.

L., J. *John Love, Jr.* Judas's younger brother manifested ... L. 1704.

L., J. *Rev. James Lukin.* The lathe and its uses ... 3d ed. L. 1871.

L., J. J. *Leadbetter.* A pilgrimage to the shrines of Buckinghamshire. By ... L. 1861.

L., J. F. de. *Don J. F. de Lizardi.* Pensador Mexicano. Mexico, 1813.

L., J. R. *James Russell Lowell.* The poetical works of J. Keats, with a life. B. 1854.

L., J. S. *John Stockton Littell.* The Clay minstrel; or, national songster ... P. 1842.

L. K. *Charles Chauncy, D.D.* A letter to the Rev. Mr. George Whitefield, publickly calling upon him to vindicate his conduct or confess his faults. B. 1745.

L. L. *Rev. George Smith.* — See "Lovechurch, Leonard."

L. L. One of the pseudonyms attributed to Junius (*q.v.*). The two letters thus signed are dated Aug. 5 and Sept. 6, 1768, and express "indignation at the dismissal of Sir Jeffery Amherst from his government of Virginia, whose services and merits are strongly described."

L. L. *Laura Loring Pratt.* Evening rest; or, the shadow of the Great Shepherd ... B. 1872.

L., L. B. *Lambert Blackwell Larking.* A description of the Heart-Shrine in Leybourne Church, with some account of Sir Roger de Leyburn, Kt. L. 1864.

L., L. E. *Mrs. Letitia Elizabeth (Landon) Maclean.* Poetical works. L. 1850.

L., L. P. *Mrs. L. P. Lewis,* German correspondent of numerous American periodicals.

L., M. E. *Miss Mary Elizabeth Lee,* who contributed to the "Rose Bud," afterwards the "Southern Rose," published at Charleston, S.C., at first under the modest signature of "A Friend," and, when this became known, under those initials of her name.

L., M. R. *M. R. Lahee.* Tim Bobbin's adventures with the Irishman ... Manchester, 1860.

L. N. *Rev. George F. Cushman,* in his contributions to the "Churchman" (N.Y.), etc.

L., R. J. *Richard J. Lane.* Spirits and water. L. 1855.

L., R. W. *Rev. Randolph W. Lowrie,* in the "Churchman," April 3, 1880, p. 383.

L., S. *Stephen Lobb.* — See "A Lover of Truth and Peace."

L., S. C. *S. C. Lampreys.* A brief historical and descriptive account of Maidstone ... Maidstone, 1834.

L. S. E. *Michael Augustus Gathercole.* Letters to a Dissenting Minister of the Congregational Independent Denomination ... L. 1834.

L. S. S. *Laura Sophia Temple.* Poems. L. 1805.

L., S. W. *Mrs. S. W. Landor.* Whisperings from life's shore : a bright shell for children. B. 1849.

L., T. *Thomas Letchworth.* A morning's meditation; or, a descant upon the times : a poem. By ... L. 1765.

L., T. H. *Thomas Henry Lowth.* Essay on architecture. L. 1776.

L. U. P——, A.M. *Thomas Edwards.* A letter to the author of a late Epistolary Dissertation ... L. 1744.

L., W., Junior. *William Lamboll, Jr.* A lamentation over Zion, on the declension of the Church. L. 1747.

L., W. B. *W. B. Lord (?).* The corset and the crinoline ... L. 1865.

L., W. F. B. *W. F. B. Lawrie.* The Idol-shrine ... L. 1851.

L., W. H. *William Henry Leeds.* A treatise on the decorative part of civil architecture. Revised, etc., by ... L. 1862.

L., W. S. *Walter Savage Landor.* Dry sticks, fagoted by W. S. L. Edinb. 1858.

This book is very scarce, having been suppressed; and it is not included in any edition of Landor's works.

L***, Mrs. *Mrs. Lefevre.* An extract of letters, — by ... Dublin, 1808.

L - - -, T. *Thomas Lewis.* English Presbyterian eloquence ... L. 1720.

L ... M ... B ..., armateur. *Louis Marie Prudhomme.* — See "Armateur."

Labourer for Peace, A. *Jane Ogilvie.* A handbook for the Churches ... Edinb. 1840.

Labourer in the Same Cause, A. One of the pseudonyms attributed to Junius (*q.v.*). The letters thus signed are dated June 27 and July 7, 1770, and are directed against Mr. Wilkes.

Labrunie, Gérard. *Gérard de Nerval.* Piquillo. Paris, 1837.

Lackland, Thomas. *George Canning Hill.* Homespun; or, five and twenty years ago ... N.Y. 1867.

Laco. *Stephen Higginson.* The writings of Laco, as published in the "Massachusetts Centinel" in ... 1789. B. 1789.

Lacon. *Rev. Caleb C. Colton.* Lacon; or, many things in few words. L. 1820–22.

Lacretie, Arnold. *Jules Claretie.* Le rocher des fiancés. 1851.

Lactantius. *Sir David Dalrymple.* Of the manner in which persecutors died; by ... Edinb. 1782.

Lactilla. *Mrs. Ann Yearsley.* Poems. L. 1785.

Lady, A. *Miss Sarah Fielding.* The adventures of David Simple ... By ... L. 1744.

Lady, A. *Mrs. (Mallet) Celisia.* Almida: a tragedy, as it is performed at the Theatre-Royal, in Drury Lane. L. 1771.

Lady, A. *Mrs. Henry Freshfield.* Alpine byways; or, light leaves gathered in 1859 and 1860. L. 1861.

Lady, A. *Mrs. Mary J. Jourdan.* The Althorp Picture Gallery, and other poetical sketches. Edinb. 1836.

Lady, A. *Miss Elizabeth Missing Sewell.* Amy Herbert ... L. 1844.

Lady, A. *Mrs. Hannah Glasse.* The art of cookery made plain and easy ... L. 1747.

The name, "Mrs. Glasse," is held by some authorities to be a pseudonym of *Dr. John Hill*, to whom the authorship of the above work is ascribed.

Lady, A. *Miss Maria Farquhar.* Biographical catalogue of the principal Italian painters. L. 1854.

Lady, A. *Mrs. Ballantyne.* Birds, British and Foreign. [Verses.] By ... 1843.

Lady, A. *Mrs. Pinchard.* The blind child; or, anecdotes of the Wyndham Family ... n.p. 1796.

Lady, A. *Mrs. Farren.* Boston Common: tale of our own times ... B. 1858.

Lady, A. *Miss Eliza Perkins,* of Warwickshire. The botanical and horticultural meeting ... Birmingham, 1834.

Lady, A. *M. E. Jackson.* Botanical lectures. By ... L. 1864.

Lady, A. *Mrs. M. E. Parker Bouligny.* Bubbles and ballast. Being a description of life in Paris, during the brilliant days of the Empire ... Balt. 1871.

Lady, A. *Mrs. (Wight) Cox.* Burton Wood. In a series of letters. Probably published at London, about 1783. See the "European Magazine," iii., pp. 120, 162.

Lady, A. *Mrs. — Stringer.* The chain of affection ... By ... 1830 ?

Lady, A. *Mrs. Anna Cora (Ogden Mowatt) Ritchie.* The character of Ham-

let, by ex-president Adams and James H. Hackett. Edited by ... N.Y. 1844.

Lady, A. *Mrs. R. Ward.* The child's guide to knowledge ... 2d ed. L. 1828.

Lady, A. *Miss Harriet M. Gunn.* Conversations on Church polity. By ... L. 1833.

Lady, A. *Mrs. Ellen Fox Crewdson.* The countries of Europe and the manners and customs of its various nations ... By ... L. 1849 (?).

Lady, A. *Mrs. James F. Palmer.* A dialogue in the Devonshire dialect (in three parts) by ... to which is added a glossary, by James F. Palmer. L. 1837.

Lady, A. *Mrs. Anna (Murphy) Jameson.* The diary of an Ennuyée. 1826.

Lady, A. *Annabella Plumptre.* Domestic management ... 1810.

Lady, A. *Mrs. Cockle.* An explanation of Dr. Watts' hymns for children ... By ... L. 1836.

Lady, A. *Mrs. — Thompson.* Family commentary ... York, 18–.

Lady, A. *— (Minifie) Gunning.* Family pictures: a novel ... By ... L. 1764.

Lady, A. *George Alexander Stevens.* The female Inquisition. L. 1753.

Lady, A. *Mrs. Elizabeth Sanders.* First settlers of New England ... B. 1822.

Lady, A. *Mrs. (Marshall) Cochrane.* Flights of fancy [poetry]. Arbroath, 1844.

Lady, A. *Mrs. Elizabeth Washington (Gamble) Wirt.* Flora's dictionary. Balt. 1829.

Lady, A. *Maria Julia Young.* Genius and fancy; or, dramatic sketches. By ... L. 1791.

Lady, A. *Mary Jane Mackenzie Geraldine;* or, modes of faith and practice. L. 1820.

Lady, A. *Mrs. H. J. Moore.* The golden legacy: a story of life's phases ... N.Y. 1857.

Lady, A. *Mrs. Elizabeth Winslow Allardyce.* The goodwife at home; in metre ... Aberdeen, 1867.

Lady, A. *Lady Elizabeth (Rigby) Eastlake.* Handbook of painting: the German, Flemish, Dutch, Spanish, and French schools. Partly translated from the German of Kugler, by ... L. 1854.

Lady, A. *Elizabeth Isabella Spence.* Helen Sinclair: a novel ... L. 1799.

Lady, A. *Albinia Gwynn.* The history of the Honourable Edward Mortimer. L. 1785.

Lady, A. *Millicent Whiteside Cook.*

How to dress on £ 15 a year as a lady ... L. 1874.

Lady, A. *Mrs. James Keir.* Interesting memoirs. By ... L. 1786.

Lady, A. *Martha Nicol.* Ismeer; or, Smyrna and its British hospital in 1855 ... L. 1856.

Lady, A. *Mrs. F. D. Bridges.* Journal of ... 's travels round the world. L. 1883.

Lady, A. *Mary Anne Hanway.* A journey to the Highlands of Scotland ... L. 1777.

Lady, A. *Lizzie Selina Eden.* A lady's glimpse of the late war in Bohemia.

Lady, A. *Mary Wray, Lady Cecil.* The ladies' library, written by ... L. 1714.

Lady, A. *Mrs. Rose Lawrence.* The last autumn at a favourite residence ... L. 1828.

Lady, A. *Mrs. Mary Wiseman.* A letter from ... to her daughter, on the manner of passing Sunday rationally and agreeably. L. 1788.

Lady, A. *Mrs. Charlotte MacCarthy.* A letter from ... to the Bishop of London. L. 1768.

Lady, A. *Thomas Amory.* A letter to the Reviewers, occasioned by their account of a book called "Memoirs." L. 1755.

Lady, A. *Mrs. Walker.* Letters from the Duchess de Crui and others on subjects moral and entertaining ... L. 1776.

Lady, A. *Mrs. — (Ward Rondeau) Vigor.* Letters from ... who resided some years in Russia, etc. L. 1775.

Lady, A. *Mrs. Julia Charlotte Maitland.* Letters from Madras during the years 1836–39. L. 1843.

Lady, A. *Miss Anne Wilson.* Letters on ancient history ... By ... 1809.

Lady, A. *Mrs. Mary Davis (Cook) Wallis.* Life in Feejee; or, five years among the Cannibals. By ... B. 1851.

Lady, A. *Mrs. Margaret (Holford) Hodson.* Lines to a boy pursuing a butterfly. By ... L. 1826.

Lady, A. *Mrs. Elizabeth (Alsager) Zornlin.* Lines addressed to Lord Nelson after the celebrated battle of the Nile. By ... L. 1805.

Lady, A. *Miss Emily Trevenen.* Little Derwent's breakfast. By ... Illustrated with engravings ... L. 1839.

"These poems were written . . . for the amusement and instruction of her [the lady's] godson, Derwent Moultrie Coleridge, son of Rev. Derwent Coleridge, and grandson of S. T. Coleridge."

Lady, A. *Mrs. Ann (Ritchie) Memes.* The lives of St. John the Baptist, the twelve apostles, and of St. Paul ... Edinb. 1824.

Lady, A. *Jane Budge.* Manual of English history simplified ... L. 1866.

Lady, A. *Rosalind St. Clair.* Marston: a novel ... L. 1835.

Lady, A. *Lady Anne Halkett.* Meditations on the twenty-fifth Psalm ... Edinb. 1771.

Lady, A. *Mrs. — M'Taggart.* Memoirs of a gentlewoman of the old school. L. 1830.

Lady, A. *Elizabeth Rolt.* Miscellaneous poems ... L. 1768.

Lady, A. *Anne Finch,* Countess of Winchelsea. Miscellaneous poems, on several occasions. L. 1713.

Lady, A. *Mrs. H. St. A. Kitching.* Moral plays ... L. 1832.

Lady, A. *Miss Charlotte Elliott.* Morning and evening hymns, for a week ... L. 1842.

Lady, A. *Mrs. — Rundell.* A new system of domestic cookery. 1808–59.

Lady, A. *Mrs. — Woodfin.* Northern memoirs; or, the history of a Scotch family. By ... L. 1756.

Lady, A. *Mrs. Harry Rawson.* Notes of Eastern travel; being selections from the diary of ... Manchester, 1874.

Lady, A. *Mrs. R. Douglas.* On the conservative elements of the American republic ... Chillicothe, 1842.

Lady, A. *Mrs. Julia Ward Howe.* Passion flowers. Poems. B. 1854.

Lady, A. *Miss Coxe.* A picture of Monmouthshire; or, an abridgment of Mr. [William] Coxe's historical tour in Monmouthshire. By ... L. 1802.

Lady, A. *Mrs. Elizabeth Griffith.* The Platonic wife: a comedy. By ... L. 1765.

Lady, A. *Mrs. Emilie Earle (Steele) Hicks.* Pocket guide to the Lizard. By ... Truro, 1876.

Lady, A. *Elizabeth Thomas.* Poems on several occasions ... L. 1726.

Lady, A. *Mrs. Sarah Greer.* Quakerism; or, the story of my life. By ... who for forty years was a member of the Society of Friends. Dublin, 1851.

Lady, A. *Mrs. Felicia Dorothea (Browne) Hemans.* The restoration of the works of art to Italy: a poem. By ... Oxf. 1816.

Lady, A. *Mrs. Dalkeith Holmes.* A ride on horseback to Florence, through France and Switzerland, described in a series of letters, by ... L. 1842.

Lady, A. *Miss Susan Fenimore Cooper.* Rural hours. N.Y. 1854.

Lady, A. *Mrs. Eliza Lee (Cabot) Follen.* Selections from the writings of Fénelon, with a memoir of his life. By ... 2d ed. B. 1829.

Lady, A. *Jane Austen.* Sense and sensibility : a novel. By ... L. 1811.

Lady, A. *Rebecca Wilkinson.* Sermons to children ... By ... L. 1830 (?).

Lady, A. *Mrs. Hannah Anderson (Chandler) Ropes.* Six months in Kansas, by ... B. 1856.

Lady, A. *C. L. Moody.* A sketch of modern France ... Written in the years 1796 and 1797, during a tour through France. By ... Edited by C. L. Moody, LL.D., F.A.S. L. 1798.

Allibone enters the work under *Dr. Moody's* name as the author.

Lady, A. *Miss Cleaver.* Some account of a new process in painting by means of glazed crayons ... By ... Brighton, 1815.

Lady, A. *Mrs. E. Throop Martin.* Songs in the house of my pilgrimage; selected and arranged by ... N.Y. 1852.

Lady, A. *Miss Sallie A. Brock.* The Southern amaranth. N.Y. 1869.

Lady, A. *William Kenrick.* The whole duty of woman ... L. 1753.

Lady, A. *Hannah Maynard Pickard.* The widow's jewels. In two stories. By ... L. 1831.

Lady, A. *Mrs. Eliza (Rotch) Farrar.* The young lady's friend ... B. 1836.

Lady, A. *Clara Jesup Moore.* The young lady's friend ... By Mrs. H. O. Ward (*pseud.*). P. 1880.

Lady at Cape François, A. *Miss — Hassall.* Secret history; or, the horrors of St. Domingo ... P. 1808.

Lady in England, A. *Thomas Tickell.* An epistle ... to a gentleman at Avignon. L. 1717.

Lady of Boston, A. *Miss Susan D. Nickerson.* The bread winners. By ... B. 1871.

Lady of Boston, A. *Elizabeth Johnson.* Pious thoughts. By ... B. 1834.

Lady of Boston, A. *Rebecca Brown.* Stories about General Warren ... B. 1835.

Lady of Charleston, S.C., A. *Mrs. Eliza Murden.* Miscellaneous poems. Charleston, 1826.

Lady of England, A [A.L.O.E.]. *Charlotte M. Tucker.*

Lady of Fashion, A. *Miss Blackwell.* Ernestine; or, the child of mystery. L. 1840.

Lady of Massachusetts, A. *Mrs. Hannah Foster.* The coquette; or, the history of Eliza Wharton: a novel ... by ... B. 1797.

This work underwent many editions, and was finally reprinted " with historical preface and memoir of the author, by A(nother) Lady of Massachusetts " (*i.e. Jane E. Locke*). P. 1866.

Lady of Massachusetts, A. *Jane E. Locke.* — See preceding.

Lady of Massachusetts, A. *Mrs. Lydia Maria Child.* The first settlers of New England; or, conquest of the Pequods, Narragansetts, and Pokanokets ... By ... B. 1829.

Lady of Massachusetts, A. *Mrs. A. M. Richards.* Memories of a grandmother ... B. 1854.

Lady of New Hampshire, A. *Mrs. Sarah Josepha (Buell) Hale.* The genius of Oblivion; and other original poems. By ... Concord, N.H., 1823.

Lady of New York, A. *Mrs. Sarah (Rogers) Haight.* Letters from the Old World ... N.Y. 1840.

Lady of Pennsylvania, A. *Miss Rebecca Rush.* Kelroy: a novel ... P. 1812.

Lady of Philadelphia, A. *Mrs. Sarah (Ewing) Hall.* Conversations on the Bible ... P. 1827.

Lady of Quality, A. *Miss Frances Williams Wynn.* Diaries of ... from 1797 to 1844. Ed., with notes, by A. Hayward. L. 1864.

Lady of Rank, A. *Mary Margaret Egerton,* the Countess of Wilton. The book of costume ... L. 1841.

Lady of Rank, A. *Lady Charlotte Maria (Campbell) Bury* (?). The murdered queen; or, Caroline of Brunswick. By ... L. 1838.

Lady of South Carolina, A. *Mrs. Mary Elizabeth (Morague) Davis.* The British partizan: a tale of the olden time. Macon, Ga., 1864.

Lady of South Carolina, A. *Mrs. Louisa S. (Cheves) MacCord.* A letter to the Duchess of Sutherland . . . in the " Charleston Mercury," July 30, 1853.

Lady of Virginia, A. *Mrs. J. W. (Brockenborough) McGuire.* Diary of a Southern refugee during the war ... N.Y. 1867.

Lady of Virginia, A. *Mrs. William Cabell Rives.* Tales and souvenirs of a residence in Europe ... P. 1842.

Lady, Resident near the Alma, A.
Mrs. Andrew Neilson. The Crimea;
its towns, inhabitants, and social customs. L. 1855.

**Lady who prefers to be anony-
mous.** *Miss Emily Jolly.* An experi-.
ence.

Her contributions to "Household Words"
and "All the Year Round" were republished in
three volumes in 1875 under the title of "A
Wife's Story, and other tales."

Laertes. *George Alfred Townsend.*
Washington, outside and inside. Hartford, 1874.

Lageniensis. *Rev. John O'Hanlon,
M.R.I.A.* Irish folk-lore . . . Glasgow,
1871.

La Girandole. *Émile le Girardin.*

He "did not gain the confidence of any considerable body of his countrymen, and has justified in every act of his public life the soubriquet
bestowed upon him of 'La Girandole,' the
Weathercock."

Laicus. *Rev. Lyman Abbott.* Laicus;
or, the experiences of a layman in a
country parish. N.Y. 1872.

Laicus. *Ira Warren* (?). Review of
the Rev. William Croswell's letter to
the Bishop of . . . Massachusetts. B.
1845.

**Laird of Torfoot, an Officer in the
Presbyterian Army, The.** *Thomas
Brownlee.* Narrative of the battles of
Drumclog and Bothwell Bridge . . .
Glasgow, 1822.

Lake, Claude. *Mathilde Blind.*
Poems by . . . L. 1867.

Lake-Elbe. *Archibald Bleloch.* A
glance at the Old World . . . Edinb.
1878.

Laker, Cecil. *Mrs. Harriette (Smith)
Bainbridge,* who uses this pen-name in
periodical literature, and published
"Irene Floss, and other poems" in
1878.

La Mara. *Marie Lipsius.* Musika-
lische Studienköpfe. 1873–80.

Lamber, Juliette. *Mme. Edmond
(Lamber) Adam.* Les poètes grecques
contemporains. Paris, 1881.

Lan, Viggo. *Hother Tolderlund,* a
Danish author, who published under this
pseudonym a collection of poems.

Lancashire Artisan, A. *Malcolm
Macleod.* Practical guide to emigrants
to the United States . . . Manchester,
1866.

Lancashire Incumbent, A. *Rev.
Abraham Hume, LL.D.,* in the "London
Times." 1857–58.

Lancashire Lad, A. *Thomas Sowden.*
The siege of Rome, and Bishop Colenso

slain with a sling and a stone . . . Manchester, 1857.

Lancashire Manufacturer, A. *Henry Bleckley.* Butler's analogy: a lay
argument by . . . L. 1876.

Lancaster, W. P. *Hon. John Byrne
Leicester Warren.* Philoctetes: a metrical drama . . . L. 1866.

Lancer. *O. C. Stouder.* Shakespeare's
biography. Does it conform to the
author of the plays? In the "Witten-
berger Magazine," Springfield, O., November, 1880.

Lancewood, Lawrence, Esq. *Rev.
Daniel Wise.* Lindendale stories . . .
B. 1868.

Lander, Jean. *Mme. Ernest Hello.*
Nouvelles et récits villageois. Paris,
1861.

Lander, Meta. *Mrs. Margarette
(Woods) Lawrence.* Fading flowers. B.
1860.

Landholder, A. *Elisha R. Potter.*
Address to the freemen of Rhode Island.
Providence, 1831.

Landholder, A. *Wilkins Updike.* An
address to the people of Rhode Island
. . . Providence, 1828.

Landholder, A. *Clement Clarke
Moore, LL.D.* A plain statement, addressed to the proprietors of real estate
in the city and county of New York . . .
N.Y. 1818.

Landor, Charles. *Caroline Stickney,*
in her contributions to "Harper's Magazine" (N.Y.).

Landowner, A. *Lord Charles Townshend.* National thoughts, recommended
to the serious attention of the public . . .
By . . . L. 1751.

Landscape Painter, A. *Charles Lanman.* Letters from . . . B. 1845.

Lane, Chancery, Esq. *James Edwin
Wilson.* A throw for a throne; or, the
Prince unmasked . . . L. 1872. — See
"Zinn, Sergeant."

Lane, Wycliffe. *Mrs. Edmond Jenings.* My good for nothing brother. L.
1862.

Lang Syne. *William McKoy,* in a
contribution to "Poulson's Daily Advertiser," 1829. — See "Historical Magazine," September, 1861 (N.Y.).

Langdon, Mary. *Mrs. Mary H.
(Greene) Pike.* Climbing and sliding:
book for boys. B. 1873.

Langenevais, F. de. *Ange Henri
Blaze de Bury.* His signature as musical
critic in the "Revue des Deux Mondes"
from 1864.

Langshank, Laurence, Gent. *Robert Mudie.* Things in general. L. 1824.

—"See N. and Q.," 4th Ser., xi. 156, 510; xii. 19.

Langstaff, Launcelot, Esq. *Washington Irving, William Irving, and James Kirke Paulding.* Salmagundi; or, the Whimwhams of . . . and others. N.Y. 1807-8.

Langston, Lawrence. *Reverdy Johnson.* Bastiles of the North. Balt. 1863.

Laon. *W. D. Le Sieur,* in his contributions to the "Canadian Monthly Magazine" (Toronto).

La Roque. *Louis Boyer,* who wrote many vaudevilles, the most of them with others, and signed them with the pseudonym "La Roque."

Larwood, Jacob. *L. R. Sadler.* Theatrical anecdotes. By . . . L. 1882.

Lascelles, Lady Caroline. *Mrs. Mary Elizabeth (Braddon) Maxwell.* The black band. L. 1866.

The pseudonym was suggested by Sir F. C. Lascelles Wraxall, who "claimed a family right in the name."—See "Wraxall, Lascelles."

Lass with the golden Locks, The. *Mrs. Anna Maria Smart,* of Reading, Berks., relict of Christopher Smart, M.A., of Pembroke Hall, Cambridge, thus celebrated in one of his ballads.

Last of the Puritans, The. *Samuel Adams.* So named by Edward Everett, in 1825.

Last Traveller, The. *Viscount George Annesley Valentia,* in Beloe's "Sexagenarian," Vol. 2, p. 77. 2d ed. L. 1818.

Late American Statesman, A. *Charles Fenton Mercer.* The weakness and inefficiency of the government of the United States . . . L. 1863.

Late Barrister at Law, A. *Sir John Strange.* A collection of select cases relating to evidence. By . . . L. 1754.

Late Chief-Secretary of that Kingdom, A. *Sir George (afterwards Earl) Macartney.* An account of Ireland in 1778. Priv. printed, 1773.

Late Eminent Prelate, A. *William Warburton,* Bishop of Gloucester. Letters from . . . to one of his friends [Hurd, Bp. of Worcester]. L. 1809.

Late Fellow of All Souls College, Oxford, A. *Rev. Arthur Philip Perceval.* A letter to the members of both Houses of Parliament, on the Dissenters' petitions . . . L. 1834.

Late Fellow of King's College, A. *Thomas Ashton, D.D.* Extract from the case of the electors of Eton College to supply all vacancies, etc. 1771.

Late Graduate of Oxford, A. *Frederick Naghten, B.A.* A metrical version

of the Song of Solomon, and other poems . . . L. 1845.

Late Learned Judge, A. *Sir Geoffrey Gilbert.* An historical account of the . . . law of devises and revocations. L. 1739.

Late Lord Lyttelton, The. *William Coombe.* Letters of . . . L. 1806.

Late Master of the Temple, The. *Caleb Fleming.* Natural and revealed religion at variance . . . L. 1758.

Late Member of the University, A. *Theophilus Lindsey.* An examination of Mr. Robinson of Cambridge's plea for the divinity of our Lord Jesus Christ . . . L. 1785.

Late Member of the University, A. *Peter Le Page Renouf.* The character of the Rev. W. Palmer . . . L. 1843.

Late Merchant, A. *Asa Greene.* The perils of Pearl Street, including a taste of the dangers of Wall Street. N.Y. 1834.

Late Noble Writer, A. *Henry St. John Bolingbroke.* A vindication of natural society. By . . . or, rather written in ridicule of his opinions, by Edmund Burke. L. 1762.

Late Officer in the United States Army, A. *Jervase Cutler.* A topographical description of the State of Ohio, Indiana Territory, and Louisiana . . . B. 1812.

Late Patriot Prisoner, A. *Thomas Jefferson Sutherland.* Loose leaves from the portfolio of . . . in Canada. N.Y. 1840.

Late President of a select Chess Club, The. *C. Pearson.* Chess exemplified in a concise and easy notation . . . L. 1842.

Late Prime Minister, A. *Duke of Portland.* Letters to a nobleman, proving . . . to have been Junius. With an appendix [by A. G. Johnston]. L. 1816.

Late Recorder of Newcastle, The. *C. Fawcett.* A letter to . . . by an old friend. 1754.

Late Resident at Bhagulpore, A. *David Hopkins.* The dangers of British India, from French invasion . . . L. 1808.

Late Resident in Bengal, A. *John Shore,* Lord Teignmouth. Considerations on the practicability . . . of communicating to the natives of India the knowledge of Christianity . . . L. 1808.

Late Resident in the East, A. *John Hobart Caunter, B.D.* The cadet: a poem, in six parts, containing remarks on British India . . . L. 1814.

Late Staff Officer, A. *Woodbourne Potter.* The war in Florida; being an exposition of its causes, and an accurate history of the campaigns of Generals Clinch, Gaines, and Scott ... By ... Balt. 1836.

Late Staff Sergeant of the 13th Light Infantry, A. *John Mac Mullen.* Camp and barrack-room ... L. 1846.

Late Steward of the Sons of the Clergy, A. *Nathaniel John Hollingsworth.* A defence of the Society of the Sons of the Clergy ... Newcastle, 1812.

Late Stipendiary Magistrate in Jamaica, A. *Stephen Bourne.* — See "A Resident in the West Indies for Thirteen Years."

Late Teacher, A. *William Singleton.* Mentor and Amander; or, a visit to Ackworth School ... By ... [In verse.] L. 1814.

Late Under Secretary of State, A. *William Knox.* Considerations on the present state of the nation ... L. 1789.

Late very learned and reverend Divine, A. *Samuel Pegge.* Anonymiana; or, ten centuries of observations on various authors and subjects ... L. 1809.

Late Vicar, A. *Rev. Robert Masters.* A short account of the parish of Waterbeach. By ... Waterbeach, 1795.

La Tenella. *Mrs. Mary Bayard (Devereux) Clarke.* The *nom de plume* she first adopted.

Latienne. *Lizzie W. Bacchus.* The Confederate dead. 1866.

Latimer, Faith. *Mrs. John A. Miller.* The children's church ... P. 1868.

Latona. *Mrs. Sallie J. (Hancock) Battey.* Rayon d'amour. Poems. P. 1869.

La Touche, Geoffrey. *Theodore William Snow,* in the "Collegian," a periodical published by a number of undergraduates of Harvard University in 1830.

Latouche, John. *Oswald John Frederick Crawfurd.* Travels in Portugal. L. 187-.

Latour, Tomline. *William Schwenck Gilbert.* Happy Land: a burlesque. L. 18-.

Laugel. The papers upon the United States, contributed to "La Revue des Deux Mondes" (Paris, 1865), and signed "Laugel," are attributed to the *Comte de Paris.*

Laun, Friedrich. *Friedrich August Schulze.* Œuvres complètes. Stuttgart, 1843–44.

Laura. *Mrs. Maria Robinson.* Signature to poems published in the "Oracle."

Laura, Maria. *Mrs. Maria Robinson,* who corresponded under the name of "Perdita," and who was called "The English Sappho." The words of the once popular song, "Bounding billow, cease thy motion," were written by her.

Laurent-Jan. *Laurent Jean Lausanne,* who to his first article, written for a satirical journal, signed only his Christian names, which, by a mistake of the printer, appeared as Laurent-Jan. This name the author afterwards signed to all his publications.

Laurie, Annie. *Mrs. Laura Brady Starr,* in several of her earlier writings.

Laval. *Rev. Bernard O'Reilly.* The two brides: a tale. N.Y. 1879.

Lavengro. *George Borrow.* Lavengro: the scholar, the gipsey, and the priest. L. 184-.

Lavigne, Jean. *Arthur de Boissieu.* Lettres du village, extraites du journal de Saône-et-Loire, 1878–80. Paris, 1880.

Law Clerk, A. *William Russell.* Leaves from the diary of ... L. 1857.

Lawrence, Slingsby. *George Henry Lewes.* Sunshine through the clouds. A drama in one act, adapted from "La joie fait peur" by Madame De Girardin. By S. L. ... L. 187-.

Lawton, Effie. *Mrs. S. May Bell.*

Lawyer, A. *Charles Cowley.* Leaves from a lawyer's life afloat and ashore. Lowell (?), 1879.

Lawyer, A. *Sir James Stewart.* The life of ... written by himself. L. 1830.

Lay Baronet, A. *Sir Henry Martin, Bart.* Archbishop Murray's Douay and Rhemish Bible ... 1848. L. 1850.

Lay Brother of the Same Society, A. *Henry Foley.* The life of blessed Alphonsus Rodriguez, Lay-brother of the Society of Jesus ... L. 1873.

Lay-dissenter, A. *John Stevenson.* A letter to a dissenting minister ... n.p. 1780.

Lay Dissenter, A. *Richard Sharp.* A letter to the public meeting of the friends to the repeal of the Test and Corporation Acts ... L. 1790.

Lay Gentleman, A. *Dr. Francis Lee.* The history of Montanism. L. 1709.

Lay-hand, A. *Thomas Lewis.* The clergy-man's advocate ... L. 1711.

Lay Hand, A. *Sir Richard Cox,* Lord Chancellor of Ireland. An enquiry into religion ... L. 1711.

Lay Hand, A. *Roger Lawrence.* Lay baptism invalid ... L. 1708.

Lay-Member of the British and Foreign Bible Society, A. *George Stokes.* Bible Society. L. 1826.

Lay Member of the Church of England, A. *John Muir.* A brief examination of prevalent opinions on the inspiration of the Scriptures . . . L. 1861.

Lay-Member of the Church of England, A. *John Stow.* Thoughts on the Gospel of Jesus Christ. By . . . Greenwich, Eng., 1846.

Lay Member of the Church of Scotland, A. — *Stevenson.* The harmony of the Bible with facts . . . Edinb. 1867.

Lay Member of the Church of Scotland, A. *Thomas Carlyle.* Letter to the Rev. Robert Burns, D.D. . . . Greenock, 1830.

Lay-member of the Committee, A. *William Rivington.* Remarks and suggestions regarding the want of parsonage houses in the parish of St. Pancras . . . By . . . L. 1849.

Lay Preacher, The. *Joseph Dennie,* who is best known for the essays which he contributed to the "Farmer's Museum," a periodical which he published at Walpole, N.H., 1795–98.

Lay Seceder, A. *George Wilson Meadley.* A letter to the Bishop [Burgess] of St. David's . . . L. 1814.

Layman, A. *Samuel Adams,* in the "Boston Gazette," March 27, 1769.

Layman, A. *John Skinner.* A L.'s account of his faith and practice. Edinb. 1836.

Layman, A. *Peter Virtue,* the younger. An address on ignorance of the Scriptures . . . By . . . 1873.

Layman, A. *Joseph Jewell.* An address to Christians, particularly those who are united in circulating the Scriptures. By . . . Oxf. 1821.

Layman, A. *John Hay Forbes.* Lord Medwyn. Address to the members of the Episcopal Church in Scotland. Edinb. 1847.

Layman, A. *Patrick Duigenan, LL.D.* An address to the nobility and gentry of the Church of Ireland . . . Dublin, 1786.

Layman, A. *Thomas Williams.* The age of infidelity . . . By . . . L. 1795.

Layman, A. *Solomon Lowe.* The antidote or full answer to Mr. Woolston's Five Discourses on the Miracles of our Saviour . . . L. 1729.

Layman, A. *William Hussey.* An appeal to the holy Scriptures themselves . . . L. 1830.

Layman, A. *S. Robinson.* An appeal to serious Dissenters . . . 1805.

Layman, A. *John Taylor.* Armageddon . . . L. 1851.

Layman, A. *Asa Wilbur.* Biblical standpoint . . . B. 1874.

Layman, A. *William Penney,* Lord Kinloch. The circle of Christian doctrine . . . Edinb. 1861.

Layman, A. *William Brown* (?). The claims of Thomas Jefferson to the Presidency examined at the bar of Christianity. P. 1800.

Layman, A. *John Osborne Sargent.* Common Sense *versus* Judicial Legislation . . . The rule in Minot's case . . . By . . . N.Y. 1871.

Layman, A. *John David Chambers.* A companion to Confession and Holy Communion. Trans. by . . . L. 1853.

Layman, A. *Goldwin Smith, M.A.* Concerning doubt . . . Oxf. 1861.

Layman, A. *John Muir.* Considerations on religion . . . Edinb. 1842.

Layman, A. *James Whatman Bosanquet.* Daniel's prophecy of the seventy weeks interpreted. L. 1836.

Layman, A. *Harold Richard Bush.* David's choice of three evils . . . A discourse on the distress in the cotton districts. By . . . L. 1862.

Layman, A. *Thomas Falconer.* Devotions for the Sacrament of the Lord's Supper . . . By . . . L. 1786.

Layman, A. *John Watts De Peyster.* A discourse on High Church doctrines. Poughkeepsie, 1860.

Layman, A. *Ralph Hodshon,* of Lintz. A dispassionate narrative of the conduct of the English clergy . . . L. 1768.

Layman, A. *William Falconer.* Dissertation on Paul's voyage from Cæsarea to Puteoli . . . Oxf. 1817.

Layman, A. *F. Bolingbroke Ribbans, LL.D.* Doctrines and duties; faith and practice. L. 1843.

Layman, A. *Rev. William Macfarlane.* Duty; or, ability and present action contrasted . . . Edinb. 1850.

Layman, A. *Sir James Allan Park, D.C.L.* An earnest exhortation to a frequent reception of . . . the Lord's Supper. L. 1804.

Layman, A. *John Allen.* Enquiry into the tripartite Division of the Tithes in England. L. 1833.

Layman, A. *Peter Waldo.* An essay on . . . the Lord's Supper . . . by . . . L. 1771.

Layman, A. *William Stevens.* An essay on the nature and constitution of the Christian Church . . . L. 1773.

Layman, A. *Thomas Carlyle.* An Essay to illustrate the foundation . . . and the evidences of Christianity . . . Edinb. 1827.

Layman, A. *Rev. John Hollis.* Essays meant as an offering in support of rational religion . . . n.p. 1790.

Layman, A. *Robert Benton Seeley.* Essays on the Church ... L. 1834.

Layman, A. *James Norton.* Essays and reflections in Australia, Sydney. L. 1852.

Layman, A. *Alexander Watson.* Essays, religious and moral ... Edinb. 1821.

Layman, A. *Caleb Fleming.* An examination of Mr. Chubb's discourse on miracles ..: L. 1742.

Layman, A. *Samuel K. Jennings, M.D.* An exposition of the late controversy in the Methodist Episcopal Church ... Balt. 1831.

Layman, A. *William Rivington.* The extent, evils, and needlessness of Sunday trading in London ... L. 1855.

Layman, A. *Capt. Matthew Montagu, R.N.* A few words on Popery and Protestantism ... L. 1854.

Layman, A. *Theodore Irving, LL.D.* The Fountain of Living Waters. N.Y. 1850.

Layman, A. *Frederick John Monson,* 5th Lord Monson. Four sermons ... L. 1842.

Layman, A. *Rev. Nathaniel Neal.* A free and serious remonstrance to Protestant Dissenting Ministers on occasion of the decay of religion ... L. 1746.

Layman, A. *Rev. Andrew Macgeorge.* The Free Church ... Glasgow, 1873.

Layman, A. *David Rowland.* An inquiry concerning the principles of the constitution of human nature. L. 1856.

Layman, A. *Arthur Ellis.* Is the vicar of Brompton a Tractarian ? ... L. 1855.

Layman, A. *George Foster Talbot, A.M.* Jesus: his opinions and character. The New Testament studies of ... B. 1883.

Layman, A. *William Rivington.* The late payment of weekly wages considered in connexion with Sunday trading in London ... L. 1854.

Layman, A. *Alexander Dunlop.* The law of the Sabbath of perpetual obligation ... Edinb. 1847.

Layman, A. *John Skinner,* Bishop of Aberdeen. A layman's account of his faith and practice. Edinb. 1801.

Layman, A. *Thomas Hughes.* A layman's faith. L. 1868.

Layman, A. *Lyman Abbott, D.D.* A L.'s story; or, the experiences of John Laicus and his wife in a country parish. N.Y. 1873.

Layman, A. *Samuel Greg.* Legacy in prose and verse. L. 1877.

Layman, A. *Thomas Gordon.* A letter of consolation and counsel to the good people of England ... L. 1750.

Layman, A. *Duncan Innes,* of Edinburgh. A letter ... to a Lay-deacon, of the Kirk of Scotland ... n.p. 1749.
The address to the reader is signed " D. I."

Layman, A. *Sir George Colebrooke, Bart.* A letter to a nobleman, containing considerations on the laws relative to Dissenters ... L. 1790.

Layman, A. *Richard Gough.* A letter to [B. Porteus] the Bishop of London. n.p. 1799.

Layman, A. *Thomas James Mathias.* A letter to the Lord Marquis of Buckingham ... chiefly on the subject of the numerous emigrant French priests and others of the Church of Rome ... L. 1797.

Layman, A. *Samuel Saunders.* A letter to the Rev. Mr. Tong, Mr. Robinson, Mr. Smith, & Mr. Reynolds. Occasion'd by the late differences amongst the Dissenters ... L. 1719.

Lay-man, A. *John Shute Barrington* A letter to the Right Revd. the Lord Bishop of ——. L. 1714.

Layman, A. *Thomas Kynaston.* A letter to Theophilus Lindsey ... L. 1785.

Layman, A. *Rev. Walter Farquhar Hook.* Letters to the authors of the " Plain tracts for critical times." L. 1839.
Also ascribed to John Sibbald Edison.

Layman, A. *Thomas Cogan, M.D.* Letters to William Wilberforce, Esq., M.P. ... L. 1799.

Layman, A. *John Lavicount Anderdon.* Life of Thomas Ken, Bishop of Bath and Wells. L. 1851.

Layman, A. *Prince Hoare, Esq.* (?). Manual of the Latin words ... of the Church service. 1822.

Layman, A. *Sir William Domville, Bart.* The Mosaic Sabbath ... L. 1850.

Layman, A. *T. M. Stevenson.* The natural or the supernatural. By ... L. 1874.

Layman, A. *Michael Dodson.* New translation of Isaiah ... by ... L. 1790.

Layman, A. *John Poynder.* Observations on the Sunday newspapers. 1820.

Layman, A. *Richard Monckton Milnes,* Lord Houghton. One tract more ... L. 1841.

Layman, A. *Stephen Colwell.* Politics for American Christians ... P. 1852.

Layman, A. *Sir John Bayley, Bart.* Prophecies of Christ ... L. 1828.

Layman, A. *James Augustus St. John.* The reasonableness of Christianity ... With a biographical essay ... and notes by ... L. 1850.

Layman, A. *John Lowell, LL.D.* The recent attempt to defeat the Constitutional provisions in favour of religious freedom ... B. 1828.

Layman, A. *Andrew Wilson, M.D.* Reflections upon some of the subjects in dispute between the author of the "Divine legation of Moses" [Warburton] and a late professor in the University of Oxford [Lowth], by ... 1767.

Layman, A. *Sir Walter Scott.* Religious discourses. Edinb. 1828.

Layman, A. *B. Bartlett.* Remarks on the proceedings of the Episcopal conventions for forming an American Constitution ... B. 1786.

Layman, A. *William Witherby.* A review of Scripture ... By ... L. 1816.

Layman, A. *Samuel Austin Allibone.* A review by ... of a work entitled "New themes for the Protestant Clergy" [by S. Colwell]. P. 1852.

Layman, A. *Samuel Heywood.* The rights of Protestant Dissenters to a compleat toleration asserted ... 2d ed. L. 1789.

Layman, A. *Edgar Taylor,* in his revision of the New Testament ... L. 1840.

Layman, A. *Sharon Turner, Esq.* Sacred meditations and devotional poems by ... L. 1810.

Layman, A. *William Peter, M.A.* Sacred songs, being an attempted paraphrase of some portions of Scripture; with other poems. By ... L. 1834.

Layman, A. *Ralph Nicholson Wornum.* Saul of Tarsus; or, Paul and Swedenborg, etc. By ... L. 1877.

Layman, A. *Sir Edward Hall Alderson.* A second letter ... 1851.

Layman, A. *Thomas Sanden, M.D.* A second letter to the Rev. Dr. Goddard. Chichester, 1815.

Layman, A. *James Wardrop.* Sermon occasioned by the death of Alexander Christie, Esq., of Townfield, late chief magistrate of Montrose ... By ... L. 1796.

Layman, A. *George Hardinge.* Three sermons. 1813.

Layman, A. *Richard Dykes Alexander.* The speech of ... at a late anniversary meeting of a Bible association in the County of Suffolk, 1826.

Layman, A. *George Griffin.* The sufferings of Christ. N.Y. 1845.

Layman, A. *Thomas Crowther Brown.* Suggestions for a Church of Unity. By ... 1862.

Layman, A. *William Oldisworth.* Timothy and Philatheus ... By ... L. 1709–10.

Layman, A. *C. N. Cumberlege Ware.* The union of Church and State ... By ... L. 1869.

Layman, A. *John Edmonds Stock.* Unitarianism tried by Scripture, etc. Bristol, 1840.

Layman, A. *John Bevans, Jr.* A vindication of the authenticity of the narratives contained in the first two chapters of the Gospels of St. Matthew and St. Luke ... By ... L. 1822.

Layman, A. *Orlando Meads.* What ought the Diocese to do ... 1845.

Layman, A. *George Brown.* Words from a layman's ministry at Barnard Castle. L. 1871.

Layman of Boston, U.S., A. *Hon. Nathan Appleton.* The doctrines of Original Sin and the Trinity; discussed in a correspondence between a clergyman of the Episcopal Church in England [*i.e.* Rev. William Edward Heygate] and ... B. 1859.

Layman of the Church, A. *William Edmonstoune Aytoun.* The Drummond Schism examined and exposed. Edinb. 1842.

Layman of the Church of England, A. *William Knox.* Considerations on the universality and uniformity of the theocracy. L. 1796.

Layman of the Church of England, A. *John Watson.* The New Testament ... with notes ... By ... L. 1822.

Layman of the Church of Scotland, A. *Thomas Blackwood.* Remarks on the Constitution of the Canadas, civil and ecclesiastical, with a view to its amendment. n.p., n.d.

Layman of the County of Suffolk, A. *P. Deck.* The advantage of a national observance of Divine and Human laws ... Ipswich, 1792.

Layman, A Leeds. *George Rawson,* known as "A Leeds Layman," was residing at that city when he contributed 15 hymns to the "Leeds Hymn Book," 1853.

Layne, Pyngle. *J. Fox Turner.* A short discourse on sermons ... L. 1855.

Layton, Lillie. *Mrs. Emeline H. (Brown) Johnson,* whose last poetical productions, written on her sick-bed, appeared in the "American Courier," Philadelphia, 1850, under the above signature.

Lazarus, Ebenezer. *Robert Mason.* Description of the town of Kelso ... Kelso, 1789.

Leal. *E. Disosway.* Fables for little folk. N.Y. 1871.

Leander, Richard. *Richard Volkmann.* Traümereien an französischen Kaminen : märchen. 1871. 12th ed. 1880.

Learned, Faithful, Zealous, and Reverend Minister of the Gospel in the Church of Scotland, A. *Rev. Ebenezer Erskine.* The groans of believers under their burdens ... Edinb. 1722.

Learned Hand, A. *Sir Matthew Hale.* History of the Common Law of England. In the Savoy, 1713.

Learned Hand, A. *Zachary Grey, LL.D.* A preface to Dean Moss's sermons. By ... L. 1732.

Learned Judge, A. *Sir Francis Buller.* An introduction to the law relative to trials at Nisi Prius. By ... L. 1768.

Lebrun, Alfred. *Alfred Hennequin.* J'attends mon oncle, 1869 ; and Trois chapeaux. Brussels, 1870.

Lebrun, Camille. *Pauline Guyot.* Une amitié de femme. Paris, 1843.

Le Clerc. *Mrs. Samuella (Mardis) Cowen,* who has written for several Southern journals under this signature, — the " New Orleans Mirror," the " Southern Literary News," etc.

Ledyard, Hope. *Mrs. F. McCready Harris,* in numerous works for young people.

Lee, Alfred. *John Clark Ferguson.* The Empire of Music ; and other poems. L. 1849.

Lee, Alice Gordon. *Mrs. Alice (Bradley Neal) Haven.* The game of checkers, published in the Philadelphia " Saturday Gazette."

Lee, Edith. *Miss Florence Burckett.* Wildmoor. P. 187-.

Lee, Griffin. *Paschal Beverley Randolph, M.D.* Pre-Adamite man. N.Y. 1863.

Lee, Holme. *Harriet Parr.* Annis Warleigh's fortunés. L. 1863.

Lee, Leila. *Miss R. Coe.* Wee Wee Songs. B. 1859.

Lee, Minnie Mary. *Julia Amanda (Sargent) Wood.* Hubert's wife: story for you. Balt. 1875.

Lee, Patty. *Miss Alice Cary,* who, under this pen-name, wrote a series of prose sketches and essays in the "National Era " (Washington, D.C.).

Lee, Sheppard. *Robert Montgomery Bird.* Sheppard Lee ... N.Y. 1836.

Lee, Stannie. *Mrs. Laura S. Webb,* who, for several years, contributed poems and sketches to various papers under this pen-name.

Lee, Vernon. *Violet Paget.* Belcaro, being essays on sundry æsthetical questions. By ... L. 1881.

Leevit, Don T. B., of Chickomango, Ohio, U.S. *James Mudie Spence, F.R.G.S.* Life on the Great Hydropathium ... L. 1877.

Lefebre, Dr. René. *Édouard Laboulaye.* Paris in America ... N.Y. 1863.

Left Hand, The. *Benjamin Franklin.* A petition of the left hand: one of the bagatelles. Written about 1778.

Le G., C. V. *Charles Valentine Le Grice.* — See Lamb's " Elia," " Christ's Hospital."

Legion. *Hon. Robert Baldwin Sullivan.* Letters on responsible government ... Toronto, 1844.

Leicester, Mrs. *Miss Mary Lamb.* Mrs. Leicester's school; or, the history of several young ladies ... L. 1808.

Leigh, Florence. *Mrs. Anne T. (Wilbur) Wood,* who wrote for papers and periodicals under this pen-name.

Leigh, Hart. *John Thomas Denny,* in his contributions to " Wideawake " (L.), etc.

Leigh, Larrie. *L. T. Warner.* The true Grecian bend. N.Y. 187-.

Leigh, Stuart. *Mrs. Mary Bayard (Devereux) Clarke,* who published considerably under this pen-name.

Leighton. *Jesse Appleton, S.T.D.,* who, under this signature, wrote for the Boston " Panoplist " and the " Piscataqua Evangelical Magazine."

Leila. *Mrs. Emma Barlow,* a frequent contributor to " Harper's Magazine," " Scribner's," and other periodicals.

Leila. *Miss Ella Campbell,* who contributed poetry to the " Louisville (Ky.) Democrat," under this pen-name.

Leina, Wil. D', Esq., of the Outer Temple. *Prof. Daniel Wilson.* Spring wild flowers. Toronto, 1870.

Leisurely Saunterer. *Rev. Edward Eggleston,* in his contributions to " Hearth and Home."

Lemage, Gaspard. *Jean Charles Taché, M.D.* La Pléiade Rouge ... Quebec, 1854.

Lemoine. *Eugene Lemoine Didier.* The life and letters of Madame Bonaparte. N.Y. 1879.

Lena. *Mrs. Mary Torrans Lathrop.* In early life her signature in the country paper.

Lennox, Mary. *Mrs. Mary Louise Cook.* Ante Bellum. P. 1869.

Leo. *J. K. Casey.* Rising of the moon. L. 18-.

Leo. *Col. — Pemberton.* The scapegoat. L. 1870.

Léo, André. *Mme. L. Champseix.* Les deux filles de Monsieur Plichon. Paris, 1865.

Leo, Dr. *Dr. Leo de Colange.* The preservation of beauty. N.Y. 1877.

Leo the Second. *Lawrence Eusden,* in a letter contributed to the "Guardian," No. 124, Aug. 3, 1713.

Leola. *Mrs. Loula (Kendall) Rogers,* whose productions consist of fugitive pieces, many of them published in the newspapers of the day.

Leoline. *Mrs. Emma B. (Sargent) Dunham,* in her contributions to the "Christian Leader" (B.), etc.

Leon. *Leonard Boitel.* Feuilles mortes. Paris, 1836.

Leoni, Leone. *Dr. John D. Osborne,* as Paris correspondent of the "World" (N.Y.).

Leontes. *James Bindley,* who was the "Leontes" celebrated by Dr. Dibdin in his "Bibliomania" and in the "Biographical Decameron."

Leroy. *Miss Annie M. Barnwell,* who, under this signature, has been a frequent contributor to "Scott's Magazine" (Atlanta, Ga.), and to the "Land we Love" (Charlotte, N.C.).

Leslie, Emma. *Mrs. Dixon.*

Leslie, Frank. *Frank Collier,* proprietor of "The Chimney Corner"(N.Y.) and numerous other publications.

Leslie, Mrs. Madeline. *Mrs. Harriet Newell (Woods) Baker.* Woodlawn Series. B. 1868.

L'Espiön Turc. *Giovanni Paolo Marana.* Letters sent by the Turkish Spy. L. 1770.

L'Estomac, Don Bilioso de. *Dr. John Woodward.* The life and adventures of . . . [A satire on Dr. John Woodward.] L. 1719. By Richard Mead, M.D.

Leto, Pomponio. *Francesco Nobili Vitelleschi.* Morale induttiva. Roma, 1882.

Letter H., The. *Charles G. Halpine.* Lyrics by . . . N.Y. 1854.

Levater, Louis. *Louis Adolphe Spach,* who has in some of his books used this pseudonym.

Leviathan of Literature, The. *Samuel Johnson.*

Levis, Jeremy. *Laughton Osborn.* Sixty years of the life of . . . N.Y. 1831.

Lewald, Fanny. *Mme. Fanny (Lewald) Stahr.* Hulda: translated . . . P. 187-.

Lewis, Augustin. *Lewis* or *Louis Austin.*

The "Nation" of July 17, 1884, points out that two chapters of the biography of Henry Irving [by Frederic Daly] are copied word for word from an article published in the "Dublin University Magazine" for September, 1877, over the signature Augustin Lewis, which it suspects to be an anagram of the real name of the author of both eulogies, *i.e.* "Louis or Lewis Austin."

Lewis, Henry. *A. H. Lewis.* The Boston boy. B. 1871.

Lewis, Monk. *Matthew Gregory Lewis.* The monk: a romance. L. 1795.

Lewtral, H. M. *Mary Hartwell.* Woman in armor. N.Y. 1875.

Lex Publica. *Augustus Granville Stapleton,* in the London "Morning Herald," 1850–55.

Libertas. *Peter Brown.* The fame and glory of England vindicated. N.Y. 1842.

Libertas. *Hon. Mrs. Caroline Elizabeth Sarah (Sheridan) Norton,* afterwards Mrs. Stirling-Maxwell. Letters to the mob . . . L. 1848.

Libertas. *Charles Mayo Ellis.* The power of the Commander in Chief to declare martial law . . . B. 1862.

Libraire, Un. *P. Chaillot, jeune.* Manuel du libraire bibliothécaire, et de l'homme de lettres . . . Paris, 1829.

Lightfoot. *John Isaac Ira Allen,* in the "Boston Traveller," 1857.

Lightfoot. *Michael Martin.* — See "Thunderbolt."

Lil. *Waterman L. Ormsby, Jr.,* in his contributions to the "Sun" (N.Y.).

Lilburne. *James Ralph,* who compiled for the "Champion" what was called an "Index to the Times," which contained the current news of the day, under the assumed name of "Lilburne."

Lilias. *Miss Carter.* Class Rimes (N.Y.), etc.

Lilly, Lambert, Schoolmaster. *Francis Lester Hawks.* The early history of the Southern States . . . P. 1832.

Limbertongue, Mr. *James Hain Friswell.* Twelve insides and one out. Edited from the papers of . . . L. 1855.

Limner, Luke, Esq. *John Leighton, F.S.A.* London cries and public edifices. L. 1847.

Lincolnshire Grazier, A. *Thomas Hartwell Horne.* The complete grazier. L. 1805.

L'Inconnue. *Mrs. Janie (Ollivar) Benson,* whose poems appeared for the years between 1861 and 1865 in the "Southern Field and Fireside," Augusta, Ga.

L'Inconnue. *Mrs. L. Virginia (Smith) French.* Kernwood; or, after many days :

a historical romance . . . Louisville, 1867.

Lindau, Heinrich. *Hermann Francke.*

Lindon, Lilia. *Mrs. Aggie Graves.*

Lington, Burr, D.LL. *Gay Humboldt.* Poems and letters to Don Brown by G. H., *alias* Burr Lington, D.LL. Albany, 1857.

Linkinwater, Tim. *Mr. Waldo*, in his contributions to the "Picayune" (New Orleans, La.).

Linois, Georges. *Charles de Batz-Trenqueléon.* A ma fenêtre. Calais, 1852.

Linwood, Lottie. *Mrs. Helen M. Cooke.*

Lion-Killer. *Cécile Jules Basile Gérard.*

Lips. *Wilhelm Oertel.*

Lisle, Fernand de. *Edmond (Demanne et de) Manne*, who used the above as one of his pseudonyms.

Listener, The. *Rev. John Macgowan.* Infernal conferences; or, dialogues of devils. By . . . L. 1772.

Listener, The. *Caroline Fry.* The listener in Oxford. L. 1839.

Literary, Mrs. *Mrs. Sallie Elizabeth (Hillyer Ballard) Maynard*, in humorous contributions to periodicals, etc.

Literary Antiquary, A. *F. W. Fairholt.* Holbein's Dance of Death. Edited by . . . L.

Literary Lounger, A. *J. H. Willis.* Scraps and sketches; or, the album of . . . Quebec, 1830.

Literary and Scientific Association of Elgin, A Member of the. *Dr. Taylor.* Edward I. of England in the North of Scotland . . . Elgin, 1858.

Little, Thomas, Esq. *Thomas Moore.* The poetical works of the late T. L., Esq. L. 1801.

Littlejohn. *Dr. R. Shelton Mackenzie.* "The present 'Weekly Times' (L.) started with some new features. One of these was an article on the leading events of the week, signed 'Littlejohn.' The name was a pseudonym, but not that of any actual person. Two of the gentlemen who under it wrote perhaps longer than any others were Dr. Shelton Mackenzie and Mr. Frederick Guest Tomlins."

Littlejohn. *Frederick Guest Tomlins.* "In his early days he was a contributor to Hetherington's 'Poor Man's Guardian,' and latterly to the 'Weekly Times,' in which the series of articles signed 'Littlejohn' were from his pen."

Littlejohn, Hugh. *John Hugh Lockhart*, son of John Gibson Lockhart and grandson of Sir Walter Scott, for whom

the latter wrote "Tales of a Grandfather." He died when a child.

Littlepage, Cornelius. *James Fenimore Cooper.* Satanstoe: a tale of the Colony. N.Y. 1860.

Littleton, Mark. *John Pendleton Kennedy.* Swallow barn. P. 1832.

Live American, A. *Henry Morford.* Over sea; or, England, France, and Scotland as seen by . . . N.Y. 1867.

Liverpool Merchant, A. *Henry Arthur Bright (?).* Free Trade Policy, examined with respect to . . . our Colonial System . . . L. 1846.

Lizard, John. *Dr. Edward Young*, in a paper to the "Guardian" (No. 86, June 19, 1713).

Llewellyn. *Robert Sanders.* — See "Spencer, Nath."

Lleyon, Gutto. *Griffith Robert Jones*, at one time of Lleyn, Carnarvonshire, was once called by a bard "Gwyrgant's Boswell."

Llucen. *Rev. John Cullen*, of Radcliffe-on-Trent, in his contributions to various British newspapers and reviews.

Local Artist, A. *John C. Fernihough.* Pen and ink sketches of Liverpool town councillors, by . . . Liverpool, 1866.

Local Preacher, A. *William Henry Rodd.* Impetus. An address to the members of the Wesleyan Methodist Association . . . By . . . Penzance, 1844.

Locke, Una. *Mrs. Una Locke Bailey.* The school at Elm Oak and the school of life. N.Y. 1861.

Locker, Arthur. *J. H. Forbes.* Sir Goodwin's Folly: a story of the year 1795 . . . L. 1864.

Lockfast. *William Henry Simmons*, in the "Collegian" of Harv. Univ. Cambridge, 1830.

Locomotive. *Rev. Moses Harvey*, of St. Johns, Newfoundland, in his contributions to various local periodicals.

Log, Abel. *Rev. Charles Butler Greatrex.* Whittlings from the West: with some account of Butternut Castle . . . Edinb. 1854.

Logan. *Townsend Ward.* Letters . . . P. 18–.

Logan. *John Neal.* Logan, a family history. P. 1822.

Logan. *Thomas Bangs Thorpe (?).* The master's house: a tale of Southern life . . . N.Y. 1854.

Logan, Olive. *Mrs. Olive (Logan) Sikes.* Get thee behind me, Satan! a home-born book of home-truths . . . N.Y. 1872.

Lola. *Mrs. Emma (Moffett) Wynne,*

who, during the civil war, occasionally contributed to the "Field and Fireside" (Augusta, Ga.) under this pen-name.

Lombard, A. *Benjamin Smart.*
"The fluctuations of our money system, Mr. Smart's occupation enabled him to consider with peculiar advantages; and accordingly, in addition to frequent communications on points of fact ('Gent. Mag.,' Nov. 1811, 424, signed 'B. S.'), he entered, under the signature of 'A Lombard,' into an extensive theoretical discussion on the subject, of which the pages of this ('Gent') Magazine from 1813 to 1820 bear proof."

Lombarda, Una. *Felicita Morandi.* Ghirlanda di fiori per l'infanzia e per l'adolescenza. 1857.

London Antiquary, A. *John Camden Hotten.* A dictionary of modern slang, cant, and vulgar words ... L. 1859–60.

London Hermit. *F. Parke.* Poetry and essays. L. 18–.

London Merchant, A. *C. W. Stokes.* An inquiry of the Home Secretary as to whether Professor Tyndall has not subjected himself [in his Belfast Address] to the "Penalty on persons expressing blasphemous opinions" ... By ... L. 1874.

London Physician, A. *James Howard.* The evils of England, social and economical. L. 1848.

London Physician, A. *Edward Smith, M.D.* How to get fat ... L. 1865.

London Physician, A. *Samuel Dickson.* Memorable events in the life of ... L. 1863.

London Physician, A. *William Augustus Guy, M.D.* Principles of forensic medicine. L. 1844.

London W. *Joseph H. Dean*, editor of "Bicycling World" (Boston).

Londoner, A. *Walter White.* A L.'s walk to the Land's End; and a trip to the Scilly Isles. L. 1855.

Londoner, A. *Charles Lamb.* "The Londoner," contributed to the "Reflector."

Long, Silent. *Rev. Thomas T. Lynch.* The ethics of quotation ... L. 1856.

Long Island Farmer Poet. *Bloodgood H. Cutter.*

Longchamps. *John C. Delille*, Paris correspondent of the "Spirit of the Times" (N.Y.).

Looker-On, A. *John Dix Ross.* Local loiterings, and visits in the vicinity of Boston ... B. 1845.

Looker On, A. *Hector Orr.* A sketch of Camden City, New Jersey, with a view to business. By ... Camden, 1873.

Looker On from America, A. *Charles Brandon Boynton.* The four great powers: England, France, Russia, and America ... Cin. 1866.

Looker-On-Here in Vienna. *Mrs. Mary E. Andersen.* The merchant's wife.

Lord and Lady there, The. *Lord George Grenville Nugent*, and *Lady Nugent.* The legends of the library at Lilies, by ... L. 1832.

Lord Bishop of Oxford. *Robert Lowth, D.D.* Sermon before the Society for the Propagation of the Gospel ... By ... L. 1771.

Lord Chief Commissioner of the Jury Court, The. *William Adam.* Extracts from a paper entitled Statement, etc., by ... Edinb. (?) 1823.

Lorenzo. *Lorenzo Dow.* Polemical works of Lorenzo. N.Y. 1814.

Lorimer, Mary. *M. O. B. Dunning.* Among the trees: journal of walks in the woods ... N.Y. 187–.

Loring, Laura. *Laura Loring Pratt.* Juveniles. B. 1874–75.

Lorm, Hieronymus. *Heinrich Landesmann.* High-life in der Vorstadt, in "Ueber Land und Meer." 1878.

Lorrain, Camille. *Hippolyte Babou*, who, under this signature, contributed to Parisian journals.

Lorraine, Mrs. Felix. *Lady Caroline (Ponsonby) Lamb.*
"Lord Beaconsfield, in 'Vivian Grey,' roughly sketched the portrait of the subject of our article in 'Mrs. Felix Lorraine.' At end of the first edition of that work (1827) ... there is a key to the novel, in which these disguised and real names amongst others are given: — 'Marquis of Carabas, *Marquis of Clanricarde*; 'Mr. Foaming Fudge,' *Mr. Brougham*; 'Mr. Charlatan Gas,' *Mr. Canning*; 'Lord Past Century,' *Earl of Eldon*; 'Mr. Liberal Principles,' *Mr. Huskisson*; 'the Duke of Waterloo,' *the Duke of Wellington*; 'Prince Hungary,' *Prince Esterhazy*; 'the Marchioness of Almacks,' *the Marchioness of Londonderry*; 'Mrs. Felix Lorraine,' *Lady Caroline Lamb*; 'Stanislaus Hoax,' *Theodore Hook*; 'Lord Prima Donna,' *Lord William Lennox*; and 'the Marquis of Grandgout,' *the Marquis of Hertford*." — See "Gent. Mag.," October, 1883, pp. 341, 42.

Lorrequer, Harry. *Charles James Lever.* Charles O'Malley. L. 1841.

Lorrimer, Laura. *Mrs. Julia (Finley) Shelton*, who, under this signature, was a contributor to various journals and magazines, "North and South," "Godey's Lady's Book," "Louisville Journal," and "Field and Fireside" among others.

Lot, Parson. *Rev. Charles Kingsley.*
"It was at one of these gatherings" at Mr. Maurice's, "towards the end of 1847 or early in 1848, when *Kingsley* found himself in a minority of one, that he said jokingly, he felt much as Lot must have felt in the Cities of the Plain when he

seemed as one that mocked to his sons-in-law. The name 'Parson Lot' was then and there suggested, and adopted by him as a familiar *nom de plume.* He used it from 1848 up to 1856; at first constantly, latterly much more rarely. But the name was chiefly made famous by his writings in 'Politics for the People,' the 'Christian Socialist,' and the 'Journal of Association,' three periodicals which covered the years from '48 to '52, by 'Alton Locke,' and by tracts and pamphlets, of which the best known is 'Cheap Clothes and Nasty.'"

Lothrop, Amy. *Miss Anna B. Warner.* Dollars and cents. P. 1860.

Loti, Pierre. *Julien Viaud.* Azyadé: le mariage de Loti and le roman du Spahi. Paris, 188-.

Lottie. *Miss C. Walker.* Leaves blown together. By ... L. 1865.

Louis. *Louis Dutens,* in Beloe's "Sexagenarian," Vol. 2, p. 100. 2d ed. L. 1818.

Louisa, Aunt. *Mrs. Richard Valentine.* Wee Wee Stories. N.Y. 187-.

Lounger, A. *Frank Fowler.* Dottings of ... L. 1859.

Lounger, A. *John Matthews.* Eloisa en dishabille. A new version of that lady's celebrated epistle to Abelard, in English metre. L. 1780.

This *jeu d'esprit* has been attributed to Porson, Coleridge, and Mathias; but Moore, in his "Life of Byron," says it was written by *John Matthews, Esq.,* of Belmont, Herefordshire, and that Porson was in the habit of reciting it, and even printed an edition.

Lounger, A. *William Bromet, M.D., F.S.A.* Perigrine in France; or ... journal. L. 18-.

Lounger, A, an Old Maid, and Lady Honora. *Alexander M'Gibbon.* Answer to the satirical poem on Stirling. In three respondendos ... Stirling, 1809.

Lounger, The. *George William Curtis,* probably his signature in some paper or periodical.

Lounger, The. *Joseph B. Gilder,* in his contributions to the "Critic and Good Literature" (N.Y.).

Lounger at the Clubs, The. *Edmund Yates,* in the "Illustrated Times" for many years, from 1855.

Lounger in the Lobby, The. *Royal W. Merrill,* in his contributions to the "Press" (P.).

Love, James. *James Dance.* Pamela: a comedy. L. 1742.

Lovechild, Mrs. *Lady Eleanor Fenn.* The child's grammar. L. 1851.

Lovechild, Solomon. *Lady Eleanor Fenn.* Sketches of little boys and girls. 1852.

Lovechurch, Leonard. *Rev. George Smith,* of Sheffield. A letter to the inhabitants of Sheffield on a subject which

has lately made, and is likely to make, much noise in the town and neighbourhood; or, a short peal on the new bells ... Sheffield, 1799.

This pamphlet, signed "L.L.," was reprinted from the "Country Spectator" (Gainsborough, 1792-93), where it was subscribed "Leonard Lovechurch."

Lovel. *John Lamb,* father of Charles. — See Lamb's "Elia," "The Old Benchers," etc.

Lovemore, Sir Charles. *Mrs. N. Manley de la Riviere.* The adventures of Rivella; or, the history of the author of the Atalantis ... L. 1714.

Lovengood, Sut. *George W. Harris.* Sut Lovengood: yarns spun by a "Nat'ral born durn'd Fool"; warped and wove for public wear. P. 187-.

Lover of Christ, A. *Rev. John Collett Ryland.* The life and actions of Jesus Christ ... By ... L. 1766.

Lover of Christian Liberty, A. *William Matthews.* Considerations on public worship ... By ... Bristol, 1808.

Lover of Episcopacy, A. *Zachary Grey, LL.D.* A century of eminent Presbyterian preachers; or, a collection of choyce sayings, from the publick sermons before the two houses, from November, 1640, to Jan. 31, 1648. (The day after the king was beheaded.) By ... L. 1723.

Lover of Free Grace, A. *John Wesley.* What is an Arminian? answered. By ... L. 1770.

Lover of her Sex, A. *Mary Astell.* A serious proposal to the ladies ... By ... L. 1695.

Lover of his Country, A. *Henry Fielding.* The crisis: a sermon on Rev. xiv. 9, 10, 11 ... L. 1741.

Lover of his Country, A. *George Ridpath.* A discourse upon the union of Scotland and England ... n.p. 1702.

Lover of his Country, A. *William Macintosh,* of Borlum. An essay on the husbandry of Scotland ... Edinb. 1732.

Lover of his Country, A. *William Smith, D.D.* An historical account of the expedition against the Ohio Indians in 1764, under the command of Henry Bouquet, Esq. ... By ... P. 1766.

Lover of his Country, A. *Caleb Fleming.* The immorality of prophane swearing demonstrated ... L. n.d.

Lover of his Country, A. *Rev. Arthur Ashley Sykes.* A letter to a friend ... L. 1717.

Lover of his King and Country, A. *S. Hayward.* A letter to the inhabitants of Great Britain and Ireland ... By ... L. 1756.

Lover of his Memory, A. *John Rhodes.* Fruits of a father's love: being the advice of William Penn to his children ... L. 1726.

Lover of History, A. *Zachary Grey, LL.D.* A caveat against Mr. Benj. Bennet, a meer pretender to history and criticism. By ... L. 1724.

Lover of Literature, A. *Thomas Green, Esq.* Diary of ... Ipswich, 1810.

Lover of Mankind, A. *Anthony Benezet.* The Mighty Destroyer displayed ... the dreadful havock made by the ... use as well as abuse of distilled spirituous liquors. By ... P. 1774.

Lover of Mankind and of Common Sense, A. *John Wesley.* The desideratum; or, electricity made plain and useful. By ... L. 1759.

Lover of Old England, A. *Daniel Defoe.* Mercurius politicus ... L. 1720.

Lover of Order, A. *Rev. Joseph Bretland,* in the "Theological Repository" (L.).

Lover of Order, A. *William Godwin* (?). Considerations on Lord Grenville's and Mr. Pitt's bills, concerning treasonable and seditious practices, etc. By ... L. 1795.

Lover of Peace and Order, A. *Esther Tuke.* An address to the inhabitants of the city of York ... By ... York, about 1794.

Lover of Peace and the Public Good, A. *John Humfrey.* Letters to Parliament-Men ... L. 1701.
Signed "J. H."

Lover of Peace and Truth, A. *Joseph Priestley.* A free address to those who have petitioned for the repeal of the late act of parliament, in favour of the Roman Catholics. L. 1780.

Lover of Peace and Truth in this Church, A. *Rev. James Adams.* Marrow-chicaning displayed ... n.p. 1726.

Lover of Stability. *Noah Webster.* Article in the "Hampshire Gazette."

Lover of that innocent and healthful diversion, A. *George Smith.* "The Angler's Magazine" ... (L. 1754).

Lover of that People, A. *John Barclay.* An affectionate address to such of the people called Friends as reside in London and its vicinity. By ... L. 1818.

Lover of the Church of England, A. *Patrick Drewe.* The Church of England's late conflict with, and triumph over, the spirit of fanaticism ... L. 1710.

Lover of the Fine Arts, A. *Maria*

(*Gowen*) *Brooks.* Judith, Esther, and other poems ... B. 1820.

Lover of the Gospel, A. *Joseph Priestley, D.D.* A familiar illustration of certain passages of scripture ... L. 1772.

Lover of the Gospel, A. *Thomas Reader.* A letter to ... [Dr. Priestley] ... L. 1772.

Lover of the Protestant Religion, A. *Rev. William Wright.* The Jacobite curse ... Glasgow, 1714.

Lover of the Publick Welfare, A. *Andrew Stevenson.* De municipum juramento ... Edinb. 1746.

Lover of the Pure Gospel, A. *Silvanus Gibbs.* The Calvinistic doctrine of election and reprobation exploded: in a letter to a friend ... Plymouth-Dock, 1820.

Lover of the Truth, A. *Jonathan Warne.* The Babel of Quakerism thrown down ... L. 1739.

Lover of the Truth in Fife, A. *Rev. William Campbell,* of Dysart. A just view of the principles of the Presbytery of Relief ... Edinb. 1778.

Lover of the Word, A. *Harvey A. Ingham.* Glad tidings; or, walks with the wonderful ... Rochester, N.Y., 1868.

Lover of Truth, A. *Thady Fitzpatrick.* — See "T. F."

Lover of Truth, A. *George Coade, Jr.,* of Exeter. A letter to a clergyman relating to his sermon on the 30th January. n.p. 1746.

Lover of Truth, A. *Rev. David Wilson.* A modest apology for the conduct of Seceders ... L. 1773.

Lover of Truth and Decency, A. *John Ewer,* Bishop of Landaff. A vindication of the Bishop of Landaff's sermon ... N.Y. 1768.

Lover of Truth and Liberty, A. *James Ralph.* The history of England during the reigns of K. William, Q. Anne, and K. George I.... L. 1744.

Lover of Truth and Mankind universally. *Francis Hatt.* Friendly advice to children and all mankind in general ... By ... n.p. 1765.

Lover of Truth and Peace, A. *Rev. Arthur Ashley Sykes.* The external peace of the Church only attainable by a zeal for Scripture in its just latitude ... L. 1716.

Lover of Truth and the British Constitution, A. *Caleb Evans, D.D.* A letter to ... John Wesley on his Calm Address to the American Colonies ... L. 1775.

Lover of Zion, A. *John Glass*, the founder of the "Glassites." A letter ... discovering the mystery of national church covenanting under the New Testament. Edinb. 1728.

Lovette, Lillie. *Mr. M. W. Torrey.*

Lowe Farmer, The. *William Law Gane*, an English and Canadian writer. He wrote for the "Royal Ladies' Magazine" in 1830, and afterwards for "Blackwood," the "New Monthly Magazine," the "Gentleman's Magazine," "Fraser," the "Tablet," "Douglas Jerrold's Magazine," "Household Words," and finally for "Punch." He also contributed to the "Metropolitan," the "Cabinet," and "Bentley's Miscellany," and was editor of the "Lady's Magazine," the "Court Magazine," and the "Town and Country Magazine"; was sub-editor of the "Morning Chronicle," and wrote for the "Sun" and other dailies and weeklies. Becoming acquainted with Cobbett, he contributed several papers to "Cobbett's Magazine." Coming to Canada in 1860, Mr. G. contributed prose and poetry to the "Saturday Reader," Montreal, and in 1865 edited a comic weekly called the "Sprite," Quebec.

Luçay, H. de. *Henri Rochefort de Luçay.* "Le mousquetaire" of Alex. Dumas. Paris, 1854.

Lucifer. *John Ball.* The baptism of fire. B. 1877.

Lucius. One of the signatures adopted by Junius (*q.v.*).

The letters subscribed "Lucius" relate exclusively to the dismission of Sir Jeffery Amherst from his post of Governor of Virginia for the sole purpose, as it should seem, of creating a post for the Earl of Hillsborough's intimate friend, Lord Botetourt, who had completely ruined himself by gambling and extravagance. — JAQUES, *Junius.*

The first of these letters appeared in the "Public Advertiser," Aug. 10, 1768.

Lucius. *Dr. Samuel Parr*, who contributed papers on Troy and the Troad to the "British Magazine" signed "Lucius."

Lucius. *Rev. James Blatch Piggot Dennis, B.A., F.G.S.* A letter to Lord John Russell ... By ... L. 1848; and another, 1850.

Ludlow, Johnny. *Ellen (Price) Wood.* Anne, and other tales. By ... 188–.

Ludlow, Park. *Theron Brown.* Nick Hardy at college; or, the wooden spoon. B. 188–.

Ludolff, M. *Luise Huyn.* Beata. 1880.

Luganski, Kosak. *Vladimer Ivanovitch Dahl.* Chmœl. St. Petersburg, 183–.

Lulu. *Miss Louise G. Hall.* Manna:

night and morning; selected and arranged by ... N.Y. 1883.

Lunar Wray, A. *Minot Judson Savage.* At the back of the moon. B. 1879.

Lunettes, Henry. *Margaret C. Conkling.* American gentleman's guide to politeness and fashion. N.Y. 187–.

Lunt, Irene. *Irene Bradbury*, in her contributions to the "Cottage Hearth."

Luola. *Mrs. Mary (Ayer) Miller*, who, under this pen-name, published poems in the youth's department of the "North Carolina Presbyterian" and the "Central Presbyterian" (Richmond, Va.), and wrote several Sunday-school books for the Presbyterian Board of Publication.

Lycurgus. *John Kent*, a frequent contributor to the "Public Advertiser" during 1769, and an opponent of the ministry. He is classed among the claimants to the "Junius Letters" (*q.v.*). See also "Private Letters of Junius," No. 5.

Lycus. *John Fitzgibbon*, 2d Earl of Clare, in Byron's "Childish Recollections" (Newark, 1807).

Lyle, Annot. *Mrs. Annot (Lyle) Saxon*, who contributed poems and sketches to the "American Courier" (P.) under this signature.

Lyle, Currer. *Mrs. M. Louise (Rogers) Crossley*, who, under this pen-name, contributed some of her most finished articles to the "Literary Companion" (published in Newnan, Ga.).

Lyn, R. *Sir Robert Walpole.* The life of Mr. R. Lyn, etc. L. 1728.

Lynceus. *Frederick Starr, Jr.* Letters for the people ... N.Y. 1853.

Lyndon. *Mrs. Matilda A. Bright.* Margaret: a story of life in a prairie home ... N.Y. 1868.

Lyndon, Barry. *George Lowell Austin.* Under the tide. B. 1870.

Lyndon, Barry, Esq. *William Makepeace Thackeray.* The memoirs of ... written by himself. L. 1856.

Lyndon, Mary. *Mrs. Mary (Neal Sergeant Gove) Nichols.* Mary Lyndon; or, revelations of a life. An autobiography. N.Y. 1855.

Lynn Bard, The. *Alonzo Lewis.* Forest-flowers and sea-shells. B. 1831.

Lynn, Ethel. *Mrs. Ethel Lynn Beers.* General Frankie: story for little folks. N.Y. 1863.

Lyon, Bonnet de. *Amédée Bonnet.* Éloge du docteur Alph. Dupasquier. Paris, 1849.

Lyrist, The. *E. Randles*, who was the lyrist mentioned by Miss Seward in her poem called "Llangollen Vale."

Lysander. *Rev. Thomas Frognall*

Dibdin, who was the "Lysander" of his own "Bibliomania."

Lysander. *James Cheetham.* Annals of the Corporation relative to the late contested elections . . . N.Y. 1802.

Lysander. *William P. Van Ness.* A correct statement of the late melancholy affair of honor between General Hamilton and Colonel Burr . . . July 11, 1804 . . . By . . . N.Y. 1804.

Lyttelton, Lord. *William Coombe, Esq.* Lord L.'s letters. L. 1784.

Lyttle, Byrd. *E. Victoria Lomax.* Mary Austin; or, the new home. P. 1870.

Lyulph. *H. R. Lumley.* Something like a nugget: a drama. By . . . L. 1868.

M.

M. *Mr. Macintosh*, editor of the "Buffalo News," in his contributions to various periodicals.

M. *Thomas Manning*, the Cambridge mathematical tutor.—See Lamb's "Elia," "Dissertation on Roast Pig," and "The Old and New Schoolmaster."

M. *Maunde*, dismissed schoolmaster.— See Lamb's "Elia," "Christ's Hospital."

M. *Maynard*, who hanged himself.— See Lamb's "Elia," "The South-Sea House."

M. *Joseph Mellish*, his signature to a paper in the "Microcosm," published at Eton College, 1787.

M. *Rev. Gerard Moultrie*, who contributed 35 hymns to the "People's Hymnal" (1867), some of which are signed "M.," others with the initials of his *nom de plume*, "D. P.," for "Desiderius Pastor"; and one is signed "The Primer."

M. *Alexander Pope.* — See "Bavius."

M. *Rev. William Lewis Rham*, his well-known signature in the London "Gardeners' Chronicle."

M. *Matthew F. Ward.*

M. *Sir George Steuart Mackenzie, Bart.* A letter to William Rae, Esq. . . . on the public execution of criminals. Edinb. 1815.

M. *Hugh Miller.* Letters on the herring fishing in the Moray Frith. Inverness, 1829.

M., Le Marquis de. *M. Moise Schwab.* Mélanges bibliographiques. Marseilles, 1880.

M., Mrs. *Mrs. Basil Montagu.* — See Lamb's "Elia," "Oxford in the Vacation."

M., A. *A. Mannington.* Footprints of the holy dead; trans. . . . L. 1863.

M., A. *Alfred Miles.* A word or two on the Liturgy. By . . . L. 1837.

M., A., Esquire. *Daniel Defoe.* — See "Moreton, Andrew, Esq."

M., A, a Layman. *Alexander Murray.* A clear display of the Trinity from Divine Revelation . . . By . . . L. 1773.

M., A. B. *Arthur Bache Matthews*, as editor of the "Riots at Birmingham, July, 1791 . . . L. 1863.

M., A. B. *Rev. Artemas Bowers Muzzey.* The Sabbath School Service and Hymn Book . . . B. 1855.

M., A. C. *Agnes C. Maitland.* Elsie: a Lowland sketch. L. 1875.

M., A. D. *Louis Charles Alfred de Musset*, as translator of De Quincey's "Confessions of an English Opium Eater" (1828), etc.

M., A. D., H.F.S.A. *Abbé Angé Denis McQuin.* A description of more than three hundred animals . . . By . . . L. 1872.

M., A. S. *A. S. Moffat.* Cedar Brook stories; or, the Clifford children . . . B. 1864.

M., A. W. *Agnes W. Mitchell.* The smuggler's son. P. 1842.

M. B. *Rev. Roger Baxter, S.J.* The Alexandria controversy; or, a series of letters between . . . and Quæro, on the tenets of Catholicity . . . Georgetown, D.C., 1817.

M., B. *Mrs. Barbara (Miller) Macandrew.* Ezekiel, and other poems. Edinb. 1872.

M., B. *Bernard de Mandeville.* Free thoughts on religion . . . L. 1720.

M., B. *Barclay de Mounteney.* Letter to Lord Brougham on the elective franchise. L. 1839.

M., B. *Bezaleel Morris.* A letter to Mr. Theobald, in verse, against Mr. P. . . . (*i.e.* Alex. Pope) contributed to the "Daily Journal," June 11, 1728.

M. B., Draper. *Jonathan Swift.* A letter to the people of Ireland. Dublin, 1729.

The letter is signed "Publicola."

M. B., Drapier. *Jonathan Swift.* The Drapier letters. 1724.

These letters were directed against the coinage of farthings and half-pence, and resulted in their

author obtaining the name of "The Copper-Farthing Dean" (*q.v.*).
See also "The Drapier" and "M. B., Draper."

M., B. A. *Brother Azarias Mullany.* An essay, contributing to a philosophy of literature. P. 1877.

M., C., J. H. G. and M. R. Respectively *Campbell Mackinnon, Joseph H. Gibbs,* and *Montgomerie Ranking,* authors of the "Quadrilateral." L. 1865.
These poems are dedicated by the above gentlemen to C. M. Crawford, whose name completes "The Quadrilateral."

M., C., Vicar of Brixworth. *Rev. Charles Marshall.* A plain and easy introduction to the knowledge and practice of gardening, with hints on fishponds. By . . . L. 1796.

M., C. B. *Mrs. Clara Barnes Martin.* Mount Desert, on the coast of Maine. Portland, 1867.

M., Mr. C. J. *Charles Julius Mickle.* A concise essay on the nature and connexion of the philosophy and mythology of Paganism . . . L. 1826.

M., C. P. *Christopher Parr Male.* Have you any fear of death? Birmingham, 1851.

M., C. R. *Rev. Charles Robertson Manning, M.A.* The canticles of the Book of Common Prayer, marked for chanting . . . L. 1858.

M.D., of Newark, Ohio, An. *Dr. J. R. Black.* Alcohol as a medicine. Syracuse, 1870.

M. D. C., C. *Claude François Xavier Mercier de Compiegne.* Histoire de Marie Stuart . . . 1820.

M., D. G. *Donald Grant Mitchell.* Dream life . . . N.Y. 1866.

M., E. *Rev. Edward Melton.* Annals of the church in Brimfield. Springfield, Mass., 1856.

M., E. *E. Magrath.* A letter on Canada in 1806 and 1817 . . . 1853.

M., E. *Edward Moxon.* Memoir of Charles Lamb, in Leigh Hunt's "London Journal."

M., E. A. *Mrs. E. A. Maddock.* The Liturgy explained. L. 1839.

M. E. B. *Mrs. Mary E. Gellie.* Clement's trial and victory . . . L. 1875.

M, E. S. *Edward Sanford Martin.* Sly ballades in Harvard China. B. 1882.

M., F. *Sir Frederick Madden.* How the goode wife thaught hir doughter. Edited by . . . L. 1838.

M., F. *Rev. Frederick Martin.* Notes on the four gospels. L. 1838.

M., F. L. *F. L. Morse.* Onward to the heights of life. B. 1880.

M., G. *George Mooar.* Historical manual of the South Church in Andover, Mass., August, 1859. Andover, 1859.

M., G. *Gervase Markham.* The young sportsman's instructor. L. 1820.

M., G. L. *Gilbert Laing Meason.* On the landscape architecture of the great painters of Italy. By . . . L. 1828.

M., G. W. *George W. Marshall.* A catalogue of pedigrees hitherto unindexed. Ed. by . . . L. 1867.

M., G. W. *George Wharton Marriott, B.C.L.* Memoir of Rev. Dr. Gaskin, in "Gent. Mag.," Vol. 99, 2d Pt., 183, 280, 643.

M., G. W. *George Wilson Meadley.* Memoirs of Mrs. Jebb. L. 1812.

M., H. *Harriet Martineau.* The martyr age of the United States . . . Newcastle-upon-Tyne, 1840.

M., Sir H. *Sir Humphrey Mackworth.* Down with the mug . . . L. 1717.

M., H. E. *Henry Edward Manning.* Dies consecrati . . . L. 1855.

M., H. L. *Mrs. Hannah L. Murray.* Florence Murray: a narrative of facts. By her mother . . . B. 1849.

M. I. D. *Richard Hengist Horne,* in his contributions to the "Monthly Repository" (L.).

M'G., J. *John M'Gilchrist, M.D.* Chatelard: a tragedy in five acts. Edinb. 1852.

M'S., J. *Dr. Joseph Macsweeny.* An essay on aërial navigation . . . Cork, 1824.

M., J. *John Muir.* The course of divine revelation . . . Calcutta, 1846.

M., J. *Josiah Martin.* The great case of tithes truly stated . . . L. 1730.

M., J. *James Morgan, D.D.* Elegy, Mark Luke Grayston. L. 1830.

M., J. *John Martin.* An inquiry into Echard's statement in his history of England . . . L. 1852.

M., J. *J. Masson.* Miscellaneous observations upon authors, ancient and modern. L. 1731–32.

M., J. *Rev. Joseph Morris, M.A.* Monuments in Feltham Church, Middlesex, in "Gent. Mag.," July, 1824, p. 39.

M., J. *James Maidment.* A new book of old ballads. Edited . . . Edinb. 1844.

M., J. *Joseph Massie.* Observations on Mr. Fauquier's "Essay on Ways and Means for Raising," etc. L. 1756.

M., J. *John Major.* Rational madness : a song for the lovers of rare and curious books. L. n.d.

M., J. *Major Moyle Sherer.* Scenes and impressions in Egypt and Italy, etc. L. 1824.

M., J. *J. Mortimer.* La Secession aux États-Unis et son origine. Paris, 1861.

M., J. *Rev. James Murray.* The travels of the imagination . . . L. 1773.

M., J., Esq., F.R.S. *John Mortimer.* The whole art of husbandry . . . By . . . L. 1707.

M., J., Rev., D.D., F.S.A. *John Milner, D.D.* A vindication of the end of religious controversy . . . L. 1822.

M., J., of the Inner Temple. *Jasper Mauduit.* The Legislative authority of the British Parliament with respect to North America . . . L. 1766.

M., Sir J., and Dr. Ja. S. *Sir John Mennis* and *Dr. James Smith.* Facetiae. Musarum deliciae . . . L. 1817.

M., J., et P., R. *James Maidment* and *Robert Pitcairn.* Nugæ derelictæ quas colligerunt . . . Edinb. 1822.

M., J. A. *Mrs. J. A. Merryweather.* The hermit of Eskdaleside ; with other poems . . . Whitby, 1833.

M., J. A. *Sir John Archibald Murray,* Lord Murray. Letter to the Judge Advocate . . . Edinb. 1850. — See "A Member of Court."

M., J. C., Esq. *J. C. Mellish.* Mary Stuart : a tragedy. Trans. by . . . L. 1801.

M., J. H. *John Herman Merivale, Esq.*— See "Gent. Mag.," November, 1837, p. 481.

M., J. H. *James Henry Monk.* Memoir of Duport . . . Cambridge, 1825.

M., J. H. B. *Jacob Henry Brooke Mountain.* A sermon preached at Blunham church . . . on . . . the completion of an east window, by M. F. Sadler, with a preface by J. H. B. M. L. 1864.

M., J. L. *J. L. Martin.* Native bards : a satirical effusion . . . P. 1831.

M., J. M. *J. M. Moore.* Lord Nial. N.Y. 1834.

M., J. R. *John Ramsay MacCulloch.* Tracts . . . on metallic and paper currency, by S. J. Lloyd. Edited by . . . L. 1858.

M., J. W. H. *John William Henry Molyneaux.* Private prayers . . . selected . . . L. 1866.

M., K. *Kate M'Clellan.* Anne and Pierre ; or, our father's letter. N.Y. 186-.

M., L. F. *Mrs. Lydia Falconer Miller.* Cats and dogs ; nature's warriors and God's workers. L. 1868.

M., L. M. *Mrs. Louise (Chandler) Moulton.*

M., M. F. *Mary Fawley Maude.* Scripture natural history, etc. L. 1848.

M., M. L. *Mary L. Meaney.* Grace Morton ; or, the inheritance . . . P. 1864.

M. M. M. *William Tooke, Esq., F.R.S.* Verses. Edited by . . . L. 1860.

See "Gent. Mag.," July, 1844, p. 2, an inquiry under this signature on the origin of the name of Tooke. On many other occasions Mr. Tooke wrote under the signature of "M. M. M.," as his father had done previously. They were the initials of the family motto, *Militia Mea Multiplex.*

M., M. M. *Miss M. M. Montgomery.* Lights and shadows of German life. P. 1833.

M., M. N. *Mrs. Mary Noel (Bleecker M'Donald) Meigs.* Poems by . . . N.Y. 1845.

M., Matt. Robinson. *Matthew Robinson Montagu.* Peace the best policy. L. 1777.

M. N. *William Wotton, D.D.,* in a letter contributed to the "Guardian." No. 93, June 27, 1713.

M., N. *Nathaniel Morren.* Annals of the General Assembly of the Church of Scotland . . . 1739–76 . . . Edinb. 1838.

M., O. *Oswald Moosmüller.* St. Vincenz in Pennsylvanien . . . N.Y. 1873.

M., P. *Rev. Patrick Middleton.* A dissertation on the power of the Church . . . L. 1733.

M. P. *Mrs. Marianne Girdlestone Filleul.* Marion ; or, the smuggler's wife . . . L. 1873.

M. P., An. *William Pollard Urquhart.* The currency question and the Bank Charter Committee of 1857–58. L. 1860.

M., P. D. *Rev. Peter Du Moulin.*— See "A Prebend of the Church of Canterbury."

M., R. *Richard Morris.* — See "One of the Excluded Members of Parliament."

M., R. C. *Robert Cotton Money.* Journal of a tour in Persia during the years 1824 and 1825. L. 1828.

M., Rose C. *Rose C. Monckton.* Letters from Futtehgurh. Clifton, 1858.

M., R. K. *Richard Kendall Mackittrick.*

M., R. S. *Dr. Robert Shelton Mackenzie,* in his contributions to the "Lady's Magazine."

M., R. W. *Robert W. McAlpine,* in his contributions to the "Press" (P.).

M., S. *Samuel Merriman, M.D.,* one of his signatures in the "Gent. Mag.," 1828–47. His others were "Correspond-

ent," " L. N.," and "'Ιλαρανθρώπος." See
"Gent. Mag.," 1853, Pt. I., pp. 207–209.

M., S. *Miss Selina Martin.* Narrative
of three years' residence in Italy. L.
1828.

M., S., and S., G. M. *Samuel Mecutchen* and *George M. Sayre.* The new
American Arithmetic. P. 1877.

M. S. A. and M. R. A. S., An. *Robert
Scott Burn.* The grammar of house
planning . . . Edinb. 1864.

M., T. *Thomas Maule.* An abstract
of a letter to Cotton Mather . . . n.p.
1701.

M., T. *Thomas Mounsey.* A brief
account of Thomas Fell of Swarthmore
Hall. By . . . Manchester, 1846.

**M., T. A suffering Presbyter of the
Church of Scotland.** *Thomas Moubray.*
A catechism, appointed in the liturgy of
the Church of Scotland . . . Edinb.
1712.

M., T. C., M.B., F.L.S. *Sir Thomas
Charles Morgan.* An expostulatory letter
to Dr. Moseley . . . L. 1808.

M., T. S. *T. S. Muir.* Notes on remains of ecclesiastical architecture and
sculptured memorials in the southern division of Scotland. Edinb. 1855.

M., W. *William Mason.* — See " A
Gentleman of Cambridge."

M., W. *Rev. William Maskell, M.A.*
Bude Haven: a pen-and-ink sketch, with
portraits of the principal inhabitants. L.
1863.

M., W. *Rev. William Marsh.* Jeho-
vah's ancient temple, city, and land.
Dublin, 1863.

M., W. *William Mackenzie.* The pyra-
mid and the Bible . . . Edinb. 1868.

M., W., a Beneficed Priest. *William
Maskell.* A letter to the Very Rev. Wil-
liam Cockburn, D.D., Dean of York . . .
L. 1842.

M., W. I. L. *W. I. L. Müller.* Ueber
London und Paris nach Rom . . . Berlin,
1853.

M., W. S. *William Shaw Mason.*
Bibliotheca Hibernica; or, a descriptive
catalogue of a select Irish library, collected for the Right Hon. Robert Peel.
Dublin, 1823.

M.***, louisianais. *Dr. Alfred Mercier.* Le fou de Palerme . . . N.O.
1873.

M***, Paul Hyppolite de. *Paul
Hyppolite de Murat.* Les paradoxes du
capitaine Marc-Luc-Roch Barole . . .
Paris, 1802.

M***e, T***y. *Thomas Moore.* The
fudger fudged; or, the Devil and
T[omm]y M[oor]e. L. 1819.

M******l, Sylvain. *Pierre Sylvain
Maréchal.* Dictionnaire des athées
anciens et modernes . . . Paris, 1800.

M*th**s, Thomas James. *Thomas
James Mathias.* The sphinx's head
broken: a poetical epistle, with notes,
to . . . Clerk to the Qu**n's Tr**s*r*r;
proving him to be the author of the
" Pursuits of Literature." By Andrew
Œdipus, an injured author. L. 1798.

M——, Mrs. *Mrs. Elizabeth Montagu,*
in Beloe's " Sexagenarian," I., 335. 2d
ed. L. 1818.

M——, H——. *Hannah More,* in Beloc's " Sexagenarian," I., 338. 2d ed.
L. 1818.

M—d, Dr. *Dr. Mead.* An account
of a strange . . . dream, etc. [A satire
on Dr. Mead]. By Dr. John Woodward.
L. 1719.

**M—e, Right Hon. Lady M—y
W—y.** *Right Hon. Lady Mary Wortley
Montague.* Letters of . . . written during
her travels in Europe, Asia, and Africa
. . . L. 1763.

Ma., Ch. El. *Charles Elkin Mathews,*
of Exeter, in his contributions to " Notes
and Queries " (L.).

Mabel. *Mary P. Hazen.* Joanna;
or, learning to follow Jesus. N.Y. 1871.

Mac. *E. A. MacClean,* in contributions to the " Library Journal " (B.), etc.

Mac (Artist). *W. McConnell.* Twice
round the clock. L. 18–.

Mac (The Danburian). *Charles E.
A. McGeachy.*

McArone. *George Arnold,* who, as a
writer of comic verse and humorous
sketches, had many pen-names, —
" McArone," " Allen Grahame," " George
Garrulous," etc.

MacArone, Mat. *Theodore P. Cook.*

Macaroni, A. *Christopher Anstey.*
Liberality; or, memoirs of a decayed
. . . L. 1788.

Macaulay. *Rev. Washington Frothingham,* in the " Rochester (N.Y.) Democrat."

Macaulay, Mr. Babbletongue.
Thomas Babington Macaulay.

" We remember the 'Times' commenting
on Lord Macaulay's too flippant address to his
constituents, dated from Windsor Castle, with
attempted humor equally reprehensible, called
the then member for Edinburgh, ' Mr. Babbletongue Macaulay,' in a poor play upon his second
name of Babington."—See ANDREW's " British
Journalism," Vol. 2, p. 221.

MacCarte, Duncan, a Highlander.
Rev. Samuel Squire. " A letter to John
Trot-Plaid, Esq.," author of the " Jaco-
bite Journal " . . . L. 1748.

McCoomb, Florence. *Mary Miller*

Meline. The Montarge's legacy. P. 1875.

MacDavus. *Herbert Mayo.* Letters on the truths contained in popular superstitions [first published in "Blackwood's Magazine," vol. 61, etc., under this signature]. 3d ed. L. 1851.

Macgillicuddy, Irene. *Laurence Oliphant.* The tender recollections of . . . N.Y. 1878. [First published in "Blackwood's Magazine."]

McGrath, Terence. *Henry A. Blake.* Pictures from Ireland. L. 1880.

MacGregor, Malcolm. *Maurice Morgan, Esq.* Ode to Mr. Pinchbeck, upon his newly invented candlesnuffers . . . L. 1776. See "Gent. Mag.," December, 1815. Also ascribed to *Rev. William Mason,* Canon of York.

McGuire, M. *Malcom McPherson,* in the "Amateur Emigrant."

Mack. *Joseph B. McCullough,* editor of the St. Louis "Globe Democrat" and "Cincinnati Commercial."

McKenzie, Christine. *Miss Annie Duffell.* In the meshes. P. 1877.

Mackworth, Humphry. *Robert Harley,* Earl of Oxford and Mortimer. A vindication of the rights of the Commons of England. L. 1715.

Macleod, the late Dr. Archibald. *Rev. William Lisle Bowles, M.A.* Ellen Gray; or, the dead maiden's curse. L. 1828.

MacPacke, Jose, a bricklayer's labourer. *James Peacock.* Οἰκίδια; or, nutshells. By . . . L. 1785.

Macrobin, Mark. *Allan Cunningham,* in "Blackwood's Magazine."

M'Rory, Rev. Rory. *James Cameron Lees, D.D.* M'Stottie's tour: a highland yarn. By the . . . minister of Tobersnory, presbytery of Dall. Edinb. 1880.

MacSarcasm, Rev. Sir Archibald, Bart. *Rev. William Shaw.* The life of Hannah More . . . L. 1802.

Macsarconica, Archy, F.R.S. *Thomas Hastings.* The book of the wars of Westminster . . . L. 1784. — See "Fox, The."

Mac-Shinie, Gillespie. *Archibald Simson.* Annals of such patriots of the distinguished family of Fraser, Frysell, Sim-son, or Fitz-simon, as have signalized themselves in the public service of Scotland . . . Edinb. 1795.

Macswell. *W. L. Russ,* in his contributions to the "Courier" (Buffalo, N.Y.).

MacWhirter, Theresa, Whistlebinkie, N.B. *William Makepeace Thackeray.* A legend of the Rhine. L. 1856.

Mace, Sloper. *Charles Godfrey Leland.* Ballads. 18–.

Mad Poet, The. *McDonald Clarke.* The elixir of moonshine; being a collection of prose and poetry, by . . . Gotham [N.Y.], A.M. 5822 [1822].

Mada. *Mary Latham Clarke.* Birthday present. B. 1869.

Madison, Virginia. *Mrs. Sallie A. (Brock) Putnam.* Kenneth, my king N.Y. 187–.

Märzroth, Dr. *Moritz Barach.* Lachende Geschichten. 1880–81.

Maevius. *Dr. Richard Russell.* — See "Bavius."

Maga. *Blackwood's Magazine.*

Magenta. *Capt. Mahon.* — See "Cavalry Officer, A."

Maggie, Aunt. *Mrs. Raymond Blathwayt,* in her contributions to various periodicals.

Maggie, Aunt. *Mrs. Henshaw.*

Magistrate, A. *Patrick Colquhoun, Esq.* A treatise on the police of the Metropolis . . . By . . . L. 1796.

Magistrate for Middlesex, A. *John Thomas Barber Beaumont.* Letters on public house licensing. By . . . L. 1816.

Maglone, Barney. *Robert A. Wilson,* in his contributions to the "Republic" (B.).

Magoogin. *John J. Jennings,* in his contributions to the "Post-Dispatch" (St. Louis, Mo.).

Magpie. *William H. Webb.* Word method primer. N.Y. 1859 (?).

Maguire, Aunt. *Mrs. Frances Miriam Berry,* in Godey's "Lady's Book."

Maharba. *John Abraham.* An imperial manifesto, and other poems. Liskeard, 1872.

Mahmut the Spy. *Giovanni Paolo Marana,* a Jesuit. The Turkish spy. The eight volumes of letters writ by Mahmut, the Spy, who lived five and forty years undiscovered in Paris, unfolding the intrigues of the Christian courts between 1637 and 1682. L. 1770.

The work has been characterized as "speculating very freely on all subjects, under a mask of bigotry."

Mairet, Jeanne. *Mme. Mary (Healy) Bigot.* Marca. Paris, 1883.

Maitland, Mrs. Margaret. *Mrs. Margaret O. (Wilson) Oliphant.* Passages in the life of . . . of Sunnytide. L. 1855.

Maitland, Thomas. *Robert Buchanan.* "The Fleshly School of Poets," contributed to the "Contemporary Review" (L. 1872).

Major, The. *Ben Perley Poore.*

Makewright, George Washington. *Frank Cahill,* in his contributions to the "Saturday Press" (P.).

Malack, Muly. *Mordecai Manuel Noah,* in the New York "Times," 1811.

Malagrowther, Malachi. *Sir Walter Scott.* Thoughts on the proposed change of currency . . . Edinb. 1826.

Malakoff. *Dr. W. F. Johnston,* in the New York "Times."

Malet, Lucas. *Mrs. (Kingsley) Harrison.* Mrs. Lorimer: a study in black and white. L. 1883.

Malone, Carroll. *M. McBurney.*

Maltitz, Hermann von. *Hermann Klencke,* who, under this name, published a long series of historical and social novels from distinguished German authors.

Mambrino. *H. D. McKinney,* Janesville (O.) correspondent of "The Spirit of the Times" (N.Y.).

Man, A. *Horace Walpole,* Earl of Orford. Reflections on the different ideas of the French and English in regard to cruelty . . . By . . . L. 1759.

Man about Town, The. The papers in the "Star" (N.Y.) under the above pseudonym, are contributed by *Charles E. File, P. McCann, William H. Muldoon, and others.*

Man in the Claret-Colored Coat, The. *Edward S. Gould.* The Sleep Rider; or, the Old Boy in the omnibus. N.Y. 1843.

Man in the Moon, The. *Captain Anstruther,* of Spencerfield. A letter . . . to Mr. Anodyne Necklace . . . L. 1725.

Man in the Moon, The. *Daniel Defoe.* A letter . . . to the author of the "True born Englishman." L. 1705.

Man in the Moon, The. *Joseph Browne.* The moon calf . . . n.p. 1705.

Man in the Moon, The. — See "Themaninthemoon."

Man of Business, A. *John Ashton.* Autumn holidays. By . . . Manchester, 1876.

Man of Business, A. *T. Dicker.* The Christian life exemplified in the memorials and remains of . . . L. 1852.

Man of Business, A. *William Rathbone, Jr.* Social duties . . . benevolence and public utility. By . . . L. 1867.

Man of Fashion, A. *John Mills* (?). D'Horsay; or, the follies of the day. By . . . L. 1844.

"The personages introduced figure under flimsy disguises, and the reader will hardly need a 'key' to indicate the originals of the Earl of Chesterlane, Mr. Pelham, General Reel, Lord George Bedtick, Mr. George Bobbins ('the Prince of Auctioneers'), the Marquis of Riverford, Lord Huntingcastle, Mister Sloughman, Joe Banks (the 'Stunner'), the Earl of Byworden, the Countess of Rivington, the Earl of Raspberry Hill, 'the circumcised driver of the cabriolet' (*Benjamin Disraeli*), and the Marquis of Hereford." — See "Maclise Portrait Gallery," p. 290.

"Man of Kent," A. *Robert Cowtan.* Passages from the autobiography of . . . 1817–1865. L. 1866. Edited by Reginald Fitz-Roy Stanley [*pseud.*].

Man of the People, The. *Charles James Fox.*

Man of the People, The. *William Thomson.* The man in the moon . . . L. 1783.

Man of the Revolution, The. *Samuel Adams,* so termed by Jefferson, in 1825.

Man of the Times, A. *John Pendleton Kennedy.* Letters of . . . to the citizens of Baltimore. Balt. 1836.

Man of the World, A. *Charles Phillips.* Napoleon the Third . . . L. 1854.

Man who wishes to be Governor of Pennsylvania, A. *George W. Woodward.* Opinions of . . . P. 1862.

Managing Clerk, A. *G. Stuart.* A concise system of book-keeping . . . By . . . L. 1862.

Manchester Layman, A. *Rev. J. Gill.* A literary curiosity. A sermon in words of one syllable only . . . Manchester, 1860.

Manchester Man, A. *Rev. J. Lamb.* Free thoughts of . . . L. 1866.

Manchester Man, A. *Richard Burn.* The present and long-continued stagnation of trade; its causes, effects, and cure . . . By . . . Manchester, 1870.

Manchester Manufacturer, A. *Richard Cobden.* England, Ireland, and America. By . . . 1835.

Manchester Poet, The. *Charles Swain.*

Manchester Prison Philanthropist, The. *Thomas Wright.*

Manchester Spinner, A. *John Cameron.* Yarns. Manchester, n.d.

Manent, Graviora. *James R. Manley, M.D.* Letters on the College of Physicians and Surgeons. N.Y. 1841.

Manetti, Fanny. *Fanny Smith.*

Manfred. — *Preston.* Lord Byron vindicated; or, Rome and her pilgrim . . . L. 1876.

Manhattan. *Charles Alexander Nelson,* as New York correspondent of the "Bookseller and Stationer." Chicago, 1881–84.

Manhattan. *Joseph A. Scoville,* who, at the time of his death in 1864, was the correspondent of the "London Herald" and "London Standard" under this signature.

Manley, Jack. The stories in the "Boys and Girls' Weekly" (N.Y.) over this pseudonym were partly written by *Alfred Trumble* and partly by *Charles Hull Webb.*

Manlius. *Christopher Gore.* Manlius; with notes and references. B. 1794.

Mann, Nellie A. *Helen A. Manville.* Heart echoes: book of poems. N.Y. 1874.

Mannering, Max. *Josiah Gilbert Holland,* in the "Springfield Republican" in 1850–51.

Mannering, May. *Mrs. Harriet P. H. Nowell.* Helping hand series. B. 187–.

Manners, Mrs. *Mrs. Cornelia H. (Bradley) Richards.* At home and abroad; or, how to behave. N.Y. 1853.

Manners, Mrs. Horace. *Algernon Charles Swinburne,* his signature in the "Tatler" (L.).

Manners, Motley. *Augustine J. H. Duganne.* Parnassus in Pillory: a satire. N.Y. 1851.

Mansfield, Walworth. *W. H. Walton.* Love for life. 18–.

Manson, James B., Bannockburn. *James Murray.* The Bible in school . . . Edinb. 1852.

Manton, Kate. *Mrs. S. G. Knight.*

Manuel, Ernest. *Ernest L'Épine.* La legende de Croque-Mitaine. Paris, 1863.

Maori. *James Inglis.* Sport and work on the Nepaul frontier; or, twelve years' sporting reminiscences of an indigo planter. L. 1878.

Maple-Knot. *Ebenezer Clemo.* The life and adventures of Simon Seek; or, Canada in all shapes. Montreal, 1858.

Mar, Helen. *Mrs. D. M. F. Walker.*

Marble, Major. *Rev. Henry T. Cheever.* The whale and its captors. N.Y. 1849.

Marcellus. *John Quincy Adams,* who, 1790–94, varied his law practice by occasional communications to the "Boston Centinel" signed "Publicola" and "Marcellus."

Marcellus. *Allan Ramsay, Jr.,* in his contributions to the "Public Advertiser" (L. about 1776), on the war with America.

Marcellus. *Amédée Marteau,* in "L'Esprit des Femmes." Paris, 1860.

Marcellus. *Noah Webster.* Letter to the Honorable Daniel Webster on the political affairs of the United States. P. 1837.

March, Anne. *Constance Fenimore Woolson.* The old stone house . . . B. 1873.

March, Marjorie. *Augusta Liebich,* in her contributions to the "Household."

March, Walter. *Orlando Bolivar Willcox.* Shoepac recollections. N.Y. 1856.

Marcliffe, Theophilus. *William Godwin.* The looking-glass: a true history of the early years of an artist [William Mulready, R.A.] . . . L. 1805.

Marcoy, Paul. *Lorenzo de Saint-Cricq.* Travels in South America from the Pacific Ocean to the Atlantic Ocean. Translated from the French. L. 1875.

Marcullus. *Philip G. Kershaw.* Reflections on itinerary parliaments . . . Montreal, 1856.

Marcus. *William Charles Wells, M.D.* In the latter part of the year 1780 he published an account of Mr. Henry Laurens, some time president of the American Congress, in the form of a letter under the signature of "Marcus," to the printer of the "Public Advertiser."

Marcus. *Oliver Wolcott.* British influence in the affairs of the United States proved and explained. B. 1804.

Marcus. *Joseph Blunt.* An examination of the expediency and constitutionality of prohibiting slavery in the State of Missouri . . . N.Y. 1819.

Marcus.* *William P. Van Ness.* Letters addressed to De Witt Clinton, Esq. . . . N.Y. 1810.

These letters originally appeared in the "Poughkeepsie Barometer," 1805.

Marcus. *Matthew L. Davis.* The plot discovered. Poughkeepsie, 1807. — See also "Philo-Cato."

Margaret, Aunt. *Miss Margaret (?) Buchan,* a well-known writer for the "St. Nicholas" in 1883, became principal of Wolfe Hall, a school for young ladies at Denver, Colorado.

Maria. *Clemens Brentano.* Satyren und poetische Spiele. Leipsic, 1800.

Maria del Occidente. *Mrs. Maria (Gowen) Brooks,* who, in "The Doctor" is styled by Southey "the most impassioned and the most imaginative of all poetesses," and who received from him the name of "Maria del Occidente."

Mariaker, Élie. *Évariste Cyprien Felix Boulay-Paty.* Odes nouvelles. Paris, 1844.

Marie. *Harriet M. Skidmore.* Beside the Western Sea: a poem. N.Y. 1878.

Marietta. *Miss Harriette Mary Bradley.* Minnie's birthday; and other juvenile stories. L. 186–.

Marine Officer, A. *Major-General Andrew Burn.* Who fares the best, the Christian or the man of the world? By ... L. 1792.

Mariotti, Luigi. *Antonio Carlo Napoleone Gallenga.* Italian grammar. L. 1858.

Maritzburg, Pieter. *Rev. T. Jackson.* The fire of London. 18–.

Marius. *Thomas Day.* The letters of ... or, reflections upon the Peace, the East India Bill, and the present crisis. L. 1784.

Marius, Claude. *Claude Marius Duplany.* A *nom de théâtre.*

Mark, Uncle. *Mark Lemon.* — See "Ponny."

Markham, Mrs. *Mrs. Elizabeth (Cartwright) Penrose.* New children's friend ... L. 1836.

Markham, Howard. *Mary Cecil Hay.* Old Myddleton's money. L. 18–.

Markham, Pauline. *Mrs. Margaret (Hale) McMahon.*

Marlay. *D. W. Chapman.*

Marling, Matt. The stories in the "Boys and Girls' Weekly " (N.Y.), over this pseudonym, were partly written by *Alfred Trumble,* and partly by *Charles Hull Webb.*

Marlinsky, The Cossack. *Alexander Bestoujeff,* a Russian poet, who, under this name, wrote small novels and sketches for the "Telegraph," a periodical of Moscow, and for some others.

Marlitt, E. *Henriette Friederike Christiane Eugenie John.* Old Mamselle's secret ... P. 187–.

Marlow, The Right Hon. Lady Harriet. *William Beckford.* Modern novel writing; or, the elegant enthusiast, and interesting emotions of Arabella Bloomville ... L. 1796.

Marmaduke, Sir. *Theodore Tilton.* The sexton's tale, and other poems. N.Y. 1867. Probably his signature to contributions to the press.

Married Critic, The. *Jules Gabriel Janin.*

Marryat, Florence. *Mrs Florence (Marryat) Ross-Church,* in her numerous works of fiction.

Marsden, Frederick. *W. A. Sliver.* Clouds: comedy. N.Y. 187–.

Marshall, ——. *Thomas Holcroft.* The German hotel: a comedy. L. 1790.

Marshall, William, Gent. *Horace Walpole.* The castle of Otranto: a story

translated by ... from the original of Onuphrio Muralto, Canon of the Church of St. Nicholas, at Otranto. L. 1765.

Martel. *Rev. Washington Frothingham,* in the New Hampshire "Statesman."

Martel, Charles. *Thomas Delf.* The principles of colouring in painting. L. 1855.

Martesia, Honoria. *Judith Sargent.*

Martext, Oliver. *James Cook Richmond,* a member of the "Polyglot Club," which consisted of the nine editors of the "Harvard Register." Camb. 1827–28.

Martin, Edward Winslow. *James D. McCabe.* History of the Grange Movement. Chic. 1874.

Martingale. *Charles White.* English country life ... L. 1843.

Martingale, Hawser. *John Sherburne Sleeper.* Mark Rowland: a tale of the sea. B. 1867.

Martlet. *Richard Bingham Davis,* in the "Drone papers " in the "New York Magazine."

Martyn, William Frederick. *Rev. William Mavor, LL.D.* Dictionary of natural history. L. 1784.

Martyne, Herbert. *William Tait Ross,* a Scottish poet.

Marvel, Andrew. *William Goddard,* printer of the "Constitutional Courant," of which only one number was issued, Sept. 21, 1765, and issued at Burlington, New Jersey. There is a copy in Harvard College library.

Marvel, Ik. *Donald Grant Mitchell.* Reveries of a bachelor ... 1851. — See "Opera Goer, An."

Mary, Aunt. *Mary A. Lathbury.* Fleda with the voice, with other stories. N.Y. 1876.

Mary, Aunt. *Miss Mary Low.* A peep into Uncle Tom's Cabin. By ... L. 1853.

Mary, Cultivator. *Miss Mary Asenath Short,* who is well known at the West, having frequently written under this signature for the "Ohio Cultivator," and for "Grace Greenwood's " "Little Pilgrim." Her later poems were signed "Fanny True."

Marylander, A. *Reverdy Johnson.* The dangerous condition of the Country ... Balt. 1867.

Mask. Probably *James Grant.* St. Stephen's; or, pencillings of politicians. L. 1839. See "Notes and Queries," 5th Ser., I., 50, 373, 396, 457.

Mason, Ida. *Eliza A. Mason Fisher,* in her contributions to "Peterson's Ladies' Magazine " (P. about 1860), etc.

Massachusettensis. *David Leonard.*

Origin of the American contest with Great Britain ... N.Y. 1775.

Also in a series of political letters (17) he contributed to the Boston newspapers, frequently reprinted. See Sabin, " Dictionary of Books relating to America," No. 40,097. In the controversy occasioned by these letters, John Adams replied, under the pseudonym of " Novanglus."

Massachusetts. *Elias Haskett Derby.* His signature in the Boston papers. See " A Rail-Road Director."

Massachusetts Lawyer, A. *John Lowell, Jr.* Review of a treatise on expatriation by George Hay, Esq. By ... B. 1814.

Massachusetts Yankee, A. *Lyman Hotchkiss Bagg.* His signature in the " Anglo-American Times" (L. 1876) and the " Nation " (N.Y. 1880).

Master Mason, A. — *Ward.* Freemasonry: its pretensions exposed ... N.Y. 1828.

Master of Arts, A. *William King, LL.D.* Elogium famæ inserviens Jacci Etonensis, sive Gigantis ; or, the praises of Jack of Eton, commonly called Jack the Giant: collected into Latin and English metre, after the manner of Thomas Sternhold, John Hopkins, John Burton, and others ... By ... L. 1749.

Master of Arts of the University of Oxford, A. *William Asplin.* Alkibla: a disquisition upon worshipping towards the east ... By ... L. 1728-31.

Master of Arts of Trinity College, Cambridge, A. *R. Allen.* The life, times, and travels of Abraham. L. 1875.

Master of the Grammar-School at Arundel, The. *Charles Caraccioli.* Antiquities of Arundel ; by ... L. 1766.

Mata. *William R. Thompson.*

Materfamilias. *Mrs. C. M. Bell.* Tales from the Odyssey, for boys and girls. N.Y. 1880.

Mathetes. *John Wilson (Christopher North),* in Coleridge's " Friend."

Soon after leaving the university (of Oxford), he purchased the beautiful estate of Elleray, on the noble lake of Windermere, which led to his intimacy with Wordsworth, Southey, Quillinan, Coleridge, and DeQuincey. Here he contributed some fine letters to Coleridge's " Friend," under the signature of " Mathetes." See " Maclise Portrait Gallery," p. 60.

Mathilde. *Henriette Friederike Amalie von Hohenhausen,* in her contributions to Lecke's " Monatrosen."

Μαθος, Θυος. *Thomas South.* Early magnetism ... L. 1846.

Matilda. *Mrs. Matilda Caroline*

(*Smiley*) *Edwards.* Poems by ... Richmond, 1851.

Matrimonial Monomaniac, A. *L. A. Abbot.* Seven wives and seven prisons ; or, experiences in the life of ... N.Y. 1870.

Matthews & Co. *Leicester Silk Buckingham.* Aggravating Sam : a comic drama ... L. 1854.

Matthey, A. *Arthur Arnould.* Zoé Chien-Chien. Paris, 1881.

Matthias Lord Bishop of Chichester. *Matthias Mawson, D.D.* A sermon ... before the ... Society for the Propagation of the Gospel in Foreign Parts ... February 18, 1742-43. By ... L. 1743.

Maude. *Miss Clotilda Jennings.* Linden Rhymes ... Halifax, 1854.

Maurice, Cæsar, Esq. *Dr. George W. Bagby.*

Maurice, Jacques. *James W. Morris.* K. N. Pepper, and other condiments. N.Y. 1859.

Mauris, Maurice. *Marquis de Caglengano,* a native of Nice, a Garibaldian, and an ardent admirer of Victor Hugo.

Mauritius, Pfaffe. *Moritz Hartmann.* Reimchronik des Pfaffen Mauritius. 1849.

Maury, J. C. F. *Auguste Tillet.* Treatise on the dental art ... P. 1842.

Mawe, Thomas. *John Abercrombie.* Every man his own gardener. L. 1767.

Mawr, Eta. *Elizabeth Colling.* Far and near ; or, translations and originals ... L. 1856.

Max. *William H. Maxwell.* Novels and tales. L. 187-.

May. *M. Porter.*

May, Cora. *Mrs. Jennie Curtis.*

May, Edith. *Anna Drinker.* Katy's story. P. 1855.

May, Mattie. *Mrs. C. R. Brown.* Ethel Dutton. B. 1880.

May, Morna. *Miss Lelia B. Bickford.*

May, Sophie. *Rebecca Sophia Clarke.* The Asbury twins. B. 187-.

Mayfield, Frank. *Daniel Starnes.*

Mayfield, Millie. *Mrs. Mary Sophie (Shaw) Homes.* Carrie Harrington ; or, scenes in New Orleans. N.Y. 1857.

Mayflower, Minnie. *Mrs. Catharine (Stratton) Ladd,* who contributed tales, sketches, essays, and poems to various journals, under the signatures " Minnie Mayflower," " Arcturus," " Alida," and " Morna."

May Fly. *Wellington Somerset.* A Continental tour ... L. 1871.

Maynard, Walter. *Thomas Willert Beale.* The enterprising impresario. L. 1867.

Mayne, Hope. *Mrs. E. Auderton.*

Mayne, Leger D. *W. B. Dick, S. A. Frost,* and *W. Taylor.* What shall we do to-night ? or, social amusements. N.Y. 1873.

Mayo, Frank. *Francis Maguire.*

Me. *H. C. Bunner.* Remarks by Me, contributed to "Puck" (N.Y.).

Me, the Hon. B. B., Esq. *Joseph Green.* Entertainment for a winter's evening ... B. 1750.

Me, Phil Arcanos, Gent., Student in Astrology. *Joseph Green.* The Grand Arcanum detected ... 1755.

Mechanic, A. *Charles Devonshire.* Clara ; or, the marriage feast ... Falmouth, 1836.

Medical Man, A. *Forbes Watson.* Flowers and gardens ; notes on plant beauty. L. 1872.

Medical Student, A. *Robert Douglas.* Reminiscences of . . . in the "New Monthly Magazine" for 1843–44.

"Several of his early effusions first appeared in the 'Glasgow Courier' with the Celtic signature of 'Sholto.'"

Medico Campo, Don Richardo de. *Gabriel Harvey.* The trimming of Thomas Nash ... L. 1871.

Medicus. *George Bott Churchill Watson.* Hints for pedestrians, by ... L. 1842.

Medicus. *John Epps, M.D.* Internal evidences of Christianity, deduced from phrenology. By . . . member of the Edinb. Phren. Soc. Edinb. 1827.

Medicus. *Forbes Benignus Winslow.* On the nature, symptoms, and treatment of cholera. By . . . L. 1831.

Medicus. *Daniel Denison Slade, M.D.* Twelve days in the saddle. A journey on horseback in New England, during the autumn of 1883 ... By ... B. 1884.

Medicus Cantabrigiensis. *John Spurgin.* Wisdom, intelligence, and science, the true characteristics of Emanuel Swedenborg ... L. 1862.

Medicus & Co. *Joshua T. Woodhead.* The golden referee, a guide to health ... By ... Liverpool, 1874.

Medius. *Benjamin Franklin.* Remarks and facts relative to the American paper money. P. about 1765.

Medlar, Momus. *James Smith.* Macbeth travestie. By . . . L. 1852. [In "Rejected addresses ; or, the new theatrum poetarum." By J. and H. Smith.]

Medlecott, Humphrey. For the supposed editor of the "Observator." L. 1718.

Medley, Matthew. *Anthony Aston.* The fool's opera. L. 1731.

Meirion. *W. Owen,* in his contributions to the "Monthly Magazine." L. 1803.

Mel, Mary. *Mary E. Bennett.* Poems and tales, by ... Mary Campbell [*pseud.*], etc. N.Y. 1851.

Mela Britannicus. *Charles Kelsall.*

Melata, Don Macario Padua. *Félix Amat.* Tratado de la Iglesia de Jesu Christo. 1793–1803.

Melena, Elpis. *Marie Espérance (Brandt) von Schwartz.* Gemma ; oder, Tugend und Laster. Munich, 1877.

Mélesville. *Baron Anne Honore Joseph Duveyrier.* Valerie : comedie. Paris, 186–.

Melissa. *Jane Hughes Brereton.*

Mellot, Claude. *Tom Taylor.* This character in Charles Kingsley's "Two Years Ago" is said by Thomas Hughes to represent *Mr. Taylor.* — See "Macmillan's Magazine" for August, 1880, "In Memoriam."

Melmoth. *Judge Saint-George Tucker,* in Wirt's "Old Bachelor."

Melmoth, Courtney. *Samuel Jackson Pratt.* The sublime and beautiful of Scripture ... L. 1777.

Mels, August. *Martin Cohn.* Baron Leo von Oberg, M.D. A story of love unspoken [trans.]. B. 1868.

Melville, Emily. *Mrs. Emily Jones Derby.*

Member, A. *Joseph Sparkes.* An affectionate address to the Society of Friends in Great Britain and Ireland. By ... L. 1834.

Member, A. *William Milnor.* An authentic historical memoir of the Schuylkill Fishing Company of the State in Schuylkill ... P. 1830.

Member, A. *Thomas Greer Jacob.* Brief remarks on the Christian Sabbath ... addressed to ... the Society of Friends ... Belfast, 1832.

Member, A. *Maria Arthington.* A few remarks addressed to the Society of Friends on the subject of a revival of religion amongst them. By ... Leeds, 1836 (?).

Member, A. *Samuel Gilman, D.D.* Memoirs of a New England village choir ... B. 1829.

Member, A. *John Faulder.* Remarks on the birthright membership of the Society of Friends. By . . . L. 1843.

Member for Chiltern Hundreds, The. *Henry W. Lucy.* Men and manners in

Parliament . . . L. 1874. Also in his contributions to the "Gent. Mag."

Member for Paris, The. *Eustace Clare Grenville Murray*, the English novelist.

Member of a Close College, A. *Augustus William Hare.* A letter to Daniel K. Sandford, Esq., Professor of Greek in the University of Glasgow . . . Oxf. 1822.

Member of a Provincial Parliament, A. *Edward Gibbon Wakefield.* View of Sir Charles Metcalfe's government of Canada . . . L. 1844.

Member of Convocation, A. *Rev. White Kennet.* Dr. Snape instructed in some matters especially relating to convocations and converts from popery. L. 1718.

Member of Convocation, A. *Rev. Thomas Vaughan.* The legality of the present academical system of the University of Oxford . . . Oxf. 1831.

Member of Convocation, A. *George Horne, D.D.* A letter to the Right Honorable, the Lord North, Chancellor of the University of Oxford, concerning subscription to the 39 articles, and particularly the under-graduate subscription in that university. By . . . L. 1773.

Also ascribed to Rev. Thomas Patten.

Member of Court, A. *John Archibald Murray*, Lord Murray. Letter to the Lord Advocate on the procedure in the court of session and jury trials . . . Edinb. 1850.

The letter is signed "J. A. M."

Member of Gray's Inn, A. *P. B. Leigh.* Law students' guide . . . L. 1827.

Member of his Privy Council, A. *Charles MacCormick, LL.B.* Secret history of the court and reign of Charles II., by . . . L. 1792.

Member of it, A. *Rowley Lascelles.* — See "Publicola."

Member of Lincoln's Inn, A. *John Raithby.* The study and practice of the law considered in their various relations to society . . . By . . . L. 1798.

Member of Lincoln's Inn, A. *John Lind, Esq.* Three letters to Dr. Price . . . By . . . L. 1776.

Member of neither Syndicate, A. *Henry Addington, M.A.*, Lord Sidmouth. A few remarks on the "New Library" question . . . Camb. 1831.

Member of one of the Societies, A. *W. Dale.* Calculations deduced from first principles . . . By . . . L. 1772.

Member of one of the Religious Societies, A. *Richard Finch.* A de-

fence of the Rev. Mr. Whitefield's doctrine of regeneration . . . By . . . L. 1739.

Member of Parliament, A. *George Ellis,* in Beloe's "Sexagenarian," Vol. 2, p. 110. 2d ed. L. 1818.

Member of Parliament, A. *Treysac de Vergy.* A defence of his royal highness the Duke of Cumberland. L. 1770.

Member of Parliament, A. *Robert Henley Ongley*, 1st Baron Ongley. An essay on the nature and use of the militia . . . By . . . L. 1757.

Member of Parliament, A. *Sir Robert Walpole.* A letter . . . concerning the duties on wine and tobacco. L. 1733.

Member of Parliament, A. *William Pulteney*, Earl of Bath. A letter . . . concerning the sum of £ 115,000 granted for the service of the Civil List. L. 1729.

Member of Parliament, A. *Sir Humphrey Mackworth.* A letter . . . giving an account of the proceedings of the Tackers . . . L. 1704.

Member of Parliament, A. *Constantine John Phipps,* Lord Mulgrave. A letter . . . on the late proceedings of the House of Commons in the Middlesex elections. n.p. 1769.

Member of Parliament, A. *Sir William Meredith.* The question stated . . . L. 1769.

A treatise upon Wilke's election.

Member of Parliament, Another. *Sir William Blackstone.* A letter to the author of "The Question Stated." By . . . L. 1769.

Member of Parliament, A Late. *Thomas Carew, Esq.* An historical account of the rights of elections of the several counties, cities, and boroughs of Great Britain . . . By . . . L. 1755.

Member of the Arcadian Academy of Rome, A. *Joseph Cooper Walker.* Historical memoir on Italian tragedy . . . By . . . L. 1799.

Member of the Association, A. *Henry Biggs.* Annals of the county and city of Cork, commencing with an abridged report of the transactions of the British Association . . . L. 1843.

Member of the Athenian Society, A. *John Dunton.* The Athenian oracle . . . By . . . L. 1703–4.

The preface is signed "Philaret, a Member of Athens."

Member of the Bar, A. *C. W. Hart.* Essay on industry, and biographical sketches of Theophilus Radcliffe and Emma Jones. By . . . Steubenville, O., 1835.

Member of the Bar, A. *Phineas*

Bacon Wilcox. Thoughts ... Columbus, O., 1836.

Member of the Bar, A. *Leonard Kip.* The Volcano Diggings: a tale of California law ... N.Y. 1851.

Member of the Boston Bar, A. *Ivers James Austin.* An account of the origin of the Mississippi doctrine of repudiation ... B. 1842.

Member of the Boston Bar, A. *John Augustus Bolles.* The affairs of Rhode Island, being a review of Dr. Wayland's "Discourse" ... B. 1842.

Member of the British Parliament, A. *Francis Ingram Seymour Conway,* Viscount Beauchamp. A letter to the First Belfast Volunteers in the Province of Ulster. By ... L. 1782.

Member of the Burton Hunt, A. *Henry Braddon,* in the "Sporting Magazine" (L.).

Member of the Church at Oxford, A. *William Palmer.* At him again! or, the fox without a tail, being another word for Mr. Bulteel. Oxf. 1832.

Member of the Church of Christ, A. *Rev. Richard Clarke.* An essay on the number seven ... By ... L. 1759.

Member of the Church of England, A. *Rev. William Hopkins, B.A.* An appeal to the common sense of all Christian people ... By ... L. 1752.

Member of the Church of England, A. *Charles Leslie.* The case truly stated, wherein the case restated is fully consider'd. L. 1714.

This work is in the form of a dialogue, and is signed "Philalethes."

Member of the Church of England, A. *Josiah Woodward.* The Christian peace maker ... L. 1710.

Member of the Church of England, A. *William Palmer, M.A.* Examination of an announcement made in the "Prussian State Gazette" ... Oxf. 1842.

Member of the Church of England, A. *J. A. Thornthwaite.* The young churchman's manual ... By ... L. 1837.

Member of the Church of England, from Birth and Education, A. *Rev. Edward Evanson.* The doctrines of a Trinity and the Incarnation of God examined ... L. 1772.

Member of the Church of God at Oxford, A. *William Palmer, M.A.* A hard nut to crack; or, a word in season to Mr. Bulteel ... Oxf. 1832.

Member of the Church of Scotland, A. *Rev. James Hog,* of Carnock.

An essay to vindicate some Scripture truths ... n.p. 1716.

Member of the Class of '67, A. *Park Benjamin.* Shakings. Etchings from the naval academy ... B. 186–.

Member of the College of Justice, A. *James Watson.* New form of process before the Court of Session ... Edinb. 1799.

Member of the College of Justice, A. *William Spink, S.S.C.* Scenes and sketches in legal life. L. 1876.

Member of the College of Physicians, A. *Jeremiah Wainewright.* An anatomical treatise of the liver, with the diseases incident to it. L. 1722.

Member of the Committee of Peace in Paris, A. *George M. Gibbs.* A letter to the American Peace Society ... Paris, 1842.

Member of the Community, and a Sincere Friend to his Country, A. *John Campbell.* The naturalization bill confuted ... L. 1751.

Member of the Congregation, A. *Joseph Moule.* A letter to the members of the congregation of St. James' chapel, Edinburgh ... Edinb. 1842.

Member of the Convention of the Royal Burghs of Scotland, A. *David Dundas Scott.* Blue-book curiosities ... Edinb. 1867.

Member of the Corporation, A. *Samuel Atkins Eliot.* A letter to the president of Harvard College ... B. 1849.

Member of the Dramatic Lunatic Asylum, A. *Crosbie Ward, Esq.* The haunted housemaid; or, the villain of the velvet veskit. Christchurch, New Zealand, 1865.

Member of the Duddingston Curling Society, A. *Rev. James Ramsay.* An account of the game of curling. By ... Edinb. 1811.

Member of the Edinburgh Photographic Society, A. — *Burnett,* of Edinburgh. Photography in colours ... By ... Edinb. 1857.

Member of the English Bar, A. *John Sibbald Edison.* "St. George for England." An address to, and correspondence with, certain persons disaffected to the established constitution ... L. 1850.

Member of the English Bar, A. *John Hodgkin.* Incumbered Estates (Ireland) Bill. Objections, by the Irish attornies and solicitors; and answers by ... L. 1849 (?).

Member of the Established Church, A. *Sir John Bayley.* The Book of

Common Prayer, with notes. L. 1813.

"The author withheld his name, not from any wish improperly to conceal it, but because it was no part of his object to draw himself into notice."

Member of the Established Church, A. *Dr. Samuel Parr.* A letter from Irenopolis to the inhabitants of Eleutheropolis . . . Birmingham, 1792.

Member of the Executive Committee, A. *Jordan L. Mott.* Report to the inventors of the United States. Morrisania, N.Y., 1854.

Member of the Faculty, A. *Robert Hannay.* Letter to the Dean of the Faculty of Advocates . . . Edinb. 1823.

Member of the Faculty of Advocates, A. *Charles Ferguson,* younger, of Kilkerran. The early history of Church Patronage . . . Edinb. 1833.

Member of the Faculty of Advocates, A. *James Starke.* An introduction to the study of the law of Scotland . . . Edinb. 1832.

Member of the Free Church, A. *James Gall.* A free Church and a free trade . . . 1844.

Member of the Gild, A. *James Augustine Stothert.* A short series of lectures on the parochial and collegiate antiquities of Edinburgh, read to the Holy Gild of St. Joseph. By . . . Edinb. 1845.

Member of the Guildry, A. *James Shirra.* An historic sketch of Cowane's Hospital, Stirling. By . . . Stirling, 1867.

Member of the Honourable Society of Writers to the Signet, A. *William Jamieson.* A letter to the Right Honourable Lord Viscount Melville . . . Edinb. 1814.

Member of the House of Assembly of Newfoundland, A. *Patrick Morris.* A short reply to the speech of Earl Aberdeen . . . Liverpool, 1839.

Member of the House of Commons, etc., A. *William Arnall.* Animadversions on a Reverend Prelate's [Bishop T. Sherlock's] remarks upon the bill . . . entitled "A Bill to prevent suits for tythes . . . By . . . L. 1731.

Member of the House of Commons, A. *John Hervey,* Lord Hervey. An answer to the Country Parson's Plea against the Quakers' Tythe-Bill . . . By . . . L. 1736.

Member of the House of Commons, A. *Archibald Hutcheson.* An estimate of the value of South-Sea stock. L. 1720.

Member of the House of Commons,

A. *Daniel Defoe.* A letter . . . relating to the Bill of Commerce . . . L. 1713.

Member of the House of Commons, A. *Robert Molesworth,* Viscount Molesworth. A letter . . . relating to the Bill of Peerage . . . L. 1719.

Member of the House of Commons, A. *Philip Carteret Webb.* Some observations on the late determination for discharging Mr. Wilkes from his commitment to the Tower of London . . . By . . . L. 1763.

Member of the House of Commons in Ireland, A. *Jonathan Swift, D.D.* A letter from . . . to a member of the House of Commons in England . . . L. 1709.

Member of the Howard Association of New Orleans, A. *William L. Robinson.* Diary of a Samaritan. N.O. 1858.

Member of the Humane Society, A. *Wendell Davis.* Barnstable, Massachusetts. A description of the eastern coast of the county of Barnstable . . . B. 1802.

Member of the Humane Society, A. *John Davis, LL.D.* The life boat: a poem . . . n.p., n.d.

Member of the Inner Temple, A. *H. Roscoe.* A discourse on the study of the laws . . . L. 1824.

Member of the Irish Bar, A. *Dennis Burrowes Kelly.* The Manor of Glenmore; or, the Irish peasant . . . L. 1839.

Member of the Irish Parliament, A. *Hervey Redmond Morres,* 2d Viscount Mountmorres. Considerations on the intended modification of Poyning's Law. L. 1780.

Member of the Late Parliament, A. *Lord Robert Grosvenor,* Baron Ebury. Leaves from my journal during the summer of 1851. L. 1852.

Member of the Legislative Assembly of Upper Canada, A. *Hon. Francis Hincks.* The Seigniorial Question: its present position . . . Quebec, 1854.

Member of the Literary and Scientific Association of Elgin, A. *Dr. Taylor.* Edward I. of England in the North of Scotland . . . Elgin, 1858.

Member of the Lower House, A. *Charles Trimnell, D.D.* An account of the proceedings between the two Houses of Convocation which met October the 20th, 1702 . . . L. MDCCIV.

Member of the Lower House, A. *Robert Walpole,* Earl of Orford. Thoughts of . . . in relation to a project for . . . limiting the power of the Crown in the future creation of peers. L. 1719.

Member of the Lower House of

Convocation, A. *Francis Atterbury.* The case of the schedule stated ... L. 1702.

Member of the Manchester Athenæum, A. *J. P. Culverwell.* Manchester in 1844 ... L. 1844.

Member of the Marine Society, A. *Jonas Hanway.* A letter ... Shewing the piety, generosity, and utility of their design ... 5th ed. L. 1757.

Member of the Maryland Legislature, A. *Lawrence Sangston.* The Bastiles of the North ... Balt. 1863.

Member of the N. E. Hist. Gen. Society, A. *Timothy Farrar.* Memoir of the Farrar family. B. 1853.

Member of the New York Bar, A. *Vine Wright Kingsley.* Reconstruction in America ... N.Y. 1865.

Member of the N.Y. Genealogical and Biographical Society, A. *William Ingraham Kip.* The olden time in New York, 1664–1775. N.Y. 1883.

Member of the Numismatic Society of Philadelphia, A. *Henry Phillips, Jr.* Historical sketch of the paper money issued by Pennsylvania ... P. 1862.

Member of the Oxford Convocation, A. *Rev. C. A. Row,* of Pembroke College. Letter to the Right Honourable Lord John Russell, M.P. .... on the constitutional defects of the University and Colleges of Oxford ... L. 1850.

Member of the Philadelphia Bar, A. *John G. Johnson.* A criticism of Mr. Wm. B. Reed's aspersions on the character of Dr. Benjamin Rush ... P. 1867.

Member of the Philadelphia Bar, A. *David Boyer Brown.* Reply to Horace Binney on the privilege of the Writ of Habeas Corpus under the Constitution ... P. 1862.

Member of the Political Economy Club, A. *Col. Robert Torrens.* The budget. L. 1841.

Member of the Press, A. *G. P. Ure.* The hand-book of Toronto ... Toronto, 1858.

Member of the Red River Conference, A. *Thomas Osmond Summers, D.D.* Post Oak Circuit. Edited by ... Nashville, 1857.

Member of the Reformed Catholic Church, A. *George Finch.* A brief reply to "A sure way to find out the true religion" ... L. 1841.

Member of the Revision Committee of the Church of Ireland, A. *H. Lloyd.* The doctrine of absolution ... By ... Dublin, 1871.

Member of the Rock County Bar, A. *J. M. Bundy.* State rights and the

appellate jurisdiction of the Supreme Court of the United States ... Beloit, Wis., 1860.

Member of the Roxburghe Club, A. *Thomas Frognall Dibdin, D.D.* Cranmer: a novel. L. 1839.

Member of the Royal College of Surgeons, A. *William Wadd.* Cursory remarks on corpulence. L. 1810.

Member of the Royal Society, and of the Society of Antiquaries, of London. *Sir James Burrow.* A few anecdotes and observations relating to Oliver Cromwell and his family ... By ... L. 1763.

Member of the Said Society, A. *White Kennet.* Bibliothecæ Americanæ primordia ... L. 1713.

Member of the Same Society, A. *Henry Foley.* English province S. J. Alphabetical catalogue ... Roehampton, 1875.

The introduction is signed "H. F."

Member of the Senate, A. *William Frend.* Considerations on the oaths required by the University of Cambridge ... L. 1787.

Member of the Society, A. *Edward Ash, M.D.* An address to the Society of Friends on ... disseminating Christian knowledge among the Heathen. By ... L. 1828.

Member of the Society, A. *Frank Arnee.* Brief remarks on an important subject; or, a parent's thoughts on the means of obtaining a guarded and religious education for youth at schools ... By ... Bristol, 1820.

Member of the Society of Antiquaries in London. *Francis Wise.* Some enquiries concerning the first inhabitants, language, religion, learning, and letters of Europe, by ... L. 1758.

Member of the Society of Antiquaries of Scotland, A. *Archibald M'Neill, W.S.* Notes on the authenticity of Ossian's poems ... 1868.

Member of the Society of Artists and Manufacturers of Philadelphia, A. *Tench Coxe.* An essay on the manufacturing interest of the United States, etc. P. 1804.

Member of the Society for Constitutional Information, A. *William Davies Shipley.* The principles of the Government ... L. 1783.

Member of the Society of Friends, A. *Joseph John Gurney.* The contribution of ... to a lady's album. 1827.

Member of the Society of Friends, A. *James Bowden.* An examination into the scriptural lawfulness of mar-

riage with a deceased wife's sister, etc.
By ... L. 1863.

**Member of the Society of Friends,
A.** *Henry Callaway.* Immediate revelation: being a brief view of the dealings of God with man in all ages ... By ... L. 1842.

**Member of the Society of Friends,
A.** *Jonathan Pim.* Is it right for a Christian to marry two sisters? By ... Dublin, 1863.

**Member of the Society of Friends,
A.** *Mary Stacey, Jun.* A letter on the Lord's Supper. By ... L. 1836.

**Member of the Society of Friends,
A.** *William Collier.* Quakerism. By ... Plymouth (?), 1837.

**Member of the Society of Friends,
A.** *Philip Thompson.* The remembrancer, for such as believe in the truth as it is in Jesus ... By ... Woodbridge, 1820.

Member of the Society of Lincoln's Inn, A. *Timothy Brecknock.* Droit le Roy ... L. 1764.

Member of the Sodality of the B. V. Mary, Church of the Most Holy Redeemer, East Boston. *James Fitton.* Influence of the Catholic doctrines on the emancipation of slaves ... B. 1863.

Member of the Suffolk Bar, A. *Harrison Gray Otis.* A letter to the Hon. Josiah Quincy ... on the law of libel ... B. 1823.

Member of the Suffolk Committee of 1829, A. *Henry Gassett.* Catalogue of books on the Masonic Institution ... B. 1852.

Member of the Synod of United Original Seceders, A. *Rev. John Graham.* Non-intrusion weighed in the balance and found wanting ... Ayr, 1843.

Member of the Twenty-Seventh Congress, A. *John Pendleton Kennedy.* Defence of the Whigs. N.Y. 1844.

Member of the University, A. *Benjamin Blayney.* An expostulatory letter to ... Dr. Randolph. Oxf. 1773.

Member of the University, A Late. *Peter Le Page Renouf.* The character of the Rev. W. Palmer, M.A., of Worcester College ... L. 1843.

Member of the University of Cambridge, A. *Richard Duppa, B.C.L.* An address to the Parliament of Great Britain, on the claims of authors to their own copyright. L. 1813.

Member of the University of Cambridge, A. *Thomas Perronet Thompson.* Catechism of the Corn Laws. Manchester, n.d.

Member of the University of Cambridge, A. *Jackson Muspratt Williams.* The elements of Euclid ... By ... 1827.

Member of the University of Cambridge, A. *Rev. Edward John Nixon.* The facts as they are ... Camb. 1844.

Member of the University of Cambridge, A. *William Burdon, M.A.* A few words of plain truth ... Camb. 1797.

Member of the University of Cambridge, A. *Prof. George Long.* Hannibal's passage of the Alps. L. 1830.

Member of the University of Cambridge, A. *Rev. Philip Stanhope Dodd, M.A.* Hints to Freshmen, from ... 1798.

Member of the University of Cambridge, A. *Benjamin Hall Kennedy, D.D.* The Psalter in English verse. Edited ... 1860.

Member of the University of Oxford, A. *John Anthony Cramer, D.D.* A dissertation on the passage of Hannibal over the Alps. Oxf. 1820.
Ascribed also to H. L. Wickham.

Member of the University of Oxford, A. *Dr. John Burton.* An introduction to the metres of the Greek tragedians.

Member of the University of Oxford, A. *Rev. Wyndham Madden Hutton.* Poems. By ... Oxf. 1851.

Member of the Vermont Bar, A. *Daniel Pierce Thompson.* The adventures of Timothy Peacock, Esq. ... Middlebury, 1835.

Member of "The Victoria Discussion Society," A. *Mrs. — Stafford.* Signs of the times: from the works of Emanuel Swedenborg. To which is added a pamphlet by ... L. 1872.

Member of the Whip Club, A. *Dr. Hewson Clarke.* Lexicon Balatronicum: a dictionary of British slang, University wit, and pickpocket eloquence. By ... assisted by Hell-fire Dick. Edited by ... 1811.

Member of the Worcester Anglers' Society, A. *William George.* An essay on angling; by ... Worcester, 1840. [Also signed "Frater."]

Member of Trinity College in Cambridge, A. *Richard Bentley.* Proposals for printing a new edition of the Greek Testament ... L. 1721.

Membre Adoptif de la Nation Onéida, Un. *J. Hector St. Jean de Crèvecœur.* Voyage dans la Haute Pennsylvanie et dans l'État de New York ... Paris, 1801.

Memor, Andreas. *Antoine Agénor Alfred, duc de Gramont.* L'Allemagne nouvelle, 1863–67 ... Paris, 1879.

Memoriter. *David Pae.* Sermon reading in the pulpits of the United Presbyterian Church . . . Edinb. 1854.

Menalcas. *Bracy Clark.* Remarks on French shoeing, by an English shoeing smith. L. n.d.

Menander. *Robert Treat Paine,* in the "American Apollo." B. 1792.

Ménard, Théophile. *Just Jean Étienne Roy.* Captain Rougemont . . . N.Y. 1875.

Méndes, Judith. *Judith Gautier.* Le dragon impérial. Paris, 1869.

Mendsoale, My-heele. *John Taylor,* the water-poet. A tale in a tub; or, a tub lecture as it was delivered by . . . an inspired Brownist. L. 1641.

Mentor. *Josiah Quincy, Jr.,* who, in 1771–72, published in the "Boston Gazette" patriotic essays under the signatures of "Mentor," "Edward Sexby," and "Marchmont Needham."

Mentor. *Ven. George O'Kill Stuart,* in his letters to the "Kingston Herald," 1839–44.

Mentor. *Nathan D. Urner.* Never, Always, and Stop, three brochures published by Carleton & Co. N.Y. 1884.

Menzies, Sutherland. *Mrs. Elizabeth Stone.* Royal favourites. L. 1865.

Mephistopheles. *John Pendleton Kennedy.* A review of Mr. Cambreling's report from the committee of commerce . . . Balt. 1830.

Méplats, Isidore. *Jean Charles Taché, M.D.* Le défricheur de Langue . . . Quebec, 1859.

Méplats, Isidore de. *F. A. H. La Rue, M.D.* French Canadian author, in 1859 contributor to "La Ruche Littéraire," under this signature.

Mercantile Man, A. *James Lumsden.* American memoranda, by . . . during a short tour in the summer of 1843. Glasgow, 1844.

Mercator. *William A. Brewer,* in his contributions to various New York and Boston periodicals.

Mercator. *Right Hon. Edward Ellice,* in his letters to the "Herald," Montreal, 1807.

Mercator. *Samuel Jones Loyd,* Lord Overstone. His papers on the Bank Charter Act, etc., in the London "Times" under this signature, attracted great attention from political economists, bankers, and the mercantile classes.

Mercator. *James Anderson.* Thoughts on the privileges and power of juries, etc. By . . . Edinb. 1793.

Mercer. *James Cheetham.* Letter

concerning the Ten Pound Court, in the city of New York. N.Y. 1800.

Merchant, A. *M. Frank Carr.* Business . . . Edinb. 1873.

Merchant, A. — *Tod,* of Kirtlands. Consolatory thoughts on American independence. By . . . 177–.

Merchant, A. *C. H. Kauffman.* The dictionary of merchandize, and nomenclature in all languages . . . L. 1803.

Merchant, A. *R. Williams.* A letter . . . relating to the danger Great Britain is in of losing her trade . . . L. 1718.

Merchant, A. *William Workman.* Letters of . . . upon "Rival routes to the ocean from the West, and docks at Montreal." Montreal, 1859.

Merchant, A. — *Breed,* of Liverpool. Local issues . . . L. 1834.

Merchant, A. *John Theodore Koster.* Observations on the pending question of additional duties on cotton . . . L. 1813.

Merchant, A. *William Colson Westlake.* Practical remarks on the Corn Laws as viewed in connexion with the corn trade . . . By . . . L. 1833.

Merchant, A. *David Henshaw.* Remarks upon the Bank of the United States . . . B. 1831.

Merchant, A. *Henry M. Bird.* A view of the relative situation of Great Britain and the United States of America . . . L. 1794.

Merchant-Citizen, A. *Robert Mein.* The Edinburgh Paradise regain'd . . . n.p. 1764.

Merchant, A Late. *Asa Greene.* The perils of Pearl Street, including a taste of the dangers of Wall Street . . . N.Y. 1834.

Merchant in London, A. *Josiah Tucker, D.D.* A letter from . . . to his nephew in North America relative to . . . affairs in the colonies. L. 1766.

Merchant of Boston, A. *Samuel Hooper.* Currency or money; its nature and uses . . . B. 1855.

Merchant of Boston, A. *James Lloyd Homer.* Short inquiry into the commercial policy of the United States. By . . . B. 1845.

Merchant Seaman's Friend, The. *Jeffrey Dennis.* An address to the Committee for the Relief of Distressed Seamen . . . L. 1813.

Merchant, Mat. *W. S. Wood.* How Bennie did it. Portland, 187–.

Merchant, T. *Thomas Dibdin.* The mad guardian; or, sunshine after rain: a farce . . . Huddersfield, 1795.

Mercurius Rusticus. *Rev. Thomas Frognall Dibdin.* Bibliophobia: remarks on the present languid and depressed state of literature... With notes by Cato Parvus (Richard Heber). L. 1832.

Mercury. *George D. Baird*, editor of "Cyclist and Athlete" (N.Y.).

Mercury. *L. C. Bruce*, in his contributions to the "Turf, Field, and Farm" (N.Y.).

Mercury. *J. Pitter.* Rhymes for the times. L. 1853.

Mercutio. *William Winter*, who, 1861–66, was dramatic critic of the "New York Albion" under this pen-name.

Merdant, Daniel. *Rev. Robert Wynell Mayow, B.A.* Tracts for the use of the poor. By... 18–.

Meredith, Owen. *The Right Hon. Edward Robert Bulwer-Lytton, Earl Lytton.* The wanderer : a poem. L. 1859.

Merlin. *Alfred Tennyson*, in two poems contributed to the "Examiner" (L. 1852).

The poems referred to are "The Third of February, 1852," and "Hands All Around."

Merlin. *Alexander Wilder, M.D.* His signature as New York correspondent of the Boston "Daily Advertiser" from 1864 to 1870.

Merriweather, Magnus. *Charles Remington Talbot.* Royal Lowrie ; or, a general misunderstanding. B. 1878.

Merry, Doctor. *J. Wyndham.* Merry companion. L. 18–.

Merry, Felix. *Evert Augustus Duyckinck*, editor of the "New York Literary World," 1847–53 *et seq.*; also of "Arcturus"; contributor to the "New York Quarterly Review," 1837–42, the "Democratic Review," the "Morning News," and other periodicals, and author of valuable works.

Mer(ton), Amb(rose), Gent., F.S.A. *William John Thoms.* Gammer Gurton's pleasant stories... Newly revised and amended by... Westminster, 1846.

Merton, Tristram. *Thomas Babington Macaulay.* Sketches and ballads in "Knight's Quarterly Magazine."

Merulan. *Dr. Robert Dwyer Joyce.* — See "Feardana."

Mesnager, Monsr. *Daniel Defoe.* Minutes of the Negociations... at the Court of England... L. 1717.

Meta. *Mrs. Mary Lewis.* Heart echoes. Balt. 1873.

Metador. *William L. Alden*, in the New York "Times."

Metaphoricus, Archimagirus. *William Kenrick, LL.D.* The Kapélion ; or, poetical ordinary... L. 1750.

Methodist, A. *Alexander Chalmers.*

Caution against a growing immorality of principle. "Gent. Mag.," May, 1801, p. 398.

Methodist, A. *John Wesley.* The contents of a folio history of the Moravians...

Methodist-Preacher in Cambridgeshire, A. *Rev. John Berridge.* A fragment of true religion. Being the substance of two letters from... to a clergyman in Nottinghamshire. L. 1760.

Preface signed "Faith Workless" [*pseud.*].

Meyer, Adolf. *Meyer Aaron Goldschmidt.* The Jew. 1845.

Middle Aged Citizen, A. *R. Russell.* London railways. L. 1867.

Middle-aged Man, A. *John Dix*, afterwards *Ross*. Passages from the history of a wasted life. By... 1853.

Middle Aged Man, A. *Mrs. Katharine (Byerley) Thomson.* Recollections of literary characters and celebrated places (which consist partly of a series of articles originally published in Bentley's Miscellany" and "Fraser's Magazine" under this signature). L. 1854.

Middlesex. *William Stevens Robinson*, his signature in the New York "Evening Post" in 1853.

Middlestitch, Giles. *William Maginn, LL.D.* Semihoræ biographicæ, in "Blackwood's Magazine," September, 1820.

Midgley, R. L. *David Pulsifer.* Inscriptions from the burying-ground in Salem, Mass. B. 1837.

Midnight, Mrs. Mary. *John Newbery (?).* An index to mankind ; or, maxims selected from wits of all nations ... By... L. 1751.

Midshipman, A. *G. Home.* Memoirs of an Aristocrat, and reminiscences of the Emperor Napoleon. By... of the Bellerophon. L. 1836.

Midshipman of the last Century, A. *Commander Robert Campbell, R.N.* Recollections of a sea-life, by... in the "United Service Magazine."

Midshipman of the United States Navy, A. *William Leggett.* Leisure hours at sea... N.Y. 1825.

Mignionette. *Miss Hume Middlemass.* The bouquet culled from Marylebone Gardens by... L. 1851–55. — See "Bluebell."

Mignonette. *Emily H. Moore.* A lost life. N.Y. 1871.

Miles. *Walter Henry, M.D.* Accounts of the rebellions in Canada, 1837–38. He also contributed letters, under this signature in the "New York Albion."

Milford Bard, The. *John Lofland.* Poems and essays. Balt. 1846.

Military Chaplain, A. *Rev. Joshua Fraser.* Three months among the moose: "a winter's tale" of the northern wilds of Canada. By . . . Montreal, 1881.

Military Officer, A. *Peter Henry Bruce.* Memoirs of . . . in the services of Prussia, Russia, and Great Britain . . . L. 1782.

Military Officer (A), J. C. *Sir James Caldwell.* Debates relative to the affairs of Ireland in the years 1763 and 1764, taken by . . . L. 1766.

Mility, Hugh. *Thomas D. Suplée,* in his contributions to various periodicals.

Mill. *William Mill Butler,* in his contributions to the "Rochester Post-Express" (N.Y.).

Miller, Joaquin. *Cincinnatus Heine Miller.* First families of the Sierras. Chic. 1876.

Miller, Joe. *John Mottley* (?). Jests; or, the wits' vade-mecum. L. 1739.

Miller, Joe. *James Bannantine.* Old Joe Miller, by the editor of the "New J. M.," two jest books. L. 1801.

Miller, Joe, Jr. *Thompson Westcott,* editor of the "Sunday Dispatch" (P.), 1848–70 *et seq.*, and author of "Life of John Fitch" . . . P. 1858.

Milton, Viscount. *William Wentworth-Fitzwilliam.* A history of the San Juan Water Boundary Question . . . L. 1869.

Miltonicus. *Mr. Henderson,* a bookseller. Furius; or, a modest attempt towards a history of the life and surprising exploits of the famous W[illiam] L[auder] . . . L. 1754.

Minister, A. *Dr. Stonhouse,* of Bristol. Hints from . . . to his curate for the management of his parish. Bristol, 1774.

Minister, A. *Donald Fraser, D.D.* Leaves from a minister's portfolio. L. 1858.

Minister, A. *Rev. James Bean.* Pastoral advice from . . . to one of his parishioners recovering from sickness. L. 1798.

Minister, A. *Archdeacon Arthur Blennerhassett Rowan, D.D.* Spare minutes of . . . [poems].

Minister, and a Layman, A. *Rev. Robert Philip and another.* No opium; or, commerce and Christianity working together for good in China. L. 1835.

Minister in Boston, A. *Cotton Mather.* A letter to a friend in the country . . . B. 1721.

Minister in the Country, A. *Philip Doddridge, D.D.* Free thoughts on the most probable means of reviving the Dissenting interest . . . By . . . 1730.

Minister in the Country, A. *Rev. Edward Welchman.* The husbandman's manuel . . . L. 1707.

The "address" is signed "E. W."

Minister of Boston, A. *Rev. William Cooper, A.M.* A reply to the Objections made against the small-pox in the way of inoculation from principles of conscience. B. 1730.

Minister of the Church of England, A. *Rev. John Newton.* Apologia . . . By . . . L. 1784.

Minister of the Church of England, A. *T. Bray.* Bibliotheca Catechetica . . . L. 1702.

Minister of the Church of England, A. *Rev. William Dodd.* An earnest address to his parishioners. — See "Gent. Mag.," September, 1777, p. 421.

Minister of the Church of England, A. *Rev. Joshua Bassett,* master of Sydney College, Cambridge. An essay towards a proposal for Catholick communion . . . L. 1704.

Minister of the Church of England, A. *Rev. Edward Wells.* A letter . . . to Mr. Peter Dowley . . . Oxf. 1706.

Minister of the Church of England, A. *Rev. John Howard.* The great duty and benefit of self-denial. By . . . L. 1710.

Minister of the Church of England, A. *Rev. George Edis Webster.* Marriage with the sister of a deceased wife . . . Ipswich, 1846.

Minister of the Church of England, A. *Josiah Woodward, D.D.* Pastoral advice to young persons in order to their being confirmed . . . By . . . L. 1778.

Minister of the Church of Ireland, A. *Rev. Arthur Philip Perceval.* The King and the Church vindicated and delivered . . . L. 1833.

Also ascribed to the *Rev. Robert J. M'Ghee.*

Minister of the Church of Scotland, A. *— M'Lean, D.D.* The claim stated . . . Edinb. 1800.

Minister of the Church of Scotland, A. *Rev. Alexander Irvine.* On clerical pluralities and non-residence . . . Edinb. 1844.

Minister of the Church of Scotland, A. *Rev. — Porteous.* A critical lecture on Daniel's prophecy . . . Edinb. 1763.

Minister of the Church of Scotland, A. *Rev. John Willison.* A defence of National Churches . . . Edinb. 1719.

Minister of the Church of Scotland, A. *Rev. William Wishart.* A discourse of suppressing vice ... Edinb. 1702.

Minister of the Church of Scotland, A. *William Wilson.* The Douay-elder unmask'd ... Probably Edinb. 1731.

Minister of the Church of Scotland, A. *Rev. Alexander Campbell.* The duty of praying for civil magistrates ... Edinb. 1726.

Minister of the Church of Scotland, A. *Rev. John Ballantyne.* An essay upon Gospel and legal preaching. Edinb. 1723.

Minister of the Church of Scotland, A. *Rev. John Bethune,* of Rosskeen. Four short discourses on funeral occasions. Edinb. 1758.

Minister of the Church of Scotland, A. *John Pollock.* Intemperate indulgence in intoxicating liquors the bane of this country ... Glasgow, 1797.

Minister of the Church of Scotland, A. *Rev. John Currie,* of Kinglassie. Jus populi divinum ... Edinb. 1727.

Minister of the Church of Scotland, A. *Rev. Andrew Thomson.* A letter to the Reverend Dr. Inglis ... Edinb. 1806.

Minister of the Church of Scotland, A. *Rev. James Bannatine,* of Edinburgh. Mistakes about religion ... Edinb. 1737.

Minister of the Church of Scotland, A. *Rev. John Bisset.* Modern Erastianism unvailed ... Edinb. 1732.

Minister of the Church of Scotland, A. *Rev. George Logan.* A modest and humble inquiry concerning the right and power of electing and calling ministers to vacant churches. Edinb. 1732.

Minister of the Establishment, A. *Lawrence Lockhart, D.D.* An answer to the protest of the Free Church ... Edinb. 1846.

Minister of the Establishment, A. *Henry Card, D.D.* A letter to the Duke of Wellington, on the reasonableness of a Church reform and its fitness to the present times. By ... L. 1830.

Minister of the Free Church of Scotland, A. *Rev. John Montgomery.* An examination of articles contributed by Prof. W. Robertson Smith to the Encyclopædia Britannica ... Edinb. 1877.

Minister of the Gospel, A. *John Bell.* An abridgement and alphabetical index to the Acts of the General Assemblies of the Church of Scotland from the year 1638 to 1706, inclusive of both. Edinb. MDCCVI.

Minister of the Gospel, A. *Rev. Joseph Wilson.* Selfishness, and its remedy. By ... N.Y. 1850.

Minister of the Gospel, A. *Rev. J. E. Cullen.* Vox veritatis; or, the voice of truth ... By ... formerly educated ... for the Catholic priesthood. L. 1833.

Minister of the Gospel, A. *Nathanael Clap.* Zebulon advised ... Newport, 1738.

Minister of the Gospel in the Church of Scotland, A. *Rev. Ralph Erskine.* Gospel-canticles; or, spiritual songs ... Edinb. 1720.

Minister of the Interior, A. *Sydney Whiting.* Memoirs of a stomach ... With notes ... by ... L. 1853.

Minister, The. *Sir Robert Walpole.* An apology for the minister [a satire]. L. 1739.

Minister, The. *Sir Robert Peel.* A letter to B. D'Israeli, M.P., upon the subject of his recent attack upon the M. By a barrister. L. 1846.

Minister of a Chapel of Ease, The. *Rev. Andrew Gray.* The Chapel Question considered ... Edinb. 1834.

Minister of a Parish, The. *Samuel Glasse, D.D.* (?). An earnest and affectionate address to his parishioners from ... Gloucester, 1785.

Minister of the Church, The. *Rev. Henry C. Leonard.* A discourse delivered ... in ... Orono, Maine, at the funeral of Mary E. Crane ... March 20, 1853. By ... Bangor, 1853.

Ministering Friend, A. *Daniel Defoe.* A declaration of truth to Benjamin Hoadly ... L. 1717.

Minister's Wife, A. *Mrs. Henry Ward Beecher.* From dawn to daylight: a simple story of a Western home. N.Y. 1859.

Minor. *Jules Graf de Carné.*

Minor, A. *William Butterworth.* Three years' adventures of ... Leeds, 1822.

Minstrel of the Border. *Sir Walter Scott.* "Great Minstrel of the Border," Wordsworth.

Minstrel Maiden of Mobile, The. *Julia Mildred Harriss.* Wild shrubs of Alabama; or, rhapsodies of restless hours ... N.Y. 1852.

Mintwood. *Miss Mary A. E. Wager.*

Minus, Mr. *Thomas Moore.* One of the portraits sketched in the "Man of Sorrow," a novel by Alfred Allendale (*pseud.* for *Theodore Hook*) is that of *Thomas Moore.*

Minute Philosopher, A. *Charles Kingsley.* Hints to stammerers. L. 1864.

Mira, Isabine de. *Paul Eymard.* Voilà l'homme . . . Paris, 1863.

Mirabaud. *Paul Thiry,* baron de Holbach. The system of nature; or, the laws of the moral and physical world. Translated . . . L. 1797.

Mirbel, Elisa de. *Baronne Decazes.*

Mirecourt, Eugène de. *Charles Jean Baptiste Jacquot,* de Mirecourt. Maison Alexandre Dumas et Comp., fabrique de romans. Paris, 1845.

Miriam. *Miss Maggie E. Heath.* — See "Neale, Nettie."

Mirliter. *A. L. Boué de Villiers,* who contributed to several journals and reviews of Paris and the Provinces, under the pseuds. of "Le Capitaine Lancelot," "Le Docteur Rouge," "Raymond de Ferrières," "Guy de Vernon," "Mirliter," "Jacques Artevelle," etc.

Miron. *Miron J. Hazeltine.* Brevity and brilliancy in chess. N.Y. 1866.

Mises, Dr. *Gustav Theodor Fechner.* Kleine Schriften von Dr. Mises. Leipsic, 1875.

Misostratus. *John Taylor.* — See "Philanar."

Missioner, A. *Rev. William Rowe.* A tract for penitents at mission services. By . . . L. 1874.

Mitchell, Joseph. *Aaron Hill.* The fatal extravagance : a tragedy. L. 1721.

Mix, Parmenas. *Albert W. Kelly,* in the "Kentucky Patriot."

Mizpah. *Henry Charles Lea.* Bible view of polygamy . . .

Mnemon. One of the signatures of Junius (*q.v.*), under which "he sarcastically opposed the ministry upon the subject of the *Nullum Tempus* Bill." See letters to the "Public Advertiser," dated Feb. 24, 1768, and March 4, 1768.

Mock Preacher, The. *Rev. George Whitefield.* The M. P. : a satyrico comical allegorical farce . . . L. 1739.

Moderate Clergyman, of the Synod of Aberdeen, A. *Rev. G. Skene Keith.* Address to the ministers of the Church of Scotland . . . 1797.

Moderator. One of the pseudonyms attributed to Junius (*q.v.*). The letter thus signed is dated Oct. 12, 1767, and attacks Lord Townshend.

Moderatus. One of the signatures adopted by Junius (*q.v.*). The letter thus signed, and dated Nov. 15, 1769, was republished in the authorized edition of Junius, with the signature of "Philo-Junius." The signature was also appended to a letter dated March 10, 1770.

Modern Antique, A. *Miss Medora Gordon Byron.* Celia in search of a husband. By . . . L. 1809.

Modern Genius, A. *John Fitzgerald Pennie.* The tale of . . . or, the miseries of Parnassus, in a series of letters. L. 1827.

Modern Greek, A. *Robert Mudie.* The Modern Athens . . . L. 1825.

Modern Lady, A. *Jonathan Swift, D.D.* The journal of . . . L. 1729.

Modern Parson Adams, The. *Rev. William Young,* in Beloe's "Sexagenarian," Vol. II., p. 139. 2d ed. L. 1818.

Modern Pythagorean, A. *Dr. Robert Macnish, LL.D.* His signature to papers in "Blackwood's" and "Fraser's Magazine."

Modern Rabelais, The. *Dr. William Maginn.*

Modestus. *John Cleland,* who was the author of long letters given in the public prints, from time to time, signed "A Briton," "Modestus," etc., etc.

Modestus. *Mr. Dalrymple,* a Scotch advocate, wrote several letters under this signature in the "Gazetteer" and the "Public Advertiser," the same being attacks upon Junius, and which provoked a reply from the latter, Nov. 15, 1769.

Modestus. *Sir William Draper.* His signature in his controversy with Junius.

Modoc. *J. E. P. Doyle,* in the Cincinnati "Inquirer."

Modus, A. *Jonathan Swift, D.D.* Some reasons against the bill for settling the tithe of hemp, flax, etc. 170–.

Mofussilite. *John Lang.* Too clever by half. L. 18–.

Mogador, Céleste. *Countess Céleste Venard de Chabrillan.* Adieux au monde : mémoires de . . . Paris, 1854.

Mohawk. *Dr. Nicholas Rowe,* in the Chicago "Field."

Mohican. *Joseph E. Fisher.*

Moile, Nicholas Thirning. *Henry Bliss.* State trials. Specimen of a new edition. By . . . L. 1838.

Moïna. *Mrs. Anna Peyre (Shackelford) Dinnies,* long known as a poet, by the sweet, wild title of "Moïna," a signature which she adopted while quite young. Since the close of the war, *Rev. Father Ryan* has used the same pseudonym.

Moïna. *Rev. Father A. J. Ryan.* The conquered banner. 186–.

Moléri. *Hippolyte Jules Demolière.* La famille Renneville. Paris, 1843.

Mon Droit. *R. E. Selden, Jr.* (?). Criticisms on the Declaration of Independence as a literary document. N.Y. 1846.

Mona, Viva. *Peter Fishe Reed*, one of the contributors, under this signature, to the "Weekly Columbian," a literary paper which flourished for two or three years from 1850, at Cincinnati, when it became absorbed into the "Daily Columbian," and was discontinued in 1856.

Moncrieff, William Thomas. *William Thomas.* The new guide to the Spa of Leamington Priors... Leamington Priors, 1822.

Monday Club, The. *Rev. John Wesley Churchill, Edwin Cone Bissell,* etc. Sermons... By... B. 1877.

Monitor. *Arthur Lee, Esq.* Monitor's letters to the inhabitants of the British colonies. Williamsburg, 1769.

Monk, Geoffrey, M.A. *J. Henry Shorthouse.* John Inglesant : a romance. L. 1881.

"Monk" Lewis. *Matthew Gregory Lewis,* so called from his novel.

"Books have given rise to a name that has met with anything like general acceptance less frequently than might have been thought. *Matthew Gregory* is indeed ' Monk ' *Lewis* ; the *Rev. Jno. Williams,* ' The Redeemed Captive'; the *Rev. Henry Taylor,* who published the ' Apology of Benjamin Ben Mordecai for embracing Christianity,' ' Ben Mordecai '; *John,* author of the ' First Century of Scandalous Malignant Priests,' etc.; ' Century,' *White; William Jones,* of Nayland, from his writings in defence of the Trinity, ' Trinity Jones,' etc." — See " Gent. Mag." for January, 1883, p. 47.

Monkey. *Frédéric du Petit-Méré.* Sapajou ; ou, le naufrage des singes ... Paris, 1826.

Monmouth, T. de. *Thomas Powell.* Edgar and Elfrida, with the defeat of Hoel, Prince of Wales. 179–.

Monmouthshire Magistrate, A. *J. H. Moggridge.* Remarks on the report of the select committee of the House of Commons on the Poor-Laws. By... Bristol, 1818.

Monsieur de l'Orchestre, Un. *Arnold Mortier.* Under this pseudonym for many years one of the dramatic critics of the "Figaro."

Mont, Ruben du. *Edmund Burton,* who was for some years a valuable correspondent of the "Gent. Mag." under this signature.

Montague, Clinton. *Miss H. Maria George.*

Montanus. *Vincenz von Zuccalmaglio.* Vorzeit der Länder Kleve, Mark, etc. 1836.

Montclair, John W. *John William Weidemeyer.* Real and ideal. P. 1865.

Monteagle, Lady. *Lady Caroline (Ponsonby) Lamb.* "Lord Beaconsfield for a second time depicts Lady Caroline Lamb in the character of ' Lady Monteagle ' in ' Venetia.' "

Montefiore, Joshua. *William Playfair.* The spirit of the Bankrupt Laws. L. 1806. — See "Oddy, J. Jephson."

Montelion, Knight of the Oracle. *Thomas Flatman.* Don Juan Lamberto ; or, a comical history of the late times. L. 1661.

Montez, Lola. *Charles Chauncey Burr.* Lectures of... N.Y. 1858.

Montgomery, Miss Betty. *William Cullen.* A funeral oration in honour of Miss Jeany Muir [*i.e.* Dr. John Clark] ... Amsterdam, n.d.

Montgomery, Gerard. *Rev. John Moultrie,* in the "Etonian" and in "Knight's Quarterly Magazine."

Monthly Nurse, A. *Mrs. Harriet Downing Oliver.* Remembrances of... in "Fraser's Magazine."

Montifaud, Marc de. *Marie Emilie Quivogne-Chartrouse.* Contes drôlatiques. 1880.

Montigny. *Adolphe Lemoine,* joint author. Le doigt de dieu... Paris, 1854.

Montmorency, Frederick Haltamont de. *William Makepeace Thackeray.* "A Doe in the City," in "Punch," Nov. 1, 1845.

Moody, Querulous. *David Henry Urquhart.*

Moore, Mollie E. *Mrs. Mollie E. (Moore) Davis.* Poems. Houston, Tex., 1872.

Moore, Thomas, Esq. *James Barlow.* The Peacock, The Baboon, and The Moneyspinners. By... Mexico, 1841.

Moore, William V. *John Frost.* Indian wars of the United States, from the discovery to the present time... P. 1840.

Moorman. *W. Carnegie,* in several works on sports and pastimes.

Moral Censor. *John Lathrop, Jun.,* in the "Polyanthos." Boston, 1812 *et seq.*

Moralisto, Poet 'Lariat' of Carthage. *J. M. Dill.* The village school : a poem. Cin. 188–.

Morar. *Sir William Augustus Fraser, Bart.* Poems. 1866.

Moray, John S. *Augustus R. Cazauran,* in the Brooklyn "Sun."

Mordaunt, Late Colonel Harry, The. *George Ogle.* A modest defence of public stews ; or, an essay upon whoring... L. 1740.

Mordaunt, John. *John Moore, M.D.* Mordaunt : sketches of life, characters, and manners in various countries . . . written by the Honourable . . . L. 1800.

Mordecai, Benjamin Ben. *Rev. Henry Taylor.* The apology of . . . to his friends, for embracing Christianity; in seven letters to Elisha Levi, merchant of Amsterdam . . . L. 1771–74.

More, Margareta. *Mrs. Anne (Manning) Rathbone.* The household of Sir Thomas More. L. 1851.

Morecamp, Arthur. *Thomas Pilgrim.* Live boys in the Black Hills; or, the young Texan gold hunters . . . B. 1880.

Morel, H. *Mme. Claude Vignon Rouvier.* The daily articles upon the sittings of the Corps Législatif from 1868 to 1870, which appeared in the "Moniteur," with this signature, are attributed to *Mme. Vignon Rouvier.*

Morell, Sir Charles. *Rev. James Ridley.* The tales of the genii . . . Trans. by . . . L. 1764. See "Horam, the Son of Asmar."

Morely, Ralph. *Henry L. Hinton,* editor and publisher of "Acting Plays of Edwin Booth." N.Y. 187–, etc.

Morenos, Ojos. *Mrs. Josephine Russell Clay.* What will he say? and Only a woman. P. 1873.

Moreton, Andrew, Esq. *Daniel Defoe.* Everybody's business is nobody's business; or, private abuses publick grievances . . . By . . . L. 1725.

Moreton, Clara. *Mrs. Clara Jessup Moore,* who under this pen-name published most of her writings.

Morganwg, Iolo. *Edward Williams.* Poems, lyric and pastoral. 1794.

Moriturus. *Charles Lamb,* on burial societies, and the character of an undertaker; contributed to the "Reflector."

Morlon, G. de. *Gaspard Georges,* le Marquis de Cherville. Le dernier crime de Jean Hiroux, par . . . Paris, 1862.

Morna. — See "Mayflower, Minnie."

Morris, Dinah. *Elizabeth Evans,* in George Eliot's "Adam Bede."

"The Wesleyans at Wirksworth are going to remove from their old chapel, where *Elizabeth Evans,* the prototype of 'Dinah Morris' in 'Adam Bede,' preached for many years. The new chapel, which is to be called 'Bede Memorial Chapel,' is 'to be erected to the glory of God, and in memory of *Elizabeth Evans,* immortalized as 'Dinah Morris' by George Eliot in her novel of 'Adam Bede.'"

Morris, John. *John O'Connor.* Wanderings of a vagabond: an autobiography. Edited by . . . N.Y. 1873.

Morris, Katherine. *Mrs. Frances West (Atherton) Pike.* Katherine Morris: an autobiography . . . B. 1858.

Morris, Dr. Peter, the Odontist.

John Gibson Lockhart. Peter's letters to his kinsfolk. Edinb. 1819.

Morris, Robert. *James S. Gibbons.* The organization of the public debt, and a plan for the relief of the treasury . . . N.Y. 1863.

Morrison, Mary. *Mary B. Washburne.*

Mortimer, Gilbert. *Montgomery Gibbs.* Six hundred Robinson Crusoes; or, the voyage of the golden fleece . . . L. 1878.

Mortimer, Grace. *Miss M. B. Stuart.* Bosom foes. N.Y. 187–.

Mortimer, Sir Henri. *Almire Gandonnière.* Les mystères de la Bastille. Dans la "Chronique." Paris, 1844.

Moschus. *Robert Lovel.* Poems by Bion [*i.e.* Southey, Robert] and . . . Bristol, 1794.

Moses. *Moses Field Fowler.* A defence of corporal punishment. B. 1873.

Most Artful Man Alive, The. *Richard Brinsley Sheridan.* — See "Albion."

Most Impudent Man Living, The. *Bishop William Warburton.* A familiar epistle to . . . L. 1749. By Henry St. John, Lord Bolingbroke.

Also ascribed to *David Mallet.* — See the "Monthly Review," Vol. 1, p. 238.

Most Unpatriotic Man Alive, The. *Charles James Fox.* — See "Albion."

Moth. *Joseph T. Buckingham.* Letters from Washington in the "Boston Courier," 1830 *et seq.*

Mother, A. *Sarah Bird.* Amy's first trial. L. 1854.

Mother, A. *Mrs. J. A. Sargant.* Letters from . . . 6th ed. L. 1843.

Mother, A. *Mrs. Crespigny.* Letters of advice from . . . to her son. L. 1803.

Mother, A. *Mrs. Abigail Mott.* Observations on the importance of female education and maternal instruction . . . By . . . N.Y. 1825.

Mother, A. *Mrs. Maria (Rowe) Gurney.* Rhymes for my children, by . . . L. 1840.

Mother and the Mistress of a Family, A. *Adelaide Sophia Kilvert.* Home discipline . . . L. 1841.

Mt. Hood. *I. N. Fleischner.*

Mountain Bard. *David Hatch Barlow,* who wrote a number of poetical pieces with this signature for the "New England Galaxy" (B.).

Mountain Minstrel, The. *Evan McColl,* a Scotch lyric poet residing in Canada.

Mountaineer. *Charles Wright.* The prospect: a view of politics. Buffalo, 1862.

Mountaineer. — *Wilson*, of Mussoorie. A summer ramble in the Himalayas; edited by . . . L. 1860.

Mountaineer, The. *Joseph Alston*, in the "Charleston (S.C.) Gazette," 1810–16.

Mousse, Alfred. *Arsène Houssaye.* De profundis. Paris, 1834.

Muehlbach, Luise. *Mme. Klara (Müller) Mundt.* Geschichtsbilder historische Novellen. Von . . . Jena, 1868.

Muehlfeld, Julius. *E. Robert Roesler.* Gegensätze. Novelle. Von . . . Altona, 1872.

Müller, Christine. *E. C. W. (Gobie) van Walrée.* Story of Wandering Willie. N.Y. 187–.

Muggins, William. *Charles Selby.* Maximums and speciments of . . . L. 1841.

Muir, Jeany. *Dr. John Clark.* — See "Montgomery, Miss Betty."

Mul. *William H. Muldoon*, in the Brooklyn "Sun."

Muldoon, Dennis. *George B. Goodwin.*

Muldoon, Major. *William H. Macartney.*

Mullian, Mordecai. This name was occasionally employed by *Prof. John Wilson* as a pseudonym, in the "Noctes Ambrosianæ." It is intended as a personification of *the inhabitants of Edinburgh.*

Mulligan, The (of Kilballymulligan). *William Makepeace Thackeray.* "The Pimlico Pavilion," in "Punch," August 9, 1845.

Mullner. *Jacques Albin Simon Collin de Plancy.*

Multatuli. *Edward Douwes Dekker.* Max Havelaar; or, the coffee auctions of the Dutch Trading Company, 1856. Edinb. 1868.

Mum, Ned. *Dr. Zachary Pearce*, Bishop of Rochester, in a letter contributed to the "Guardian," No. 121, July 30, 1713.

Mungo, the minstrel. — *Darkison.* The Border Gipsy . . . An operatic drama. 1868.

Munster, Minnie. *Harriet E. Burleigh.*

Munster Farmer, A. *Thomas Moore.* Captain Rock detected. L. 1824.
Also ascribed to *Farrar O'Sullivan* and *J. Jebb*, Bishop of Limerick.

Muralto, Onuphrio. *Horace Walpole.* The castle of Otranto, translated by William Marshall, Gent., from the original Italian of Onuphrio Muralto, canon of the church of St. Nicholas at Otranto. 1765. — See "Marshall, William."

Murdock, Frank. *Francis Hitchcock.*

Murphy, Dennis Jasper. *Rev. Robert Charles Maturin.* Fatal revenge; or, the House of Montorio: a novel. L. 1807.

Murray. *Robert Sanders.* — See "Spencer, Nath."

Murray, Dominick. *Dominick Moran.*

Murray, Hamilton. *Henry Malden.* Origin of universities and academical degrees. L. 1835. Also in his contributions to "Knight's Quarterly Magazine" (L.), 1835.

Murray, Herbert. *Rev. Francis Charles Hingeston-Randolph, M.A.* The curse of Trecobben. By . . . in the "New Monthly Magazine," 1859.

Musæus. *John Morrison, D.D.*, who, in early life, contributed verses to the "Edinburgh Weekly Magazine" under this signature.

Muscipula, Sen. *John Collier*, of Urmston. Curious remarks on the history of Manchester [by J. Whitaker]. L. 1771.

Musgrave, Philip. *Rev. Joseph Abbott, M.A.* Philip Musgrave; or, the adventures of a missionary in Canada. L. 184–.

Musical Professor, A. *Edward Holmes.* A ramble among the musicians of Germany, giving some account of the operas of Munich, Dresden, Berlin, etc. . . . L. 1828.

Musical Small-coal Man. *Thomas Britton.*

Musidorus. *B. Way.* His signature to a letter in the "Microcosm" (published at Eton College, 1787).

Mutual Friend, A. *Mrs. Grote.* The case of the Poor against the Rich . . . L. 1850.

Myers, Ned. *Lemuel Bryant*, in one of Cooper's novels.

Mylius, Otfried. *Karl Müller.* Für Frauenhand. 1875.

Myra. *Mrs. A. W. Fairbanks*, European correspondent of the "Herald" (Cleveland, O.).

Myrtle, Annie. *Miss Annie M. Chester.*

Myrtle, Harriet. *Mrs. Mary (Gillies) Miller.* More fun for our little friends. L. 1864.

Myrtle, Mrs. Harriet. *Mrs. Lydia Falconer Miller.* A day of pleasure . . . L. 1853.

Myrtle, Lewis. *George Canning Hill.* Our parish; or, pen paintings of village life. P. 187–.

Myrtle, Marmaduke, Gent. *Sir Richard Steele,* in the "Lover." L. 1713.

Myrtle, May. *Mrs. Maria Holden.*

Myrtle, Minnie. *Mrs. Sarah Morgan (Bryan) Piatt.* Mrs. Piatt early in life wrote for the "Louisville Journal" and the "New York Ledger"; but after her marriage, for the "Galaxy," "Our Young Folks," and other periodicals.

Myrtle, Minnie. *Mrs. Anna C. Johnson Miller.* The myrtle wreath; or, stray leaves recalled. N.Y. 1854.

Myrtle, Mollie. *Miss Julia Bacon,* who has published prose and verse under several *noms de plume,* the most popular of which was "Mollie Myrtle."

Myrtle, Mollie. *Miss Agnes Leonard.* Myrtle blossoms. 1863.

Mystery. *Mrs. Maria Elizabeth (Jourdan) Westmoreland,* whose many and valued contributions to the Southern press have appeared under this pen-name.

N.

N. *C. B. Northrup.* Political remarks by . . . Charleston, 1861.

N., Earl. *Rev. William Nelson,* 1st Earl Nelson, in Beloe's "Sexagenarian," Vol. II., p. 156. 2d ed. L. 1818.

N. of Arkansas. *Col. C. F. M. Noland.*

N. A. B. *Charles Alexander Nelson.* His signature to a description of the Cornell University library in the "Evening Post" (N.Y.), Sept. 13, 1883.

N., C. *John Wilson and others.* Christmas chit-chat: poetry in "Blackwood's Magazine," Vol. 10, p. 493 *et seq.*

N., C., C.F.P.D. *Cornelius Nary.* New Testament translated . . . Dublin, 1718–19.

N., C. A. *Charles Alexander Nelson,* as Boston correspondent of the "American Bookseller" (N.Y. 187– to 1881).

N. C. M. S. C. *Humphrey Cotes.* An enqviry into the condvct of a late Right Honovrable Commoner [Mr. Pitt]. L. 1766.

N., E. D. *Edward Duffield Neill.* Maryland not a Roman Catholic colony . . . Minneapolis, 1875.

N., E. D. E. *Emma D. E. (Neville) Southworth.*

N., H. *Henry Norris.* The Royal Merchant; or, the beggar's bush. A comedy. L. 1706.

N., Honoria. *Miss Marguerite A. Power.* — See "Honoria."

N., H. J. B. *Henry J. B. Nicholson.* The Abbey of St. Alban. Some extracts from its early history . . . By . . . L. 1851.

N., J. *John Nichols.* Bibliotheca topographica Britannica. L. 1780–90.

N., J. *Joachim Navarro.* Études législatives. Paris, 1836.

N., J. *John Nichol.* Leaves. [Poem by] J. N. Edinb. 1854.

N., J. B. *John Bowyer Nichols.* The life and errors of John Dunton . . . L. 1818.

N., J. H. *John Henry Newman.* The dream of Gerontius. L. 1865.

N. J. N. *Mrs. A. G. Wilson.* Time will tell. By . . . 1868.

N. N. *Rev. John Strachan,* in his contributions to the "Canadian Magazine."

N. N. *Charlwood Lawton.* Civil comprehension, etc., in a letter to a friend . . . L. 1705.

N. O. *Lieut. Edward Thompson.* The demi-rep. By . . . author of the "Meretriciad." L. 1756.

N. O. Ancien Missionaire. *Rev. Jean André Cuoq.* Études philologiques sur quelques langues sauvages de l'Amérique. Montreal, 1860.

N., R. *Randal Norris,* sub-treasurer, Inner Temple. — See Lamb's "Elia," "The Old Benchers," etc.

N. R. *John Hunter.* Miscellanies . . . 1843.

N. R. S. *John Bowyer Nichols, Esq. F.S.A.* "Among his duties from an early age, was that of assisting in the editorship of this [the "Gent."] Magazine; and the contributions which he made to its pages, when not signed with his initials, had usually the signature "N. R. S." being the final letters of his name."

N. S. G. *Lyman Hotchkiss Bagg.* His signature in "Oliver Optic's Magazine," and N.Y. "Citizen," 1869.

N., T., Philomath. *Jonathan Swift.* A famous prediction of Merlin, the British Wizard . . . Edinb. 1708.

N., W. *William Noy.* His signature in "Notes and Queries," etc., 1865–71.

N., W. *William Naish.* George Fox and his friends . . . L. 1859.

N., W. *Rev. William Nind.* The German lyrist; or, metrical versions from the principal German lyric poets ... Camb. 1856.

N., W. D. *William Dummer Northend.* Catalogue of the officers and students of Dummer Academy. By . . . Salem, Mass., 1844.

N****m, T****s.** *Rev. Thomas Newenham.* — See "One of the Laity," etc.

Nadar. *Gustave Felix Tournachon,* an aëronaut, who, in 1842, wrote in "la Vogue," "le Negociateur," and "l'Audience," at Paris, under this signature.

Nadir, William, S.X.Q. *William Douglass, M.D.* Mercurius Novanglicanus. [An almanac.] By . . . B. 1743–44.

Nagrom. — *Morgan,* Boston correspondent of the "Cleveland (O.) Leader."

Nancy, A. P. F. *Anne Philibert François Claude.* Alphonse de Coucy; ou, quelques scenes de la campagne de Russie. Metz, 1819.

Nankin Man, A. *Abbé Evariste Régis Huc.* "Letters from . . . of Science," in the "Gazette de France."

Nasby, Petroleum Vesuvius. *David Ross Locke.* Nasby: divers views, opinions, and prophecies of yours trooly . . . lait paster in the Church of the Noo Dispensashun. 1863.

Natali, Agnes and Fanny. *Agnes and Fanny Heron.* A nom de théâtre.

Native and Inhabitant of that Place, A. *Robert Beverley.* The history and present state of Virginia . . . By . . . L. 1705.

Native, and Member of the House of Burgesses, A. *Thomas Jefferson.* A summary view of the rights of British America . . . Williamsburg, 1774.

Native of America, A. *Lt.-Col. John Parke.* The lyric works of Horace, translated into English verse. To which are added a number of original poems . . . P. 1786.

Native of Boston, A. *Jonathan Jackson.* Thoughts upon the political situation of the United States . . . Worcester, 1788.

Native of Craven, A. *William Carr, B.D.* Horæ momenta Cravenæ; or, the Craven dialect ... L. 1824.

Native of Denmark, A. *Andreas Anderson.* A tour in Zealand, in . . . 1802 ... By ... 1804.

Native of New England, A. *Daniel Leonard.* The present political state of the province of Massachusetts-Bay in general, and the town of Boston in particular ... N.Y. 1775.

Native of Pennsylvania, A. *Joseph Sansom.* Letters from Europe, during a tour through Switzerland and Italy, 1801–2 ... P. 1805.

Native of Pennsylvania, A. *Isaac Grey.* A serious address to such of the people called Quakers . . . as profess scruples relative to the present government ... written ... by ... P. 1778.

Native of Pennsylvania, A. *George McHenry.* Why Pennsylvania should become one of the Confederate States of America ... L. 1862.

Native of Philadelphia, A. *David McClure.* A system of education for the Girard College for Orphans ... P. 1838.

Native of Scotland, A. — *Bruce.* Poems, chiefly in the Scottish dialect, originally written under the signature of the "Scots-Irishman ... Washington, Pa., 1801.

Native of that Colony, A. *Carter Braxton.* Address to the Convention of the Colony ... of Virginia ... P. 1776.

Native of the Forest, A. *William Apes.* The experience of ... written by himself. N.Y. 1831.

Native of the South, A. *Dr. Thomas Cooper,* or *A. S. Johnson.* Memoirs of a Nullifier, written by himself ... Columbia, 1832.

Native of Virginia, A. *William Branch Giles.* Public defaulters brought to light, etc. N.Y. 1822.

Native of Virginia, A. *Daniel McLeod.* The rebellion in Tennessee ... Washington, 1862.

Native of Virginia, A. *Moncure Daniel Conway.* The rejected stone; or, insurrection vs. resurrection in America ... B. 1861.

Native African, A. *Quobna Ottobouh Cugoano.* Thoughts and sentiments on the evil of slavery ... L. 1791.

Native American, A. *Richard Hildreth.* Native Americanism detected and exposed ... B. 1845.

Native American, A. *E. Hutchinson.* "Young Sam"; or, native American's own book ... N.Y. 1855.

Native Artist, A. *Edward Pugh.* Cambria depicta: a tour through North Wales ... By ... L. 1816.

Native Born Citizen of the United States, A. *Oliver Evans.* Exposition of part of the patent laws ... 1816.

Native Brahmin, A. *Joguth Chunder Gangooly.* Juthoo and his Sunday-school. By ... B. 1861.

Native Canadian, A. *Lt.-Col. George T. Denison, Jr., LL.B.* Canada : is she prepared for war ? . . . Toronto, 1861.

Native Citizen and Servant of the State, A. *Alexander Contee Hanson.* Political schemes and calculations, addressed to the citizens of Maryland . . . Annapolis, 1784.

Native Georgian, A. *Augustus Baldwin Longstreet.* Georgia scenes, characters, incidents, etc., in the first half century of the republic . . . N.Y. 1840.

Nat'ral Born Durn'd Fool, A. *George W. Harris.* Sut Lovengood : yarns spun by a . . . N.Y. 1867.

Naturalist. *Philip Lutley Sclater.* Naturalist's impressions of Spain. L. 1861.

Naturalist, A. *George Edwards.* A discourse on the emigration of British birds . . . L. 1795.

Naturalist, A. *Robert Garner, F.L.S.* Holiday excursions of . . . L. 1867.

Naturalist, A. *John Leonard Knapp, Esq., F.S.A., F.L.S.* Journal of . . . L. 1829.

Naturalist, A. *William John Broderip, Esq., F.L.S.* Leaves from the note-book of . . . L. 1852.

Naturalist, A. *Count Valerian Krasinski.* Monachologia ; or, handbook of the natural history of monks . . . Edinb. 1852.

Naturalist, A. *Arthur Adams.* Travels of . . . in Japan and Manchuria. L. 1870.

Naturalist, The. *John Matthew Jones.* The Naturalist in Bermuda . . . L. 1859.

Naufragus. *Mr. Horne.* The adventures of . . . L. 1827.

Nava, Franz. *Edward Francis Rimbault.* A number of musical compositions, arrangements, etc., under this pseudonym, after 1852.

Naval Officer, A. *Augustus Collingridge.* The lieutenant and the crooked midshipman : a tale of the ocean. L. 1844.

Naval Officer, A. *Captain William Harwar Parker.* Recollections of . . . N.Y. 1883.

Naval Officer, A. *James B. West.* Shall we continue to drown our sailors ? By . . . Tunbridge Wells, 1875.

Navarin, Charles. *Charles Henri Ternaux-Compans.* Les aventures de Don Juan de Vargas . . . Translated by . . . P. 1853.

Navery, Raoul de. *Mme. Marie (de Saffron) David.* Un erreur fatale. Paris, 1882. Also in contributions to periodcals.

Neafie. *Edwin R. Purple.*

Neale, Flora. *Mrs. Georgie A. (Hulse) McLeod,* a constant contributor to magazines, etc., North and South, under this and other signatures.

Neale, Nettie. *Miss Maggie E. Heath,* who was favorably known to the readers of the "Field and Fireside" (Raleigh, N.C.) under this pen-name. She also contributed to the Richmond "Christian Advocate" and the Nashville "Home Circle," under the pseud. of "Miriam," both prose and verse.

Near Observer, A. *Mr. Bentley.* A few cursory remarks upon the state of parties, during the administration of the Right Hon. Henry Addington. L. 1803.

Near Observer, A. *M. Montagu.* Friendly remarks upon some particulars of his administration, in a letter to Mr. Pitt. L. 1796.

Necessitarian, A. *John Allen, M.D.* Illustrations of Mr. Hume's essay concerning liberty and necessity . . . L. 1795.

Neck, Mr. Vander. *James Burgh.* An account of the first settlement, laws, form of government, and police of the Cessares, a people of South America. In nine letters, from . . . one of the senators of that nation, to his friend in Holland . . . L. 1764.

Neckar. *R. Fisher.* Seventeen numbers . . . upon the causes of the present distress of the country . . . N.Y. 1837. — See "Citizen of New York, A."

Needham, Marchamont. *Josiah Quincy, Jr.,* who, under this signature, commenced a series of papers in the Boston "Gazette," June 7, 1772, which were ended in January, 1774.

Neighbor, A. *Nathan Fiske, S.T.D.* — See "General Observer, The."

Neighbour, A. *Sir Charles Morell.* The contrast : a familiar epistle to Mr. C. Churchill, on reading his poem called "Independence." By . . . L. 1764.

Neighbour, A. *Ebenezer Chaplin.* A treatise on Church government. B. 1773.

Neighbouring Minister, A. *William Fleetwood,* Bishop of St. Asaph. A funeral sermon upon Mr. Noble. L. 1713.

Neil, Rose. *Miss Isabella Harwood.*

Nella. *Miss E. Ward.* Cousin Winifred. L. 18–.

Nellerto, Don Juan. *Juan Antonio Llorente.* History of the Inquisition of Spain. L. 1827.

Nellie. *Miss E. Marsh.* Issy and her lovers. L. 18–.

Nemesis. A pseudonym of Junius (*q.v.*). The letter thus signed is dated

May 12, 1772. It is directed against Lord Barrington, and is the last of all the public letters of Junius.

Nemesis. *James Beal,* in the London "Dispatch."

Nemesis. *Alfred Farthing Robbins.* Five years of Tory Rule. 1879.

Nemmersdorf, Franz von. *Franziska,* Baronin von Reitzenstein. Gebt Raum! 1880.

Nemo. *Rev. Moses Harvey,* of St. John's, Newfoundland, in his contributions to various local periodicals.

Nemo. *Roland F. Coffin.* Straws by Nemo. Camb. 1859.

Nemo, Mrs. *Miss — Roberts.*

Neptune. *Benjamin Ogle Taylor.*

Neptunus. *Benjamin Bruce.*

Nereus. *John Wilson Croker.* The letters on the subject of the naval war with America, which appeared in the "Courier" under the signature of "Nereus." L. 1813.

Nero, Caius Claudius. *Earl of Winchelsea.* — See "Florus, Julius."

Nerva. *Hon. Samuel Gale.* A collection of papers published in the "Montreal Herald." Montreal, 1814.

Nessmuk. *George W. Sears.* Woodcraft. N.Y. 1884.

Nestor. *Hugh Barclay.* Rambling recollections of Old Glasgow. By ... Glasgow, 1880.

Nettement, Alfred. *Étienne Léon,* Baron de Lamothe-Langon. Memoires historiques de ... Duchesse de Berri ... Paris, 1837.

Nettle, H. *William Jackson.* Sodom and Onan: a satire inscribed to Samuel Foote, Esq. L. 1776.

Neuvil, Jules. *Jules Hocédé.* Illusions, poésies. Paris, 1840.

Neuville, Auguste. *Félix Dubourg.* Le portefeuille d'un comédien de province ... Amiens, 1849.

Nevers, C. O. *Charles Crozat Converse.* Spring and holiday: a cantata. 1855.

Neville, Mary. *Miss Mary A. Foster,* for some years a frequent contributor to the "Cincinnati Gazette," the "Cincinnati Commercial," and the "Ohio Statesman."

Neveu de mon oncle. *Jacques Albin Simon Collin de Plancy.* Légendes des philosophes. Paris, 1849.

New England Bride, A. *Mrs. Caroline (Howard) Gilman.* Recollections of ... Charleston, 1852.

New England Farmer, A. *John Lowell.* A dispassionate enquiry into the reasons alleged by Mr. Madison for declaring an offensive and ruinous war against Great Britain ... B. 1812.

New England Housekeeper, A. *Mrs. Caroline (Howard) Gilman.* Recollections of ... B. 18–.

New England Man, A. *James Kirke Paulding.* Sketch of Old England ... N.Y. 1822.

New England Man, A. *Benjamin Franklin.* Toleration in Old England and New England, contributed to the "London Packet," June 3, 1772.

New England Minister, A. *Bennet Tyler, D.D.* Letters on ... the New Haven theology ... N.Y. 1837.

New (A) England Minister, A.B. *Rev. Edward Everett Hale.* Margaret Percival in America: a tale. Edited by ... Being a sequel to Margaret Percival: a tale [by Miss Elizabeth Missing Sewell] ... Edited by ... B. 1850.

New Englander, A. *Rufus B. Sage.* Scenes in the Rocky Mountains, and in Oregon, California, New Mexico, Texas, and the grand prairies ... P. 1846.

New Englander Over the Sea, A. *John Neal.* Authorship: a tale ... B. 1830.

New Lord Chancellor, The. *Richard West.* A poem on ... Dublin, 1725.

New Member of the House of Commons, A. *Mr. Callaghan.* A letter on the probable safety in resuming cash payments. L. 1819.

New Writer, A. *Mrs. Frances E. (Ternan) Trollope.* Aunt Margaret's trouble. By ... L. 1866.

New Yorker, A. *John McVickar, D.D.* Hints on banking ... N.Y. 1827.

New Yorker, A. *Henry Wikoff.* A New Yorker in the Foreign Office, and his adventures in Paris. L. 1858.

New Yorker, A. *William Gillespie Mitchell, LL.D.* Rome as seen by ... 1843–44. N.Y. 1845.

New Yorker, A. *Charles Astor Bristed.* The upper ten thousand: sketches of American society, by ... reprinted from "Fraser's Magazine." L. 1852.

New Yorker, A. *Charles Fenno Hoffman.* A winter in the West ... N.Y. 1835.

Newberry, My Uncle. *George Mogridge.*

Newbury, Herbert. *Sarah A. F. Herbert.* May Bell. B. 1869.

Newdigate Prizeman, A. *William Hurrell Mallock.* Every man his own poet ... Oxf. 1872.

Newfoundland Missionary, A. *Archdeacon Edward Wix.* Six months of ... 's journal, from February to August, 1835. L. 1836.

Newil, Charles. *Adrien Charles Alexander Basset.* Contes excentriques. Paris, 1834.

Newlight, Rev. Aristarchus, Phil. Dr. of the University of Giessen. *Richard Whately, D.D.* Historic certainties respecting the early history of America. L. 1851.

Newte, Thomas. *William Thomson.* Prospects and observations in a tour in England and Scotland ... L. 1791.

Niade, Hippolyte. *Hippolyte Édain.* Six années de mariage. Paris, 1832.

Nicander. *Rev. Morris Williams.*

Nichols, T. Nickle. *Thomas Nichols.* "What's in a name?" Being a popular explanation of ordinary Christian names of men and women. By ... L. 1859.

Nicholson, My Aunt Margaret. *Percy Bysshe Shelley.* Posthumous poems of ... Oxf. 1810.

Nick. *Jonas E. Whitley.*

Nicolai. *Carl Henrik Scharling.* Ved Nytaarstid i Nöddebo Prastegaard. 1874.

Nidrah. *L. S. Hardin.*

Nil. *Henry John Whitling.* Heidelberg and the way thither ... L. 1845.

Nil Admirari, Esq. *Rev. Frederick William Shelton.* The Trollopiad; or, travelling gentleman in America: a satirical poem ... N.Y. 1837.

Nilense, le baron de. *Jacques Albin Simon Collin de Plancy.* Les deux Robinsons. Paris, 1849.

Nilense, le frère Jacques. *Jacques Albin Simon Collin de Plancy.* Guirlande catholique des douze mois de l'année. Paris, 1849.

Niles, Willys. *J. F. Hume.* Five hundred majority; or, the days of Tammany ... N.Y. 1872.

Nilla. *Mrs. Abby (Allin) Carter.* Home ballads. N.Y. about 1850.

Nimble-Chops, Aquiline, Democrat. *Brockholst Livingston.* Democracy: an epic poem ... N.Y. about 1790.

Nimini, Notus. *George W. Ogden.* A letter to Hull Barton ... By his friend ... New Bedford, 1823.

Nimrod. *Charles James Apperley.* The horse and the hound. Edinb. 1858.

Nimrod. *John Hamilton Reynolds.* Sporting by ... L. 1838.

Nina, Miss. *Mlle. Nina Duff.* La Marquise de Senneville ... Paris, 1844.

Nitgenockle. *William Hamilton Galt.*

No Author. *Mortimer M. Thompson.* Plu-ri-bus-tah: a song that's by no author. N.Y. 1856.

No Bel-Esprit. *John Lowell, LL.D.*

Gov. Strong's calumniator reproved ... B. 1814.

No Bigot to, nor against the Church of England. *Rev. Samuel Cooper.* A full refutation of the reasons advanced in defence of the petition which is intended to be offered to Parliament ... for the abolition of subscription to the Articles. By ... L. 1772.

No Genius. *Alexander Chalmers.* Increase of geniuses, in "Gent. Mag." March, 1799, p. 199.

No Jacobin. *Alexander Hamilton.* — See "Pacificus."

No Name. *Cecil Burleigh.*

No-Party Man, A. *Henry Hayes.* What is baptism? Is it a fiction? Considered by ... Holloway, 1859.

No Tithe Gatherer. *Rev. Samuel Cooper.* A letter to the clergy of the county of Norfolk ... By ... Norwich, 1773.

Noakes, John. *Tom Taylor.* Barefaced impostors. A farce ... By J. D., Richard Roe, and ... L. 1854.

Noble Author, A. *George Gordon Noël, Lord Byron.* Hours of idleness: a series of poems ... By ... L. 1822.

Noble Lord, A. *George Gordon Noël, Lord Byron.* Lines addressed to a noble lord. 1815.

Noble Lord and Eminent Lawyer, A. *J. Gore,* Baron Annaly. Cases argued and adjudged in the Court of King's Bench ... L. 1770.

Noble-man, A. *Ford, Lord Grey.* Love-letters between a noble-man and his sister [Henrietta, Countess of Berkeley]. (Letters signed "Philander" and "Silvia.") L. 1693. By Aphra Behn.

Nobleman, A. *John Hervey,* Lord Hervey of Ickworth. An epistle from ... to a Doctor of Divinity [Dr. Sherwin]. L. 1733.

Nobleman, A. *Oliver Goldsmith.* An history of England, in a series of letters from ... to his son. L. 1764.

Nobleman, A. *Edward Howard,* 8th Earl of Suffolk. Musarum deliciæ ... L. 1728.

Nobleman, A. *Robert Sanders.* Roman history ... L. 17–.

Noble-man abroad, A. *George Granville,* Lord Lansdowne. A letter to ... his friend in England. L. 1722.

Nobody. *Rev. James Cook Richmond.* No slur, else slur: a dancing poem, or satyr ... N.Y. 1840.

Nobody. *William Stevens.* Οὐδενός ἔργα. The works of Nobody. L. 179–.

Nobody. *James Robinson.* Poems,

consisting of tales, fables, epigrams, etc.,
by ... L. 1770.

Nobody, Nemo, Esq. *James Fennell.*
Something. Edited by ... B. 1810.

Nobody, Nothing of Nowheres.
Rev. James Alexander Young.

Nolands, Robert. *Robert William
Essington.* The legacy of an Etonian.
Edited by ... Camb. 1846.

Nomentino. *John McCosh, M.D.*
Nuova Italia: a poem. L. 1872.

Nomistake. *W. B. or W. P. Partee.*
Science of money. P. 187-.

Non Clericus. *James Cottle* (?).
Romanism in an Apostate Church ...
L. 1852.

Non-Combatant, A. *George Alfred
Townsend.* Campaigns of ... and his
romaunt abroad during the war. N.Y.
1866.

Non-Combatant, A. *Henry Jeffreys
Bushby.* A month in the camp before
Sebastopol. L. 1855.

Nonagenarian, A. *Richard Graves.*
The invalid: with the obvious means of
enjoying health and long life. By a ...
editor of the "Spiritual Quixote,"
"Columella," "Reveries of Solitude,"
etc. L. 1804.

Nonagenarian, A. *Mrs. Sarah Anna
(Smith) Emery.* Reminiscences of ...
Newburyport, 1879.

Noncathoni. *John Canton.* Electri-
cal properties of the tourmaline, in the
"Gent. Mag.," September, 1759, p. 424.

Noncommissioned Officer, A. *George
W. Driggs.* Opening of the Mississippi:
or, two years' campaigning in the South-
West ... Madison, Wis., 1864.

Non-Intrusionist, A. *Prof. George
Dunbar.* The Non-Intrusionists; their
principles, conduct, and their consequences. Edinb. 1842.

Non-juror, A. *Nathaniel Spinckes.*
No just grounds for introducing the new
Communion Office ... L. 1719.

Nonsence, Sir Gregory. *John Taylor,* the water-poet. Sir G. N., his newes
from no place. L. 1622.

Norb. *P. N. Myers,* a bicycler of
Covington, Ky.

Nore, Alfred de. *Le Marquis Adolphe
de Chesnel.* Coutumes, mythes, et traditions des provinces de France. Paris,
1846.

Norfolk Clergyman, A. *Rev. Samuel Hobson.* The nature and design of
the new poor laws explained ... Norwich, 1834.

Norlac, Jules. *Claude Antoine Jules
Cairon.* Les mémoires d'un baiser.
Paris, 1863.

Norman, Lucia. *Mrs. S. M. Heaven.*
Youth's history of California ... San
Fran. 1867.

Norna. *Mrs. Mary Elizabeth (Akin)
Brooks,* who from an early age was a
writer of verse for periodicals, under this
signature.

Norris, Dr. Robert. *Jonathan Swift,
D.D.* The narrative of ... concerning
the ... frenzy of Mr. John Dennis ...
L. 1713.
Also ascribed to Alex. Pope.

North, Christopher. *John Wilson.*
The critical and miscellaneous articles
of ... P. 1842. Under this pseudonym,
John Wilson edited "Blackwood's Magazine."

North, Danby. *Daniel Owen Madden.*
The Mildmayes; or, the clergyman's secret ... L. 1856.

North, W. Savage. *William S. Newell.*

North American, A. *John Dickinson.*
An address to the Committee of Correspondence in Barbados ... P. 1766.

North American, A. *Myles Cooper.*
The American querist ... N.Y. 1774.
*Also ascribed to Thomas Bradbury Chand-
ler, D.D.*

North-British Protestant, A. *Rev.
Archibald Bruce,* of Whitburn. The interest and claims of the Church and Nation of Scotland in the settlement of
religion in India ... Edinb. 1813.

North Briton, A. *William Burns.*
What's in a name? By ... Glasgow,
1861.

North Country Angler, A. *Thomas
Doubleday.* The Coquet-dale fishing
songs ... By ... Edinb. 1852.

Northamptonshire Poet, The. *John
Plummer.* Songs of labour, and Northamptonshire rambles. L. 1860.

Northamptonshire Rector, A. *Rev.
Granville Hamilton Forbes, A.B.* Village
sermons. By ... L. 1863.

Northelia. *Lord North.* The Coalition rencontre anticipated: a poetical
dialogue ... Dramatis personæ ... and
"Carlo Khan" [Charles James Fox]. L.
1785.

Northern Man, A. *Calvin Colton.*
Abolition a sedition, by ... N.Y. 1838.

Northern Man, A. *Charles Ingersoll
or Joseph Reed Ingersoll.* The diplomatic
year ... P. 1863.

Northern Man, A. *James Kirke
Paulding.* Letters from the South by
... N.Y. 1815.

Northern Man, A. *William Bradford
Reed.* Review of Mr. Seward's diplomacy, by ... P. 1862.

Northern Man with American

Principles, A. *Thomas Robinson Hazard.* A Constitutional manual for the National American party ... Providence, 1856.

Northern Presbyter, A. *Nathan Lord, D.D.* A letter of inquiry to ministers of the Gospel ... on slavery. B. 1854.

Norval. *James Scrymgeour.* The Ferns ... Dundee, 1867.

Norval. *E. H. Noyes.* Steamship notes ... N.Y. 1875.

Norwich Weaver-boy, A. *William Johnson Fox.* Letters of ... in the newspapers of the " Anti-Corn-Law League."

Nostrodamus, Merlin. *Miss Frances Power Cobbe.* The " Age of Science ": a newspaper of the twentieth century. By ... L. 1877.

Notelrac. *Fanny E. Carleton.* Operas: their writers and their plots. P. 1882.

Nothus, Cornelius Scriblerus. *Thomas Burgess,* Bishop of St. David's. Ode on the present state of English poetry ... By ... Oxf. 1779.

Also attributed to *Rev. Alexander Crowcher Schomberg, M.A.*

Notional, Nehemiah. *John Lovering,* in .the " Polyanthos," Boston, 1806–7.

Notitia Literaria. *Edward Tuckerman,* contributor of 54 papers under the title of " Adversaria " and ... " Notitia Literaria " to the " New York Churchman."

Nouel, Edmond. *Edmond de Manne.* La femme de chambre ... Paris, 1831.

Nourma, Cousin. *Dr. J. E. Nagle.*

Nova Scotian, A. *Miss Eliza Frame.* Descriptive sketches of Nova Scotia ... Halifax, 1864.

Nova Scotian, A. *C. B. Owen.* Epitome of the history, statistics, etc., of Nova Scotia ... Halifax, 1842.

Novalis. *Friedrich Ludwig von Hardenberg.* Heinrich von Ofterdingen. 1800.

Novanglus. *John Adams, LL.D.,* who wrote under this signature, in 1774, a series of effective papers in reply to " Massachusettensis."

Novelist, A. *Eliza Tabor.* Diary of ... L. 1871.

Novice, A. *Henry Victor.* The whimsical bachelor ; or, married at last : a comedy ... Written by ... who has never beheld the interior of the green room. Penzance, 1869.

Nox, Owen. *Charles B. Cory.* Southern rambles. Florida. By ... 188–.

Nugator. *St. Leger L. Carter.* Nugæ, by ... or, pieces in prose and verse. Balt. 1844.

Nuitter, C. L. E. *Charles Louis Étienne Truinet.* Les bavards ; Vert-Vert ; La princesse de Trebisonde.

Nullifier, A. *Dr. Thomas Cooper.* Memoirs of ... Columbia, S.C., 1832.

Numa. *Rowley Lascelles, Esq.* — See " Yorick."

Nun of Kenmare. *Mary Frances Cusack.* Advice to Irish girls in America. N.Y. 187–.

Nunnery, Fabricia, Spinster. *Peter Coxe.* Another word or two ; or, architectural hints, in lines to those Royal Academicians who are painters, addressed to them on their re-election of Benjamin West, Esq., to the president's chair, 10th December, 1806. By ... with notes, etc. L. 1807.

Nurse and Spy. *S. Emma E. Edmonds.* In the Union army, 1861–63. Hartford, 1865.

Nye, Bill. *E. W. Nye,* in his contributions to the " Free Press " (Detroit, Mich.), etc.

Nye, Columbus, pastor of a church in Bungtown Corner. *James Russell Lowell.*

O.

Ω. *Dr. J. Thirlby.* Miscellaneous observations on authors ancient and modern. L. 1731–32.

O. *Rev. Henry Coventry,* in his contributions to the " Athenian Letters " ... L. 1741–43.

O. *J. Moffatt.* The ferns of Moffat ... Moffat, 1863.

O., Jr. *Waterman L. Ormsby.* Cycloidal configurations ; or, the harvest of counterfeiters ... N.Y. Also in his contributions to the " New York Sun."

O. B. *Samuel Griswold Goodrich.*

Five letters to my neighbor Smith touching the Fifteen Gallon Jug ... B. 1838.

O., C. *Cæsar Otway.* Sketches in Ireland descriptive of interesting and hitherto unnoticed districts in the north and south of Ireland. By ... Dublin, 1827.

"Mr. Otway was a large contributor to the 'Dublin Christian Examiner' and the 'Dublin University Magazine'; the former, indeed, principally owed its fame to the articles signed 'C. O.'"

O. F. and A. K. *Judah Lee Bliss.* The triplet : Church, State, and Vassalage. "Tria juncta in uno." B. 1872.

Of these papers the first, signed "An Old Fogy" (of which O. F. is probably an abbreviation) will be found under this pseudonym; the second, likewise a reprint, under "Curtus Gallus." The concluding paper, "with some uni-lateral opinions and angular reflections," is signed "Democritus Junior."

O., G. E. *George Edmund Otis.* Thurid; and other poems. By... B. 1874.

O., H. U. *Henry Ustick Onderdonk, M.D.* Regeneration. By... n.p., n.d.

O., J. *John Oldmixon.* The life and posthumous works of Arthur Maynwaring, Esq.... L. 1715.

O., J. (Jacob Omnium). *Matthew James Higgins.* The story of the Mhow Court Martial. L. 1864.

O., J. C. *John Cardell Oliver.* Guide to Newquay and neighborhood, including Perran and Bedruthen Steps. By... Truro, 1872.

O. K. *Olga de Kiréef Novikoff,* in a series of letters in the Darlington "Northern Echo" and the London "Daily News"; in 1877 published in a collected form under the title of "Is Russia Wrong? by a Russian lady."

O. P. *William Maginn, LL.D.* "Chevy Chase: a poem, idem Latine redditum," in "Blackwood's Magazine." November, 1819.

O. P. Q. *Rev. Caleb Charles Colton,* who was at one time correspondent of the London "Morning Chronicle," under this signature.

O., S. G. *Rev. Lord Sydney Godolphin Osborne,* long known for his letters on social and philanthropic subjects, published under this signature in the London "Times."

O., W. *William Oldys.* A dissertation upon pamphlets... L. 1732.

O. W. *Rev. John Bridle,* of Hardwick. A letter to the Rev. Dr. Lowth, prebendary of Durham... L. 1758.

O——, W——, Esq. *William Owen.* A brief memoir of... L. 1841.

Oakes, A. H. *H. C. Bunner,* in New York "Puck."

Oakey, Miss. *Mrs. T. W. Deering.* Beauty in dress. N.Y. 188-.

Oakly. *David Garrick.* His signature to letters in the "St. James's Chronicle."

Oakum, John. *Walter P. Phillips.*

Oakwood, Oliver. *Stacy Gardner Potts.* Village tales... Trenton, 1827.

Oates, Felix. *George L. Catlin.*

Oberon. *Nathaniel Hawthorne.* — See "Royce, Ashley Allen."

Oberon. *Mrs. Mary Robinson.* Signature to poems published in the "Oracle."

Obiter Dictum. *James Anderson.* The union of the British North American provinces considered... Montreal, 1859.

O'Brien, Edward Stevenson. *Isaac Butt,* who was for some time editor of the "Dublin University Magazine," and contributed to it, under this signature, "Chapters of college romance," which were afterwards published separately.

Obscure Individual, An. *Aedanus Burke.* Observations upon a late pamphlet entitled "Considerations upon the Society or Order of the Cincinnati... P. 1783.

Observateur, Un. *L. H. Huot.* Le Rougisine en Canada... Quebec, 1864.

Observateur Résident sur les Lieux, Un. *Berquin DuVallon.* Vues de la colonie espagnole du Mississippi... Paris, 1803.

Observator. *Samuel Adams,* in the "Boston Gazette," Sept. 27, 1773.

Observator. *David Wells, Esq.,* in "Gent. Mag.," November, 1784, p. 814.

Observator. *Rev. John Evans, M.A.* Letters of... Whitchurch, Salop. 1837.

Observator, Charles. *Rev. Elijah Robinson Sabin.* The life and reflections of... B. 1816.

Observer. *Francis J. Grund,* in the Philadelphia "Ledger."

Observer, An. *Stedman Wright Hanks.* The Black Valley Railroad... An allegory, in "The Nation," etc. N.Y. 1865.

Observer, An. *Sir John James Rutlidge.* The Englishman's fortnight in Paris... L. 1777.

Observer, An. *J. McNaughton.* An enquiry into the present system of medical education, in the State of New York... Albany, 1830.

Observer, The General. *Nathan Fiske, S.T.D.,* who wrote essays for the "Massachusetts Spy," under the title of "The Worcester Speculator" and "A Neighbor;" and for the "Massachusetts Magazine" under that of "The General Observer."

Observer of the Times, An. *Alexander Shand.* An explanation of the interesting prophecy respecting the two apocalyptic Witnesses... L. 1817.

Obsolete Author, An. *James Kirke Paulding.* Odds and ends, in the New York "Literary World."

O'C., E. *E. O'Conor.* A grammar of the Gaelic language... Dublin, 1818.

O'C., E. M. *Eva M. O'Connor.* Analytical index to the works of Hawthorne. B. 1882.

O'Cataract, Jehu. *John Neal.* Battle of Niagara. A poem . . . Balt. 1818.

Occasional. *Col. Sanders D. Bruce,* in the New York "Turf, Field, & Farm."

Occasional. *John Weiss Forney,* in the Philadelphia "Press."

῎Οχος. *John Coglan.* The confessions of an Unfermented Wine Communicant . . . Edinb. 1877.

Ockside. *Mortimer M. Thompson.* History and records of the Elephant Club, by Doesticks and . . . N.Y. 1856.

Oconomowoc. *James A. Henshall,* who used this signature, while residing in Wisconsin, in contributing numerous articles to the press on the "Bass." Author of "Book of the black bass," 1881.

Octavia. *Mrs. Mary Alice (Ives) Seymour.* Christmas holidays at Cedar Grove. B. 1865.

Octogenarian, An. *James Roche.* Critical and miscellaneous essays, by . . . Cork, 1850–51.

Octogenarian, An. *John Mathew Gutch, Esq.* The Eagles of Bristol; father and son. "Gent. Mag.," February, 1856, p. 148.

Octogenarian, An. *Walter Savage Landor.* Hebrew lyrics . . . L. 1859.

Octogenarian, An. *Sir Brenton Halliburton, Knt.* Reflections on passing events: a poem . . . Halifax, 1856.

Octogenarian, An. *Richard Lower.* Stray leaves from an old tree: selections from the scribblings of . . . 1862.

Octogenarian Architect, An. *George L. Taylor.* The autobiography of . . . L. 1870–72.

Octogenarian Lady of Charleston, S.C., The. *Mrs. E. A. Poyas.* The olden time of Carolina . . . Charleston, 1855.

Octogenary. *Rev. Daniel Huntington.* Memories, counsels, and reflections . . . Camb. 1857.

Oculatus, Testis. *Rev. Richard Treffry.* The Chatham races: in three letters to a friend, by . . . Maidstone, 1824.

Odd Boy. *John Tillotson.* Palestine: its holy sites and sacred story. L. 1871, etc. Also contributions to "The Boys' Magazine" (L.).

Odd Fellow, An. *Peter M'Kenzie,* editor of the "Glasgow Gazette," *James Wallace,* of Glasgow, *Dr. James Brown* and *Robert Kay* of Dumbarton, *Joseph Souter* of Aberdeen, *Alexander M'Neill,* advocate, and *James Duncan,* a bookseller of Glasgow, were the joint authors of "Gotham in alarm: a farce in three acts" . . . 9th ed. Glasgow, 1816. Published under the above pseudonym.

Odds and Ends. *Walter C. Quevedo,* in the New York "Dispatch."

Oddy, J. Jephson. *William Playfair.* European Commerce. L. 1805.

"These two works (this of Oddy and the 'Spirit of the Bankrupt Laws,' of Joshua Montefiore) though published under the names of both gentlemen last mentioned, were written by *Mr. Playfair*." — "Gent. Mag," June, 1823.

Odman, Jeremiah. *D. H. Atkinson.* Old Leeds; its bygones and celebrities. By an Old Leeds Cropper. Leeds, 1868.

O'Doherty, Sir Morgan, Bart. *William Maginn.* Maxims of . . . Edinb. 1849. Was also a constant contributor to "Blackwood's Magazine" under this signature.

O'Donald, Peregrine. *William King, LL.D.* — See "Scheffer, Frederick."

O'Donnor, Andrew. *A. Fontaney.* Le Parlement anglais en 1835 . . . in the "Revue des Deux Mondes," 1835.

O'Dowd, Cornelius. *Charles James Lever.* Cornelius O'Dowd upon men and women and other things in general. Edinb. and L. 1864.

Reprinted from "Blackwood's Magazine."

Officer, An. *John Fitch.* Annals of the Army of the Cumberland . . . P. 1864.

Officer, An. *Capt. William Edward Montague.* Campaigning in South Africa. Reminiscences of . . . in 1879. Edinb. 1880.

Officer, An. *Dr. John Gordon Smith.* The English Army in France . . . L. 1830.

Officer, An. *Harry Austin.* Guards, hussars, and infantry . . . By . . . L. 1838.

Officer, An. *Lieut. Douglas.* A general essay on military tactics . . . trans. by . . . L. 1781.

Officer, An. *M. J. Home.* A letter . . . to his son in Parliament. L. 1776.

Officer, An. *Major Alexander Jardine.* Letters from Barbary, France, Spain, Portugal, etc. By . . . L. 1788.

Officer, An. *Sir Robert Ker Porter.* Letters from Portugal and Spain . . . L. 1809.

Officer, An. *Arent Schuyler Depeyster.* Miscellanies . . . Dumfries, 1813.

Officer, An. *Thomas Anbury.* Travels through the interior parts of America . . . By . . . L. 1789.

Officer employed in his Army, An. *John Fane,* 11th Earl of Westmoreland. Memoir of the early campaigns of the Duke of Wellington, in Portugal and Spain. By . . . L. 1820.

Officer employed on the Expedition, An. *William Smith.* An impartial narrative of the reduction of Belleisle . . . L. 1761.

Officer in His Majesty's service, An. *Robert Grenville Wallace.* Fifteen years in the Indies; or, sketches of a soldier's life ... by ... L. 1822.

Officer in the Army of Wolfe, An. *James Athearn Jones.* Memoirs of ... L. 1831.

Officer in the East India Company's Service, An. *James Kerr.* A short historical narrative of the rise and rapid advancement of the Mahratta State ... Translated by ... L. 1782.

Officer in the Field, An. *Charles P. Kirkland.* The coming contraband ... N.Y. 1862.

Also attributed to *Charles C. Nott.*

Officer in the Guards, An. *George Edward Ayscough.* Letters from ... to his friend in England, containing some accounts of France and Italy. L. 1778.

Officer in the Hon. E. I. Co.'s Bengal native infantry, in civil employ, An. *Major John Butler.* A sketch of Assam ... By ... L. 1847.

Officer in the Military and Civil Service of the Hon. East India Company, An. *Maj.-Gen. Sir William Henry Sleeman.* On taxes on public revenue ... By ... L. 1829.

Officer in the Service of the Hon. E. I. Co., An. *John Clunes.* An historical sketch of the princes of India ... Edinb. 1833.

Officer in the U. S. Army, A Late. *Jervase Cutler.* A topographical description of the State of Ohio, Indiana Territory and Louisiana ... B. 1812.

Officer of Colonel Baillie's Detachment, An. *William Thomson.* Memoirs of the late war in Asia ... L. 1788.

Officer of Rank, An. *Capt. William Nugent Glascock, R.N.* Naval sketch book; or, the service, afloat and ashore. L. 1826.

Officer of the Army, An. *Capt. Hall.* The history of the civil war in America. By ... L. 1780.

Officer of the Army, An. *Capt. Edwin D. Phillips.* Texas, and its military occupation and evacuation. By ... N.Y. 1862.

Officer of the Army at Detroit, An. *Henry Whiting.* Ontwa, the son of the forest. A poem, by ... N.Y. 1822.

Officer of the British Army, An. *Maj. Edward Drewe.* A letter to a young officer, written in the year 1776 ... N.Y. 1778.

Officer of the Chancery of the ... Order of St. Joachim, An. *Sir Levett Hanson.* An accurate historical account of all the orders of knighthood at present existing in Europe ... L. 1802.

Officer of the First Regiment of Ohio Volunteers, An. *L. Giddings.* Sketches of the campaign in Northern Mexico, in 1846–47 ... N.Y. 1853.

Officer of the Household Brigade of Cavalry, An. *Col. George Greenwood.* Hints on horsemanship ... L. 1839.

Officer of the Line, An. *John L. Gardner.* Military control; or, command and government of the army. Washington, 1839.

Officer of the Rear-Guard, An. *Edward M. Boykin.* The falling flag, evacuation of Richmond, retreat and surrender at Appomattox. By ... N.Y. 1874.

Officer of the Royal Engineers, An. *Charles Edmund Webber.* — See "W., C. E."

Officer of the Royal Navy, An. *John Matthews.* Twenty-one plans ... of different actions in the West Indies, during the late war. By ... Chester, 1784.

Officer of the United States Army, An. *Maj.-Gen. George C. Strong.* Cadet life at West Point ... B. 1862.

Officer of the United States Army, An. *Lieut. Richard Bache.* Notes on Colombia, taken in the years 1822–23, etc. ... P. 1827.

Officer of the United States Army, An. *James H. M'Culloh, Jr., M.D.* Researches in America ... Balt. 1816.

Officer of the United States Navy, An. *Horatio Bridge.* Journal of an African cruiser, 1843–44. N.Y. 1845.

Officer of the United States Navy, An. *William S. W. Ruschenberger.* Three years in the Pacific, by ... 1835.

Officer of this Establishment at Charlestown, An. *Gamaliel Bradford, Senior.* Some ... remarks and documents relating to the Massachusetts State Prison. By ... Charlestown, 1821.

Officer on the Staff, An. *Hon. Somerset John Gough Calthorpe.* Letters from headquarters; or, the realities of the war in the Crimea ... L. 1857.

Officer serving as Quarter-Master General. *De Lacy Evans.* Facts relating to the capture of Washington ... L. 1829.

Officer under that General, An. *Henry Adams Bullard.* The history of Don Francisco de Miranda's attempt to effect a revolution in South America ... B. 1808.

Officer who served in the Expedition, An. *Rev. George Robert Gleig.* A narrative of the campaigns of the British army at Washington and New Orleans ... 1814 and 1815. L. 1821.

Officer who served there. *William W. Ireland, M.D.* History of the siege of Delhi ... Edinb. 1861.

Officer's Wife, An. *Mrs. M. J. Carrington.* Ab-sa-ra-ka Home of the Crows ... P. 1868.

Officier Américain, Un. — See "An American Officer in the Service of France."

O'Gotham, Bob. *Robert H. Greely.*

O'Hannegan, Larry. *Lee O'Harris.*

O'Hara, Abel. *Michael Banim.* The "Abel O'Hara" of the O'Hara Family.

O'Hara Family, The. *John Banim.* The bit o' writin' and other tales. L. 1838.

Ohio Volunteer, An. *James Foster.* The capitulation; or, a history of the expedition conducted by William Hull, Brigadier-General of the North-Western army .. Chillicothe (O.), 1812.

O'Keefe, Cornelius. *Thomas Francis Meagher,* in his contributions to "Harper's Magazine" (N.Y.).

Oksaselta, A. *August Engelbrekt Alqvist.* Säkeniä [Sparks] ... 4th ed. Helsingfors, 1881.

In 1847, Prof. Alqvist, with some other young men, founded, at Helsingfors, "Suometar," a literary periodical, for which he wrote under the signature of "Oksanen."

O'Lanus, Corry. *John Stanton,* in his letters to the "Brooklyn Daily Eagle."

Old Acquaintance, An. *George McHenry.* A familiar epistle to Robert J. Walker ... From ... L. 1863.

Old Amateur, An. *Richard Edgcumbe,* 2d Earl of Mt. Edgcumbe. Musical reminiscences of ... L. 1827.

Old and Experienced Trader, An. *Alexander Cluny.* The American traveller; or, observations on the present state, culture, and commerce of the British colonies in America. By ... L. 1769.

Old Angler and Bibliopolist, An. *Thomas Boosey.* Piscatorial reminiscences and gleanings, by ... L. 1835.

Old Author, An. *J. Johnson.* The advantages and disadvantages of the marriage state ... from ... L. 1830.

Old Bachelor, An. *E. Carrington.* Confessions of ... 18–.

Old Bachelor, An. *George William Curtis.* Manners on the road, by ... in "Harper's Bazaar."

Old Bachelor, The. *William Wirt.* The old bachelor. Balt. 1818.

Old Bard, The. *Edward Jerningham.* The old bard's farewell: a poem. 2d ed. ... L. 1812.

Old Block. *Alonzo Delano.* Live woman in the mines: play. N.Y. 1857.

Old Bookseller, An. *William West.* Fifty years' recollections of ... with anecdotes, etc., of authors, artists, actors, books, booksellers, etc. L. 1837.

Old Bookworm, An. *William John Thoms.* Gossip of ... in the "Nineteenth Century," July, 1881.

Old Boomerang. *John Richard Houlding.* Australian capers; or, Christopher Cockle's colonial experience. L. 1867.

Old Boy. *Edward Leman Blanchard.* Children's pantomime. L. 186–.

Old Boy, An. *John W. Steel.* A sketch of the life and professional services of Isaac Sams ... a distinguished teacher ... [By Henry S. Doggett.] With some reminiscences by an old boy. Cin. 1880.

Old Boy, An. *Thomas Hughes.* Tom Brown's schooldays ... Camb. 1857.

Old Boy in Specs, The. *Matthew L. Davis,* thus familiarly known to politicians.

Old Burchell. *Elihu Burritt.* Old Burchell's pocket for the children. L. 1868.

Old Bushman, An. *Horace William Wheelwright.* Sporting sketches. Home and abroad. By ... L. 1866.

Old Cartman, An. *Isaac S. Lyon,* in his letters to the "Daily Journal" (Newark, N.J.), 1871.

Old Cayen. *Alexander Chalmers.* The dress of the ladies medicinally considered. "Gent. Mag.," October, 1802, p. 916.

Old Celt, An. *William Bottrell, Jr.* Traditions and hearthside stories of West Cornwall. Penzance, 1870.

Old Chalk. *Henry Chadwick,* in his contributions to "The Union" (Brooklyn, N.Y.).

Old Chatty Cheerful. *William Martin.* "The Boy's Own Annual." L. 1861.

Old Cheltonian, An. *Paul Ward.* Reminiscences of Cheltenham College. By ... L. 1868.

Old Cicerone of Elgin Cathedral, The. *John Shanks.* Elgin, and a guide to Elgin cathedral ... By ... L. 1866.

Old Citizen, An. *Col. William L. DeBeck.* Murder will out ... Cin. 1867.

Old Citizen, An. *Samuel Mordecai.* Richmond in by-gone days ... Richmond, Va., 1856.

Old Colonist, An. *George Wright.* Wattle blossoms: some of the grave and gay reminiscences of ... Melbourne, 1857.

Old Colony. *Rev. F. N. Zabriskie.* Golden fruit from Bible trees. N.Y. 1862.

Old Conservative, An. *John Gorham Palfrey.* Letter to a Whig neighbor on the approaching State election, by . . . B. 1855.

Old Cormorant, An. *Constance Burdett.* Flight of fancy, folly, and fun . . . L. and Edinb. 1878.

Old Cornish Boy, An. *Dr. Samuel Woolcock Christophers.* From out of the deeps. [A Cornish tale.] By . . . L. 1875.

Old Corporal. *Rev. Leander S. Coan,* of Alton, N.H., in miscellaneous dialect poems.

Old Correspondent, An. *Mr. Fox,* the second son of Lord Holland, in a communication to the "Public Advertiser" (October, 1771), which occasioned a reply from Junius, under the signature of "Anti-Fox" (*q.v.*).

Old Diplomatic Servant, An. *David Urquhart.* British diplomacy illustrated in the affair of the "Vixen." By . . . L. 1838.

Also ascribed to *H. H. Parish.*

Old Dissector, An. *James Browne.* The "Life" of the Ettrick Shepherd anatomized . . . Edinb. 1832.

Old Ebony. *William Blackwood,* in his contributions to "Blackwood's Magazine."

Old Etonian, An. *Bracebridge Hemyng.* Eton school days . . . L. 1864.

Old Farmer, An. *John Lowell, LL.D.* The road to peace, commerce, wealth, and happiness . . . B. 1813.

Old File, An. — See "Waverley."

Old Fogy, An. *Judah Lee Bliss.* On reform in general and prison reform in particular (N.Y. 1853); and Footprints of travel in France and Italy, with occasional divagations, by an old fogy. B. 1858.

The latter pamphlet is signed "Curtus Gallus." *Conf.* also "O. F. and A. K."

Old Friend, An. *Miss Jane Louisa Willyams.* The reason rendered. A few words addressed to the inhabitants of M[awgan], in Cornwall, by . . . L. 1847.

Old Friend and Servant of the Church, An. *William Jones, F.R.S.* A letter to the Church of England . . . L. 1798.

Old Friend of the Society for Promoting Christian Knowledge, An. *Rev. Edward Ward.* A letter on the subject of the British and Foreign Bible Society, addressed to Dr. Gaskin. By . . . L. 1810.

Also attributed to *William Ward, D.D.,* Preb. of Salisbury.

Old Gardener, An. *Edward Beck.* A packet of seeds saved by . . . L. 1861.

Old Georgia Lawyer, An. *Garnett Andrews.* Reminiscences of . . . Atlanta, Ga., 1870.

Old Hand on Board, An. *Arthur Benoni Evans, D.D.* Britain's wreck; or, breakers ahead . . . L. 1853.

Old Harlo. *Rev. Charles Edwards Abbott.*

Old Harrovian, An. *Douglas Straight.* Harrow recollections. L. 1867.

The preface is signed "Sidney Daryl."

Old Hickory. *Andrew Jackson.*

Old Humphrey. *George Mogridge.* Old Humphrey's walks in London and its neighborhood. L. 1843.

Old Inhabitant, An. *James Horsburgh,* provost of Pittenweem. A glance at the historical traditions of Pittenweem . . . Pittenweem, 1851.

Signed "J. H."

Old Inhabitant of British North America, An. *Sir Brenton Halliburton.* Observations on the importance of the North American colonies to Great Britain . . . Halifax, 1825.

Old Inspector of Schools, An. *Joseph Bentley.* Religious training for the people . . . L. 1862.

Old Itinerant, An. *Rev. Henry Smith.* Recollections and reflections of . . . N.Y. 18–.

Old Jonathan. *David Alfred Doudney, D.D.* Try and try again . . . L. 1864.

Old Knick. *Edward Dubois.* Old Knick's pocket book; or, hints for "a Rhyghte Pedantique and Manglynge" Publication to be called "My Pocket Book." By himself. L. 1808.

This and "My Pocket Book by a Knight Errant" were humorous attacks upon the "Tours" of Sir John Carr.

Old Lady, An. *Frank Cahill,* in his contributions to the "Saturday Press" (P.), etc.

Old Lady, An. *A. Dawson.* A guide to the musical tuition of very young children. By . . . L. 1868.

Old Lady in Threadneedle Street, The. The bank of England.

Old Leeds Cropper, An. *D. H. Atkinson.* — See "Odman, Jeremiah."

Old Maid, An. — See "Lounger, A," etc.

Old Maid, An. *Miss Phillips.* My life and what I shall do with it. By . . . L. 1864.

Old Man, An. *Josiah Quincy, Jr.,* in the "Boston Gazette," Aug. 6, 1770.

Old Man, An. *Sir Francis Bond*

Head, Bart. Bubbles from the Brunnen of Nassau ... L. 1833.

Old Man, An. *Richard Malcolm Johnston.* Georgia Sketches ... Augusta, Ga., 1864.

Old Man, An. *Joseph M. White* (?). The presidency [political essays, subscribed ... reprinted from the "Baltimore Chronicle"]. Balt. 1831.

Old Man, An. *Rev. Philip Skelton.* Senilia; or, an old man's miscellany. L. 1786.

Old Man, An. *Alexander Dalrymple.* Thoughts of ... of independent mind though dependent fortune. L. 1800.

Old Man, The. *Samuel West, S.T.D.* Essays of the Old Man, in the "Columbian Centinel," 1806–7.

Old Man Eloquent, The. *John Quincy Adams.*

Old Man of Business, An. *Charles Lloyd.* An examination of the principles and boasted disinterestedness of a late Right Honourable Gentleman [W. Pitt, Earl of Chatham]. In a letter from ... to a noble lord. L. 1766.

Old Man of the Mountain, The. *Nathaniel Peabody Rogers,* some of whose most popular pieces were published in the New York "Tribune" under this signature.

Old Man well-known on the Derbyshire streams a century ago, An. *W. H. Aldam.* A quaint treatise on "Flees and the art a' artyficiall flee making," by ... L. 1876.

Old Mariner, An. *Mrs. Mary Cowden Clarke.* Kit Bam's adventures; or, the yarns of ... L. 1849.

Old Member of Parliament, An. *Richard Glover.* An appeal to the justice and interests of the people of Great Britain in the present dispute with America. By ... L. 1776.

Also ascribed to *Arthur Lee, Lord Chatham,* and *Dr. Franklin.*

Old Member of Parliament, An. *Sir Richard Hill.* Remarks on a charge delivered by the Right Reverend the Lord Bishop of London ... in May and June, 1803 ... By ... L. 1804.

Old Member of the Society, An. *John Annesley Colet.* A letter to the Rev. Thomas Coke, LL.D., and Mr. Henry More ... to which is added an appeal and remonstrance to the people called Methodists. L. 1792.

Old Merchant, An. *Hon. John Nesmith.* Thoughts on the currency ... Lowell, 1866.

Old Merry. *Edmund Hodder.* Bookstall boy of Batherton. B. 1873.

Old Mountaineer, An. *J. P. Scribner* (?). Laconia; or, legends of the White Mountains ... B. 1856.

Old New Yorker, An. *William Alexander Duer, LL.D.* Reminiscences of ... N.Y. 1867.

Old Nick. *Paul Émile Daurand Forgues.* La Chine ouverte: aventures d'un Fan-kouei dans le pays de Tsin ... Paris, 1845.

Old Noll. *Jules Barbey d'Aurevilly,* who, under this signature, first published in the "Nain Jaune" the portraits afterwards collected under the title of "Quarante médaillons de l'Academie." Paris, 1864.

Old Officer, An. *Rev. Philip Skelton.* A letter to the authors of "Divine Analogy and the Minute Philosopher," from ... L. 1744.

Old, Old Bachelor, An. *Nathan Stone Reed Beal.* Diamond leaves from the lives of the Dimond family, etc. By ... Macedon, N.Y., 1872.

Old Paris Man, An. *William Makepeace Thackeray.* "Paris revisited," "Punch," 1849.

Old Parishioner, An. *Mrs. H. Madden.* Personal recollections of ... Robert Daly, late Bishop of Cashel, at Powerscourt and Waterford. By ... Dublin, 1872.

Old Parochial Clergyman, An. *Rev. Dr. John Duncan* (?). The libertine led to reflection by calm expostulation ... By ... L. 1794.

Old Pioneer, An. *John Mason Peck, D.D.* "Father Clark"; or, the pioneer preacher ... N.Y. 1855.

Old Planter, An. *Lieut. Gordon Turnbull.* Letters to a young planter ... n.p. 1785.

Old Pop. *Thomas Popplewell,* a celebrated singer of Covent Garden, well known to the choice spirits of London, the latter part of the last century, for his scientific skill and the comic fashion with which he sung his songs.

Old Prob. *Albert J. Myers.* Manual of signals for U. S. army and navy. 1868.

Old Reporter, An. *Walter Henry Watts.* My private note book; or, recollections of ... L. 1862.

Old Republican, An. *Rev. Joseph Lyman,* in the "Hampshire Gazette" (Northampton, Mass.), who wrote a series of articles in that paper, in 1786, against Shay's Rebellion.

Old Resident, An. *Andrew Burke.* Burke's guide; or, the visitor's companion to Niagara Falls ... Buffalo, 1850.

Old Resident in the Parish of Staverton, An. *Charles Wildegoose.* A short and plain address to his cottage neighbors. By ... Daventry, 1840.

Old Rugbæan, An. *R. N. Hutton.* Recollections of Rugby ... L. 1848.

Old Sailor, An. *Nathaniel Ames.* An old sailor's yarns. N.Y. 1835.

Old Sailor, An. *Isaac Carter.* On Quakerism ... By ... L. 1800.

Old Sailor, The. *Roland F. Coffin.* Archibald the cat, and other sea yarns. N.Y. 1878.

Compiled from Mr. Coffin's tales in the "World" (N.Y.), to which he was a frequent contributor under the same pseudonym.

Old Sailor, The. *Frederick Chamier.* Topsail sheet blocks; or, the naval foundling. L. 1838.

Old Sailor, The. *Matthew Henry Barker, R.N.* Tough Yarns. L. 1852. Greenwich hospital: a series of naval sketches, descriptive of the life of a man-of-war's man (L. 1826), by the same author, was published under the pseudonym of "An Old Sailor."

Old Scout. *H. R. Merrill.*

Old Seaman, An. *Admiral William Swiney.* Causes of the numerous shipwrecks on the Scilly Islands ... in the "Literary Panorama," 1817.

Old Servant, An. *George Heathcote.* A letter to the Right Hon. the Lord Mayor, the Worshipful Aldermen, and the Common Council, the merchants, citizens, and inhabitants of the city of London. From ... L. 1762.

Old Shekarry, The. *Henry A. Leveson.* Wrinkles; or, hints to sportsmen and travellers on dress, equipment, and camp life. By ... L. 1874.

Old Si. *Samuel W. Small,* formerly editor of the "Atlanta (Ga.) Constitution," in his contributions to various periodicals.

Old Simon. *Alexander Chalmers.* The present state of our current monies. "Gent. Mag.," September, 1802, p. 809.

Old Slyboots. *James Scott, D.D.,* who, in 1769 *et seq.,* wrote essays under this signature which were afterwards collected and published in a small volume.

Old Smoker, An. *John Stock, LL.D.* Confessions of ... L. 1872.

Old Smoker, An. *James Parton.* Does it pay to smoke, by ... B. 1868.

Old Soldier, An. *General Sir George Bell.*

Old Soldier, An. *Major Edward Moor.* The gentle sponge; being a safe ... and just mode of reducing ... the national debt of England ... By ... L. 1829.

Old Soldier, An. *Gen. John Armstrong.* Hints to young generals ... Kingston, 1812.

Old Soldier, An. *Capt. David Perry.* Recollections of ... Windsor, Vt., 1822.

Old South. *Benjamin Austin.* Constitutional Republicanism in opposition to Federalism ... B. 1803.

Benjamin Austin was long known as a writer in the "Independent Chronicle," Boston, under the signatures of "Honestus" and "Old South."

Old Stager, An. *Munsell B. Field.*

Old Stager, An. *James Aspinall.* Liverpool a few years since, by ... Liverpool, 1869.

Old Statesman, An old. *David Williams.* Lessons to a young prince by ... Dublin, 1791.

Old Straws. *Joseph M. Field,* in his contributions to the "Picayune" (New Orleans).

Old Student, An. *Daniel Dana, Jr.* (?). Baptology. My bootmaker and I on modes of baptism. N.Y. 1860.

Old Style, Oliver. *Dr. James Beattie,* in the "Aberdeen Journal," 1768.

"On the first publication of the poem [Ross's 'Helenore; or, the Fortunate Shepherdess'], a letter highly laudatory of it appeared in the 'Aberdeen Journal' under the fictitious signature of 'Oliver Old Style,' accompanied by an epistle in verse to the author from the pen, it is understood, of *Dr. Beattie,* being the latter's only attempt in the Scots' vernacular."—See ANDERSON's *The Scottish Nation,* Vol. 3, p. 370.

Old Teacher, An. *George Barrell Emerson.* Reminiscences of ... B. 1878.

First published in the "Journal of Education," and then in book form with the author's name.

Old Teacher, An. *Mrs. Margaret Hosmer.* A year in Sunday school. From the journal of ... By ... P. 1869.

Old Times. *James D. Davis.* Old times papers. Memphis, 1873.

These papers were first published in the "Memphis Daily Appeal" over this signature.

Old Townsman, An. *James Bisset.* Comic strictures on Birmingham's "Fine arts and converzationes," by ... Leamington (?), 1829.

Old Tradesman, An. *Benjamin Franklin.* Advice to a young tradesman. P. 1748.

Old Tradesman, An. *Thomas Bailey.* Recreations in retirement. L. 1836.

Old Traveller, An. *Henry Llewellyn Williams.* Gay life in New York. By ... N.Y. 1866.

Old Traveller, An. *Thomas Brown.* Reminiscences of . . . throughout different parts of Europe. Edinb. 1840.

Old 'Un, The. *Francis Alexander Durivage*, in his contributions to the "Turf, Field, and Farm" (N.Y.), etc. He is also the author of "Stray subjects arrested and bound over, being the fugitive offspring of the 'Old Un' and the 'Young Un' (*q.v.*), that have been 'lying round loose,' and are now 'tied up' for fast keeping." P. 1848.

Old Unitarian, An. *Thomas Sanden.* Unitarianism, old and new exemplified . . . in three letters [the first and third by "An Old Unitarian," the second by W. J. Fox] . . . With a preface by . . . Chichester, 1817.

Old Vicar, An. *Rev. John Wood Warter.* The sea-board and the down; or, my parish in the South, by . . . L. 1860.

Old Vicar, The. *John Samuel Bewley Monsell, LL.D.* Lights and shadows; or, double acrostics . . . L. 1870.

Old Whig, The. *Joseph Addison.* "Steele endeavoured to alarm the nation by a pamphlet called 'The Plebeian'; to this an answer was published by *Addison*, under the title of 'The Old Whig.'"

Old Yorkshire Turfman, An. *Henry William Herbert.*

Oldacre, Cedric, of Sax-Normanbury. *Rev. John Wood Warter.* The last of the old squires: a sketch. L. 1854.

Oldbuck, Obadiah. *Rodolphe Töpffer* (?). Mishaps and adventures of . . . N.Y. 187-.

Oldbug, John, Esq. *Leonard Withington, D.D.* The puritan: a series of essays . . . B. 1836.

Oldcastle, Humphrey. *Henry St. John*, Viscount Bolingbroke. Remarks on the history of England. From the minutes of . . . L. 1743.

Oldest Inhabitant, The. *Mrs. Julia Mayo Cabell.* Sketches and recollections of Lynchburg, Va. By . . . Richmond, Va., 1858.

Oldest School Inspector, The. *Joseph Bentley.* The best uninspired book for teaching children how to become "well off" in this world, and happy in the next. L. 1864.

Oldfellow, Polywarp, M.D. *Charles Smart, M.D.* Driven from the path . . . N.Y. 1873.

Oldfield, Traverse. *Rev. George Whitefield Samson.* To daimonion; or, spiritual medium . . . B. 1852.

Oldham, Dr., at Greystones. *Caleb*

Sprague Henry, D.D. Dr. Oldham at Greystones, and his talk there. N.Y. 1860.

Oldpath, Obadiah. *James Robinson Newhall.* Liñ; or, jewels of the third plantation . . . Lynn, 1862.

Oldschool, Oliver. *Joseph Dennie.* The poetry of the portfolio . . . P. 1818.

Oldschool, Oliver. *Nathan Sargent.* Public men and events, 1817-53. P. 1875.

Oldstyle, Jonathan, Gent. *Washington Irving.* Letters on the drama. N.Y. 1802. [First published in the N.Y. "Daily Chronicle."]

Oldys, Francis, of the University of Pennsylvania. *George Chalmers.* Life of Thomas Paine. L. 1791-92. *Conf.* Sabin, "Bibliotheca Americana," No. 11,763, note.

Oleander. *David M'Culloch.* Darkness and sunshine. Glasgow, 1876.

Olim Oxoniensis. *George Wilmot.* A letter to ******* *****, M.D. . . . L. 1752.

O'Lincoln, Robert. *George C. Mason.* George Ready; or, how to live for others . . . N.Y. 1857.

Olive-Branch, Rev. Simon. *William Roberts.* The looker-on: a periodical paper . . . L. 1795.

Oliver, Nathan, Esq. *Robert Blakey, Ph.D.* A few remarkable events in the life of the Rev. Josiah Thomson, a Secession minister . . . L. 1836.

Oliver, Stephen, the younger, of Aldwark, in Com. Ebor. *William Andrew Chatto.* Scenes and recollections of fly fishing, in Northumberland, Cumberland, and Westmoreland. L. 1834.

Oliver, William Pynchon. *Peter Oliver.* His signature in the N.Y. "Church Review."

Olivia. *Emily Edson Briggs*, in her contributions to periodical literature.

Olivia. *Olivia Wilmot Serres.* Olivia's letters of advice to her daughters. L. 1806.

Ollapod. *Willis Gaylord Clark*, who contributed "Ollapodiana" to the "Knickerbocker Magazine" (N.Y.).

Ollapod. *Thomas A. Edwards*, editor of cycling column in the "Melbourne Bulletin" (Australia); also in his contributions to "Springfield Wheelmen's Gazette" and "Outing" (B.).

Olla Podrida. *Frank M. Pixley*, who, since 1877, has contributed sketches, under this pseudonym, to the San Francisco

"Argonaut"; is also editor of the same.

Omega. *Rev. Dr. Blackburn,* President of the Presbyterian College, Danville. — See "Omikron."

Omicron. *Rev. John Otho West, M.A.* Church reform . . . By . . . L. 1871.

Omicron, Mr., "the Unborn Poet." *John Oldmixon,* who was ridiculed in the "Tatler," under this name.

Omikron. *Francis Patrick Kenrick,* who, in 1828, wrote a series of articles in an ironical vein to the Rev. Dr. Blackburn, who had opposed his church on the subject of the Eucharist, in a number of articles signed "Omega," entitled, "Letters of Omikron to Omega."

Omnium, Jacob. *Matthew James Higgins.* Letters on military education. L. 1856.

Omnivagant. *Rufus Wyman, M.D.,* in the "Polyanthos" (B. 1806–7).

Ompax, Konx. *Richard Whately.* Historic doubts relative to Napoleon Buonaparte . . . Cambridge, U.S., 1832. This is given in the Brit. Mus. Catalogue.

O'N., D. *Daniel O'Neill,* in the Pittsburg "Dispatch."

On-the-go. *Francis Alfred Steimer.*

One formerly possessed of the Place. *Willoughby Lacy.* The Garden of Isleworth: a sketch . . . by . . . L. 1794.

One from the Plough. *G. Mitchell,* in the London "Times."

One not of the Association. *Theodore Parker.* Answers to questions contained in Mr. Parker's letter to the Boston Association. B. 1845.

One of a Literary Family. *Mrs. Anna Letitia (Aikin) Le Breton.* Memories of seventy years, by . . . L. 1883.

One of her Ladies. *Lady Frances Erskine.* Memoirs relating to the Queen of Bohemia. About 1772.

One of her Majesty's Surgeons. *James Handley.* Colloquia chirurgica . . . L. 1705. The preface and dedication are signed "J. H."

One of her Sisters. *Miss R. Bolton.* The lighted valley; or, the closing scenes of the life of a beloved sister [Abby Bolton]. N.Y. 1850.

One of her Sons. *Alfred Owen Legge.* A life of consecration. Memorials of Mrs. Mary Legge. By . . . L. 1883.

One of her Sons. *Jacob Abbot.* New England and her institutions. B. 1835.

One of His Children. *Mrs. M. E. (Harding) White.* My egotistigraphy. By Chester Harding. Prepared for his family and friends. By . . . Camb. 1866.

One of his Constituents. *Henry Drummond, Esq.* Cheap corn best for farmers, proved in a letter to G. H. Sumner, Esq., M. P. for Surrey. By . . . L. 1826.

One of his Constituents. *Henry Boase.* A letter to Sir Richard R. Vyvyan, Bart. . . . Penzance, 1826.

One of his Constituents. *Rev. Edward Copleston,* Bishop of Llandaff. A letter to the Right Hon. Robert Peel . . . 2d ed. Oxf. 1819.

One of his Constituents, and a Magistrate of the County of Surrey. *John Ivatt Briscoe.* A letter on the nature and effects of the tread-wheel . . . addressed to the Right Hon. Robert Peel . . . L. 1824.

One of his Countrymen. *Caleb Cushing.* A reply to the letter of J. Fenimore Cooper . . . B. 1834.

One of his Descendants. *Lorenzo D. Johnson.* A Boston merchant of 1745; or, incidents in the life of James Gibson . . . B. 1847.

One of His Majesty's Chaplains. *Rev. Arthur Philip Perceval.* A letter to the Right Honourable Earl Grey, on the obligation of the coronation oath. L. 1833.

One of His Majesty's Justices of the Peace. *W. Wilshere* or *Samuel Parr, LL.D.* Considerations on the Poor Laws . . . By . . . 1817.

One of his Majesty's Justices of the Peace. *Robert Owen.* A new view of society . . . 1813.

One of H. M.'s Justices of the Peace for the County of Somerset. *Rev. John Langhorne.* The country justice: a poem. By . . . L. 1774–77.

One of H. M.'s Justices of the Peace for the Three Inland Counties. *John Weyland, Esq.* A short inquiry into the policy, humanity, etc., of the Poor Laws. By . . . L. 1807.

One of His Majesty's Servants. *Rev. Arthur Philip Perceval.* A letter to Earl Grey . . . L. 1832.

One of his Sons. *F. H. West.* Memorial sketch of . . . Francis Athon West. By . . . L. 1873.

One of its Members. *Edward Ash, M.D.* Reasons for objecting to the republication and circulation of Barclay's Apology, addressed to the Society of Friends, by . . . L. 1849.

One of No Party. *James Grant.* Random recollections of the House of Commons. L. 1856.

One of Our Club. *Rev. Richard Farquhar Wise.* Clerical papers. By . . . L. 1861.

One of ourselves. *Richard Marrack,* assisted by *Rev. E. G. Harvey.* How we did them in seventeen days! To wit, Belgium, the Rhine, Switzerland, and France, described and illustrated by ... aided, assisted, and abetted by the other. Truro, 187-.

One of Plutarch's Men. *Samuel Adams.* "Samuel Adams," said a distinguished divine, "was one of Plutarch's men. Modern times have produced no character like his that I can call to mind."

One of·the Alumni. *John Inglis, D.D.* Memoranda respecting King's College at Windsor, Nova Scotia... L. 1836.

One of the Authors of "Rejected Addresses." *Horace Smith.* Gaieties and gravities : a series of essays, comic tales, and fugitive vagaries. By ... L. 1826.

One of the Barbarous Blockheads of the Lowest Mob. *William Pettman.* A letter to Robert Heron, Esq., containing a few brief remarks on his Letters of Literature ... L. 1786.

One of the Barclays. *Mrs. Harrison Gray Otis.* The Barclays of Boston. B. 1854.

One of the Bible Readers. *Miss Sarah Start.* Extracts from the report of ... in the mission of the Church of the Ascension. n.p. 1864.

One of the Board of Managers. *William Richards Lawrence, M.D.* A history of the Boston Dispensary. Compiled by ... B. 1859.

One of the Boys. *Percy Hetherington Fitzgerald.* School days at Saxonhurst. By ... L. 1869.

One of the Churchwardens. *Charles Westerton.* A letter to ... the Lord Bishop of London ... L. 1853.

One of the Commissioners. *Sir Charles Edward Grey.* Remarks on the proceedings as to Canada in the present session of Parliament ... L. 1837.

One of the Company. *Miss A. Fletcher.* Within Fort Sumter; or, a view of Major Anderson's garrison family for one hundred and ten days. By ... N.Y. 1861.

One of the Convention. *Harrison Gray Otis.* Letters developing the character and views of the Hartford Convention ... W. 1820.

One of the Country Party. *Rev. James Webster.* A letter ... to his friend of the Court Party. n.p. 1704.

One of the Craft. *Cornelius Moore, A.M.* Masonic biography ... Cin. 1862.

One of the Crew. *John Bolton.* Account of the loss of the [American] ship "Omartal" [on "The Banks"]. By ... n.p. 1860 (?).

One of the Crowd. — *Greenwood.* Signature to papers in the "Telegraph" (L.).

One of the Defeated. *Frederick Hallard.* The catalogue question in the Advocates' Library ... Edinb. 1872.

One of the Directors. *Nathan Matthews.* An address to the stockholders of the Winnisimmet Company, by ... B. 1852.

One of the Editors of the New York Mirror. *Theodore Sedgwick Fay.* Dreams and reveries of a quiet man ... N.Y. 1832.

One of the "Eighteen Millions of Bores." *Elizur Wright.* Perforations in the "Latter-Day Pamphlets." By ... Edited [written] by ... B. 1850.

One of the 80,000 incorrigible Jacobins. *Sir John Colman Rashleigh, Bart.* The case of the people of England addressed to the "Lives and fortune men" both in and out of the House of Commons as a ground of national thanksgiving. By ... L. 1798.

One of the Family. *R. Channing M. Page.* Genealogy of the Page family in Virginia ... N.Y. 1883.

One of the Fancy. *Thomas Moore.* Tom Crib: his memorial to Congress, with a preface ... by one of the fancy. 4th ed. L. 1819.

One of the Firm. *Anthony Trollope.* The struggles of Brown, Jones, and Robinson. L. 1870.

One of the Fools. *Albion Winegar Tourgée.* A fool's errand ... N.Y. 1880.

One of the Fraternity. *Capt. William Morgan.* Illustrations of Masonry ... N.Y. 1826.

One of the Idle Classes. *William Thompson.* Labor rewarded ... L. 1827.

One of the Inspectors of the Prison. *Thomas Eddy.* An account of the state prison, or penitentiary house, in the city of New York. By ... N.Y. 1801.

One of the Jurymen. *Philip Thicknesse.* An account of the four persons found starved to death at D(atchworth) in Hertfordshire. L. 1769.

One of the Laity. *Miss Hannah More.* An estimate of the religion of the fashionable world ... L. 1791.

One of the Laity of the Church of

England. *Rev. Thomas Newenham.* The family scripture reader ... L. n.d.

The dedication is signed " T****s N******m."

One of the Memorialists. *William Augustus Muhlenberg.* An exposition of the memorial of sundry Presbyters of the Protestant Episcopal Church ... N.Y. 1854.

One of the Million. *J. E. Grey.* Decimal coinage ... L. 1854.

One of the Ministers in Boston. *Cotton Mather.* A good character ... B. 1723.

One of the Ministers of Edinburgh. *Rev. John Inglis.* An examination of Mr. Dugald Stewart's pamphlet ... Edinb. 1806.

One of the Ministers of this Present Church. *Rev. G. Hamilton.* Just reflections upon a pamphlet entitled " A modest reply to a letter from a friend of Mr. John M'millan ... ." n.p. 1712.

One of the Old School. *William West.* Tavern anecdotes ... By ... L. 1825.

One of the Party. *F. Taylor.* Ella V—; or, the July Tour. N.Y. 1841.

One of the Party. *Miss E. Tuckett.* How we spent the summer; or, a "Voyage en Zigzag" in Switzerland and Tyrol, with some members of the Alpine Club: from the sketch book of one of the party. L. 1864.

One of the Party. *William H. Young.* Journal of an excursion from Troy, N.Y., to Gen. Carr's headquarters ... Troy, N.Y., 1871.

One of the People. *William Hussey.* An appeal to the plain sense and calm judgment of the people ... L. 1829.

One of the People. *Abraham Lansing.* Brief remarks ... March 11, 1837 ... touching the nomination of a candidate for the Boston collectorship. B. 1837.

One of the People. *Churchill C. Cambreling.* An examination of the new tariff proposed by the Hon. Henry Baldwin, a member of Congress ... N.Y. 1821.

One of the People. *Dr. William Glover.* Letter to Her Most Gracious Majesty the Queen, upon the Papal question ... Edinb. 1851.

One of the People. *Hon. Tristram Burges.* Reasons why the Hon. Elisha R. Potter should not be a senator in Congress ... Providence, 1834.

One of the People called Christians. *George Horne.* A letter to Adam Smith, LL.D., on the life, death, and philosophy of his friend, David Hume, Esq. By ... Oxf. 1777.

One of the People called Quakers. *Daniel Defoe.* A friendly rebuke to one Parson Benjamin ... L. 1719.

One of the People called Quakers. *Joseph Besse.* A letter to Stephen Clarke, rector of Burythorpe, in Yorkshire ... By ... L. 1740.

One of the Raiders. *G. W. Atkinson.* After the moonshiners. Wheeling, W. Va., 1881.

One of the Rhode Island People. *John Pitman.* A reply to the letter of the Hon. Marcus Morton, late Governor of Massachusetts, on the Rhode Island question. Providence, 1842.

One of the Scotch People. *Hugh Miller.* A letter from ... to Lord Brougham. Edinb. 1843.

One of the Seventeenth. *Thomas Kirwan.* Soldiering in North Carolina ... B. 1864.

One of the Sons of the Clergy. *Julius Brockman Backhouse.* The Second Advent; the Seventh Vial; and the First Resurrection. By ... Deal, 1865.

One of the Special Constables in London. *Arthur Helps.* A letter ... on the late occasion of their being called out to keep the peace. L. 1848.

One of the Working Clergy. *Bishop Charles James Blomfield.* A remonstrance addressed to Henry Brougham, by ... L. 1823.

One of their Number. *Cotton Mather.* The minister: a sermon ... B. 1722.

One of their own Order. *R. W. Smiles.* The education question: an appeal to the Evangelical Dissenting laity. Manchester, 185–.

One of them. *Emily Peart.* A book for governesses. Edinb. 1869.

One of them. *Mrs. Cornelia C. (Joy) Dyer.* A brief history of the Joy family. By ... N.Y. 1876.

One of them. *Mrs. W. H. White.* Some women of to-day ... N.Y. 1880.

One of themselves. *Henry Mudge, M.R.C.S., and L.A.C.* Alcoholics: a letter to practitioners in medicine. By ... L. 1856.

One of themselves. *John Fielder Mackarness, M.A.* A few words to the country pastors touching the election for the Univ. of Oxford ... L. 1847.

One of themselves. *Charlotte Montefiore.* A few words to the Jews ... L. 1853.

One of themselves. *Robert Michael Ballantyne.* How not to do it. A manual for the awkward squad ... Edinb. 1859.

One of themselves. *C. Penrhyn Aston.* A letter to the working men of England, from ... L. 1866.

One of themselves. *Theodore Compton.* A letter to the young men of the Society of Friends. By ... L. 1840.

One of themselves. *William Makepeace Thackeray.* "The snobs of England." "Punch," 1846.

One of us. *Edward Gandy.* Moods and tenses ... L. 1827.

One Unconcerned. *Rev. William Daddo, A.M.* The Tiverton woolcombers' defence. By ... but a friend to liberty. L. 1750.

One under a Hood. *John Major.* Poetical description of Bartholomew Fair. L. 1837.

Also ascribed to *Thomas Hood.*

One very near a Kin to the Author of the Tale of a Tub. *John Oldmixon.* The history of addresses. L. 1709.

One who has a Tear for Others, as well as himself. *Rev. A. Currie,* of Abercorn. God's bottle for believers' tears. Edinb. 1854.

One who has been there. *James Delavan* (?). Notes on California and the placers ... N.Y. 1850.

One who has done it and can do it again. *Francis Cowley Burnand.* How to get out of Newgate. By ... L.

One who has never quitted him for fifteen years. *Charles Doris.* Secret memoirs of Napoleon Bonaparte. 1815.

One who has recently crossed. *J. W. Carrington.* The passage of the Isthmus; or, practical hints to persons about to cross the Isthmus of Panama. N.Y. 1849.

One who has Seen and Describes. *Charles Frederick Henningsen.* Revelations of Russia; or, the Emperor Nicholas and his empire, in 1844. L. 1844.

One who has seen them. *A. R. Middletoun Payne.* Rambles in Brazil; or, a peep at the Aztecs ... N.Y. 1854.

One who has stood behind the Counter. *David Pae.* George Sandford; or, the draper's assistant. Edinb. 1853.

One who has served under the Marquis of Dalhousie. *Charles Allen.* A few words anent the "Red" Pamphlet [by Colonel G. B. Malleson] ... By ... L. 1858.

One who has served under Sir Charles Napier. Probably *Henry Charles Bunbury.* The mutiny of the Bengal army ... L. 1857.

One who has whistled at the Plough. *Alexander Somerville.* The autobiography of a working man (L. 1848), reprinted from the "Manchester Examiner."

The author employed the signature "The Whistler" in the newspapers to which he contributed.

One who is also an Elder. *Rev. Richard Mant,* Bishop of Down and Connor. A letter to the Rev. Henry Hart Milman ... Oxf. 1830.

One who is but an Attorney. *George Butt.* A peep at the Wiltshire assizes: a serio-ludicrous poem. By ... Salisbury, 1819.

One who is neither Jacobite nor Republican, Presbyterian nor Papist. *Zachary Grey.* A letter of thanks to Mr. Benja. Bennet ... L. 1723.

One who is not a Doctor of the Sorbonne. *John Louis De Lolme.* History of the flagellants; or, memorials of human superstition ... By ... L 1783.

One who is really an Englishman. *C. W. Smith.* Letters published in the "Sun" by C. W. S. ... L. 1853.

One who keeps his eyes and ears open. *Henry Ward Beecher.* Thoughts as they occur; by ... A series of papers in the "New York Ledger," afterwards published in Boston, 1862, with the title "Eyes and ears."

One who knew him many years *Charles Deane.* A brief memoir of Robert Waterson, a Boston merchant .. B. 1869.

"One who knew him well." *Richard Green Parker.* A tribute to the life and character of Jonas Chickering ... B 1854.

One who Knows. *Arnold Foster,* in a pamphlet attack on the Irish Land League, 1882.

One who Knows. *W. A. Coffey.* Inside out; or, an interior view of the New York State prison ... N.Y. 1823.

One who knows. *Charles James Wahab.* Workman! What of your house? ... By ... Edinb. 1867.

One who Knows it. *Hardwick Shute, M.A.* Cuddesdon College. 1858.

One who Knows them. *Thomas L. V. Wilson* (?). The aristocracy of Boston ... being a history of the business and business men of Boston for the last forty years ... B. 1848.

One who Loves the Souls of the Lambs of Christ's Flock. *Rev. Richard Marks.* English history for children ... L. 1832–33.

"One who was thar." *B. F. Scribner.* A campaign in Mexico, by . . . P. 1850.

One who Went to It. *Rev. Warren Burton.* The district school as it was . . . N.Y. 1838.

One who wishes well to all Mankind. *Charles Chauncy, D.D.* Divine glory brought to view in the final salvation of all men . . . By . . . B. 1783.

One who wishes well to the whole Human Race. *Charles Chauncy, D.D.* The mystery hid from ages and generations made manifest by the Gospel Revelation; or, the salvation of all men the grand thing aimed at in the scheme of God, as opened in the New Testament writings and entrusted with Jesus Christ to bring into effect. In three chapters. By . . . L. 1784.

O'Neddy, Philothée. *Auguste Marie Dondey,* called *Théophile Dondey.* Poésies posthumes. Paris, 1878.

O'Neddy, Vitreuil. *Théophile (?) Dondey-Dupré, fils.* Le pays Breda. Paris, 1853.

Oneiropolos. *Charles Johnston.* Cobbler of Preston: a farce. N.Y. 1857 (?).

Onesimus. *Peter L. Courtier.* Memoirs of the life of the Rev. W. Huntington . . . L. 1813.

Ontologos. *William Kenrick, LL.D.* The grand question debated . . . By . . . Dublin, 1751.

Onyx. *Miss Elizabeth Stuart Phelps.* Silent partner. B. 1871.

O'Pagus, Arry. *H. B. Sommer,* joint author. Our show: one hundred years a republic . . . P. 1876.

O'Pake. *William M. Mallison,* in the "Brooklyn Eagle."

O'Pake, Mr. *Samuel W. E. Beckner,* in the New York "Corner Stone."

Opera Goer, An. *Donald Grant Mitchell.* The lorgnette; or, studies of the town. N.Y. 1832.

The prefaces and introductory remarks of the various editions are signed sometimes "John Timon," and sometimes "Ik. Marvel."

Optic, Oliver. *William Taylor Adams,* who for some years edited "Oliver Optic's Magazine for Boys and Girls," and is the author of many books for the young.

Optimist, An. *John William Kaye.* Essays of . . . P. 1871.

O'Quill, Maurice. *Martin Van Buren Denslow.*

Or—d. *Sir Robert Walpole.* A letter from Or[for]d in the Shades to . . . the D[uk]e of C[umberlan]d in Flanders. L. 1745.

Oran. *F. N. Otis,* in his contributions to "Harper's Magazine" (N.Y.)

O'Random, Mem. — See "Waverley."

O'Reilly, Private Miles. *Charles Grahame Halpine.* Poetical works . . . N.Y. 1869.

O'Rell, Max. *Paul Blouet.* John Bull's Womankind. L. 1884.

"'Max O'Rell,' whose writings have aroused a natural curiosity as to the identity of their author, stands revealed to the public in the person of *M. Paul Blouet.* He is the French master at Westminster School, and editor of the Clarendon volumes on French Oratory."

Orellana. *William Drennan, M.D.* Letters of . . . an Irish Helot . . . Dublin, 1785.

Orient. *Frederic Kidder,* who contributed articles to the "Boston Daily Advertiser," in 1866, on the Popham Colony, which were afterwards collected in book form under the title of "The Popham Colony." B. 1866.

Oriental Student, An. *Andrew Archibald Paton.* The modern Syrians . . . L. 1844.

Original Editor, The. *John Wade.* The extraordinary black book . . . By . . . L. 1831.

Originator of the Shetland Fishery Company, The. *Mr. Anderson.* — See "A Brother Fish Dealer," etc.

Orinda. *Mrs. Katherine (Fowler) Philips.* Letters from . . . to Poliarchus [*i.e.* Sir Charles Cotterel]. L. 1705.

Orion. *Héctor F. Varela.* Elisa Lynch . . . Buenos Ayres, 1870.

Orion. *J. Hammerton.* Orion's Almanack. L. 18–.

Orlando. *James Hall,* who edited the "Illinois Intelligencer," wrote letters for the "Portfolio," and poems and sketches for Flint's "Western Review" at Cincinnati, signing himself "Orlando."

Orleanian. *George F. Wharton.* War of the bachelors. N.O. 1882.

Orme, Mary. *Mrs. Mary (Neal Sergeant Gore) Nichols, M.D.* Uncle John; or, is it too much trouble? N.Y. 185–.

Orsin, Florio. *Alice Townsend.*

Orsini, Mme. Virginie. *Mme. Virginie (Mortemart Boisse) Baudoin.* Heures de l'énfance: poésies. Paris, 1839.

Ort, Ivan. *Ossian E. Dodge.*

Orthodox, Moses. *John Boyle,* Earl of Cork and Orrery. — See "G. K."

Orthodox Divine, An. *Rev. Joseph Smith.* A clear and comprehensive view of the being, nature, and attributes of God. L. 1754.

Orthodox Minister of the Gospel, An. *Rev. James Morris Whiton.* Is "eternal" punishment endless ... B. 1876.

Ortis, Jacopo. *Nicolò Ugo Foscolo.* Ultime lettere di ... Paris, 1824.

Ortyx. *David H. Eaton.*

Orwell. *Walter Chalmers Smith.* The bishop's walk and the bishop's times. Camb., Eng., 1861.

Ory, Stéphanie. *Just Jean Étienne Roy.* Lucille. N.Y. 1873.

Osander. *Rev. Benjamin Allen*, editor of the "Christian Magazine" (P.). Also in miscellaneous poems. N.Y. 1812.

Osborn, George, Esq. *John Huddleston Wynne,* who was also the "Mother Osborn" of Sir Robert Walpole's time.

Osborne, Edward. *Mrs. Anne Manning Rathbone.* The colloquies of ... citizen and cloth worker of London ... L. 1860.

Osborne, Jane. *Mme. Léonie d'Aunet.* Feuilletons insérés dans le journal "la Presse" en 1856.

Osborne, Sandy. *Alexander McGrew,* in his letters to various Western periodicals.

Oscar. *Gerald Griffin, Esq.,* whose first literary efforts appeared in the "Literary Gazette," when he was not twenty, under this signature.

Oscar. *Mrs. Leman Grimstone.* Zayda: a Spanish tale in three cantos; and other poems, stanzas, and canzonets. L. 1820.

Oscotian, An. *William Charles Mark Kent.* Catholicity in the dark ages, by ... L. 1847.

O'Squarr. *Oscar Charles Flor.* La guerre dans la Baltique. Brussels, 1854.

Ossola. *Clement Le Neve Foster.* The Feast of St. Anthony in the Val Anzasca, in "Land and Water." L. 1869.

Other, The. *Rev. Edmund George Harvey.* — See "One of ourselves."

Other Gentleman of Lincoln's Inn, The. *Thomas Edwards.* The canons of criticism, and glossary, being a supplement to Mr. Warburton's edition of Shakspeare ... By ... L. 1748.

Otis, Belle. *Caroline H. Woods.* Diary of a milliner. N.Y. 1867.

Otis, James. *James Otis Kaler,* in his contributions to "Harper's Young People" (N.Y.).

Otter. *H. J. Alfred.* A complete guide to spinning and trolling ... By ... L. 1859.

Otway, Sylvester. *John Oswald.* Euphrosyne: an ode to beauty. L. 1788.

Oudenarde, Dominie Nicholas Ægidius. *James Kirke Paulding.* The book of Saint Nicholas ... N.Y. 1836.

Ouida. *Mlle. Louise de la Ramé,* author of "Granville de Vigne" and numerous other works of fiction. The pseudonym is said by some authorities to be an infantile corruption of her baptismal name (Louise), while others translate it as a slang French equivalent of "Why, certainly," *Oui-dà!*

Ouno. *T. M. Ashworth,* joint author. Tom Chips. P. 187-.

Our Boy Jack. *Albert Charles Wildman,* in the "Western Counties Herald" (English).

Our Member for Paris. *Henry Du Pré Labouchere.*

Our Own Correspondent. *James O. Noyes, M.D.*

Our Own Correspondent. *Michael Burke Honan.* The personal adventures of ... in Italy. L. 1852.

Our Special Correspondent. *G. F. Atkinson.* Indian spices for English tables ... being the adventures of ... 18-.

Outcast, The. *C. B. Northrup.* Southern Odes ... Charleston, 1861.

Outis. *J. C. Ward.* The Jesuits [by William Waterworth]. Reviewed. By Outis. L. 1852.

Outis, U. Donough. *Richard Grant White.* Chronicles of Gotham. N.Y. 1871.

Over Forty. *Nathan Green.* The tall man of Winton and his wife ... Nashville, Tenn., 1872.

Overtheway, Mrs. *Juliana Horatia Ewing.* Six to sixteen. B. 1875.

Owanda. *Miss Emma Robinson* (?). Only a tramp. N.Y. 186-.

Owen. *Jesse Appleton, S.T.D.,* in the Boston "Panoplist."

Owen, Ashford. *Annie Ogle.* A lost love ... L. 1862.

Owen, Junior. *George Hardinge.* Chalmeriana ... arranged and published by ... of Paper Buildings, Inner Temple; assisted by his friend and clerk, Jasper Hargrave ... L. 1800.

Owen, J. P. *Samuel Butler.* The fair haven ... L. 1872.

Owen, Tom, the Bee-Hunter. *Thomas Bangs Thorpe.* The hive of the "Bee-Hunter." N.Y. 1853.

Owenson, Miss. *Lady Sydney (Owenson) Morgan.* The lay of the Irish harp; or, metrical fragments. By ... L. 1807.

Owl, The. *Charles Henry Bennett.* — See "Woodensconce, Papernose, Esq." "Notes and Queries," Oct. 21, 1876, p. 333.

Owl, Eugene. *Thomas Pilgrim.* Old Nick's camp-meetin' ... N.Y. 1880.

Oxford Graduate, An. *Edwin Arnold.* — See "A., E."

Oxford Man and a Wykehamist, An. *Robert Blackford Mansfield.* The log of the Water Lily . . . L. 1852.

Oxonian, An. *Samuel Reynolds Hole.* A little tour in Ireland . . . L. 1859.

Oxonian, An. *Stephen Weston.* A trimester in France and Switzerland. By . . . L. 1821.

Oxonian, The. *Frederick Metcalfe.* The Oxonian in Thelemarken, 1856–57. L. 1858.

Oxoniensis. *Rev. John Pickford, M.A.* Memoir of Percy, Bishop of Dromore, 1837, contributor to the "Athenæum" and "Once a Week," and writer of various articles in "Notes and Queries," as "Oxoniensis."

Oxoniensis. *Henry Brooke.* An appeal to the publick from an unappellate tribunal . . . L. 1740.

Oxoniensis. *Rev. Thomas Monro.* Philoctetes in Lemnos : a drama in three acts, to which is prefixed a green-room scene . . . inscribed . . . to the managers of Covent-garden and Drury-lane theatres, by . . . L. 1795.

P.

Π. *Rev. Joseph Wasse.* Miscellaneous observations upon authors, ancient and modern. L. 1731–32.

P. *Rev. Richard Polwhele*, his signature in the "Gent. Mag.," 1793 *et seq.*

P. *William Frederick Poole*, in the "Boston Advertiser" in 1866.

P. *Hon. Philip Yorke*, Earl of Hardwicke, in his contributions to the "Athenian letters" . . . L. 1741–43.

P., Mr. *Rev. Robert Potter*, in Beloe's "Sexagenarian," Vol. I., p. 298. 2d ed. L. 1818.

P., Professor. *Professor William Pole*, in an essay upon the game of whist, contributed to a work on that subject by C. B. Coles. — See "A*****, Major."

P., A. *Anthony Parkinson.* Collectanea Anglo-Minoritica ; or, a collection of the antiquities of the English Franciscans or Friers Minors, commonly call'd Gray Friers . . . Collected by . . . L. 1726.

P., A. *Arthur Pember.* Mysteries and miseries of the Great Metropolis . . . N.Y. 1874.

P., A. *A. Penfield.* Yet another plan for the resumption of specie payments easy and early. Wash. 1869.

P., A., M.D. *Dr. Alexander Pennecuik*, of Newhall. A geographical historical description of the Shire of Tweeddale . . . Edinb. 1715.

P., A. E. *Ann Eaton Polglase.* The shipwreck : a tale of Arabia ; and other poems. By . . . L. 1827.

P. A. R. *Stephen Weston.* A supplement to the grammar for the use of students in the German language. By . . . L. 1808.

P., A. S. *Ann S. Paschall.* The home circle. P. 18–.

P., B. K. *Rev. Bradford Kinney Peirce.* Stories from life, which the chaplain told. B. 1866.

P., B. W. *Bryan Waller Procter.* William Jerdan says : "Mr. *Procter's* first appearance in print was, as far as I am aware, in No. 45, Nov. 29th, 1817 [in the 'London Literary Gazette']. It was signed with the initials of his real name . . . and not Barry Cornwall . . . It was some time before he adopted the signature by which he is so well known, and his numerous charming productions which appeared in the 'Gazette' were signed 'B.,' or 'W.,' or 'O.,' or 'X. Y. Z.,' etc."

P., C. H. *Charles Henry Parry.* Memoir of Peregrine Bertie, 11th Lord Willoughby de Eresby . . . L. 1838. — See "Descendant in the Fourth Generation, A."

P. D. *Prof. Thomas C. James, M.D.*, who contributed to the Philadelphia "Port-Folio," under this signature, translations in verse of the "Idyls" of Gessner, which were highly commended.

P., D. *Daniel Parsons.* Arms in St. Winnow church, signed . . . Stuart's lodge, Malvern wells, in "Notes and Queries." 1867.

P., D. *Daniel Puseley.* Dan's political note book. Session 1871. L. 1871.

P. D. *R. Bentley.* A full and true account of the dreadful and melancholy earthquake . . . L. 1750.

P. E. *Samuel Pegge.* Explanation of the expression, a "White Crow." "Gent. Mag.," 1754, p. 305.

"P. E." are the first and last letters of *Paul* Gemsege. — See "Gent. Mag.," LXVI., p. 979.

P., E. *Rev. Edward Pearson.* A letter to a member of the Senate of the University of Cambridge. Camb. 1799.

P., F. E. *Rev. Francis Edward Paget.*

Caleb Kniveton, the incendiary: a tale ... Oxf. 1833.

P., F. J. *F. J. Pakenham.* Life lines; or, God's work in a human being. L. 1862.

P., F. M. *Frances Mary Peard.* The wood-cart; and other tales of the south of France ... L. 1867.

P., G. *Mrs. Gertrude (Hext) Parsons.* How I became a hero. By ... in "Once a Week." 1852.

P. G. *Samuel Pegge.* On Godmersham church, in Kent, "Gent. Mag.," 1789, p. 420.

"*P. G.*," initials of *Paul Gemsege.* — See "Gent. Mag.," LXVI., p. 1083.

P., G. F. *George Frederick Pardon.* Games for all seasons. L. 1869.

P., G. W. *George William Pettes.* American or standard whist. B. 1880.

P. H. *Richard Derby Ness,* in his contributions to "Notes and Queries" (L.).

P., H. *Henry Pownall.* A word from the Bible ... on behalf of enslaved British subjects ... L. 1829.

P., H. E. *Harriet Eleanor Phillimore.* Violet Stuart: a tale of the Gibraltar, and the heir of Cholmeley's Dene. L. 1878.

P., H. F. *Helen F. Parker* (?). Constance Aylmer: a story of the 17th century ... N.Y. 1869.

P., H. K. *Mrs. H. K. Potwin.* Paul and Margaret, the inebriate's children ... N.Y. 1869.

P., H. W. *Henry Webster Parker.* Verse by ... B. 1862.

P., J. *Miss Jane Porter.* Biographical account of the late Rev. Percival Stockdale, in "Gent. Mag.," October, 1811, pp. 384–390.

P., J. *James Pycroft, B.A.* Cricketana. L. 1865.

P., J. *J. B. Papworth.* Poetical sketches of Scarborough (with text signed ... text signed "W" [by the Rev. Francis Wrangham], and text unsigned, by W. Coombe). L. 1813.

P., J. *Jonathan Pereira.* Selectis è præscriptis ... L. 1844.

P., J. *James Pedder.* The yellow shoestrings ... P. n.d.

P., J., Esq., F.R.S. *James Postlethwayt, Esq.* A collection of the yearly bills of mortality from 1657 to 1758 inclusive ... By ... L. 1759.

P., J., Student in Astrology. *John Phillips.* The English fortune-tellers ... L. 1703.

P., J. B. *J. Bertrand Payne.* The gossiping guide to Jersey. L. 1865.

P., J. B. *J. B. Peat.* Sure; or, it pays ... B. 1872.

P., J. C. *James C. Parsons.* The living word; or, Bible truths and lessons. B. 1872.

P., J. G. *John Gorham Palfrey, D.D.* Notice of Professor Farrar. [From the "Christian Examiner" for July, 1853.] B. 1853.

P., J. H. *Rev. James H. Potts,* editor of the "Michigan Christian Advocate," Detroit.

P., J. H. *John Henry Parker.* A guide to the architectural antiquities in the neighbourhood of Oxford. Edited by ... Oxf. 1842–46.

P., E. J. *E. J. Pringle.* Notes on Spain and the Spaniards, 1859 ... Charleston, 1861.

P., J. V. *J. V. Prichard* (?). Who wrote "Shakspere"? By ... In "Fraser's Magazine," August, 1874.

P., K. *Kenrick Prescott.* Mildenhall. n.p. 1771.

P., L. *Count Leon Potocki.* Sketch of the social life of the city of Warsaw ... Posen, 1854. In Polish.

P. P., M.A., The Rev. *Richard Graves.* The farmer's son: a moral tale. L. 1795.

P. P., A parish clerk. *Dr. John Arbuthnot.* Memoirs, written in imitation of Burnet's "History of my own Times."

P. P., Poet Laureate. *George Daniel.* R—l stripes; or, a kick from Yar—h to Wa—s, with particulars of an expedition to Oatlands, and the sprained ankle. L. 1812.

P. P. C. R. *Thomas Watts,* Keeper of Printed Books, British Museum, who under these initials wrote letters in the "Mechanic's Magazine," 1836–73, on the British Museum library.

P. P. P. *William Maginn,* in the London "Literary Gazette," 1820.

P. Q. *William Coombe.* The Fastday: a Lambeth eclogue. L. 1780.

P., R. *Robert Paltock.* The life and adventures of Peter Wilkins ... L. 1816.

P., R., An Honorary Associate. *Rev. Richard Polwhele.* An epistle to an archdeacon [Nares], Vice President of the Royal Society of Literature, from ... an Honorary Associate. L. 1824.

P., R. A. *Mrs. Rhoda Ann (Paige) Falkner.* Wild notes from the backwoods ... Cobourg, 1850.

P., R. B. *Robert Bateman Paul.* History of Germany from the invasion of Germany by Marius ... L. 1847.

P., R. de Venezuela. *Ramon Paez.* Ambas Americas contrastes ... N.Y. 1872.

P., S. *Samuel Pegge.* "Les brandons" explained. "Gent. Mag.," 1754, p. 508; and a few other articles.

S. P., his initials. — See " Gent. Mag.," LXVI., p. 979, *ss.*

P., S. *Mrs. S. Pennington.* Letters on different subjects, in four volumes ... L. 1766–67.

P., S. *Samuel Pegge.* On the Sordid Philosophers. "Gent. Mag.," 1756, p. 330.

P. S., initials reversed. — See " Gent. Mag.," LXVI., p. 981.

P., S. B. *Samuel Browning Power.* Some school and children's books, under his initials.

P., S. R. *Miss S. Rugeley Powers.* Why do not women swim? A voice from many waters. L. 1859.

P., S. W. *S. W. Partridge.* Rhymes worth remembering, for the young. L. 1848.

P., T. *Thomas Parsons.* Christianity, a system of peace ... Bath, 1804.

P., T. *Thomas Poyser, Esq.* List of contributors to the "Quarterly Review," in "Gent. Mag.," February, 1844, pp. 137, *ss.*; and other articles.

P., T. *Theophilus Parsons.* Remarks upon "Swedenborgianism reviewed, by Enoch Pond, D.D...." By ... B. 1846.

P., V. W. *Rev. Vyvyan Wallis Popham.* All my heart this night rejoices: a Christmas carol ... L. 1874.

P. W. *Rev. Pierce William Drew.* An account of the present state of Youghal church ... Cork, 1848.

P., W. *William Peck.* A topographical history and description of Bawtry and Thorne, with the villages adjacent, by ... Doncaster, 1813.

P., W. & I., A. *W. Pamplin and Alexander Irvine.* Botanical tour in ... Perthshire. L. 1857.

P., W. F. *W. F. Palmer.* Memoirs of S. S. Jamison. P. 1878.

P., W. P. *Willard P. Phillips.* Wenham water-works. Statements, by ... Salem, 1867.

P., W. S. *William Stevens Perry, D.D.* A memorial of the Rev. Thomas Mather Smith, D.D.... By ... Camb. (Mass.) 1866.

P., Z. (Pundison, Zachary). *L. W. Mansfield.* Up-country letters [by Z. P.]. Edited by Prof. B. [William W. Benedict], National Observatory. N.Y. 1852.

P*. *Rev. Joseph T. J. Hewlett.* — See "Priggins, Peter."

P*****, Mrs. *Mrs. Hester Lynch (Thrale) Piozzi*, in Beloe's "Sexagenarian," I., 384. 2d ed. L. 1818.

P*******, Miss. *Miss Anne Plumptre*, in Beloe's "Sexagenarian," I., 362. 2d. ed. L. 1818.

P***, J. A. S. C*** de. *Jacques Albin Simon Collin de Plancy.*

P*****, P****, Esq., F.G.H. *John Colls.* The Bouselliad; or, an apology for Aminadab Shoe's (John Bousell) apostacy. By ... Norwich, 1786.

P****m, Mr. *Right Hon. Henry Pelham.* The discovery. An ode to ... L. 1752.

P——, Mrs. C——. *Mrs. Constantia Phillips.* The happy courtezan ... L. 1735.

P——, Miss Susan. *Miss Susan Pierson.* — See Lamb's "Elia," "The Old Benchers of the 'Inner Temple.'"

P——, P——. *Poet Laureate, i.e.* **Peter Pindar.** *George Daniel.* Modern Dunciad, Virgil in London, and other poems. L. 1835.

P—s, The. *The Pitcairns*, in Beloe's "Sexagenarian," Vol. I., p. 306. 2d ed. L. 1818.

P—y, William. *William Pudsey.* The constitution and laws of England consider'd; by ... L. 1701.

Pacificator. *Murray Hoffman.* A letter to the clergy and laity of the Protestant Episcopal Church in the Diocese of New York ... N.Y. 1850.

Pacificator. *Richard Dykes Alexander.* Observations on the subject of war. 1817.

Pacificus. *Alexander Hamilton.* The Federalist ... with an appendix containing the Letters of ... and Helvidius [James Madison] on the proclamation of neutrality of 1793 ... Hallowell (Me.), 1837.

Pacificus. *Joshua R. Giddings.* The rights and privileges of the several States in regard to slavery ... 1842.

Packard, Mrs. Clarissa. *Mrs. Caroline (Howard) Gilman.* Recollections of a housekeeper. Charleston, 183–.

Paddy. *Henry McCluskey*, in the "Eagle" (Brooklyn, N.Y.).

Paets, Cornelius. *Rev. Arthur Ashley Sykes.* An humble apology for St. Paul and the other apostles ... L. 1719.

Page of the Presence, A. *Philip Withers.* History of the royal malady [of George III.] ... By ... L. 1789.

Page, Abraham, Esq. *John Saunders Holt.* What I know about Ben Eccles. P. 1869.

Page, H. A. *Alexander Hay Japp.*
Leaders of men ... L. 1880.

Page, Henri. *William Duckett.* Les
petites ouvrières. Paris, 1862.

Page de la Cour Impériale, Un.
Émile Marco de Saint Hilaire. Mémoires
and révélations de ... de 1802 à 1815.
Paris, 1830.

Pagès, Emile. *Louis Bergeron.* Fables
démocratiques. Paris, 1839.

Painsworth, W. Harassing, Professor Strongfellow, G. P. R. Jacobus, &c., and other eminent Authors.
William Harrison Ainsworth, and others.
Our Miscellany [which ought to have
come out, but didn't] : containing contributions by ... L. 1856.

Painter, A. *Sir Joseph Noel Paton,
R.S.A.* Poems by ... Edinb. 1861.

Painter, A. *Sir Martin Archer Shee.*
Rhymes on art ; or, the remonstrance of
... L. 1805.

Paix, Le prince de la. *Don Manoel
Godoy.* Memoires. Paris, 1836–37.

Pakeha Maori, A. *Judge Maning (?).* Old New Zealand ... L.
1863.

Paleface, Hugh. *Sir Hugh Palliser.*
So called in the English newspapers
about 1770.

Palemon. *Leonard Welsted.* The
Triumvirate ; or, a letter in verse from
Palemon to Celia from Bath. L. 1718.

Palermo. *John North, Esq.,* in Dibdin's "The Bibliographical Decameron."

Palestinensis. *Eli Smith.* Reply to
the letters of ... by James Silk Buckingham.

Palette, Peter. *Thomas Onwhyn.* Mr.
and Mrs. Brown's visit to the Exhibition.
L. 1851.

Palinurus of the Revolution, The.
Samuel Adams. So termed by Jefferson,
in 1825.

Pall, Etienne. *Félix Platel.* Les
echos de Hombourg. Paris, 1856.

Pallet, Peter Paul. *Rev. Richard
Warner.* Rebellion in Bath ; or, the
battle of the upper rooms. Bath,
1807.

Pallette, Peter Paul. *William Hall,*
in his contributions to Birmingham periodicals, etc. See "N. & Q.," 6th series,
viii. 494.

Palliser, Francis. *Mrs. Mary Wilson.* Glenerne ... Glasgow, 1863.

Palliser, Mr. Plantagenet. *Lord
Carlingford,* in Trollope's "The Prime
Minister."

Palman, Eugène de. *Hippolyte Regnier d'Estourbet.* L'Histoire de tout le
monde. Paris, 1829.

Palmer, Lynde. *Mrs. Mary L. Peebles.* The good fight. B. 186–.

Palmer, Pot-Pie. *Edward Sanford.*
Charcoal sketch of ... N.Y. 18–.

Pamela. *Lady Edward Fitzgerald.*

Panajot. *Panajot Chitov.* Heiduck-
enführer-Balkanheiducken. 1878.

Pansy. *Mrs. Isabella M. Alden.* Ester
Reid ; or, asleep and awake. Cin. 1870.

Pantarch. *Stephen Pearl Andrews.*
The basic outline of Universology. N.Y.
1872.

Pantheist, A. *John Toland.* Indiffer-
ence in disputes recommended by ...
to an orthodox friend. L. 1705.

Paoli, Betty. *Elizabeth Glück.* Neu-
este Gedichte. 1870.

Papinian. *Rev. Charles Inglis.* Letters of ... N.Y. 1779.

Papirius, Cursor. *Caleb Whitefoord.*
" His essays, poems, and cross-readings (a
species of humour, to which he gave the apt
signature of ' Papirius Cursor ') evince the
sprightliness of his satire and the novelty of
his wit."

Parallax. *John Hampden.* Zetetic
astronomy ... L. 1865.

Parameny, K. *Anna Kempe.*

Parens. *Henry Craik.* An easy introduction to the Hebrew language on
the principles of Pestalozzi ... L. 1831.

Pariah, A. *Caroline Frances Cornwallis.* Philosophical theories and philosophical experiences ... L. 1841.

Paris, H. *Mlle. de Haza.* Tablettes
grammaticales ... Paris, 1842.

Parish Minister, A. *Lawrence Lockhart, D.D.* Facts, not falsehoods ; or, a
plain defence of the Church of Scotland
... Edinb. 1845.

Parish Priest, A. *Rev. Frederick
William Faber.* The Blessed Sacrament
... L. 1845.

Parish Priest, A. *Rev. Michael
Maughan Humble, M.A.* Methodistic
Catholicism ... L. 1852.

Parish Priest in the Diocese of
Chichester, A. *Rev. James Munro Sandham, M.A.* The wonders of to-morrow,
and the crown of life ... Brighton,
1853.

Parishioner of St. Chad's, A. *Rev.
Job Orton.* Diotrephes re-admonished ...
By ... and author of "Diotrephes ad-
monished." L. 1770.

Parishioner of St. George's Parish,
Edinburgh, A. *Rev. James Bryce.* A
letter to the Rev. Robert S. Candlish.
Edinb. 1841.

Parishioner of the Doctor's, A. *Rev.
Caleb Fleming.* A letter to the Revd.
Dr. Cobden, rector of St. Austin's and
St. Faith's and of Acton ... L. 1738.

Parisienne, Une. *Mme. Juliette (Lamber) Adam.* Le siége de Paris: journal d'une Parisienne. Paris, 1873.

Parker, Bently. *Park Benjamin.*

Parlante, Priscilla. *Hon. Mary Ann Cavendish Bradshaw.* Ferdinand and Ordella: a Russian story ... L. 1810.

Parley, Peter. *John Bennett.*

Parley, Peter. *W. Tegg.*

Parley, Peter. *Samuel Griswold Goodrich.* Fireside education. 1838.

Parley, Peter. *William Martin.* P. P.'s annual: a Christmas and New Year's present for young people. Edited by ... L. 1867.

Parley, Peter. *George Mogridge.* Tales about shipwrecks and disasters at sea. L. 1827.

Parliamentary Secretary, A. *Arthur Symonds.* Practical suggestions for the internal reform of the House of Commons. By ... L. 1832.

Parochial Bishop, A. *Rev. John Willison.* A letter ... concerning the government of the Church ... Edinb. 1714.

Parresiastes. *Rev. C. E. De Coetlogon.* The temple of truth; or, the best system of reason, philosophy, virtue, and morals, analytically arranged. L. 1806.

Parsee Merchant. — See "Curiosibhoy, Adersey."

Parsonus Rusticus. *Samuel Walton McDaniel.* His signature, 1856–60, in the "Christian Messenger" (N.Y.).

Partington, Mrs. *Benjamin Poore Shillaber.* The sayings and doings of ... B. 1854.

In the Rev. Sydney Smith's speech at Taunton, on the Lords' rejection of the Reform Bill, October, 1831, is this passage:—
"The attempt of the Lords to stop the progress of reform, reminds me very forcibly of the great storm of Sidmouth, and of the conduct of excellent Mrs. Partington on that occasion. In the winter of 1824, there set in a great flood upon that town, the tide rose to an incredible height, the waves rushed upon the houses, and everything was threatened with destruction. In the midst of this sublime and terrible storm, Dame Partington, who lived upon the beach, was seen at the door of her house with mop and pattens, trundling her mop, squeezing out the sea-water, and vigorously pushing away the Atlantic Ocean. The Atlantic was roused, Mrs. Partington's spirit was up; but I need not tell you that the contest was unequal. The Atlantic Ocean beat Mrs. Partington. She was excellent at a slop or a puddle, but she should not have meddled with a tempest."

Partington, Ruth. *Benjamin Poore Shillaber.* Knitting-work: a web of many textures. B. 1859.

Partridge, Simon. *Henry Woodward.* A letter to Henry Woodward, comedian, occasioned by his letter to the Inspector. By ... L. 1753.

Parvus. *Rev. Frederick Heesom.* Polperro games. Blame not before thou hast examined the truth, consider. By ... 1827.

Pascal, l'abbé Stanislas. *L'abbe Henri Congnet.* Mois de Marie ... Paris, 1835.

Pascal the younger. *Pierce Connelly.* Moral theology of Liguori; or, cases of conscience ... L. 1856.

Pascarel. *Rev. B. Ellison Warner,* in his contributions to the "Springfield Republican" (Mass.).

Pasquin, Anthony. *John Williams.* The life of Alexander Hamilton ... B. 1804.

Pasquin, Paul. *Alexander Fraser Tytler.*

Pasquino. *J. Fairfax McLaughlin.* The American Cyclops, the Hero of New Orleans, and Spoiler of Silver Spoons. Dubbed LL.D ... Balt. 1868.

Passant, Le. *Ernest d'Hervilly,* who, in 1872, wrote in the "Rappel," under this signature.

Passenger in the Ship, A. *George Buchan,* of Kelloe, Berwickshire. A narrative of the loss of the Winterton East Indiaman ... Edinb. 1820.

Pastel. *George Frederick Pardon.* Dramatic criticisms. L. 186–.

Pastor. *Abel Stevens, D.D., LL.D.* Pastor's stories. B. 184–.

Pastor, A. *Joshua Noble Danforth.* Gleanings and groupings from a pastor's portfolio. N.Y. 1852.

Pastor, A. *Rev. Alexander Dallas.* My church-yard ... L. 1844.

Pastor, A. *John Whitley Stokes.* A P.'s advice to a young member of his flock on going out to service. L. 1861.

Pastor, A. *Ichabod Smith Spencer, D.D.* A pastor's sketches. 1851, 1853.

Pastor, A. *Rev. Thomas Frognall Dibdin.* A word of caution and comfort to the middle and lower classes of society ... L. 1831.

Pastor, The. *Rev. Jason Morse.* Annals of the church in Brimfield. By ... Springfield, Mass. 1856.

Pastor, The. *Rev. Edward Dafydd Morris.* Five years of ministerial life: being a discourse ... at the Second Presbyterian Church, Columbus, Ohio. By ... Columbus, 1861.

Pastor, The. *John Boswell Spotswood, D.D.* An historical sketch of the Presbyterian church in New Castle, Delaware, by ... P. 1859.

Pastor of St. Paul's, Haggerstone, The. *Rev. William Stone.* Thirty-six

plain maxims on the way to live and die
in peace. From . . . to his flock. L.
1864.

Pastor, Tony. *Harlan Halsey.* 201
Bowery songster. N.Y. 1867.

Pastorini, Sig. *Bishop Charles Walmesley.* The general history of the Christian Church . . . Dublin, 1812.

Pastor's Wife, A. *Mrs. Martha Stone
Hubbell.* The shady side ; or, life in a
country parsonage . . . B. 1853.

Pater. — *Evans,* of Bradbury &
Evans.— See " Ponny."

Paterfamilias. *Matthew James Higgins.* Papers on public school education
in England in 1860 . . . L. 1865.

**Pathfinder of the Rocky Moun-
tains, The.** *John Charles Frémont.*

Patrice, Saint. *James Harden-Hickey.*

Patricius. *R. Geoghigan.* Thoughts
of . . . Dublin, 1785.

Patricius, Aberdonensis. *Patrick
Forbes,* Bishop of Aberdeen.

Patriot, A. *S. O. Townsend.*

Patriot, A. *Joseph Priestley.* An address to the inhabitants of Birmingham
: . . Birmingham.

Patrioticus. *W. P. Russel.* A patriotic letter to the Right Hon. Henry Addington, exhorting him to firmness . . .
L. 1804.

Patrolman, A. *George S. Mc Watters*
employed this signature in his letters,
which ultimately created the " Mutual
Aid Fund " for the police.

Pattieson, Peter. *Sir Walter Scott.*
Tales of my landlord. Edinb. 1830.

Patty, Aunt. *Mrs. Caroline Lee
(Whiting) Hentz.* Aunt Patty's scrap
bag. 1846.

Paturot, Jérôme. *Marie Roch Louis
Reybaud.* Le coq du clocher. Paris, 1845.

Paul. *Sir Walter Scott.* Paul's letters to his kinsfolk. L. 1816.

Paul, John. *Charles Henry Webb.*
Parodies, prose and verse . . . N.Y. 1876.

Paul, Richard. *Richard Paul Wurst.*

Paul, Uncle. *Samuel Burnham, Jr.*
Uncle Paul's stories for boys and girls.
B. 186–.

Pauline. *Mme. Kathinka (Halein)
Zitz.*

Paulinus. *John Jebb, M.D., F.R.S.*
Letters on the subject of subscription to
the liturgy, etc. First printed in the
" Whitehall Evening Post," under the
signature of "Paulinus " . . . L. 1772.

Paulus Silentiarius. *George P.
Philes,* who contributed to literary journals under this signature.

Pavo. *Mr. Langley,* in his contributions to the "Morning Post " (L.).

Pax. *Hugh F. McDermott,* in the
Boston " Courier."

Paxton, Philip. *Samuel A. Hammett.*
A stray Yankee in Texas . . . N.Y. 1853.

Paymaster, The. *Henry Fox,* 1st
Baron Holland. The Fox unkennelled ;
or, the paymaster's accounts laid open,
etc. 1769.

Peabody, Mrs. Mark. *Mrs. Metta
Victoria (Fuller) Victor.* A woman's
heart. N.Y. 186–.

Peace & Justice. *Noah Webster.*
Article in the " Hampshire Gazette,"
March 24, 1813, against the war of
1812.

Peacock, Timothy, Esq. *Daniel
Pierce Thompson.* The adventures of . . .
Middlebury, 1835. — See " Member of the
Vermont Bar, A."

Peale, Patrick. *Gustav Anton von
Seckendorf,* known by this pseudonym,
the author of dramas and prose essays.

Pearl, Christie. *Ellen M. Perkins.*
Every day lessons. B. 186–.

Peasant Bard, A. *Robert Burns.*

Peasant Bard, The. *Josiah D. Canning.* The harp and the plow . . . Greenfield, Mass., 1852.

**Peasant Poet of Northampton-
shire, The.** *John Clare.*

Pecherel, Jules. *Jules Chabot de
Bouin.* Le moutard des faubourgs . . .
Paris, 1836.

Peck, I. X. *Thomas Mason.*

Pedasculus, Paulus Purgantius.
William Warburton, D.D. Distress upon
distress ; or, tragedy in true taste . . .
By George Alexander Stevens . . . And
notes, critical, classical, and historical,
by . . . Dublin, 1752. See "Humm, Sir
Henry."

Pedestrian. *Robert Wilson.* Travels
of that well-known . . . L. 1807.

Pedestrian, The. *John Aiton, D.D.*
Eight weeks in Germany . . . Edinb.
1842.

Pedestrian, The. *Edward Payson
Weston.* Journal of a walk from Boston
to Washington, 1861. N.Y. 1862.

Pedestrian Traveller, A. *Comte Armand Bon Louis Maudet de Penhouët.* Letters describing a tour through part of
South Wales. By . . . L. 1797.

Peebles, Paul. *Augustus Maverick,* in
various periodicals.

Peeping Tom. *Rev. Henry Ryder
Knapp,* " author of several fugitive poems
and essays ; and, particularly, of a short
series, under the title of ' Peeping Tom,'
which appeared about 25 years since
(1792) in the ' Leicester Herald.' "

Peeping Tom. *Samuel Kettell.* "Peeping Tom's Letters," in the "Boston Courier," 184–.

Peer of Scotland, A. *Patrick Murray*, 5th Lord Elibank. Considerations on the present state of the peerage of Scotland ... By ... Edinb. 1771.

Peer of the Realm, A. *Patrick Murray*, 5th Lord Elibank. Eight sets of queries ... upon the subject of wool and of the woolen manufacture. Edinb. 1775.

Peer's Son, A. *George Douglas Campbell*, Duke of Argyle. Letter to the peers ... Edinb. 1842.

Pelham, M. *Sir Richard Phillips.* The parent's and tutor's first catechism ... 18–.

Pellegrin. *Baron Friedrich Heinrich Karl La Motte Fouqué*, who, under this pseudonym, published his first literary essays.

Pellegrino. *Rev. Gaudentius Rossi.* The Christian trumpet. Compiled by ... B. 1873.

Pembroke, Morgan de. *Morgan Evans.* Poems. L. 1860.

Penciller, A. *Henry C. Wetmore.* Hermit's Dell, from the diary of ... N.Y. 1854.

Pendennis, Arthur, Esq. *William Makepeace Thackeray*, as imaginary editor of "The Newcomes: memoirs of a most respectable family." L. 1853–55.

Pendennis, Launcelot. *Rev. Duke John Yonge.* Cornish carelessness. Poems ... L. 1830.

Pendragon. *Henry Sampson.* Modern boxing ... L. 1878.

Pen-Dragon, Anser, Esq. *Samuel William Henry Ireland.* Scribbleomania; or, the printer's devil's polichronicon. A sublime poem, edited by ... L. 1815.

Pendrea, W. *William Noy* ("Noy, of Cornwall"), in "Notes and Queries," 1865.

Penholder. *Rev. Edward Eggleston*, in his contributions to the "Independent" (N.Y.).

Peninsula Officer, A. *J. D. Williams.* The army: its traditions and reminiscences. By ... L. 1857.

Penman. *Charles Hallock.*

Penmarch, Gustave de. *Jules Duplessis Kergomard, de Morlaix.* Les feux follets, vers par ... Paris, 1851.

Penn, Arthur. *James Brander Matthews.* The home library. N.Y. 1883.

Penn, Mr. W. *Stephen Colwell.* A letter to the members of the legislature of Pennsylvania, on the removal of the deposits from the Bank of the United States ... P. 1834.

Penn, William. *Jeremiah Evarts.* Essays on ... the American Indians. P. 1830.

Pennec, le R. P. Cyrille. *D. L. Miorcec de Kerdanet.* Le dévôt pèlerinage de Notre Dame de Folgoët. Rennes, 1825.

Penniman, Major. *Charles Wheeler Denison.* The Tanner Boy: life of U. S. Grant. B. 1864.

Pennot, Rev. Peter. *William M. F. Round.* Achsah: a New England life study. B. 1876.

Pennsylvania Farmer, A. *John Dickinson.* Letters to the inhabitants of the British colonies. B.·1767.

Pennsylvania Sailor, A. *John Macpherson.* A P. S.'s letters, alias the farmer's fall: with extracts from a tragic comedy, called "Hodge Podge improved; or, the race fairly run" ... P. 1771.

Pennsylvanian, A. *Benjamin Rush.* Address upon slave-keeping ... P. 1772.

Pennsylvanian, A. *John Kintzing Kane.* A candid view of the presidential question. P. 1828.

Pennsylvanian, A. *Mathew Carey.* Extracts from "The Crisis" ... P. 1823.

Penrose, Llewellin. *Rev. John Eagles.* Journal of ... a seaman. L. 1815.

Pensilis. *Charles Lamb.* On the inconveniences resulting from being hanged: essay contributed to "The Reflector."

Pensioner, The. *James Abercrombie.* Extracts from the ... progress: showing how a patriot may pocket £2000 a year, by looking wise and doing nothing. Edinb. 1832.

Pentweazle, Ebenezer of Truro, in the county of Cornwall, Esq. *Christopher Smart.* The Horatian canons of friendship ... L. 1750.

People's Friend, The. *Daniel Drake.* The people's doctors. A review by ... Cin. 1830.

Pepper, K. N. *James W. Morris.* Poems. L. 18–.

Pepper, Tom. *Charles F. Briggs.* The trippings of ... an autobiography. N.Y. 1844.

Pepper-box, Peter. *Thomas Green Fessenden.* Pills. P. 1809.

Peppercorn, H., M.D. *Rev. Richard Harris Barham.* The dark-looking man. Verses first published in the London "Globe and Traveller."

Peppercorn, Peter. *Emanuel Price.* Poems. P. 1884.

Peppercorn, Peter, M.D. *Thomas Love Peacock.* Rich and poor; or, saint and sinner. Verses first published in the "Globe and Traveller."

Peppergrass, Paul. *John Boyce.* Mary Lee; or, the Yankee in Ireland. B. 186–.

Pequot. *Charles March*, who wrote for the New York "Tribune" and "Times," and the Boston "Courier," under this signature.

Perch, Mr. Philemon. *Richard Malcom Johnston.* Georgia sketches . . . Augusta, Ga., 1864.

Percy, Florence. *Mrs. Elizabeth Akers Allen.* Story of Thomas Fish. [Poem.] B. 186–.

Percy, Reuben. — See "Percy, Sholto and Reuben."

Percy, Sholto and Reuben. *Joseph Clinton Robertson* and *Thomas Byerley.* The Percy anecdotes, by . . . Brothers of the Benedictine Monastery, Mont Berger. L. 1820–23.

Perdita, The Fair. *Mrs. Mary (Darby) Robinson*, who used this signature in her amatory correspondence.

Peregrina. *Gertrudis Gomez de Avellanèda.* Poesias liricas. 1841.

Peregrine. *Rev. Gage Earle Freeman,* a writer on Falconry, etc., in the London "Field."

Peregrine, Brother. *John Octavian Blewitt,* in "Fraser's Magazine."

Périgord, A. B. de. *Horace Raisson.* Cuisine naturelle . . . Paris, 18–.

Period, Pertinax, & Co. *Joseph Tinker Buckingham,* who wrote the articles under this head for the "New England Galaxy," Boston, 1817, *et seq.*

Periwinkle, Paul. *Percy Bayle St. John.* Adventures of . . . L. 186–.

Periwinkle, Peter. *Thomas Green Fessenden.* Peter Periwinkle to Tabitha Towzer. A most delicate love song, printed in the "Farmer's Museum." Walpole, N.H., 179–.

Periwinkle, Tribulation. *Louisa May Alcott.*

Perk, Abner. *Alexander Stevenson Twombly.* Merry maple leaves; or, a summer in the country . . . L. 1873.

Perkins, Abigail. *James Otis Kaler,* in his contributions to the "Globe" (B.).

Perkins, Eli. *Melville D. Landon.* Eli Perkins (at large): his sayings and doings. N.Y. 1875.

Perley. *Benjamin Perley Poore,* correspondent of the Boston "Journal" for many years, from 1854, under this signature.

Perriwig, Sir J. *Amédée Pichot.* Littérature retrospective. I. La semaine de Du Bartas, in the "Revue de Paris," 1833.

Persian, A. *Lord George Lyttelton.* Letters from . . . in England to his friend at Ispahan. L. 1735.

Persic, Peregrine. *James Morier.* The adventures of Hajji Baba of Ispahan. L. 1824.

Persimmons. *M. Bennett, Jr.,* in his contributions to various periodicals, on insurance subjects.

Persimmons. *W. L. Russ,* in his contributions to the "Courier" (Buffalo, N.Y.).

Person Abroad, A. *William Mercer.* A letter . . . to a lady in Scotland. Edinb. 1785.

Person Concern'd, A. *Rev. John Colbatch.* Jus Academicum . . . L. 1722.

Person, late Apprentice to Messrs. Negri and Witten, of Berkley Square, A. *F. Nutt.* The complete confectioner . . . L. 1789.

Person lately about Town, A. *Cornelius Webbe.* The posthumous papers . . . of . . . L. 1828.

Person of Distinction, A. *Patrick Murray,* 5th Lord Elibank. An inquiry into the original and consequences of the public debt. L. 1754.

Person of Honor, A. *Daniel Leonard.* Massachusettensis; or, a series of letters containing a faithful state of facts which laid the foundation of the present troubles in Massachusetts-Bay. By . . . upon the spot. L. 1776.

Person of Honour, A. *Charles Howe.* Devout meditations . . . By . . . Edinb. 1751.

Person of Honour, A. *Hon. Roger North.* A discourse of fish and fish ponds. Done by . . . L. 1713–14.

Person of Honour, A. *Charles Ancillon.* Eunuchism display'd . . . L. 1718.

The above is an unacknowledged translation from the French of *Charles Ancillon.* The original was published in 1707 under the pseudonym of "C. D'Ollincan," an anagram of the author's name.

Person of Honour, A. *Jonathan Swift, D.D.* Some advice humbly offered to the Members of the October Club. L. 1711–12.

Person of Honour, A. *John Dalrymple,* 1st Earl of Stair. A vindication of the divine perfections . . . By . . . 1695.

Person of Quality, A. *John Pomfret.* The choice: a poem. L. 1700.

Person of Quality, A. *Mrs. Sarah Scott.* A journey through every stage of life . . . By . . . L. 1754.

Person of Quality, A. *Jonathan Swift, D.D.* A letter to a young gentleman lately enter'd into holy orders ... writ ... by Dr. S. L. 1721.

Person of Quality, A. *Edward Howard*, 8th Earl of Suffolk. Miscellanies in prose and verse. L. 1725.

Person of Quality, a Native of France, A. *Mons. de Souligné.* A comparison between old Rome in its glory ... and London as at present. L. 1706.

Person who lived there ten years, A. *Philippe Fermin.* An historical and political view of the present and ancient state of the colony of Surinam, in South America ... L. 1781.

Person who travelled through that country at the close of the year 1811. *Rev. Thomas Jones.* The Welsh looking glass; or, thoughts on the state of religion in North Wales. By ... L. 1812.

Personne. *Edward G. P. Wilkins*, the dramatic critic of the "New York Herald."

Personne. *F. G. De Fontaine.* Gleanings from a Confederate Army note-book. Columbia, S.C., 186-.

Pertinax, Anobium. *William Hand Browne.* "Convict Indexes," in the N.Y. "Nation," February, 1883.

Pestalozzi. *Bernard Peters*, in the Brooklyn "Times."

Peter. *Peter Zinzan, M.D.* — See "Friar, The."

Peter. *George Alexander Stevens.* The birth-day of Folly: an heroi-comical poem. By ... L. 1755.

Peter. *John Gibson Lockhart.* Peter's letters to his kinsfolk. Edinb. 1819.

Peter, Brother. *John Wolcot.* Brother Peter to Brother Tom [*i.e.* Thomas Warton]. L. 1789.

Peter, Parson. *Rev. Samuel Andrew Peters*, in Trumbull's "McFingal."

Peter, Lord Bishop of Cork and Rosse. *Peter Browne.* A discourse of drinking healths. L. 1716.

Peter of Pontefract. *Richard Graves.* Lucubrations ... L. 1786.

Peterson, Charles J. *J. Thornton Randolph.* The cabin and the parlor; or, slaves and masters. P. 1852.

Peterson, Paul. *Capt. Hugo Playfair, R.N.* Brother Jonathan ... edited by Paul Peterson. L. 1840–41. [Published collectively as "The Playfair Papers; or, the Americans in 1841." L. 1841.]

Petitioner, A. *Benjamin Thomas.* A letter to the Right Rev. Father in God, Shute, Lord Bishop of Landaff, from ... Marlborough, 1774.

Petrus. *Pierre Borel d'Hauterive.* Rhapsodies. Paris, 1831.

Petscherstij, Andrei. *Pawel Iwanowitsch Melnikow.* In den Bergen. 1876.

Peuchet, J., archiviste de la police. *Étienne Léon*, Baron de Lamothe-Langon. Mémoires ... pour servir à l'histoire de la morale et de la police, depuis Louis XIV. Paris, 1838.

Peudemots, M. de. *William Howison.* Fragments and fictions. Edinb. 18-.

Pfaal, Hans. *Edgar Allan Poe.* Adventures of ... N.Y. 1864.

Phalaris. One of the pseudonyms attributed to Junius (*q.v.*).
The letter thus signed is dated Decb'r 17, 1770, and is directed against Lord Mansfield.

Phantastes. *William Hazlitt*, in the "New Monthly Magazine," 1822.

Phazma. *Matthew C. Field*, who, under this signature, contributed many poetical and other articles to the Southern journals.
"'Who were the editors?' [of the 'New Orleans Picayune'] asked the outsiders. 'Phazma and Straws,' replied the Crescenter.
"'Not know the Brothers Field? — Jim Field [Jos. Field], who had kept audiences in boxes, and pit, on the roar by the hour, and who had turned editor? or Mat. Field, his sedater brother, whose heart was like a well, and deep enough for any honest human bucket to descend and take a draught of pure, reviving, sparkling friendship.'"

Phebe. *Miss Joanna Bentley*, daughter of the celebrated Dr. Bentley. See "Byrom, John."

Philadelphian, A. *W. Williams.* A handbook for the stranger in Philadelphia ... By ... P. 1849.

Philadelphus. *Samuel Whelpley.* Compend of history ... N.Y. 1835.

Philagathus. *John Haven Dexter.* Waltzing. B. 1868 (?).

Philalethes. *Nicholas Amhurst*, as contributor to the London "Evening Post."

Philalethes. *William Hazlitt*, in the "Monthly Repository."

Philalethes. *Johann Nepomuk Maria Joseph*, King of Saxony, who, under this name, published, in 1849, a German edition of the "Divina Commedia" of Dante.

Philalethes. *Thomas Morgan*, in works on moral philosophy, 1738.

Philalethes. *Samuel Spring, D.D.* — See "Toletus."

Philalethes. *Joseph Besse.* The Clergy's plea for a settled and forced maintenance from the Quakers ... L. 1737.
Also attributed to *Joseph Ollive*, of Bromley, Middlesex.

Philalethes. *Rev. John Gough.* A discourse concerning the resurrection bodies ... L. 1788.

Philalethes. *Rev. Thomas Twining.* A discourse on baptism ... 1788.

Philalethes. *John Jones, LL.D.* The epistles of St. Paul . . . a new version . . . L. 1819.

Philalethes. *Rev. William Goode, M.A.* The Established Church. Reply to letters on the Voluntary principle, by "A Quiet Looker-on" [Rev. John Foster], published in the "Morning Chronicle," Oct. 2 and 3, 1834.

Philalethes. *John Hancock.* The Examiner; or, Gilbert against Tennent . . . B. 1743.

Philalethes. *Matthias Earbery.* Impartial reflections upon Dr. Burnet's posthumous history. By . . . L. 1724.

Philalethes. *Henry Portsmouth.* An index to William Penn's works. Signed . . . About 1730.

Philalethes. *Rev. John E. Blox.* Justo Ucundono, Prince of Japan . . . Balt. 1854.

Philalethes. *Cotton Mather.* A letter of advice to the Churches of the Non-Conformists . . . L. 1700.

Philalethes. *James Beezley.* A letter to Dr. Formey, F.R.S., Professor of Philosophy, etc. By . . . L. 1766.

Philalethes. *Rev. John Wesley.* A letter to Dr. Priestley, respecting his late publication of Mr. Wesley's letters . . . L. 1791.

Philalethes. *Richard Bentley.* A letter to the Reverend Master of Trinity College in Cambridge . . . L. 1721.

Philalethes. *Hon. Archibald Campbell.* A letter to the most reverend the Lord Archbishop of Canterbury, concerning the validity of Lay-Baptism . . . L. 1738.

Philalethes. *Sir Richard Hill.* A letter to the Rev. Dr. Adams of Shrewsbury . . . L. 1770.

Philalethes. *Rev. Nathaniel Lardner.* A letter writ in the year 1730. Concerning the question, whether the Logos supplied the place of a human soul in the person of Jesus Christ . . . L. 1759.

Philalethes. *George Turner.* Methodist class leaders not New Testament pastors or elders . . . L. 1858.

Philalethes. *Sir R. J. W. Horton.* On colonies. L. 1839.

Philalethes. *Rev. William Stothert.* Plain reasons for adhering to the Church of England . . . L. 185–.

Philalethes. *Alexander Greaves.* Reflections on the statements and opinions published in the "Free Engineer" . . . N.Y. 1829.

Philalethes. *Charles Leslie.* The rehearsal; or, a view of the times, their principles and practices: a weekly journal, from Aug. 2, 1704, to March 26, 1709. By . . . L. 1750.

Philalethes. *Albertus Samuel Carpentier Alting,* in his reply to J. I. Doedes' "Modern of apostolisch Christendom?" . . . Leiden, 1861.

Philalethes. *Rev. Reuben Sherwood.* The reviewer reviewed; or, Doctor Brownlee vs. The Bible . . . Poughkeepsie, N.Y., 1840.

Philalethes. *Thomas Kingsmill Abbott, M.A.* Revision of the authorized version: the English Bible and our duty with regard to it . . . Dublin, 1857.

Philalethes. *Col. F. Webb.* Shakspeare's manuscripts in the possession of Mr. Ireland examined, etc. By . . . L. 1796.

Philalethes, M.A., Oxon. *Robert Fellowes.* History of Ceylon . . . L. 1817.

Philalethes, Mencius. *Peter Annet.* The history of Joseph consider'd . . . L. 1744.

Philalethes Candaliensis. *Thomas Lancaster.* An examination of a discourse on baptism with the Holy Ghost; lately published by James Rudd . . . Kendal, 1741.

Philalethes Cantabrigiensis. *Rev. John Jackson.* Farther remarks on Dr. Waterland's farther vindication of Christ's divinity. L. 1724.

Philalethes Cantabrigiensis. *James Jurin, M.D.* Geometry no friend to infidelity. L. 1734.

Philalethes Cantabrigiensis. *Thomas Turton, D.D.* A letter to Edward Copleston, D.D., Provost of Oriel College, Oxford . . . by . . . L. 1822.

Philalethes Cantabrigiensis. *Zachary Grey, LL.D.* Schismatics delineated from authentic vouchers, in reply to Neal, with Dowsing's Journal, etc. By . . . L. 1739.

Philalethes Londiniensis. *Caleb Fleming, D.D.* Civil establishments in religion a ground of infidelity . . . By . . . L. 1767.

Philalethes Rusticus. *Edward Aspinwall.* The impertinence and imposture of modern antiquaries display'd . . . By . . . L. 1839.

Also ascribed to *William Asplin,* Vicar of Banbury.

Philaleutheros. *Caleb Fleming, D.D.* St. Paul's heretic . . . L. 1735.

Philanar and Misostratus, Two London-Apprentices. *John Taylor,* in ΙΠΠ-ΑΝΘΡΩΠΟΣ . . . n.p. 1648.

Philanax, Calvin. *Samuel Young,* who published tracts under this name, and that of "Trepidantium Malleus." L. 1698–1700.

Philander. *Ford, Earl Grey.* The amours of ... and Silvia [Countess of Berkeley] ... By Aphra Behn. L. 1693.

Philander. *Rev. James Wright.* Capital punishment ; is it defensible ? By ... L. 1865.

Philander. *David Williams.* Letters concerning education ... L. 1785.

Philanglia. *James Scott, D.D.*, who published the essays in the London "Public Advertiser," under this signature, 1765 *et seq.*

Philanthropist, A. *W. P. Russell.* British liberty and philanthropy ... L. 1808.

Philanthropist, A. *Josiah Harris.* A voice from the ocean grave ... Truro, 1859.

Philanthropos. *William Ladd.* Brief illustration of the principles of war and peace. Albany, 1831.

Philanthropos. *Thomas Mortimer, Esq.* Every man his own broker ... By ... L. 1761.

Philanthropos. *John Fellows.* Grace triumphant: a sacred poem ... By ... L. 1770.

Philanthropos. *John Dove.* Rational religion, distinguish'd from that which is enthusiastic ... L. 1757 or '58.

Philanthropos. *Thomas Wakefield* (?). Reflections on faith ... By ... L. 1790.

Philanthropos. *John Forster.* Remarks, occasioned by a sermon on the "Reasonableness of the Established Church of England" ... by Johnson Grant, M.A. ... Liverpool, 1807.

Philanthropos, Theophilus. *David Hall.* An essay on intemperance, particularly hard drinking ... By ... 1742.

Philanthropus. *Joseph Besse.* An enquiry into the validity of a late discourse, intituled, "The nature and duty of self-defence." L. 1747.

Philanthropus. *Thomas Bott* (?). Remarks upon Dr. Butler's sixth chapter of the "Analogy of Religion," etc. L. 1737.

Philanthropus Oxoniensis. *Dr. Morgan.* A letter to the Rev. Dr. Waterland, occasioned by his late writings in defence of the Athanasian hypothesis. L. 1722.

Philarchaismos. *Thomas Sharp, Esq.*, in "Gent. Mag." for 1793, p. 690, article on St. Michael's Church, Coventry.

Philaret, a Member of Athens. *John Dunton.* — See "Member of th Athenian Society, A."

Philaretes. *John Gilbert Cooper.* Poems on several subjects. L. 1764.

Originally contributed to "Dodsley's Museum," under this signature.

Philaretes, Philippus, A.C.C. *Thomas Comber.* Adultery analyzed ... 1810.

Philaretus. *Thomas Letchworth.* An essay on liberty and necessity : in answer to Augustus Toplady's tract ... By ... L. about 1776.

Philargyrus. *Rev. William Rider*, who was a writer of verses in the "Gent. Mag." under this signature. 176–.

Phileleutheros. *Rev. John Fell.* The justice and utility of penal laws for the direction of conscience, examined ... L. 1774.

Phileleutheros Londinensis. *John Burton, D.D.* Remarks on Dr. King's speech before the University of Oxford, at the dedication of Dr. Radcliff's library, on the 13th of April, 1748. L. 1749.

Phileleutherus Anglicanus. *Rev. John William Donaldson.* A vindication of Protestant principles. L. 1847.

Phileleutherus Cantabrigiensis. *Thomas Herne, M.A.* Three discourses on private judgment ... by ... L. 1718.

Under this name he was one of the writers in the Bangorian controversy, of which he began, in some measure, the history, by publishing an account of all the considerable pamphlets to which it gave rise ... to the end of the year 1719, by the name of "Philonagnostes Criticus." See *Chalmers*, Vol. 17.

Phileleutherus Christianus. *Rev. Thomas Broughton.* Christianity distinct from the religion of nature ... L. 1732.

Phileleutherus Devoniensis. *Thomas Northmore* (?). Memoirs of Planetes; or, a sketch of the laws and manners of Makar. By ... L. 1795.

Phileleutherus Lipsiensis. *Richard Bentley, D.D.* Remarks upon a late discourse of free-thinking, in a letter to F. H., D.D. [Francis Hare, D.D.] L. 1713.

Phileleutherus Norfolciensis. *Samuel Parr, D.D.* A discourse ... on the late fast. L. 1781.

Phileluth. Bangor, V.E.B. *Thomas Foxcroft.* Eusebius incramatus ... B. 1733.

Philemon. *Henry Coventry.* Letters of ... to Hydaspes. L. 1736–44.

Philenia, a Lady of Boston. *Mrs. Sarah Wentworth (Apthorp) Morton.* Ouâbi; or, the virtues of nature. An Indian tale ... B. 1790.

Philidor, A. D. *François André Dan-*

ican. Analyse du jeu des échecs . . . Paris, 1749.

Philindus. *Dr. Frederick Max Müller.* Correspondence relating to the establishment of an Oriental college in London . . . L. 1858. See "Indophilus."

Philip. *Rev. Philip Pyle,* in Beloe's "Sexagenarian," Vol. II., p. 146. 2d ed. L. 1818.

Philip, Uncle. *Francis Lister Hawks.* The American forest . . . N.Y. 186–.

Philipe, frère. *Mathieu Braussi,* the joint author of about 30 elementary works for the use of schools.

Philips, docteur J. P. *J. P. Durand.* Cours théorique et pratique de braidisme, ou hypnotisme nerveux . . . Paris, 1860.

Phillatins. *David Storer.*

Philo. *Rev. Joseph Proud.* The incendiary corrected; or, injured virtue and honesty defended. A satyric poem. Being an answer to . . . "The Bouseliad" . . . By . . . Norwich, 1786.

Philo. *Ellis Ballou* (?). The patent hat : for the use of mankind in general, and the clergy in particular . . . N.Y. 1855.

Philo-Cato. *Matthew L. Davis* (?). Letters of Marcus and . . . addressed to DeWitt Clinton, Esq., mayor of the city of New York. A new edition, containing one letter of Marcus and several numbers of Philo-Cato, never published before. N.Y. 1810.

Said to be " A caustic, and sometimes comical *exposé* of the political quarrels arising out of the Burr Union, etc., formed about the year 1806, between the Clintonians and Burrites, by *Matthew L. Davis.*"

Philo-Criticus. *Rev. Francis Hare.* The clergyman's thanks to Phileleutherus [*i.e.* Bentley] . . . L. 1713.

Philo-Junius. One of the signatures adopted by Junius (*q.v.*).

In his preface to Woodfall's edition, Junius says : "The auxiliary part of Philo-Junius was indispensably necessary to defend or explain particular passages in Junius, in answer to plausible objections; but the subordinate character is never guilty of the indecorum of praising his principal. The fraud was innocent, and I always intended to explain it."

The following are the dates of the letters signed " Philo-Junius " : —

June 12, 1769.	May 1, 1771.
June 22, 1769.	May 22, 1771.
Aug. 1, 1769.	May 25, 1771.
Aug. 14, 1769.	May 28, 1771.
Sept. 4, 1769.	Aug. 26, 1771.
Oct. 19, 1769.	Oct. 15, 1771.
Nov. 14, 1769.	Oct. 17, 1771.
(See " Moderatus.")	Oct. 18, 1771.
Feb. 6, 1771.	

Philo-Malthus. *George Hancock.* A consideration in political economy . . . L. 1832.

Philo Musa. *Dr. James Currie,* in his contributions to the "Weekly Herald." Liverpool, 1789.

Philo-Nauticus. *Henry Nugent Bell,* whose celebrated research into the Huntingdon Peerage made him as high an authority in genealogical cases, as Sir Harris Nicholas was as his successor in practice.

Philo-Nauticus. *Rev. Lawrence Hynes Halloran, D.D.* The female volunteer; or, the dawning of peace : a drama . . . By . . . L. 1801.

Philo Pacificus. *Noah Worcester.* The friend of peace : containing a special interview between the President of the United States and Omar, an officer dismissed for duelling. Six letters . . . Camb. 1815.

The letters are signed " Omar."

Philo-Roskelynsis. *Robert Forbes,* Bishop Caithness and Orkney. An account of the Chapel of Roslin. Edinb. 1774.

Philo Ruggles. *John Adams,* of the Middle Temple. A treatise on the principles and practice of the action of ejectment . . . N.Y. 1821.

Philo-Scotus. *Duncan Forbes.* Copy of a letter from a gentleman in Edinburgh to his friend in the country, upon the subject of the malt tax. 1725.

Philo-Scotus. *Philip Barrington Ainslie.* Reminiscences of a Scottish gentleman, commencing in 1787 . . . L. 1861.

Philo-Tragicus. *Thady Fitzpatrick.* — See " F., T."

Philo-Veritas. *Thomas D'Arcy M'Gee.* " In 1857, Mr. M'Gee got into a controversy with the Roman Catholic Archbishop Hughes; his communications in the New York 'Times,' over the signature of 'Philo-Veritas,' attracted general attention."

Philobiblius. *Linus Pierpont Brockett.* History and progress of education . . . N.Y. 1859.

Philobiblos. *Alexander Ireland.* The book-lover's enchiridion . . . By . . . L. 1883.

Philobiblos. *Thomas Rodd.* A defence of the veracity of Moses . . . L. 1820.

Philochelidon. *Dr. Thomas Forster.* Observations on the Brumal retreat of the swallow, by . . . L. 1808.

Philochristus. *Rev. Edwin Abbott Abbott.* Memoirs of a disciple of the Lord. L. 1878.

Philocrin, Sampfilius. *William Sampson.* Beasts at law; or, Zoölogian jurisprudence : a poem [by S. Woodworth], trans. from the Arabic of . . . N.Y. 1811.

Philodemus. *Joseph Clegg.* A correct translation of the charter of Liverpool . . . Liverpool, 1757.

Philoglottus. *Richard Parker.* An essay on the usefulness of Oriental learning. L. 1739.

Philojuvenis. *C. J. Hambro.* Edda; or, tales of a grandmother . . . Edited by . . . L. 1847.

Philokalist, A. *Felix Paul Wierzbicki.* The ideal man . . . B. 1842.

Philolegis, Tyro. *Gov. William Livingston,* who, in 1745, published two essays under this signature in Parker's "New York Weekly Post Boy" on the mode of studying law which then prevailed.

Philomath, J. J. *Joseph Jenkins.* A lecture on future punishment. Penzance, 1867.

Philomath: Oxoniensis. *Richard Walker, B.D.* A few words in favour of Professor Powell . . . Oxf. 1832.

Philomauri. *James Moore Smith,* in a communication to the "Daily Journal" (L., Mar. 18, 1728) relative to Alexander Pope.

Philomirth, Aaron. *John Hamilton Parr.* My book . . . Liverpool, 1821.

Philomneste, Junior. *Gustave Brunet.* La bibliomanie en 1878. Paris, 1878.

Philomorus. *Rev. John Howard Marsden.* Philomorus: an examination of the Latin poems of Sir Thomas More. L. 1842.

Πιλόμουσος. *Charles Wallington.* Ismael: an Oriental tale; with other poems. [Of Bulwer-Lytton. With a preface signed . . .] L. 1820.

Philonagnostes Criticus. *Thomas Herne, M.A.* — See "Phileleutherus Cantabrigiensis."

Philonomus Eleutherus. *Dr. John Arbuthnot.* — See "Eminent Lawyer of the Temple, An."

Philopatria. *Thomas Paine.* A discourse shewing that the real first cause of the straits and difficulties of this province of the Massachusetts Bay is its extravagancy . . . B. 1721.

Philopatria. *Rachel Fanny Antonina Lee.* An essay on government by . . . L. 1808.

Philopatris. *Rev. Thomas Burgess.* Letters . . . to Dr. Phillimore . . . L. 1819.
Reprinted from the "Morning Post."

Philopatris Varvicensis. *Samuel Parr, D.D.* Characters of the late Charles James Fox . . . L. 1809.

Philopenes. *John Dormer.* Usury explained . . . L. 1818.

Philopis. *Prof. James Marsh,* who, under this signature, published papers in the "Vermont Chronicle," 1829, on "Popular Education."

Philopolites. *William Pettman.* A letter to W. A. Miles . . . L. 1808.

Philopolities. *Rev. Benjamin Prescott.* Free and calm consideration of the misunderstandings between the Parliament of Great Britain and the American colonies. Salem, 1774.

Philopropos. *William Duncombe.*

"In 1728, a letter by *Mr. Duncombe,* signed 'Philopropos,' was printed in the 'London Journal' of March 30, containing some animadversions on the 'Beggar's Opera' . . . And the same popular entertainment having been soon after most seasonably condemned in a sermon preached at Lincoln's-Inn chapel by Dr. Herring . . . in a subsequent letter on the same subject in the 'London Journal' of April 20, subscribed 'Benevolus,' he paid a just compliment, etc."

Philopyrphagus Ashburniensis. *Ellis Farneworth.*

"*Mr. Farneworth* is supposed to have been the author of a ludicrous and pleasant account of Powell, the fire-eater, in 'Gent. Mag.,' 1755 [p. 59], signed 'Philopyrphagus Ashburniensis.'" — See CHALMERS, Vol. 14.

Phil-orthos. *George Johnstone.* The eternal obligation of natural religion . . . L. 1732.

Philorthos. *William Frederick Poole.* The orthographical hobgoblin . . . Springfield, Mass., 1856.

Philos. *Rev. James Challen,* in his contributions to reviews, periodicals, etc.

Philosopher, A. *Charles Babbage.* Passages from the life of . . . L. 1864.

Philosopher of Wimbledon, The. *John Horne Tooke.*

Philostratus. *Thomas Foster, F.R.S., M.B.* Somatopsychonoologia . . . L. 1823.

Philotesis. *Daniel Roberts.* Reasons why the Society of Friends should not vote for Members of Parliament, etc. L. 1804.

Philotheorus. *Samuel Dexter, Sr.*

Philotheorus. *Caleb Fleming.* Religion not the magistrates' province . . . L. 1773.

Philoxenus Secundus. *Rev. Stephen Weston.* Persian recreations . . . L. 1812.

Phiz. *Hablot Knight Browne.* Hunting bits . . . L.

Phiz, Francis. *Francis Edward Smedley.* Lewis Arundel. L. 1855.

Phlogobombus, Terentius. *Samuel B. H. Judah.* The buccaneers: a romance of our own country in its ancient days . . . B. 1827.

Phocion. *William Loughton Smith, LL.D.* American arguments for British rights. L. 1866.

Phocion. *Alexander Hamilton.* Letter from ... to the citizens of New York on the politics of the times ... P. 1784.

Phocion. *George Ticknor Curtis.* Letters of ... First printed in the "Boston Daily Advertiser and Courier," August to November, 1853.

Phocion. *Thomas Hartley.* Observations on the propriety of fixing upon a central and inland situation for the permanent residence of Congress ... N.Y. 1789.

Phœnix. *Sir Henry William Martin. Bart.* Archbishop Murray's Douay and Rhemish Bible ... L. 1850.

Phœnix, John. *Capt. George Horatio Derby.* Phœnixiana; or, sketches and burlesques. N.Y. 1856.

Photius, Junior. *W. Sherlock.* Letters on literature. Brussels, 1836.

Phrenologist, A. *Thomas Tichborne.* The amendment of the law of lunacy: a letter to Lord Brougham. L. 1840.

Physician, A. *Sir Philip Crampton.* An attempt to explain ... the cures ... of Miss Lalor and Mrs. Stuart. Dublin, 1823.

Physician, A. *J. Hoskyns.* A commentary on "The Revelation of Jesus Christ." Dublin, 1863.

Physician, A. *Andrew Wilson, M.D.* An essay on the autumnal dysentery. By ... L. 1761.

Physician, A. *Dr. James Mackenzie.* Essays and meditations on various subjects. Edinb. 1762.

Physician, A. *Joseph Bullar, M.D.* Evening thoughts ... L. 1850.

Physician, A. *John Rutty, M.D.* A faithful narrative of a remarkable visitation. By ... L. 1776.

Physician, A. *Thomas Foster Barham, M.B.* Genuine Christianity; or, the Unitarian doctrine briefly stated. Penzance, 1824.

Physician, A. *John Ayrton Paris, M.D.* A guide to Mount's Bay and the Land's End. L. 1824.

Physician, A. *James Warburton Begbie.* Handy book of medical information and advice ... L. 1859.

Physician, A. *D. E. Smith.* Leaves from a physician's journal. N.Y. 1867.

Physician, A. *Samuel Dickson* (?). London medical practice, its sins and its shortcomings. L. 1860.

Physician, A. *Thomas Forster.* Medicina simplex ... Chelmsford, 1829.

Physician, A. *Dr. Wurderman.* Notes on Cuba, by ... B. 1844.

Physician, A. *John Darby.* Odd hours of ... P. 1871.

Physician in Hertfordshire, A. *Francis Bragge.* A full confutation of witchcraft ... L. 1712.

Physician in the West Indies, A. *James Grainger, M.D.* An essay on the more common West India diseases ... L. 1764.

Physician in Town, A. *Daniel Cox, M.D.* A letter from ... to a friend in the country, on the subject of inoculation ... L. 1757.

Physician of Philadelphia, A. *William E. Horner, M.D.* Observations on the mineral waters in the south-western part of Virginia ... P. 1834.

Physician's Wife, A. *Mrs. Madeline Leslie.* Revelations of ... B. 1859.

Physicien voyageur, Un. *Thomas Forster.* Annales d' ... volume contenant les années 1831–34. Bruges, 1851.

Physico-Theologus. *Rev. Thomas Tregenna Biddulph, M.A.* Thirteen letters on Christian philosophy, in the "Christian Guardian," 1819–20.

Physicus. *George J. Romanes.* A candid examination of Theism. L. 1878.

Pianist, A. *Louis M. Gottschalk,* in the "Atlantic Monthly."

Picard, Léon. *Antoine Bayard.* Le bonheur dans la retraite ... Paris, 1838.

Piccadilly. *Pierre Girard,* European correspondent of the N.Y. "World" for several years, including the Franco-German war.

Picciola. *Miss Angelina S. Mumford,* who published a number of poetical pieces under this pen name.

Pick, Mr. *Joseph A. Scoville.*

Pick and Pen. *Henry Rosales.* Essay on the origin and distribution of gold in quartz veins ... Melbourne, 1861.

Pickaway. *Allen O. Myers,* in his contributions to the "Enquirer" (Cin., O.).

Picket. *B. W. Tomlinson,* in his contributions to the "News and Courier" (Charleston, S.C.), and the "World" (N.Y.).

Pickle, Peregrine. *George P. Upton.* Letters of ... Chic. 1869.

These letters first appeared in the Chicago "Tribune," under the above signature.

Pickle, Prometheus. *William Bush.*

Pictor Ignotus. *William Blake.* Selections from poems. L. 1863.

Piedfort, Athanase. *Charles Gille.* Histoire de M. Louis Bonaparte ... Paris, 1848.

Pierce, Dod, M.S. Probably *Dr. Barrowby* and *Dr. Schomberg, Jr.* A letter to the real and genuine Pierce Dod, M.D., actual physician of St. Bartholomew's Hospital ... L. 1746.

Pierre et Paul. *Paul de Lourdoueix.* Histoire de trente heures ... Paris, 1848.

Pigmy, Sir Minimus. *John Kent,* who, under this signature, published in a Canadian periodical a humorous paper entitled "A Defence of Little Men." — See "Fairford, Alan."

Pikestaff. *Thomas Baker.* Plain papers by ... L. 1866.

Pikromel, Timotheus, Esq. *Thomas Clarke.* Erotophuseos; or, the love of nature ... L. 1840.

Pilgrim, A. *Frederick Wright.* Lays of ... Brockville, Can., 1864.

Pilgrim, A. *David Addison Harsha.* Wanderings of ... N.Y. 1854.

Pilgrim, A. *Mrs. Fanny (Parkes) Parlby.* Wanderings of ... in search of the picturesque during four-and-twenty years in the East ... L. 1850.

Pilgrim of 1851, A. *Rev. Frederic West Holland.* Scenes in Palestine, by ... B. 1852.

Pilgrim, A. *George Barrell Cheever.* Wanderings of ... in the shadow of Mont Blanc and the Jungfrau Alp. N.Y. 1845.

Pilgrim, Peter. *Robert Montgomery Bird, M.D.* Peter Pilgrim; or, a rambler's recollections. N.Y. 1838.

Pilot who has hitherto weathered the Storm, A. *James Brown.* General hints for improving the merchant service of the United Kingdom ... Glasgow, 1825.

Pimpernel. *Rev. W. H. Beaver,* in London "Live Stock Journal."

Pindar, Jonathan. *Saint George Tucker.* Liberty, Days of my youth, and other poems, some of them political satires under the title of "Jonathan Pindar."

Pindar, Paul, Gent. *John Yonge Akerman.* London legends ... L. 1862.

Pindar, Peter. *C. F. Lawler.* Selim: a tale. L. 1803.

Pindar, Peter, Esq. *John Wolcot.* The fat knight and the petition; or, cits in the dumps. L. 1815.

Pindar, Peter, Jun. *Henry S. Ellenwood,* the writer of a number of poetical trifles in the Peter Pindaric style, some of them signed as above, and others "Cape Cod Bard," for the "New England Galaxy," Boston, 1817 *et seq.*

Pine, Cuyler. *Ellen Peck.* Ecce Femina; or, the woman Zoe. N.Y. 186–.

Pinkney, Miles. *Thomas Carre.*

Pinneberg, Rentier. *Carl Hauser,* in his contributions to the German edition of "Puck" (N.Y.).

Piomingo. *John Robinson.* The savage. P. 1810. — See "American Hist. Record," III., pp. 373, 466.

Pioneer of the Wilderness, A. *Rev. — Rose.* The emigrant churchman. L. 1849.•

Pious Jeems. *Col. James Gordon.*

Pious Lawyer (A), late Lieutenant in the American Navy. *Daniel Murray.* Extract from a letter written by ... n.p., n.d.

Pipes, Jeemes, of Pipesville. *Stephen C. Massett.* Drifting about; or, what J. P. of P. saw-and-did: an autobiography ... N.Y. 1863.

Pippen, Parley. *M. R. Bartlett (?).* The orator's ladder, in three parts ... N.Y. 1843.

Pips, Mr. *Percival Leigh,* in "Punch" (L.).

Piscator. *William Elliott,* who published essays by "Piscator" and "Venator," which were afterwards enlarged and embodied in "Carolina Sports."

Piscator. *Thomas Pike Lathy, Esq.* The angler: a poem in ten cantos ... L. 1819.

Piscator. *Robert Lascelles.* Angling .·. L. 1815.

Piscator. *William Hughes.* Fish, how to choose and how to dress. L. 1843.

Piscator. *Alfred Ronalds.* Fly fisher's entomology ... L. 1856.

Piscator. *George P. R. Pulman.* Rustic sketches: being poems on angling ... By ... Taunton, 1842.

Piscator. *Walter Henry.* Salmon fishing in Canada, letters under this signature in the New York "Albion."

Piscator Fluviatulus. *Rev. John Seccombe.*

Pisistratus. *William Black.*

Piso, Lucius Manlius. *Rev. William Ware.* Letters of ... N.Y. 1837.

Pitarra, Serafi. *Frederick Soler.* Lo dir de la gent. 1880.

Pitt, William. *Robert Wickliffe, Jr.* Letters to the Hon. James T. Morehead, on Transylvania University ... By ... Smithland, Ky., 1837.

Place, Benjamin. *Edward Thring, M.A.* Thoughts on life science ... L. 1869.

Plain, Timothy. *G. W. Blaikie.* Fire: a poem ... Edinb. 1828.

Plain, Timothy. *Moncrieff Threepland.* Letters respecting the perform-

ances at the Theatre Royal, Edinburgh
... Edinb. 1800.

Plain, Honest, Lay-man, A. *Edward King, F.R.S., F.A.S.* Honest apprehensions; or, the unbiassed and sincere confession of faith of ... L. 1803.

Plain Man, A. *William Coombe, Esq.* Plain Thoughts of ... L. 1797.

Plain Woman, A. *Catharine Barter.* Alone among the Zulus ... L. 1866.

Plantagenet. *William Bromet, M.D., F.S.A.* His usual signature in the "Gent. Mag."

Planter, A. *Edward Long.* Candid reflections upon the judgment, lately awarded by the Court of King's Bench, in Westminster-Hall, on what is commonly called the Negro Cause. By ... L. 1772.

Planter and Distiller in Bengal, A. *John Prinsep.* An account of the method and expence of cultivating the sugar cane in Bengal ... L. 1793.

Platonist, The. *Thomas Taylor.*

Plautus. *Alexander Wilder, M.D.* His signature as legislative correspondent of the "Evening Post" (N.Y.), from 1859 to 1871.

Play-goer, A. *Joseph N. Ireland.* Fifty years of ... or, annals of the New York stage from A.D. 1798 to A.D. 1848 ...

Plinius Secundus. *John Rumsey.* Curiæ Canadenses; or, the Canadian Law Courts ... Toronto, 1843.

Plough, Peter. *James S. Barty, D.D.* P. P.'s letters to the Right Hon. Lord Kinniard on high farming and free trade. Edinb. 1850.

Ploughist, A. *Samuel Pegge.* Against Faunists. "Gent. Mag.," 1792, p. 1002. See "Gent. Mag.," LXVI., p. 1084.

Ploughman, John. *Rev. Charles Hadden Spurgeon.* John Ploughman's talk: plain advice to plain people. N.Y. 1869.

Ploughshare, Peter. *Samuel B. Beach* (?). Considerations against continuing the great canal west of the Seneca ... By ... Utica, N.Y., 1819.

Plover. *John S. Wise,* in the "American Field."

Plowshare, John. *Alfred Sharples,* a writer on agricultural subjects.

Plume, Porte. *W. M. Harding.* Trans-atlantic sketches ... N.Y. 1870.

Pl—sh, Je—mes, Esq. *William Makepeace Thackeray.* Crinoline. "Punch," 1847.

Plymley, Peter. *Rev. Sydney Smith.* Letters on the subject of the Catholics, to my brother Abraham, who lives in the country. L. 1838.

Pocahontas. *Mrs. C. H. Pearson.* Cousin Franck's household; or, scenes in the Old Dominion ... B. 1853.

Poche. *Pierre Deschamps.* Bibliographie Molièresque de ... Paris, 1879.

Podgers. *R. L. Ogden,* in the New York "Forest and Stream."

Poet, A. *Laughton Osborn.* Confessions of a poet. P. 1835.

Poet, A. *James Montgomery.* A poet's portfolio; or, minor poems ... 1835.

Poet at the Breakfast Table, The. *Oliver Wendell Holmes,* in the "Atlantic Monthly."

Poet of Kirkintilloch, The. *Walker Watson.* Jockie's far awa', and other popular songs.

Poet of Nature, The. *William Wordsworth.* "Poet of Nature, thou hast wept to know." To Wordsworth, by Percy Bysshe Shelley.

Poet of Poets, The. *Percy Bysshe Shelley.*

Poet of the Poor, The. *George Crabbe.*

Poet Laureate of the New Town Dispensary, The. *Douglas Maglagan, M.D.* Nugæ canoræ medicæ: lays by ... Edinb. 1850.

Poet Laureat of Westminster, The. *George Bridgman.*

Poeta, Enginæ Societatis [of Harvard College, Cambridge, Mass.]. *Augustus Peirce.* The Rebelliad; or, terrible transactions at the seat of the Muses: a poem in four cantos, auctore ... Edited and patronized by the Pi Tau. B. 1842.

ACTEURS (College Faculty in 1819).

"Lord Bibo," *Pres. Kirkland, D.D., LL.D.*; "Dr. Pop," *Dr. Popkin,* Prof. of Greek; "Sikes," *Rev. Henry Ware, D.D.,* Prof. of Divinity; "Touchy," *Rev. John Brazer, A.M.,* Prof. of Latin; "Logic," *Levi Hedge, LL.D.,* Prof. of Logic, etc.; "Screwem," *John Farrar, LL.D.,* Prof. of Mathematics, etc.; "Gad Norton," *Andrews Norton, A.M.,* Librarian and Prof. of Sacred Literature; "Willard," *Sidney Willard,* Prof. of Hebrew, etc.; "Sparks," *Jared Sparks, A.M.,* Tutor; "Barnwell and Nathan," *Robert W. Barnwell,* Sophomore, *post* Col. Carol. Austr. Pres.; "Abijah," a Freshman; "Caleb," *Caleb Stetson,* a Sophomore, afterwards the Rev. Caleb Stetson; "Goody" and "Goody Muse," *Mrs. Morse;* "Wallis," *Charley Wallis,* Musician.

"This poem was written by Augustus Peirce of the class [Harv. Coll.] of 1820, and was delivered before the 'College Engine Club,' in July, 1819 ... At the time it was written, Peirce was not seventeen years of age, and was the youngest member of his class ... The next day, Pres. Kirkland called Peirce to his study ... for 'cutting prayers' ... and said, 'Peirce, I think you would be more regular in attending morning prayers, if you ... did not sit up so late *writing poor poetry.*' Nothing more was said to him on the subject by any of the faculty."

Poetaster, A. *George Hughes.* Rhymes by ... L. 1846.

Polesworth, Sir Humphry. *Jonathan Swift, D.D.* Law is a bottomless pit; or, the history of John Bull ... 1712–13.

Poliarchus. *Sir Charles Cotterel.* — See "Orinda."

Policeman X. 54. *William Makepeace Thackeray.* A Bow Street ballad ... "Punch," Nov. 25, 1848.

Political Apothecary, A. *W. P. Russell.* An anodyne to soothe Catholic intemperance ... L. 1812.

Polluto. *Frank B. Wilkie.* Petrolia; or, the oil regions of the United States. Chic. 1865.

Polko, Elise. *Elise Vogel.* Musical sketches. Translated. P. 1864.

Pollock, Guy. *Robert Douglas Hamilton, M.D.*, who, under this signature, contributed several series of letters on literary, political, and other subjects, to the "Canadian Literary Magazine," York, 1833; and the "Courier of Upper Canada," the "Herald," the "Palladium," and the "British Colonist," all of Toronto.

Polyanthus. *John Wilson.* The Parisian mirror; or, letters from Paris, in "Blackwood's Magazine," Vol. XI., p. 217 *et seq.*

Polypus. *Eaton Stannard Barrett.* All the talents. A satirical poem ... L. 1807.

Polyxena. *Philip Thicknesse, Esq.* in the "Gent. Mag."

Pomeroy, "Brick." *Mark M. Pomeroy.* Sense; or, Saturday night musings ... N.Y. 1868. Nonsense; or, hits and criticisms on the follies of the day ... N.Y. 1868.

Pomeroy, Eugene. *Thomas F. Donnelly.*

Pomfret, Peter. *Rev. Richard Graves.* Lucubrations ... in prose and verse. L. 18–.

Pomona. One of the pseudonyms attributed to Junius (*q.v.*).

The letter thus signed, is dated July 1, 1768; it is directed "to Master Harry, in Black Boy Alley," and relates to his "duplicity in promising a place to Lord Rockingham and to another person."

Pomponio, Leto. *Marchese Francesco Vitelleschi.* Vatican council. L. 1876.

Ponder, Rev. Peter. *Rev. William Bell.* Kirkcumdoon ... Edinb. 1875.

Ponny. *Horace Mayhew.*

"'Ponny' was a nickname. Most of the men [writers for 'Punch'] were known to each other by some familiar pseudonym. They call *Mr. Percival Leigh* 'Professor' to this day, *Mark Lemon* was 'Uncle Mark,' and old *Evans* 'Pater.'"—See HATTON'S "Journalistic London," pp. 19, 20.

Pontiac. *Oliver Knight*, in "Harper's Weekly."

Pontoosuc. *Ensign H. Kellogg.* The Johnson protocol and international good neighborhood ... Pittsfield, Mass., 1869.

Poor-Rich Man, A. *John Berrien Lindsley, M.D.* Our ruin: its causes and cure. By ... Nashville, Tenn., 1868.

Poor Richard. *Benjamin Franklin.* — See "Saunders, Richard."

Poor Robert the Scribe. *Charles Miner.* Essays from the desk of ... P. 184-.

Popinack. *Mrs. Virginia Durant Covington.* — See "Fabian."

Poplar, Anthony. *Rev. Charles Stuart Stanford*, editor of the "Dublin University Magazine."

Poplicola. The earliest signature adopted by Junius (*q.v.*). The attack on Lord Chatham, which was signed as above, was published in the "Public Advertiser," April 28, 1767. The signature was only once more employed, *viz.* in the letter dated May 28, 1767, which was the celebrated reply to Sir William Draper's defence of Lord Chatham.

Poplicola, in April, 1767, depicts Lord Chatham as aspiring to a political dictatorship, and that the Tarpeian rock or a gibbet would be enough for the "carcase of such a traitor." But observe the contrast: Junius, in a letter addressed to the Earl of Chatham in the following January, marked "private and secret, to be opened by Lord Chatham only," sets himself forth as a warm admirer of that statesman, and anxiously cautions him against the underhand practices of his colleagues, especially of Lord Northington and Mr. Conway, concluding as follows :—

"My Lord, the man who presumes to give your Lordship these hints admires your character without servility, and is convinced that, if this country can be saved, it must be saved by Lord Chatham's spirit, by Lord Chatham's abilities."—"Correspondence of the Earl of Chatham," vol. iii., p. 305.

Upon this Wade remarks: —

"So that the 'dictator' of Poplicola is the saviour of Junius, both one writer. Impossible! Who then, it may be asked, was Poplicola? a question probably not very material to answer if he were not Junius. But I will mention one conjecture by an American editor, namely, that Poplicola was Horne Tooke, which seems not unlikely. About this period Mr. Horne Tooke returned from a tour in Italy as travelling tutor; on his way he spent some weeks with Mr. Wilkes in Paris, and imbibed his rancour against Grafton and Chatham; the latter, in the full bloom of place, peerage, and pension, having haughtily rejected Wilkes's application for compensation or public employment, and disowned his quondam friend 'as the blasphemer of his God and libeller of his king.' In retaliation, Wilkes addressed a bitter, inculpatory letter to the Duke of Grafton, and Mr. Tooke is surmised to have lent his auxiliary aid by the two letters signed 'Poplicola.'"

Poplicola, Valerius. *Samuel Adams,* in the "Boston Gazette," Oct. 28, 1771; Oct. 5, 1772.

Popular Author, A. — *Montgomery* (?). Essays and tales by . . . L. 1833.

Porcupine, Peter. *William Cobbett.* The rush-light. N.Y. 1800.

Porcustus. *Henry Swinburne, Esq.,* who, under this signature, communicated a Roman inscription to the "Gent. Mag."

Porson of Old English and French Literature, The. *Francis Douce.*

Porte. *G. H. Mathews.* Diary of a summer in Europe . . . N.Y. 1866.

Portia. *Mrs. Abigail Adams.* — See "Diana."

Portius. *Samuel Pegge.* A short letter referring to p. 25, "Gent. Mag.," 1785, p. 176. — See "Gent. Mag.," LXVI., p. 1082.

Porus, King. *John Proby,* the reporter for the London "Morning Chronicle."

Positive, Paul. *James Montgomery.* Prison amusements, by . . . 1797.

'Possum, Peter. *Richard Rowe.* P. P.'s portfolio. Sydney, 1858.

Postman Poet, The. *Edward Capern.*

Potion, Paul. *William Phillips* or *Shearsmith.* A poetical picture of Worthing and its vicinity. Worthing, 1814.

Potiphar, Paul. *George William Curtis.* The Potiphar papers. N.Y. 1854.

Potter, Maj. Roger Sherman. *Frederic Colburn Adams.* Life and adventures of . . . N.Y. 186–.

Potts, Pipsey. *Miss Rosella Rice,* in her contributions to "Arthur's Magazine."

Pounce, Peter, Esq. *Richard Lewis.* The Robin Hood Society : a satire . . . By . . . L. 1756.

Powel, R., the Puppet-Show Man. *Sir Thomas Burnet.* A second tale of the tub . . . [A satire on the Earl of Oxford.] L. 1715.

Powell, Mary. *Mrs. Anne Manning Rathbone.*

Poyntz, Launce. *Frederick Whittaker.* Numerous mediæval tales contributed to the "Fireside Companion" (N.Y. about 1870).

Practical Banker, A. *James B. Congdon.* A defence of the currency of Massachusetts. B. 1856.

Practical Farmer, A. *David Henry.* The complete English Farmer . . . By . . . and a friend of the late Mr. Jethro Tull . . . L. 1772.

Practical Gardener, A. *Thomas*

Green Fessenden. The American kitchen gardener. N.Y. 1852.

Practical Hand, A. *John Hill Burton.* Convicts. Edinb. 1865.

Practical Printer, A. *John Mitchell.* A manual of punctuation . . . Manchester, 1859.

Practical Teacher, A. *Benjamin Greenleaf.* Key to the new practical arithmetic . . . B. 1867.

Practical Teacher, A. *George Bettany.* Murby's Scripture manuals. The book of Genesis . . . L. 1867, etc.

Practitioner of more than Fifty Years' Experience in the Art of Angling. *John Bartlett.* A catalogue of books on angling . . . From the library of . . . Camb., Mass., 1882.

Prairie Bird. *Mary W. Wellman.* Poems and other thoughts. B. 1854.

Prattle, Mrs. For the supposed editor of the "Parrot." L. 1728.

Prawda, Franz. *Adalbert Klinka,* who, during a literary career of 30 years, has written a whole library of popular histories.

Preacher of the Gospel, A. *Peter Hately Waddell.* A letter to R. Wardlaw . . . By . . . L. 1844.

Prendergast, Paul. *Douglas William Jerrold.* The heads of the people. L. 182–.

Presbyter. *Samuel Hurlbeart Turner, D.D.* Strictures on Archdeacon Wilberforce's doctrine of Incarnation, etc. L. 1851.

Presbyter. *John Morgan.* Trinity Church case . . . N.Y. 1856.

Presbyter, A. *Rev. Berkely Addison, A.M.* An earnest and solemn remonstrance . . . Edinb. 1843.

Presbyter, The. *Rev. Thomas Haweis, LL.B., M.D.* Plain truths; or, the . . . reply to all his anti-Calvinist opponents . . . L. 1805.

Presbyter Anglicanus. *Joseph Hemington Harris.* Auricular Confession : not the rule of the Church of England. 1852.

Presbyter Catholicus. *Rev. William Harness.* Visiting Societies and Lay Readers. L. 1844.

Presbyter Cicestrensis. *Henry Latham.* Anthologia Davidica . . . L. 1846.

Presbyter in the Diocese of Canterbury, A. *Rev. and Hon. Arthur Philip Perceval.* An address to the deans and chapters of the cathedral churches in England and Wales . . . L. 1833.

Presbyter of the Church in Philadelphia, A. *Rev. J. P. Lundy.* Review of Bishop Hopkins' Bible view of slavery ... 1863.

Presbyter of the Church of England, A. *John Jackson.* An answer to a book entitled, Things divine and supernatural conceiv'd by analogy with things natural and human ... L. 1733.

Presbyter of the Church of England, A. *Rev. John Hancock.* An answer to some things contain'd in Dr. Hicks's Christian priesthood asserted ... L. 1709.

Pre[s]byter of the Church of England, A. *Matthew Hole.* An antidote against infidelity ... L. 1702.

Presbyter of the Church of England, A. *Mr. Sharp.* An appeal of the clergy of the Church of England to the bishops ... L. 1706.

Presbyter of the Church of England, A. *William Robertson, D.D.* An attempt to explain the words, reason, substance, person, creeds, orthodoxy, Catholic Church, subscription, and Index Expurgatorius ... By ... L. 1766.

Presbyter of the Church of England, A. *John Pittis.* The character of a primitive bishop ... L. 1709.

Presbyter of the Church of England, A. *Rev. Augustus Montague Toplady.* The Church of England vindicated from the charge of Arminianism ... By ... L. 1769.

Presbyter of the Church of England, A. *Rev. Francis Hare.* The difficulties and discouragements which attend the study of the Scripture ... L. 1714.

Presbyter of the Church of England, A. *Rev. — Tremellier.* The divine right of Episcopacy asserted ... L. 1708.

Presbyter of the Church of England, A. *Rev. Samuel Walker.* The doctrine of the Eucharist stated . . . By ... L. 1720.

Presbyter of the Church of England, A. *Robert Hall.* Four sermons upon most important topicks ... L. 1715.

Presbyter of the Church of England, A. *Joseph Pitts.* Immortality preternatural to human souls ... L. 1708.

Presbyter of the Church of England, A. *William Asplin.* A letter to [Edmund Gibson] the Bishop of London ... L. 1730.

Signed "W. A.," and also ascribed to *W. Austin.*

Presbyter of the Church of England, A. *William Sclater, D.D.* An original draught of the Primitive Church ... By ... L. 1717.

Presbyter of the Church of England, A. *Rev. James Creighton* (?). The reciprocal duty of the ministers of Christ and of the people ... By ... L. 1790.

Presbyter of the Church of England, A. *Rev. William Jones.* Reflections on the growth of Heathenism among modern Christians, in a letter to a friend at Oxford. L. 1776.

Presbyter of the Church of England, A. *Zachary Grey, LL.D.* A vindication of the Church of England, in answer to Mr. Pearce's vindication of the Dissenters; by ... L. 1720.

Presbyter of the Diocese of Maryland, A. *Norris M. Jones.* A letter to a Methodist, by ... Balt. 1844.

Presbyter of the Diocese of Toronto, A. *Rev. William Stewart Darling.* Sketches of Canadian life, lay and ecclesiastical ... L. 1849.

Presbyterian, A. *Rev. Alexander Blaikie.* The schools . . . New, old, older, and oldest schools of Presbyterians in the United States ... B. 1860.

Presbyterian Minister in the Countrey, A. *Rev. James Bannatyne.* A letter ... concerning toleration and patronages. n.p. 1703.

Presbyterian Scot, A. *Alexander P. Stewart, M.D.* "Divide and conquer"; or, diplomacy and the Church of Scotland ... L. 1843.

Presbyterus. *Rev. Robert Hussey.* A help to young clergymen ... Oxf. 1839.

President, The. *Sir John Sinclair.* Account of the Origin of the Board of Agriculture, and its progress for three years after its establishment. L. 1796.

President, The. *John Alderson, M.D.* An address to the subscribers to the library at Hull at the opening of the new rooms ... Hull, 1801.

President, The. *Amos Binney.* Remarks made at the annual meeting of the Boston Society of Natural History, June 2, 1845 ... B. 1845.

President, The. *Thomas Sanden, M.D.* Three discourses ... delivered at Chichester. L. 1802.

President, The. *John Jay.* Union League Club of New York. Address of ... Paris, 1866.

President of Kenyon College, The. *Philander Chase.* Facts and circumstances relating to the endowment of the Theological Seminary of Ohio. By ... Gambier, Ohio, 1849.

Presto. *Jonathan Swift* refers to himself at times under this pseudonym.

"It was bestowed upon him by the Duchess of Shrewsbury, who, being a foreigner, could not pronounce 'Swift' properly, and thus translated it."

Preston, Laura. *Mrs. S. M. Heaven.* Aldeane. San Fran. 1868.

Preston, Paul. *Thomas Picton* (?). The fireside magician; or, the art of natural magic made easy ... N.Y. 1870.

Pretzel, Karl. *Charles H. Harris.*

Prevost, Katherine. *E. M. Olcott.* Margaret Worthington ... B. 1872.

Priam. *C. J. Collins.* Dick Diminy; or, the life and adventures of a jockey ... L. 1855.

Priest, A. *Francis Lloyd Bagshawe.* A catechism of the sacraments of the Catholic church. Compiled by ... L. 1871.

Priest of the Church of England, A. *Rev. Luke Milbourne.* A letter to [Lawrence] the author of lay baptism invalid ... n.p. 1713.

Priest of the Church of England, A. *Rev. Hilkiah Bedford.* A vindication of the Church of England from the aspersions of a late libel intituled "Priestcraft in perfection," etc. By ... L. 1710.

Priest of the Congregation of the Most Holy Redeemer. *Rev. J. H. Cornell.* The little vesper-book ... Balt. 1860.

Priest of the English Church, A. *Rev. Clement Ogle Smith.* Family prayers for morning and evening ... L. 1862.

Priggins, Peter. *Rev. Joseph T. J. Hewlett,* the author of "Peter Priggins," "College Life," and "Parsons and Widows," the two former of which appeared in the "New Monthly Magazine," 1840–42. He sometimes signed "P*" instead of "P. P."

Primcock, A. *James Ralph.* The taste of the town; or, a guide to all publick diversions ... L. 1731.

Prime Minister, A. *Robert Folkestone Williams.* Mephistopheles in England; or, the confessions of ... L. 1835.

Prince. *Leon N. Salmon.*

Prince de la critique, Le. *Jules Gabriel Janin.*

Prince of the Infernal Regions, The. *John Campbell.* A letter ... to a spiritual lord on this side the great gulf ... L. 1751.

Principiis Obsta. *Samuel Adams,* in the "Boston Gazette," Oct. 17, 1768.

Pringle, Seth. *Charles Francis Barnard,* a member of the "Polyglot Club," consisting of the nine editors of the "Harvard Register," Camb., 1827–28.

Prior, Samuel. *John Galt.* All the voyages around the world ... L. 1820.

Priscilla. *Mrs.* (*Torkington*) *Jebb,* widow of John Jebb, M.D., who died in 1786. "The doctor, it is well known, engaged in some very serious controversies with the University [of Cambridge] ... *Mrs. Jebb* was not content with being a silent observer; she became an active opponent of Dr. Powell ... It was in reference to the force of argument contained in a smart pamphlet written by *Mrs. Jebb* ... under the signature of 'Priscilla' ..." — See "Gent. Mag.," January, 1812, p. 94.

Prison Matron, A. *Miss Mary Carpenter.* Female life in prison ... L. 1862.

Prisoner on the Common Side, A. *Simon Wood.* Remarks on the Fleet Prison; or, lumber-house for men and women. Written by ... L. 1733.

Prisonnier d'État Canadien en 1838, Un. *Felix Poutré.* Souvenirs d' ... Montreal, 1861.

Private. *Rev. Benjamin Franklin De Costa,* in his letters to the "Advertiser" (B.) during 1861–62.

Private Gentleman, A. *Daniel Defoe.* Christian conversation; in six dialogues ... L. 1720.

Private Gentleman, A. *Edward Synge,* Archbishop of Tuam. A Gentleman's religion ... By ... Dublin, 1693.

Private Gentleman, A. *Thomas Allan.* Sketch of Mr. Davy's lectures in Geology ... From notes taken by ... Edinb. 1811 (?).

Private Man, A. *Rev. Francis Wolaston, LL.D.* The secret history of ... [An autobiography.] L. 1795.

Private Person, A. *Thomas Rogerson.* The controversy about restoring some prayers, etc. ... L. 1719.

Private Soldier, A. *J. P. Blessington.* Campaigns of Walker's Texas Division; by ... 1875.

Private Soldier, A. *C. S. McClenthen.* Narrative of the Fall and Winter campaign ... Syracuse, N.Y., 1863.

Private Tutor, A. *David James Vaughan.* A few words about private tuition ... Camb. 1852.

Private of the 38th Artists', and Member of the Alpine Club, A. *John Barrow.* Expeditions on the glaciers ... L. 1864.

Privateer. *Charles J. Foster,* in the "New York Sportsman."

Probationer of the Church of Scotland, A. *William Rae.* The Dissenters and Voluntary Church-men ... Edinb. 1835.

Probus. *Thomas Chatterton,* in the "Political Register."

Probus. *David Lee Child.* The Texan revolution ... W. 1843.

Probus Britannicus. *Samuel Johnson, LL.D.* Marmor Norfolciense ... L. 1739.

Procul. *Rev. Robert Stephen Hawker, M.A.* The Cell. verses. Signed ... Monasterium Morwennæ in the year of the church, 1840. "British Mag.," xvii., 622–23. 1840.

Professor. *Percival Leigh.* — See "Ponny."

Professor, A. *John Gwilliam.* The delicious amour ... By ... L. 1812.

Professor at the Breakfast Table, The. *O. W. Holmes,* in the "Atlantic Monthly."

Professor of Surgery, A. *John O. Justamond.* Notes on chirurgical cases and observations, by ... L. 1773.

Profit and Loss. *James Loring Baker.* A review of the tariff of 1846 ... in a series of articles contributed to the "Evening Transcript," under this signature. B. 1858.

Prog. *Thomas J. Scott,* in the "Turf, Field, & Farm."

Prolix, Peregrine. *Philip Houlbrooke Nicklin.* A pleasant peregrination through the prettiest parts of Pennsylvania ... P. 1835.

Prometheus. *Francis Alfred Steimer,* in the "Turf, Field, & Farm" (N.Y.).

Prominent London Journalist, A. *Frank Harrison Hill.* Political portraits, by ... P. 1873.

Promotion by Merit. *William Angers.* Purchase in the Church ... Manchester, 1878.

Prophet James, The. *James Smith Buck.* The chronicles of the Land of Columbia, commonly called America ... By ... Milwaukee, Wis., 1876.

Proprietor of Bank Stock, A. *Peter Carey.* A letter to Wm. Huskisson, Esq., M.P. ... L. 1811.

Proprietor of Indian Stock, A. *James Silk Buckingham.* A second letter to Sir Charles Forbes, Bart., M.P., on the suppression of public discussion in India ... By ... L. 1824.

Proprietor of said Church, A. *Benjamin B. Mussey.* Letter to Rev. Frederick T. Gray ... at the "Bulfinch Street Church." By ... 1842.

Proprietor of that Work, A. *Philip Nichols.* The castrated letter of Sir Thomas Hanmer, in the sixth volume of the Biographia Britannica ... By ... L. 1763.

Prospero. *Francis Douce,* in the "Bibliomania" of T. F. Dibdin.

Protectionist, A. *John Lettsom Elliot.* A letter to the electors of West-minster. L. 1848.

Protestant, A. *Robert Shirra.* Antichrist's inquest ... Dundee, 1781.

Protestant, A. *Charles William Twort.* The Christian corrector corrected. Lambeth, 1829.

Protestant, A. *Robert Daly,* Bishop of Cashel. A correspondence which arose out of the discussion at Carlow, between ... (R. D.) and a Roman Catholic clergyman (W. Cloury). To which are annexed notes ... by ... R. D. L. 1825.

Protestant, A. *Rev. Caleb Fleming.* The Jesuit unmask'd ... L. 1737.

Protestant, A. *Rev. David Wilson.* A letter to the ... Lord Chancellor concerning the mode of swearing, by laying the hand upon and kissing the Gospels. By ... L. 1778.

Protestant, A. *Mr. Cooke.* Letters addressed to Lord Grenville and Lord Howick, upon their removal from the councils of the king ... L. 1807.

Protestant, A. *Rev. Edward Smedley.* Lux renata: a Protestant epistle, with notes ... L. 1827.

Protestant, A. *Rev. Calvin Colton.* Protestant Jesuitism ... N.Y. 1836.

Protestant Churchman, A. *J. Ballard.* A few strictures addressed to Mr. Alderman Sadler ... Oxf. 1851.

Protestant Clergyman, A. *Rev. Michael Vicary, B.A.* Notes of a residence at Rome in 1846, by ... L. 1847.

Protestant Dissenter, A. *Rev. William Wood.* Brief (A) enquiry concerning the dignity of the Ordinance of the Lord's Supper ... Written in 1732 ... and now reprinted ... by ... Leeds, 1790.

Protestant Dissenter, A. *William Christie.* An essay on ... Establishments in religion ... L. 1792.

Protestant Dissenter, A. *Dr. Thomas Morgan.* The nature and consequences of enthusiasm consider'd ... L. 1720.

Protestant Dissenter of Old England, A. *Rev. Caleb Fleming.* The claims of the Church of England seriously examined ... L. 1764.

Protestant-dissenting-minister, A. *Rev. Caleb Fleming.* A letter ... occasioned by the alarming growth of Popery in this kingdom ... L. 1768.

Protestant Episcopalian, A. *Francis Lister Hawks.* Auricular confession in the Protestant Episcopal Church ... N.Y. 1850.

Protestant Lady, A. *Ann Adams.*

Convent-tales, during the reigns of Henry the Eighth of England, Louis the Sixteenth of France, Napoleon Buonaparte ... By ... L. 1838.

Protestant Layman, A. *Alexander Copland.* Mortal life; and the state of the soul after death ... L. 1833.

Protestant Nonconformist, A. *Edward Ash, M.D.* Thoughts on the State Church question ... By ... L. 1861.

Protestant Rector of Tixall, The. *Rev. William Webb.* A correspondence between ... and the Catholic chaplain of Sir C. Constable, etc. L. 1834.

Protesting Catholic, A. *Alexander Geddes.* An answer to [Gibson] the Bishop of Comana's pastoral letter. L. 1790.

Proteus. *S. S. Carvalho.*

Proussinalle, M. De. *Pierre Joseph Alexis Roussel.* Histoire secrète du tribunal révolutionnaire. Paris, 1815.

Prout, Father. *Rev. Francis Sylvester Mahony.* The reliques of ... late P. P. of Watergrasshill, in the county of Cork, Ireland. Collected and arranged by Oliver Yorke, Esq. (Rev. Francis S. Mahony). Illustrated by Alfred Croquis, Esq. [D. Maclise, R.A.]. L. 1866.

Prowler, The. *Archibald Gordon,* in his contributions to the "Weeks' Doings" (N.Y.).

Pry, Paul. *Thomas Hill,* the "Paul Pry" of Poole and Liston, the "Hull" of *Gilbert Gurney,* the "Jack Hobbleday" of *Little Pedlington,* the "thrice-centenarian TOM HILL," the "TOM HILL of all the realm of Cockayne."

Pry, Solomon. *Thomas Bailey Fox,* a member of the Polyglot Club, consisting of the nine editors of the "Harvard Register" (Camb. 1827–28).

Prynne, Arthur. *Joel Munsell.* Prynne's almanac for 1841 ... Albany, 1840.

Pryor, Paul. *E. T. Taggard.*

Psalm-Singer, The. *Samuel Adams.* So called in a letter from a loyalist in Boston to Dr. Church, in allusion to his having often assisted in the choir of the New South church, Boston.

Publicola. *John Quincy Adams.* — See " Marcellus."

Publicola. *Pierre Jean Baptiste Chaussard* in his youth adopted this name.

Publicola. *William Johnson Fox,* in the London "Dispatch."

Publicola. *Mr. Smith,* in his contributions to the "Weekly Dispatch" (L. 1838).

Publicola. *Jonathan Swift.* — See " M. B. Draper."

Publicola. *Ferris Pell.* Letter to ... Albert Gallatin, Esq., on the doctrine of gold and silver ... N. Y. 1815.

Publicola. *Rowley Lascelles.* Letters of ... or, a modest defence of the established church. By a member of it. Dublin, 1816. See "Yorick."

Publicola. *William David Evans* (?). Six letters ... on the liberty of the subject. L. 1810.

Publicus Severus. *Sir John Joseph Dillon.* Horæ Icenæ: being the lucubrations of a winter's evening, on the result of the general election, 1835. n.p., n.d.

Publisher, A. *Edward Marston.* Copyright, national and international, from the point of view of ... L. 1879.

Publius. *Alexander Hamilton,* who, under this signature, contributed to the "Federalist" the papers numbered 1, 6–9, 11–13, 15–17, 21–36, 59–61, 65–85.

Publius. *John Jay,* who, under this signature, contributed to the "Federalist" the papers numbered 2–5, 64.

Publius. *James Madison,* who, under this signature, contributed to the "Federalist" the papers numbered 10, 14, 18–20, 37–63.

Publius. *James De Peyster Ogden.* Remarks on the currency of the United States ... N. Y. 1840.

Puck. *John Proctor.* Caricature cartoons. L. 186–.

Puff, Brevet Major Pindar. *Gulian Crommelin Verplanck, LL.D.* Epistles of ... N. Y. 1819.

Pulteney, The Rt. Hon. William. *Jonathan Swift, D.D.* The answer of ... to the Right Hon. Sir Robert Walpole. 1730.

Pumpkin, Miss Harriet. *Mrs. Harriet (Mellon) Coutts,* afterwards the most noble Harriet, Duchess of St. Albans. Memoirs of ... L. 1822.

A libellous work.

Pun-sibi, Tom. *Jonathan Swift, D.D.* Ars punica; sive, flos linguarum; the art of punning; or, the flower of languages ... Dublin, 1719.

Said to have been written by *Dr. Thomas Sheridan,* and only revised by Dr. Swift.

Punch. *Sir Robert Walpole.* Politicks in miniature; or, the humours of Punch's resignation, etc. L. 1742.

Punch. *Douglas William Jerrold.* Punch's letters to his son. Punch's complete letter writer. L. 1853.

"Punch's" Commissioner. *Wil-*

liam Makepeace Thackeray. Beulah Spa, etc., "Punch," 1845.

Punchinello, Plato. *Abbé Antoine Martinet.* Ark of the people ... trans. from the French. P. 1873.

Punever, Peter. *Lawrence N. Greenleaf.* King Sham, in verse ... N.Y. 1868.

Pungent, Pierce. *Thomas Powell.* Chit chat ... N.Y. 1858.

Punjabee. *William Delafield Arnold.* Oakfield; or, fellowship in the East ... L. 1853.

Pupils of the City of London School. *John Robert Seeley, William Young,* and *Ernest Abraham Hart.* Three essays on Shakespeare's tragedy of King Lear. By ... L. 1851.

Pupils of the City of London School. *William Young.* On the character of the religious belief and feeling which pervade the tragedy of King Lear ... L. 1851.

Pupils of the City of London School. *John Robert Seeley.* A parallel between Shakespeare's tragedy of King Lear and the Œdipus in Colono of Sophocles ... L. 1851.

Pupils of the City of London School. *Ernest Abraham Hart.* On the tragedy of King Lear ... By ... L. 1851.

Purdy. *Mrs. Emily Huntington Miller.*

Puritan, A. *Rev. Edward Cornelius Towne.* Question of Hell: an essay in the New Orthodoxy. By ... New Haven, 1873.

Puritan of the Nineteenth Century, A. *Rev. Joseph Warren Alden.* Vaticanism unmasked in the United States. Cambridgeport, 1877.

Purves, George, LL.D. *Simon Gray.* All classes productive of national wealth ... L. 1817.

Putnam, Say. *Anna A. Pratt.* Little Freddie feeding his soul ... N.Y. 1869.

Puzzle, Peter. *Joseph Addison,* in a paper to the "Guardian," No. 106, July 13, 1713.

Pylades. *Richard Gwinnett, Esq.,* once affianced to Mrs. Elizabeth Thomas, Junr. (Corinna). — See "Corinna."

Pylodet, L. *Friedrich Leypoldt.* Beginner's French reader ... N.Y. 1876.

Pym, Arthur Gordon, of Nantucket. *Edgar Allan Poe.* The narrative of ... N.Y. 1838.

Pynnshurst. *Xavier Donald Macleod.* Pynnshurst, his wanderings and his ways of thinking. N.Y. 185-.

Pythagorean, A. *Fitz-Hugh Ludlow.* The hasheesh-eater : being passages from the life of a Pythagorean. N.Y. 1857.

Python. *Major John Tyler.*

Q.

Q. *Thomas Purnell,* "who excited the ire of poor Mr. Tom Taylor by some fierce attacks upon his plays, in 'The Athenæum.'" See "Journalistic London," p. 9.

Q. *Edmund Hodgson Yates,* in the London "Evening Star" the papers preceding "Readings by Starlight."

Q. *Alfred Barron.* Foot notes; or, walking as a fine art. Wallingford, 1875.

Q. in the Corner. *John Harris.* Tit for tat. Original poems for juvenile minds. By ... L. 1830.

Q. Q. *Miss Jane Taylor.* Contributions to the "Youth's Magazine" or "Evangelical Miscellany." L. 1816-22.

Q., T. *Samuel Young.* Wall Street bear in Europe ... By ... N.Y. 1855.

Q——, T——. *Thomas Quincey.* A tour in the midland counties of England, performed in the summer of 1772. By

... In the "Gent. Mag.," 1774, pp. 206, 253, 299, 353, 410.

"The editor of the 'Gent. Mag.,' in the plenitude of his power, made a number of alterations in the Ms., greatly to the disgust of T—— Q——, who therefore printed it in an independent form." L. 1775.

Quad, M. *Charles B. Lewis.* Quad's odds ... Detroit, 1875.

Quadragenarian, A. *Rev. Robert Weaver.* The Reconciler; or, the harmony and glory of the Divine Government. By ... in the ministry. L. 1841.

Quadratus, Pileus. *Prof. Stephen Reay, B.D.* Observations on the defence of the Church Missionary Society against the objections of the Archdeacon of Bath [the Rev. Josiah Thomas]. L. 1818.

Quadroon, A. *David F. Dorr.* A colored man round the world ... 1858.

Quæro. *William H. Wilmer, D.D.*

Quaker, A. *Josiah Forster.* A Q.'s

reasons for opening his shop on that called Christmas Day. n.p. 1789.

Quallon. *Stephen Henry Bradbury*, editor of the "Nottingham Review," and contributed poetry under this signature.

"Quantum Mutatis." *William Bigg.* An essay on the causes of the decline of the Society of Friends ... L. 1859.

Quarles. *Edgar Allan Poe*, in the "American Review," 1845.

Quatrelles. *Ernst L'Epine.* Casse Cou! 1881 ... Paris, 1881.

Queen of Hearts. *Mrs. E. M. (Patterson) Keplinger*, contributed poetry to the "New Orleans Sunday Times." 1866 *et seq.*

Queerfellow, Quintin. *Charles Clark.* A doctor's "Do"-ings; or, the entrapped heiress of Witham. Totham, 1848.

Quercus. *Rev. O. A. Kingsbury.*

Querno, Camillo, Poet-laureat to the Congress. *George Cockings.* The American times: a satire ... L. 1780. Also ascribed to *J. Odell.*

Query. *James Topham Brady*, contributor to the old "Knickerbocker Magazine" and author of "A Christmas Dream."

Query, Peter. *Martin Farquhar Tupper.* Rides and reveries of the late Mr. Æsop Smith ... L. 1858.

Quévilly, Valentin de, and **Quévilly, vicomte de.** *Edmond About*, in "Figaro." Paris, 1856–57.

Quick, Jeremy. For the supposed editor of the "Medley; or, Daily Tatler." L. 1715.

Quid. *Robert Allan Fitzgerald.* Jerks in from Short-leg ... L. 1866.

Quid-pro-quo. *Charles John Smyth, M.A.* Defence of religious establishments ... Norwich, 18–.

Quiet, Charles. *Charles Henry Noyes.* Studies in verse. P. 1878.

Quiet George. *George Frederick Pardon.* The juvenile museum ... L. 1849.

Quiet Looker-on, A. *Rev. John Foster.* Letters on the Voluntary principle, by ... in the "Morning Chronicle" (L.),

Oct. 2 and 3, 1834. — See "Philalethes" [for Rev. William Goode].

Quiet Man, A. *Alexander Wheelock Thayer*, his signature to musical and other letters published in the "Boston Courier" in 1857–58.

Quiet Man, A. *Theodore Sedgwick Fay.* Dreams and reveries of ... N.Y. 1832.

Quill, Timothy. *Arthur Warren*, when English correspondent of the "Boston Herald."

Quillibet, Philip. *George E. Pond.*

Quilp, Jr. *William H. Halstead.* Little pieces: verse and prose. Norfolk, Va., 1868.

Quince, Peter, Esq. *Isaac Story.* A Parnassian shop opened in the Pindaric style, by ... P. 1801.

Quincey, Vernon H., Esq. *Jonathan Mitchell Sewall.* Parody on some passages in a pamphlet entitled "A letter to a Federalist." Portsmouth, 1805.

Quintus, Tertius Quartus. *W. Samsom.* The Conciliad; or, the triumph of patriotism: a poem. Translated from the Latin of ... 3d ed. L. 1762.

Quip. — *Dickenson.* Vincent Eden; or, the Oxonian, by ... in "Bentley's Miscellany," III., 1839, p. 313, 390, 583.

Quir, Peter de. *John Henley*, "Orator Henley," who, while an undergraduate at St. John's Coll., Camb., wrote a letter to the "Spectator," dated from that college, Feb. 3, 1712, signed "Peter de Quir," abounding with quaintness and local wit. In No. 396, June 4, 1712.

Quiver. *Timothy J. Dyson*, in the Brooklyn "Union Argus."

Quiz. *Rev. Edward Caswall.* Sketches of young ladies. L. 1846.

This is generally ascribed to *Charles Dickens*, but probably incorrectly. — See "Notes and Queries," Sept. 14, 1867, p. 219.

Quod, John. *John Treat Irving.* "The Attorney" and "Harry Harson" originally appeared in the New York "Knickerbocker Magazine" under this signature.

Quondam Oxonian and Carthusian, A. *Daniel Cabanel.* British scenery: a poetical sketch ... L. 1811.

R.

R. — *Ramsay*, of the London Library, Ludgate Street, now extinct. See Lamb's "Elia," "All Fools' Day."

R. *Rev. George Henry Rooke*, of Christ's College, Cambridge, in his con-

tributions to the "Athenian Letters" ... L. 1741–43.

R. *A. E. T. Watson*, London correspondent of the "Spirit of the Times" (N.Y.).

R. *Bishop Zachary Pearce.* Miscellaneous observations upon authors ancient and modern. L. 1731–32.

R., Major. *Major James Rennell,* in Beloe's "Sexagenarian," Vol. II., p. 50. 2d ed. L. 1818.

R., Mr. — *Roche,* in Beloe's "Sexagenarian," Vol. I., p. 329. 2d ed. L. 1818.

R., A. B. *Arthur Blennerhassett Rowan.* Lake lore; or, an antiquarian guide to some of the ruins and recollections of Killarney. Dublin, 1853.

R., A. G. *Alida G. Radcliffe.* Daily hymns . . . N.Y. 1867.

R. C. *Dr. Richard Laurence.* On the existence of the soul after death. By . . . L. 1834.

R., C. *Miss Clara Reeve.* Original poems . . . L. 1769.

R., C. A. *Caroline Alice Roberts.* Isabel Trevithoe : a poem. L. 1879.

R., C. H. *Charles H. Ross.* Ye comical rhymes of ancient times dug up into jokes for small folks. L. 1862.

R., E. *E. Reed.* Gold, frankincense, and myrrh. P. 1872.

R., F. *Francis Russell.* A short history of the East India Company . . . L. 1793.

R., F., Barrie. *Francis Rye.* The so-called Shakespearean myth. In the "Canadian Monthly" for July, 1879.

R., F. M. *Frederick Mansell Reynolds.* The coquette . . . L. 1865.

R., F. W. *Fannie W. Rankin.* True to him ever . . . N.Y. 1874.

R., G. *George Ripley.* The doctrines of the Trinity and Transubstantiation compared. B. 1833.

R., G. E. *George Edward Rice.* Ephemera, and Nugamenta. B. 1852.

R., G. W., Jr. *George Washington Riggs, Jr.* The narrative of Alvar Nuñez Cabeça de Vaca, translated by Buckingham Smith [with a preface by G. W. R., Jr.]. Wash. 1851.

R., H. *Henry Robson.* Figures in rhymes; or, metrical computations . . . By . . . Newcastle, 1814.

R., H. *Henry Reeve.* Graphidæ; or, characteristics of painters . . . n.p. 1838.

R., H., A Minister of the Church of England. *Hugh Ross.* An essay for a new translation of the Bible . . . L. 1702.

R., H. E., Trin. Coll. Camb. *H. E. Reynolds.* Freaks, follies, fancies, and fashions. L. 1868.

R., J. *James Rice.* — See "B., W. and J. R."

R., J. *James Roche.* His signature in the "Gent. Mag."

R., J. *John Ruskin.* His signature in the "Magazine of Natural History," conducted by J. C. Loudon, 1834, 1836.

"Mr. Loudon was the first literary patron who sent words of mine to be actually set up in print, in his 'Magazine of Natural History,' when I was sixteen," says Mr. Ruskin. Also his signature in "Friendship's Offering," 1833, 1836, 1837, 1841. "My first verse-writing in 'Friendship's Offering' at fifteen." Also to poems in the "Amaranth." L. 1839; and in the "London Monthly Miscellany," 1839.

R., J. *Rev. John Rogers.* Critical remarks on the third chapter of Habakkuk . . . L. 1854. Also a letter (Penzance Chapel) under this signature, in "Gent. Mag.," 1830, C. 304.

R., J. *James Relly.* Epistles; or, the great salvation contemplated . . . L. 1776.

R., J. *John Rickman.* Historical curiosities relating to St. Margaret's Church, Westminster. L. 1837.

R., J. *Joseph Reed.* A pastoral on the death of Alexander Pope, Esq.; in imitation of Allan Ramsay. "Jemmie, Simie, Patie," in the "Gent. Mag.," August, 1744, p. 445.

R., J. *Joseph Ritson.* The quip modest : a few words . . . on the text and notes of the last edition of Shakspeare . . . L. 1788.

R., J. Christ Church, Oxon. *John Ruskin,* in "Friendship's Offering," 1838–44; in the "Keepsake," 1845, 1846; and in "Heath's Book of Beauty," 1845, 1846.

R., J., D.D. *John Ross, D.D.* A brief admonition to the members of the Church of England . . . 2d ed. L. 1711.

R., J., Jun. *John Ryland, D.D.* His signature in the magazines.

R., J. D. *John Dix, afterwards Ross.* A handbook of Newport and Rhode Island. By . . . 1852.

R., J. J. *J. J. Reid.* [Gladstone's] Political speeches in Scotland, November and December, 1879, etc. With preface by . . . Edinb. 1879.

R., L. *Leander Richardson,* in letters to the "Journalist" (N.Y.).

R. L. B. *Harriet G. Storer.* An autobiography : being passages from a life now progressing in the city of Boston . . . Camb., Mass., 1871.

R., L. N. *Mrs. Ellen Ranyard.* The book and its story . . . L. 1853.

R., M. *B. Montgomerie Ranking.* Fair Rosamond, and other poems. L. 1868.

R., M. W. *M. W. Rooney.* Hamlet first edition [1603]. The last leaf of the lately discovered copy, carefully re printed, with a narrative of its discovery, etc. By . . . Dublin, 1856.

R., N. *Nicholas Rowe*, in a letter communicated to the "Guardian," No. 118, July 27, 1713.

R., O. *Olive Rand.* A vacation excursion from Massachusetts Bay to Puget Sound, by . . . Manchester, N.H., 1884.

R., P. *Patrick Robertson*, Lord Robertson, in "Leaves from a Journal." n.p. 1844.

R., S. *Mrs. Susanna Rowson*, whose contributions, chiefly of a religious and devotional character, were published in the "New England Galaxy," usually over her initials "S. R.," 1817 *et seq.*

R. S. *John Scott.* "Epidemick Mortality, from Ecclesias. XII.," in the "Gent. Mag.," December, 1753. "Verses occasioned by the Description of the Æolian Harp, in the "Gent. Mag.," February, 1754, XXIV., p. 525.

R., S. *Samuel Robinson, Esq.* Flowers culled from the Gulistan or Rose Garden, and from the Bostan or Pleasure Garden of Sadi, a Persian poet . . . L. 1876.

R. S., a Passenger. *Robert Paltock.* — See " Wilkins, Peter."

R., T. *T. Rud.* Miscellaneous observations upon authors ancient and modern. L. 1731–32.

R., T., M.D. *Dr. Thomas Reeve.* A cure for the epidemical madness of drinking tar water . . . L. 1744.

R. T. S. *William Maginn, LL.D.* His first signature in "Blackwood's Magazine."

R. V. *James Harvey.* Interest of money a legalized robbery . . . By . . . Liverpool, 1875.

R., W. B. *William Bradford Reed.* Haud immemor: a few personal recollections of Mr. Thackeray in Philadelphia. P. 1864.

R., W. E. *William Esdaile Richardson.* A letter . . . on the establishment of ragged school churches. L. 1852.

R., W. H. *W. H. Royston.* The rowing almanack. L. 1861–68.

R., W. H. *William Harris Rule.* The Wesleyan Methodist Sunday hymn-book. L. 1851.

R., W. J. *William James Robson.* September 1, 1850. Fresh waters from a fresh spring. Wave the first . . . Westminster.

R., W. J. D. *W. J. D. Ryder.* Chronicles of Charter-House . . . L. 1847. See "Carthusian, A."

R. W. L. *Rev. Rowland Connor*, who contributed " The Radical Club " and several social articles to the N.Y.

"Tribune," under this signature, which he also used in some of his contributions to the "International Review," "Lippincott's Magazine," etc.

R., W. M. *W. M. Russell.* The truth . . . L. 1852.

R., W. P., a political observer. *W. P. Russel.* A few valuable hints for the new ministry . . . L. 1806.

R., W. P. Verbotomist. *W. P. Russel.* An address intended to have been delivered to The Literary Fund . . . April 12th, 1804 . . . By . . . L. 1804.

R., W. S. *Walter S. Raleigh.* Scheme for the establishment of a national theatre . . . 1878.

R., W. S. *William Stewart Rose.* Thoughts and recollections . . . L. 1825.

R., W. S. W. *William S. W. Ruschenberger.* The principles of naval staff rank, etc. P. 1869.

R., W. U. *William Upton Richards.* Familiar instructions on mental prayer . . . Edited by . . . L. 1852.

R***, E—l of O*****.** *Robert, Earl of Orford.* An authentic copy of the last will and testament of . . . With remarks. L. 1745.

R**, J. J.** *Joseph Jules Rovel.* Des institutions militaires de la troisième république. Paris, 1878.

R****, Maria.** *Maria Riddell.* Voyages to the Madeira . . . Edinb. 1792.

R***, S*****.** *Samuel Rogers*, who published eight papers in the "Gent. Mag." for 1781, pp. 68, 119, 168, 218, 259, 306, 355, and 405, entitled, "The Scribbler," of which the first number is signed " S***** R*****."

Mr. Rogers was still in his 'teens when he contributed these papers to the "Gent Mag."

R—— H——, Esq. *Thomas Carte.* A full answer to the Letter from a Bystander . . . wherein his false calculations and misrepresentations of facts in the time of King Charles II. are refuted . . . L. 1742.

R—r, Lord. *John Wilmot*, Earl of Rochester. Windsor, by . . . L. 1703.

R—— H——, (The) Lord C. *The Right Hon. William Lord Craven.* The heroic epistle answered by . . . L. 1776.

Rachel, Mlle. *Elizabeth Rachel Felix.*

Raconteur. *Benjamin Perley Poore.*

Radical. *Col. Leslie Grove Jones*, the author of powerful but violent letters in the "Times" (L.) during the progress of the Reform Bill under this signature.

Rae, Leonard. *John Douglas.* Hal o' the Wynd. L. 18–.

Rag, Tag, and Bobtail. *James Cameron Lees, D.D.*

Ragged Philosopher, A. *John J. Proctor*, a Canadian poet, author of the "Essays of a Ragged Philosopher" in the "Freeman" (Sherbrooke).

Railroad Director, A. *Elias Hasket Derby*. Two months abroad; or, a trip to England, France, Baden, Prussia, and Belgium ... By ... of Massachusetts. B. 1844.

Railway King, The. *George Hudson.*

Raimond. *William Henry Hurlbut.*

Raimund, Golo. *Georg Dannenberg.* Ein neues Geschlecht. Roman, 1879.

Rain-Water Doctor, The.

"Was a German who landed in Philadelphia in the early part of the year 1811, and went shortly to Brooklyn, N.Y., where he remained for about a year. In 1812 he removed to Providence, R.I., where he had a large practice; then went, in 1813, to East Hartford, Conn., where he enjoyed an extraordinary success, but again returned to Providence, and died there in 1814-15. He was an educated physician, honest, skilful, extremely eccentric, and noted for many deeds of charity. While he resided in the village of Brooklyn he was consulted by thousands from the city of New York and from Long Island. The recommendation to all his patients to use *rain-water* as a drink won for him the cognomen of the 'Rain-Water Doctor.' Although he gave himself no distinct name, he sometimes signed himself 'Sylvan, Enemy of human diseases.' — See STILES's "Hist. of Brooklyn, N.Y.," Vol. I., p. 393.

"He must not be confounded with his evident imitators. The 'Rain-Water Doctor,' *alias* Sylvan Gardener, who flourished awhile about 1817 at Roxbury, Mass., and elsewhere (see 'Hist. Mag.,' February, 1862, or *Octavius Plinth*, the Rain-Water Doctor, or *Dr. C. Humbert*, *alias* Sylvan Gardener, who died in the vicinity of Philadelphia in June, 1825, at 'the supposed age of one hundred years' [see 'Long Island Star,' June 9, 1839]."—See STILES's "Hist. of Brooklyn," Vol. I., note, pp. 393, 394.

Rajah of Vaneplysia, The. *William Penn, Esq.*, his signature in the "Gent. Mag." — See "Gent. Mag.," February, 1818, p. 122, July, 1823, and elsewhere. "Vaneplysia" is an anagram of Pennsylvania.

Raleigh, Richard. *W. H. Kister*, in his contributions to various periodicals of Chicago, Ill.

Rambaud, Yveling. *Frédéric Gilbert*. Little walks in London ... L. 1875.

Rambler. *Luther L. Holden*, in the Boston "Journal" (?).

Rambler. *George H. Fullerton.* Persis: a tale of the White Mountains. N.Y. 1879.

Rambler, A. *Joseph Budworth.* A fortnight's ramble to the lakes in Westmoreland, Lancashire, and Cumberland. By ... L. 1796.

Rambler, A. *Robert Montgomery Bird.*

Peter Pilgrim; or, a rambler's recollections ... B. 1838.

Rambler, A. *G. A. Simcox.* Recollections of a rambler. L. 1874.

Rambler in Mexico, The. *Charles Joseph Latrobe.* The rambler in Mexico in 1834. L. 1836.

Rambler, Jacques. *Gabriel Peignot.* Le nouvelliste des campagnes ... Dijon, 1816.

Ramsay, Grace. *Miss Kathleen O'Meara.* A woman's trials. L. 1867.

Ramsbottom, Mrs. *Theodore Edward Hook.* Ramsbottom Papers, contributed to the "John Bull" newspaper (L.), in 1829.

Ramsneb, T. *Benjamin Smart.* Saturday night. By a journeyman mechanic, in the "Gent. Mag.," August, 1806, p. 751.

Randall, Anne Frances. *Mrs. Maria (Darby) Robinson.* A letter to the women of England ... L. 1799.

Randol, Louis. *Eusèbe Salverte.* Un pot sans couvercle et rien dedans ... Paris, 1799.

Ranger. *Luther L. Holden.* A thrilling balloon voyage ... B. 1870.

Ranger, The. *Capt. — Flack.* The life of a Texan hunter. L. 1866.

Ranger, Charles, Esq. *Arthur Murphy.* The Gray's Inn journal. L. 1753-54.

Raoul, Maximilien. *Charles Letellier*, de Saint-Malo. Histoire pittoresque du mont Saint-Michel et de Tombelène ... Paris, 1833.

Raphael. *R. C. Smith.* A manual of astrology; or, the book of the stars ... L. 1828.

Also attributed to *J. Palmer.*

Rapidan. *Daniel Connelly*, in his contributions to the "Buffalo Courier" (N.Y.).

Rapier, Rob. *Dr. O. C. Alexander.* Aleora.

Ratclyffe, Sir Isaac, of Elbow-lane. *Rev. John Henley* (Orator Henley).

"The 'Hyp Doctor' was written by that 'a little more knave than fool,' Orator *Henley*, under the name of 'Sir Isaac Ratclyffe, of Elbow-lane.'"

Rational Christian, A. *Alexander Leopold*, Prince of Hohenlohe, Bishop of Sardica. An exposure of the late Irish miracles ... Dublin, 1823.

Rational Mystic, A. *W. Belcher.* Intellectual electricity, novum organum of vision, and grand mystic secret ... By ... L. 1798.

Rationalis. *William Hazlitt*, in the London "Monthly Repository."

Rationalist, The. *William Baker.* Peregrinations of the mind ... by ... L. 1770.

Rattlehead, David, M.D. *M. Lafayette Byrn.* Rattlehead's travels; or, the recollections of a backwoodsman ... P. 1852.

Rattler, Morgan. *Percival Weldon Banks*, in "Fraser's Magazine," 1851.

Rattler, Corporal Morgan. *Dennis O'Sullivan*, in his contributions to various periodicals.

Rattler, Raby, Gent. *Thomas Hall.* "Effects" and adventures. L. 1845.

Rausse, J. H. *H. F. Franke.* Miscellanies to the Græfenburg Water-Cure. N.Y. 1848.

Ravelin, Humphrey, Esq. *Col. George Proctor.* The lucubrations of ... late major in the ... regiment of infantry. L. 1823.

Raven, Ralph. *George Payson.* Golden dreams and leaden realities. N.Y. 1853.

Ravenswood. *Charles Washington Beebee.* Edmund Dawn; or, ever forgive. N.Y. 1873.

Rayland, Rose. *Mrs. N. E. Mortimer.*

Raymond, Élie. *Élie Bertrand Berthet.* La Veilleuse. Romans. Paris 1835.

Raymond, Henry Augustus, Esq. *Mrs. Sarah Scott.* The history of Gustavus Ericson, King of Sweden ... L. 1761.

Raymond, Ida. *Mary T. Tardy.* Southland writers. P. 1870.

Raymond, John T. *John O'Brien.* A *nom de théâtre.*

Raymond, Malone. *Richard Malone.* A *nom de théâtre.*

Raynor, George. *George James Rea.* A *nom de théâtre.*

Raynor, Leslie. *Maria A. Barlow.* in her contributions to the "Household."

Reader Therein, A. *Andrea Crestadoro.* The art of making catalogues of libraries ... L. 1856.

Reader, A Desultory. *Alexander Graydon*, a number of whose essays, under the title of "Notes of a Desultory Reader," will found in the Phila. "Portfolio," 1813-14.

Réal, Antony. *F. Fernand Michel.* Les atomes, les rêves. Paris, 1865.

Real Lover of Freedom, A. *W. P. Russel.* Important proposals for national and universal peace ... L. 1812.

Rebel, A. *George Cary Eggleston.*

Rebel War Clerk, A. *John B. Jones.* Diary, 1861-65. P. 1866.

Rebenstein, A. *Aaron Bernstein.* Hohen Liedes. Berlin, 1834.

Recapper. *Thomas C. Abbott.*

Reckoner. *Rt. Rev. John Strachan, D.D.*, a Canadian divine. As a writer, *Bishop Strachan* is known as the author of 70 essays, embracing various subjects, which appeared in the "Gazette" (Kingston), in 1811, under this signature.

Recluse, A. *Mrs. Anne Charlotte (Lynch) Botta.* Leaves from the diary of ... in "The Gift" (N.Y.) for 1845.

Recluse, A. *Rev. John Brewster, M.A.* Meditations of ... L. 1800.

Recluse, A. *John Barton Derby.* Musings of ... B. 1837.

Recluse, A. *Rev. Francis Jacox.* Recreations of ... L. 1870.

Recluse, A. *Mrs. Mary Ann Kelty.* Visiting my relations, and its results: a series of small episodes in the life of ... L. 185–.

Recorder of the City of New York, The. *Daniel Horsmanden.* A journal of the proceedings in the detection of the conspiracy formed by some white people, in conjunction with negro and other slaves, for burning the city of New York ... and murdering the inhabitants. By ... N.Y. 1744.

Rector, The. *John H. Egar.* The Christian patriot ... Quincy, Ill., 1863.

Rector, The. *Rev. Asa Eaton.* Historical account of Christ Church, Boston ... B. 1824.

Rector, The. *Rev. Francis Vyvyan Jago Arundell, M.A.* Some notices of the church of Landulph, by ... Devenport, 1840.

Rector, and Bishop of the Diocese, The. *George W. Doane.* The way of the Church with children ... Burlington, N.J., 1848.

Rector of Calverton, Bucks. *Hon. and Rev. C. G. Perceval.* A serious address to persons recovered from dangerous illness ... By ... L. 184–.

Rector of St. Timothy's Church, Philadelphia, The. *J. Grigg.* A pastoral address to young women ... P. 1843.

Red Spinner. *William Senior.* Travel and trout in the Antipodes. L. 1879.

Red Wing. *Frederic Eugene Pond*, in his contributions to the "Turf, Field, and Farm" (N.Y.).

Reddik. *Joseph Kidder*, in his contributions to newspapers.

Reden, Benno. *Oskar Meding.*

Reden, Karl. *Charles Crozat Converse.* The voice of praise: a selection of hymns and tunes. Richmond, 1872.

Redgap. *George Frederick Pardon.* The faces in the fire: a story for the season. L. 1849.

Redivivus, Quevedo, Jr. *Robert W. Wright.* Vision of judgment; or, the South Church ... N.Y. 1867.

Rednaxela. *Hon. Mrs. Cropper.* The hermit of the Pyrenees; and other miscellaneous poems ... L. 1858.

Redruth, E. *Richard Edmonds, Jun.* Proposed reformation of the laws of England, in the "Cornish Magazine," 1828.

Redwin. *Richard E. Day,* in his contributions to the "Syracuse Standard" (N.Y.).

Redwood, Ralph. *J. G. P. Holden.*

Reedwater Minstrel, The. *Robert Roxby.* The lay of the ... Newcastle, 1809.

Reformator. *Charles Clarke.*

Reformed Stock Gambler, A. *William Armstrong.* Stocks and stock-jobbing in Wall Street ... N.Y. 1848.

Reformer, A. *Rev. Frederick Nolan.* Fragments of a civic feast ... L. 1826.

Refugee, A. *Frederick Augustus Porter Barnard.* A letter to the President of the United States. N.Y. 1863.

Refugitta. *Mrs. Constance Cary Harrison,* who is best known to Southern literature under this pen-name, which she first assumed in Richmond.

Regimental Officer, A. *Capt. Hawker.* Journal ... during the recent campaign in Portugal and Spain ... L. 1810.

Regina. "Fraser's Magazine."

Regis, Thorpe. *Frances M. Peard.*

Register, Seeley. *Mrs. Metta Victoria (Fuller) Victor.* Dead letter. N.Y. 186-.

Registrar of the Birmingham County Court, The. *Charles Waterfield.* The Bankruptcy Act, 1861 ... A summary of the new practice in the County courts in bankruptcy ... By ... Birmingham, 1862.

Reid, Christian. *Miss Frances C. Fisher.* Carmen's inheritance. P. 1873.

Reid, Hartebor. *Robert Hardie.* Rational cookery. L. 18-.

Reimar, Reinald. *Adolf Glaser.* Kriemhildens Rache [drama]. 1853.

Reinmar, Freimund. *Friedrich Rückert.* Deutsche Gedichte. Heidelberg, 1814.

Reinwald, Theodor. *Therese von Hansgirg.* Dunkle Fügungen, 1862, and Novellen, 1874.

Relative, A. *William Thomas Brande (?).* The life and adventures of the celebrated Walking Stewart ... By ... L. 1838.

Religious Politician, A. *Samuel Adams.* Address to the people in general, February, 1775.

Remus, Uncle. *Joel Chandler Harris.* Uncle Remus; his songs and his sayings. The folk-lore of the old plantation. N.Y. 1880.

Rena. *Mrs. M. Louise (Rogers) Crossley,* who frequently wrote for the newspapers under this pen-name.

Renaud. *L. Desloges.* Grandeurs et gloires de la France et de la maison de Bourbon ... Paris, 1849.

Renault, Ernest. *Léon Pillet.* L'obstiné; ou, les Bretons ... Paris, 1837.

René. *Mlle Léonie Larouc.* Marie Touchet, drame ... Montpellier, 1848.

René, Jules. *Marquis de Casamajor,* in the "National" (Paris).

Rengade, J. *Aristide Roger.* La vie normale et la santé ... Paris, 1881.

Repandunum. *John Adey Repton, Esq., F.S.A.* "In August, 1799 ["Gent. Mag."] is a view from his pencil of Ingworth Church, Norfolk, taken before its round tower fell down. The accompanying letter is signed 'Repandunûm.'"

Repmah. *William Hamper, F.S.A.* "In his younger days he was much attached to music, and was a composer as well as a performer; he set to music one or more songs, which were published under the assumed name of 'Repmah,' being his own reversed."

Reporter of the "Boston Morning Post," The. *William Beals.* Trial of W. B. and C. G. Greene for an alleged libel ... on A. W. Pike ... By ... B. 1835.

Reporter of the New Orleans "Picayune," The. *D. Corcoran.* Pickings from the portfolio of ... P. 1846.

Representative Peer, A. *Charles John Gardiner,* Earl of Blessington. A letter to ... the Marquis of Wellesley ... on the state of Ireland. By ... L. 1822.

Republican, A. *Charles Pinckney,* in the Charleston (S.C.) "City Gazette," 1810-16.

Republican, A. *Jonathan Russell.* To the freemen of Rhode Island ... n.p., n.d.

Resident, A. *Rev. Andrew Bonar.* The Canongate, ancient and modern ... 2d ed. Edinb. 1856.

Resident, A. *Rev. William Agar Adamson, D.C.L.* Salmon fishing in Canada ... L. 1860.

Resident, A. *Isabel Massary.* Social life and manners in Australia ... L. 1861.

Resident, A. *Newton H. Chitten-*

den (?). **Strangers' guide in Minneapolis and surrounding country** ... By ... Minneapolis, Minn., 1869.

Resident beyond the Frontier, A. *William Joseph Snelling.* Tales of the Northwest; or, sketches of Indian life and character. By ... B. 1830.

Resident in the West Indies for Thirteen Years, A. *Miss Bourne.* The British West India colonies in connection with slavery ... With an introduction and concluding remarks by a late stipendiary magistrate in Jamaica [*i.e.* Stephen Bourne]. L. 1853.

Resident of San Domingo, A. *J. W. Fabens.*

Resident of Twelve Years at Marietta, in that State, A. *Return Jonathan Meigs.* A brief sketch of the State of Ohio ... Glasgow, 1822.

Resident There, A. — *La Corte.* Letters from Spain, 1863 to 1866. By ... L. 1868.

Resident, who has never possessed either Land or Slaves in the Colony, A. *Mr. Telfair* (?). Representation of the state of government slaves and apprentices in the Mauritius; with observations. L. 1830.

Resident M.A., A. *Frederick Edward Weatherly, M.A.* Oxford days; or, how Ross got his degree. L. 1879.

Resident Member of Convocation, A. *Rev. Edward Hawkins.* A letter to the Earl of Radnor upon the oaths, dispensations, and subscription to the xxxix articles ... Oxf. 1835.

Residuary Legatee, The. *Henry Jackson Sargent.*

Restless, Tom. *Thomas Tyers.*

"It is said that the character of 'Tom Restless' (in the 'Idler,' No. 48) was intended by Dr. Johnson for *Mr. Tyers.*"—CHALMERS, Vol. 30.

Resurgam. *Charles Pettitt.*

Retired Barrister, A. *Charles Ambler.* A review of the proceedings and arguments in a cause in chancery, between J. Fox and R. Mackuth ... by ... L. 1792.

Retired Captain, R.N. *George H. Gardner, R.N.* Suggestions for forming a reserve of seamen ... L. 1871.

Retired Common Councilman, A. *James Kirke Paulding.* Chronicles of the City of Gotham ... N.Y. 1830.

Retired Editor, A. *Dorus Clarke, D.D.* Fugitives from the escritoire of ... B. 1864.

Retired Governor of the Island of Juan Fernandez, The. *Thomas Sut-*

cliffe. Sixteen years in Chili and Peru, from 1822 to 1839. By ... L. 1841.

Retired Guardian, A. *William Bradley.* Sketches of the poor. L. 18–.

Retired Officer, A. *William Coombe, Esq.* Letter of ... a defence of Colonel Cawthorne. L. 1801.

Retired Officer, A. *J. Spens.* Memoir of the life and character of the late Lieut. Colonel John Campbell ... Edinb. 1836.

Retnyw, Werdna. *Andrew Wynter, M.D.* Odds and ends from an old drawer. L. 1855.

Retort, Dick. *William Cobbett.* Tit for tat; or, a purge for a pill ... By ... P. 1796.

Retort, Jack, Student in Scurrility. *William Franklin.* A humble attempt at scurrility, in imitation of those great masters of the art, the Rev. Dr. S—th [Smith], the Rev. Dr. Al—n [Allison], the Rev. Mr. Ew—n [Ewing], the Rev. D. J. D—ve [Dove], and the heroic J—n D—n [John Dickinson] Esq.: being a full answer to the observations in Mr. H—s's [Hughes] advertisement ... Quilsilvania [Pennsylvania], 1765.

A defence of Dr. Franklin, by his son.

Returned Australian, A. *William H. Thomes.* The gold hunter's adventures; or, life in Australia. By ... B. 1872.

Returned Californian, A. *J. M. Letts.* Pictorial view of California ... N.Y. 1853.

Returned Missionary, A. *Rev. Thomas Laurie.* Woman and her Saviour in Persia ... B. 1863.

Reuben. *Rev. Robert Stephen Hawker, M.A.* Tendrils by ... Cheltenham. L. 1821.

Revel. *Adolphe Volleau.* Fastes de Henri IV., surnommé le Grand ... Paris, 1815.

Reverend Author of the Rosciad, The. *Charles Churchill.* The Church Iliad; or, a few modest questions proposed to ... L. 1761.

Reverend Dean, A. *William Vincent, D.D.,* in Beloe's "Sexagenarian," Vol. II., 91. 2d ed. L. 1818.

Reverend Divine, A. *Rev. Archibald Bruce.* Poems, serious and amusing, by ... 1812.

Reverie, Reginald. *Grenville Mellen.* Glad tales and sad tales. B. 1829.

Réville, Édouard. *Guillaume Amédée Fauvel.* Guibray au temps de Louis XII. Caen, 1841.

Revilo. *Oliver P. Marshall.*

Revilo, E. B. *Oliver Byrne.* The creed of St. Athanasius proved by a mathematical parallel. L. 1839.

Revolutionary Soldier, A. *James Collins.* Autobiography of . . . Clinton, La., 1859.

Revolutionary Soldier, A. *James Sullivan Martin.* A narrative of the adventures [in the battle of Long Island], dangers, and sufferings of . . . Hallowell, Me., 1830.

Revons, E. C. *Charles Crozat Converse.* Sayings of sages . . . N.Y. 1864.

Revorg, Trebla. *Albert Grover.* Monkey vs. Man . . . L. 1878.

Rexdale, Robert. *Robert F. Barbour.*

Reybaud, Madame Charles. *Henriette Arnaud.* Madame de Rieux. Paris, 185–.

Reynard. *Myron Fox*, in the New York "Telegram."

Reynard. *Frank Foxcroft.* Transcript pieces. North Adams, Mass., 1856.

Reynaud, Jacques. *Gabrielle Anne (de Cisternes de Coutiras)*, marquise de Poilow de Saint-Mars ("Comtesse Dash"). Portraits contemporains. Paris, 1859–61.

Reynolds, Beatrice. *Elizabeth Sara Sheppard.* My first season; by . . . Edited [or rather written] by . . . L. 1855.

Reynolds, Francis. *F. Reginald Statham.* Alice Rushton, and other poems . . . L. 1868.

Rhéal, Sébastien. *Sébastien Gayet.* Les chants du Psalmiste, odes, hymnes, et poëmes . . . Paris, 1839.

Rhode Islander, A. *Mrs. Catherine R. Williams.* Might and right; by . . . Providence, 1844.

R'Hoone, Lord. *Honoré de Balzac.* Clotilde de Lusignan ; ou, le beau Juif . . . Paris, 1822.

Rhymer, A. *Thomas Bell*, of Fifeshire (Scotland). Verses for the people. Glasgow, 1844.

Ricard, Adolphe. *Gustav Sandré.* L'amoureux des onze milles vierges. Paris, 1846.

Ricard, Adolphe. *Xavier Eyma.* Cascarinette, roman comique. Paris, 1846.

Richard. *J. M. V. Audin.* English and German dialogues. P. 187–.

Mr. Audin was assisted in this work by another.

Richard, Lord Bishop of Cloyne. *Richard Woodward, LL.D.* Remarks on a pamphlet entitled, "The present state

of the Church of Ireland." By . . . Dublin, 1787.

Richard, Lord Bishop of Litchfield. *Richard Hurd.* A sermon . . . December 13, 1779 . . . L. 1779.

Richards, Ezek. *John Savage*, in his contributions to the "Press" (P.).

Richards, Parke. *Miss Laura R. Fewell*, who contributed to Godey's "Lady's Book" under this pen-name.

Richelieu. *William E. Robinson*, in the Brooklyn "Eagle."

Richmond. *Jacob R. Shepherd.*

Richmond Lady, A. *Mrs. Sarah A. (Brock) Putnam.* Richmond during the war. N.Y. 1867.

Richmondiensis. *Christopher Clarkson, Esq.*, in "Gent. Mag.," September, 1823, p. 201; February, 1824, 113; June, 1824, 489; December, 1827, 593; and December, 1832, 601.

Richmondiensis. *Rev. Matthew Dawson Duffield, F.S.A.*, who, in the early part of his life, was a frequent contributor to the "Gent. Mag.," sometimes under this signature.

Riddinge, Amias, B.D. *William King, LL.D.* (?) Key to the Fragment, by . . . with a preface by Peregrine Smyth, Esq. L. 1751.

Riderhood, Pleasant. *Mrs. M. Slaughter.*

Ridges, B. *Bridges W. Smith.*

Rie, May. *Miss Mary Walsingham Crean*, whose "career as a writer commenced as a school-girl, and opened with a series of lively, dashing, and piquant articles, prose and verse, in the New Orleans "Sunday Delta."

Riesler, Ulrich. *Wilhelm Molitor.* Die Blume von Sizilien. 1880.

Rieux, A. de. *Alexandre Carrat de Vaux.* Eudoxe ; ou, l'homme du XIXᵉ siècle ramené à la foi de ses pères. Paris, 1840.

Rieux, Georges de. *Xavier de Montépin.* Les mystères du Palais-Royal . . . Paris, 1863.

Rifleman, A, Esq., Gent. *A. M. Keiley.* Prisoner of war ; or, five months among the Yankees . . . Richmond, Va., 1865.

Rigby. *Rt. Hon. John Wilson Croker*, in Disraeli's "Coningsby."

Rigdum, Drunken. *Rt. Hon. Richard Rigby*, so called in the English newspapers. 1779.

Right Honourable Mendicant, The. *Charles James Fox.* A looking-glass for . . .

Right Honourable Person, A. *William Pitt.* A letter from . . . and the answer to it [by William Beckford, Lord Mayor of London]. L. 1761.

Right Rev. the Lord Bishop of Natal, The. *Rt. Rev. John William Colenso, D.D.* The Pentateuch and Book of Joshua critically examined. By ... L. 1862–65.

Rigolo. *Nicolas Léon Thieblin*, in the Monday financial article of the N.Y. "Sun."

Rinaldo. *James Edwards*, in Dibdin's "Bibliomania."

Ring, Ivar. *Alfhilda (Svenson) Mecklenburg.* Fortällinger, 1871–72 and 1878–80.

Ringbolt, Captain. *Capt. John Codman.* Sailors' life and sailors' yarns ... N.Y. 1847.

Ringletub, Jeremiah. *Rev. John Styles.* The legend of the velvet cushion ... L. 1815.

Rinmon. *Simon Blocquel.* Nouvel album pittoresque ... Lille, 1835.

Ripon, John Scott. *John Scott Byerley.* Buonaparte; or, the freebooter. A drama. L. 1803.

Rit Toujours, M. *A. Peccatier.* Le véritable farceur perpétuel; ou, propos comiques de ... Paris, 1851.

Rita. *Mrs. Eliza M. J. Gollan von Booth.* My Lord Conceit. L. 1884.

Rivers, Dio. *Samuel H. Dixon*, in his contributions to various periodicals of Texas, etc.

Rivers, Pearl. *Mrs. A. M. Holbrook.*

Rivers, Pearl. *Mrs. Eliza Jane (Poitevent) Nicholson.* Lyrics ... P. 1873. Also in her contributions to the "Times-Democrat" (New Orleans, La.).

Rob Roy. *John Macgregor.* The Rob Roy on the Baltic. L. 1879.

Robert. *John T. Bedford*, member of the Corporation of the City of London, in his contributions to "Punch" (L.).

Robert, Lord Bishop of Sarum. *Robert Drummond.* Sermon before the Society for Propagation of the Gospel in Foreign Parts. L. 1754.

Robert, Jules. *Jean Baptiste Marie Augustin Challamel.* Une visite à la Galarie Aguado, in "la France littéraire," 1841.

Robert, Karl. *Eduard von Hartmann.* Dramatische Dichtungen. 1871.

Robert, Karl. *Georges Meusnier.* Le fusain. Charcoal drawing without a master. Cin. 1881.

Robert, Ludwig. *Georg, Baron von Oertzen.* Erlebnisse und Studien in der Gegenwart. 1875.

Robertjeot. *John Sanderson*, who, in letters signed with this name, insisted upon classical culture in Girard College.

Roberts, Capt. Hon. *Augustus Charles Hobart*, generally known as Hobart Pasha. Never caught: personal adventures in blockade running, 1863–64. L. 1867.

Roberts, George. *Robert Walters.*

Robertson, Ignatius Loyola, LL.D. *Samuel Lorenzo Knapp.* Sketches of public character ... N.Y. 1830.

Robin, Commodore. *William Harding*, in his contributions to the "Clipper" (N.Y.).

Robin. *Sir Robert Walpole.* Robin's panegyrick, etc. L. 1729.

Robineau. *Alexandre Louis Bertrand Beaunoir.* L'amour quêteur, Vénus pèlerine. Paris, 1778.

Robinson, Doctor. *Dennis Hannegan.*

Robinson, Jack. *Archibald Michie.* The Hamlet Controversy. Was Hamlet mad ... L. 1867.

Robinson, Jack, Junior. *David Blair.* The Hamlet Controversy ... L. 1867.

Robinson, Ralph. *His Majesty Geo. III., of England.*

Huish, in his "Memoirs of George the Third," p. 562, states that "The king's letters were seven in number, all of considerable length, and displaying a most profound knowledge of the subject." The first letter is printed in Young's "Annals of Agriculture," vol. vii., p. 65, entitled "On Mr. Duckett's Mode of Cultivation," and dated Jan. 1, 1787. The second letter occurs at p. 332, of the same volume, and is entitled "Further Remarks on Mr. Duckett's Mode of Cultivation," dated "Windsor, March 5, 1787." The other letters will probably be found in the subsequent volumes.—See "Notes and Queries," 2d Ser., V., May, 1858, p. 439.

Robson, Frederick. *Frederick Robson Brownhill.* Nom de théâtre.

Rochester, Mark. *William Charles Mark Kent.* The Derby Ministry ... L. 1858.

Rochfort, Alfred. *Major Alfred R. Calhoun.*

Rock, Captain. *Roger O'Connor.* Letters to H. M. George the Fourth. L. 1828.

Rock, Captain. *Mortimer O'Sullivan.* Memoirs of ... the celebrated Irish chieftain ... L. 1824.

Also attributed to *Thomas Moore.*

Rock, Captain, in London. *J. M. Whitty.*

Rock-man, Constant, M.A. *Rev. Nicholas Bowes.* Modest account concerning the salutations and kissings in ancient times ... B. 1768.

Rockingham, Sir Charles. *Le Comte de Jarnac de Rohan-Chabot.* Le Dernier d'Egremont. Paris, 1851.

Rodenberg, Julius von. *Julius Levy.* The Island of the Saints ... L. 1861.

Roderick. *William Davis Gallagher.* In 1827 Mr. *Gallagher* and Otway Curry, as "Roderick" and "Abdallah," maintained a friendly rivalry in the columns of the "Cincinnati Chronicle" and "Cincinnati Sentinel."

Rodman, Ella. *Mrs. Eliza Rodman (McIlvaine) Church.* Flights of fancy. N.Y. 1851.

Roe, Richard. *F. G. B. Ponsonby.* Barefaced impostors ... By J. D., Richard Roe, and John Noakes [*i.e.* Tom Taylor]. L. 1854.

Roger, Aristide. *Le docteur Jules Rengade.* Voyage sous les flots. Paris, 1868.

Rollicker, Harry. *William Makepeace Thackeray.* Phil Fogarty. A tale of the Fighting Onety-Oneth. "Punch," August, 1847.

Rollingpin, Commodore. *John Hanson Carter.* Log of ... N.Y. 1874.

Romain, Jules. *Jules Girette.* La paix ou la guerre, choisissez! ... Paris, 1840.

Romaine, Robert Dexter. *George Payson.* The new age of gold; or, the life and adventures of ... B. 1856.

Roman Catholic, A. *Rev. Hardinge Furenzo Ivers.* Important questions affecting the existence of the Catholic Church in England ... L. 1854.

Roman Catholic Clergyman, A. *Rev. W. Cloury.* A correspondence, etc. L. 1825.—See "Protestant, A."

Romano, Enotrio. *Giosuè Carducci.* Odi barbare. Bologna, 1877.

Romeo. *George W. Fellowes.*

Romer, Jonathan. *William Starbuck Mayo, M.D.* Kaloolah; or, journeyings to the Djébel Kumri: an autobiography of ... N.Y. 1849.

Rooke, Thomas Elbridge, Esq. *John Player.* Considerations on the present dearness of provisions and corn, in Great Britain ... Devizes, 1772.

Rooney, Alderman. *Daniel O'Connell Townley.* His signature in "Scribner's Magazine."

Rooney, Barney. *William Garvie.* Letters on confederation, botheration, and political transmogrification. Halifax, N.S., 1865.

Roper, Abel. *Jonathan Swift, D.D.* Cursory but curious observations of ... L. 1711.

Rosa. *Mrs. Rosa Vertner (Griffith Johnson) Jeffrey.* Poems. B. 1858.

Rosa Matilda. *Mrs. Charlotte Dacre Byrne.* Hours of solitude: poems. L. 1805.

Rosalba. *Kathinka (Halein) Zitz.*

Rosalind. *Miss Rosalind Davis.* Garibaldi; or, the rival patriots. A dramatic operetta ... L. 1860.

Rosavella. *Mad. Blanche (Tucker) Marochetti.*

Roscoe, Deane. *Frederic B. Yates.* Glendover. N.Y. 1880.

Roscoe of Cork, The. *James Roche.* —See London "Athenæum," 1853, 448 (obituary); Prout papers.

Roseau, Emie. *Emeline Reed.*

Roseau, Marie. *Mary J. Reed,* who contributed to periodicals under this pen-name.

Roseharp. *James M. Cawdell,* in his contributions to "Fothergill's Weekly Register" (Toronto, Can., 1824), etc.

Roselinda. *Mrs. Rose C. (King) White.* The little white cot. B. 1872.

Rosen, Julius. *Nikolaus Duffek.* Sämtliche Werke. Vienna, 1870–79.

Roset, Hipponax. *Joseph Rupert Paxton.* Jewelry and the precious stones ... P. 1856.

Rosicrucian. *Rev. Washington Frothingham,* in the Utica "Herald."

Rosicrucian. *Paschal Beverley Randolph.* Dealings with the dead ... Utica, N.Y., 1861–62.

Rosicrucius. *Thomas Frognall Dibdin* concealed his identity with · the authorship of "Bibliomania; or, Book Madness: a Biographical Romance in Six Parts" (1809), for a short time, under this pseudonym.

Roslyn, Guy. *Joshua Hatton.* Poems. L. 18–. Also ascribed to *George Barnett.*

Ross, John. *Koo-wes-koo-we.* His Indian name.

Rossi, Émile. *Émile Chevalet.* Amélie; ou, la Grisette de province. Paris, 1832.

Rothenfels, Emmy von. *Emilie von Ingersleben.* Eleanore. P. 1872.

Rouillon, Paul. *Auguste Paul Poulet-Malassis.* Apropos d'une faïence républicaine à la date de 1868. Paris, 1868.

Roumany Rei. *Tom Taylor.* "Gipsey Experiences," in the "Illustrated London News," November and December, 1851.

Roundelay, Roger, Esq. *William Biglow (?).* "The Occupations of a Social Recluse" (poetry), in the "Federal Orrery" (B. 1795).

Rover, Ralph. *Robert Michael Ballantyne.*

Roving Editor, The. *James Redpath.* The roving editor; or, talks with slaves in the Southern States. N.Y. 1859.

Roving Englishman, The. *Eustace Clare Grenville Murray.* Pictures from the battle-fields. L. 1856. [Reprinted from "Household Words" (L. 1854).]

Roving Printer, A. — *Jones.* Life and adventures in the South Pacific. N.Y. 1861.

Row, T. *Samuel Pegge.* "A Letter in Behalf of the Wives of Excise-men," "Gent. Mag.," 1757, p. 559; and 124 other articles, from 1758 to 1795.

"T. Row," *i.e.* the Rector of Whittington.— See "Gent. Mag." LXVI., p. 981.

Rowe, Saville and Bolton. *Clement Scott,* who writes dramas under this double *nom de plume.*

Rowlands, Cadwalader. *John Camden Hotten.* Life of H. M. Stanley. L. 18-.

Rowley, Thomas. *Thomas Chatterton.* An examination of the poems attributed to ... By Thomas Warton. L. 1782.

Roxbury Farmer, A. *John Lowell.*

Roy. *Nathaniel Parker Willis,* who, while in college, 1823-27, published several religious pieces of poetry under this signature.

Roy, Luxymon. *Samuel H. Homan.*

Royce, Ashley Allen. *Nathaniel Hawthorne,* in the "Salem Gazette," and the "New England Magazine."

Mr. Lathrop says of the "Twice Told Tales," "The earlier pieces appeared in the 'Salem Gazette' newspaper and in the 'New England Magazine' (published in Boston from 1831 to 1834). Sometimes they bore the author's real name, and sometimes a pseudonym was attached. Several among them purported to have been written by 'Ashley Allen Royce,' or the 'Rev. A. A. Royce.' Another pen-name used by the young romancer was 'Oberon,' the choice of which may be explained by the fact that, as the late Henry W. Longfellow recalled, some of the college friends of *Hawthorne* have nicknamed him 'Oberon,' in allusion to his personal beauty and the imaginative tone of his conversation."

Rozier, Jacques. *Mme. Émilie Paton.*

Rubek, Sennoia. *John Burke.* The burden of the South, in verse; or, poems on slavery ... N.Y. 18-.

Rudorff, E. *Franziska Julie (Schlesius) Jarke.* Stunden der Erhebung. Aussprüche von K. J. Nitzsch, 1877.

Rugby, Nym. *Nugent Robinson,* in his contributions to the "Boys and Girls' Weekly" (N.Y.).

Ruhamah. *Miss Lily Scudamore,* in the Washington "Republic."

Ruhamah. *Harriet M. Skidmore,* in her contributions to the "Globe-Democrat" (St. Louis, Mo.), etc.

Ruling Elder of the Church of Scotland, A. *Bishop Forbes.* An essay on the nature of the human body ... Edinb. 1767.

Runnymede. *Benjamin Disraeli,* Earl of Beaconsfield.

In 1836, "A series of letters ... appeared in the 'Times,' signed 'Runnymede,' which were in professed imitation of 'Junius's Letters,' but which could only be compared to them in point of violence and personality. These letters were written by D'Israeli, and contained fierce and unscrupulous attacks upon Lord Melbourne's government. Lord John Russell is called 'an infinitely small scarabæus, an insect'; Lord Palmerston and Grant, 'two sleek and long-tailed rats'; and Lord William Bentinck (... who had just returned from the government of India, 'one of those mere lees of debilitated humanity and exhausted nature which the winds periodically waft to the hopeless breezes of their native cliffs, — a drivelling Nabob, of weak and perplexed mind and grovelling spirit.' The appearance of the Marquis of Lansdowne is described as 'the ox-like form of the Lansdowne Apis'; and O'Connell as 'towering, like a crocodile, above, above them all.' These letters were, in August, 1836, reprinted in a volume entitled, 'The Letters of Runnymede,' and dedicated to the late Sir Robert Peel."— See ANDREWS's "British Journalism," vol. 2, p. 223.

Rural. *M. L. Dunlap,* in the New York "Tribune."

Rural D.D., A. *David Esdaile, D.D.* Contributions to natural history ... Edinb. 1865.

Rural Dean, A. *Rev. Arthur Tatham, M.A.* "O pray for the peace of Jerusalem." A few psalms, collects, and prayers selected for the daily use of the Church of England during her present troubles. By ... L. 1851.

Rusco. *Mary Ann Smith.* Teone; or, the magic maid: a poem. Milwaukee, 1862.

Rushton, Wattie. *A. Watson Atwood.*

Russ-Ockside, Knight. *Mortimer M. Thompson.* The history and records of the Elephant Club ... N.Y. 1856.

Russell. *Col. Russell H. Conwell,* in the Boston "Traveller."

Russell, Margaret. *Mrs. Eleonora Louisa Montagu Hervey.* Margaret Russell: an autobiography. L. 1849.

Russelli, L. *Léon Rousseau.* Les suivantes de Jésus ... Genève, 1866.

Russian, A. *Alexis Eustaphieve.* Sketch of the internal condition of the United States of America ... By ... Balt. 1826.

Russian, A, quondam civis bibliothecæ Edinensis. — *Davidoff.* An appeal on the Eastern Question ... Edinb. 1854.

Russian Lady, A. *Olga de (Kiréef) Novikoff.* Is Russia wrong? By ... L. 1877.

Russian Noble, A. *Nicolas Gogol.* Home life in Russia ... L. 1854.

Rustic Bard, The. *Robert Dinsmoor.* Incidental poems ... Haverhill, Mass., 1828.

Rustic Maiden, A. *Miss Stevenson.* Homely musings. Kilmarnock, 1870.

Rusticus. *Dr. Linnœus B. Anderson,* in his contributions to "The State" (Richmond, Va.).

Rusticus. *Rev. Samuel Denne.* Curate's bill. "Gent. Mag.," September, 1797.

Rusticus. *Caleb Fleming.* The devout laugh ... L. 1750.

Rusticus. *Edward Newman.* Letters of ... on the natural history of Godalming. L. 1849.

Rusticus. *George Hickling.* Mystic land, and other poems. 188-.

Rusticus, Gent. *Gerrit-Maspeth Furman.* Long Island miscellanies. By ... 1847.

Rustifustius, Trismagistus, D.D. *Thomas Moore.* An ode upon nothing, with notes. By ...

A poetical extravagance which, while the author was a student at Trinity College, Dublin, gained the medal of the Historical Society.

Ruth. *Mrs. A. P. (Dawson) Hill.* New cook-book ... N.Y. 1870.

Rutherglen. *Robert Macfarlane,* in various writings on Scottish antiquities and the history of Scottish emigration to America.

Ruy-Blas, Eugène. *Eugène Lebeau.* Chansons de ... Paris, 1844.

Ryse, Sherwood. *Alfred B. Starey,* in his contributions to "Harper's Young People" (N.Y.).

Rytter, Poul. *Parmo Karl Ploug.* Poul Rytters Viser og Vers. 1861.

S.

Σ. *Thomas Sharp, Esq.,* his signature in the "Gent. Mag." — See the volume for 1793, pp. 1103 and 1162, and elsewhere.

S. *Rev. Dr. Samuel Salter,* master of Charter House, in his contributions to the "Athenian Letters" ... L. 1741-43.

S. — *Scott,* who died in Bedlam. — See Lamb's "Elia," "Christ's Hospital."

S. *Percy Bysshe Shelley.* — See "V——, Emilia."

S. *Thomas Sharp, Esq.,* in "Gent. Mag." for 1800, p. 817, his signature to an article on "Antient British Torques."

S. *Royall Tyler,* his signature to poetical contributions to the "Polyanthos," Boston, 1806-7.

S. *Samuel Webber, M.D.,* his signature to poetical articles published in the "New England Galaxy," Boston, 1817 *et seq.*

S., Dean. *Jonathan Swift, D.D.* Dean S.'s true ... copy of that most strange ... prophecy written by Saint Patrick ... 1740.

S., Dr. *Jonathan Swift, D.D.* The celebrated Mrs. Pilkington's jests ... to which is ... added a ... variety of bons mots ... of ... Dr. S., etc. 1764.

S., Lord. *Henry Addington,* Viscount Sidmouth, in Beloe's "Sexagenarian," Vol. II., p. 155. 2d ed. L. 1818.

S., Mrs. *Mrs. Spinks.* — See Lamb's "Elia," "A Chapter on Ears."

S., Révérend Mr. J. *Jonathan Swift, D.D.* Les trois just-au-corps, conte bleu, tiré de l'Anglois du ... 1721.

S., A. *Anna Shipton.* The child minister. L. 1866.

S., A. *Anna Swanwick.* The complete works of Shakespeare, edited by ... L. 1851.

S., A. *Abraham Shackleton.* The court of Apollo ... Cork, 1815.

S., A. *A. Seton.* Poems, by ... Stockholm, 1827.

S., A., K. *A. Stansfield, Kersal.* Ground flowers and fern leaves: being a selection of poems ... By ... Manchester, 1876.

S., A., Philomath. *Abraham Sharp.* Geometry improv'd. L. 1717.

S. A. L. E. M. *Mrs. John C. Wyman,* of Fall River.

S., A. M. *Alexander Mackay Smith.* Ariadne in Naxos. Hartford, Conn., 1872.

S., A. W. and H., M. W. *A. W. Smith* and *M. W. Hallett.* The Thames angler. By ... L. 1846.

S., Barbara. *Miss Frances Maria Kelly,* in the "Essays" of "Elia."

S.B. *Charles St. Barbe,* one of his signatures in the "Gent. Mag." — See September, 1813, p. 231, February, 1815, p. 109, and 1828, ii., p. 603, and elsewhere.

S.B. *Charles Augustin Sainte-Beuve.* Volupté. Paris, 1834.

S.B., C. *Charles St. Barbe,* one of his signatures in the "Gent. Mag." — See March, 1823, p. 198; October, 1824, p. 296; July, 1828, p. 17, etc.

S., C. *Charles Shadwell.* The fair Quaker of Deal . . . A comedy . . . L. 1710.

S., C. *C. Staunton.* Life and humours of Falstaff. L. 1829.

S., C. *Charles Stanley.* Plain words by . . . L. 1861.

S., C. *Charles Sackville,* 2d Duke of Dorset. A treatise concerning the militia . . . By . . . L. 1753.

S., Sir C. *Sir Charles Sedley.*

S., Sir C. E., Bart. *Sir Claude Edward Scott, Bart.* Comic illustrations to T. Moore's "Irish Melodies." L. n.d.

S., C. W. *Charles William Smith.* The big bulls of Europe and the blasphemous "Te Deum." L. 1855.

S., C. W. *Charles William Short.* A treatise on swimming . . . 1846.

S., E. *Edward Seymour,* in his contributions to the "Times" (N.Y.).

S., E. *Elkanah Settle.* The Lady's triumph: a comi-dramatic opera . . . L. 1718.

S., E. *Miss Emily Sharp.* Outlines of sermons, taken chiefly from the published works of Unitarian writers. [Edited by E. S.] L. 1872.

S., E. *Epes Sargent.* Planchette; or, the despair of science . . . B. 1869.

S., E. *Mrs. William Stewart* (?). Sketches of home. Hale Parsonage. 1843.

S., E. B. *Ephraim Baynard Seabrook.* Ariel refuted . . . By . . . Charleston, S.C., 1867.

S., E. B. *Eliza B. Swan.* Once a year; or, the doctor's puzzle. 1881.

S., E. H. *Edward Henry Smith,* Lord Stanley. Six weeks in South America. L. 1850.

S., E. L. *Mrs. E. L. Saxon,* in the New Orleans "Picayune" and "Times."

S., E. R. *Ernest R. Seymour.* Mignonette: a sketch . . . L. 1858.

S., E. S. *E. S. Seward.* Columbiad poems. Balt. 1840.

S., F. (Felix Summerly). *Sir Henry Cole.* The most delectable history of Reynard the Fox. Edited by . . . L. 1846.

S., F. *Frederic Saunders.* Salad for the solitary . . . L. 1853.

S., F. M. F. *Felicia M. F. Skene.* A memoir of Alexander, Bishop of Brechin . . . L. 1876.

S., G. *George Slater,* in his contributions to the "Mail" (N.Y.).

S., G. *George Smith.* A defence of the communion-office of the Church of England . . . Edinb. 1744.

S., G. *Sir George Stephen.* The guide to service . . . L. 1844.

S., G. *George Sewell.* An introduction to the life and writings of G—t Lord Bishop of S—m . . . L. 1714.

S., G. *George Stronach, M.A.* Shakespeare and Bacon. By . . . In the "Hornet" (L.), Aug. 11, 1875.

S., G. A. *George Augustus Sala,* in newspaper contributions.

S., G. O. *George O. Seilhamer,* in his contributions to "Truth" (N.Y.).

S., G. W. *George W. Smalley,* the London correspondent of the New York "Tribune."

S. H. *James Tidmarsh.* National religious education . . . L. 1852.

S., H. H. A. *Hely H. A. Smith.* The duke and the doctors. L. n.d.

S., H. P. *Miss Helen P. Strong,* in her contributions to "Harper's Young People" (N.Y.).

S., H. S. *Henry Sewell Stokes.* The plaint of Morwenstowe. Verses signed . . . Bodmin, 1876.

S., H. W. *Mrs. Horace Wemyss Smith* (?). Records of a happy life . . . P. 1873.

S., I. T. *John Talwin Shewell.* A tribute to the memory of William Cowper . . . By . . . Ipswich, 1808.

S., J. *Sir John Stoddart,* who wrote his first contribution for the "Times" in the shape of a series of letters, in 1810, under this signature.

S., J. *John Sympson.* The age of the world, collected in all its periods from the sacred Scriptures, and other histories of undoubted veracity . . . n.p. 1707.

S., J. *John Small.* An apology for the true Church of Scotland . . . Edinb. 1719.

S., J. *Joseph Sutton.* The character of the true Gospel ministry, and the liberty of the children of God, etc. By . . . L. 1836.

S., J. *Joseph Sykes.* Detached thoughts. Brighton, 1865.

S., J. *Josiah Swett, D.D.,* compiler. Forms of prayer to be used in families, as set forth in the prayer-book . . . Claremont, N.H., 1861.

S., J. *Jonathan Swift, D.D.* A letter of advice to a young poet. 1720.

S., J. *J. Smith.* The mirror of merit and beauty. N.Y. 1808.

S., J. *J. Stephens.* Monody on the death of the Rev. Sir Hugh Molesworth,

Bart., of St. Petroc Manor, Cornwall. Wadebridge, Cornwall, 1862.

S., J. *Miss Jessy Stewart.* Ode to Dr. Thomas Percy. Edinb. 1804.

S., J. *James Smith.* Shakespeare, not Bacon, in the "Daily Argus" (Melbourne, Australia), Aug. 20, 1881.

S., J. *John Sarjeant, Sargeant, or Sergeant,* sometimes called *Smith,* sometimes *Holland.* Transnatural philosophy; or, metaphysicks ... By ... L. 1700.

S., J. *Major John (Scott) Waring.* Two letters to the Right Hon. Edmund Burke ... By ... L. 1783.

S., J., A.C. *John Sleech,* Archdeacon of Cornwall. Mr. Pitfield's reason for charging Dr. Andrew ... Exeter, 1762.

S., J., D.D.D.S.P.D. *Jonathan Swift, D.D.* The mishap: a poem. Written by the late Rev. Dr. ... Dublin, 1750 (?).

S., J., of Dale. *Frederic Jesup Stimson.* Guerndale: an old story. N.Y. 1882.

S., J., a Layman. *James Sullivan.* Strictures on the Rev. Mr. Thatcher's pamphlet entitled "Observations upon the State of the Clergy of New England" ... By ... B. 1785.

S., J., A Presbyter of the Episcopal Church of Scotland. *John Small.* The fourth commandment of the Decalogue considered ... Edinb. 1713.

S., Dr. J. *Jonathan Swift, D.D.* The sermons of ... L. 1790.

S., J., D.S.P. *Jonathan Swift.* The beast's confession to the priest ... 2d ed. Dublin, 1738.

S., J. A. *James Alexander Smith.* God and man L. 1861.

S., J. H. *J. H. Shorthouse.* John Inglesant: a romance. L. 1882.

S., J. R. *John Russell Smith,* the London publisher, in his contributions to Hamst's "Handbook of fictitious names," etc. 1868.

S., L. *Lister Smith.* The cruise of the "Zephyr"; or, the humorous adventures of some Halstead navigators, by land, river, and sea. By ... Halstead, 1860.

S., the late J. J., Esquire. *John Anstey.* The pleader's guide: a didactic poem ... By ... 4th ed. L. 1804.

S., L. *Leslie Stephen.* The "Times" on the American civil war ... L. 1865.

S., L. C. *Lucy Coffin Starbuck.* Seaweeds from the shores of Nantucket. P. 1853.

S., L. H. *Lewis Henry Steiner, M.D.* The history of Guilford, Conn., from the Mss. of Hon. Ralph D. Smith. [Pref-

ace signed "L. H. S.," as editor.] Albany, 1877.

S., Mario. *Isabella Scopoli-Biasi.* Versi e prose. 1866.

S., M. *Mary J. Safford,* in the N.Y. "Home Journal."

S., M. *Miss Margaret MacNair Stokes.* The Cromlech on Howth. A poem [by Sir Samuel Ferguson] ... With ... drawings from nature by M. S. ... L. 1864.

S., M. *Menella Bute Smedley.* A very woman. L. 1846.

S., M. C. *Mrs. Mary (Crowinshield) Sparks.* Hymns, home, Harvard. B. 1883.

S., M. E. W. *Mrs. Margaret Elizabeth (Wilson) Sherwood.* Home amusements. N.Y. 1881.

S., M. H. *Mary H. Seymour,* in the "St. Nicholas."

S., M. L. R. & W. *M. L. R. and W. Satterlee.* Two legions of the Christ Child: for Christmas Tide. N.Y. 186–.

S., M. S. *Marie Sophie (Birath) Schwartz.* Förtalet, 1855.

S., N. *Nehemiah Strong.* An astronomical diary or almanack for ... 1783 ... By N. S. ... Springfield, Mass., 1782.

S. N. *Bishop Thomas Elrington.* Miscellaneous observations on J. K. L.'s letter to the Marquess Wellesley ... Dublin, 1824.

S., N. B. *Nathaniel Bradstreet Shurtleff.* John Beal, of Hingham, and one line of his descendants. B. 1865.

S. P. *Thomas Carlyle.* Varnhagen von Ense's memoirs, in the "London and Westminster Review" for December, 1838.

S. P. A. M. *Jonathan Swift, D.D.* The seventh epistle of the first book of Horace, imitated ... Dublin, 1749.

S., P. C. S. *Rt. Hon. Percy Clinton Sydney Smythe,* 6th Lord Viscount Strangford. He was a frequent correspondent of the "Gent. Mag." under the initials of his name, "P. C. S. S.," and the same signature has often appeared in "Notes and Queries."

S., P. R. *Peter Remsen Strong.* "Awful," and other jingles ... N.Y. 1871.

S. P., Y. B. *Samuel Parker, Yeoman Beadle.* A chiding letter to ... in defence of Epistola Objurgatoria. L. 1744. By Dr. William King.

S., R. *Robert Percy Smith,* in the "Museum Criticum," 1826, in which also "W. F." is *William Frere;* "H. V. B.," *Henry Vincent Bayley;* "J. P.," *James Parke;* and "J. K.," *John Keate.*

"Robert Smith ... wrote, in the style of Lucretius, such Latin poetry as is fairly worth all the rest in that language since the banishment of Ovid." — W. S. LANDOR, letter to R. W. Emerson, Bath, 1856.

"We introduce him here on the strength of his famous Cambridge Latin Triposes verses, in Lucretian rhythm, on the three systems of Plato, Descartes, and Newton." — ALLIBONE.

S., R. B. *Robert Bissett Scott, Esq.* Roman remains at Lisbon, in "Gent. Mag.," April, 1832, p. 291.

S., R. H. *Richard Henry Stoddard.* Life, travels, and books of A. Von Humboldt ... N.Y. 1860. [Introduction by Bayard Taylor.]

S., R. H. *Richard Herne Shepherd.* Tennysoniana ... L. 1866.

S., R. J. *Richard Joseph Sulivan.* Observations made during a tour through parts of England, etc. L. 1780.

S., R. P. *Robert Pearsall Smith.* Walking in the light ... B. 1872.

S., R. T. *William Maginn.*

"For a considerable time Dr. Maginn corresponded with Mr. Blackwood under the signature of 'R. T. S.'; and he gradually withdrew the incognito so far as to subscribe himself 'Ralph Tuckett Scott,' and Mr. Blackwood sent him a cheque, payable to that gentleman. Dr. Maginn wrote a very humorous letter, quizzing Mr. B. for being gulled, and exaggerating the difficulty he had in getting the cheque cashed, with the endorsement of an imaginary person."

S., R. V. *Robert Vernon Smith.* Early writings of Robert Percy Smith, with a few verses in later years; edited by ... his surviving son. Chiswick, 1850.

S., R. W. *R. W. Smiles.* The war; is it just or necessary ? L. n.d.

S., S. *Sarah Sheppard.* Illustrations of Scripture, the Hebrew converts, and other poems ... L. 1837.

S., S. *Stephen Salisbury.* Remarks on the report of the Committee of Examiners at the Commencement of the Worcester Co. Free Inst. of Industrial Science. Worcester, Mass., 1877.

S. S. (Sinner Saved). *William Huntington.*

He said of himself: "As I cannot get a D.D., for the want of cash, neither can I get an M.A., for the want of learning; therefore I am compelled to fly for refuge to S. S., by which I mean 'Sinner Saved.'"

S., S., Your Bible Reader. *Miss Sarah Start.* To the children of the Sunday-School ... of the Church of the Ascension. N.Y. 1866.

S., S. S. *S. S. Simpson.* Aunt Sophie's stories ... B. 1859.

S. T. *Rev. William Fleetwood.* — See "Curate of Wilts, A."

S., T. *E. W. Krackowizer,* of Normal Park, Ill., in his contributions to various periodicals.

T. S. = Theophrastus Schopenhauer.

S. T. *Charles Knight.* His signature

to poetry entitled "Typhus and Cholera — An Eclogue," published in the "Times," London, Sept. 24, 1854.

S., T. *Thomas Shillitoe.* An abstract from an English edition of the meditations of Thomas A'Kempis on the life and loving-kindness of Jesus Christ. By ... L. n.d.

S., T. *Thomas Stratton.* Aureæ sententiæ: select sentences ... By ... L. 1768.

S., T. *Thomas Story.* To the saints in Sion: a song of praise ... L. 1740.

S., T. F., an old Piscator. *Thomas Frederick Salter.* Hints to anglers ... By ... L. 1808.

S., W. *William Shippen.* Four speeches against continuing the army ... L. 1732.

S., W. *William Sandys, F.S.A.* The hornpipes of Cornwall, mentioned in "Le Roman de la Rose." Letter signed "W. S.," in "Gent. Mag.," 1824; and The Christmas drama of St. George, "Gent. Mag.," 1830.

S., W. *William Spalding.* On Shakspeare's authorship of "The two noble kinsmen": a drama commonly ascribed to John Fletcher. Edinb. 1833.

S., W. *Whitley Stokes.* Three Irish glossaries ... L. 1862.

S., Sir W. *Sir William Symonds.* Holiday trips, etc. L. 1847.

S., W., M.P. *Rev. William Stewart.* A letter to the Reverend Professor Campbell ... Glasgow, 1731.

S., W. G. *Rev. William G. Shaw.* Memorials of the clan Shaw ... n.p. 1868.

S., W. S. *Rev. William Samuel Symonds, B.A.* Malvern Chase: an episode of the Wars of the Roses and the Battle of Tewkesbury. An autobiography. Edited [or rather written] by ... Tewkesbury, 1881.

S., W. W. *William Wetmore Story.* "Ginevra da Siena" [a poem], in "Blackwood's Magazine," June, 1866, p. 673. "A Roman lawyer in Jerusalem — first century," in "Blackwood's Magazine," October, 1868, p. 479.

S ..., Eugène. *Marie Joseph* (called "Eugène") *Sue,* in several dramatic pieces.

S**, B.** *Benjamin Smart.* Cloathing society, in "Gent. Mag.," July, 1815, p. 39.

S** W***** N., Major.** *Major Selwyn.* The speech of ... the first day of the session ... 18 Nov. 1746. L. 1746.

S — — — — — — n, A — — — w. *Andrew*

Stevenson. A letter to the Reverend Mr. James Fisher . . . Edinb. 1747.

S——, ——. — *Stewarton.* Memoirs of C. M. Talleyrand de Perigord. L. 1806.

S——, **Granville.** *Granville Sharp.* — See Lamb's " Elia," " All Fools' Day."

S——, **Major.** *Major Michael Symes,* in Beloe's " Sexagenarian," Vol. II., p. 70. 2d ed. L. 1818.

S——, J——, Esq., **Poetry Professor for the University of Oxford.** *Rev. Joseph Spence.* A full and authentick account of Stephen Duck, the Wiltshire poet . . . L. 1731.

S——, R——, **Esq.** *Robert Southey, Esq.* — See Lamb's " Elia," " The tombs in the abbey," in a letter to R—— S——, Esq.

S——, **Sir R——.** *Sir Robert Sibbald.* A letter . . . to Dr. Archibald Pitcairn. Edinb. 1709.

S—le, **Sir R—d.** *Sir Richard Steele.* A letter to the Earl of O—d [Oxford], concerning the Bill of Peerage. L. 1719.

S——, **W., Esq.** *James Kirke Paulding.* The lay of the Scotch fiddle: a poem . . . N.Y. 1813.

S—t, **D—n.** *Jonathan Swift, D.D.* A soldier and scholar . . . Captain —— —— and D—n S—t. L. 1732.

S—t, **Dr.** *Jonathan Swift, D.D.* The wonderful wonder of wonders . . . By . . . Dublin, 1722.

S—t, **Rev. D—n.** *Jonathan Swift, D.D.* The history of Martin . . . L. 1742.

S—t, **Rev. Dr.** *Jonathan Swift, D.D.* The lady's dressing room . . . L. 1732.

S.-W., **R. W.** *Rev. and Hon. Reginald Windsor Sackville-West,* 7th Earl of De-la-Warr. Historical notices of the parish of Withyham . . . with a description of the church and Sackville Chapel . . . By . . . L. 1857.

S—y. *Robert Southey.* Peter Pindar's ghost; or, poetic epistles . . . to S—y. 1821.

S—— Y——, **T., Esq.** *Richard Finch.* A congratulatory letter to the Rev. Dr. Trapp . . . By . . . L. 1739.

Sabaroth, Ludwig de. *Isnard de Sainte-Lorette.* L'enfant du coche. Paris, 1822.

Sabbath-School Superintendent, A. *Alexander S. Arnold.* Uncle Timothy Taber . . . Augusta, Me., 1868.

Sabbath School Teacher, A. *Robert Frame.* Leaves from . . . L. 1859.

Sabino. *Edward Ballard, D.D.,* in the Boston " Daily Advertiser," in 1866, on the Popham Colony.

Sacheverellio, Don. *Dr. Henry*

Sacheverell. A character of . . . Knight of the Firebrand. In a letter to Isaac Bickerstaff, Esq. Dublin, 1710.

Sackett, Harry. *Andrew Dixon.*

Sadie. *Miss Sarah Williams.* Twilight hours : a legacy of verse . . . L. 1869.

Särkilax. *Emil von Quanten.* Fennomani och Skandinavism. 1855.

Sagadahoc. *Frederic Kidder,* in the Boston " Daily Advertiser," 1866, on the Popham Colony.

Sagittarius. *John Mein.* S.'s letters and political speculations. Extracted from the " Public Ledger " . . . B. 1775.

Sailer, Frederick. *Frederick Israel.*

Sailor. *Captain Edward Thompson.* Sailor's letters from 1754–1759. L. 1766.

Sailor, A. *Rev. Joshua Larwood.* Erratics ; by . . . L. 1800.

Sailor, A. *Franklin Fox.* Glimpses of the life of . . . L. 1862. New edition. Brighton, 1875.

Sailor, A. *Charles Reece Pemberton* (?). The Nautilus, in five cantos . . . a voyage . . . Liverpool to Buenos-Ayres and Monte-Video . . . 1825 and 1826, by . . . L. 1829.

Sailor, A. *Charles Nordhoff.* Nine years . . . N.Y. 1857.

Sailor Boy, A. *Charles Nordhoff.* The merchant vessel . . . 's voyage to see the world. Cin. 1855.

Saint-Albin, J. S. C., et Jacques Saint-Albin. *Jacques Albin Simon Collin de Plancy.* Les contes noirs ; ou, les frayeurs populaires . . . Paris, 1818.

Saint-Aubin, Horace de. *Honoré de Balzac.* Le Vicaire des Ardennes. Paris, 1822.

St. Clair, Mabel. *Miss Carrie S. Hibbard,* who, under this pen-name, contributed to the " Ohio State Journal," " Toledo Blade," and " Athens Messenger."

St. D., T. *Rev. Thomas Burgess.* Hebrew elements . . . L. 1807.

St. Denis Le Cadet. *E. Denison.* The lottery. Balt. 1815.

Saint-Germain, J. T. de. *Jules Romain Tardieu.* Pour un épingle . . . Paris, 1858.

Saint-Hermel. *Elme Marie Caro.* Vie de Pie IX. 1850.

Saint-Hermidad, Emanuel. *Valdemar Thisted.* Familienschatz. 1856.

St. Ives. *James Lawrence, Esq.* History of the antient family of Lawrence, in " Gent. Mag.," July, 1815, p. 12.

St. John, J. Hector. *Hector St. John Crevecœur.* Letters from an American farmer . . . P. 1794.

St. John, Mrs. Eugenia. *Mrs. Mar-*

tha Eugenia Berry. Bella; or, the cradle of liberty ... B. 1875.

St. John, Theophilus, LL.B. *Rev. Samuel Clapham, M.A.* Original sermons (L. 1790); Practical sermons (L. 1803); and Charges of Masillon, from the French. L. 1805.

St. Kames. *S. Nugent Townshend.* Colorado : its agriculture, stock-feeding, scenery, and shooting (which originally appeared in letters to the "Field" (L.), under this signature). N.Y. 1879.

St. Leon, Count Reginald de. *Edward Dubois* (?). St. Godwin: a tale of the sixteenth, seventeenth, and eighteenth century. By ... L. 1800.
This is a satire of W. Godwin's "St. Leon."

Saint Meva. *Josiah Harris.* A voice from the police court; or, the danger of too much punch. Plymouth, 18-.

Saint Sylvestre, P. D. de. *Pierre François Parent-Desbarres.* Gerbe de l'âge d'or. Paris, 1877.

St. Ursula. *Mary E. Blair.*

Saintine, X. B. de. *Joseph Xavier Boniface.* Picciola; or, the prisoner of Fenestrella. P. 1857.

Salar, Salmo, Esq. *George Rooper.* The autobiography of the late ... L. 1867.

Salem, Ahab. *Rev. James Murray.* The new maid of the oaks. A tragedy ... By ... L. 1778.

Salem, Hezekiah. *Philip Freneau,* who frequently described himself by this name.

Salvage, Jonas. *Rev. James Walker, B.C.L.* A dialogue between a captain of a merchant ship and a farmer ... L. 1768.

Sam. *Samuel Henri Berthoud.* Articles in periodical publications.

Sam, Invisible. *Reuben Vose* (?). Despotism; or, the last days of the American republic ... N.Y. 1856.

Sam the Malster. *Samuel Adams,* in the lampoons of the Hudibrastic poet, Green.

Samaritan, A. *William L. Robinson.* Diary of ... N. Orleans, 1858.

Samarow, Gregor. *Oscar Meding.* Held und Kaiser. Stuttgart, 1876.

Same Author, The. *Richard Whately, D.D.* Introductory lessons on the history of religious worship. Being a sequel to the "Lessons on Christian Evidences," by ... L. 1849.

Sampfilus Philocrin, ZYXW etc. *William Sampson.* Beasts at law; or, Zoölogian jurisprudence: a poem ... N.Y. 1811.

Sampleton, Samuel. *Luigi Monti.* Adventures of a consul abroad. B. 1878.

Sampson Short and Fat. *Samuel Kettell.* Quozziana; or, letters from Great Goslington, Mass., giving an account of the Quoz dinner ... B. 1842.

Samuel the Publican. *Samuel Adams.* Thus derisively styled by the royalists, in allusion to his office as tax-collector, 1763 *et seq.*

San-Marte. *Albert Schulz.* Leben und Dichtungen Wolframs von Eschenbach. 1858.

Sana. *Mrs. Anna Holyoke (Cutts) Howard,* in her contributions to the "Household" (Brattleboro, Vt.), etc.

Sancho. *Rev. J. W. Cunningham.* Sancho; or, the proverbialist. L. 1816.

Sand, George. *Mme. Amandine Lucile Aurore (Dupin) Dudevant,* in her numerous publications.
The name is said to have been given to her by Jules Sandeau, the academician, and was adopted by her to denote a masculine style in her writings.

Sand, Jules. *Jules Léonard Sylvain Sandeau.* Rose et Blanche. Paris, 1833.
Although the title-page bears only the name "Jules Sand," the author was assisted by Mme. Dudevant.

Sand, Maurice. *Jean François Maurice Arnauld Dudevant.* Six mille lieus à toute vapeur. Paris, 1862.

Sandette. *Miss Marie A. Walsh.* My queen. N.Y. 1879.

Sandrié, Pierre. *Pierre Marie Augustin Filon.* Les mariages de Londres. Paris, 1875.

Sands, John. *William Hutchinson,* in his contributions to the "Newark Journal" (N.J.).

Sanftleben, Adolar. *Carl Hauser,* in his contributions to the German edition of "Puck" (N.Y.).

Sans-Peur, Jean. *Hippolyte Babou.* L'homme à la lanterne. Paris, 1868.

Sans Souci. *Mrs. Nelly (Marshall) McAfee.* Gleanings from fireside fancies. 1866.

Sarti, Signor. *Ashton Knight.*

Sass, Job. *George. A. Foxcroft,* in his contributions to the Boston "Herald" about 1850.

Satanella. *Mrs. Mary (Hewins) Burnham.*

Satanella. *Mrs. Jennie (Cunningham) Croly,* in her letters to the "Call" (San Francisco, Cal.), 1856.

Sator. *Mrs. Leigh.* "Not quite a peck of P—s": a domestic story for girls. L. 1881.

Sault, R. O. *Charles F. Swain.* Captain Waters, and Bill his bo'sun. A tale of the ocean and the farm. N.Y. 1877.

Saunders, Jefferson, Esq. *Horace Smith.* The tin trumpet ... by the late Paul Chatfield, M.D. Edited by ... L. 1836.

Saunders, Richard. *Benjamin Franklin.* Almanacks. P. 1732–57.

Saunterer. *Hewson Clarke,* who, in 1804 and 1805, published in the "Tyne Mercury," a Newcastle paper, a series of essays called the "Saunterer," which were afterwards issued in book-form. 1806.

Savid. *James David,* in his contributions to the "World" (N.Y.), etc.

Savile. *Henry Sotheran.*

Saville, & Bolton Rowe. *Clement Scott,* who, according to the London letter in the "New York Times," 1878, "was making his way as a dramatist under this double *nom de plume.*"

Saville Row. *Saville Clarke.* Peril. L. 18–.

Savin, Una. *Mrs. George Hughes Hepworth.* Little gentleman in green: American fairy story. B. 187–.

Savonarola, Don Jeremy. *Francis Sylvester Mahony.* Facts and figures from Italy, by ... Benedictine monk, addressed ... to Charles Dickens, Esq. ... 1847. L. 1847.

Sawney. *William Douglass, M.D.* A friendly debate; or, a dialogue between Academicus and ... and Mundungus, two eminent physicians, about some of their late performances. B. 1722.

Sawney, 'Squire. *William Biglow.* His signature to "Assology" (poetry), in the "Columbian Centinel" (B. 179–).

Saxifrage. *Sheldon B. Thorne.*

Saxon. *E. Herbert Noyes,* in his contributions to the "Hotel Mail" (N.Y.)

Saxon, Isabelle. *Mrs. Redding Sutherland.* Five years within the golden gate. L. 1868.

Say. *Langdon Cheeves,* whose essays on the subject of the United States Bank, published under this signature, attracted much attention.

Scæva. *Prof. Isaac William Stuart.* Hartford in the olden time ... Hartford, 1853.

Scævola. *John Allen.* Letters of ... L. 1807.

Scævola, Mutius. *Joseph Greenleaf,* in the Massachusetts "Spy," 1771 *et seq.*

Scalpel, M.D. *Edward H. Dixon.* The terrible mysteries of the Ku-Klux-Klan ... N.Y. 1868.

Scavenger, John, M.D. *Elias Bockett.* A rod for the author of the little

switch; or, Mr. Wm. Gibson's picture drawn to the life ... By ... L. 1728.

Scelter, Helter van. *James Ridley.* The schemer; or, universal satirist. By that great philosopher ... L. 1763.

Schartenmeyer. *Friedrich Theodor Vischer.* Heldengedicht. P. 1874.

Scheffer, Frederick. *William King, LL.D.* The toast: an heroick poem, written originally in Latin by F. S.; now done into English with notes by Peregrine O'Donald. L. 1736.

Schlemihl, Peter. *George Wood.* Peter Schlemihl in America. P. 1848.

Schliemann der jüngere. *August Ebrard.* Cheirisophos' Reise durch Böotien. 1872.

Schnake. *Carl Hauser,* in his contributions to the German edition of "Puck" (N.Y.).

Schneider, Uncle. *C. M. Conolly.*

Schollar, A. *Rev. Samuel Wesley.* Maggots; or, poems on several subjects never before handled. By ... L. 1685.

Scholto. — See "Medical Student, A."

Schoolmaster, A. *William Alexander Alcott, M.D.* Confessions of ... Andover, Mass., 1839.

Schoolmaster, A. *D'Arcy Wentworth Thompson.* Day dreams of ... Edinb. 1864.

Schoolmaster in the Eastern Country, A. *Asa Humphrey.* Personal satire; or, satirical epistle. Written by ... B. 1804.

Schoolmaster of twenty years' standing. A. *Rev. Charles Alexander Johns.* The governess: a first lesson book for children ... L. 1854.

Schrader, August. *August Simmel.* Das testament des Grafen Hamilton. 1842.

Schreier, Capt. *Leopold Schenck,* editor of the German edition of "Puck" (N.Y.), in his contributions to that periodical.

Schubin, Ossip. *Miss L. Kirschner.* Our own set: a novel ... N.Y. 1884.

Scipio. *Uriah Tracy.* Reflections on Monroe's "View of the Conduct of the Executive," 1794–96. B. 1798.

Also ascribed to *Alexander Hamilton.*

Sclavonian Nobleman in London, A. *Sir John Hill.* A dissertation on royal societies, in a letter from ... to his friend in Sclavonia. L. 174–.

Scot., Quod Ar. *Allan Ramsay.* The vision ... [in verse]. Edinb. 1748.

Scotch Episcopalian, A. *H. Robertson.* A letter to the laymen of the Scotch Episcopal church. Edinb. 1848.

Scotch Family, A. *Mrs. John Hill*

Burton. Our summer in the Harz forest. By ... Edinb. 1865.

Scotch Granite. *Mrs. Hannah (McLaren) Shepard,* in her contributions to periodical literature, etc.

Scotch Minister's Daughter, A. *Mrs. S. R. Whitehead.* Rose Douglas; or, sketches of a country parish ... L. 1851.

Scotch Physician, A. *Francis Adams, M.D., LL.D.* Arundines devæ; or, poetical translations on a new principle ... Edinb. 1853.

Scoto-Britannus. *Thomas M'Crie, D.D.* Free thoughts on the late religious celebration of the funeral of ... Princess Charlotte of Wales ... Edinb. 1817.

Scots Gentleman, A. *Archibald Pitcairne, M.D.* The assembly: a comedy. By ... L. 1722.

Scots Gentleman, A. *Mr. Gray.* The memoirs, life, and character, of the great Mr. Law ... L. 1721.

Scots Gentleman, in the Swedish Service, A. *Daniel Defoe.* History of the wars of his present Majesty, Charles XII., King of Sweden ... L. 1715.

Scots-Irishman, The. *D. Bruce.* Poems, chiefly in the Scottish dialect ... Washington, 1801.

Scott, Julia. *Miss Mary O'Brien,* of St. Joseph, Mo.

Scott, Leader. *Mrs. Lucy E. Baxter,* under this pseudonym, has been the Italian correspondent of the "Magazine of Art" since its commencement.

Scott, Ralph Tucker. *William Maginn, LL.D.*

"*Maginn,* in his earlier communications with Blackwood, did not make his personality known, and corresponded with him under the signature of 'R. T. S.,' or, later, as 'Ralph Tucker Scott.'" —See "The Maclise-Portrait Gallery," Appendix, p. 520.

Scott, Robert. *James Robins.* The history of England during the reign of George the Third. L. 1820–24.

Scott, Sir Walter, Bart. *J. H. Allan.* The bridal of Caölchairn, and miscellaneous poems. L. & Edinb. 1822.

Scott, William Henry. *John Lawrence.* British field sports ... L. 1818.

Scott, T., Esq. *Robert Smith Surtees.* Hawbuck grange; or, the sporting adventures of ... By ... L. 1847.

Scott, Walter, Esq. *James Kirke Paulding.* The lay of the Scottish fiddle: a tale of Havre de Grace. Supposed to be written by Walter Scott, Esq. N.Y. 1813.

Scottish Barrister, A. *John Borthwick.* A letter to the representatives of

Scotland in Parliament, respecting the state of our law ... Edinb. 1830.

Scottish Boz, The. *Robert Mackenzie Daniel.*

Scottish Farmer and Land Agent, A. *John Claudius Loudon.* The utility of agricultural knowledge to the sons of the landed proprietors of Great Britain, etc. By ... L. 1809.

Scottish Hogarth, The. *David Allan.*

Scotty. *C. H. Urquhart,* in the Chicago "Times."

Scotus. One of the pseudonyms of Junius (*q.v.*). The letter thus signed is dated May 4, 1772, and severely censures Lord Barrington.

Scotus. *David Burn,* in his letters on educational topics to the "Gazette" (Hamilton, Can., about 1850).

Scotus. *John Gibson.* Strictures upon the letter of Lucius to the Rev. Andrew Thompson ... Edinb. 1817.

Scratch, Harry. *H. W. Burton,* in the "Norfolk Virginian" in 1877.

Scratchley, Harry. *John D. Sherwood.* Comic history of America ... B. 1870.

Scribble, Timothy. *A. Cowper.* The Norfolk poetical miscellany ... L. 1744.

Scribe, Simon, Senior. *Adam Black.* Maynooth ... L. 1852.

Scribe, Sylvan. *Seloftus D. Forbes,* in "Turf, Field, and Farm," of N.Y.C.

Scriber, Peter. *Charles Augustus Davis.* Peter Scriber on protection. n.p. 1844. Also his contributions to the New York "Commercial Advertiser."

Scriblerus, Johannes. *William Coombe.* Cogitations of ... in the "Repository of Arts," etc. L. 1814–16.

Scriblerus, Martinus. *Jonathan Swift, D.D.* The art of sinking in poetry. 1727. With Pope and Arbuthnot.

Scriblerus, Martinus. *Alexander Pope.* The Dunciad. L. 1727.

Scriblerus, Martinus. *Rev. Robert Morehead.* Explanations and emendations of some passages in the text of Shakespeare ... Edinb. 1814.

Scriblerus, Martinus. *John Arbuthnot, M.D.* The first book of ... L. 1714.

Scriblerus Maximus. *James Love.* Cricket: an heroic poem, illustrated with the critical observations of ... 1770.

Scriblerus Quartus. *Thomas Cooke.* The boys' miscellany; or, Colley triumphant ... L. n.d.

Scriblerus Secundus. *Rev. Thomas*

Burgess. Bagley: a descriptive poem . . . Oxf. 1777.

Also ascribed to *Rev. Alexander Crowcher Schomberg.*

Scriblerus Secundus. *Henry Fielding.* The author's farce; and the pleasures of the town . . . by . . . L. 1730.

Scricci. *John Swaby.* Philosophy of the opera . . . P. 1852.

Scrub, Timothy, Esq., of Rag Fair. *John Kelly.* The fall of Bob; or, the oracle of gin . . . 1736.

Scrutator. — See "Antiquarius."

Scrutator. *Henri Du Pré Labouchere,* in his contributions to "Truth" (L.).

Scrutator. *John S. Rarey.*

Scrutator. *Rev. John Tucker.* The apparition; or, the ghost of Archbishop Cranmer deciding the baptismal and predestinarian controversy. By . . . L. 1850.

Scrutator. *K. W. Horlock.* The country gentleman. L. 1852.

Scrutator. *Rev. Malcolm Maccoll.* Mr. Gladstone and Oxford. L. 1865.

Scrutator. *Charles Pennell Measor.* Irish fallacies and English facts . . . L.

Scrutator. *Charles Jerram, A.M.* Letters to an Universalist . . . Clipstone, 1802.

Scrutator. *David Macallan.* The mode of Christian baptism . . . L. 1858.

Scrutator. *Walter Henry, M.D.* The politics of Nova Scotia. Letters dated Halifax, 1843–44, in the New York "Albion" under this signature.

Scrutator. *Charles Rivington.* Strictures on Mr. N. E. S. A. Hamilton's inquiry into the genuineness of the Ms. corrections in Mr. J. J. Collier's annotated Shakespeare, folio, 1632. L. 1860.

Sculler, The. *John Taylor,* the Water-poet. Taylor's water-works; or, the sculler's travels from Tyber to Thames, with epigrams, etc. L. 1614.

Sculptor, Satiricus, Esq. *Samuel William Henry Ireland.* Chalcographimania; or, the portrait-collector and print-seller's chronicle, with infatuations of every description: a humorous poem . . . By . . . L. 1814.

Sea. *Roland F. Coffin.*

Sea Officer, A. *Lieut. Richard Pickersgill, R.N.* A concise account of voyages for the discovery of a North-West passage . . . By . . . L. 1782.

Sea Officer, A. *Francis V. Vernon.* Voyages and travels of . . . Dublin, 1792.

Seab, Lenial. *D. S. B. Johnston.*

Seacole. *William G. Hudson,* in the Brooklyn "Eagle."

Seafarer, A. *Clark Russell.* My watch below. Yarns by . . . L. 1883.

Seafield, Frank, M.A. *Alexander H. Grant, M.A.* The literature and curiosities of dreams . . . L. 1865.

Sealsfield, Charles. *Karl Postel.* Gesammelte Werke. Stuttgart, 1843–46.

Seaman, A. *John Stevenson.* An address to the Hon. Admiral Augustus Keppel . . . L. 1779.

Seaman, A. *Thomas Cochrane,* Earl of Dundonald. Autobiography of . . . L. 1860.

Seaman, A. *Lieut. Weaver.* Journals of the ocean, and other miscellaneous poems; by . . . N.Y. 1826.

Seaman's Friend, A. *Samuel Baker.* A few words of advice to the mariners of England . . . L. 1854.

Search, Edward. *William Hazlitt.*

Search, Edward, Esq. *Abraham Tucker.* The light of nature pursued; by . . . L. 1769–70.

Search, John. *Rev. Mr. Mursell.*

Search, John. *Rev. Thomas Binney.* The great Gorham case . . . With a preface by J. S. L. 1850.

Search, John. *Archbishop Richard Whately.* Considerations on the law of libel (L. 1833), and Religion and her name, a metrical tract (1841).

"In resuming on this occasion the signature prefixed by him some years ago to a pamphlet on the subject of Religious Libel, the author of these stanzas takes the opportunity of stating that, except in the present instance and in that of the pamphlet alluded to, he is not accountable for anything that may have appeared under the signature of 'John Search.' He is led to mention this from the circumstance of some other writer having assumed the same signature about a twelvemonth, more or less, after *he* had adopted it; and forthwith prefixed it to sundry publications of his own." — Preface, "Religion and her Name."

Search, Sappho. *Rev. John Black.* A poetical review of Miss H. M.'s [Hannah More] strictures upon female education, in a series of anapestic epistles. By . . . L. 1800.

Search, Sarah. *F. Nolan.* Marriage with a deceased wife's sister . . . L. 1855.

Search, Warner Christian, LL.D., F.R.S., and M.R.I.A. *Sir William Cusack Smith, Bart.* Metaphysic rambles . . . Dublin, 1835.

Searcher, Leland. *William Wallace Hebbard, M.D.* Will it come? a story. Hyde Park, Mass., 1870.

Searle, January. *George Searle Phillips.* Memoirs of W. Wordsworth . . . L. 1852.

Seaworthy, Captain Gregory. *James Gregory.* Nag's Head; or, two months among " The Bunkers " . . . P. 1850.

Second Childhood. *Edmund Burke.*
— See " Albion."

Secondsight, Solomon. *Thomas Berkeley Greaves.* The insurgent chief; or, O'Halloran. P. 1824.

Secondsight, Solomon. *Dr. James McHenry.* The wilderness; or, Braddock's times. A tale of the West. N.Y. 1823. Also under this signature contributed to the "American Quarterly Review," 1827–37.

Secondthoughts, Solomon, Schoolmaster. *John Pendleton Kennedy.* Quodlibet: containing some annals thereof . . . P. 1840.

Secretary and General Agent. *Rev. N. Sayre Harris.* Journal of a tour in the "Indian Territory," performed by order of the Domestic Committee of the Board of Missions of the Protestant Episcopal Church, in the Spring of 1844, by their . . . N.Y. 1844.

Secretary of an Auxiliary Bible Society, A. *Rev. George Clayton.* Considerations respectfully submitted to the Committee of the British and Foreign Bible Society, on the present crisis of its affairs. By . . . L. 1831.

Secretary of State, The. *Timothy Pickering.* Letter from . . . to Charles C. Pinckney, Esq. . . . N.Y. 1797.

Secretary of the Boston Society, The. *Rev. Seth Bliss.* Letters to the members, patrons, and friends of the Branch American Tract Society in Boston . . . B. 1858.

Secretary to the Board, The. *Arthur Young.* On the advantages which have resulted from . . . the Board of Agriculture . . . L. 1809.

Secunder. *Alexander Chalmers.* Hyperbole in conversation justly censured. "Gent. Mag.," August, 1801, p. 704.

Secundus, Theophilus. *Rev. Stephen Jenner.* Wilberforce's doctrine of the Eucharist refuted. L. 1854.

Sedley, F. *Theodore Sedgwick Fay.*

See, Gustav vom. *Gustav Otto von Struensee.* Die Philosophie des Unbewussten. 1876.

See, Henricus vom. *William Dilg,* of Milwaukee, in several poetical works.

Seeburg, Franz von. *Franz Hacker.* Die Fugger und ihre Zeit, ein Bildercyklus. 1879.

Seedy, Alfred. *Charles Rowcroft.* Chronicles of "The Fleet prison" . . . L. 1847.

Segdirboeg. *George Bridges.* A letter upon the decay of the woollen manu-

factories in Great Britain and Ireland . . . L. 1739.

Seidlitz, Julius. *Isaak* or *Itzig Jeitteles.* Die Poesie und die Poeten in Österreich. 1837.

Select Vestryman of the Parish of Putney, A. *Rev. William Carmalt.* A letter to the Right Honourable George Canning on the principle and the administration of the English Poor Laws. L. 1823.

Selim. *Samuel Woodworth.* Quarter Day. N.Y. 1812.

Selkirk, J. B. *James Brown.* Ethics and æsthetics of modern poetry. L. 1878.

Semilasso. *Hermann,* Fürst von Pückler-Muskau. Semilassos vorletzter Weltgang, 1835; Semilasso in Afrika, 1836.

Senate of Lilliput, The. *Parliament* [both houses of]. This important article in the "Gent. Mag." was for several years executed by Mr. William Guthrie, born, 1708, at Brechin, and died in 1770; afterwards it was done (1740–43) by Dr. Samuel Johnson from scanty (or no) notes furnished by persons employed to attend Parliament.

Senator of thirty-years, A. *Thomas Hart Benton.* Thirty years' view . . . By . . . N.Y. 1857.

Seneachie. *Lachlan Maclean.* An historical and genealogical account of the clan Maclean . . . L. 1858.

Seneca. *Lord Neaves,* of "Maga."

Seneca. *Noah Webster.* Article in " Hampshire Gazette."

Senectus. *Gideon Granger,* who, under this signature, published some essays on the New York school fund.

Senex. *James Anderson,* who, 1790–94, wrote essays in the "Bee" (L.) under this signature.

Senex. *William A. Brewer,* in his contributions to various New York and Boston periodicals.

Senex. *Alexander Chalmers, Esq.* During the American war " Mr Chalmers acquired considerable fame as a political writer. He also contributed to the other popular journals of the day. In the ' St. James Chronicle ' he wrote numerous essays, many of them under the signature of ' Senex.' "

Senex. *Lord Grey,* in the London " Times."

Senex. *Canon Josiah Bateman.* Clerical reminiscences. L. 1882.

Senex. *Samuel Pegge.* On the hopes of a general index to the "Gent. Mag.," " Gent. Mag.," 1786, p. 757. — See "Gent. Mag.," LXVI., 1083.

Senex. *Edward Rowland.* The psalms of David attempted in verse ... L. 1826.

Senilis, Johannes. *John Nelson.* Pinaceæ: being a handbook of firs and pines ... L. 1866.

Senior, A. *John Penrose, M.A.* A familiar introduction to the Christian religion ... L. 1831.

Senior Curate of St. Luke's, Berwick Street, The. *Rev. Henry Whitehead.* The cholera in Berwick Street. By ... L. 1854.

Senior Member of Convocation, A. *Rev. B. P. Symons.* A letter to a non-resident friend upon subscription to the thirty-nine articles ... Oxf. n.d.

Senior of the National Era. *Dr. William Elder.*

Sensitive, Samuel, and Testy, Timothy. *James Beresford.* The miseries of human life; or, the groans of ... with a few supplementary sighs from Mrs. Testy ... L. 1807.

Sentimental Idler, A. *Henry Harewood Leech.* Letters of ... 1866.

Sentimental Philosopher, A. *Washington Irving.* Fragment of a journal of ... during his residence in the city of New York. N.Y. 1809.

Sentinel. *William Henry Bogart.* Who goes there? or, men and events ... N.Y. 1866. Also his signature in the N.Y. "World."

Sepia. *Fanny Fryatt.*

Septuagenarian, A. *Selina E. Means.* Reminiscences of York, by ...

Septuagenarian, A. *Emma Sophia Cust*, Countess Brownlow. Slight reminiscence of ... from 1802 to 1815. L. 1867.

Septuagenarian, A. *James Forbes Dalton, Esq.* Some of my contributions in rhyme to periodicals in bye-gone days, by ... Edinb. 1860.

Seraph. *Stephen Fiske.* His signature in the N.Y. "Spirit of the Times." etc.

Sergeant of the ** Regiment of Infantry, A. *J. Donaldson.* The eventful life of a soldier ... Edinb. 1827.

Serulan. — *Laurens.* Poems. By ... Charleston, S.C., 1854.

Servati, Erich. *Heinrich Sautier.* Warum soll ich ein freymäurer werden? Basel, 1786.

Servetus, Michael, M.D. *Dr. Patrick Blair.* Thoughts on nature and religion ... L. 1774.

Servington, Quintus. *Henry Savary.* Quintus Servington: a novel. Hobart-Town, 1830.

Settler, A. *Richard Arthur Seymour.* Pioneering in the Pampas; or, the first four years of a settler's experience in the La Plata camps. L. 1869.

Settler, A. *John W. Bannister.* Sketch of a plan for settling in Upper Canada a portion of the unemployed labourers of England. L. 1821.

Settler in Santo Domingo, A. *Joseph Warren Fabens.* In the tropics, by ... N.Y. 1863.

Preface by Richard Burleigh Kimball.

Seven Years' Resident, etc., A. *G. Nettle.* A practical guide for emigrants to North America ... By ... L. 1850.

Several American Authors. *Miss Catharine Maria Sedgwick, James Kirke Paulding, William Cullen Bryant, William Leggett,* and *R. C. Sands.* Tales of Glauber-Spa. N.Y. 1832.

Several Young Persons. *Jane Taylor,* assisted by her sister *Anne* (afterwards *Mrs. Gilbert) and others.* Original poems for infant minds. L. 1807.

Severne, Christine. *Mrs. Anne Boulton.*

Seward, W. *William Maginn.* Letter from ... "Ullaloo, Gol; or, lamentation over the dead," in "Blackwood's Magazine," Vol. VII., pp. 194–197.

Sexagenarian, A. *The Hon. and Rev. Robert Liddell.* "The lay of the last angler"; or, a tribute to the Tweed at Melrose ... By ... Kelso, 1867–74.

Sexagenarian, The. *Rev. William Beloe.* The sexagenarian; or, the memoirs of a literary life. L. 1817.

For key to the above, see "Notes and Queries," 2d Ser., IX., 300; X., 33, 93.

Sexagenarius. *John Holland.* The old arm chair; or, recollections of a bachelor. B. S. Sheffield, 1824.

Sexagenary, The. *S. De Witt Bloodgood.* Reminiscences of the American Revolution. Albany, 1833.

Sexby, Edward. *Josiah Quincy, Jr.,* who, under this and other signatures, 1771–72, published patriotic essays in the Boston "Gazette."

Sexton of the Old School, A. *Lucius Manlius Sargent.* Dealings with the dead, contributed to the "Boston Transcript" (repub. 1856).

Seymour, Robert. *John Mottley.* A survey of the cities of London and Westminster ... By ... L. 1734–5.

Seymour, W. *Cuthbert Shaw.* Odes on the four seasons. L. 1760.

Shadow, John. *John Byrom, A.M., F.R.S.*

Whilst at Trin. Coll., Camb., 1707–11, "he held a correspondence with some of the *literati* of that time, and wrote some papers in the

'Spectator' on 'Dreaming' signed 'John Shadow.' He was also the author of that much admired pastoral, 'My time, O ye Muses, was
happily spent,' which appeared in the 8th volume of the same work.'

**Shahcoolen, a Hindu Philosopher
residing in Philadelphia.** *Samuel
Lorenzo Knapp.* Letters of ... to his
friend El Hassan, an inhabitant of
Delhi. B. 1802.

Shaker. *F. W. Adams*, in his contributions to the "Atlantic Monthly."

Shallow, Master. *Rev. Dr. Thomas
Ford.*

"He was an enthusiastic admirer of the
'Sweet Swan of Avon.' Of this, his numerous
and admirable imitations of that matchless dramatist, inserted in several volumes of the 'Gent.
Mag.,' under the signature of 'Master Shallow,'
bear abundant testimony." — "Gent. Mag.,"
June, 1821.

Shamrock. *R. D. Williams*, in poems.

Shandon, Capt. *C. Smith Cheltnan*,
in London "Belgravia."

Shandon, Captain. *Dr. William Maginn*, the Captain Shandon of Thackeray's "Pendennis."

Shandy, Tristram, Gentleman.
Laurence Sterne. The life and opinions
of ... L. 1760–67.

Sharp, Conversation. *Richard Sharp.*
Letters and essays in prose and verse.
L. 1834.

**Sharp, Gustavus, Esq., of the late
firm of Flint and Sharp.** Probably
Samuel Warren. The confessions of an
attorney. N.Y. 1852.

**Sharpe, Jérôme, professeur de phy-
sique amusante.** *Henri Decremps.* Cod-
icile de ... Paris, 1787.

Shatt, Montague. *Latham C. Strong.*

Shaver, The. *Rev. John Macgowan.*
[C. Churchill's] Night: a satire on the
manners of the rich and great ... with
notes by ... L. 1768.

Sheelah. *A. Fletcher.* The mother's
request. 18–.

Sh—lb—ne, L—d. *Lord Shelburne.*
— See "F., Hon. C. J."

Shelley, A. Fishe. *James W. Gerard.*
Aquarelles [poetry]. N.Y. 1858.

Shenandoah. *Lewis H. Morgan.* His
signature to papers on the "Iroquois,"
in Cotton's "American Quarterly Review," in 1847.

Shepherd, The. *James Hogg.* The
S.'s calendar. Edinb. 1829. [First published in "Blackwood's Magazine."]

Shepherd, Dorothea Alice. *Mrs.
Ella (Farnam) Pratt.* How two girls
tried farming. B. 1879.

Shepherd Tom. *Thomas Robinson
Hazard.* Recollections of olden times.
1879.

Sheridan, Right Hon. R. B. *John
Hall Stevenson.* Crazy tales. By the
late ... L. 1825. — See "Eugenius."

Sherlock. *Solomon Southwick.* A
layman's apology ... Albany, 1834.

Sherry, Charles. *John Osborne Sargent*, who wrote the versatile papers,
signed with this name, in the "Collegian," a periodical published by a number of undergraduates of Harvard University in 1830.

Shingle, Solon. *Caleb Dunn.*

Shippen. *Samuel Adams*, in the
"Boston Gazette," Jan. 30, 1769.

Shirley. *John Skelton.* Nugæ criti-
cæ: occasional papers written at the sea-
side by ... Edinb. 1862.

Shoddy, Gretchen. *Carl Hauser*, in
his contributions to the German edition
of "Puck" (N.Y.).

Shoe, Aminidab. *John Bousell.* —
See "P*****, P****, Esq."

Shoeboy, A. *Jonathan Swift, D.D.*
A vindication of the libel; or, a new
ballad, written by ... on an attorney
who was formerly a shoeboy.

Sholto. *Robert Douglas*, in his contributions to the "Courier" (Glasgow).

Sholto. *Dr. Robert Shelton Mackenzie*,
in his contributions to the "London
Magazine."

Short, Bob. *Alexander Pope*, in his
contributions to the "Guardian," Nos.
91 and 92, June 25 and 26, 1713.

Short, Bob. *Augustus Baldwin Longstreet, LL.D.*, whose "Bob Short" articles exerted great influence in nullification times, and who established at that
time the Augusta (Ga.) "Sentinel."

Short, Joshua. *Frederick Oakley.*

Shortcut, Daisy. *D. S. Cohen and
another.* Our show; one hundred years
a republic ... P. 1876.

Shortfellow, Harry Wandsworth.
*Mrs. Mary (Victoria Novello) Cowden
Clarke.* The song of drop o' wather: a
London legend. L. 1856.

Shrewsbury, B. de, Esq. *William
Makepeace Thackeray.* Codlingsby.
"Punch," 1847.

Shropshire Gentleman, A. *Daniel
Defoe.* The history of the civil wars in
Germany ... Newark, 1782.

Shufflebottom, Abel. *Robert Southey.*
Minor poems. Bristol, 1797–99.

Shuttle, Job. *Thomas Weaver.*

Siberian Exile, A. *Rufin Pietrowski.*
Story of ... 1843–46. L. 1863.

Sibyl. *Mrs. Sallie M. (Davis) Martin*, who contributed to various journals
of the South, especially to "Scott's Mag-

**azine," Atlanta, Ga., under this pen-name.

Siddons, J. H. *J. H. Stocqueler.* Norton's handbook to Europe. N.Y. 1860.

Sidney. *Ebenezer Smith Thomas;* in the Charleston (S.C.) "City Gazette," 1810–16.

Sidney. *Noah Webster.* Articles in "Commercial Advertiser" and "Spectator," Nov. 20 and 22, 1837.

Sidney, Algernon. *Gideon Granger,* who, in 1808 and 1809, published a number of papers with this signature in favor of the administration of President Jefferson.

Sidney, Algernon. *Salma Hale.* The administration and the opposition. Concord, N.H., 1826.

Sidney, Algernon. *Samuel Ferrand Waddington.* Address to the people of the United Kingdom. 2d ed. L. 1812.

Sidney, Margaret. *Mrs. Harriet Mulford (Stone) Lothrop.* The Pettibone name. B. 1882.

Sidrophel. *Sir Paul Neal.*

Sic, Paul. *Louis Amédée Eugéne Achard,* and others.

Sieg, W. M. *Sigismund Wulff.* Griseldis : a drama. Translated by . . . L. 1871.

Siegmey. *Siegbert Meyer.* Quousque tandem Catilina. 1879.

Siegvolk. *Albert Mathews.* Bundle of papers. N.Y. 1879.

Sièrebois, R. P. *Jean Baptiste Prudence Boissière.* Psychologie realiste . . . Paris, 1876.

Sigma. *James Sinclair.* The free public library question discussed. Aberdeen, 1883.

Sigma. *Lucius Manlius Sargent.* Reminiscences of Samuel Dexter [originally written for the Boston " Evening Transcript "]. B. 1858.

Sigma. *Samuel Newington, M.D.* Thick and thin feeding ; or, a new and scientific method of feeding grain . . . L. 1856.

Silalicum. *W. A. Perry,* of Seattle, Washington Territory, in his contributions to the "American Field."

Silentiarius, Paulus. *George P. Philes.* His signature in literary journals.

Silly-Billy. *Duke of Gloucester,* in the "John Bull," about 1827. See " Wilberforce, Samuel."

Siluriensis. *John Wilson.* Lord Byron, in "Blackwood's Magazine," Vol. XI., pp. 212 *et seq.*

Silverpen. *Miss Eliza Meteyard.* The little museum keeper. L. 1861.

This pseudonym was bestowed upon *Miss Meteyard* by Douglas Jerrold, and afterwards adopted by her.

Silverstar. *John Thomas Denny,* in his contributions to the "Weekly Budget" (L.), etc.

Silvertongue, Gabriel, Gent. *James Montgomery.* The whisperer ; or, hints and speculations by . . . 1797.

Silvervale, Lumina. *Mrs. H. A. B. Suddoth.* An orphan of the Old Dominion. P. 1873.

Silvia. *Henrietta,* Countess Berkeley. — See " Noble-man, A," and " Philander."

Silvicola. *William Haughton,* a Canadian poet, whose fugitive pieces have appeared in the newspaper press under this signature.

Silvius. *John Balguy,* who took part in the Bangorean controversy, and published three pamphlets in defence of Dr. Hoadley, under the name of "Silvius."

Simkins, Jonas. *E. G. Jewett.* Reveries of a wood sawyer . . . N.Y. 1872.

Simon the Wagoner. *John Downey,* author of a series of humorous sketches written for the press, under this signature.

Simpkin the second, poetic recorder. *Ralph Broome.* The letters of . . . of all the proceedings, upon the trial of Warren Hastings, Esq. . . . L. 1789.

Simple, Sam. *George T. Wilburn.*

Simplex. One of the pseudonyms attributed to Junius (*q.v.*).

The letter thus signed is dated June 6, 1769, and attacks the Duke of Grafton and Sir William Blackstone for the pardon of M'Quirk.

Simplex. *John Young.* An inquiry into the constitution, government, and practices of the churches of Christ . . . Edinb. 1808.

Simplicius. *Sir Charles Grant.*

Simpson, Maria. *Frank Cahill,* in his contributions to the "Saturday Press" (P.), etc.

Sincere Admirer of True Liberty, A. *Zachary Grey.* An examination of Mr. Samuel Chandler's "History of persecution . . . L. 1736.

Sincere Friend of Mankind, A. *Francis Eyre, Esq.* A short essay on the Christian religion . . . L. 1795.

Sincere Friend of the People, A. *Maurice Lothian.* The expediency of a secure provision for the ministers of the Gospel . . . Edinb. 1834.

Sincere Lover of our present Con-

stitution, A. *Zachary Grey.* A caveat against the Dissenters . . . L. 1736.

Sincere Lover of the Church and State, A. *Rev. James Webster,* of the Tolbooth Church, Edinburgh. An essay upon toleration. n.p. 1703.

Sincere Protestant, A. *Zachary Grey, LL.D.* Serious address to Lay-Methodists to beware of the false pretences of their teachers. By . . . L. 1745.

Sincerus. *Samuel Adams.* An earnest appeal to the people, Feb. 12, 1775.

Sinclair, Eugene. *Frederick A. Moore.* A book of gems. Manchester, 1854.

Sindera. *Mrs. Eliza Elliott (Lewis) Harper,* whose early publications were in the "Louisville Journal" under this pen-name.

Singing Sibyl. *Mrs. Metta Victoria (Fuller) Victor,* a Western poetess, who, in 1847, "made a brilliant *début* in the New York "Home Journal."

Single, Celia. *Benjamin Franklin,* in a letter contributed to the "Pennsylvania Gazette" (P.), July 24, 1732.

Singleton, Arthur, Esq. *Henry Cogswell Knight.* Letters from the South and West. B. 1824.

Singleton, Mary, Spinster. *Mrs. Frances Morne Brooke,* editor of the "Old Maid," a periodical (L. 1755–56), and the author of novels, poems, dramas, and translations.

Singleton, Captain Tom. *Alfred Follin,* in his contributions to the "Boys and Girls' Weekly" (N.Y.).

Singular Man, A. *Samuel W. Francis, M.D.* "Inside out": a curious book . . . N.Y. 1862.

Singularity, Thomas, Journeyman Printer. *Henry Junius Nott.* Novelettes of a traveller; or, odds and ends from the knapsack of . . . N.Y. 1834.

Sinner Saved. *Rev. William Huntington.* — See "S. S." (Sinner Saved).

Sionara, a Japanese Traveller. *Laurence Oliphant.* "Political Reflections" and "Moral Reflections," — articles in the "North American Review," 1877.

Sir ***. *Sir Robert Walpole.* Sir *** speech upon the peace. To the tune of the Abbot of Canterbury. L. 1739.

Sir Bob. *Sir Robert Walpole.* The congress of beasts. To which is annex'd the advice of Sir Bob, etc. L. 1730 (?).

Six. *Rev. A. H. Potter,* in the New York "Examiner."

Skenandoah. *Lewis H. Morgan,* in Cotton's "American Review," papers on the Iroquois.

Sketcher, The. *Rev. John Eagles, M.A.,* in "Blackwood's Magazine," 1833–35.

Sketcher from nature. *Mary Stanley.* True to life: a simple story. L. 1873.

Sketchley, Arthur. *Rev. George Rose.* Mrs. Brown at the play . . . L. 186–.

Sk–ff–ingt–n, Esq. *Sir Lumley St. George Skeffington,* Bart. Letter VIII. of the "Twopenny Post Bag" [Thomas Moore] is addressed from Col. Th–m–s to . . .

Skillet, Joseph. *Earl Russell.* — See "Gentleman who has left his Lodgings, A."

Skitt. *H. E. Taliaferro.* Fisher's River: North Carolina scenes and characters; by "Skitt," who was rais'd thar. N.Y. 187–.

Slater, Nic. *Charles M. Connolly.*

Slender, Mr. *Philip Freneau.* Tracts and essays . . . by Mr. Slender; essays, tales, and poems, by . . . P. 1788.

Slender, Robert, Stocking Weaver. *Philip Freneau.* A journey from Philadelphia to New York . . . P. 1787.

Slick, Sam, of Slickville. *Thomas Chandler Haliburton.* The clockmaker . . . L. 1849.

Slick, Sam, in Texas. *Samuel A. Hammitt.* Piney Woods Tavern; or, . . . P. 1858.

Slingsby, Jonathan Freke. *Dr. John Francis Waller.* The Slingsby papers. Dublin, 1852.

Slingsby, Philip. *Nathaniel Parker Willis,* who, about 1835, published in England, his "Inklings of Adventure," a collection of tales and sketches originally written for a London magazine, under this signature.

Slocum, Sal. *E. R. Kidder.*

Slokumb, Si. *Henry P. Cheever.*

Slop, Dr. *Sir John Stoddart, D.C.L.* Dr. Slop's shave at a broken Hone (in verse). L. 1820.

"In the political satires and caricatures of that day [in the earlier part of the present century], *Dr. Stoddart* was continually introduced as ' Dr. Slop'; and the pencil of George Cruikshank, when employed for Mr. Hone, frequently represented him."

Sloper, Ally. *Charles H. Ross,* in London "Judy," 1864 *et seq.*

Sloper, Joel. *W. A. Peters,* editor of the "American Bottler" (N.Y.).

Sloper, Mace. *Charles Godfrey Leland.* Ballads. P. 185–.

Sloth. *Robert Thom.* Wang Keaou-Lwan Pih Nëen Hän; or, the lasting resentment of Miss Keaou Lwan Wang: a Chinese tale . . . Translated by . . . Canton, 1839.

Small Courtier, A. *Jonathan Swift, D.D.* The new way of selling places at court. In a letter from . . . to a great stock-jobber. L. 1712.

Smalltalk, Quicksilver. *William Gray Swett,* a member of the "Polyglot Club," which was composed of the nine editors of the "Harvard Register," Camb., 1827–28.

Smelfungus. *Patrick Proctor Alexander.* Carlyle redivivus . . . Glasgow, 1881.

Smiff, Philander, O.P.Q. *A. A. Dowty,* in the London "Figaro." "Journalistic London" gives the name "Doughty." — See "Alma Viva."

Smith, A. *Charles Smith.* Sparks from a smith's forge. N.Y. 1852.

Smith, Bell. *Mrs. Louisa (Kirby) Piatt,* author of a series of essays in the "Home Journal" over this pen-name. Her letters from Paris were published with the title, "Bell Smith Abroad." N.Y. 1855.

Smith, Grandfather. *Charles Knight,* who wrote a short series of articles for the "Town and Country Newspaper" (L. 185-), which he entitled "Grandfather Smith's Lectures." — See his "Passages of a Working Life," Vol. III., p. 153.

"Smith, Neighbor." *Moses Williams.* The cracked jug; or, five answers to my neighbor Parley's five letters . . . B. 1838.

Smith, Brown, Jones, and Robinson, Messrs. *James Smith, Dr. Neild, Charles Bright, David Blair,* and *Archibald Michie.* Was Hamlet mad? or, the lucubrations of . . . Melbourne, 1868.

Smith, Mrs. *Mrs. Martha (Savory) Yeardley.* Pathetic tales, founded on facts. By . . . L. 1813.

This work was originally published under the title "Poetical Tales," founded on facts, L. 1808, and suppressed by the author, Miss Martha Savory.

Smith, The Late Mr. Æsop. *Martin Farquhar Tupper, D.C.L.* Rides and reveries of . . . L. 1857.

Smith, the late Ben. *Cornelius Mathews.* The motley book: a series of tales and sketches . . . N.Y. 1838.

Smith, Elephant. *Cave Underhill.*

Smith, Gamaliel. The work Not Paul, but Jesus (L. 1823), usually attributed to *Jeremy Bentham,* was compiled at the latter's request by *Francis Place.*

Smith, Gerald. *William McCrillis Griswold.* — See "Venner, Arthur."

Smith, J. *William Black,* in his contributions to the "Daily News" (L.).

Smith, J., Gentleman. *Charles Baring.* Letters on the prophecies selected from eminent writers. L. 1810.

Smith, John, Esq. *Seba Smith.*

Smith, John (of Smith-Hall). *John Delaware Lewis.* Sketches of Cantabs. By . . . L. 1849.

Smith, Mrs. John. *Mrs. Celia M. (Kellum Burr) Burleigh,* who, under this signature, wrote sprightly letters for the "Great West," a weekly journal published at Cincinnati, 1849 *et seq.*

Smith, Mrs. John. *Timothy Shay Arthur.* Confessions of a housekeeper. P. 1851.

Smith, John, Jr., of Arkansas. *Sylvester S. Southworth.*

Smith, John, Jr. *Brantz Mayer.* Romanism in Mexico: being a reply to an article . . . against Mayer's "Mexico" in "U.S. Catholic Magazine," March, 1844, by . . . Balt. 1844.

Smith, John, late Fellow of Queen's College. *Sir David Dalrymple.* Select discourses (in number nine), by . . . Edinb. 1756.

Smith, Margaret. *John Greenleaf Whittier.* Leaves from . . . journal. B. 1849.

Smith Matthew. *Charles Mordaunt.*

Smith, Shirley. *Miss E. J. Curtis.* All for herself. 1877.

Smithies, William, Junior Rector of St. Michael, Mill End, Colchester. *Daniel Defoe.* The coffee-house preachers . . . L. 1706.

Smitts, Oude Neer, Mr. *Mark Prager Lindo.* Dutch stories. L. 18-.

Smoko, Puffo. *Harry J. Shellman.* "Smoke wreathes," contributed to various Indianapolis papers in 1870-74, etc.

Smuggler, A. *John Rattenbury.* Memoirs . . . compiled from his diary and journal . . . Sidmouth, 1837.

Smyth, Peregrine, Esq. *William King, LL.D.* A key to the fragment. By Amias Riddinge, B.D. With a preface. By . . . L. 1751. See "Riddinge, Amias, B.D."

Smythe, Samuel. *Rufus Dawes.*

Snake, William. *Jean Raymond Eugène d'Araquy.* Les mondes habités . . . Paris, 1859.

Snap. *Melville Phillips,* Philadelphia correspondent of "Texas Siftings" (N.Y.).

Snap, Sylvanus. *Albert E. Bergh.*

Snapshot. *Lewis Clements.* Shooting adventures, canine love, and sea-fishing trips. L. 1878.

Snekul, Heinrich Yalc. *Henry Clay Lukens.* Lean' Nora: a supernatural, though sub-pathetic ballad . . . P. 1870.

Snift, Pollexenes Digit. *Benson Earle Hill.* A pinch of snuff. L. 1840.

Snob, Mr. *William Makepeace Thackeray.* Mr. Snob's remonstrance with Mr. Smith. "Punch," 1848.

Snoggins. *Henry M. Putney.* His signature as correspondent of the Manchester (N.H.) "Mirror" from 1860 to 1870.

Snooks, Peter. *John C. Moore.* His signature in the "Boston Journal."

Society called the Oziosi, A. *Robert Merry, — Roscoe, etc.* Arno miscellany. Florence, 1784.

Society of Gentlemen, A. *Thomas Morgan.* A brief examination of the Rev. Mr. Warburton's divine legation of Moses . . . L. 1742.

Society of Gentlemen, A. *John Stone.* The history of Faringdon . . . Faringdon, 1798.

Socius, Ol. *Thomas Humphrey Ward.* Brasenose ale . . . Ed. by . . . Boston, Eng., 1878.

Sohailee. *Ahmed Ibn Hemdem.* Turkish evening entertainments.

Sojourner, A. *Rev. John Gay Copleston.* Lynmouth; or, sketchings and musings in North Devon . . . L. 1835.

Sol. *A. M. Soteldo,* Albany correspondent of the "Sun" (N.Y.).

Sola. *Olive San Louie Anderson.* An American girl, and her four years in a boy's college. N.Y. 1878.

Soldier, A. *Major Ranken.* Canada and the Crimea : sketches of a soldier's life. L. 1862.

Soldier, A. *Joseph Donaldson.* Recollections of . . . Edinb. 18–.

Soldier, A. *J. H. Wilton.* Scenes in a soldier's life . . . 1839–43 . . . Montreal, 1848.

Soldier, The. *Warren Lee Goss.* The soldier's story of his captivity at Anderson, Belle Isle, etc., 1862–64. B. 1867.

Soldier of 1812, A. *Orrin Abbott.* Appeal of . . . to the soldiers who suppressed the Rebellion. Chic. 1867.

Soldier of Fortune, A. *William Hamilton Maxwell.* Rambling recollections of . . . L. 1842.

Soldier's Daughter, A. *Lady Nicholas Harris Nicolas.* The cairn : a gathering of precious stones from many hands. Ed. by . . . L. 1846.

Soldier's Friend, The. *Mrs. Maud J. (Fuller) Young,* who, during the late civil war, under this signature addressed thrilling appeals to the Confederate soldiers.

Sole Survivor, The. *George Fracker.* A voyage to South America, with an account of a shipwreck in the river La Plata, in the year 1817. By . . . B. 1826.

Solicitor, A. *Edwin Wilkins Field.* Observations of . . . on the equity courts. L. 1840.

Solitaire. *John S. Robb,* who contributed humorous pieces to the Western periodicals, and in 1856 published, in conjunction with Madison Tenzas, M.D., "The swamp doctor's adventures in the Southwest" (P. 1856), and other sketches.

Solitaire, A. *Edwin S. Rickman.* The diary of . . . or, sketch of a pedestrian excursion through part of Switzerland . . . L. 1835.

Solitaire, Un. *Hippolyte Barbier.* Biographie populaire du clergé contemporain . . . Paris, 1840–51.

Solitary Wanderer, A. *Mrs. Charlotte (Turner) Smith.* Letters of . . . L. 1801.

Solomon of Streetsville. *Rev. Robert Jackson MacGeorge,* who contributed to the "Commercial Advertiser" (Montreal, 1854), and to other Canadian journals, under this signature.

Solomons, Ikey, Esq., junior. *William Makepeace Thackeray.* Catherine: a story. "Fraser's Magazine," 1839–40.

Solymos, B. *B. E. Falkonberg.* Desert life. Recollections of an expedition in the Soudan. L. 1879.

Sombre, Samuel. *J. W. Gerard.* Ostrea. N.Y. 1857.

Some Unknown Foreigner. *Charles Jared Ingersoll.* Inchiquin : the Jesuit's letters on American literature and politics. P. 1810.

Somebody. *William Donaldson.* The life and adventures of Sir Bartholomew Sapskull, Baronet . . . 1768.

Somebody, M. S. *John Clutton.* A letter to Dr. Joseph Priestley . . . Birmingham, 1787.

Somebody who is not Doctor of the Sorbonne. *John Louis Deloîne.* The history of the Flagellants . . . L. n.d.

Somers, Felix. *Julius Chambers.* A mad world and its inhabitants. L. 1877.

Somers, Miss Rosalie. *Mrs. Harriet Marion Stephens,* who appeared on the stage under this name until 1851, and was afterwards well known by the contributions of her pen under the signatures of "Marion Ward" and "H. M. S."

Somerset Herald, The. *James Robinson Planché.*

Sommers, Jane R. *Cornelia Jones.* Heavenward led ; or, the two bequests. P. 1870.

Somnambulus. *Sir Walter Scott,* in some political satires, entitled the "Visionary," contributed to the "Edinburgh Weekly Journal" in 1819.

Son of Bon-Accord in North America, A. *James Riddel.* Aberdeen and its folk, from the 20th to the 50th year of the present century. Aberdeen, 1868.

Son of Candor, A. *George Grenville.* The principles of the late changes impartially examined, in a letter from ... to the "Public Advertiser." L. 1764.

Son of Liberty, A. *Benjamin Church, M.D.* An address to a provincial Bashaw ... B. 1781.

A poem. Gov. Barnard is the Bashaw.

Son of Liberty, A. *Silas Downer.* A discourse delivered in Providence, in the colony of Rhode Island, on the 25th day of July, 1768 ... Providence, 1768.

Son of Mary Moore, A. — *Brown.* The captives of Abb's valley : a legend of frontier life. By ... P. 1854.

Son of Reed, A. *Robert Roxby.* The lay of the Reedwater minstrel ... Newcastle, 1809.

Son of the Church of England, A. *Arthur Browne.* Remarks on Dr. Mayhew's incidental reflections relative to the Church of England ... Portsmouth, 1763.

Son of Truth and Decency, A. *Rev. Charles Inglis.* A vindication of the Bishop of Landaff's sermon ... N.Y. 1768.

Sonica. *Robert W. McAlpine,* in his contributions to the "Sun" (N.Y.).

Sophronia, Aunt. *Mrs. Julia (McNair) Wright.*

Sophronius. *François Marie Bertrand,* who, in 1864, published five letters under this signature on the question of liturgies.

Sopht, Ensign. *Robert Michael Ballantyne.* The volunteer levee; or, the remarkable experiences of ... Edinb. 1860.

Sorbiere, Monsieur, Samuel de. *Dr. William King.* A journey to London in the year 1698, written ... by ... L. 1699.

"It was never ' written originally in French by Monsieur Sorbiere' ... but was the production of the witty *Dr. William King,* advocate of Doctors' Commons, in facetious imitation of the 'Journey to Paris,' in the same year, by Dr. Martin Lister."—See "Notes and Queries," February, 1865, p. 98.

Sosiosch. *Edward Byron Eaton.* Manifest destiny ... N.Y. 1869.

Sothern, Edward Askew. *Douglas Stewart.*

Souffrant, Jacques, ouvrier. *Louis*

Ulbach. La politique de l'atelier ... Troyes, 1850.

South, Elma. *Miss Essie B. Cheesborough,* who commenced her literary career at an early age, writing under the pen-names of "Motte Hall," "Elma South," "Ide Delmar," and her initials, "E. B. C."

South, Simeon. *John M'Gregor.* S.'s letters to his kinsfolk, etc. L. 1841.

South, Theophilus, Gent. *Edward Chitty.* The fly fisher's text book. By ... L. 1841.

South-American, A. *Mons. Palacio.* Outline of the Revolution in Spanish America ... L. 1817.

South Carolina Planter, A. *Charles Pinckney.* Three letters ... on the case of Jonathan Robbins ... on the recent captures of American vessels ... etc. P. 1799.

Reprinted from a Charleston (S.C.) newspaper.

South-Carolinian, A. *Henry Middleton.* Economical causes of slavery in the United States, and obstacles to abolition ... L. 1857.

South-Carolinian, A. *Charles Pinckney.* Observations to shew the propriety of the nomination of Colonel James Monroe, to the Presidency of the United States ... By ... Charleston, 1810.

South-Carolinian, A. *Robert Pleasants Hall.* Poems. Charleston, 1848.

South-Carolinian, A. *Edwin C. Holland.* A refutation of the calumnies circulated against the Southern and Western States ... Charleston, 1822.

South-Carolinian, A (who had nothing else to do). *William M. Bobo.* Glimpses of New York City. Charleston, S.C., 1852.

South Sea Bard, The. *Hector A. Stuart,* in his contributions to various California periodicals.

Southern Barrister, A. *Alexander Hamilton Sands.* Recreations of ... P. 1859.

Southern Citizen, A. *Reverdy Johnson.* Remarks on popular sovereignty. Balt. 1855.

Southern Lady, A. *Mrs. Catharine Ann (Ware) Warfield.* The household of Bouverie; or, the elixir of gold: a romance ... N.Y. 1860.

Southern Man, A. *John Pendleton Kennedy.* Slavery the mere pretext for the Rebellion, not its cause ... P. 1863.

Southern Matron, A. *Mrs. Caroline (Howard) Gilman.* Recollections of ... Charleston, 1852.

Southern Planter, A. *N. A. Ware.*

Notes on political economy, as applicable to the United States . . . N.Y. 1844.

Southern Pre-Emptor, A. *Thomas B. Winston.* Minnesota; or, a "bundle of facts," going to illustrate its great past, the grand present, and her glorious future; by . . . New Orleans, 1858.

Southern Spy, The. *Edward A. Pollard.* Letters of . . . in Washington and elsewhere. Balt. 1861.

Southerner, A. *James M. Smythe.* Ethel Somers; or, the fate of the Union. By . . . Augusta, Ga., 1857.

Southerner, A. *Seymour R. Duke.* Osceola; or, fact and fiction. A tale of the Seminole war. N.Y. 1838.

Southernwood. *Charles Sotheran.*

Southron, A. *William Gilmore Simms.* South Carolina in the Revolutionary War . . . By . . . Charleston, 1853.

Southwell, Henry, LL.D. *Robert Sanders.* New book of martyrs . . . L. 1775.

Sparkle, Richard. *William Mee.* Much of the poetry which he wrote appeared in periodicals under this signature. "Winter," "The rose bud," "Flaccus," and other pieces were thus brought out.

Sparkle, Sophie. *Jennie E. Hicks.* Sparkles from Saratoga. N.Y. 1873.

Sparkle, Tom. *Thomas Sheridan.*
"In 'Pen Owen' Mr. Hook has sketched his friend Tom Sheridan, son of *the* Sheridan, under the name of ' Tom Sparkle.' "

Sparks, Godfrey. *Charles Dickens.* The Bloomsbury christening. L. 186–.

Sparks, Timothy. *Charles Dickens.* Sunday under three heads: as it is; as Sabbath bills would make it; as it might be made. By . . . L. 1836.

Sparrowgrass, Mr. *Frederic Swartwout Cozzens.* The Sparrowgrass papers . . . N.Y. 1856.

Spartacus. *William James Linton.* Poems. L. 1845.

Spavery. *Samuel P. Avery.* The harp of a thousand strings; or, laughter for a lifetime. Konceived, kompiled, and komically konkokted by Spavery, etc. N.Y. 1868.

Spec. *William Makepeace Thackeray.* Travels in London. "Punch," 1847.

Special Correspondent, A. *W. L. McFarlan.* Behind the scenes in Norway, by . . . Glasgow, 1884.

Special Correspondent, A. *Alfred Arthur Reade.* My trip to Paris . . . Manchester, 1878.

Special Reporter, A. *Rev. John Allan.* A council canticle . . . Aberdeen.

Spectacles, Timothy. *William C. Foster.* Poetry on different subjects, written under the signature of T. S. . . . Salem, N.Y., 1805.

Spectator. *David W. Bartlett,* in the Boston "Congregationalist."

Spectator. *W. H. Wingate.* The goal of life: a poem by . . . L. 1867.

Spectator, A. *Cyrus Augustus Bartol.* Influence of the ministry at large in the city of Boston. B. 1836.

Spectator, A. *John Nelson Darby.* New opinions of the brethren. L. n.d.

Spectator, The. *Joseph Addison and others.* Sir Roger de Coverley. By . . . L. 1850.

Spectator of the Past, A. *C. G. Memminger.* The book of nullification . . . Charleston, 1830.

Spectator of the Scenes, A. *Rev. John Carroll.* Past and present . . . or, Canadian Methodism for the last 40 years . . . Toronto, 1860.

Spen, Kay. *H. C. Selous.* True of heart. L. 1868.

Spencer, Edward. *Caroline Seymour,* in her contributions to "Harper's Magazine" (N.Y.).

Spencer, Nath. *Robert Sanders.* The complete English traveller. L. 17–.
This work was republished in England under the name of "Burlington," in Scotland under that of "Murray," and in Wales under that of "Llewellyn."

Spenser, Edmund, the Poet. *Gilbert West.* A canto of the Fairy Queen. Written by Spenser. L. 1739.

Speranza. *Lady Jane Francesca Speranza Wilde.* Her first literary efforts were some verses signed with this pseud. in the "Irish Nation" in 1847.

Spermaceti, Marcus, the Elder. *Major Downs.* Specimen of a new jest book . . . L. about 1810.

Sperry, Charles. *John Osborne Sargent.* His signature in the Harv. Coll. "Collegian," 1830, and in the "Token and Atlantic Souvenir" of fifty years ago.

Sphinx. *Mrs. Sarah (Hustler) Fox.* Catch who can; or, hide and seek. Original double acrostics. L. 1869.

Spicer, Nicholas. *Col. Alban S. Payne,* in his contributions to the "Turf, Field, and Farm" (N.Y.).

Spicer, Seth. *Benjamin F. Gould.*

Spike, Ethan. *Matthew Francis Whittier,* who was many years ago known to the reading public as Ethan Spike, whose satirical letters appeared in the Portland "Transcript," and were widely copied.

Spikes. *Randolph Botts,* of Albany (N.Y.), in his contributions to various periodicals.

Spindrift. *Sir Joseph Noel Paton.* Poems. L. 1867.

Spiral Groove. *Wilson MacDonald,* in his contributions to the "Turf, Field, and Farm" (N.Y.).

Spiridion. *John Dunlap Osborne.*

"Mr. Osborne was a contributor to the press for more than forty years, and his letters under the signature of 'Spiridion' were familiar to Boston readers through the columns of the Boston 'Atlas,' Boston 'Traveller,' and the 'Saturday Evening Gazette.' He contributed to the latter paper for nearly ten years, and during the war it was his only American newspaper, for communication with New Orleans was so irregular that he was obliged to suspend his correspondence with the 'Picayune' of that city. Articles from his pen have appeared in the 'Century.'"

Spirit of Hampden, The. *Dr. Robert Fellowes,* in periodical contributions. 1821.

Spiritual Watchman, A. *Rev. C. D. Hawtrey.* The nature of the first Resurrection ... L. 1830.

Splene, Megathym, B.A., Oxon. *John Cockburn Thomson.* Almæ matres ... L. 1858.

Spokes. *W. J. Morgan,* a professional bicycle racer.

Sponge, Mr. *Robert Smith Surtees.* Mr. Sponge's sporting tour. L. 1853.

Spoopendyke. *Mr. Stanley Huntley.* Mr. and Mrs. Spoopendyke. N.Y. 1881.

Sportsman, A. *Charles Clarke.* Crumbs from a sportsman's table. L. 1865.

Sportsman and Naturalist, A. *Charles William George Saint John.* Field notes of ... with a tour in Switzerland. L. 1849.

Sportsman of Berkshire, A. *Peter Beckford.* Essays on hunting ... By ... L. (?) 1785.

Spot, Dick, the Conjuror. *Richard Morris.*

Spriggs. *Edward Payson Tenney.* Jubilee essays: a plea for an unselfish life. B. 1862.

Sproule, Ziba. *Lucius Manlius Sargent.* The diary of Solomon Spittle. B. 1847.

Sprouts. *Richard Whiteing.* Mr. Sprouts; his opinions. L. 1867. Also in his contributions to the London "Evening Star."

Spruggins, Richard Sucklethumkin. Not by *Morley,* the Dowager-Countess of, who only lithographed the drawings. Portraits of the Spruggins family. L. 1829.

Spunkey, Simon. *Thomas Green Fessenden,* in the "Farmer's Weekly Museum," Walpole, N.H., 1796 *et seq.*

Spur, Mercurius, Esq. *Cuthbert Shaw.* The race: a poem. L. 1766.

Spy. *Pelligrini,* in "Vanity Fair."

Spy in Washington, The. *Matthew L. Davis,* in the New York "Courier and Inquirer."

Squatter, A. *John B. Jones.* Wild Western scenes: a narrative of adventures ... P. 1869.

Squibob. *George Horatio Derby.* Squibob papers. N.Y. 187-.

Staats. *William Staats.* A tight squeeze; or, the adventures of a gentleman who undertook to go from New York to New Orleans in three weeks without money, as a professional tramp. B. 1879.

Staff, Jack. *James Henry Harris,* in his contributions to the "Central Baptist" (St. Louis, Mo.), etc.

Staff Officer, A. *Major Thomas Fourness Wilson.* The defence of Lucknow: a diary ... By ... L. 1858.

Staff Officer, A. *Hon. Somerset John Gough Calthorpe.* Letters from headquarters; or, realities of the Crimea. L. 1856.

Staff Officer, A. *James T. Lyon.* War sketches from Cedar Mountain to Bull Run ... Buffalo, 1862.

Staff Officer, A late. *Woodburne Potter.* The war in Florida ... Balt. 1836.

Staff-Officer who was there, A. *Sir Anthony Coningham Sterling.* Letters from the army in the Crimea ... 1854, 1855, and 1856. n.p., n.d.

Staff Surgeon, A. *Walter Henry, M.D.* Trifles from my portfolio ... Quebec, 1839.

Stahl. *Pierre Jules Hetzel.* Les pêcheurs ennemis ... Paris, 1881.

Stahl, Arthur. *Valeska Voigtel.* Historische Bilder aus der alten Welt. 1870.

Stahl, Pierre Jules. *Pierre Jules Hetzel.* Histoire d'un âne et de deux jeunes filles ... Paris, 1874.

Stampede. *Jonathan Kelly,* a humorist, known as "Falconbridge," "Jack Humphries," and "Stampede."

Standfast, Joshua. For the supposed editor of the "Political Tatler." L. 1716.

Standfast, Silas. *George Stillman Hillard.* Letters of, to his friend Jotham. B. 1853.

Stanfield, Agnes. *Mrs. Jane McElhinney Noyes* (Ada Clare).

St**pe.** *Earl Stanhope.* The noble sans-culotte: a ballad occasioned by a certain Earl's styling himself a sans-culotte citizen in the House of Lords. L. 1794 (?).

Stanley, Frank. *Mary Gibson* (?). The power of gentleness; and other tales ... P. 1864.

Stanley, Reginald Fitz-Roy, M.A. *Robert Cowtan.* Passages from the autobiography of a "Man of Kent," 1817–65. Edited ... L. 1866.

St–nn–d, E–t–n. *Eaton Stannard.* The ghost of Walter Alexander, to E–t–n St–nn–d, Esq., late Recorder of the City of Dublin ... Dublin, 1751 (?).

Stanser, Robert. *Sir Alexander Croke, D.C.L.* An examination of the Rev. Mr. Burke's letter of instruction to the Catholic missionaries of Nova Scotia. Halifax, 1804.

"States"man, A. *Edward Vernon Childe.* Letters to the "London Times," "New York Courier and Inquirer"; by ... B. 1857.

. Statutophilus. *Dr. John Speed.* An impartial by-stander's review of the controversy concerning the wardenship of Winchester College. L. 1759.

Stawel, Augustus. *Alfred Owen Legge.* Manslaughter: a chronicle ... L. 1876.

Stchedrin, Nikolai. *N. Saltikoff.* Sketches of provincial life. L. 1861.

Steady. *Allan Ramsay, Jr.* A letter to Edmund Burke, Esq. ... L. 1780.

Stedman. *Mrs. Elizabeth C. Dodge Kinney,* who commenced publishing under this pen-name, dating from "Cedar Brook," her father's residence, near Newark, N.J.

Stedman, Charles. *William Thomson, LL.D.* The history of the origin, progress, and termination of the American War ... By ... L. 1794.

Stein, Adam. *Robert Springer,* author of other valuable works, and of numerous popular books for the young, partly published under this pseudonym.

Stein, Johann Saville. *John Saville Stone.* Fantasia. L. 1855.

Stella. *Mrs. Bowen-Graves,* "the author of some verses called 'My Queen,' which, allied to a charming melody by Blumenthal, have had, and still have, a wide-spread popularity.

Stella. *Penelope Devereau.*

Stella. *Miss Esther Johnson.*

Stella. *Mrs. N. C. Iron.* Minna Monte. P. 187–.

Stella. *Miss Anna C. Johnson.* Peasant life in Germany. N.Y. 1858.

Stella. *Mrs. Estella Anna Blanche (Robinson) Lewis.* Records of the heart. N.Y. 1844.

Stendhal. *Marie Henri Beyle.* Chroniques italiennes, par de ... Paris, 1855.

Stenne, Georges. *David Schornstein,* who contributed to all the Jewish papers published in France, and was on the staff of the "Petit Journal" from its foundation, and was the author of novels and translations.

Stephanie. *Kathinka (Halein) Zitz.*

Stephanowitch, Dmtri. *J. Girard de Rialle.* La mythologie comparée. Paris, 1878.

Stephens, George. *John Lloyd Stephens.* Incidents of travel in Egypt, Arabia Petræa, and the Holy Land. By ... L. 1838.

Stephens, "Kit." *Charles Asbury Stephens.* Camping out ... B. 1872.

Stern, Daniel. *Comtesse Marie (de Flavigny) d'Agoult.* Études littéraires ... Paris, 1844.

Sterne, Carus. *Ernst Ludwig Krause.* Werden und Vergehen. 1880.

Sterne, the late Rev. Laurence. *William Coombe, Esq.* Original letters of ... L. 1788.

Sterne, Stuart. *Miss Gertrude Bloede.* Giorgio, and other poems. B. 1881.

Stevenson, Pearce. *Mrs. Caroline E. S. (S. Norton) Maxwell.*

Stevin, Adam. *James Richardson.* Eyes right. B. 1878.

Steward, A. *Thomas Yates.* The hospital ... By ... L. 1830.

Stewart, Catherine. *Kate M. Zeigle.*

Stewart, J. C. *J. S. Crossey* (?). Ethiopian dramas. N.Y. 187–.

Stewart, Margaret Caroline. *Margaret Caroline Rudd.* Mrs. Stewart's case, written by herself ... L. 1788.

Stewart, Mary Clementina. *Mrs. Hibbert Ware.* Dr. Harcourt's assistant: a tale of the present day. L. 1868.

Stille, Carl. *Hermann Christoph Gottfried Demme.* Abendstunden ... Gotha, 1804.

Stilling, Margaret. *Mrs. Mary Evans Wiley,* who, during the civil war, contributed both prose and verse to the Southern journals.

Stilton, W., Horologist. *Peter Annet* (?). A view of the life of King David ... L. 1765.

Stirling, John. *Mrs. (Mary Neal) Sherwood,* the translator of E. Zola's "L'Assommoir."

Stirrup. *Henry J. Brent,* in Porter's "Spirit of the Times."

Stock le baron. *Princesse Marie Studolmine (Bonaparte, dame de Solms) Ratazzi.* La belle Juive: épisode du siège de Jerusalem. Paris, 1882.

Stolz, Mme. de. *Countess Fanny de Bégon.* Blanche and Beryl; or, the two sides of life. L. 1873.

Stonecastle, Henry. *William Oldys.* "The Universal Spectator." By . . . and others. L. 1747.

The other editors were J. Kelly (?), Sir J. Hawkins (?), etc.

Stonehenge. *John Henry Walsh.* The greyhound . . . L. 1853.

Stonemason of Cromartie, The. *Hugh Miller.* Poems. L. 18–.

Storer, R. E. *Capel Lofft.* New Testament: suggestions for reformation of the Greek text . . . By . . . L. 1868.

Story, Sydney A., Jr. *Mrs. Mary H. (Greene Pike) Atherton.* Pearl. B. 1868.

Stothard, Kempe. *Mrs. Anna Eliza Bray.* De Foix: or, sketches of the manners and customs of the XIV. century. L. 1845.

Strada. *Thomas Barnes,* who, in 1812, wrote a series of critical essays, under this signature, for the London "Champion."

Stradling, Matthew. *Martin Francis Mahony.* The Irish bar sinister . . . By . . . (author of "Cheap John's auction"). L. 1872.

Strahan, Edward. *Earl Shinn.* The new Hyperion . . . P. 1875.

Stranger, Sir Peter, Bart. *Japhet Crook.*

Stranger, The. *Charles William Janson.* The stranger in America . . . L. 1807.

Stranger, The. *Francis Lieber.* The stranger in America. P. 1835.

Stranger in Parliament, The. *Edward Michael Whitty,* who contributed to the "Leader" (L.) the series of papers entitled "The stranger in Parliament." 185–.

Strangford, Viscountess. *Emily Anne (Beaufort) Smythe,* Viscountess Strangford. The eastern shores of the Adriatic in 1863. With a visit to Montenegro. L. 1864.

Strap, Hugh. *Hugh Hewson,* whom Dr. Smollett has rendered conspicuously interesting in his "Life and adventures of Roderick Random," and who for more than 40 years kept a hair-dressing shop in Villiers Street, London.

Stratford, Edmund. *E. Lechmere.*

Strathesk, John. *John Tod.* Bits from Blinkbonney; or, Bell o' the Manse: a tale of Scottish village life, 1841–51. 1882.

Strauss, Leedle Yawcob. *Charles Follen Adams.* Leedle Yawcob Strauss, and other poems. B. 1878. Also in his contributions to the "Detroit Free Press."

Straws. *Joseph M. Field,* in the New Orleans "Picayune," where "he acquired great celebrity, contributing for some years fugitive pieces of poetry to its columns, of great merit."

Straws, Jr. *Kate Field,* in the "Springfield Republican."

Strebor, Elggam. *Maggie Roberts.* Home scenes during the Rebellion. N.Y. 1875.

Strephon. *Edward Bradbury.*

Stretton, Hesba. *Hannah Smith.* The Clives of Burcot. L. 1866.

Strickland, Joe. *George W. Arnold.* (Pub. 1826–28.) Conf. Hudson, "Journalism in America," p. 688.

Strike but Hear. *John Horne Tooke,* in the London "Public Advertiser." 1774.

Strix. *George W. Howes,* in the "Evening Post" and the "Dial" (N.Y.).

Stroling Player, A. *John Roberts.* An answer to Mr. Pope's preface to Shakespeare . . . L. 1729.

This pamphlet is signed "Anti-Scriblerus Histrionicus."

Stroller in Europe, A. *W. W. Wright.* Doré. N.Y. 1857.

Strongfellow, Professor. *H. W. Longfellow.* — See "Painsworth, H. Harassing."

Strutt, Lord. *Spain.* Law is a bottomless-pit: exemplify'd in the case of . . . John Bull [Great Britain and Ireland], Nicholas Frog [the United Provinces of the Netherlands], and Lewis Baboon [France], who spent all they had in a law-suit. By John Arbuthnot. Edinb. 1712.

Stuart, Charles Edward. *Charles Hay Allan,* joint author. The costume of the clans . . . Edinb. 1845.

Stuart, John Sobieski Stolberg. *John Hay Allan,* joint author. The costume of the clans . . . Edinb. 1845.

Stuart, Robert. *Robert Meikleham.* A descriptive history of the steam engine . . . L. 1824.

Stubble, Sir Hector. *Sir Stratford Redcliffe,* in the "Roving Englishman," which appeared in "Household Words," written by Grenville-Murray.

Student, A. *S. Brookes.* The Church

of Abraham, Isaac, and Jacob. By ...
L. 1864.

Student, A. *Ebenezer Forsyth.* Shakspere: some notes on his character and
writings. By ... Edinb. 1867.

Student at Law, A. *Frederick
Knight.* Twilight: a poem. By ...
N.Y. 1813.

Student at Oxford, A. *Nicholas
Amhurst.* An epistle ... to the Chevalier ... L. 1717.

Student in Divinity, A. *Thomas
Rennell, B.D.* Animadversions on the
Unitarian ... version of the New Testa-
ment. L. 1811.

**Student in the University of Edin-
burgh, A.** *Charles Kerr.* Juvenile performances in poetry ... Edinb. 1788.

**Student of Harvard University,
A.** *Thaddeus Mason Harris, D.D.* Triumphs of superstition: an elegy. B.
1790.

Student of History, A. *Edward
Denham.* Why is history read so little?
... New Bedford, 1876.

Student of Marischal College, A.
Charles Keith. Farmer's Ha': a Scots
poem ... Aberdeen, 1776.

Student of the Temple, A. *Charles
Leslie.* The best answer ever was made
... L. 1709.

Student of the Temple, A. *Jonathan Bleuman.* A letter to the Rev. Mr.
Brydges, Rector of Croscombe ... L.
1715.

Stukeley, Simon. — *Wills.* The
hermit in Van Diemen's Land. 1829.

Stultifex, Academicus. *Edmond
Malone.*

"The consequence was a pamphlet, published
by the Provost [John Hely Hutchinson, Provost
of the Univ. of Dublin], in which he defended his
conduct; but this only served as food for his ene-
mies. The pamphlet was turned, grammatically,
into ridicule, by an anonymous writer under the
signature of 'Stultifex Academicus,' supposed
to be *Mr. Malone*, the commentator on Shakespeare." — "Gent. Mag.," Vol. 64, Pt. 2, p. 867.

Sturdy, Tristram, Esq. *John James
Gilchrist,* member of the "Polyglot Club,"
composed of the nine editors of the "Harvard Register" (Camb. 1827–28).

Stutter, Poet. *Thomas D'Urfey.* Wit
for money; or, Poet Stutter: a dialogue
between Smith, Johnson, and Poet Stutter ... L. 1691.

Subaltern, A. *William Cobbett* (?).
The soldier's friend ... Written by ...
L. 1793.

Subaltern, A. *Edward Thomas Coke.*
A subaltern's furlough in the United
States, 1832. L. 1833.

Subscriber, A. *Charles Dickens,* in
the "Daily News," 1846, calling atten-

tion to typographical errors, etc.; by
whom, also, the editorial rejoinder was
also written, and signed "Your Constant
Reader."

Subscriber, A. *Benjamin Franklin.*
An economical project to the authors of
the Journal of Paris, one of the Bagatelles (written about 1778).

Suburban Clergyman, A. *Rev. John
Owen,* of Fulham. A letter to a country
clergyman [Thomas Sikes], occasioned
by his address to Lord Teignmouth ...
L. 1805.

Sue, Aunt. *Mrs. Susanna Newbould.*

Sue, Cousin. *S. A. Wright.* Wild
roses ... P. 1868.

Sue, Eugène. *Marie Joseph Eugène
Sue.* Le diable médicin ... Paris,
1860.

Sufferer, A. *John Howell.* A concise ... account of the accident that
occurred at the sale of the late Lord
Eldin's pictures ... Edinb. 1833.

Sufferer, A. *R. Copithorne.* The English Cotejo; or, the cruelties, depredations,
and illicit trade charg'd upon the English
... n.p. 1730.

Sufferer, A. *Thomas Wilson, D.D.* A
review of the project for building a new
square at Westminster; said to be for the
use of Westminster School ... Part I.,
L. 1757.

Sufferer for Truth, A. *Caleb Fleming.* A harmony in Christianity: being
an answer to "The true Gospel of Jesus
Christ." By ... L. 1738.

**Suffering Presbyter of the Church
of Scotland, A.** *Thomas Mawbrey.* An
apology for the religious observation of
the anniversary festival of our blessed
Saviour's nativity. Edinb. 1711.

Suffolk Clergyman, A. *Rev. John
Whitmore.* An address to my parishioners ... L. 1828.

Suffolk Freeholder, A. *Rev. Charles
Edward Stewart.* Thoughts on the letter
of Buonaparte, etc., on the pacific principles and last speech of Mr. Fox. By ...
L. 1796.

Suffolk Yeoman, A. *James Bird.*
The beauty of Suffolk vindicated, "Gent.
Mag.," September, 1833, p. 229.

Suggs, Simon. *Berd H. Young,* in
the New York "Clipper."

Suggs, Capt. Simon. *Johnson J.
Hooper.* Some adventures of ... P.
1845.

Sui generis. *Thomas Man.* Picture
of a factory village. Providence, 1833.

Sulpicius. *Augustus Granville Stapleton,* in the London "Times." 1833.

Summer, Marie. *Charlotte Foucaux.*

Les héroïnes du poète Kalidasa comparées aux héroïnes de Shakespeare. Paris, 1879.

Summerfield, Charles. *Theodore Foster.* The desperadoes of the South-West . . . N.Y. 1847.

Summerfield, Charles, late Judge of the Rio Grande District. *Alfred W. Arrington.* The rangers and regulators of the Yanaha; or, life among the lawless . . . N.Y. 1856.

Summerly, Felix. *Sir Henry Cole, K.C.B.* Home treasury of books, pictures, toys . . . L. 1844.

Summerly, Mrs. Felix. *Mrs. Henry Cole.* The mother's primer. L. 1844.

Sunavill, J. F. & Hogo-Hunt, J. W., Messrs. *James Frank Sullivan and John William Houghton.* The gnome hatter; or, the elfinish wife and the well-finished tile. A "moral" impossibility. By . . . n.p., n.d.

Sunbeam, Susie. *Matilda Anne (Planché) Mackarness.* Susie Sunbeam's series. N.Y. 1856.

Sunday. *Mrs. Catherine Talbot,* in a paper contributed to the "Rambler." No. 30, June 30, 1750.

Sunday Scholar, A. *W. Todd.* The teacher rewarded; or, the memoir of . . . L. 1852. By Daniel Sutcliffe.

Sundry Whereof. *Richard Porson, M.A.* Panegyrical epistles on Hawkins v. Johnson, in "Gent. Mag.," 1787, pp. 652, 751, 847.

Sunshine, Silvia. *Abbie M. Brooks.* Petals plucked from sunny climes. By . . . Nashville, Tenn., 1880.

Supernumerary, A. *J. Pring.* Six letters to a brother curate . . . L. 1839.

Surfaceman. *Alexander Anderson.* Ballads and sonnets. L. 1879.

Surgeon, A. *Henry Mudge.* Dialogues, etc., against the use of tobacco. By . . . L. 1861.

Surgeon, A. *William S. W. Ruschenberger.* An examination of the legality of the general orders which confer assimilated rank on officers of the civil branch of the United States navy. P. 1848.

Surgeon, A. *B. Abrahams.* A treatise on the hair and teeth . . . by . . . New Hampton, N.H., 1849.

Surgeon in the U.S. Navy, A. *George Clymer.* The principles of naval staff rank . . . 1869.

Surrebutter, the late John, Esq., Special Pleader and Barrister at Law. *John Anstey.* The pleader's guide: a didactic poem . . . By . . . L. 1796.

"In lecture the seventh, the author, under the pseudonym of 'Mr. Surrebutter,' gives this account of his professional education : —
'Whoe'er has drawn a special plea
Has heard of old Tom Tewkesbury,
Deaf as a post and thick as mustard,
He aim'd at wit, and bawl'd, and bluster'd,
And died a Nisi Prius leader,
That genius was my Special Pleader.'"

Surry, Col., of Eagle's Nest. *John Esten Cooke.* Surry of Eagle's Nest; or, the memoirs of a staff-officer serving in Virginia. Edited from the Ms. of . . . N.Y. 1866.

Survivor, The. *Capt. Thomas Fernyhough.* Military memoirs of four brothers . . . L. 1829.

Susan, Aunt. *Mrs. Elizabeth Prentiss.* Urbané and his friends. N.Y. 1874.

Sussexiensis. *G. G. Stonestreet.* Reasons of a subscriber for opposing Mr. Wyatt's plan for a monumental trophy to the late King George III. L. 1822.

Sutton. *Sir John Sutton.* Short account of organs built in England from the reign of Charles II. to 1847. By . . .

Swammerdam, Martin Gribaldus. *William Mudford.* The life and adventures of Paul Plaintive, Esq., an author. Compiled . . . by . . . L. 1811.

Swan, Sir Simon, Bart. *Rev. Joseph Fawcett.* The art of poetry according to the latest improvements . . . L. 1797.

Swan of Lichfield, The. *Miss Anna Seward.*

Swětlá, Karolina. *Johanna Mužáková.* The love of the poet. Prague, 1860.

Sw—t. *Jonathan Swift.* The metamorphosis . . . or, the canine appetite . . . in the persons of P-pe [Pope] and Sw-t. Dublin, 1730.

Sw-ft, Dr. *Jonathan Swift.* The blunderful blunder of blunders . . . L. 1721.

Swift, Dean, of Brasen-nose. *Benson Earle Hill.* The pinch of snuff . . . By . . . L. 1840.

Swift, Jonadab, M.D. *John Henley.* The hyp doctor. By . . . L. 1730.

Swift, Patrick. *William Lyon Mackenzie,* in his contributions to the "Colonial Advocate" and his numerous almanacs (1827–34).

Occasionally we find the pseudonym varied to "Mr. Patrick Swift."

Swiss Gentleman, A. *Mark Akenside.* A letter from . . . in Dodsley's "Museum," Vol. II.

Swiss Minister, A. *Jean Henri Merle D'Aubigné.* Germany, England, and Scotland, recollections of . . . 1848.

Sx. *Oliver Johnson Schoolcraft.* Arsicsis; and other poems. N.Y. 1881.

Sydenham, Edward. *James Boaden.* The man of two lives: a narrative, by himself. L. 1828.

Sydney, Algernon. *Spencer Roane,* who was the author of some political essays published under this signature.

Sydney, Algernon. *Benjamin Watkins Leigh.* Address to the people of New England ... W. 1808.

Sydney, Edward William. *Nathan Beverley Tucker.* The partisan leader: a tale of the future, by ... W. 1837.

Sylva, Carmen. *Elizabeth,* Queen Consort of Charles I., King of Roumania. Sappho [a poem]. Leipsic, 1880.

Sylvan, Enemy to Human Diseases. Formula of prescriptions ... Providence, 1813. [Written by a quack generally known as the "Rainwater doctor."]

Sylvan. *Samuel Hobbs.* Fire-side melodies. A love dream, etc. L. 1859.

Sylvander. *Robert Burns.* The name under which he corresponded with a Mrs. Maclehose ("Clarinda"). The letters were published in 1802, and immediately suppressed; but republished in 1845.

Sylvanus. *Robert Colton.* Rambles in Sweden and Gottland. L. 1847.

Sylvaticus. *J. F. Pennie.* The tale of a modern genius; or, the miseries of Parnassus ... L. 1827.

Sylvester, C. *Lady Emma Caroline (Michell) Wood.* Rosewarn: a novel. L. 1866.

Sylvester, Joshua. *John Camden Hotten.* A garland of Christmas carols ... L. 1861.

Sylvestris. *Rev. Jehoida Brewer,* in the "Gospel Magazine," 1776, when and where he published the hymn, "Hail! Sovereign Love, that first began."

Sylvius. *Edmond Texier.* La physiologie du poète. Paris, 1841.

Symington, Maggie. *Miss Charlotte Symington.* Working to win. L. 1872.

Sympathes. *Joseph Willard.* Poetical elegy: sacred to the memory of Dr. Wigglesworth. B. 1760.

Symposiast, Our. *Edmund Burke* (?), in Beloe's "Sexagenarian," Vol. II., p. 119. 2d ed. L. 1818.

Syndas, Kate. *Miss Kate Sandys.* Songs and music. L. 18–.

Syndercombe. *Rt. Hon. Henry Flood.* "The 'Freeman's Journal' [started by Henry Brooke in 1763] became the organ, in 1770, of Flood, Grattan, and the other opponents of the administration of Lord Townshend, who was defended by Jephson and Simcox in Hoey's 'Mercury.' Flood's letters to the 'Freeman' appeared under the signature of 'Syndercombe'; and the various essays and *jeux d'esprit* published in this journal against Lord Townshend were collected and reprinted in 1773 under the title of 'Baratariana,' to which Grattan contributed his celebrated character of Pitt."—See GILBERT'S "History of the City of Dublin," Vol. I., p. 294.
The principal authors of "Baratariana," were *Sir Hercules Langrishe, Mr. Grattan,* and *Mr. Flood.* For a key to "Baratariana," see "Notes and Queries," 2d Ser., VIII., 211.

Syntax, Dr. *William Coombe.* Tour of ... in search of the picturesque ... L. 1821.

Syntax, Dr., Jr. *S. Kimber, Jr.* A new "Sartor Resartus" ... 1862.

Syntax, Peregrinus. *Friedrich Ferdinand Hempel.* Allgemeines deutsches Reimlexicon ... Leipsic, 1726.

T.

θ. *William Makepeace Thackeray.* "An Essay on the Genius of George Cruikshank," contributed to the "Westminster Review" (L.).

T. *Dr. Samuel Johnson,* in his contributions to the "Adventurer" (L. 1753).

T. *Mrs. Catherine Talbot,* in her contributions to the "Athenian Letters" ... (L. 1741–43).

T. *Alfred Tennyson.* "The War," a poem contributed to the "Times" (L., May 9, 1859).

T. *Martin Farquhar Tupper.* A hymn for all nations. 1851.

T. *George McCall Theal.* "Kafir Nursery Tales," "Cape Monthly Magazine," 1877.

T. *William Henry Trenwith.* Truth. Signed ... N.Y. 1873.

T., A. *Mrs. Ann (Mallett) Thomas.* "Clavigo: a tragedy, from the German of Goethe," in the "Monthly Magazine," for September and October, 1834.

T., A. D., Merton College. *Amhurst Daniel Tyssen.* "Cornish Bell Inscriptions," in "Notes and Queries," 1865.

T., A. F. *Anne Fraser Tytler.* Mary and Florence; or, grave and gay ... L. 1835

T., B. *M. R. Lahee.* "Latest Intelligence from the Planet Venus," in "Fraser's Mag.," December, 1874, p. 763.

T. C. D. *John Wilson Croker.* Familiar epistles to F. J[one]s, Esq., on the present state of the Irish stage. Dublin, 1804.

T., D. O'C. *D. O'C. Townley.* Alderman Rooney at the Cable banquet. N.Y. 1866.

T., E. *E. Tasker.* Catalogue of [his] private library . . . N.Y. 1880.

T., E. *Emilio Teza.* Il canto di Ivan Vasilévici . . . Bologna, 1870.

T., E. C. *Rev. Edward C. Towne.* "Bacon-Shakespeare Theory," in the "Christian Register" (B., May, 1875).

T., F. *Mrs. Frances Trollope.* The mother's manual . . . L. 1833.

T. F., Taylor's Friend. *Rev. George Ashby,* "best known to literary history as 'T. F.,' the author of many spicy notes in Nichols's 'Life of Bowyer.'"

T., G. W. *George Watson Taylor.* Pieces of poetry: with two dramas . . . Chiswick, 1830.

T., H. S. *Mrs. Harriet Smith Tolman.* James Tolman . . . B. 1869.

T., I. *Isaac Taylor.* Home education. L. 1837.

T., J., D.D. *Rev. Joseph Trapp.* The ministerial virtue . . . L. 1738.

T. J., of Bristol. *Josiah Tucker.* An impartial inquiry into the benefits and damages . . . from the present very great use of low-priced spirituous liquors . . . L. 1751.

T., James, of B. Castle. *James Townsend,* in Beloe's "Sexagenarian" Vol. II., p. 20, 2d ed. (L. 1818).

T., J. E. *J. E. Tuel.* Saint Clair; or, the protégé: a tale of the Federal City. By . . . Washington, 1846.

T., J. F. *Joseph Farrand Tuttle.* Interesting reminiscences: two papers on the battle of Gettysburgh. Dated, Crawfordsville, Ind., Aug. 12, 1874.

T., J. J. *Rev. John James Tayler.* Forms of prayer for public worship. 3d ed. L. 1851.

T., J. O. *John Orville Terry.* The poems of . . . N.Y. 1850.

T., L. *Louisa Twining.* Dress. L. 187-.

T., L. *Lewis Theobald.* Miscellaneous observations upon authors, ancient and modern. L. 1731–32.

T., L. B. *Lawrence Buckley Thomas.* Autograph poems. 18-.

T., M. A. *Mary Agnes Tincker.* The house of Yorke . . . N.Y. 1872.

T., M. M. D. L. *M. Maître De La Tour.* The history of Ayder-Ali-Khan, Nabob Bahader . . . by . . . L. 1784.

T., M. W. *William Tennant.* Papistry storm'd . . . L. 1827.

T., M. W. *Mary W. Tileston.* The wisdom series. B. 1876–7.

T., Marmaduke. *Marmaduke Thompson.* — See Lamb's "Elia," "Christ's Hospital."

T., P., Esq. *Philip Thicknesse.* Junius discovered. L. n.d.

T. P. A. P. O. A. B. I. T. C. O. S. [The Precentor And Prebendary Of Alton Borealis In The Church Of Sarum.] *Rev. Arthur Ashley Sykes.* An enquiry into the meaning of demoniacks in the New Testament. 2d ed. L. 1737.

T. Q. *Samuel Young.* A Wall Street bear in Europe . . . by . . . N.Y. 1855.

T. Q. Z., Esq. *Major John Scott.* An epistle from Oberea, Queen of Otaheite . . . L. 1774.

T., R. *Ralph Thomas.* "Abolition of imprisonment for debt," contributed to the "Monthly Magazine." L. 1832.

T., R. *Rev. Robert Tyas, M.A.* Sentiment of flowers. L. 1835.

T., R., gent. of London. *Robert Tofte.* Laura. The toyes of a traveller . . . n.p. 1597.

T. R. D. J. S. D. O. P. I. I. The *Rev. Dr. Jonathan Swift,* "Dean of Patrick's in Ireland." Miscellaneous works, comical and diverting. n.p. 1720.

T., S. *Samuel Timmins.* Lord Spencer's library . . . n.p., n.d. but 1870.

T., S. *Sarah Tucker.* South Indian missionary sketches . . . L. 1842.

T., S. C. *Rev. Samuel Cooper Thatcher.* Elements of religion and morality . . . B. 1813. [Co-author with Rev. W. E. Channing, D.D. — See "C., W. E.," and "T., S. C."]

T., St. D. *Thomas Burgess.* The Samaritan and Syriack alphabets, with a praxis to each. By . . . L. 1814.

T., S. E. *Samuel E. Thomas.* The row in Dame Albion's Church school; or, high, low, and broad ideas of essentials. In two scenes. By . . . L. 1871.

T., W. *Dr. William Thomson.* Bacon, not Shakespeare. By . . . Melbourne, Australia, 1881.

T., W. *William Trotter.* Five letters on worship . . . L. 1857.

T., W. *William Thornton, M.D.* Political economy; founded in justice and humanity . . . W. 1804.

T. W., a Bostonian. *Charles Chauncy.* A letter to a friend, giving a concise but just representation of the hardships and sufferings the town of Boston is exposed to ... B. 1774.

T., W. B. D. D. *William Barclay David Donald Turnbull.* ˙ Remarks on the Hussey peerage. Edinb. 1842.

T., W. F. *W. F. Taylor.* Suitable bathing dresses, as used in Biarritz ... Windsor, 1864.

T., W. M. *William Makepeace Thackeray.* "Going to see a man hanged." "Fraser's Magazine," August, 1840.

T. Z. *Samuel Adams,* in the "Boston Gazette," Jan. 9, 1769.

T***e, Citizen H. *John Horne Tooke.* A political eclogue. Citizen H. T***e, Citizen T**rn*y [George Tierney], and R. B., Esq. L. 1797.

T**r**w, L**d. *Edward,* 1st Baron Thurlow. A dressing for ... prepared by a surgeon. L. 1797.

T**rn*y, Citizen. *George Tierney.* — See " T**ke, Citizen H."

T——, Mrs. *Mrs. Sarah (Kirby) Trimmer,* in Beloe's "Sexagenarian," I., 344. 2d ed. L. 1818.

T——, J——, Esq. *John Wilson Croker.* An intercepted letter from ... Dublin, 1804.

T——, The R—v—d D——. *Rev. William Thom,* of Govan. The happiness of dead clergymen ... Glasgow, 1769.

T—e, Dr. *Rev. William Trollope.* — See Lamb's "Elia," "Christ's Hospital."

T—n, J——. *Dr. William Maginn.* Extracts from a lost (and found) memorandum book, in "Blackwood's Magazine," March, 1821.

Tabitha. *Edward Taylor Fletcher.* — See "Korah."

Tacitus. *De Witt Clinton.* The canal policy of the State of New York. Albany, 1821.

Tacitus. *Thomas Evans.* A series of letters addressed to Thomas Jefferson ... P. 1802.

Tag, Rag, and Bobtail, Messieurs. *Isaac D'Israeli.* Flim-flams! Or, the life and errors of my uncle and the amours of my aunt ... L. 1805.

Talis Qualis. *Karl Wilhelm-August Strandberg.* Sanger i pansar. 184–.

Tally Tom. *George Barham.* The merry days of coaching ... By ... L. 1857.

Talmon, Thrace. *Mrs. Ellen T. H. Putnam.* Captain Molly : the story of a brave woman. N.Y. 1857.

Talvi. *Mrs. Thérèse Albertine Louise (von Jacob) Robinson.* Heloise ; or, the unrevealed secret. N.Y. 1850.

Tam. *Thomas MacKellar.* Tam's fortnight ramble, and other poems. P. 1847.

Tan Chau Qua of Quang Chew Fu, gent. *Sir William Chambers.* An explanatory discourse by ... annexed to " A dissertation on oriental gardening." L. 1774.

This was attacked and burlesqued in the admirable "Heroic Epistle," generally ascribed to Rev. William Mason, the poet.

Tandem, K. Felix. *Karl Spitteler.* Extramundana, Von ... Leipsic, 1883.

Tanhäuser, der neue. *Eduard Grisebach.* Der neue Tanhäuser. 1869.

Taoalttbob. — *Graham.* Diana great at Ephesus ... A sermon ... By ... L. 1755.

" Taoalttbob" seems to be a name composed, as an acrostic, of the initials of the words forming the following sentence, " The Author Of A Letter To The Bishop Of Bangor."

Tasma. *Miss Jessie Fraser,* in several works of fiction.

Taswert. *John Allan Stewart,* in his contributions to the "Times" (No. Springfield, Mo.).

Tatem, H. M. *Helen Hazlett.* Glenair ; or, life in Scotland. P. 1869.

Taubert, A. *Agnes (Taubert) von Hartmann.* Der Pessimismus und seine Gegner. 1873.

Taylor, George. *Joseph Archer Crowe.* Antinous. 1880.

Taylor, George. *Prof. Adolf Hausrath.* Klytia, and other novels.

Also attributed to *Joseph Archer Crowe.*

Taylor, Theodore. *John Camden Hotten.* Thackeray, the humorist and the man of letters ... L. 1864.

Teacher, A. *Charles W. Sanders.* Metrical stories in chemistry and natural philosophy. By ... N.Y. 1842.

Teacher, A. *Henry Russell Cleveland.* Remarks on the classical education of boys. B. 1834.

Teacher, A. *Miss Elizabeth P. Peabody.* Theory of teaching ... B. 1841.

Teacher in Boston, A. *Nathaniel Peabody.* First lessons in grammar on the plan of Pestalozzi. By ... B. 1830.

Teacher of thirty years' experience, A. *N. W. Starr.* The arithmetical assistant ... N.Y. 1863.

Tekeli. *Theodore Edward Hook (?).* Poems, by ... L. 1809.

Tela, Josephus. *Joseph Webb.* Philosophical library. Edited by ... L. 1818.

Telarius. *Foster Webb,* who contributed translations from the Latin classics, particularly "Ovid" and "Homer," to the "Gent. Mag.," 1740 *et seq.*, under the signatures of "Telarius" and "Vedastus."

Telba. *William Ablett.* The road to riches; or, plain directions for securing wealth . . . L. 1857.

Tell, Muni. *Mrs. Alice (McClure) Griffin.* — See "Glenmore, Addie."

Temperate Drinker, A. *William Gauntley.* Animadversions on a treatise published on behalf of teetotalism. Bakewell, 1857.

Templar, A. *William Charles Mark Kent.* The Gladstone government, being cabinet pictures . . . L. 1866.

Temple, Rev. Allan. *Rev. Charles Benjamin Tayler.* The will-forgers. L. 1847.

Temple, Launcelot, Esq. *John Armstrong.* Sketches; or, essays on various subjects. By . . . L. 1758.

Temple, Neville. The *Hon. Julian Charles Henry Fane.* Tannhäuser; or, the battle of the bards (1861), conjointly with "Edward Trevor" (*pseud.*), *q.v.*

The authorship, which was intended to be a profound secret, was discovered by Fane's use of his family motto, "Ne Vile Fano," as a pseudonym.
In his "Julian Fane: a Memoir" (1871, p. 173), Lord Lytton writes as follows: "The little poem of 'Tannhäuser,' which, whilst at Vienna, he [Fane] published under a feigned name, and which was written in conjunction with myself, grew naturally out of his enthusiasm for . . . Wagner's great opera of 'Tannhäuser.'" He then, after explaining that the pseudonym "Neville Temple" refers to the motto of the Fanes, *ne vile fano*, proceeds to give in full those parts of the poem which were composed by *Fane.*

Templeton. *George H. Monroe.* Musical entertainment. B. 1845. Also in his contributions to the Hartford "Courant," and other papers.

Templeton, Faith. *Harriet Boomer Barber.* Wrecked, but not lost. P. 1880.

Templeton, Laurence. *Sir Walter Scott.* Ivanhoe: a romance. Edinb. 1820.

Templeton, Timothy. *Charles Adams,* of Washington. — See "Brit. Mus. Cat."

Templeton, Tristram. *Nicholas Francis Flood Davin.* Charles Kavanah: a story of modern life, character, and adventure, in the London "Monthly Journal," 1866–67.

Temporary Inhabitant, An. *Johann Jakob Grümbke.* A tour through the Island of Rügen, in the Baltic, 1805 . . . L. 1807.

Temporum Felicitas. One of the pseudonyms attributed to Junius (*q.v.*).

The letter thus signed is dated Oct. 12, 1768, and satirizes the correspondents who had supported the ministry.

Tenella, La. *Mrs. Mary Bayard (Devereux) Clarke,* who first adopted this pen-name in her contributions to Southern literature.

Tennessean, A. *Randal W. Mac-Gavock.* A T. abroad; or, letters from Europe, Africa, and Asia, 1851–52.

Tennessean. *D. W. Marsh.* Tennessean in Persia and Koordistan. P. 18–.

Ten-Pounder, A. *P. Mackenzie.* An exposure of the spy-system pursued in Glasgow during the years 1816, 17, 18, 19, and 20 . . . Edited . . . Glasgow, 1833.

Termagant, Madame Roxana. *Bonnel Thornton.* Have at you all; or, the Drury Lane journal . . . L. 1752.

Terræ Filius. *Robert Edward Garnham.* A letter to the Right Rev. Lewis [Bagot], by divine permission, Lord Bishop of Norwich . . . L. 1789.

Terræ Filius. *Rev. Stephen Weston.* Werneria; or, short characters of Earth's . . . By . . . L. 1805.

Terry, Money, Esq. *James B. Congdon.* New Bedford money matters . . . B. 1859.

Ter-Tisanthrope. *William Honyman Gillespie.* The origin of evil: a celestial drama. L. 1873.

Testiculus. One of the pseudonyms attributed to Junius (*q.v.*).

The letter thus signed is dated Nov. 24, 1770, and consists of an ironical defence of Lord Barrington.

Testis. One of the pseudonyms attributed to Junius (*q.v.*).

The letter thus signed is dated Nov. 19, 1770, and reflects upon the army.

"Testudo, Totty." *Mrs. Flora Frances Wylde.* The life and wonderful adventures of . . . an autobiography. Edinb. 1873.

Testy, Tim. *Alden Spooner.* His signature, Sept. 4, 1811, to lines "Crossing the Ferry," in the "Long Island Star" (Brooklyn, N.Y.).

Testy, Timothy. — See "Sensitive, Samuel," and —.

Teutha. *William Jerdan,* who used this signature from his first to his last contributions to the press.

Th. *Thomas Thornton* (?). — See Lamb's "Elia," "Christ's Hospital."

Thacker, Page. *Lettie M. Burwell.* Plantation reminiscences. 1878.

Thanelian. *N. W. Coffin,* in the Boston "Journal."

Thanet, Octave. *Miss Alice French,*

of Davenport, Iowa, in her contributions to magazine literature.

Their Chairman. *Benjamin Franklin Hallett.* The Sears Fund connected with St. Paul's Church in Boston. Report of a committee of the proprietors, by . . . Easter, 1854. B. 1854.

Their Latest Victim. *John Habberton.* Helen's babies; by . . . B. 1876.

Their Nephew. *John Penrose.* Lives of Vice-Admiral Sir Charles Vinicombe Penrose, and Capt. James Trevenen. By . . . L. 1850.

Their Wellwisher. *Simeon Ide.* The young Franklinsonian . . . written for the children of mechanics and farmers . . . Hartford, 1872.

Thekla. *Mrs. Caroline Atherton (Briggs) Mason.* Three of us. B. 1880.

Themaninthemoon. *Rev. John Eagles.* Felix Farley; Rhymes, Latin and English. Bristol, 1826.

Themistocles. *Harvey Redmond Morres,* 2d Lord Viscount Mountmorres. Letters of . . . with appendix, containing the character of Dr. Franklin . . . L. 1795.

Theodelinda. *Mrs. Charles E. Kelsey.* The Vail family; or, doing good . . . P. 1862.

Theodosia. *Anne Steele.* Poems on subjects chiefly devotional. L. 1780.

Theophanes Cantabrigiensis. *Bishop Samuel Squire.* The ancient history of the Hebrews vindicated; or, remarks on . . . the third volume of the Moral Philosopher. By . . . Camb. 1741.

Theophilanthropist, A. *William R. Peck.* Discourses on the diversity of theological opinions . . . Doncaster, 18-.

Theophilus. — See "Layman, A." (*P. Duigenan*).

Theophilus. *Samuel Spring, D.D.* (?). Essay on the discipline of Christ's house . . . Newburyport, 1816.

Theophilus Secundus. *Rev. Stephen Jenner.* Answer to Archdeacon Wilberforce, on the doctrine of the Holy Eucharist. L. 1854.

Theophrastus, Sylvanus. *John Thelwall.* The peripatetic; or, sketches of the heart, of nature, and society . . . of . . . L. 1793.

Theoptes. *Job Durfee.* The Panidèa . . . B. 1846.

Theoria. *Digby Pilot Starkey.* Theoria; poems. Dublin, 1847.

Théotime. *L'Abbé Marc Antoine Bayle.* Les chants de l'adolescence, poésies religieuses. Marseille, 1846.

Therapeutes. *David Brodie.* The

healing art the right hand of the Church . . . Edinb. 1859.

Theron. *John Pierpont.* His signature to a prize poem for the Boston Theatre, in 1827.

Theseus. *Edward Hamilton.* Death of our Minotaur. B. 1868.

Theta. *Julia Putnam Henderson.* Annie Balfour and her friends . . . N.Y. 1870.

Theta. *Miss Maria Theresa Hoblyn.* The fisherman's daughter, and dreams of the past. L. 1869.

Theta. *William Thorn.* The thorntree: being a history of thorn worship of the Twelve Tribes of Israel, but more especially of the Lost Tribe, and House of David. L. 1863.

The full pseudonym reads, "Theta, a lineal descendant of the Hereditary Standard Bearers of Normandy and England. 'The Knights of the Swan.'"

The work is dedicated to the Bishop of Natal, by ⊙, presumably the author.

Theta, Lancastriensis. *Rev. Thomas Hayes,* in the "British Magazine."

Thinker, Theodore. *Francis Channing Woodworth.* Jack Mason, the old sailor. N.Y. 18-.

Thinkingmachine, John. *James Ferdinand Mallinckrodt.* Novissimum organon. St. Louis, Mo., 1882.

Thinks-I-To-Myself, Who? *Edward Nares, D.D.* Thinks-I-to-myself. A serio-ludicro-tragico-comico tale. L. 1811.

Third Member of this "Symposium," A. *William Gifford,* in Beloe's "Sexagenarian," Vol. II., p. 114. 2d ed. L. 1818.

Thirty-One, The. *Rev. Leonard Withington.* Penitential tears; or, a cry from the dust. 1845.

Thistle. *R. Hume Middlemass, Senior.* — See "Bluebell."

Thistle, Timothy. *O. Ellsworth.* A single gentleman. Designs by the author . . . B. 1867.

Thistleton, the Hon. Francis, late Governor of the Island of Cacona. *William Henry Fleet.* How I came to be governor of the island of Cacona . . . Montreal, 1853.

Thomas, Father. *Thomas Doyle.* His signature to letters in the London "Tablet."

Thomas, Caroline. *Mrs. Julia Caroline (Ripley) Dorr.* Farmingdale: a tale. N.Y. 1854.

Thomas, Karl. *Karl Thomas Richter.* As a poet, under this pseudonym, he was quite fruitful.

Thoninonca. *John Canton.* Number

of Mr. Whitefield's hearers calculated and justified, in the "Gent. Mag.," August, 1739, p. 416, and September, p. 472.

Thorne, Kate. *Miss Louisa M. Gray.* Nelly's teachers, and what they learned ... L., Edinb. & N.Y.

Thorne, P. *Mrs. Mary Prudence (Wells) Smith.* Jolly good times; or, child life on a farm. B. 1875.

Thorne, Tom. *Robert Merry,* in the London "Argus."

Thornton, Harold. *Cecil Offord.* Cry of Humanity. L. 18–.

Thorpe, Kampa. *Mrs. E. W. Bellamy.* Little Joanna. N.Y. 187–.
Other authorities give this pseud. as " Kamba Thorpe." Mrs. Tardy, " Kampa Thorpe."

Those who Knew. *T. R. DeForest.* Olden time in New York ... N.Y. 1833.

ΘΥΟΣ ΜΑΘΟΣ. *Thomas South.* Early magnetism in its higher relations to humanity ... L. 1846.

Three Friends. *H. H. Weston, C. Clark,* and *L. Gibbons.* The fairy egg and what it held. By ... B. 1870.

Three Friends. *Rev. Thomas Raffles, James Baldwin Brown,* and *Jeremiah Holmes Wiffen.* Poems by ... L. 1813.

Three Sisters. *Ellin Isabelle, Mary Frances,* and *Margaret Elenore Tupper.* Poems by ... L. 1864.

Thumb, Thomas, Esq. *Benjamin Church, M.D.* The monster of monsters ... B. 1754.

Thumb, Tom. *Charles S. Stratton.* Sketch of the life of ... N.Y. 1847.

Thunderbolt. *John Doherty.* An authentic account of Thunderbolt and Lightfoot [Michael Martin], two notorious highwaymen. B. 1847.

Thunder-Ten-Tronckh, Baron Arminius von. *Matthew Arnold,* in the London "Pall-Mall Gazette."

Thurland, Bilberry. *Charles Hooton.* Adventures of ... L. 1836.

Thurston, Henry J. *Francis Turner Palgrave.* The passionate pilgrim; or, Eros and Anteros. L. 1858.

Thwackus, Herman. *Jonas Clopper.* Fragments of the history of Bawlfredonia, containing an account of the discovery and settlement of that great Southern continent ... By ... Translated from the original Bawlfredonian manuscript into the French language by Monsieur Traducteur, and rendered into English by a citizen of America. n.p. 1819.

Tibbs. *Charles Dickens.* Scenes and characters, in "Bell's Life in London and Sporting Chronicle" for 1835–36.

Tichebourne, Cheviot. *William Harrison Ainsworth.* Poems. L. 1824.

Tickle, Timothy, Esq. *B. F. Kendall.* The doleful tragedy of the raising of Jo. Burnham; or, the "Cat let out of the bag" ... Woodstock, Vt., 1832.

Tickler, Timothy. *Robert Sym,* in the "Noctes Ambrosianæ," and a contributor under the same name to " Blackwood's Magazine," 1818 *et seq.*

Tickletoby, Timothy. *Samuel F. Bradford.* The imposter detected; or, a review of some of the writings of "Peter Porcupine" ... P. 1796.

Tickletooth, Tabitha. *Charles Selby.* The dinner question. L. 1860.

Tidy, Theresa. *Mrs. Elizabeth Susanna (Davenport) Graham.* Eighteen maxims of neatness and order. L. 184–.

Tim, Uncle. *Richard Lower.* Tom Cladpole's journey to Lunnun ... Brighton, 1831.

Tim, Tiny. *H. T. Jenkins,* of Southsea, in his contributions to "Notes and Queries," etc.

Times, The London ("The Thunderer," "The Jupiter of the Press"). An English newspaper started in 1785 under the title of the "Daily Universal Register," and adopted its present name in 1788. It was originated by Mr. John Walter, grandfather of the late Mr. John Walter.

Times Bee-Master, The. *John Cumming, D.D.* Bee-keeping. L. 1864.

Timoleon. *Isaac Orr,* in the "Boston Courier."

Timoleon. *William Bollan.* Epistle from ... to all the honest freeholders, and other electors of Members of Parliament ... L. 1768.

Timon. *Vicomte Louis Marie (de la Haye) de Cormenin.* Études sur les orateurs parlementaires. Paris, 1836.

Timon, John. *Donald Grant Mitchell.* Signature of his preface to "The Lorgnette." See "Opera Goer, An."

Timothy. *Thomas Worcester.* Letter to the moderator of the N. Hampshire Association. B. 1812.

Timothy, Master. *George W. M. Reynolds.* Master Timothy's bookcase. L. 1843.

Tinker, T. *Jonathan Swift, D.D.* Wood's [Wiiliam, hardware dealer] plot discover'd. 1724.

Tinklarian Doctor, The. *William Mitchel.* The T. D.'s funeral sermon ... Edinb. (?) 1737.

Tinto, Dick. *Frank Boott Goodrich,* for several years the Paris correspondent of the New York "Times" under this signature, and author of "Tri-colored sketches in Paris, during the years 1851 to 1853." N.Y. 1855.

Tinto, Dick. *Charles A. Jones,* who wrote a series of poems for the "Cincinnati Gazette," under this signature.

Tinto, Gabriel. *G. W. Anthony.* The wise judgment . . . Manchester, 1853.

Tirabecque. *Modesto Lafuente,* who, under the pseuds. "Fray Gerundio" and "Tirabecque," published the periodical works, "Coleccion de capilladas y disciplinarzos," 16 vols., etc.

Titcomb, Timothy, Esquire. *Josiah Gilbert Holland.* Titcomb's letters to young people, single and married. 1859. Letters to the Joneses. N.Y. 1864.

Titian, Onyx. *Miss Sarah Woodward.* The apple blossom; or, a mother's legacy. L. 186–.

Titmarsh, Michael Angelo. *William Makepeace Thackeray.* The Paris sketch book. L. 1840.

"Michael Angelo" is said to be a nickname bestowed upon *Thackeray* by a friend, probably in allusion to his youthful aspirations, whilst "Titmarsh" was perhaps "added as a sort of humorous anti-climax."

"Doctor Birch and his young friends" (L. 1849), and several other minor pieces are signed "Mr. M. A. Titmarsh."

Titterwell, Timothy, Esq. *Samuel Kettell.* Yankee notions. A medley . . . B. 1838.

Toby. *Jonathan Swift, D.D.* A town eclogue; or, a poetical contest between Toby and a minor poet [Steele] of B—tt—n's coffee-house.

Toby, Abel's Kinsman. *Jonathan Swift, D.D.* The character of Richard St—le [Steele], Esq.; with some remarks . . . L. 1713.

Toby, M. P. *Mr. Lucy.* Essence of Parliament, contributed to "Punch" (L. 1881), etc.

Toby, Uncle. *Rev. Tobias H. Miller.*

Toby, Uncle. *Elisha North, M.D.* The pilgrim's progress in phrenology . . . New London, Conn., 1833.

Toby, Simeon. *George Trask.* Thoughts and stories on tobacco, for American lads; or, Uncle Toby's anti-tobacco advice to his nephew, Billy Bruce. B., 5th ed., 1852.

Todd, Laurie. *Grant Thorburn.* Sketches from the note-book of . . . N.Y. 1847.

Todkill, Anas. *John Esten Cooke.* My Lady Pokahontas . . . With notes by . . . [or, rather, written by . . .] B. 1885.

Toletus. *David Tappan, D.D.* Two friendly letters from Toletus to Philale-

thes [the Rev. Samuel Spring, D.D.] . . . Newburyport, Mass., 1785.

Tom, Brother. *Thomas Warton.* — See "Peter, Brother."

Tom, Captain. *Daniel Defoe.* A letter . . . to the mobb, now rais'd for Dr. Sacheverel. L. 1710.

Tom of Bedlam. *Luke Milbourne.* Tom of Bedlam's answer to Hoadly. L. 1698.

Tom-Tit, Ebenezer. *Charles Smith.* Letter, addressed to the dean and chapter of Norwich . . . Norwich, 1824.

Tomkins, Isaac, Gent. *Henry,* Lord Brougham and Vaux. Thoughts on the aristocracy of England . . . L. 1834.

Ton. *E. Kingman.*

Tonson, Monsieur. *John Taylor.* Monsieur Tonson. L. 1830.

Topping, Godfrey. *Dr. John Robertson.* Educational voluntaryism . . . Manchester, 1854.

Tory, A. *Samuel Adams,* in the "Boston Gazette," May 1, 1769.

Total Abstainer, A. *Susanna Corder* (?). Friendly cautions addressed to the advocates of total abstainance from all intoxicating beverages. By . . . Lindfield, n.d.

Touchatout. *Léon Bienvenu.* Histoire de France tintamarresque, par . . . Paris, 1869.

Touch'em, Timothy. *Thomas Beck.* The age of frivolity: a poem. L. 1807.

Touchstone. *John Savage.*

Touchstone. *M. Booth.* Roadside sketches in the south of France and Spanish Pyrenees. By three wayfarers; with 24 illustrations by . . . L. 1859.

Touchstone, Timothy. *Oliphant* and — *Allen,* of Trinity Coll., Camb., and the *Hon. W. Aston,* and — *Taunton,* students of Christ Church, Oxford. The trifler: a new periodical miscellany. By . . . of St. Peter's College, Westminster. L. 1788.

Toupius, Joannes. *Jonathan Toup.* Emendationes in Suidam. L. 1760.

Tourist, A. *J. Talboys Wheeler.* Adventures of . . . from Calcutta to Delphi. Calcutta, 1868.

Tourist, A. *Charles Lanman.* Haw-ho-noo; or, records of . . . P. 1851.

Town, Mr., Critic and Censor-general. *George Colman* and *Bonnel Thornton.* The Connoisseur. By . . . L. 1856.

Town, Mr., junior, Critic and Censor General. *James Henry Leigh Hunt,* in the London "Traveller," afterwards the "Globe."

Town Listener, The. *Leander Rich-*

ardson, in his contributions to the "World" (N.Y.).

Towne, Tracy. *Mrs. E. W. Sawtelle.* Pen and pencil sketches. B. 1878.

Toxophilite. *G. F. Lanigan*, a Canadian writer, who, under this signature, contributed to Wilkes' "Spirit" and Porter's "Spirit of the Times" (N.Y.).

Tractarian British Critic, A. *Rev. George Herbert Townsend.* The life and defence of the conduct and principles of the venerable and calumniated Edmund Bonner, Bishop of London ... L. 1842.

Trader, An Old and Experienced. *Alexander Cluny.* The American traveller ... By ... L. 1769.

Tradesman, A. *John Drinker.* Observations on the late popular measures ... P. 1774.

Tradesman of Oxford, A. *G. S. Green.* The images of the antients, particularly those in the University of Oxford ... a poem. By ... Oxf. 1758.

Tradesman of Philadelphia, A. *Benjamin Franklin.* Plain truth ... P. 1747.

Tradleg, Nitram. *Martin Geldart.* A son of Belial ... L. 1882.

Traducteur, Monsieur. *Jonas Clopper.* — See "Thwackus, Herman."

Trafford, F. G. *Mrs. Charlotte Eliza Lawson (Cowan) Riddell.* The moor and the fens. L. 1858.

Tramp. *Charles M. Skinner*, in the Brooklyn "Times."

Translator, The. *Henry Crude Murphy.* Poetry of Nieuw-Neder-Landt, comprising translations of early Dutch poems relating to New York, etc. ... By ... Williamstadt, 1866.

Translator, The. *John Kesson.* Travels in Scotland, translated from the German. With notes by ... L. 1844.

Translator of "Lady Catesby's Letters," The. *Mrs. Frances (Moore) Brooke.* The history of Lady Julia Mandeville. By ... Dublin, 1763.

Translator of the "Caledonian Bards," The. *John Clark, F.S.A.* A letter ... on the late mutinies in the Highland regiments ... Edinb. 1780.

Translator of the "New Atalantis," The. *Mrs. N. De la Rivière Manley.* Memoirs of Europe towards the close of the eighth century. Written by Eginhardus, secretary and favourite of Charlemagne, and done into English by ... L. 1710.

Translator of the "Niebelungen Treasure." *Madame (Phillips) de Pontes.* A selection from the poems and dramatic works of Theodor Körner. L. 1850.

Translator of the "Pattern of Modesty," The. *Elias Bockett.* The wit and honesty of James Hoskins, etc., consider'd in remarks on their late pamphlet call'd "The Pennsylvania Bubble." By ... L. 1726.

Translator of "Wilhelm Meister," etc., The. *Thomas Carlyle.* German romance; specimens of its chief authors ... By ... Edinb. 1827.

Trash. *Royall Tyler*, in the "Polyanthos," a literary monthly, published and edited by Joseph T. Buckingham, 1806–7. B.

Traun, Julius von der. *Julius Schindler.* Excursionen eines Osterreichers, 1840–79, 1880.

Traveler, A. C. *Mrs. H. K. U. Clark.* Teachings of the ages. By ... San Francisco, 1874.

Traveller, A. *De Witt Clinton.* An account of Abimelech Coody and other celebrated writers of New York ... N.Y. 1815. — See "Coody, Abimelech."

Traveller, A. *Charles E. Kells* (?). California, from the discovery by the Spaniards to the present time ... N.Y. 1848.

Traveller, A. *John Banim.* Contributions chiefly on "Theatrical topics," in the "Limerick Evening Post."

Traveller, A. *Henry Salt.* Egypt: a descriptive poem. Alexandria, 1824.

Traveller, A. *Dinah Maria (Mulock) Craik.* Fair France. Impressions of ... L. 1871.

Traveller, A. *Benjamin C. Clark.* Geographical sketch of St. Domingo ... B. 1850.

Traveller, A. *Mrs. Ann (Hinton) Taylor.* Itinerary of ... in the wilderness. B. 1825.

Traveller, A. *Henry Russell Cleveland.* A letter to the Hon. Daniel Webster, on the causes of the destruction of the steamer "Lexington" ... B. 1840.

Traveller, A. *William Cullen Bryant.* Letters of ... 1857–58. N.Y. 1859.

Traveller, A. *George William Curtis.* Nile notes. L. 1851.

Traveller, A. *Samuel Laing.* Notes of ... in France, Prussia, Switzerland, etc. L. 1841.

Traveller, A. *H. C. Todd* (?). Notes upon Canada and the United States, from 1832 to 1840. By ... Toronto, 1840.

Traveller, A. *George W. Carleton.* Our artist in Cuba: fifty drawings on wood. Leaves from the sketch-book of ... during the winter of 1864–65. N.Y. 1867.

Traveller, A. *A. V. Kirwan.* The

ports, arsenals, and dockyards of France. L. 1841.

Traveller. A. *Thomas Victor.* Sir Humphry Davy's monument. A midnight tale. By . . . Penzance, 1875.

Traveller, A. *Silas Pinckney Holbrook.* Sketches by . . . B. 183–.

Traveller, A. *Edmund Flagg.* Sketches of . . . in 1836, published in the "Louisville Journal"; afterwards, in book form, under the title, "The far West; or, a tour beyond the mountains . . . N.Y. 1838.

Traveller, A. *Mrs. Anne Royall.* Sketches of history, life, and manners in the United States. New Haven, 1826.

Traveller, A. *Sir John Malcolm.* Sketches of Persia, from the journals of . . . in the East. L. 1828.

Traveller, A. *Mrs. Sarah (Wallis Bowdich) Lee.* Stories of strange lands, and fragments from the notes of . . . L. 1835.

Traveller, A. *Sir William Draper.* The thoughts of . . . upon our American disputes. L. 1774.

Traveller, A. *Frank Starr.* Twenty years of . . . 's life: being extracts from his journal. L. 1851.

Traveller, A. *Thomas Jefferson Hogg, Esq.* Two hundred and nine days; or, the journal of . . . on the Continent. L. 1827.

Traveller and Teacher, A. *Alonzo Tripp.* Crests from the ocean world . . . By . . . B. 1855.

Traveller in the Tropics, A. *Maturin M. Ballou.* History of Cuba; or, notes of . . . etc. B. 1854.

Traveller, The. *Isaac Story,* in some contributions to the "Columbian Sentinel."

Travelling Bachelor, A. *James Fenimore Cooper.* Notions of the Americans, picked up by . . . P. 1838.

Travelling Physician, A. *Sir George William Lefevre, Knt.* Life of . . . L. 1843.

Treasurer of a Corporation, A. *Thomas Greaves Cary.* Profits on manufactures at Lowell . . . B. 1845.

Treasurer of the Wimbledon Local Museum, The. *Joseph Toynbee.* Hints on the formation of local museums. By . . . L. 1863.

Trebor. *Robert S. Davis.* As it may happen. P. 1879.

Trebor, Eidrah. *Robert Hardie.* Hoyle made familiar. Edinb. 1830.

Treddlehoyle, Tom. *J. Rogers.* Tom Treddlehoyle's peep at t'Manchester art treasures exhebishon e 1857. Leeds, 1857.

Treenoodle, Uncle Jan. *William Sandys, F.S.A.* Transactions of the Loggerville Literary Society. L. 1867.

Trefoil. *Gen. F. F. Millen,* in his contributions to the "Golden Era" (San Francisco, Cal.), etc.

Tregenna, the late James Hamley. *Ven. Robert Bateman Paul, M.A.* The autobiography of a Cornish rector. By . . . L. 1872.

Trelawny, Anne. *Mrs. Anne (Trelawny) Gibbons.* An Easter offering. By . . . L. 1845.

Tremaine, Canon. *Rev. Robert Stephen Hawker, M.A.*

The character of Canon Tremaine in Mortimer Collins's "Sweet and Twenty," a novel, L. 1875, was intended for *Rev. R. S. Hawker.*

Trenchard, Asa. *Henry Watterson.* Comic sketches. L. 18–.

Trepidantium, Malleus. *Samuel Young,* who published tracts under this name and that of "Calvin Philanax." L. 1698–1700.

Trepolpen, P. W. *William Prideaux Courtney.* His signature in "Notes and Queries," 1864–69.

Tressilian. *Edward William Brydges Willyams,* in Lawrence's "Silverland."

Tretane. *John Brendon Curgenoen, M.R.C.S.* London riots in 1780. Light horse volunteers. By T., in "Notes and Queries," 1860.

Trevor, Edward. *The Right Hon. Edward Robert Bulwer-Lytton,* Baron Lytton, joint-author. Tannhäuser; or, the battle of the bards: a poem. L. 1861.

Trevylyan, Mrs. Kitty. *Mrs. E. R. Charles.* Diary of . . . N.Y. 1864.

Tricotrin. *A. J. Henderson,* in the New York "Tribune."

Trifle and the Editor. *Warren Tilton* and *William A. Crapts.* Trifleton papers . . . B. 1856.

Trigger, George. *W. H. Florio Hutchisson.* Pen and pencil sketches, being reminiscences during eighteen years' residence in Bengal. L. 1883.

Trim. *Rev. Edward Baldwyn.* A critique on the poetical essays of the Rev. William Atkinson . . . 1787.

Trim. *Louis Gustave Fortuné Ratisbonne.* Les petits hommes, 1868; Les petites femmes, 1871.

Trimalcion. *Félix d'Amoreux* (called *Jules de Saint-Félix*). Etudes parlementaires, morales, et pittoresques . . . Paris, 1850.

Trimble, Esther J. *Esther J. T. Lippincott.* A handbook of English and American literature, historical and critical. By . . . P. 188–.

Trimester, A. *Rev. Stephen Weston.* A Trimester in France and Switzerland. L. 1821.

Trimm, Timothée. *Léo Lespès.* Promenades dans Paris. Paris, 1867.

Trimmer, Tim. *Albion H. Redford.* Fred Brenning. Nashville, 1876.

Trimsharp. *Harvey A. Fuller.* Trimsharp's account of himself. Ann Arbor, Mich., 1873.

Trimstave, Tyro, M.D. *Christopher Reid.* Killvillian. A catechetical ode by the late . . . With preface and notes by Cosmo Caustic, Gent. Edinb. 1835.

Trinculo. *Andrew C. Wheeler,* in dramatic criticisms contributed to the "Leader" (N.Y.).

Trinitarian, A. *John Penrose, M.A.* Of God or of the divine mind, and of the doctrine of the Trinity ; also of Pantheism. Oxf. 1849.

Trinity Man, A. *Thomas Wright.* Alma Mater ; or, seven years at Cambridge University. Edinb. 1827.

Trinity Undergraduates [One of]. *W. C. Borlase.* Leaves from the Lime-Walk. By . . . Oxf. 1867.
Contains " A West Country ditty," and other pieces signed " B.," *i.e. W. C. Borlase.*

Trip, Tom. *Giles Jones.* The history of Giles Gingerbread . . . N.Y. 1880.

Tripe, Dr. Andrew. *Jonathan Swift, D.D.* A letter from the facetious . . . at Bath, to the venerable Nestor Ironsides (the name under which Steele wrote " The Guardian "). L. 1714.

Tripe, Dr. Andrew. *Dr. William Wagstaffe.* A letter . . . to his loving brother, the profound Greshamite. n.p. 1725.

Trismegistus. *Thomas Manning,* the " Trismegistus " of Lamb's " Letters."

Trismegistus. *Moses Whitney, Jr.,* in the " New England Galaxy." B. 1828 et seq.

Triton, Willie. *Alonzo Tripp.* The fisher boy. B. 1857.

Trognon, A. *Le Prince de Joinville.* Campagne de l'année du Potomac . . . N.Y. 1862.

Trois Etoiles. *Eustace Clare Grenville Murray.* The Boudoir cabal. L. 1875.

Trollopp, Sir Francis. *Paul Féval.* Les mystères de Londres. Paris, 1844.

Trooper, A. *John A. B. Williams.* Leaves from a trooper's diary. P. 1869.

Trooper, A. *Frederick Colburn Adams.* Story of . . . campaign on the Peninsula, 1861–62. N.Y. 1865.

Trotandot, John. *George P. R. Pul-*man. Rambles, roamings, and recollections . . . L. 1870.

Trott, John, Yeoman. *Henry St. John,* Viscount Bolingbroke. A letter to Caleb D'Anvers, Esq., concerning the state of affairs in Europe as published in the " Craftsman " . . . L. 1730.

Trottplaid, John, Esq. *Henry Fielding,* who in 1747 brought out the " Jacobite Journal " as the production of J. T., Esq.

Trovata, Ben. *Samuel Lover.* Rival rhymes in honour of Burns . . . L. 1859.

Trovator. *William Francis Williams.* Letters from Europe, in " Dwight's Journal of Music." 1861.

Trowel, Adjutant. *Thomas Dawes.* Proposals for printing by subscription the history of Adj. Trowell and Bluster [*i.e.,* James Otis]. B. 1761.

Truck, Bill. *John Howell.* The man-of-war's-man, originally published in " Blackwood's Magazine," commencing in Vol. X., p. 161.

True, Fanny. *Miss Mary Asenath Short,* who contributed poems to " Arthur's Home Magazine " and " Beadle's Home Monthly " under this *nom de plume.*

True Lover of Presbyterian Principles, A. *Rev. John Malcome,* of Dunmurry. More light . . . n.p. 1721–22.

True Quaker, A. *William Singleton.* A letter addressed to Joseph John Gurney . . . By . . . Nottingham, 1824.

True Son of the Church of England, A. *William Asplin.* The anatomy of the Kebla ; or, a dissection of the defence of Eastward adoration . . . L. 1729.

True Son of the Church of Scotland, A. *William Cheyne.* The friendship of Christ . . . Edinb. 1718.
The dedication is signed " W. C."

Trumbull. *Noah Webster.* Article in " Hampshire Gazette," Feb. 14 and 21, 1838.

Trumps. *William Brisbane Dick* (?). The American Hoyle . . . N.Y. 1868.

Trusta, H. *Mrs. Elizabeth* (*Stuart*) *Phelps.* A peep at " Number Five." B. 1852, etc.

Truth. *James Stephen,* in various letters to the " Courier " (L. 1816) upon the Crown Estates in the West Indies.

Tub, Elder Triptolemus. *Rev. George Rogers.* Adventures of . . . B. 1846.

Tugmutton, Timothy. *Charles Chorley.* Letter [on Governor Eyre's case] offered to the " Times," and placed among its " Rejected Addresses." Signed . . . " Christmas, 1868." Truro, 1868.

Turdus Merula. *Frau Emil von Quanten,* who, under this name, has obtained a reputation as a translator.

Turkish Spy, A. *Giovanni Paolo Marana.* Letters writ by ... L. 1770. — See "Mahmut the Spy."

Turnham, Trevelyan, Esq. *James Flamank.* Tracings of men and things ... L. 1854.

Tutor, A. *William Jones, F.R.S.* Letters ... to his pupils. L. 1780.

Tutor, and Fellow of a College in Oxford, A. *Rev. Edward Bentham.* A letter to a young gentleman. n.p. 1748.

Tuvar, Lorenzo. *Wilson Armistead.* Tales and legends of the English lakes and mountains ... Compiled by ... L. about 1855.

Twain, Mark. *Samuel Langhorne Clemens.* The Innocents abroad; and other works. 1871–85.

In 1877 the "San Francisco (Cal.) Alta" published the following letter from *Mr. Clemens* to Mr. John A. McPherson of that city, in which the former gentleman explains how he came to adopt the pseudonym:—

"DEAR SIR,—'Mark Twain' was the *nom de plume* of one Capt. Isaiah Sellers, who used to write river news over it for the New Orleans 'Picayune.' He died in 1863, and as he could no longer need that signature, I laid violent hands upon it without asking permission of the proprietor's remains. That is the history of the *nom de plume* I bear. Yours truly,

"May 29.   SAMUEL L. CLEMENS."

Twig, Timothy, Esq. *Joseph Moser, Esq.* The adventures of ... in a series of poetical epistles. L. 1794.

Twig, Timothy, Esq. *Alexander Campbell.* The guinea note: a poem. Edinb. 1797.

Twist-wit, Christopher, Esq. *Christopher Anstey.* Madge's addresses to C. W., Esquire, Bath-laureat, and Miller's PLUMIAN professor. L. 1777.

Twitcher, Jemmy. *Lord Sandwich,* the "Jemmy Twitcher" of the newspapers during the latter part of the last century.

Two Americans. *Arthur* and *Augustus Beaumont.* Adventures of ... in the siege of Brussels, September, 1830. By one of them. L. 1830.

Two Brothers. *A.* and *George Henry Mooney.* Sevastopol: our tent in the Crimea. L. 1856.

Two Brothers. *Julius Charles* and *Augustus William Hare.* Guesses at truth. L. 1827–48.

Two Brothers. *Alfred* and *Charles Tennyson.* Poems. L. 1827.

Two Candidates for the Bachelor's Degree. *Theodore Parsons* and *Eliphalet Pearson.* A forensic dispute on the legal-ity of enslaving the Africans, held at the public Commencement in Cambridge, New England, July 21st, 1773. B. 1773.

Two Children. *Elaine* and *Dora Goodale.* Verses by ... N.Y. 1878.

Two Clergymen. *Rev. James Ellaby* and *Rev. A. S. Thelwall.* Anti-mammon; or, an exposure of the unscriptural statements of "Mammon" ... L. 1837.

Two English Gentlemen. *W. R.* and *Eustace Chetwood.* A tour through Ireland, in several entertaining letters. Dublin, 1748. See "N. & Q.," 3d Ser., II., 148, 258.

Two Englishmen. — *Rivington* and — *Harris.* Reminiscences of America in 1869. L. 1870.

Two Friends. *John James Piatt* and *William Dean Howells.* Poems of ... N.Y. 1860.

Two Gentlemen of Harvard. *John Tyler Wheelwright* and *Frederic Jesup Stimson.* Rollo's journey to Cambridge. B. 1880.

Two Merry Men. *Francis Edward Smedley* and *Edmund Hodgson Yates.* Mirth and metre. By ... L. 1855.

Two Mounted Sentries. *Lt.-Col. John Josiah Hort.* The Horse Guards ... L. 1851.

Two Oxford Men. *Rev. Robert Stephen Hawker, M.A.* A ride from Bude to Boss. By ... "Belgravia," iii. 328–37 (1867).

Two Priests of the Church of England. *John Mason Neale* and *Rev. Joseph Haskoll.* The history and fate of sacrilege. Edited by ... L. 1853.

Two Private Soldiers. *Lemuel Lyon* and *S. Haws.* Military journals of ... 1758–1775 ... Poughkeepsie, N.Y., 1855.

Two Sisters. *Madeline Wallace* and *Rosalind Dunlop.* The timely retreat. By ... L. 1858.

Two Sisters, The. *Eliza* and *Sarah G. Walcott.* The two sisters' poems and memoirs. New Haven, 1830.

Two Sisters of the West. *Mrs. Catherine Ann (Ware) Warfield* and *Mrs. Eleanor Percy (Ware) Lee.* Poems by ... N.Y. 1843.

Two of themselves. *Mrs. Elizabeth (Rundle) Charles.* Chronicles of the Schönberg-Cotta family; by ... L. 1864.

Tydus-Pooh-Pooh. *Sir John Bowring,* in the "Maclise Portrait Gallery."

"To a grateful and discerning public ... we gladly submit the effigy of our MAN OF GENIUS ... 'Tydus-Pooh-Pooh, the translator of the poetry of the Sandwich Islands.'

"Further on in the pages of Fraser (vol. xxi.,

p. 22), it may be read that this queer, enigmatical plate is merely a joke, the point of which is now forgotten ... I would, however, just hint ... that the original of this odd caricature portrait was no other than the celebrated scholar, linguist, and political economist, *Dr.* — more recently *Sir John — Bowring*, so well known by his translations from the Russian, Servian, Polish, Magyar, Danish, Swedish, Frisian, Dutch, Esthonian, Spanish, Portuguese, and Icelandic poetry." — See the "Maclise Portrait Gallery," pp. 74, 75.

Tyne, William de. *William Sidney Gibson, F.S.A.* The day after to-morrow; or, fata morgana ... L. 1858.

Tynt, R. *Harcourt Brown.* Streetology of London; or, the metropolitan papers of the Itinerant Club. L. 1837.

Typo, A. *John S. Robb.* The Western wanderings of ... P. 1846.

Tyro Phileleutherus. *John Duncan, D.D.* An address to rational advocates for the Church of England. L. 1766.

Tyro Philolegis. *William Livingston.* He was studying law in New York City, with Mr. James Alexander, when two essays which he published under this signature, in Parker's New York "Weekly Post Boy," 1745, offended his instructor, and led to his withdrawal to the office of Mr. William Smith.

Tytler, C. C. Fraser. *Mrs. Edward Slidell.* Jasmine Leigh. L. 1871.

Tytler, Sarah. *Miss Henrietta Keddie.* Modern painters and their paintings. L. 1874.

U.

U. *A. W. and J. C. Hare.* — See "Two Brothers."

U., C. *Charles Usher.* A letter to a member of the Convocation of the University of Oxford ... L. 1699.

U., E. *Edward Upham.* Rameses: an Egyptian tale, etc. L. 1824.

U., E. V. *Edward Vernon Utterson.* A little book of ballads. Edited by ... Newport, 1836.

U., J. *James Usher.* Clio; or, a discourse on taste. L. 1772.

U., J. *John Upton.* Miscellaneous observations upon authors ancient and modern. L. 1731–32.

U., M. *Mary Uniacke.* The dolls' pic-nic. By ... L. 1860.

U. S. E. *W. Spear.* Emanuel Swedenborg ... by ...

U. U. *Cyrus Redding.* The sword song of Körner. Translated closely from the German. Signed ... in "Blackwood's Magazine," xii., 585–86. 1862.

U—d, T. *T. Underwood.* A dialogue in Hudibrastic verse. Occasioned by the publication of a volume of poems by ... L. 1768.

"Ubique." *Parker Gillmore.* Accessible field sports; the experiences of a sportsman in North America. By ... L. 1869.

Ulsterman, An. *George Sigerson.* Modern Ireland ... L. 1868.

Ulysses. *George Newman Bliss*, in the Providence papers. 1861–65.

Ulysses. *Samuel Graves.* A letter to the Right Hon. George Canning ... 1814.

Ulysses Cosmopolita. *George Berkeley, D.D.*, in his contributions to the "Guardian," No. 35, Apr. 21, 1713; No. 39, Apr. 25, 1713.

Umbra. *Charles Cavendish Clifford, M.P.* Hotch-pot ... Edinb. 1866.

Una. *Mrs. Mary (Hall) Lawrence.* "Distinguished for her beauty, she was pourtrayed by West in two of his most admired pictures: first, as Una; and secondly, as Fidelia, in his 'Fidelia and Speranza.'" — See "Gent. Mag.," February, 1815, p. 184.

Una. *Miss Mary A. McMullen.* Snatches of song. St. Louis, 1874.

Uncle Tom's Nephew. *Thomas Driver.* The slavery of the pulpit ... Salem, Mass., 1860.

Uncommercial Traveller, The. *Charles Dickens.* Notes by ... in "All the Year Round." L. 1861–68.

Unda. *Thomas S. Muir.* Inchcolm, Aberdour, North Rona, Sula Sgeir ... Edinb. 1872.

Undergraduate, An. *Rev. Thomas Whytehead, M.A.* College life. Letters by ... 1845.

Undergraduate, An. *Rev. Thomas Agar Holland, M.A.* (?). The colossal statue of William Wallace: a poem. By ... Oxf. 1824.

Undergraduate, An. *Rev. Richard Polwhele.* The follies of Oxford; or, cursory sketches on a university education from ... to his friend in the country. L. 1785.

Undergraduate, An. *George Horne*, Bishop of Norwich. A letter to the Reverend Doctor Priestley. By ... Oxf. 1787.

Undergraduate, An. *John Delaware Lewis.* Our college, leaves from ... Scribbling book. L. 1857.

Undergraduate, An. *William Penn.* Vindiciæ Britannicæ ... By ... L. 1794.

Undergraduate of the University of Oxford, An. *Benjamin Bailey.* A discourse inscribed to the memory of the Princess Charlotte Augusta. L. 1817.

Underhill, Doctor Updike. *Royall Tyler.* The Algerine captive; or, the life and adventures of ... Walpole, N.H., 1797.

Underwriter, An. *Samuel A. Wells.* Opinion of the Supreme Judicial Court of Massachusetts in the case of W. Eager v. the Atlas Ins. Co. With remarks ... by ... B. 1833.

Uneducated Man, An. *Thomas Flindell.* Prison recreations ... Exeter, 1822.

Unfeigned Admirer of genuine British Jurisprudence, An. *Henry Constantine Jennings.* A free enquiry into the enormous increase of attornies ... Chelmsford, 1785.

Unfortunate Nobleman, An. *Thomas Christopher Banks.* The detection of infamy ... n.p. 1816.

Uniche. *Mrs. R. A. Heavlin.* The mysteries of Isis, by ... N.Y. 1858.

Unitarian, A. *L. Foot.* A few words of plain truth ... By ... 1832.

Unitarian, The. *Lant Carpenter, LL.D.* The Unitarian's appeal ... Bristol, 1817.

Unitarian Clergyman, An. *Henry Ware, Jr., D.D.* Reply of ... to the "Letter of a gentleman in Boston" [L. Tappan]. B. 1828.

Unitarian Layman, A. *H. J. Huidekoper.* Unitarianism the doctrine of the Bible ... By ... Pittsburgh, Penn., 1843.

University Man, A. *George Carrington.* Colonial adventures and experiences. By ... L. 1871.

University Pen, An. *Luke Howard.* Extracts from the Spiritual Bee ... L. 1823.

University Professor, An. *Alexander Harvey, M.D.* Man's place and bread unique in nature, and his pedigree human not semian ... Edinb. 1865.

Unknown, An. *George Mollett Murphy.* The slave among pirates; or, "Uncle Tim's" many editors: a satire. By ... L. 1852.

Unknown Friend, An. *Rev. George Garden.* A letter to the Episcopal clergy in Scotland ... Edinb. 1703.

Dated M.DC.III., but published in 1703.

Untaught Minstrel, An. *Elizabeth N. Lockerby.* The wild brier ... Charlottetown, 1866.

Unus quorum. *William Wadd, Esq., F.L.S.* Nugæ canoræ; or, epitaphian mementoes (in stone-cutter's verse) of the Medici family of modern times. By ... L. 1827.

Unworthy Member of that Community, An. *John Rutty.* The liberty of the spirit and of the flesh distinguished: in an address to those captives in spirit among the people called Quakers, who are commonly called Libertines. By ... P. 1759.

Upholsterer, An. *A. J. Kay.* The age of gold; and other poems. By ... L. 1851.

Upper Graduate, An. *Rev. Alexander Geddes.* A letter to the Right Rev. the Archbishops and Bishops of England ... By ... L. 1790.

Upper Servant, An. *Jonathan Swift, D.D.* Advice to servants, by ... 172-.

Upper Servant, An. *John Jones.* Hints to servants: being a poetical and modernized version of Dean Swift's "Directions to Servants" ... L. 1843.

Urban, Sylvanus. The pseudonym adopted by the managing editor of the "Gent. Mag.," from its commencement in 1731 to the present day.

"It is intended to typify the interest taken by the periodical in both town and country affairs."
—— trifles for the "Morning Post,"
And nothing for Sylvanus Urban.
— W. M. PRAED, "The Vicar."

Utis, U. Donough [you don't know who 'tis]. *Richard Grant White.*

Utopiensis, Bernardus. *John Rutty.* A second dissertation on the liberty of preaching granted to women by the people called Quakers ... By ... Dublin, 1739.

Uvedale, Christian, M.D. *Sir John Hill.* The construction of the nerves ... L. 1758.

V.

V. *Orville J. Victor.* The American Rebellion. N.Y. 1862.

V. *Mrs. Caroline (Wigley) Clive.* Poems. L. 1872.

V., A. J. *Abraham John Valpy.* Q. Horatii Flacci opera. Edited by ... L. 1818.

V., C. *Charles Vallancey, LL.D.* An essay towards illustrating the ancient history of the Britannic Isles ... L. 1786.

V., C. M. *C. M. Vaughan.* An advanced reading book. L. 1866.

V. D. C. *Ch. Fr. Valentin de Cullion.* Examen de l'esclavage ... Paris, 1802.

V., F. E. J. *Francis Edward Jackson Valpy.* Sacræ historiæ veteris epitome ... L. 1862.

V., G. *Gilbert Venables.* Facts and comments bearing on Mr. Morgan's Burials Bill. L. 1873.

V., G. *George Vivian.* Some illustrations of the architecture of Claverton and of the Duke's house, Bradford, etc. L. 1837.

V., G. G. *G. G. Vaudoncourt.* Letters on the internal political state of Spain during 1821–23. L. 1825.

V., G. L. *Mrs. G. L. Vanderbuilt.* A kite story. A birthday festival ... N.Y. 1871.

V., H. *H. Vizetelly.* Christmas with the poets: a collection of songs ... Embellished ... by Birket Foster, etc. Edited by ... L. 1851.

V., H. *Herbert Vaughan.* Devotions for Advent, Christmas, and the Epiphany (Paschal Time ... Whitsuntide) ... L. 1867.

V., H. F. *Henrietta F. Valpy.* Autumnal leaves, etc. L. 1834.

V., I. *Mrs. Isabella Jane (Houlton) Vivian.* To Mrs. Henry Austin Bruce. The midnight watch. Words and music by ... L. 1876.

V., J. *John Vizard.* Narrative of a tour through France, Italy, and Switzerland ... L. 1872.

V., L. *Louis Viardot.* Apologie d'un Incrédule. Paris, 1868.

V., L. *Mrs. Laura (Jewry) Valentine.* Beautiful bouquets gathered from the poets of all countries ... Selected and edited by ... L. 1869.

V., Mary V. *Thomas Jefferson (?).* A dialogue between a Southern delegate and his spouse, on his return from the Grand Continental Congress. A frag-ment, inscribed to the married ladies of America, by ... N.Y. 1774.

V., R. *Richard Valpy.* The second part of King Henry the Fourth, altered by ... L. 1801.

V. S. N. *David Dakers Black.* Legal reform in Scotland proposed ... Edinb. 1731.

The letters "V. S. N." are the initials of *Virtus sola nobilitas,* the notarial docquet of D. D. B.

V., T. *T. Veasey.* Hours of solitude; or, poetical recreations of a bachelor. By ... L. 1851.

V——, Emilia. *Emilia Viviana.* Epipsychidion. Verses addressed [by P. B. Shelley] to the noble and unfortunate lady ... now imprisoned in the convent of —— (St. Anne, Pisa. With an advertisement signed S., *i.e.* P. B. Shelley]. L. 1821.

V., Lady V—ss. *Lady Viscountess Vane.* A letter to ... occasioned by the publication of her memoirs in the "Adventures of Peregrine Pickle." L. 1751.

V*, Mr. de.** *François Marie Arouët de Voltaire.* Histoire de Charles XII., Roi de Suède, par ... Basle, 1731.

Vagabond. *Adam Badeau.* The vagabond. N.Y. 1859.

Vagabondia. *Mrs. Frances Hodgson Burnett.*

"At seven, Frances' 'Stories' were the delight of her brothers and sisters. We can well imagine no day dreary, and no evening could be long in that household, a circle which in later years has become familiar through her pen as 'Vagabondia.' The first essay at a story that might go beyond the approving audience of 'Vagabondia' was attempted in her 13th year; written and read, not told, to her two sisters, when she was nearly 15." — From the Boston "Sunday Herald."

Valbert, G. *Victor Cherbuliez.* Hommes et choses d'Allemagne. 1877.

Valdarfer, Cristofer. *Joseph Haslewood.* Bibliomaniac ballad. L. 1815 (?).

Vale, Ferna. *Miss E. V. Hallett.* Natalie; or, a gem among the sea-weeds ... Andover, Mass., 1858.

Valens. *Richard Burke.* About 1770 *et seq.* The three Burkes, Edmund, Richard, and William, wrote for the London "Evening Post." Richard was the principal contributor, under the signature of "Valens."

Valentine. *Rev. Joseph Holden Pott, M.A.* The tour of ... L. 1786.

Valentine. David T. *William I.*

Paulding. History of the City of New York. By ... N.Y. 1853.

This work was compiled by *Mr. Paulding,* though published under the name of Mr. Valentine.

Valentine, Floyd. *Floyd Vail,* in contributions to the "Freeman's Journal" (1884), etc.

Valérie. *Mme. Wilhelmine Joséphine Simonin Fould.*

Valerius. One of the pseudonyms attributed to Junius (*q.v.*).

The first letter, signed as above, is dated May 12, 1768, and relates to the Duke of Portland's case, in reply to a defence of the grant to Sir James Lowther. Another letter, dated August 23, 1768, relates to Sir Jeffery Amherst.

Valerius. *William Coombe.* The letters of ... on the state of parties, etc. Originally published in the "Times." L. 1804.

Valery. *Antoine Claude Pasquin.* Italy and its comforts. Manual of tourists. By ... L. 1841.

Valmy, Alfred de. *Julius Stinde.* Die Opfer der Wissenschaft. 1879.

Valrey, Max. *Mme. Miller.* Les confidences d'une Puritaine. Paris, 1865.

Van. *David W. Bartlett,* in the "Springfield Republican."

Van Augustine. *John G. Abbott,* in letters to the Boston "Herald," from Maine and later on from Cuba.

Van Engelgom. *Jules Lecomte.* Lettres sur les écrivains français. Brussels, 1837.

Van Scelter, Helter. *Rev. James Ridley.* The schemer; or, universal satirist. By that great philosopher ... L. 1763.

Van Tromp. *Lucius Manlius Sargent.* No. 1 of the new milk cheese; or, the comi-heroic thunderclap. B. 1807.

Van Truesdale, Pheleg. *Frederic Colburn Adams.* Life and adventures of Maj. Roger Sherman Potter. N.Y. 1858.

Van West, Rupert. *Daniel C. Eddy.* Rip Van Winkle's travels in Asia and Africa. 188–.

Vanbustle, Timothy, M.D. *John Woodward, M.D.* The art of getting into practice in physic, etc. [A satire on Dr. Mead.] L. 1722.

Vance, Clara. *Mrs. Mary A. Denison.* Andy Luttrell. B. 1869.

Vandegrift, Margaret. *Margaret Janvier.*

Vandelli, Dominick, LL.D. *James Cavanah Murphy.* A general view of the state of Portugal ... L. 1798.

Vanderdecken. *William Cooper.* Yachts and yachting ... L. 1873.

Vane, Paul. *Frank W. Potter.*

Vane, Violet. *Mrs. Jane L. Howell* Justine's lovers. N.Y. 1878.

Vanella. *The Hon. Anne Vane.* The fair concubine; or, the secret history of the beautiful Vanella. Containing her amours with Albimarides [J. Hervey, Baron Hervey], P. Alexis [*i.e.* Frederick, Prince of Wales], etc. L. 1732.

Vanessa. *Miss Esther Vanhomrigh,* a lady acquaintance of Dean Swift.

Vanished Hand, A. *Mortimer Collins.* Pen sketches by ... L. 1879.

Varina. *Miss Jane Warying,* a friend of Dean Swift.

Varney. *Thomas Griffiths Wainewright,* the prototype of "Varney" in Bulwer's "Lucretia."

Varvicensis, Philopatris. *Samuel Parr, D.D.* Characters of the late Charles James Fox. L. 1809.

Vaughn, Mrs. Marion. *Mrs. Stella (Scott) Gilman.* Mothers in council. N.Y. 1884.

Vedastus. — See "Telarius."

Velasques. *Harvey D. Little,* who, about 1830, contributed poetry, under this signature, to an obscure paper published in the interior of Ohio, at St. Clairsville.

Vely, Emma. *Emma (Couvely) Simon.* Gratiana. Herzberg, 1880.

Venator. *William Elliott.* — See "Piscator."

Venerable Nestor Ironsides. *Richard Steele.* The name under which he wrote "The Guardian."

Venerated Nobleman, A. *William Wentworth, Earl of Fitzwilliam.* A letter ... to the Earl of Carlisle ... Dublin, 1795.

Veni Vidi. *Mrs. Jennie (Cunningham) Croly,* in her contributions to various periodicals.

Venner, Arthur. *William McCrillis Griswold.* His signature in the magazines.

Verax. *Morris Moore.* The abuses of the National Gallery ... L. 1847.

Verax. *Rev. Francis A. Fleming.* The calumnies of Verus; or, Catholics vindicated ... in a series of letters published in different Gazettes at Philadelphia. Collected and revised by ... P. 1792.

Verax. *Thomas Foster.* Christian Unitarianism vindicated ... L. 1808.

Verax. *Henry Dunckley.* The Crown and the Cabinet: five letters on the biography of the Prince Consort, etc. L. 1878.

Verax. *Dr. Edward Carbutt.* The letters of ... on the currency ... Manchester, 1829.

Verax. *William Godwin.* Letters of ... to the Morning Chronicle, on the assumed grounds of the present war. L. 1815.

Verax. *Robert Blakey* and *George Herbert Townsend.* No Popery: stanzas, in two cantos. Edited by ... L. 1854.

Verax. *Samuel Alexander.* Remarks on Dr. Adams Clarke's discourse on the nature, institution, and design of the Holy Eucharist ... By ... Stockport, 1819.

Verdad. *Gen. F. F. Millen,* in his contributions to various California periodicals.

Verdello, Cordrac. *Richard Harris.* The English press and its poets: a satire. L. 1856.

Verdery, Emily. *Mrs. Emily Verdery Battey,* in the New York "Sun," the "Woman's World," etc. 1870.

Verena, Sophie. *Sophie (Mödinger) Alberti.* Altes und Neues. 1879.

Veridicus. *Richard Whitworth, M.P.* for Stafford, a frequent contributor to the "Public Advertiser" during 1769. — See the Private Letters of Junius, No. 6.

Veritas. *George S. McWatters* employed this signature in a letter exposing some existing evils of Bellevue Hospital (N.Y.).

Veritas. *E. C. Walker,* in his contributions to the "Spirit of the Times" (N.Y.).

Veritas. *Rev. Andrew MacGeorge.* The Church of Scotland and the Free Church ... Glasgow, 1870.

Veritas. *Hon. John Richardson.* The letters of ... Montreal, 1822.

Verité, Auguste. *Jules Fournier,* a Montreal merchant, who, since 1864, has occasionally contributed to "La Minerve," Montreal, under the signature above.

Verité sans Peur. *Frederic James Prouting,* in his contributions to various English periodicals.

Vermond, Paul. *Eugène Guinot.* — See "Durand, Pierre."

Vernon, Judge. *E. C. Tuttle,* in his contributions to various Western periodicals.

Vernon, Henry. *George Wightwick.* The life and remains of Wilmot Warwick. Ed. by ... L. 1828.

Vernon, Ruth. *Stopford J. Ram.* Unseen hand ... Cin. 1863.

Versatile, Val. *Harry Enton,* in his contributions to the "Sun" (Baltimore, Md.).

Vertaur. *J. H. Trumbull,* in "Notes and Queries" and elsewhere.

Verus. *Francis Webb, Esq.,* who "wrote a series of letters in the 'Diary,' under the signature of 'Verus,' on the subject of the dispute with Spain respecting Nootka Sound. These were reprinted in a pamphlet."

Verus. *Edward Burton.* An address to his fellow-countrymen, in a letter from ... in allusion to some of the popular doctrines agitated at the present time, and guarding his countrymen against delusion. L. 1820.

Verus. *John Taylor.* Currency explained ... L. 1843.

Verus. *Timothy Pickering.* Letters of ... to the native Americans. P. 1797.

Verus. *Sir James Bland Burges Lamb, Bart., D.C.L.* Letters on the Spanish Aggression at Nootka. L. 1790.

Verus. *Don Luis Onis.* Observations on the existing differences between the government of Spain and the United States. P. 1817.

Very Exalted Subject in his Majesty's Dominions, A. *George,* Prince of Wales. — See "Albion."

Very learned Man of the Church of England, A. *Henry Dodwell, D.D.* An abstract of common principles ... out of the "Vindication of the deprived bishops, etc., by ... By Edward Stephens. L. 1700.

Vestris, Mons., Sen. *Dr. John Nott.* An heroic epistle ... to Mademoiselle Heinel in France. With notes. n.p. 1781.

Veteran. One of the pseudonyms attributed to Junius (*q.v.*).

The letters thus signed (January to May, 1772) are all directed against Lord Barrington.

Vétéran de 1812, Un. *Sir Étienne Paschal Taché, Knt., M.D.* Quelques réflexions sur l'organisation des volontaires et de la milice de cette province ... Quebec, 1863.

Veteran Observer, A. *Edward Deering Mansfield,* editor at Cincinnati, 1835–51, and at N.Y.C. from 1853–71.

Veteran Soldier, A. *John Frost (?).* The heroes and battles of the American Revolution ... P. 1845.

Veteran Stager, A. *G. Grant.* An essay on the science of acting. L. 1828.

Veteran Traveller, A. *William Rae Wilson.* Notes abroad and rhapsodies at home, by ... L. 1837.

Veto. *Theodore Sedgwick, Jr.,* in the New York "Evening Post."

Vetus. *Edward Sterling,* in his letters contributed to the "Times" (L. 1812–13).

"Voluntary letters, I suppose, without payment or pre-engagement, one successful letter calling out another, till 'Vetus' and his doctrines came to be a distinguishable entity, and the business amounted to something; but of my own earliest newspaper reading, I can remember the name 'Vetus' as a kind of editorial hacklog, on which able editors were wont to chop straw now and then."— THOMAS CARLYLE.

Vetus. *Charles Marsh.* The famous letters of "Vetus" in the "Times" have been confidently ascribed to his pen. These letters were republished in 1812 in two parts, with a preface and notes.

Vetus. *Benjamin Bailey, D.D.* Six letters of ... to the editor of the "Ceylon Times" ... Columbo, 1852.

Vey, Elinor. *Mrs. Elliot Glover,* in the New York "Independent."

Viator. *William Beckford,* in his contributions to the "Literary Gazette" (L. 1823).

Viator. *Jonathan Huntington Bright,* who was for several years a writer for the public journals and literary magazines under this signature.

Viator. *William Jerdan,* in the London "Sun." 1814 *et seq.*

Viator. *George Lipscomb, M.D.,* by whose hand numerous articles appeared in the "Gent. Mag.," chiefly under this signature.

Viator. *Thomas D'Oyly.* Edward Somers ... L. 1843.

Viator. *Joseph B. Varnum, Jr.* Washington sketch-book. N.Y. 1864.

Viator, John, Esq. *Samuel Andrew Peters.* An answer to Dr. Inglis's defence of his character against certain false and malicious charges ... By ... L. 1785.

Viator, Vacuus. *Thomas Hughes,* the writer of the series of letters in the London "Spectator," describing the new settlement at Rugby, Tennessee. These letters were afterwards published as the 2d part of a pamphlet entitled "Rugby, Tennessee ... N.Y. 1881.

Viator Verax. *Rev. George Musgrave, M.A.* Cautions to tourists ... L. 1863.

Vicar, A Late. *Rev. Robert Masters, B.D.* A short account of the parish of Waterbeach, in the diocese of Ely ... Camb. 1795.

Vicar of Cudham. *Samuel Ayscough.* Account of the parish of Cudham, in Kent, in "Gent. Mag.," September, 1804, p. 830.

Vicar of Frome-Selwood, The. *T. Clissold.* Swedenborg's writings and Catholic teaching; or, a voice from the new church porch, in answer to a series of articles on the Swedenborgians, by ... [Rev. William James Early Bennett] in "The old church porch." L. 1858.

Vicar of Holbeach, The. *Cecil Willis, D.D.* The nature of Agistment Tithe of unprofitable stock, illustrated in the case of the Vicar of Holbeach. 1778.

Vicar of Morwenstow, The. *Rev. Robert Stephen Hawker, M.A.* Rural synods. By ... Cornwall. L. 1844.

Vicar of Napton, The. *Rev. Henry Windsor Villiers Stuart.* The royal wedding [of the Prince of Wales], and the national festivities. A sermon preached by ... L. 1863.

Vicar of the Church of England, A. *Rev. Joseph Bosworth.* The Episcopal Church of Scotland proved to be in full communion with the Church of England ... L. 1849.

Vicarius Cantianus. *Samuel Pegge.* "A stricture of D. Ducarel's repertory." "Gent. Mag.," 1763, p. 441. See "Gent. Mag.," LXVI., p. 982.

Victim, A. *George Chittenden Benham.* A year of wreck. A true story ... N.Y. 1880.

Victor. *Percy Bysshe Shelley.* Original poetry by Victor and Cazire. 1810.

"Cazire" is the poet's friend, Miss Grove. "Some of the pieces are borrowed bodily from Matthew Gregory Lewis."

Victor, Verity. *E. M. Wright.* Behind the scenes: a story of the stage. B. 1870.

Videbimus, Joannes. *Jacques Albin Simon Collin de Plancy.* Trésor de la chanson ... Paris, 1849.

Video. *Jonathan Couch.* Words and phrases common at Polperro in Cornwall, but not used elsewhere, in "Notes and Queries." 1854.

Vidette. *Jefferson E. P. Doyle,* in the New York "Globe Democrat."

Vidette. *J. J. Elliott,* in his contributions to the "Picayune" (New Orleans, La.).

Vidocq. *Col. Charles Ashton Hawkins* (?). "The great ether question ... "National Police Gazette" (N.Y. 1852).

Vierge. *Virginia Beecroft.*

Vieux garçon, Un. *Alphonse Cynosuridis.* Mémoires d' ... Montreal, 1865.

Vieux Moustache. *Clarence Gordon.* Boarding-school days. N.Y. 1873.

Vigilans. *Rev. Charles Valentine Le Grice, M.A.* Letters on Church questions. Truro, 1845.

Vigilant. *R. Mitchell,* in his contributions to the "Sportsman" (L.).

Vigilant. *F. W. Vosburgh,* in his contributions to the "Spirit of the Times" (N.Y.).

Vigilant and Wizard. *John Corlett.*

"Racing Prophet," in "Sporting Times" and "Sportsman."

Vigornius. *Samuel Melancthon Worcester, D.D.* Essays on slavery . . . 1826.

Vigors, N. A., Jun. *Rev. Frederick Nolan, LL.D., F.R.S.* An inquiry into the nature and extent of poetick. licence. L. 1810.

Village Apothecary, A. *W. F. Deacon.* Murder will out; or, confessions of . . . St. John, 186–.

Village Curate, A. *Rev. William Glenn.* Temperance lecture, by . . . [in verse]. L. 1877.

Village Schoolmaster. *Charles M. Dickinson,* in several tales.

Villard, Henry. *Heinrich Hilgard,* correspondent of the New York "Tribune" just before the civil war, and rose to eminence as a newspaper writer during that period.

Villiers, Lt. Wainwright, U.S.N. *Frank Cahill,* in his contributions to the "Saturday Press" (P.), etc.

Vincent, Ellerton. *M. C. Logan.* The artist's dream. 18–.

Vincent, John, Esq. *Jedediah Vincent Huntington.* The pretty plate . . . N.Y. 1852.

Vincent, William, of Gray's Inn. *Thomas Holcroft.* Plain and succinct narrative of the late riots and disturbances in the cities of London and Westminster, and the borough of Southwark. L. 1780.

Vindex. — See "Antiquarius."

Vindex. One of the signatures adopted by Junius (*q.v.*).

The two letters thus signed are dated February 22 and March 6, 1771, and treat upon the Spanish declaration.

Vindex. *Samuel Adams,* in the "Boston Gazette," 1768, 1770, 1771, April 20, 1772.

Vindex. *John Butler,* Bishop of Hereford. Some of his political tracts in defence of Lord North's measures are said to have appeared under the name of "Vindex."

Vindex. *Dr. John Loveday,* in "Gent. Mag.," Vol. LVII., p. 135, notice of Bacon's "Liber Regis."

Vindex. *E. J. Newell,* in his contributions to the "Evening Post" (N.Y.).

Vindex. *Lorenzo Sabine.* His signature to a discussion in the "Home Journal," 1848, between him, "Vindex," and H. C. Van Schaack, and H. Onderdonk, Jr., in regard to General De Lancey's conduct to General Woodhull.

Vindex. *Rev. John Poage Campbell.* Answer to Stone's reply. 1806.

Vindex. *Patrick Ellison.* Candid animadversions respecting a petition to the late General Assembly of Maryland, in behalf of the Episcopal ministers in the same. Balt. 1783.

Vindex. *Very Reverend Thomas Maguire.* Clergé Canadien vengé par ses ennemis . . . Quebec, 1834.

Vindex. *Henry Rogers.* The eclipse of faith . . . L. 1852.

Vindex. *Joseph Gurney Bevan.* An examination of the first part of a pamphlet called "An appeal to the Society of Friends." By . . . L. 1802.

Vindex. *Sir Frederick Morton Eden, Bart.* On the maritime rights of Great Britain. L. 1807.

Vindex. *Mr. Hannay,* of Marylebone Bank. Letter to William Clay, Esq. . . . L. 1836.

Vindex. *Thomas Maguire.* Observations d'un Catholique sur l'histoire du Canada . . . Quebec, 1827.

Vindex. *John M. Gordon.* Tableau No. 16; or, a box on both ears. Norfolk, Va., 1872.

Vindicator. *Rev. William Woodis Harvey.* An impartial view of the state of religion in Penzance and its vicinity . . . Penzance, 1824.

Vindicator of Mr. Wesley's Minutes, The. *Rev. Mr. — Fletcher,* of Madeley Co., Salop. A third check to Antinomianism, in a letter to the author of "Pietas Oxoniensis" [Sir Richard Hill]. By . . . L. 1772.

Vinegar, Captain Hercules. *Henry Fielding,* who, in 1739, wrote for "Champion" under this signature.

Viola. *Mrs. Fanny (Murdaugh) Downing,* who began to write for the public under this signature. Author of "Five Little Girls and Two Little Boys." Evanston, 1878.

Viola. *Mrs. Laura M. (Hawley) Thurston,* who, under this signature, published her poems in the "Louisville Journal," and in Gallagher's "Hesperian," Columbus, O.

Viola. *Kathinka (Halein) Zitz.*

Viola, Le. *Col. Thomas Picton.*

Violet, Corporal or **Daddy** (Fr. Caporal la Violette *or* Papa la Violette). *Napoleon Bonaparte.*

"A name given to the Emperor by his partisans in France after his banishment to Elba, and designed to express their hope that he would return in the spring (of 1815)."

Violet, Monsieur. *Frederick Marryat.* The narrative of . . . in California, Sonora, and Western Texas. L. 1839.

Violette. *Mrs. Marion Eva Garrick.* Her *nom de théâtre.*

Virginia. *Miss Virginia E. Davidson,* who, under this signature, wrote for the "Southern Opinion" (Richmond, Va.).

Virginia, Cousin. *Virginia W. Johnson.* Calderwood secret. N.Y. 187–.

Virginia Confederate, A. *A. M. Keiley.* In vinculis; or, the prisoner of war ... N.Y. 1866.

Virginia Physician, A. *P. S. Ruter, M.D.* Reminiscences of ... Louisville, 1849.

Virginian, A. *Robert Tyler.* Ahasuerus: a poem. N.Y. 1842.

Virginian, A. *George Tucker.* A defence of the character of Thomas Jefferson against a writer in the New York "Review" [Dr. F. L. Hawks]. By ... N.Y. 1838.

Virginian, A. *James H. Price.* Don Paez; and other poems ... N.Y. 1847.

Virginian, A. *William A. Carruthers.* The Kentuckian in New York; or, the adventures of three Southerners. N.Y. 1834.

Virginian, A. — *Gardner.* The life and death of Sam, in Virginia ... Richmond, 1856.

Virginian, A. *John Esten Cooke.* The life of Stonewall Jackson from official papers ... by ... N.Y. 1863.
Usually, but incorrectly, attributed to *John M. Daniel.*

Virginian, A. *Francis W. Gilmer, Esq.* Original and miscellaneous essays, by ... Richmond, 1829.

Virginian, A. *John H. Gilmer.* Southern politics; what we are and what we will be ... Richmond, 1867.

Virginian, A. *Angus W. Macdonald.* The two rebellions; or, treason unmasked ... Richmond, 1865.

Visionary, The. *Sir Walter Scott,* who, in 1821, contributed some political lucubrations to the "Edinburgh Weekly Journal" under the head of "The Visionary."

Visiter, A. *Stephen Weston.* A slight sketch of Paris ... by ... L. 1814.

Visitor, A. *Dr. John Croghan.* Rambles in the Mammoth Cave in 1844 ... Louisville, 1845.

Vissch. *William L. Visscher,* in his contributions to various Western periodicals.

Visto. *W. S. Jordan,* of San Francisco, Cal., in his contributions to various European periodicals.

Vitalis. *Erik Sjöberg.* Poésies completes. Stockholm, 1828.

Viva. *Miss Eva Williams,* in her contributions to the "Evening Journal" (Jersey City, N.J.).

Vive Valeque. *Rev. John Eagles.* "Once upon a time," in "Blackwood's Magazine," Vol. 77, p. 685 *seq.*
Other articles in "Blackwood's Magazine" under the same signature are by him.

Vivian. *George Henry Lewes,* in the London "Leader," 1852.

Voice from Kentucky, A. *William Coleman.* Appeal to the people of the North. Louisville, Ky., 1861.

Voluntary Advocate, A. *Adam Thomson, D.D.* Appeal from Scotland ... Edinb. 1834.

Volunteer, A. *Col. George Chesney.* Battle of Dorking, reminiscences of ... Edinb. 1871.

Volunteer, A. *B. F. Scribner.* Camp life of ... A Campaign in Mexico. P. 1847.

Volunteer, A. *John Beatty.* The citizen-soldier; or, memoirs of a volunteer. Cin. 1879.

Volunteer, A. *Anna Letitia Barbauld.* Sins of government, sins of the nation ... By ... L. 1793.

Volunteer in the United States Service, A. *Henry Howard Brownell.* Lyrics of a day; or, newspaper poetry by ... N.Y. 1866.

Vouziers, M. de. *P. D. Moithey.* Marie Antoinette d'Autriche, reine de France et de Navarre. Paris, about 1816.

Voyager, A. *George Hill.* The ruins of Athens; with other poems. By ... W. 1831.

Voyager, A. *William Scoresby.* Tales of ... to the Arctic Ocean. L. 1826.

Voyageur, Un. *Amandine Lucile Aurore (Dupin) Dudevant.* Lettres d' ... Paris, 1857.

Voyageur, Un. *Xavier Marmier.* Poésies d' ... 1834–78. Paris, 1882.

Voyageur, Anglois, Un. *Martin Sherlock.* Lettres d' ... Geneva, 1779.

Vyse, Bertie. *Arthur William A'Beckett.* On strike. L. 1873.

W.

W. *Sir John Bowring.* His signature to the postscript to an article in the "Westminster Review" for January, 1841.

W. *William Hazlitt,* in the London "Examiner," Dec. 24, 1815.

W. *William Cowper Prime,* in the New York "Journal of Commerce."

W. *Hon. William B. Whitehead,* in his meteorological contributions to the "Daily Advertiser" (Newark, N.J.).

W. *Henriette (Guizot) de Witt,* known for her educational works, and her translations from the English, signed at first with this initial.

W. *Rev. Francis Wrangham.* — See "P. J."

W. *Thomas Webster.* The Holy Bible ... With short notes, etc. Ed. by ... L. 1810.

W. *Richard Walker.* The legend of Cosmo ... By Basil. L. 1860.

W. *Samuel Hurd Walley.* National finances. B. 1863.

W. *W. Elliot Woodward.* Records of Salem witchcraft, copied from the original documents, by ... 1864.

W., A. *Alexander Wilder, M.D.* His signature in the "Young Men's Mag.," and similar periodicals.

W., A. *A. Wilkinson, M.D.* Brief historical notices of the parishes of Hurstbourn Priors and St. Mary Bourn, etc., Hampshire ... By ... L. 1861.

W., A. *William Atkinson Warwick.* The clergyman's companion. Ed. by ... L. 1846.

W., A. *Aaron West.* A plain address ... to the Churches of Christ ... In two letters. By ... L. 1797.

W., A. *Ambrose Weston.* Two letters describing a method of increasing the quality of circulating-money, etc. 1799.

W., Mrs. A. *Mrs. Anna Weamys.* — See "Young Gentlewoman, A."

W., A., farmer. *Rev. Isaac Wilkins.* Congress canvassed. N.Y. 1775.
Also ascribed to *Samuel Seabury.*

W., A., M.D., Reg. Coll. Med. Edin. Soc. *Andrew Wilson.* Bath waters: a conjectural idea of their nature and qualities, in three letters ... L. 1788.

W., A. C. Q. *Mrs. Anna C. (Quincy) Waterston.* Verses. B. 1863.

W., A. D. T. *Mrs. Adeline D. (Train) Whitney.* Faith Gartney's childhood. By .. B. 1863.

W., A. L. *Miss Anna Letitia Waring.*
Hymns and meditations. By ... L. 1850.

W., A. M. *Mrs. Ann Michell Wood.* Verses with imitations and translations. By ... L. 1842.

W., A. O. *A. O. Wheeler.* Eyewitness; or, life scenes in the Old North State ... By ... B. 1865.

W., B. *Basil Woodd.* The Psalms of David ... Ed. by ... L. 1800.

W., C. *Christopher Wordsworth.* Defensio Ecclesiæ Anglicanæ, etc. Ed. by ... L. 1847.

W. C. *Charles Clarke.* "The Fresh Water Whale," contributed to the "Monthly Magazine" (L. 1832).

W., C. *Charlotte White.* Hymns for the cottage. By ... L. 1840.

W., C. *Charles Winston.* An inquiry into the difference of style observable in ancient glass paintings, especially in England. By C. W. Oxf. 1847. — See "Amateur, An."

W., C. *Rev. Charles Walker.* Plain suggestions for a ceremonial after Sarum use ... L. 1867.

W., C. *Rev. Charles Woodward.* Reminiscences of an interesting event, presented to his friends by the late Churchwarden of St. Mary's Islington. L. 1832.

W., C. *Charles Wildegoose.* A short and plain address to his cottage neighbours. By an old resident in the parish of Staverton. Daventry, 1840.

W., C. *Charles Wordsworth,* Bishop of St. Andrews. Tres hymni ad usum scholarium Wiccamicorum ... Latine redditi by ... L. 1845.

W., C. *Rev. Charles Wooley.* A two years' journal in New York: and part of its Territories in America. By ... L. 1701.

W., C., A.M. *Charles Wooley.* Poems. By ... L. 1868.

W., C., M.D. *Clifton Wintringham.* Observations on Dr. Friend's history of Physick ... By ... L. 1726.

W., Mrs. Charles. *Mrs. Charles Wightman.* Haste to the rescue; or, work while it is day. By ... L. 1859.

W., C. A. *C. A. Wheeler.* Sportscrapiana. Cricket and shooting ... L. 1867.

W., Captain the Honble C. S. *Captain and the Hon. Charles Stuart Wortley.* Journal of an excursion to

Antwerp, during the siege of the citadel in December, 1832. By . . . L. 1833.

W., C. E. *Charles Edmund Webber.* Military work by military labour. By an officer of the Royal Engineers . . . L. 1869.

W., C. H. *Charles H. Wharton, D.D.* A reply to an address to the Roman Catholics of the United States of America. By . . . P. 1785.

W., C. J. *Rev. Charles James Wilding.* A sermon on the rainbow . . . Preached at Arley . . . 1870. By . . . Bewdley, 1870.

W., C. K. *Charles King Whipple.* The American Tract Society. B. 1859.

W., C. R. *C. R. Williams.* Home letters, etc. Compiled by . . . L. 1878.

W., C. S. *Charles Stearns Wheeler.* Biographical notices of . . . C. Hayward . . . and . . . S. Hildreth. Camb. 1839.

W., C. T. *C. T. Wheler.* The Crystal Hive; or, the first of May, 1851. By . . . L. 1852.

W., C. W. *Charles W. Wood.* "A Drive to the Land's End," in the "Argosy," 1874.

W. D. *Rev. Samuel Denne.* His signature in the "Gent. Mag.," 1771–99.

W. D. *Richard Derby Ness*, in his contributions to "Notes and Queries" (L.).

W., D. *Daniel Wilson*, Bishop of Calcutta. Letters from an absent brother . . . L. 1824.

W., D. *David Walther.* A serious expostulation addressed to Mr. A— J— [*i.e.* Andrew Jukes] on the subject of his recent book . . . By . . . L. 1869.

W., E. *Lady E. Wallace.* A letter to a friend, with a poem called the Ghost of Werter. By . . . L. 1787.

W., E. *Edward Ward.* The mourning prophet . . . L. 1714.

W., E. *Edward West.* Observations . . . L. 1835.

W., E. *Edward Wynne.* Observations touching the antiquity and dignity of the degree of Serjeant of Law. 1765.

W., E., and L., A. Say and seal . . . L. 1860.

The preface is signed "E. W." [*i.e.* Elizabeth Wetherell]; pseud. for *Susan Warner*, and "A. L." [*i.e.* Amy Lothrop], pseud. for *Anna B. Warner.*

W., E. H. *E. H. Watson.* Child-life in Europe . . . By . . . B. 1874.

W., E. J. *Miss E. Jane Whately.* [Richard Whately's] The judgment of conscience, and other sermons. Ed. by . . . L. 1864.

W., E. S. *E. S. Waters.* Inter-State . . . Exposition. Handbook to the bric-a-brac collection, etc. Compiled by . . . Chic. 1877.

W., F. *Forbes Benignus Winslow.* On the nature, symptoms, and treatment of cholera. By Medicus. L. 1831.

W., F. *Rev. Francis Wrangham.* Psychæ; or, songs of butterflies, by T. H. Bayly, Esq. Attempted in Latin rhymes, to the same airs; with a few additional trifles. Malton, 1828.

W., F. *Francis Wharton.* A reminiscence of Gambier. Camb. 1868. — See "L., E." [*i.e.* Lewis, Emma].

W., F. *Francis Wilson.* Where shall I worship when I am saved? In verse. By . . . L. 1879.

W., F., R.L. *Francis Wise*, Radcliffe Librarian. History and chronology of the Fabulous Ages, considered . . . L. 1764.

W., F. C. *F. C. Westley.* The new guide to Cheltenham . . . By . . . L. 1867.

W., F. G. *Francis Godolphin Waldron.* The Holy Vengeance: a Scottish ballad, by . . . 1802.

W., G. *G. Wall.* A catalogue of ferns indigenous to Ceylon . . . L. 1873.

W., G. *George Woodley.* Mount-Edgcumbe: a descriptive poem . . . Dock, 1804.

W. G. *William Frederick Deacon.* Warreniana . . . B. 1851.

W., Gilbert. *Gilbert Wakefield*, in Beloe's "Sexagenarian," Vol. 1, Chap. XIV., p. 84.

W., G. R. *George Robert Wynne.* Overton's question, and what came of it. By . . . L. 1868.

W. H. *Henry Wash.* Adelphi series [of school books]. By . . . L. 1871.

W., H. *H. Wigram (?).* Digest of rules and orders of the High Court of Judicature at Madras . . . Corrected up to 20th October, 1873, by H. W. Madras, 1874.

W., H. *H. Whately (?).* Life in a Swiss chalet, etc.: a tale by . . . L. 1878.

W., H. *Horace Walpole.* The magpie and her brood . . . Probably Strawberry Hill, 1758.

W., H. *Henry Wix.* On roach fishing . . . By . . . L. 1860.

W., H. A. *Henry Austin Whitney.* A brief account of the descendants of John and Elinor Whitney. By . . . B. 1857.

W., H. B. *Harry Brown Wilkinson.* Handbook of guaranteed furnished apartments and hotels at home and abroad. By ... L. 1873.

W., H.E.C. *Nicholas Patrick Stephen Wiseman.* Hymnus S. Casimiri in honorem Deiparæ Virginis Mariæ ... Trans. ... by ... [*i.e.*, His Eminence Cardinal Wiseman]. L. 1859.

W., H. L. *Henry L. Williams, Jr.* Bryant's new songster, etc. Ed. by ... L. 1864.

W., H. L. *Henry Lovett Woodward.* Poems of a religious kind in the "Christian Observer." L. 1835–36.

W., H. N. F. *H. N. F. Woodburn.* Senatorial functions ... By ... L. 1822.

W., H. P. *Mrs. H. P. Warner.* Our baby [poems]. N.Y. 1872.

W., H. S. *Henry Stevenson Washburn.* The vacant chair ... Words by ... Music by G. F. Root. Chicago, 1861.

W., I. *Isaac Williams.* Hymns on the catechism [of the Church of England]. By ... L. 1843.

W., J. *James White.* — See Lamb's "Elia," "The Praise of Chimney Sweepers."

W., J. *John Washington.* The Baltic pilot. Edited by ... L. 1855.

W., J. *John Wade.* The cabinet lawyer ... L. 1866.

W., J. *Rev. James White.* John Savile of Haysted: a tragedy ... By ... L. 1847.

W., J. *Jean Wallon.* M. Cousin. Paris, 1859.

W., J. *John Wilson.* The music of the soul ... in verse. L. 1829.

W., J. *John Wauchope.* The whole doctrine of the Sabbath ... Edinb. 1850.

W., J., C—t—ss of R—s—g. *Justine Wynne*, Countess of Rosemberg. Moral and sentimental essays ... L. 1785.

W., J., deceased, in usum Amicorum. *John Wilson*, of Islington, in the "Music of the Soul" ... L. 1829.

W. J., Mrs. *Mrs. J. Williamson.* Hymns for the household of faith, and lays of the Better Land ... L. 1867.

W., J., M.D. *Dr. James Wallace.* The history of the kingdom of Scotland ... Dublin, 1724.

W., J., M.O.S.B. *Joseph Wyche.* The creed expounded ... L. 1735.

W., J., of Tysoe. *John Wright.* Cottagers' family prayers. By ... Cheltenham, 1845.

W., J. E. *Jonas E. Whitley*, in his contributions to the "World" (N.Y.)

W., J. E. *John Ernest Weekes.* Lectures on art [by Henry Weekes, R.A.], with sketch of the author's life [by J. E. W.] ... L. 1880.

W., J. F. W. *Rev. John Fothergill Waterhouse Ware.* [Sadler's] Silent pastor, etc. By ... B. 1848.

W., J. H. *John Huddlestone Wynne.* Tales for youth; in thirty poems ... L. 1794.

W., J. I. *John Iliffe Wilson.* A brief history of Christ's Hospital ... By ... L. 1820.

W., J. J. *James Jacob Welsh.* A brief notice of Mr. T. Taylor, the ... Platonist ... By ... L. 1851.

W., J. J. G., of St. John's Wood. *James John Garth Wilkinson.* Improvisations from the spirit [in verse]. L. 1857.

W., J. L. *Jean L. Watson.* Bygone days in our village. Edinb. 1864.

W., J. L. *Miss Jane Louisa Willyams.* Passing hours [poems]. By ... Truro, 1863.

W., J. P. *John Philip Wood.* A sketch of the life and projects of John Law ... Edinb. 1791.

W., J. R. *Rev. John Rowland West.* A catechism on the Church. L. 1848.

W., J. R. *Rev. John Ryle Wood.* Some recollections of the last days of ... King William the Fourth. L. 1837.

W., J. S. *Rev. Joseph Stone Williams.* All nations. England. The chronology of the world ... L. 1871.

W., J. T. *J. Talboys Wheeler.* An analysis and summary of Thucydides. By ... L. 1852.

W., J. W. *J. W. Woolgar.* Catalogue of the library of the Royal Astronomical Society. November, 1850. By ... L 1850.

W., L. *Leonard Welsted.*
"'L. W.,' characterized in the 'Bathos; or, the Art of Sinking,' as a didapper, and after as an eel, is said to be this person, by Dennis, 'Daily Journal' of May 11, 1728." — CHALMERS, Vol. 31.

W., L. *Mrs. L. Whitney.* The burning of the convent ... as remembered by one of the pupils. Camb., Mass., 1877.

W. L. *Robert Lang.* The father's catechism ... Glasgow, 1726.

W., L. *Leonard Waldo.* Standard public time ... Camb. 1877.

W., L. *Sir Frederick Charles Lascelles Wraxall, Bart.* The trappers of Arkansas ... Trans. ... L. 1864.

W., L. P. *Mrs. Lucy Pauline (Wright)*

Hobart. The changed cross [in verse].
Birmingham, 1855.

W., M. *Mary Williams.* Little Ella
and the Fire King, and other tales.
Edinb. 1861.

W., M. *Maxwell Woodhull.* Our
navy . . . W. 1854.

W., M. E. C. *Rev. Mackenzie Edward
Clarke Walcott, B.D.* Leaflets [in verse].
By . . . L. 1872.

W., M. J. *M. J. Wilkinson.* Memorials of an Indian missionary; or, a
memoir of M. Wilkinson. Compiled by
a member of his family . . . L. 1859.

W., M. S. *M. S. Woodman.* Choice
receipts . . . B. 1875.

W., N. B. *Nathaniel Bagshaw Ward.*
Aspects of nature. Clapham, 1864.

W., N., C. *Nicholas Wiseman, Cardinal.*
A retrospect of many years, being verses
. . . by . . . L. 1864.

W. P. *Charles Dickens.* The "Goings
on" at Bramsby Hall. In the "Monthly
Magazine," etc., for September, 1834.

W., P. C. *Philip Carteret Webb.* A
short account of Danegeld, etc. By . . .
L. 1756.

W., R. *Richard Wharton.* Cheviot:
a poetical fragment. By R. W. Newcastle-upon-Tyne, 1817.

W., R. *Robert Walker.* From Tap-
low to Taunton. By . . . Weymouth,
1868.

W., R. *Robert White.* Going home
[a poem]. By . . . Newcastle-upon-
Tyne, 1850.

W., R. *Robert Wright.* An humble
address to the commissioners appointed
to judge of all performances relating to
the longitude . . . L. 1728.

W., R. *Robert Whatley.* A short history of a ten years' negotiation between
a prime minister [Sir R. Walpole] and a
private gentleman . . . L. 1737.

W., R., Jr. *Robert Wickliffe, Jr.*
Machiavel's political discourses . . .
Louisville, 1840.

W., R., D.P. *R. Wetham.* New Testament, translated from the Latin Vul-
gate . . . Douay, 1730–33.

W., R., M.D. *Robert Willis.* [Les-
sing's] Nathan the Wise . . . with an
introduction, etc. By . . . L. 1868.

W., R. C. *Rev. Robert Cassie Waterston.* Service book . . . B. 1846.

W., R. E. E. *Rowland Eyles Egerton
Warburton.* Hunting songs, ballads, etc.
By . . . Chester, 1834.

W., R. G. *Richard Grant White,* in
his contributions to the "New York
Times," etc.

W., R. P. *Robert Plumer Ward.*

Illustrations of human life. By . . .
L. 1837.

W. S. *Charles Chauncy,* in the "Antigionian and Bostonian beauties . . . B.
1754.

W., S. *Samuel Warren.* Cotton. By
. . . L. 1874.

W., S. *Rev. Samuel Walker.* The
doctrine of the Eucharist stated . . .
By a Presbyter of the Church of England. L. 1720.

W., S. *Susan Warner.* The letter of
credit. By . . . N.Y. 1882.

W., S. *Miss S. Waring.* The meadow
queen; or, the young botanists with the
wild-flower alphabet. By . . . L. 1836.

W., S. *S. Watts.* The religion of
Jesus . . . By . . . L. 1838.

W., S. *Stephen Weston.* A supplement to the German grammar. By . . .
L. 1829.

W., S., A.B. *Charles Chauncy, D.D.*
The Antigionian and Bostonian beauties :
a poem. Occasion'd by seeing the Assembly at St. John's, Antigua . . . and
afterwards at Boston, in King-street. By
. . . B. 1754.

W., S., A.B. *S. Walker, A.B.* Tradi-
tion is no rule now to Christians, either
of faith or practice . . . By . . . L. 1721.

W., S., F.R.S., F.S.A. *Rev. Stephen
Weston.* The praise of Paris . . . By . . .
L. 1803.

W., S. A. *Rev. Samuel Abraham
Walker.* Absolution. L. 1874.

W., S. B. *Stephen B. Wickins.* The
life of the Rev. Legh Richmond . . .
N.Y. 1842.

W., S. D. *S. D. Waring,* in his translation of "Charcoal drawing, by Auguste
Allongé." N.Y. 1876.

W., S. M. *S. M. Warren.* A compendium of the . . . works of Emanuel
Swedenborg . . . With many new extracts . . . added by the present compiler
. . . L. 1875.

W., T. — See "Amateur, An" (Wilson).

W., T. *Thomas Walters.*

"He was the author of numerous letters, under anonymous signatures, in various magazines
and public journals, for the space of half a century; more particularly as ' T. W.,' in the pages
of Sylvanus Urban." — In the "Gent. Mag."

W., T. *Thomas Warton.* "Student"
(The); or, the "Oxford and Cambridge
Monthly Miscellany." 1750–51.

"Its principal writers were Mr. Bonnell
Thornton and Mr. Coleman. Dr. Johnson contributed to it ' The Life of Dr. Francis Cheynel,'
which is subscribed with the initials, S. J—n.
The opening number has some lines by Pope.
Other authors (as Christopher Smart and Somerville) give their names . . . The articles signed

'T. W.,' are, I presume, by **Thomas Warton.**"
—"Notes and Queries," 2d Ser., Vol. IV., p.
206.

W., T. *Thurlow Weed.*

W., T. *Thomas Wilson.* A descriptive catalogue of the prints of Rembrandt, by an amateur. L. 1836.

W., T. *T. Wilkins.* An elegy on the death of A. M. Toplady. By . . . L. 1778.

W., T. *Thomas Williams.* An historic defence of experimental religion . . . L. 1795.

W., T. *Rev. Thomas Webster.* On honouring God. A sermon . . . Thames Ditton, 1835.

W., T. D. *Theodore Dwight Weld.* In memory. A. G. Weld . . . B. 1880.

W.,T. H. *Thomas H. Wynne.* [Byrd's] History of the dividing line, and other tracts, etc. Edited by . . . L. 1866.

W. W. *Thady Fitzpatrick.* — See "F., T."

W., W. *William West.* Fifty years' recollections of an old bookseller. Cork, 1835.

W., W. *William Whewell.* English hexameter translations from Schiller, Goethe, etc. By . . . L. 1847.

W., W. *W. Wileman.* The Lord's controversy with England. L. 1880.

W., W. *William Winstanley.* The new help to discourse . . . 5th ed. L. 1702.

W., W. *William Walker Wilkins.* [Quarles's] Emblems . . . With a sketch of the life and the times of the author, by . . . L. 1858.

W., W. A. *William A. Wallace.* The Great Eastern's log . . . L. 1860.

W., W. B. *William Burt Whitmarsh.* Lyra Biblica; or, Scriptural lyrics on the New Testament. By . . . L. 1873.

W., W. C. *Rev. William Chalmers Whitcomb.* The early saved . . . Compiled by . . . B. 1861.

W., W. C. B. *William Charles Bonaparte Wyse.* Sonnet: à T. Aubanel. By . . . Plymouth, 1877.

W., W. C. T. *W. C. T. Wilkinson.* The Islanders and their crowns: an allegory. By . . . L. 1874.

W., W. E. *W. E. Walker.* Proportional parallel lines . . . By . . . L. 1849.

W., W. F. *William Francis Wilkinson.* The articles of the Church of England . . . By . . . L. 1847.

W., W. G. *William George Ward.* A few words in support of No. 90 of the "Tracts for the Times" . . . Oxf. 1841.

W., W. H. *Walter Henry Watts,* a gentleman connected with the fine arts, and a member of the London press.

W., W. H. *W. H. Wyman.* The Bacon-Shakespeare literature. By . . . in the Madison (Wis.) "State Journal," April 24, 1882.

W., W. H. *William Henry Whitmore.* The Norton family . . . B. 1859.

W., W. H. J. *William Henry James Weale.* Flores ecclesiæ: the saints of the Catholic Church . . . with the flowers dedicated to them. L. 1849.

W., W. J. D. *Rev. W. J. D. Waddilove.* Report of the late Bishop of Quebec's Upper Canadian Mission Fund. To October 31st, 1838. Hexham, 1838.

W., W. L. *William Locock Webb.* The public telegraph companies (with chart). By . . . L. 1868.

W., W. W. *W. W. Wright.* A narrative of facts; with several reflexions relative to the erecting two meeting-houses at Belford . . . n.p. 1777.

W., Z. L. *Zebulon L. White,* in his contributions to the "Tribune" (N.Y.), etc.

W******, H*****. *Horace Walpole,* in Beloe's "Sexagenarian," Vol. I., Chap. 42, p. 265.

W********, J. B. *James Brydges Willyams.* Compendious treatise of modern education . . . by the late Joel McCringer, D.D. . . . with colored designs, delineated by . . . L. 1804.

W****s [*i.e.* Willibald Alexis]. *Georg Wilhelm Heinrich Haering.* Walladmor, Frei nach dem englischen von . . . 1824.

W*****cks. — *Willcocks.* Observations on the conduct of Messrs. . . . and D****n [Dawson], late bankers of the city of Dublin, towards Mr. R**d B**r [Brewer], their cashier. Dublin, 1755.

W****le, R. *Robert Walpole.* A letter . . . directed to the E[arl] of Sun-[derlan]d [respecting the report of the Committee of Secrecy]. L. 1715.

W***m, Sir. *Sir William Waller.* Plot or no plot; or . . . and his spy foil'd. L. (?) 1679 (?).

W****n, Lord. *Lord Wharton.* A letter of thanks from my . . . to the Lord Bishop of S. Asaph [W. Fleetwood] in the name of the Kit-Kat Club. [By J. Swift]. L. 1712.

W****s. *John Wilkes.* W****s feast; or, Dryden Travesti, etc. L. 1774.

W——, Mrs. *Mrs. Mary (Wollstonecraft) Godwin,* in Beloe's "Sexagenarian," I., 347. 2d ed. L. 1818.

W——, H—— M——. *Helen Maria Williams,* in Beloe's "Sexagenarian," I., 356. 2d ed. L. 1818.

W——, J——, Esq. *John Wilkes,*

Esq. Rebellion : a poem, addressed to ... late L—d M—r [Lord Mayor] of the city of L—n [London]. L. 1775.

W—'s, Mr. *William Warburton, D.D.* An answer to certain passages in ... preface to his edition of Shakspear ... L. 1748.

W——, G——. *George Wollaston, Esq.* The life and history of a pilgrim. Dublin, 1753.

W——, M——. *John M. Whitelaw.* Hours of quiet thought ... L. 1865.

W——, R. E. E. *R. E. Egerton Warburton.* Hunting songs, ballads, etc. Chester, 1834.

W—b—r, A., M.A. *Alexander Webster, D.D.* Haman's deserv'd end : a sermon ... By ... L. 1740.

W—dw—d, Hal. *Henry Woodward.* Faddle found out; or, the draining of Hal W[oo]dw[ar]d's coffee-pot. Dublin, 1748.

W—le, Hon. H—ce. *Horace Walpole.* The genuine copy of a letter found Nov. 5, 1782, near Strawberry Hill, Twickenham. Addressed to ... L. 1783.
Horace Walpole, respecting Thomas Chatterton.

W—p—le, R——, Esq. *Sir Robert Walpole.* The speech of ... at his election at Lynn-Regis ... August 31, 1713. L. 1713.

W—lp—le, Sir R—t. *Sir Robert Walpole.* A short history of a ten years' negociation between a Prime Minister and a private gentleman ... and Mr. W. L. 1738.

W—m, Sir W—m. *Sir William Wyndham* (?). A letter to ... By a modern Tory. L. 1736.

W—n, Mr. *Rt. Hon. Thomas Winnington.* An apology for the conduct of a late second-rate minister ... from ... 1729 ... till ... his death in 1746. Written by himself and found among his papers. L. 1747.

W—n, Alice. *Alice Winn,* afterwards Mrs. Bartrum, wife of the pawnbroker of Princes Street, Coventry Street. See Lamb's " Elia," " Dream children."

W—n, M—s. *Marquis of Wharton.* A short character of the late ... Extracted from an Irish manuscript, by the author of the " Tale of a tub " [Jonathan Swift]. L. 1711.

W—n, W—m. *William Warburton,* Bishop of Gloucester. A proclamation : a poem. A satire upon ... L. 1750.

W—r, Sally. *Sally Winter.* — See Lamb's " Elia, " The praise of chimney sweeps."

W—te—d, Rev. Mr. G——. *Rev.*

George Whitefield. A letter of consolation to the Rev. Mr. Romaine ... By ... L. 1759.

W—tt—n, William. *William Wotton.* A tale of a tub ... with notes by ... L. 1724.

Wade. *Charles Asbury Stevens.* Off the geysers ... B. 1872.

Waggle, Sam. *Mrs. Matilda A. Bailey.* — See " Forlorn Hope."

Wagoner, Hank. *L. E. Mosher,* in his contributions to the "Graphic" (N.Y.), etc.

Wagstaff, Lancelot, Esq. *William Makepeace Thackeray.* "The partie fine," in the " New Monthly Magazine." 1844–45.

Wagstaff, Simon, Esq. *Jonathan Swift, D.D.* A complete collection of genteel and ingenious conversation ... L. 1738.

Wagstaff, Théophile. *William Makepeace Thackeray.* Flore et Zephyr. Ballet ... L. 1836.

Wagstaff, Walter, Esq. *William Oldisworth.* Annotations on the Tattler ... L. 1710.

Wagstaffe, Jeoffry, Esq. *John Jephson, John Courtenay, — Burroughs,* etc. Select essays from the Batchelor; or, speculations of ... Dublin, 1772.

Wagstaffe, John, Esq., of Wilbye grange. *Charles Mackay.* The gouty philosopher ; or, the opinions, whims, and eccentricities of ... L. 1862.

Wagstaffe, Launcelot, Jr. *Dr. Charles Mackay.* The gouty philosopher. L. 1872.

Waking, Elizabeth. *Miss Sue Harry Clagett,* of Keokuk (Iowa), in her contributions to various periodicals.

Wallbridge, Arthur. *Arthur Wallbridge Lunn.* Bizarre fables ... L. 1842.

Waldau, Max. *Richard Georg Spiller von Hauenschild.* Ein Elfenmaerchen. Heidelberg, 1847.

Waldbrühl, Wilhelm von. *Florentin von Zuccalmaglio.* Kinderkomödien. 1870.

Waldmüller, Robert. *Edouard Charles Duboc,* in his translation of " Enoch Arden " etc.

Waldow, Ernst von. *Lodoiska von Blum.* Die Hexe von Wrostava. 1880.

Wales, Peleg. *William A. Croffut.*

Walford, Flora. *Bessie G. Walford.* Sketches from Flemish life. L. 1843.

Walker, Henry (?). *John Taylor,* the water-poet. An answer to a foolish pamphlet entitled "A Swarme of Sectaries and Schismaticks." L. 1641.

Walker, Patricius. *William Alling-ham.* Rambles by ... L. 1873. [His signature in "Fraser's Magazine" from 1847.]

Walker in the Pines, The. *General Henry Hastings Sibley,* in his contributions to various sporting papers.

This pseudonym is a translation of "Wa-ze-o-man-nee," a name given to Gen. Sibley by the Sioux Indians, and by which he is generally known among them.

Walking Gentleman, A. *Thomas Colley Grattan.* High-ways and bye-ways; or, tales of the roadside ... L. 1825.

Wall Street Bear, A. *Samuel Young.* A ... in Europe ... N.Y. 1855.

Wallah, A Competition. *George Otto Trevelyan.* Letters from ... "Macmillan's Magazine," 1863–64; signed J. Broughton. Reprinted as "The Competition Wallah." L. 1864.

Wallner, Franz. *Franz Leidesdorf.* Rückblicke ... Berlin, 1864.

Walneerg. *Thomas Knox.* Rhymed convictions; in songs ... L. & Edinb. 1852.

Walsingham. *Will Stuart.*

Walsingham, C. *Mrs. F. Howell.*

Walsingham, Francis, of the Inner Temple, Esq. *William Arnall.* The free Briton extraordinary ... L. 1730.

Walter, Uncle. *Walter T. Sleeper.* Walks and talks ... B. 187–.

Walter, Emile, a worker. *Alexander Delmar.* What is free trade? N.Y. 1867.

Walter, Judith. *Mme. Judith (Gautier) Mendès.* Le livre de Jade. Paris, 1867.

Walton. *Henry Thorpe.*

Wanderer. *E. H. d'Avigdon.* Fair Dianas. 188–.

Wanderer, A. *Philip Thicknesse, Esq.,* in the "Gent. Mag.," 1791, and "St. James Chronicle."

Wanderer, A. *I. Peirce.* The Narraganset chief; or, the adventures of ... N.Y. 1832.

Wanderer, A. *Carroll Ryan.* The songs of ... Ottawa, 1867.

Wanderer, A. *R. M. Beverley.* Thoughts in the night: a poem written in Auvergne. By ... L. 1852.

Wanderer, A. *A. Moberley.* Varieties [in prose and verse]. By ... L. 1849.

Wanderer in Egypt, H. *Henry T. Wace.* Palm leaves from the Nile; being a portion of the diary of ... Shrewsbury, 1865.

Wanderer, The. *John Keast Lord.* At home in the wilderness ... L. 1867.

Wanderer, The. *Matthew Henry Barker.*

Wanderer, The. *George Watterston.* The wanderer in Washington. W. 1827.

Wandering Bard, The. *Nathan Withy.* The present case of ... (epitaph on the Wandering Bard, wrote by himself) [in verse]. L. (?) 1790 (?).

Wandering Minstrel, The. *Frederick Wilson,* in his contributions to the "Republican" (St. Louis, Mo.). P. 1878.

Wandering Patentee, The. *Tate Wilkinson.* The Wandering Patentee; or, a history of the Yorkshire theatres ... York, 1795.

War-horse, The. *Alderman Purdy* (?). War-horsiana; or, an authentic report of ... sayings and doings of the war-horse and his ponies from the year 1847 to the present time ... N.Y. 1851.

Warbler, Forest. *M. R. McCormick.* The Duke's chase; or, the diamond ring vs. the gold ring ... Cin. 1871.

Warburtonian, A. *Richard Hurd,* Bishop of Worcester. Tracts of Warburton and ... L. 1789.

Ward, Artemus. *Charles Farrar Browne.* Artemus Ward in London: a new comic book. N.Y. 1867.

Ward, Mrs. Betsey Jane. *Charles Farrar Browne.* Hur book of Goaks. N.Y. 1866.

Ward, Mrs. ·Harriette Oxnard. *Mrs. Clara Jessup Moore.* The young lady's friend. By a lady. P. 1880.

This book was written and first published by Mrs. Farrar, of Cambridge, Mass.

Ward, Ireland. *Irene Widdemer.* Daisy Brentwell. N.Y. 1876.

Ward, Marion. *Mrs. Harriet Marion (Ward) Stephens.* One of the signatures to her contributions to literature.

Warhawk. *William Palmer.* English correspondent.

Waring. *Alfred Domett.* "Browning immortalized *Domett* many years ago, under the name of 'Waring,' in one of his early dramatic poems: —

  "' What's beoome of Waring
  Since he gave us all the slip —
  Chose land, travel, or seafaring,
  Boots and chest, or staff and scrip,
  Rather than pace up and down
  Any longer London town ?'"

Warmley, Ernest, M.A. *James B. Manson.*

Warneford, Lieut. Robert. *Wil-*

liam Russell. The phantom cruiser . . .
L. 1865. See "Waters."

**Warner, Warren, Esq., of the Inner
Temple.** Probably *Samuel Warren,* in
"The experiences of a barrister." N.Y.
1852.
Originally published in " Blackwood's Magazine."

Warren. *James Cheetham.* An antidote to John Wood's poison. N.Y.
1802.

Warren, Esther. *Miss Esther Robinson,* in the New York "Independent."

Warrington. *William Stevens Robinson.* His signature in the "Springfield
(Mass.) Republican," 1856–76; in the
"N.Y. Tribune," 1857–60; and in the
"Boston News," 1875–76; and to an article in the "Atlantic Monthly" for December, 1871, on "General Butler's campaign in Massachusetts."

Warton, John, Dr. *Rev. William
Wood.* Death-bed scenes, etc. L. 1830.

Warwick. *C. J. McDonough.*

Warwick. *Frank B. Ottarson.*

Warwick, Eden. *George S. Jabet,*
of Birmingham. The poet's pleasaunce;
or, garden of all sorts of pleasant flowers,
which our pleasant poets have, in past
time, for pastime, planted. L. 1847.

Wash. *Charles Asbury Stevens.* Left
on Labrador . . . B. 1872.

Washingtonian, A. *John Lovett.*
Washington's birthday: an historical
poem, with notes and an appendix. By
. . . Albany, 1812.

Wastle, William. *John Gibson Lockhart,* in several contributions to "Blackwood's Magazine."

Watcher, A. *Mrs. Worsley.* The house
of Joseph in England. By . . . L. 1881.

Water Drinker, A. *Basil Montagu,
Esq.* Inquiries as to the effects of fermented liquors, by . . . L. 1814.

Water Drinker, A. *William Dunlap.* Memoirs of a . . . N.Y. 1837.

Water-poet, The. *John Taylor.*

Waters. *William Russell.* The game
of life. L. 1857.

Waters, John. *Henry Cary,* whose
signature of "John Waters" was well
known to the readers of the "New York
American" and the "Knickerbocker
Magazine."

Waters, Thomas. *William Russell.*
The recollections of a policeman. By . . .
an inspector of the London detective
corps. N.Y. 1853.

Watson, George. *George Watson
Taylor.* England preserved: an historical play, by . . . L. 1795.

Waugh, Mansie. *David Macbeth*

Moir. The life of . . . taylor in Dalkeith . . . Edinb. 1828.
" Waugh," not " Wauch," is according to
Brit. Mus. Catalogue.

Wave. *Eugene Batchelder.* A romance
of the sea-serpent, or the ichthyosaurus.
. . . Camb., Mass., 1849.

Waverley. *A. J. Wilson,* a London
tricycler; under this signature contributes monthly to the "Springfield Wheelmen's Gazette."
He is a voluminous writer in the London cycling press, chiefly over signature of " Faed,"
which he also used in " American Bicycle Journal" (B. 1879), and by which he is best known.
He also signs " Axis," " Mem O'Random," and
" An Old File."

**Waverley, Edward Bradwardine,
Esq.** *John Wilson Croker.* Two letters
on Scottish affairs from . . . to Malachi
Malagrowther, Esq. [Sir Walter Scott].
L. 1826.

Waybridge, W. *Elias Nason.*

Wayfarer, A. *Moses H. Sargent.*
Traditions of Palestine; or, scenes in the
Holy Land in the days of Christ. By . . .
B. 1863.

Wayfarer, A. *Cuthbert G. Young.* A
wayfarer's notes on the shores of the
Levant, and the valley of the Nile . . .
L. 1848.

Wayfaring Man, A. *Clinton G. Gilroy.* Inner life; or, the joys of my
Father's house . . . P. 1865.

Wayne, Gladys. *Miss Julia Von
Valkenburg,* in her contributions to the
"Household" (Brattleboro, Vt.).

Wayne, Olive. *Mrs. Mary E. Connell.*

Weathercock, Janus. *Thomas Griffiths Wainewright,* the "Janus Weathercock" of the "London Magazine."

Weaver, A. *T. Bakewell.* The moorland bard; or, poetical recollections of
. . . in the moorlands of Staffordshire.
Hanley, 1807.

Weaver Poet, The. *William Thom.*

Webber, Frank. *William H. Bushnell.* Prairie fire: a novel. Chic. 184–.

Webfoot. *W. D. Phelps.* Fore and
aft; or, letters from the life of an old
sailor. B. 1870.

Webster, Leland A. *Robert S. Hamilton.* Present status of the philosophy
of society . . . N.Y. 1866.

**Wednesday's Club in Friday-street,
The.** *William Paterson.* An enquiry
into the state of the union of Great Britain . . . L. 1717.

Wehl, Feodor. *Feodor Zu Wehlen.*
Von Herzen zu Herzen. 1867.

Weiss, Lynde. *Thomas Bangs Thorpe.*
Lynde Weiss: an autobiography. P.
1854.

Welby, Horace. *John Timbs.* Predictions realized in modern times ... L. 1862.

Welch Freeholder, A. *David Jones.* A letter to the Right Reverend Samuel [Horsley], Lord Bishop of St. David's ... L. 1790.

Welch Member of Parliament, A. *Chase Price.* Dialogue in the shades, between Dr. Dodd and .. By William Coombe. L. 1777.

Wells, Thornton. *Thomas Williams.* Poems. L. 1869.

Well-wisher, A. *Mary Maw.* An exhortation or warning to the inhabitants of Woodbridge ... n.p. 1778.

Well-wisher of the Good-old-way, A. *Rev. John Pollock.* An answer to the first part of Humble Pleadings; or, a vindication of the Church of Scotland ... Dumfreis, 1717.

Well-wisher to all Mankind, A. *William Dover.* Useful miscellanies; or, serious reflections respecting men's duty to God, and one towards another ... L. 1739.

Well-wisher to both Governments, A. *Francis Makemie.* A plain and friendly perswasive to the inhabitants of Virginia and Maryland ... L. 1705.

Well-wisher to his Country, A. — *Reynolds.* The hardships occasioned by the oaths to the present government considered ... L. 1716.

Well-wisher to Mankind, A. *Rev. Joseph Townsend.* A dissertation on the Poor Laws. L. 1786.

Well-Wisher to the Good People of Great Britain, A. *Sir Mathew Decker.* Serious considerations on the several high duties which the nation in general, as well as trade in particular, labours under, etc. By ... L. 1743.

Well-wisher to the Peace of Britain, A. *Daniel Defoe.* A modest vindication of the present ministry ... L. 1707.

Well-wisher to Trade, A. *Alexander Justice.* A general treatise of monies and exchanges ... L. 1707.
The dedication is signed "A. J."

Wells, Charles J. *H. L. Howard.* Joseph and his brethren. 1824.

Wells, Thornton. *Thomas Williams.* Poems. By ... L. 1869.

Welp, Treumund. *Eduard Pelz.* Petersburger Skizzen. Leipzig, 1842.

Welsh Curate, A. *Edward Davies.* Eliza Powell; or, trials of sensibility ... n.p. 1795.

Welsh, W. *William Baxter.* The land question. Whose is the land? A dialogue. By ... Glasgow (?), 1870.

Wensleydale Poet, The. *W. G. M. J. Barker.* The three days of Wensleydale ... L. 1854.

Wentworth, May. *Mrs. Mary W. Newman.* Golden Gate series of fairy tales. N.Y. 1867.

Werner, Ernst. *Elisabeth Bürstenbinder.* Um hohen Preis. Roman. Leipsic, 1879.

Werner, Hans. *Ange Henri Joseph Castil Blaze de Bury,* in the "Revue des Deux Mondes."

Werter, Max. *Frank Smyth,* of Richmond, Va., in his contributions to the "Capitol" (Washington, D.C.), etc.

Wesleyan Methodist Missionary, A. *Rev. Robert Cooney, D.D.* The autobiography of ... Montreal, 1856.

West, Marion. *Mrs. G. S. Hoyt.* Sunday-school concert book ... B. 187–.

West, Willa. *Mary S. F. Slocum (?).* Lucy Gelding: a tale of land and sea ... Chic. 1862.

West End, Sir Warwick. *Sir Strafford Northcote,* in Trollope's "The Three Clerks."

West India Merchant, A. *William Innes.* Slave trade indispensable ... L. 1790.

West India Proprietor, A. *Matthew Gregory Lewis.* Journal of ... L. 1834.

West Indian, A. *Samuel Estwick, LL.D.* Considerations on the negro cause, commonly so called ... By ... L. 1772.

West Indian, A. *Richard Nisbet.* Slavery not forbidden by Scripture ... P. 1773.

West-Yankee-Elf, A. *L. A. Wood.* John Bull's scientific (?) "man-machine"; or, American "common-sense" vs. Huxley's paradoxical nonsense ... Louisville, 1871.

Westbrook, Raymond. *William Henry Bishop,* who, in 1878, over this signature published six "Open Letters from New York" in the "Atlantic Monthly."

Westchester Farmer, A. *Samuel Seabury, D.D.* Letters of ... 179–. Also in a pamphlet advocating loyalty to the Crown, 1775.

Western Memorabilia. *William Gowan,* who "published many catalogues of books on American history, which are enlivened by his own notes, written under the pseudonym of 'W. M.'"

Western Tourist, A. *Elbert H. Smith.* Ma-ka-tai-me she-kai-kiah; or, Black Hawk and scenes in the West: a national poem ... N.Y. 1849.

Westman, Hab, K.O. *Thomas Ewbank.* The spoon, with upwards of 100 illustrations. N.Y. 1844.

Wetherell, Misses. *Susan* and *Anna B. Warner.*

Wetherell, Elizabeth. *Miss Susan Warner.* The wide, wide world. N.Y. 1852.

Wh††††††d. *George Whitefield.* The amorous humours and audacious adventures of one ... by a Muggletonian. [A satire in verse.] L. 1760 (?).

Whachum. *Albert Charles Wildman,* in the "Cornwall (Eng.) Gazette."

Whack, Paddy. *John Fitzgibbon,* Earl of Clare. No union, but unite and fall. By ... of Dyott Street, London ... L. 1799.

Wharton, Grace. *Mrs. Katharine (Byerley) Thomson,* joint-author. The wits and beaux of society ... L. 1860.

Wharton, Philip. *John Cockburn Thomson,* joint-author. The wits and beaux of society. L. 1860.

Whatshisname. *E. C. Massey.* The green-eyed monster: a Christmas lesson. L. 1854.

What-You-Call-Him, John. *Matthias Symson.* The Caledonian almanak ... By ... 1700.

Whats-you-call-him, Clerk to the same. *Patrick Anderson.* The copie of a Barons court, newly translated. (Printed at Helicon, beside Parnassus, and are to be sold in Caledonia.) n.d.

Wheaton, Campbell. *Mrs. Helen C. Weeks.* Six sinners; or, schooldays in Bantam Valley. N.Y. 1877.

Mrs. Weeks now signs her name to periodicals "Helen Campbell."

Wheeler, Stern. *Charles S. Wheeler,* editor of the "Pontiac Jacksonian," and contributor to periodicals under this signature, published at Boston, in 1851, a volume of poems entitled "The Winnowing."

Whetstone, Pete. *Charles Fenton Mercer Noland.*

Whig, A. One of the signatures attributed to Junius (*q.v.*).

The letter thus signed is dated April 9, 1771, and relates to the privileges of Parliament.

Whig, A. *John Butler,* Bishop of Hereford. An answer to the cocoa-tree (a pamphlet so called), from ... L. 1762.

Whig, A. *Major John Scott,* afterwards *Waring.* Seven letters to the people of Great Britain. By ... L. 1789.

Whig of the Old School, A. *Charles Francis Adams.* An appeal from the new to the old Whigs ... B. 1835.

Whig of '76, A. *Robert Macomb.* A reply to the resolutions and address of a meeting convened at Martlings, in ... New York, Feb. 4, 1811 ... N.Y. 1811.

Whimsy, Sir Finical. *Sir Richard Worsley.* Memoirs of ... and his lady ... L. 1782.

Whimsical Man, A. *Frederic Townsend* (?). Fancies of ... N.Y. 185-.

Whip, The. *Claudius Bradford,* who wrote four or five poetical articles with this title for the "New England Galaxy" (B.).

Whipem, Benedick. *Richard Harris.* New nobility: a novel ... L. 1867.

Whipple, Wade. *George Stevens.* Revenge; or, woman's love: a melodrama. L. 1857.

Whirlwind, Captain. *Captain Edward Sterling,* at one time principal leader-writer for the London "Times." Carlyle says of him: "An impetuous man, full of real energy, and immensely conscious of the same; who transacted everything, not with the minimum of fuss and noise, but with the maximum: a very 'Captain Whirlwind,' as one was tempted to call him."

Whistlecraft, William and Robert, of Stow Market, in Suffolk, Harness and Collar Makers. *Rt. Hon. John Hookham Frere.* Prospectus and specimen of an intended national work ... L. 1818.

Whistler, The. *Alexander Somerville.* His signatures in the newspapers. — See "One who has whistled at the Plough."

White, Babington. *Mrs. Mary Elizabeth (Braddon) Maxwell,* in a novel entitled "Circe" (L. 1867), which has been described as being plagiarized from Octave Feuillet's "Dalilah." Miss Braddon has denied the authorship of the work.

See the controversy in the "Pall Mall Gazette," "London Review," "Globe," and "Belgravia" (September to December, 1867).

White, Blythe, Jr. *Solon Robinson.* Green Mountain girls: a story of Vermont. N.Y. 1856.

White, Century. *John White.*

White, Charles Erskine, D.D. *Laughton Osborn.* The dream of Alla-Ad-Deen ... N.Y. 1831.

White, James. *Robert B. Seeley.* Is the Bible true? Seven dialogues between J. W. and E. Owen, concerning the "Essays and Reviews." By ... L. 1862.

White, L. C. *Lucy C. Lillie.* The story of English literature for young readers ... B. 1878.

White, Matthew, Jr. *William L. Alden,* in his contributions to various periodicals.

White, Mr. Thom. *Charles Wyllys Elliott.* Wind and whirlwind: a novel. N.Y. 1868.

White Mountain Pilgrim, The. *E. B. Rollins.* A brief illustration of the prophecies and promises of God's Word ...

White Republican, The. *Hiram Fuller.* North and South ... L. 1863.

Whitecross, James William. *Michael Pius de Wisniewski.* Sketches and characters; or, the natural history of the human intellect ... L. 1853.

Whitefeather, The Late Captain Barabbas. *Douglas William Jerrold.* The handbook of swindling. By ... Edited by John Jackdaw. L. 1839.

Whitehead, Grandfather. *Thomas Powell.*

Whitehook. *Edward Kellogg.* Remarks upon usury and its effects ... N.Y. 1841.

Whitewell, A. M. *John Close.* A month in London ... L. 1844.

Whitney, Harry, Philomath. *Patrick Kennedy.* Legends of Mount Leinster ... L. 1856.

Why? One of the pseudonyms attributed to Junius (*q.v.*).

The letter thus signed is dated Oct. 26, 1768, and contains "a high eulogium on the Earl of Rochford, pointing out his peculiar fitness for conducting affairs with France."

Wiar, W. *John Adey Repton, Esq., F.S.A.* "It was quite in his boyish days, that Mr. Repton first became a correspondent of the "Gent. Mag." In the number for June, 1795, is a view of the round-towered church of Witlingham, in Norfolk. The signature is W. WIAR, being the conjoint initials of William Wilkins and *John Adey Repton*.

Wickham, Martha. *Miss Cornelia Huntington,* of East Hampton, L.I. Sea Spray. A Long Island village. N.Y. 1857.

Wickliffe. *John Stuart Mill,* in his letters contributed to the "Morning Chronicle" (L. 1823), advocating the free publication of all opinions concerning religion.

Wickliffe. *Rev. Samuel Gover Winchester.* The people's right defended ... P. 1831.

Widow in Blue, The. *Mrs. George Clinton Smith,* in her contributions to the "Household."

Widow of a Clergyman of the Church of England, The. *Mrs. Walter Birch.* Job; or, the Gospel preached to the patriarchs ... L. 1838.

Widowed Wife, A. *M. G. Derenzy.* A whisper to a newly-married pair from ... Wellington, Salop, 1824.

Wife of an Emigrant Officer, The. *Mrs. Catharine (Parr) Traill.* The backwoods of Canada: being letters from ... L. 1838.

Wife of a Mormon Elder, The. *Mrs. Maria Ward.* Female life among the Mormons ... N.Y. 1855.

Also attributed to *Mrs. Benjamin G. Ferris.*

Wilbur, Homer, A.M., pastor of the first church in Jaalam, &c. *James Russell Lowell.* — See "Biglow, Hosea."

Wild Methodist, The. *Isaac Abrams.* The truths come out at last. A true history of ... or, odd man's experience, written by himself. P. 1831.

Wildfire, Madge. *Esther Graham,* from whom Sir Walter Scott drew that character in the "Heart of Mid-Lothian."

Wildfowler. *Lewis Clements.* Shooting adventures ... L. 1878.

Originally published in Bell's "Life in London," under the signature of "Wildfowler," and in the "Sporting Gazette," under that of "Snapshot." — See "Snapshot."

Wildgoose, Geoffry. *Richard Graves.* The spiritual Quixote; or, the summer's ramble ... a comic romance. L. 1773.

Wilding, Ernest. *J. Fitzgerald Molloy.*

Wildrake. *George Tattersall.* Pictorial gallery of English race-horses, by ... L. 1844.

Wildwood, Will. *Frederick Eugene Pond,* in his contributions to the "Turf, Field, and Farm" (N.Y.).

Wilhelm. *William A. Brewer,* in his contributions to various New York and Boston periodicals.

Wilhelmi, Alexander Viktor. *Alexander Viktor Zechmeister.* Lustspiele. 1879.

Wilkes, Mr. *Samuel Derrick.* A general view of the stage. L. 1759.

Wilkins, Caleb. *George Sheppard.* What have the Whigs done? ... Newark, Eng., 1838.

Wilkins, Peter. *Cyrus Redding.* A

letter from . . . to Isaac Tomkins [*i.e.*
Lord Brougham]. L. 1839.

This was published in reference to " Thoughts
upon the aristocracy of England." By Isaac
Tomkins, Gent. [*i.e.* Lord Brougham]. L.1835.

Wilkins, Peter. *Robert Paltock.* The
life and adventures of Peter Wilkins, a
Cornish man, taken from his own mouth,
in his passage to England, from off Cape
Horn in America in the ship Hector.
By R. S., a passenger in the Hector. L.
1750.

The dedication is signed " R. P.," the initials
of the author.

Will, Deep. *William Pitt.* A political dictionary for the guinea-less pigs;
or, a glossary of emphatical words made
use of by that jewel of a man . . . in his
administration . . . L. 1790 (?).

Will, Uncle, V.M. *Rev. W. F.
Crafts.*

Will, Uncle. *Prof. William Wells.*

Will-Will-be so. *W. Hall.* Sketch
of local history : being a chain of incidents relating to the state of the Fens,
by . . . Lynn, 1812.

Willard, Oscar. *O. Carpenter.*

William. *William Ewart Gladstone.*
William's workingman and his representative, etc. L. 1874.

William, de Worfat. *Rev. Hutton Beetham.* A bran new wark, by . . . containing a true calendar of his thoughts concerning good nebborhood . . . L. 1879.

William, the Fourth. *William Pitt,*
afterwards Earl of Chatham. Speech of
. . . to both Houses of P . . . [Parliament]
L. 1757.

William, Lord Archbishop of York.
Most Rev. William Markham. A sermon
preached before the Incorporated Soci-
ety for the Propagation of the Gospel in
Foreign Parts . . . February 21, 1777.
By . . . L. 1777.

William and Charles. *William Pitt
and Charles James Fox.* Whig and no
Whig. A political paradox. [A dialogue between . . .] L. 1789.

Williams, Barney. *Barney O'Flaherty.* A *nom de théâtre.*

Williams, Katherine. *Mrs. Laura
A. Buck.* Tiptoe. N.Y. 1871.

Williams, Tummus a. *John Collier.*
A view of the Lancashire dialect . . .
By . . . L. 1770.

Willis, Hal, Student-at-Law. *Charles
Robert Forrester,* whose literary contributions were issued under this pseud. and
that of " Alfred Crowquill."

Willis, Julia A. *Julia A. Kempshall.*
What a boy ! problems concerning him.
P. 187-.

Willis, Kate. *Sarah E. Coolidge.*
Ambition. B. 1856.

Willis, Uncle. *Stephen Willis Tilton.*
Songs for our darlings. B. 1873.

Wilson, Alf. *John Alfred Wilson.*
Adventures of . . . Toledo, O.,
1880.

Wilson, J. Arbuthnot. *Grant Allen.*
His signature in "Belgravia" and in
"Longman's Magazine" to a series of
stories reprinted as "Strange stories."
L. 1884.

Wilson, James. *Andrew Park.* Silent
love: a poem . . . Paisley, 1845.

Wilson, Jasper, Esq. *Dr. James
Currie.* A letter . . . Addressed to
the R^t H$^{onble.}$ William Pitt . . . L.
1793.

Winchester, Arnold or Carroll.
Mrs. Caroline G. Curtis. From Madge
to Margaret. B. 1880.

Windle, Mary Jane. *Mary Jane
McLane.* Truth and fancy: tales
legendary, historic, and descriptive . . .
P. 1850.

Winkey. *Wells Egelshem.* Winkey's
whims. L. 1769.

Winnefred. *Mary Frances Gibson.*

Winter, Amalie von. *Amalie (von
Saebach) von Gross.* Pictures of German
life. 1838.

Winter, Frank. *N. A. Trueblood,* of
Philadelphia, as correspondent of various
newspapers.

Winterbotham. *Mrs. Ann Sophia
(Winterbotham) Stephens.* Norton's Rest.
P. 1877.

Wintertown Democrat, The. The
Springfield Republican. — See "Benson,
Carl."

Winthrop, Sophy. *Mrs. Sophy (Winthrop) Weitzel.* Miss Robert's fortune.
N.Y. 1875.

Winwood, Brent. *John Thomas
Denny,* in his contributions to numerous English provincial journals.

"I used the *nom de plume* 'Rett Winwood'
for a drama entitled 'The Dead Letter'; but,
finding that it was used by another author in
America, I changed it to 'Brent Winwood.'"
—Extract from a letter to A. R. Frey, Oct. 31,
1884.

Wise, Jonathan B. *Stephen Colwell.*
The relative position in our industry of
foreign commerce, domestic production,
and internal trade. P. 1850.

Wisewood, Solomon. *Rev. Duncan
Ross,* who contributed a series of valuable letters, entitled "Busy Body," to
the "Acadian Recorder" (Halifax, 1826-
27), under this signature.

Wishit, Mr. *Thomas Spence.* A supplement to the history of Robinson Cru-

soe. Being the history of Crusonia, or Robinson Crusoe's island, down to the present time ... Copied from a letter sent by ... Newcastle, 1782.

Witherne, Raven. *Mary Parkinson.* Giles Witherne; or, the reward of disobedience: a village tale for the young, founded on fact. [In verse.] L. 1859.

Wittitterly, John Altrayd. *Miss Elizabeth T. Carne.* Three months' rest at Pau, in the winter and spring of 1859. L. 1860.

Wizard. *John Corlett,* in the London "Sportsman."

Wolfe, Reginalde, Esq. *Thomas Frognall Dibdin, D.D.* Francis Quarles's: — Judgment and mercy for afflicted souls; or, meditations, soliloquies, and prayers, edited by ... L. 1807.

Wolfram, Leo. *Ferdinand Prantner.* Wiener Federzeichnungen. 1871.

Woman, A. *Frances (Wright) D'Arusmont.* England, the civilizer ... By ... L. 1848.

Woman, A. *Mrs. Mary Clemmer.* "A Woman's Letters from Washington," a series of letters in the N.Y. "Independent," 1866.

Woman, A. *Mrs. Sarah Morgan (Bryan) Piatt.* A woman's poems. B. 1871.

Woman, A. *Mrs. Dinah Maria (Mulock) Craik.* A woman's thoughts about women. L. 1758.

Woman of Quality, A. *James Ralph.* The other side of the question; or, an attempt to rescue the characters of the two royal sisters, Q. M. and Q. Anne, out of the hands of the D—s D—— of —— [i.e. the Duchess Dowager of Marlborough] ... In a letter to Her Grace, by ... L. 1742.

Wonder, Jak. *Peter K. Ferguson.* Ugliness and its uses: a lecture delivered before the "Y. L. Circulating Library Association," by ... N.Y. 1852.

Wonderful Quiz, A. *James Russell Lowell.* Reader! walk up at once (it will soon be too late), and buy at a perfectly ruinous rate: a fable for critics ... N.Y. 1848.

Wons, Mailliw. *William Snow.* John Bull all agog. [Song.] L. 1803.

Wood, Will. *Jonathan Swift, D.D.* Petition to the people of Ireland: being an excellent new song ... by William Wood, iron monger and halfpenny monger. 1725.

Woodbine, Jenny. *Miss Annie R. Blount,* who, under this name, in 1859

received a one-hundred-dollar gold medal for "The Sisters," in the "Newbern Gazette."

Woodensconce, Papernose, Esq. *Robert Barnabas Brough.* The wonderful drama of Punch and Judy and their little dog Toby ... By ... With illustrations by "The Owl." L. 1854.

Woodfall, Wilfred, Esq. *Sir Samuel Egerton Brydges, Bart.* My note-book; or, sketches from the gallery of St. Stephen's: a satirical poem ... L. 1821.

Woodfern. *Mary W. Stanley Gibson.*

Woodville, Jennie. *Jennie Latham Stabler,* in "Left to Herself" (P. 1871).

Worcester Speculator, The. *Nathan Fiske, D.D.,* in the "Massachusetts Spy."

Working Clergyman, A. *Rev. Erskine Neale.* The life-book of a labourer. L. 1850.

Working Man, A. *Alexander Somerville.* The autobiography of ... L. 1848.

Working-Man, A. *Andrew Stewart.* The clodpole; or, the normal condition of agricultural labourers. Dundee, 1858.

Working Man, A. *John Overs.* The evenings of ... L. 1844.

Working Man, A. *John Lash Latey.* Letters to working people on the new poor law ... L. 1841.

Working Man, A. *James Carter.* Memoirs of ... L. 1845.

Working-Man, A. *Thomas Dixon.* Time and tide by Weare and Tyne. Twenty-five letters to ... of Sunderland, on the laws of work. L. 1867. By John Ruskin.

Working Man, A. *Johann Georg Eccarius.* A working man's refutation of Stuart Mill. L. 1867.

World's Child, The. *Warren Chase.* The life-line of the lone one; or, autobiography of ... B. 1857.

Worth, Mrs. L. L. *Mrs. Ellsworth.* Smith's saloon; or, the Grays and the Grants. N.Y. 1871.

Worthy, Will. *William Pulteney, Earl of Bath.* Bob-Lynn [i.e. Sir R. Walpole] against Franck-Lynn; or, a full history of the controversies ... occasioned by the quarrel of Bob-Lynn and ... 1732.

Wotton, William, D.D. *Mary Astell.* Bart'lemy fair; or, an enquiry after wit, in which due respect is had to a letter [by A. A. Cooper, Earl of Shaftesbury] concerning enthusiasm, to my lord ... By ... L. 1709.

Would be Cromwell of America, The. *Samuel Adams.* So called by the Loyalist printer, James Rivington, 1776.

Wounded Officer, A. *Capt. — Gibney.* My escape from the mutinies in Oudh ... L. 1858.

Wraxall, Lascelles. *Sir Frederick Charles Lascelles Wraxall, Bart.,* a contributor to the "Athenæum" (L.), etc. — See "Lascelles, Lady Caroline."

Wray, A. Lunar. *Rev. Minot Judson Savage* (?).

Wraythe, Hope. *Miss Edith Hawtrey.* Talent in tatters. L. 1877.

Wren, Jenny. *Jane Atkinson.* Facts and fancies, in prose and verse. L. 1864.

Wright, Saul. *T. T. Wilson.* Surf: a summer pilgrimage. N.Y. 1881.

Writer of a Glance behind the Grilles, The. *Mrs. William Pitt Byrne.* Flemish interiors. L. 1856.

Writer of the Parodies in the Gentleman's Magazine. *Thomas Ford.* "Confusion's masterpiece; or, Paine's labour's lost ... "Gent. Mag.," May, 1794, p. 456; June, 1821, p. 565.

Writer of these Tracts, The. *Isaac Williams.* A few remarks on the charge of the Bishop of Gloucester and Bristol, on the subject of reserve in communicating religious knowledge, as taught in the "Tracts for the Times," Nos. 80 and 87; by ... 1841.

Writer to the Signet, A. *A. Kennedy.* The high price of food, butcher-meat, meal, and bread-stuffs, etc., stated and illustrated ... Edinb. 1860.

Writewell, A. M. *John Close.* A month in London; or, the select adventures of S. Dowell ... Edited by ... L. 1844.

Wykehamist, A. *J. Ashley.* The church of the period; or, the Church of England in my own time. By ... a "Priest" of 1824. L. 1871.

Wykehamist, A. *G. J. Davies.* Papers on preaching and public speaking. By ... L. 1861.

Wylde, Hazel. *Miss Ella A. Hotchkiss,* in her contributions to the "Household" (Brattleboro, Vt.), etc.

Wyseman, Demetrius, Gent. *Duke Willis.* The quality papers; edited by ... L. 1828.

Wythe. *Theodore Dwight Weld.* The power of Congress over the District of Columbia. N.Y. 1838.

X.

X. *Eustace Budgell.* "All the papers marked with an X [in the 'Spectator'] were written by him, and the whole eighth volume is attributed to Addison and himself, without the assistance of Steele." — See CHALMERS, Vol. 7.

X. *Henry S. Ellenwood,* who contributed articles of a serious tone to the "New England Galaxy" over this signature.

X. *Sir John Bowring.* Anglo-Turkish war: Egypt and Syria. L. 1841.

X. *Rev. Robert Stephen Hawker, M.A.* A legend of Cornwall, in Sharpe's "London Magazine," 1846.

X. *William Ware.* Sketch of a petition proper to be presented to the legislature of the United Kingdom ... by the friends of peace and justice in Ireland. By X., author of "Letters on Slavery," under that signature, etc. L. 1832.

X, author of Nothing. *Major — Ranken.* The experiment: a farce in one act ... Quebec, 1854.

X. A. P. *John Peace.* A descant upon railroads. L. 1842.

X. H. *Mrs. Brewster Macpherson.* Gifts for men ... Edinb. 1870.

XX. *John Canton.* "The year's length," in the "Gent. Mag.," June, 1752, p. 255.

X. X. X. *Bryan Waller Procter,* in the London "Literary Gazette."

X. Y. *John Rickman.* Eight letters concerning the pavement of the Metropolis and the adjoining turnpike road. L. 1817.

X. Y. Z. *Thomas De Quincey,* in the "London Magazine," 1785–1859.

X. Y. Z. *Bryan Waller Procter,* in the London "Literary Gazette."

X. Y. Z. *William Purton, M.A.* Gradus ad Homerum; or, the A. B. C. D. of Homer ... Oxf. 1862.

X. Y. Z. Club. *John Godfrey Saxe, A. Livien Douglas,* and *George W. Pettes.* Euchre; or, the game of life. 18–.

X. Z. *Rev. John Sylvester John Gardiner.* Remarks on the Jacobiniad, first published in the "Federal Orrery," Boston, 1794 or 95, and afterwards republished in a 12° volume in Boston, 1795–98, *embellished* with caricature likenesses of many of those against whom its satire was directed. This book is in the Boston Athenæum Library.

X*****, Le Chev., O.A.S.D.S.M.S. *Le Comte Xavier de Maistre.* Voyage autour de ma chambre. Par ... Hamburg, 1796.

"O.A.S.D.S.M.S." = Ancien officier au service de S. M. Sarde.

Xariffa. *Mrs. Mary Ashly (Van Voorhis) Townsend.* Xariffa's poems. P. 1870.

Xenette. *Miss Pamela S. Vining,* known to the literary world by this penname, has contributed to Wellman's "Literary Miscellany" (Detroit), has written for New York magazines, and for the "Ladies' Repository" (Cin.).

Xo Ho. *Horace Walpole, Earl of Orford.* A letter from ... a Chinese philosopher at London, to his friend Lien Chi at Peking. L. 1757.

Xylo. *John Homer Bliss,* in the "Printer's Miscellany," St. John's, N.B., 1877–78.

Y.

Y. — See "Alcæus."

Y. *E. V. Kenealy.* E. W. Montagu: an autobiography. Edited [or rather written] by ... L. 1869.

Y., A. *Arthur Young, Esq.* Letters to the yeomanry .. L. 1797.

Y., E. *Edward Yardley (?).* A letter to a friend [giving some account of the life and works of C. Hayes]: by ... L. 1761.

Y., E. A. G. *Mrs. E. A. G. Young.* Last leaves from the journal of Julian Charles Young. Edited by ... L. 1875.

Y., E. J. *Edward James Young.* George Harris. B. 1875.

Y., J. *John Yardley (?).* [Rickli's] The Swiss peasant. Trans. by ... L. 1856.

Y. J. O. *Mrs. Sarah S. Black.* Rambling chats and chatty rambles. N.Y. 1872.

Y. M. *William Pengelly.* "The late W. J. Henwood, F.R.S.," in "Nature." 1875.

Y., M. J. *Mrs. Maud J. (Fuller) Young.* The legend of Sour Lake. Houston, 186–.

Y. N. *John Fry.* Pieces of ancient poetry ... Edited by ... Bristol, 1814.

Y. N. L. *Rev. Timothy Horton Ball.* The Lake of the Red Cedars; or, will it live? Thirty years in Lake ... By ... Crown Point, Indiana, 1880.

Y., R. *Robert Young.* Rabbinical vocabulary ... By ... Edinb. 1853.

Y., W. *William Yates.* The Hitopadesa; or, Salutary instruction, etc. Edited by ... 1841.

Y. Z. One of the pseudonyms attributed to Junius (*q.v.*).

The letter thus signed was contributed to the "Public Advertiser," and was dated Dec. 5, 1767. It contained a copy of Burke's speech against the Ministry, but the printer was afraid to insert the same.

Y****, A., Esq. *Arthur Young, Esq.* Reflections on the present state of affairs at home and abroad. By ... L. 1759.

Yankee, A. *Richard Grant White.* American correspondence in the "Spectator" (L. 1863–67).

Yankee, A. *William H. Thoms.* The bushranger: a Yankee's adventures during his second visit to Australia. B. 1866.

Yankee, A. *John Kearsley Mitchell, M.D.* Saint Helena: a poem, by ... P. 1821.

Yankee, A. *Joseph Holt Ingraham.* The South-west ... N.Y. 1835.

Yankee, A. *Asa Greene.* A Yankee among the Nullifiers. N.Y. 1835.

Yankee, A. *Henry David Thoreau.* A Yankee in Canada ... B. 1866.

Yankee Conscript, The. *George Adams Fisher.* The Y. C.; or, eighteen months in Dixie, 1861–62. P. 1864.

Yankee Farmer, A. *John Lowell, LL.D.* Peace without dishonour — war without hope ... B. 1807.

Yankee Ned. *George Edward Clark.* Seven years of a sailor's life ... B. 1867.

Yankee Officer, A. *Henry L. Estabrooks.* Adrift in Dixie; or ... among the Rebels, 1865. N.Y. 1866.

Yankee Prisoner, A. *John James Geer.* Beyond the lines ... loose in Dixie, 1862–63. P. 1864.

Yanko-Sequor. *Martin Regul Pilon.* The Yanko-Sequor: disquisitions upon several things in America ... N.Y. 1874.

Yarmouth. *Isaac H. Bailey.*

Yates, M. *Mary Anne Yates Corkling.* Bread reform league. Wheatmeal bread. L. 1882.

Y–ll–wpl–sh, Ch—s, Esq. *William Makepeace Thackeray* to Sir Edward Lytton Bulwer, Bart. . . . "Fraser's Magazine," January, 1840.

Yellowplush, Charles, Esq. *William Makepeace Thackeray.* The Yellowplush correspondence, in "Fraser's Magazine," 1837–38.

Yelmarb, H. E. *H. E. Bramley.* Phrenological stump orations, etc. [with a preface signed . . .]. L. 1868.

Yenda, Mit. *Timothy Adney.*

Yendys, Sydney. *Sydney Thompson Dobell.* The Roman : a dramatic poem. L. 1850.

Yeoman, A. *Sir William Cusack Smith, Bart.* A letter to the Right Honourable William Wickham . . . 3d ed. Dublin, 1803.

Yewrownckie, Aunt. *Mrs. Henry G. Blinn.* Eyes and ears ; or, how I see and hear. P. 1877.

Ylloss. *Samuel Solly, Esq.,* who was an occasional contributor to the "Gent. Mag.," on subjects of currency particularly, under this signature.

Yonge, A. de. *Miss A. Watson.* Joy, and other poems. L. 18–.

Yonge, Remington. *Robert Remington Doherty.* Miscellaneous writer. 1847.

Yorick. *Piero Francesco Leopoldo Ferrigni,* who, as a spirited *Feuilletonist* under the pseud. of "Yorick," borrowed from Shakespeare's "Hamlet," became a favorite with the Tuscan public.

Yorick. *Rowley Lascelles, Esq.* Letters of . . . or, a good-humoured remonstrance in favour of the Established Church. By a very humble member of it, in three parts . . . Dublin, 1817.

The letters in the Second Part appeared, the first three of them in the "Dublin Evening Post," and the remainder in "Freeman's Journal," under the signature of "Numa"; those in Part III., in the "Correspondent" newspaper, January, 1817, under the signature of "Publicola." The First Part, under the title of "Letters of 'Publicola,' . . . was published in Dublin, 1816. An article signed "Yorick," in the "Gent. Mag." for March, 1835, was written by *Mr. Lascelles.*

Yorick. *Laurence Sterne.* Letters from Eliza [Mrs. Elizabeth Draper] to . . . By William Coombe. L. 1775.

Yorick. *James Warren Ward.* Yorick, and other poems. Cleveland, 1838.

Yorick, Mr. *Laurence Sterne.* A sentimental journey through France and Italy . . . L. 1768.

Yorke, Oliver, Esq. *Francis Sylvester Mahony,* as editor of "Fraser's Magazine''; and still the assumed name of its editor.

Yorke, Onslow. *William Hepworth Dixon.* Secret history of "The International" Working Men's Association. L. 1871.

Yorke, Stephen. *Miss Linskill.* Tales of the North Riding. L. 1871.

Yorke, Zaida, and Una Locke. *Mrs. Una Locke Bailey, and another* (?). The Fourth of July in New England, and the fifth of November in Old England . . . N.Y. 1870.

Yorkel, Hans. *A. Oakey Hall.* Ballads. N.Y. 1880.

"I have a dim recollection of signing some newspaper letters 'Hans Yorkel,' but those were ephemeral." — Letter to A. R. Frey, Sept. 29, 1884.

York's Tall Son. *William Trotter Porter.* An appellation playfully applied to him by his friends.

Yorkshire Clergyman, A. *Rev. Francis Orpen Morris, B.A.* Archdeacon Wilberforce on supremacy. By . . . L. 1854.

Yorkshire Freeholder, A. *Samuel Bailey.* A discussion of parliamentary reform. L. 1831.

Young American, A. *Isaac F. Coffin.* Journal of a residence in Chili . . . 1817–18–19. B. 1823.

Young American, A. *Alexander Slidell, U.S.N.* (*Slidell-Mackenzie,* after 1837), in "A Year in Spain" (L. 1836), etc.

Young and Happy Husband, A. *A. A. Dowty.* Connubial bliss. L. 18–.

Young Artist, A. *A. B. Cochrane.* A young artist (L. Holme)'s life. L. 1864.

Young Clergyman, A. *Joseph Butler,* Bishop of Durham. A letter of thanks . . . to the Rev. Dr. Hare . . . L. 1719.

Young English Positivist, A. *John Morley,* in Robert Buchanan's "Masterspirits." L. 1873.

Young Englishman of Rank, A. *William Wirt* (?). The British spy ; or, letters of . . . written during a tour through the United States. Newburyport, Mass., 1804.

Young Gentleman, A. *Benjamin Church, M.D.* The choice : a poem after the manner of Mr. Pomfret . . . B. 1757.

Young Gentleman, A. *Thomas Dawes.* The law given at Sinai : a poem . . . B. 1777.

Young Gentleman, A. *Thomas Green.* The micthodion ; or, a poetical olio . . . L. 1788.

Young Gentleman, A. *Richard Valpy, D.D., F.A.S.* Poetical blossoms . . . By . . . of the Royal Grammar School, Guildford. L. 1772.

Young Gentleman, A. *Thomas Rodd, Senior.* The Theriad: an heroic-comic poem . . . by . . . L. 1790.

Young Gentleman, A. *Fortescue Hitchins.* Vision of memory, and other poems. By . . . Plymouth, 1803.

Young Gentleman of Cambridge, A. *Rev. Henry Etough*, of Therfield, Hertfordshire. A letter to [Henry Dodwell] the author of Christianity not founded on Argument. L. 1742.

Young Gentleman of New York, A. *John Blair Linn, D.D.* Miscellaneous works, prose and poetical, by . . . N.Y. 1765.

Young Gentleman of Seventeen, A. *A. Pitman.* Eugenio; or, the man of sorrow . . . L. 1780.

Young Gentleman of Sixteen, A. *B. Allen.* Modern chastity; or, the agreeable rape: a poem; by . . . in vindication of the Right Hon. Lord B—e [*i.e.* Frederick Calvert, Lord Baltimore]. L. 1768.

Young Gentleman of Truro School, A. *Richard Polwhele.* The fate of Lewellyn; or, the druid's sacrifice . . . L. 1778.

Young Gentleman of Winchester School, A. *Robert Lowth*, afterwards bishop of London. The genealogy of Christ; as it is represented in the east window in the college chappel at Winchester: a poem. L. 1729.

Young Gentlewoman, Mrs. A. W., A. *Mrs. Anna Weamys.* A continuation of Sir Philip Sydney's Arcadia . . . L. 1651.

Young Greek Lady, A. *Pauline Adelaide Alexandre Panam.* Memoirs of . . . L. 1823.

Young Lady, A. *Helen Maria Williams.* Edwin and Eltruda: a legendary tale. L. 1782.

Young Lady, A. *Mary Julia Young.* Horatio and Amanda: a poem. By . . . L. 1777.

Young Lady, A. *Gertrude Wyatt.* Miscellaneous poems. By . . . L. 1829.

Young Lady, A. *Miss J. Harvey.* A sentimental tour through Newcastle. By . . . Newcastle, 1794.

Young Lady, A. *William Coombe, Esq.* "A series of letters from . . . on a visit in London, to a sick mother in the country," contributed to Ackerman's "Literary Repository."

Young Lady, lately deceased, A. *Miss Elizabeth Smith.* Fragments in prose and verse. Bath, 1808.

Young Man, A. *Henry Revell Reynolds.* An address to the ladies. n.p. 1796.

Young Nobleman, A. *Lord George Lyttelton.* Poems by . . . of distinguished abilities, lately deceased . . . in a letter from an American traveller, dated from the ruinous portico of St. Paul's, in the year 2199, to a friend settled in Boston, the metropolis of the Western Empire . . . 2d ed. L. 1780.

Young Man of Massachusetts, A. *Benjamin Waterhouse, M.D.* Journal of . . . captured at sea by the British, May, 1813. B. 1816.

Young Painter, A. *John Russell.* Letters from . . . abroad to his friends in England. L. 1750.

Young Peer of the Highest Rank, just returned from his travels, A. *Francis Russell, 5th Duke of Bedford.* A descriptive tour through the interior parts of Germany and France . . . L. 1786.

Young Pilgrim, A. *Mrs. Anne (Hindley) Woods.* Life in the tent; or, travels in the desert and Syria, in 1850 . . . L. and Ashton-under-Lyne.

Young Rapid. *Col. T. Allston Brown.*

Young Roscius. *William H. W. Betty.*

Young Scots Gentleman, A. *Adam Thomson.* The disappointed gallant . . . Edinb. 1738.

Young Southern Lady, A. *Mrs. Emma (Moffett) Wynne.* Cragfont. N.Y. 1867.

Young 'Un. *George P. Burnham.* Stray subjects arrested and bound over, being the fugitive offspring of the "Old 'Un" [F. A. Durivage] and the Young 'Un, etc. B. 1848.

Young Woman, A. *Susannah Harrison.* Songs in the night, by . . . Burlington, N.J., 1788.

Younger Brother, A. *Samuel Bailey, Esq.* The right of primogeniture examined, in a letter to a friend. By . . . L. 1837.

Younger Son, A. *Edward John Trelawny.* The adventures of a younger son. L. 1831.

Youngest member, The. *Annie T. Slosson.* The China-hunter's club . . . N.Y. 1878.

Your Constant Reader. *Charles Dickens*, in the "Daily News," January, 1846.—See "Subscriber, A."

Your Real Friend. One of the pseudonyms attributed to Junius (*q.v.*).

The letter thus signed is dated May 6, 1769, and censures the Marquis of Granby.

Youth of Thirteen, A. *William*

Cullen Bryant. The embargo; or, sketches of the times: a satire, by ... B. 1808.

Yrubslips, F. *Francis Spilsbury.* The art of etching and aqua tinting ... By ... L. 1794.

Z.

Z. *H. Wilberforce.* — See " α " (under Alpha).

Z. *Samuel Adams,* in the "Boston Gazette," Oct. 11, 1773.

Z. *George Horne,* Bishop of Norwich. His signature to papers in the "Olla Podrida," a periodical work, at Oxford.

Z. *John Gibson Lockhart,* in "Blackwood's Magazine."

Z. *Rev. Joseph Warton,* in his contributions to the "Adventurer." L. 1752–54.

Z. *Hannah More.* The lady and the pye ... and the plum-cakes. L. 1800.

Z. *Col. G. W. Prosser.* A letter ... on the Royal Military College at Sandhurst. L. 1848.

Z. *Samuel Edmund Sewall, LL.B.* Remarks on slavery in the United States ... B. 1827.

Z., A. *William Lucas.* A five weeks' tour to Paris, Versailles, Marli, etc. By ... L. 1765.

Z., A. *Rev. John Clayton.* Four letters occasioned by two pamphlets ... L. 1805.

Z., A. *Benjamin Gale, M.D.* The present state of the Colony of Connecticut considered ... New London, 1755.

Z——, Mrs. B. M. *Mrs. Bettie M. Zimmerman.* "It was in 1863, that the ' Southern Illustrated News ' (Richmond, Va.) contained creditable poems by ' Mrs. B. M. Z——,' and in 1864, the ' Southern Field and Fireside ' (Augusta, Ga.) published some poems by the same pen."

Z., E. S. *Hon. Elizabeth Susan Law,* afterwards *Lady Colchester.* Miscellaneous poems ... By ... L. 1832.

Z., J. V. *Joseph Veazie.* Asphalt ... B. 1875.

Z., T. Q., Esq. *Major John Scott,* afterwards *Waring.* An epistle from Oberea, Queen of Otaheite, to Joseph Banks, Esq. Translated by ... professor of the Otaheite language in Dublin, and of all the languages of the undiscovered islands in the South Sea ... L. 1774.

Zadig. *Hon. Chief Justice J. H. Hogarty,* in his contributions to various Canadian periodicals.

Zadkiel. *William Lilly.* Astrology, and a grammar of astrology. L. 1832.

Zadkiel. *Lieut. Richard James Morrison.* An essay on love and matrimony. L. 1851.

Zadkiel, Tao Sze. *Lieut. Richard James Morrison.* Zadkiel's almanack for 1851, etc. L. 1851.

Zadkiel, the Seer. *Lieut. Richard James Morrison.* The horoscope ... Edited by ... L. 1834 and 1841.

Zaphaniel. *George Alexander Stevens.* The dramatic history of Master Edward, Miss Ann, Mrs. Llwhuddwhydd, and others. The extraordinaries of these times. Collected from Z.'s original papers, etc. L. 1743.

Zara. *Miss Ponsonby.* "Zara's look serene," in Anna Seward's "Llangollen Vale."

Zarah. *Sarah,* Duchess of Marlbourough. The secret history of Queen Zarah and the Zarazians: being a looking glass for ... in the kingdom of Albigion ... Albigion [L.]. By Mrs. De la Riviere Manley (?).

Zell. *Mrs. H. O'Brien.* Social influence; or, take care of the boys. P. 1865.

Zell, Ira. *Robert Barnwell Roosevelt.*

Zeno. *Thomas M'Grugar.* Letters ... addressed to the citizens of Edinburgh, on Parliamentary representation ... Edinb. 1783.

Zeokinizul. *Louis XV.,* King of France. The amours of ... king of the Kofirans. Translated from the Arabic of the famous traveller Krinelbol. With a key. [From the French of Claude Prosper Jolyot de Crébillion.] L. 1749.

Zepa. *D. Hulburt, M.D.* An eye-opener. "Citateur, par Pigault" ... B. 1871.

Zero. *Allan Ramsay.* A succinct review of the American contest ... L. 1782.

Zeta. *John Lovell,* in his contributions to the "Graphic" (L.).

Zeta. *James Anthony Froude.* Shadows of the clouds [tales]. By ... L. 1847.

Zianitzka, K. Th. *Kathinka (Halein) Zitz.* Schiller's Laura, etc. Mainz, 1855

Zigzag, Mr., the Elder. *John Wyke*

ham Archer. The recreations of . . . L. 18–.

Zinn, Serjeant. *James Edwin Wilson.* A throw for the throne; or, the prince unmasked. L. 1872.

Zion. *John Ward.* The standard of Zion . . . Birmingham, 1831.

Ziska. *Amos Jay Cummings,* in the New York "Sun."

Zulano. *Jerome Alfred Harte,* who, under this pseudonym, for four years contributed to the San Francisco "Argonaut" *feuilleton,* with the title "Echoes from Everywhere"; also sketches and translations.

ZZ—, J——. *Rev. John Butler.* The genuine will of a clergyman lately deceas'd . . . L. 1750.

ADDITIONS.

******. *William Maginn.* Letter from . . . inclosing hymn to Christopher North, Esq. [with the hymn], in " Blackwood's Magazine," Vol. IX., pp. 59–64.

A., C. C. *Rev. C. C. Adams.*

"A," "H," "B," "M," "F," "N," and **"E."** Letters from the Irish Highlands. L. 1825.

The letters signed "H" were written by *Henry Blake, Esq.,* of Renvyle; the others by *Mrs. Blake and her sisters.*

A., H. and R. *Harriet and Rose Acton.* Poems. L. 1846.

A., J. *Dr. John Aiken,* in " Gent. Mag."; Nichols' " Literary Anecdotes, 18th Century," IX., 384.

A. R. *Richard Allen* (?). The fortune hunter's guide, etc. By . . . 1840 (?).

A. S. *Rev. Thomas Russell.*

In Allibone's " Critical Dictionary of English Literature," Vol. II., under *Joseph Ritson,* on p. 1812, about one-third down on first column, I find,—

" The controversy was carried on by different parties in London ' Gent. Mag.,' 1782, etc. ('A. S.' stands for *Rev. Thomas Russell*)."

A. W., Farmer. Free thoughts on the proceedings of the Continental Congress held at Philadelphia, September 5th, 1774, etc. By . . . n.p., n.d.

Said by Mr. John Russell Bartlett to be the joint production of *Dr. Seabury,* afterwards Bishop of Connecticut, and *Mr. Isaac Wilkins,* a West-Chester farmer.

A., W. G. *G. W. Allen.* Two ghost tales: poems. Nottingham, 1870.

Absentee, An. *Rev. Edward Mangin.* Utopia found: being an apology for Irish absentees . . . by . . . Bath, 1813.

Achates. *Thomas Pinckney.* Reflections occasioned by the late disturbances [by negroes] in South Carolina. By . . . Charleston, 1822.

Acorn. *James Oakes.*

In the Boston " Sunday Herald " for Dec. 7, 1884, is an article called " Passing Away," which gives an account of " The Place where the ' Scarlet Letter' was written." In this article a bit of information is given about *James Oakes.* He was something of a literary man, a good theatrical critic, and wrote for the Boston " Post" and New York papers over the signature of " Acorn." He was a friend of Edwin Forrest.

Agricola. *Rev. Percival Stockdale.*

In the summer of 1779, *Rev. Percival Stockdale* wrote several political letters with the signature " Agricola." They were published by Mr. H. S. Woodfall in the " Public Advertiser." " Literary Anecdotes of 18th Century," Nichols, Vol. VIII., p. 25, note at foot. The opening of the note is on p. 18, and is signed on p. 29 as " J. P." The next sentence says written by *Jane Porter.*

Albens, le vicomte d'. *Mme Urbain Rattazzi.* Articles in the journal " Le Pays," notably *parisiennes* " Lettres," and among other novels, " Le quartrième larron," published in 1862.

Alceste. *Louis Amédée Eugéne Achard.* Lettres parisiennes, the first of which appeared in " L'Assemblée Nationale," April 14, 1849, and several of the following appeared signed " Alceste."

Allen, Grant. *Charles Grant Blair-findie Allen.* Physiological æsthetics. L. 1877.

Alphonso. *John Nichols.*

In August, 1778, *John Nichols* became associated with David Henry in the management of the " Gent. Mag.," and from that time not a single month elapsed in which he did not write several articles in that miscellany, some with his own name or his initials, and some anonymously. A note to the above says, under these signatures, " Alphonso " = *John Nichols;* " Eugenio " = *John Nichols;* " M. Green " = *John Nichols;* " A London Antiquary " = *John Nichols;* " J. N." = *John Nichols.* — " Literary Anecdotes of 18th Century," NICHOLS, Vol. VI., p. 628 and note.

Amateur, An. *Hon. E. S. Abbot,* afterwards *Baroness Colchester.* Views in London [in verse], sketched from a window in the " Palais de la Vérité," etc. Chiswick, 1833.

American, An. *Henry Pickering.* Poems by . . . B. 1830.

Ancient Brahmin, An. *Philip Dormer Stanhope,* 4th Earl of Chesterfield. The œconomy of human life. Translated from an Indian manuscript, written by ... To which is prefixed an account of the manner in which the said manuscript was discover'd. In a letter from an English gentleman now residing in China, to the Earl of – – – – – – . L. 1761. See "Notes and Queries," Vol. X., pp. 8, 74, and 318.

Angelo, Master Michael. *Oliver Goldsmith* (?). The drawing school for little masters and misses ... By ... L. 1777.

Goldsmith is believed to have written the "History of Little Goody Two Shoes ... From the original Ms. in the Vatican at Rome, the cuts by Michael Angelo." L.

Angeloni, Battista, a Jesuit. *John Shebbeare, M.D.*

Indeed that gentleman, whatever objections were made to him, had knowledge and abilities much above the class of ordinary writers, and deserves to be remembered as a respectable name in literature, were it only for his admirable "Letters on the English Nation," under the name of "Battista Angeloni, a Jesuit." This was John Shebbeare, in 1755. — BOSWELL'S "Life of Johnson," edition of London (Bell), 1876, Vol. VIII., p. 90, year 1781.

Anti-Janus. *Dr. Phil Hergenroether.* An historico-theological criticism of "The Pope and the Council," by "Janus." N.Y. 1871.

Anti-Sejanus. *James Scott.*

Dr. James Scott wrote, in 1765, the letters signed "Anti-Sejanus," which were published in the "Public Advertiser," and were so popular that they raised the sale of the paper from 1500 to 3000 a day ... There are likewise some others signed "Philanglia," written by *Dr. Scott.* — NICHOLS, "Literary Anecdotes of 18th Century," Vol. IX., p. 725.

Antiquarian. *Henry Phillips, Jr.* A review of an article on Continental money, in "Harper's Magazine" for March, 1863. n.p. 1863.

Armenian, An. *Judge Robert Hellen.* Letters from ... in Ireland to his friends at Trebisond ... L. 1757. Also ascribed to *Edmund Sexton Pery, Esq.,* afterwards speaker of the Irish House of Commons.

Artist, An. *John Beugo.* Poetry, miscellaneous and dramatic. By ... Edinb. 1797.

Ashleigh, Rose. *Mrs. Rose Aldrich,* in contributions to the "Weekly" (N.Y.).

Augustinus. *William Maginn.* Latin prosody from England. To Christopher North, Esq., dated St. Andrews, Sept. 13, 1821, in "Blackwood's Magazine," Vol. X., pp. 383–388.

Autolycus. *John Edwards,* in his contributions to the "Springfield Wheelmen's Gazette."

Azamat Batuk. *Nicolas Léon Thiéblin.*

"The pseudonym of 'Azamat Batuk' was used by me for fancy sketches in the 'Pall Mall Gazette' (L.); the pseudonym of 'Rigolo' was used for the last seven or eight years in the 'Sun' for my Monday Wall Street articles only, and is being used still. I have occasionally used some other pseudonyms, including that of 'John Collins' in the 'Sun,' giving sketches of Wall Street men (Vanderbilt, Gould, Woerishoffer, and others), in the years 1877 and '78." — Letter to A. R. Frey, Jan. 18, 1885.

B., C. K. *Charles K. Bishop,* in "Harper's Monthly."

B., E. B. *Elizabeth (Barrett) Browning.* "Victoria's tears," in the "Athenæum" for July 8, 1837, p. 506.

B., O. B. *Oliver Bell Bunce,* in various periodicals.

B., S. J. *Mrs. Sallie J. (Hancock) Battey.*

Barrett, Rev. J., D.D.S.F.T.C.D., Professor of Hebrew in Trinity College, Dublin. *William Maginn.* A Hebrew dirge over Sir Daniel Donnelly. By ... in "Blackwood's Magazine," Vol. VII., pp. 197–199.

Beauchamp, Philip. *George Grote.* Analysis of the influence of natural religion on the temporal condition of mankind. L. 1822.

The "British Museum Catalogue" thus ascribes this work to *Mr. Grote,* and not to *Mr. Bentham.*

Beauvoir, Roger de. *Édouard Roger de Bully.* L'ecolier de Cluny; ou, le sophisme, 1315. Paris, 1832.

Belle, Clara. *Frank File,* in various periodicals.

Benedick. *Joseph Reed.*

"*Joseph Reed* wrote letters under the signature 'Benedick' (in defence of Mr. Garrick, on the publication of Kendrick's 'Love in the suds'), printed originally in the 'Morning Chronicle.'" — NICHOLS, "Literary Anecdotes of the 18th Century," IX., 118

Bernard, Camille. *Mme Urbain Rattazzi.*

Bessie. *Mrs. Kent.* — See Clark's "Recollections of Writers."

Bienaise, Jacques. *Louis Labarre.* Un mois à Paris; ou, le fameux petit tour en France du poëte Marie-Amour Janvier, recueilli et mis en lumière, par ... Liége, 1838.

Bigwig's Friend, The. *Henry George Herbert,* Lord Porchester and 2d Earl of Carnarvon. A letter to the "Oxford Spy," from ... 1818.

Birch, Rev. Busby, LL.D., F.R.S., F.A.S., F.G.C., and M.S.E.A.M.C. [*i.e.*

Member of the Society for the Encouragement of Arts, Manufactures, and Commerce]. *Bonnel Thornton.* City Latin; or, critical and political remarks on the Latin inscription on laying the first stone of the intended new bridge at Black Fryars ... By ... L. 1760.

"This sparkling, frisky squib from the pen of *Bonnel Thornton* was let off more in merriment than rancour. The witty author followed up his whimsical strictures in another droll pamphlet," for the title of which, see "A Deputy."—See "Notes and Queries," July, 1865, pp. 41, 42.

Bluggen, Vander von. *Charles Knight.* "The Bœotian order of architecture," in Knight's "Quarterly Magazine," 1824.

Boythorn. *W. S. Landor,* in Dickens's "Bleak House."

Bridges, Sallie. *Mrs. S. B. Stebbins,* of Philadelphia, in poems contributed to various periodicals.

Brown, Edward, Esq. *John Campbell, LL.D.* The travels and adventures of ... L. 1739.

Buller, Bob. *William Maginn.* A Latin version of Will's [see W. Seward] "Ullaloo," in "Blackwood's Magazine," Vol. VII., p. 197.

C., Mrs. *Maria (Little) Child,* in her contributions to literary journals.

C., C., C.A.D.A. [Carolus Cordell, Catholicæ Academicæ Duacenæ Alumnus]. *Rev. Charles Cordell.* The Divine Office for the use of the laity. Newcastle (?), 1763.

C., G. T. *George Ticknor Curtis,* in "Harper's Weekly," Aug. 9, 1884, and in other periodicals.

C., H., Esq. *Henry Coventry.* The history of Pompey the Little. L. 1751.

C., M. A. *Miss Mary Ann Cursham.* Emanuel Swedenborg; and other poems. L., n.d. Also poems in Colburn's "New Monthly," about 1834.

Calcroft, John William. *J. W. Cole.* A defence of the stage. L. 1809.

Campana. *Right Hon. Frederick Richard Chichester, Earl of Belfast,* who, under this signature, contributed to the "Northern Magazine" for February, 1852, an article headed "Twelfth-day at Cannes," written in a style of lively reminiscence and graceful sentiment.

Carlton, Carrie. *Mary Booth.*

Celeste. *Mrs. George C. (Bowlin Jenkins) Brown.*

Champlin, Virginia. *Miss Grace Virginia Lord.*

"Many have read with pleasure the translations in different papers and magazines furnished

by "Virginia Champlin." They were the work of a scholar, and, by the beauty of their composition, showed a familiarity with the original that could only come from long years of study."

Chromo, Polly. *Miss Lizzie F. Schuster,* in contributions to the "Household" (Brattleboro, Vt.) *et al.*

Citizen of Massachusetts, A. *Willard Phillips.* An appeal to the good sense of the Democrats and the public spirit of the Federalists. By ... B. 1814.

Citizen of New York, A. *Mathew Adgate.* A northern light; or, new index to the Bible ... Troy, 1800.

Citizen of South Carolina, A. *William Smith.* Candid examination of the objections to the Treaty of Amity, Commerce, and Navigation between the United States and Great Britain ... By ... N.Y. 1795.

Clergyman of the Episcopal Church in England, A. *Rev. William Edward Heygate.* — See "Layman of Boston, A."

Clyde, Kate. *Miss C. G. Tharin,* in contributions to the "Weekly" (N.Y.).

C—o. *Rev. John Spicer,* in "Gent. Mag.," Vol. LIV., 825; Nichols' "Literary Anecdotes of 18th Century," IX., 545.

Crito. *John Duncombe.*

"In the 'Gent. Mag.,' *John Duncombe's* communications in biography, poetry, and criticism, during the last 20 years of his life, were frequent and valuable. Many of them were without a name, but his miscellaneous contributions were usually distinguished by the signature 'Crito'; and the 'Review of Books' ... was nearly all his own."—NICHOLS, "Literary Anecdotes of the 18th Century," Vol. VIII., p. 277 at top.

Crookleg, W. *William Tennant.* The Anster concert. Cupar, 1811.

Crossman, P. J. *William Maginn,* in the "Literary Gazette," in 1819.

See "Noctes Ambrosianæ," edited by Mackenzie, Vol. V., p. iv.

"O. P." = *Wm. Maginn.*—See same book, Vol. V., p. v. This pseudonym was changed to "Olinthus, Petre, D.D." = *Wm. Maginn.*—See same book, Vol. V., p. vii.

Curio. *Mark Akenside.*

"His stay at Northampton, however, was fertile in a literary respect, for he published two of his more remarkable works while there; his 'Epistle to Curio,' in November, 1744, and his 'Odes on Several Subjects.' Under the pseudonym of 'Curio,' the former of these works was a very spirited attack on Wm. Pulteney."

Custom-House Officer, A. *William Russell.* Leaves from the journal of ... L. 1868.

D., A. *Dr. Andrew Douglas.* Notes of a journey from Berne to England through France, made in the year 1796. By ... (with supplement by M. D.). L. 1797.

D., C. W. *Charles W. Deans.*

D., W. *W. Derham.* Artificial clock-maker ... 4th ed. L. 1734.

D'Anvers, Caleb. *Nicholas Amhurst.*

"In 1726, Dec. 5th, Nicholas Amhurst issued, under the pseudonym of 'Caleb D'Anvers of Gray's Inn,' the first number of the famous 'Craftsman,' the most successful of all the political journals of this age."—STEPHEN, "Dict. of Nat. Biog.," p. 362, col. 2.

"He was also, in all probability, author of a poem, 'The Protestant Session' ... By a member of the Constitutional Club of Oxford, 1719."—STEPHEN, "Dict. of Nat. Biog.," p. 362, col. 1.

Dapiferus, Jacobus, Corcagiensis. *William Maginn.* Adventus in Hiberniam, etc. "Blackwood's Magazine," Vol. IX., pp. 319–20.

Ascribed to *Dr. Maginn* as well as to *Mr. Murphy.*

Debruel, Louis. *Louis Amédée Eugène Achard* issued several vaudevilles under this pseudonym.

Delta. *David Macbeth Moir.*

Under "Δ" he contributed 395 poems to "Blackwood's." See a note in "Noctes Ambrosianæ," J. Wilson; edited by R. Shelton Mackenzie, pub. by W. J. Widdleton, N.Y. 1875. Vol. II., p. 21.

Allibone says he contributed articles from 1817 (when the magazine was established) till 1851, the year of his death.

Denton, H. B. *Edgar Taylor.* Lord Brougham's local courts' bill examined. By ... L. 1833.

Deputy, A. *Bonnel Thornton.* Plain English in answer to city Latin; or, critical and political remarks on the Latin inscription on laying the first stone of the intended new bridge at Black-Fryars ... By ... L. 1761.

Divine of the University of Cambridge, A. *George Smith, D.D.* An epistolary dissertation addressed to the clergy of Middlesex ... By ... L. 1739.

Dixon, Helena. *Adeline E. Story,* in contributions to the "Weekly" (N.Y.).

Dowden, Richard. *William Maginn.* Letter from ... Cork, 1820; and A new song ... in lamentation for ... Sir Daniel Donnelly, Kt. C.I. [Champion of Ireland]; also, Speech delivered at the Cork Institution, in "Blackwood's Magazine," Vol. VII., pp. 200–205.

E., M. E. *Mrs. Mary Ellen Edwards Staples,* whose first essay in wood-drawing appeared on the title-page of the "Illustrated Times," 1859.

Earle, Sidney. *Mrs. Sallie J. (Hancock) Battey.*

Earnshaw, Catharine. *Maria L. Pool,* in contributions to the "Weekly" (N.Y.).

Edwards, Leon. *Alfred R. Calhoun,* in contributions to the "Weekly" (N.Y.).

Elbon, Barbara. *Leonora B. Halsted.* Bethesda.

Emerald Isle. *Duncan D. Hepburn.* Stray rhymes. 1885 (?).

Eminent Hand, An. *Alexander Pope.* The impertinent; or, a visit to the Court. A satire. By ... L. 1733.

English Gentleman, An. *Philip Dormer Stanhope,* 4th Earl of Chesterfield. — See "Ancient Brahmin, An."

English Officer, An. *John Banks.* The history of Francis Eugene, Prince of Savoy ... By ... L. 1741.

European Traveller, The. *Rev. Thomas Brockway* (?). The E. T. in America, contained in three letters to his friend in London. Hartford, 1785.

Ex-Hussar, An. *A. Heron,* in the "United Service Magazine." 1885.

Fairie, Fanny. *Mrs. Mary T. Waqgamon,* in contributions to the "Weekly" (N.Y.).

Father, A. *William Tighe, Esq.* Observations on the Lord's Prayer, in the form of a letter from ... to his son. Dublin, 1816.

Federal Republican, A. — *Richards.* Politics of Connecticut. Hartford, 1817.

Fielding, Henry. *Samuel William Henry Ireland.* Fielding's proverbs. L. 18–.

Fine Arkansas Gentleman, The. *Albert Pike.* The life-wake of ... who died before his time. W. 1859.

"This pamphlet commemorates a reception given to *Albert Pike* by his friends, subsequent to a premature announcement of his death which appeared in the Washington papers."

Fisherman and Zoölogist, A. *Francis Trevelyan Buckland.* The log-book of ... L. 1875.

Fitztravesty, Blaise, Esq. *William Maginn.* "A midsummer night's dream, in blank verse, by ... In "Blackwood's Magazine," Vol. X., pp. 557–562.

Flat Enlightened, A. — *Deale.* Life in the West; or, the curtain drawn ... By ... L. 1827.

This work afterwards appeared, with the title, "Crockfords; or, life in the West," L. 1828.

Fledger, Aaron. *Addison Fletcher Andrews,* in the New York journals.

Flora. *Miss Payne,* correspondent of the "Herald" (Cleveland, O.).

Footman, A. *Robert Dodsley.* Servitude: a poem ... Written by ... L. about 1725.

Forager, Philip. *William Maginn.* Ode to Marshal —, on his return. By an Irish gentleman lately deceased. In

"Blackwood's Magazine," Vol. VII., pp. 587, 588.

Forester, Fleta. *Mrs. S. C. Stone,* in her contributions to "St. Nicholas" (N.Y.) *et al.*

Fow. *F. O. Ward,* leader-writer on the "London Times."

Foxhall. *Miss Molly Elliott Seawell,* in her contributions to the "Mail and Express" (N.Y.).

Friend in the North, A. *Stephen Colwell.* The South: a letter from . . . With special reference to the effects of disunion on slavery. P. 1856.

Friend to the West India Colonies and their Inhabitants, A. *James Tobin* (?). Cursory remarks upon the Reverend Mr. Ramsay's "Essay on the treatment and conversion of African slaves in the sugar colonies." By . . . L. 1785.

Gentleman at Cambridge, A. *Francis Bragge.* Two odes of R. Rapin, imitated in English Pindaricks. By . . . L. 1710.

Gentleman Here, A. *John Macky.* A journey through Scotland; in familiar letters from . . . to his friend abroad . . . By . . . L. 1723.

Gentleman in the Country, A. *Adam Ferguson, LL.D.* Remarks on a pamphlet lately published by Dr. Price, intitled "Observations on the nature of civil liberty . . . In a letter from . . . to a member of Parliament. L. 1776.

Gentleman of the Middle Temple, A. *Thomas Babington Macaulay.* Conversation between Mr. Abraham Cowley and Mr. John Milton touching the great Civil War, in Knight's "Quarterly Magazine," 1824.

Gentleman, resident there, A. *Thomas Clio Rickman.* Emigration to America candidly considered. In a series of letters from . . . to his friend in England. L. 1798.

George, Uncle. *Frederick George Pardon.* Parlour pastimes, containing charades, etc. L. 1857.

Graduate of 1794, A. *Ezekiel Bacon, LL.D.*— See "B., E."

Graham, Ennis. *Mrs. Mary Louisa Molesworth.* "Carrots": just a little boy . . . L. 1876.

Greatest Hypocrite in England, The. *John Wesley.* Perfection: a poetical epistle, calmly addressed to . . . L. 1778.

"He, like our hypocrite brother,
Professes one thing, does another;

Thus all things where they're most profest
Are found to be regarded least."
—BUTLER, upon P. Nye's "Thanksgiving Bard."

"This epistle seems to be aimed at the Rev. John Wesley, in answer to his 'Calm Address.'"

H. E., Esq. *Samuel William Henry Ireland.*

H., J. *Rev. John Hutton, B.D.* A tour to the caves in the environs of Ingleborough and Settle . . . L. 1781.

H. M. *Sir Samuel Egerton Brydges.*

"In 1832, *Sir Egerton Brydges* contributed some letters to the "Times" newspaper, during the discussion of our legislative constitution, on the Peerages, signed 'H. M.,' and dated Leipsic."—"Gent. Mag.," November, 1837, Vol. VIII., N.S., Pt. II., p. 538.

H., M. W. *M. W. Hallett.*

Hastler, Doctor, M.R.S.P.Q. *John Whitley Boswell.* Συλλεγομενα of the antiquities of Killmackumpshaugh, in the County of Roscommon and Kingdom of Ireland. Written by . . . Dublin, 1790.

Hincks, Rev. E., F.T.C.D. *William Maginn.* Translation of Hebrew dirge in "Blackwood's Magazine," Vol. VII., pp. 198, 199.

His Sister. *Miss Angeline M. Cudworth.* A memorial of Rev. Warren H. Cudworth. By . . . B. 1885.

Holt, Wm. *William Maginn.* Report of the "Speech delivered at the Cork Institution," in "Blackwood's Magazine," Vol. VII., pp. 202–205.

Irish Clergyman, An. *Rev. Spencer Knox.* Pastoral annals. By . . . L. 1840.

Irish Gentleman, lately deceased, An. *William Maginn.* An ode to Mrs. Flanagan. By . . . in "Blackwood's Magazine," Vol. VI., pp. 628–630.

Ixion. *Llewelyn H. Johnson.*

J., R. *Richard Jones.*

[NOTES BY MR. A. R. FREY.]

I have before me a book with the following title, "Six Old Plays," on which Shakspeare founded his "Measure for Measure," "Comedy of Errors," "Taming of the Shrew," "King John," "King Henry IV. and V.," and "King Lear." Two Vols. bound in one. L. 1779. Sometimes called "Nichols Steevens' edition." In it I find several initials, and I have looked them up with the following result. The first play is,—
"Historye of Promus and Cassandra," by Geo. Whetstones. It opens with an address by the author, and signed with his name. Then follows "The Printer to the Reader," signed "R. I." In Collier's "Shakspere Library," edited by Hazlitt, I find that this "R. I." = *Richard Jones,* who printed the edition of the play in 1578. His whole name appears at the close of the play in the above book.
The next play is "Menæcmi," a pleasant and fine conceited comoedie, taken out of the most excellent wittie poet, Plautus . . . written in English by W. W. London, 1595. "W. W.," says Knight, in his introductory notice to the

"Comedy of Errors" (on the authority of Wood) was *William Warner.*

Born, probably 1558; died, March 9 or 10, 1608–9. Allibone, under *William Warner.*

The next play is the "First and Second Part of the Troublesome Reign of John, King of England," etc., written by W. Sh. Imprinted by Valentine Simmes for John Helme, 1611.

" W. Sh." = *William Shakespeare,* but I find "On the title of the reprint of 1611, the bookseller placed the initials W. Sh., ostensibly for the purpose of creating a belief that the play was Shakespeare's."—See "Shakespeare's Library," by COLLIER, edited by Hazlitt, Pt. II., Vol. I., p. 222; edition London, 1875.

Next comes the "Taming of a Shrew," printed by V. S. for Nicholas Ling.

"V. S." = *Valentine Simmes* (a printer), who printed "King John."

Here ends all the initials that I find in the "Six Old Plays, etc."; but I find a reference to another initial.

"The Whole Contention between the two Famous Houses, Lancaster and York. With the Tragicall ende of the good Duke Humphrey, Richard, Duke of York, and King Henrie the sixt. Divided into two Parts, and newly corrected and enlarged. Written by William Shakspeare, Gent. Printed at London, for T. P."

This contains the "First Part of the Contention" as well as the "True Tragedie." " T. P." was *Thomas Pavier,* the publisher of other plays.

See "Shakspere's Library," Collier, edited by Hazlitt, Pt. II., Vol. I., p. 386. L. 1875.

Jacobus, G. P. R. *G. P. R. James.* — See " Painsworth, W. Harassing."

Jacques. *Robert W. Ewing,* a severe censor of the stage under this signature during the years 1825 and '26.

Jennings, Thomas, Soda Water Manufacturer. *William Maginn.* Letter from . . . Cork, 1820, and a dirge over Sir Daniel Donnelly ; by . . . in "Blackwood's Magazine," Vol. VII., pp. 199, 200.

Johnny the Bear. *John Abernethy.*

"Has any one who knows Johnny the Bear heard his name thus anagrammatised without a smile? We may be sure he smiled and growled at the same time when he first heard it himself."—SOUTHEY's "Doctor," ch. clxxix., p. 468.

Junius Redivivus. *William Bridges Adams.* A tale of Tucuman, with digressions, English and American [a political poem]. L. 1831. He also contributed " On the Working Classes" to Tait's "Edinburgh Magazine," 1834, pp. 79, 701.

Keen, Royal. *F. F. Schrader,* in his contributions to various Western periodicals.

Kettle, Rosa Mackenzie. *Mary Rosa Stuart Kettle.* The Carding-Mill Valley. L. 1882.

L., A. H. *Alexander H. Laidlaw, M.D.,* in contributions to Philadelphia journals, 1854, etc.

Author of an English dictionary, in which *demote* appears for the first time as opposite of *promote.*

Laboring Man, A. *Thomas Robinson Hazard.* Facts for the laboring man. By . . . Newport, R.I., 1840.

Lady, A. *Mrs. Hannah Glasse.* The art of cookery. L. 1747.

This is ascribed, not only to *Dr. John Hill,* but also to the witty *Dr. William King.*

Lady, A. *Mrs. — Salmon.* Jeptha: a dramatic poem, by . . . L. 1846.

Lady, A. *Miss Mary Ann Cursham.* Norman Abbey: a tale of Sherwood Forest. L. 1832.

Lady, A. *Miss Anna Jane Vardill.* Poems by . . . L. 1809.

Lady, A. *Lady Charlotte Maria (Campbell) Bury.* Poems on several occasions, by . . . Edinb. 1797.

Lady lately Deceased, A. *Miss Henrietta Bowdler.* Poems and essays by . . . 2d ed. Bath, 1786.

Lancelot, le Capitaine. *Amable Louis Boué de Villiers.* Les pompiers peints par eux-mêmes. Paris, 1868.

Lang, S. *Richard Henry Stoddard,* in his contributions to the "Aldine" (N.Y.).

Late Celebrated Genius Deceased, A. *Richard Griffiths.* The posthumous works of . . . L. 1770.

Late Eminent Divine of the Church of England, A. *John Lawson, D.D.* Occasional sermons. 2d ed.

Le Ros, Christian. *W. J. Sorel.* Christmas Day, and how it was spent, by . . . L. 1854.

Libera Clavis, Gul. [*i.e.* Free Key, *i.e.* Freke]. *William Freke.* An essay towards an union between divinity and morality. L. 1687.

Licius. *Sir Francis Freeling,* in Dibdin's " Bibliophobia."

London, Thomas. *Philip Thicknesse,* in the "Gent. Mag.," 1748–49.

Lover of Peace and Good Government, A. *James Stewart.* Letter to the Rev. Dr. Price, F.R.S., wherein his observations on the nature of civil liberty . . . are candidly examined . . . By . . . L. 1776.

M.A. of Balliol College, Oxford, An. *A. D. Thomson.* On mankind: their origin and destiny. L. 1872.

McC., J. L. *James Law McCance,* contributor to "Notes and Queries."

The following are what I have so far sent:—
6th Ser., Vol. IX., p. 107, a paragraph under name "J. L. McC.," referring to F. Ford, an artist.
6th Ser., Vol. IX., p. 389, under name "McC.," referring to N. Tull, an artist.
6th Ser., Vol. X., p. 125, under name "J. L. McC.," a folk-lore note.

6th Ser., Vol. X., p. 295, under same initials, on an epitaph.

Also there are various — more than two dozen — letters to the editor, answers to queries, etc., scattered through Vols. 24 to 28 of the "English Mechanic and World of Science"; these are almost all on astronomical subjects, and are signed "Mac." — Letter to Mr. A. R. Frey, dated Jan. 26, 1885.

McFlimsey, Flora. *Miss Ebelyn Kimball Johnson.* Associate Editor of the "Bar Harbor Tourist," at Mt. Desert. 1885.

M., J., of T. *John Moncrieff.* Tippermalluch's receipts . . . written by that worthy and ingenious gentleman . . . Leith, 1775.

M., Paul. *Paul Möbius.* Hundert Charaden und Rätsel. 1875.

M., R. *Prof. Robert Manning.* The rise and fall of the heresy of iconoclasts; or, image-breakers . . . Collected by . . . L. 1731.

Macaroni, A. *Mr. "Sun" Taylor.* Theatrical portraits epigrammatically delineated. About 1775. See "Notes & Queries," 2d Ser., xii., 473; 3d Ser., i., 39.

Malagrowther, Malachi. *Sir Walter Scott.*

In 1826, Sir Walter Scott wrote "Three Letters by Malachi Malagrowther," first published in "Edinburgh Weekly Journal," and subsequently in a pamphlet by Blackwood. These were on paper money, etc. In 1830, when the Reform Ministry came in, Scott wrote a fourth "Letter of Malachi Malagrowther."

See Allibone, "Dict. of Eng. Lit.," under "Scott," 1826; "Noctes Ambrosianæ," edited by Mackenzie, N.Y. 1875, Vol. II., pp. 194, 195, note; "Life of Sir Walter Scott," R. Shelton Mackenzie, B. 1871, p. 391, etc.

Marc, A. *Marc Antoine Bayle.* Causeries littéraires, in "Le Messager de la Semaine."

Mel, Mary, should be not *Bake, M. E.,* but *Bennett, Mary E.* — See "B.," M. E."

Melmoth, Courtney. *Samuel Jackson Pratt.*

"*Samuel Jackson Pratt* commenced his literary course very early in life under the name of 'Courtney Melmoth.' The first of his publications which attracted notice was the 'Tears of Genius,' 1774, on the death of Goldsmith." — NICHOLS, "Literary Anecdotes of 18th Century," IX., p. 722.

Member of that Institution, A. *Ezekiel Porter Belden, A.M.* Sketches of Yale College . . . By . . . N.Y. 1843.

Member of the Church of England, A. *Rev. Ernest Silvanus Appleyard.* Proposals for Christian union. By . . . L. 1846.

Member of the Massachusetts Bar, A. *John Pickering.* National rights and State rights . . . By . . . B. 1841.

Member of the University of Cam-

bridge, A. *Rev. Edward Valpy, B.D.* (?). Academic errors; or, recollections of youth. By . . . L. 1817.

Minister of the Church, The. *Rev. Henry C. Leonard.* Discourse delivered in Orono, Me., at the funeral of Mary E. Crane, March 20, 1850. Bangor, 1853.

Minor, A. *G. W. M. Reynolds* (?). Rodolph: a dramatic fragment, etc., by . . . L. 1832.

Moggridge, Major Spencer, of the Prince's Own. *Captain Thomas Hamilton* (?), in "Blackwood's Magazine."

Mulligan, Morty Macnamara. *William Maginn.* Irish melodies, in "Blackwood's Magazine," Vol. X., pp. 613–622.

N., J. H. *John Henry Newman.*

"The 'Manual of Devotion in Greek and Latin' by Lancelot Andrews, was translated by J. H. N., in the 'Tracts for the Times.'" — STEPHEN, "Dict. of National Biography," p. 405, col. 1.

N. S. *Sir Samuel Egerton Brydges.*

"N. S." in "Gent. Mag.," Vol. LVIII., p. 698, and in "Gent. Mag.," Vol. LIX., p. 584, is *Sir Egerton Brydges.* — "Literary Anecdotes of 18th Century," Vol. VIII., p. 560.

N. Y. *John Fry.* Pieces of ancient poetry . . . [Edited by "N. Y."] Bristol, 1814.

Native of Algiers, A. *Peter Markoe* (?). The Algerine spy in Pennsylvania; or, letters written by . . . on the affairs of the United States of America . . . P. 1787.

Naturalist, A. *Andrew Leith Adams.* Wanderings of . . . in India, the western Himalayas, and Cashmere. Edinb. 1867.

Naval Officer, A. *Captain G. Boid.* Travels through Sicily and the Lipari Islands in . . . 1824. By . . . L. 1827.

Nemo. *Henry Gardiner.*

Noble Duke, A. *Henry St. John, Lord Bolingbroke.* A collection of political tracts. Dublin, 1748.

"The tracts are signed as if by different writers, but the style of all is so alike as to lead one to the conclusion that they are all by the same hand . . . Some of the names found at the end of the various papers [are] : — 'The Occasional Writer,' 'From my Garret,' 'John Trot,' 'Phil-Athenus.' The following names appear in one of the articles . . . 'Benjamin, Lord Bishop of ******,' 'Ben,' 'Robin,' 'Numb Fish,' 'Raleigh,' 'Publicola,' 'A Person.'" — See "Notes and Queries," February, 1865, p. 156.

"By 'Robin of notable memory' is probably meant *Robert Harley,* Earl of Oxford; and 'Benjamin, Lord Bishop of ******,' is clearly *Benjamin Hoadly,* Bishop of Bangor." — See "Notes and Queries," February, 1865, p. 157.

Nobleman of the other Kingdom, A. *Sir John Perceval,* 1st Earl of Egmont. The question of the precedency of the peers of Ireland in England fairly stated. A letter to an English lord, by ... Dublin, 1739.

No Zoo, Lord. *John Swinton.*

Octavius. *Rev. William Hales.* Pursuits of literature : translations by ... Dublin, 1799.

O'Doherty, Sir Morgan, Bart. *William Maginn.* — See "Notes and Queries," Vol. viii., pp. 11, 12; Vol. ix., p. 209; Vol. x., pp. 96, 150, 151, 233.

For a list of Dr. Maginn's writings, see "Dublin University Magazine," Vol. XXIII., pp. 80 *et seq.*

Officer in the Field, An. *Charles C. Nott.*

O'Fogarty, Fagarty, Esq., of Blarney. *Samuel Gosnell.* Daniel O'Rourke : an epic poem, in six cantos, in "Blackwood's Magazine," Vol. VII., pp. 476-481, and later volumes.

Also ascribed to *Dr. William Maginn.*

Oinophilus de Monte Frasconi, Boniface, A.B.C. *Robert Samber.* Ebrietatis encomium ; or, the praise of drunkenness ... By ... L. 1723.

"This is not an original work ... but a translation from the French. The original is entitled "L'Eloge de l'Yvresse (á la Haye ... MDCCXIV.)," and is by Sallengre, Henri Albert de. — See "Notes and Queries," November, 1865, p. 442.

Oliver, Pen, F.R.C.S. *Sir Henry Thompson.* Charley Kingston's aunt. By ... L.

One of the Rhode-Island People. *John Pitman, Jr., Esq.* A reply to the letter of the Hon. Marcus Morton ... on the Rhode Island question ... By ... Providence, 1842.

One who has seen the Elephant. *B. F. Scribner.* Camp life of a volunteer : a campaign in Mexico ... By ... P. 1847. — See "One who was thar."

One who Respects them. *James Bury.* Little bits from workingmen. By ... Manchester, 1874.

Our Bard. *Frank Waters,* contributor to the "Weekly Courant," of Columbia, Penn.

P. *Hon. Philip Yorke.*

The "Athenian Letters" were first published for the private use of a limited number of friends, in 4 Vols., 8vo., 1741-43. In 1781, they were again printed in 4to (100 copies only), but not published. An edition having afterwards been surreptitiously printed in Ireland, this Lord Hardwick, in 1810, published them in two handsome quarto volumes for general circulation. The several writers were thus designated : —
"P.," *Hon. Philip Yorke,* afterwards Earl of Hardwick; "C." *Hon. Charles Yorke;* "R.," *Rev. Dr. G. H. Rooke,* Master of Christ's College; "G.," *Rev. Dr. John Green,* afterwards Bishop of Lincoln; "W.," *Daniel Wray,*

Esq.; "H.," *Rev. Mr. John Heaton,* of Bene't College; "E.," *Dr. Heberden;* "O.," *Henry Coventry;* "L.," *Rev. John Lawry,* Prebendary of Rochester; "T.," *Mrs. Catherine Talbot;* "B.," *Rev. Dr. T. Birch;* "S.,"*Rev. Dr. Samuel Salter,* late member of the Charter House. — See " Illustrations of the Literary History of the 18th Century," JOHN NICHOLS. Vol. I., pp. 15, 23, 33, 73, 92. Allibone, under "Yorke, Philip, Second Earl of Hardwick," also speaks of it.

P. R., Gent. *Robert Paltock* (?). Memoirs of the life of Parnese, a Spanish lady ... By ... L. 1751.

P. T. T. [Post ten tumblers]. *William Maginn.* To Thomas Campbell, Esq. An expostulatory epistle ... signed ... Cork, 1820, in "Blackwood's Magazine," Vol. VI., pp. 504, 505.

P. W. *Wyatt Papworth,* in "Notes and Queries," 1869; "Dic. of National Biog.," p. 59, col. 1.

Palatine, Tom. *Thomas Nash.* A long lane. L. 1883. Also in his literary contributions.

Pallet, Peter Paul. For key to Bath characters, see "Notes and Queries," 2d Ser., Vol. II., 1856, pp. 253, 254.

Parallax. *Alfred Russell Wallace.*

Parallax. *Samuel Birley Robotham.*

The immediate predecessor of John Jasper, the colored philosopher of Richmond, Va., whose recent assertion that " the sun do move " has shaken the world of science from centre to circumference. Robotham taught that Earth was a circular plain over which the sun moved. In 1885 the editor of the " Pillory " published at No. 12, Catherine St., Strand, London, offered 100 guineas to the rash man or woman who could disprove the truth of the Robotham theory.

Parenthenopeus Hereticus. *William Gordon.* Popery against Christianity; or, an historical account of the present state of Rome, etc. L. 1719.

Pastor, The. *William Wirt Phillips, D.D.* Memorial of the goodness of God, in two discourses, delivered at the opening of the First Presbyterian Church in the city of New York, Jan. 11, 1846. By ... N.Y. 1846.

Pastor of Hollis Street Society, The. *Rev. John Pierpont.* A letter from ... to his parochial friends, with their reply [by Edmund Jackson] ... October and November, 1841. B. 1841.

Pedestrian, A. *Thomas Alexander Boswell.* Recollections of ... L. 1826.

Pennsylvanian, A. *Benjamin Rush.* An address to the inhabitants of the British settlements in America upon slave-keeping ... By ... P. 1773.

Perambulating Philosopher, The.

Gilbert Abbott à Beckett, in the London "Times" and "Morning Herald."

Petre, Dr. Olinthus. *William Maginn.* Letter from . . . to Christopher North, signed Trinity College, Dublin, Nov. 10, 1820, in "Blackwood's Magazine," Vol. VIII., pp. 207–209.

Philalethes. *Dr. Edward Young* employed this pseudonym in his contributions to periodicals, 1718–20.

Philalethes. *Rev. Thomas Stackhouse,* author of "The History of the Bible," employed this pseudonym in several of his minor works.

Philalethes. *Arthur Ashley Sykes.* Moral philosophy. 1715.

Phileleutherus Devoniensis. *Thomas Northmore.* Memoirs of Planetes; or, a sketch of the laws and manners of Makar. By . . . L. 1795.

Phileleutherus Dubliniensis. *Patrick Delany.* Reflections upon polygamy . . . L. 1739.

Phileleutherus, Londinensis. *John Burton, D.D.*

It is asserted that *John Burton, D.D.,* was the author of a work under the title of "Phileleutherus Londinensis," which work was "Remarks on Dr. King's Speech before the University of Oxford at the Dedication of Dr. Radcliff, on the 13th of April, 1749." — "Illustrations of the Literary History of 18th Century," NICHOLS, Vol. II., p. 223.

The above was answered by Dr. William King himself, in "Elogium Famæ inserviens Jacci Etoniensis, sive Gigantis," under the name of "A Master of Arts."

"Jacci Etoniensis," namely, *John Burton,* of Eton, commonly called "Dr. Jack."

Philo-Cato. *Matthew L. Davis.* The celebrated letters of . . . with an introduction to them. By Aristides. N.Y. 1811.

Piece of an Antiquary, A. *Philip Thicknesse,* in the "Gent. Mag.," 1790.

Pipes, Thomas. *William Maginn.* Ancient national melodies . . . in "Blackwood's Magazine," Vol. X., pp. 554–557.

Ploughman, A. *Tristam Burges (?).* What . . . said about the "Hints to farmers" made last April by men of "trade." Kingston, R.I., 1829.

Polyxena. *Philip Thicknesse, Esq.*

In 1785, Mr. Thicknesse published "A letter to the Earl of Coventry," 8vo, and in that year commenced his correspondence with Mr. Urban, under the signature of "Polyxena," which he continued under that of "A Wanderer," his own initials, and other designations, till nearly the day of his death. See Nichols' "Literary Anecdotes of the 18th Century," Vol. IX., p. 267.

Porcustus. *Henry Swinburne.*

A letter of *Mr. Swinburne,* under the assumed name of "Porcustus," in answer to some remarks on his travels, and describing a Roman altar then in his possession, is printed in "Gent. Mag.," 1784, Vol. LIV., p. 974.

Positive, Paul. *James Montgomery.* Prison amusements, by . . . L. 1797.

President, The. *Thomas Sanden, M.D.* Three discourses . . . delivered at the anniversary meetings of the Library Society at Chichester, January, 1800, 1801, 1802. By . . . L. 1802.

Protestant Nonconformist, A. *Edward Ash.* Thoughts on the State-Church Question. By . . . 2d ed. L. 1861.

Queerquill. *Mrs. Mary T. Waggamon,* in contributions to the "Weekly" (N.Y.).

Quongti, Richard. *Thomas Babington Macaulay.* A prophetic account of a grand national poem, to be entitled "The Wellingtoniad," and to be published, A.D. 2824. Knight's "Quarterly Magazine," 1824.

In the introductory account of Quongti, noticing his travels "to the United States of America," he says, "That tremendous war, which will be fatal to American liberty, will, *at that time* [2824], be raging through the whole federation. At New York the travellers will hear of the final defeat and death of the illustrious champion of freedom, Jonathan Higginbottom, and of the elevation of Ebenezer Hogsflesh to the perpetual presidency."

R. F. P. *William Maginn.* "Bacchus; or, the pirates" [a short Homeric hymn, in the metre of Sir Walter Scott], in "Blackwood's Magazine," Vol. IX., pp. 264–266.

R., J. R. *J. R. Randall,* author of "My Maryland," 1839.

Randolph, J. Thornton. *Charles J. Peterson.* "Cabin and Parlor" . . . P. 1852.

Regryph. *Rev. Henry G. Perry,* of Chicago, in his contributions to various periodicals.

Retlaw. *Walter S. Waldie,* in his contributions to the "Journal of Commerce" (Chic. 1875–77), *et al.*

Richards, Henry. *Richard Henry Stoddard,* in his contributions to the "Aldine" (N.Y.).

Rigby. *John Wilson Croker,* in Disraeli's "Coningsby."

Mr. Charles Knight says, "I think . . . the 'Rigby' of 'Coningsby' is an ebullition of personal spite."

Rosamond. *Sophia Edna Thomson.* 1883.

Rusticus. *John Duncombe.*

"*John Duncombe* was also the author of a letter signed 'Rusticus' in the 'World,' Vol. I., No. 36, and of several letters in the 'Connoisseur,' being the 'Gentleman of Cambridge, A.B.' mentioned." — "Literary Anecdotes of the 18th

Century," NICHOLS, Vol. VIII., pp. 276, 277, note.

S. *Titus Strong.* Candid examination of the Episcopal Church ... Newburyport, Mass., 1820.

S., E. *Elias Smith.* An essay on the fall of angels and men ... 3d ed. B. 1812.

S., G. B. *Giles Badger Stebbins.* Alliance of British cotton spinners and slave-holding cotton lords to build up "free trade." Detroit, Mich., 1871.

S., H. S. *H. S. Stevens,* correspondent of the "Herald" (Cleveland, O.).

S., J. S. *J. S. Sargent,* correspondent of the "Herald" (Cleveland, O.).

S., W. O. *W. O. Stillman, M.D.,* author of a book on Saratoga Springs, and many articles in magazines and newspapers.

Seaton, Mrs. *Edmund H. Yates.* "Five O'clock Tea," in the "Queen," 1872.

Seneca. *Mr. Paskco,* in his contributions to "Truth" (N.Y.).

Spectator. *George Wetherspoon, Jr.,* in his contributions to the "Mail and Express" (N.Y.).

Spike, Ethan. *Matthew F. Whittier.*

Stereo. *Mrs. S. G. Humphrey,* in contributions to the "Weekly" (N.Y.).

Sydney. *Miss Molly Elliott Seawell,* in her contributions to the "Mail and Express" (N.Y.).

Tallyho, Ben. *Henry Alken,* drafts-

man and engraver. His earliest productions were published anonymously under the signature "Ben Tallyho," 1816–31.

Teufelsdroeckh, Herr. *Thomas Carlyle.* Sartor Resartus: the life and opinions of ... 3d ed. L. 1849.

First appeared in " Fraser's Magazine," 1830.

Tukesbury, Joe. *Joseph X. Wright,* of the "Republican" (St. Louis).

Umbra Oxoniensis. *Sir William Palmer.* Results of the expostulation of the Rt. Hon. W. E. Gladstone. L. 1875.

Vaughn, Kate. *Mrs. Helen Kestin,* in contributions to the "Weekly" (N.Y.).

Verdery, Emily. *Mrs. Emily V. Battey,* in contributions to the "Woman's World," etc. 1870.

Vernon, Louis de. *Louis Énault,* who wrote for various French journals, either under his own name, or under this pseudonym.

This is the reading of Vapereau, 1880; Quérard has it Louis de Vermont; others, Louis de Vermond.

W., T. H. *Thomas White,* in "Gent. Mag."

Warwick, Elsie. *Mrs. E. J. Fullilove,* in contributions to the "Weekly" (N.Y.).

Winwood, Rett. *Frank Corey,* in contributions to the "Weekly" (N.Y.).

INITIALS AND PSEUDONYMS.

PART II.

Abbot, ——. *An Irish Bachelor.* An Irish novelist.

Abbot, the Hon. E. S., afterwards Baroness Colchester. *An Amateur.* An English poet.

Abbot, Ezra, D.D., LL.D., 1819–84. *E. A.* An American biblical scholar. b. at Jackson, Me.; Bowdoin Coll., 1840; he was ass't librarian of Harv. Univ. Library, 1856–72, and Bussey Prof. of New Test. Criticism and Interpretation, 1872–84. The "Literary World," Sept. 11, 1880, says: "Dr. Ezra Abbot ... has the learning of a library, the eye of a microscope, and the coolness of a surgeon operating under fire." Died in Cambridge, Mass.

Abbot, L. A. *A Matrimonial Monomaniac.* An English writer.

Abbott, Austin, 1831–. *Benauly.* An American lawyer of New York City.

Abbott, Benjamin Vaughan, 1830–. *Benauly.* An American lawyer of New York City.

Abbott, Rev. Charles Edwards, 1811–80. *Old Harlo.* An American teacher at Pittsfield, Mass.; Hartford, Conn.; in Boston and New York City.

Abbott, Rev. Edwin Abbott, D.D., 1833–. *Philochristus.* An English Epis. divine and educator; from 1865, headmaster of the City of London School.

Abbott, Rev. Jacob, 1803–79. *J. A.; One of her Sons; One of them; Erodore.* An eminent American author; b. in Hallowell, Me.; from 1838 a resident of New York City; devoted to literary work; d. at Farmington, Me.

Abbott, Jennie A. — See "Johnson, Mrs. Jennie (Abbott)," wife of Oliver Johnson.

Abbott, John G., –1884. *Van Augustine.*

Abbott, Rev. Joseph, M.A., 1789-1863. *An Emigrant Farmer; Philip Musgrave.* A Canadian missionary from 1818; d. at Montreal.

Abbott, Lawrence Frazer. *Lawrence Frazer.*

Abbott, Lyman, D.D., 1835–. *Benauly; Laicus; A Layman.* An American author, clergyman, and journalist; b. in Roxbury, Mass.

Abbott, Rev. Thomas Kingsmill, M.A. *Philalethes.* An English clergyman; Fellow of Trinity College, Dublin.

Abdy, Mrs. Maria Smith, 1818-67. *M. A.* An English poet; niece of James and Horace Smith; b. in London. Miss Smith was in early life married to the Rev. John Channing Abdy, Rector of St. John's, Southwark. Died at Margate.

A'Beckett, Arthur William, 1844–. *Bertie Vyse.* An English journalist and miscellaneous writer. Since 1874, on the staff of London "Punch."

Abeken, Bernhard Rudolf, 1780–1866. *Ernst Andolt.* A German writer; b. at Osnabruck; tutor to the children of Schiller, and afterwards professor in his native town.

Abercrombie, John, 1726–1806. *Thomas Mawe.* A Scottish gardener; he published his first two works under the name of Mr. Mawe, the gardener of the Duke of Leeds; for which privilege he paid him twenty guineas.

Abercromby, James, First Baron Dunfermline, 1776–1858. *Signor Abacrombi; The Pensioner.* A British peer, called to the bar at Lincoln's Inn in 1800; Speaker of the House of Commons, 1835; and on retiring from that office in 1839, created Baron Dunfermline, in the peerage of the United Kingdom.

Abingdon, Willoughby Bertie, Earl of, 1740-99. *E—l of A—n.* An English nobleman.

Ablett, William. *Telba.* An English writer.

About, Edmond François Valentin, 1828–85. *Valentin de Quevilly; Vicomte de Quevilly.* A French novelist, politician, and journalist.

Abraham, John, 1798–. *Maharba.* An English poet; in 1878 a resident of Liskeard, Cornwall.

Abrahams, B. *A Surgeon.* An American physician.

Abrams, Isaac. *The Wild Methodist.*

Aby, Joseph C. *Buck Saw.*

Achard, Louis Amédée Eugène, 1814–75. — *Grimm.* A French novelist and journalist at Paris.

Acland, Henry Wentworth, M.D., F.R.S., D.C.L., 1815–. *H. W. A.* An English physician, educ. at Harrow and Christ Church, Oxford; Regius Prof. of Med. from 1858; and Radcliffe Librarian.

Acland, Rev. Peter Leopold Dyke, M.A. *A Clergyman.* An English divine, Christ College, Oxford, 1841. Vicar of Broad-Clyst, Exeter, 1845–80 *et seq.*

Acton, Harriet. *H. A.* An English poet.

Adair, James Makittrick, M.D., 1728–1802. *Benjamin Goosequil; Peter Paragraph.* A Scottish physician; b. at Inverness; resided some time in the West Indies; was *opposed* to the abolition of the slave-trade.

Adam, Mme **Edmond,** 1836–. *Juliette Lamber.* A French author; b. at Berberic (Oise); first married the physician La Messine, then Edmond Adam, who d. a senator in 1877. In 1879 she founded the "Nouvelle Revue."

Adam, William, 1751–1839. *Lord Chief Commissioner.* An eminent Scottish jurist; b. in Edinburgh; Lord Chief Commissioner of the Jury Court of Scotland, 1816–33; d. in Edinburgh.

Adami, Friedrich, 1816–. *Paul Frohberg.* A German writer; b. at Suhl, Prussia; studied at Berlin; and from 1838 led a literary life in that city.

Adams ——. *A Friend to the Sex.* An English writer.

Adams, Mrs. **Abigail (Smith),** 1744–1818. *Diana; Portia.* An American lady; wife of Pres. John Adams.

Adams, Alexander Maxwell. *An Antiquary.*

Adams, Andrew Leith. *A Naturalist.* A Scottish author.

Adams, Ann. *A Protestant Lady.* An English writer.

Adams, Mrs. **Ann Olivia.** *Astarte.* An American poet.

Adams, Arthur. *A Naturalist.* An English writer; a staff surgeon in the Royal Navy.

Adams, Charles. *Timothy Templeton.* An American writer of Washington.

Adams, Charles Follen. *Leedle Jawcob Strauss.* An American humorous poet, of Boston, Mass., "adorns mercantile circles, and at the same time relieves the tedium of business by modest indulgence in literary avocations."

Adams, Charles Francis, LL.D., 1807–. *A Whig of the Old School.* An eminent American statesman; b. in Boston, Mass.; Harv. Univ., 1825; U.S. Minister to England, 1861–68; is a lawyer of Boston, residing at Quincy, Mass.

Adams, Charlotte. *C. A.* An American novelist.

Adams, Rev. **C. C.** *C. C. A.* An American clergyman; rector of St. Mary's church, New York (?).

Adams, Capt. **E. G.** *E. G. A.* An American author; an officer in the American forces at Fort Rice, Dacotah Territory, 1865.

Adams, Francis, M.D., 1797–1861. *A Scotch Physician.* An eminent Scottish physician and classical scholar, during his whole life a resident of Banchory-Ternan, a parish of Scotland, Co. of Kincardine, near Aberdeen, on Deeside.

Adams, Francis Colburn. *Justia, a Know-nothing; Major Roger Sherman Potter; Pheleg Van Truesdale; A Trooper.* An American miscellaneous writer, in 1853 he styled himself late of Charleston, S.C.

Adams, Frederick W. *Shaker.* An American writer, of the Shaker denomination.

Adams, Henry Gardiner. *Nemo.* An English naturalist.

Adams, J. B. *Kit.* An American journalist, of Colorado.

Adams, Rev. **James.** *A Lover of Peace and Truth in this Church.* A Scottish Minister at Kinnaird.

Adams, John, of the Middle Temple. *Philo-Ruggles.*

Adams, John, LL.D., 1735–1826. *An American; An American Citizen; A Gentleman; Novanglus.* An eminent American statesman; second President of the U.S.; b. and d. in Quincy, Mass.

Adams, John Isaac Ira, A.M., 1826–57. *Izak; Lightfoot.* An American teacher and journalist; Yale Coll., 1850; for a short time Western correspondent of the Boston "Traveller" and the Boston "Republican."

Adams, John Quincy, LL.D., 1767–1848. *Algernon Sidney; Publicola; The Old Man Eloquent.* An eminent American statesman; sixth President of the U.S.

Adams, Nehemiah, D.D., 1806–78. *Her Father.* An eminent American Congr. clergyman; b. at Salem, Mass.; pastor at the Essex Street Church in Boston from 1834.

Adams, Richard Newton, D.D. *Pergamos.* An English Epis. divine; rector of Rempstone, Loughborough, 1839–60 *et seq.*

Adams, Samuel, LL.D., 1722–1803. An eminent American patriot and statesman. John Adams says of him, "For fifty years his pen, his tongue, his activity, were constantly exerted for his country without fee or reward. During that time he was almost an incessant writer." His biographer, Mr. Wells, says, "How many signatures he adopted during the long period between the commencement of the revenue system and the Declaration of Independence, it is impossible to say. Twenty-five have been collected, of his use of which there is absolute proof . . . Some of his essays over one signature extend, in consecutive series, through several years . . . while with different names he kept up contests simultaneously with the Crown writers on different subjects . . . His writings over the following signatures have been collected: *Determinatus; Principiis Obsta; T. Z.; A Layman; A. B.; Cedant Arma Togae; E. A.; A Bostonian; A Tory; Populus; An Impartialist; Alfred; Candidus; Vindex; A Chatterer; An Elector in* 1771; *An American; A.; Valerius Poplicola; A Son of Liberty; Shippen; Z.; Observation; Sincerus; A Religious Politician.*" Besides the pseudonyms, the following nicknames and epithets were given him: *Sam the Maltster; Samuel the Publican; The Father of America; Instar omnium; The Chief Incendiary of the House; One of Plutarch's men; The first Politician in the World; The Psalmsinger; The Palinurus of the Revolution; The Man of the Revolution; The Would-be-Cromwell of America; The Cromwell of New England; The Last of the Puritans; The American Cato; Father of the American Revolution; Political Parent;* etc.

Adams, William Bridges. *Junius Redivivus.* An English civil engineer; b. in London. He joined Lord Dundonald in his mining expedition to South America, and whilst there wrote "A Tale of Turcoman."

Adams, William Henry Davenport, 1828–. *A.; W. H. D. A.; Walter Clinton.*

An English journalist and miscellaneous writer; b. in London; after many years of literary work in that city, since 1870 he has resided in Scotland, till 1877, editing a weekly religious newspaper.

Adams, William Taylor, 1822–. *Oliver Optic; Warren T. Ashton.* An American writer for the young; b. in Medway, Mass.; became a teacher, but, in 1863, left the profession, to devote himself to literary labor.

Adamson, John, Esq., 1787–1855. *J. A.* An English literary antiquary; b. at Gateshead; Under Sheriff of Newcastle, 1811–36; for many years Fellow of the Society of Antiquaries of London; d. at Newcastle-upon-Tyne.

Adamson, Rev. **William Agar,** D.C.L., 1800–. *A Resident.* A Canadian clergyman; from 1867, Afternoon Lecturer at Christ's Church, Ottawa.

Addington, Antony, M.D., 1714–90. *Dr. Ad***gt*n.* An English physician; b. at Fringford, Oxfordshire; practised his profession in London from 1754 to 1780; spent the last years of his life in Reading, and died there.

Addington, Henry, Lord Sidmouth, 1757–1844. *A Member of neither Syndicate.* An English statesman; son of the preceding; d. at White Lodge, Richmond Park.

Addison, Rev. **Berkeley,** M.A. *A Presbyter.* An English Epis. divine; St. Peter's Coll., Camb., 1839; Vicar of Jesmond, Newcastle-on-Tyne, 1861–80 *et seq.*

Addison, Henry Robert. *A Half-Pay Officer; An Irish Police Magistrate.* An English novelist and dramatist; an officer of the 2d Dragoon Guards.

Addison, Joseph, 1672–1719. *C. L. I. O.; The Old Whig; Peter Puzzle; The Spectator.* An eminent English author; b. at Milston, near Ambrosbury, Wilts, and d. at Holland-House, London.

Adee, Hon. **Alvey A.** *A. A. A.* An American Shakesperian scholar.

Adlersparre, Karl August, Count, 1810–62. *Albano.* A Swedish author of Stockholm.

Adney, Timothy. *Mit Yenda.*

Ady, John, 1744–1812. *J. A.* An English Friend or Quaker; recording clerk of the Society; d. in London.

Agassiz, Alexander. *A. Ag.* An American naturalist; son of Louis J. R. Agassiz; succeeded his father in 1874 as Curator of the Museum of Comp. Zoölogy, connected with Harv. Univ. at Cambridge, Mass.

Agassiz, Mrs. **Elizabeth (Cary).** *E*

C. A.; Actœa. An American lady; widow of Louis J. R. Agassiz; for many years a resident of Cambridge, Mass.

Agg, John, -1813. *J. A.* An English poet and novelist.

Agnew, Rev. **David Carnegie A.** *A Free Church Minister.* A Scottish writer.

Agnew, Miss **Emily C.** *E. C. A.* An English writer on religious subjects, and poet.

Agoult, Marie de Flavigny, Comtesse d', 1805–76. *Daniel Stern.* A French author; b. at Frankfort-on-the-Main; married Comte d'Agoult in 1827; spent a long time travelling in Switzerland, Germany, and Italy, then settled in Paris, where she died.

Aguilar, Miss **Grace,** 1816–47. *G. A.* An English Jewish writer of religious fiction; the daughter of Emanuel Aguilar, of Hackney; d. at Frankfort.

Ahlqvist, August Engelbrekt, 1826–. *A. Oksaselta; Oksanen.* A Finnish poet and philologist; b. at Kuopio; studied at Helsingfors; Professor of the Finnish Language and Literature at Helsingfors. His Finnish name is Oksanen.

Ahmed Ibn Hemdem Kiäya. *Sohailes.* A Turkish writer; translated by J. P. Brown [and edited by E. E. Salisbury], N.Y. 1850.

Aigner, Lajos. *Lajos Abafi.* A Hungarian writer.

Aiken, Clementina Edith. *C. E. A.* An English writer.

Aiken, Peter Freeland. *The Grandson of R. Aiken.* An English author; admitted a member of the Faculty of Advocates in 1822.

Aikin, John, M.D., 1747–1822. *J. A.; Uncle John.* An English physician and miscellaneous writer; b. at Kibworth, Leicestershire; settled in London in 1792; d. at Stoke-Newington.

Aikin, Lucy, 1781–1864. *Mary Godolphin.* An English miscellaneous writer; daughter of the preceding; b. at Warrington; d. at Hampstead.

Ainley, ——. *Ajax.* An English writer.

Ainslie, George Robert, 1776–1839. *A Fellow of the Antiquarian Society; A Fellow of the Antiquarian Societies of London and Scotland.* A Scottish numismatologist; b. in Edinb.; appointed Governor of Dominica in 1813, but soon after retired, having been made lieutenant-general; d. in Edinb.

Ainslie, Philip Barrington. *Philo-Scotus.* An English gentleman of "The

Mount," Guilford, Surrey; member of the Surrey Archæological Society.

Ainslie, Robert, 1766–1838. *A Father.* A Scottish author; b. at Berrywell, near Dunse; Writer to the Signet, 1789; a friend of Robert Burns, and a contributor to the "Edinburgh Magazine," and other periodicals, for forty years.

Ainslie, Whitelaw, M.D., M.R.A.S. *Caledonicus.* A Scottish physician of the Medical Staff of Southern India.

Ainsworth, William Harrison, 1805–82. *Cheviot Tichebourne; W. Harassing Painsworth.* An English novelist; b. in Manchester; in 1824, removed to London; d. at St. Mary's Road, Reigate, Surrey.

Airy, George Biddell, M.A., 1801–. *The Astronomer Royal; G. B. A.* An eminent English astronomer; b. at Alnwick; from 1835 astronomer royal.

Aitken, Rev. **Robert,** 1800–73. *A Parish Priest.* An English Epis. divine; Univ. of Edinburgh; Vicar of Pendeen, Penzance, Cornwall, 1849–73.

Aiton, Rev. **John,** D.D. *A Clergyman of the Old School; A Pedestrian.* A Scottish divine; Minister of Dolphinton, Lanark County, Scotland.

Akenside, Mark, M.D., 1721–70. *A Swiss Gentleman.* An eminent English poet; b. at Newcastle-upon-Tyne, and d. in London.

Akerman, John Yonge, 1806–73. *J. Y. A.; Paul Pindar, Gent.* An English numismatist and miscellaneous writer of London.

Akers, Mrs. **Elizabeth (Chase).**— See "Allen, Mrs. Elizabeth (Chase Akers)."

Albee, John. *J. A.* An American *littérateur;* Harv. Univ. Div. School, 1858; resides at "Jaffrey Cottage," on Newcastle or Great Island, in the mouth of the Piscataqua River, near Rye, N.H.

Alberdingk-Thym, Josephus Albertus, 1820–. *Paul Forestier.* A Dutch poet and prose-writer; b. at Amsterdam; devoted himself almost entirely to art and literature. His first poems appeared in 1844. From 1855 he has published "De dietsche Warande," a journal of art and literature.

Alberti, Sophie (Mödinger), 1826–. *Sophie Verena.* A German author; b. in Potsdam; married Robert Alberti, who died in 1870; and now (1882) lives in her native town.

Alby, Ernest François Antoine, 1809–68. *Anatole de France.* A French writer; b. at Marseilles; about 1837 he devoted himself to literary pursuits, at Paris.

Alcott, Miss Louisa May, 1833–. *Tribulation Periwinkle.* An American miscellaneous writer; b. at Germantown, Pa.; for many years chiefly a resident of Concord, Mass.; devoted to literary pursuits.

Alcott, William Alexander, M.D., 1798–1859. *A Schoolmaster.* An American author and lecturer; b. at Wolcott, Conn.; wrote and edited more than 100 volumes; d. at Auburndale, Mass.

Aldam, W. H. *An Old Man, &c.* An English angler, and writer on angling.

Alden, Mrs. Isabella M. *Pansy.*

Alden, Rev. Joseph Warren. *A Puritan of the 19th Century.* An American Cong. minister.

Alden, William L. *Matthew White, Jr.; Metador.* An American journalist, of New York.

Alderson, Sir Edward Hall, Baron, 1787–1857. *A Layman.* An eminent English jurist; b. at Great Yarmouth; was Judge of the Court of Exchequer, 1834–57; d. in London.

Alderson, John, M.D., 1758–1829. *The President.* An English physician; b. at Norwich; practised his profession at Hull for more than 40 years, and died there.

Aldred, Rev. Ebenezer. *Ebenezer; A Unitarian Minister.* An English minister.

Aldrich, Mrs. Rose. *Rose Ashleigh.* An American writer.

Aldrich, Thomas Bailey, 1836–. *T. B. A.* An American poet; b. in Portsmouth, N.H.; in 1885 editor of the "Atlantic Monthly," Boston.

Aldridge, Ira, 1805–1867. *The African Roscius.* An African actor; son of a chief of Senegal, brought to New York by an American missionary. The son played "Othello," "Macbeth," and "Shylock," with great success, in London, Edinburgh, Liverpool, Dublin, etc., on the Continent, and especially in Russia. Some account of his performance in Russia, by Bayard Taylor, in "Atlantic Monthly," January, 1865. D. at Lodz, Polonia.

Alexander, Mrs. Cecil Francis. *C. F. A.* An English poet and hymnwriter; wife of the Rt. Rev. William Alexander, D.D., Bishop of Derry and Raphoe from 1867.

Alexander, Charles. *Wesley Bradshaw.* An English author.

Alexander, Miss Francesca. *Francesca.* An American author; a lady

artist, from Boston, now (1883) residing in Florence.

Alexander, James Lynne. *A Canadian.* A British American writer, of Toronto (?).

Alexander, James Waddel, D.D., 1804–59. *Cæsariensis.* An eminent American Presbyt. divine, of the Fifth Avenue Presbyt. Church, New York City.

Alexander, Dr. O. C. *Rob Rapier.*

Alexander, Patrick Proctor. *Smelfungus.* A Scottish author.

Alexander, Richard Dykes. *A Layman; Pacificator.* An English Friend, or Quaker, of Ipswich, Suffolk.

Alexander, Samuel, 1749–1824. *Aquila; Verax.* An English Friend, or Quaker; b. at Needham Market, Suffolk, where he also died.

Alexander, Rev. Samuel Davies, D.D., 1819–. *S. D. A.* An American Presbyt. divine; b. at Princeton, N.J.; pastor in New York City, 1856–81 *et seq.*

Alexander, W. *W. A.* An English writer.

Alexander, William, 1768–1841. *Amicus.* An English Friend, of Needham Market, Suffolk; for many years a bookseller and publisher, of York, where he died.

Alfieri, Count **Vittorio Amadeo**, 1749–1803. *Count Asmodei.* An Italian poet; b. at Asti, in Piedmont; d. at Florence.

Alford, Mrs. Fanny. *A Clergyman's Wife.* An English lady; wife of Henry Alford, Dean of Canterbury.

Alford, Very Rev. Henry, B.D., 1810–71. *The Dean of Canterbury; H. A.* An English clergyman; b. in London; Trin. Coll., Cambridge, 1832; Dean of Canterbury, 1857–71.

Alfred, H. J. *Otter.*

Alison, William Pulteney, M.D., 1790–1859. *Academicus.* A Scottish political economist, physician, and Professor of the Practice of Medicine in the Univ. of Edinb., and brother of the historian; b. and d. in Edinburgh.

Allan, Charles Stuart Hay, –1880. *Charles Edward Stuart.* A Scottish (?) author.

Allan, David, 1744–96. *The Scottish Hogarth.* An eminent Scottish painter; b. at Alloa, on the Forth, 25 miles from Edinburgh; studied in Glasgow, and for 14 years in Italy; practised his art in London, 1777–80, and in Edinburgh the remainder of his life, and d. near that city.

Allan, Rev. **J. A.** *A Butterfly.* A Canadian poet, in 1867, of Ardath, Wolfe Island.

Allan, James MacGrigor. *A Bachelor.* An English miscellaneous writer.

Allan, Rev. **John.** *A Special Reporter.*

Allan, Rev. **John.** *Beefeater, Domestic Chaplain to Fill Pots.* A Scottish minister of the Union Church, Aberdeen.

Allan, Rev. **John.** *Kn.-Oxonian.* A Scottish minister of Potterton, Belhelvie Co., Aberdeen.

Allan, John Hay, –1872. *Sir Walter Scott, Bart.; John Sobieski Stolberg Stuart.* A Scottish poet; brother of Charles Stuart Hay (?).

Allan, Thomas, 1777–1833. *A Private Gentleman.* A Scottish banker in Edinburgh; b. and d. in that city.

Allardyce, Mrs. **Elizabeth (Winslow).** *A Lady.* A Scottish poet. — See "Allderdyce, Mrs. Eliza (Winslow)."

Allderdyce, Mrs. **Eliza (Winslow).** *E. W. A.* A Scottish poet.—See "Allardyce, Mrs. Elizabeth (Winslow)."

Allen, ——. *Timothy Touchstone.* An English scholar; one of the editors, under this pseud., of the "Trifler," at Westminster School, in 1788; afterwards a student of Trin. Coll., Cambridge.

Allen, Rev. **Benjamin,** 1789–1829. *Osander.* An American Epis. clergyman; b. at Hudson, N.Y.; Rector of St. Paul's Church, Philadelphia, 1821–29; d. on board ship, on the return voyage from Liverpool.

Allen, Charles. *One who has served under the Marquis of Dalhousie.* A British civilian in the Bengal Civil Service.

Allen, Mrs. **Elizabeth (Chase Akers).** 1832–. *Florence Percy.* An American poet; b. in Strong, on Sandy River, Maine; passed her girlhood at Farmington, in the same State; early became devoted to literary pursuits. In 1866, she married Mr. E. M. Allen, and since 1872 has resided with her husband in Greenville, New Jersey.

Allen, G. W. *W. G. A.* An English poet of Nottingham.

Allen, Rev. **George,** 1792–1883. *A Freeman.* An American clergyman; b. in Worcester, Mass.; Yale Coll., 1813; pastor at Shrewsbury, Mass., 1823–40; chaplain at the Worcester Insane Asylum, 1843–72; d. at Worcester.

Allen, Grant. *J. Arbuthnot Wilson.* An English author and journalist of London.

Allen, John. *Scævola.*

Allen, John, M.D., 1770–1843. *A*

Necessitarian. A Scottish philosopher; b. at Redford, near Edinburgh; contributed largely to the "Edinburgh Review"; was an inmate of Holland House for more than forty years; d. in London.

Allen, Rev. **John.** *A Citizen of Maryland.* An American writer of Baltimore (?).

Allen, Rev. **John.** *A British Bostonian.* An American author.

Allen, John, 1771–1839. *A Layman.* An English schoolmaster; b. at Truro, in Cornwall; for more than 30 years conducted a private academy at Hackney, and d. there.

Allen, Mrs. **M.** *M. A.* An English writer.

Allen, Richard. *R. A.* An English writer and printer at Nottingham.

Allen, Rev. **Robert,** M.A. *A Master of Arts of Trinity College, Cambridge.* An English clergyman; Trin. Coll., Cambridge, 1859; Vicar of Christ Church, Eastbourne, 1877–83 *et seq.*

Allen, Stephen Merrill, 1819–. *Alpha; S. M. A.* An American merchant and banker; b. at Burton, N.H.; in 1836 removed to Boston, Mass., where, in 1884, he was still engaged in business, residing in Roxbury.

Allen, Rev. **Thomas.** *An Impartial Hand.* An English country clergyman.

Allen, Rev. **Wilkes,** A.M., –1845. *A.* An American Cong. minister, of Chelmsford, Mass., from 1803; b. in Sterling, Mass.; Harv. Univ., 1801.

Allen, William. *W. A.* An English writer.

Allibone, Samuel Austin, LL.D., 1816–. *S. A. A.; Bibliophile; A Layman.* An eminent American bibliographer; since 1879, librarian of the Lenox Library, New York City.

Allin, Miss **Abby.** *Nilla.* An American poetess, of Pomfret, Connecticut. — See "Carter, Mrs. Daniel A."

Allingham, William, about 1828–. *Patricius Walker.* An Irish author; b. at Ballyshannon; editor of "Fraser's Magazine," 1874–79. Mr. Allingham was for several years in the Custom's service, from which he retired about 1872.

Allsop, Robert. *R. A.* An English littérateur.

Almon, John, 1738–1805. *An Independent Whig.* An English bookseller, author, and editor; b. in Liverpool; early became at London the publisher of political tracts, for which he was several times prosecuted and punished; he more than once retired from business to his pleasant villa at Boxmoor, but the want of an active life and of its excitement drew him again to London; d. at Boxmoor, near Hemel Hempsted, Herts.

Alsop, Alfred. *A Delver.* An English missionary in Manchester.

Alsop, Richard, A.M., 1761–1815. *R. A.* An American poet and journalist; b. at Middletown, Conn.; was first known to the public as the author of satires on public characters and events entitled the "Echo," the "Political Greenhouse," etc. Alsop, Dwight, Hopkins, Trumbull, and others were called "The Hartford Wits." He d. at Flatbush, L.I.

Alston, Alfred Henry. *The Captain of the "Cumberland."* An English naval officer and poet.

Alston, Joseph, 1778–1816. *The Mountaineer; A Southern Planter.* An American statesman; son-in-law of Aaron Burr; Governor of South Carolina in 1812.

Alting, Albertus Samuel Carpentier. *Philalethes.* A Dutch writer.

Amalia, Herzogin von Sachsen, 1794–1870. *Amalie Heiter.* A German dramatic poet; b. at Dresden; daughter of Duke Maximilian, and sister of John, king of Saxony.

Amat, Felix, 1750–1824. *Don Macario Padua Melata.* An eminent Spanish ecclesiastic and writer; Archbishop of Palmyra in 1803, and confessor to Charles IV. in 1806.

Ambler, Charles. *A Retired Barrister.* An English lawyer; practised for nearly forty years in the Court of Chancery; and was Attorney-General to the queen when he died, in 1794, at Maidenhead-thicket.

Ames, Mrs. Eleanor, 1830–. *Eleanor Kirk.* An American novelist.

Ames, Fisher, LL.D., 1758–1808. *An American, formerly a Member of Congress; Brutus; Camillus; Falkland.* An eminent American orator and statesman; b. in Dedham, Mass.; Harv. Univ., 1774. "He drew his eloquence," says Allibone, "from the best source." "I will hazard the assertion," was his own expression, "that no man ever did or ever will become truly eloquent without being a constant reader of the Bible, and an admirer of the purity and sublimity of its language." He was an M.C. from Massachusetts, 1789–97, when he returned to his farm in Dedham, and d. there.

Ames, Nathan, –1865. *Señor Alguño.* An American poet; Harv. Univ., 1848; among other works, he was the author

of the "Bards of Lind," etc., consisting of ten parodies of Longfellow and others, purporting to be "expressly written for the 'Greeting to America' of Jenny Lind."

Ames, Nathaniel, –1835. *An Old Sailor; N. A.* An American sailor, and writer of sea sketches; the son of Fisher Ames.

Amhurst, Nicholas, 1706–42. *Caleb D'Anvers; A Student at Oxford; Philalethes.* An English journalist; was connected with Bolingbroke and Pulteney in the management of the "Craftsman." Being expelled from St. John's Coll., Oxford, he satirized his *alma mater* in his "Oculus Britanniæ" and his "Terræ Filius."

Amicus, C. B. C. *C. B. C. A.* An English writer.

Amner, J. T. *A Head Master under the London School Board.* An English educator.

Amory, Thomas, about 1691–1789. *An Antiquarian Doctor; A Lady; John Buncle, Esq.* An English humorous writer.

Anbury, Thomas. *An Officer.* An English traveller and writer; was an officer in Burgoyne's army, and taken prisoner by the Americans; returned to England soon after the surrender of Cornwallis.

Ancillon, Charles, 1656–1715. *A Person of Honour.* A French lawyer and judge; b. at Metz; spent the greater part of his life in Berlin, and d. there.

Anderdon, John Lavicount. *J.L.A.; A Layman.* An English writer.

Anderdon, Rev. William Henry. *Owen Evans.* An English R. C. clergyman, a convert from the Church of England.

Andersen, Carl Christian Thorvaldus. *Christian Adam.* A Danish writer.

Andersen, Mrs. Mary E. *A Looker-On-Here in Vienna.* An English (?) writer.

Anderson, ——. *A Brother Fish Dealer; The Originator of the Shetland Fishery Company.* A Scottish writer.

Anderson, Adam. *A. A.* An Irish writer; member of the Royal Irish Academy; d. 1867.

Anderson, Alexander. *A Gent.; Surface Man.* A Scottish poet; Asst. Librarian in the Univ. of Edinburgh.

Anderson, Andreas. *A Native of Denmark.* A Danish traveller.

Anderson, Mrs. Galusha. *Dorothy Doe.* An American writer; wife of Galusha Anderson; from 1878 Pres. of the Univ. of Chicago.

Anderson, George. *Cyclos, a Member of the Glasgow Skating Club.* A Scottish writer, of Glasgow.

Anderson, Henry. *A Gentleman of Lincoln's Inn.* An early English writer.

Anderson, James, LL.D., 1739–1802. *Agricola; Alcibiades; Aristides; Candid Enquirer; Cimon; E. Aberdeen; A Farmer; Germanicus; Henry Plain; Impartial Hand; Mercator; A Scot; Scoto-Britannicus; Senex; Timothy Hairbrain.* An eminent Scottish author; b. at Hermiston, near Edinburgh; wrote for Ruddiman's "Edinburgh Weekly Magazine," and published the "Bee," 1790–94. About 1797 he removed to London, and there conducted a journal called "Recreations in Agriculture," etc.; 1799–1802, corresponded with Washington.

Anderson, James, F.R.S.E. *Obiter Dictum.* A Canadian farmer and journalist; editor of the "Farmer's Journal," Montreal.

Anderson, Rev. John, – ab. 1722. *A Countreyman.* A Scottish Presbyt. minister; for 25 years a schoolmaster in Edinburgh; about the beginning of the eighteenth century became the minister at Dumbarton, and afterwards at Glasgow.

Anderson, John. *Aednr-Nos-Seer I'Noh.* A Scottish writer.

Anderson, Dr. Linnæus B. *Elon-Rusticus.* An American writer of Virginia.

Anderson, Olive San Louie, 1842–. *Sola.* An American writer; b. at Lexington, O.; a graduate of the Univ. of Michigan of 1875; and Professor in Santa Barbara Coll., California.

Anderson, Patrick. *Whats-You-Call-Him, Clerk to the Same.* A Scottish (?) poet; physician to Charles I.

Andersson, Anna. — See "Wastberg, Mme H. E."

André, Major John, 1751–80. *A Dreamer.* An English officer; b. in London; educ. at Geneva; joined the British army in America, and was executed as a spy, Oct. 2, 1780, at Tappan, N.Y.

Andrews, Addison Fletcher, 1857–. *Aaron Fledger.* An American journalist of New York City; Dart. Coll., 1878.

Andrews, Rev. Elisha, 1768–1841. *Gimel.* An American Baptist minister; b. at Middletown, Conn.; after leading a faithful and laborious life as a minister in other places, his last years were spent in Hinsdale, N.H., where he died.

Andrews, Miss Fanny. *Elzey Hay.*

An American writer; daughter of a lawyer of Washington, Ga.; has written for New York papers, "Godey's Lady's Book," and "Scott's Magazine," Atlanta, Ga. In 1870 she resided in her native place.

Andrews, Garnett. *An Old Georgia Lawyer.* An American writer.

Andrews, Miles Peter, Esq., –1814. *Arley.* An English dramatist; b. in London; M.P. for Bewdley, 1790–1814; suddenly d. in London.

Andrews, Sidney, 1837–80. *Dixon.* An American journalist; secretary of the Massachusetts Board of Charities, 1872–80.

Andrews, Stephen Pearl, 1812–. *Pantarch.* An American miscellaneous writer; b. in Massachusetts; has been a contributor to the London "Times" and other journals.

Angas, George Frederick. *G. F. A.* A British writer on New Zealand and Australia.

Angove, Miss Emily, 1837–. *Emily.* An English religious writer; b. at Redruth, Cornwall.

Angus, William, A.M. *Promotion in the Church.* A Scottish educational writer, of Glasgow.

Anley, Charlotte. *C. A.* An English writer.

Annet, Peter, –1778. *A Certain Free Enquirer; Free Inquirer; Mencius Philalethes; W. Stilton, Horologist.* An English Deist; was pilloried and imprisoned for publishing the "Free Inquirer."

Anselmi, Teodoro. *Leo Velleita.* An Italian miscellaneous writer.

Anstey, Christopher, 1724–1805. *C. A., Esq.; Mr. Inkle; A. Macsaroni; Christopher Twist-Wit, Esq., Bath Laureat.* An English humorous poet; b. at Trumpington, near Cambridge; was a frequent resident in the city of Bath; d. at the house of a friend in Harnage, Wilts.

Anstey, John, 1796–1867. *J. A.; The Late J. J. S., Esq.; The Late John Surrebutter, Esq.* An English humorous poet, son of the preceding; was a barrister-at-law, of Lincoln's Inn, and a commissioner for auditing Public Accounts.

Anstruther, Capt., of Spencerfield. *The Man in the Moon.*

Anthony, ——. *A.* An English poet.

Anthony, G. W. *Gabriel Tinto.*

Anthony, Louisa. *L. A.* An English writer of history, etc.

Anthony, W. B. *W. B. A.* An English writer of educational works.

Anti-Theatre, supposed editor. *Sir John Falstaff.*

Antrobus, Benjamin. *B. A.* An early English religious writer.

Apes, William. *A Native of the Forest.* An American Indian, and Indian preacher of the Pequot tribe.

Apperley, Charles James, 1777–1843. *Nimrod.* A popular English writer on sporting subjects; second son of Thomas Apperley, Esq., of Woottonhouse, Gloucestershire; d. in Upper Belgrave-place, London.

Appleton, Jesse, D.D., 1772–1819. *Leighton; Owen.* An American Cong. minister; b. at New Ipswich, N.H.; Dart. Coll. 1792; second Pres. of Bowd. Coll., 1807–19; d. at Brunswick, Me.

Appleton, John Reed. *J. R. A.* An English writer; a humorous poet of Yorkshire.

Appleton, Nathan, LL.D. 1779–1861. *A Layman of Boston.* An American statesman; b. in New Ipswich, N.H.; M.C., 1831–33 and 1843–45; d. in Boston.

Appleton, Col. Nathan, A.M., 1843–. *N. A.* An American author and financier; b. in Boston; Harv. Univ., 1863; in 1866 purchased a cotton plantation in Edisto Island, S.C., and, since that event, calls himself a planter; at the North, resident in Boston.

Appleyard, Rev. Ernest Silvanus, M.A. *E. S. A.; A Member of the Church of England.* An English clergyman; Caius Coll., Cambridge, 1827.

Apthorp, Sarah Wentworth. — See "Morton, Mrs. Perez."

Arago, Étienne, 1803–. *Jules Ferney.* A French poet and journalist; b. at Perpignan; brother of François Arago; became a chemist, at Paris, but soon turned his attention entirely to literature; he was engaged in the public service from 1848 to 1867, when he returned to his literary pursuits.

Araguy, Jean Raymond Eugène d', 1808–. *William Snake.* A French writer; b. at Newark, N.J.; was educated in Paris, and devoted himself there to literary pursuits.

Arbuckle, James, 1700–34. *Hibernicus.* An Irish or Scottish writer; said by Watt to have been born in Glasgow, by others to have been born in Ireland, where he is supposed to have kept an academy.

Arbuthnot, ——. *A Farmer.* An English economist.

Arbuthnot, John, M.D., 1675–1734-5–. *J. A.; Doctor Bantley; An Eminent Lawyer of the Temple; Martinus Scriblerus; P. P., A Parish Clerk; Philonomus Eleutherus.* A Scottish physician; b. at Ar-

buthnot, near Montrose; studied at Aberdeen; removed to London, and there "his uncommon powers of wit and ripe scholarship introduced him to the society of the principal literary characters of the day."

Archbold, John Flather. *John Flather.* An eminent English writer on law.

Archer, Edward, 1816–. *E. A.* An English agriculturist.

Archer, Frederick. *F. A.* An American writer, of New York City.

Archer, George W. *Hesper Bendbow.* An American novelist.

Archer, John Wykeham, 1809–64. *Mr. Zigzag, the Elder.* An English artist and antiquary; b. at Newcastle-on-Tyne; spent some years in that town, but resided in London 1830–64; d. at Kentish-town.

Argles, Mrs. Maggie. *The Duchess.* An English novelist.

Argyle, Duke of, 1682–1769. *The D*** of A****e.* A Scottish nobleman; —John Campbell, 4th Duke.

Armistead, Wilson. *A Friend of the Negro; Lorenzo Tuvar.* An English Friend and philanthropist, of Leeds, Yorkshire.

Armroyd, George. *A Citizen of the United States.* An American merchant, in the first quarter of the century, of Philadelphia; a writer on commerce, statistics, etc.

Armstrong, Miss Frances Charlotte. *F. C. A.* An English writer of stories for the young; residing, 1878, at the Royal Terrace, Weymouth.

Armstrong, John, M.D., 1709–79. *Launcelot Temple, Esq.; A Free-Thinker.* A Scottish poet and physician; b. at Castleton, in Roxburghshire; in 1735 settled in London as a physician; but was a physician in the army, 1760–63, where his half-pay supported him.

Armstrong, Gen. John, 1758–1843. *An Old Soldier.* An American general; b. at Carlisle, Pa.; entered the army when he was only eighteen years old; U. S. Senator, 1801–4; Minister to France, 1804–10; Brigadier-General, 1812; U.S. Secretary of War, 1813. He d. at Red Hook, Dutchess Co., N.Y.

Armstrong, Rev. John, 1771–1797. *Albert.* A Scottish poet; d. at Leith, near Edinb., and educ. at the Univ. of that city. In 1790 he removed to London, and devoted himself to literary pursuits; d. at his father's house in Leith.

Armstrong, Miss Katherine. *Kate*

De Courcy. An American contributor to periodicals.

Armstrong, Rev. **Skeffington,** B.A. *A Clergyman.* An English (?) clergyman; Trin. Coll., Dublin, 1845; rector of Bessingham, Hanworth, 1872–83 *et seq.*

Armstrong, William. *A Reformed Stock Gambler.* An American writer, of New York City.

Arnall, William, 1715–1741. *Sir Francis Walsingham; Solomon Abrabanel; A Member of the House of Commons.* An English journalist; a zealous supporter of the administration of Sir Robert Walpole, and was the editor of the "True Briton." "He boasted to have received in four years, out of the treasury, the sum of ten thousand nine hundred and ninety-seven pounds six shillings and eight pence for abusing every one opposed to Walpole. Still he died in debt, in 1741, aged twenty-six."

Arndt, Ernst Moritz, 1769–1860. *E. M. A.* An eminent German patriot, poet, and miscellaneous writer; b. in the island of Rugen, in the Baltic. He was a strong opponent of Napoleon, and by pamphlets, poems, and songs he sought to communicate his own love of liberty to his countrymen. He was professor of history at Bonn, 1818–19 and 1840–41, and rector of the Univ. from 1841. With rare freshness and vigor he continued to lecture and write, and on his 90th birthday received from all parts of Germany good wishes and love-tokens. About a month later he died.

Arnee, Frank, 1767–1858. *A Member of the Society.* An English Friend and minister, of Bristol.

Arnim, Elisabeth (Brentano) von, 1785–1859. *Bettina.* A German lady; wife of L. A. (J.) von Arnim, and friend of Goethe; b. at Frankfort-on-the-Main; removed with her husband to Berlin, and became the star of fashion, as well as the literary star, in the brilliant circles of that city. After the death of her husband, in 1831, she devoted herself to charity and literature at Berlin, and d. there.

Arnold, Alexander S. *A Sunday School Superintendent.* An English writer.

Arnold, Edwin, 1832–. *E. A.* An English poet; son of Robert Coles Arnold, and brother of Arthur; graduated at Univ. Coll., Oxford, with honors, in 1854, and was then elected Second Master in the English division of King Edward the Sixth's School in Birmingham, and subsequently appointed Prin-

cipal of the Government Sanscrit College at Poonah, in the Bombay Presidency, and Fellow of the Univ. of Bombay, which offices he held during the mutiny, and resigned in 1861. Since 1861 he has been on the editorial staff of the "Daily Telegraph," London. Mr. Arnold married the daughter of the late Rev. W. H. Channing, our countryman.

Arnold, Rev. **Frederick,** 1833–. *F. A.* An English journalist and miscellaneous writer, of London; b. at Cheltenham; Ch. Ch., Oxford, 1858.

Arnold, George, 1834–65. *Allen Grahame; George Garrulous; McArone.* An American poet and journalist; d. at Strawberry Farms, N.J., in 1865. He served with honor in the Union army during the late Civil War. "Some of his poems are of remarkable sweetness."

Arnold, George W. *Joe Strickland.*

Arnold, Henry Thomas. *Henry T. Arden.* An English dramatist.

Arnold, M. E. *M. E. A.* An English poet.

Arnold, Matthew, LL.D., 1822–. *A.; M. A.; Arminius von Thundertentroncle.* An eminent English author, the eldest son of Dr. Thomas Arnold, Head-Master of Rugby School; b. at Laleham, near Staines; Balliol Coll., Oxford, 1844; but in 1845, Fellow of Oriel Coll.; was private secretary to Lord Lansdowne, 1847–51; Lay Inspector of Schools, 1851–79 *et seq.;* Prof. of Poetry at Oxford, 1857–67; has within a few years visited this country, and given very valuable and interesting lectures.

Arnold, Rev. **Thomas Kerchever,** M.A., 1800–53. *T. K. A.* An English classical scholar; b. at Stamford; Trin. Coll., Cambridge, 1821; Rector of Lyndon, Rutlandshire, 1830–53. In 1838 he published the first of a numerous list of introductory and other books for the study of the Greek, Latin, Hebrew, German, French, and Italian languages, which have been extensively used in England and this country. He d. at his rectory, at Lyndon.

Arnold, William Delafield, 1828–59. *Punjabee.* An English novelist, brother of Matthew Arnold; an officer in the British army in India; afterwards director of public instruction in the Punjab; d. at Gibraltar, on his passage home from India.

Arnot, Hugo, 1749–86. *A Citizen; Eugene.* A Scottish historian; b. at Leith; his name was Pollock, but he adopted that of Arnot on succeeding to the maternal estate of Balcormi in Fifeshire; member of the Faculty of Advocates in Edinburgh, 1752.

Arnot, Rev. William. *John Bunyan, Junior.* An eminent minister of the Free Church in Scotland; pastor of St Peter's in Glasgow.

Arnould, Arthur, 1833-. *A. Matthey.* A French journalist and *littérateur*; b. at Dieuze (Meurthe); has made himself favorably known by his contributions to various literary and political journals.

Arnoux, Charles Albert d', 1820-. *Bertall.* A French artist and *littérateur*; b. in Paris. His works, disseminated everywhere, and of which the first date from 1843, have appeared under the pseud. of "Bertall," a sort of anagram of *Albert*, which was suggested to him by Balzac, the kind protector of his *débuts.*

Arriazza, Don Juan Bautista de, 1770-1837. *D. J. B. de A.* A Spanish poet; b. and d. in Madrid. He took an active part in politics, advocating an absolute monarchy, and thus gained the favor of Ferdinand VII.

Arrington, Alfred W., 1810-67. *Charles Summerfield.* An American lawyer, statesman, and *littérateur*; b. in Iredell Co., N.C.; became a Methodist preacher, and was an itinerant in Missouri, 1832-33, where his remarkable mental powers, and his glowing, fiery eloquence everywhere drew crowds to hear him. He then studied law. In 1857, he went to Chicago, where he was remarkably successful in his profession, and drew much attention by his contributions to the "Democratic Review" and the "Southern Literary Messenger." D. in Chicago.

Arrom, Cecilia (Böhl de Faber), 1797-1877. *Fernan Caballero.* A Spanish novelist; b. at Morges, in Switzerland; in 1813 followed her father to Spain; married the Marquis von Arco-Hermoso, and after his death in 1835, the Advocate Arrom, in Seville, where she afterwards lived and died.

Arrowsmith, R. G. *Juvenis.* An English writer.

Arthington, Maria, -1863. *A Member.* An English Friend, of Leeds.

Arthur, Timothy Shay, 1809-85. *Uncle Herbert; Mrs. John Smith.* An American author; b. near Newburg, Orange Co., N.Y.; has resided in Philadelphia since 1841, devoted to literary work.

Arundell, Rev. Francis Vyvyan Jago, M.A., 1780-1847. *The Rector.*

An English traveller and antiquary; b. at Launceston; Rector of Landulph, Cornwall, 1804-47, where he died.

Arundell, William Arundell Harris, 1794-1865. *Arundell Harris.* An English poet; b. at Kenegie, near Penzance, Cornwall; assumed the name of Arundell in 1822; sheriff of Cornwall, 1817; d. at Lifton, Devon.

Ascher, Isidore G., 1835-. *Isidore.* A Canadian poet; b. in Glasgow, Scot.; came to Canada in 1843, and educ. at Montreal, and became a lawyer. Since 1864 he has resided in England, contributing regularly to one or two leading London magazines.

Ash, Edward, M.D. *A Member of the Society; One of its Members; A Protestant Nonconformist.* An English Friend and physician, of Bristol.

Ashe, Thomas, -1835. *T. A.; T. A., Gent.; Captain Light Dragoons.* An English writer (the well-known Captain); author of several works; was in Oxford a few weeks before his death, in a very distressed state, and received alms from the Anti-Mendicity Society. He d. in Bath, at an advanced age.

Ashhurst, William Henry, Esq., -1855. *John Search.* An English writer; a solicitor of the Old Jewry, who had at one time a large proportion of business in bankruptcy; d. at Wimbledon Park, county of Surrey.

Ashley, Florence Emily. *F. E. A.* An English poet.

Ashley, Rev. George, 1724-1808. *Dr. Taylor's Friend.* An English divine and antiquary; St. John's Coll., Cambridge; an able contributor to several important works; d. in the parsonage house at Lytchet, Maltravers, Co. Dorset.

Ashley, John, LL.D. *A Wykehamist.* An English writer.

Ashley, John. *A Barbadoes Planter.* A West Indian gentleman; member of the Council of Barbadoes.

Ashley, Rev. John Marks, S.C.L., LL.B. *J. M. A.* An English Epis. divine, and voluminous writer; Caius Coll., Cambridge, 1856; Vicar of Feuston, Otley, 1873-83 *et seq.*

Ashton, John. *A Man of Business.* An English writer, of Manchester (?).

Ashton, Thomas, D.D., 1716-1775. *A Late Fellow of King's College, Cambridge.* An English clergyman, of Eton and Cambridge; b. at Lancaster; preacher at Lincoln's Inn, 1762-64.

Ashworth, T. M. *Ouno.* An American writer.

Aspinall, W. B. *An Invalid.* An English writer.

Aspinwall, James. *An Old Stager.* An English writer.

Aspland, Rev. Robert, R.A., 1782–1845. *The Editor of the "Monthly Repository."* An English Unitarian minister; b. at Wicken, Co. of Cambridge; was for 40 years pastor of the Gravel-Pit Chapel, Hackney, London.

Asplin, Rev. William, M.A. *W. M.; A Master of Arts of the University of Oxford; Philalethes Rusticus; A Presbyter of the Church of England; A True Son of the Church of England.* An English clergyman, Vicar of Banbury.

Assheton-Craven, Rev. Charles Audley, M.A. *A Gentleman.* An English clergyman; Ass't Chaplain to the Forces, Chatham.

Assolant, Jean Baptiste Alfred, 1827–. *Alcofribas, le Magicien; Lord Claudius Hastings Cumbermere.* A French feuillitonist; b. at Aubusson Creuse; was professor in the Normal School for several years; visited the United States, and, on his return to France, contributed to the "Revue des Deux Mondes" an article on "Walker and the Americans." He also published "Scenes de la Vie des États-Unis."

Astell, Mrs. Mary, 1668(?)–1731. *A Daughter of the Church of England; A Lover of her Sex; William Wotton, D.D.* An English writer of considerable note in her day.

Astley, Francis Dukinfield, Esq. *An Admirer of the Fine Arts.* An English poet, of Dukinfield Hall, Cheshire.

Aston, Anthony. *Matthew Medley; Tony Aston.* An English "gentleman, lawyer, poet, actor, soldier, exciseman, and publican" of first half of the 18th century. He was bred an attorney, but left the law for the stage. He played in all the theatres in London, but never long in any of them. In 1735 he petitioned the House of Commons to be heard against the bill then pending for regulating the stage, and was permitted to deliver a ludicrous speech, which was afterwards published in folio, 1735. He is thought to have been living in 1749, and travelling in some part of the kingdom.

Aston, C. Penrhyn. *One of themselves.* An English workingman.

Aston, Joseph. *Editor of the "Manchester Herald."* An English journalist and dramatist.

Aston, the Hon. W. *Timothy Touchstone.* An English scholar; one of the

editors of the "Trifler"; at Westminster school in 1788; afterwards a student of Christ Church, Oxford.

Atcherley, James. *A Drapier.* An English teacher, Master of Shrewsbury school.

Atcheson, Rev. Alfred S. *A. S. A.* An English clergyman; rector of Teigh, Rutlandshire.

Atcheson, Thomas. *Broad Church.* An American writer, of Louisville, Kentucky.

Atkins, Mrs. Anna. *A. A.* An English novelist.

Atkinson, D. H. *Jeremiah Odman; An Old Leeds Cropper.* An English writer.

Atkinson, Edward. *E. A.; A Cotton Manufacturer.* An American gentleman; president of the Boston Manufacturers' Mutual Fire Insurance Company, etc.

Atkinson, G. W. *One of the Raiders.* An American writer.

Atkinson, George Francklin. *Our Special Correspondent.* An English writer in India; Captain Bengal Engineers.

Atkinson, Jane. *Jenny Wren.* An English author.

Atkinson, Sir Jasper, Knt., 1790–1856. *I. A.* An eminent English financier; was Provost of the Royal Mint, 1804–51, when a change in its management caused his retirement; he d. at his country residence at North Frith, Tunbridge Wells, Kent.

Atkinson, John. *I. A.* An English financier; father (?) of the preceding; and, like him, an official of the Royal Mint.

Atkinson, William, M.A. *The Enquirer; The Inquirer.* An English political writer, of Bradford.

Atterbury, Francis, 1662–1732. *A Member of the Lower House of Convocation.* An English clergyman; b. near Newport-Pagnell; Bishop of Rochester, 1713–23; d. in Paris.

Atteridge, Andrew Hilliard. *A. H. A.* An English writer.

Atthill, Rev. Lombe. *L. A.* An Irish clergyman; Domestic Chaplain to the Earl of Bantry, and clerk in orders at Trinity Church, Hull, Yorkshire.

Attwell, Henry. *H. A.* An English writer of educational works.

Attwood, J. S. *J. S. A.* An English writer.

Atwood, A. Watson. *Wattie Rushton.*

Aubert, Albert. *Desiré Hazard.* A

French writer who, together with Octave Feuillet and Paul Bocage, under this pseudonym, in 1845, published "Le Grand Viellard" in "Le National."

Aubry, Philippe Charles, 1744–1812. *P. C. A****.* A French poet and translator; b. at Versailles; for a time held a situation in the Ministry of Marine at Paris; but in 1798 returned to Versailles, and was a teacher of languages till his death.

Audin, J. M. V., 1793–1851. *Richard.* A French historian and biographer; b. at Lyons; removed to Paris; he d. suddenly in his carriage between Marseilles and Avignon.

Audran, Prosper Gabriel, 1744–1819. *P. G. A.* A French lawyer; b. in Paris; Professor of Hebrew in the University of Paris from 1799; d. in Paris.

Auersperg, Anton Alexander, Count von, 1806–1876. *Anastasius Grün.* A popular German poet; b. at Laybach; in 1831 he retired to his family estate, and occupied himself exclusively with agriculture and literary labor.

Auger, Louis Simon, 1772–1827. *L. S. A.* An eminent French critic and journalist; b. in Paris; after filling various important positions, he was, in 1827, made perpetual secretary of the French Academy. He was accidentally drowned in the river Seine.

Aulnay, Louise d'. *Julie Gouraud.* A French writer.

Aurevilly, Léon Louis Frédéric, dit Jules, Barbey d', 1809–. *Old Noll.* A French *littérateur;* b. at Saint-Sauveur-le-Vicomte, Manche; from 1851 a journalist at Paris.

Austen, Jane, 1775–1817. *A Lady.* An English novelist; b. at Steventon, Hampshire, where her father was rector for more than 40 years. Miss Austen resided at Chawton while publishing her novels, but d. at Winchester, to which city she was removed for her health.

Austin, Benjamin, 1752–1820. *Honestus; Old South.* An American political writer; b. in Boston; was a merchant and an earnest political writer of Boston.

Austin, Miss Eliza Howard, –1849. *Miss Betty Austin.* An English colonial lady; for many years proprietor of the Clarence Hotel, at Bridgetown, Barbadoes, where she died.

Austin, George Lowell, M.D., 1849–. *Barry Lyndon.* An American miscellaneous writer, of Cambridge and Boston; b. in Lawrence, Mass.; spent three years at Harv. Univ., 1868–71; in 1875, studied medicine, and adopted it as his profession; has, however, devoted much time to literary labor.

Austin, Harry. *An Officer.* An English writer.

Austin, Ivers James, M.A. 1808–. *A Member of the Boston Bar.* An American lawyer; b. in Boston; West Point, 1828; Honorary A.B. at Harv. Univ. in 1831; A.M. in 1852; practised his profession in his native city, 1831–71.

Austin, James Trecothick, LL.D., 1784–1870. *A Citizen of Massachusetts.* An American lawyer; b. in Boston; Harv. Univ. 1802; editor of the "Emerald"; County Attorney for Suffolk, 1812–32; Attorney-General of Massachusetts, 1832–43; a fine political and miscellaneous writer; d. in Boston.

Austin, Lewis. *Augustin Lewis; Frederic Daly.* An English author; private secretary of Mr. Henry Irving, the celebrated actor.

Austin, Mary Therese, 1849–. *Betsy B.* An American writer; b. at Greenbay, Wis.; since 1876, dramatic critic of the "San Francisco Argonaut."

Austin, William. *A Presbyter of the Church of England.* An English clergyman.

Austin, Rev. Wiltshire Stanton, Jr. *V. Dayrell.* An English Epis. divine and *littérateur;* Exeter Coll., Oxford; Rector of Allhallows, Lombard Street, London.

Avellanèda, Gertrudis Gomez de. 1816–1873. *Peregrina.* A distinguished Spanish poet; b. at Puerto Principe in the island of Cuba; in 1840 settled in Madrid. In 1846 she married the Deputy, Pedro Sabadon; became a widow in a few months; in 1854 again married, the Deputy Masieu, whom she lost in 1860, when she removed to Seville, where she died.

Avery, Jane Greenough. *A. Jane Greenough.* An American writer for the young.

Avery, Samuel P. *Spavery.* An American artist and humorous writer of New York City.

Avril, Baron Adolphe d'. *Cyrille.* A French writer.

Axon, William Edward Armitage. *W. E. A. A.; The Author; Dudley Armitage.* An eminent English bibliographer, of Manchester; a constant correspondent of "Notes and Queries."

Aynge, G. A. *G. A. A.* An American poet.

Ayrton, William, Esq., F.R.S., F.S.A.,

1777–1858. *A Friend of the Family.* An English musical and literary critic, of the London "Morning Herald," 1813–26; and in the "Examiner," 1837–51; was editor of the "Harmonicon," 1823–33; wrote the musical articles in the "Penny Cyclopædia," 1833–44; d. in London.

Ayscough, George Edward, Esq., –1779. *An Officer in the Guards.* An English lieutenant and writer who, after a few years' service, was compelled by ill health to relinquish his profession; travelled in Italy, but without benefit.

Ayscough, Samuel, 1745–1804. *S. A.; Vicar of Cudham.* An English clergy-man and bibliographer; for about 20 years assistant librarian in the British Museum, where he d.; he was b. in Nottingham, and was Vicar of Cudham, Kent, 1803–4.

Aytoun, William Edmonstoune, 1813–65. *W. E. A.; Ane of that Ilk; Augustus Dunshunner; A Layman of the Church; T. Percy Jones.* An eminent Scottish poet and essayist; b. and educ. at Edinburgh; Prof. in the Univ. of Edinburgh, 1845–65; for many years, from 1839, a contributor to "Blackwood's Magazine"; d. at Blackhills, Elgin.

Aytoun, W. E., and **Martin, Theodore.** *Bon Gaultier.*

B.

Baärnhielm, Miss **E. W.** — See "Barnes, Miss E. W." Her father was a Swede, who, when he came to this country, changed his name to Barnes.

Babb, C. E. *Uncle Jesse.* An American writer.

Babbage, Charles, 1792–1871. *A Philosopher.* An eminent English mathematician; b. at Teignmouth, in Devonshire; Trin. Coll., Cambridge, 1814; Prof. in the Univ. of Camb., 1828–39. During his latter years he resided in London, and d. in that city.

Babeuf, François-Noel, 1764–1797. *Caius Gracchus.* A French political writer and conspirator; b. at Saint-Quentin; at Paris he became one of the most violent Revolutionists, and with another being condemned to death for a conspiracy against The Directory, he poignarded himself, and was borne dying to the scaffold.

Babington, Charles Cardale, M.A., F.R.S., etc., 1808–. *C. C. B.* An eminent English botanist; b. at Ludlow; St. John's Coll., Cambridge, 1830; Prof. of Botany in his *alma mater.*

Babington, Mrs. **E.** *E. B.* An English editor of C. Elliott's poems.

Babou, Hippolyte, 1824–1878. *Camille Lorrain; Jean Sans-Peur.* A French journalist; b. at Peyriac (Aude); wrote for the principal French journals, and was one of the most active editors of the "Athenæum française" and of the "Revue française"; d. in Paris.

Babron, J. E. *J. E. B.* An English editor of Lamb's "Eliana." etc.

Babson, Joseph E., ab. 1831–75. *Tom Folio.* An American *littérateur;* b. at Newburyport, Mass.; for many years a resident of Melrose, Mass.; and it was his custom to visit Boston twice a week to put himself *au courant* with the literary news, and to indulge in pleasant talks in the publishing houses and in the "Transcript" office, of which paper he was a frequent correspondent.

Bacchus, Miss **Lizzie W.** *Latienne.* An American poet; b. at Wilmington, N.C.; a teacher at Eufaula, Ala., in 1872.

Bache, Benjamin Franklin. *The Editor of the "Aurora."* An American journalist; b. in Philadelphia; was carried when a boy to Paris, and placed in the printing-office of the well-known printer, Didot; on his return, in 1785, he studied in the Philadelphia Coll., and in 1790 commenced the "General Advertiser," afterwards called the "Aurora," which long exerted considerable political influence.

Bache, Richard, 1794–1836. *An Officer of the U.S. Army.* An American; b. in Philadelphia; Univ. of Penn., 1812; Captain of Ordnance, 1819–36; d. at Washington, D.C.

Backhouse, James. *J. B.* An English Friend, of Yorke; a missionary in 1839 *et seq.* to Australia and South Africa.

Backhouse, Rev. **Julius Brockman.** *One of the Sons of the Clergy.* An English clergyman.

Backus, Rev. **Isaac,** 1724–1806. *A Countryman.* An American Baptist minister, of Massachusetts; b. at Norwich, Conn.; Honorary A.M. at Brown Univ., of which he was a trustee for more than 30 years, 1765–99.

Bacon, Ezekiel, LL.D., 1776–1870. *E. B.; A Graduate of* 1794. An eminent American lawyer and statesman; b. in Boston; Yale Coll., 1794; from 1815, a resident of Utica, N.Y., and for some years the oldest living graduate of Yale Coll.; d. at Utica.

Bacon, Miss **Julia.** *Mollie Myrtle.* An American writer of prose and verse; b. at Macon, Ga.; in 1871 a resident of Howard, Taylor Co., Ga.

Bacon, Phanuel, D.D., 1700–83. *The Friar.* An English clergyman; of Magdalen Coll., Oxford; Vicar of Bramber, Sussex, and Rector of Balden, Oxfordshire, where he died.

Bacon, Rev. **Thomas.** *An American Pastor.* An American Epis. clergyman, of St. Peter's, Md.

Badcock, John. *John Bee, Esq.* An English journalist, of London; "Editor of the 'Fancy,' 'Fancy Gazette,' 'Living Picture of London,' and the like of that."

Badcock, Rev. **John.** *J. B.* An English Epis. divine; with two others left England, in 1850, to found a Christian Mission in Terra del Fuego, where they starved to death (?).

Badcock, Rev. **Samuel,** 1750–88. *Cam.; Justinophilus.* An English clergyman; b. at South Moulton, Devon.; in 1787 he joined the Church of England, and became Curate of Broad Clyst; contributor to the "London Review," "London Magazine," etc., and especially to the "Monthly Review"; d. in London.

Badeau, Adam. *The Vagabond.* An American officer and author; b. in New York City; Consul-General at London, 1874 *et seq.*, more recently at Havana, Cuba; resigned in 1884.

Badgley, Jonathan. *Uncle Jonathan.* An American author of educational works.

Badham, Charles, M.D., –1845. *An Amateur.* An English physician and poet; b. in London; educ. at Edinburgh and Oxford; Prof. of Med. in the Univ. of Glasgow, 1827–45; d. in London; he was a contributor to "Blackwood's Magazine."

Badia y Leblich, Domingo, 1766–1818. *Ali Bey, El Abassi.* A Spanish adventurer; b. in Biscay; received the best education Europe could afford; passed through many strange adventures in a professed attempt to found a colony of Europeans between Algiers and Morocco; d. on his way to Mecca.

Badin, Rev. **Stephen Theodore,** 1768–1853. *A French Clergyman.* An R. C. divine; b. at Orleans, France; came to Baltimore, 1792; ordained by Dr. Carroll in 1793; d. in Cincinnati.

Bagby, Dr. **George W.,** 1828–1883. *Moses Adams; Mozis Addums.* An American humorous writer, of Richmond, Va., where he died.

Bagehot, Walter, M.A., 1826–77. *W. B.* An English economist; b. in Longport, Somersetshire; for a time Examiner in the Univ. of London; contributor of essays and reviews to the periodical press, and editor of the "Economist"; d. in his native town.

Bagg, Lyman Hotchkiss, 1846–. *A Yale Graduate of '69; Karl Kron; El Atchby; A Massachusetts Yankee; N. S. G.* An American author and journalist, of New York City; college chronicler for the New York "World," 1876–82; b. in West Springfield, Mass.

Bagley, Miss **Sarah G.** *S. G. B.* An American writer, of Meredith (now Laconia), N.H.; contributed to the "Lowell Offering."

Bagnold, Miss **E. S. H.** *E. S. H. B.* An English author.

Bagot, A. G. *Bagatelle.* An English sporting writer, in the "Country Gentleman and Sporting Gazette" in 1881.

Bagot, Very Rev. **Daniel,** D.D. *D. B.* An eminent Irish (?) Episcopal divine; Trin. Coll., Dublin, 1827; Dean of Dromore, Ireland, 1850–75; in 1880, resident at St. James Road, Surbiton, Surrey.

Bagot, Lewis, D.D., 1740–1802. *Bishop B****.* An eminent English clergyman; educ. at Westminster School and at Christ Church, Oxford; successively Bishop of Bristol, Norwich, and St. Asaph, 1782–1802; d. at his house in Oxford Street.

Bagshawe, Francis Lloyd. *A Priest.* An English Roman Catholic writer.

Baikie, William Balfour, M.D. *W. B. B.* An English naturalist and bibliographer.

Bailey, Ven. **Benjamin,** D.D., 1791–1853. *An Undergraduate of the Univ. of Oxford; Vetus.* An English Episcopal divine; archdeacon of Colombo; for forty years a missionary at Travancore, India; d. in London.

Bailey, Ebenezer, –1839. *Grins and Gripes.* An American educator; Yale Coll., 1817; for many years an eminent teacher in Boston; d. at Lynn, Mass.

Bailey, Rev. Henry, D.D., 1815-. *H. B.* An English Episcopal divine; b. at North Leverton, Notts; St. John's Coll., Cambridge, 1839; Vicar of W. Tarring *w.* Dur.ington, 1878–80 *et seq.*

Bailey, Isaac H. *Yarmouth.*

Bailey, James Montgomery, 1841-. *Danbury News Man.* An American journalist and humorous writer, of Danbury, Conn.; b. in Albany, N.Y.

Bailey, Peter, -1823. *Giorgione di Castel Chiuso.* An English poet and journalist; editor of the " Museum," London.

Bailey, Samuel, 1791–1870. *An Egyptian Kafir ; A Yorkshire Freeholder ; A Younger Brother.* An eminent English philosopher and *littérateur;* b. at Sheffield; the "Bentham of Hallamshire," as he was called; devoted the greater part of his life to his literary pursuits; he d. suddenly, and left £ 90,000 to his native town.

Bailey, Thomas. *An Old Tradesman.* An English writer, of Basford, near Nottingham.

Bailey, Mrs. Una Locke. *Una Locke.* An American writer.

Baillie, Mrs. E. C. C. *E. C. C. B.* An English poet and prose writer.

Baillie, Hugh. *A Doctor of Laws.* An English jurist; at one time Judge of the Court of Admiralty.

Baillie, Miss Joanna, 1764–1851. *J—— B——.* An eminent Scottish writer; b. at the Manse of Bothwell, in the upper dale of the Clyde; for the principal part of her life a resident of Hampstead, near London, where she died.

Baillie, Matthew, M.D., 1761–1823. *Dr. B—e.* An eminent Scottish physician; brother of Joanna Baillie; b. in the Manse of Tholy, near Hamilton, Scotland; Balliol Coll., Oxford; practised his profession in London; d. at his seat at Duntisbourne, near Cirencester.

Bailliere, Jean Baptiste Émile, 1831-. *J. B. E. B.* A French journalist; b. in Paris; contributor to the "Chronique" of the "Journal de la Librairie."

Bailly, Mme Emma Berenger. *Claire de Chandeneux.* A French novelist; a prolific writer of romances suitable for the young.

Bainbridge, Mrs. Harriette (Smith). *Cecil Laker.* An English (?) poet.

Baird, George D. *Mercury.* An American bicycle journalist and writer, of New York City.

Baird, Henry. *Nathan Hogg.* An English philologist and dialect poet.

Baird, Thomas H., 1787–1866. *Alethes.* An eminent American jurist; b. in Washington, Penn.; after more than 30 years of active life as a judge and lawyer, he returned to his farm near Monongahela City, Washington Co., Penn.; d. in Alleghany City, Penn.

Baker, Frank Leslie. *Grip Fast.* An American journalist.

Baker, Mrs. Delphine P. *Delphine.* An American philanthropist, the chief object of whose life for years was to provide a home for the men disabled in the late war.

Baker, Mrs. Harriette Newell (Woods). *Aunt Hattie; Mrs. Madeline Leslie.* An American writer of books for children.

Baker, Henry. *A Gentleman late of the Inner Temple.* An English writer; son of Henry Baker.

Baker, Henry, 1703–74. *Henry Stonecastle.* An English poet and naturalist; b. in London; devoted his life chiefly to teaching the deaf and dumb; d. in London.

Baker, Rev. Sir Henry Williams, 3d Bart., 1821–77. *H. W. B.* An English Epis. divine; Vicar of Monkland, near Leominster, Hertfordshire, 1851–77.

Baker, James Loring. *Profit and Loss.* An American economical writer, of Boston.

Baker, Leonard. *Maistre Drekab.* An English humorous writer.

Baker, Samuel. *A Seaman's Friend.* An English writer; member of the Board of Trade, and Hon. Sec. to the Committee of Inquiry into the Merchant Seamen's Friends.

Baker, Mrs. Sarah S. (Tuthill). *Aunt Friendly.* An American writer of books for the young; a daughter of Mrs. Louisa C. Tuthill, late of Princeton, N.J.; now (1885) residing in Sweden.

Baker, T. M. *T. M. B.* An American novelist.

Baker, Thomas, 1656–1740. *A Gentleman.* A learned English antiquary; b. at Crook, in the parish of Lancaster, in the bishoprick of Durham; Fellow of St. John's Coll., Cambridge, 1679, but in 1717 was deprived of his fellowship, and afterwards was wont to add to his signature *Socius Ejectus;* he resided at his college till his death, devoted to studies in history, biography, and antiquities.

Baker, Thomas. *Pikestaff.* An English barrister-at-law.

Baker, Rev. Thomas Bagnall. *T. B. B.* An English Epis. clergyman; Minister of Woburn Chapel, St. Pancras.

Baker, William, 1742–1785. *The Rationalist.* A learned English printer, of London; son of a schoolmaster at Reading, where he died.

Baker, William Deal, A.M., 1812–76. *Hyton Hosmot.* An American lawyer and editor; Univ. of Penn., 1830; Member of the Const. Conv. in 1873; b. and d. in Philadelphia.

Baker, William E. S. *An Eye-Witness.* An American writer.

Baker, Rev. William Munford, 1825–1883. *George F. Harrington.* An American Presbyt. clergyman, of Newburyport, Mass., 1873 *et seq.*

Bakewell, T. *A Weaver.* An English weaver, of Cheadle, Staffordshire; "the Moorland Bard."

Balch, William Ralston. *C. C. C.* An American journalist and compiler.

Baldwin, Henry. *H. B.* An English printer, and publisher of "St. James's Chronicle," London, 1761.

Baldwin, John Loraine. *A Glow-worm.* An English whist player, and editor, of London (?).

Baldwyn, Rev. Edward. *Trim.* An English Epis. divine; educ. at Jesus Coll., Oxford; resident first in Yorkshire, then at Ludlow, Shropshire.

Baleson, J. E. *J. E. B.* An American editor and compiler, of Chelsea, Mass.

Balguy, Rev. John, 1686–1748. *A Clergyman; A Country Clergyman; Silvius.* An English clergyman; b. at Sheffield, in Yorkshire; Vicar of North-Allerton, Yorks, 1729–48; d. at Harrowgate.

Ball, Edward. *Edward Fitzball.* An English dramatist.

Ball, Henry William. *H. W. B.* An English author.

Ball, John. *Lucifer.* An English writer.

Ball, Rev. Timothy Horton. *Y.N.L.* An American Bapt. minister; b. at Agawam, Hampden Co., Mass.; graduated at Franklin Coll., Ala.; studied theology at Newton (Mass.) Sem., 1861–63; minister for some years at Crown Point, Ind.

Ballance, John. *His Father.* An English writer, father of Mr. John des Carrieres Ballance, of Queen's Coll., Cambridge.

Ballantyne, Mrs. ——. *A Lady.* An English poet and naturalist.

Ballantyne, James, 1772–1833. *Aldiborontiphoscophornio.* A Scottish journalist and publisher, of Edinburgh; b. in

Kelso; a schoolfellow and friend of Sir Walter Scott; d. in Edinburgh.

Ballantyne, James R., LL.D. *J.R.B.* An English Orientalist; in 1850, Principal of the Benares Coll.; from 1862, Librarian of the India Office, London.

Ballantyne, John, 1774–1821. *Rigdum-Funnidos.* A Scottish printer and publisher, of Edinburgh, brother of James, like him the friend of Scott and publisher of his works.

Ballantyne, Rev. John. *A Minister of the Church of Scotland.* A Scottish clergyman of the early part of the 18th century.

Ballantyne, Rev. John, 1778–1830. *A Dissenter.* A Scottish clergyman; minister of Stonehaven, Kincardineshire, 1805–30.

Ballantyne, Robert Michael. *One of themselves; Ensign Sopht; Comus; Ralph Rover.* A popular Scottish author of fiction and adventure for the young.

Ballard, Anna. *Annibale.* An American writer and musician.

Ballard, Rev. Edward, D.D., 1805–70. *Sabino.* An American P. E. clergyman; b. at Hopkinton, N.H.; Rector of St. Paul's Church, Brunswick, Me., where he died.

Ballard, Edward George, Esq., 1791–1860. *E. G. B.; Γ.* An English antiquary and student of Ecclesiastical history; b. in Salisbury; from 1817 he devoted himself entirely to literary pursuits; d. at Compton-terrace, Islington.

Ballard, J. *A Protestant Churchman.* An English author.

Ballard, Mrs. Julia P. *Kruna.* An American writer for the young.

Ballou, Rev. Adin. *A. B.* An American minister; pastor at Mendon, Mass., 1831–42; afterwards at Milford, where he became the founder of the Hopedale (Mass.) Community.

Ballou, Ellis. *Philo.* An American humorist.

Ballou, Maturin Murray, 1822–. *A Traveller in the Tropics.* An American author and journalist; son of Rev. Dr. Hosea Ballou; b. in Boston; editor and proprietor of "Ballou's Pictorial" and the "Flag of our Union."

Ballow, Henry. *H. B.* An English writer on law early in the 18th century.

Balsamo, Giuseppe, 1743–95. *Comte di Alessandro Cagliostro.* A Sicilian impostor; b. at Palermo, Sicily; assumed the title of Count; travelled in many countries under various names; professed alchemy and free-masonry; practised medicine and sorcery, and raised money by various forms of imposture; he d. at Rome in prison.

Baltimore, Frederick Calvert, 7th Lord. *Right Hon. Lord B—e.* An English nobleman; a poet, etc.; in 1751 he became the proprietor of Maryland; about 1767 he became a resident of Naples, and d. there.

Balzac, Honoré de, 1799–1858. *Henri B***; Horace de Saint Aubin; Lord R'Hoope.* An eminent French novelist; b. at Tours; after struggling for ten years at Paris with poverty and starvation, he at last obtained appreciation, and with appreciation what ought to have been wealth. But he spent his gains as freely as he made them. At length he married a wealthy Russian lady; but just at the culmination of his fame, and at the beginning, as it seemed, of the rest and satisfaction to which he had always looked forward, he died.

Bampfield, Rev. Robert Lewis, 1819–. *R. L. B.* An English clergyman; Trin. Coll., Oxford, 1842; Vicar of West Anstey, Devon, 1868–83 *et seq.*

Bangs, J. K. *J. K. B.* An American journalist, of New York.

Banim, John, 1798–1842. *A Traveller.* An Irish novelist; b. at Kilkenny; at 18 years of age was editor of the "Leinster Journal"; at 18 produced a successful play; at 20 was married, proceeded to London, and became editor of the "Literary Register." Though the author of the "O'Hara Tales" was exceedingly popular, he found literature a precarious subsistence, and in 1832 he was reduced to such distress at Boulogne that a public subscription was raised for his relief, which enabled him to return to Kilkenny in the summer of 1835. In 1837 a pension of £150 a year was granted to him by Government, which was afterwards increased by the addition of £40 a year for the education of his only child, a daughter. He d. at Windgap Cottage, near Kilkenny.

Banim, Michael, 1796–1874. *Abel O'Hara.* An Irish novelist; brother of the preceding; b. at Kilkenny; aided his brother in the composition of the "O'Hara Tales," etc., etc. For many years he filled the office of Postmaster in his native town, and was at one time its Mayor. Fortunately, the Royal Literary Fund came to the aid of narrow means, and after his decease a pension was given to his widow by Mr. Disraeli. He d. at Kilkenny.

Bank of England, The. *The Old Lady in Threadneedle Street.*

Banks, John, 1709–51. *An English Officer.* English writer, of Sunning, Berks.; was successively a weaver, a bookseller, a book-binder, and an author, chiefly at London. From 1742 he was chiefly occupied as both writer and editor for the "Old England" and "Westminster Journals."

Banks, Joseph. *Uncle Joseph.* An English humorous writer.

Banks, Percival Weldon, M.A., 1806–50. *Morgan Rattler.* An Irish lawyer and journalist, of London; called to the bar at Gray's Inn in 1835; d. in London.

Banks, Thomas Christopher, 1765–1854. *T. C. B.; An Unfortunate Nobleman.* An English lawyer and genealogist; he practised for some years, 1813–20, at Lyon's Inn, and afterwards at an office which he called the Dormant Peerage Office, in John St., Pall Mall, London; d. at Greenwich.

Bannatine, James. *Joe Miller.* An English writer; at one time resident in Honduras; author of several papers in the "Monthly Magazine."

Bannatine, Rev. James. *A Minister of the Church of Scotland.* A Scottish minister, of Edinburgh.

Banning, Edmund P. *Goldlace.* An American naval officer; appointed 2d Lieutenant in the Marine Corps in 1864; resigned in 1870.

Bannister, John William. 1794–1829. *A Settler.* An English jurist; b. in Steyning, Sussex; served in the Royal Navy till the end of the American war. In 1819 he settled in Upper Canada; later he returned to England, studied law, was called to the bar at the Middle Temple in 1826. He was Chief Justice at Sierra Leone, 1828–29, when he d. there.

Banville, Théodore Faullain de, 1823–. *Bracquemond.* A French poet; b. at Moulins (Allier); in early life went to Paris, and there engaged in literary pursuits.

Barach, Moritz, 1818–. *Dr. Märzroth.* A German poet and prose writer; b. at Vienna; studied there; and from 1834 has devoted himself exclusively to a literary career with great and marked success.

Barbauld, Mrs. Anna Letitia (Aikin), 1743–1825. *A. L. B.; A Volunteer.* An eminent English female writer; b. at Kibworth, Leicester; in 1774 she married Rev. Rochemont Barbauld, who, in 1802, became pastor of a congregation, and a resident of Stoke-Newington, but d. in 1808, when Mrs. Barbauld devoted herself chiefly to literary pursuits; d. at Stoke-Newington.

Barber, Harriet Boomer. *Faith Templeton.* An American novelist.

Barber, John. *The Alderman.* An English character; city-printer, common councilman, alderman, and lord-mayor of London, during the earlier part of the last century.

Barber, Joseph. *Disbanded Volunteer.* An American humorist, who says of himself, "My life, as the kentry is aware, hes been full of wunderful vississytoods from the time I was Disbanded arter the Mexican war, to the present crysis. First I made my pile in the airly days of Californy . . . then I pardizzipated in the revolushionary movements in Payris; arterwards I figgered around a wile in London; next I visited Constantinopul . . . subsekwently I emmygrated to Australy . . . later I tuck up my abode in New York . . . still later I went on an eggscarsion to Springfield, Illanoy; and finally brort up at Washington, where I hang out at present."

Barber, W. R. *Chincapin.* An American journalist, of New York City.

Barber-Beaumont, John Thomas. Esq., F.S.A., F.G.S., 1771–1841. *A Magistrate for Middlesex.* An English gentleman; founder, and for many years managing director of the County Fire Office and Provident Life Office, and Magistrate for Middlesex; b. in the parish of St. Marylebone, and d. at his official residence in Regent Street, London.

Barbier, Abbé Louis Stanilas Hippolyte, 1808–64. *Un Solitaire.* A French ecclesiastic and biographer; b. at Orleans; went to Paris, and devoted himself to literature; d. in that city.

Barbour, John Gordon. *Caledonius; Cincinnatus.* A Scottish writer, of the earlier part of the century.

Barclay, Anthony, Esq. *Græculus.* An English civilian; at one time British Consul at New York City; for 50 years never failed to spend some portion of each year at Savannah, Ga.

Barclay, Hugh, LL.D. *An Elder of the Church of Scotland; Nestor.* A Scottish writer; sheriff-substitute, Perth.

Barclay, John, M.D., 1756 or 60–1826. *Jonathan Dawplucker, Esq.* A Scottish physician; Lecturer on Anatomy; Fellow of the Roy. Coll. of Physicians and of the Roy. Soc. of Edinburgh.

Barclay, John, 1797–. *A Lover of that People.* An English Friend or Quaker; b. in Clapham, Surrey; in 1820 he removed to Poole, in Dorsetshire; afterwards to Alton, Croydon; and last to Stoke-Newington.

Barclay, Robert, 1648–1747. *R. B., a Servant of the Church of Christ.* An eminent Scottish Friend; b. at Gordonstown, in the Shire of Murray; was distinguished for his religious writings; d. at his house of Springhall, and interred in the family's burying-place.

Barclay, Robert, 1779–1854. *Allerdyce.* A British pedestrian, the first who walked 1000 miles in 1000 hours.

Bardwell, William. *An Architect.* An English architect, of London (?).

Bardwood, Rev. James. *John Bunyan.* An English minister of the Gospel, of the last century.

Barère de Vieuzac, Bertrand, 1755–1841. *The Anacreon of the Guillotine.* A French Jacobin demagogue. The flowery style with which he adorned the measures of a merciless proscription procured him this designation.

Barham, Francis, 1808–71. Δ; *Alist.* An eminent English poet and scholar; b. at Leskinnick, Penzance, and d. at Bath.

Barham, George. *Tom Tally.* An English poet.

Barham, Rev. Richard Harris, 1768–1845. *Thomas Ingoldsby; H. Peppercorn, M.D.; Peter Peppercorn.* A celebrated English humorist; b. at Canterbury; held a country curacy, 1813–21; Minor Canon of St. Paul's, London, 1821–45. In 1826 he first contributed to "Blackwood's Magazine"; and in 1837 began to furnish the "Ingoldsby Legends" to "Bentley's." He also wrote for the "Edinburgh Review" and the London "Literary Gazette." D. in London.

Barham, Thomas Foster, M.B., 1766–1844. ΕΛΑΧΙΣΤΟΣ; *A Bible Student; A Physician.* An English poet and dramatist, of Cornwall.

Barinetti, Charles. *An Italian.*

Baring, Charles, Esq., 1743–1829. *J. Smith, Gentleman.* An eminent English merchant, of a Devonshire family; devoted the latter part of his life to literary pursuits; d. at Exmouth.

Barker, Lady Catherine, 1815–. *A Plain Woman.* An English lady, daughter of the 1st Earl of Ducie; in 1841, married John Raymond Barker, Esq.

Barker, Edmund Henry, Esq. 1788–1839. *Aristarchus Anti-Blomfieldianus.* An English philologist; b. at Hollym vicarage, Yorkshire; Trin. Coll.,

Cambridge, 1807, but did not graduate; for 20 years a contributor to the "London Classical Journal"; d. in London.

Barker, Rev. Edward Waller. *E. W. B.* An English Epis. divine; Vicar of Legsby, Market Rasen, 1882–83 *et seq.*

Barker, Jacob, 1779–1871. *Investigator.* An American financier; b. at Swan Island, Kennebec Co., Me.; went to New York City when he was 16; in 1834 removed to New Orleans; d. at Philadelphia.

Barker, Joseph. *J. B.* An English Radical (?), of Newcastle.

Barker, Mrs. L. J. *A Former Resident of Slave States.* An American author.

Barker, Matthew Henry, 1790–1846. *Old Sailor; Father Ambrose; The Wanderer.* An English writer; b. at Deptford; spent some years in the Royal Navy; was editor of the "Demerara Gazette," 1815–23, and of the "Nottingham Mercury," 1828–41. He made hundreds of communications, in prose and verse, to the "Literary Gazette," "Bentley's Miscellany," various annuals, and, near the close of his life, to the "Pictorial Times" and "United Service Gazette."

Barker, Samuel. *S. B.* An English writer of the earlier part of the last century, of Lyndon.

Barker, Rev. Thomas, M.A. *T. B.* An English clergyman; Queen's Coll., Oxford, 1848; Vicar of Revesby, Boston, 1867–83 *et seq.;* and Rector of Wilksby *w.* Claxby, Pluckacre, 1874–83 *et seq.*

Barker, William Gideon Michael Jones, 1817–55. *The Wensleydale Poet.* An English poet; d. at Leeds.

Barkly, A. M. *A. M. B.* An English botanist.

Barlow, Rev. David Hatch, A.M., –1864. *Mountain Bard.* An American Unit. minister, of Brooklyn, N.Y.

Barlow, Mrs. Emma, 1854–83. *Leila.* An American writer.

Barlow, Henry Clark. *H. C. B.* An English *littérateur,* the "Dantopholist"; resident, in 1866, of Newington, Butts-Surrey; representative from England at the Sixth Centenary Festival of Dante, in Florence and Ravenna, Italy, 1864–65.

Barlow, James. *Thomas Moon, Esq.* An American poet.

Barlow, Maria A. *Leslie Raynor.*

Barlow, Samuel L. M. *S. L. M. B.* An English author and editor.

Barnard, Rev. Charles Francis. *Seth Pringle.* An American Unitarian minister; for many years minister of the Warren-Street Chapel, and from 1869, of the Harvard (Charlestown) Chapel, Boston.

Barnard, Charles Francis, Jr. *Jane Kingsford; Maria Gilman.* An American miscellaneous writer, of Boston.

Barnard, Mrs. Charlotte A., –1869. *Claribel.* An English composer and lyric poetess; wife of Rev. C. C. Barnard, rector of Brocklesby, Ulceby, Lincs.

Barnard, Frederick Augustus Porter, D.D., LL.D., 1809–. *A Refugee.* An eminent American scholar and educator; b. in Sheffield, Mass.; Yale Coll., 1828; President of Columbia Coll., New York City, 1864–83 *et seq.*

Barnes, Alfred (?) **C.** *Barnacle.* An American writer, publisher, of New York City (?).

Barnes, Miss E. W. *E. W. B.* An American writer of prose and verse in annuals and magazines; resident of Portsmouth, N.Y.

Barnes, Rev. Richard William. *Alazon.* An English Epis. divine; Queen's Coll., Oxford, 1834; Vicar of Probus, Cornwall, 1849–83 *et seq.*; Prebendary of Exeter, 1853–83 *et seq.*

Barnes, Thomas, 1786–1841. *Strada.* An English journalist; Pembroke Coll., Camb., 1808; editor of the London "Times," 1830–41; d. at his house in Soho-Square, London.

Barnett, George. *Guy Roslyn.*

Barnum, Augustine. *Fax.* An American editor, of New York City.

Barnwell, Miss Annie M. *Leroy.* An American "Southland writer"; b. at Beaufort, S.C., in 1872; was a teacher in Waynesboro, Burke Co., Ga.

Barr, Rev. James. *Aliquis.* An English writer.

Barrett, Charlotte. *Her Niece.* An English lady, niece of Madam D'Arblay.

Barrett, Eaton Stannard, about 1785–1820. *Cervantes Hogg; Polypus.* An Irish writer of satire and fiction; a student of the Middle Temple; d. in Glamorganshire, Wales.

Barrett, Jonathan, 1791–1860. *J. B.* An English Friend, of Croydon, Surrey; d. at Hastings, Sussex.

Barrett, Richard. *R. B.* An Irish clergyman (?).

Barrett, Thomas Squire. *T. S. B.* An English metaphysician, of London.

Barrington, John Shute, 1st Viscount, 1678–1734. *A Layman.* An English nobleman; son of Benjamin Shute, of London; in 1723, retired from public life, and devoted himself to theological researches.

Barron, Alfred. *Q.* An American editor and writer, of the Oneida Community, N.Y. (?).

Barrow, Mrs. Fanny. *Aunt Fanny.* An American writer of books for children.

Barrow, John. *A Private of the 38th Artists*, etc.

Barrow, John, F.R.S. *J. B.* An English writer; son of Sir John Barrow.

Barrowby, Dr. ——. *Dod Pierce; M. S.*

Barrows, Charles Henry, 1853-. *Eleven Sophomores.* An American lawyer; b. in Springfield, Mass.; Harv. Univ., 1876; settled in his native town; Ass. Attor.-Gen. of Massachusetts, 1881-.

Barry, Joseph. *Josephus, Jr.* An American annalist.

Barry, William Whittaker. *An Englishman.* An English barrister, of Lincoln's Inn.

Barstow, Amos C. *A. C. B.* An American manufacturer; head of the firm, A. C. Barstow & Co., stove-founders of Providence, R.I.; travelled in Europe in 1873, and wrote letters to the "Providence Journal" over the signature "A. C. B.," which were afterwards issued in a separate form.

Barter, William George Thomas. *T. E. Cour.* An English lawyer and poet.

Barthélemy, Jean Jacques, 1716-95. *Anacharsis.* A French scholar; b. near Aubagne, in Provence. Removing to Paris, having obtained several lucrative offices through the favor of the Duke of Choiseul, he devoted himself to literary pursuits. D. in Paris.

Bartlett, Bailey, 1750-1830. *A Layman.* An American patriot; b. in Haverhill, Mass.; a friend of John and Samuel Adams, and was with them at Philadelphia in 1776, when the Declaration of Independence was declared; a member of the Mass. Convention to adopt the U.S. Constitution; held the office of sheriff of Essex Co. for about 40 years; and was an M.C. from Massachusetts 1797-1801.

Bartlett, David W. 1828-. *D. W. B.; Van; Spectator.* An American journalist; b. in Bloomfield, Hartford Co., Conn. In 1857 he went to Washington to assist Dr. Bailey in editing the "National Era." For more than 20 years he was correspondent of the "Springfield Republican," over the signature of "Van"; for nearly the same period for the New York "Independent" as "D. W. B."; and for the Boston "Congregationalist" as "Spectator"; in 1878 he became American Secretary of Legation of the Chinese Legation at Washington.

Bartlett, John. *J. B.; Practitioner of more than Fifty Years' Experience in the Art of Angling.* An eminent American publisher and bookseller, of Boston.

Bartlett, M. R. *Parley Pippin.* An American writer.

Bartol, Rev. Cyrus Augustus, D.D., 1813-. *A Spectator.* An eminent American clergyman; b. at Freeport, Me.; Bowd. Coll., 1832; Harv. Univ. Div. School, 1835; since 1837, pastor of the West Church, Boston.

Barton, Bernard, 1784-1849. *B. B.* An English "Quaker poet"; b. in London; was a bank clerk, 1810-47; the friend of Southey, Lamb, and Byron; received a donation of £1200 from a reading-club which he had established at Woodbridge, his place of residence, and a pension of £100 from the Government. D. at Woodbridge.

Barton, William, A.M. *An American.* An American lawyer; b. at Lancaster, Penn.; was educ. chiefly in England; returning home in 1779, he was soon admitted to the Lancaster bar; in 1789 he was appointed by Washington one of the judges of the Western Territory; he was then President Judge of his district in Penn.; in 1800 was appointed Prothonotary of Lancaster Co., and Clerk of the Orphans' Court, 1803-9; afterwards removed to Philadelphia, where he was Secretary to the American Philosophical Society of that city.

Barton, Rev. Evelyn, A.M. *E. B.* An American clergyman; b. in Brooklyn, N.Y.; Col. Coll., 1869; Assistant and Assistant Priest, Mt. Calvary Church, Baltimore, from 1872.

Barty, Rev. James S. *Peter Plough.* A Scottish minister, of the parish of Bendochy.

Basset, Adrien Charles Alexandre, 1822-69. *Charles Newil.* A French littérateur; b. in Paris; began to make himself known in 1845 under the pseud. of "Adrien Robert."

Bassett, Rev. Edward Barnard, 1819-. *Beta.* An American Cong. minister; b. at Newburyport, Mass.; pastor at Warwick, Mass., 1869-72 et seq.

Basté, Eugène Pierre. *Eugène Grange.* A French dramatic author.

Bastide, Mme Jenny (Dufourquet), 1792-1854. *Camille Bodin; Thalaris Du-*

fourquet. A French poet and novelist; b. at Rouen; commenced her literary career in 1821; d. in her native city.

Batchelder, Eugene. *Wave.* An American poet; b. in New Ipswich, N.H. ; grad. at the Harv. Univ. Law School, 1845; resided at Cambridge, Mass.; d. at Dover, N.H.

Batchelder, James L. *A Chicagoan.* An American writer.

Bateman, Charles. *Ch— B—n.* An English surgeon, of Chertsey.

Bateman, James, M.A., F.R.S. *J. B.* An English author; member of Magdalen Coll., Oxford; M.A., 1834.

Bateman, Rev. Josiah, M.A. *Senex.* An English clergyman; Queen's Coll., Cambridge, 1828; Hon. Canon of Canterbury, 1863; Rector of Southchurch, St. Albans, 1873–83 *et seq.*

Bateman, Virginia Francis. *Virginia Francis.* An American author, sister of Isabella Bateman; a native of New York City.

Bateman, Rev. William Fairbairn, M.A. *W. F. B.* An English Epis. divine; Perpetual Curate of St. John Evang., Upper Norwood, 1875–83 *et seq.*

Bates, Miss Fanny D. *Beulah.* An American writer of books for the young, of Westfield, Mass.

Bates, G. W. *A. Haöle.* An English traveller.

Bates, Lewis James, 1832–. *B.; President Bates.* An American poet and journalist; b. at Catskill; has passed much of his active life in the Mississippi Valley; was in 1860 one of the most promising poets of the West, who could set type as well as make rhymes; his poems were chiefly published in the "Grand River Eagle," at Grand Rapids, Mich., where he resided for many years; is now (1885) on the editorial staff of the "Detroit Post and Tribune," and a distinguished bicycle journalist, writing for the "Outing," Boston, etc.

Bates, Mrs. M. V. *Margaret Holmes.*

Bates, Thomas. *T. B.* An English writer.

Bath, William Pulteney, the Earl of, 1682–1764. *Marcus Cato.* An English statesman; educ. at Christ Church, Oxford; was at first a personal friend of Walpole, but afterwards one of his most bitter opponents; acted as chief assistant to Bolingsbroke, in the "Craftsman"; was prime minister for two days, in 1746; and thenceforth took little part in public affairs.

Bathurst, Charles, M.A. *C. B.* An

English lecturer and educator, of Rochester.

Bathurst, Rev. William Hiley, M.A., 1796–. *W. H. B.* An English clergyman and hymn-writer; b. at Cleve Dale, near Bristol; Christ Church Coll., Oxford, 1818; from 1863, residing at Lydney Park, Gloucestershire.

Battay, Mrs. Emily Verdery. *Emily Verdery.*

Battersby, W. J. *W. J. B.* An Irish Catholic, of Dublin (?).

Battey, Mrs. Sallie J. (Hancock). *Cecil; Latona.* An American Southland writer; b. at Evanside, near Jeffersontown, Ky.; in 1870 married Mr. Manfred C. Battey, formerly of Buffalo, N.Y., and more recently of Washington, D.C.; in 1871 her address was Evanside.

Batty, Christopher, 1715–97. *C. B.* An English hymn-writer; b. at Newby Cote, near Settle, in Yorkshire, and d. at Kendal.

Batz-Trenqueléon, Charles de, 1835–. *Georges Linois.* A French author and journalist; b. at Mas d'Agenais (Lot et Garonne); was co-editor of several provincial journals, and then the author of a comedy which was brought out at Bordeaux.

Baudoin, Mme Virginie (Mortemart-Boisse). *Mme Virginie Orsini.* A French writer, wife of the proprietor of the "Moniteur parisien."

Baudouin, Jean Marie Théodore. *D'Aubigny.* A French dramatic author, of Paris.

Bauer, Klara, 1836–76. *Karl Detlef.* A German novelist; b. at Swinemunde, Pomerania; after the death of her father, spent some time in St. Petersburg; returning, she devoted herself to literary pursuits, at Dresden; d. at Breslau.

Bauerle, Adolf, 1787–1859. *Otto Horn.* A German humorous author and dramatist; b. at Vienna; published his first two romances under the above pseud.; d. at Bâle.

Baxter, Rev. John Alexander. *J. A. B.* An English Epis. divine; Perpetual Curate of Christ Church, Coseley.

Baxter, Mrs. Lucy E. (Barnes). *Leader Scott.* An English author; the daughter of the Rev. W. Barnes, the well-known author of poems in the Dorsetshire dialect; was educ. principally at home, occasionally attending a morning school at Dorchester. All her married life has been spent in Italy, and her attention has been turned chiefly to artistic and antiquarian subjects.

"Leader Scott" has been the Italian correspondent of the "Magazine of Art," London, since its commencement.

Baxter, Robert M., 1851-. *Arlington.* An American journalist, of New York.

Baxter, Rev. Roger, S.J., 1793-1827. *M.B.* An American R.C. divine and Jesuit, of Alexandria, D.C.; b. in Lancashire, England; d. in Philadelphia.

Baxter, Sylvester. *S. B.* An American journalist.

Baxter, William. *W. Welsh.* A Scottish poet, of Glasgow.

Baxter, Wynne Edwin. *Llewellin Acton.* An English lawyer.

Bayard, Antoine, 1807-72. *Léon Picard.* A French vaudeville writer; b. in Paris; under the above pseud. he assisted in editing the works of his more celebrated brother, Jean F. A. Bayard; d. in Paris.

Bayard, Mrs. Elise Justine. *E. J. B.* An American poetess, of New York.—See "Cutting, Mrs. Elise Justine (Bayard)."

Bayer, Karl Emmerich Robert von, 1835-. *Robert Byr.* A German writer; b. at Bregenz, Tyrol, Austria; served for a time in the army; in 1862 settled in Bregenz, where he now lives, as an author.

Bayle, Marc Antoine, 1825-79. *A. Marc; A. Marc Theotime.* A French theologian and professor of sacred eloquence; b., lived, and d. at Marseilles.

Bayle, Mouillard, Mme Élisabeth Félicie (Canard), 1796-1865. *Élisabeth Celnart.* A French authoress; b. at Moulins; wife of Jean Baptiste Bayle Mouillard.

Bayley, Francis. *F. B.; A County Court Judge.* An English barrister.

Bayley, Frederic W. N., 1807-52. *Alphabet Bayley.* An English journalist; editor of the "Omnibus," and first editor of the "London Illustrated News"; d. at Birmingham.

Bayley, Henry Vincent. *H. V. B.* An English clergyman; Archdeacon of Stow and Prebendary of Westminster.—See "S., R."

Bayley, Sir John, Bart., 1763-1841. *A Layman; A Member of the Established Church.* An eminent English jurist and special pleader, of London; called to the bar in 1792; Judge of the Court of King's Bench, 1809-34; d. at Vine House, near Seven Oaks, Co. Kent.

Baylie, Rev. John. *J. B.* An English Epis. divine; Perpetual Curate of Bloxwich, Walsall, Staffs., 1826-60 *et seq.*

Bayly, Anselm, Mus.D. *Anti-Socinus.* An English musician; Mus.D. at the Univ. of Cambridge, 1783; sub-dean of H. M.'s Chapel Royal towards the end of the 18th century.

Bayly, James Dudgeon. *J. D. B.*

Bayman, Mrs. A. Phelps. *An English Lady.* An English lady who wrote a series of letters in defence of the American Union in 1862-63; a sister of Robert Bayman.

Bayne, A. *A. B.* A Scottish (?) writer on music early in the 18th century.

Beach, Charles. *Cannibal Jack.* An English novelist; said in the "British Museum Catalogue" to be a pseudonym.

Beach, John Wesley. *John.* An American journalist.

Beach, Samuel B. *Peter Ploughshare.* An American writer.

Beaconsfield, Benjamin Disraeli, 1st Earl of, LL.D., 1805-81. △; *Mr. Daubeny; Runnymede.* A celebrated English novelist and statesman; son of Isaac D'Israeli, of Bradenham Manor, Bucks.; M.P., 1837-76; Chancellor of the Exchequer, 1852, 1858-59, 1868, and 1874-80; Lord Privy Seal, 1876; rector of Glasgow Univ., 1872 and 1874; d. in London.

Beadle, John Hanson, 1840-. *Beadle; Hanson.* An American author and journalist; b. at Liberty Township, Parke Co., Ind.; Univ. of Mich., 1867; in 1880 *et seq.* he resided at Rockville, Ind.

Beal, James, 1829-. *Father Jean; Nemesis.* A prominent English politician and lecturer; b. in Chelsea, and educ. at private schools; has contributed largely to the "Freeholder" and "London Dispatch."

Beal, Nathan Stone Reed. *An Old, Old Bachelor.* An American writer, of Macedon, N.Y.

Beale, John. *I. B.* An early English writer.

Beale, Thomas Willert, 1831-. *Walter Maynard.* An English lawyer and *littérateur*; b. in London; called to the bar at Lincoln's Inn in 1863, and since chiefly engaged in literary pursuits.

Beals, William. *The Reporter of the "Boston Morning Post."*

Bean, Rev. James. *A Minister.* An English clergyman; Vicar of Olney, Buckinghamshire; Curate of Carshalton, Surrey; Ass't Minister of Welbeck Chapel, St. Marylebone, and one of the librarians in the British Museum.

Beard, John Reilly, D.D. *A Dis-*

senting Minister. An English Unit. Minister, of Manchester.

Beasley, Rev. Frederick Williamson, D.D., 1808–78. *Caspar Almore.* An American clergyman, of Philadelphia; b. at Albany, N.Y.; Univ. of Penn., 1827; rector at Eddington, Penn.; d. in Philadelphia Co.

Beattie, James, LL.D., 1735–1803. *Oliver Old Style.* A Scottish poet; b. at Laurencekirk, Kincardineshire; was Prof. of Moral Philosophy and Logic in Marischal College at Aberdeen, 1760–180–.

Beatty, Anne. *A. B.* An English poetess, of Manchester (?).

Beatty, John. *A Volunteer.*

Beaufort, Rear Admiral Sir **Francis,** Knt., K.C.B., F.R.S., etc., 1774–1857. *F. B.* A British hydrographer; b. at Collon, Co. Louth, Ireland; entered the navy, 1787; retired in 1846; hydrographer to the Admiralty, 1832–55; d. at Brighton.

Beauchamp, Francis Ingram Seymour Conway, Viscount, 1719–94. *A Member of the British Parliament.* An English nobleman; created Viscount Beauchamp in 1750; Lord Lieut. of Ireland, 1765; Earl of Yarmouth, 1794.

Beaufoy, ——. *A British Subject.* An English writer.

Beaufoy, Henry, of Hackneywick. *H. B. H. B.; A Corporal of Riflemen.* An English gentleman.

Beaumont, George Duckett Barber. *George Barber; George Beaumont.* An English lawyer; Trin. Coll., Cambridge, 1824.

Beaumont, Rev. James Akroyd, M.A. *A Former Curate of Hunslet.* An English clergyman; Trin. Coll., Cambridge, 1841; Rector of Poughill, Crediton, Devon., 1850–61; Domestic Chaplain to the Earl of Fitzwilliam, 1842–83 *et seq.*

Beaumont, John Thomas Barber, Esq., F.S.A., 1774–1841. *Hastatus; A Magistrate for Middlesex.* An English gentleman; Managing Director of the Provident Institution, Southampton Street, London; b. in the parish of Marylebone; d. in London.

Beaunoir, Alexandre Louis Bertrand, 1746–1823. *Robineau.* A French dramatist; b. in Paris; he became successively director of the theatre of Bordeaux; of the theatres of Saint Petersburg, during the Revolution; and on his return to Paris in 1804 was employed in the literary division of the ministry of the police, supplying all the theatres of Paris with successful pieces.

Beauvoir, Edouard Roger (de Bully) de, 1809–66. *Eugène.* A French writer of poetry and romance; b. and d. in Paris; he published numerous romances and also wrote for the theatre.

Beaver, Rev. W. H. *Pimpernel.* An English writer.

Beazeley, Samuel, 1786–1851. *Beaseley.* An English architect and author; b. in London; besides erecting many great buildings, he wrote more than 100 dramas, and two novels; d. at Tunbridge Castle, in Kent.

Beck, Edward, 1804–61. *An Old Gardener.* An English Friend, of Worton Cottage, Isleworth, Middlesex.

Beck, Nicholas F., –1830. *A Citizen of New York.* An American lawyer; b. in Schenectady, N.Y.; Union Coll., 1813; settled in his profession at Albany, N.Y.

Beck, Paul, Jr., about 1760–1844. *A Citizen of Philadelphia.* An American merchant and philanthropist; b. in Philadelphia; served in the Revolutionary War; for many years Port Warden at Philadelphia, where he died.

Beck, Rev. Thomas, 1765–1808. *Timothy Touch'em.* An English poet and Dissenting Minister, of London.

Beckford, Peter. *A Sportsman of Berkshire.* An English sportsman; a relative of the famous William Beckford, of Bristol Hot Wells.

Beckford, William, Esq., 1760–1844. *A Gentleman; Viator; The Right Hon. Lady Harriet Marlow; Jacquetta Agneta Mariana Jenks, of Belgrove Priory in Wales.* An eminent but eccentric English author; b. in London; after travelling and residing some years on the Continent, he built a magnificent residence at Fonthill, which cost £273,000, which he sold in 1822, but built another near Bath, where he lived till his death, and d. there.

Beckner, Samuel W. E. *Belle Z. Bubb; Mr. O'Pake.* An American editor, of New York City.

Bedford, Rev. Hilkiah, 1663–1724. *A Priest of the Church of England.* An English non-juring divine.

Bedford, John T. *The City Waiter; Joseph Greenhorn; Robert.* An English writer; Member of the Corporation of the City of London.

Beebee, Charles Washington. *Ravenswood.* An American novelist.

Beecher, Mrs. Eunice W. (Bullard). *A Minister's Wife.* An American writer; wife of Henry Ward Beecher.

Beecher, Rev. Henry Ward, 1813–. *; *One who keeps his Eyes and Ears open.* An American clergyman; b. at Litchfield, Conn.; Amherst Coll., 1834; since 1847, minister of the Pilgrim Church, Brooklyn, N.Y.

Beer, Georg Joseph, M.D., 1763–1821. *An Experienced Oculist.* A celebrated German oculist; b., lived, and d. in Vienna.

Beers, Mrs. **Ethelinda (Elliott)**, 1827–79. *E. B.; Ethel Lynn.* An American poetess; b., educ., and d. at Goshen, Orange Co., N.J.

Beetham, Rev. **Hutton.** *Dr. William De Worfat.* An English writer.

Beeton, Samuel Orchart. *S. O. B.* An English editor and publisher, of London.

Beets, Nikolaus, 1814–. *Hildebrand.* A Dutch poet and prose-writer; b. at Haarlem; studied theology at Leyden; and since 1854 has been a preacher and professor at Utrecht. His poetic works were collected and published in three volumes in 1873–75.

Beever, Rev. **William Holt**, M.A. *An Amateur Farmer.* An English clergyman; Jesus Coll., Oxford, 1849; Examining Chaplain to the Bishop of Llandyssil, 1859; Prebendary of Fairwell in Llandyssil Cathedral, 1866; Rector of Llandyssil, 1879 *et seq.*

Beezley, James, 1739–1811. *J. B.; Philalethes.* An English Friend, of Tokenhouse Yard, London, and a Member of Gracechurch Street Monthly Meeting (?).

Beffroy de Reigny, Louis Abel, 1757–1811. *Cousin Jacques.* A French dramatist and writer, and composer of songs and operas; b. at Laon; d. at Charenton (Seine).

Begbie, James Warburton, M.D., F.R.S.E., about 1823–76. *A Physician.* An eminent Scottish medical writer; educ. at Edinburgh; lived and d. in that city.

Begg, ——. *Walter Bentley.* A Scottish actor; b. in Edinburgh.

Bégon, Fanny, Comtesse de. *Madame de Stolz.* A French novelist.

Behrens, Bertha. *W. Heimburg.*

Belcher, William. *A Rational Mystic.* An English bookseller, poet, and incoherent writer, of London. The pamphlet shop which he opened he called "The Asylum of Genius."

Belden, Ezekiel Porter, A.M. *A Member of that Institution.* An American

writer; b. in Wethersfield, Conn.; Yale Coll., 1844; studied law at New Haven, 1844–45; engaged in the construction and exhibition of models of New Haven and New York, 1845–47.

Belden, G. H. *Concivis.* An American writer.

Belden, N. H., 1810–. *N. H. Belden Clarke, Esq.* An American actor and dramatist; b. in Connecticut; first appeared on the stage at the old Chatham Garden, New York, in 1830.

Beldene, W. W. *W. W. B.* An American writer.

Belfast, Frederick Richard Chichester, Earl of, 1827–53. *Lord B—; Lord B******; Campana.* An Irish nobleman; educ. at Eton; early evinced a taste for literature and art, and was a successful cultivator of music; he devoted the proceeds of his literary and musical efforts to the relief and elevation of the working classes; d. at Naples.

Belfour, Rev. **Hugo John**, 1802–27. *St. John Dorset.* An English poet and dramatist; admitted to holy orders in 1826, and appointed to a curacy in Jamaica, where he died.

Belknap, Andrew Eliot, 1780–1858. *A Boston Boy.* An American merchant, of Boston, son of Rev. Dr. Jeremy Belknap.

Belknap, Jane. *J. B.* An American biographer, daughter of the Rev. Dr. Jeremy Belknap.

Bell, Mrs. **C. M.** *Materfamilias.* An English novelist; wife of Rev. Edward Bell, of Wakefield.

Bell, Catharine Douglass, –1861. *Kate; Cousin Kate.* A Scotch novelist, of Edinburgh, where she died.

Bell, Major **Evans.** *Indicus.* An East Indian officer and historian.

Bell, General Sir **George**, K.C.B., 1794–1877. *An Old Soldier.* An eminent English soldier; entered the army in 1811, and served with great distinction; author of "Rough Notes, by an Old Soldier." L. 1867.

Bell, Henry Nugent, Esq., 1773–1822. *Philo-Nauticus.* An English law student of the Inner Temple, London; d. at Whitehall-place, sincerely regretted by his numerous friends.

Bell, J. *John Hinds.* An English veterinary surgeon.

Bell, J. Forsyth. *A Canadian.*

Bell, Rev. **John.** *A Minister of the Gospel.* A Scottish minister, early in the 18th century.

Bell, John Montgomerie, 1804–62.

J. M. B. A Scottish lawyer; b. in Paisley; Univ. of Glasgow; admitted to the bar, 1825; sheriff of Kincardineshire, 1851; d. at Linnhouse.

Bell, N. R. E. *N. D'Anvers.* An English artist.

Bell, Thomas. *A Rhymer.* A Scottish poet, of Ceres, Fife, who acquired considerable popularity in Glasgow.

Bell, William, D.D., 1732–1816. *Rev. Peter Ponder.* An eminent English divine; Cambridge Univ., 1753; Prebendary of Westminster and Treasurer of St. Paul's, 1765–1816; d. at Westminster.

Bellak, James Blumtal. *James Blumtal.* A musical composer.

Bellamy, Mrs. E. W. *Kampa Thorpe.* An American "Southland" writer; in 1872, a teacher at Eutaw, Greene Co., Ala.

Bellemane, Eugène Louis Gabriel de Ferry de. *Gabriel Ferry.* A French voluminous writer, and contributor to the "Revue des Deux Mondes," 1846–52.

Bellett, John George. *J. G. B.* An Irish (?) writer.

Bellows, John, 1831–. *J. B.* An English printer and publisher, of Gloucester, from 1858; b. at Liskeard, Cornwall; is a Friend, or Quaker.

Beloe, Rev. William, 1756–1817. *A Sexagenarian.* An English miscellaneous writer; b. at Norwich; Bennet Coll., Cambridge, 1779; one of the assistant librarians to the British Museum from 1804.

Belsham, Rev. Thomas, 1750–1829. *T. B.* An English Unit. minister; b. at Bedford; succeeded Dr. Priestley at Hackney, when the latter removed to America in 1794, and was the successor of Mr. Lindsey, in Essex Street, in 1808; d. at Hampstead.

Belton, ——. *An Englishman.* An English angler.

Beltz, George Frederick, Esq., K.H., –1842. *L.* An eminent English genealogist; Lancaster Herald, Gentleman Usher of the Scarlet Rod and Brunswick Herald of the Order of Bath; Knight of the Royal Hanoverian Guelphic Order, and F.S.A.; d. at Basle while on his return home from Italy.

Benedict, David, D.D., 1778–1874. *John of Enon.* An eminent Bapt. clergyman; b. at Norwalk, Conn.; Brown Univ., 1806; for 25 years minister of the Bapt. church in Pawtucket, R.I., and in 1870, at the age of 92, preached in that city.

Benezet, Anthony, 1713–84. *A Farmer; A Lover of Mankind.* An American Friend and philanthropist; b. at St. Quintin, Picardy; resided at Philadelphia (where he established a school for the colored people), 1731–84.

Bengo, John. *An Artist.* A Scottish poet and engraver, of Edinburgh.

Bengough, J. D. *Grip.* A Canadian writer, of Toronto.

Benham, Daniel. *D. B.* An English writer.

Benham, George Chittenden. *A Victim.* An English (?) writer.

Benjamin, Park, 1809–64. *Bentley Parker; Flaneur; Member of the Class of '67.* An American poet; b. in British Guiana; Trin. Coll., Hartford, 1829; removed to New York City in 1837, and devoted himself to journalism and literary pursuits; d. in New York City.

Benjamin, Walter Romaine, 1854–. *Dud Jermyn.* An American reporter, of New York City.

Bennet, Philip. *A Gentleman of Cambridge.* An early English poet.

Bennett, Charles, 1854–. *Daniel Daddow.* An English humorist, of Cornwall; b. at Treverbyn Vicarage; in 1879 resident at Treverbyn Street, Anstell.

Bennett, Charles Henry. *The Owl* (?). An English artist.

Bennett, J. *A Detective.* An English writer.

Bennett, J. W. *A Fellow of the Linnæan and Horticultural Societies.* An English writer.

Bennett, John. *Peter Parley.* An English compiler.

Bennett, M., Jun. *Persimmons.*

Bennett, Mrs. Mary E. *M. E. B.; Mary Campbell; Mary Mel.* An American poet.

Bennett, Mrs. William. *Getty Gay.*

Bennett, William. *W. B.* An English Friend, or Quaker, first of London; in 1867, of Brockham Lodge, Betchworth, near Reigate, Surrey.

Bennett, Rev. William James Early, M.A. *The Vicar of Frome-Selwood; W. J. E. B.* An English clergyman; Ch. Ch., Oxford, 1827; Vicar of Frome-Selwood w. Woodlands, 1852–80 *et seq.;* editor of the "Old Church Porch."

Benson, Mrs. Janie (Ollivar). *L'Inconnue.* An American "Southland" poet, of Augusta, Ga.

Bentham, Edward, D.D., 1707–76. *E. B.; E. B——, D.D.; A Tutor and Fellow of a College in Oxford.* A learned divine of the Church of England; Regius Professor of Divinity at Oxford, from 1763.

Bentham, Jeremy, 1747–1832. *J. B.; Gamaliel Smith; Philip Beauchamp.* An English philosopher and legal reformer; b. in London; B.A. at Oxford, 1763; d. in London in the house where he had lived for 50 years.

Bentinck, Rt. Hon. George Augustus Frederick Cavendish, 1821–. *John Doe.* An English lawyer; Trin. Coll., Cambridge, 1843; called to the bar at Lincoln's Inn, 1846; judge advocate general from 1875 and of the Privy Council.

Bentley, ——. *A Near Observer.* An English political writer.

Bentley, Edwin. *E. B.* An English poet.

Bentley, Joseph. *J. B.; The Oldest School Inspector.* An English educator, of London.

Bentley, Richard, D.D., 1661–62–1742. *A Member of Trinity College, Cambridge; Philalethes; Phileleutherus Lipsiensis.* An eminent English Grecian; b. at Oulton, near Wakefield, in the West Riding of Yorkshire; Master of Trin. Coll., Cambridge, 1700–42.

Bentley, Richard, Esq., –1782. *P. D.; R—— B——, Esq.* An English poet and prose writer; educ. at Trin. Coll., Camb.; resided for many years in the south of France, and for some time at Teddington, near Twickenham, being a friend of Horace Walpole.

Benton, Mrs. C. C. *C. C. B.* An American writer.

Benton, Thomas Hart, 1782–1858. *A Senator of Thirty Years.* An American statesman; b. at Hillsborough, N.C.; was a lawyer at St. Louis from 1815, and U.S. Senator, 1820–50; d. at Washington, D.C.

Benwell, John. *An Englishman.* An English traveller in America.

Béraud, Antoine Nicolas, 1792–1860. *Antony.* A French miscellaneous writer; b. at Aurillac (Cantal); Director of the Prison of Belle-Isle-en-Mer, 1849–52; d. at Paris.

Berens, Rev. Edward, 1778–1859. *A Churchman; A Country Clergyman.* An English divine; Oriel Coll., Oxford, 1804; Vicar of Shrivenham, and Archdeacon of Berks.; d. at Shrivenham.

Beresford, Rev. James, 1764–1840. *An Aspirant; Ignoto Secondo; Timothy Testy and Samuel Sensitive.* An English clergyman and humorous writer; b. at Upham, Hants.; educ. at Oxford Univ.; Rector of Kibworth, Leicestershire.

Bergh, A. E., 1855–. *Sylvanus Snap.* An American writer.

Berguin, H. K. *A Citizen of North Carolina.*

Berkeley, George, D.D., 1684–1753. *The Bishop of Cloyne; Ulysses Cosmopolite.* An Irish prelate; b. in Kilcrin, Co. Kilkenny; Bp. of Cloyne, 1734–53.

Berkeley, Hon. George Augustus Grantley Fitzhardinge, 1800–81. *The English Sportsman; A Huntsman.* An English author; a younger son of the Earl of Berkeley; served for a time in the army; was an M.P., 1832–47; and in 1836 commenced his literary career by his novel of "Berkeley Castle."

Berkeley, George Monck, Esq., LL.B., F.A.S., –1793. *Bard; A Gentleman of the Inner Temple.* An English writer, only son of Dr. Berkeley, Prebendary of Canterbury; d. at Cheltenham.

Berkeley, Henrietta, Countess. *Silvia.* An English lady; one of the younger daughters of the Rt. Hon. George, Earl Berkeley.

Bernard, Sir Francis, 1st Bart., 1714–79. *F—— B——.* An English lawyer; Governor first of New Jersey, then of Massachusetts, 1760 *et seq.*

Bernard Du Grail de la Villette Charles, 1804–50. *Charles de Bernard.* A French writer; b. at Besançon; removed to Paris, and met the pleiad of the young authors of the day, Hugo, Dumas, Musset, Sainte Beuve, etc., and became one of the most brilliant; d. at Sablonville.

Berneck, Karl Gustav von, 1803–71. *Bernd von Guseck.* A German novelist; b. at Kirchhain, Prussia; Professor of Mathematics in the School of Engineers at Berlin, where he died.

Bernstein, Aaron, 1812–. *A Rebenstein.* A German author; b. at Dantzic; the son of a Jewish elder; was educ. for the office of Rabbi, and completed his education at Berlin, where he became favorably known by his literary work.

Berridge, Rev. John, 1716–93. *A Methodist Preacher in Cambridgeshire.* An English divine; b. at Kingston, Notts.; Clare Hall, Cambridge, 1738; Vicar of Everton, 1755–93; adopted the views and became the friend of Wesley, Whitefield, and Lady Huntington, and his labors resembled theirs.

Berry, Frances Miriam.— See "Whitcher, Mrs. Frances (Berry)."

Berry, Mrs. Martha Eugenia. *Eugenia St. John.* An American writer of religious fiction.

Berthet, Élie Bertrand, 1815-. *Élie Raymond.* A French novelist; b. at Limoges; in 1834 he went to Paris and devoted himself to literature, and is the author of about one hundred volumes.

Berthoud, Eugène. *Gontran Borys.* A French writer of the day.

Berthoud, Samuel Henri, 1804-. *Sam.* A French *littérateur;* b. at Cambrai (Nord); in 1832 removed to Paris, and from 1848 he wrote scientific articles for "La Patrie," Paris, under the pseudonym of "Sam."

Bertram, James G. *Rev. William U. Cooper, B.A.* An English miscellaneous writer.

Bertrand, L'Abbé François Marie, 1807-. *Sophronius.* A French Orientalist; b. at Fontainebleau (Seine-et-Marne); Canon of the Cathedral of Versailles.

Besant, Walter, 1838-. *W. B.* An English novelist, of London; b. at Portsmouth; Christ's Coll., Cambridge, 1859; devoted to literary pursuits.

Besemeres, Jane. *Janet Byrne.* An English religious writer.

Besemeres, John. *John Daly.* An English writer, of Calcutta.

Besly, Rev. John, M.A. *J. B.* An English Epis. divine; Rector of Aston Subedge, Gloucs., 1831–60 *et seq.*

Besse, Joseph, about 1683–1757. *J.B.; Irenicus; One of the People called Quakers; Philalethes; Philanthropos.* An English Friend; a writing-master of Colchester, but afterwards of Clerkenwell, London, and Chelmsford; still later removed to Ratcliffe, London, where he died.

Bestoujéff, Alexandre, 1793–1837. *Marlinsky, the Cossack.* A Russian novelist, the famous conspirator of 1825.

Bethune, George Amory, M.D. *A Certain Traveller.* An American physician; Harv. Univ. in 1831; Harv. Med. School, 1834; practises his profession in Boston.

Bethune, Rev. John. *A Minister of the Church of Scotland.* A Scottish minister, of Rosskeen.

Bethune, John. 1812–39. *Fifeshire Forester.* A Scottish peasant-poet; b. in the parish of Monimail, Fifeshire; never was but one day at school, and passed his short life chiefly at Lochend, near the loch of Lindores.

Bettany, George, 1819-. *A Practical Teacher.* An English teacher and journalist; b. at Cheadle; Master of the Wesleyan School at Penzance, 1847–74; editor and manager of the "Methodist," 1874–75; on the staff of the "Western Morning News" from 1875.

Betty, William Henry West, 1791-. *The Young Roscius.* A young English actor, who was wonderfully successful on the stage, 1804–7.

Bettziech, Heinrich, 1813–76. *H. Beta.* A German writer and journalist; b. at Werben, near Delitsch, in Prussian Saxony; from 1838 engaged at Berlin on various journals.

Beudin, Jacques Félix, 1796-. *Dinaux.* A French banker and man of letters; b. in Paris; although at the head of a great Parisian banking-house, he was a successful writer of romance and the drama.

Bevan, E. F. *E. F. B.* An English poet and translator.

Bevan, Joseph Gurney, 1753–1814. *Cryptonimus; Editor of that Journal; Vindex.* An English chemist and druggist; b. in London; a member of the Society of Friends; d. at Stoke-Newington.

Bevan, Robert Casper Lee. *R. C. L. B.* An English writer.

Bevan, Samuel. *Cavendish.* An English artist (?); son of Paul Bevan; a Friend, of Tottenham.

Bevan, Thomas. *Custos.* An English Friend; son of Thomas Bevan, M.D., of London.

Bevans, John, Jr., 1773–1836. *Christicola; A Layman.* An English Friend, of London.

Beverley, Robert, -1716. *A Native and Inhabitant of that Place.* An American historian; b. and d. in Virginia; was the son of Major Robert Beverley, clerk of the council of Virginia.

Beverley, Rev. Robert Mackenzie. *A Wanderer; Rev. Rabshakeh Gathercoal, late Vicar of Tuddington.* An English Epis. divine; at one time Vicar of Tuddington.

Bewick, Miss Jane, 1787–1881. *J. B.* An English lady; daughter of Thomas Bewick, and editor of his memoirs; d. at Gateshead.

Bewley, Henry. *H. B.* An Irish Friend, of Dublin.

Beyle, Marie Henri, 1783–1842. *A. M. B. A.; Alexandre César Bombet; De Stendhal.* An accomplished French *littérateur;* b. at Grenoble; removed to Paris in 1802, and devoted himself to study and literary work; d. in that city.

Biard, Mme Auguste François, 1820–79. *Leonie d'Aunet.* A French literary lady, of Paris; became the wife of the celebrated painter, and accompanied him to Spitzbergen; but separated from him in 1843; d. in Paris.

Bibby, E. *E. B.* An English poet.

Biber, Rev. George Edward, Ph.D., LL.D., 1801–74. *G. E. B.* An eminent German-English theologian and educator; removed to England in 1826, and took holy orders; Rector of West Allingham, 1872–74; for some years was editor of the "John Bull" (L.).

Bickersteth, Mrs. C., afterwards **Wheeler.** *C. B.* An English poet.

Bickersteth, Rev. Edward, 1786–1850. *E. B.; A Churchman.* An English lawyer till 1815, when he took holy orders, and was minister of Walton, 1830–50. B. at Lonsdale, Westmoreland; d. at Watton, Herts.

Bickersteth, Rev. Edward Henry, 1825–. *E. H. B.* An eminent English poet and divine; son of the preceding; Rector of Christ Church, Hampstead, from 1855; editor of "Evening Hours" (L.).

Bickham, William D. *W. D. B.* An American writer; correspondent of the "Cincinnati Commercial."

Bicknell, John Laurens, Esq., F.R.S., F.S.A., 1786–1845. *The Late Joel Collier, Licentiate in Music.* An English attorney, author, and musician of London.

Biddle, Miss Beatrice. *Beatrice B.* An American journalist, of New York City.

Biddle, Richard, 1796–1847. *An American.* An American author, jurist, and statesman, of Pennsylvania; b. in Philadelphia; became the leader of the Pittsburg bar; M.C., 1837–41; d. at Pittsburg.

Biddulph, Rev. Thomas Tregenna, M.A., 1763–1838. *Physico-Theologus.* An English Epis. divine; b. at Claines, Worcestershire; B.A., Oxford, 1784; minister of St. James's, Bristol, 1798–1838; d. in that city.

Bienvenu, Charles Léon, 1835–. *Touchatout.* A French journalist and littérateur; b. in Paris; chief editor of the "Tintamarre," a Paris journal; in 1866, one of the principal editors of the "Charivari," and in 1868, founded a humorous review, under the title of the "Touchatout Review."

Bierce, M. H. *Dod Grile.* An American humorist; at one time a writer in the San Francisco "News-Letter."

Bigelow, Josiah. *A Factory Hand of Waltham.* An American workman, of Waltham, Mass.

Bigg, Jeremiah. *An Embryo "Harvest Man."* An English Friend, son of Thomas Bigg, of Swansea; d. 1830, at Llantwit Major, Glamorganshire.

Bigg, William. *W. B.; "Quantum Mutatis."* An English Friend; brother of Jeremiah Bigg; formerly of Banbury, but in 1867 *et seq.,* of Luton, Bedfordshire.

Biggs, Henry. *A Member of the Association.* An Irish author.

Biggs, James. *A Gentleman who was an Officer under that General.* An American adventurer; a friend and officer of Don Francisco de Miranda, in his attempt to effect a revolution in South America in 1806–7.

Biglow, William, A.M., 1773–1844. *A Brother; Charles Chatterbox; Roger Roundelay; Square Sawney.* An American humorous writer; b. in Natick, Mass.; Harv. Univ., 1794; was a teacher, a wit, a poet, an editor, an author, and a proof-reader. He was principal of the Boston Latin School several years; and for many years connected with the press at Cambridge, Mass. D. in Boston.

Bigot, Mme Mary (Healy). *Jeanne Mairet.* An American novelist; daughter of the American artist, Healey; wife of Charles Bigot.

Binckes, William, D.D. –1712. *A Country Divine; A Presbyter of the Church of England.* An English clergyman; Dean of Lichfield, 1703–12.

Bindley, Charles, 1798–1859. *Harry Hieover.* An English sporting-writer; d. at Brighton.

Bindley, James, Esq., F.S.A. *Leontes.* A Senior Commissioner of the English Stamp Office, London; one of the most eminent bibliomaniacs, and collector of rare prints, of his day.

Bingham, Sir Charles. *A Country Gentleman.* An Irish (?) writer.

Bingham, Frances Lydia. *A Clergyman's Daughter.* An English writer, eldest daughter of the Rev. Richard Bingham; d. at Harwood parsonage, Bolton-le-Moors, in 1847.

Binney, Amos, M.D., 1803–47. *The President.* An American merchant and naturalist; b. in Boston; Brown Univ., 1821; was one of the founders of the Boston Natural History Society, and its president 1843–47; d. in Rome.

Binney, Horace, LL.D., 1780–1875. *H. B.* An eminent American lawyer; b. in Philadelphia; Harv. Univ., 1797; admitted to the bar in 1800, and was for many years the leader of the Philadelphia bar; d. in that city.

Binney, Mrs. Juliette Patterson. *Mrs. J. G. Binney.* A missionary in Burmah for twenty years (?).

Binney, Thomas, D.D., 1798–1874. *Fiat Justitia; John Search.* An eminent English Dissenter; b. at Newcastle-on-Tyne; minister of the Weigh House Chapel, London, 1829–71.

Birch, Jonathan, Esq., –1847. *Johann Abrtcht; Job Crithannah.* An Englishman of considerable literary attainments, chiefly known for his translation of Goethe's "Faust"; was enthusiastic for everything German; d. at the Palace of Bellevue, near Berlin.

Birch, Mrs. Walter. *The Widow of a Clergyman of the Church of England.* An English religious writer.

Bird, Henry Merttins, Esq. *A Merchant.* An English economist, of London.

Bird, Miss Isabella. — See "Bishop, Mrs. I. (B.)."

Bird, James, 1789–1839. *A Suffolk Yeoman.* An English poet; in early life a miller, but, failing in business, his friends set him up in a stationer's shop and small circulating library in the village of Yoxford, Suffolk, where he died.

Bird, Robert Montgomery, M.D., 1803–54. *Peter Pilgrim; A Rambler; Sheppard Lee.* An American physician and miscellaneous writer; b. at Newcastle, Del.; practised in Philadelphia; after some years of successful literary labor, after 1839 he gave it up, in great measure, for the life of an extensive farmer; d. in Philadelphia.

Bird, Sarah. *A Mother.* An English writer.

Birdsall, A. F., 1858–. *Hall-Hildebrand.* An American writer.

Birdwood, James. *J. B., a Servant of Jesus Christ.* An early English religious writer.

Birkbeck, Morris, 1764–1825. *Jonathan Freeman.* An early English emigrant to Illinois, in 1817, the son of an English Quaker; he founded the town of New Albion, and resided there; when the State was organized, in 1818, he opposed the introduction of slavery; he was drowned, while returning from a visit to Robert Owen at New Harmony, in 1825.

Bischoff, Joseph Edward Konrad, 1828–. *Konrad von Bolanden.* A German novelist; b. at Gailbach, in the Rhine Palatinate; studied Catholic theology, and became a clergyman at Börrstadt, and afterwards at Berghausen near Spire; in 1857 began his literary career.

Bishop, Mrs. Isabella (Bird). *The Englishwoman.* An English author.

Bishop, William Henry, 1847–. *Ray-* mond Westbrook. An American novelist; b. in Hartford, Conn.; Yale Coll., 1867; for some years a journalist at Milwaukee, Wis.; since 1877 has been engaged at New York City in literary work.

Bissell, Rev. Edwin Cone, D.D., 1832–; *The Monday Club.* An eminent American Cong. clergyman; b. at Schoharie, N.Y.; Amherst Coll., 1855; Professor of the Hebrew Language and Literature, at Hartford, Conn., since 1881.

Bisset, James, 1762–1832. *An Old Townsman.* A Scottish gentleman; b. at Perth; removed to Birmingham, where he established a museum and shop for curiosities, which in 1813 he removed to Leamington, where he opened a news-room and picture gallery; and d. there.

Bisset, Rev. James. *A Minister of the Church of Scotland.* A Scottish minister, of Aberdeen.

Bitzius, Albert, 1797–1854. *Jeremias Gotthelf.* A celebrated Swiss novelist; b. at Murten, canton of Freiburg; pastor at Lützelfluh, not far from Berne, 1832–54.

Black, Adam, 1784–1874. *Simon Scribe.* A Scottish bookseller and publisher; b. in Edinburgh, and educ. at the Univ. there. For many years he published the "Edinburgh Review" and Scott's works. He was Lord Provost of Edinburgh, 1843–48, and M.P. from that city, 1856–65.

Black, Alexander. *Jefferson Brick.* An American journalist.

Black, David Dakers. *V. S. N.* A Scottish local historian, of Brechin (?).

Black, James R., M.D., 1827–. *M.D. of Newark, Ohio.* An American physician, of Newark, O.; b. near Glasgow, Scotland; is Prof. of Hygiene in Columbus (O.) Med. Coll.

Black, Rev. John. *Sappho Search.* An English clergyman, of Butley, Suffolk.

Black, Mrs. Sarah S. *J. O. Y.*

Black, William, 1841–. *Pisistratus Brown; J. Smith.* A popular Scottish novelist; b. at Glasgow; for a time studied to become an artist, but eventually drifted into journalism, becoming connected with the "Glasgow Weekly Citizen" while yet in his teens. In 1864 he removed to London, and has since that time been devoted to literary work in that city.

Blackburn, Charles F. *A Journeyman.* An English author.

Blackburn, Rev. Gideon (?), D.D., 1772–1838. *Omega.* An eloquent American Presbyterian clergyman; b. in Augusta Co., Va.; educ. in Tenn.; minister of Louisville, Ky., 1823–27; President of Centre Coll., Ky., 1827–30; in 1833 he removed to Illinois, and did much there for education, literary and theological; d. at Carlinville, Ill.

Blackburn, Mrs. J. B. *J. B.* An English writer; wife of Hugh Blackburn, Prof. of Math. at the Univ. of Glasgow.

Blacker, Rev. Beaver Henry, M.A. *B. H. B.* An English Epis. divine; Trin. Coll., Dublin, 1843; in 1883 *et seq.* resident at Meridian-place, Clifton, Bristol.

Blackham, George E., M.D. *Cyclos.* An American physician of Dunkirk, N.Y.

Blackstone, Sir **William,** 1723–80. *Another Member of Parliament.* An eminent English lawyer and law-writer; b. in London; practised in London from 1759, visiting Oxford to give his lectures as Law Professor; Judge of the Court of Common Pleas, 1761–80.

Blackwell, Miss ——. *A Lady of Fashion.* An English novelist.

Blackwell, E. H. *E. H. B.* An English lawyer.

Blackwell, Henry. *H. B.* An English teacher (?) of fencing, in the early part of the last century.

Blackwell, Robert. *R. B.* An English writer of the earlier part of the last century.

Blackwood, Thomas. *A Layman of the Church of Scotland.*

Blackwood, William, 1776–1834. *Ebony; Old Ebony.* An eminent Scottish publisher; b. in Edinburgh; in 1804 he settled in Edinburgh; in 1817 he commenced the famous "Blackwood's Magazine"; d. at Edinburgh.

"Blackwood's Magazine." *Maga.*

Blades, R. H. *R. H. B.* An English writer.

Blades, William, 1824–. *W. B.* An English printer and writer; b. at Clapham, Surrey; succeeded his father as a printer in London, where he has edited early-printed books, and contributed to the literature of the day.

Blagdon, Francis William, 1778–1819. *Æschines; Aristides.* An English journalist; originally a horn-boy, employed to sell the "Sun"; studied grammar and French under Mr. Willich; after quite a successful career as an editor and translator, he unfortunately started the "Political Register" in opposition to William Cobbett, but was ru-

ined by the speculation. Incessant hard work broke up his constitution, and he died poor, in London.

Blakie, Alexander, D.D. *A Presbyterian.* An American Presbyt. minister; b. at Pictou, N.S.; for some years pastor at Boston, and from 1867 a resident of that city.

Blakie, G. W. *Timothy Plain.* A Scottish poet and artist.

Blair, David. *Jack Robinson, junior.* An English colonial Shakespearian critic, of Melbourne, Australia.

Blair, Mary E. *St. Ursula.* An American teacher, of Boston.

Blair, Patrick, M.D. *Michael Servetus, M.D.* A Scottish physician, originally of Dundee; imprisoned in 1715 on account of his attachment to the Stuart family; removed to London, and afterwards to Boston, in Lincolnshire.

Blake, Henry A. *Terence McGrath.* An Irish author of the day.

Blake, Rev. James Vila, 1842–. *J. V. B.* An American Unit. minister; b. in Brooklyn, N.Y.; Harv. Univ., 1862; Pastor at Quincy, Ill., from 1877.

Blake, Mrs. Lillie Devereux. *Æsop.* An American "woman-rights" advocate; b. at Raleigh, N.C.; educ. at New Haven, Conn.; in 1877 a resident of New York City.

Blake, William, 1757–1827. *W. B.; Augur; Pictor Ignotus.* An excellent, but eccentric, English artist; b. and d. in London.

Blakeslee, Mrs. Mary N. *Mary Blake.* An American writer; wife of a Connecticut minister.

Blakesley, Very Rev. Joseph William, B.D., 1808–85. *A Hertfordshire Incumbent.* An eminent English divine; b. in London; Trin. Coll., Camb., 1831; Fellow and Tutor there till 1845; Dean of Lincoln, 1872–85; during these years he lived a quiet and retired life.

Blakey, Robert, Ph.D., 1795–1878. *Nathan Oliver, Esq.; Palmer Hackle; Verax.* An eminent English miscellaneous writer; b. at Morpeth, Northumberland; early devoted to literature and philosophy; for a time Prof. at King's Coll.; Belfast, from 1835; d. at Blomfield Road, Shepherd's Bush.

Blanc, Jean Joseph Louis, 1811–82. *A Freeman.* A French political theorist and writer; b. at Madrid; when nineteen years of age, went to Paris; has chiefly resided in Paris, writing for the press.

Blanc, Mary Thérèse, 1840–. *Thérèse Bentzon.* A French writer; b. at Seine-Porte; in 1871 she decided to make literature her profession, and is a regular contributor to the "Revue des Deux Mondes."

Blanch, John. *J. B.; A Clothier; A Gentleman in Gloucestershire.* An English dramatist of the early part of the last century.

Blanchard, Edward Leman, 1820–84 (?). *E. L. B.; Old Boy.* An English *littérateur;* son of William Blanchard; for many years on the staff of the London "Daily Telegraph."

Blanchard, Rev. Joshua Pollard, 1782–1868. *J. P. B.* An eminent American philanthropist; for more than 50 years a chief supporter and advocate of the cause of peace; d. in Boston.

Bland, J. Harcourt. *J. Harcourt B.* An English writer; a comedian.

Bland, Sir James Bland Burges. *Sergeant Bradshaw, Esq.* An English lawyer and poet. — See "Lamb, Sir J. B. B."

Bland, Rev. Robert, B.A., 1779–1825. *B.* An English clergyman; curate of Kenilworth, 1816–25. He possessed high classical and literary attainments, and was greatly accomplished in music. D. at Leamington, near Warwick.

Bland, Thomas, 1740–1818. *A Friend to Accuracy.* An English Friend, or Quaker; b. in London; for 44 years connected, first as an assistant, and afterwards as an active partner in the commercial establishment, for some years under the firm of "Gurneys and Bland." D. at Norwich.

Blane, William Newnham. *An English Gentleman.* An English traveller.

Blathwayt, Mrs. Raymond. *Aunt Maggie.*

Blauvelt, ——. *Sir Anthony Avalanche.* An American poet.

Blayney, Benjamin, D.D., 1728–1801. *A Member of the University.* An English clergyman, of Worcester Coll., Oxford, afterwards of Hertford Coll.; Regius Prof. of Hebrew, Oxford, 1787–1801. D. at Polshot, Wilts.

Blaze, François Henri Joseph, 1784–1857. *Castil Blaze.* A French composer and writer on music; b. at Cavaillon (Vaucluse). Under the Empire he was successively a painter, an *employé,* chief of bureau at the prefecture of Vaucluse, an inspector of libraries, and a wholesale wine-merchant. He played upon several instruments, and had composed many romances, and published fugitive pieces under a feigned name. In 1819 he removed to Paris, and devoted

himself to musical journalism and literature. D. in Paris.

Blaze de Bury, Ange Henri, 1813–. *Henri Blaze; Hans Werner; F. de Langenevais.* A French *littérateur,* contributor of poetry and musical criticisms to the "Revue des Deux Mondes" from 1864.

Blaze de Bury, Mme Marie Pauline Rose (Stewart). *Arthur Dudley; Maurice Flassan.* A French literary lady of an old Scottish family; wife of Ange Henri; a contributor to the "Revue des Deux Mondes," the "Revue de Paris," and the "North American Review."

Bleckley, Henry. *A Manchester Manufacturer.*

Bleloch, Archibald. *Lake-Elbe.* A contemporary Scottish philosopher.

Blessington, Charles John Gardiner, Earl of, 1782–1829. *A Representative Peer.* An Irish nobleman; married, in 1817, Marguerite (Power Farmer), Countess of Blessington. He d. in Paris.

Blessington, J. P. *A Private Soldier.* An American adventurer.

Blessington, Marguerite (Power Farmer) Gardiner, Countess of, 1789–1849. *Idler.* An Irish novelist and miscellaneous writer; daughter of Mr. Edmund Power, of Curragheen, Co. Waterford; when only 15 she married M. St. Leger Farmer, Esq., of Poplar Hall, Co. Kildare, and 14 years after, the Earl of Blessington; for many years was a contributor to literature; d. at Paris.

Bleuman, Jonathan. *A Student of the Temple.* An English writer, of Christ Church, Oxford, 1706.

Blewitt, John Octavian, 1810–84. *Brother Peregrine.* An English *littérateur;* b. in London; edited for 29 years the "newspaper side" of the "Gardeners' Chronicle," and contributed numerous articles to "Fraser's Magazine" and "St. Paul's Magazine"; Secretary of the Royal Literary Fund, 1839–84; d. at Elgin Crescent.

Bleyer, Julius. *Cæsar.* An American journalist, of Milwaukee, Wis.

Blind, Mathilde. *Claude Lake.* An English poet.

Blinn, Mrs. Henry G. *Aunt Yewrowyckie.* An American writer.

Bliss, E. M. *E. M. B.* An American writer.

Bliss, Florence. *Cousin Florrie.* An American writer.

Bliss, George Newman, LL.B., 1837–. *Ulysses.* An American lawyer and journalist; b. at Tiverton, R.I.;

Union Coll., 1860; and at the Albany Law School, 1861; Trial Justice at East Providence, R.I., 1872–80 *et seq.*

Bliss, Henry, Q.C. *Nicholas Thirning Moile.* An English barrister-at-law; b. in New Brunswick; of Lincoln's Inn; for many years English agent for Nova Scotia; 1867 *et seq.* resident in London.

Bliss, John Homer, 1832–. *Xylo.* An American printer and genealogist; b. at Oswego, N.Y.; resided in Conn., 1836–54; in 1879 removed to Boston, Mass.

Bliss, Judah Lee, M.D., 1803–. *O. F. and A. K.; Curtus Gallus; Democritus, junior; An Old Fogy.* An eccentric American author; b. in North Wilbraham, Mass.; Yale Coll., 1822; was a merchant in Canada, and New York City, till 1830; was then a teacher in or near Natchez, Miss.

Bliss, Rev. Seth, 1793–1879. *The Secretary of the Boston Society.* An American Cong. minister; b. in Springfield, Mass; Yale Div. School, 1825; pastor at Jewett City, Conn., 1825–32; Secretary of the American Tract Society at Boston, 1833–57; and of the Society of the same name at New York City, 1857–79; residing at various places.

Blocquel, Simon, 1780–1863. *Rinmon.* A French author and lithographer; b. at Douai; d. at Lille, where he was a publisher and bookseller.

Bloede, Victor Gertrude. *Stuart Sterne.* An American poetess.

Blomfield, Charles James, D.D. 1786–1857. *One of the Working Clergy.* An eminent English clergyman; b. at Bury St., Edmund's; Trin. Coll., Cambridge, 1808; Lord Bishop of London, 1828–57; d. at the palace, Fulham.

Blomfield, H. *H. B.* An English writer.

Bloodgood, Simeon DeWitt, 1799–1866. *The Sexagenarian.* An American merchant and politician; b. in Utica, N.Y.; Union Coll., 1818; first resided in Albany, then in New York City, devoting much of his time to literary pursuits; d. in New York City.

Bloom, Rev. John Hague, B.A., *Cicerone.* An English clergyman; Caius Coll., Cambridge, 1827; Vicar of Castleacre, Brandon, Norfolk, 1835–70 *et seq.*

Bloomfield, J. K. *J. K. B.* An American writer for the young.

Bloomfield, Robert, 1766–1823. *R. B.; The Farmer's Boy.* An English poet; b. at Hornington, Suffolk; was

brought up as a farmer's boy; then removed to London, and worked as a shoemaker till 1800. Of his "Farmer's Boy" 26,000 copies were sold; d. in poverty at Shefford, in Bedfordshire.

Blouet, Paul. *Max O'Rell.* A French writer; French master at Westminster School, and editor of Clarendon volumes on "French Oratory."

Blount, Miss Annie R. *Jenny Woodbine.* An American "Southland" poetess; b. in Richmond Co., Va.; graduated at the Madison Female Coll., Ga.; in 1869 *et seq.* she resided at Augusta, Ga.

Blower, Miss Elizabeth, 1763–. *E. B.* An English novelist; b. at Worcester; early engaged in literary work for the benefit of her family.

Blox, Rev. John E. *Philalethes.* An American writer.

Blum, Lodoiska von, 1842–. *Ernst von Waldow.* A German author; b. at the Castle Caczevice in Poland; daughter of a Prussian officer; until that time living in Berlin; in 1869 she settled in Vienna.

Blundell, Henry. *H. B.* An English art amateur and collector, of Ince, near Liverpool.

Blundell, John. *A Gentleman, Native Thereof.* An English antiquary, of Tiverton, early in the 18th century.

Blunt, Arthur Cecil. *Arthur Cecil.* An English actor; b. near London; made his *début* in that city in 1869, where he has since constantly distinguished himself.

Blunt, George William, 1822–78. *G. W. B.* An American hydrographer; b. at Newburyport, Mass.; Harbor Commissioner at New York City from 1867; d. in New York City.

Blunt, Joseph, 1792–1860. *Marcus.* An American lawyer and politician; b. at Newburyport, Mass.; brother of the preceding; editor of the "American Annual Register," N.Y., 1827–35.

Blunt, Wilfrid Scawen, Esq., 1840–. *W. S. B.* An English diplomatist and traveller, of Crabbet, Sussex; Secretary of Legation at Berne, 1869–70.

Boaden, James, 1762–1839. *Edward Sydenham.* An English author; b. at Whitehaven; devoted himself to literature; d. in London.

Boardman, James. *A Citizen of the World.* An English writer.

Boase, Rev. George Clement, 1810–80. *G. C. B.; A Brother; Britannicus.* An English bibliographer; cashier of the bank, Dundee; after his retirement from business he became the pastor of the Catholic Apostolic church at Brighton; d. at Fairlie House, Bridge of Allan.

Boase, Henry, 1763–1827. *A Freeholder; Britannicus; One of his Constituents.* An English financier; father of the preceding; b. at Madron; d. at Penzance, Cornwall.

Boase, John Josias Arthur, 1801–. *Johannes Buritonensis.* An English antiquary; son of the preceding; b. in London; Librarian of the Geological Society of Cornwall.

Boase, William Millett, M.D., 1802–. *Delta; Gregory Hopeful; A Wayfaring Man.* An English physician and antiquary, of Cornwall; b. at Penzance; Univ. of Edinburgh, 1823.

Boaz, Mrs. Eliza. *His Widow.* An English lady; widow of the Rev. Thomas Boaz, LL.D., of Calcutta.

Boaz, H. *H. B.* An English poet.

Bobo, William M. *A South Carolinian.*

Bock, Cornelius Peter, 1804–70. *Christodor.* A German archæologist; Hon. Prof. at Freiburg, about 11 years before his death.

Bockett, Elias, 1695–1735. *E. B.; Alexander Blunt; Damon; A Friend; A Gentleman; John Scavenger, M.D.; The Translator of the Pattern of Modesty.* An English Friend; a distiller of Georgeyard, Lombard Street, London; b. and d. in that city.

Bocock, Willis H. *Cigarette; Erceldoune.* An American poet, of the Univ. of Virginia; contributed to Richmond journals.

Bogardus, Adam H. *The Champion Wing Shot of America.* An American sharpshooter; Captain to the American Rifle Team.

Bogart, Miss Elizabeth. *Adelaide; Estelle.* An American poetess; daughter of the Rev. David Schuyler Bogart; b. in New York City, where she has chiefly resided.

Bogart, William H. *Sentinel.* An American journalist, of New York City.

Boid, Captain G. *An Amateur; A Naval Officer.* An English writer.

Boissière, Jean Baptiste Prudence, 1806–. *R. P.; Sièrebois.* A French grammarian; b. at Valogne (Manche); was engaged in teaching in France and England till 1856, but since that time in philological and lexicographal works.

Boissieu, Arthur de. *Jean Lavigne.* A French journalist; contributed to "Figaro" and the "Gazette de France."

Boitel, Leonard, 1806–55. *Léon.* A

French *littérateur* and journalist, of Lyons.

Bolde, Rev. Samuel, 1674–1737. *A Clergyman in the Country.* An English clergyman; Vicar of Shapwicke, Dorsetshire, 1674; Rector of Steeple, in the same county, 1682.

Boles, W. *Alexander the Coppersmith.* An Irish writer.

Bolingbroke, Henry St. John, Viscount, 1678–1751. *Humphrey Oldcastle; A Late Noble Writer; Lord B——; Lord B–ke.* An eminent English statesman; b. at Battersea, in Surrey; was distinguished for his talents, brilliancy of conversation, fascinating manners, and great personal beauty; was a rival of Sir Robert Walpole through life; d. at Battersea.

Bollan, William. *Timoleon.* An English political writer; agent of the Massachusetts colony in Great Britain, 1745–62.

Bolland, Sir William, Knt., M.A., 1773–1840. *Hortensius.* An English literary antiquary; Trin. Coll., Cambridge, 1795; d. at his residence, Hyde Park Terrace, London.

Bolles, John Augustus, LL.D., 1809–78. *A Member of the Boston Bar.* An American lawyer; b. at Eastford, Conn.; Brown Univ., 1829; admitted to the Boston Bar, 1833; Mass. Secretary of State, 1843; Judge Advocate on the staff of Gen. John A. Dix, 1862–65; Brev. Brig.-Gen., 1865; d. at Washington, D.C.

Bolton, John. *One of the Crew.* An American seaman; carpenter on board the ship *Omartel,* which was lost on the voyage from London to New York City in 1860.

Bolton, Miss R. *One of her Sisters.* An English lady; granddaughter of Rev. William Jay.

Bolton, Rev. Robert, A.M., 1814–77. *R. B.* An English American clergyman, brother of the preceding; b. at Bath, Somerset Co., England; came to this country in 1836; after being engaged in farming and teaching for some years, in 1868 he was ordained to the Episcopal ministry, and took charge of St. John's Church, Lewisboro, N.Y.; d. in Pelham, N.Y.

Bonaparte, Prince Louis Lucien, 1813–. *L. L. B.* An English philologist; b. at Thorngrove, county of Worcester; in 1852 he was appointed Senator under the French Empire; is deeply interested in philological researches and work.

Bonar, Rev. Andrew. *A Resident.* A Scottish clergyman.

Bonavino, Christoforo, 1821–. *Ansonio Franchi.* An Italian philosopher; b. at Pegli, near Genoa. He was a priest in his youth, but renounced that profession. About 1854, he founded at Turin a journal called "La Ragione."

Boniface, Joseph Xavier, 1797–1865. *X. B. Saintine.* A French littérateur and dramatic author, of Paris; b. in Paris; about 1823 he devoted himself to dramatic composition, and produced more than 200 dramas. His "Picciola" (1836), a work of different kind, was peculiarly successful, it having been reprinted more than twenty times, and translated into all languages. This work, in 1837, procured for him the cross of honor and the Montyon prize of 3000 francs. D. in Paris.

Bonnet, Amédée, about 1795–1858. *Bonnet de Lyon.* A French physician; b. at Ambérieux (Ain); from about 1840 a professor at the Medical School of Lyons, where he was also an editor.

Bonnet, I. E. *Un Citoyen des États-Unis.* A French writer.

Bonnye, J. H. *Michel Carlin.* An English physician, of Preston.

Boodle, E. *A Barrister of Lincoln's Inn.* An English writer.

Boosey, Thomas. *An Old Angler and Bibliopolist.* An English publisher and miscellaneous writer, of London.

Booth, Mrs. Eliza M. J. (Gollan) von. *Rita.* A Scottish writer; b. at Gollanfield, Inverness; spent the greater part of her early life in Australia; is a contributor to "Temple Bar" and other London magazines.

Booth, M. *Touchstone.* An English writer on geography.

Booth, M. I. *M. I. B.* An English artist.

Booth, Miss Mary.—See "Wright, Mrs. Mary (Booth)."

Boott, William. *A Bostonian.* An American musical critic.

Borel d'Hauterive, Pierre, 1809–59. *Petrus,* or *Peter Borel.* A French writer of romance; b. at Lyons; early went to Paris; first worked as an architect, then wrote for the literary journals; for a long time, however, he abandoned literature, and was inspector of colonization at Mostaganem, in Algeria, and d. there.

Borlase, William Copeland, M.A., F.S.A., 1848–. *B.* An English antiquary; b. at Castle Horneck; Trin. Coll., Oxford, 1870; Pres. of the Roy. Instit. of Cornwall, 1877.

Borrow, George, 1803–81. *Lavengro.* An English traveller and miscellaneous writer; b. at East Dereham, near Norwich, Norfolk; Univ. of Edinburgh.

Borthwick, John. *A Scottish Barrister.*

Bosanquet, James Whatman, 1803–78. *A Layman.* An English chronologist; son of Samuel Bosanquet, Esq., of Dingeston Court, County Monmouth; educ. at Westminster; and is a banker in London; resident at Claysmore, Middlesex.

Boston, ——. *A Friend of the Secession.* A Scottish writer, of Falkirk.

Boswell, Sir Alexander, Bart., 1775–1822. *Simon Gray.* A Scottish antiquary and song writer, of Edinburgh; a friend of Sir Walter Scott. He spent much time writing for the journals of the day; and having in one of these communications imputed cowardice to Mr. James Stuart, a leading Whig of Edinburgh, he was challenged by him to a duel, in which he was mortally wounded.

Boswell, James, 1740–95. *Bozzy.* A famous Scottish biographer; father of the preceding; b. at Edinburgh; educ. at Edinburgh and Glasgow; in 1773, settled in London, and d. there.

Boswell, John Whitley. *Doctor Hastler, M.R.S.P.Q.* An Irish antiquary.

Boswell, Thomas Alexander. *An Exile; A Pedestrian.* An English writer.

Bosworth, John. *John, of Manchester.* An English editor.

Bosworth, Rev. Joseph, D.D., LL.D., F.R.S., F.A.S., 1788–1876. *A Vicar of the Church of England.* An eminent English Anglo-Saxon scholar; b. in Devonshire; educ. at Aberdeen, Cambridge, and Leyden; Professor of Anglo-Saxon at Oxford, 1858–76, where he died.

Botsford, Charles H. *Cornwall.* An American journalist, of New York City.

Bott, Edmund. *A Barrister at Law of the Inner Temple.* An English lawyer.

Bott, Rev. Thomas, 1688–1754. *Philanthropus.* An English clergyman of the Established Church.

Botta, Mrs. Anne Charlotte (Lynch). *A Recluse.* An American poetess; b. at Bennington, Vt.; removed to New York City about 1841, where her house became the resort of persons connected with art and literature; in 1855, married Prof. V. Botta.

Bottrell, William, 1816–81. *An Old Celt.* An English literary antiquary; b. at Raftra, Cornwall; after travelling in Spain, Canada, and Australia, he finally came back to his native country to lead the life of a recluse at Hawke's Point, Lelant. D. at St. Ives.

Botts, Randolph. *Spikes.* An American writer, of Albany.

Boucher de, Crèvecœur de Perthes, Jacques, 1788–1868. *M. Christophe, vigneron.* A French archæologist and miscellaneous writer; b. at Rethel (Ardennes); was employed by Napoleon in various foreign missions; is regarded as the father of the science of "archæology"; d. at Abbeville.

Boudreaux, F. J. *A Father of the Society of Jesus.* An American Jesuit.

Boué de Villiers, Amable Louis, 1834–. *Le Capitaine Lancelot; Le Docteur Rouge; Raymond de Ferrières; Guy de Vernon; Mirliter; Jacques Artevelle.* A French journalist and romancer; b. at Villiers-le-Bel (Seine-et-Oise); edited and wrote for journals in Paris and the provinces, under various pseudonyms, and published several novels.

Boulay-Paty, Évariste Cyprien Félix, 1804–64. *Elie Mariaker.* A French poet; b. at Donges (Ille-et-Vilaine). Having studied law, his literary tastes led him to Paris, where he was appointed librarian of the Palais-Royal, as successor of Alexander Dumas. He acquired many honors by his literary efforts. D. at Paris.

Bouligny, Mrs. M. E. Parker. *A Lady.* An American writer.

Boulton, Mrs. Anne. *Christine Severne.* An English writer.

Bourdillon, Rev. **Francis,** M.A. *F. B.* An English Epis. divine; Emmanuel Coll., Cambridge, 1845; Vicar of Old Warden, Biggleswade, 1880–83 *et seq.*

Bourn, Rev. **Samuel.** *Belzebub.* An English minister, of Norwich; an assistant to John Taylor. He was the founder of a sect of Universalists, called after him, Bourneans.

Bourne, Miss ——. *A Resident in the West Indies for 13 years.* An English writer.

Bourne, Rev. **George.** *A Citizen of Virginia; A Virginian Presbyter.* An American clergyman and writer.

Bourne, Henry Richard Fox. *H. R. F. B.* An English biographer.

Bourne, John George Hamilton, 1804–46. *J. G. H. B.* An eminent English jurist; Chief Justice of Newfoundland, 1838–46.

This is according to the "Gent. Mag.," March, 1846; the list of Oxford graduates has it *John Gervase Hutchinson.*

Bourne, Stephen. *A Late Stipendiary Magistrate in Jamaica.*

Bousell, John. *Aminidab Shoe.* An English Friend; for more than 20 years a leather-cutter of Norwich; was a person of strange opinions.

Bowden, James. *A Member of the Society of Friends.* An English Friend, of London; many years Recording Clerk.

Bowden, John, D.D., 1751–1817. *A Churchman.* An eminent American P. E. clergyman; b. in Ireland; graduated at Columbia Coll. (then King's) in 1772; professor in Columbia Coll., New York City, 1802–17; d. at Ballston Spa.

Bowden, John William, M.A., 1798–1844. *A* (alpha). An English poet and prose writer; b. in London; Trin. Coll., Oxford, 1820; Commissioner of Stamps, 1826–40.

Bowditch, Nathaniel Ingersoll, A.M., 1805–61. *Gleaner.* An eminent American conveyancer, of Boston; b. in Salem, Mass.; Harv. Univ., 1822; admitted to the Suffolk bar, 1825; in 1858, retired from business, and took up his residence in Brookline, Mass., where he died.

Bowdler, Miss **Henrietta,** 1743–84. *A Lady lately deceased.* An English poet and prose writer; daughter of Thomas Bowdler, Esq., of Ashley, Co. Somerset; d. at Bath.

Bowdler, Thomas, Esq., F.R.S., F.S.A., 1754–1825. *T. B.; A Friend to Both.* An English *littérateur*; editor of the "Family Shakespeare"; d. at his residence, the Rhyddings, Swansea.

Bowdoin, James, LL.D., 1727–90. *A Citizen of Massachusetts.* An eminent American statesman; b. in Boston; Harv. Univ., 1745; devoted his life to literary and scientific research; was Governor of Massachusetts in 1785–86; d. in Boston.

Bowen, C. E. *C. E. B.* An English writer for the young.

Bowen, Rev. **C. J.** *C. J. B.* An English Catholic priest.

Bowen, Francis, LL.D., 1811–. *F. B.* An American metaphysician; b. in Charlestown, Mass.; Harv. Univ., 1833; professor there, 1853–85 *et seq.*

Bowen, Sir George Ferguson, D.C.L., G.C.M.G., 1821–. *G. F. B.* An eminent Irish statesman; Brasenose Coll., Oxford, 1844; admitted to the bar at Lincoln's Inn, 1844; Governor of Victoria from 1873.

Bowen-Graves, Mrs. ——. *Stella.* An English poet.

Bowes, James Stuart, Esq., 1789–1864. *Alfred Dubois.* An English journalist; for 40 years editor of "Galignani's Messenger." D. in Paris.

Bowes, Rev. **Nicholas**, M.A., –1755. *Constant Rock-man.* An American Cong. minister; Harv. Univ., 1725; pastor at Bedford, Mass.

Bowles, Thomas Gibson. *John, Junior.* An English (?) journalist; editor of "Vanity Fair."

Bowles, Rev. **William Lisle**, M.A., 1762–1850. *The Late Dr. Archibald Macleod.* An English clergyman and man of letters; b. at King's Sutton; Canon Residentiary of Salisbury, and Rector of Dumbleton, Gloucestershire. D. at his residence in the Close, Salisbury.

Bowring, Sir **John**, LL.D., 1792–1872. *Tydus-Pooh-Pooh; W.; X.* An English translator; b. at Exeter; served his Government ten years in China, as Plenipotentiary and Chief Superintendent of Trade; he, himself, estimated the number of languages which he knew, at *two hundred,* of which he spoke *one hundred;* d. at Mount Radford, near Exeter.

Bowser, Miss **Lucinda.** *Lucinda B.* An English writer.

Boyce, G. W. *A Cape Correspondent.* An English poet.

Boyce, Rev. **John.** *Paul Peppergrass.* An American R. C. priest and novelist; b. in Ireland; educ. at Maynooth; pastor and assistant pastor at Worcester, Mass., from 1847.

Boyce, Rev. **John Coxe**, M.A. *J. C. B.* An English Epis. divine; Chaplain of the West Riding Lunatic Asylum, 1869–80 *et seq.*

Boyce, Rev. **William Birmington.** *W. B. B.* An English writer; a Wesleyan missionary.

Boyd, Rev. **Andrew Kennedy Hutchison**, D.D., 1825–. *A Country Parson.* An eminent Scottish essayist; b. in Auchinleck, in Ayrshire; educ. at King's Coll., London, and at the Univ. of Glasgow; minister at the Univ., City of St. Andrews, 1875 *et seq.*

Boyd, S. S. *Jurisconsult.* An American lawyer.

Boyer, Louis, 1810–1866. *La Roque.* A French dramatic author; b. in Paris; in 1848, with two others, he founded "Le Lampion, ou Eclaireur politique"; in 1851–54, was first inspector, then censor, of the theatres, and was manager of the "Vaudeville" Theatre, 1854–56; d. in Paris.

Boykin, Edward M. *An Officer of the Rear-Guard.* An American officer.

Boyle, Hon. **Eleanor Vere** (**Gordon**), 1825. *E. V. B.* A Scottish artist; b. at Auchlunies, Kincardineshire;

chiefly self-educated; in 1845 was married to the Hon. and Rev. Richard Boyle; and since 1851 has been much devoted to artistic pursuits.

Boyle, John, Earl of Cork and Orrery, 1706–62. *G. K.; Goliah English; Reginald Fitzworm; Michael Krawbridge; Moses Orthodox; Thomas Vainall.* An eminent British peer and author.

Boyne, William, F.S.A. *B. W.* An English numismatist; Hon. member of the Literary and Philosophical Society of Leeds.

Boynton, Charles Brandon, D.D., 1806–83. *A Looker-on from America.* An American minister, who served as pastor of the Vine Street Cong. Church in Cincinnati twenty-five years; he also preached in Eastern churches, and served two terms as Chaplain of the House of Representatives in Washington, beginning in 1865; he was a native of Pittsfield, Mass., and graduated at Williams Coll. in 1827; d. in Cincinnati.

Boynton, Harry Free. *Harry B. Free.* An American journalist, of New York City.

Boyrie, Arthur. *Aristophanes.* An American dramatist.

Boyse, Samuel, 1708–49. *Alcæus; Y.* An English poet, idle and improvident, befriended by Dr. Johnson, and employed by Mr. Cave of the "Gent. Mag."

Brackenridge, Henry Hugh, 1748–1816. *Democritus; A Gentleman of Maryland.* An American jurist; b. in Scotland; was brought to this country when a child; graduated at New Jersey Coll., 1771; removed to Pittsburg in 1781; judge of the Supreme Court of Pennsylvania, 1799–1816; wrote one humorous and satirical novel, and many essays and fugitive verses; d. at Carlisle, Penn.

Brackenridge, Henry M., Esq., 1786–1871. *A Friend of Truth and Sound Policy.* An American statesman; b. at Pittsburgh, Penn.; admitted to the bar, 1806; M.C., 1841; d. in his native city.

Bradbury, Edward. *Strephon.* An English writer (?).

Bradbury, Irene. *Irene Lunt.*

Bradbury, Stephen Henry. *Quallon.* At English editor, of Nottingham.

Bradbury, Rev. **Thomas**, 1677–1759. *T. B.* An English Dissenting minister, of London, celebrated for his facetiousness.

Braddon, Henry. *Gilbert Forrester; A Member of the Burton Hunt.* An English sporting writer in the old London "Sporting Magazine."

Braddon, Miss **Mary Elizabeth.** — See "Maxwell, Mrs. M. E. (B)."

Bradford, Alden, LL.D., 1765–1843. *A Citizen of Boston.* An American author; b. in Duxbury, Mass.; Harv. Univ., 1786; tutor there, 1791–93; minister of Pownalborough (now Wiscasset), Me., 1793–1801, then removed to Boston; Secretary of State of Massachusetts, 1812–24; engaged in literary work, 1824–43; d. in Boston.

Bradford, Rev. **Claudius.** *The Whip.* An American Unit. minister and social reformer.

Bradford, Capt. **Gamaliel,** A.M., 1763–1824. *An Officer of this Establishment at Charlestown.* An American seaman; b. in Duxbury, Mass.; served in the Revolutionary War, 1776–83; followed the sea, 1783–1808; was warden of the Charlestown (Mass.) State Prison, 1813–24.

Bradford, Gamaliel, M.D., 1795–1839. *A Gentleman of Massachusetts.* An American physician; b. in Boston; Harv. Univ., 1814; Superintendent of the Massachusetts General Hospital, 1833–39.

Bradford, Samuel F. *Timothy Tickletoby.* An American printer, bookseller, and stationer, of Philadelphia, son of Thomas Bradford.

Bradlaugh, Charles, 1833–. *Iconoclast.* An English Radical; b. in London; was successively an errand-boy in a solicitor's office, a wharf-clerk and cashier to a firm of coal merchants, and a Sunday-school teacher in a Church of England school; about 1849 he adopted radical views, and became a public lecturer and pamphleteer; in 1858 he became editor of the "Investigator," and afterwards projected the "National Reformer," of which he became the editor; chosen M.P. for Northampton in 1880, and again, in 1881, but has not been permitted to take his seat; resident in St. John's Wood, London.

Bradley, Rev. **Edward,** B.A., 1827–. *Cuthbert Bede.* An English Epis. divine, and miscellaneous writer; b. at Kidderminster; Univ. Coll., Durham, 1848; Rector of Stretton, Oakham, 1871–83 *et seq.*

Bradley, Miss **Harriette Mary.** *Marietta.* An English writer.

Bradley, T. Waldron. *Shelsley Beauchamp.* An English writer.

Bradley, Mrs. **Thomas.** *Hannah Cook.*

Bradley, Warren Ives, 1847–68. *Glance Gaylord.* A gifted young American author. Within a space of three or four years he gave to the public 13 books, besides numerous articles for papers and magazines. His "Culm Rock" took a prize of $350, over 72 competitors. D. at Bristol, Conn.

Bradley, William. *A Retired Guardian.* An English writer.

Bradshaw, Hon. **Mary Ann Cavendish.** *Priscilla Parlante.* An Irish biographer and novelist; wife of the Hon. Augustus Cavendish Bradshaw, M.P. for Castle-Riding. She was the daughter of James St. John Jeffereyes, Esq., of Blarney Castle, County Cork; was married in 1784 to the Earl of Westneath, from whom she was divorced in 1790, when she married Mr. Cavendish Bradshaw.

Brady, James Topham, 1815–69. *Query.* An American lawyer; b. in New York City; admitted to the bar in 1835, and became distinguished for ability, legal learning, and eloquence; d. in New York City.

Brae, Andrew Edmund. *A Detective.* An English writer, of Leeds.

Bragg, H. A. *Braganza.* An American novelist.

Bragg, Jane. *J. B.* An English poet and prose writer.

Bragge, Francis. *A Physician in Hertfordshire; A Gentleman of Cambridge.* An English clergyman and poet; Vicar of Hitchin, and Prebendary of Lincoln.

Braham, John, 1774–1856. *B.* An English singer; b. in London; for 40 years, from 1801, his powers continued unimpaired, and he occasionally appeared in public till his death. D. in London.

Braley, A. B. *A. B. B.* An American Shakespeare scholar, of Madison, Wis.

Bramley, H. E. *H. E. Yelmarb.* An English writer.

Branch, Thomas. *T. B.* An English law-writer, of the last century.

Brande, William Thomas, 1788–1866. *D. C. L.; A Relative.* An eminent English chemist; b. in London; Professor of Chemistry in the Royal Institution, 1813–25; Superintendent of the Die Department, Royal Mint, 1825–66; d. at Tunbridge Wells.

Braman, William Penn, 1825–66. *Vandyke Brown.* An American poet-painter, of Chicago; b. in Cincinnati; self-instructed as a scholar and as an artist; d. in his native city.

Brannigan, Larry, 1836–. *Lawrence Barrett.* An American actor; b. in New York City; served in the late civil war as captain in the 28th Massachusetts Regiment; in 1866–67 visited England, and in 1867–63, California.

Brash, Richard. *Richardus Incognitus.* An English writer.

Braussi, Mathieu. *Philippe, frère.* A French theologian, Superior-general of the Christian "Frères des Écoles."

Braxton, Carter, 1736–97. *A Native of that Colony.* An American patriot; b. at Newington, Va.; one of the signers of the American Declaration of Independence.

Bray, Mrs. Anna Eliza, 1790–1883. *Kempe Stothard.* An English novelist; b. in the county of Surrey; married in 1818 to Charles Stothard, and after his death, in 1821, to the Rev. Edward A. Bray, vicar of Tavistock, who died in 1859.

Bray, Rev. Thomas, D.D., 1656–1730. *A Minister of the Church of England.* An English clergyman; b. at Martin, Shropshire; educ. at Hart Hall, Oxford; in 1699 he was sent to America as Ecclesiastical Commissary for Maryland and Virginia; was minister of St. Botolph, Aldgate, London, 1706–30.

Brazer, John, D.D., 1787–1846. *J. B.* An American minister; b. in Worcester, Mass.; Harv. Univ., 1813; pastor in Salem, Mass., 1820–46; d. in Charleston, S.C.

Brecknock, Timothy. *A Member of the Society of Lincoln's Inn.* An English lawyer, of the last century.

Breckinridge, Robert Jefferson, D.D., 1800–71. *R. J. B.* An American Presbyt. minister; b. at Cabell's Dale, Ky.; studied at Princeton, Yale, and Union Colls.; practised law in Kentucky, 1823–31; having studied theology, he was pastor in Lexington from 1847, and President of Theology at Danville, 1853; in the civil war he was a firm Union man, and in 1864 presided over the National Convention that nominated Mr. Lincoln for the Presidency; d. at Danville, Ky.

Breed, ——. *A Merchant.* An English writer, of Liverpool.

Brennan, Mrs. R. A. *Hope Arden.* An American poet.

Brent, Henry J., 1811–80. *Stirrup.* An American journalist; b. in Washington, D.C.; the associate of Lewis Gaylord Clark in founding and editing the "Knickerbocker" Magazine; d. in New York City.

Brentano, Clemens, 1777–1842. *Maria.* A German novelist and poet, brother of Elisabeth von Arnim; b. at Frankfort-on-the-Main; studied at Jena, and afterwards lived in Heidelberg, Vienna, and Berlin, and still later at Dülmen, and still later at Ratisbon, Frankfort, and Munich; d. at Aschaffenburg.

Brentano, Elisabeth. *Bettina.* — See "Arnim, Elisabeth (Brentano) von."

Brereton, Jane Hughes. *Melissa.*

Bretland, Rev. Joseph, 1742–1819. *Adjutor; Garon; A Lover of Order.* An English Dissenter; b. in Exeter, and spent there the whole of a long-protracted life, in literary retirement, and d. there: he was a Unit. minister.

Breton, William. *W. B., Gent.* An English writer.

Brett, Robert. *R. B.* A Laymember of the English Church.

Brett, Rev. Thomas, 1667–1743. *T. B.* An English clergyman; Rector of Bettishanger, 1703, and of Ruckinge, 1705.

Breval, John Durant de, –1738–39. *Joseph Gay.* An English officer, a captain under the Duke of Marlborough; he was the son of Francis Durant de Breval, D.D., Prebendary of Westminster; graduated at Trin. Coll., Cambridge, in 1700; in 1708 entered the army; he was the author of several poems and dramas.

Brewer, George, 1766. *G. B.* An English naval officer; then lawyer and miscellaneous writer, of London.

Brewer, Rev. Jehoida, 1752–1817. *Sylvestris.* An English Cong. minister; b. at Newport, Monmouthshire; of Birmingham, 1798–1817, and d. there.

Brewer, William A. *W. A. B.; Amicus; Apex; Guildhelm; Justitia; Mercator; Senex; Wilhelm.* An American writer; was for many years a merchant of Boston, now (1885) of New York City.

Brewster, Sir David, LL.D., etc., 1781–1868. *A Calm Observer.* A Scottish physicist, of Edinburgh; b. at Jedburgh; M.A., Univ. of Edinburgh, 1800; editor of the "Edinburgh Encyclopædia"; editor and co-editor of the "Edinburgh Philosophical Journal," 1819–, etc., etc.; Principal of the Univ. of Edinburgh, 1838–68.

Brewster, Rev. John, M.A., 1754–1843. *A Recluse.* An English clergyman; b. at Heighington, Co. Durham; M.A. at Lincoln Coll., Oxford, 1778; Rector of Egglescliffe, Co. Durham, 1814–43, and a magistrate for the county; d. at his rectory.

Brewster, Rev. Samuel. *S. B.* An

English clergyman, early in the 18th century.

Brickwood, Edwin D. *Argonaut.* An English writer on rowing, training, etc., of London; a contributor to the London "Field."

Bridge, Horatio, 1806–. *An Officer of the United States Navy.* An American lawyer; b. in Augusta, Me.; Bowdoin Coll., 1825; studied and practised law, 1825–38; entered the navy as paymaster, 1838–54; Chief of the Bureau of Provisions and Clothing at Washington, 1854–69, and Inspector of the same, 1869–73.

Bridge, J. *A Fellow Townsman.* An English writer, of Manchester.

Bridges, Mrs. F. D. *A Lady.* An English traveller of to-day.

Bridges, George. *Segdirboeg.* An English writer.

Bridges, Thomas. *Caustic Barebones.* An English humorist; b. in Yorkshire; at one time a wine-merchant in Hull; was also member of a banking house.

Bridgman, George, –1832. *Poet Laureat of Westminster.* An Englishman who, during the latter part of the reign of George III., was court newsman. For several years before his death he was designated as above; d. at the Cat and Bagpipe public house, London.

Bridle, Rev. **John.** *O. W.* An English clergyman, of Hardwick.

Brierley, Benjamin. *A.; Ab; Ab hissel; AB-o'-the-Yate.* An English dialect writer, of Manchester (?).

Briggs, Charles Frederick, about 1810–77. *C. F. B.; Harry Franco; Tom Pepper.* An American journalist; b. at Nantucket, Mass.; early removed to New York City, and engaged in literary work as editor of some of the most important of the New York journals.

Briggs, Emily Edson. *Olivia.*

Bright, Charles. *Thomas Jones.* An English writer, of Australia, on Shakespeare.

Bright, Henry Arthur, 1830–84. *A Cambridge Man; A Liverpool Merchant.* An English economist; b. at Liverpool; educ. at Rugby, and at the Univs. of Cambridge and London; became a merchant; devoted much time to literary pursuits. "There are many personal touches in these books ['Year in a Lancashire Garden' and the 'English Flower Garden'], as, for instance, his acquaintance with Hawthorne, who, on his part, has left some notices of his Lancashire

friend." In 1877 *et seq.* resident at Ashford, Knotty Ash, Liverpool.

Bright, Jonathan Huntington, 1804–37. *Viator.* An American poet and journalist; b. in Salem, Mass.; resided in New York City, Albany, and Richmond, Va.; in 1836 he sailed for New Orleans, and soon after his arrival was induced to ascend the Mississippi to take part in a mercantile interest at Manchester, where he suddenly died.

Bright, Rev. **William,** D.D., 1824–. *W. B.* An English Epis. divine; b. at Doncaster; Univ. Coll., Oxford, 1846; Canon of Christ Church and Regius Professor of Eccles. History at Oxford, 1868–83 *et seq.*

Brightwell, Thomas. *T. B.* An English writer.

Briscoe, John Ivatt, 1791–. *One of his Constituents and a Magistrate of the County.* An English civilian; b. at Twickenham; B.A., Oxford, 1812; M.P., 1830–41, and from 1857.

Bristed, Charles Astor, 1820–74. *Carl Benson; A Broken-down Critic; A New Yorker.* An American author; b. in New York City; Univ. of Cambridge, England, 1845; afterwards spent many years in Europe; wrote much for the newspapers and magazines, and published several books; d. at Washington, D.C.

Britton, John, F.S.A., 1771–1857. *Hilaris Benevolus & Co.* An English antiquary, of London; a writer on topography and architecture; b. at the village of Kingston in Wiltshire; in 1787 went to London, where he was apprenticed to a wine-merchant, meanwhile cultivating his taste for reading; after various adventures and struggles with life, he engaged in the pursuits which occupied the last 50 years of his life. "He was the originator of a new class of literary works. Before his time popular topography was unknown."

Britton, Thomas, about 1650–1714. *Musical Smallcoal Man.* An English eccentric; b. near Higham Ferrers, Northants; set up the trade of smallcoal in London, which he continued to the end of his life. In the "Guardian," No. 144, Steele says: "We have a smallcoal man who, beginning with two plain notes, which made up his daily cry, has made himself master of the whole compass of the gamut, and has frequent concerts of music at his own house for the entertainment of himself and friends."— See CHALMERS, Vol. 7.

Broadhead, James. *A Citizen of the World.* An English writer.

Brock, Miss Sallie A. — See "Putnam, Mrs. Sallie A. (Brock)."

Brockett, John Trotter, 1788–1842. *J. T. B.* An English antiquary; b. at Witton Gilbert, Co. Durham; admitted to the bar, and practised many years at Newcastle, but gave his leisure time to literary and scientific pursuits. He was one of the founders of the Newcastle Typographical Society; d. at his residence in Albion Place, Newcastle-upon-Tyne.

Brockett, Linus Pierpont, M.D., 1820–. *An American Citizen; Philobiblius.* An American writer; b. at Canton, Conn.; Yale Med. Coll., 1843; after practising his profession for some years, he devoted himself to literary pursuits at Hartford, Conn.; was partner in a publishing house in that city, 1847–57; in 1856 resumed his literary work, and had charge of several departments in the "American Annual Encyclopædia," 1862–77 *et seq.*

Brockway, Rev. Thomas, 1744–1807. *The European Traveller.* An American Cong. minister; b. in Lyme, Conn.; Yale Coll., 1768; pastor at Lebanon, Conn., 1772–1807. He was an ardent friend of his country, and when New London was burnt, as soon as the news reached him, he started off with his long gun, and deacons, and parishioners, to assist in doing battle with the enemy. D. at Lyme.

Broderick, A. B. An English poet.

Broderip, William John, Esq., F.L.S., 1787–1859. *A Naturalist.* An English lawyer; b. in Bristol; graduated at Oriel Coll., Oxford; called to the bar in 1817; was a police magistrate in London for 34 years; devoted his leisure time to the study of natural history, and became distinguished as a zoölogist; d. in London.

Brodrib, John Henry, 1838–. *Henry Irving.* An English actor; b. at Keinton, near Glastonbury, Somersetshire; educ. in London; became professionally connected with the stage in 1856, and has since been eminently successful in his dramatic career.

Broekel, Johanne Antonie, 1819–. *A. Broek.* A Danish teacher and writer; b. at Tondern, in Schleswig; founded in 1844, at Keil, a boarding-school for young women, which she continued till 1875. ·

Bromet, William, M.D., F.S.A.,

–1850. *A Lounger; Plantagenet.* An English surgeon and antiquary; Asst. Surgeon, 1st Regt. Life Guards, 1814–35; and Surgeon, 1835–47; d. at Bologna.

Bromfield, William, 1712–92. *W. B.* An English writer; an eminent surgeon; b. in London; lectured with great success in that city; became surgeon to George III.; invented the "tenaculum," by which the operator could separate, extend, and tie a divided artery.

Bromley, M. I. *M. I. B.* An English poet.

Bromley, William. *A Gentleman.* An English statesman; Speaker of the House of Commons in 1710.

Brontë, Anne, 1820–49. *Acton Bell.* An English poet and novelist; b. at Thornton, near Bradford. Her poems are of a deeply religious character, and most beautiful in sentiment.

Brontë, Charlotte. *Currer Bell.* — See "Nicholls, Mrs. C. (B.)."

Brontë, Emily Jane, 1818–48. *Ellis Bell.* An English novelist; b. at Thornton, near Bradford, Yorkshire. At Haworth she divided her time between homely domestic duties, studies, and rambles.

Brook, Mary, about 1726–82. *M. B.* An English Friend; b. at Woodstock, in Oxfordshire; joined the Friends about 1753, and was married to Joseph Brook, of Leighton Buzzard, in 1759. She was a minister of the Friends about 27 years.

Brooke, E. *E. B.* An English bibliographer.

Brooke, Mrs. Frances (Moore), 1745–89. *Mary Singleton; Spinster; Translator of Lady Catesby's Letters.* An English novelist and dramatist; daughter of Rev. Mr. Moore and wife of the Rev. John Brooke, Rector of Colney in Norfolk.

Brooke, Henry, 1706–83. *Farmer; Oxoniensis.* An Irish poet; b. at Rantavan, County Cavan; educ. at the Univ. of Dublin; spent some years in London; the friend of Swift, Pope, and Lord Lyttelton; in 1740 he retired to his native town, and was for the rest of his life chiefly engaged in literary work; d. in Dublin.

Brooke, John Charles, 1748–94. *J. B.* A professed English antiquary; published the "Somerset Herald," and wrote for the "Gent. Mag." under the signature "J. B."

Brooke, Richard (?). *R. B.* An English writer.

Brooke, Major William (?). *A Gen-*

tleman of the Committee. An English philanthropist, of Bath.

Brookes, S. *A Student.* An English writer.

Brooks, Abbie M. *Silvia Sunshine.* An American writer, of the South.

Brooks, Charles Shirley, 1815–74. *Epicurus Rotundus.* An English journalist, lecturer, dramatist, and novelist; b. in Oxfordshire; studied law, but preferred a literary life, which he passed chiefly in London, where he died; editor of "Punch," 1870–74.

Brooks, Rev. Charles Timothy, 1813–83. *C. T. B.; Carrier Boy; Carrier Mercury.* An American poet and clergyman; b. in Salem, Mass.; Harv. Univ., 1832; for many years, from 1837, minister of the Unit. Society at Newport, R.I., where he died.

Brooks, James Gordon, 1801–41. *Florio.* An American poet; b. at Claverack, N.Y.; Union Coll., 1819; studied law; removed in 1823 to New York City, and was successively the editor of the "Minerva," the "Literary Gazette," the "Athenæum," and the "Morning Courier"; in 1830 he removed to Winchester, Va., in 1838 to Rochester, N.Y., and afterwards to Albany, where he died.

Brooks, Rev. Joshua William. *Abdiel.* An English Epis. divine; Rector of Great Ponton, Grantham, 1864–80 *et seq.*

Brooks, Mrs. Maria (Gowen), 1795–1845. *A Lover of the Fine Arts; Maria del Occidente.* An American poet; b. at Medford, Mass.; married Mr. Brooks, a Boston merchant; at the death of her husband in 1823, she removed to Cuba; in 1830, visited London and Paris; d. at Matanzas, Cuba.

Brooks, Martha. *Martha Caroll.* An American writer for the young.

Brooks, Mrs. Mary Elizabeth (Akin). *Norna.* An American writer and skilful designer; b. in New York City; married James Gordon Brooks in 1828; resided in New York City in 1854, where she made drawings to illustrate books.

Brooks, Seth. *An Alient Baptist Dissenter.*

Brooks, Vincent. *V. B.* An English lithographer.

Broom, W. W. *Eboracus.* An English reformer and politician; in 1859 he wrote for the "Morning News," of Liverpool; in 1865 he visited New York City, and wrote for New York and Boston papers, and gave addresses on "Reconstruction" at Newark, N.J., and New York City.

Broome, Frederick Napier, 1842–. *F. N. B.* An English poet, civilian, and journalist; b. in Canada; emigrated to New Zealand in 1857; Colonial Secretary of Natal, 1875 *et seq.*

Broome, Captain Ralph. *Simpkin the Second, Poetic Recorder.* An English miscellaneous writer; was once a captain in the service of the E. I. Co., and Persian translator to the army on the frontier station; wrote in defence of Warren Hastings.

Broome, William, LL.D., about 1689–1745. *Chester.* An English poet; b. at Cheshire; rector of Pulham in Norfolk *w.* Oakley Magna in Suffolk from 1733, and Vicar of Eye, in Suffolk; d. at Bath.

Brosböll, Karl, 1820–. *Carit Etlar.* A Danish poet; b. at Fredericia; when he was 16 years old he went to Copenhagen, and after passing through all the schools of the Art Academy, he devoted himself to literature. In 1853 he received an appointment in the Royal Library; in 1867 he travelled in North Africa, and in 1869 in Western Europe.

Brough, Fanny Whiteside. *Mrs. R. S. Boleyn.* An English actress; wife of Richard Smith Boleyn.

Brough, Robert Barnabas, 1828–60. *Papernose Woodenscone, Esq.* A wellknown English writer of burlesque dramas; b. in London; passed his early years in Monmouthshire, and his schooldays at Newport. He was first employed on a publication at Liverpool, and afterwards, with Mr. Angus B. Reach, on a comic periodical in London; d. at Manchester.

Brougham and Vaux, Henry Peter Brougham, Lord, F.R.S., etc., 1778–1868. *Lord B********; Isaac Tomkins, Gent.* An eminent British man of science, lawyer, orator, and statesman, of London; b. in Edinburgh; educ. at the Univ. of that city; settled there as an advocate for a few years; removed to London in 1806; M.C. for the burgh of Camelford, 1810; for Yorkshire, 1830; Lord Chancellor and a Peer, 1830–34, and never held public office afterwards. He is to be ranked as a philanthropist, statesman, orator, philosopher, and savant, among the most illustrious men his country has ever produced. In 1848 he purchased an estate at Cannes, and d. there.

Brougham, John, 1810–80. *Diogenes, Jr.* An Irish American comedian; b. in Dublin; studied for a time at the Dublin and Oxford Univs., but did not graduate;

made his first appearance on the stage in London in 1830; came to this country in 1842, and for 38 years was not only a favorite on the stage, but outside the theatre; d. in New York City.

Broughton, John Cam Hobhouse, Lord, G.C.B., F.R.S., 1786–1869. *An Englishman.* An English nobleman and writer; b. near Bristol; Trin. Coll., Camb., 1808; travelled with Lord Byron; M.P., 1820–33 and 1834–51; in 1851 elected to the peerage as Lord Broughton; held public office much of the time, 1832–41, and 1846–52, but from that time took no active part in politics; d. in London.

Broughton, Rev. Thomas, 1704–74. *Phileleutherus Christianus.* An English clergyman; b. in London; Vicar of Bedminster, near Bristol, 1774, and Prebendary in Salisbury Cathedral.

Brown, ——. *A Son of Mary Moore.* An American writer; son of Rev. Samuel Brown, who married Mary Moore.

Brown, Mrs. C. R. *Mattie May.* An American novelist, of Concord, N.H.

Brown, Charles. *Carlone; Carluccio.* An English writer, whose name is well known in connection with Keats, and whose invitation to "domesticate with him" Keats accepted. Contributed to the "Liberal" and other periodicals.

Brown, Charles Brockden, 1771–1810. *C. B. B.* An American novelist and journalist; b. of Quaker parents, at Philadelphia; founded, in 1803, the "Literary Magazine and American Register," which he conducted for nearly five years. Richard H. Horne, of London, wrote me a few years ago: "In early life I read all his novels with an interest that has made a lasting impression. Certainly, they are very unlike any that preceded them; and they have exercised a quiet, but peculiar influence, more especially in a tender melancholy, producing something like tears in the heart, rather than tears in the eyes."

Brown, Charles John, D.D. *A Clergyman of the Church of Scotland.* A Scottish minister, of the Free New North Church, Edinburgh.

Brown, David. *Amicus.* A Scottish bookseller, of Edinburgh, 1826.

Brown, David Boyer. *A Member of the Philadelphia Bar.* An American lawyer, of Philadelphia.

Brown, Miss Emma Elizabeth. *E. E. B.* An American poet, of Concord, N.H.; has, since she was a school-girl, contributed a large number of papers to a large number of newspapers, and is the author of several books. She studied painting, and has had charge of the art department at Maplewood Institute, Pittsfield, Mass., and St. Catherine's Hall, Augusta, Me. Through the winter of 1876–77 she was art critic of the Boston "Advertiser."

Brown, George, 1810–67 (?). *A Layman.* An English barrister-at-law.

Brown, Harcourt. *R. Tynt.* An English writer, of London.

Brown, Irving. *Cream Curdle; W. Ord Hunter.* A writer on Shakespeare.

Brown, J. E. *J. E. B.* An English poet.

Brown, James. *J. B.; Selkirk.* A Scottish poet, and Shakespearian scholar, of Selkirk.

Brown, James. *A Pilot who has hitherto weathered the Storm.* A Scottish writer, of Glasgow.

Brown, James Baldwin, Esq., LL.D., 1785–1843. *Three Friends.* An English barrister-at-law, called to the bar at the Inner Temple in 1816; Judge of the Oldham Court of Requests, 1840–43; d. in London.

Brown, Rev. James Baldwin, LL.D., 1820–. *Epsilon.* An eminent English Independent minister; b. in London; educ. at Univ. Coll., London; studied for the bar at the Inner Temple; and then for the ministry at Highbury Coll.; Minister of the London Road Independent Chapel, Derby, 1843, and of Clayland's Independent Chapel, Clapham Road, London, 1846; removed to a new church at Brixton, 1870.

Brown, John J. *An American Angler.* An American writer.

Brown, Capt. John Murray. *An Eye-Witness.* An English historian.

Brown, Joseph. *The Man in the Moon.* An English writer, early in the 18th century.

Brown, Miss Josephine. *His Daughter.* An American colored woman; daughter of William Wells Brown; educ. in France, and returned home in 1855.

Brown, Peter, about 1784–1863. *Libertas.* A Canadian journalist; b. in Scotland; was first a merchant in Edinburgh; came to New York City in 1838, where he wrote for the "Albion," and afterwards established the "British Chronicle." In 1843 he removed to Toronto, and established the "Banner." He also wrote largely for the "Globe." D. in Toronto.

Brown, Rebecca. *A Lady of Boston.* An American writer.

Brown, Richard. *R. B.* An Eng-

lish architect and draftsman. He devoted himself to the theory and teaching
of his profession; exhibited at the
Academy from 1793.

Brown, Robert Lundin. *A Friend.*
A Scottish teacher, early in the 18th
century.

Brown, Samuel, M.D., 1817–56.
Alumni of the Univ. of Edinburgh. A
Scottish poet, chemist, and essayist;
b. at Haddington; educ. at the Univ.
of Edinburgh; devoted himself chiefly
to chemistry; d. at Edinburgh.

Brown, Samuel. *Crito.* An English journalist; writer for the London
"Insurance Magazine."

Brown, Theron. *Park Ludlow.* An
American (?) novelist.

Brown, Col. T. Allston. *Young
Rapid.* An American journalist.

Brown, Thomas, 1770–1851. *An Old
Traveller.* An English merchant, at St.
Petersburg; d. at Edinburgh.

Brown, Thomas Crowther. *A Layman.* An English religious writer; a
Friend, or Quaker, of Cirencester.

Brown, William. *W. B., Gent.* A
Scottish poet, early in the 18th century.

Brown, William, 1769–1846. *Ahiezer.* An English Friend, of Houghton,
near Huntingdon.

Brown, William. *W. B.* A Scottish
surgeon and biographer, of Edinburgh.

Brown, William. *A Layman.* An
American (?) political writer.

Brown, William Linn. *A Fisher in
Small Streams.* An English miscellaneous writer.

Browne, Albert Gallatin, Jr., A.M.
A. G. B., Jr. An American writer;
Harv. Univ., 1853; Ph.D., Heidelberg,
1855.

Browne, Rev. Arthur. *A Son of the
Church of England.* An English clergyman; Vicar of Marham, Downham Market, Suffolk.

Browne, Charles Farrar, 1834–67.
Artemus Ward; Mrs. Betsy Jane Ward.
An American humorist; b. at Waterford,
Me.; became first a printer, then wrote
and lectured under the pseud. of "Artemus Ward"; d. at Southampton, England.

Browne, Charles Thomas, 1825–68.
Alexandre de Comyn. An English poet;
b. at Wellington, Somersetshire; educ.
at Trin. Coll., Dublin; first published a
poem in "Blackwood's Magazine."

Browne, Hablot Knight, about
1815–83. *Phiz.* An English artist and
comic designer; educ. at a private
school, and at an early age began to

draw caricatures with great spirit; in
1825 he became the illustrator of "Pickwick," and his success at once established his reputation as one of the first
artists of the day.

Browne, Lady Hester Georgiana,
1837–. *Bluebell.* An Irish lady, daughter of the 2d Marquis of Sligo.

Browne, James, LL.D., 1793–1841.
An Old Dissector. An eminent Scottish
writer; b. at Coupar-Angus; educ. at
Edinburgh and St. Andrews; in 1826
became a member of the Faculty of
Advocates; editor of the "Caledonian
Mercury," 1828, and in 1830 sub-editor
of the "Encyclopædia Britannica; d. at
Edinburgh.

Browne, Peter, –1735. *Peter, Lord
Bishop of Cork and Rosse.* An Irish cler-
gyman; was at first Provost of Trin.
Coll., Dublin, and afterwards Bishop of
Cork.

Browne, Thomas. *The Comet Literary and Patriotic Club.* An Irish writer.

Browne, William, 1807–. *W. B.,
Fowey.* An English geologist, of Cornwall.

Browne, William Hand. *Anobium
Pertinax.* An American bibliographer;
librarian of Johns Hopkins Univ., Baltimore.

Brownell, Henry Howard, M.A.,
1820–72. *A Volunteer in the U. S. Service.* An American poet; b. in East
Hartford, Conn.; Trin. Coll., Hartford,
1841; studied law, but devoted himself
to literature; friend and secretary of
Admiral Farragut; d. in his native
city.

Brownhill, Frederick Robson,
1821–64. *Frederick Robson.* An English comic actor; b. at Margate; d. in
London.

**Browning, Mrs. Elizabeth (Bar-
rett),** 1809–61. *E. B. B.* An eminent
English poet; b. in London; in 1846
married Robert Browning; resided with
him in Italy; d. in Florence.

Browning, Robert, 1812–. *Dervish
Serivœ Ferishtah.* An eminent English
poet; b. at Camberwell; educ. at the
London Univ.; began his literary career
in 1835; in 1846 married Elizabeth Barrett, and afterwards resided in Florence,
Italy.

Brownlee, Thomas. *The Laird of
Torfoot, an Officer in the Presbyterian
Army.* A Scottish writer.

Brownlow, William Gannaway,
1805–77. *Parson Brownlow.* An American Methodist minister and politician;
b. in Virginia; editor of the "Knoxville

Whig" about 1837; Governor of Tennessee, 1865 and 1867; U.S. Senator, 1869–75.

Bruce, Capt. **Alexander**. *Don A. B.* A writer of the earlier part of the 18th century.

Bruce, Rev. **Archibald**, 1746–1816. *Calvianus Presbyter; Calvinus Minor; A Reverend Divine; Scoto-Britannus.* An eminent Scottish Secession minister; b. at Broomhall, near Denny, Stirlingshire; minister at Whitburn.

Bruce, Benjamin. *Neptunus.*

Bruce, D. *A Native of Scotland; The Scots-Irishman.*

Bruce, Leslie C. (?). *Mercury.* An American publisher, of New York City.

Bruce, Peter Henry, Esq., 1692–1757. *A Military Officer.* An English traveller; b. in Westphalia; devoted himself to a military life in the service of Prussia, Russia, and Great Britain.

Bruce, Col. **Sanders D.** *Occasional.* An American publisher, of New York City; partner of Leslie C. Bruce; editor of the New York "Turf, Field, and Forest."

Bruce, William, D.D. *W. B.* An English classical scholar; senior minister of the first Presbyterian congregation, Belfast.

Bruckner, Rev. **John.** 1726–1804. *J. Cassander.* A Lutheran divine; b. on the island of Cadsand, near Belgium; studied at Francker and Leyden; preacher at Norwich, England, 1753–1804; from 1766 he was also minister of the Dutch church while any members were living.

Bruen, Rev. **Mathias**, A.M., 1793–1829. *An American.* An American Presbyt. minister; b. at Newark, N.J.; Columbia Coll., 1812; licensed to preach in 1816; after travelling in Europe, he was a missionary and minister in New York City, 1822–29, and d. there.

Brummel, George Bryan, 1778–1840. *Beau Brummel.* An English gentleman.

Brunet, Pierre Gustave, 1807–. *Dom Catalogus; Philomneste, Junior.* A French bibliographer; b. at Bordeaux, where he has been for a long time assistant to the Mayor, meanwhile very industrious in his bibliographical and editorial labors.

Bryan, George S., Esq. *G. S. B.* An American jurist; b. in Pennsylvania; received a liberal education, and settled in Charleston, S.C.; in 1866 appointed United States Judge for that district.

Bryant, Lemuel, 1794–1883. *Ned*

Myers. An American sailor; d. at Portland, Me. He was in the war of 1812, wounded, shipwrecked, and taken prisoner on Lake Ontario and confined in Dartmoor Prison.

Bryant, William Cullen, LL.D., 1794–1880. *Francis Herbert, Esq.; A Traveller; A Youth of Thirteen.* An eminent American poet; b. at Cummington, Mass.; entered Williams Coll. in 1810, but withdrew in 1812, and commenced the study of law, and was admitted to the bar in 1815; practised his profession at Great Barrington, Mass., till 1825, when he removed to New York City, and commenced his career as a journalist, which he continued till his death; d. in New York City.

Bryce, James, D.D., 1785–1866. *A Parishioner of St. George's Parish, Edinburgh.* A Scottish clergyman; b. at Aberdeen; educ. there and in Edinburgh; Chaplain at Calcutta, 1814–35; d. in Edinburgh.

Brydges, Sir **Samuel Egerton**, Bart., 1762–1837. *N. S.; S. E. B.; Sir Cosmo Gordon; Wilfred Woodfall.* An English miscellaneous writer; b. at Wootton; Queen's Coll., Cambridge, 1783; called to the bar at the Middle Temple in 1787; M.P., 1812–18; removed to the continent and resided there, 1818–37; d. at Campagne Gros Jean, near Geneva.

Bubier, Rev. **George Burden**, 1823–. *B.* An English Cong. minister and hymn-writer; was educ. for the ministry at Homerton Coll., and entered upon his duties as a pastor at Orsett, Essex, in 1844. In 1864 he became Professor of Theology and Philosophy in Spring Hill (Congregational) College at Birmingham.

Buccleugh, The Duke of, 1746–1812. *D.* A Scottish peer; succeeded his grandfather in 1751, and the 4th Duke of Queensbury in 1810.

Buchan, Right Hon. **David Stewart Erskine**, 11th Earl of, 1742–1829. *Albanicus.* An eminent and eccentric Scottish nobleman; d. at Dryburgh Abbey, Roxburghshire.

Buchan, George. *A Passenger in the Ship.* A Scottish writer, of Kelloe, Berwickshire.

Buchan, Miss **Margaret**. *Aunt Margaret.* An American writer for the young in "St. Nicholas"; in 1883 became principal of Wolfe Hall, a young ladies' school at Denver, Col.

Buchanan, Robert, 1841–. *Caliban; Thomas Maitland.* An eminent Scottish poet; educ. at Glasgow; commenced his literary career in 1860; at the commencement of 1869 he gave in London a series of "Readings" of selections from his poetical works.

Buchanan, W. B. *W. B. B.* An American poet, of Ellendale, Va., in 1852.

Buck, Henry. *Hotspur.* An English journalist, of London.

Buck, James Smith. *The Prophet James.* An American writer, of Milwaukee, Wis.

Buck, Mrs. Laura A. *Katherine Williams.* An American novelist.

Bucke, Charles, 1781–1847. *C. B.* An English miscellaneous writer; b. at Worlington, Suffolk; for more than 40 years he prosecuted his literary labors in the midst of great poverty; d. at Poulteney-terrace, Islington.

Buckingham, James Silk, 1786–1855. *A Proprietor of India Stock.* An English author and traveller; b. at Flushing, near Falmouth; passed his early life at sea, but afterwards adopted the profession of literature. In 1815 he went to India, and established a newspaper, but, attacking the India government, he was summarily expelled, and his journal suppressed. He went to India a second time, when the restrictions on the press had been removed; and, on his way to and from that country, visited various other countries, and published narratives of his travels. At a later period he made other tours, and published accounts of them. In 1825 he established, in London, "The Oriental Herald." He was M.P. for Sheffield, 1832–37. He was the founder of the London "Athenæum," which was the "Asineum" of Bulwer's "Paul Clifford." D. in London.

Buckingham, Joseph H. *J. H. B.* An American journalist, of Boston; the son of the following; was an efficient assistant of his father in the editorial department of the "Boston Courier" for almost 20 years. While connected with that paper he made two voyages to Europe, and furnished letters from England and France. He was on board the ill-fated ship "Poland," when it was burnt at sea in 1840, and was the last passenger to leave its flaming deck.

Buckingham, Joseph Tinker, 1779–1861. *J. T. B.; Cobweb; Moth; Pertinax Period & Co.* An American journalist; b. at Windham, Conn.; at the age of 16, he entered a printing-office at Walpole, N.H., and a few months later became a printer at Greenfield, Mass.; and in 1800 removed to Boston, where

he distinguished himself as an editor and publisher, till 1848, a period of nearly half a century. D. at Cambridge, Mass.

Buckingham, Leicester Silk, 1825–67. *Matthews & Co.* An English dramatist; son of James Silk Buckingham; b. at Cornwall Terrace, Regent's Park, London, and d. at Margate. He wrote, translated, and adapted a large number of farces, burlesques, and comic dramas, for the English stage, from 1854 to 1866.

Buckinghamshire, John Sheffield, Duke of, 1649–1721. An English nobleman and poet.

Buckland, Francis Trevelyan, M.A., 1826–80. *A Fisherman and Zoölogist; Irondequoit.* An eminent English surgeon and naturalist; educ. at Winchester and Christ Church, Oxford; served in the Life Guards as assistant surgeon, 1854–63; in 1866, with Mr. W. Pfennell, projected and started "Land and Water," and aided in its conduct till the very day before his death; d. at his residence in Albany Street, Regent's Park, London.

Buckley, Rev. Theodore William Alois, M.A., 1825–56. *Horace Fitzjersey; Tom Hawkins.* An English *littérateur;* sent to Oxford, but wasted his opportunities there; then repaired to London, and became a "bookseller's hack" and a journalist, and wrote or edited a large number of books, and contributed a vast amount of matter to periodicals. D. in London.

Budd, G. H. *G. H. B.* An English author.

Budd, Rev. James. *J. B.* An English clergyman, of West Horsley.

Budge, Rev. Edward, B.A., 1800–65. *E. B.* An English Epis. divine; Christ Church, Oxford, 1824; Rector of Bralton-Clovelly, Okehampton, Devonshire, 1846–65.

Budge, Jane, 1832–. *A Lady.* An English educational writer; b. at Camborne, Cornwall.

Budge, John, 1787–1864. *J. B.* An English Friend, or Quaker, of Camborne, Cornwall; a minister.

Budgell, Eustace, 1685–1736. *X.* An English writer; friend of Addison; b. at St. Thomas, near Exeter; lost £20,000 in 1720, in the famous South Sea scheme; drowned himself in the river Thames.

Budgen, Miss L. M. *Acheta; Acheta Domestica.* An English writer on insect life.

Budworth, Joseph. *A Rambler.* An English poet and officer.

Bürstenbinder, Elisabeth, 1838–. *Ernst Werner.* A German novelist; b. at Berlin, where she has always lived in the house of her mother.

Bulkeley, Sir Richard, Bart. *A Gentleman of the University of Cambridge.* An English writer, of the first part of the 18th century.

Bullar, Joseph, M.D. *A Physician.* An English physician.

Bullard, Henry Adams, A.M., 1788–1851. *An Officer under that General.* An eminent American jurist; b. in Groton, Mass.; Harv. Univ., 1807; studied and practised law in Philadelphia for a time; joined General Toledo in an expedition to New Mexico; after its defeat in 1812, escaped to Natchitoches, where he opened a law-office; served as an M.C., a judge, and a professor of law, in Louisiana, from 1831 till his death in New Orleans, to which city he removed in 1847.

Bullen, William. *Hibernicus; An Irish Catholic.* An Irish lawyer (?).

Buller, Sir Francis, Bart., 1745–1800. *A Learned Judge.* An English jurist; b. at Morval or Crediton; called to the bar at the Inner Temple, 1772; 1778–94, of the Court of King's Bench; and of Common Pleas, 1794–1800; d. in Bedford Square, London.

Bullock, C. *C. B.* An English editor.

Bulwer, Sir Edward Lytton. *E. L. B.* — See "Lytton, Lord."

Bunbury, Henry, Esq. *Geoffrey Gambado.* An English humorous artist ("the Hogarth of his day"), of London.

Bunbury, Henry Charles. *Lieut. Col. B****; One who has served under Sir Charles Napier.* An English officer, and a writer on whist.

Bunbury, Sir Henry Edward, 7th Bart., 1778–1860. *E. H. B.* An English soldier and writer; b. in London; served in the army, 1794–1809; Under Secretary of State for War, 1809–16; M.P. for Suffolk, 1830–36; passed in retirement and literary work, 1836–60; d. at his seat, Barton Hall, Bury St. Edmunds.

Bunce, Cyprian Rondeau. *A Citizen.* An English writer, of Canterbury.

Bunce, Oliver Bell. *B.; Bachelor Bluff; Censor.* An American journalist, editor of "Appleton's Journal."

Bundy, J. M. *A Member of the Rock County Bar.* An American lawyer, of Wisconsin.

Bunn, Alfred, –1860. *Conrad.* An English dramatist and theatrical mana-ger. In 1852, appeared at Niblo's Saloon, New York City, in a literary and dramatic entertainment. D. at Boulogne-sur-mer.

Bunner, H. C. *Me; V. Hugo Dusenbury; A. H. Oakes.* An American journalist, editor of N.Y. "Puck."

Burckett, Miss Florence. *Edith Lee.* An American novelist.

Burdett, Constance. *An Old Cormorant.* A Scottish (?) writer.

Burdette, Robert J., 1844–. *Burlington Hawkeye-Man.* An American journalist; b. at Greensborough, Penn.; in 1852 his parents removed to Peoria, Ill.; served in the late Civil War, 1862–65; in 1870 became editor of the Peoria "Transcript," and afterwards of the Peoria "Review"; in 1874 he took charge of the "Burlington (Ia.) Hawkeye," with which his name has ever since been associated, and to which he has imparted a world-wide reputation.

Burdick, Miss H. H. *Alice Irving Abbott.* An American writer.

Burdon, Thomas. *The Governor of White Cross Street Prison.* An English Attorney-at-law, of London.

Burdon, William, M.A., 1764–1818. *A Member of the University of Cambridge.* An English writer; b. at Newcastle-upon-Tyne; Emmanuel Coll., Cambridge, 1782; as a coal-owner he resided a part of the year at Hartford, near Morpeth, and the remainder in London, where he died.

Burge, William, Esq., D.C.L., F.R.S., F.S.A., 1786–1849. *W. B.* An English lawyer; called to the bar at the Inner Temple, 1808, and nominated a Queen's Counsel, 1834; Local Bankruptcy Judge in the Leeds District from 1846; d. in London.

Burges, George, Esq., 1786–1864. *Cato.* An English editor and publisher; b. in Bengal; Trin. Coll., Cambridge, 1807; edited several Greek works, and contributed to periodicals numerous articles on classical literature; d. at Ramsgate, Co. of Kent.

Burges, Sir James Bland. *Alfred.* — See "Lamb, Sir J. B. B."

Burges, Tristram, LL.D., 1770–1853. *A Farmer; A Ploughman; One of the People.* An American statesman; b. in Rochester, Mass.; Brown Univ., 1796; became a leader of the Rhode Island bar, practising at Providence; M.C., 1825–35. "He used sarcasm with great effect in debate, especially in his famous dispute with John Randolph." D. in Providence.

Burgess, Henry, LL.D., Ph.D., 1808–. *A Baptist.* An eminent Scottish divine; b. in Glasgow; educ. at Stepney; entered the Church of England, 1850; P.C. of Clifton Reynes, Bucks., 1854–61; Vicar of St. Andrew, Whittlesey, Cambs., 1861–83 *et seq.*; editor of the " Classical Journal," 1854–68, and for some years of the " Journal of Sacred Literature."

Burgess, James. *J. B.* An English biographer.

Burgess, Thomas, D.D., 1756–1837. *T., St. D.; Cornelius Scriblerus Nothus; Philopatris; Scriblerus Secundus.* An eminent English prelate; b. at Odiham, Hampshire; Bishop of St. David's, 1803–25, of Salisbury, 1825–37; d. at Southampton.

Burgess, W. H. *A Governor.* An English writer, of Bethlehem Hospital, London.

Burgh, James, 1714–75. *J. B.; Mr. Vander Neck.* A Scottish teacher; b. at Madderty, Perthshire; kept a school at Stoke-Newington (removed to Newington Green in 1750), Middlesex, 1747–71, then resided at Islington till his death.

Burgh, William, LL.D., 1741–1808. *An Humble Expectant of the Promise.* An Irish writer on theology; educ. at Trin. Coll., Dublin; was a member of the English parliament, where he took an active part in the debates on the American War and the French Revolution.

Burgoyne, Gen. John, 1730–93. *Sir Jack Brag.* An English general in the Revolutionary War; Oct. 17, 1777, surrendered his army to Gen. Gates at Saratoga.

Burk, Edward. *An Eye-Witness.* An English poet.

Burke, Ædanus, 1743–1802. *Cassius; An Obscure Individual.* An American jurist; b. at Galway, Ireland; came to South Carolina, and served in the Revolutionary War; M.C., 1789–91; Chancellor of South Carolina; d. in Charleston. " He was witty, accomplished, upright, and eccentric."

Burke, Andrew. *An Old Resident.* An American publisher, of Buffalo, N.Y.

Burke, Edmund, 1730–97. *E. B.; A Gentleman in the English House of Commons; Our Symposiast; Second Childhood.* A celebrated British statesman; b. in Dublin; M.P., 1766–94; the king wished to make him a peer under the title of Lord Beaconsfield, but the sudden death of his son so distressed him that he would not accept the merited honor; d. in London.

Burke, Hon. **Edmund,** 1809–82.

Bundelcund. An American statesman; b. at Westminster, Vt.; after being admitted to the bar, he removed to New Hampshire, and was so successful as a lawyer and as an editor, that he was elected to Congress for three terms of service, 1839–45; was Commissioner of Patents, 1845–47; in 1850, he returned to Newport, which had been his principal place of residence in New Hampshire, resumed the practice of his profession, and engaged to a considerable extent in literary pursuits. In his latest years, his greatest happiness was in the reading of literary works, and in collecting rare works for his library.

Burke, Harry. *H. B.* An English religious writer, of London.

Burke, John. *Sennoia Rubek.* An American poet.

Burke, Michael Honan. *Our own Correspondent.* An English journalist.

Burke, Richard. *Valens.* An English journalist; brother of Edmund Burke; wrote in the " London Evening Post." He was the principal contributor, occasionally assisted by his brothers William and Edmund.

Burleigh, Cecil, 1850–. *Albert J. Booth; Caleb Burt; Capt. Will Dayton; No Name.* An American poet and journalist, of New York City; son of William Burleigh; b. in Syracuse, N.Y.; educ. at Brooklyn, in 1880 *et seq.*; was on the staff of the " New York Witness."

Burleigh, Mrs. Celia M. (Kellum Burr), about 1825–75. *Celia; Mrs. John Smith.* An American poet and journalist; b. at Cazenovia, N.Y.; became a school-teacher; in 1844 married Mr. C. B. Kellum, of Albany; removed with him to Cincinnati, was divorced from him, and in 1851 married Charles Chauncey Burr; was divorced from him, and married Mr. Burleigh in 1865; d. at Syracuse, N.Y.

Burleigh, Francis Julius Le Moyne, 1845–. *Donatello.* An American journalist; son of W. H. Burleigh; b. in Hartford, Conn.; served in the late Civil War; and in 1867 went into journalism, and has been on the staff of several New York papers; in 1880 *et seq.*, on the " Witness."

Burleigh, Harriet E. *Minnie Munster.*

Burleigh, William Henry, 1812–71. *Burleigh.* An American journalist and reformer; b. in Woodstock, Conn.; removing to Pittsburgh, Penn., in 1837, he published the " Christian Witness," then the " Temperance Banner "; in 1843 he–

removed to Hartford, Conn., and in 1849 to Syracuse, N.Y., and still later to Albany, in all these places acting as journalist or lecturer. He was Harbor Master of New York City for some years till 1871, residing at Brooklyn, N.Y., where he died.

Burn, Andrew, –1814. *An Eye-Witness; A Marine Officer.* A Scottish writer; Maj.-Gen. in the East India service; d. at Exeter, England.

Burn, David. *Scotus.* A Canadian lawyer; Deputy Register of the Co. of Wentworth, Upper Canada.

Burn, James Dawson. *A Beggar-Boy.* An English working man; spent three years among the working classes in this country during the recent Civil War.

Burn, John Ilderton, Esq., 1774–1848. *J. I. B.* An English lawyer, of London; for some years honorary solicitor to the Literary Fund Society; d. in London.

Burn, Richard. *A Manchester Man.* An English writer on trade, commerce, etc., of Manchester.

Burn, Robert Scott. *M. S. A. and M. R. A. S.* A Scottish architect, etc.

Burnaby, Edwyn Sherard. *E. S. B.* An English novelist; entered the British Army in 1846; Lieut.-Col. of the Grenadier Guards, 1857; served in the Eastern campaign of 1854, including the battle of Inkerman and the siege of Sebastopol.

Burnand, Francis Cowley, 1837–. *Cecil Colvin; Amateur Dramatic Club.* An English dramatist; educ. at Eton and Trin Coll., Cambridge; called to the bar in 1862; is the author of about 100 dramatic pieces; has been long on the staff of "Punch," and in 1880 succeeded Tom Taylor as its editor.

Burnell, Arthur Coke, –1882. *A. C. B.* An eminent English Sanscrit scholar; was employed in the south of India; weakened by overwork in 1879; he returned to England for medical advice, and again in 1880 was compelled to leave India; spent some time in Italy for his health and for study; d. in England.

Burnet, Thomas, D.D., –1750. *A Divine of the Church of England.* An English clergyman; rector of West Kingston and Prebendary of Sarum; educ. at New College, Oxford.

Burnet, Sir Thomas, –1753. *Sir Iliad Doggrel; R. Powel, the Puppet-Show Man.* An eminent English lawyer; son of Bp. Burnet, a Justice of the Court of Common Pleas, 1741–53.

Burnett, ——. *A Member of the Edinburgh Photographic Society.* A Scottish photographer, of Edinburgh.

Burnett, Mrs. Frances (Hodgson). *Vagabondia.* An American novelist; b. at Manchester, England; came to this country with her mother and brothers and sisters about 1866; resided at New Market and Knoxville, Tenn., till in 1872 she was married to Dr. Swan M. Burnett, of New Orleans.

Burnett, George. *G. B.* A Scottish author; Lyon king-at-arms.

Burney, Edward. *E. B.* An English admiral; half-brother of Miss Fanny Burney, Madame D'Arblay.

Burnham, Benjamin Franklin, 1830–. *A men der.* An American lawyer; b. in Groton, Mass.; Wesleyan Univ., 1853; practised his profession in Chicago, 1857–60; in Newberry, Vt., 1862; served in the late Civil War, 1863–65; a lawyer in Boston, 1867–85 *et seq.*

Burnham, Mrs. Clara Louise. *Edith Douglas.* An American novelist, of the West.

Burnham, George P. *Young 'Un.* An American journalist, of Boston; served in the late Civil War, 1862–64; was three years in the U.S. Detective Service.

Burnham, Mrs. Mary (Hewins). *M. H. B.; Satanella.* An American writer, of the West.

Burnham, Samuel. A.M., 1833–73. *Uncle Paul.* An American journalist and miscellaneous writer; b. in Rindge, N.H.; Williams Coll., 1855; soon after, came to Boston, and entered upon that career of literary industry which continued till his death; one of the editors and proprietors of the "Congregational Quarterly," 1869–73; his home was at North Cambridge for several years, and he d. there.

Burns, Robert, 1759–96. *Bard of Ayrshire; A Peasant Bard; Sylvander.* A celebrated Scottish poet; b. near the town of Ayr; his first volume of poetry was published in 1786, and "with his poems, old and young, grave and gay, learned and ignorant, were alike transported"; d. at Dumfries.

Burns, Robert, Jr., 1786–1857. *His Son.* A Scottish compiler; son of the poet; b. at Mauchline; became Clerk in the office of the Comptroller of Stamps,

Somerset House. He was an accomplished scholar, was a proficient in music, and possessed a theoretical and practical knowledge of art. D. at Dumfries.

Burns, William. *A North Briton.* A Scottish theological writer.

Burr, Charles Chauncey, 1817–83. *Lola Montez.* An American schoolteacher, lawyer, lecturer, preacher, author, elocutionist, political orator, and journalist; b. in Maine; graduated at Bowd. Coll.; d. at his residence in Hoboken, N.J.

Burr, Enoch Fitch, D.D., 1818–. *A Connecticut Pastor.* An American Cong. minister; b. at Green's Farms, in Westport, Fairfield Co., Conn.; Yale Coll., 1839; Yale Theol. Sem., 1842; Pastor at Hamburg (in Lyme), Conn., 1850–73 *et seq.;* is distinguished for his attainments in the higher mathematics and astronomy.

Burritt, Elihu, 1811–79. *The Learned Blacksmith; Old Burchell.* An eminent American linguist and reformer; b. in New Britain, Conn.; besides Greek and Hebrew, he acquired in the intervals of labor, French, Spanish, Italian, German, Portuguese, Flemish, Danish, Swedish, Norwegian, Icelandic, Welsh, Gaelic, and Russian, and a good knowledge of English literature and mathematics. In 1846 he went to England, and resided there nearly 25 years. D. in his native town.

Burroughs, Samuel, Esq. *Everard Fleetwood, Esq.* An English master in chancery, of the earlier part of the 18th century.

Burrow, Sir **James,** 1701–82. *J. B.; A Member of the Royal Society and of the Society of Antiquaries.* An English lawyer; Master of the Crown Office, from 1724 till his death, the long period of 58 years.

Burt, Capt. **Edward.** *A Gentleman in the North of Scotland.* An English officer, stationed at Inverness about 1730, whose book is constantly quoted by Sir Walter Scott.

Burt, Thomas Seymour. *T. S. B.* An English miscellaneous writer, some time resident in India.

Burt, William. *Danmoniensis.* An English attorney, of Plymouth; Secretary of the Chamber of Commerce of that city.

Burton, Edmund, Esq. *E. B.; Ruben du Mont.* An English lawyer and classical scholar; Fellow of Trin. Coll., Cambridge. He attacked and ridiculed

Dr. Bentley, who was defended by Dr. Parr.

Burton, Edward, D.D., 1794–1836. *Verus.* An eminent English divine; b. at Shrewsbury; Christ Church Coll., Oxford, 1815; Regius Prof. of Divinity, and Rector of Ewelme, in Oxfordshire, 1829–36; d. at Ewelme.

Burton, H. W. *Harry Scratch.* An American journalist, in Virginia.

Burton, John, D.D., 1696–1771. *Phileleutheros Londinensis.* An eminent English divine; b. at Wembworthy, Devonshire; Rector of Worplesdon, Surrey, 1766–71.

Burton, John, 1773–1822. *J. B., Nottingham.* An English hymn-writer, of Nottingham.

Burton, Dr. **John.** *An Englishman; A Member of the Univ. of Oxford.* An English classical scholar.

Burton, John Hill, LL.D., F.R.S.E., 1809–81. *The "Ex-officio" Superintendent of the Department; A Practical Hand.* A Scottish historian and biographer; b. at Aberdeen; "Historiographer Royal" for Scotland from 1868; Commissioner under the Prisons (Scotland) Act from 1877; d. at Morton House, near Edinburgh.

Burton, Mrs. **John Hill.** *A Scotch Family.* An English lady, wife of the preceding.

Burton, Joseph. *J. B.* An English satirist.

Burton, Richard Francis, 1821–. *F. R. G. S.; Frank Baker, D.O.N.* An Irish traveller; b. at Tuam, Galway; proceeded to Bombay, under Sir Charles Napier, in 1842, and to Sindh in 1843, and served for some years in the Bombay survey; after spending many years in extensive travels, he was British Consul at Damascus, 1861–71, and at Trieste, 1872–75 *et seq.*

Burton, Rev. **Robert,** 1576–1639,40. *Democritus, Junior.* A quaint and famous old English writer.

Burton, Rev. **Warren,** A.M., 1800–66. *One who went to it.* An American Unit. minister; b. at Wilton, N.H.; Harv. Univ., 1821; Harv. Div. School, 1826; he became, in the later years of his life, a most earnest student and apostle of the "New Church" doctrines, but chiefly devoted himself to the cause of domestic education and home culture; d. at Salem, Mass.

Burtt, John, 1788–1859. *J. B.; A Friend to the Aborigines' Protective Society.* An English Friend, of London; b. at

Fulbeck, Lincolnshire; during the latter part of his life, he resided at Stockport, Cheshire.

Burtt, Thomas. *T. B.* An English poet.

Burwell, Adam Hood. *Erie-us.* A Canadian poet.

Burwell, Lettie M. *Page Thacker.* An American writer, of the South.

Bury, Lady Charlotte Susan Maria (Campbell), 1775–1861. *A Flirt; A Lady of Rank.* An English lady, daughter of the 5th Earl of Argyll; in 1796 married Colonel John Campbell, and in 1818 Rev. Edward John Bury; after his death, she devoted much time to writing for the press, with remarkable success.

Bury, James. *An Englishman; One who respects them.* An English writer, of Manchester (?).

Busbey, Hamilton. *H. B.* An American sporting writer-publisher, in New York City.

Bush, Harold Richard. *A Layman.* An English writer.

Bush, William. *Prometheus Pickle.* An American writer, of Chicago.

Bushby, Henry Jeffreys, 1820–. *A Non-Combatant.* An English civilian in the Bengal Civil Service, 1839–45; Police Magistrate at Worship Street, London, from 1870.

Busk, Hans, LL.D., F.R.G.S., 1815–. *Beaujolais.* An English author, son of Hans Busk, Esq., of Glenalder, Radnorshire; Trin. Coll., Cambridge, 1839; called to the bar at the Middle Temple, 1841; founded, and for several years edited, the "New Quarterly Review"; is "the Founder of England's Volunteer Army."

Bute, John Stuart, the 3d Earl of, 1713–92. *Earl of B—e.* An unpopular British statesman; *played* himself into the favor of the Prince of Wales, and took refuge from the arrows of "Junius" in his Paradise of Shrubs.

Butler, Charles, Esq., 1750–1832. *C. B.* An English jurist and miscellaneous writer; b. in London; educ. at Douay; called to the bar at Lincoln's Inn, 1791; the first Roman Catholic barrister since the Revolution; his literary activity was enormous, and the number of his published works very great; d. in London.

Butler, Hon. Lady Eleanor, –1829. *Eleonora.* A celebrated Irish lady.

Butler, John, 1717–1802. *A Country Clergyman; Vindex; A Whig.* An emi-

nent English divine; b. in Hamburg; Bishop of Hereford, 1788–1802.

Butler, Rev. John. *J— ZZ—.* An English clergyman.

Butler, Major John. *An Officer in the Hon. E. I. Co.'s Bengal Native Infantry in Civil Employ.* An English writer.

Butler, Joseph, D.D., 1692–1752. *A Young Clergyman.* An eminent English prelate; b. at Wantage, in Berkshire; Oriel Coll., Oxford, 1718; Bishop of Durham, 1750–52.

Butler, Robert. *Sergeant B—.* A Scottish lawyer.

Butler, S. *A Gentleman of Bristol.*

Butler, Samuel, 1612–80. *John Canne.* An English humorous poet; b. at Strensham, a parish in Worcestershire; became steward of Ludlow Castle. Sir Samuel Luke, a gentleman of Bedfordshire and a commander of note under Cromwell, was the original of "Hudibras."

Butler, Samuel. *J. P. Owen.* An English author, of St. John's College, Cambridge.

Butler, Rev. William John, M.A. *W. J. B.* An English clergyman; Trin. Coll., Cambridge, 1840; Canon of Worcester, 1880–83 *et seq.*

Butler, William Mill. *Mill.* An American journalist, of Rochester, N.Y.

Butt, Mrs. E. O. *E. O. B.* An English religious writer; author of "A Sequel to Mrs. Sherwood's Easy Questions for a Little Child."

Butt, George. *One who is but an Attorney.* An English poet and solicitor.

Butt, Isaac, LL.D., 1813–79. *Edward Stevenson O'Brien.* An eminent Irish politician; b. in Stranorlar, Co. Donegal; Univ. of Dublin, 1835; called to the Irish bar, 1838; M.P. for 1852–65, and for Limerick from 1871. D. at Dundrum, near Dublin, at the residence of his son-in-law.

Butterworth, William. *A Minor.* An English writer.

Butts, Mrs. M. F. *Fanny M. Barton.*

Bye, Deodatus, 1745–1826. *D. B.* An eminent English printer in St. John's square, Clerkenwell, London; d. in Camden-row, Peckham.

Byerley, John Scott. *John Scott Ripon.* An English dramatist; b. at Ripon, Yorkshire.

Byerley, Thomas. *Stephen Collet; Sholto Percy.* An English miscellaneous writer.

Byles, Rt. Hon. Sir John Barnard, 1801–84. *A Barrister.* An eminent English lawyer; b. at Stowmarket, Suffolk; called to the bar at the Inner Temple in 1831; one of the Judges of the Court of Common Pleas, 1858–73; d. at Harefield House, near Uxbridge.

Byrn, M. Lafayette. *David Rattle-head.* An American author.

Byrne, Mrs. Charlotte (Dacre). about 1783–. *Rosa Matilda.* An English poet.

Byrne, Mrs. Fanny. *His Widow.* An Irish lady; widow of Miles Byrne, an Irish exile of 1798.

Byrne, May. *A Cape Colonist.* An English writer.

Byrne, Oliver. *E. B. Revilo.* An English mathematician and engineer; "Inventor of the Art and Science of Dual Arithmetic."

Byrne, Mrs. William Pitt. *The*

Writer behind the Grille. An English artist and art-critic; daughter of Hans Busk, of Great Cumberland Place. She wrote at an early age for many of the periodicals of the day, but always anonymously. Many of her works have been illustrated by her own pencil.

Byrom, John, 1691–1763. *John Shadow.* An English poet; b. at Kersall, near Manchester.

Byron, George Gordon Noël, Lord, 1788–1824. *Abbé; Harold; Horace Hornem; A Noble Author; A Noble Lord.* A celebrated Scottish poet; b. about thirty miles from Aberdeen; d. at Missolonghi, Greece.

Byron, Miss Medora Gordon. *A Modern Antique.* An English novelist.

C.

Cabanel, Daniel, Esq. *A Quondam Oxonian and Carthusian.* An English poet and lawyer, of Lincoln's Inn.

Cabell, Mrs. Julia (Mayo). *The Oldest Inhabitant.* An American lady, of Lynchburg, Va.

Caglengano, Marchése d'. *Maurice Mauris.* An Italian, of Nice.

Cahill, Frank. *John Agg; Mark Conway; Maria Simpson; An Old Lady; Lieut. Wainwright Villiers, U.S.N.; George Washington Makewright.* An American journalist.

Caillot, Antoine, about 1757–1830. *A. C.; Ant. C.* A French priest and writer; was imprisoned during the Reign of Terror, and escaped death only through a confusion of names.

Cairon, Jules, 1827–. *Jules Noriac.* A French author; b. at Limoges; was at first a Feuilletonist in the old "Figaro"; then in some sheets edited by himself as the "Soleil," "Nouvelles," etc. He was Director of the "Théâtre des Variétés" and of the "Bouffes-Parisiens," 1862–70.

Calamy, Adam. *A Consistent Protestant.* An English attorney; son of Dr. Edmund Calamy.

Calder, John, D.D., 1733–1815. *Annotator.* A Scottish divine, and miscellaneous writer; b. at Aberdeen, and educ. at the Univ. there. He for some time had charge of a congregation at Alnwick, Northumberland, and thence removed to London to succeed Dr. Price in the afternoon service, Jewry Lane,

London; after the dissolution of this society, Dr. Calder retired to Hammersmith, where he devoted himself cniefly to literary labor; d. at Paddington.

Calder, Rev. Robert, 1658–. *R. C.* A Scottish Epis. clergyman; refused to acknowledge William and Mary, and was deprived of his curacy; in 1689 he was imprisoned for eleven months in the Edinburgh jail for exercising his ministry.

Calderon de la Barca, Madame Frances Erskine (Inglis). *Attaché; Mme C—— de la B——.* A Scottish lady; passed her earlier years in Normandy; with her mother and sisters came to the United States, and established a school in Boston. In 1838 she married Don Calderon de la Barca, the Spanish minister at Washington, and went with him to Mexico. In 1873 *et seq.* she resided in Spain, and received a pension.

Caldwell, Sir James, 3d Bart. *A Military Officer, J. C.* An Irish gentleman, of Castle Caldwell, Co. Fermanah. He was created a Count of Milan in the Holy Roman Empire.

Caldwell, Joseph, D.D., 1773–1835. *Carlton.* An eminent American scholar; b. at Leamington, N.J.; New Jersey Coll., 1791; Prof. in the Univ. of North Carolina, 1796–1804; and President, from 1804 till his death, at Chapel Hill, N.C.

Calef, John, 1725–1812. *J. C., Esq., a Volunteer.* An American loyalist. After the American Revolution he resided at St. Andrews, New Brunswick.

Caley, John, F.R.S., 1763–1834. *An Illused Candidate.* An English antiquary, of London; Secretary of the National Record Commission, 1801–31; d. in London.

Calhoun, Major **Alfred R.** *Alfred Rochfort; Leon Edwards.* An American writer.

Calkins, Hiram. *Deacon.* An American journalist, of New York City.

Callaghan, ——. *A New Member of the House of Commons.* An English statesman and financial writer.

Callaway, Henry. *A Member of the Society of Friends.* An English Friend, of London.

Callender, James Thomson, –1803. *Tom Callender, Esq., Citizen of the World.* An American political writer; b. in Scotland; came to Philadelphia, where he published the "Political Register," 1794–95, the "American Annual Register," 1796–97; afterwards edited the "Richmond Recorder"; d. in Richmond, Va.

Calthorpe, Hon. **Somerset John Gough**, 1831–. *An Officer on the Staff.* An English officer, aide-de-camp to Lord Raglan in the Crimea.

Calthrop, John Alfred Clayton, 1845–. *John Clayton.* An English actor; b. at Gosberton, Lincolnshire.

Calverley, Charles Stuart, –1884. *C. S. C.* An English poet, hymn-writer, and translator; Fellow of Christ's Coll., Cambridge; removed to London in 1863.

Calvert, George Henry, 1803–. *An American.* An eminent American writer; a descendant of Lord Baltimore and the painter Rubens; b. in Baltimore; Harv. Univ., 1823; in 1843 he took up his residence at Newport, R.I., and devoted himself to literary pursuits.

Cambreling, Churchill C., 1786–1862. *One of the People.* An American statesman; b. in Washington, N.C.; removed to New York City in 1802, which was afterwards chiefly his home. He engaged at an early day in mercantile pursuits with John Jacob Astor; was an M.C. from New York, 1821–39; in 1840 was appointed Minister to Russia, and on his return home he retired to private life. D. at West Neck, Long Island.

Cambridge, Richard Owen, 1717–1802. *Cantabrigius.* An English poet; resided at Twickenham, 1750–1802, where he entertained the literary stars of the day.

Camelford, Thomas Pitt, Lord, 1775–1804. *Lord C.* An English nobleman and a lieutenant in the Royal Navy; b. in Cornwall; succeeded his father in 1793; he "was not only inclined to the more enlightened pursuits of literature, but his chemical researches and his talents as a seaman were worthy of the highest admiration." He was wounded in a duel with Capt. Best, and d. in London.

Cameron, Alexander, 1748–1828. *A. C.* An eminent Scottish prelate; Bishop of Maximianopolis and Vicar Apostolic of the Lowland district of Scotland; d. at Edinburgh.

Cameron, John. *A Manchester Spinner.*

Campbell, Alexander. *Timothy Twig, Esq.* A Scottish poet and musician; b. at Tombea, on the banks of Loch Lubnaig, above Callendar; removed to Edinburgh and became a teacher of music; in 1816 he published two parts of a collection of native Highland music, for which Sir W. Scott and others contributed modern verses.

Campbell, Hon. **Archibald.** *Philalethes.* A Scottish prelate, consecrated, 1711, at Dundee.

Campbell, George John Douglas, 8th Duke of Argyle, 1823–. *A Peer's Son.* A Scottish nobleman; b. at Ardencaple Castle, Dunbartonshire; succeeded his father in 1847; Secretary of State for India, and President of the Council of India, 1868–74.

Campbell, Miss **Ella**, 1842–. *Leila.* An American poet, of Jeffersonville, Ind.

Campbell, Sir **Ilay**, Bart., 1734–1823. *I. C.* A Scottish advocate; Lord President of the Court of Session, 1789–1808.

Campbell, John, LL.D., 1708–75. *J. C.; Edward Brown, Esq.; John Claridge, Shepherd; An English Merchant; A Gentleman of the Inner Temple; A Gentleman who resided five Years on the Island; A Member of the Community and a Sincere Friend to his Country; The Prince of the Infernal Regions.* A Scottish miscellaneous writer; b. in Edinburgh; in early life removed to England, and devoted himself to authorship; d. in London.

Campbell, John F. *The Editor of "Life in Normandy."* A Scottish author and traveller; known in his own country as "Iain Ileach." "My Circular Notes" (L. 1876) has the dedication dated from Niddry Lodge, Kensington.

Campbell, Rev. **John Poage**, M.D., 1767–1814. *Vindex.* An American Presbyt. minister; b. in Augusta Co.,

Va.; Hampden Sidney Coll., 1790; d. at Chillicothe, Ky.

Campbell, Mrs. **Juliet H. (Lewis)**, 1823-. *Judith Canute.* An American poet; b. at Williamsport, Lycoming Co., Penn.; in 1843 she married Mr. Campbell, a lawyer of Pottsville, where they afterwards resided, and where she became an occasional contributor to the best periodicals.

Campbell, Commander **Robert**, R.N., -1832. *A Midshipman of the Last Century.* An English naval officer; held the command of the Isle of Ascension, 1818-20; d. at Gunley, near Welch Pool, Montgomeryshire.

Campbell, **Thomas**, Esq., LL.D., 1777-1844. *The Bard of Hope.* A celebrated Scottish poet; b. in Glasgow; resident in London, 1803-44; d. in Boulogne.

Campbell, **William**, D.D. *A Lover of the Truth in Fife.* A Scottish clergyman, of Dysart.

Candler, Isaac. *An Englishman.* An English traveller.

Canler, ——. *A French Detective.*

Canning, Rt. Hon. **George**, D.C.L., 1770-1827. *B.; Gregory Griffin; Solomon Grilding.* An eminent English orator and statesman; b. in London; d. at Chiswick.

Canning, **Josiah D.** *The Peasant Bard.* An American poet, of Gill, Mass.

Canton, John, 1718-72. *Amicus; J. C.: Indagator; Noncathoni; Thoninonca; XX.* An English physician, astronomer, and natural philosopher; b. at Stroud, Gloucestershire.

Capell, Edward, 1713-81. *E. C.* An eminent English Shakespearian scholar; b. in Suffolk. After the labor of 40 years he died without seeing his great work in print; but it was published, by the care of Mr. Collins, in 1873, with the title, "Notes and Various Readings to Shakespeare."

Capen, Rev. **Lemuel**, A.M., 1789-1858. *L. C.* An American minister; b. in Dorchester, Mass.; Harv. Univ., 1810; Pastor in South Boston, 1822-39, and d. there.

Capern, Edward, 1819-. *The Bideford Postman; The Devonshire Poet; The Postman Poet.* An English rural poet; b. at Tiverton, in Devonshire; spent much of his life as a postman at Bideford; now lives at Harborne, near Birmingham.

Cappe, Rev. **Newcome**, 1732-1800. *A Doughty Champion in Heavy Armour.* An English Unit. minister; b. in Leeds; minister at York, 1756-96.

Capper, Edward. *C.* An early English critical writer.

Cappot, Jean Gabriel, 1800-63. *Capo de Feuillide.* A French poet; b. at the Antilles; went to France, studied law, and admitted to the bar of Toulouse in 1821. In 1831 he devoted himself chiefly to political journalism at Paris.

Capron, Mary J. *Archie Fell.* An American novelist.

Caraccioli, Charles. *The Master of the Grammar School at Arundel.* An English teacher, probably an Italian by birth.

Carbutt, Dr. Edward. *Verax.* An English writer.

Card, Henry, D.D., F.R.S., 1779-1844. *A Minister of the Establishment.* An English clergyman; b. at Egham, Surrey; Vicar of Great Malvern, 1815-44; and of Donnington, Hereford, 1832-44; d. at Great Malvern, Worcestershire.

Carducci, Giosuè. *Enotrio Romano.* An Italian compiler, biographer, and bibliographer.

Carew, Hugh. *Hugh C****.* An English biographer.

Carew, Thomas. *A Late Member of Parliament.* An English compiler; once M.P. for Minehead, Somersetshire.

Carey, David, 1782-1824. *Chronon-hotonthologos.* A Scottish poet and novelist; b. in Arbroath; was engaged during his life in literary labor at Edinburgh and London; d. at his father's house, in Arbroath.

Carey, Henry Charles, 1793-1879. *A Citizen of Burlington.* An American political economist; a publisher of Philadelphia, 1821-36; he then retired from business with a considerable fortune, and forthwith commenced his writings on political economy; d. in his native city.

Carey, Mathew, 1760-1839. *C.; M. C.; Caius; A Catholic Layman; A Citizen of Philadelphia; A Citizen of the World; A Clergyman of the Church of England; Colbert; Hamilton; Jefferson; A Pennsylvanian.* An American author and publisher, of Philadelphia; b. in Dublin, Ireland; came to Philadelphia in 1784, and was actively engaged in business as a political writer in that city till his death.

Carey, Peter. *A Proprietor of Bank Stock.* An English financial writer.

Carey-Brock, Mrs. **Frances Elizabeth Georgina (Baynes)**, 1827-. *A Clergyman's Wife.* An English writer of books for the young; b. at Guernsey;

in 1848, married Rev. Carey-Brock, the Dean of Guernsey; her chief work has been the compilation of the "Children's Hymn Book," of which 200,000 copies have been sold.

Carlén, Emilie Schmidt (Flygare Dalin), 1807–. *Fru F.* A Swedish novelist; b. at Strömstad, where her father was a merchant. She married A. Flygare at Kronbergslän, in 1727; after his death she returned to her native town and married the young lawyer, J. R. Dalin. This union, also, was soon broken by his death. She then removed, at the wish of her father, to Stockholm, where she married the author, Gabriel Carlén. The profits of a long course of successful authorship, Frau Carlén has devoted to benevolent purposes.

Carleton, Fanny E. *Notelrac.* An American writer (?).

Carleton, George W. *A Traveller.* An American publisher and author, of New York City.

Carleton, Capt. John William. *Craven.* An English sporting-writer.

Carlingford, Rt. Hon. Chichester Samuel Parkinson-Fortescue, Lord, 1823–. *Mr. Plantagenet Palliser.* An Irish peer and statesman; b. at Ravensdale Park, Co. Louth; Christ Church, Oxford, 1845; M.P. for the County of Louth, 1847–74; President of the Board of Trade, 1870–79 *et seq.*

Carlisle, Nicholas, 1771–1847. *N. C.* An English topographer; b. at York; Secretary to the Society of Antiquaries, 1807; d. at Margate.

Carlisle, Thomas. *Haroun Alraschid.* An English writer.

Carlos, Edward John, Esq., 1798–1851. *E. J. C.* An English antiquary, chiefly interested in ecclesiastical and monumental antiquity; b. and educ. at Newington; admitted to practice as an attorney, and managed the business of Mr. Reynell, of the Lord Mayor's Court Office, London, for more than 33 years; d. at York Place, Yarmouth.

Carlyle, Alexander, D.D., 1721–1805. *Jupiter Carlyle.* A Scottish Presbyt. minister; for 58 years engaged in the ministry, but passed the latter part of his life in London.

Carlyle, Thomas, 1795–1881. *T. C.; S. P.; The Censor of the Age; Dr. Pessimist Anticant; Herr Teufelsdroeck; A Layman; A Lay-member of the Church of Scotland; The Translator of Wilhelm Meister,* etc. A celebrated British essayist; he resided at Chelsea, near London, 1834–81.

Carlyon, Edward Augustus. *Cœ-*

lebs, M.A. A British colonial lawyer, second son of Col. Edward Carlyon, of Tregrehan; in 1874 resident in New Zealand.

"Cœlebs" is also regarded as the *nom de plume* of *Major Thomas Tristem Spry Carlyon*, an officer in the 3d Dragoon Guards, who retired from service in 1854.

Carmalt, Rev. William. *A Select Vestryman of the Parish of Putney.* An English Clergyman.

Carmichael, Andrew. *Catholicus Verus.*

Carmichael, Archibald N., –1847. *A. N. C.; An Amateur.* A Scottish genealogist; Parochial schoolmaster, 1817; Classical Master in the Royal Academy, Inverness, and afterwards in the Edinburgh Academy.

Carne, Miss Elizabeth, 1817–73. *John Altrayd Wittitterly.* An English writer; b. at Penzance; for some years a contributor to the London "Quarterly Review"; and was thoroughly versed in geology and mineralogy.

Carné, Comte Jules de, 1835–. *Henri Karl; Minor.* A French novelist; b. at Mériel.

Carnegie, James, Earl of Southesk, 1827–. *J. E. S.* A Scottish novelist; educ. at Sandhurst; sits in the House of Peers as Baron Balinhard, U.K. (cr. 1869); is a Deputy Lieutenant for Co. Forfar; . late Lord-Lieutenant for Co. Kincardine; formerly Lieutenant, Grenadier Guards; residence, Kinniard Castle, Brechin, N.B.

Carnegie, W. *Moorman.* An English sporting-writer of London.

Caro, Elme Marie, 1826–. *Saint-Hermel.* A French author and philosopher; b. at Poictiers; studied at the Normal School in Paris; taught philosophy in various provincial towns; then, in 1837, returned to the Normal School as Conference-master; ten years later he was Professor in the Sorbonne; was Fellow of Moral and Political Sciences; and finally, in 1876, Fellow of the Academy.

Carpenter, Frank. *Carp.* An American journalist, of Washington.

Carpenter, Lant, LL.D., 1780–1840. *The Unitarian.* An eminent English clergyman; b. at Kidderminster; Minister at Bristol, 1817–40; he fell from a vessel, between Naples and Leghorn, while on a tour for his health, and was drowned in the Mediterranean.

Carpenter, Miss Mary, 1807–77. *A Prison Matron.* An English philanthropist, of Bristol, daughter of the preceding; b. in Bristol; devoted her life to the improvement of the condition of women in England and the world; she visited the United States in 1873.

Carpenter, Rev. Philip Pearsall, Ph.D., 1819–77. *P. P. C.* An eminent English naturalist, son of Dr. Lant Carpenter; b. in Bristol; in 1865 he settled in Montreal, Canada, where he died.

Carpenter, Rev. Russell Lant. *R. L. C.* An English Unit. minister; son of Lant Carpenter, D.D.; was successively pastor at Birkenhead and at Hull. In 1850 he spent a year in the United States.

Carpenter, Stephen Cullen, –about 1820. *Donald Campbell.* An American journalist; b. in England; came to the United States in 1803; commenced as journalist at Charleston, S.C., in 1805, and in Philadelphia in 1810.

Carr, Dabney, 1743–73. *Dr. Cecil.* An American statesman; wrote for Wirt's "The Old Bachelor"; was a distinguished member of the Assembly of Virginia, and foremost in supporting revolutionary measures. He married a sister of Thomas Jefferson; d. at Charlottesville, Va.

Carr, Elias F. *Hari Kari.* An American writer (?).

Carr, Frank. *Launcelot Crosse; A Merchant.* An English merchant, of Newcastle-on-Tyne.

Carr, Gouverneur. *Epistleographos.* An English writer (?).

Carr, Rev. William, B.D. *A Native of Craven.* An English Epis. divine; Vicar of Aldbrough, Hull, Yorks, 1834–60 *et seq.*

Carrat de Vaux, Alexandre. *A. de Rieux.* A French novelist.

Carre, Thomas. *Miles Pinkney.*

Carrick, John. *J. C.* A Scottish (?) writer.

Carrington, E. *An Old Bachelor.* An English writer.

Carrington, George, R.N. *An University Man.* An English naval officer; Trin. Coll., Cambridge, 1832.

Carrington, Mrs. Margaret Jirvin. *M. J. C.; An Officer's Wife.* An American lady, wife of Col. Henry B. Carrington, Prof. of Military Science, etc., in Wabash Coll., Crawfordsville, Ind.

Carroll, Charles, 1737–1832. *The First Citizen.* An eminent American patriot; b. at Annapolis, Md.; educ. at St. Omer and at Rheims, in France; studied law at Bourges, Paris, and London; resided and d. in Baltimore.

Carroll, Howard. *H. C.* An American journalist, of New York City.

Carroll, John, D.D., LL.D., 1735–1815. *A Catholic Clergyman.* An American R. C. prelate; b. in Maryland; educ. in France; Bishop of Baltimore, 1789–, and Archbishop a few years before his death.

Carroll, Rev. John. *A Spectator of the Scenes.* A Canadian Wesleyan Methodist minister, of Guelph, Upper Canada.

Carroll, T. G. *T. G. C.* An Irish author.

Carruthers, Robert, LL.D., 1799–1878. *R. C.* A Scottish journalist, publisher, and miscellaneous writer; b. at Dumfries. After serving his time to a bookbinder, he removed to England, and resided some years in Huntingdon, and became master of the national school. In 1828, he returned to Scotland to conduct the "Inverness Courier." He afterwards chiefly wrote and published the "Cyclopædia of English Literature," and contributed numerous articles to the "Encyclopædia Britannica." For more than 40 years he labored to promote the literary and general improvement of the Highlands of Scotland.

Carruthers, William A., 1818– about 1850. *A Virginian.* An American novelist; b. in Virginia; studied at Washington Coll.; removed to Savannah, Ga., where he practised medicine, devoting his leisure time to literary pursuits, and where he died.

Carson, Christopher, 1809–68. *Kit Carson.* An American mountaineer, trapper, and guide; b. in Madison County, Ky. "For half a century, his name has been a household word all along the frontier, for daring deeds and all that constitutes a man in Western eyes ... He was Fremont's right-hand man in his explorations." D. in New Mexico.

Carte, Rev. Thomas, 1686–1754. *R— H—, Esq.* An English Nonjuring divine; b. at Clifton, in Warwickshire; was a learned and industrious scholar and writer, but suffered much persecution for his opinions.

Carteaux, Félix. *F. C***.***

Carter, Miss ——. *Lilias.* An American poet.

Carter, Mrs. ——. *Elsie Gorham.* An American writer.

Carter, Mrs. Abby (Allin). *Nilla.* An American writer; b. in Pomfret, Conn.; wife of Daniel A. Carter.

Carter, Mrs. Elizabeth, 1717–1806. *Mrs. E. C.; Eliza; Chariessa.* A celebrated English scholar, and translator of the works of Epictetus; b. at Deal, in

Kent; was learned herself, and the friend of the most learned men of England; d. in London.

Carter, Isaac. *An Old Sailor.* An English writer, of Portsea, Hants.

Carter, James, 1792-1853. *A Working Man.* An English tailor; b. at Colchester. In 1836 he removed to London, and there engaged in literary work. D. at St. John's Place, Camberwell, a suburb of London.

Carter, John, 1748-1817. *An Architect.* An eminent English architect and antiquary; b. and d. in London.

Carter, John Hanson. *Commodore Rolling-Pin.* An American writer, of New York City.

Carter, St. Leger L. *Nugator.* An American poet.

Carter, Samuel. *S. C.; S. C., Barrister-at-law.* An English lawyer, of the earlier part of the last century.

Cartwright, Miss Frances Dorothy. *His Niece.* An English author, niece of Major John Cartwright.

Cartwright, George, Esq., 1739-1819. *G. C., Esq.* An English traveller and poet; b. at Marnham, Notts.; served in the British army from the age of 14 years till he became Captain in the 37th Foot; he afterwards made five voyages to the coast of Labrador, and resided there nearly 16 years; d. at Mansfield, Notts.

Cartwright, Major John, 1740-1824. *Constitution.* An English friend of America, who refused to fight against her liberties; b. at Marnham., Notts.; d. in London.

Cartwright, W. *Clericus; A Flyfisher.* An English writer.

Caruelle, Claude Félix Théodore, 1798-. *Aligny.* A French historical painter.

Cary, A. B. *A. B. C.* An American poet, of Brooklyn, N.Y.

Cary, Alice, 1820-71. *Patty Lee.* An American poet; b. in Hamilton Co., O., near Cincinnati; till 1850 resided at Clovernook, when she removed to New York City, and from that time she and her sister became regular contributors to the leading magazines and journals of America.

Cary, Henry, 1793-1858. *John Waters.* An American poet, essayist, and humorist; b. in Boston, Mass., but for many years a resident of New York City; he d. at Florence, Italy.

Cary, Thomas, 1751-1823. *Juniolus Canadensis.* A Canadian journalist, of Quebec.

Cary, Thomas Greaves, A.M., 1791-1859. *T. G. C.; A Treasurer of a Corporation.* An American merchant; b. in Chelsea, Mass.; Harv. Univ., 1811; studied law, and admitted to the bar in 1814; in 1821 he removed to New York City, and engaged in the Canton trade, but in eight or nine years he returned to Boston, and joined the house of T. H. Perkins & Co.; he was afterwards Treasurer of the Hamilton and Appleton manufacturing companies, at Lowell, Mass., till his death; d. at his summer residence at Nahant, Mass.

Casamajor, Marquis de, -1878. *Jules René.*

Casey, Miss Elizabeth, 1848-. *E. Owens Blackburne.* An Irish writer; b. in Slane, Co. Meath; at the end of 1874 she removed to London, and became a contributor to "Belgravia," "London Society," "The Argosy," "Graphic," and many other periodicals.

Casey, J. K. *Leo.* An English author.

Cass, Lewis, LL.D., 1782-1866. *An American.* An American statesman; b. at Exeter, N.Y.; when 17 years old, he sought a home at the West, travelling on foot, and settled at Marietta, O.; studied law, and began the practice at Zanesville, O., in 1802; from 1807 till his death, he held public office in his State or the United States, and distinguished himself as a most eminent statesman.

Castlen, Mrs. Epple (Bowdre). *Chiquita.* An American poet; b. at Thomaston, Ga.; passed her earlier life in New Orleans; married Dr. F. G. Castlen, of Macon, Ga., where she resided in 1870 *et seq.*

Castro, Dr. J. *J. C., M.D.* An English writer.

Casway, R. *An Impartial Inquirer.* An English writer.

Caswell, Rev. Edward, 1814-. *Quiz.* An English poet and clergyman; b. at Yately, Hants.; Brasenose Coll., Oxford, 1836; after preaching some years, in 1847 he and his wife became Roman Catholics at Rome; in 1850 he joined the Congregation of the Oratory, established by Dr. Newman, at Birmingham, where he afterwards remained.

Cate, Miss Eliza Jane, 1812-84. *The Author of "Susie L—'s Diary."* An American author; b. in Sanbornton, N.H.; began her literary career in 1842; d. at Poughkeepsie, N.Y.

Catherwood, Mrs. Mary (Hartwell). *Mary Hartwell.* An American writer.

Catlin, George Lynde. *Felix Oates*

An American translator; at one time U.S. Consul at La Rochelle, France.

Cattermole, Rev. **Richard,** B.D. *R. C.* An English Epis. divine; Vicar of Little Marlow, Bucks.

Caunter, Rev. **John Hobart,** B.D., 1794–1850. *A Late Resident in the East.* An English Epis. divine; b. at Dittisham, in Devonshire; incumbent of St. Paul's chapel, Fetty-place, Marylebone, 1827–46; d. in London.

Cavalho, E. N., 1817–. *Frank Falconer.* An American journalist, of New York City.

Cavan, Ford, 5th Earl, –1772. *A General Officer.* An Irish peer.

Cave, Edward, 1691–1754. *Sylvanus Urban.* An English journalist; founder of the "Gent. Mag.," and its editor, 1731–54.

Cavenagh, Gen. Sir **Orfeur,** 1821–. *An Indian Official.* A British colonial officer and civilian; educ. at the Military Coll. at Addiscombe; served in India with distinction from 1837,

Cavender, C. H. *H. C. Decanver.* An American bibliographer.

Cawdell, James M., –1842. *Roseharp.* A Canadian journalist; at one time an English officer; d. at Toronto.

Cawston, A. W. *Chippenham Crœsus.* An English writer.

Cawthorne, Joseph. *Cincinnatus.* An English writer.

Cazauran, Augustus R. *Matthew Carey, Jr.; John S. Moray.* An American journalist, of Brooklyn, N.Y.

Cecil, Robert Arthur Talbot Gascoyne, Viscount Cranborne, Marquis of Salisbury, M.A., 1830–. *Anti-Cotton.* An English nobleman; succeeded his father in 1868; educ. at Eton and Christ Church, Oxford (B.A., 1850); M.P. for Stamford, 1853–68; Secretary of State for India, 1866–67 and 1874.

Chabot de Bouin, Jules, 1805–57. *Jules Pécherel.* A French dramatist, of Paris.

Chabrillan, Countess **Céleste Venard de,** 1824–. *Céleste Mogador.* A French authoress; b. in Paris. She became an actor and circus-rider under the name of "Mogador." She married the Count Lionel de Chabrillan, afterwards Consul at Melbourne; resides at Paris; manager of the Folie's Marigny, and a writer of dramas.

Chadwick, Henry, 1824–. *Old Chalk.* An American base-ball player; base-ball reporter to the principal New York City papers.

Chaillot, P., **jeune.** *Un Libraire.* A French publisher, at Avignon.

Chaise de Cahagne, François Arsène, 1806–. *Arsène de Cey.* A French novelist and dramatist, of Paris.

Challamel, Jean Baptiste Marie Augustin, 1818–. *Jules Robert.* A French *littérateur* and journalist, of France.

Challen, Rev. **James,** 1802–78. *Philos.* An American Campbellite minister; b. in Hackensack, N.J.; educ. at Transylvania Univ., Lexington, Ky.; was pastor of churches in Cincinnati, Philadelphia, etc., from 1837; d. in Cincinnati, O.

Challoner, Right Rev. **Richard,** 1691–1781. *R****** C*********; A Convert.* An English R. C. prelate; b. in Lewes, Sussex; titulary Bishop of London and Salisbury, and Vicar Apostolic of the London District, 1741–81.

Chalmers, Alexander, Esq., F.S.A., 1759–1835. *C.; A. C.; C. L. M.; Amerus; A Bartholomew-Lane Man; A Churchman; Ferdinando Fidget; A Methodist; No Genius; Old Cayen; Old Simon; Secunder; Senex.* An eminent Scottish biographer; b. at Aberdeen; led a literary life in London, from about the year 1777 till his death there in 1835; d. in Throgmorton Street.

Chalmers, George, F.R.S., F.A.S., 1742–1825. *Francis Oldys, of the University of Pennsylvania.* A Scottish antiquary and miscellaneous writer; clerk to the Privy Council at London, 1786–1825.

Chalmers, Rev. **William,** M.A. *A Friend of the People.* An English Presbyt. minister at Marylebone, London.

Chamberlain, Henry. *H. C.* An English topographer.

Chamberlayn, Dr. ——. *A Friend to Britain.* An early Scottish writer.

Chambers, Augusta. *Gussie.*

Chambers, George, LL.D., 1786–1866. *A Descendant.* An American jurist; b. in Chambersburg, Penn.; N.J. Coll., 1804; M.C., 1833–37; Judge of the Penn. Supreme Court, 1851–66; d. in his native city.

Chambers, John David, M.A., 1805–. *J. D. C.; A Layman.* An English lawyer; Recorder of Salisbury from 1842.

Chambers, Robert, LL.D., 1802–71. *R. C.* A Scottish author and publisher; b. in Peebles; removing to Edinburgh in 1818, he with his brother William engaged in the business of bookselling, which, with that of publishing, they continued as long as they lived, at the same time constantly occupying themselves as authors and editors.

Chambers, Sir William, Knt., 1726–96. *Tan Chau Qua of Quang Chew Fu, Gent.* An eminent English architect; b. in Sweden; resident in London, where he died, and was interred in Poets'-corner, Westminster Abbey.

Chambers, William, LL.D., 1800–83. *W. C.* An eminent Scottish publisher of Edinburgh; b. at Peebles.

Chamerovzow, Louis Alexis. *Bertaudière.*

Chamier, Capt. Frederick, R.N., 1796–1870. *A Captain in the Navy.* An English novelist; b. in London; in 1833, retired to Waltham Hill, where for some time he acted as a justice of the peace, then devoted himself to literary labor.

Champion, Maurice, 1824–78. *Gaston d'Arc.* A French *littérateur*, of Paris.

Champlin, E. R. *John Gossip.*

Champney, James Wells, 1843–. *Champ.* An American painter of *genre* pictures, of Boston.

Champseix, Madame L., 1828–. *André Leo.* A French author; b. at Lusignan; in 1848 married the journalist Champseix (who died in 1861), and is the author of a number of novels.

Chandler, Rev. Benjamin. *B. C.* An English clergyman, of the earlier part of the 18th century.

Chandler, Peleg Whitman, 1816–. *P. W. C.* An American lawyer; b. in New Gloucester, Me.; Bowd. Coll., 1834; has for many years practised his profession in Boston.

Chandler, Thomas Bradbury, D.D., 1726–90. *A North American.* An American P. E. divine; b. at Woodstock, Conn.; Yale Coll., 1745; was for many years rector of St. John's Church, Elizabethtown, N.J.

Channing, William Ellery, D.D., 1780–1842. *W. E. C.* An eminent American Cong. minister; b. at Newport, R.I.; Harv. Univ., 1798; pastor of the Federal-street Church (Unit.), Boston, 1803–42; d. at Stockbridge, Mass.

Chanter, Mrs. Charlotte (Kingsley). *C. C.* An English novelist; daughter of Charles Kingsley, and the wife of John Mill Chanter.

Chanter, Rev. John Mill, M.A. *J. M. C.* An English Epis. divine; Oriel Coll., Oxford, 1831; Vicar of Ilfracombe *w.* Lee C., 1836–83 *et seq.*

Chantrey, Sir Francis, R.A., D.C.L., F.R.S., L. & E.F.S.A., and M.G.S., 1781–1841. *The British Phidias.* An eminent English sculptor; b. at Norton, near Sheffield, and d. at Eccleston-street, Pimlico, London.

Chaplin, Alonzo Bowen, D.D., 1808–58. *Juris Consultus.* An American P.E. divine and journalist; b. in Somers, Conn.; practised law six years; entered the ministry, 1838; spent the latter part of his life in Hartford, Conn.

Chaplin, Ebenezer. *A Neighbour.*

Chapman, D. W. *Marlay.* An American writer.

Chapman, Edwin O. *Uncle John.* An American writer, editor of the "New York Directory"; in 1881 *et seq.* still of New York City.

Chapman, Isaac A. *A Gentleman of Wilkesbarre.* An American local historian.

Chapman, Nathaniel, M.D., 1780–1853. *Falkland.* An American physician, of Philadelphia; Univ. of Penn., 1750; for many years editor of the "Philadelphia Journal of Medicine and Physical Sciences."

Charles, Mrs. Elizabeth (Rundle), 1828–. *Mrs. Kitty Trevylyan; Two of themselves.* An English writer; b. at Tavistock, Devonshire; in 1851 married Andrew Paton Charles, Esq., who d. in 1868. She commenced her literary career in 1850.

Charles, Mrs. Emily Thornton. *Emily Hawthorne.* An American writer; b. in Indiana; long resident in Washington.

Charlesworth, Miss Maria Louisa, –1880. *A Clergyman's Daughter.* An English religious writer.

Charlton, Robert M., 1807–54. *A Georgia Lawyer.* An American lawyer, of Savannah, Ga.; U.S. Senator, 1852–54.

Charteris, Col. Francis. *Colonel Fr—nc–s Ch—rt—s.* A Scottish officer.

Chase, Miss Eliza Brown. *E. B. C.;*

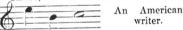 An American writer.

Chase, Philander, D.D., 1775–1852. *The President of Kenyon College.* An eminent American P.E. clergyman; b. at Cornish, N.H.; Bishop of Ohio, 1819–31; of Illinois, 1835–52; for a time President of Kenyon Coll., O., and d. at Robin's Nest, Ill.

Chase, Warren, 1813–. *The World's Child.* An American writer and reform lecturer.

Chastenay de Lanty, Mlle Louise Marie Victorine de, 1771–1855. *Mlle. V. de C**.* A French miscellaneous writer; b. in Paris; the author of various works, all anonymous.

Chatelaine, Anatole Julien, 1817–. *David Didier.* A French statistician; Chief of the Bureau of Statistics, under M. Walenski.

Chatterton, Thomas, 1752–80. *T. C.; Decimus; Probus; T. Rowley.* An English poet; b. in Bristol. In October, 1768, then only 15 years of age, he contributed some articles to "Felix Farley's Bristol Journal," and early in 1770 he commenced writing in the "Middlesex Journal" under the signature of "Decimus," in the "Political Register" under that of "Probus," and in the "Freeholder's Magazine" with the initials "T. C."

Chatto, William Andrew, 1800–64. *W. A. C.; Pay Fisher; Stephen Oliver, the Younger, of Aldwark, in Com. Ebor.* An English sporting writer; d. at the Charterhouse, London.

Chauncy, Charles, D.D., 1705–87. *L. K.; W. S., A.B.; T. W., a Bostonian; Canonicus; A Gentleman in Boston; One who wishes well to all Mankind; One who wishes well to the whole Human Race.* An American clergyman; b. in Boston; Harv. Univ., 1721; colleague and sole pastor of the First Church in Boston, 1727-87.

Chaussard, Pierre Jean Baptiste, 1766–1823. *Publicola.* An ingenious and prolific French writer, of Paris, 1807–23.

Cheesborough, Miss Essie B. *E. B. C.; Ide Delmar; Motte Hall; Elma South.* An American "Southland" writer; b. in Charleston, S.C.; educ. in that city and in Philadelphia, and commenced her literary career at an early age.

Cheetham, James, 1773–1810. *A Citizen of New York; Lysander; Mercer; Warren.* An American journalist; editor of the New York "Citizen," 1798 *et seq.*

Cheever, George Barrell, D.D., 1806–. *A Pilgrim.* An American Cong. minister; b. at Hallowell, Me.; Bowd. Coll., 1825; pastor of the Church of the Puritans, New York City, 1846–70; afterwards resided in Eaglewood, N.J.

Cheever, Henry P. *Don Carlos; Si Slokumb.* An American journalist, of Philadelphia (?).

Cheever, Rev. Henry Theodore, 1814–. *Major Marble.* An Amer. Cong. minister; b. in Hallowell, Me.; Bowd. Coll., 1834; Theol. Sem., Bangor, 1839; pastor of the Mission Chapel, Worcester, Mass., 1864–73; afterwards resided in that city without charge.

Cheeves, Langdon, 1776–1857. *Say.* An American lawyer and statesman, of South Carolina; President of the U.S. Bank at Philadelphia, 1819–22.

Cheltnan, Charles Smith. *Capt. Shandon.* An English dramatist.

Cherbuliez, Victor, 1832–. *G. Valbert.* A French writer; b. in Geneva; settled in Paris about 1862, where he published a number of novels, many of which first appeared in the "Revue des Deux Mondes."

Cherville, Gaspard Georges, Marquis de, 1821–. *G. de Morlon.* A French writer; co-laborer of Alexandre Dumas, 1850–62.

Chesbrough, E. S. *Chief Engineer of the Board of Sewerage Commissioners.* An American civil engineer, of Chicago.

Chesnel de la Charbouclais, Marquis **Louis Pierre François Adolphe** de, 1791–1862. *Alfred de Nore.* A French officer; b. in Paris; published quite a number of works under his own name, or different pseudonyms, such as "Malvius," "Alphenor," "Alfred de Nore," "Darbéci," etc.

Chesney, George. *A Volunteer.* An English writer; Lieut.-Col. of the Royal Engineers.

Chester, Miss **Annie M.** *Annie Myrtle.*

Chester, Joseph Lemuel, LL.D., 1821–82. *Julian Cramer.* An American genealogist and journalist; for some time assistant clerk of the U.S. House of Representatives; spent many years in England, where his primary pursuit was the history of the early New England settlers; d. in London.

Chetwood, Eustace, Esq., –1766, and His Brother. *Two English Gentlemen.* The former was of Harristown, Co. Kildare.

Chetwood, W. R., and His Brother. *Two English Gentlemen.*

Chevalet, Émile, 1813–. *Émile Rossi.* A French *littérateur;* b. at Levreux (Indre); in 1832 he removed to Paris, and devoted himself to literary pursuits.

Chevalier, L'Abbé Casimir, 1825–. *Jacques Duverney.* A French antiquary; b. at Saché (Indre et Loire); Secretary of the Archæological Society of Touraine.

Chevalier, Sulpice Paul, 1801–66. *Paul Gavarni.* An eminent French designer and caricaturist, of Paris.

Cheyne, William. *W. C.; A True Son of the Church of Scotland.*

Chezy, Wilhelmine Christine von. *Helmina.* A German writer.

Chibborn, E. *H.* An Irish journalist.

Child, David Lee, A.M., 1794–1874. *Probus.* An American lawyer; b. at West Boylston, Mass.; Harv. Univ., 1817; an editor of the "Massachusetts Whig," and later co-editor of the "Anti-Slavery Standard."

Child, Mrs. Lydia Maria (Francis), 1802–80. *An American; A Lady of Massachusetts.* An American writer; b. at Medford, Mass.; commenced her literary career in 1824; in 1828 married David Lee Child; in 1841 they went to New York City, and became co-editors of the "Anti-Slavery Standard"; d. at Wayland, Mass.

Child, Mrs. Maria (Little), 1797–1877. *C.; Delafield.* An American occasional writer for magazines; b. at Marshfield, Mass.; in 1822 married Simeon Child, of Boston; resided many years at Delafield, Wis., and afterwards at Dunellen, N.Y., where she died.

Child, Theodore. *Th. C.* An American journalist.

Childe, Edward Vernon, A.M., 1804–61. *E. V. C.; A "States"-man.* An American journalist; b. in Boston; Harv. Univ., 1823; studied law, but never practised; from 1834 he resided chiefly in Paris, devoting himself to literature; was correspondent of the London "Times" for ten years, and of the New York "Courier and Inquirer," 1846–56; d. in Paris.

Childs, George Borlase, F.R.C.S., 1816–. *Cirujano, M. M. C.* An English surgeon; surgeon to the London Police Force.

Chittenden, Lucius E. *Adirondack.* An American civilian; Register in the U. S. Treasury, 1861–67.

Chittenden, Newton H. *A Resident.* An American writer, of Minneapolis, Minn.

Chitov, Panajot, 1830–. *Panajot.* A Bulgarian heiduck and author, known under the name of H. Panajot; describes in his writings the manners and customs of the Bulgarians and his own life experiences.

Chitty, Edward, Esq., 1804–63. *Theophilus South, Gent.* An English barrister-at-law; called to the bar at the Inner Temple in 1829, and d. at Walham Green.

Chorley, Charles, 1810–74. *C. C.; Timothy Tugmutton, Esq.* An English journalist; b. at Taunton; sub-editor of the "Cornwall Gazette" for 30 years; d. at Truro.

Chorley, Henry Fothergill, 1808–72. *H. F. C.* An English author, art critic, and journalist; b. at Blackley Hurst, in Lancashire; in 1830 he settled in London, and was placed on the staff of the "Athenæum," for which he continued to write till his death.

Christian, Charles. *A Citizen.* An American writer, of New York City.

Christie, Rev. William, 1750–1823. *A Protestant Dissenter.* A Scottish American Unit. minister; pastor at Philadelphia, 1807–8.

Christine, Friderik, 1844–. *Ada Christen.* A German poet; b. at Vienna; married, in 1864, Herrn von Newpauer, but soon became a widow, her husband dying insane. She returned to Vienna, and was again married to Herrn von Breder.

Christison, Rev. Robert, M.A. *A Dissenting Minister; An Ex-Dissenting Minister.* An English clergyman, of Orrell, Lancashire.

Christophers, Dr. Samuel Woolcock, 1810–. *An Old Cornish Boy.* An English Wesleyan minister; b. at Falmouth; in 1879 resident in Formby, near Liverpool.

Christy, David, 1802–. *An American; Agent of the American Colonization Society.*

Christy, Edwin Byron, 1838–66. *E. C. B.; Charley Fox.* An American comic singer.

Chrystal, Thomas B. *Bernadino; Krys.* An American journalist, of New York City.

Church, Benjamin, M.D., 1734–76. *An American; Elizaphan of Parnach; A Son of Liberty; A Young Gentleman; Thomas Thumb, Esq.* An eminent American scholar, physician, poet, and politician; b. at Newport, R.I.; graduated at Harv. Univ. in 1754; studied medicine in London, and practised his profession in Boston; was proscribed and banished.

Church, Edward, Jr., 1779–1845. *A Gentleman formerly of Boston.* An American business man and political writer; passed many years of his life in Europe, but the latter part at Northampton, Mass.

Church, Mrs. Eliza Rodman (McIlvaine). *Ella Rodman.* An American writer.

Church, Thomas. *T. C.* An American writer of the first part of the 18th century.

Churchill, Charles, 1731–64. *Mr. C—— Ch—ch—ll; The Reverend Author of the "Rosciad."* An English poet; b.

in the parish of Westminster; lived a profligate life in London; d. at Boulogne.

Churchill, Mrs. Charles. *His Step-mother.* An English writer.

Churchill, Rev. John Wesley, 1839–. *The Monday Club.* An American Cong. clergyman; b. at Fairlee, Vt.; Harv. Univ., 1865; Prof. of Elocution in the Andover Theol. Sem., from 1868.

Churlton, Walter, M.D. *Carleton.* An American writer.

Clacy, Mrs. Ellen. *Cycla; A Clergyman's Daughter.* An English writer.

Cladel, Léon, 1835–. *Omikron.* A French author; b. at Montauban; made his *début* in literature in 1862, and was afterwards attached to several literary journals.

Clagett, Miss Sue Harry. *Elizabeth Waking.* An American writer, of Keokuk, Iowa.

Clap, Rev. Nathaniel, A.M., 1668–1745. *A Minister of the Gospel.* An American minister, of Newport, R.I.; graduated at Harv. Coll. in 1690.

Clapham, Rev. Samuel, M.A., 1755–1830. *Theophilus St. John, LL.B.* An English clergyman; b. at Leeds, Clare Hall, Cambridge, 1778; Vicar of Christ Church, Hampshire; of Great Ouseburn, Yorkshire; and Rector of Gussage St. Michael, Dorsetshire; d. at Sidmouth.

Clapp, Rev. Alexander Huntington, D.D., 1818–. An American Cong. minister; Secretary of the Home Missionary Society, N.Y., 1865–75 *et seq.*

Clapp, Henry, Jr., 1814–1875. *Figaro; King of the Bohemians.* An American journalist; b. in Nantucket, Mass.; was in early life a sailor. His first appearance as a journalist was in editing an anti-slavery paper at Lynn, Mass.; but he was best known as the founder of the "Saturday Press" and "Vanity Fair" in New York City. D. in New York City.

Clapp, William Warland, Jr., 1826–. *W. W. C.* An American journalist; b. in Boston; succeeded his father, in 1847, as editor of the "Boston Saturday Evening Gazette"; afterwards became proprietor of the "Boston Journal."

Clare, Ada. *Queen of Bohemia.* See "Clare, Ada," pseudonym.

Clare, John, 1793–1864. *The Peasant Poet of Northamptonshire.* An English poet; b. at Helpstone, near Peterborough; he was a farm-servant, but the hardships of his life induced a mild insanity, and he d. at the Northampton General Hospital.

Clare, John Fitzgibbon, Earl of,

1749–1802. *Lyceus; Paddy Whack.* An Irish nobleman; Lord High Chancellor of Ireland for 12 years; and later Governor of Bombay.

Clarendon, George William Frederick Villiers, 4th Earl of, 1800–70. *Un Flaneur.* An English nobleman; b. in London; after serving his country some years as a diplomatist, he was Secretary of State for Foreign Affairs, 1853–58, 1865–66, and 1868–70; d. in London.

Claretie, Jules Arnaud Arsène, 1840–. *Caliban; Candide; Arnold Lacretie.* A French journalist; b. at Limoges; has devoted his life chiefly to journalism at Paris.

Claris, John Chalk, Esq., 1797–1866. *Arthur Brooke.* An English poet and journalist; for nearly 40 years editor of the "Kent Herald." Besides "Dunvernum," he was the author of other poetical works, published under the name of "Arthur Brooke," between the years 1814 and 1824.

Clark, Bracy, F.R.S., 1770–1860. *B. C.; B. C., Vestryman of Marylebone; Menalcas.* An English veterinary surgeon of London; was a Friend, or Quaker.

Clark, C. *Three Friends.* An American writer.

Clark, Charles. *C. C., or Chilly Charley; Snarley Charley; An Amateur; Doggrel Drydog; Quintin Queerfellow; Thomas Hood, the Younger.* An English poet and amateur printer, of Totham Hall, Essex.

Clark, Charles, Esq. *A Barrister.* An English lawyer.

Clark, Mrs. Charlotte (Moon). *C. M. C.; Charles M. Clay.* An American novelist.

Clark, Dana Boardman, 1831–. *The Beardless Yankee; The Mysterious Bachelor.* An American humorist; b. in Parkman, Me.; in 1866, resident at Lostant, La Salle Co., Ill.

Clark, George Edward. *Yankee Ned.* An American sailor.

Clark, Mrs. H. K. U. *A. C.; Traveler.* An American author, of the West.

Clark, Hugh A. *Robert Boggs.* An American novelist.

Clark, J. *J. C.* An English bookseller, of Newcastle-upon Tyne.

Clark, Rev. James. *I. C., M.D.; M. J. C., Minister of the Gospel at Dirletown; M. J. C., Minister of the Gospel at Glasgow.* A Scottish minister, early in the 18th century.

Clark, John, F.S.A. *The Translator*

of the Caledonian Bards. A Scottish writer.

Clark, Lewis Gaylord, 1810–73. *An Editor.* An American journalist; b. at Otisco, N.Y.; editor of the "Knickerbocker Magazine" for many years from 1834; resided for many years at Piermont on the Hudson, N.Y.

Clark, Mary, 1791–1841. *A Friend of Youth.* An American lady; daughter of Daniel Clark (?) of Concord, N.H.; was a friend of John Farmer, Esq.

Clark, Robert. *R. C.* An English writer.

Clark, William Adolphus. *Anicetus.* An American poet.

Clark, Willis Gaylord, 1810–41. *Ollapod.* An American poet and journalist; brother of Lewis Gaylord; b. at Otisco, N.Y.; in 1830 he went to Philadelphia, and became a journalist, a profession which he pursued the rest of his life.

Clarke, Capt. ——, R.M. *The Author.* An English author.

Clarke, Benjamin. *The Editor of "Kind Words."* An English journalist, of London.

Clarke, Charles, Esq., –1842. *Indagator; Indagator Roffensis.* An English architect; author of various architectural essays; d. in Camden or Kentish Town, a suburb of London.

Clarke, Charles. *C.; W. C.; A Sportsman.* An English novelist and sporting writer; editor of the "Flying Scud."

Clarke, Charles, 1826–. *Reformator.* A Canadian journalist; editor of the Hamilton "Journal and Express," 1848–50.

Clarke, Dorus, D.D., 1797–1883. *A Retired Editor.* An American Cong. minister; b. in Westhampton, Mass.; from 1868, historiographer of the New England Historic, Genealogical Society; d. in Boston.

Clarke, Edward Daniel, LL.D., 1769–1822. *Heraclides.* An eminent English traveller; b. at Willington, in Suffolk; educ. at Jesus Coll., Cambridge; Professor of Mineralogy at Cambridge, 1808–22; d. in London.

Clarke, Dr. Hewson. *A Member of the Whip Club; Saunterer.* An English writer; of Emmanuel Coll., Cambridge; and afterwards editor of "The Scourge," a monthly publication, of London.

Clarke, James Freeman, D.D., 1810–. *J. F. C.* An American Unit. minister; b. in Hanover, N.H.; Harv. Univ., 1829; pastor of the Church of the

Disciples, Boston, 1841–59 and 1862–83 *et seq.*

Clarke, Miss Lilian Rebecca. *L. C.* An American lady; daughter of the preceding.

Clarke, M'Donald, 1798–1842. *The Mad Poet.* An eccentric American poet; b. at New London, Conn.; "for many years his blue cloak, cloth cap, erect military air, and thoughtful, beaming countenance, made him one of the features of Broadway"; d. in New York City.

Clarke, Mrs. Mary Bayard (Devereux). *A Busy Woman; Stuart Leigh; La Tenella.* An American "Southland" writer, of North Carolina; b. in Raleigh, N.C.; at an early age married William J. Clarke, Esq., of the same State, and resided with him for some time at San Antonio de Bexar, in Western Texas; but afterwards returned to her native State.

Clarke, Mrs. Mary (Latham). *Mada.* An American writer for the young.

Clarke, Mrs. Mary (Victoria Novello) Cowden, 1809–. *An Old Mariner; Harry Wandworth Shortfellow.* An English miscellaneous writer, of London; in 1828 married Mr. Charles Cowden Clarke; she spent 16 years in preparing her "Complete Concordance to Shakespeare."

Clarke, Rebecca Sophia. *Sophie May.* An American writer for the young.

Clarke, Rev. Richard. *A Member of the Church of Christ.* An English clergyman; for some time rector of St. Philip's church, Charleston, S.C.; returned to England in 1759; and in 1768 was curate of Cheshunt, in Hertfordshire.

Clarke, Samuel, D.D., 1675–1729. *A Clergyman in the Country.* A celebrated English philosopher and divine; rector of St. James's, Westminster, 1709–29.

Clarke, Saville. *Saville Row.* An English writer.

Clarke, Thomas. *Timotheus Pikromel.* An English poet of the 19th century.

Clarkson, Christopher, Esq., F.S.A., 1758–1833. *Richmondiensis.* An English local historian, of Richmond, Yorkshire, where he died.

Claude, Anne Philibert François. *A. P. F.; Nancy.* A French miscellaneous writer; director of the central *dépôt* of Artillery at Paris, at Saint-Thomas-d'Aquin.

Claudius, Matthias, 1743–1815.

Asmus. A German poet and journalist; resided chiefly at Wandsbeck, near Hamburg.

Clay, James, Esq., 1804–73. *J. C.* An English merchant, statesman, and accomplished whist-player.

Clay, Mrs. Josephine (Russell). *Ojos Morenos.* An American novelist.

Clayton, Rev. George. *A Secretary of an Auxiliary Bible Society.* An English Cong. minister.

Clayton, Rev. John. *A. Z.* An English dissenter; Minister of the Poultry Yard, London.

Cleaveland, Rev. John, A.M., 1722–99. *A Friend of Truth.* An American Cong. minister; b. in Canterbury, Conn.; Yale Coll., 1745; pastor of the parish of Chebacco, in Ipswich, Mass., 1747–99.

Cleaver, Miss ——. *A Lady.* An English artist.

Clegg, Joseph. *Philodemus.* An English antiquary.

Cleghorn, Hugh. *H. C., M.D.* A British colonial botanist.

Cleland, James. *A Citizen.* A Scottish writer, of Glasgow.

Cleland, John, 1710–89. *A Briton; Modestus.* An English etymologist; son of the "Will Honeycomb," of "Spectator."

Clemens, Samuel Langhorne, 1835–. *Mark Twain.* An American humorist; b. at Florida, Monroe Co., Mo. In 1885 he resided at Hartford, Conn., engaged in literary work.

Clements, Lewis. *Snapshot; Wildfowler.* An English sporting writer.

Clemmer, Mrs. Mary. *A Woman.* An American author; b. in Utica, N.Y.; has devoted her life, chiefly at Washington, to literary labor.

Clemo, Ebenezer, about 1831–60. *Maple-Knot.* A Canadian novelist and inventor.

Cleveland, Charles Dexter, LL.D., 1802–69. *C. D. C.* An American scholar; b. at Salem, Mass.; Dartmouth Coll., 1827; Professor in the Univ. of New York City, 1833–34; teacher of a school for young ladies at Philadelphia, Penn., from 1834.

Cleveland, Henry Russell, 1808–43. *A Teacher; A Traveller.* An American scholar; b. in Lancaster, Mass.; Harv. Univ., 1827; kept a classical school for boys in Boston, 1834–38; afterwards resided chiefly at Roxbury, engaged in literary work; d. at St. Louis, Mo.

Cliffe, John Henry. *An Angler.* An English writer.

Clifford, Charles Cavendish, M.P.,

1821–. *Umbra.* An English lawyer and civilian; M.P. for the Isle of Wight from 1857.

Cliffton, William, 1772–99. *An American Gentleman.* An American poet, son of a wealthy Quaker of Philadelphia.

Clift, William. *Timothy Bunker, Esq.* An American writer.

Clinton, De Witt, LL.D., 1769–1828. *Atticus; Grotius; Hibernicus; Tacitus; A Traveller.* An American statesman; b. at Little Britain, Orange Co., N.Y.; Columbia Coll., 1786; was in public life till 1815, when he withdrew; but was recalled again, and was governor of New York till his death at Albany.

Clissold, Rev. Augustus, M.A., 1797–. *Clericus.* An English Epis. divine; Exeter Coll., Oxford, 1819; in 1880 *et seq.* he resided at "The Park," Stoke-Newington, and at Broadwater Down, Tunbridge Wells.

Clive, Mrs. Caroline (Wigley), 1801–73. *V.* An English poet and novelist; b. at Shakenhurst, Worcestershire; in 1840 married Rev. Archer Clive, rector of Solihull. With her husband, she spent 33 years of her life at his estate at Whitfield, near Hereford, where, while sitting alone in the library, her dress caught fire, and she was so severely burned that she died in a few hours.

Clive, Hon. Robert Henry, M.A., 1785–1854. *R. H. C.* An English gentleman; educ. at St. John's Coll., Cambridge; M.P., 1817–54; d. at Shrewsbury.

Clopper, Jonas. *Monsieur Traducteur; A Citizen of America; Herman Thwackus.* An American writer.

Close, John. *Samuel Dowell; Timothy Caxton; A. M. Writewell.* An English writer.

Close, Richard Colama. *R. C. C.* A Shakespeare scholar; a barrister, of Sydney, New South Wales.

Cloury, Rev. W. *A Roman Catholic Clergyman.* An Irish (?) priest.

Clowes, Rev. John, M.A., 1743–1831. *A Clergyman of the Church of England; A Clergyman of the Established Church.* An English divine; b. in Manchester; Trin. Coll., Cambridge, 1766; rector of St. John's Church, Manchester, 1769–1831. He was a Swedenborgian, and did much to defend and spread the writings of Swedenborg; d. at Warwick.

Clunes, John. *An Officer in the Hon. E. I. Co.* An English civilian.

Cluny, Alexander. *An Old and Ex-*

perienced Trader. An English traveller in America.

Clute, Oscar. *John Allen.* An American (?) writer.

Clutton, John. *A Friend to Emancipation; M. S. Somebody.* An English writer.

Clymer, George, M.D. *A Surgeon in the United States Navy.* An American physician; b. in Pennsylvania; entered the U.S. naval service in 1829; member of the Medical Board, Washington, 1869–71.

Coad, George, Jr. *An Impartial Hand; A Lover of Truth.* An English writer, of Exeter.

Coad, Joseph. *Gregory Greendrake, Esq.* An Irish journalist; editor of the "Dublin Warder," 1824.

Coan, Rev. Leander S. *Old Corporal.* An American dialect poet, of Alton, N.H.

Coates, James Foster. *J. F. C.* An American journalist, of New York City.

Cobb, Clarence F. *Bloc.* An American poet, of Washington (?).

Cobb, Enos. *Lord Hail-fair.* An American writer.

Cobb, Gerard Francis, M.A. *A Fellow of *** College, Cambridge.* An English scholar; Trinity College, Cambridge, 1861.

Cobbe, Miss Frances Power. *Merlin Nostrodamus.* An English writer; b. and educ. at Brighton; has spent the greater part of her life in London, engaged in literary work.

Cobbett, William, 1762–1835. *An American; An American Farmer; A Brother of the Birch; Dick Retort; Franklin; A Gentleman from Connecticut; Peter Porcupine; A Subaltern.* A well-known English Radical.

Cobbold, Rev. Richard, M.A., 1797–1877. *Margaret Catchpole.* An English poet and novelist; Caius Coll., Cambridge, 1820; Rector of Wortham, 1825–77; and, for a time, Rural Dean of Hartismere.

Cobbold, Rev. Spencer. *A Country Rector.* An English Clergyman.

Cobden, Richard, 1804–65. *A Manchester Manufacturer.* An English political reformer; b. at Dunford, Sussex; M.P. for Stockport, 1841–47, and for West Riding, 1847–57; d. in London.

Coburn, Charles F. *Autograph.* An American journalist, of Lowell, Mass.

Cochrane, Mrs. Martha J. *Sydney Dare.* An American writer for the young.

Cock, Simon. *A British Merchant.*

An English merchant, of London, and commercial agent, of Liverpool.

Cockburn, Henry Thomas, Lord Cockburn, 1779–1854. *A Fellow Citizen.* An eminent Scottish jurist; called to the Scottish bar in 1800; Solicitor-General, 1830; Justice of the Court of Session, 1834; a Lord Commissioner of Justiciary, 1837–54; d. in Edinburgh.

Cockfield, Joseph, 1741–1816. *Christianus.* An English Friend, of Upton, near Plaistow and West-Ham.

"He was a contributor to the 'Christian Magazine' and other periodicals, and, under the signature of 'Christianus,' wrote a series of letters on Dr. Hawkesworth's preface to Cook's 'Voyages.'" — See SMITH's "Catalogue of Friends' Books."

Cockings, George. *Camillo Querno, Poet-Laureat to the Congress.* An English satirical poet, who aimed his darts against the American cause, in Revolutionary times.

Cockle, Mrs. ——. *A Lady.* An English writer.

Codding, Milo Defonz. *Milo Defonz.* An American writer.

Codman, Capt. John. *Ringbolt.* An American writer.

Cody, Hon. William F. *Buffalo Bill.* An American frontiersman, scout, and showman.

Coe, Miss R. *Leila Lee.* An American writer.

Coffey, W. A. *One who knows.* An American writer.

Coffin, Charles Carleton. *Carleton.* An American miscellaneous writer; Hon. A.M. at Amherst Coll., 1870.

Coffin, J. F. *A Young American.*

Coffin, Nathaniel W., 1815–69. *Thanelian.* An American poet and politician, of Boston; b. in Newburyport, Mass.; d. at Dorchester, Mass.

Coffin, Robert Barry, 1826–. *Barry Gray; An Irritable Man.* An American poet; wrote for the New York "Home Journal," 1858, and became a clerk in the New York Custom House, 1862.

Coffin, Robert Stevenson, 1797–1827. *The Boston Bard.* An American poet; b. at Brunswick, Mass.; was at first a printer at Newburyport, then a sailor during the War of 1812, then a prisoner on board a British frigate, and finally worked on newspapers in Boston, New York, and Philadelphia; d. at Rowley, Mass.

Coffin, Roland F. *Howard; Nemo; Old Sailor; Sea.* An American writer.

Cogan, John. *C.* An American journalist, of Brooklyn, N.Y.

Cogan, Rev. Thomas, M.D., 1736–

1818. *A Layman.* An English physician; b. at Rowell, Northants.; practised chiefly in London; founder of the London Humane Society; d. at Walthamstowe.

Coghlan, Charles. *C. C.* An English dramatist.

Coghlan, John. Ὄξος. An English writer.

Cohen, D. S. *Daisy Shortcut.* An American humorist.

Cohn, Martin, 1829-. *August Mels; Don Spavento.* A German writer; b. at Berlin, and educ. there; after holding several high positions, now resides in Paris.

Coke, Lieut. **Edward Thomas.** *A Subaltern.* An English officer who travelled in the United States and the British colonies in 1832.

Coker, Richard. *Signor Della Rosa.* An English writer.

Colange, Auguste Leo de, 1819-. *Dr. Leo.* A French poet and journalist; b. in the old province of Auvergne; made his *debut* in literature with a poem in 1838; coming to the United States, and residing in Philadelphia and New York, he devoted himself chiefly to the charge of "The Popular Encyclopædia" and the "National Encyclopædia"; afterwards he became editor of "Zell's Monthly Magazine."

Colban, Marie Sophie (Schmidt), 1814-. *Une Barbare.* A Norwegian novelist; for many years a resident of Paris, and devoted herself to literary pursuits. In 1884 *et seq.* lived at Rome.

Colbatch, Rev. **John.** *J. C., M.D.; A Person Concer'n'd.* An English writer, of the early part of the 18th century.

Colchester, Hon. **Elizabeth Susan (Law),** Lady, 1799-. *E. S. L.* An English poet; third daughter of Edward Law, 1st Lord Ellenborough; in 1836, married Charles Abbot, 2d Baron Colchester, who died in 1867.

Cole, Comyns. *Bras de Fer.* An English (?) journalist.

Cole, Rev. **Francis Edward Baston,** 1813-. *A Cornish Curate.* An English Epis. divine; b. at Sundridge, Kent Co.; Vicar of Pelynt, Liskeard, 1858-70 *et seq.*

Cole, Francis Sewell. *Effessea; F. S. C.* An English writer.

Cole, Mrs. **Harriet Adelia Ann (Burleigh),** 1836-65. *June Guare.* An American writer; wife of Augustus Graham Cole, of Albany.

Cole, Sir **Henry,** 1808-82. *Denarius; F. S; Felix Summerly.* An eminent English publicist: b. in Bath, and educated at Christ's Hospital; and for a time was in the Record Office in London.

Cole, Mrs. **Henry.** *Mrs. Felix Summerly.* An English novelist; wife of the preceding.

Cole, James L., 1799-1823. *Adrian.* An American poet, of Detroit, Michigan; he died at Canandaigua, N.Y., where he was born.

Cole, John Webb, -1872. *James Colcroft.* An English translator.

Cole, Miss **L. M.** *L. M. C.* An English writer; daughter of Sir Henry Cole.

Cole, Rev. **William.** *Rev. W. C.* An English clergyman and poet.

Colebrooke, Sir **George,** Bart. *A Layman.* An English writer; M.P.; and Chairman of the Court of Directors of the E. I. Company.

Coleman, Lyman, D.D., 1796-1881. *L. C.* An American educator and Cong. clergyman; b. in Middlefield, Mass.; Yale Coll., 1817; tutor at Yale, 1820-25; Professor of German in the New Jersey Coll., 1847-49; and afterwards of Greek and Latin in Lafayette Coll.; d. in Easton, Penn.

Coleman, William. *A Voice from Kentucky.* An American political writer.

Colenso, Right Rev. **John William,** D.D., 1814-83. *Bishop of Natal; The Rt. Rev. the Lord Bishop of Natal.* An eminent English clergyman; b. at St. Anstell, Cornwall; took high mathematical honors at Cambridge; was successively a master at Harrow, a resident fellow and private tutor at St. John's Coll., Cambridge, and Rector of Forncett St. Mary's, near Norwich; and Bishop of Natal, 1853-83, where he died.

Coleridge, Rev. **Derwent,** M.A.,1800-83. *Davenant Cecil.* An English Epis. divine; b. at Greta Hall, Keswick; passed some of the happiest years of his life as head master of Helston Grammar School; was Principal of St. Mark's Coll., Chelsea, 1841; Rector of Hanwell, Middlesex, 1864-80 *et seq.;* but retired from active life a year or two before his death; d. at Eldon Lodge, Torquay.

Coleridge, Henry Nelson, Esq., M.A., 1800-43. *Joseph Haller.* An English lawyer; nephew to the poet; educ. at Eton, and King's Coll., Cambridge; B.A., 1823; called to the bar in the Middle Temple, 1826, and practised in London; d. in Chester-place, Regent's Park, London.

Coleridge, Rt. Hon. Sir **John Taylor,** D.C.L., 1790-1876. *A Barrister.* An eminent English jurist; b. at Tiverton; Corpus Christi Coll., Oxford, 1813;

called to the bar at the Inner Temple, 1819; one of the judges of the Queen's Bench, 1835–58; for some time an editor of the "Quarterly Review," and afterwards an occasional contributor.

Coleridge, Samuel Taylor, 1773–1834. *C.* A celebrated English poet, essayist, and moral philosopher; b. at Ottery, St. Mary, Devon; educ. at Christ's Hospital and at Cambridge; from 1812 to 1830 he was engaged in literary labor. The latter years of his life were made easy by his residence in the family of his friend, Mr. Gilman, of Highgate Grove, and he received a pension of £100 a year. D. at Highgate.

Coles, Charles Barwell. *Major A*****.* An English writer.

Coles, Mrs. Clara. *Clara.* An American poet, of Nashville, Tenn.

Coles, John. *Civis.* An English lawyer (?).

Colet, John Annesley. *An Old Member of the Society.* An English writer; grand-nephew of John Wesley.

Collard, John, 1769–1810. *John Dralloc.* An English writer.

Colliber, Samuel. *S. C.* An English religious writer, of the earlier part of the 18th century.

Collier, Frank. *Frank Leslie.* An American publisher, of New York City.

Collier, John. *Tim Bobbin; Falcon Feather; Muscipula, Sen.; Tummus a Williams.* An English comic draughtsman; b. near Warrington; is best remembered for his little books in the Lancashire dialect. He lived to the age of 80 years.

Collier, John Payne, 1789–1883. *J. P. C.; Amicus Curiæ.* An eminent English Shakespearian scholar; b. in London; early turned to journalism, and soon after struck into the line of antiquarian lore; became librarian to the Duke of Devonshire; "it is impossible to enumerate half the volumes either written or edited by Mr. Collier in connexion with Shakespeare and the Elizabethan drama"; d. at Maidenhead, Co. of Berks., on the Thames, not far from London.

Collier, William, 1770–1856. *A Member of the Society of Friends.* An English Friend, of Woodside, Plymouth.

Collier, William Bengo, D.D. *An Evangelical Preacher.* An English writer.

Collin de Plancy, Jacques Albin Simon, 1793–. *Brindamour; Byron and Moore; Croquelardon; Ensamada; Glananville; Hormisdas Peath; Mullner; le frère Jacques Nilense; baron Nilense; Neveu de mon Oncle; Saint-Albin; Videbimus.* A French writer; b. at Plancy; went to Paris in 1812, and worked from that time for various publishers, but for a while started on his own account as a printer and publisher; and failing in Paris, carried on his business for some years in Belgium, returning to France in 1837.

Colling, Elizabeth. *Eta Mawr.* An English hymn-writer.

Collingridge, Augustus. *A Naval Officer.* An English writer.

Collins, Anthony, Esq., 1676–1729. *A—— C——, Esq.* An English free-thinker; b. at Heston, near Hounslow, in Middlesex; educ. at Eton and King's Colls., Cambridge; devoted himself to a literary life at London.

Collins, C. J. *Priam.* An English novelist.

Collins, Francis, 1801–34. *Editor of the "Canadian Freeman."* A Canadian journalist, of York; b. in Ireland; d. in Toronto.

Collins, George C. *An Irish Adopted Citizen.* An American political writer, of Baltimore (?).

Collins, Miss J. *Gooseberry Greene.* An American writer, of Mount Liberty, O.

Collins, J. L. *Jonquil.* An American novelist.

Collins, James. *A Revolutionary Soldier.* An American writer, of Louisiana (?).

Collins, Mortimer, 1827–76. *Robert Turner Cotton.* An English poet; b. at Portsmouth. He early became a writer, and published several novels; but has especially made himself by his collections of light and pleasing verses, as "Summer Songs," 1860; "Idyls and Rhymes," 1863; etc.

Colls, John. *P**** P*****, Esq., F.G.H.* An English satirical poet, of Norwich.

Collyer, Mrs. Mary Mitchell, –1763. *Felicia.* An English poet, wife of Joseph Collyer, Esq., Senior Associate Engraver of the Royal Academy.

Colman, George, and another, 1733–94. *Mr. Town.* An English poet and dramatist, of London; with Bonnel Thornton, editor of the "Connoisseur"; b. at Florence, Italy; educ. at Westminster and Oxford; studied law at Lincoln's, but deserted law for journalism, poetry, and the drama; d. in London.

Colman, George, the Younger, 1762–1836. *Arthur Griffinhoof, of Turnham Green.* An English dramatist, son of the preceding; educ. at Westminster,

Oxford, and Aberdeen; he was the author of numerous dramas, more marked for wit than decorum; d. in London.

Colman, Mrs. Julia. *Aunt Julia.* An American writer on ornithology.

Colquhoun, John Campbell, 1793–1874. *A Freeholder and Landholder of Scotland.* A Scottish statesman; b. in Edinburgh; educ. at the High School, and at Oriel Coll., Oxford; M.P., 1832, 1837, 1842–47, when he retired, from ill-health.

Colquhoun, Patrick, Esq., LL.D., 1745–1820. *A Magistrate.* A Scottish writer; b. in the borough of Dunbarton; spent in Virginia 1761–66, when he settled in Glasgow; in 1789 he removed to London, and was one of the Magistrates of the Police Office from 1792 till his death in that city.

Colquhoun, Sir **Patrick MacChambaich de,** 1815–. *Honorary Secretary of the " Leander Club."* An English lawyer; educ. at Cambridge; called to the bar at the Inner Temple, 1838; Chief Justice of the Ionian Islands, 1861–64.

Coltman, Eliza. *E—— C——.* An English Friend, of Spa, near Leicester.

Colton, Rev. **Caleb Charles,** about 1780–1832. *C. C. C.; Lacon; O. P. Q.* An eccentric English poet, journalist, etc.; educ. at Eton and King's Colls., Cambridge; after holding two parochial charges, in 1828 he lost the second; for two years then travelled in America; then removed to Paris, where he became a gamester, and was so successful that in a year or two years he acquired £25,000, but soon lost it all, and became a beggar, and finally blew out his brains to avoid a painful surgical operation; d. at Fontainebleau.

Colton, Rev. **Calvin,** 1789–1857. *An American Gentleman; An American in London; Junius; A Northern Man; A Protestant.* An American clergyman and miscellaneous writer; b. at Longmeadow, Mass.; Yale Coll., 1812; Andover Theol. Sem., 1815; devoted much time to literary pursuits; was for a few years Professor of Political Economy at Trin. Coll., Hartford, till his death; d. at Savannah, Ga.

Colton, Robert. *Sylvanus.* An English traveller and writer.

Colton, Rev. **Walter,** 1797–1851. *Bertram.* An American clergyman and journalist; b. in Rutland, Vt.; Yale Coll., 1822; Andover Theol. Sem., 1825; chaplain in the U. S. Navy, 1831–51; d. at Philadelphia.

Colvill, Rev. **Robert,** –1788. *R. C.* A Scottish writer; Minister at Dysart.

Colwell, Stephen, 1800–71. *A Friend in the North; A Layman; William Penn; Jonathan B. Wise.* An American merchant, political economist, and philanthropist; b. in Brooke Co., Va.; Jefferson Coll., Penn., 1819; studied law, and admitted to the bar, 1821; and practised his profession for some time in Pittsburg, Penn.; but was for many years a merchant in Philadelphia, where he died.

Comber, Rev. **Thomas,** B.A., 1765–. *Philippus Philaretes, A.C.C.* An English Epis. divine; b. in Yorkshire; Rector of Oswald-kirk from 1813.

Comins, Lizzie B. *Laura Caxton.* An American novelist.

Commerson, Joseph Jacques, 1802–79. *Joseph Citrouillard.* A French comic journalist, of Paris; in 1839 founder of the "Tam-Tam"; later, the "Tintamarre."

Compton, Theodore. *One of themselves.* An English Friend, of Stoke Newington, near London; now of ——.

Comstock, Mrs. Elizabeth A., 1817–60. *Elizabeth Emmet.* An American poet and prose writer; b. in New York City; the wife of Joseph E. Comstock; her literary productions were published in various New York magazines and papers.

Comyn, Rev. **Henry,** 1775–1851. *A Clergyman of the Church of England.* An English Epis. divine; Vicar of Sancreed, 1837–51; d. there.

Conant, Samuel Stillman, 1831–. *S. S. C.* An American journalist; b. in Waterville, Me.; besides a classical education at home, he studied several years at German Univs.; on his return from Europe, he became connected with the press of New York City, and devoted himself to the profession of a journalist.

Conder, Rev. **Eustace R.,** M.A. *E. R. C.* An English Dissenter.

Congdon, Charles Tabor. *A Journalist.* An American journalist, of New Bedford, Mass.

Congdon, James B., 1802–80. *A Citizen; Money Terry, Esq.; A Practical Banker.* An American writer; b. in New Bedford, Mass.; cashier of the National Bank of that city, 1825–58, and city treasurer and collector, 1859–79; d. in New Bedford.

Congnet, l'abbé Louis Henri, 1795–1870. *L'abbé Stanislas Pascal.* A French grammarian; honorary canon at Soissons (Aisne).

Conkling, Miss **Margaret C.** *Henry*

Lunettes. An American lady; sister of Roscos Conkling.

Connell, Mrs. M. E. *Olive Wayne.* An American lady.

Connelly, Daniel. *Rapidan.* An American journalist, of Buffalo, N.Y. (?).

Connelly, Rev. Pierce, A.M., 1804–. *Pascal the Younger.* An American Epis. divine; Univ. of Penn., 1821; Rector of Trinity Church, at Natchez, Tenn., for a time; then joined the Roman Catholics; but afterwards returned to the Prot. Epis. Church, and became Domestic Chaplain to the Earl of Shrewsbury, at Alton Towers.

Conner, Mrs. E. A. *Eliza Archard.* An American writer, of New York City (?).

Connolly, Charles M. *Uncle Schneider; Nic Slater.*

Connolly, James H. *J. H. C.* An American journalist, of New York City (?).

Connor, Rev. Rowland, 1842–. *R. C.; R. W. L.* An American writer; b. in New York City; at one time an editor of the "Nation" (N.Y.), and contributor to the "Tribune"; "International Review," from 1880 to 1885 *et seq.*; minister at East Saginaw, Mich.

Constable, John. *Clerophilus; Alethes.* An English writer, of the 18th century.

Constable, Michael. *M. C.; A British Soldier.* An Irish poet.

Conté, Xavier. *H. Axtern.* A French writer.

Converse, Charles Crozat, 1834–. *Karl Reden; C. O. Nevers; E. C. Revons.* An American musician and lawyer; b. in Warren, Mass.; studied music at Leipzic in 1857, and law at Albany, N.Y., in 1861.

Conway, Gen. **Henry Seymour,** 1720–95. *A General Officer.* An English soldier and statesman; Secretary of State, 1765–68.

Conway, Moncure Daniel, 1832–. *M. D. C.; A Native of Virginia.* An American writer; b. in Stafford Co., Va.; Dickinson Coll., Carlisle, Penn.; was for a time a Methodist itinerant; then studied theology at the Harvard Divinity School, and returned to his native State hoping to be able to preach his new views, but was met by a mob of gentlemen who ordered him to leave the State. Afterwards he was the minister of the Unit. societies at Washington and Cincinnati, 1854–56. He was settled as pastor of the South Place Chapel, London, in 1864, and remained there till the last year.

Conwell, Col. Russell H. *Russell.* An American lawyer and writer.

Cook, Dutton, 1832–83. *D. C.* An English dramatic critic; b. in Grantham, Lincs.; educ. at King's Coll., London, and studied law, but turned his attention to art and literature; ass't editor of the "Cornhill Magazine," 1868–71, and dramatic critic to the "Pall Mall Gazette," 1867–75, and the same to the "World" newspaper, 1875–83; d. in London.

Cook, Ebenezer. *E. C., Gent.* An American satirical writer, of Maryland (?), early in the 18th century.

Cook, Joel. *J. C.* An American author; Special Correspondent of the "Philadelphia Press" with the Army of the Potomac.

Cook, Mrs. Mary Louise (Redd). *Mary Lennox.* An American "Southland" poet and prose writer, of Georgia, where she was b., and at an early age married Mr. James C. Cook, a planter. In 1871 their residence had been for a number of years at Columbus.

Cook, Millicent Whiteside. *A Lady.* An English writer.

Cook, Theodore P. *Mat MacArone.*

Cooke, ——. *A Protestant.* An English political writer.

Cooke, Charles Wallwyn Radcliffe. *Angelina Gushington.* An English writer.

Cooke, Mrs. Helen M. *Lottie Linwood.* An American writer.

Cooke, John. *A Devonshire Dog-Trot.* An English author, of Exeter.

Cooke, John, M.D. *J. C., M.D.* An English physician; practised at Newbury, in Berkshire.

Cooke, John Esten, 1830–. *Anas Todkid; C. Effingham, Esq.; Col. Surry, of Eagle's Nest; A Gentleman; A Virginian.* An American author of distinction; b. at Winchester, Va.; studied law, but has devoted his life chiefly to literature; now resides at "The Briars," near Boyce, Va.

Cooke, Thomas, 1702(?)–56. *Atticus; Scriblerus Quartus.* An English poet; b. in Braintree, Essex; satirized by Pope in the "Dunciad."

Coole, Benjamin, –1717. *Eclea-Nobjmoni; A Father; A Gentleman in the City.* An English Friend, of Wiltshire, afterwards of Bristol.

Cooley, Adelaide J. *Addie.* An American writer.

Coolidge, Sarah E. *Kate Willis.* An American writer.

Coombe, William, Esq., 1741–1823. *The Honourable Mr. ——; P. Q.; Bel-*

phegor; Walter Boyd, Esq.; Count Coombe; A Country Gentleman; Dr. Dodd and Chace Price; Dr. Syntax; An Italian Nun; The Late Rev. Laurence Sterne; The Late Lord Lyttelton; A Plain Man; A Retired Officer; Johannes Scriblerus; Valerius; Yorick and Eliza; A Young Lady. An English humorous and satirical writer; resided abroad for many years, and was called "Count Coombe."

Coon, Spencer Wallace. *The Growler.*

Cooney, Robert, D.D., about 1800–. *A Wesleyan Methodist Minister.* A Canadian clergyman; b. in Ireland; a convert from the Catholic Church; has written extensively for the secular and religious press in Canada, where he has exercised his ministry.

Cooper, Sir **Astley Paston**, Bart., 1768–1841. *Sir A. C.* An eminent English surgeon; b. at Brooke, Norfolk; commenced his medical career under Mr. Turner, an apothecary at Yarmouth, in 1782; in 1784 went to London to attend the hospitals, and in 1787 removed to Edinburgh, but soon returned to London, where he practised till the year 1822, when his income was no less than £21,000, the largest sum ever known to be realized by a medical practitioner. After a short period of retirement in the country, however, he returned to London to resume his professional avocations. D. in London.

Cooper, Charles Purton, Esq., LL.D., –1873. *C. P. C.* An eminent English lawyer; educ. at Oxford. After a successful career as a lawyer his business fell off, and some years before his death he was compelled to retire to Boulogne, where he died.

Cooper, Edward. *An English Connaught Ranger.*

Cooper, James Fenimore, 1789–1851. *An American; Cornelius Littlepage; A Travelling Bachelor.* A celebrated American novelist; b. at Burlington, N.J.; spent three years (1802–5) in Yale Coll.; then entered the U. S. Navy, — first as a common sailor, then as a midshipman, from which position he rose to be lieutenant; in 1811 he left the navy, and settled at Mamaroneck, Westchester Co., N.Y., and devoted the rest of his life chiefly to literary labor and travel; d. at Cooperstown, N.Y.

Cooper, John Gilbert, 1723–69. *Aristippus; Philaretes.* An English writer devoted to classical literature; educ. at Trin. Coll., Cambridge.

Cooper, Mrs. Maria Susanna (Bransby), –1807. *Mrs. C.* An English writer, relict of the Rev. Dr. Samuel Cooper, of Great Yarmouth; d. at Ferney-hill, Co. Gloucester; author of many publications.

Cooper, Myles, D.D., LL.D., about 1735–85. *A North American.* An American P. E. divine; President of King's (now Columbia) Coll., New York City, 1763–75.

Cooper, Rev. Samuel, S.T.P., 1740–1800. *Dr. C.; No Bigot to, nor against, the Church of England; No Tithe Gatherer.* An English clergyman; curate of Great Yarmouth; and Rector of Morley and Yelverton, Norfolk, 1765–1800; d. at Great Yarmouth.

Cooper, Miss **Susan Fenimore**, about 1815–. *A Lady.* An American miscellaneous writer, daughter of James Fenimore Cooper.

Cooper, Thomas, LL.D., 1759–1849. *A Gentleman in America; A Native of the South; A Nullifier.* An English American; b. in London; President of Columbia Coll., S.C., 1820–34, where he died.

Cooper, Thomas, 1805–. *Adam Hornbook.* An English Radical, called the "Chartist"; b. at Leicester; taught the trade of a shoemaker at Gainsborough, Leics.; diligently applying himself to study, he became a schoolmaster at twenty; he became the leader of the Leicester Chartists in 1841; in 1848 he became an active political and historical lecturer in London; at first a Skeptic, in 1856 he became a Christian believer; and from 1858 he has travelled through England and Scotland, preaching and lecturing on the "Evidences of Christianity."

Cooper, Rev. **W.** *A Certain Unknown Vicar.* An English clergyman; Rector of Kirkby Wiske.

Cooper, Rev. **William**, A.M., 1694–1743. *A Minister of Boston.* An American clergyman; Harv. Univ., 1712; settled in Boston, Mass.

Cooper, William, Esq. *Vanderdecken.* An English yachtsman, of London; a famous reporter of regattas.

Cope, Robert L. *Arrelsee.* An American writer.

Copeland, W. C. *Cope.* An American journalist, of Brooklyn, N.Y.

Copland, Alexander. *A Protestant Layman.* An English advocate.

Copithorne, R. *A Sufferer.* An English writer, of the earlier part of the 18th century.

Copleston, Edward, D.D., 1776–1849. *One of his Constituents.* An eminent English prelate; b. at Offwell, Devon; Corpus Christi Coll., Oxford, 1794; Bishop of Llandaff, and Dean of St. Paul's, 1827–49; d. at Hardwick House, near Chepstow, Co. of Monmouth.

Copleston, Rev. John Gay, M.A. *A Sojourner.* An English clergyman; Oriel Coll., Oxford, 1824; Rector of Offwell, Horniton, 1841–83 *et seq.*

Coram, Robert. *Brutus.* An American politician, of Delaware.

Corbett, Thomas. *T. C.* An English author, early in the 18th century.

Corcoran, Dennis, –1858. *The Reporter of the New Orleans "Picayune."* An American journalist, of New Orleans; b. in Ireland; came to this country in 1834; after being on the staff of the "Picayune," he helped found the "New Orleans Delta," and was its proprietor and editor till 1858, when he established the "Sunday Magazine," which continued about one year; killed by the explosion of the steamer "Pennsylvania."

Cordell, Rev. Charles. *C. C.; C. A. D. A.* An English Catholic priest; missionary at Newcastle-upon-Tyne.

Corder, Susanna, 1788–1864. *A Total Abstainer.* An English Friend, of Stoke-Newington, near London; last of Chelmsford, Essex, where she died.

Corey, John, about –1721. *J. C.* An English dramatist; b. at Barnstaple, Devonshire; became a player, and followed that profession for 20 years, to the time of his death.

Corfield, Frederick. *F******** C*******.* An English miscellaneous writer.

Corkling, Mary Anne (Yates). *M. Yates.* An English writer, of the day.

Corlett, John. *Vigilant; Wizard.* An English sporting journalist, of London.

Cormack, John Rose, M.D. *J. R. C.* A Scottish physician; at one time, of the Royal Infirmary, Edinburgh.

Cormenin, Louis Marie (de la Haye), Vicomte de, 1788–1868. *Timon.* A French political writer; b. in Paris; studied law and was chosen advocate. While chiefly devoted to a political and business life, he exhibited an excellent taste for poetry, and some of his early verses appeared in the French journals.

Cornell, Rev. J. H. *A Priest of the Congregation of the Holy Redeemer.* An American Roman Catholic priest, of Maryland (?).

Corner, George Richard, Esq., F.S.A., 1801–63. *G. R. C.* An English attorney and antiquary; b. in the parish of Christ Church, Blackfriar's Road; and educ. at Gordon House, Kentish Town; Vestry Clerk of the parish of St. Olave, Southwark, from 1835; d. at Camberwell.

Cornu, Mme Hortense (Lacroix). *Sébastien Albin.* A French author; sister of the architect, Eugène Lacroix, and god-daughter of Queen Hortense; married, in 1834, M. Sébastien Melchior Cornu, a distinguished painter. Besides her translations from the German, etc., Mme Cornu, under this pseudonym, furnished articles to the "Revue du Nord," of Metz; she also wrote for other periodicals; etc.

Cornwall, Ebenezer. *E. C.* An English religious writer.

Cornwallis, Caroline Frances, 1786–1858. *A Pariah; Thomas Brown, redivivus.* An English writer, of London.

Corvo de Camões, João de Andrade, 1824–. *Andrade.* A Portuguese poet and professor; b. at Torres Novas; Prof. at Lisbon.

Cory, Charles B. *Owen Nox.* An American writer.

Cosel, Charlotte von, 1818–. *Adelheid von Auer.* A German poet; b. in Berlin; since 1848 has resided at Schwedt-on-the-Oder, and in 1856 began to make literature her profession.

Cotes, Humphrey. *N. C. M. S. C.* An English political writer.

Cotterel, Sir Charles. *Poliarchus.* An English translator; Master of Requests to Charles II.

Cotton, Henry, D.D., 1790–1879. *Catholicus.* An eminent English clergyman; Christ Church, Oxford, 1810; sub-librarian of the Bodleian Library, 1814–22; Archdeacon of Cashel, 1824–72.

Cotton, William Charles, M.A. *W. C. C.* An English translator; Christ Church, Oxford; B.A., 1836; M.A., 1838.

Couch, Jonathan, 1789–1870. *Ipolperroc; Video.* An English naturalist; b. and d. at Polperro, Cornwall; F.L.S., 1824.

Coues, Samuel Elliott, –1867. *Elliott.* An American philanthropist; b. at Portsmouth, N.H.; was educ. for mercantile pursuits, but was a lover of books, and took an active part in promoting public education, and a strong advocate of peace principles. In 1853 Mr. Coues received an appointment in the Patent Office at Washington; but his health failing, he returned to Portsmouth in 1866, and d. there.

Coulson, H. B., 1850–. *H. B. Conway.* An English actor; educ. at Rossall

School and the Univ. of Berlin; made his first appearance on the stage in London in 1872, where he has since remained.

Courtarey, Rev. John. *J. C.; A Clergyman.* An English writer.

Courtauld, S. *S. C.* An English botanist.

Courtenay, Rt. Hon. Thomas Peregrine, 1782–1841. *Decius.* An English civilian; M.P. for Totnes, 1810–31; Vice-Pres. of the Board of Trade, 1828–30. He was drowned while bathing at Torquay.

Courtier, Peter L. *Onesimus.* An English poet and biographer, of London; for some years an assistant at Rivingtons', Booksellers, Paternoster Row.

Courtland, Mrs. Grace. *Gypsy.* An English writer; a clairvoyant.

Courtney, William Prideaux, 1845–. *P. W. Trenpolpen.* An English antiquary; 5th son of John Sampson Courtney; b. in Penzance; one of the authors of "Bibliotheca Cornubiensis," 1874–78.

Cousin, Charles. *Charles C.; Charles C***.* A French novelist of the time.

Cousin d'Avalon, Charles Yves, 1769–1840. *M. C**.* A French compiler; b. at Avalon (Yonne); in 1789 and soon after sought his living in literary labor.

Coventry, Henry, –1752. *H. C., Esq.; Philemon.* An English writer, of Magdalen Coll., Cambridge. He took orders, and became vicar of Edgware, Middlesex; one of the authors of the "Athenian Letters."

Cowan, Charles. *The Head of a Family, etc.* A Scottish physician.

Coward, William, M.D., 1656–1725. *W. C., M.D., C.M., L.C.; A Doctor of Physick.* An English physician and poet; educ. at Hart Hall and Wadham Coll., Oxford. He is best known by his "Second Thoughts concerning the Human Soul," by Estibius Psychalettres, 1702. This work was burnt by the common hangman in 1704.

Coward, William C. *W. C. C.* An English political writer.

Cowen, Mrs. Samuella (Mardis), 1842–. *Le Clerc.* An American "Southland" poet and prose writer, of New Orleans.

Cowles, T. Z. C. *Buttons.* An American writer (?).

Cowley, Charles. *Historicus; A Lawyer.* An American lawyer, of Lowell, Mass.

Cowley, Mrs. Hannah Parkhouse, 1743–1809. *Anna Matilda.* An English poet and dramatist; d. at Tiverton.

Cowley, William. *W. C.* An English poet.

Cowper, A. *Timothy Scribble.* An English poet.

Cowper, William, 1731–1800. *The Bard of Olney.* An eminent English poet; b. at Berkhampstead, Herts.; d. at Dereham, Norfolk.

Cowtan, Robert. *A "Man of Kent"; Reginald Fitz-Roy Stanley, M.A.* An English author, of the British Museum.

Cox, Daniel, M.D. *A Physician in Town.* An English physician, of London.

Cox, Irvine E. B. *I. E. B. C.* An English writer on angling, etc.

Cox, Sir Richard, 1650–1733. *A Lay Hand.* A British jurist; Lord Chancellor of Ireland in 1763.

Cox, Mrs. S. B. (Hughes). *Beverley.* An American "Southland" writer, of New Orleans; b. in Warren Co., Miss.; at an early age married Mr. Cox, and has devoted much time to literary work.

Cox, Rev. Samuel. *Carpus.* An English writer.

Cox, Rev. Thomas. *An Impartial Hand.* An English clergyman, of Broomfield, Essex, early in the 18th century.

Cox, Mrs. Wight. *A Lady.* An English writer of the last century.

Cox, William, –1851. *An Amateur.* An English artist and writer; came to the United States early in life as a printer; after writing several years for the "New York Mirror," returned to England.

Cox, Mrs. William N. *Percy Curtiss.* An American novelist.

Coxe, Miss ——. *A Lady.* An English lady; sister of Mr. William Coxe (1747–1828).

Coxe, Rt. Rev. Arthur Cleveland, D.D., 1818–. *A——; A.C.C.; C.* An American poet and clergyman; b. at Mendham, N.Y.; educ. at the Univ. of New York; after holding several charges as rector, he was, in 1864, chosen Bishop of the Western Diocese of New York.

Coxe, Rev. Henry Octavius, M.A., 1811–81. *H. O. C.* An eminent English bibliographer; Worcester Coll., Oxford, 1833; sub-librarian of the Bodleian Library, 1838; and chief librarian, 1860–81.

Coxe, Peter, Esq., 1753–1844. *Fabricia Nunnery, Spinster.* An English writer; b. in London; educ. at the Charter house; was once an eminent auctioneer in London; but for many years retired from business; d. in Wilmot street, Brunswick Square, London.

Coxe. Rev. Richard Charles, about 1799–. *R. C. C.* An English clergyman and poet ; Worcester Coll., Oxford, 1821 ; became successively Fellow of his college, honorary Canon of Durham, Chaplain to Archbishop Tenison's Chapel, London, Vicar at Newcastle-on-Tyne, Select Preacher at Oxford, Archdeacon of Lindisfarne, and Canon of Durham.

Coxe, Richard Smith, LL.D., –1865. An American lawyer; New Jersey Coll., 1808 ; U.S. District Attorney for New Jersey.

Coxe, Tench, 1755–1824. *Juriscola ; Member of the Society of Artists, &c., of Philadelphia.* An American economist; b. in Philadelphia ; Assistant Secretary of the Treasury, 1790 ; Commissioner of the Revenue in 1792 ; Purveyor of Public Supplies, 1803–12 ; is said to have been a Loyalist during the Revolution ; d. in Philadelphia.

Cozzens, Frederic Swartwout, 1815–69. *Dr. Bushwacker ; Richard Haywarde.* An American humorist; b. in New York City, and educ. there; a leading wine-merchant, he published in connection with his business the "Wine Press" ; d. in Brooklyn, N.Y.

Crabbe, Rev. George, 1754–1832. *The Poet of the Poor.* An English descriptive poet ; minister at Trowbridge, 1815–32.

Crafton, William Bell. *W. B. C.* An English Friend, of West Hill, Sheffield, last of Tewkesbury.

Crafts, Wilbur Fisk, 1850–. *Uncle Will, V.M.* An American Meth. Epis. minister; b. in Fryeburgh, Me. ; Wesleyan Univ., 1869 ; Boston Univ., 1869–72 ; in 1873 travelled in Europe.

Cragin, Louisa T. *Ellis Gray.* An American writer for the young.

Cragin, Mary A. *Joy Allison.* An American writer.

Cragoe, Thomas Adolphus, 1840–. *T. A. C.* An English author; b. at Trevaster, Kea; travelled in Europe and North America, 1866–71 ; in 1879 resident at Woodbury villa, Truro.

Craig, Rev. James, 1682–1744. *J. C.* A Scottish clergyman and poet; b. in East Lothian ; one of the most popular preachers of Edinburgh.

Craig-Knox, Mrs. Isa, 1831–. *Isa.* A Scottish poet; b. at Edinburgh; at an early age began to write for several periodicals, and at length sent her poetical contributions to the "Scotsman"

under the above signature. In 1857 she went to London, and was employed in organizing the National Association for the Promotion of Social Science, and was its Secretary till her marriage with Mr. John Knox. In 1859 she won the first prize for her ode, recited at the Burn's Centenary Festival, over 620 competitors.

Craik, Mrs. Dinah Maria (Mulock), 1826–. *A Woman.* An English novelist ; b. at Stoke-upon-Kent, Staffordshire ; in 1865 married George Lillie Craik, the younger.

Craik, Rev. Henry, 1805–66. *Parens.* An English Baptist minister, of Bristol.

Cramer, Very Rev. John Anthony, D.D., 1793–1848. *A Member of the Univ. of Oxford.* An English clergyman; b. in Switzerland ; Christ Church, Oxford, 1816 ; Regius Professor of History at Oxford from 1842, and Dean of Carlisle from 1844.

Cramp, John Mockett, D.D., 1791–. *A Bereaved Husband.* A Canadian Baptist minister and journalist; b. at St. Peter's, Isle of Thanet, Co. Kent, England; came to Canada in 1844, and was editor of the "Pilot," Montreal, 1840–51 ; President of Acadia Coll., N.S., 1851–53 and 1860–69.

Crampton, Sir Philip, 1st Bart., M.D., F.R.S., 1777–1858. *A Physician.* An Irish physician and naturalist; b. in Dublin ; Surgeon-General of the Forces ; d. in Dublin.

Cranbourne, James Emilius William Evelyn Gascoyne Cecil, Viscount, 1821–65. *The Blind Traveller.* An English nobleman, of London, contributor to the "St. James's Medley."

Cranch, William, LL.D., 1769–1855. *Lucius Junius Brutus.* An American jurist; b. at Weymouth, Mass. ; Harv. Univ., 1787 ; for 55 years Judge of a U.S. court ; d. at Washington.

Crane, John. *A Bird at Broomsgrove.* An English poet.

Crane, John. *Jacia.* An English numismatist.

Craven, the Right Honourable **William**, Lord, 1737–91. *The R—— H—— Lord C.* An English nobleman ; Baron of Hamstead Marshall, Lord Lieut. of the Co. of Berks., Recorder of Newbury, etc. ; d. at Lausanne, Switzerland.

Crawford, E. M. *Genesee.* A sporting writer.

Crawford, Rev. Francis, LL.D. *A Celtophile.* An English Epis. divine; Trin. Coll., Dublin, 1834 ; Rector of Milton Bryant, Woburn, Beds., 1879 *et seq.*

Crawford, G. W., and **J. Apple-white.** *A Committee.* American rail-road men, of Washington.

Crawfurd, Oswald John Fred-erick. *John Dangerfield; John Latouche.* An English miscellaneous writer, of Merton Coll., Oxford; at one time, H. B. M. Consul at Oporto.

Crawfurd, Thomas. *T. C.* A Scot-tish writer, in the early part of the 18th century; Professor of Philosophy in the Univ. of Edinburgh.

Crawley, George John Lloyd. *A Convert from Anglicism.* An English theological writer.

Crean, Miss Mary Walsingham. *May Rie.* An American "Southland" poet; b. in Charleston, S.C.; but since childhood resident in the Crescent City.

Crébillion, Claude Prosper Jolyot de, 1707-77. *Krinelbol.* A French nov-elist; b. in Paris; wrote licentious novels.

Creech, William, 1745-1815. *A Jury-man.* An eminent Scottish bookseller; son of a clergyman of Newbattle; was liberally educ.; and was in business in Edinburgh from 1771 till his death, a period of 44 years. He was frequently in the Magistracy of the City; and in 1811, Lord Provost; d. in Edinburgh.

Creighton, Rev. James. *A Presbyter of the Church of England.* An English clergyman; B.A. at Trin. Coll., Dublin, 1764.

Crespigny, Mrs. Champion de. *A Mother.* An English author.

Crestadoro, Andrea, 1808-79. *A Reader therein.* An eminent English bibliographer; Chief Librarian of the Manchester Free Library, from about 1864; d. in that city.

Creswell, Mrs. Julia (Pleasants). *Adrienne.* An American poet and nov-elist; b. at Huntsville; in 1854, married Judge David Creswell, a wealthy planter near Shreveport, La., but who lost his property in the late civil war, and after-wards resumed the practice of the law. In 1870, Mrs. Creswell was teaching a village school. "Greenwood," her home, is near Shreveport.

Cresswell, Mrs. R. E. *R. E. C.* An English biographer; wife of Francis Cresswell, and daughter of Mrs. Caroline Fry.

Crevecœur, Hector St. John, 1731-1813. *An American Farmer; Un Culti-vateur; Un Membre Adoptif de la Nation Oneida.* A French economist; b. at Caen, Normandy, of a noble family; set-tled in America, 1754; French Consul in New York City, 1783-93, when he re-turned to France; d. at Sarcelles, France.

Crewdson, Mrs. Ellen (Fox), 1807-. *A Lady.* An English lady; b. at Perran-ar-worthal; married, in 1831, G. B. Crewd-son; in 1879 resided at "The Wood," Windermere.

Crickmore, Henry G. *Krik.* An American journalist, of New York City.

Crippen, William G., 1820-63. *In-visible Green, Esq.* An American humor-ist; editor of the "Cincinnati Times."

Crisp, J. *A Gentleman of Gray's Inn.* An English lawyer, of London.

Crisp, Stephen, 1628-92. *S. C.* An English Friend, of Colchester, in Essex; d. at Wandsworth, near London.

Critchett, Richard Claude. *R. C. Carton.* An English actor; b. in Lon-don; first appeared on the stage in 1875; has also acted at Liverpool.

Crittenden, William Butler. *W. B. C.* An American writer, of Rochester, N.Y.

Crocker, Rev. A. B. *A Freethinker.* An American Presbyt. preacher.

Croffut, William A. *W. A. C.; Peleg Wales.* An American journalist, of New York City.

Croft, Mrs. S. *S. C.* An English religious writer.

Crofton, Walter Cavendish. *Uncle Ben; Erienensis.* An English writer for the young; a Clerk in the Court of Chancery, Upper Canada; was at one time in the Canadian civil service.

Croghan, Dr. John. *A Visitor.* An American writer.

Croke, Sir Alexander, Knt., D.C.L., 1758-1843. *Robert Stanser.* An English lawyer and miscellaneous writer; Judge of the Vice-Admiralty Court, at Halifax, N.S., 1801-15; d. at Studley Priory.

Croker, Rt. Hon. John Wilson, LL.D., F.S.A., etc., 1780-1857. *C.; Crawley, Junior; J—— T——, Esq.; Nereus; Rigby; T. C. D.; Edward Bradwardine Waverley.* An eminent Irish statesman and miscellaneous writer; b. in the Co. of Galway; educ. at Trin. Coll., Dublin; and in 1802 called to the Irish bar; M.P., 1807, for eight parliaments; but devoted much time to literary work; d. at the house of Sir William Whiteman, St. Alban's-bank, Hampton.

Croly, David Goodman, 1829-. *C. G. David; David Goodman.* An American journalist; b. in New York City; became a silversmith; was for a time a student in the Univ. of New York; taught phonography; was employed on the New York "Evening Post" and the New York "Herald," 1854–58; was editor and proprietor of the Rockford (Ill.) "Daily News"; city editor of the New York "World" when it was first started; then managing editor till 1871; and from 1871 managing editor of the "Graphic."

Croly, Mrs. Jennie (Cunningham). *Jennie June; Satanella; Veni Vidi.* An American journalist; b. at Market Harborough, Leicestershire; removed to America with her father; and when quite a girl, edited a Lyceum paper in Southbridge, Mass.; soon after 1855 she managed the ladies' column in two weekly papers; and since that time, under the signature of "Jennie June," Mrs. Croly has been constantly engaged in journalism; in addition to her editorial duties, she contributes regularly to 27 publications outside of New York City; Mrs. Croly was the founder of the "Sorosis," in 1868; she is the wife of the preceding, whom she married in 1856.

Cronin, David E. *Seth Eyland.* An American author, of Binghampton, N.Y.; eminent, for some years, in that town, for ability, courage, and force of character.

Crook, Japhet. *Sir Peter Stranger, Bart.*

Cropper, Hon. Margaret (?), 1815–. *Rednaxela.* An English poet, daughter of 1st Baron Denman; first (1841) married Henry William Macaulay, Esq., who d. 1846; secondly (1848), Edward Cropper, Esq.

Cross, Joseph, D.D., 1813–. *An Army Chaplain.* An American Meth. clergyman; b. at Brent, Somersetshire, England; came to the United States in 1825; and commenced his ministry in 1829; contributor to the "Southern Meth. Quarterly," etc.

Crossey, J. S. *J. C. Stewart.* An American dramatist.

Crossley, Mrs. M. Louise (Rogers). *Rena; Currer Lyle.* An American "Southland" writer; b. at Athens, Ga.; in 1866 was married to J. T. Crossley, Esq.; and in 1869 resided at Columbus, Fla.

Croswell, Harry, D.D., 1778–1858. *His Father.* An American clergyman and journalist; b. at West Hartford, Conn.; after having been a vigorous journalist for some years, he entered the Epis. ministry; and was Rector of Trinity Church, New Haven, Conn.; and d. in that city.

Crouch, Nathaniel, 1681–1736. *Rich-*

ard Burton. An English writer of popular historical and miscellaneous compilations.

The British Museum Catalogue makes the pseud. "Richard," and not "Robert, Burton."

Crowe, Joseph Archer, 1825–. *George Taylor.* An English writer on art; b. in London; is now, 1882, British consul at Düsseldorf.

Crowley, ——. *Sir John Anvil.* An English manufacturer.

Crowley, Thomas. *T. C.* An English Friend, of London, and Walworth, Surrey.

Crowley, Thomas. *Amor Patriæ.* An English writer.

Croxall, Samuel, D.D., –1752. *A Gentleman-Commoner of Oxford.* An English divine, poet, and miscellaneous writer; b. at Walton-upon-Thames, in Surrey; Rector at Sellick, Herts., 1737–52.

Crozier, Henry Acheson, 1801–75, M.R.C.S. *H. A. C.* An English writer, resident at Penzance, Cornwall, 1840–50 (?); d. in London.

Cruden, Alexander, 1701–70. *Alexander the Corrector.* A Scottish author; b. in Aberdeen; in 1732 he settled in London, opened a bookstore, and became a corrector of the press. He prepared his "Concordance" in the short period of four years, 1733–37.

Cruger, Lewis. *Justinian, of South Carolina.* An American politician.

Crull, Jodocus. *J. C., M.D.* An English physician; b. in Hamburgh; M.D. at Cambridge, 1681; Licentiate of the Coll. of Phys., 1692.

Cruse, Miss Mary Anne. *M. A. C.* An American novelist; b. at Huntsville, Ala.; is a teacher in her home, at the foot of Monte Saño.

Cugoano, Quobna Ottobouh. *A Native African.* A slave in La Grenade, and free in England.

Cullen, Rev. J. E. *A Minister of the Gospel.* An English divine.

Cullen, Rev. John, B.A. *Llucen.* An English divine; Trin. Coll., Dublin, and at St. Aidans in 1863; Vicar of Radcliffe-on-Trent, Notts., 1874–83 et seq.

Cullen, William, M.D., 1712–90. *Miss Betty Montgomery.* An eminent Scottish physician; b. in Lanarkshire; settled at Hamilton as a surgeon; afterwards Prof. of Med., first in Glasgow, and afterwards in Edinburgh, where he died.

Culverwell, J. P. *A Member of the Manchester Athenæum.*

Cumberland, His Royal Highness the Duke of, 1721–65. *His R. H. the D——.*

A member of the English Royal Family, Prince William Augustus, 3d son of George II.

Cumming, John, D.D., F.R.S.E., 1810–81. *The "Times" Bee-Master.* An eminent minister of the Scottish Church; b. in Aberdeenshire; became a resident of London in 1833, and a popular preacher; d. in that city.

Cummings, Amos Jay. *Ziska.* An American journalist, of New York City.

Cummings, Elizabeth. *E. C.* An American writer, of Terre Haute, Indiana.

Cummings, M. J. *Capt. Carnes.* An American writer for the young.

Cummins, Mrs. Alexandrine (Macomb). *His Wife.* An American lady; widow of George David Cummins, D.D.

Cunningham, Allan, Esq., 1784–1842. *Hid-Allan; Mark Macrobin.* A Scottish poet and miscellaneous writer; b. at Blackwood, Dumfriesshire; removed to London in 1810, and while devoting much time to literature, held a position in the studio of Sir Francis Chantrey till his death; d. in London.

Cunningham, H. S. *H. S. C.* An English writer of the day.

Cunningham, Rev. John William, M.A., 1780–1861. *A Country Clergyman; Suncho.* An English clergyman; Vicar of Harrow for more than 50 years, and d. there. He was a poet and a writer of religious fiction.

Cunningham, Timothy, Esq. *A Gentleman of the Middle Temple.* An English lawyer, of London, of the 18th century.

Cuoq, Rev. Jean André. *N. O., Ancien missionaire.* A French Canadian priest and philologist; in 1867 became attached to the Seminary of St. Sulpice, Montreal.

Curgenoen, John Brendon, M.R.C.S., 1831. *Tretane.* An English physician; b. at Tretane, St. Kew; Fellow of the Med. Chir. Society, 1865–73.

Curran, H. G., Esq. *H. G. C., Esq.* An Irish lawyer; a writer of the day.

Currie, Rev. E. *One who has a Tear for Others as well as himself.* A Scottish minister, of Abercorn.

Currie, James, M.D., F.R.S., 1756–1805. *Caius; Philo Musa; Jasper Wilson.* An eminent Scottish physician; b. at Kirkpatrick, Fleming, in Dumfriesshire; came to Virginia, and spent some time in a commercial capacity; returned to Scotland, and studied medicine at Edinburgh; settled in Liverpool; a short

time before his death removed to Bath for his health, and d. there.

Currie, Rev. John. *A Minister of the Church of Scotland.* A Scottish minister, of Kinglassie, Co. of Fife.

Curry, Otway, 1804–55. *Abdallah.* An American poet and journalist; b. on a farm where is now the village of Greenfield, Highland Co., O.; was chiefly self-educated; in 1823 he went to Lebanon, and learned the trade of a carpenter; worked at his trade in several towns, and wrote poetry for the newspapers till 1829, when he settled as a farmer in Union Co.; in 1838 he united with W. D. Gallagher in editing the "Hesperian," at Columbus, O.; in 1839 removed to Marysville, and began to study law; in 1842 purchased the "Greene County Torchlight," published at Xenia, whither he removed the next year; in 1845 he returned to Marysville, and from that time was devoted to his profession, except that in 1853–54 he edited the "Scioto Gazette," residing in the meantime at Chillicothe. D. at Marysville, O.

Cursham, Miss Mary Ann. *M. A. C.; A Lady.* An English poet and novelist, of Nottinghamshire.

Curtis, Mrs. Caroline G. *Arnold Winchester; Carroll Winchester.* An American novelist, of Boston, wife of Charles Pelham Curtis, Esq.

Curtis, Miss E. J. *Shirley Smith.*

Curtis, George Ticknor, 1812–. *G. T. C.; Phocion; A Citizen of Massachusetts.* An eminent American lawyer; b. in Watertown, Mass.; Harv. Univ., 1832; has for many years practised his profession in New York City.

Curtis, George William, 1824–. *Howadji; The Lounger; Old Bachelor; Paul Potiphar; A Traveller.* An American journalist and miscellaneous writer; b. at Providence, R.I.; when he was 15 years old, the family removed to New York City; in 1842 he went with an elder brother, and resided at the Brook Farm, at Roxbury, for 18 months; then to Concord, Mass., where they lived with a farmer, and worked on his farm, for another 18 months; in 1846 he went to Europe, resided in Germany and Italy, and travelled in Egypt and Syria; on his return home, he soon became connected with the New York "Tribune" and has since been devoted to authorship and journalism in New York City, being from 1857 the editor of "Harper's Weekly."

Cusack, Miss Mary Frances, 1832–.

C. F. M.; Sister Mary Frances Clare;
The Nun of Kenmare. An Irish author;
b. in Dublin; in 1861 joined the Order
of Poor Clares, taking the name of Sister Mary Frances Clare; she is the author of about 40 volumes.

Cushing, Caleb, LL.D., 1800–79. *One*
of his Countrymen. An eminent American statesman; b. in Salisbury, Mass.;
Harv. Univ., 1817; studied law, and practised, at Newburyport, 1822–29; M.C.,
1835–43; Minister to China, 1843–44;
served as Colonel in the Mexican War,
1847–48; Attorney-General of the United
States, 1853–57; and Minister to Spain,
1873–77; d. at Newburyport.

Cushman, Frederick E. *F. E. C.*
An American soldier, of Massachusetts;
was private in Company E in the 58th
Regiment, in the late civil war.

Cushman, George Francis, D.D.,
1819–. *L. N.* An American P. E.
clergyman; b. at Pawtucket (now R.I.);
Amherst Coll., 1840; was a teacher and
Epis. missionary in Alabama, 1844–63;
Pastor at Pawtucket, 1863–65; Syca-
more, Ill., 1865–69; Princeton, Ill., 1869–
74; at Chicago, Ill., 1874–81; assistant
rector in New York City from 1881; associate editor of the "Province," 1874–
78; associate editor of the "Living
Church," 1878–83 *et seq.;* resident in
New York City.

Cust, Emma Sophia (Edgecombe),

Countess Brownlow. *A Septuagenarian.*
An English lady.

Cutler, Mrs. Helen (Conant Tracy),
1815–. *An American Woman.* An American physician; in 1834, married Rev.
J. M. Tracy, and was matron of the Deaf
Mute Asylum in Ohio; went to Europe
and was European correspondent of the
"Ohio Statesman," 1851; lectured in
London on Woman's Rights; married
Samuel Cutler and settled in Illinois,
1852; graduated at the Woman's Med.
Coll., Cleveland, O., 1869; visited Europe,
again, 1873–75; and on her return home
settled in Cobden, Ill., where she practises her profession.

Cutler, Jervase, 1768–1844. *A Late*
Officer in the U. S. Army. An American
pioneer; b. in Hamilton, O. In 1788, at
the early age of 19, he was one of the
little band of 48 who emigrated from
Massachusetts, under Gen. Rufus Putnam, and pitched their tents at Marietta,
O., in the very centre of the Indian bat-
tle-grounds of that day; d. at Evansville,
Ind.

Cutter, Bloodgood H. *The Long*
Island Farmer Poet. An American poet.

Cutter, Mrs. J. H. *I. Heard.* An
American writer.

Cutts, Mary. *Idamore.* An American poet.

Cynosuridis, Alphonse. *Un vieux*
garçon.

D.

Daddo, Rev. William, A.M., 1707–65.
One Unconcerned. An English clergyman; b. at West Looe, Cornwall; Head
Master of Blundell's School, Tiverton,
1743–57; d. at Calverleigh.

Dafforne, James, –1880. *J. D.* An
English writer on art; for many years
associate editor of the London "Art
Journal."

Daggett, John. *A Freeman of Massa-*
chusetts. An American lawyer, writer,
and local historian; b. at Wrentham,
Mass.; settled in Attleborough, Mass.

Dagley, Miss Elizabeth Frances.
E. F. D. An English writer for the
young; daughter of Richard Dagley, an
English artist, from 1815, of London.

Dahl, Vladimir Ivanovitch, 1802–
72. *Kosak Luganski.* A Russian novelist and philologist.

Dahlgren, John Adolphus Ber-
nard, 1809–70. *Blue Jacket.* An Amer-

ican naval officer, of Swedish descent;
b. in Philadelphia; entered the U.S.
Navy in 1826; invented the "Dahlgren"
shell-gun, 1847, and rose to the highest
positions in the U.S. Navy.

Dale, Thomas, M.A. *T. D.* An
English poet and clergyman; C.C.C.,
Cambridge, 1821; Canon of St. Paul's,
1843–70 *et seq.*

Dale, W. *A Member of one of the*
[Benefit] Societies. An English accountant, of London.

Dale, William Kelynack, 1833–.
***. An English poet; b. at Newlyn,
Cornwall.

Dallas, Rev. Alexander, A.M. *A*
Pastor. An English clergyman; rector
of Wonston, Hants.

Dallas, Rev. Alexander Robert
Charles, 1791–1869. *The Country Curate.*
An English clergyman; for many years
an officer in the English army; then

took holy orders in the Church of England.

Dallas, Eneas Sweetland. *The Editor of " Once a Week."* A Scottish journalist; b. in the West Indies; passed his life chiefly in London; was for a time on the staff of the London "Times"; d., comparatively young, in London.

Dallas, Rev. Marmaduke. *Rev. M–rm–d–ke D–ll–s.* An Irish clergyman.

Dallas, Mary Kyle. *Miss Charity Grinder.* An American writer of the day.

Dallaway, Harriet. *H. D.* An English artist. — See "Dallaway, Rev. James, B.M., Prebendary of Ferring."

Dallaway, Rev. James, M.A., F.S.A., 1763–1834. *J. D.; E. M. S.* An English clergyman; b. in Bristol; Vicar of Letherhead, Surrey, 1801–34, and of Slynfold, Sussex, and Prebendary of Ferring; Secretary to the Earl Marshal, 1797–1834; d. at Letherhead.

Dallinger, J. *An Englishman.* An English economist.

D'Almaine, Thomas, & Co. *An Eminent Tuner.* English music publishers, of London.

D'Almeïda, Anna. *Anna D'A.* An English traveller.

Dalrymple, ——. *Modestus.* A Scottish advocate; a political writer.

Dalrymple, Alexander, 1737–1808. *Aretophilos; A Christian Believer; An Old Man.* An eminent Scottish hydrographer; b. at Hailes, Haddingtonshire; Hydrographer to the Admiralty, 1795–1808; d. in London.

Dalrymple, Sir David, Lord Hailes, 1726–1792. *Marcus Minucius Felix; Lactantius; John Smith, Late Fellow of Queen's College.* An eminent Scottish lawyer, antiquary, and historian; b. in Edinburgh; one of the Lords Justiciary of Scotland, 1776–92; d. at New Hailes.

Dalrymple, Gilbert, D.D. *A Christian.* An English clergyman of the first part of the 18th century.

Dalrymple, John, 1st Earl of Stair, 1619–95. *A Person of Honour.* A Scottish Lord of Session; President Judge of the Court of Session; Lord Advocate and Secretary of State.

Dalsheimer, Mrs. Alice. *Salvia Dale.* An American "Southland" writer; b. in New Orleans. She was in 1870 *et seq.* a teacher in her native city.

Dalton, Rev. Charles Browne. *C. B. D.* An English clergyman; Wadham Coll., Oxford, 1833; Prebendary of Neasden in St. Paul's Cathedral, 1845–83 *et seq.*

Dalton, Cornelius Neale. *A Cambridge Graduate.* An English poet, of Trin. Coll., Cambridge.

Dalton, James Forbes, Esq., 1785–1862. *A Septuagenarian.* An English man of letters; b. at Great Stanmore, Middlesex; passed several years on the Continent; on his return settled near London, and was well known in the literary circles of that time; d. at High Cross, Tottenham, near London.

Dalton, Rev. John Neale, Jun., M.A. *J. N. D.* An English clergyman; Clare Coll., Cambridge, 1863; Chaplain R.N., 1879–83 *et seq.,* H.M.S. "Bacchante."

Dalton, Rev. William, M.A. *W.D.* An English clergyman; Trin. Coll., Dublin, 1823; Vicar of St. Paul, Wolverhampton. 1856–63; Vicar of St. Philip, Penn., 1859–74 *et seq.;* Prebendary in Lichfield Cathedral, 1856–74 *et seq.*

Daly, Robert. *A Protestant.* An eminent clergyman of the Church of England; Bishop of Cashel.

Dalziel, Hugh. *Corsincon.* An English writer of to-day.

Dana, Daniel, Jr., 1815–. *An Old Student.* An American publisher and bibliographer, of New York City; b. in Newburyport, Mass.

Dana, Richard Henry, Jr., LL.D., 1815–82. *R. H. D., Jr.* An eminent American lawyer; b. in Cambridge, Mass.; Harv. Univ., 1837, and Harv. Law School, 1839, and admitted to the bar, 1840, and held the highest position among his brother lawyers; d. in Rome, Italy.

Dance, James, –1774. *James Love.* An English actor and dramatic author; b. in London; under the name of Love he appeared in several strolling companies of actors; afterwards performed at Dublin and Edinburgh, and at the latter place resided some time as manager; d. in London.

Danforth, Joshua Noble, D.D., 1792–1861. *A Pastor.* An American Presbyt. clergyman; b. in Pittsfield, Mass.; graduated at Williams Coll., 1818; was for some years agent of the American Col. Society; d. at Newcastle, Del.

Dani, G. *G. D.* An English writer of the day.

Danican, François André, 1727–95. *A. D. Philidor.* A French composer and famous chess-player. In 1777 he visited London, and beat everybody at the game.

Daniel, George, about 1790–1864. *D—— G.; D. G.; Democritus; P——*

P——, *Poet Laureate* [*i.e.*, *Peter Pindar*]. An English poet and antiquary, of London. His library was one of the most remarkable private collections in the kingdom, and after his death was sold by Sotheby, Wilkinson and Hodge, of London. For an account of the sale, etc., see "Gent. Mag.," Oct., 1864, pp. 450 *seq.*

Daniel, Henry John, 1818–. *A Cornubian.* An English poet; b. in Lostwithiel.

Daniel, John M., –1865. *A Virginian.* An American journalist, of Richmond, Va.; Minister to Sardinia, 1854–58; afterwards editor of the Richmond "Examiner." The Life of "Stonewall" Jackson, published in his name, was written by John Esten Cooke. He d. in Richmond.

Daniel, Robert Mackenzie, 1814–47. *The Scottish Boz.* An eminent Scottish novelist; b. in Inverness-shire; removed to London in 1836, and devoted himself to literary work; and in 1844 again removed to Jersey, and became editor of the "Jersey Herald"; d. in London.

Daniell, Charles Addison. *D. C. Addison.* An American poet of the day.

Daniell, Miss G. F. S. *Her Daughter.* An English writer of the day; daughter of Mrs. Daniell, the soldiers' philanthropist, at Aldershot.

Daniell, Rev. John Mortlock. *Amor Veritatis.* An English minister, of Ramsgate.

Dannenberg, Georg, 1823–. *Golo Raimund.* A popular German novelist; b. at Magdeberg; studied law at Halle and Bonn; did not practise, but devoted himself to authorship; he lives chiefly at Reisen.

Dansey, Rev. William, M.A., M.B. *A Graduate of Medicine.* An English clergyman; Rector and Vicar of Donhead St. Andrew, Wilts., 1820–56.

Darby, A. *A. D.* An English writer, of the 18th century.

Darby, John. *A Physician.* An American writer of the day. [John Darby is a *pseudonym* for James E. Garretson, which see.]

Darby, John Nelson, 1800–. *J. N. D.; A Spectator.* An English clergyman and miscellaneous writer; b. in Westminster; Trin. Coll., Dublin, 1819, and then called to the bar; he afterwards took orders, but exercised his ministry, that of the so-called Plymouth Brethren, all over Great Britain and Ireland, many of the Continental Countries, and later in America and the West Indies; in

1875 *et seq.*, Mr. Darby visited the United States.

Darby, William H. *W. H. Dy.* An English religious writer.

Dargan, Miss Clara V. *Claudia; Esther Chesney.* An American "Southland" writer; b. at Winnsboro', S.C.; resided at Columbia, S.C., 1852–65; in 1871 was a teacher in Yorkville, S.C.

Darkison, ——. *Mungo, the Minstrel.* An English writer of to-day.

Darley, George, 1785–1849. *G. D.* An Irish poet and mathematician; b. in Dublin; Trin. Coll., 1811; went to London in 1825, and became attached to the "Literary Gazette" and the "Athenæum"; d. in London.

Darling, Charles John. ******s ***n ******g, *Esq.; An Habitual Criminal.* An English lawyer.

Darling, Rev. William Stewart. *A Presbyter of the Diocese of Toronto.* A Canadian clergyman of the Church of England; assistant minister of the Church of Holy Trinity, Toronto; contributed much prose and poetry to Canadian journals and periodicals.

D'Arusmont, Madame **Frances (Wright)**, 1795–1852. *An Englishwoman; A Woman.* A Scottish reformer; b. in Dundee; resided many years in the United States, and d. at Cincinnati.

Darwin, Erasmus, M.D., 1731–1802. *D——; Erasmus D——n.* An English poet and physician; grandfather of Charles Robert Darwin; b. at Elston, near Newark, Notts.; educ. at Cambridge and Edinburgh; first settled in Nottingham as a physician; afterwards went to Lichfield. The latter part of his life he resided at Radbourne and Darby, and finally at a house called "The Priory," about five miles from Darby, and d. there.

Dashwood, Rev. George Henry. *G. H. D.* An English clergyman; Vicar of Stowe-Bardolph *w.* Wimbotsham, Norfolk.

D'Aubigné, Jean Henri Merle, D.D., D.C.L., 1794–1872. *A Swiss Minister.* A Swiss Church historian and theologian; b. at Geneva, and educ. in that city and in Berlin; Prof. of Church History at Geneva, 1831–72, and d. there.

Daudet, Alphonse, 1840–. *Baptistet; Jean Froissart; Marie Gaston.* A French novelist, poet, journalist, and dramatist, of Paris; b. at Nismes; removed to Paris in 1857.

Daumer, Georg Friedrich, 1800–75. *Eusebius Emmeran.* A German poet and philosopher; b. at Nuremburg. He was

Professor in his native city a few years between 1822 and 1830. D. at Würzburg.

Daunt, William Joseph O'Neill, 1807-. *An Ex-M.P.* An Irish writer; eldest son of Joseph Daunt, of Kilcascan; M.P. for Mallow, 1832–33.

Daurand-Forgues, Paul Émile, 1813-. *Old Nick.* A French miscellaneous writer; b. in Paris; a contributor to the "National," and one of the editors of the "Revue des Deux Mondes."

Davenport, Mrs. E. A. *E. A. D.* An English writer for the young.

Davenport, John Marriott, F.S.A. *J. M. D.* An English writer of the day.

David, J. B., 1761–1841. *A Catholic Clergyman of Baltimore.* An American R.C. clergyman; b. near Nantes, France; came to this country in 1792, and was consecrated Bishop Coadjutor to Dr. Flaget, of Bardstown, Ky., in 1819.

David, Mme Marie (de Saffron), 1834-. *Raoul de Navery.* A French writer; b. near Ploermel (Morbihan).

Davidoff, ——. *A Russian, quondam Civis Bibliothecæ Edinensis.*

Davidson, Mrs. Harriet Miller. *H. D.* A Scottish writer for the young; wife of Henry Davidson.

Davidson, James Wood, 1829-. *Corsair.* An American educator; b. in Newberry District, S.C.; educ. at the Univ. of S.C., 1852; Prof. of Greek in Mount Zion Coll., Winnsboro', S.C., 1854–59, and has been since an instructor, except while serving in Virginia, in Lee's army.

Davidson, John. *J. D.* A Scottish law-writer, of Halltree, N.S.

Davidson, R., Esq. *An American.* An American writer.

Davidson, Miss Virginia E. *Virginia.* An American "Southland" writer; b. in Petersburg, Va. She published, during the late civil war, the "Bloody Footprints," some of the incidents of the volume having been printed in the "Southern Opinion," under the name of "Virginia."

Davidson, W. *W. D.* A Scottish writer.

Davies, Rev. Edward, 1756–1831. *A Welsh Curate.* A British clergyman; b. in Radnorshire; in 1801, he was Curate at Olveston, near Thornbury in Gloucestershire, where his essays on Celtic antiquities attracted notice; he was for some time master of the Grammar School of Chipping Sudbury, near Bristol. At the time of his death he was Chancellor of Brecon, Rector of Bishop-

ston and Llanwair Orlledyn, and Perpetual Curate of Llanbedr Painscastle; and d. at Bishopsgate, Co. Glamorgan.

Davies, Elizabeth. *His Widow.* An English editor of the day; widow of Robert Davies.

Davies, Rev. G. J. *A Wykehamist.* An English clergyman; Curate of Charlbury, Co. Oxford, in 1857.

Davies, Henry. *H. D.* An English publisher, of Cheltenham.

Davies, Rev. J. H. *J. H. D.* An English clergyman.

Davies, John, M.D. *Iater.* An English physician, of Bath.

Davies, Rev. Myles. *A Gentleman of the Inns of Court.* A Welsh clergyman; b. in Tre'r-Abbot, in Flintshire.

D'Avigdon, E. H. *Wanderer.* An English writer of the day; a nephew of the late Sir Francis Goldsmid.

Davin, Nicholas Francis Flood. *F.; Tristram Templeton.* An English lawyer of the Middle Temple, and a journalist of London. Mr. Davin, with Mr. Black and Mr. E. Yates, was the first to write "Readings by Starlight," in the "Evening Star," London, 1866.

Davis, Mrs. Caroline E. Kelly. *C. E. K.* An American writer.

Davis, Charles Augustus, 1795–1867. *Major Jack Downing; Peter Scriber.* An American merchant, of New York City, and political writer; well versed in finance and commerce, and a writer on those subjects.

Davis, James. *Savid.* An American journalist, of New York City.

Davis, James D. *Old Times.* An American journalist and miscellaneous writer, of Memphis, Tenn.

Davis, J. F. *J. F. D.* An English East Indian philologist.

Davis, Hon. John, LL.D., 1761–1847. *A Member of the Humane Society.* An eminent American jurist; b. at Plymouth, Mass.; Harv. Univ., 1781; practised law in his native town till 1795, when he removed to Boston; Judge of the U.S. District Court for Massachusetts, 1801–41.

Davis, Mrs. Mary Elizabeth (Moragne). *A Lady of South Carolina.* An American novelist; b. at Oakwood, S.C.

Davis, Matthew L., 1766–1850. *A Genevese Traveller; Marcus; The Old Boy in Specs; Philo-Cato; The Spy in Washington.* An American journalist; b. in New York City; was at first a printer by trade, but afterwards became the correspondent at Washington of the New York "Courier and Enquirer," and of the London "Times"; d. at Manhattanville.

Davis, Mrs. Mollie E. (Moore). *Mollie E. Moore.* An American "Southland" poet; b. on the banks of the Coosa, Texas.

Davis, Richard Bingham, 1771–99. *Martlet.* An American poet; b. in New York City; educ. at Columbia Coll., but did not graduate; was a wood-carver; editor of the "Diary," a daily gazette of New York City, writing for it during a year; then engaged in mercantile affairs; d. in New York City.

Davis, Robert S. *Trebor.* An American novelist.

Davis, Miss Rosalind. *Rosalind.* An English dramatist and composer.

Davis, Mrs. Sarah Matilda. *S. M. D.* An American biographer.

Davis, Thomas, 1814–45. *The Celt.* An Irish poet and political writer, of Ireland; the leader of "Young Ireland."

Davis, Wendell, A.M., 1776–1830. *A Member of the Humane Society.* An American; b. in Plymouth, Mass.; Harv. Univ., 1796; admitted to the bar, 1799, and settled in Sandwich, Mass.

Davis, William Augustus, M.D. *W. A. D.* An American physician; Harv. Univ., 1837; Med. School, 1840; in 1875 resided in Virginia.

Davison, Rev. Edward. *E. D.* An English clergyman; Univ. Coll., Oxford, 1816; Rector of Harlington, Middlesex, 1822–60 *et seq.*, and Incumbent of St. Nicholas, Durham, 1825–60 *et seq.*

Davy, Christopher. *An Architect.* An English architect.

Davy, David Elisha, Esq., 1769–1851. *D. A. Y.* An English antiquary; b. at Rumburgh, in Suffolk; educ. at Yoxford and Pembr. Hall, Cambridge; B.A., 1790; resided at Yoxford for many years; d. at Ufford, near Woodbridge, Suffolk.

Davy, Sir Humphry, Bart., 1778–1829. *An Angler.* An English chemist; b. at Penzance, Cornwall; in 1795 he was apprenticed to a surgeon and apothecary of his native town; in 1798 was placed in charge of the Pneumatic Institution at Bristol; and in 1799 began to publish his essays and papers; Professor at the Royal Institution, London, 1801–14; and its Vice-President from 1814; President of the Royal Academy, 1820–27; travelled on the Continent for his health, and d. at Geneva.

Davy, John, M.D., 1790–1868. *J. D.* An English physician; brother of Sir H. Davy; b. at Penzance; studied med-

icine at Edinburgh; M.D., 1814; entered the army as a surgeon, and rose to be inspector-general of army hospitals; d. at Lesketh How, near Ambleside.

Dawes, Matthew. *M. D.; A Gentleman of the Inner Temple.* An English lawyer, of London.

Dawes, Rufus, 1803–59. *Samuel Smythe.* An American poet and journalist; b. in Boston; studied at Harv. Univ., but was refused his degree; studied law, but never practised; passed the later years of his life as a government clerk at Washington, and d. in that city.

Dawes, Thomas, 1757–1825. *A Young Gentleman; Adjutant Trowell.* An American poet; b. in Boston; Harv. Univ., 1777; jurist-judge of the Municipal Court of Boston; of the Probate Court and of the Supreme Court of Massachusetts.

Dawes, William. *Elijer Goff.* An English architect and humorist, of Manchester.

Dawson, ——. *A Friend of his Age.* An English writer.

Dawson, ——. *Messrs. W*****cks and D—n.* An Irish banker, of Dublin.

Dawson, A. *A. D.; An Old Lady.* An English writer and music teacher, of London.

Dawson, Rev. Benjamin, LL.D., 1729–1814. *Anonymous; A Clergyman of the Church of England.* An English clergyman; Rector of Burgh, Suffolk, where he died.

Dawson, Charles Carroll, 1833–. *C. C. D.* An American genealogist; b. at Nelson, N.Y.; in 1857 removed to Des Moines, Ia., and engaged in business; graduated in the law department of the Univ. of Michigan, 1866; in 1878 became connected with the firm of J. C. Ayer & Co., of Lowell, Mass.

Dawson, Edward Walter, 1840–. *Benedict.* An American lawyer; b. in New Haven, Conn.; graduated at the Washington Institute at Orange, Conn., and studied law; he is prominently connected with the Order of the Knights of Pythias, in New England, and with the Odd Fellows and Freemasons; in 1871–72 travelled in Europe.

Dawson, Henry Barton, 1821–. *H. B. D.* An English-American historian and journalist; b. in Gosberton, Lincolnshire; came to the United States with his parents in 1834; in 1881 resident in New York City.

Dawson, John William, LL.D., 1820–. *J. W. D.* A British colonial geologist and naturalist; b. at Pictou,

Nova Scotia; studied in the Univ. of Edinburgh; and returning home, devoted himself to the study of the natural history and geology of Nova Scotia and New Brunswick; he has been Superintendent of Education for Nova Scotia, 1850–75 *et seq.*; and Principal of' McGill Univ. at Montreal from 1855; and is now (1875) its Vice-Chancellor.

Day, Charles William. *Agogos.* An English art and miscellaneous writer.

Day, Richard E. *Redwin.* An American journalist, of Syracuse, N.Y.

Day, Samuel Phillips. *An Englishman.* An English author and newspaper correspondent; correspondent in Canada for the "Herald" in 1863–64, and for the "Morning Post," London, in 1865.

Day, Thomas, Esq., 1748–89. *Marius.* An English poet, philanthropist, and political writer; b. in London; educ. at the Charterhouse; d. at Anningsley.

Day, W. *W. D.* An English editor and compiler.

Dayman, John, 1778–1859. *A Forreyner.* An English economist, of Padston; b. at Maer in Poughill; undersheriff of Cornwall, 1804; d. at Brighton.

Deacon, William Frederick, 1799–1845. *W. G.; William Gifford; A Bashful Irishman; The Editor of a Quarterly Review; A Village Apothecary.* An English novelist and journalist; b. and d. in London.

Dean, John. *J. D—n.* An English writer of Scarborough.

Dean, Joseph H. *London W.* An American journalist; studied in the Harvard Law School; admitted to the Boston Bar.

Deane, Mrs. A. *A. D.* An English traveller in the East.

Deane, Charles, LL.D., 1813–. *One who knew him.* An American literary antiquary; b. at Biddeford, Me.; was for many years a merchant in Boston; now an author and editor of numerous historical papers; in 1883 *et seq.* a resident of Cambridge, Mass.

Deane, Rev. William John, M.A. *W. J. D.* An English clergyman; Oriel Coll., Oxford, 1847; Rector of Ashen, Clare, Suffolk, 1853–83 *et seq.*

Deans, Charles W, 1831–73. *C. W. D.* A prominent educator, of Pennsylvania; one of promoters of Soldiers' Orphan Schools.

Dearborn, Benjamin, 1755–1838. *A Friend of Industry.* An American teacher; b. in Portsmouth, N.H.; served his time as a printer with Daniel

Fowle; taught an academy for girls at Portsmouth, and afterwards at Boston, where he died.

De Beck, Col. **William L.** *An Old Citizen.* An American writer.

De Bow, James Dunwoody Brown-son, 1820–67. *J. D.; A Citizen.* An American journalist and statistican; b. at Charleston, S.C.; Charleston Coll., 1843; called to the bar, 1844; and became the same year chief editor of the "Southern Quarterly Review"; in 1845 he removed to New Orleans, and established "De Bow's Commercial Review"; from 1855 he devoted himself to literary pursuits.

Decazes, Baronne Elisa (de Mirbel). *Eliza de Mirbel.*

Deck, P. *A Layman of the County of Suffolk.* An English writer; postmaster at Bury.

Decker, Sir **Matthew,** –1749. *A Well-Wisher to the Good People of Great Britain.* An English merchant; settled in London in 1702; was made a baronet in 1716; and an M.P. in 1719.

De Coetlogon, Rev. **Charles Edward,** –1820. *Parrestiastes.* An eminent Calvinistic divine; Rector of Godstone and a Magistrate for the Co. of Surrey; educ. at Christ's Hospital, and at Pembroke Hall, Cambridge.; B.A., 1770. Being appointed assistant chaplain to the celebrated Martyn Madan at the Lock Hospital, he soon became eminent as a popular preacher; and published a large number of sermons, 1773–1809.

De Cordova, Raphael J. *De Cordova.* An American writer; a broker of New York City.

De Costa, Benjamin Franklin, D.D. *; ***; D.; B. F. D.; Bunker Hill; Private.* An American Epis. clergyman; Rector of the Church of St. John the Evangelist, of New York.

De Courcy, Rev. **Richard,** 1743–1803. *R. D.; The Good Vicar.* An Irish clergyman and hymn-writer; educ. at Trin. Coll., Dublin; Vicar of S. Alkmond's, Shrewsbury, 1774–1803.

Decremps, Henri, 1746–1826. *Jérôme Sharpe.* A French writer.

Deems, Charles Force, D.D., 1820–. *C. F. D.* An eminent Methodist minister; b. in Baltimore, Md., and educ. at Dickinson Coll. He served his ministry at the South for several years; has been Prof. in the Univ. of North Carolina and in Randolph Macon Coll., and Pres. of the Greensboro' and Centenary Colleges, and in 1873 was the successful pastor of the Church of the Strangers, New York City.

Deering, Mrs. T. W. *Miss Oakey.* An American writer of to-day; contributor to "Harper's Monthly," December, 1881.

De Fivas, Sidney, 1846–. *Augustus Glover.* A Scottish actor; b. in Edinburgh; first appearance on the London stage in 1864.

Defoe, Daniel, 1661–1731. *D. F.; Daniel, the Prophet; A British Officer in the Service of the Czar; Capt. George Carleton; Captain Tom; A Citizen who continued all the while in London; Robinson Crusoe; Heliostropolis, etc.; A Jobber; A Lover of Old England; The Man in the Moon; A Member of the H. of C.; A Ministering Friend; Monsr. Mesnager; Andrew Moreton, Esq.; One of the People called Quakers; A Private Gentleman; A Scots Gentleman in the Swedish Service; A Shropshire Gentleman; William Smithies, Junior Rector of St. Michael, Mill End, Colchester; A Well-wisher to the Peace of Britain.* An English writer; intended for a Presbyt. minister, but became successively a soldier, a hosier, a tile-maker, a woolen-merchant, and a miscellaneous writer; b. and d. in London.

De Fontaine, Felix G. *Personne.* An American journalist, of New York City.

De Forest, T. R. *Those who Know.* An American writer, of New York City.

De Guines, Louis Alexandre Gosset. *M. Andre Gill.* A French caricaturist.

Dehon, Theodore, D.D., 1776–1817. *Japheth.* An eminent American P.E. clergyman; b. in Boston, Mass.; Harv. Univ., 1795; Rector of Trinity Church, Newport, R.I., 1798–1809; and of St. Michael's Church, Charleston, S.C., 1809–17; in 1812 he was consecrated Bishop of South Carolina.

De Kay, Charles, 1848–. *Louis Barnaval.* An American poet and novelist; b. in Washington, D.C.; Yale Coll., 1868.

De Kay, James E., 1792–1851. *An American.* An American physician and naturalist; b. in New York City; d. at Oyster Bay, Long Island, N.Y.

Dekker, Eduard Douwes, 1820–. *Multatuli.* A Dutch author; b. at Amsterdam; went to Java when he was 20 years old, and was commissioner of taxes for 17 years, when he was deprived of his office on account of his opposition to the abuses of the Colonial administration. Returned to Holland, he turned

his attention henceforth to authorship.

De la Cour, James, 1709–81. *J*** D***, T.C., D.* An Irish poet; b. at Killowen, near Blarney, Co. Cork; educ. at Trin. Coll., Dublin; and entered into orders, but did no credit to his profession. His habits were irregular, and he associated with dissipated company, till at length he obtained the name of the "Mad Poet."

De Laet, Jean Jacques, 1815–. *Johan Alfried; Félix Bogaerts.* A Belgian writer; b. at Antwerp; devoted himself to literature, and engaged in journalism in Brussels and Antwerp.

De La Motte, Col. **Philip,** –1805. *An Antiquary.* An English officer; Lieut.-Col. of the 21st Regt. of Light Dragoons; d. at Batsford, Co. Gloucester.

Delano, Alonzo. *Old Block.* An American dramatist.

Delany, Patrick, D.D., 1686(?)–1768. *Phileleutherus Dubliniensis.* An eminent Irish clergyman; Dean of Down, and friend of Dean Swift.

De La Ramée, Louisa, 1840–. *Ouida.* An English novelist; b. at Bury St. Edmunds, of French extraction on the father's side. At an early age she came with her family to reside in London, and soon began, under the pen-name of "Ouida" (a child's mispronunciation of Louisa), to write for periodicals. In 1879 resided near Florence, Italy.

De La Rocca, Countess **Irene.** *Cordula; Camille Henry.* An Italian writer, of Paris; b. in Castiglione; since 1863 has devoted herself to the education of her children.

De Larra, Mariano José, 1809–. *Figaro.* A Spanish writer, of Madrid.

Delavan, James. *One who has been there.* An American writer.

De La Touche, Janet. *Isaline.* An English novelist.

Delaune, Thomas. *T. D.* An English Nonconformist of the 17th and 18th centuries.

De La Warr, George John, 5th Earl of, 1791–1869. *Euryalus.* An English nobleman; an early friend of Lord Byron.

Delepierre, Joseph Octave, 1804–79. *M. Aude; Un grave homme.* A Belgian historian and antiquary; b. at Bruges; studied law at the Univ. of Ghent, and practised as an advocate at Brussels. After the revolution of September he entered the diplomatic service, and in 1849 was appointed Secretary of the Legation and Consul General for Belgium at Brussels. D. at the Upper Hamilton Terrace, London.

Delf, Mrs. **H. F.** *H. F. D.* An English writer.

Delf, Thomas, 1812–66. *Charles Martel.* An English author, publisher, and bookseller; for some years employed in New York City, but the greater part of his life in London, where he was born and died.

Delille, John C. *Longchamps.* An American correspondent in Paris.

Delius, Nicholaus, 1813–. *Dr. D.* A German scholar and Shakespearian; b. at Bremen; Professor at Bonn from 1855.

Delmar, Alexander, 1836–. *Emile Walter; Kwang Chang Ling.* An American economist and journalist, of Spanish descent; b. in New York City; editor of the "Social Science Review," 1864–66; organized the United States Bureau of Statistics, 1866, and was director, 1867–68.

Delmotte, Henri Florent, 1779–1836. *Tridace Nafé Théobróme de Kaout 'l' Chouk.* A Belgian miscellaneous writer; member of the Academy of Brussels.

De Lolme, John Louis, 1745–1807. *One who is not a Doctor of the Sorbonne.* A Swiss lawyer, who resided for some years in England; d. in Switzerland.

De Milly, Mrs. **Augusta.** *Ethel Dean.* An American writer; b. in New York City; has passed the greater part of her life in Florida; in 1868 she resided in Jacksonville, Fla.

Demme, Herman Christoph Gottfried, 1760–1822. *Karl Stille.* A German poet and theologian; b. at Mülhausen; became the chief director of the ecclesiastical and educational department of the Duchy of Altenburg; and wrote tales, novels, and religious songs; d. at Altenburg.

Demolière, Hippolyte Jules, 1802–78. *Moléri.* A popular French writer; author of dramas, romances, guide-books, and botanical works; d. in Paris.

De Morgan, S. *C. D.* An English spiritualist.

Denham, Edward. *E. D.; Delta; Epsilon; A Student of History.* An American author and journalist, of New Bedford, Mass.

Denham, Michael Aislabie, –1859. *M. A. D.; Archœus; Autolycus.* An English literary antiquary; b. near Bowes, in Yorkshire; engaged in business at Hull during the early part of his life, but ultimately settled at Piersebridge, on the Tees; d. at Piersebridge.

Denison, Charles Wheeler, 1809–. *An Ex-Consul; Major Penniman.* An American poet and journalist; b. in New London, Conn.; was for a time an editor in London, and also United States Consul in British Guiana.

Denison, Eliza Freeman. *Christie Crust.* An American writer.

Denison, Lieut.-Col. **George T.,** Jr., LL.B., 1839–. *Junius, Jr.; A Native Canadian.* A Canadian volunteer officer; b. at Bellevue, Toronto; graduated at Trin. Coll.; and LL.B. in Toronto in 1861; served as an officer of the Volunteer Cavalry from 1854.

Denison, Mrs. **Mary (Andrews),** 1826–. *M. A. D.; Clara Vance.* An American miscellaneous writer; wife of Charles Wheeler Denison; b. in Cambridge, Mass.

Dennant, Edward. *E. D.* An English religious writer, of Ipswich.

Denne, Rev. **Samuel,** M.A., F.S.A., 1730–99. *W. D., Rusticus.* An English clergyman; b. at the Deanery in Westminster; Vicar of Darent, and of Wilmington, near Dartford, Kent; d. at Wilmington.

Dennie, Joseph, 1768–1812. *The American Addison; The Lay Preacher; Oliver Oldschool.* An eminent American journalist; b. in Boston; Harv. Univ., 1790; studied law, but never practised; in 1795 removed to Walpole, N.H., and wrote for the "Farmer's Weekly Museum"; in 1797 he went to Philadelphia; and in 1800, with Asbury Dickins, commenced the publication of the "Portfolio," and continued his connection with it till his death; d. at Philadelphia.

Dennis, Rev. **James Blatch Piggot,** B.A., F.G.S., 1816–61. *Lucius.* An English clergyman, microscopist, and ornithologist; resided at Bury St. Edmunds, Co. of Suffolk, 1849–61, and d. there.

Dennis, Jeffrey. *The Merchant Seaman's Friend.* An English writer, of London.

Dennis, John, 1657–1734. *Sir Andrew Artlove.* An English poet, critic, and political writer; b. in London; Caius Coll. and Trin. Hall, Cambridge; obtained considerable notoriety by his writings.

Dennis, Rev. **Jonas,** B.C.L., 1775–1846. *Bathoniensis.* An English clergyman; b. at Exeter; Exeter Coll., Oxford, 1800; Prebendary of Carswell, in the castle of Exeter, 1799–1846; d. at Polsloe-park, Devon.

Dennistoun, James, Esq., 1803–55.

A Conservative. A Scottish biographer and writer on art; b. in Dumbartonshire; educ. at the Coll. of Glasgow; studied law at Edinburgh, but devoted himself to the fine arts and literature.

Denny, John Thomas. *A Free Lance; Hart Leigh; Silverstar; Brent Winwood.* An English dramatist and journalist.

Dennys, Nicholas Belfield, Ph.D., F.R.G.S., etc. *N. B. D.* An English civilian; entered the civil department of the navy in 1855; student interpreter in China, 1863–65; edited the Hong Kong "China Mail," 1866–76; assistant protector of emigrants, 1877, at Singapore; J. P. for Straits Settlements, 1877; secretary, librarian, and curator of the Raffles Public Library and Museum, 1877.

Denslow, Martin Van Buren. *Maurice O'Quill.* An American biographer.

Dent, Charles. *C. D.* An English poet.

De Peyster, Arent Schuyler, 1736–1832. *An Officer.* An American loyalist; a Canadian by birth; served in various parts of North America; commanded British forces at Detroit, 1776–85; afterwards Colonel of the Volunteers of Scotland.

De Peyster, John Watts, 1821–. *Anchor; A Layman.* An American historical writer; b. in New York City; principal contributor to the "Eclaireur," a military journal, 1853–54, and its editor, 1854–58; in 1872 resident at Rose Hill, Tivoli, N.Y.

De Puy, Henry Walter, 1820–76. *An Indian Agent.* An American journalist; b. at Pompey Hill, N.Y.; studied law and came to the bar, but preferred journalism, and settled in Indianapolis; d. in New York City.

De Quincey, Thomas, 1786–1859. *An English Opium Eater; X. Y. Z.* An English essayist; b. at Greenhay, near Manchester; passed the latter part of his life at Lasswade, 12 miles from Edinburgh.

Derby, Edward Henry Smith Stanley, Earl of, 1826–. *Lord De Terrier.* An eminent English statesman; succeeded his father, the 14th Earl, in 1869; Secretary of State for Foreign Affairs, 1866–68, and again in 1874.

Derby, Elias Hasket, 1803–80. *E. H. D.; A Citizen of Boston; Massachusetts; A Railroad Director.* An American lawyer; b. in Salem, Mass.; Harv. Univ., 1824; practised his profession in Boston.

Derby, Mrs. Emily Jones. *Emily Melville.* An American actress.

Derby, George Horatio, 1824–61. *John Phœnix; John P. Squibob.* An American humorist; b. in Norfolk County, Mass.; West Point, 1846; Capt. U. S. Topog. Engineers; brevetted at Cerro Gordo; afterwards stationed in California, where he produced his "Phœnixiana"; d. in New York City.

Derby, John Barton, 1793–1867. *A Recluse.* An American lawyer and politician; b. in Salem, Mass.; Bowdoin Coll., 1811; was the father of Lieut. George Derby ("John Phœnix"); held an office in the Boston Custom House for some time; d. in Boston.

Derenzy, M. G. *A Widowed Wife.* An English lady.

Derham, William, D.D., F.R.S., 1657–1735. *W. D., M.A.* An English divine and philosopher; b. near Worcester; Canon of Windsor.

Dering, Heneage. *H. D., Ripensis.* An English clergyman; Dean of Ripon.

Derrick, Samuel, 1724–69. *Mr. Wilkes.* An Irish dramatist; Master of the Ceremonies at Bath.

Desaussure, Henry William, 1764–1839. *A Federal Republican.* An American jurist; appointed by Washington Director of the U. S. Mint; practised law in Charleston, S. C., and became Chancellor of South Carolina, 1808–37; d. at Charleston.

Deschamps, Emile, 1791–1871. *Le jeune moraliste.* A French poet, dramatist, essayist, and novelist; b. at Bourges, and educ. at Paris, where he continued to reside; d. at Versailles.

Deschamps, Pierre Charles Ernest, 1821–. *Un Bibliophile; Poche.* A learned French bibliographer, of Paris; b. at Magny-en-Vexin (Seine et Oise); was, 1845–54, editor of the "Gazette musicale."

Desloges, L. *Rénaud.* A French libraire-éditeur at Paris.

Desnoyens, Edmond, 1814–. *De Bieville.* A French "vaudevilliste," of Paris.

Deuchar, Alexander. *A Genealogist.* A Scottish writer.

De Vere, Albert. *Winning Hazard.* An English writer on billiards.

Devereux, Penelope. *Stella.*

Devlin, J. Dacres. *Alfred Kent.* An English poet and local historian; a shoemaker.

Devonshire, Charles, 1783–1851. *A Mechanic.* An English dramatist; b. in

Falmouth, England, and d. in Indiana, U.S.A.

Devonshire, William Cavendish, 1st Duke of, 1640–1707. *Duke of D——.* An English peer, poet, and statesman.

Dewey, Orville, D.D., 1794–1882. *D.; An English Traveller.* An American clergyman; b. in Sheffield, Mass.; Williams Coll., 1814; from 1862 a resident of Sheffield, Mass., where he died.

Dewhurst, Jane. *J. D.* An English poet.

De Wint, Mrs. C. A. *C. A. D.* An American poet.

Dexter, Franklin, LL.D., 1793–1857. *Hancock.* An American lawyer; b. at Charlestown, Mass.; Harv. Univ., 1812; admitted to the Suffolk bar, and practised in Boston with eminent success. D. at Beverly, Mass.

Dexter, John Haven, 1791–1876. *Philagathus.* An American merchant; b. in Marlboro, Mass.; was in business in Boston till 1833, when he employed his leisure in collecting facts concerning persons and places in Boston, where he died.

Dexter, Samuel, Sr., LL.D., 1761–1816. *Philotheorus; A Junior Sophister.* An American jurist and statesman; b. in Boston; Harv. Univ., 1781; admitted to the bar, 1784, and after practising a few years in several country towns, removed to Boston; d. while on a journey to Athens, N.Y.

Dibdin, Thomas, 1771–1841. *T. Merchant.* An English dramatist and song-writer, of London; d. at Pentonville.

Dibdin, Thomas Frognall, D.D., 1775–1847. *T. F. D.; Lysander; A Member of the Roxburghe Club; Mercurius Rusticus; A Pastor; Rosicrucius; Reginald Wolfe, Esq.* An English bibliographer; b. in Calcutta; educ. at Oxford; studied law, but afterwards took orders, and was rector of St. Mary's, Bryanstone-square, 1824–47.

Dick, John. *A Fellow of the Society of Antiquaries of Scotland.* A Scottish writer.

Dick, William Brisbane, 1828–. *Joshua Jedediah Jinks; Leger D. Mayne; Trumps.* An American writer and publisher, of New York City.

Dickens, Charles (Huffam), 1812–70. *Boz; Godfrey Sparks; Timothy Sparks; A Subscriber; Tibbs; The Uncommercial Traveller; Your Constant Reader; W. P.* An English novelist; b. at Landport, Hants.; was for some years a reporter

for the London press, but in 1837 was known as a popular writer.

Dickenson, ——. *Quip.* An English writer, of London, where he became very profligate, but was suddenly converted, and went out as a Wesleyan missionary to a savage tribe, by whom he was slain.

Dicker, Thomas. *The Catholic Bishop of Bantry; A Man of Business.* An English satirical writer, of Lewes.

Dickinson, Rev. Charles Albert, 1849–. *Eleven Sophomores.* An American clergyman; b. at Westminster, Vt.; Harv. Univ., 1876; Pastor of the Second Parish Church, Portland, Me., 1879.

Dickinson, Charles M. *A Village Schoolmaster.*

Dickinson, John, LL.D., 1732–1808. *D.; Anticipation; Fabius; A Gentleman in Philadelphia; A North American; A Pennsylvania Farmer.* An American statesman; b. in Maryland; studied law in Philadelphia and in London; M.C., 1776–77 and 1779–80; d. at Wilmington.

Dickinson, Rev. Moses, 1696–1778. *An Aged Minister.* An American Cong. minister; b. in Hatfield, Mass.; Yale Coll., 1717; Pastor at Norwalk, Conn., 1727–78; d. at Plymouth, Conn.

Dickinson, Mrs. T. P. *Hester A. Benedict.* An American writer.

Dickinson, W. L. *W. L. D.* An English writer of to-day.

Dickson, Miss ——. *Dolores.* An English musical writer.

Dickson, Samuel, M.D. *A London Physician; A Physician.* An English physician.

Didier, Eugène Lemoine. *Lemoine.* An American writer.

Diekenga, I. E. *Don.* An American novelist.

Digges, Leonard, 1588–1635. *L. D.* An English poet and orator; son of Thomas, and brother of Sir Dudley.

Dilg, William. *Henricus vom See.* An American poet, of Milwaukee, Wis.

Dill, J. M. *Moralisto, Poet "Lariat" of Carthage.* An American poet.

Dill, Rev. James Reid. *J. R. D.* An English religious writer.

Dillon, Sir John Joseph, Knt., –1837. *A Barrister; Hiberno-Anglus; Publicus Severus.* An English lawyer, of Lincoln's Inn, 1801; d. at Ipswich.

Dillon, John Talbot. *An English Traveller in Spain.* An English writer; Knight and Baron, etc., of the Sacred Roman Empire.

Dillon, Robert Crawford, D.D., 1795–1848. *The Chaplain to the Mayoralty.* An English clergyman; b. in the rectory-house of St. Margaret's, Lothbury; St. Edmund's Hall, Oxford, 1817; held an independent service in London, 1845–48; d. at Spitalfields.

Dingé, Antoine, 1759–1832. *Joseph Ripault Desormeaux.* A French scholar and historian.

Dingle, Edward, 1814–. *E. D—e.* An English religious writer; b. in Callington; resided there, 1832–52; and at Tavistock, 1852–79 *et seq.*

Dinnies, Mrs. Anne Peyse (Shackelford). *Moïna.* An American "Southland" poet; b. at Georgetown, S.C.; educ. at Charleston; married, at the early age of fourteen, Mr. J. C. Dinnies, of St. Louis, Mo.; and 1846–68 *et seq.* resided in New Orleans.

Dinsmoor, Robert, 1759–1836. *The Rustic Bard.* An American poet; b. at Windham, N.H.; served in the Revolutionary War; then became a farmer in his native town.

Dircks, Henry, LL.D., 1806–. *H. D.* An English engineer and miscellaneous writer; b. at Liverpool; was a consulting engineer, 1842–58; afterwards travelled extensively on the Continent.

Disney, John, D.D., 1746–1816. *Anti-Draco.* An English minister; b. at Lincoln, and educ. at Cambridge; was for some years minister of the Unit. Chapel, in Essex Street, London.

Disosway, E. *Leal.* An American writer for the young.

Disraeli, Benjamin. *Beakitorius; Runnymede.* — See Beaconsfield, Earl of.

D'Israeli, Isaac, Esq., D.C.L., 1766–1848. *I. D'I.; Euterpe; Messrs. Tag, Rag, and Bobtail.* An English man of letters; b. at Enfield, near London; devoted his life to literary pursuits, and d. at Bradenham House, Buckinghamshire.

Disturnell, John, 1801–77. *J. D.* An American printer and bookseller, of New York City; b. at Lansingburg, and d. in New York City.

Ditcher, Selina. *S. D.* An English writer.

Diver, Jenny. *Mrs. Jane Jones.* An American writer.

Dix, John. *Chirurgus; J. D., Chirurgus.* An English surgeon, of Bristol; d. in America.

Dix, John Ross. *J. D.; J. D. R.; A Cosmopolitan; A Looker-On; A Middle-Aged-Man.* An American artist and author.

Dix, William Giles, A.M. *W. G. D.* An American poet; Harv. Univ., 1845.

Dixon, Mrs. ——. *Emma Leslie.* An American author.

Dixon, Andrew. *Harry Sackett.* An American writer.

Dixon, Edward Henry, M.D. *Scalpel.* An American surgeon, of New York.

Dixon, Henry Hall. *The Druid.* An English sporting writer of to-day.

Dixon, Rev. Henry John, M.A. *A Clergyman.* An English divine; St. Mary's Hall, Oxford, 1840; Vicar of Yarnscombe, Barnstaple, 1872–80 *et seq.*

Dixon, James Henry, LL.D., 1803–76. *Stephen Jackson, Esq., of The Flatts, Malham Moor.* An English literary antiquary, of Skipton.

Dixon, Samuel H. *Dio Rivers.* An American journalist, of Texas.

Dixon, Thomas. *A Working Man.* An English laborer, of Sunderland.

Dixon, William Hepworth, 1821–79. *Onslow Yorke.* An English critic, historian, and traveller, of London; b. in Yorkshire; editor of the London "Athenæum," 1853–69.

Doane, George Washington, D.D., LL.D., 1799–1859. *The Rector and Bishop of the Diocese.* An American Epis. clergyman; b. at Trenton, N.J.; Union Coll., 1818; Bishop of New Jersey, 1832–59; d. at Burlington, N.J.

Doane, Rev. William Croswell, M.A., 1832–. *His Son.* An American clergyman; second son of Bishop G. W. Doane; is a pleasing poet; has written his father's memoir, and edited his poetical works, sermons, and miscellaneous writings; Bishop of Albany from 1869.

Dobell, Sydney Thompson, 1824–74. *Sydney Yendys.* An English poet; b. at Peckham Rye; in 1868 *et seq.*, resided on the Cotswold Hills, near Gloucester.

Dodd, George. *G. D.* An English writer.

Dodd, Rev. Philip Stanhope, M.A., 1775–1852. *A Member of the University of Cambridge.* An English clergyman; nephew of the famous Dr. William Dodd; b. in Cowley, Middlesex; Magdalen Coll., Cambridge, 1796; rector of Penshurst, Kent, 1819–52.

Dodd, William, LL.D., 1729–77. *A Gentleman of One of the Inns of Court; A Minister of the Church of England.* An English clergyman; b. at Bourne, Lincolnshire, and educ. at Clare Hall, Cambridge. He was ordained in 1753, and distinguished as one of the most eloquent preachers in London. In 1777 he forged the name of his former pupil, Lord Ches-

terfield, to a bond for £4200, and for
that crime was executed at Tyburn.

Doddridge, Philip, D.D., 1702–51.
A Minister in the Country. An eminent
English Dissenting clergyman; b. in
London; Minister at Northampton,
1829–51; d. at Lisbon.

Dodge, Miss **Mary Abigail,** 1830–.
Gail Hamilton. An American writer; b.
at Hamilton, Mass.; has been a teacher,
but is now an author and journalist;
since 1876 has lived chiefly at Washington.

Dodge, Mrs. **Mary (Mapes).**
M. M. D. An American journalist;
daughter of Prof. Mapes; editor of the
"Saint Nicholas"; earlier name, Mary
E. Dodge.

Dodge, Nathaniel Shatswell, 1810–
74. *John Carver, Esq.* An American
educator; b. in Haverhill, Mass.; studied at Dartmouth Coll., but did not
graduate; and spent one year (1833–
34) at the Andover Theol. Sem.; was
afterwards a teacher at Pittsfield, Mass.;
in London, England, 1851–61; quartermaster in the late war, 1862–66; d. in
Boston.

Dodge, Ossian E. *Ivan Ort.* An
American musician; in 1870 Secretary
of the St. Paul (Minn.) Chamber of
Commerce.

Dodgson, Rev. **Charles Lutwidge,**
M.A. *Lewis Carroll.* An English clergyman and miscellaneous writer: Christ
Church Coll., Oxford, 1854; Mathematical Lecturer of his college.

Dodington, George Bubb, Lord Melcombe, 1691–1762. *B**b L**n.* An English statesman.

Dodsley, Robert, 1703–64. *An Ancient Brahmin; A Footman; Nathan Ben
Saddi; Belshazzar Kapha, the Jew.* An
English author and bookseller, of London; b. in Mansfield, Notts.; he purchased of Johnson, in 1738, "London"
(Johnson's first original composition),
for ten guineas, and in 1749 gave him
fifteen guineas for "The Vanity of
Human Wishes."

Dodson, Michael, M.A., 1732–99. *A
Layman.* An English lawyer; b. at
Marlborough, in Wiltshire; practised
many years in London, where he died.

Dodwell, Henry, D.D., 1641–1711.
*A Very Learned Man of the Church of
England.* An Irish clergyman; b. in
Dublin; and educ. at Trin. Coll., in that
city; in 1674 he removed to London;
and in 1788 was chosen Camden Professor at Oxford; but lost his place in
1691, because he would not take the

oaths of allegiance to William and
Mary.

Dodwell, Rev. **William,** 1709–85.
A Country Clergyman. An English
clergyman; b. at Shottesbrooke, in
Berkshire; Archdeacon of Berks.

Doe, Charles Henry, 1838–. *Samuel
Blotter.* An American journalist, of
Worcester, Mass.

**Döllinger, Johann Joseph Ignaz
von,** 1799–. *Janus.* A German theologian; b. at Bamberg, in Bavaria; is
a leader of the "Old Catholics"; Rector of the Univ. of Munich from 1871.

Doherty, Hugh. *H. D., Esq.* An
English dramatist; late of the 23d Light
Dragoons.

Doherty, John. *Thunderbolt.* An
English highwayman.

Doherty, Robert Remington. *Remington Yonge.* An English miscellaneous
writer.

Dole, Nathan Haskell, 1852–. *N.
H. D.; The Cerberus.* An American
journalist; b. in Chelsea, Mass.; Harv.
Univ., 1874; is now (1885) Art, Dramatic, and Literary editor of the "Philadelphia Press."

Domett, Alfred, about 1815–. *Waring.* An English poet, of a Dorsetshire
family; studied at Cambridge; called to
the bar, 1841, but never practised; in
1880 was still living in London.

Domett, Henry W. *Delta.* An
American journalist.

Domville, Sir **William,** 2d Bart., 1774–
1860. *A Layman.* An English civilian;
b. in London, and succeeded his father
in 1833; Lord Mayor of London, 1813–
14; d. at Southfield-lodge, Eastbourne.

Donald, George, 1801–52. *The Glasgow Unfortunate.* A Scottish cotton-spinner, who gained some celebrity as a
poet; lived and d. at Glasgow.

Donaldson, J. *A Sergeant of the **
Regiment of Infantry.* A British soldier.

Donaldson, John William, D.D.,
1812–61. *J. W. D.; Phileleutheros Anglicanus.* An English biblical critic and
philologist; b. in London; educ. at the
London Univ.; Trin. Coll., Cambridge,
1834; master of King Edward's School
at Bury St. Edmunds, 1841–52; d. in
London.

Donaldson, Joseph, 179–1830. *A
Soldier.* A Scottish writer; b. in Glasgow; went to Paris in 1830; took an
active part in the Revolution of July;
and died of disease and fatigue.

Donaldson, William. *Somebody.*
An English writer.

Dondey, Auguste Marie (called

"Theophile" Dondey). *Philotee O'Neddy.* A French poet, of Paris.

Dondey-Dupré, Theophile, fils. *Vetreuil O'Neddy.* A French writer.

Donnelly, Thomas F. *Bookworm; Eugene Pomeroy.* An American journalist and publisher, of New York City.

Doris, Charles. *Le Baron B***; One who has never quitted him for 15 years.* A French friend of Napoleon.

Dorman, William H. *W. H. D.* An English writer.

Dormer, John. *Philopones.* An English writer, of the Society of Jesus.

Dorr, Benjamin, D.D., 1796–1869. *B. D.* An American clergyman; b. in Salisbury, Mass.; Dart. Coll., 1817; Rector of Old Christ Church, Philadelphia, 1837–69; d. at Germantown, Penn.

Dorr, David F. *A Quadroon.* An American colored man.

Dorr, Mrs. **Julia Caroline (Ripley),** 1825–. *Caroline Thomas.* An American poet and prose writer; b. at Charleston, S.C.; in 1847 married Seneca M. Dorr, then of New York, but for the last 20 years a resident of Vermont. In 1880 the family resided at "The Maples," near the city of Rutland.

Dorr, Thomas Wilson, A.M., 1805–54. *Aristides.* An American politician; b. in Providence, R.I.; Harv. Univ., 1823; became a lawyer in his native city, 1827; was a leader of the Suffrage Party of Rhode Island in 1841; d. in Providence.

Dorset, Charles Sackville, Duke of, 1711–69. *D. of D——.* An English peer; author of a number of prose and poetical compositions.

Dorsey, Mrs. **Sarah Anne (Ellis),** 1829–79. *Filia Ecclesiæ.* An American "Southland" writer; b. on her father's plantation, just below Natchez; in 1853 married Samuel W. Dorsey, of Tensas Parish, La.; from 1875 resided at Beauvoir, on the Gulf Shore, and at her death left her estate to Jefferson Davis.

Douay, Edmond. *E. D.* A French editor.

Doubleday, Thomas, 1790–1870. *A North Country Angler.* An English poet and miscellaneous writer, of Newcastle; the associate editor of a little volume of verse published in 1818; afterwards rose to eminence as a writer on political, social, and financial subjects.

Douce, Francis, F.A.S., 1762–1834. *The Porson of Old English and French Literature; Prospero.* An eminent English literary antiquary, of London; for a time keeper of the Mss. in the British Museum; d. in London.

Doudney, Rev. **David Alfred.** *Alfred; Old Jonathan.* An English clergyman; P.C. of St. Luke, Bedminster, Bristol, 1859–83 et seq.; editor of the "Gospel Magazine" and "Old Jonathan," both monthly.

Doughty, G. *G. D.* An old English writer.

Douglas, Lieut. ——. *An Officer.* An English translator.

Douglas, A. Livien, and Two Others. *X, Y, Z, Club.* — See "Saxe, John Godfrey," and "Pettes, George W."

Douglas, D. *A Gentleman of Lincoln's Inn.* An English lawyer.

Douglas, Rev. **James John,** B.D. *J. J. B.* A Scottish clergyman; incumbent of St. Mary, Kirriemuir, Dio. St. Andrews, 1851–83 et seq.

Douglas, John, D.D., 1721–1807. *Leonard Rae; An Honest Man.* A Scottish clergyman; b. at Pittaween, Fifeshire; B.A., Oxford, 1741; Bishop of Salisbury, 1791–1807, where he died.

Douglas, Rev. **Niel.** *Britannicus.* A Scottish minister at Cupar, near Fife.

Douglas, Mrs. **R.** *A Lady.* An American writer.

Douglas, Robert. 1820–44. *Sholto; A Medical Student.* A Scottish surgeon, in the Royal Navy; b. in Glasgow; d. on board the coasting packet, H. M. Steamer "Albion."

Douglass, Frederick, 1817–. *Bailey.* An American orator and journalist; b. at Tuckahoe, Maryland; after many years of slavery, he escaped to the North; Marshal of the District of Columbia from 1877.

Douglass, William, –1752. *W. D.; William Nadir, S.X.Q.; Sawney.* An American physician; b. in Scotland; settled in Boston about the year 1716; was opposed to inoculation, and the public measures of the colonial government; d. in Boston.

Dove, John. *Philanthropos.* An English Friend; a tailor of London.

Dover, Thomas. *A Gentleman of Trinity College, Cambridge.* An early English writer.

Dover, William. *A Well-Wisher to all Mankind.* An English Friend, of London.

Dow, Lorenzo, 1777–1834. *Cosmopolite; Lorenzo.* An eccentric American Meth. preacher; b. at Coventry, Conn.; d. at Georgetown, D.C.

Dowdall, John. *John at Stiles.* An English Shakespearian.

Dowling, J. L. *J. L. D.* An English writer of to-day.

Downer, Silas, A.M., –1785. *A Son of Liberty.* An American patriot; Harv. Univ., 1747.

Downey, John, 1770–1827. *Simon the Wagoner.* An American educator; b. at Germantown, Penn.; in 1795 opened a Latin and grammar school at Harrisburg, Penn.; and afterwards held important civil offices in that city, and d. there.

Downing, Mrs. **Fanny (Murdaugh).** *Viola.* An American "Southland" writer; b. at Portsmouth, Va.; in 1851, married Charles W. Downing, Esq., of Florida; in 1869 she resided in Charlotte, N.C.

Downing, Frank L. *The Editor of "Bell's Life in London."*

Downs, Major ——. *Marcus Spermaceti, the Elder.* An English compiler; d. on board the Bewick packet, on his passage to London.

Dowson, Emerson. *E. D.* An English writer.

Dowson, Susanna. *S****** D*****.* An English poet.

Dowty, A. A. *Young and Happy Husband; Philander Smiff, O. P. Q.* An English journalist, in the London "Figaro."

Doyle, Hannah. *H. D.* An English Friend, of Crimplesham, Norfolk.

Doyle, Jefferson E. P., 1837–. *Major Jep Joslyn; Modoc; Vidette.* An American journalist, of New York City and of Cincinnati.

Doyle, J. Dixie. *Dixie.* An American journalist, of Washington, D.C.

Doyle, Rt. Rev. **James Warren,** D.D., 1786–1834. *J. K. L.; An Irish Catholic.* An Irish R. C. prelate; b. near New Ross, Co. Wexford; educ. in Portugal; Bishop of Kildare and Leighlin, 1819–34; d. in Carlow.

Doyle, John, 1797–1868. *HB.* An Irish caricaturist; b. in Dublin; his works from 1829 to 1840 aroused a degree of interest in England, which more than approached the proportions of a *furore;* d. at his residence in Clifton Gardens.

Doyle, Richard, 1826–. *Dick Kitcat.* An English artist; son of the preceding; b. in London; first attracted attention by his designs for "Punch"; but in 1850 he severed his connection with that journal on account of its incessant attacks on the Roman Catholics.

Doyle, Thomas, about 1799–1879.

Father Thomas. An eminent R. C. priest, of London.

D'Oyly, Sir **Charles,** 7th Bart., 1781–1845. *A Civilian, an Officer in the Bengal Establishment.* An English gentleman, of Shottisham; early in life entered the East India Service, and remained in India for 40 years; d. at Adenza, near Leghorn.

D'Oyly, Thomas. *Viator.* An English poet and prose writer.

Drake, Daniel, M.D., 1785–1852. *The People's Friend.* An American physician; b. in Plainfield, N.J.; a resident of Cincinnati, and d. there.

Drake, Joseph Rodman, and Another, 1795–1830. *Croaker & Co.* An American poet; b. in New York City; studied at Columbia Coll., but did not graduate; resided and d. in his native city.

Drake, Samuel Adams, 1833–85. *S. A. D.* An American journalist; brother of Samuel Gardner Drake; b. in Boston; was a newspaper editor and correspondent at the West from 1858; returned to Massachusetts in 1871; resided at Melrose.

Drake, Samuel Gardner, 1798–1875. *S. G. D.; The Editor of that Periodical.* An American literary antiquary; b. in Pittsfield, N.H.; kept an Antiquarian Bookstore in Boston from 1828.

Drake, Swaine. *The Clerk of the "California."* An English writer.

Draper, Mrs. **Elizabeth.** *Eliza.* An English lady; correspondent of Laurence Sterne.

Draper, Sir **William,** K.B., 1720–87. *Modestus; A Traveller.* An English officer and statesman; Lieut.-Gov. of Minorca, 1779 *et seq.*

Drayton, William Henry, 1742–99. *A Carolinian; Freeman.* An American patriot and statesman; b. at Dayton Hall, on Ashley River, S.C.; educ. in England; in 1775 President of the Provincial Congress; and M.C., 1778–90; d. in Philadelphia.

Drennan, William, M.D., 1754–1820. *Orellana.* An Irish physician; b. at Belfast; M.A. at Glasgow Coll. in 1771; studied medicine, and began to practise at Belfast; but soon removed to Newry, and then to Dublin; but in 1807 returned to Belfast.

Drew, Benjamin. *Dr. E. Goethe Digg.* An American writer ["an old 'Boston Post' joker"]; visited Canada, and wrote an interesting book about fugitive slaves there.

Drew, Jacob Halls, 1793–1875. *His Eldest Son.* An English publisher; b. at

St. Austell; removed to Bodmin in 1859; and to Bath in 1865, where he died.

Drew (afterwards **Bickersteth**), **Mona.** *M. B.* A British poet.

Drew, Pierce William. *P. W.* An Irish (?) antiquary.

Drewe, Edward. *An Officer of the British Army.* An English writer; Major of the 35th Regt. Foot.

Drewe, Patrick. *A Lover of the Church of England.*

Driggs, George W. *G. W. D.; A Non-Commissioned Officer.* An American officer, in the 8th Wisconsin Volunteers.

Drinker, Anna. *Edith May.* An American poet; a native of Pennsylvania.

Allibone has the name *Drinker;* others, *Drinkwater.*

Drinker, John. *A Tradesman.* An English writer.

Driver, Thomas. *Uncle Tom's Nephew.* An American writer.

Drohojowska, Countess **Antoinette Joséphine Françoise Anne** (Symon de Latreiche), 1822-. *Chevalier A. de Doncourt.* A French writer; b. at St. Chily (Lozère); in 1847 married Count Félix de Drohojowski, an Austrian officer.

Drummond, Mrs. ——. *Mrs. D—m—m—d.* A Scottish poet.

Drummond, Henry, Esq., 1786-1860. *H. D.; One of his Constituents.* An English gentleman; son of Henry Drummond, Esq., of the Grange, Hants; was founder (1825) of the chair of Political Economy in the Univ. of Oxford; M.P. for West Surrey, 1847-1859; d. at Albury Park, Guildford.

Drummond, Robert Hay, D.D., 1711-76. *Robert, Lord Bishop of Sarum.* An English prelate; b. in London; Christ Church, Oxford; Bishop of Salisbury, 1761; Archbishop of York, 1761-76.

Drummond, Rev. **Spencer Rodney,** M.A. *S. R. D.* An English clergyman; Christ Church, Oxford, 1813; in 1880, resident at St. George's Place, Brighton.

Drummond, Sir **William,** -1828. *Another Considerable Personage.* A Scottish author, and a profound and elegant scholar, of Logie, Almond, North Briton; d. at Rome.

Drummond, William Abernethy. *W. A. D.* A Scottish bishop.

Drury, Henry Joseph Thomas, M.A., F.R.S., F.S.A., 1779-1841. *Detector.* An English clergyman; King's Coll., Cambridge, 1801; Rector of Fingest, Bucks., 1820-41; and lower master of Harrow School; d. at Harrow-on-the-Hill.

Dryden, John, 1631-1700. *Mr. D—n.* A celebrated English poet.

Drysdale, William. *W. D.* An American journalist, of New York City.

Duane, William, 1760-1835. *Anti-Monopoly; Camillus; Jasper Dwight.* An American politician and journalist; b. near Lake Champlain, N.Y.; educ. in Ireland; editor of the Philadelphia "Aurora," 1795-1822; d. in Philadelphia.

Duane, William, 1808-. *W. D.* An American lawyer; b. in Philadelphia; grandson of the preceding.

Duboc, Karl Edward, 1822-. *Robert Waldmüller.* A German author; b. at Hamburg; was for some years engaged in commerce, but in 1856 devoted himself entirely to literature; in 1859 he settled at Dresden.

Du Bois, Edward, Esq., 1775-1850. *A Knight Errant; Count Reginald de St. Leon; Old Knick.* An English lawyer and *littérateur;* called to the bar at the Inner Temple in 1809; editor, for a time, of the "Monthly Mirror"; was for many years Deputy Judge of the Court of Requests in Holborn; d. in London.

Du Bose, Mrs. **Catherine A.** (Richards), 1828-. *Leila Cameron.* An American "Southland" writer; b. in a village in Oxfordshire, England; her family came to the United States and settled in Georgia; then removed to South Carolina; in 1848, she married Charles W. Du Bose, a lawyer of Sparta, Ga., where in 1867 she resided.

Dubourg, Félix. *Auguste Neuville.* A French dramatic artist, first in the provinces, later in the Théâtre des Variétés; b. in Champagne.

Dubuison, Paul Ulrich, 1746-94. ****, Américain.* A French dramatist and ardent revolutionary; b. at Laval; beheaded at Paris.

Duché, Jacob, D.D., 1739-98. *Tamoc Caspipina; A Gentleman of Foreign Extraction; A Gentleman who resided Some Time in Philadelphia.* An American clergyman; educ. at the Univ. of Penn., and at Cambridge, Eng.; his loyalty became suspected, and he fled to England in 1777, but returned in 1790; d. in Philadelphia.

Duchesne, Henri Gabriel, 1739-1822. *D****.* A French naturalist; b. in Paris; keeper of the archives of the clergy before the Revolution; and from 1807 counsellor at the Court of Accounts.

Duck, Rev. **Stephen,** -1756. *S—n D—k.* An English uneducated poet;

originally a thresher, but became a clergyman of the Church of England; drowned in the Thames.

Ducket, George, and Another. *Sir Iliad Doggrel.*

Duckett, William, 1805–63. *Henri Page.* A French writer; the son of an English teacher in Paris; in 1848 he became a journalist.

Du Couret, Louis. *Hadji Abd-el-Hamid Bey.* A French traveller; ex-lieutenant of the Emirs of Mecca, of Yemen, and of the king of Persia.

Dudevant, Mme **Amandine Lucile Aurore (Dupin du Franceuil),** 1804–76. *Blaise Bonin; George Sand; Un Voyageur.* A celebrated French novelist; b. in Paris; in 1822 married the Baron Casimir Dudevant, but soon separated from him; devoted her life at Paris to literary pursuits; and d. there.

Dudley, Rev. Sir **Henry Bate,** Bart., LL.D., 1745–1824. *A Gentleman.* An English "tutor, *littérateur,* play-writer, topographer, farmer, agriculturist, land-drainer, magistrate, sportsman, pugilist, diner-out, clergyman, baronet, and canon of a cathedral; also an orator, and the founder of two London newspapers."

Dudley, Paul, 1675–1751. *A Gentleman.* An American jurist; Harv. Coll., 1690; Chief Justice of Massachusetts.

Duer, William Alexander, LL.D., 1780–1858. *An Old New Yorker.* An eminent American lawyer; brother of John Duer, LL.D.; b. in Dutchess Co., N.Y.; admitted to the bar, 1802; in 1818 removed to Albany; afterwards to New York City; was President of Columbia Coll., 1829-42; and d. in that city.

Duff, Andrew Halliday. *Andrew Halliday.*

Duff, Miss **Henriette A.,** –1879. *H. A. D.* An English poet and prose writer, of London; daughter of Admiral Duff; d. at Brighton.

Duff, Mlle **Nina.** *Miss Nina.* A French writer; sister of Mme la Comtesse A. d'Adhémar.

Duff, William, M.A. *An Impartial Hand.* A Scottish writer; Professor of Philosophy at Aberdeen.

Duffek, Nikolaus, 1833–. *Julius Rosen.* A Bohemian dramatist; b. at Prague; studied at the Univ. there philosophy and jurisprudence; entered the public service, and was Police Commissioner for some time, till in 1867 he was suspended as being friendly to Prussia; he was afterwards restored, and then resigned in order to devote himself en-

tirely to literature; he now (1882) resides at Vienna.

Duffell, Miss **Anne.** *Christine McKenzie.* An American novelist.

Dufferin, Helen Selina (Sheridan), Baroness (afterwards Countess of Gifford), 1807–67. *Hon. Impulsia Gushington.* An Irish writer; author of the "Irish Emigrant's Lament"; granddaughter of Richard Brinsley Sheridan.

Duffield, Rev. **Matthew Dawson,** F.S.A., 1792–1866. *Richmondiensis.* An English clergyman; b. at Middleham, Yorkshire; Canon and Chaplain of the Collegiate Church of Middleham, 1843–66; d. at Stebbing Vicarage, Essex (to which he was instituted in 1842).

Duffield, Rev. **Samuel W.** *Anselmus.* An American minister, of Bloomfield, N.J.

Duffy, J. W. *J. W. D.* An English translator of to-day.

Duganne, Augustine Joseph Hickey, 1823–84. *Motley Manners.* An American poet and novelist; b. in Boston; wrote 20 or 30 novellettes, and was a frequent contributor to periodical literature; d. in New York City.

Duigenan, Patrick, LL.D., 1735–1816. *A Layman; Theophilus.* An Irish civilian and lawyer; M.P. for Armagh; d. in London.

Duke, Alfred. *Broomstraw; Hewletts.* An American journalist, of Richmond, Va.

Duke, Seymour R. *A Southerner.* An American novelist.

Dulany, Daniel, 1721–97. *Antilore.* An American lawyer and loyalist, of Annapolis, Md.; survived the Revolution many years.

Dulaure, Jacques Antoine. *J. A. D****.** A French historian.

Dumas, Alexandre, 1803–70. *Davy.* A French novelist and dramatist; b. at Villiers-Cotterets (Aisne); resided at Paris, devoted to his literary work; d at Puys, near Dieppe.

Dunbar, George, M.A., F.R.S.C. 1774–1851. *G. D.; A Non-Intrusionist* A Scottish classical scholar; b. at Cold ingham, Berwickshire; Professor of Greek in the Univ. of Edinburgh, 1805–51; d. in Edinburgh.

Dunbar, Margaret Juliana Maria *M. J. M. D.* A Scottish writer (?).

Duncan, Mrs. **Florence I.** *F. I. D* An American writer, of Philadelphia.

Duncan, Rev. **George J. C.** *His Son.* A Scottish minister; son of Henry Duncan, D.D.

Duncan, James, –1811. *An Odd Fel*

low. A Scottish writer; a bookseller, of Glasgow.

Duncan, John. D.D., 1720–1808. *J**n D****n; John Brighte; Richard Brisk: An Old Parochial Clergyman: Tyro-Phileleutherus.* An English divine; Rector of South Warmborough, Hants.; d. at Bath.

Duncan, W. *W. D.* A Scottish poet.

Duncan, William James. *W. J. D.* A Scottish financial writer, of Glasgow.

Dunckley, Henry, M.A. *Verax.* An English author and journalist; editor of the "Manchester Examiner and Times."

Duncombe, Rev. John, 1730–85. *Another Gentleman of Cambridge; Crito: Rusticus.* An English clergyman; Vicar of Herne; a contributor to the "Gent. Mag." for 20 years, under the signature of "Crito."

Duncombe, William, 1689–1769. *Benevolus; Philopropos.* An English translator and miscellaneous writer; b. in London; devoted his life chiefly to literary pursuits in that city; and d. there.

Dundas, J. Hamilton. *J. H. D.* A Scottish poet.

Dundas, Wedderburn. *W. D.* A Scottish poet.

Dundonald, Thomas Cochrane, 10th Earl of, 1775–1860. *A Seaman.* An English admiral, commander-in-chief of the North American and West India Station, 1848–51; M.P. for Westminster, 1807–8.

Dunham, Mrs. Emma B. (Sargent). *Leoline.* An American writer.

Dunham, Robert Carr. *C—s D—s; Bellamy Brownjohn.* An English writer.

Dunlap, M. L. *Rural.* An American journalist, of New York City.

Dunlap, William, 1766–1839. *A Water Drinker.* An American painter and dramatic author, of New York City; b. at Perth Amboy, N.Y.; founder of the N.Y. Academy of Design.

Dunlop, Rev. Alexander. *Civis; A Layman; A Country Minister.* A Scottish religious writer.

Dunlop, Madeline Wallace and **Rosalind.** *Two Sisters.* English writers; daughters of an Indian official, and b. in India.

Dunlop, William, M.D., 1795–1848. *A Backwoodsman; Colin Ballantyne.* A Scottish and Canadian *littérateur;* b. at Greenock, Scotland; came to Canada in 1826; d. at Lachine, near Montreal.

Dunn, Caleb, 1834–. *Solon Shingle.* An American writer (?).

Dunning, Mrs. A. K. *Nellie Grahame.* An American writer.

Dunning, M. O. B. *Mary Lorimer.* An American writer (?).

Dunning, Miss Susan C. *Shirley Dare.* — See "Power, Mrs. Susan C. (Dunning)."

Dunster, Rev. Charles, M.A., –1816. *A Country Clergyman.* An English clergyman; an elegant scholar and ingenious poet; Trin. Coll., Oxford, 1771; Rector of Petworth, 1783–1816, and Rural Dean of Western Sussex.

Dunton, John, 1659–1733. *A Bookseller; His Grace, John, Duke of . . . ; A Member of the Athenian Society; Philaret, a Member of Athens.* An English bookseller; turned author; in 1685 visited New England, and resided 8 months in Boston.

Du Parquet, Mme ——. *Mme de Chabreul.*

Dupetit-Méré, Frédéric, 1785–1827. *M. Frédéric.* A French dramatic author; b. in Paris.

Duplany, Claude Marius, 1850–. *Claude Marius.* A French actor.

Duplessis-Kergomard, Jules de Morlaix. *Gustave de Penmarch.* A French poet.

Duppa, Richard, B.C.L., 1767–1831. *R. D.; Member of the Univ. of Camb.* An English lawyer and miscellaneous writer; d. in London.

Durand, Mme **Alice Marie Céleste (Henry),** 1842–. *Henri Gréville.* A French novelist; b. in Paris; passed some years, till 1872, at St. Petersburg, when she returned to her native city.

Durand, J. P. *J. P. Philips, docteur.* A French physicist, of Paris.

Durfee, Job, LL.D., 1790–1847. *Theoptes.* An American jurist; b. at Tiverton, R.I.; Brown Univ., 1813; admitted to the bar, 1814; M.C., 1821–25; Associate Justice and Chief Justice of the Supreme Court of Rhode Island, 1835–47; d. at Tiverton.

D'Urfey, Thomas, –1723. *Mr. D'Uffey; Poet Stutter.* An English poet, song-writer, and dramatist; b. in France.

Durgin, Miss ——. *Elizabeth Conover.*

Durivage, Francis Alexander, 1814–81. *The Old 'Un.* An American miscellaneous writer; d. in New York City.

Durward, Bernard Isaac. *Porte Crayon.* An American poet and artist; adopted the *nom de plume* of "Porte Crayon," not knowing that it had already been appropriated by another writer.

He began contributing to the press about the time Gen. Strother's "Virginia Illustrated" first appeared in "Harper's," and published a collective edition of his poems in 1872 under the title "Wild Flowers of Wisconsin."

Du Sollé, John S. *Knickerbocker.* An American journalist, of Philadelphia.

Dutens, Rev. Louis, 1729–1812. *Louis; Duchillon.* An English writer; b. in Tours, France; took orders in the Church of England, and became rector of Elsdon, Northumberland; d. in London.

Dutt, Shoshee Chunder. *J. A. G. Barton.* A Hindoo writer of to-day, of Calcutta.

Dutton, Anne. *A. D.* An English writer of the early part of the 18th century.

Dutton, George. *Bank Crash, Esq.* An American writer on finance.

Du Vallon, Berquin. *Un Observateur résident sur les lieux.* A French resident in Louisiana early in the century.

Duveyrier, Anne Honore Joseph, 1787–1865. *Mélesville.* A French dramatist; b. in Paris; studied law, but preferred to work for the theatre.

Duyckinck, Evert Augustus, A.M., 1816–78. *Felix Merry.* An American editor and essayist; b. in New York

City; Columbia Coll., 1835; admitted to the bar, 1837, but devoted himself to literary pursuits; d. in his native city.

Dwight, Timothy, D.D., LL.D., 1752–1817. *An Inhabitant of New England.* An American divine; b. at Northampton, Mass.; Yale Coll., 1769; President of his *alma mater*, 1795–1817; d. at Philadelphia.

Dyer, Mrs. Cornelia C. (Joy). *One of them.* An American writer.

Dyer, Hon. Eliphalet, LL.D., 1721–1807. *E. D.* An American lawyer and politician; b. at Windham, Conn.; Yale Coll., 1740; chief justice of Connecticut, 1789–97.

Dyer, Rev. George, 1755–1841. *G. D.* An English classical scholar and antiquary; b. in London, and from 1792 a resident in that city; a friend of Charles Lamb; d. in London.

Dyson, Rev. Charles, 1787–1860. *D.* An English scholar; for a short time Professor of Anglo-Saxon, Oxford; successively incumbent of Nunburnholme in Yorkshire, Nasing in Essex, and finally of Dogmersfield in Hampshire, where he died.

Dyson, Mrs. Charles. *C. D.* An English writer; wife of the preceding.

Dyson, Timothy J. *Quiver.* An American journalist, of Brooklyn, N.Y.

E.

Eagles, Rev. John, M.A., 1784–1855. *Llewellin Penrose; The Sketcher; Themaninthemoon; Vive valeque.* An English clergyman; was for five years curate of Rev. Sydney Smith at Halburton; and resided at Bristol, his native place, 1841–55, without pastoral charge, devoted to artistic and literary pursuits.

Earbery, Matthias, A.B. *M. E.; Anonymous Londinensis; Philalethes.* An old English writer of the first part of the 18th century.

Early, Miss M. A. *Cousin May Carleton.* — See "Fleming, Mrs. M. A. (Early)."

Easby, J. *A Citizen of the World.* An English writer, of Manchester.

Eastlake, Lady Elizabeth (Rigby), 1816–. *A Lady.* An English writer; b. in Norwich; widow of Sir Charles Locke Eastlake.

Eastwick, Edward Backhouse, C.B., F.R.S., 1814–83. *An Ex-Political.* An English orientalist; b. in London;

M.A., Oxford; called to the bar, 1840; M.P. for Penryn and Falmouth, 1868–74.

Eaton, Asa, D.D., 1778–1858. *The Rector.* An American clergyman; b. at Plaistow, N.H.; Harv. Univ., 1803; Rector of Christ Church, Boston, 1805–37; Instructor at Burlington, N.J., 1837–41; Rector at Bridgewater, Mass., 1841–58, residing in Boston.

Eaton, Mrs. Charlotte Ann (Waldie), –1859. *An Englishwoman.* A Scottish writer; second daughter of George Waldie, Esq., Hendersyde-park, Roxburghshire, and wife of Stephen Eaton, Esq., of Ketton-hall, Rutland; d. in Hanover-square, London.

Eaton, Edward Byron. *Sosiosch.* An American writer.

Eaton, George B. *Jacobstaff.* An American editor, of New York City.

Eaton, William, 1764–1811. *W. E.* An American soldier; b. at Woodstock, Conn.; Dartmouth Coll., 1790; United States Consul at Tunis, 1798–1803; Navy

Agent for the Barbary States, 1804–5; d. at Brimfield, Mass.

Eber, General ——. *Un Flaneur.* A Hungarian officer.

Ebersberg, Ottokar Franz, 1833–. *O. F. Berg.* A German dramatist; b. at Vienna; in 1859 founded the satirical sheet "Tritsch-Tratsch"; and in 1862 joined the illustrated "Kikeriki."

Ebhardt, G. *Justus.*

Ebhardt, Olga. *Mme Louise d'Alq.*

Ebrard, Johann Heinrich August, 1818–. *Christian Deutsch; Schliemann der jüngere.* A German theologian; b. at Erlangen, and educ. there and at Berlin. Since 1875 has been pastor of the French Reformed congregation in his native town.

Eccarius, Johann Georg, 1818–. *A Working Man.* A German-English tailor and labor reformer, of London. In 1867 elected General Secretary of the International Working Men's Association.

Eccles, Ambrose, –1809. *The Editor.* An Irish Shakespearian; educ. at Trin. Coll., Dublin; travelled on the Continent, going from France to Italy, where he studied the language with great success. On his return he devoted himself chiefly to literary pursuits, the fruits of which appeared in his illustrated editions of Shakespeare's plays.

Édain, Hippolyte. *Hippolyte Niade.* A French novelist.

Eddy, Caleb, 1788–1859. *The Agent of the Corporation.* An American merchant, long a resident of Boston; early in life of the firm of Bemis & Eddy, merchants on Long Wharf. He was superintendent of the Middlesex Canal many years, a member of the Board of Aldermen, 1823 and 1824, and Democratic candidate for Mayor in 1828 and 1838. D. at Chicopee, Mass.

Eddy, Daniel Clarke, S.T.D. *Rupert Van West.* An eminent American Baptist clergyman; b. in Salem, Mass.; Minister of the First Baptist Church in Brooklyn, N.Y., 1881–84 *et seq.*

Eddy, Thomas, 1758–1827. *One of the Inspectors of the Prison.* An American Friend; b. in Philadelphia; a merchant and insurance broker in New York City, where he died.

Eden, ——, 1844–. *William Herbert.* An English actor.

Eden, Hon. **Eleanor,** 1826–78. *L. E.* An English artist, daughter of 3d Baron Auckland.

Eden, Sir **Frederick Morton,** Bart., about 1766–1809. *Vindex.* An English diplomatist and writer on political econ-

omy; ambassador to Berlin, Vienna, and Madrid, 1792–96, and at the time of his death Chairman of the Directors of the Globe Insurance Company, Pall Mall, in whose house he died.

Eden, Lizzie Selina. *A Lady.* An English writer.

Edgcumbe, Richard, 2d Earl of Mount Edgcumbe, D.C.L., F.R.S., F.S.A., 1764–1839. *An Old Amateur.* An English nobleman; M.P. for the borough of Fowey, 1786–95, when he succeeded his father as Earl and member of the House of Lords. At the time of his death, at his residence on Richmond Hill, he was a Privy Councillor, Lord Lieutenant, Vice-Admiral, and Custos Rotulorum of the Co. of Cornwall, High Steward of Plympton, etc.

Edmonds, Richard, Jun., 1801–. *Epsilon; E. Redruth.* An English antiquary and hymn-writer; b. at Penzance, Cornwall; admitted to the bar, 1823; practised at Plymouth, 1861.

Edmonds, S. Emma E. *Nurse and Spy.* An American writer.

Edmonds, Thomas Rowe, B.A., 1803–. *Junius.* An English writer on vital statistics; brother of Richard; b. at Penzance; resident in London, 1879 *et seq.*

Edwards, Rev. ——. *A Country Parson.* An English poet, of Aldwinkle, Northamptonshire.

Edwards, Rev. Edward. *The Archdeacon.* An English clergyman; Archdeacon of Brecon, Wales.

Edwards, George, F.R.S., F.A.S., 1694–1773. *A Naturalist.* An English naturalist; b. in Essex; after travelling for several years, returned to his native country, and was librarian to the Royal College of Physicians.

Edwards, James, Esq., 1756–1816. *Rinaldo.* A London bookseller and bibliographer; sold his valuable library in 1815.

Edwards, John. *Autolycus.* An American bicycle writer.

Edwards, Joseph. *Agrikler.* An English dialect poet of to-day.

Edwards, Mrs. L. *L. E.* An English religious writer.

Edwards, Mrs. Matilda Caroline (Smiley). *Matilda.* An American "Southland" poet; b. at Grape Hill, Nelson Co., Va.; married Rev. A. S. Edwards, of Washington City. During the late war she lived at Richmond; but after its close, she opened a girls' school at Grape Hill, but the country was so poor that it did not succeed.

Edwards, Thomas, 1699–1757. *T. E.; Another Gentleman of Lincoln's Inn; The Other Gentleman of Lincoln's Inn.* An English critic, poetical writer, and Shakespeare scholar; b. at or near London; the earlier part of his life was spent in that city and at Pitzhanger; but he resided at Turrick, in the parish of Ellesborough, Bucks., 1739–57.

Edwards, Thomas A. *Ollapod.* An Australian bicycle journalist, of Melbourne, Aus.

Edwards, Tryon, D.D., 1809–. *Everard Berkeley.* An American theologian and miscellaneous writer; b. at Hartford, Conn.; Yale Coll., 1828; studied law in New York City; then theology at Princeton; Pastor at New London, Conn., 1844–57; Hagerstown, Md., 1866–73; Philadelphia, 1874–79; Gouverneur, N.Y., 1880–.

Edwards, William. *A Bengal Civilian.* An English colonial writer.

Egan, John. *Junius Hibernicus.* An Irish journalist.

Egan, Pierce, 1772–1849. *An Actor; An Amateur.* An English author; the veteran historian of the ring and sporting journalist; d. in London.

Egar, Rev. **John H.** *The Rector.* An American clergyman; in 1882, of Rome, N.Y.

Egelshem, Wells, –1786. *Winkey.* An English printer and humorous poet, of London; having from nature a remarkable squint, he assumed the name of "Winkey."

Egerton, Mary Margaret, the Countess of Wilton. *A Lady of Rank.* — See "Wilton, The Countess of."

Eggleston, Edward, D.D. *Leisurely Saunterer; Zoraster Higgins; Penholder.* A Methodist clergyman and literary worker; b. at Vevay, Ind.; joined the Meth. ministry in his 19th year, and preached ten years in Minnesota; in 1870 removed to New York City, and became editor of the "Independent" and the "Hearth and Home."

Eggleston, George Cary, 1839–. *A Rebel.* An American author, brother of the preceding; b. in Vevay, Ind. In 1875 he joined the editorial staff of the New York "Evening Post," and in 1876 became its literary editor. In 1878 resided in Brooklyn, N.Y.

Egmont, John, Earl of, 1711–70. *J., E—l of Eg—t.* An English nobleman; held several public offices, and was the author of political tracts.

Eichelberger, Thomas W. *Ike L. Berger.*

Elder, Mrs. **Susan (Blanchard).** *Hermine.* An American "Southland" writer; b. at an extreme Western military station, where her childhood was passed; educ. in New Orleans, and married Charles D. Elder, of that city; resided at Thibodeaux, La.

Elibank, Patrick Murray, 5th Lord. *A Peer of Scotland.* A Scottish nobleman.

Eliot, Francis Perceval, 1755–1818. *Falkland.* An English writer on finance; one of the Commissioners for auditing Public Accounts; d. in London.

Eliot, Samuel Atkins, A.M., 1798–1862. *A Member of the Corporation.* An American merchant; b. in Boston; Harv. Univ., 1817; M.C., 1850–51; Mayor of Boston, 1837–39; d. in Cambridge, Mass.

Elizabeth. *Carmen Sylva.* A European poet; Queen Consort of Charles I., King of Roumania.

Ellaby, Rev. **James,** and Another. *Two Clergymen.* An English clergyman. — See "Thelwall, Rev. A. S."

Ellenborough, Jane Elizabeth (Digby), 1807–82. *Ianthe.* An English lady; the wife of an Arab chief, who was her 4th husband; d. at Damascus.

Ellenwood, Henry S. *Cape Cod Bard; Peter Pindar, Jr.; X.* An American writer; contributor to the "New England Galaxy," in the earlier part of the century.

Ellice, Rt. Hon. **Edward,** 1787–. *Mercator.* An English gentleman; b. in London; M.P., 1818–26, and from 1830.

Elliot, Mrs. **Frances (Minto).** *An Idle Woman.* An English lady.

Elliot, John Lettsom. *An Aristocrat; A Conservative; A Protectionist.*

Elliott, Charles Wyllys, 1817–. *Mr. Thom White.* An American miscellaneous writer; a descendant of John Eliot; was a landscape gardener at Cincinnati, 1840–48; then in New York City, he devoted himself chiefly to literary and philanthropic labors; in 1875 et seq. he resided in Cambridge, Mass.

Elliott, Miss **Charlotte,** 1789–1871. *C. E.; A Lady.* An English hymnwriter; at one time resided at Torquay, and afterwards at Brighton; d. at Torquay.

Elliott, Ebenezer, 1781–1849. *The Corn-law Rhymer.* An English poet; b. at Masborough, in Yorkshire; labored many years in an iron-foundry; in 1821 he settled in business at Sheffield; but in 1841, retired with a competency, and passed the remainder of his life at a villa near Barnsley, where he died.

Elliott, J. J. *Vidette.* An American journalist, of New Orleans.

Elliott, Miss Lillie (Peck), –1878. *Ruth Elliott.* An English writer; daughter of Rev. James B. Peck, of Chelmsford, England.

Elliott, William, 1788–1863. *Agricola; An American; Piscator; Venator.* An American politician; b. at Beaufort, S.C.; Harv. Univ., 1809; devoted himself to the care of his estates; was opposed to secession, and wrote against it; d. in his native town.

Ellis, Arthur. *A. E.; A Layman.* An English writer.

Ellis, Brabazon. *A Churchman.* An English writer.

Ellis, Charles Mayo, Esq., 1818–78. *Libertas.* An American lawyer; b. in Boston; Harv. Univ., 1839; admitted to the Suffolk bar, and practised his profession in Boston; d. in Brookline, Mass.

Ellis, George, 1745–1815. *Sir Gregory Gander; A Member of Parliament.* An English literary antiquary; was a contributor to the "Rolliad" and the "Probationary Odes," and editor of "Early English Poets" and "Early English Romances."

Ellis, Rev. John, D.D. *A Member of Brazen-Nose College, Oxford.* An English clergyman; Vicar of St. Catharine's, Dublin.

Ellis, Jonathan. *J. E.* An American writer.

Ellis, Rev. Robert Stevenson, M.A. *Anglicanus.* An English clergyman, of St. Peter's Coll., Cambridge; in 1834 appointed Chaplain to the British Legation at Copenhagen.

Ellis, Thomas T., M.D. *An Army Surgeon.* An American physician; served in the late Civil War; Post Surgeon at New York City, and Acting Medical Director at White House, Va.

Ellison, Henry. *A Bornnatural.* An English poet, of Christ Church, Oxford.

Ellison, Rev. John. *A Certain Northern Vicar.* An English clergyman; curate of Wellingborough.

Ellison, Patrick. *Vindex.* An American political writer.

Ellsworth, Mrs. ——. *Mrs. L. L. Worth.* An American novelist.

Ellsworth, O. *Timothy Thistle.* An American publisher, of Boston.

Elrington, Rt. Rev. Thomas, D.D., about 1760–1835. *S. N.* An Irish mathematician; b. near Dublin; Fellow of the Univ. of Dublin, 1781; Provost

of the Univ., 1811–20; Bishop of Limerick, 1820–22, and of Leighlin and Ferns., 1822–35.

Elsum, John. *J. E., Esq.* An English artist and poet.

Elton, Sir Arthur Hallam, Bart., 1818–. *An English Landowner.* An English poet and politician, of Clevedon Court, Somerset; M.P. for Bath, 1857–59.

Ely, Miss ——. *Shirley Keeldar.* An English poet.

Embury, Mrs. Emma Catharine (Manley), 1806–63. *Ianthe.* An American poet and prose writer; daughter of James R. Manley, M.D., of New York City; in 1828 married Mr. Daniel Embury, of Brooklyn.

Emerson, George Barrell, LL.D., 1797–1881. *An Old Teacher.* An eminent American educator; b. in Kennebunk, Me.; Harv. Univ., 1817; for 40 years a teacher in Boston, Mass., where he died.

Emerson, George Samuel, –1848. *G. S. E.* An American scholar; Harv. Univ., 1845.

Emerson, Ralph Waldo, 1803–82. *R. W. E.* An eminent American essayist; b. in Boston; Harv. Univ., 1821; passed his life chiefly in Concord, Mass., where he died.

Emery, Mrs. Sarah Anna (Smith). *A Nonagenarian.* An American lady, of Newburyport, Mass.

Enault, Louis, 1824–. *Louis de Vernon.* A French miscellaneous writer, traveller, and journalist; b. at Isigny (Calvados); studied law, and was called to the bar in Paris; in 1851 engaged in literary pursuits.

Endean, James Russell, 1826–76. *Councillor Dreenan.* An English publisher, of London; b. at Cambridge, and educ. at Truro, Cornwall.

Engel, Louis. *L. E.* An English musical critic.

Englefield, Sir Henry Charles, F.R.S., F.S.A., about 1752–1822. *H. E.* An English antiquary and astronomer; b. in Englefield, and d. in London.

Englehardt, Frederick J. *Drahlegne; Gray Eagle.* An American journalist, of New York City.

Engleheart, N. B. *An Amateur.* An English writer.

English, Mrs. Frances Mary, 1783–1858. *A Descendant of the Plantagenet.* An English lady; widow of John English, Esq., Bath; d. in London.

English, George Bethune, A.M., 1789–1828. *An American in the Service* *of the Viceroy.* An American writer, of Boston, Mass.; Harv. Univ., 1807; was the son of Thomas English, Boston.

Ensor, George, Esq., 1769–1843. *Christian Emanuel, Esq.* An Irish writer; b. in Dublin, and d. at Ardress, Co. Armagh.

Ensworth, Mrs. Kate. *Kathleen.* An American writer, of the West.

Enton, Henry. *Val Versatile.* An American journalist.

Epps, John, M.D. *Medicus.* A Scottish physician and phrenologist.

Erck, John Caillard, LL.D. *J. C. E.* An Irish lawyer.

Ericsson, Prof. **Olaf A.** *O. A. E.* An American author, of Richmond, Va. His work, it is said, "may appropriately be called ' Modern Canterbury Tales in Prose.' "

Ermatinger, Edward. *A British Canadian.* A Canadian journalist; was for 10 years in the service of the Hudson Bay Company, and traversed the territory from the Atlantic to the Pacific several times.

Erskine, Sir **David.** *D. E.* A Scottish advocate.

Erskine, Rev. **Ebenezer,** A.M., 1680– 1754. *A Learned, Faithful, Zealous, and Reverend Minister of the Church of Scotland.* A Scottish divine; b. in the Prison of the Bass; first minister of Portmoak, Co. of Fife; afterwards one of the ministers of Stirling.

Erskine, John, D.D., 1721–1803. *A Freeholder; A Friend in the Country.* An eminent divine of the Church of Scotland; minister of New Greyfriars, Edinburgh.

Erskine, Rev. **Ralph,** 1685–1752. *A Minister of the Gospel in the Church of Scotland.* An esteemed Scottish Dissenter; b. in Northumberland; Minister at Dunfermline, in Fifeshire.

Erskine, Thomas Erskine, Baron, 1750–1823. *E.; Alexander, the Coppersmith, LL.D.* A Scottish peer, lawyer, orator, and wit; Lord Chancellor, 1806– 7; d. at Almondell, near Edinburgh.

Escoffier, Marie Henri Amédée, and Others, 1837–. *Thomas Grimm.* A French journalist and romance writer; b. at Serignon (Vaucluse); commenced his literary career at Paris in 1857.

Esdaile, David, D.D. *D. E.; A Rural D.D.* A Scottish minister, of Rescobie.

Essington, Rev. **Robert William,** M.A. *An Etonian; A Kingsman; Robert Nolands.* An English clergyman; King's Coll., Cambridge, 1841; Vicar of Shenstone, Lichfield, 1848–83 *et seq.*

Estabrooks, Henry L. *A Yankee Officer.*

Estourbet, Hippolyte Regnier d'. *Eugène de Palman.* A French historian.

Estwick, Samuel, LL.D. *A West Indian.* An English clergyman.

Etches, John. *Argonaut.* An English writer.

Etough, Rev. **Henry.** *A Young Gentleman of Cambridge.* An English clergyman; Rector of Therfield, Hertfordshire.

Ettingsall, Thomas. *Geoffrey Greydrake.* An Irish writer on angling.

Eusden, Rev. **Lawrence,** –1730. *Leo the Second.* An English poet; b. at Spotsworth, Yorkshire; educ. at Trin. Coll., Cambridge; took orders, and became chaplain to Richard, Lord Willoughby de Broke; d. at Coningsby, Lincolnshire.

Eustace, John Skey, 1760–1805. *An American Officer in the Service of France.* An American officer of the Revolution; after the war he resided some time in Georgia; in 1794 he visited France, and, entering the army, became Major-General; he returned to the United States in 1800, and, settling in Orange Co., N.Y., devoted himself to literary pursuits till his death, at Newburgh.

Eustaphieve, Alexis. *A Russian.* A Russian gentleman, long resident in the United States.

Evans, —— [of Bradbury & Evans]. *Pater.* English publisher, of London.

Evans, Arthur Benoni, D.D. 1781– 1855. *Barnaby Fungus, Esq.; An Old Hand on Board.* An English clergyman, poet, and miscellaneous writer; b. at Compton, Beauchamp; head master of the Free Grammar School, Bosworth, Leicestershire, 1829–55; and d. there.

Evans, Caleb, D.D., 1737–91. *Americanus; A Lover of Truth and the British Constitution.* An English Bapt. minister; b. in Bristol; was for many years President of the Baptist Academy, and Pastor of the Prot. Dissenters in that city; d. at Downend, near Bristol.

Evans, Gen. Sir **De Lacy,** D.C.L., G.C.B., 1787–1870. *Officer serving as Quarter-Master General.* An Irish soldier; b. at Moig; entered the army in 1807, and, in 1846, rose to be Major-General; M.P., 1831, 1833–34, and 1846–65.

Evans, Elizabeth. *Dinah Morris.* An English Meth. preacher, at Wirksworth.

Evans, Estwick. *Belarius of Cymbeline.* An American writer.

Evans, Rev. **Evan,** 1732–79. *Ad-*

vena. A Welsh divine and poet; b. in Cardiganshire; educ. at Jesus Coll., Oxford; took orders, and officiated as curate in several places; d. in his native place.

Evans, Frederick White, 1808–. *A Friend of Youth and Children.* An American Shaker; b. in Leominster, England; came to the U.S. in 1820; was a hatter, but occupied his leisure hours in study; became a socialist; but finally joined the Shakers, and became a presiding elder at Mt. Lebanon, N.Y.

Evans, Rev. John, M.A. *Observator.* An English clergyman; Christ Church, Oxford, 1816; Vicar of Whixhall, Whitchurch, Salop, 1844–83 *et seq.*

Evans, Rev. Jonathan, 1749–1809. *Coventry.* An English Cong. minister and hymn-writer; b. at Coventry; was engaged in secular pursuits, but seized every opportunity to preach the Gospel.

Evans, Leo C. *Grin.* An American journalist, of New York City.

Evans, Morgan. *Morgan de Pembroke.* An English poet.

Evans, Oliver, 1755–1819. *Native Born Citizen of the U.S.* An American inventor; b. at Newport, R.I.; resided chiefly in Philadelphia; d. in New York City.

Evans, Robert. *Adam Bede.* The father of "George Eliot"; steward to Sir Roger Newdigate and other landed proprietors. The original of "Adam Bede" in his daughter's novel. — See "Littell," No. 2072.

Evans, Samuel. *Seth Bede.* An English writer; uncle of "George Eliot," a carpenter and undertaker; follower of Wesley, and class-leader and preacher among the Methodists. The original of "Seth Bede" in his niece's novel. — See "Littell," No. 2072.

Evans, Thomas. *Tacitus.* An American political writer.

Evans, Sir William David, Knt., –1821. *Publicola.* A British colonial lawyer; Recorder of Bombay, and afterwards Stipendiary Magistrate of Manchester.

Evanson, Rev. Edward, 1731–1805. *A Member of the Church of England.* An English clergyman; Vicar of South Minns in 1768, and Rector of Tewkesbury in 1770. In 1778 he became a school-master, and was soon after regarded as an infidel.

Evarts, Jeremiah, A.M., 1781–1831. *William Penn.* An American journalist and philanthropist; b. in Sunderland, Vt.; Yale Coll., 1802; admitted to the bar, 1806, and practised at New Haven about 4 years; was Corresponding Secretary of the A.B.C.F.M., 1821–31; d. in Charleston, S.C.

Evelyn, John, F.R.S., 1620–1705 or 6. *J. E.* An English philosopher and patriot, particularly skilled in natural history; b. at Wotton, Co. of Surrey; resided at Say's Court, near Deptford, and d. there (?).

Everett, Alexander Hill, LL.D., 1792–1847. *An American; A Citizen of the United States; Un Ciudadano de los Estados Unidos.* An American diplomatist; b. in Boston; Harv. Univ., 1806; Commissioner to China, 1846–47; d. in Canton, China.

Everett, David, 1769–1813. *An American; Junius Americanus.* An American journalist; b. in Princeton, Mass.; Dartmouth Coll., 1795; was engaged in journalism in Boston till 1813, he removed to Marietta, O., where he d. the same year.

Everist, Miss M. L. *Emma.* An American writer, of the West.

Evers, ——. *A Gentleman, late an Officer in the Service of the Hon. E. I. Co.*

Ewbank, Thomas, 1792–1870. *Hab. Westman, K.O.* An American inventor; b. at Barnard Castle, Durham, England; came to this country in 1820, and settled in New York City.

Ewer, John. *A Lover of Truth and Decency.* An English divine; Bishop of Llandaff, 1761–69.

Ewing, Mrs. Juliana Horatia, –1885. *Mrs. Overtheway.* An English writer of children's stories.

Ewing, Robert W., –1834 or 35. *Jacques.* An American dramatic critic; a merchant of Philadelphia; d. at Mobile, Alabama, in the fall of 1834 or 1835.

Eyma, Louis Xavier, 1816–76. *Amey.* A French *littérateur*, of Paris; b. at Saint Pierre (Martinique); d. at Paris.

Eymard, Paul. *Isabine de Mira.* A French writer.

Eyre, Francis, Esq., 1732–1804. *A Gentleman; The Gentleman who is particularly addressed, &c.; A Sincere Friend of Mankind.* An English Catholic, of Warkworth Castle, Co. Northampton; d. in London.

Eytinge, Margaret. *Madge Elliot.*

F.

Fabens, Joseph Warren. *Resident of San Domingo; A Settler in Santo Domingo.* An American adventurer; secretary of emigration to William Walker, the filibuster.

Faber, Frederick William, D.D., 1814–63. *A Parish Priest.* An English poet and clergyman; b. at Calverley, Yorks.; educ. at Harrow School and Oxford; B.A., 1836; in 1846 he became a Roman Catholic; and in 1849 established at London a brotherhood of "Oratorians," or "Priests of the Congregation of St. Philip Neri," which in 1854 was removed to Brompton, where he died.

Fairbairn, Sir **Thomas,** 2d Bart., 1823–. *Amicus.* An English civilian; b. in Manchester; resided a long time in Italy; is a magistrate and dep.-lieut. for Lancashire and Hampshire; and in 1870 was High Sheriff of the latter county; country residence, Brambridge House, Hants.

Fairbanks, Mrs. **A. W.** *Myra.* An English writer.

Fairbanks, Charles Bullard, 1827–59. *Aguecheek.* An American writer, of Boston.

Fairholt, Frederick William, Esq., F.S.A., 1814–66. *A Literary Antiquary; An Archæologist.* An English artist; b. in London; won for himself an eminent position as an antiquarian draftsman; d. at Brompton.

Fairs, John. *John Hare.* An English actor, of London; first appearance in 1865.

Falconer, R. W. *R. W. F.* An English botanist.

Falconer, Thomas, 1736–92. *A Layman.* A learned English writer; a native and resident of Chester.

Falconer, William, M.D., F.R.S., 1743–1824. *A Layman.* An English physician, of Bath.

Falkner, Mrs. **Rhoda Ann (Paige),** 1826–63. *R. A. P.* A Canadian poet; b. at Hackney, near London; removed to Canada when six years old.

Falkonberg, B. E. *B. Solymos.* A Hungarian civil engineer, who was appointed, in 1875, a member of an exploring party sent from the Upper Nile to Darfour.

Falmouth, Mary Frances Elizabeth Boscawen, Viscountess, 1822–. *M. F. E. F.* An English lady; b. in Westminster; in 1845 married Evelyn Boscawen, 6th Viscount Falmouth.

Fane, Hon. **Julian Charles Henry,** 1827–70. *Neville Temple.* An English "poet, musician, linguist, diplomatist, eloquent speaker, wit, mimic, and delightful talker"; b. in London.

Fanning, Nathaniel, –1805. *An American Navy Officer.* An American writer; lieutenant, 1804.

Fargus, Frederick J., –1885. *Hugh Conway.* An English writer; b. in Bristol; in 1884 removed to London.

Faris, William S. *Harvey Howard.*

Farley, Mrs. **Helen H.** *Ernest Gilmore.*

Farneworth, Rev. **Ellis,** –1762. *Philopyrphagus Ashburiensis.* An English translator; b. at Bonteshall, in Derbyshire; Rector of Carsington, in that county, 1762–3; and d. there.

Farnie, Henry. *A Keen Hand.* A Scottish sporting writer, etc.

Farquhar, Miss **Maria.** *A Lady.* An English art biographer.

Farrar, Mrs. **Eliza Ware (Rotch),** 1791–1870. *A Lady.* An American writer; b. in Flanders, Europe; in 1828 married Prof. John Farrar, of Harv. Univ.; and d. in Springfield, Mass.

Farrar, Frederic William, D.D., F.R.S., 1831–. *F. T. L. Hope.* An English clergyman; b. in Bombay; educ. in London and Cambridge; Chaplain to the Queen from 1873.

Farrar, Timothy, LL.D., 1788–1874. *A Member of the New England Hist. Gen. Society.* An American jurist; b. at New Ipswich, N.H.; Dartmouth Coll., 1807; Judge of the New Hampshire Court of Common Pleas, 1824–33; d. at Mount Bowdoin, Boston.

Farren, Mrs. ——. *A Lady.* An American novelist.

Farrer, Henrietta Louisa. *H. L. F.* — See "Lear, Mrs. H. L. (F.)."

Fast, Edward G. *Ben Horst.* An American dramatist and miscellaneous writer.

Faulder, John, 1801–63. *A Member.* An English Friend, of Bristol.

Fauquier, Francis. *F. F.* An English writer on finance.

Fauvel, Guillaume Amédée, 1808–41. *Édouard Réville.* A French lawyer, of Normandy.

Favell, ——. *F.* An English student at Cambridge Univ.

Fawcett, C. *The Late Recorder of Newcastle.*

Fawcett, Edgar. *E. F.; Karl Drury.* An American novelist, of New York City; editor of the "Family Star Paper"; and contributor, both as poet and novelist, to many of the leading periodicals of the day.

Fawcett, Rev. Joseph, –1804. *Sir Simon Swan, Bart.* An English Dissenting clergyman; lecturer at the Old Jewry Meeting, London; afterwards a farmer; d. in Essex.

Fawkes, Francis, 1721–77. *A Gentleman of Cambridge.* An English clergyman, poet, and classical scholar; b. in Yorkshire.

Fay, Joseph Dewey, M.A., 1780–1825. *Howard.* An American lawyer; b. in Bennington, Vt.; Williams Coll., 1798; studied law, and settled in New York City, where he died.

Fay, Theodore Sedgwick, 1807–. *F. Sedley; One of the Editors of the N.Y. "Mirror"; A Quiet Man.* An American journalist and miscellaneous writer; b. in New York City; Minister to Switzerland, 1857–61.

Fechner, Gustav Theodor, 1801–. *Dr. Mises.* A German writer on physics and philosophy; b. at Gross-Gärchen, near Moskau; studied the natural sciences at Leipsic; became in 1834 Prof. of Physics, but afterwards exchanged to the chair of Natural Philosophy and Anthropology.

Feist, Charles, 1795–. *An East Anglian.* An English poet.

Feist, Henry Mort. *Augur; Hotspur.* An English sporting writer of to-day.

Felix, Elizabeth Rachel, 1820–58. *Mlle Rachel.* A famous French actress, a Jewess.

Fell, Edward, Jr., 1804–35. *E. F., Jr.* An English author; was well versed in heraldic matters; d. at High Holborn.

Fell, Rev. John, 1735–97. *Phileleutheros.* An English Dissenting minister; b. in Cumberland; tutor in the academy at Homerton, near Hackney.

Fellowes, George W. *Romeo.*

Fellowes, Rev. Robert, LL.D., 1770–1847. *Philalethes, M.A., Oxon.; The Spirit of Hampden.* An English journalist; b. in Norfolk; educ. at Oxford, and in 1795 took orders; d. in London.

Fellows, John, – about 1770. *Philanthropos.* A Methodist poet and hymn-writer; most of his works date from Birmingham.

Fenety, George E. *A Bluenose.* A New Brunswick journalist; in 1839 established the "Commercial News" at

St. John, the first tri-weekly or penny newspaper started in the Maritime Provinces, which he continued till 1863, when he was appointed Queen's printer for New Brunswick.

Fenn, Lady Eleanor (Frere), 1743–1813. *Mrs. Lovechild; Solomon Lovechild.* An English lady and writer for the young; widow of Sir John Fenn; d. at Dereham, Norfolk.

Fennell, Greville. *Greville F., of Barnes.* An English writer of guide-books, of London.

Fennell, James, Esq. *Nemo Nobody.* An American writer.

Fenton, Richard, Esq., F.R.S., –1821. *A Barrister.* A Welsh lawyer; in the early part of his life he spent much of his time in London, during which period he associated with Goldsmith, Glover, Garrick, and many wits of that age. He d. at Glynamel, near Fishguard, Pembrokeshire.

Fenwick, John Ralph, M.D. *Ralph Bigod.* An English physician, of Durham.

Fenwick, Rev. Thomas. *Blue Bonnet; Hydrophilus.* A Canadian Presbyt. clergyman, of Metis, Lower Canada.

Ferguson, Adam, LL.D., 1724–1816. *A Gentleman in the Country.* A Scottish historian; b. in the parish of Logierait, Perthshire; Professor in the Univ. of Edinburgh, 1759–84; d. at St. Andrews.

Ferguson, C. *C. F—n; C. F–r–n.* An English writer.

Ferguson, Charles. *Member of the Faculty of Advocates.* A Scottish lawyer, of Kilkerran.

Ferguson, J. E. *Jeff Josslyn.* An American journalist, of Washington, D.C.

Ferguson, James Frederick, Esq., 1807–55. *F. & J. F. F.* A literary antiquary; b. in Charleston, S.C.; went to Dublin in 1820; was employed there in the Record Office; d. in Dublin.

Ferguson, John Clark. *Alfred Lee.* An English poet.

Ferguson, Peter K. *Jak Wonder.* An American humorist.

Ferguson, Samuel, 1815–. *Mr. Michael Hefferman.* An Irish lawyer and poet; b. in Belfast, Ireland; educ. at the Univ. of Dublin; and from 1838 practised his profession in Dublin.

Fermin, Philippe. *A Person who lived there Ten Years.* A British colonial writer of the last century.

Fernihough, John C. *A Local Artist.* An English artist, of Liverpool.

Fernyhough, Thomas. *The Survivor.* An English officer.

Ferrier, William W. *Baconian.* An American Shakespeare scholar, of Angola, Indiana.

Ferrigni, Piero Francesco Leopoldo, 1836-. *Yorick.* An Italian lawyer, author, and journalist; b. at Livorno; after the peace of Villafranca he became private secretary to Garibaldi; later, lived in Florence.

Ferris, Mrs. Benjamin G. *Wife of a Mormon Elder.* An American lady, whose husband was Secretary of Utah Territory.

Fessenden, Thomas Green, 1771-1837. *Christopher Caustick; Peter Pepperbox; Peter Periwinkle; A Practical Gardener; Simon Spunkey.* An American journalist and satirical writer, of Boston; b. at Walpole, N.H.; Dart. Coll., 1796; in 1804 settled in Boston; and in 1822 commenced the publication of the "New England Farmer"; d. in Boston.

Fessenden, William. *Peter Dobbins, Esq., R.C., U.S.A.* An American politician.

Feuillet, Octave, 1812-. *Désiré Hazard.* A French dramatist and novelist; b. at Saint Lo (Manche); has devoted himself at Paris to literary pursuits.

Feuillet de Conches, Baron **Félix Sébastien,** 1798-. *Un curieux septuagénaire.* A French writer; b. in Paris; entered, in 1820, the Ministry of Foreign Affairs; then was, under the 2d empire, master of ceremonies, retiring in 1874.

Féval, Paul Henri Corentin, 1817-. *Sir Francis Trolopp.* A popular French novelist; b. at Rennes; devoted himself at Paris to literature.

Fewell, Miss **Laura R.** *Parke Richards.* An American "Southland" writer; b. in Brentsville, Prince William Co., Va., and spent most of her life there; when she was sixteen her father died, and she commenced teaching, and contributed to "Scotts Magazine" and other journals.

Fibiger, Johannes Henrik Tauber, 1821-. *Diodoros.* A Danish poet; b. at Nykjobing; studied theology; and in 1874 became pastor at Vallensved, in Soroe.

Field, Barron, Esq., 1787-1846. *F.; B. F.; A Barrister.* An English jurist; called to the bar at the Middle Temple, 1814; at one time, Advocate Fiscal at Ceylon; afterwards, Chief Justice of New South Wales; and finally, Chief Justice of Gibraltar; after his retirement from his judicial functions and return to England, he devoted considerable attention to dramatic literature; d. at Meadfoot House, Torquay.

Field, Cyrus West, 1819-. *Harry Hunter.* An American merchant; b. at Stockbridge, Mass.; at New York City much engaged in promoting the interests of ocean telegraphs, having crossed the Atlantic more than fifty times for this purpose.

Field, E. *E. F.* An English religious writer.

Field, Mrs. E. B. *Blanche.* An American journalist.

Field, Edwin Wilkins, 1804-71. *E. W. F.; A Solicitor.* An English lawyer; b. in Warwick; admitted to the bar, 1826; and practised law in London; drowned in the river Thames.

Field, Rev. **John Edward,** M.A. *A Graduate of Dame Europa's School.* An English clergyman; C. of Burnham w. Boveney, 1878-83 et seq.

Field, Joseph M., -1856. *Everpoint; Straws; Old Straws.* An American actor, writer, editor, and manager; b. in England; came to the United States at an early age.

Field, (M.) Kate. *Straws, Jr.* An American actress and journalist; daughter of the preceding; in 1874, first appearance at Booth's Theatre, New York City.

Field, Matthew C., 1812-44. *Phazma.* An American poet and prose writer; brother of Joseph M.; b. in London; contributor to Southern journals; d. on the passage from Boston to Mobile.

Field, Maunsell Bradhurst, A.M., 1822-75. *An Old Stager.* An American lawyer; b. in New York City; Yale Coll., 1841; admitted to the New York bar in 1848; Judge of the 2d District Court in New York City, 1873-75; d. in his native city.

Field, Richard M. *Ager.* An American writer; manager of the Boston Museum.

Field, Rev. **William,** 1787-1851. *W. F.* An English local historian; b. in London; educ. for the ministry, and was Pastor at Warwick for 54 years; d. at Leamington, near Warwick.

Fielding, ——. *Hamet the Moor.* An English poet; son of the following.

Fielding, Henry., 1707-54. *Sir Alexander Drawcansir, Knight; Habbakkuk Hilding, Justice, Dealer, and Chapman; Joseph Andrews; John Trottplaid, Esq.; Scriblerus Secundus; A Lover of his Country.* An eminent English novelist; b. at Sharpham Park, Somersetshire; engaged in literary pursuits in London; and died in Lisbon, Portugal.

Fielding, Miss **Sarah**, 1714–68. *A Lady.* An English lady; third sister of Henry Fielding; lived and died unmarried at Bath.

File, Charles E., 1843–. *C. F.; Titus A. Brick.* An American journalist, of New York City.

File, Charles E., P. McCann, and **William H. Muldoon**, and Others. *The Man about Town.*

Fillebrown, Edward. *F.; E. F.* An American Shakespearian scholar, of Brookline, Mass.

Filleul, Mrs. Marianne (Girdlestone), 1828–. *M. P.* An English novelist; b. in London; the wife of Rev. Philip V. M. Filleul, of Biddisham, Somerset.

Fillias, Achille Étienne, 1821–. *Charles Besson.* A French author and journalist.

Filon, Pierre Marie Augustin, 1841–. *Pierre Sandrié.* A French writer; b. at Paris; was at first Professor of Rhetoric at the Lyceum of Grenoble; was appointed tutor of the Prince Imperial in 1867; and in 1870 followed him into exile.

Finch, Anne, Countess of Winchelsea, –1720. *A Lady.* An English poet.

Finch, George. *A Member of the Reformed Catholic Church.* An English religious writer.

Finch, Richard. *R. F.; T. S——Y——, Esq.; A Member of One of the Religious Societies.* An English Friend; a clock-maker, of White-Hart-Court, Lombard-street, London.

Findlay, Mrs. Robert (Markland), –1851. *One of the " Belles of Mauchline."*

For an account of the " Belles of Mauchline," see " Gent. Mag.," November, 1851, p. 557.

Findley, William, 1750–1821. *A Citizen.* An American politician; b. in Ireland; came to this country while young; served in the Revolutionary War; settled in Pennsylvania; M.C., 1791–99 and 1803–17; d. at Unity Township, Greensburg, Penn.

Finerty, Hon. John F., 1846–. *J. F. F.* An American journalist; b. in Galway, Ireland; came to this country, 1864; settled at Chicago, Ill.; M.C., 1883–85.

Finlay, K. J. *K. J. F.*

Finley, Miss Martha. *Martha Farquharson.* An American writer of children's books; b. in Chillicothe, O.; in 1853 she went to New York City, and there commenced her literary career.

For several years past (1881) she has resided in Elkton, Cecil Co., Md.

Finn, Henry James; James W. Miller; Moses Whitney, Jr.; and **Oliver C. Wyman.** *Four of Us.* American writers, of Boston.

Firebrace, Rev. **John**, B.A. *A Clergyman of the Church of England.*

Fisher, Charles Edward. *Cecil.* An American writer.

Fisher, Eliza A. Mason. *Ida Mason.* An American writer.

Fisher, Miss Frances C. *Christian Reid.* An American novelist of the day.

Fisher, G. C. *Horus.*

Fisher, George Adams. *A Yankee Conscript.* An American writer; a compulsory soldier in the Rebel army.

Fisher, Joseph E., 1856–. *Mohican.*

Fisher, Rev. **R.** *A Citizen of New York; Neckar.* An American writer on politics.

Fisher, Thomas, Esq., F.S.A., 1772–1836. *An Abolitionist; Antiquitatis Conservator.* An English antiquary; b. in Rochester; clerk at the India House, 1786–1816, and Searcher of Records, 1816–34, when he retired on a pension; d. at Stoke-Newington.

Fisk, Rev. **Samuel**, A.M., 1828–64. *Dunn Browne.* An American clergyman; b. at Shelburne, Mass.; Amherst Coll., 1848; Pastor at Madison, Conn., 1857–61; served with distinction in the late Civil War, and was killed in the battle of the Wilderness.

Fiske, Nathan, D.D., 1733–99. *The General Observer; A Neighbor; The Worcester Speculator.* An American Cong. minister; b. in Weston, Mass.; Harv. Univ., 1754; Pastor of the Third Church in Brookfield, Mass., 1758–99.

Fiske, Stephen, 1840–. *An American; Ariel; Seraph.* An American journalist; b. in New Brunswick, N.J.; Rutger's Coll., 1861; editor of the New York " Star," and editor of the dramatic department of the New York " Spirit of the Times."

Fitch, John. *An Officer.* An American writer.

Fitton, S. M. *S. M. F.* An English writer.

Fitz-Gerald, Lady **Edward**, –1831 *Pamela.*

Fitz-Gerald, Maurice. *The Knight of Kerry.* An Irish writer on religious matters.

Fitzgerald, Percy Hetherington, M.A., F.S.A., 1834–. *Gilbert Dyce; One of the Boys.* An Irish novelist; b. at Fane Valley, Co. Louth; educ. at Stony hurst Coll., Lancashire, and at Trin. Coll., Dublin, after which he was called to the bar, and appointed a Crown Prosecutor on the North-Eastern Circuit.

Fitzgerald, Robert Allan. *Quid.* An English sporting writer.

Fitzgibbon, Edward, 1803–57. *Ephemera.* An English sportsman; editor of "Bell's Life in London."

Fitzpatrick, Thady. *T. F.; Antitheatricus; Candidus; Ingenuus; A Lover of Truth; Philo-Tragicus; Theatricus; W. W.* An English journalist, of London.

Fitzpatrick, William John, LL.D., 1830–. *W. J. F.* An Irish miscellaneous writer; Professor of History and Archæology in the Royal Hibernian Academy from 1876.

Fitzwilliam, Richard Fitzwilliam, 7th Viscount. *Atticus.* An English writer.

Flack, Capt. ——. *A Hunter; The Ranger.* An English sporting writer; a hunter in the Southern United States.

Flagg, Edmund, 1815–. *A Traveller.* An American lawyer and journalist; b. in Wiscasset, Me.; Bowdoin Coll., 1835; chief clerk of a commercial bureau in the State Department at Washington from 1854.

Flagg, Elizabeth E. *E. E. F.; Robert Bloomfield.* An American religious writer.

Flagg, Mary. *Emeff.* An American journalist, of New York City.

Flaherty, W. E. *W. E. F.* An English historian.

Flamank, James. *Trevelyan Turnham, Esq.* An English miscellaneous writer; b. in Exeter; resident some time at St. Austell, and many years at Penzance, Cornwall.

Flatman, Thomas, 1633–72. *T. F.; Montelion, Knight of the Oracle.* An English author; b. in London; educ. at Oxford; was skilled in law, painting, and poetry.

Fleet, William Henry. *The Hon. Francis Thistleton.* A Canadian journalist; editor of the "Montreal Transcript" for some years.

Fleetwood, William, D.D., 1656–1723. *S. T.; Curate of Wilts.; A Neighbouring Minister.* An English divine; b. in London; successively Bishop of St. Asaph and Ely.

Fleischner, I. N. *Mt. Hood.*

Fleming, Caleb, D.D., 1698–1779. *An Advocate of the Christian Revelation; Credens; An English Catholic of the Metropolitan Diocese; Philalethes Londonien-* sis; *Philaleutheros; Philotheorus; The Late Master of the Temple; A Layman; A Lover of his Country; A Parishioner of the Doctor; A Protestant; A Protestant Dissenter of Old England; A Protestant Dissenting Minister; Rusticus; A Sufferer for Truth.* An English Dissenter; b. at Nottingham; succeeded Dr. James Foster at Pinner's Hall, London.

Fleming, Rev. Francis A., –1793. *Verax.* An American Catholic clergyman; a Jesuit father.

Fleming, John, about 1786–1832. *A British Settler.* A Canadian merchant; b. in Aberdeenshire, Scotland; was a resident of Montreal for 29 years.

Fleming, Mrs. May Agnes (Early), 1840–79. *Cousin May Carleton.* An American writer; b. at Portland, St. John, New Brunswick; after her marriage with Mr. Fleming, a civil engineer, in 1865, resided and d. at Brooklyn, N.Y.

Fleming, Rev. Robert, –1716. *F. T.* A Scottish divine; Pastor of a Scotch church, in Lothbury, London.

Fletcher, Rev. ——. *The Vindicator of Mr. Wesley's Minutes.* An English Meth. preacher, of Madeley, Co. Salop.

Fletcher, Miss A. *One of the Company.* An American lady; one of the inmates of Fort Sumter.

Fletcher, A. *Sheelah.*

Fletcher, Mrs. E. *E. F.* An English writer.

Fletcher, Edward Taylor. *Korah; Tabitha.* A Canadian poet, ethnologist, linguist, and translator; holds an appointment in the Surveyor's Branch of the Crown Land Dept., Canada.

Fletcher, Julia Constance. *Dudu; George Fleming.* An American novelist.

Fletcher, Mrs. Maria Jane (Jewsbury), 1800–33. *M. J. J.* An English poet and prose writer; b. in Measham, Warwickshire; in 1833, married Rev. William Fletcher, missionary to India, and d. almost immediately on her arrival with him at Bombay.

Fletcher, Rev. William., F.R.A.S. *A Country Clergyman.* An English writer; Rector of Foscott, Bucks.

Fletcher, William, Esq., –1845. *A Country Gentleman; Junius Secundus.* An Irish gentleman of great literary taste, of Merrion Square, Dublin.

Fleuriot, Mlle Zenaïde Marie Anne. *Anna Edianez.* A French novelist; b. at Saint Brieuc.

Fleury-Husson, Jules, 1821–. *Champfleury.* A French author and journalist; b. at Laon; entered a publishing house in Paris, and afterwards devoted himself to literature.

Flindell, Thomas, 1767–1824. *An Uneducated Man.* An English journalist and publisher; b. at Helford; d. at Exeter.

Flint, Charles Louis, and Others. *Eminent Literary Men.* American writers.

Flint, Henry M., –1868. *The Druid.* An American journalist and miscellaneous writer; d. in Camden, N.J.

Flint, Miss **Sarah A.** *S. A. F.* An American writer for the young.

Flint, William. *Henry Druit.* An English writer on the management of horses.

Flood, Henry, 1732–91. *Syndercombe.* An Irish poet, orator, and politician; Member of the Irish H. of C., 1759, and in 1761 of the British H. of C.; d. at Farmley, Co. Kilkenny.

Flor, Oscar Charles. *O'Squarr.* A Belgian novelist, of Brussels.

Floyd, Mrs. **Cornelia.** *Neil Forrest.* An American writer for the young.

Foley, Henry. *H. F.; A Lay Brother of the Same Society; A Member of the Same Society.* An English Jesuit.

Folger, William C. *F.* An American writer, of Nantucket, Mass.

Follen, Mrs. **Eliza Lee (Cabot),** 1787–1860. *A Lady.* An American author; b. in Boston; in 1828 married Charles Follen; d. in Brookline, Mass.

Follett, Oran. *O. F.* An American Shakespeare scholar, of Sandusky, O.

Follin, Alfred. *Captain Tom Singleton.* An American writer for the young.

Fonnereau, Thomas George. Esq., 1789–1850. *H. E. O.; A Dutiful Son.* An English writer; d. at Watford, Herts.

Fontaney, A. *Andrew O'Donnor.* A French writer; contributor to the "Revue des Deux Mondes," 1835.

Foot, L. *A Unitarian.* An English writer.

Foote, John P. *His Brother.* An American writer; brother of Samuel E. Foote.

Forbes, ——. *A Barrister.* An English traveller.

Forbes, Alexander Penrose, D.C.L., 1817–75. *A. P. F.* A Scottish clergyman; Episcopal Bishop of Brechin, Dundee.

Forbes, Duncan, 1685–1747. *Philo-Scotus.* A Scottish jurist; b. at Culloden, Co. Inverness; Lord President of the Court of Session.

Forbes, Rev. **Granville Hamilton,**

B.A. *G. H. F.; A Northamptonshire Rector.* An English clergyman; Downing Coll., Cambridge, 1847; Rector of Broughton St. Andrew, Kettering, 1849–83 *et seq.*

Forbes, J. H. *Arthur Locker.* An English novelist, of London.

Forbes, James David, D.C.L., LL.D., 1809–68. *Glacier Forbes.* A Scottish naturalist; b. at Colinton, near Edinburgh; educ. at the Univ. of Edinburgh; Principal of St. Salvator's and St. Leonard's Coll., Saint Andrews, 1860–68; d. at Clifton.

Forbes, John Hay, Lord Medwyn, 1776–1854. *A Layman.* A Scottish jurist; a judge of the Court of Session, 1825–52; d. at Edinburgh.

Forbes, Patrick, D.D., –1848. *Patricius Aberdonensis.* A Scottish clergyman; Minister of Old Machar Parish; Professor of Humanity in King's Coll., Aberdeen; and d. in that city.

Forbes, Robert, Gent. *R. F., Gent.; R—— F——, Gent.* A Scottish poet.

Forbes, Robert, D.D. *Philo-Roskelynsis; Ruling Elder of the Church of Scotland.* A Scottish clergyman; Bishop of Caithness and Orkney.

Forbes, Seloftus D. *Oliver Echo; Sylvan Scribe.* An American journalist.

Forbes, Mrs. **Simelde.** *Jessie June.*

Ford, Alfred. *Balloonist.*

Ford, Thomas, D.D., 1743–1821. *Master Shallow.* An eminent English clergyman; b. in Bristol; Christ Church, Oxford, M.A., 1765; Vicar of Melton-Mowbray, 1773–1819; resided in Bristol, 1819–21; and d. in that city.

Ford, Thomas. *T. F.* An English printer, of London.

Ford, Tom. *A Boston Supernumerary.* An American writer.

Forgues, Paul Émile (Daurand), 1813–. *Old Nick.* A French philosopher and journalist, of Paris.

Forney, John Weiss, 1817–82. *Occasional.* An American politician and journalist, of Philadelphia; b. in Lancaster, Penn.; Secretary of the U.S. Senate, 1861–68; d. in Philadelphia.

Forrest, Frederick. *Young D'Urfey.* An English writer, of the last century.

Forrester, Alfred Henry, 1805–72. *Alfred Crowquill; The Ghost of Harry the Eighth's Fool.* An English humorous artist and author; b. in London; resided and d. there.

Forrester, Andrew. *The Female Detective; The Private Detective; The Detective; The City Detective.* An English writer, of London.

Forrester, Charles Robert, 1803-50. *Alfred Crowquill; Hal Willis, Student-at-Law.* An English humorist; brother of Alfred Henry Forrester. The two, under the pseudonym of "Alfred Crowquill," — Charles as author, and Alfred as artist and illustrator, — united their forces for about 18 years, 1827-44, in their literary career, when Charles discontinued his literary work, and Alfred became himself both author and artist.

Forshall, Rev. Josiah, M.A., F.R.S., 1797-1863. *A Fellow of the Royal and Antiquarian Societies.* An English biblical scholar; grad. at Exeter Coll., 1818; Asst. Keeper of the Mss. in the British Museum, 1824; afterwards Keeper and Secretary; d. at his residence, Woburn Place, London.

Forster, Johann Georg Adam, 1754-92. *J. G. A. F.* A German naturalist; b. in Dantzic, and went with his father to England when he was about 12 years of age; Professor of Natural History in the Univ. of Cassel, 1779 *et seq.*, whence he removed to Wilna; d. in Paris.

Forster, John. *Philanthropos.* An English Friend, of Warrington, Lancashire.

Forster, John, 1812-76. *J. F.* An English lawyer, author, and journalist; b. at Newcastle; educ. at the London Univ., and called to the bar at the Inner Temple; devoted himself to literary work in London.

Forster, Josiah, 1726-90. *A Quaker.* An English Friend; a linen draper, of Paul's Church Yard, London; d. at Plaistow.

Forster, Samuel. *A Gent.* An English writer, of the first part of the 18th century.

Forster, Thomas, M.D., F.L.S., 1789-1860. *F.; Alumnus Cantabrigiensis; The Hon. Foreign Secretary to the Annual Friends' Society; Philochelidon; A Physician; Un Physicien Voyageur; Verax.* An English astronomer, naturalist, and meteorologist; b. in London.

Forster, Thomas Ignatius Maria. — See "Forster, Thomas."

Forsyth, Ebenezer. *E. F.; A Student.* A Scottish Shakespearian writer of to-day.

Forteguerri, Nicolò, 1674-1735. *Nicolò Carteromaco.* An Italian priest and poet; Bishop of Ancyra.

Fortis, Abbate Giovanni Battista, 1741-1803. *Albert.* An Italian poet, naturalist, journalist, and biographer.

Fosberry, Rev. Thomas Vincent, M.A. *T. V. F.* An English clergyman; Trin. Coll., Dublin, 1830; Vicar of St. Giles, Reading, 1857-70 *et seq.*

Foscolo, Niccolò Ugo, 1777-1827. *Dedimo Chierico; Jacopo Ortis.* An eminent Italian poet and miscellaneous writer; b. in the Island of Zante; resided in England, 1816-27; d. at Turnham Green, near London.

Fosdick, Charles A. *Harry Castlemon.* An American novelist.

Foss, Edward, F.S.A., 1787-1870. *John Gifford.* An English lawyer and biographer; b. in London; was a Magistrate for Kent and Surrey, and Dep. Lieut. for Kent.

Foster, Arnold. *One who knows.* An English writer.

Foster, Catharine. *C. F.* An English poet and hymn-writer.

Foster, Charles J. *Privateer.* An American journalist and sporting writer, of New York City.

Foster, Clement le Neve, 1841-. *Ossola.* An English geologist and mining engineer; H. M. Inspector of Mines for Cornwall, etc., from 1873-.

Foster, George G. *An Experienced Carver.* An American author and publisher, of New York City.

Foster, Mrs. Hannah (Webster). *A Lady of Massachusetts.* An American novelist; daughter of Grant Webster, of Boston, and wife of Rev. Dr. John Foster, of Brighton; wrote the first American novel.

Foster, Mrs. I. H. *Faye Huntington.* An American novelist.

Foster, James. *An Ohio Volunteer.* An American soldier; present at Hull's surrender in 1812.

Foster, Rev. John, 1770-1843. *A Quiet Looker-on.* An eminent English essayist; passed the last 18 or 20 years of his life at Stapleton, near Bristol, in literary pursuits.

Foster, Miss Mary A., 1823-. *Mary Neville.* An English-American poet and prose writer; b. near Oxford, England; came to this country and settled at Columbus, Ohio.

Foster, Mrs. Olive (Leonard), 1819-81. *O. L. F.* An American poet and hymn-writer, of Raynham, Mass.; in 1847 married Theodore Foster.

Foster, Theodore. *Charles Summerfield.* An American author and journalist; husband of the preceding.

Foster, Thomas, M.D. *Julius Juniper; Philostratus.* An English writer; Poet Laureat to the Royal College of Physicians.

Foster, William, 1772–1863. *Franklin.* An American merchant; b. in Boston; spent some years at Cadiz, in Spain; was in business at Bordeaux, France, for several years, till 1807, when he settled in Boston.

Foster, William C. *Timothy Spectacles.* An American poet.

Foucaux, Charlotte, 1842–. *Marie Summer.* A French author; b. at Paris; wife of the orientalist, Édouard Foucaux; engaged early in literary criticism; but since her marriage, has turned her attention chiefly to Indian studies.

Fouillie, Alfred Jules Émile, 1838–. *G. Bruno.* A French writer; b. at Pouëze (Maine-et-Loire); in 1872 he was called to Paris to the Higher Normal School; but ill-health soon compelled him to retire, and he was admitted to the Retreat in 1879.

Fould, Mme **Wilhelmine Joséphine Simonin,** 1836–. *Gustave Haller; Valérie.* A French actress, sculptor, and writer; b. in Paris.

Fournel, François Victor, 1829–. *Bernadille.* A French *littérateur;* b. at Cheppy, near Varennes; devoted himself to literary work at Paris.

Fournier, Antoine. *Jean Dolent.* A French novelist of to-day.

Fournier, Jules. *Auguste Verité.* A Canadian merchant; b. in France; settled in Montreal.

Fowle, Mrs. **Mary,** 1703–84. *Immortal Molly.* A lady of Cambridge, England; youngest daughter of Alderman Fowle, woolen draper of that town, and d. there.

Fowle, Rev. **Thomas Welbank,** M.A. *Cellarius.* An English clergyman; Oriel Coll., Oxford, 1858; rector of Islip, Oxford, 1875–83 *et seq.*

Fowler, Frank, 1833–63. *Harper Atherton; A Lounger.* An English journalist, author, and secretary of the Library Company. In 1855 left England for New South Wales, and started the "Month" at Sydney; but soon returned to England, and in 1862 was editor of the "Literary Budget," London; d. at Oakley-cottage, Hammersmith.

Fowler, Moses Field. *Moses.* An American writer, of Boston.

Fowler, William. *The Butcher.* An English writer.

Fox, Charles H. *Urastix Bust.* An American compiler of Ethiopian songs.

Fownes, Sir **William.** *Sir W. F.* An Irish gentleman, of Dublin.

Fox, ——. *An Old Correspondent.*

An English political writer; second son of Lord Holland.

Fox, Hon. **Charles James,** 1749–1806. *Carlo Khan; Cnœus Fulvius; The Cub; The Fox; Right Honourable Mendicant; The Man of the People; The Most Unpatriotic Man Alive.* A celebrated English orator and statesman; b. in London; Univ. of Oxford, 1766; d. at Chiswick-house.

Fox, Edward, Esq., 1829–62. *Lynn Erith.* An English poet, of Wellington, Somerset; was drowned while bathing.

Fox, Mrs. **Emily.** *Toler King.* An American novelist, of Oregon.

Fox, Franklin. *A Sailor.* An English writer.

Fox, Henry Richard Vassall, 3d Baron Holland, 1773–1840. *A Disciple of Selden; An Englishman.* An English statesman; b. at Winterslow-house, in Wiltshire; d. at Holland-house, Kensington.

Fox, Myron. *Reynard.* An American journalist, of New York City.

Fox, Mrs. **Sarah (Hustler),** 1800–82. *S. H. F.; Sphinx.* An English poet; b. at Bradford, Yorkshire; in 1825 married to Charles Fox, who d. at Swathmore, near Ulverstone; and after that her home was at Trebah, near Falmouth, where she died.

Fox, Rev. **Thomas Bayley,** A.M., 1808–76. *Solomon Pry.* An American clergyman and journalist; b. in Boston; Harv. Univ., 1828; Pastor at Newburyport, Mass., 1831–45; then in Boston for some years; for many years editor of the Boston "Transcript"; d. in Dorchester, Mass.

Fox, Rev. **William Johnson,** 1786–1864. *A Norwich Weaver Boy; Publicola.* An English divine, writer, and statesman; b. at Uggeshall Farm, near Wrentham, Suffolk; for many years was a preacher at the South-street Chapel, Finsbury; M.P. much of the time from 1847 till 1862; d. in London.

Foxcroft, Francis [Frank]. *Reynard.* An American poet and editor; grad. at Williams Coll. in 1871; ass't editor of the "Boston Journal." In 1883 resident in Cambridge.

Foxcroft, George Augustus, 1815–75. *Job Sass.* An American humorist; b. in Boston; in 1837 bought a farm in Dedham, Mass., and lived there till 1846, when he returned to Boston.

Foxcroft, Rev. **Thomas,** A.M., 1697–1769. *T. F.; An Impartial Hand; Phileleuth. Bangor, V.E.B.* An American

Cong. minister, of Boston; Harv. Univ., 1714.

Fracker, George. *The Sole Survivor.* An American sailor.

Frame, Miss Eliza. *A Nova Scotian.* A Nova Scotian writer of prose and poetry.

Frame, Robert. *A Sabbath School Teacher.* A Scottish (?) poet.

France. *Lewis Baboon.*

Francis, Henry Ralph, M.A. *H. R. F.* An English writer on angling; St. James' Coll., Cambridge, 1834.

Francis, Sir Philip, K.B., 1740–1818. *A Distinguished Living Character; The Cocoa-Tree; Junius.* An Irish politician; b. in Dublin; educ. chiefly at St. Paul's School, London; resided in India, 1774–81; M.P. for Yarmouth, Isle of Wight, 1784–; received the Order of Bath, 1806; d. in London.

Francis, Samuel Ward, M.D., 1835–. *A Singular Man.* An American miscellaneous writer; b. in New York City; Columbia Coll., 1857; M.D., 1860; began to practise in New York City, but afterwards removed to Newport, R.I., where he resided in 1879 *et seq.*

Francke, Hermann, –1882. *Heinrich Lindau.* A German poet and dramatist.

Francklin, Thomas, D.D., 1721–84. *T. F.* An English poet and Greek scholar; b. in London; educ. at Westminster School and Trin. Coll., Cambridge; Rector of Brasted, in Kent, 1776–84; d. in London.

Franke, H. F. *J. H. Rausse.*

Franklin, ——. *Fr. ——.* An English grammar master, of Hertford.

Franklin, Benjamin, D.C.L., 1706–90. *A. B.; Father Abraham; Anthony Afterwit; B. B.; The Busybody; Mrs. Silence Dogood; A Good Conscience; Historicus; The Left Hand; Medius; Poor Richard; Richard Saunders, Philomath; Celia Single; A Subscriber; A Tradesman of Philadelphia.* A celebrated American philosopher and statesman, of Philadelphia.

Franklin, Gov. William, 1731–1813. *Jack Retort.* An American loyalist; the natural son of the preceding; Governor of New Jersey, 1763–76; d. in England.

Franks, Rev. James. *A Clergyman.* A British colonial minister, of Halifax, N.S.

Frankum, R. *R. F.* An English poet.

Fransham, John. *J. F.* An English statistical writer, of Norwich.

Fraser, Donald, D.D. *A Minister.*

A Scottish Presbyt. minister, of the Marylebone Presbyt. Church, London.

Fraser, Miss Jessie. *Tasma.*

Fraser, Rev. Joshua. *A Military Chaplain.* A Canadian clergyman.

Fraser, Patrick, LL.D. *A Bystander.* A Scottish lawyer, of Edinburgh (?).

Fraser, W. *Father Fitz-Eustace, a Mendicant Friar; Randolph Fitz-Eustace.* A Scottish (?) miscellaneous writer.

Fraser, Sir William Augustus, 4th Bart., 1826–. *The Knight of Morar.* An English baronet; M.P. for Barnstaple, 1852–53 and 1857–59; for Ludlow, 1863–65, and for Kidderminster from 1874.

Fraser's Magazine (*Regina*) was founded, February, 1830, by Hugh Fraser and Dr. William Maginn, and ceased to be published, November, 1882.

Frazaer, Mary. *Sarah Marshall Hayden.* An American writer. This is according to Ralph Thomas.

Frazer, John. *J. de Jean.* An Irish poet; b. in King's Co.; resided for many years in Dublin, where he worked as a cabinet-maker.

Frazer, Rev. P. *Aristogeiton.* An English Baptist minister.

Frearson, John. *M. Justitia.* An English writer.

Free, John, D.D. *An Antigallican; A Bishop of the Church of England.* An English clergyman; Vicar of East Croker, Somersetshire.

Freeland, Mrs. Carrie J. *G. C. J.* An American novelist.

Freeling, Sir Francis, Bart., 1764–1836. *Licius.* An English baronet; b. in Redcliff parish, Bristol; employed in the General Post-Office, 1787–1836; d. in London.

Freeman, Rev. Gage Earle, M.A. *Peregrine.* An English clergyman and writer on falconry in the London "Field"; of Wild Boar Clough, Macclesfield, 1883 *et seq.*

Freeman, James, D.D., 1759–1835. *J. F.* An American clergyman; b. at Charlestown, Mass.; Harv. Univ., 1777; Minister of King's Chapel, Boston, 1782–1835, and d. in that city.

Freeman, Julia Deane. *Mary Forrest.* An American writer.

Freind, John, M.D., 1675–1728. *J. Byfielde.* An English classical scholar; b. at Croton, Northamptonshire, and educ. at Christ Church, Oxford.

Freke, William, Esq., –1767. *W. F., Esq.; Gul. Libera Clavis.* An English Unit.; b. at Hannington, Wilts.; Wadham Coll., Oxford; afterwards a barrister of law; was fined £500 for publishing a book against the Trinity, and sentenced to make a recantation in the four courts in Westminster Hall. He resided at the Chapelry of Hinton St. Mary, Co. Dorset, where he died.

Frémont, John Charles, 1813–. *The Pathfinder of the Rocky Mountains.* An American explorer and general; b. in Savannah, Ga.; candidate for the U.S. presidency in 1856.

French, Miss Alice or Olive. *Octave Thanet.* An American writer, of Davenport, Ia.; educ. at the Abbot Academy, Andover, Mass.

French, Benjamin Franklin, 1799–. *A Gentleman of Philadelphia.* An American poet and scholar; b. in Virginia; studied law; in 1830 became a planter and merchant of Louisiana; afterwards removed to New York City.

French, James Clark, and **Edward Carey.** *A Committee appointed by the Passengers of the "Oceanus."*

French, Mrs. L. Virginia (Smith), 1820–81. *L'Inconnue.* An American "Southland" writer; b. in Virginia; educ. in Pennsylvania, and married in Tennessee; d. at McMinnville, Tenn.

French, Nicholas. *N. F.* An Irish clergyman; R. C. Bishop Ferns.

French, Robert. *A Friend to his Country.* An Irish writer.

Frend, William, Esq., M.A., 1757–1841. *A Member of the Senate.* An English writer; b. in Canterbury; Christ Church Coll., Cambridge, 1780; fixed his residence in London, and aided in forming the Rock Life Assurance Co., and was its Actuary till 1827; d. in London.

Freneau, Philip, 1752–1832. *Tomo Cheeki; Hezekiah Salem; Robert Slender.* An American poet and journalist; b. in New York City; grad. at Nassau Hall, then known as the New Jersey "Log College," in 1771; passed his life chiefly in Philadelphia, devoted to literary work; perished in a snowstorm, near Freehold, N.J.

Frere, B. *A Dramatist.* An English writer.

Frere, John. *D.* An English scholar, of Eton Coll.; one of the editors of the "Microcosm," 1787.

Frere, John Hookham, M.A., 1769–1841. *William and Robert Whistlecraft.* An English poet and diplomatist; b. in Norfolk; M.P., 1796; Minister to Spain, 1818–19; passed his last years at Malta, where he died.

Frere, Rev. R. L. *R. L. F.* An English clergyman.

Frere, William. *W. F.* An English writer; Serjeant-at-Law; master of Downing Coll. — See " S., R."

Freshfield, Mrs. Henry. *A Lady.* An English traveller.

Frey, Albert R. *Caxton.* An American bibliographer, of the Astor Library, New York City.

Frey, Friedrich Hermann, 1839–. *Martin Greif.* A German poet; b. at Spires; studied at Munich; entered the army; became an officer in 1859; resigned in 1867; and now (1882) lives in Munich.

Friswell, James Hain, 1827–78. *Jaques; Mr. Limbertongue.* An English miscellaneous writer; b. in Newport, Shropshire; devoted himself chiefly to literature; d. at Fair Home, Bexley Heath.

Fritts, Charles. *Excelsior.*

Frost, John, LL.D., 1800–59. *William V. Moore; A Veteran Soldier.* An American educator; b. in Kennebunk, Me.; Harv. Univ., 1822; in 1828 he settled in Philadelphia, devoting himself to teaching and literary work.

Frothingham, Nathaniel Langdon, D.D., 1793–1870. *N. L. F.* An American clergyman; b. in Boston; Harv. Univ., 1811; Pastor of the First Church, Boston, 1815–50, and afterwards lived and d. there.

Frothingham, Rev. Washington. *Hermit; The Hermit of New York; Macaulay; Martel; Rosicrucian.* An American journalist, at different times at Portsmouth or Concord, N.H., and Rochester, Troy, and Utica, N.Y.

Froude, James Anthony, LL.D., 1818–. *Zeta.* An English historian and journalist; b. at Dartington, Devon; Exeter Coll., Oxford; lectured in the United States, 1872–73; has written for "Fraser" and "Westminster Review."

Fry, Caroline. *The Listener.* — See "Wilson, Mrs. Caroline (Fry)."

Fry, John, 1792–1822. *Y. N.; J—n F—y; J. F.* An English poet and bibliographer, of Bristol; was a publisher and bookseller.

Fry, Joseph Storrs, 1767–1835. *Peter Bullcalf.* An English Friend, of Frenchay, and afterwards of Redland, near Bristol.

Fryatt, Fanny. *Sepia.*

Fuhrmann, Wilhelm David. *W. D. F.* A German classical scholar and writer on the Greek and Latin classics.

Fuller, Hiram, about 1815–80. *Belle Brittan; The White Republican.* An American journalist (b. in Halifax, Mass.), of New York City; afterwards at

London in support of the "Confederates."

Fuller, James Franklin. *Ignotus.* An Irish architect, of Dublin.

Fuller, J. J. *Uncle John.* An American writer.

Fuller, John James Gibson, 1804–. *Curiosus.* An English antiquary, of Cornwall.

Fuller, Rev. **P.** *P. F.* An English minister of the first part of the 18th century.

Fuller, Hon. **Timothy**, A.M., 1778–1835. *A Citizen.* An eminent American lawyer and statesman; b. at Chilmark, Mass.; Harv. Univ., 1801; M.C., 1817–25; d. at Groton, Mass.

Fullerton, Rev. **George Humphrey**, 1838–. *Rambler.* An American Presbyt. clergyman; Madison Univ., N.Y., 1858; Pastor at Walnut Hills Church, Cincinnati, 1879–81 *et seq.*

Fullilove, Mrs. **E. J.** *Elsie Warwick.* An American writer.

Furly, Benjamin, –1714. *B. F.* An

English Friend, of Colchester; afterwards of Rotterdam, in Holland.

Furman, Gerrit Maspeth. *Rusticus, Gent.* An American poet, etc., of Brooklyn, N.Y. (?)

Furniss, Louise E. *Chollet.* An American writer.

Furniss, William. *Will De Grasse.* An American writer.

Fusinato, Arnoldo, 1817–. *Don Fuso; Fra Fusina.* An Italian poet; b. in Schio, in the district of Vicenza; studied law at Padua; in 1865 he went to Florence with his family, and in 1870 to Rome.

Fyers, Lieut.-Col. **William Augustus.** *W. A. F.* An English officer; entered the army in 1834; Lieut.-Col. of the Rifle Brigade in 1859.

Fysh, Frederic. *F. F.* An English writer on religion and theology.

Fyvie, Isabella. *Edward and Ruth Garrett.* — See "Mayo, Mrs. Isabella (Fyvie)."

G.

Gage, Mrs. **Frances Dana (Barker)**, 1808–. *Aunt Fanny.* An American writer; b. at Marietta, O.; in 1828 was married to James L. Gage, of McConnelsville, where she lived for 25 years, when, in 1853, the family removed to St. Louis, Mo.

Galaher, Rev. **George Fitzgerald**, M.A. *Rev. A—m.* An English clergyman; Trin. Coll., Dublin, 1839; P. C. of St. Mark, Horseleydown, 1845–70.

Gale, Benjamin, M.D., 1715–90. *A. Z.* An American physician; b. in Long Island; Yale Coll., 1733; settled in Killingworth, Conn.

Gale, Frederick. *F. G.* An English writer on school matches and the laws of cricket.

Gale, Hon. **Samuel**, 1783–1865. *Nerva.* A Canadian jurist; for many years a Judge of the Court of Queen's Bench, Lower Canada.

Gale, William. *Aura.* An English journalist, of London.

Gall, Rev. **James.** *A Member of the Free Church.*

Gallagher, William Davis, 1808–. *W. D. G.; Roderick.* An American poet and journalist; b. in Philadelphia; chiefly resident at Cincinnati; and afterwards lived on a farm near Louisville.

Gallatin, Albert, LL.D., 1761–1849. *A Citizen of Pennsylvania.* An American statesman; b. at Geneva, Switzerland; came to this country in 1780; U.S. Minister to France, 1816–23; special envoy to Great Britain, 1826; d. at Astoria, Long Island.

Galloway, Joseph, about 1730–1803. *Cicero; Fabricius.* An American loyalist; b. in England; became a lawyer in Philadelphia; went with his daughter to England in 1778, and there passed the rest of his life.

Galt, John, 1779–1839. *Archibald Jobbry; Rev. T. Clark; Rev. Michael Balwhidder; Samuel Prior; Thomas Duffle.* A popular Scottish writer; b. in Ayrshire; devoted himself chiefly to authorship.

Galt, William Hamilton, 1856–. *Nitgenocle.*

Gandonniere, Almire. *Sir Henri Mortimer.* A French writer; author of articles in the "Chronique."

Gandy, Edward. *One of Us.* An English writer.

Gane, William Law, 1815–. *The Lowe Farmer.* An English and Canadian writer; came to Canada in 1860.

Gangooly, Joguth Chunder. *A Native Brahmin.* A Hindoo convert of Rev.

C. II. Dall; came to this country to study.

Garcia, Eduarda. *Daniel.* A South American novelist; niece of Juan Manoel de Rosas.

Garczynski, J. *Gar.* An American journalist, of New York City.

Garden, Rev. George. *An Unknown Friend.* A Scottish minister.

Gardener, Sylvan. *The Rain-Water Doctor.* An American quack; flourished a while about 1817 at Roxbury, Mass., and elsewhere.—See "Hist. Mag.," February, 1862.

Gardiner, John Sylvester John, D.D., 1765–1830. *X. Z.* An American P. E. clergyman; b. in Haverford West, South Wales; after a previous visit to Boston, he came to the United States in 1787; and was Rector of Trinity Church, Boston, 1805–30; d. at Harrowgate, England.

Gardiner, R. *R. G., a Clerk of the Court of Common Pleas.* An English lawyer.

Gardiner, Richard. *William Honeycomb, Esq.* An English writer.

Gardiner, W. *A Gentleman of the Inner Temple.* An English translator.

Gardiner, William, Esq., 1770–1853. *A Dilettante.* An English writer on music; b. in Leicester, where he lived and died.

Gardiner, Mrs. William. *Her Mother.* An American writer.

Gardner, ——. *A Virginian.* An American writer, of Richmond, Va.

Gardner, Alexander. *A. G.* A Scottish writer on religious subjects.

Gardner, George H. *A Retired Captain, R.N.* A British naval officer.

Gardner, John. *Aurelius.* An American political writer.

Gardner, John Lane, 1793–1869. *An Officer of the Line.* An American officer; b. in Boston; served in the army with distinction, 1812–62; d. at Washington.

Gardner, Samuel Jackson, 1788–1864. *Decius.* An American journalist and miscellaneous writer; b. at Brookline, Mass.; editor of the Newark (N.J.) "Daily Advertiser."

Gardner, William. *W. G.* An English gentleman, of Richmond.

Garner, Robert, F.L.S. *A Naturalist.* An English naturalist of to-day.

Garnham, Rev. Robert Edward, 1753–1802. *Terræ Filius.* An English divine; b. at Bury St. Edmunds.

Garnier, Jean Joseph, 1816–. *Jules.* A French chemist; in 1855 removed to Turin, Italy.

Garretson, James Edmund, 1828–. *John Darby.* An American writer; b. in Wilmington, Del.; Prof. of Med. in the Univ. of Pennsylvania.

Garrick, David, 1716–79. *D. G.; Oakly.* A famous English actor; b. in Hereford; passed his life in London; and left an estate valued at £140,000.

Garrick, Mrs. Marion Eva, 1725–1822. *Violette.* A German lady; wife of the preceding.

Garvie, William. *Barney Rooney.* A Nova Scotian journalist at Halifax, having previously acted as such at Edinburgh.

Gaspey, Thomas. *George Godfrey.* An English author and journalist; commenced his literary career in 1809, as reporter on the "Morning Post" (London).

Gassaway, Frank. *Derrick Dodd.* An American writer.

Gassett, Henry, 1813–. *A Member of the Suffolk Committee.* An American bibliographer; b. in Boston; Harv. Univ., 1834; in 1884 resided in Braintree, Mass.

Gaston, Mrs. A. F. *A. F. G.* An English writer on domestic economy.

Gathercole, Rev. Michael Augustus. *L. S. E.* An English divine; Vicar of Chatteris, Cambs., 1845–77, and resident at the Manor House, Chatteris, 1877–83 *et seq.*

Gatty, Alfred, D.D., 1813–. *A. G.* An English clergyman and miscellaneous writer; b. in London; B.A., Oxford, 1836; Vicar of Ecclesfield, near Sheffield, 1839–83 *et seq.*

Gatty, Mrs. Margaret (Scott), 1809–73. *Aunt Judy.* An English writer; wife of the preceding; b. in Burnham, Essex; editor of "Aunt Judy's Magazine," 1866–73; d. at Ecclesfield.

Gaume, François. *F. G.* A French writer.

Gauntlett, Rev. Henry. *Detector.* An English clergyman; Vicar of Olney, Bucks.; for many years teacher of a college for the instruction of candidates for the ministry.

Gauntley, William, 1775–1860. *W. G.; A Temperate Drinker.* An English Friend, of Bakewell, Derbyshire; an elder.

Gautier, Judith.—See "Méndes, Judith (Gautier)."

Gavin, Antoine, 1680–. *Gabriel d'Emiliane.* A French secular R.C. priest at Saragossa, and from 1715 minister of the English Church.

Gaye, Selina. *A Clergyman's Daughter.* An English writer for the young.

Gayet, Sébastien. 1815–. *Sébastien*

Rhéal. A French clerk in the publishing house of Gide *fils*, and, it is said, a dramatic artist.

Gayette-Georgens, Jeanne Marie, 1817-. *Jeanne Marie.* A German author; b. at Kolberg; passed her youth in Breslau and Hirschberg; later married the teacher Jan Daniel Georgens, with whom, 1856–63, she kept a school for weak-minded children at Vienna, and has since 1867 resided in Berlin.

Gazley, Allen W. *Cephas Broadluck.* An American humorous writer.

Geddes, Rev. **Alexander,** 1737–1802. *Theomophilus Brown; H. W. C(oulthurst), D.D.; A Protesting Catholic; An Upper Graduate.* A Scottish R.C. divine; b. in the parish of Ruthven, Co. Banff; was suspended from his clerical office on account of his translation of the Bible; d. in London.

Geer, John James. *A Yankee Prisoner.* An American officer in the late civil war.

Geiger, Annie, about 1850-. *Maria Bogor.* A French writer; b. at Strasbourg; in 1870 she went to Java, and spent three years; in 1874 took up her residence at Florence, and devoted herself to literary pursuits.

Geldart, Martin. *Nitram Tradleg.* An English writer of the day.

Gell, Sir **William,** 1777–1836. *W. G.* An eminent English classical antiquary; after 1820 resided at Rome or Naples.

Gellie, Mary E. *M. E. B.* An English writer for the young; wife of William Gellie (?).

Gemmer, Caroline M. *Gerda Fay.* An English writer of to-day for the young.

Genet, Edmond Charles, 1765–1834. *A Citizen of New York.* A French diplomatist; b. at Versailles; ambassador to the United States, 1792; d. at Schodac, N.Y.

Genlis, Mme **S. F. D. de Saint-Aubin,** 1746–1830. *S. F. Brulart de Sillery.* An eminent French author; b. near Autun, in Burgundy; passed her life chiefly in Paris, engaged in literary labor.

Gent, Mrs. **L. C.** *G.* An English compiler.

Gentleman, Francis, 1728–84. *The Authors of the " Dramatic Censor."* An Irish actor and poet; b. in Dublin; first appearance in that city; after playing in London and some provincial towns, he settled at Malton; but soon returned to London, and thence to Ireland, where he d. in poverty.

Geoghigan, R. *Patricius.* An Irish writer.

George (William Frederick) III., 1738–1811. *Farmer George; Ralph Robinson.* King of Great Britain.

George (Augustus Frederick) IV., 1762–1830. *Admiral George Carlton.* King of Great Britain.

George, Prince of Wales [afterwards George IV. of England]. *A Very Exalted Subject in His Majesty's Dominions.*

George of Prussia, Prince, 1826-. *Georg Conrad.* A German dramatic poet; b. at Berlin; son of Prince Friedrich; has lived from his early life in Düsseldorf, where his father held his court. His latest drama is "Katharina von Medici," 1881.

George, Miss **H. Maria.** *H. M. G.; Clinton Montague.*

George, William. *Frater; A Member of the Worcester Anglers' Society.* An English writer on angling; now editor of the " Worcester Herald."

Gerard, Cécile Jules Basile, 1817–64. *The Lion-Killer.* A French officer; killed 25 lions, 1844–55.

Gerard, James Watson, LL.D. *A. Fishe Shelley.* An American lawyer and poet, of New York City; Columbia Coll., 1811.

Gérard, Jean Ignace Isidore, 1803–47. *J. J. Grandville.* A French caricaturist; b. at Nancy; in 1824 went to Paris to exercise his art; and d. there.

Gerhard, Dagobert von, 1831-. *Gerhard von Amyntor.* A German poet; b. at Liegnitz; since 1871 has resided at Potsdam.

Germa, Maurice, 1825-. *Maurice Cristal.* A French journalist.

Gerry, Mrs. **H. B.** *H. B. G.* An American writer.

Getchell, Miss **Florence B.** *Florence B. Hallowell.* An American writer.

Gib, T. *T. G.* An English religious writer, of the earlier part of the 18th century.

Gibbon, Rev. **Charles.** *C. G.* A Scottish minister, of Lonmay, Co. Aberdeen.

Gibbons, Mrs. **Anne Trelawny,** 1813-. *Anne Trelawny.* An English author, of Cornwall; b. at Penquite, near Fowey.

Gibbons, James S. *Robert Morris.* An American writer on banks and finance, of New York City.

Gibbons, L. *Three Friends.* An American writer.

Gibbs, George M. *Un Citoyen des États-Unis; A Member of the Committee of*

Peace in Paris. An American writer, of Springfield, Mass. (?).

Gibbs, Joseph H. *J. H. G.* An English poet.

Gibbs, Montgomery. *Gilbert Mortimer.* An English miscellaneous writer, of the day.

Gibbs, Silvanus. *A Lover of the Pure Gospel.* An English controversial writer, of Cornwall; son of Rev. Silvanus Gibbs, minister of the Unit. Congregation, at Devonport, 1820–57.

Giberne, Agnes. *A. G.* An English writer of the day, for the young.

Gibney, Capt. ——. *A Wounded Officer.* An English East Indian officer.

Gibson, Atkinson F., 1764–1829. *A. F. G.* An English Friend, of Saffron Walden, Essex.

Gibson, Edmund, D.D., 1669–1748. *Rev. Dr. Codex.* An eminent English prelate; b. in Bampton, Westmoreland; Bishop of London, 1723–48.

Gibson, Henry. *Harry Hunter.*

Gibson, John. *Scotus.* A Scottish writer.

Gibson, Mary. *Frank Stanley.* An American writer.

Gibson, Mary Frances. *Winnefred.*

Gibson, Mary W. Stanley. *Winnie Woodfern.*

Gibson, William. *A Friend in the Country.* An English Friend, of London.

Gibson, William Sydney, F.S.A. *William de Tyne.* An English writer; formerly Bankruptcy Registrar at Newcastle.

Or, *William Bainbridge, Esq.*, of Newcastle-on-Tyne, barrister, who died Dec. 13, 1869, about 60 years old.

Giddings, Hon. Joshua Reid, 1795–1864. *Pacificus.* An eminent American statesman; b. at Athens, Penn.; M.C., 1838–59; d. at Montreal, Canada.

Giddings, Luther. *An Officer of the 1st Regt. of Ohio Vols.*

Giffard, Pierre. *Henri Charlet.* A French writer.

Gifford, Rev. Richard, 1725–1807. *R. Duff.* An English clergyman; Rector of North Okendon, Essex, 1772–1807, and Vicar of Duffield, in Derbyshire, 1759–1807, where he chiefly resided and where he died.

Gifford, William, 1756–1826. *A Third Member of this "Symposium."* An eminent English critic; b. at Ashburton, Devon.; editor of the "Anti-Jacobin," 1797–98; and of the "London Quarterly Review," 1809–24.

Gilbart, James William, F.R.S., 1794–1863. *A Fellow of the Royal Society.*

An English writer; general manager of the London and Westminster Bank.

Gilbert, Frédéric. *Yveling Rambaud.* An English writer.

Gilbert, G. *Gurth.* An English writer.

Gilbert, Sir Geoffrey, 1674–1726. *A Late Learned Judge.* A British jurist; Chief Baron of the Exchequer in Ireland, 1715 or 1716, and in England, 1725.

Gilbert, James Anthony. *A Friend.* An English officer; Captain in the Royal Artillery, 1837.

Gilbert, John T. *An Irish Archivist.* An Irish writer of the day.

Gilbert, Mrs. R. L. *Charles D. Knight.* An American writer of fiction, of the day.

Gilbert, Richard, Esq., 1794–1852. *R. G.* An English printer, of London; b. and d. in that city.

Gilbert, William Schwenck, 1836–. *Bab; Tomline La Tour.* An English dramatist and contributor to periodical literature, of London; b., educ., and lives in that city.

Gilchrist, John James, LL.D., 1809–58. *Tristram Sturdy, Esq.* An American jurist; b. at Medford, Mass.; Harv. Univ., 1828; Chief Justice of the U.S. Court of Claims at Washington, where he died.

Gilder, Miss Jeanette L. *Brunswick; Erasmus.* An American journalist; editor of the New York "Critic," and correspondent of the "Boston Saturday Evening Gazette" and "Philadelphia Press."

Gilder, Joseph B. *The Lounger.* An American journalist, of New York City.

Gilder, Richard Watson, 1844–. *Old Cabinet.* An American poet and journalist; associate editor from 1870, and editor of the "Century," N.Y., from 1881; was b. in Bordentown, N.J.; served a short time in 1863 in the 1st Philadelphia Artillery in the defence of Carlisle, etc.

Giles, Alfred E. *A Citizen of Massachusetts.* An American writer of the day.

Giles, William Branch, 1762–1830. *A Native of Virginia.* An American statesman; b. in Amelia Co., Va.; M.C., 1790–98 and 1801–2; U.S. Senator, 1805–15, and Governor of Virginia, 1827–30; d. at "The Wigwam," in his native county.

Gill, Rev. J. *A Manchester Layman.* An English writer.

Gille, Charles Eugène, 1820–56.

Athanase Piedfoot. A French lyric poet and dramatist.

Gillespie, William Honyman. *Ter-Tisanthrope.* A Scottish (?) theological writer of the day.

Gillespie, William Mitchell, LL.D., 1816–68. *A New Yorker.* An American civil engineer; b. in New York City; Union Coll., 1834; Prof. in Union Coll., Schenectady, N.Y., 1845–08; d. in his native city.

Gillies, Mary. *Harriet Myrtle.* — See "Miller, Mrs. Mary (Gillies)."

Gillies, Robert Pearce. *Kemperhausen.* A Scottish journalist; lived near Edinburgh; first editor of the "Foreign Quarterly Review"; a friend of Sir Walter Scott.

Gillmore, Parker. *Ubique.* An English (?) sporting writer.

Gilman, Mrs. Caroline (Howard), 1794–. *Mrs. Clarissa Packard; A New England Bride; A New England Housekeeper; A Southern Matron.* An American lady; b. in Boston, Mass.; in 1819 married Samuel Gilman, D.D., of Charleston, S.C.; in 1883 *et seq.* lived in Cambridge, Mass.

Gilman, Samuel, D.D., 1791–1850. *S. G.; A Member.* An American clergyman; b. in Gloucester, Mass.; Harv. Univ., 1811; in 1819 married the preceding; Pastor at Charleston, S.C., 1819–58; d. at Kingston, Mass.

Gilman, Mrs. Stella (Scott), 1844–. *Mrs. Marion Vaughn.* An American author; b. in Alabama; in 1885 a resident in Cambridge, Mass.

Gilmer, Francis W., Esq. *A Virginian.* An American lawyer; at one time reporter to the Court of Appeals of Virginia; d. early.

Gilmer, John Harmer. *A Virginian.* An American writer on finance, etc.

Gilmore, James Roberts, 1823–. *Edmund Kirke.* An American writer; b. in Boston; in 1857 retired from business, and engaged in journalism and authorship.

Gilmore, Rev. Joseph Henry, A.M., 1834–. *Genesee.* An American divine and educator; b. in Boston; Brown Univ., 1858; Prof. at the Univ. of Rochester, N.Y., 1867–83 *et seq.*

Gilmour, Rev. James, M.A. *Hoïnos.* An American clergyman; Union Coll., 1850; in 1868 of Brooklyn, N.Y.

Gilpin, Rev. William, 1724–1804. *Josiah Frampton.* An English clergyman; b. at Carlisle; Queen's Coll., Oxford; Vicar of Boldre and Prebendary of Salisbury.

Gilroy, Clinton G. *A Wayfaring Man.* An English writer.

Girard, Pierre, –1882. *Piccadilly.* A French journalist of the day.

Girardin, Delphine Gay de, 1804–55. *Delphine Gay; Vicomte Delaunay.* A popular French writer; b. at Aix-la-Chapelle; wife of the following; of Paris, where she died.

Girardin, Émile de, 1802–81. *Émile Delamothe; La Girandole, i.e. Weathercock.* An eminent French journalist and politician; b. in Switzerland; removed to Paris and engaged in literary work, from which he retired in 1880 at San Remo, where he died.

Girette, Jules. *Jules Romain.* A French writer; secretary of M. de Mackau, Minister of Marine.

Gladstone, John. *An Edinburgh Burgess of* 1786.

Gladstone, Thomas H. *The Englishman.* An English traveller.

Gladstone, William Ewart, D.C.L., 1809–. *Bartholomew Bouverie; The Chancellor of the Exchequer; Etonian; Etoniensis; Gladiolus; Mr. Gresham; William.* An English statesman; b. at Liverpool; educ. at Eton and Oxford; B.A., 1831; prime minister, 1868–74 and 1880–85.

Glascock, William Nugent. *An Officer of Rank.* An English novelist; a captain in the Royal Navy.

Glaser, Adolf, 1829–. *Reinald Reimar.* A German author; b. at Wiesbaden; attended there the Royal Gymnasium, and later the Univ. of Berlin; edited the Berlin "Monatshefte," 1856–78; at present (1882) lives in Darmstadt.

Glass, Rev. John, 1698–1773. A Scottish clergyman; b. and d. at Dundee.

Glassbrenner, Adolf, 1810–76. *Adolf Brennglas.* A German satirical poet and writer; b. at Berlin; passed his life there in literary pursuits, and d. there.

Glasse, Dr. ——. *A Country Magistrate.* An English law writer.

Glasse, Mrs. Hannah. *A Lady.* An English author.

Glasse, Samuel, D.D. *The Minister of a Parish.* An English clergyman; Rector of Wanstead, Essex.

Glassford, James, Esq. *J. G.* A Scottish advocate, of Dougalston.

Gleig, Rev. George Robert, 1796–. *G. R. G.; An Eyewitness; An Officer who served in the Expedition.* A Scottish clergyman; served in the Peninsula War, and in the War of 1812–15 in America.

Glenn, Rev. William. *A Village Curate.* An Irish clergyman; Trin. Coll.,

Dublin; C. of Derryloran, Cookstown, Co. Tyrone, 1880–83 *et seq.*

Gloag, J. A. Lake. *Ekal Gaolg.* A Scottish novelist of the day.

Glossop, Maria Elizabeth, 1851–. *Maria Harris.* An English actress.

Glover, Mrs. Elliot. *Elinor Vey.* An American journalist.

Glover, Richard, 1712–85. *A Celebrated Literary and Political Character; An Old Member of Parliament.* An English merchant and famous poet and Greek scholar; M.P. from 1760.

Glover, William, M.D. *One of the People.* A Scottish physician.

Glubb, Rev. **Peter Southmead,** B.D., 1819–. *P. S. G.* An English clergyman; b. at Liskeard; Sidney Sussex Coll., Cambridge, B.D., 1857; Vicar of St. Anthony-in-Meneage, 1858–83 *et seq.*

Glück, Elizabeth, 1815–. *Betty Paoli.* A German poet and prose writer; b. in Vienna; the daughter of a physician; since 1852 has resided in her native city.

Goddard, William, 1740–1817. *Andrew Marvel.* An American journalist; at Providence, 1762; at Philadelphia, 1767; Baltimore, 1773–92, when he returned to Rhode Island; d. at Providence.

Godolphin, William, Marquis of Blandford. *An English Traveller at Rome.*

Godwin, Mrs. Mary Wollstonecraft, 1759–97. *Mrs. W——.* An English author; b. in London; d. in Somerstown.

Godwin, William, 1756–1836. *Rev. Edward Baldwin; Theophilus Marcliffe; A Lover of Order; Verax; The Sir Hildebrand Horrible of the English Novelists.* An English novelist; b. in Cambridgeshire; studied theology at Hoxton; after preaching five years, removed to London, and began his career as an author; and d. in that city.

Goetz, Mrs. Angelina (Levy). *Angelina.* An English song-composer.

Gogol, Nikolai Vasilievich, 1809–52. *V. Alof; A Russian Noble.* A celebrated Russian *littérateur;* passed his later years in Moscow.

Goldicutt, John, 1793–1842. *J. G.* An English architect; studied at the Royal Academy in Paris, and in Rome; was one of the secretaries of the Institute of British Architects.

Goldschmidt, Meyer Aaron. *Adolf Meyer.* A Danish poet and journalist, of Copenhagen.

Goldsmith, James Carleton [or Jay Carlton]. *Goldie; Jay Carlton* [or *Charleton*]. An American writer.

Goldsmith, Oliver, 1728–74. *Master Michael Angelo; The Citizen of the World; A Chinese Philosopher; A Nobleman.* An eminent Irish author; b. in Leinster; from 1756 led a literary life in London.

Gonzalès, Louis Jean Emmanuel, 1815–. *Caliban.* A French journalist and romance writer; b. at Saintes (Niedercharente); studied in Paris; then devoted himself to literary pursuits.

Goodale, Elaine, and **Dora Reed.** *Two Children.* American poets, of Sky-Farm, South Egremont, Mass.; Elaine, b. 1863; Dora Reed, 1866.

Goodale, Miss Mary Green. *Edith Alston.* An American "Southland" poet; b. in New Orleans; began to write poetry at the age of twelve years.

Goode, Very Rev. **William,** D.D., F.S.A., 1801–68. *A Clergyman; Philalethes.* An English clergyman; Trin. Coll., Cambridge, 1825; Dean of Ripon, 1860–68; editor of the "Christian Observer."

Goodman, Miss Margaret. *An English Sister of Mercy.* An English lady; a Sister of Mercy at Devonport.

Goodrich, Frank Boott, 1826–. *Dick Tinto.* An American writer; b. in Boston; Harv. Univ., 1845; for several years the Paris correspondent of the New York "Times."

Goodrich, H. Newton. *Beelzebub.* An English poet.

Goodrich, Samuel Griswold, 1793–1863. *O. B.; Peter Parley.* An American popular and miscellaneous writer, chiefly for the young; b. at Ridgefield, Conn.; U.S. Consul at Paris, 1848–52; d. in New York City.

Goodridge, Mrs. Mary Williams (Greeley). *Dorothy Dudley.* An American writer.

Goodwin, George B. *Dennis Muldoon.*

Goodwyn, Maj.-Gen. **Julius Edmund,** C.B. *Gershom.* An English officer; entered the army, 1844; Lieut.-Col. 41st Foot, 1854; Colonel, 1858; distinguished himself in the Eastern campaign of 1854–55.

Goorbeyre, Dr. **Imbert.** *Un Ethophile.* A French physician; nephew of Admiral Goorbeyre; d. Guadeloupe.

Gordon, Archibald D. *The Prowler.* An American journalist, of New York City.

Gordon, Clarence. *Vieux Moustache.* An American novelist of the day.

Gordon, George. *Will Honeycomb.*

Gordon, James. *Amicus.* A Scottish advocate, of Craig.

Gordon, Col. James. *Pious Jeems.* An American writer.

Gordon, John M. *Vindex.* An American writer.

Gordon, Thomas, 1684(?)–1750. *Cato; An Englishman; A Layman.* A Scottish religious and political writer; b. at Kirkcudbright, Galloway; and settled in London.

Gordon, William. *A Citizen of Aberdeen; Parenthenopeus Hereticus.*

Gore, Mrs. **Catherine Frances Grace (Moody),** 1799–1861. *C. F. G.; A Desennuyée.* An English novelist; b. at East Retford, Notts.; in 1823 married Capt. Charles A. Gore; devoted her life chiefly to literary work; d. at Linwood, Lyndhurst.

Gore, Christopher, LL.D., 1758–1827. *Manlius.* An American statesman; b. in Boston; Harv. Univ., 1776; Governor of Massachusetts, 1809–14; United States Senator, 1814–17; d. at Waltham, Mass.

Gore, John, Baron Annaly. *A Noble Lord and Eminent Lawyer.* An English jurist.

Gorman, Charles O. *An Irish Catholic Whig.* An American politician.

Gorman, Rev. **Thomas Murray,** M.A. *T. M. G.* An English clergyman; Hertford Coll., Oxford, 1863; in 1883 resident at Invermore, Woodstock-road, Oxford.

Gorst, Gilpin. *The Deputy Governor.* An English author.

Goslin, S. B. *S. B. G.* An English writer of the day.

Gosling, Charles, about 1657–1747 or 48. *The British Timon.* An English woman-hater; b. in London, and d. there. — See "Gent. Mag.," November, 1784, p. 814.

Gosnell, Samuel. *Fagarty O'Fogarty, Esq., of Blarney.* An English poet; contributor to "Blackwood."

Goss, Elbridge Henry, 1830–. *Elhegos.* An American author; b. in Boston; Treasurer of the Melrose (Mass.) Savings Bank.

Goss, Warren Lee. *A Soldier.* An American soldier of the 2d Mass. Reg't of Heavy Artillery in the late civil war.

Gottschalk, Louis Moreau, 1829–69. *A Pianist.* An American musician; b. at New Orleans; educ. in Paris; made professional tours in Europe and the United States; d. near Rio Janeiro.

Gough, Rev. **Benjamin.** *A Brother Methodist.* An English Wesleyan Methodist.

Gough, John. *An Englishman.*

Gough, Rev. **John.** *Philalethes.* An English clergyman; Rector of Kirk-Ireton, Derbyshire.

Gough, Richard, 1735–1809. *Clio; R. G.; D. H.; A Layman; R. G., junior.* An eminent English antiquary; "the Camden of the 18th century"; b. in London; devoted his life to antiquarian research; d. at Wormley, Herts.

Gould, Benjamin F. *Seth Spicer.*

Gould, Edward S., 1808–. *Cassio; The Man in the Claret Colored Coat.* An American merchant, of New York City, and *littérateur*; b. at Litchfield, Conn.

Gould, James L. *Harry Hunter.* An American writer, of New York City.

Gould, Sylvester C., 1840–. *Godfrey.* An American journalist; b. in Weare, N.H.; now (1885) publisher of "Notes and Queries," Manchester, N.H.

Gould, Rev. **William,** A.M. *Commoner.* An English clergyman of the 18th century.

Gowan, William. *Western Memorabilia.* An American bookseller and bibliographer, of New York City.

Gower, Foote, M.D. *A Fellow of the Antiquarian Society.* An English physician.

Graff, John Franklin. *Graybeard.* An American novelist of the day.

Graham, Rev. ——. *Taoalttbob.* An English writer; a clergyman of the 18th century.

Graham, Mrs. **Elizabeth Susanna (Davenport),** 1763–1844. *Theresa Tidy.* An English writer for children; daughter of John Davenport, Esq., and widow of Thomas Graham, Esq., of Edmond Castle, Cumberland, and of Lincoln's Inn, London; d. at Clapham Common, a suburb of London.

Graham, Esther, –1859. *Madge Wildfire.* A Scottish rustic beauty; made insane by her wrongs; dwelt in the old Quarry Hill of Melrose; d. in the road, near Ellwand-bridge.

Graham, Sir **James Robert George,** 2d Bart., LL.D., 1792–1861. *A Cumberland Land-owner.* An English statesman; a member of the English Ministry most of the time, 1830–55.

Graham, Rev. **John.** *A Member of the Synod of United Original Seceders.* A Scottish minister of the 18th century.

Graham, Robert, M.D., 1786–1845. *R. G.* A Scottish physician and botanist; b. at Sterling; Professor of Botany at Glasgow, about 1818; in the Univ. of Edinburgh, 1820.

Graham, Rev. **William.** *A Friend*

to the *Natural and Religious Rights of Mankind*. An English clergyman, of Whitehaven.

Grahame, James, 1765–1811. *Calvinus*. A Scottish poet and advocate; b. at Glasgow, and educ. at the Univ. there; was till 1809 an advocate at Edinburgh; was a curate at Shipton, Gloucester, England, 1809–11; d. at Glasgow.

Grainger, James, M.D., 1723(?)–67. *A Physician in the West Indies*. A Scottish physician; b. in Dunse, Co. Berwick; practised his profession first in London; then at St. Christophers, West Indies, where he died.

Gramont, Antoine Agénor Alfred, Duc de, 1819–. *Andreas Memor*. A French diplomatist.

Granger, Gideon, 1767–1822. *Algernon Sidney; Senectus; Epaminondas*. An American lawyer and statesman; b. at Suffield, Conn.; Yale Coll., 1787; in 1814 removed to Canandaigua, N.Y., where he died.

Grant, Alexander H., M.A. *A. H. G.; Frank Seafield*. An English poet of the day.

Grant, Mrs. Anne (McVickar), 1755–1838. *An American Lady*. A Scottish writer; b. at Glasgow; spent some years with her father in America; in 1779 married Rev. James Grant of Laggan, in Invernesshire; in 1810 removed to Edinburgh, and d. there.

Grant, Sir Charles. *Simplicius*. An English statesman.

Grant, Sir Francis, Lord Cullen, about 1660–1726. ****; A Magistrate in the Country; A Country Gentleman*. An eminent Scottish lawyer and judge.

Grant, G. *A Veteran Stager*. An English writer.

Grant, Gertrude, –1883. *Gerald Grant*. An English novelist; d. at Goritz, Austria.

Grant, James. *J. G., Late Serrishtehdar of Bengal*. A British colonial civilian.

Grant, James, about 1805–. *Mask; One of No Party*. A Scottish journalist and miscellaneous writer; b. at Elgin, Morayshire; removed to London in 1834; editor of the "Morning Advertiser," 1850–70.

Grant, Judith T. *J. T. G.* An English religious biographer.

Grant, William, and Brothers. *Cheeryble Brothers*. An English mercantile firm of Manchester. W. Grant (1775–1842) d. at Springside, near Bury; was a magistrate and dep.-lieut. of his county.

Granville, Augustus Bozzi, M.D., 1783–1872. *A. B. G********; An English physician and traveller; b. at Milan; resided chiefly in London when not travelling; d. at Dover.

Granville, George, Lord Viscount Lansdowne, 1667–1735. *A Nobleman Abroad*. An English poet.

Grasberger, Hans, 1836–. *Karl Birkenbuhl*. An Austrian poet; b. at Marktflecken, Obtach; studied law at Vienna, 1856–60; studied art in Italy, 1867–73; since 1870 the art-editor of the Vienna "Presse."

Grascome, Samuel. *S. G.* An English religious writer.

Gratacap, Paul Antoine, 1788–. *Cap.* A French naturalist and scientific writer.

Grattan, Thomas Colley, 1796–1864. *A Walking Gentleman*. A popular Irish novelist; b. in Dublin; British consul at Boston, 1839–53.

Graves, Rev. Richard, 1715–1804. *The Editor of "Columella," "Eugenius,"* etc.; *The Editor of the "Spiritual Quixote"; Euphrosyne; A Nonagenarian; An Intimate Friend of His; Rev. P. P., M.A.; Peter Pomfret; Peter of Pontefract; Geoffrey Wildgoose*. A popular English poet and novelist; Rector of Claverton, near Bath, 1750–1804.

Graves, Samuel, 1788–. *Ulysses*. An English political writer, of Colleton.

Gray, ——. *A Scots Gentleman*. A Scottish writer of the first part of the 18th century.

Gray, Rev. Andrew. *A Free Churchman; A Minister of a Chapel of Ease*. A Scottish minister, of Perth.

Gray, Asa, M.D., LL.D., 1810–. *A. G.* An eminent American botanist; b. at Paris, Oneida Co., N.Y.; Fisher Prof. of Natural History at Harv. Univ., 1842–84 *et seq.*

Gray, Harrison. *A Friend to Peace and Good Order*. An American loyalist; Receiver General of Massachusetts; in 1776 went to England, and d. there. He was the grandfather of Harrison Gray Otis, of Boston.

Gray, Miss Louisa M. *Kate Thorne*. A Scottish (?) novelist.

Gray, Rt. Rev. Robert, D.D. *The Bishop of Capetown*. An English clergyman; Univ. Coll., Oxford, 1831; Bishop, 1847.

Gray, Simon. *George Purves*. An English miscellaneous writer.

Gray, W. *A Forfarian*. A Scottish writer.

Graydon, Alexander, 1752–1818. *A Desultory Reader.* An American writer; b. at Bristol, Penn.; resided in Philadelphia, 1816–18, where he died.

Grayson, William J., 1788–1863. *Curtius.* An American poet and politician, of Charleston, S.C.; b. in Beaufort, S.C.; South Carolina Coll., 1809; M.C., 1833–37; d. at Newbern, N.C.

Great Britain and Ireland. *John Bull.*

Greatrex, Rev. **Charles Butler.** *Abel Log.* An English clergyman; Curate in charge of Echinswell *w.* Sydmonton, Hants., 1878–79; in 1880 *et seq.* resided at Burghclere, Newbury.

Greaves, Alexander. *Philalethes.* An American writer.

Greaves, Rev. **Thomas Berkeley.** *Solomon Secondsight.* An English poet and novelist.

Greeley, Horace, 1811–72. *H. G.* An American journalist; b. in Amherst, N.H.; went to New York City in 1831; and was there engaged in journalism till his death at his country residence near Chappaqua, N.Y.

Greeley, Miss **Mary Williams.** *Dorothy Dudley.* — See " Goodridge, Mrs. Mary Williams (Greeley)."

Greely, Robert H. *Bob O'Gotham.*

Green, Duff, 1794–1875. *An American.* An American lawyer, journalist, and politician, of Georgia; where he was born, and died.

Green, G. *G. G.* An American poet.

Green, George Smith. *A Gentleman of Oxford; A Tradesman of Oxford.* An English poet; a watchmaker, of Oxford, in the 18th century.

Green, John. *J. G.* An English traveller of the 18th century.

Green, John, D.D., about 1706–79. *G.* An English clergyman; b. at Beverly, in Yorkshire; Bishop of Lincoln, 1761–79.

Green, John Richards, 1758–1818. *John Gifford; Humphrey Hedgehog.* An English author and journalist; having become deeply in debt by his excesses, in 1782 fled to France under the assumed name of John Gifford. He died a magistrate of Worshipstreet police-court, at Bromley, in Kent.

Green, Joseph, 1706–80. *Me, Phil Arcanos, Gent.; Me, the Hon. B. B., Esq.* An American wit and satirical poet, of Boston; resided in England, 1775–80.

Green, Nathan. *Over-Forty.* An American writer of religious fiction, of the day.

Green, Rupert. *R. G.* An English writer, of Worcester.

Green, Mrs. **S.** *A Cockney.* An Irish novelist.

Green, Thomas, Esq., 1769–1825. *A Lover of Literature; A Young Gentleman.* An English man of letters, of Ipswich; entered the Middle Temple, but devoted his time to travel and literary research.

Greene, Albert Gorton, 1802–68. *Old Grimes.* An American poet; b. at Providence, R.I.; Brown Univ., 1820; for many years President of the R.I. Hist. Soc.

Greene, Annie Douglas. *Marion Douglas.* — See " Robinson, Mrs. Annie Douglas (Greene)."

Greene, Asa, M.D., –1837. *Elnathan Elmwood, Esq.; A Late Merchant; A Yankee; Dr. Dodimus Duckworth, A. N. Q.; Ex-Barber Fribbleton.* An American bookseller and journalist, of New York City; for a time editor of the New York " Evening Transcript."

Greene, Charles Gordon, 1804–. *Flaneur.* An American journalist; b. in Boscawen, N.H.; editor of the " Morning Post," Boston, 1831–; Naval Officer at the Port of Boston, 1853–57; resides in Boston.

Greene, Edward Burnaby, –1788. *E. B. G.* An English poet.

Greene, Nathaniel, 1797–1876. *Boscawen.* An American journalist; b. at Boscawen, N.H.; founder of the " Boston Statesman," 1821; Postmaster at Boston, 1829–41 and 1844–49; and d. in that city.

Greenleaf, Benjamin, 1786–1864. *A Practical Teacher.* An American educator; b. at Haverhill, Mass.; Dart. Coll., 1813; Principal of Bradford (Mass.) Academy, 1814–36; of Bradford Teachers' Sem., 1839–48; d. at Bradford.

Greenleaf, Joseph. *Mutius Scævola.* An American lawyer and political writer, of Boston.

Greenleaf, Lawrence N. *Peter Punever.* An American poet of the day.

Greenleaf, Simon, LL.D., 1783–1853. *S. G.* An American jurist; b. at Newburyport, Mass.; Royall Professor of Law in Harv. Univ., 1834–46; Dane Professor, 1846–48; and Emeritus, 1848–53; d. in Cambridge, Mass.

Greenwood, George. *An Officer of the Household Brigade of Cavalry.* An English officer; Colonel of the 2d Life Guards; retired from service in 1838.

Greenwood, James. *Amateur Cas-*

ual; One of the Crowd. An English journalist, of London.

Greer, Mrs. **Maria.** *Armar Greye.* An English writer of to-day.

Greer, Mrs. **Sarah.** *An Irish Lady; A Lady.* An Irish Friend; wife of John R. Greer, of Monkstown, near Dublin.

Greg, Samuel, 1804–76. *A Layman.* An English poet and prose writer, of Manchester; brother of William Rathbone Greg.

Greg, William Rathbone, 1809–83. *W. R. G.* An English economist and writer on social science, of London; b. at Manchester.

Gregory, Alexander Tighe. *An Englishman Abroad; An Englishman in Switzerland.* An English traveller.

Gregory, J. *Captain Gregory Seaworthy.* An American (?) writer.

Gregory, John, M.D., 1724–73. *A Father.* An eminent Scottish physician; Prof. of Physic in the Univ. of Edinburgh, 1766–73.

Grenville, A. S. *A. S. G.* An American poet, of Dedham, Mass. (?).

Grenville, George, 1712–70. *G. G.; A Son of Candor.* An English statesman; Chancellor of the Exchequer, 1763.

Grenville, George, Lord Nugent, 1788–1850. *John Hampden; The Lord and Lady there.* An English nobleman; educ. at Brazenose Coll., Oxford; D.C.L., 1810; d. at his seat, Lillies, Bucks.

Grenville, Hon. **Robert Fulke,** 1800–67. *An Invalid.* A English officer and civilian, of Pembrokeshire; d. at Milford.

Grey, Sir **Charles Edward,** Knt., 1785–1865. *One of the Commissioners.* An eminent English jurist; Governor of Jamaica from 1846; d. at Tunbridge Wells.

Grey, Ford Grey, Earl. *A Nobleman.* An English lord.

Grey, Rev. **Harry.** *H. G.*

Grey, Henry, 3d Earl, 1802–. *G. C.* An English statesman; b. at Howick House; Trin. Coll., Cambridge, M.A., 1823; succeeded his father in 1845; Secretary of State for the colonies, 1846–52.

Grey, Isaac. *A Native of Pennsylvania.*

Grey, J. E. *One of the Million.* An English writer.

Grey, Jeannie H. *Hearton Drille.* An American (?) novelist.

Grey, Zachary, LL.D., 1687–1766. *An Admirer of Monarchy and Episcopacy;*

A Country Curate; A Country Gentleman; A Friend; A Gentleman and No Knight; A Gentleman of the University of Cambridge; A Learned Hand; A Lover of Episcopacy; A Lover of History; One who is neither Jacobite nor Republican, Presbyterian nor Papist; Philalethes Cantabrigiensis; A Presbyter of the Church of England; A Sincere Admirer of True Liberty; A Sincere Lover of the Present Constitution; A Sincere Protestant. An eminent English clergyman, literary critic, and controversialist; Rector of Houghton Conquest, Beds., and Vicar of St. Peter's and St. Giles's, Cambridge; d. at Ampthill, near Houghton Conquest.

Grey-Egerton, Sir **Philip De Malpas,** 10th Bart., 1806–. *P. G. E.* An English gentleman; M.P. for Chester City, 1830; South Cheshire, 1835–68; and Cheshire West from 1868–81.

Griesebach, Eduard, 1845–. *Tanhäuser der neue.* A German author; b. at Göttingen; studied law there; chose the diplomatic career, and rose to be consul at St. Petersburg in 1881.

Griffin, Mrs. **Alice (McClure).** *Muni Tell; Addie Glenmore.* An American "Southland" poet; b. in Boone Co., Ky.; grad. at the Wesleyan Female Sem., Cincinnati, at the age of sixteen; married at Newport, Ky., in 1861, Mr. G. W. Griffin, an American author, and they have since resided at Louisville.

Griffin, George. *A Layman.* An American religious writer.

Griffin, Gerald, Esq., 1805–40. *Oscar.* An Irish poet; b. in Limerick; the latter part of his life he spent in a Catholic monastery, devoting himself to religious exercises, and d. there.

Griffin, John Quincy Adams. *Azarias Bumpus; A Bunker Hill Boy.* An American lawyer, of Boston.

Griffith, Acton Frederick. *A. F. G.* An English bibliographer.

Griffith, Mrs. **Elizabeth (Griffith),** –1793. *Frances.* A Welsh lady; a writer of novels and plays; married Richard Griffith; d. at Millecent, Co. of Kildare.

Griffith, Richard. *Henry.* — See "Griffith, Mrs. Elizabeth."

Griffith, William, Esq. *Eumenes.* An American political writer, of New Jersey.

Griffiths, Mattie. *A Female Slave.* An American colored poet; b. in Louisville, Ky. (?); in 1860 resided in Boston, writing for the "Anti-Slavery Standard," and other Boston and New York journals.

Griffiths, Richard. *A Late Cele-*

brated Genius Deceased. An English author.

Grigg, Rev. **John,** A.M. *The Rector of St. Timothy's Church, Philadelphia.* An American clergyman; Columbia Coll., 1817.

Griggs, Miss ——. *H. N.* An American religious poet.

Grimani, Julia C. *J. C. G.* An English poet.

Grimston, William Hunter, 1843-. *W. H. Kendal.* An English actor; b. in London; entered the dramatic profession at London in 1861, where he has since chiefly remained.

Grimston, Mrs. **W. H.,** 1848-. *Mrs. W. H. Kendal.* An English actress; neé Margaret ["Madge"] Robertson; wife of the preceding.

Grimstone, Mrs. **Leman.** *Oscar.* An English poet.

Grinfield, Charles Vaughan, M.D. *C. V. G.* An English physician and writer, of Clifton.

Griswold, A. Minor, 1837-. *The Fat Contributor.* An American journalist, of Cincinnati (?).

Griswold, Almon W. *A Bibliomaniac.* An American lawyer, of New York City.

Griswold, Miss **Mary Caroline.** *Carrie.* An American "Southland" poet and prose writer, of Charleston, S.C.

Griswold, William McCrillis. *Gerald Smith; Arthur Venner; P. Q. Index.* An American journalist and bibliographer; Harv. Univ., 1875; employed in the Library of Congress at Washington.

Gross, Amalie (von Saebach) von, 1803-. *Amalie von Winter.* A German poet and novelist, of Weimar; a friend of Goethe.

Grosvenor, Lord **Robert,** Baron Ebury, 1801-. *A Member of the Last Parliament.* An English nobleman; b. at Millbank House, Westminster; Christ Church, Oxford, 1821; M.P., 1822-57; residence, Moor Park, Rickmansworth, Herts.

Grote, Mrs. ——. *A Mutual Friend.* An English writer.

Grouvelle, Philippe Antoine, 1758-1806. *Ph. G***.* A French poet and diplomatist; b. at Paris; engaged in politics; was Secretary of the Provisory Executive Council, and obliged to read the sentence of death to Louis XVI.; was afterwards Minister to Copenhagen; d. at Varennes.

Grover, Albert. *Trebla Revorg.* An English writer of to-day.

Gruau de la Barre, Modeste, Count. *Eliakim.*

Grümbke, Johann Jakob. *A Temporary Inhabitant.*

Grund, Francis J., about 1803-63. *A German nobleman; An Observer.* An American author; b. in Germany; resided many years in Philadelphia, and d. there.

Gruppe, Otto Friedrich, 1804-76. *Absolutus von Hegelingin.* A German poet and critical writer; b. at Dantzic; and d. in Berlin.

Guénard de Méré, Elisabeth, Baroness, 1751-1829. *M. de Boissy.* A French novelist, of Paris.

Guernsey, Miss **Lucy Ellen.** *L. E. G.* An American writer for the young.

Guernsey, Roscellus S. *R. S. G.* An American lawyer and Shakespearian scholar, of New York City.

Guidickins, F. W. *F. W. G., of the Middle Temple.* An English lawyer of the last century.

Guild, Mrs. **Caroline Snowden (Whitmarsh),** 1817-. *Hetty Holyoke.* An American author and compiler, of Boston (Roxbury) Mass.; b. in that city.

Guines, Louis Alexandre Gosset de. *André Gill.* A French caricaturist and writer.

Guinot Eugène, 1812-61. *Pierre Durand; Paul Vermond.* A French littérateur and journalist; b. and d. in Paris.

Gunn, Miss **Harriet M.** *A Lady.* An English writer.

Gunn, Rev. **Henry Mayo.** *H. M. G.* An English Cong. minister; studied at Coward Coll.; and entered upon his ministry at Warminster in 1839.

Gunning, Mrs. —— **(Minifie),** -1800. *A Lady.* An English writer; widow of General Gunning; d. in London.

Gurney, Hudson, Esq., F.R.S., F.S.A., M.P., 1774-1864. *H. G.* An English poet and antiquary; b. in Norwich, and d. in that city.

Gurney, Rev. **John Hampden,** A.M., 1802-62. *J. H. G.* An English clergyman and hymn-writer; b. in London; Trin. Coll., Cambridge, 1824; Rector of St. Mary's, Marylebone, London, 1847-62.

Gurney, Joseph John, 1788-1847. *A Member of the Society of Friends.* An English Friend; b. in Earlham, near Norwich; travelled in this country, 1837-40.

Gurney, Mrs. **Maria (Rowe),** 1802-68. *A Mother.* An English poet; b. at Launceston; married Charles Gurney of Trebursye, South Petherwin, where she died.

Gurney, Miss Priscilla Hannah, 1757–1828. *A Cordial Well-wisher to the Cause of Universal Truth and Righteousness.* An English Friend; daughter of the youngest son of Joseph Gurney, and great-granddaughter of Robert Barclay, the Apologist; and b. in Norwich.

Gutch, John Mathew, Esq., 1777–1861. *The Bristol Junius; Cosmo; An Octogenarian.* An English journalist, of Bristol; editor and proprietor of "Felix Farley's Bristol Journal" for nearly 50 years.

Guthrie, F. Anstey. *F. Anstey.* An English novelist.

Guy, William Augustus, F.R.S., 1810–. *A London Physician.* An eminent English physician; b. at Chiches-ter; Pembroke Coll., Cambridge, 1837; connected with King's Coll., London, from 1838.

Guyot, Mlle Pauline. *Mme Camille Lebrun.* A French novelist.

Guyton de Morveau, N. *Brumore.* A French writer; brother of Baron Louis Bernard Guyton de Morveau, the Chemist.

Gwilliam, John. *A Professor.* An English poet.

Gwin, Thomas, 1656–1720. *T. G.* An English Friend; son of Thomas Gwin, of Falmouth, Cornwall.

Gwinnett, Richard, Esq., –1717. *Pylades.* An English gentleman; once affianced to Mrs. Elizabeth Thomas, Jr. ("Corinna").

Gwynn, Albinia. *A Lady.*

H.

Habberton, John, 1842–. *H. A. Burton; Uncle Harry; Their Latest Victim.* An American author and journalist, of New York City; b. on Long Island.

Habersham, Robert, –1832. *Mr. Airy; Deloraine Digress.* An American scholar; Harv. Univ., 1831.

Haberstich, Samuel, 1821–72. *Arthur Bitter.* A Swiss writer; b. at Dörschen, in the Canton Bern; spent his life chiefly in Bern, and d. there.

Habich, Edward. *An American.* An American writer, not by birth, but from love of the cause of liberty.

Hack, James, Jun., 1758–1829. *A Citizen.* An English Friend, of Chichester.

Hack, Maria, 1778–1844. *M. H.* An English Friend, of Chichester; d. at Southampton.

Hack, Mary P. *Claudia.* An English writer of the day.

Hacker, Franz, 1836–. *Franz von Seeburg.* A German Catholic popular writer; b. at Nymphenburg; studied philosophy, jurisprudence, and theology, and became cathedral vicar at St. Cajetan, in Munich.

Haderman, Miss Jeannette R. *Ann Atom.* An American "Southland" writer, of Lake St. Joseph, Tensas Parish, La.; b. in New Jersey; the daughter of an Epis. clergyman.

Häberlin, Karl Ludwig, 1784–. *H. E. R. Belani.* A German novelist; b. at Erlangen.

Haering, Georg Wilhelm Heinrich, 1798–1871. *Wilibald Alexis; W*****s.* A popular German novelist; had a seat called Häringsford, to which he gave something of the celebrity of the Isle of Monte-Christo.

Haeselbairth, A. C. *A. C. H.* An American journalist, of New York City.

Hagarty, The Hon. **John Hawkins,** D.C.L., 1816–. *Zadig.* A British colonial jurist; b. in Dublin; spent two years at Trin. Coll., 1832–34; then emigrated to Canada, where he studied law; Chief Justice of Ontario from 1878.

Hahn-Hahn, Ida Maria Louisa Frederika Gustava, Gräfinn, 1805–79. *A German Countess.* A German novelist; was divorced in 1829; became a Roman Catholic about 1850.

Haight, Mrs. **Sarah (Rogers).** *A Lady of New York.* An American traveller; wife of Richard K. Haight, of New York City.

Haines, F. E. H. *F. E. H. H.* An American biographer.

Haines, Rev. **Herbert,** M.A. *H. H.* An English writer; Exeter Coll., Oxford, 1848; second master of the Gloucester Collegiate School.

Haines, Zenas T. *Corporal.* An American soldier of the 44th Mass. Reg't in the late civil war.

Hakewell, James Ridgway. *J. R. H.* An English writer of the day on athletics.

Hakewill, Arthur William, 1808–56. *An Architect.* An English archi tect, of London; lecturer to the Architectural Society, 1848.

Haldeman, Samuel Stehman, LL.D., 1812–80. *Felix Ago.* An American philologist and naturalist; Prof. of Comp. Philology in the Univ. of Penn., 1869–80.

Hale, Rev. Edward Everett, 1822–. *Col. Frederic Ingham; A New England Minister, A.B.* An American clergyman; b. in Boston; Harv. Univ., 1839; Pastor at Worcester, Mass., 1846–56; in Boston, 1856–85 *et seq.*

Hale, John Mc., D.D. *Hierophilus.* An Irish prelate; Roman Catholic Archbishop of Tuam.

Hale, Sir Matthew, 1609–1676. *A Learned Hand.* An eminent English jurist; b. at Alderley, in Gloucestershire; Lord Chief Justice of England, 1671–76.

Hale, Capt. Nathan, 1755–76. *The American Spy.* An American soldier; b. in Coventry, Conn.; executed as a spy in New York City.

Hale, Nathan, LL.D., 1784–1863. *The Editor of the Boston Daily Advertiser; A Gentleman of Boston.* An American journalist; b. in Westhampton, Mass.; William's Coll., 1804; removed to Boston in 1810.

Hale, Salma, 1787–1866. *Algernon Sidney; A Citizen of Massachusetts.* An American lawyer; b. at Alstead, N.H.; M.C., 1817–19; practised law at Keene, N.H., 1834–66, and d. there.

Hale, Mrs. Sarah Josepha (Buell), 1790–1879. *A Lady of New Hampshire.* An American author and journalist; b. in Newport, N.H.; was the widow of David Hale; d. in Philadelphia.

Hales, Thomas, 1740–about 1780. *D'hele.* An English dramatic writer; settled in Paris about 1770, and wrote in French with ease and elegance.

Hales, William, D.D., –1831. *Octavius.* An Irish clergyman; Fellow of Trin. Coll., Dublin; and Rector of Killesandra.

Halford, Sir Henry, Bart., M.D., 1766–1844. *Sir H. H., Bart.* An English poet and physician; b. at Leicester; educ. at Rugby and Oxford; practised his profession and died in London.

Halfpenny, F. W. *F. W. H.* An English bibliographer, of London.

Haliburton, Thomas Chandler, 1796–1865. *A Colonist; Sam Slick of Slickville.* A British colonial judge and humorist, of Nova Scotia; b. at Windsor, N.S.; but removed to England in 1850; and d. at Gordon House, Isleworth.

Haliburton, William. *A Bostonian.*

An American writer upon the influence of the stage.

Halkerstoun, H. *A Country Gentleman.* A Scottish writer, of Rathillet, Fifeshire.

Halkett, Lady Anne. *A Lady.*

Hall, Capt. ——. *An Officer of the Army.* An English officer; supposed to have been a major in General Howe's army.

Hall, A. Oakey. *Hans Yorkel.* An American journalist, of New York City.

Hall, Rev. Baynard Rust, D.D., 1798–1863. *Robert Carlton.* An American writer, of Brooklyn, N.Y., from 1852.

Hall, Blakely. *Flaneur.* An American journalist, of San Francisco.

Hall, Chambers. *C. H.* An English writer on art.

Hall, David, 1682–1756. *Theophilus Philanthropos.* An English Friend, of Skipton, Yorkshire; a schoolmaster.

Hall, Mrs. F. (Howe). *F. H.* An American writer.

Hall, Fitzedward, A.M., J.U.D. *F. E. H.* An American Anglo-Sanskrit scholar; Harv. Univ., 1846; Prof. in London; Librarian of the India Office till 1869.

Hall, George. *G. H.* An English antiquary and traveller.

Hall, James. *An Amateur.* An English writer, of London (?).

Hall, James, 1793–1868. *Orlando.* An American lawyer, financier, journalist, and *littérateur;* b. at Philadelphia; in 1833 removed to Cincinnati, and d. near that city.

Hall, John E., 1783–1829. *The Editor of the "Port Folio."* An American lawyer and journalist; editor of the "Port Folio," Philadelphia, 1816–27; d. in Philadelphia (?).

Hall, Miss Louise G. *Lulu.* An American literary lady of the day.

Hall, Rev. Robert. *A Presbyter of the Church of England.* An English clergyman of the first part of the 18th century.

Hall, Robert Pleasants, 1825–54. *A South Carolinian.* An American lawyer and poet; b. in Chester District, S.C.; in 1849 removed to Macon, Ga., and d. there.

Hall, Mrs. Sarah (Ewing), 1761–1830. *A Lady of Philadelphia.* An American writer; b. in Philadelphia.

Hall, Spencer. *S. H.* An English bibliographer.

Hall, Spencer T. *Sherwood Forester.* An English biographer and miscellaneous writer.

Hall, Thomas. *Raby Rattler, Gent.* An English writer.

Hall, W. *Will-Will-be-so.* An English author; a singular character.

Hall, William. *Peter Paul Pallette.* An English writer, of Birmingham (?).

Hall-Stevenson, John, –1785. *Cosmo.* An English writer; a kinsman of Laurence Sterne, and the "Eugenius" of his "Tristram Shandy"; lived in "Crazy Castle."

Hallard, Frederick. *One of the Defeated.* A Scottish lawyer; connected with the Edinburgh Advocates' Library.

Halle, Hughes R. P. Fraser, LL.D. *R. F. Brancassine.* An English writer on philosophy, etc.

Halleck, Fitz-Greene, 1790–1867. *A Connecticut Farmer's Boy.* An eminent American poet; b., lived, and d. in Guilford, Conn.

Hallet, John. *J. H.* An English writer of the first part of the 18th century.

Hallett, Benjamin Franklin, A.M., 1797–1862. *Their Chairman.* An American lawyer and politician; b. in Barnstable, Mass.; Brown Univ., 1816; a member of the Boston bar, and d. in that city.

Hallett, Miss **E. V.** *Ferna Vale.* An American writer.

Hallett, M. W. *M. W. H.* An American writer.

Halley, Edmund, LL.D., 1656–1742. *An Infidel Mathematician.* An eminent mathematician and astronomer; b. at Haggerston, Shoreditch, London; Astronomer Royal, 1719–42.

Halliburton, Sir **Brenton,** Knt., 1775–1860. *Anglo-American; An Octogenarian; An Old Inhabitant of British North America.* A British colonial jurist; Chief Justice of Nova Scotia, 1833–60.

Halliwell-Phillipps, James Orchard, LL.D., F.R.S., etc., 1820–. *A Fellow of the Royal Society; J. O. H.* An English literary antiquary; b. in Chelsea; studied for a time at Cambridge; and entered upon his work in London in 1839.

Hallock, Charles. *Penman.* An American sporting writer, of New York City.

Halloran, Lawrence Hynes, D.D., 1766–1831. *Philo-Nauticus.* An Irish clergyman; in 1818 convicted of forging a frank, by which he defrauded the revenue of 10d., and sentenced to transportation for seven years; d. at Sydney, New South Wales.

Halpine, Charles Graham, 1829–68. *Charles Broadbent; The Letter H; Private Miles O'Reilly.* An Irish-American

writer; b. at Oldcastle, Co. Meath, Ireland; Univ. of Dublin, 1846; in 1847 came to this country; and was a journalist in New York City, 1847–68.

Halsey, Harlan, 1835–. *Tony Pastor.* An American comic vocalist, of New York City.

Halstead, Murat, 1829–. *M. H.* An American journalist; b. in Butler Co., O.; in 1851 went to Cincinnati; and from 1853 has been connected with the "Cincinnati Commercial."

Halstead, William H. *Quilp, Jr.* An American poet, of Norfolk (?), Va.

Halsted, Leonora B. *Barbara Elbon.* An American writer, of St. Louis.

Hambro, Mrs. **C. J.** *A Grandmother; Philojuvenis.* An English writer for the young.

Hamel, ——. *H.* A German musical writer.

Hamilton, Alexander, LL.D., 1757–1804. *An American; Camillus; Cato; Lucius Crassus; Pacificus; Phocion; Publius; Scipio.* An American statesman; b. in the West India island, Nevis; Columbia Coll. (then King's Coll.), 1774; U.S. Secretary of the Treasury, 1789–95; d. in New York City.

Hamilton, Alexander. *Cuthbert Clutterbuck of Kennaquhair.* A Scottish novelist; writer to the Signet.

Hamilton, Mrs. **Alice (King).** *Alice King.* An American writer.

Hamilton, Charles G. *C. G. H.* An English writer on grammar, etc.

Hamilton, Edward. *Theseus.* An American engineer (?).

Hamilton, Miss **Elizabeth,** 1758–1816. *Geoffrey Jarvis; A Hindoo Rajah.* An English lady; author of several useful and elegant works; d. at Harrogate.

Hamilton, Frank E. *Fern.* An American writer.

Hamilton, Rev. **G.** *One of the Ministers of this Present Church.* A Scottish (?) minister of the first part of the 18th century.

Hamilton, Gavin. *G. H.* A Scottish poet of the day.

Hamilton, Harris, D.D. *A Beneficed Clergyman of the Established Church.* An English clergyman.

Hamilton, John Church, 1792–1882. *His Son.* An American lawyer; b. in Philadelphia; Columbia Coll., 1809; aide to Gen. Harrison till 1814; d. at Long Branch, N.J.

Hamilton, Miss **Kate W.** *Fleta.* An American writer for the young.

Hamilton, Robert Douglas, M.D., 1783–1857. *Mungo Coulter Goggle; Guy*

Pollock. A Canadian physician, and frequent contributor to the newspaper press, and author of several works.

Hamilton, Robert S. *Leland A. Webster.* An American writer.

Hamilton, Captain **Thomas,** 1789–1842. *T. H.; Major Spencer Moggridge of the Prince's Own.* An English officer; served in the Peninsula War, and that with the United States of 1812–15; d. at Pisa, Italy.

Hamilton, William, Esq., 1704–54. *Hamilton.* A Scottish poet, of Bangour.

Hammerton, J. *Orion.* An English almanac maker.

Hammitt, Samuel A., 1816–. *Philip Paxton; Sam Slick in Texas.* An American humorist; from 1848 resident in New York City.

Hammond, Mrs. ——, 1847–. *Louise Capsadell.* An American writer.

Hammond, Anthony, Esq., 1688–1738. *A Gentleman.* An English writer; b. in Huntingdonshire; a Commissioner of the Navy, and a man of note among the wits, poets, and parliamentary writers of his time.

Hammond, Charles, 1779–1840. *Hampden.* An American lawyer and journalist, of Cincinnati, 1825–40.

Hammond, Mrs **E. H.** *Henri Daugé.* An American writer of the day.

Hammond, Mrs. **J. S.** *Belle Boyd.* An American writer.

Hammond, Samuel H., 1809–. *A Journalist.* An American writer; b. at Bath, N.Y.

Hampden, John. *Parallax.* An English writer.

Hamper, William, Esq., 1776–1831. *H. D. B.; M. R.; Repmah.* An English poet and antiquary; b. in Birmingham, where he spent his life, and was a Justice of the Peace for the Counties of Warwick and Worcester; d. at Highgate, near Birmingham.

Hancock, George. *Philo-Malthus.* An English economist.

Hancock, John, 1737(?)–93. *Johnny Dupe.* An American patriot; b. in Quincy, Mass.; Harv. Univ., 1754; President of the Continental Congress, 1775; Governor of Mass., 1780–84 and 1787–93.

Hancock, Rev. **John,** 1703–44. *Philalethes.* An American minister, of Braintree, Mass.

Hancock, John, D.D. *A Presbyter of the Church of England.* An English clergyman; Rector of St. Margaret's, Lothbury; Prebendary of Canterbury; and Chaplain to the Duke of Bedford.

Handley, James. *J. H.; One of Her Majesty's Surgeons.* An English writer of the first part of the 18th century.

Hanks, Rev. **Stedman Wright.** *An Observer.* An American writer of the day on theology; agent Seaman's Friend Society, Congregational House; living at Cambridge.

Hannay, ——. *Vindex.* An English writer, of Marylebone Bank, London.

Hannay, Robert, 1789–1868. *A Member of the Faculty.* A Scottish lawyer.

Hannegan, Dennis. *Doctor Robinson.* An American writer.

Hannett, John. *John Andrews Arnett.* An English writer, of London, on bookbinding.

Hansgirg, Therese von. *Theodor Reinwald.* A Bohemian novelist; wife of Karl Viktor, Ritter von Hansgirg, a Bohemian author (1823–77), who died at Joachimsthal.

Hanson, Alexander Contee, –1819. *Aristides; A Native Citizen and Servant of the State.* An American lawyer and statesman, of Maryland.

Hanson, Sir **Levett.** *An Officer of the Chancery, &c.* An English writer.

Hanson, Sir **Richard Davis.** *C. V. S.* An English colonial jurist; went to New Zealand, 1846; Advocate-General of South Australia, 1851–56; Attorney-General, 1856–61; Chief-Justice from 1861.

Hanway, Jonas, 1712–86. *Mr. H*****; A Gentleman of the Partie; A Member of the Marine Society.* An English merchant; b. in Portsmouth; resided for some years in Russia, engaged in mercantile business.

Hanway, Mary Anne. *A Lady.* An English novelist; resided at Blackheath.

Happer, A. P. *Inquirer.*

Harbin, Rev. **George.** *A Gentleman.* A Non-juring English clergyman of the first part of the 18th century.

Harcourt, Sir **William George Granville Vernon,** LL.D., Q.C., 1827–. *Historicus.* An eminent English publicist; M.P. for Oxford City from 1868.

Hardenberg, Friedrich Ludwig von, 1772–1801. *Novalis.* A German poet and philosopher; b. at Wiederstett, Prussian Saxony; the friend of Schlegel, Fichte, and Schelling; d. at his native place.

Hardham, John, –1772. *Abel Drugger.* An English dramatist; b. at Chichester; removed to London, and was at first a lapidary, or diamond-cutter; afterwards possessed the greatest snuff-trade anywhere about; and was for some years under-treasurer to the theatre in Drury Lane; d. in London.

Hardie, Robert. *Eidrah Trebor;* *Hartebor Reid.* A Scottish writer on chess.

Harding, W. M. *Porte-Plume.* An American writer.

Harding, William. *Bashi-bazouk; Commodore Robin; Fac et Spera.* An American journalist, of New York City.

Hardinge, Mrs. Belle (Boyd). *Belle Boyd; A Friend to the South.* An American woman, of Martinsburg, Va.; a spy for "Stonewall" Jackson and other Rebel generals; married one Hardinge, an officer of the U.S. Navy, who deserted to the "Confederates."

Hardinge, George, F.R.S., F.S.A., 1744–1816. *Owen Junior; Jasper Hargrave; A Layman; Minutius Felix.* An English lawyer; Attorney General to the Queen; and H. M.'s Justice for the Counties of Glamorgan, Brecknock, and Radnor; d. at Presteigne.

Hardwick, the Rt. Hon. Philip Yorke, 1st Earl of, 169 –1764. *Rt. Hon. P—p E—l of H—k.* An eminent English statesman; Lord High Chancellor, 1737–56.

Hardy, Arthur Sherburne, 1847–. *A. S. H.* An American civil engineer; b. in Mass.; Professor at Dartmouth Coll., 1873–83 *et seq.*

Hardy, Mrs. Janet (Gordon). *Janet Gordon.* An English novelist of the day.

Hardy, John Stockdale, Esq., F.S.A., 1793–1849. *Britannicus.* An English ecclesiastical lawyer; b. at Leicester; Registrar of the Archdeaconry Courts of Leicester; d. at his residence in the Newarke, Leicester.

Hare, Rev. Augustus William, 1792–1834. *A Member of a Close College.* An English clergyman; Rector of Alton Barnes, Wiltshire, 1829–34; d. in Rome.

Hare, Rev. Francis, D.D., –1740. *A Citizen; The Clergyman; An Impartial Hand; Philo-Criticus; A Presbyter of the Church of England.* An eminent English clergyman; b. in London; Bishop of Chichester, 1731–40.

Hare, Julius Charles. *Julius Hirsutus.*

Hare, Julius Charles, and **Augustus William.** Julius Charles, 1795–1855; Augustus William, 1792–1834. *Two Brothers.* English theologians, of the Church of England.

Hare, Robert, M.D., 1781–1858. *Eldred Grayson, Esq.* An eminent American chemist; b. in Philadelphia; Professor in the Univ. of Penn., 1818–47; d. in his native city.

Harel, Marie Maximilién, 1749–1823. *Élie, le Père.* A French ecclesiastic, of Saint-Germain-des-Prés.

Harland, John, F.S.A. *Iota.* An English literary antiquary, of Manchester (?).

Harley, Robert, Earl of Oxford and Mortimer, 1661–1724. *Humphry Mackworth.* A distinguished English statesman and an eminent patron of letters, and a great collector of literary treasures; b. in London; Lord High Treasurer, 1711–14.

Harness, Rev. William, M.A., 1790–1869. *Presbyter Catholicus.* An English clergyman; b. at Wickham, Hants.; B.A., Cambridge, 1813; Prebendary of St. Paul's, London.

Harper, Mrs. Eliza Elliott (Lewis), 1834–. *Sindera.* An American "Southland" writer, of Minden, Claiborne Parish, La.; b. in James Co., Ga., and removed to Louisiana in 1846, and at an early age married Dr. James D. Harper.

Harper, Mrs. Frances Ellen (Watkins). *Effie Afton.* An American poet, of Baltimore.

Harper, John. *Hautboy.*

Harper, Rev. Samuel Brown. *An English Priest.* An English clergyman; Curate of Dalton.

Harring, Paul, 1798–. *Harro.* A Danish adventurer, poet, and novelist; visited the United States about 1844.

Harrington, George N., 1827–68. *George Christy.* An American minstrel singer.

Harrington, John A. *John Carboy.* An American novelist of the day.

Harris, Alexander. *An Emigrant Mechanic.* An English emigrant to Australia.

Harris, Charles H. *Karl Pretzel.* An American writer, of New York City (?).

Harris, Miss E. F. S. *E. F. S. H.; A Companion Traveller.* An English writer, of Windsor.

Harris, Emily Marion. *Estelle; E. M. H.* An English writer.

Harris, Mrs. F. (McCready). *Hope Ledyard.*

Harris, George W., 1805–69. *Sut Lovengood; A Nat'ral Born Durn'd Fool.* An American jurist and humorist; b. in Tennessee; d. near Knoxville, Tenn.

Harris, James Henry. *Jack Staff.* An American writer, of St. Louis, Mo. (?).

Harris, Joel Chandler, 1848–. *Uncle Remus.* An American negro-dialect writer; b. in Georgia.

Harris, John, 1784–1858. *Q. in the Corner.* An English Friend, of Ratcliff, afterwards of Wapping, and lastly of Kingston-upon-Thames.

Harris, John. *Kuklos.* A Canadian writer on natural philosophy, etc.

Harris, Rev. Joseph Hemington, M.A. *Anglicanus Presbyter.* An English clergyman; Vicar of Tor-Morhun *w.* Cockington, Devon., 1848–79; resident at Sorèl, Torquay, 1880 *et seq.*

Harris, Josiah, 1821–. *Cantabar; Ishmael; A Philanthropist; Saint Meva.* An English journalist and miscellaneous writer, of Cornwall.

Harris, Mrs. Lilly C. *Chrysanthea.* An American hymn-writer; wife of Thomas Lake Harris.

Harris, Rev. N. Sayre. *Secretary and General Agent.* An Epis. clergyman; in 1882 of New York City.

Harris, Richard. *A Barrister.* An English lawyer.

Harris, Richard, 1833–. *Benedick Whipem; Cordrac Verdello.* An English miscellaneous writer of the day.

Harris, Mrs. Sydney S., 1834–. *Miriam Coles.* An American novelist; b. in Long Island.

Harris, Thaddeus Mason, D.D., 1768–1842. *A Student of Harvard University; Dorcastriensis.* An American Cong. minister, of Dorchester, Mass., 1793–1839; b. in Charlestown, Mass.; Harv. Univ., 1787; d. in Dorchester.

Harris, Thomas Lake, 1823–. *Chrysantheus.* An American poet and spiritualist; b. in England; founder of the order "The Brotherhood of the New Life" at Passaic, N.J., 1861–67, and at Brocton, N.Y., 1867–75 *et seq.*

Harris, W. C. *A Ball's Bluff Prisoner.* An American soldier.

Harrison, Mrs. —— (Kingsley). *Lucas Malet.* An English novelist; a daughter of Charles Kingsley.

Harrison, Mrs. Constance (Cary). *Refugitta.* An American "Southland" writer; b. in Mississippi (?); in 1866 married Mr. Burton N. Harrison, and in 1870 was residing with him in New York City.

Harrison, George. *His Grandson.* An English Friend, of Lancashire; son of George Harrison, of Wandsworth, near London.

Harrison, John, 1796–1852. *J. H.* An English Friend, of Manchester.

Harrison, Susannah. *A Young Woman.* An English poet of the last century.

Harriss, Julia Mildred. *The Minstrel Maiden of Mobile.* An American poet.

Harsha, David Addison, 1827–. *A Pilgrim.* An eminent American author; b. in Argyle, Washington Co., N.Y.; since 1851 has devoted himself to literary work in New York City.

Hart, Adolphus M., 1834–. *A Hoosier.* A Canadian writer and lawyer, of Montreal, from 1857.

Hart, C. W. *A Member of the Bar.* An American lawyer, of Steubenville, O.

Hart, Charles B. *Mr. Benjamins.* An English writer.

Hart, Ernest Abraham. *Pupils of the City of London School.* An English Shakespearian scholar.

Hart, Mrs. Fanny (Wheeler). *A Clergyman's Wife.* An English writer.

Hart, W. C. *Chevalier.* An American journalist.

Harte, Francis Bret. *Bret Harte.* An American writer; b. in Albany, N.Y.; went to California, dug for gold, taught school, engaged in the express business, set type, edited the "Californian," was Secretary of the U.S. Mint at San Francisco in 1864, started the "Overland Monthly" in 1864, was Professor of Modern Literature in the Univ. of California, 1870–71; then returned to the East, and for some years has been United States Consul at Glasgow.

Harte, Jerome Alfred, 1854–. *Zulano.* An American writer; b. at San Francisco, Cal.; has been for several years a contributor to the San Francisco "Argonaut," of feuilletons, sketches, and translations.

Hartley, Mrs. May Laffan. *The Irish Charles Dickens.* An Irish writer; b. in Dublin; her first essay in literature was a paper in "Fraser's Magazine" for 1876, on "Convent Schools."

Hartley, Rev. Thomas, 1707–84. *Un Ami.* An English clergyman; Rector of Winwick, Northamptonshire; was a translator of Swedenborg.

Hartley, Thomas, 1748–1809. *Phocion.* An American soldier and statesman; b. at Reading, Penn.; practised law in York; M.C., 1789–1800; d. at York.

Hartmann, Agnes (Taubert) von. *A. Taubert.* A German writer; wife of Eduard von Hartmann.

Hartmann, Eduard von, 1842–. *Karl Robert.* A German philosopher; b. in Berlin; and there devoted himself to the study of philosophy and natural science.

Hartmann, Moritz, 1821–72. *Pfaffe Mauritius.* A German poet and prose-writer; b. at Duschnik in Bohemia; studied in Prague and Vienna; in 1868 he settled in Vienna; and d. there.

Hartshorne, B. F. *B. F. H.* An English poet.

Hartwell, Mary. *H. M. Leutral.* An American novelist.

Harvey, Alexander, M.D. *A University Professor.* A Scottish physician; Professor at Aberdeen.

Harvey, Rev. Edmund George, B.A., 1828-. *The Captain; The Other.* An English clergyman; b. at Penzance; Vicar of Mullyon-Helston, 1865-83 *et seq.*

Harvey, Gabriel, LL.D., about 1545-about 1630. *Don Richardo de Medico Campo.* An old English writer; a caustic wit, during the reign of Elizabeth.

Harvey, Miss J. *A Young Lady.*

Harvey, James. *R. V.* An English financial writer of the day.

Harvey, Rev. Moses. *Delta; Locomotive; Nemo.* An American Presbyt. minister, of St. John's, Newfoundland; b. at Armagh, Ireland; studied in Belfast Coll.; came to Newfoundland in 1852.

Harvey, Rev. Richard, M.A. *R. H.* An English clergyman and hymn-writer; St. Catharine Coll., Cambridge, 1818; Rector of Hornsey, Middlesex, 1829-80.

Harvey, William, 1800-66. *Aleph.* An English artist; b. at Newcastle-on-Tyne; was an apprentice of Thomas Bewick; in 1817 went to London.

Harvey, William Henry, M.D., 1811-66. *W. H. H.* An Irish botanist; b. at Limerick; Professor at Trin. Coll., Dublin, 1856-66.

Harvey, Rev. William Woodis, M.A., 1798-1864. *Vindicator.* An English clergyman; b. at Penzance; Prebendary of Exeter, 1839-64; d. at Torquay.

Harwood, Miss Isabella. *Rose Neil.*

Harwood, Thomas. *Clio.* An English author; educ. at Eton, and Univ. Coll., Oxford; Master of Lichfield School; in 1787 resided at Lavenham, near Sudbury, Suffolk.

Haseltine, Mayo H. *M. H. H.* An American writer.

Haseltine, W. H. H. *W. H. H. H.* An American journalist.

Haslewood, Joseph, 1769-1833. *Eu. Hood; Gridiron Gabble; Christofer Valdarfer.* An English editor and bibliographer; b. in London; one of the founders of the Roxburghe Club.

Hassall, Miss ——. *A Lady at Cape François.*

Hassan, A. B. *A. B. H.* An American poet.

Hassard, John R. G., 1836-. *J. R.*

G. H. An American journalist; b. in New York City; educ. at St. John's, Fordham, N.Y., 1855; since 1866, employed in his native city.

Hasselt, André Henri Constant van, 1806-74. *Alfred d'Avaline.* A Belgian miscellaneous writer; member of the Royal Academy of Brussels.

Hastings, Thomas, -1800. *Archy Macsarconica, F.R.S.* An English itinerant bookseller and pamphleteer; b. in the bishopric of Durham; lived chiefly in London, where he died. His travelling name was "Dr. Green."

Hatfield, John, -1803. *A Gentleman.* An English impostor, swindler, and forger; during a visit to Keswick, in Cumberland, he called himself the Hon. Alex. Aug. Hope; M.P. for Dumfries; married, in 1802, a young lady of fortune, not his only wife; forged Hope's name; was convicted of forgery, and hung for that crime.

Hatfield, Miss Julia. *The Idle Scholar.* An American compiler.

Hatheway, Calvin. *An Inhabitant of the Province.* An American writer, of New Brunswick.

Hatt, Francis, 1691-1767. *A Lover of Truth and Mankind universally.* An English Friend, of Ratcliff, London; a member of the Southwark Monthly Meeting; d. in Clerkenwell.

Hatton, Mrs. Anne Kemble, 1764-1838. *Anne of Swansea.* An English lady; sister of Mrs. Siddons; d. at Swansea. — See "Kemble, Ann."

Hatton, Joshua. *Guy Roslyn.* An English (?) poet.

Hauenschild, Richard Georg Spiller von, 1822-55. *Max Waldau.* A German poet; b. at Breslau.

Haug, Johann Christoph Friedrich, 1761-1829. *Friedrich von Hophthalmos.* A celebrated German epigrammatist; Librarian at Stuttgart, 1817-29; b. in Würtemberg; d. in Stuttgart.

Hauser, Carl. *Rentier Pinneberg; Adolar Sanftleben; Schnake; Gretchen Shoddy.* An American journalist, of New York City.

Hausrath, Prof. **Adolf.** *George Taylor.*

Havard, Jean Alexandre d'Albanès-Havard. *Albanès Havard d'; A. d'Albanès.* A French writer; in the public service.

Haven, Mrs. Alice (Bradley Neal), 1828-63. An American writer; b. in Hudson, N.Y.; married Joseph C. Neal, of Philadelphia, in 1846; and in 1853, Samuel L. Haven; and afterwards resided at Mamaroneck, N.Y.; and d. there.

Havers, Miss **Dora.** *Theo. Gift.* An English novelist of the day.

Hawarden, Rev. **Edward.** *E. H.* An English Roman Catholic writer, of the earlier part of the 18th century.

Haweis, Rev. **Thomas,** LL.B., M.D., 1733–1820. *The Presbyter.* An English clergyman; b. at Redruth; Rector of All Saints, Aldwinkle, Northamptonshire; d. at Bath.

Hawes, Mrs. **Joel.** *Her Mother.* An American writer; wife of Rev. Dr. Hawes, of Hartford, Conn.

Hawes, William Post, 1821–41. *J. Cypress, Jr.* An American journalist, of New York City.

Hawke, Lady **Annabella Eliza Cassandra,** 1787–. *The Right Honourable Lady H****.* An English poet; sister of the Hon. Martin Bladder Hawke.

Hawker, Capt. ——, R.A. *A Regimental Officer.* An English soldier; Captain of the 14th Light Dragoons.

Hawker, Mrs. **Charlotte E. (l'Ans),** –1863. *C. E. H.* An English translator; wife of Rev. Robert Stephen Hawker, M.A., Vicar of Morwenstow, Cornwall.

Hawker, Admiral **Edward,** 1782–1860. *A Flag Officer.* An English seaman; entered the navy in 1793; became captain in 1804; d. at Brighton.

Hawker, Rev. **Robert,** 1753–1827. *R. H.* An English Calvinistic minister; b. at Exeter; Magdalen Coll., Cambridge; for fifty years vicar of a church in Plymouth.

Hawker, Rev. **Robert Stephen,** M.A., 1804–75. *R. S. H.; Breachan; A Cornish Vicar; Procul; Reuben; Canon Tremaine; The Vicar of Morwenstow; Two Oxford Men; X.* An English clergyman; b. at Stoke Damerel; Vicar of Morwenstow, Cornwall, 1834–75; d. in Plymouth.

Hawkes, James. *A Citizen of New York.* An American writer.

Hawkes, W. R. *W. R. H.* An English poet and dramatist, of the early part of the present century.

Hawkesworth, John, LL.D., 1715 or 19–1773. *Greville,* or *H. Greville.* An eminent English author and critic; b. in London, where he chiefly passed his literary life, and where he died.

Hawkins, Col. **Charles Ashton.** *Vidocq.* An American writer of the day.

Hawkins, Edward, D.D., 1789–. *A Resident Member of Convocation.* An English clergyman; St. John's Coll., Oxford, 1811; Provost of Oriel Coll., 1828.

Hawkins, Sir **John,** 1719–89. *J. H.* An English attorney and solicitor; in 1753 retired from business, and devoted himself to literary pursuits; from 1777 resided in Westminster, where he died.

Hawkins, Rev. **John.** *A Fair Inquirer.* An English Catholic priest; joined the Protestants in 1782–84.

Hawks, Francis Lister, D.D., LL.D., 1798–1866. *Frater; Lambert Lilly: A Protestant Episcopalian; Uncle Philip.* An eminent American clergyman and author; b. at Newbern, N.C.; Univ. of North Carolina, 1815; Rector of the Calvary Church, New York City, 1850–66, where he died.

Hawling, Francis. *A Citizen of London.* An English dramatist.

Haws, L. *Two Private Soldiers.* An American soldier, 1758–75.

Hawthorne, Nathaniel, 1804–64. *Oberon; Ashley Allen Royce.* An eminent American romancer; b. in Salem, Mass.; d. at Plymouth, N.H.

Hawtrey, Rev. **C. D.** *A Spiritual Watchman.* An English clergyman.

Hawtrey, Miss **Edith.** *Hope Wraythe.* An English writer of the day.

Hay, Dr. ——. *An Episcopal Divine.* An English clergyman of the first part of the 18th century.

Hay, Sir **Andrew Leith,** F.R.S., 1785–1862. *A British Officer.* A Scottish soldier; b. at Aberdeen; M.P. for the Elgin burghs, 1832–38 and 1841–47; d. at his seat, Leith Hall, Aberdeenshire.

Hay, George, –1830. *Hortensius.* An American jurist; many years U.S. Attorney, and afterwards Judge of the U.S. Court for the Eastern District of Virginia; d. at Richmond.

Hay, Mary Cecil. *Howard Markham.* An English novelist.

Hayden, Rev. **John.** *J. H.* An English clergyman; Archdeacon of Surrey.

Haydon, Benjamin Robert, 1786–1846. *B. R. H.* An eminent English artist; b. in Plymouth; committed suicide in London.

Hayes, ——. *Thomas Bishop.* An English writer; a footman to Lord Belgrave.

Hayes, Henry. *A No-Party Man.* An English religious writer.

Hayes, Isaac Israel, M.D., 1832–81. *John Hardy, Mariner.* An American Arctic explorer; b. in Chester Co., Penn.; Univ. of Penn., 1853; surgeon of the second Grinnell expedition, 1853–55; commander of another expedition, 1860–61; d. in New York City.

Hayes, P., M.D. *A Gentleman of the Faculty.* An English physician.

Hayes, Rev. **Thomas,** M.A. *Theta;*

Lancastriensis. An English clergyman; St. John's Coll., Cambridge, 1834; Rector of Duntsbourn-Abbots, 1861–73.

Hayley, William, 1745–1820. *A Friend to the Sisterhood.* An English poet and miscellaneous writer; the friend and biographer of William Cowper.

Haynes, John Edward, 1825–. *John H. Edwards.* An American publisher and writer, of New York City.

Hays, Mrs. Mary. *M—— H——.* An English novelist.

Hayward, Edward Dykes. *E. D. H.* An English Friend, of Southwark, London; son of William Hayward, of Malden, Essex.

Hayward, S. *A Lover of his King and Country.* An English writer of the 18th century.

Haywood, Mrs. **Eliza (Fowler),** 1693(?)–1756. *A Celebrated Author of that Country; Explorabilis.* An English writer; b. in London; the author of several loose novels, and some respectable books.

Haza, Mlle —— de. *H. Paris.* A French author.

Hazard, Rowland Gibson, LL.D., 1801–. *H.; Heteroscian.* An American manufacturer; b. in South Kingston, R.I.; resident at Peacedale, R.I.; devoted much time to literary pursuits.

Hazard, Thomas Robinson, 1784–. *A Northern Man with American Principles; Shepherd Tom.* An American writer, of Rhode Island; brother of the preceding; b. in South Kingston, R.I.

Hazeltine, M. W. *M. W. H.* An American writer; literary editor of the New York "Sun."

Hazeltine, Miron J. *Miron.* An American writer on games.

Hazen, Mary P. *Mabel; Marion Haven.* An American writer of the day on religious topics.

Hazlett, Helen. *M. H. Tatem.* An American (?) novelist.

Hazlitt, William, 1778–1830. *W. H.; Boswell Redivivus; Edward Search; Phantastes; Philalethes; Rationalis; W.* An English essayist; b. at Wem, in Shropshire; went to London before 1804, and devoted himself to literary pursuits; d. in that city.

Head, Edward Francis. *An Admirer of Chivalry.* An English (?) dramatist.

Head, Sir **Francis Bond,** 1st Bart., 1793–1875. *A British Subject.* An English politician; b. at Rochester; served for a time in the army; afterwards travelled, and wrote accounts of his travels;

received a pension of £100, 1867–75; d. at Croydon.

Head, Truman. *California Joe.* An American sportsman (?).

Headley, Henry, 1766–88. *C. T. O.* An English poet and literary critic; b. at Instead, in Norfolk; educ. at Trin. Coll., Oxford.

Heady, Morrison. *Uncle Juvinell.* An American writer.

Hearne, Mary Anne. *Marianne Farningham.* An English writer; b. at Farningham, in Kent.

Hearne, Thomas, 1678–1735. *A Gentleman of Cambridge; Phileleutherus Cantabrigiensis.* An English antiquary, collector, and editor; b. in Berkshire; resided chiefly at Oxford.

Heath, Miss **Maggie E.** *Miriam; Nettie Neale.* An American "Southland" writer, of Oakland, Va.; b. at Petersburg, Va.

Heath, W. McKendree. *R. E. Ducaigne.* An English author.

Heathcote, George. *An Old Servant.* An English gentleman; once an Alderman of London.

Heathcote, Ralph, D.D., 1721–95. *A Gentleman of the Commission.* An English clergyman; b. in Barrow-upon-Soar, Leicestershire; educ. at Jesus Coll., Cambridge; Prebendary of Southwell, 1768–95.

Heathcote, Rev. **William Beadon.** *W. B. H.* An English clergyman; Chaplain to the Bp. of Salisbury, 1850–60 *et seq.*

Heaton, Ellen Marvin. *E. M. H.* An American writer of the day.

Heaton, Rev. **John.** *H.* An English clergyman.

Heaven, Mrs. **S. M.** *Laura Preston; Lucia Norman.* An American writer, of San Francisco (?).

Heavlin, Mrs. **R. A.** *Uniche.* An American writer, of North Carolina.

Hebbard, William Wallace, M.D. *Leland Searcher.* An American novelist.

Heber, Richard, 1773–1883. *Atticus; Cato Parvus.* An English man of letters; half-brother of Reginald; b. in Westminster; educ. at Oxford; spent £180,000 for books; d. in London.

Heberden, Dr. ——. *E.* An English author of the 18th century.

Hector, Mrs. **Annie F.** *Mrs. Alexander.* An English novelist; in 1877 was living in Dresden, Germany.

Hedge, Edward Holyoke, –1837. *Jeremiah Grimes, Jun., Gent.* An American graduate of Harv. Univ., 1828.

Heesom, Rev. **Frederick.** *Parvus.*

An English author; b. at St. Veep; Schoolmaster at Polperro; local preacher.

Hello, Mme **Ernest.** *Jean Lander.* A French novelist.

Helps, Sir **Arthur,** 1817–75. *One of the Special Constables in London.* An English author; Trin. Coll., Cambridge, 1835; was in the public service, 1840–59; Secretary of the Privy Council, 1859–75.

Hemans, Mrs. **Felicia Dorothea (Browne),** 1793–1835. *Clara Balfour; A Lady.* An English poet; b. in Liverpool; the last years of her life were passed in Dublin, where she died.

Hemmings, Rev. **Joseph.** *A Disciple of the Prince of Peace.* An English minister.

Hempel, Friedrich Ferdinand. *Peregrinus Syntax.* A German philologist of the first part of the 18th century.

Hemyng, Bracebridge. *An Old Etonian; Jack Harkaway.* An English novelist of the day.

Henderson, Andrew. *A Christian; An Impartial Hand; Miltonicus.* A Scottish writer; once kept a bookseller's shop in Westminster Hall; styled himself A.M.

Henderson, Miss **Florence Leslie,** 1859–. *F. L. H.* An English poet; b. at Truro; educ. under masters in Brussels and Normandy.

Henderson, Julia Putnam. *Theta.* An American writer of the day.

Henderson, N. J. *Tricotrin.* An American journalist.

Henderson, Thulia Susannah. *T. S. H.* An English writer.

Henley, Rev. **John,** 1692–1756. *Peter de Quir; Jonadab Swift; Sir Isaac Ratcliffe, of Elbow-lane.* An English lecturer who, for 30 years, delivered his famous orations in London upon theology, etc.

Hennequin, Alfred, 1842–. *Alfred Lebrun.* A French dramatist; b. at Luttich; studied there, and became an engineer; from 1875 devoted himself, at Paris, entirely to dramatic poetry.

Hennessy, John C. *Irraghticonner.* An American publisher, of New York City.

Henningsen, Charles Frederick. *One who has Seen and Describes.* An English writer.

Henry, Caleb Sprague, D.D., 1804–83. *Dr. Oldham at Greystones.* An American clergyman; b. at Rutland, Mass.; Dart. Coll., 1825; in 1874 removed to Stamford, Conn.

Henry, David, 1710–92. *A Practical Farmer.* A Scottish writer; b. near Aberdeen; resided in London; was connected with the "Gent. Magazine" for more than half a century.

Henry, H. L. *H. L. H.* An American writer for the young.

Henry, Mrs. **Ina M. (Porter).** *Ethel Hope.* An American "Southland" writer; in 1872 resided near Greenville, Butler Co., Ala.

Henry, Capt. **J.** *Camillus.* A Canadian writer.

Henry, Mrs. **Mary H.** *Howe Benning.* An American novelist of the day.

Henry, Walter, M.D., 1791–1860. *Miles; Piscator; Scrutator; A Staff Surgeon.* An Irish journalist; b. at Donnegal; was stationed in Canada, 1827–41; at Halifax, 1841–52; in Canada again till his death at Belleville, Upper Canada.

Henshall, James A. *Oconomowoc.* An American writer of the day, of Wisconsin.

Henshaw, Mrs. ——. *Aunt Maggie.*

Henshaw, David, 1791–1852. *A Merchant.* An American politician; b. at Leicester, Mass.; in 1814 settled in Boston; Collector of the port of Boston, 1830–38; d. in his native town.

Henshaw, Mrs. **Sarah Edwards.** *Sidney E. Holmes.* An American writer of the day.

Hentz, Mrs. **Caroline Lee (Whiting),** 1800–56. *Aunt Patty.* An American writer; b. in Lancaster, Mass.; in 1825 married Prof. N. M. Hentz; d. at Marianna, Fla.

Hepworth, Mrs. **George Hughes.** *Una Savin.* An American writer; wife of Rev. G. H. Hepworth, of New York City.

Herbert, David. *Daryl Holme.* A Scottish translator of the day.

Herbert, Henry George, Lord Porchester, and 2d Earl of Carnarvon, 1772–1833. *The Bigwig's Friend.* An English nobleman; d. in London.

Herbert, Henry William, 1807–58. *W. H. H.; Dinks(?); F. F. of the Cedars; Frank Forester; Mr. Sponge; Old Yorkshire Turfman.* An English-American writer; came to the United States in 1831; his last years were passed at Newark, N.J.

Herbert, Sarah A. F. *Herbert Newbury.* An American(?) writer.

Hereford, John Butler, D.D., Bishop of, 1717–1802. *Vindex.* An English clergyman; b. at Hamburg; Bishop of Hereford, 1788–1802, where he died.

Herne, Thomas, 1722-. *Phileleutherus Cantabrigiensis; Philonagnostes Criticus.* An English controversialist; b. in Suffolk; a man of learning, virtue, and spirit; d. at Woburn.

Heron, A. *An Ex-Hussar.*

Heron, Agnes and Fanny. *Agnes and Fanny Natali.* American lyric artists; made their *début* in Philadelphia in 1848; in 1870 were in Europe.

Heron, Mrs. Emily (Manning). *Australie.* An English colonial poet; daughter of Sir William Montague Manning, Vice-Chancellor of the Sydney University.

Heron, Robert, 1764-1807. *Ralph Anderson.* A Scottish miscellaneous writer; b. at New Galloway; wrote and translated a number of works, and was editor and contributor to several periodicals.

Herrick, Edward Claudius, 1811-62. *B. F.* An American scholar; b. in New Haven, Conn.; Yale Coll., 1862; Librarian there, 1843-58, and Treasurer, 1852-62; d. in New Haven.

Herrick, N. *N. H.* An English writer of the first part of the 18th century.

Hervey, Mrs. Eleonora Louisa (Montagu), 1811-. *Margaret Russell.* An English author; b. in Liverpool; the wife of Thomas Kibble Hervey.

Hervey, John, Lord Hervey of Ickworth, 1696-1743. *A Member of the House of Commons; A Nobleman.* An English political and poetical writer; Lord Privy Seal, 1740-42; he was the "Sporus" of Pope's Satires.

Hervey, Thomas Kibble, 1804-59. *Jack Ketch.* A Scottish poet; b. at Paisley; engaged in literary work in London; d. at Kentish Town.

Hervilly, Ernest d', 1839-. *Le Passant.* A French author; b. in Paris; became a railroad engineer, but soon devoted himself entirely to literature and journalism.

Herzen, Alexander, 1812-70. *Iskander.* A Russian socialist and able republican writer; d. at Paris.

Heslop, R. O. *Harry Haldane.* An English dialect writer.

Hesse, Lépold Auguste Constantin, -1844. *L. A. Constantin.* An old bookseller and bibliographer, of Amsterdam.

Hetzel, Pierre Jules, 1814-. *Pierre Jules Stahl.* A French author and publisher, of Paris; in 1851 removed to Brussels.

Heun, Karl Gottlob Samuel, 1771-1854. *H. Clauren.* A German novelist; b. at Dobrilugk; spent his life chiefly in Berlin.

Hewerdine, Rev. Thomas, M.A. *T. H.* An English clergyman; Rector of Abington, and Vicar of Basingbourn, Cambridge.

Hewetson, William. *A Christian.* An English Friend.

Hewins, Miss C. M. *C. M. H.* An American bibliographer, of Hartford, Conn.

Hewitt, Harry S., 1856-. *Keld.* An American journalist, of Syracuse, N.Y.

Hewitt, John. *I. H.* An English antiquary.

Hewitt-Stebbins, Mrs. Mary Elizabeth (Moore), 1808-. *Ione; Jane.* An American poet; b. in Malden, Mass; married Mr. James L. Hewitt, and in 1854 Mr. R. Stebbins; has resided chiefly in New York City.

Hewlett, Rev. Joseph T. J., 1800-47. *P*; Peter Priggins.* An English divine; b. in London; Worcester Coll., Oxford; a teacher, 1828-40; an Epis. clergyman, 1823-28 and 1840-47; d. at Little Stambridge, Essex.

Hewson, Hugh, 1724-1809. *Hugh Strap.* An English hair-dresser, of Villiers-street, London; the original of the character of "Hugh Strap" in Smollett's "Roderick Random."

Heygate, Rev. William Edward, M.A., 1816-. *W. E. H.; A Clergyman of the Episcopal Church, in England.* An English divine; St. John's Coll., Oxford, 1839; Rector of Brightstone, Newport, Isle of Wight, 1869-83 *et seq.* — See "A Layman of Boston, U.S.A."

Heywood, James. *James Easy.* An early English writer.

Heywood, Samuel. *A Layman.* An English barrister-at-law.

Hibbard, Miss Carrie S., 1833-. *Mabel St. Clair.* An American poet; in 1860 resided at Spring Hill, Fulton Co., O.

Hickes, George, D.D., 1642-1715. *A Dignify'd Clergy-man of the Church of England.* An English divine; b. in Yorkshire; Dean of Worcester.

Hickes, T. *T. H., Pharmacop., Rustican.* An early English pharmacist.

Hickey, James Harden. *Saint Patrice.*

Hickey, Rev. Ross, 1790-. *Martin Doyle.* An Irish clergyman and rural economist; b. in Co. Cork.

Hickling, George. *Rusticus.* An English poet of the day.

Hicks, Mrs. Emilie Earle (Steele), 1820-. *A Lady.* An English author; b. at Penryn; in 1842, married William Briddlecombe Hicks, at St. Glavis.

Hicks, Jennie E. *Sophie Sparkle.* An American writer of the day.

Hiffernan, Paul, M.D., 1719–77. *P. H., M.D.* An Irish physician; b. in the Co. of Dublin; went to London in 1753; and for the rest of his life was a hack author.

Higgins, Matthew James, 1810–68. *J. O.; Jacob Omnium; Civilian; Paterfamilias.* An Irish journalist; for 20 years a constant contributor to the London "Times," and afterwards to the "Pall-Mall Gazette."

Higginson, Stephen, 1743–1828. *Cato; Laco.* An American merchant and politician; b. in Salem, Mass.; M.C., 1782–3; d. in Boston.

Higham, Mrs. **Mary R.** *M. R. H.* An American writer of the day.

Higham, T. R. *T. R. H.* An English dialect writer, of Cornwall.

Highmore, Joseph, 1692–1780. *J. H.* An English painter; b. and d. in London; was a writer of considerable merit.

Hildreth, Rev. **Hosea,** A.M., 1782–1835. *A Father.* An American minister, of Gloucester, Mass.; b, at Chelmsford, Mass,; Harv. Univ., 1803.

Hildreth, James. *A Dragoon.* An American soldier; served in the Western country, 1833–34.

Hildreth, Richard, 1807–65. *A Native American.* An American journalist and miscellaneous writer; b. at Deerfield, Mass.; Harv. Univ., 1826; d. at Florence, Italy.

Hildrop, John, D.D., 1725–56. *An Impartial Hand.* An English clergyman; Rector of Wath, near Rippon, Yorkshire.

Hildyard, Rev. **James,** B.D. *Ingoldsby.* An English clergyman; Christ Coll., Cambridge, 1833; Rector of Ingoldsby-Grantham, 1846–83 *et seq*.

Hilgard, Heinrich, 1834–. *Henry Villard.* A German-American financier; emigrated to this country from Munich in 1853, and at first settled at Belleville, Ill.; in 1878 was a millionaire and railroad king in New York City.

Hill, Mrs. **A. P. (Dawson).** *Ruth.* An American "Southland" writer; in 1872, Superintendent of the "Orphans' Free School" at Atlanta, Ga.

Hill, Benson Earle, 1795–1845. *Pollexenes Digit Snift; Dean Swift, of Brazennose.* An English author and comedian; at one time editor of the "Old Monthly"; and afterwards co-editor, with Theodore Hook, of the "New Monthly"; d. in London, in penury and distress.

Hill, F. S. *F. S. H.* An American poet.

Hill, Frank Harrison. *A Prominent London Journalist.* An English writer; successively editor of the "Northern Whig" at Belfast, and the "Daily News," London.

Hill, George, 1796–1871. *A Voyager.* An American poet; b. at Guilford, Conn.; Yale Coll., 1816; Librarian, etc., of the State Dept., Washington, 1831–55; then spent the rest of his life in his native town; d. in St. Vincent Hospital, New York City.

Hill, George Canning, 1825–. *Lewis Myrtle; Thomas Lackland.* An American writer; b. in Norwich, Conn.; Yale Coll., 1845.

Hill, Henry Scrine, 1845–. *H. S. H.* An English journalist; b. at Exeter; Reporter of the "Western Daily Mercury," 1863–77.

Hill, Isaac, 1788–1851. *A Citizen of New England.* An American journalist and politician; b. in Cambridge, Mass.; resided in Concord, N.H., from 1809; U.S. Senator, 1830–36; d. at Washington, D.C.

Hill, Sir John, M.D., 1716–1775. *George Crine, M.D.; Mrs. Glasse; An Impartial Hand; The Inspector; Abraham Johnson; A Lady; A Sclavonian Nobleman in London; Christian Uvedale.* An English author; a singular character and voluminous writer; resided in London. . .

Hill, L. C. *L. C. H.* An American novelist of the day.

Hill, Sir Richard, 1733–1808. *A Friend; A Gentleman of the University of Oxford; An Old Member of Parliament; Philalethes.* An English Calvinistic Methodist; sometimes preached in their chapels; at one time M.P. for Salop.

Hill, Thomas, about 1760–1841. *Paul Pry, etc.* An English eccentric; b. and d. in London; was styled by Lockhart "the most innocent and ignorant of bibliomaniacs."

Hillard, George Stillman, LL.D., 1808–79. *An Idler; Sylvanus Dashwood; Silas Standfast.* An American lawyer and writer; b. at Machias, Me.; Harv. Univ., 1828; practised law in Boston; d. in Brookline, Mass.

Hiller, Rev. **Thomas Oliver Prescott.** *An American.* An American poet; a Swedenborgian minister.

Hilliard, Kate. *Lucy Fountain.* An American (?) poet.

Hincks, Edward, D.D., 1795–1866. *E. H.* An Irish archæologist; b. in Cork; Trin. Coll., Dublin, 1812; celebrated for his knowledge of Assyrian inscriptions.

Hincks, Sir Francis, K.C.B., 1807-. *A Member of the Legis. Assem. of Upper Canada.* A Canadian statesman; b. at Cork, Ireland; settled in Canada in 1832; Financial Minister of Canada, 1869-73.

Hindley, Miss Anne. — See "Woods, Mrs. A. (H)."

Hingeston-Randolph, Rev. **Francis Charles,** M.A., 1833-. *A Country Parson; Herbert Murray.* An English clergyman; b. at Truro; Rector of Ringmore, Kingsbridge, Devon., 1860-83 *et seq.;* Rural Dean of Woodleigh, 1879.

Hinkley, Holmes, 1853-. *Eleven Sophomores.* An American educator; b. in Boston; Harv. Univ., 1876; a teacher in Boston in 1881-82 *et seq.*

Hinman, Royal Ralph, 1785-1868. *An Antiquarian.* An American biographer; b. in Southbury, Conn.; Yale Coll., 1804; Secretary of State for Conn., 1835-42; spent the last years of his life in New York City, and d. there.

Hinton, Henry L., 1840-. *Ralph Morely.* An American actor, dramatist, and publisher; b. in New York City; first appearance on the stage, 1864.

Hinton, Howard. *Hd. H.* An American novelist and publisher, of New York City.

Hippisley, John, -1748. *A Gentleman.* An English comic actor and dramatist; built a theatre at Bristol, and had commenced another at Bath, when he d. at Bristol.

Hislop, Rev. **Alexander.** *Godfrey Golding.* A Scottish Free Church minister, of Arbroath.

Hitchcock, Ethan Allen, 1798-1870. *E. A. H.* An American author; b. at Vergennes, Vt.; West Point, 1817; d. at Hancock, Ga.

Hitchcock, Francis. *Frank Murdock.* An American writer.

Hitchins, Fortescue, 1784-1814. *A Young Gentleman.* An English poet; b. at St. Hilary; Solicitor at St. Ives; d. at Marazion.

Hlinka, Adalbert, 1817-. *Franz Prawda.* A Bohemian author; b. at Nekrasin; studied theology at Vienna and Prague; and is at the present time (1882) Castle chaplain at Hradet.

Hoare, Rev. **Edward Newenham,** M.A. *Decanus.* An English clergyman; Trin. Coll., Dublin, 1862; Rector of Acrise, Canterbury, 1879-83 *et seq.*

Hoare, Prince, Esq., 1755-1834. *A Layman.* An English artist and dramatist; b. at Bath; Secretary to the Royal Academy from 1799; d. in his native city.

Hoare, Sir Richard Colt, Bart., F.R.S., F.S.A., F.L.S., 1758-1838. *R. C. H.* An English antiquary; b. and d. at Stourhead.

Hoare, Miss Sarah, 1767-1855. *A Friend to Youth.* An English Friend, of Bath; b. in Bristol.

Hobart, Augustus Charles, 1822-. *Capt. A. Roberts.* An English naval officer; known as Hobart Pasha, being on half pay; he commanded a swift blockade runner, the "Don," 1861-65, along the coasts of North Carolina.

Hobart, John Henry, D.D., 1775-1830. *Corrector.* An American clergyman; b. at Philadelphia; New Jersey Coll., 1793; Asst. Bishop and Bishop of New York, 1811-30; d. at Auburn, N.Y.

Hobbs, Samuel. *Sylvan.* An English poet.

Hobhouse, Sir Benjamin, 1757-1831. *A Barrister at Law.* An English statesman; M.P., 1797-1818; and filled several important posts.

Hobhouse, John Cam, Lord Broughton, 1786-1869. *An Englishman resident at Paris.* An English author; b. near Bristol; Trin. Coll., Cambridge, 1808; accompanied Lord Byron to Greece; M.P., 1820-51; raised to the peerage in 1851.

Hoblyn, Miss Maria Theresa. *Theta.* An English poet and musical composer, of Cornwall; b. at Mylor Vicarage.

Hobson, Robert. *R. H.* An English writer.

Hobson, Rev. **Samuel,** LL.D. *A Norfolk Clergyman.* An English divine; LL.D., Cambridge, 1831; Vicar of Tuttington, Norwich, 1853-74 *et seq.*

Hocédé, Jules. *Jules Neuvil.* A French poet.

Hodder, Edwin. *Old Merry.* An English writer of the day.

Hodge, Thomas Hounsell. *H. T. Devon.* A Canadian writer.

Hodges, Sydney, 1829-. *George Budock.* An English portrait painter; b. at Worthing; resident, 1880, in London.

Hodgkin, John. *A Member of the English Bar.* An English Friend, of Tottenham; afterwards of Lewes; son of John Hodgkin, of Tottenham.

Hodgkin, John Eliot, F.S.A. *J. E. H.* An English artist of the day.

Hodgkinson, ——. *A Gentleman lately returned from America.* An English writer.

Hodgman, Rev. **Stephen A.** *A Chaplain of the U. S. A.* An American clergyman.

Hodgson, William, Jr. *W. H., junr.*
An English writer.

Hodshon, Ralph. *A Layman.* An
English writer of the 18th century.

Hodson, Mrs. **Margaret (Holford).**
A Lady. An English poet; daughter of
Mrs. M. Holford, of Chester.

Hoffman, Charles Fenno, 1806–84.
A New Yorker. An American poet; b.
in New York City; in 1824 entered upon
literary pursuits; in 1849 was seized with
a mental disorder, and was compelled to
retire from the world; d. at Harrisburg,
Penn.

Hoffman, David, LL.D., 1784–1854.
*Cartaphilus; Anthony Grumbler, Esq., of
Grumbleton Hall.* An American lawyer;
b. in Baltimore; Professor of Law in the
Univ. of Maryland, 1817–36; practised
his profession in Philadelphia, 1838–47;
d. in New York City.

Hoffman, David Murray, LL.D.,
1791–1878. *Pacificator.* An American
jurist; b. in New York City; Columbia
Coll., 1809; Judge of the Superior Court
of New York, 1853–62.

Hofland, Mrs. **Barbara (Wreaks
Hoole),** 1770–1844. *An Englishwoman.*
An English writer; b. in Sheffield; d. at
Richmond.

Hog, Rev. **James.** *A Member of the
Church of Scotland.* A Scottish minister,
of Carnock.

Hog, James Maitland. *A Barrister.*
A Scottish lawyer.

Hogan, Rev. **Edmund.** *E. G.* An
Irish editor.

Hogarth, Mrs. **Georgina.** *His Sister-
in-law.* An English lady; sister-in-law of
Charles Dickens.

Hogarth, T. B., R.A. *T. B. H., R.A.*
An English artist.

Hogarth, William, 1697–1764. *Giles
Grinagain.* A celebrated English painter;
b., lived, and d. in. London.

Hogg, James, 1772–1835. *J. H. Craig,
of Douglas, Esq.; The Ettrick Shepherd;
The Shepherd; Jamie the Poeter; A Jus-
tified Sinner; Robert Wringham Colwan.*
A famous Scottish poet; b. at Ettrick in
Selkirk; in 1810 removed to Edinburgh;
d. at his residence on the banks of the
Yarrow.

Hogg, James. *J. H.* A Scottish publisher, of Edinburgh.

Hogg, Thomas Jefferson, Esqr., 1792–
1862. *John Brown, Esqre.; A Traveller.*
An English lawyer; b. at Norton, Co.
Durham; called to the bar at the Middle
Temple, 1817; for more than 20 years
was Revising Barrister for Northumberland, etc.; d. at St. John's Wood, London.

Holbach, Paul Thiry, Baron von,
1723–89. *Mirabaud.* A German philosopher.

Holberg, Baron **Ludwig von,** 1684–
1754. *Niels Klim.* A Danish poet and
dramatist, of Copenhagen.

Holbrook, Mrs. **A. M.** *Pearl Rivers.*

Holbrook, Silas Pinckney, 1796–
1835. *A Boston Merchant; Jonathan Farbrick; A Traveller.* An American writer;
b. in Beaufort, S.C.; studied law in Boston, and practised at Medfield, Mass.; d.
at Pineville, S.C.

Holcroft, Thomas, 1744–1809. *William Vincent, of Gray's Inn; —— Marshall.* An English actor and dramatist;
b. in London, and chiefly practised his art
there; but spent the principal part of the
years 1799–1801 in Germany and France.

Holden, J. G. P. *Ralph Redwood.*

Holden, Luther L. *Rambler; Ranger.*
An American journalist; correspondent
of the Boston "Journal."

Holden, Mrs. **Maria.** *May Myrtle.*

Holden, Oliver, –1831. *A Citizen of
Massachusetts.* A popular American composer of sacred music; was a carpenter;
then a music-teacher and bookseller; d.
at Charlestown, Mass.

Hole, Matthew, D.D., about 1640–
about 1730. *A. B.; A Presbyter of the
Church of England.* An English clergyman; Rector of Exeter Coll., Oxford,
1715–30.

Hole, Rev. **Samuel Reynolds,** M.A.
An Oxonian. An English clergyman; Brasenose Coll., Oxford, 1844; Vicar of Caun-
ton, Newark-on-Trent, 1850–83 *et seq.*

Holford, Miss **Margaret.** — See
"Hodson, Mrs. M. (H.)."

Holland, Edwin Clifford, about
1793–1824. *A South Carolinian.* An
American poet, essayist, and journalist,
of Charleston, S.C.

Holland, Rev. **Frederic West,**
1811–. *A Pilgrim of 1851.* An American clergyman; b. in Boston; Harv.
Univ., 1831; has been pastor in many
places; is now (1885) resident in Concord, Mass.

Holland, Henry Fox, 1st Baron,
1705–74. *The Paymaster.* An English
nobleman and politician.

**Holland, Henry Richard Vassall
Fox,** 3d Baron, 1773–1840. *A Disciple
of Selden; An Englishman.* An eminent
English statesman; b. at Winterslow
house, in Wiltshire; d. at Holland house,
Kensington.

Holland, John, 1794–1872. *A Christian Poet; Sexagenarius.* An English
author and journalist; b. in Sheffield,

Yorks. Co.; was for a time an optician, but afterwards devoted his life in his native city to literary pursuits, and d. there.

Holland, Josiah Gilbert, 1819–81. *Dr. Henry Halford; Max Mannering; Timothy Titcomb.* An American author and journalist; b. at Belchertown, Mass.; was connected with the "Springfield Republican," 1849–66, and editor of "Scribner's Monthly," 1870–81; d. in New York City.

Holland, Rev. Thomas Agar, M.A. *An Undergraduate.* An English clergyman; Worcester Coll., Oxford, 1825; Rector of Poynings, Sussex, 1846–83 *et seq.*

Holley, Marietta. *Josh. Allen's Wife.* An American novelist of the day.

Holley, Myron, 1779–1841. *A Citizen of New York.* An American lawyer and journalist.

Hollingbery, R. H. *An Indian Official.* An English colonial writer of the day.

Hollingsworth, Rev. Nathaniel John. *A Late Steward of the Sons of the Clergy.*

Hollis, Rev. John. *A Layman.* An English clergyman.

Hollis, William. *A Contributor to "Bentley."* An English scholar and poet.

Holloway, Laura Carter. *L. C. H.* An American writer of the day.

Holman, James, 1787–1857. *The Blind Traveller.* An English traveller; entered the navy in 1798; was made lieutenant, 1807; at the age of 25 was compelled by blindness to leave the service, but afterwards travelled all over the world; d. in London.

Holme, L. *A Young Artist.* An English artist.

Holmes, Cecil Frederick. *C. F. H.; A Harrow Tutor.* An English writer of the day.

Holmes, Mrs. Dalkeith. *A Lady.* An English writer.

Holmes, Edward. *A Musical Professor.* An English writer.

Holmes, Mrs. Elizabeth (Emra), –1843. *A Country Parson's Daughter.* An English writer; daughter of Rev. John Emra, Vicar of St. George's, Bristol, and wife of Marcus Holmes, Esq., of Westbury-on-Trym; was a frequent contributor to periodicals; d. at Westbury.

Holmes, Nathaniel, A.M. *N. H.* An American Shakespearian scholar; Harv. Univ., 1837; Royall Professor of Law, 1868–72; in 1885 resident at Cambridge, Mass.

Holmes, Oliver Wendell, M.D.,

1809–. *Autocrat of the Breakfast Table; The Poet at the Breakfast Table; The Professor at the Breakfast Table.* An eminent American poet; b. at Cambridge, Mass.; Harv. Univ., 1829; Professor of Anat. and Physiol. in his *alma mater*, 1847–82; and Professor *Emeritus* from 1882.

Holroyd, Rev. James John, M.A. *I. J. H.* An English clergyman; Christ Coll., Cambridge, 1830; Rector of Abberton, Essex, 1830–70 *et seq.*; resident at White Hall, near Colchester.

Holt, John. *A Gentleman formerly of Gray's Inn.* An English Shakespearian scholar of the last century.

Holt, John Saunders, 1826–. *Abraham Page, Esq.; John Capelsay.* An American lawyer and novelist, of Woodville, Miss.; b. at Mobile, Ala., and educ. in New Orleans and at Centre Coll., Danville, Ky.

Holthaus, P. D. *A Journeyman Taylor.* An American traveller.

Holyoake, George Jacob. 1817–. *The Editor of the "National."* An English Radical and journalist, of London; b. at Birmingham; claims to be the founder of "Secularism"; was the editor of the "Reasoner."

Homan, Samuel H., 1842–. *Homer; Luxymon Roy.* An American writer.

Home, Sir Everard, Bart., 1756–1832. *E. H.* An eminent Scottish surgeon; President Royal Coll. of Surgeons; practised in London for many years.

Home, G. *A Midshipman.*

Home, M. J. *An Officer.* An English writer.

Homer, James Lloyd. *A Merchant of Boston.* An American printer and publisher, of Boston.

Homes, Mrs. Mary Sophie (Shaw). *Millie Mayfield.* An American poet; b. in Frederick City, Md.; has resided most of her life in New Orleans; in 1864 married Mr. Luther Homes, of that city.

Honan, Michael Burke. *Our own Correspondent.* An Irish journalist.

Hone, William, 1779–1842. *Cecil.* An English satirist, antiquary, and publisher, of London; b. in Bath.

Honeywood, St. John, Esq., 1765–98. *S. J. H., Esq.* An American lawyer; b. at Leicester, Mass.; Yale Coll., 1782; was a teacher at Schenectady, and a lawyer at Salem, N.Y.

Hook, James, LL.D., 1771–1828. *Fitz-Harding.* An English writer; brother of Theodore Edward Hook; b. in London; Dean of Worcester, 1825–28; d. at the Deanery.

Hook, Theodore Edward, Esq., F.S.A., 1788–1841. *Alfred Allendale, Esq.; Vicesimus Blenkinsop, LL.D., F.R.A., A.S.S., etc.; Mrs. Ramsbottam; Tekeli.* An English novelist; b. in London; spent his life there in literary work, and d. at his house, near Fulham Bridge, near London.

Hook, Rev. Walter Farquhar, D.D., F.R.S., 1798–1875. *A Layman.* An English clergyman; b. in London; B.A., Oxford, 1821; Dean of Chichester, 1859–75; d. in London.

Hooke, Josiah. *A Citizen of New England.* An American educator.

Hooker, Edward William, D.D., 1794–. *Her Father.* An eminent American divine; b. in Goshen, Conn.; Middlebury Coll., 1814; Prof. in Connecticut Theological Institute, 1844–48.

Hooker, John. *An Eminent Lawyer of Connecticut.* An American lawyer.

Hooper, Col. George W. *An Amateur.* An American writer.

Hooper, Henry. *Ducdame.* An English novelist of the day.

Hooper, Johnson J., Esq., –1863. *A Country Editor; Capt. Simon Suggs.* An American lawyer and journalist; b. and educ. in North Carolina; removed to Alabama; Secretary of the Provisional Congress of the Confederate States, 1861; resided at Lafayette, Ala.

Hooper, Miss Lucy, 1816–41. *L. H.* An American poet; b. in Newburyport, Mass.; resided at Brooklyn, N.Y., 1831–41, and d. there.

Hooper, Samuel, A.M., 1808–75. *A Merchant of Boston.* An American merchant and statesman; b. at Marblehead, Mass.; M.C., 1851–75; d. at Washington.

Hooper, Miss Susan C. *Adrienne.* An American "Southland" writer; b. in Richmond, Va.; in 1871 a teacher in the Richmond Female Institute.

Hooton, Charles. *Bilberry Thurland.* An English novelist.

Hope, Alexander James Beresford, LL.D., 1820–. *D. C. L.* An English statesman; son of "Anastasius" Hope; M.P. for the Univ. of Cambridge from 1868.

Hope, John. *An Advocate of the Cause of the People.* A Scottish writer; "M.P. for Linlithgow in 1768 on the nomination of his kinsman, the Earl of Hopetown, but lost his seat and allowance of £200 a year by giving offence to the Earl in his vote on the expulsion of Wilkes."

Hopkins, David, –1814. *A Late*

Resident at Bhagulpore. A British colonial civilian, of the Bengal Medical Establishment; d. at Samarang, Island of Java.

Hopkins, Samuel Miles, 1772–1837. *A House Holder.* An American lawyer; Yale Coll., 1791; M.C., 1813–15; lived and d. at Geneva, N.Y.

Hopkins, Rev. William, B.A., 1706–86. *A Member of the Church of England.* An English Arian clergyman; b. in Monmouth; of All Souls Coll., Oxford; Curate of Slaugham, Co. of Sussex, 1766–86.

Hopkinson, Francis, Esq., LL.D., 1737–91. *Peter Grievous, Esq.; A. B. C. D. E.* An American jurist; b. in Philadelphia; Univ. of Penn., 1757; U.S. Judge of the District of Pennsylvania, 1790–91; d. in his native city.

Hopkinson, J. *The Honorary Secretary.* An English naturalist, of Watford, Co. of Herts.

Hopkinson, Joseph, LL.D., 1770–1842. *An American.* An eminent American poet and jurist; b. in Philadelphia; Univ. of Penn., 1786; Judge of the U.S. Court for the Eastern District of Pennsylvania, 1828–42; d. in his native city.

Hopley, Miss Catherine C. *A Blockaded British Subject.* An English writer.

Hopper, Clarence. *Ithuriel.* An English writer.

Hoppin, Augustus, 1828–. *C. Auton.* An American artist; b. at Providence, R.I.; Brown Univ., 1848; studied law; then art, in Europe.

Horbery, Rev. Matthew, D.D., 1707–73. *A Clergyman in the Country.* An English clergyman; b. at Haxay, Lincolnshire; Rector of Standlake, and Prebendary of Lichfield.

Horlock, K. W. *Scrutator.* An English sporting writer.

Horne, ——. *Naufragus.* An English writer.

Horne, George, D.D., 1730–92. *A Clergyman; One of the People called Christians; An Undergraduate; Z.* An eminent English divine; b. at Otham, near Maidstone, in Kent; Bishop of Norwich, 1789–92; d. at Bath.

Horne, Henry, Jr. *An American Indian.*

Horne, Richard Hengist, –1884. *The Farthing Poet; M. I. D.; Salem Ben Uzāir.* An English poet and critic; educ. at Sandhurst; went to Australia, in 1852, with William Howitt; has of late years resided in London, where he died.

His name was *Richard Henry;* in 1864 he adopted that of *Richard Hengist.*

Horne, Thomas Hartwell, D.D., 1780–1862. *John Clarke; A Lincolnshire Grazier.* An English biblical critic; educ. in London; Prebendary of St. Paul's, 1841; and Librarian of the British Museum, 1824–60; d. in London.

Horner, William Edmunds, M.D., 1793–1853. *A Physician of Philadelphia.* An American anatomist; b. at Warrenton, Va.; Prof., etc., of Anatomy in the Univ. of Penn., 1816–53; d. in Philadelphia.

Hornihold, John. *J... H.....,* C. A. D. S. An English religious writer of the last century.

Horsburgh, James. *J. H.; An Old Inhabitant.* A Scottish writer; Provost of Pittenweem.

Horsburgh, Matilda. *M. H.* A Scottish novelist of the day.

Horsley, Samuel, D.C.L., 1733–1806. *The Archdeacon of St. Albans; A Clergyman.* An eminent English divine; b. in London; Archdeacon of St. Albans, 1780; Bishop of St. Asaph's, 1802–6.

Horsmanden, Daniel, 1691–1778. *The Recorder of the City of New York.* An American jurist; b. in England; Chief Justice of New York, 1763–78; d. at Flatbush, N.Y.

Horsnell, William. *W. H.* A Canadian poet, of Montreal.

Hort, John Josiah. *Two Mounted Sentries.* An English officer; entered the service, 1840; Lieut.-Col., 36th Foot, 1855; served in the Eastern campaign of 1854–55 with the 4th Regiment.

Horton, Sir Robert John Wilmot, 2d Bart., 1784–1841. *Philalethes.* An English statesman; b. at Ormaston, Co. Derby; Christ Church Coll., Oxford, 1806; M.P., 1818–20 and 26–; d. at Sudbrooke Park, Petersham.

Hoshour, S. K. *Lorenzo Altisonant.* An American writer.

Hoskins, Mrs. Josephine R. *Hildegarde; Jacqueline.* An American "Southland" writer, of New Orleans; b. in New York State.

Hoskyns, Chandos Wren, 1812–76. *C. W. H.* An English lawyer; educ. at Balliol Coll., Oxford; called to the bar at the Inner Temple, 1838; M.P. for Hereford, 1869–75.

Hoskyns, J. *A Physician.*

Hosmer, Miss Harriet G., 1830–. *Kilosa.* An American sculptor; b. at Watertown, Mass.; has for some years resided at Rome.

Hosmer, Mrs. Margaret. *An Old Teacher.* An American religious writer.

Hostrup, Jens Christian, 1818–. *Jens Christrup.* A Danish lyric and dramatic poet; b. at Copenhagen; studied theology; in 1856 became pastor at Silkeborg in Jutland, and in 1863 at Frederiksborg in Seeland.

Hotchkiss, Miss Ella A. *Hazel Wylde.* An American writer.

Hotton, John Camden, 1832–73. *Cadwalader Rowlands; A London Antiquary; Joshua Sylvester; Theodore Taylor; Titus A. Brick.* An English bookseller, of London, where he died.

Houghton, John William. *J. W. Hogo-Hunt.* An English humorist of the day.

Houghton, Richard Monckton Milnes, 1st Baron, D.C.L., F.R.S., 1809–85. *A Layman.* An English poet; Trin. Coll., Cambridge, 1831; M.P. for Pontefract, 1837–63, when he was raised to the peerage.

Houlding, John Richard. *An Old Boomerang.* An English writer, of Australia.

Houssaye, Arsène, 1815–. *Alfred Mousse; Arsène Housset; Pierre de l'Estoile.* A French man of letters; b. at Bruyères; settled in Paris; his works embrace romance, the theatre, poetry, and criticism.

Houston, George. *An Israelite; Nathan Joseph.* An American writer.

Hovey, William Alfred, 1842–. *Causeur.* An American journalist; b. and educ. in Boston; editor of the Boston "Transcript," 1875–81.

Howard, Mrs. Anna Holyoke (Cutts). *A. H. H.; Anna Holyoke; Edith Elliot; Lux Dux; Sana.* An American writer.

Howard, Edward, 8th Earl of Suffolk, –1731. *A Person of Quality.* An English peer.

Howard, Rev. John, M.A. *A Minister of the Church of England.* An English clergyman; Rector of Marston Trussel, Northampton, and afterwards Vicar of Kidderminster, Worcestershire.

Howard, Joseph, Jr. *Dead Beat; Diabolus; Howard of the "Times"; M. T. Jugg.* An American journalist.

Howard, Luke, 1773–1864. *Eccletus; H.; A Friend; An University Pen.* An English Friend, of Plaistow, Essex; last of Tottenham, Middx., and Ackworth, Yorkshire; d. at Tottenham.

Howard, Martin, –1781. *A Gentleman of Halifax.* An American loyalist; his house at Newport, R.I., was destroyed and his person injured; he fled to North Carolina, and was there Chief Justice for a short time; in 1778 he went to England, where he died.

Howe, Charles, 1661–1745. *A Person of Honour.* An English writer; b. in Gloucestershire; a diplomatist under James II.

Howe, Elias, Jr., 1819–67. *Gumbo Chaff.* An American inventor; b. at Spencer, Mass.; invented his sewing machine in 1846; from that time lived chiefly in Boston.

Howe, Mrs. Julia (Ward), 1819–. *A Lady.* An American poet; b. in New York City; in 1843 married Dr. Samuel G. Howe, and has since lived chiefly in Boston.

Howe, Miss Maud. *Halcyon.* An American novelist, of Boston; daughter of the preceding.

Howell, Mrs. F. *C. Walsingham.* An American writer.

Howell, John. *A Sufferer.* A Scottish writer.

Howell, John, 1788–1863. *Bill Truck.* A Scottish author, of Edinburgh; a "polyartist," as he called himself. He was a printer and book-binder, and invented the plough for cutting the leaves of books, etc., etc.; d. in Edinburgh.

Howells, William Dean, and Another, 1837–. *Two Friends.* A popular American editor and author; b. at Martinsville, O.

Howes, Osborne. *F. A. C. T.* An American writer.

Howison, William. *M. de Peudemots.* A Scottish writer; protegé of Sir Walter Scott.

Howitt, William, 1795–1879. *Dr. Cornelius.* An English author; b. at Heanor, Derbyshire; has chiefly devoted his life to literary pursuits.

Howlett, Robert, Esq. *R. H., Esq., near Forty Years a Practitioner in this Art.* An early English writer on angling.

Hows, George W. *Strix.* An American journalist, of New York City.

Howse, Mrs. Rebecca (Wildgoose Hedges), 1737–1818. *Mother Goose.* An English woman, of Oxford.

Hoyle, Edmond, 1672–1769. *A Gentleman.* An English writer of London, on games.

Hoyt, Charles H. *His Majesty Himself.* An American journalist; on the staff of the Boston "Post."

Hoyt, Mrs. G. S. *Marion West.* An American religious writer.

Hubbell, Mrs. Martha Stone, 1814–56. *A Pastor's Wife.* An American writer; b. at Oxford; d. at North Stonington; both of Connecticut.

Huber, Johann Nepomuk, 1830–79. *Janus.* A German theologian; b. at Munich; Professor of Philosophy there, 1859–79; was an old "Catholic."

Huc, Abbé Evariste Regis, 1813–60. *A Nankin Man of Science.* A French literary man of world-wide celebrity; a native of Toulouse, and became a missionary in 1839; d. in Paris.

Huddesford, George, 1751–1809. *The Editor of "Salmagundi."* An English clergyman and humorous poet; M.A. of New Coll., Oxford, 1780; Vicar of Loxley, Co. Warwick; d. in London.

Hudson, George, 1800–71. *The Railway King.* An Englishman; b. in York; M.P. for Sunderland, 1845–59.

Hudson, Rev. Henry Norman, 1814–. *A Chaplain.* An American Shakespearian scholar; b. in Cornwall, Vt.; Middlebury Coll., 1840; has for some years resided in Cambridge, Mass.

Hudson, William G. *Cadwalader.* An American journalist.

Hülsen, Helene (von Häseler), Gräfin von, 1829–. *Helene.* A German author; b. at Blankenfelde; in 1849 married the theatrical Von Hülsen at Berlin.

Hughes, Catherine. *C. H.* An English writer.

Hughes, George, M.A. *A Graduate of Oxford; A Poetaster.* An English poet; Christ Church, Oxford, 1811.

Hughes, John, Esq., 1790–1858. *Buller of Brasenose.* An English literary antiquary, of Donnington-priory, Berks.

Hughes, T. M. *An English Resident.* An English poet and prose writer; in 1845 resident in Spain.

Hughes, Thomas, 1823–. *A Layman; An Old Boy; Vacuus Viator.* An English writer; b. at Donnington-priory, near Newbury, Berks.; Oriel Coll., Oxford, 1845; called to the bar at Lincoln's Inn, 1848; M.P., 1865–74; visited the United States in 1870.

Hughes, William, 1803–61. *Piscator.* An English lawyer; Auditor of the Poor Law Union District of Cornwall and Devon.; b. at Maker Vicarage; d. at Millbay Grove, Plymouth.

Hugo, Le Comte Victor Marie, 1802–85. *Aristide; Hierro.* A French poet and novelist; b. at Besançon; resided at the islands of Jersey and Guernsey, 1851–71; d. in Paris.

Huidekoper, H. J., 1776–1854. *A Unitarian Layman.* A Dutch-American; b. in the Netherlands; came to the United States in 1795; in 1804 removed to Meadville, Penn., where he lived and died.

Huish, H. *A Blue.* An English novelist.

Hulburt, D., M.D. *Zepa.* An American writer.

Hull, Rev. **Joseph Darling,** A.M., 1818–. *A Connecticut Pastor.* An American teacher and minister; b. in New Haven, Conn.; Yale Coll., 1837; Yale Div. School, 1842; Pastor at Essex, Conn., 1844–48; Principal of the Murray Hill Institute, New York City, from 1864.

Hull, Thomas, 1728–1808. *A Gentleman.* An English actor and dramatist; b. in London; for a time an apothecary; and an actor at Covent Garden Theatre, 1759–1808; d. in Westminster.

Hullah, Mrs. **M.** *M. H.* An English musician, or writer on music.

Humbert, Dr. **C.,** *alias* **Sylvan Gardner.** *The Rain-Water Doctor.* D. in the vicinity of Philadelphia, in June, 1825, at "the supposed age of one hundred years." — See "L. I. Star," June 9, 1839.

Humble, Rev. **Michael Maughan,** M.A. *A Parish Priest.* An English clergyman; Emman. Coll., Cambridge; Rector of Sutton *w.* Duckmanton, 1839–83 *et seq.*

Humboldt, Gay. *Burr Lington, D.LL.* An American writer.

Hume, Rev. **Abraham,** D.C.L., F.R.S., about 1815–. *A Lancashire Incumbent.* An Irish clergyman and antiquary; Vicar of Vauxhall, Liverpool, 1847–83 *et seq.*

Hume, J. F. *Willys Niles.* An American writer.

Hume, Rev. **James Deacon,** 1774–1842. *H. B. T.* An English civilian; b. at Newington, Surrey; Assistant Secretary to the Board of Trade, 1829–40; d. at Reigate.

Hume, Miss **Sophia,** 1702–74. *S. H.* An English Quaker lady, of London; b. in South Carolina; d. in London; was a minister about 25 years.

Humfrey, John. *J. H.; A Grave Author of Middle and Unparty Principles; A Lover of Peace and the Public Good.* An English political writer, of the first part of the 18th century.

Humphrey, Asa, 1781–1841. *A Schoolmaster in the Eastern Country.* An American poet; b. and d. at North Yarmouth, Me.; by occupation a chairmaker (?).

Humphrey, E. A. *A Churchman.* An English writer.

Humphrey, George. *A Collector.* An English conchologist.

Humphrey, Rev. **John.** *His Respect-*

ful Neighbour, J. H. An English clergyman, of Frome.

Humphrey, Mrs. **S. G.** *Stereo.* An American writer.

Humphreys, Col. **David,** LL.D., 1753–1818. *A Gentleman of the Army.* An American poet, soldier, and diplomatist; b. at Derby, Conn.; Yale Coll., 1771; lived and d. at New Haven, Conn.

Humphreys, Edward Rupert, LL.D. *A British Commoner; The Head Master of an English Grammar School.* An English writer and educator; now, 1883, a classical teacher of Boston.

Humphreys, Henry Noel, 1810–. *H. N. H. An Archæologist.* An English numismatist; b. at Birmingham; educ. in England and on the Continent, where he resided several years, chiefly at Rome.

Hunt, Freeman, 1804–58. *An American; A Citizen of New York.* An American printer, editor, author, and publisher; b. at Quincy, Mass.; in 1831 settled in New York City; d. at Brooklyn, N.Y.

Hunt, Helen. *H. H.* — See "Jackson, Mrs. H. (F. H.)."

Hunt, (James Henry) Leigh, 1784–1859. *The Editor of "The Examiner"; Henry Honeycombe; Mr. Town, Junior, Critic and Censor-General.* An English poet and prose writer; b. at Southgate, near London; resided chiefly in London; d. at Putney.

Hunt, Jedediah, 1815–. *Cresinus.* An American merchant; in 1860, at Chilo, Clermont Co., O.; also a poet and prose writer; b. at Candor, Tioga Co., N.Y.; removed to Ohio about 1840.

Hunt, Mrs. **Margaret.** *Averil Beaumont.* An English writer.

Hunt, Rev. **Robert Shapland,** M.A. *R. S. H.* An English clergyman; Exeter Coll., Oxford, 1841; Vicar of Mark-Beech, Edinbridge, 1852–83 *et seq.*

Hunt, Rowland, Esq. *An Independent Voter.* An English political writer, of Shrewsbury.

Hunt, Thornton, 1810–73. *T. H.* An English journalist, of London, after 1840; son of (James Henry) Leigh Hunt.

Hunt, William. *W. H., Gent.* An English dramatist; a Collector of Excise; wrote one play, of which the following line is a specimen: —

"As the tall trees stood *circling* in a *row*."

Hunter, Mrs. **Anne (Home),** 1742–1821. *Mrs. J. H.* An English poet; wife of Dr. John Hunter, and sister of Sir Everard Home; b. and d. in London;

Hunter, John. *N. R.* A Scottish writer.

Hunter, Rev. Joseph, F.S.A., 1783–1861. *J. H.; An English Traveller.* An English antiquary; b. at Sheffield; Asst. Keeper of the Public Records, 1838–61; d. in London.

Huntington, Miss **Cornelia.** *Martha Wickham.* An American writer, of East Hampton, L.I.

Huntington, Rev. Dan, M.A., 1774–1864. *Octogenary.* An American Cong. minister; for many years resident at Hadley, Mass.

Huntington, Emily. *E. H.* An American writer for the young.

Huntington, Frederic Dan, D.D., 1819–. *F. D. H.* An American clergyman; b. in Hadley, Mass.; Amherst Coll., 1839; Bishop of Central New York, 1869–83 *et seq.*

Huntington, Rev. **George,** M.A. *A Clerical Friend.* An English clergyman; St. Bees, 1846; Rector and Vicar of Tenby, 1867–83 *et seq.*

Huntington, Jedediah Vincent, M.D., 1815–62. *John Vincent, Esq.* An American poet and novelist; b. in New York City; Univ. of New York, 1838; became a Roman Catholic in 1850; was then a journalist at Baltimore, 1853–54, and at St. Louis, 1855–57; d. at Pau, France.

Huntington, Joseph, D.D., 1735–95. *A Gentleman of Connecticut.* An American Cong. minister; b. at Windham, Conn.; Yale Coll., 1762; pastor at Coventry, Conn.

Huntington, Rev. **William,** 1744–1813. *S. S., Sinner Saved.* An English Meth. preacher, of London; b. in Kent; d. at Tunbridge.

Huntley, Mrs. **E. D.** *Fannie Grey.*

Huntley, Stanley, 1845–85. *Spoopendyke.* An American journalist; b. in New York City; for many years connected with the press at Chicago, Ill.; about six years ago returned to New York City; and d. there.

Huntt, Henry, M.D. *An Annual Visitor.* An American physician.

Huot, L. H. *Un Observateur.* A French-Canadian writer.

Hurd, Richard, D.D., 1720–1808. *A Warburtonian.* An English prelate; b. at Congreve, Staffs.; Bishop of Worcester, 1781–1808; d. at Hartlebury.

Hurlbut, William Henry, 1827–. *Raimond.* An American journalist; b.

at Charleston, S.C.; Harv. Univ., 1847; Div. School, 1849; Law School, 1852; since 1855 has been connected with the periodicals and newspapers of New York City.

Hussey, Edward Law. *E. L. H.* An English *littérateur* of the day.

Hussey, Rev. Robert, B.D., 1801–56. *Presbyterus.* An English scholar; b. at Sandhurst, Kent; Christ Church, Oxford, 1825; Professor of Ecclesiastical History at Oxford, 1842–56; d. in Oxford.

Hussey, William. *A Layman; One of the People.* An English writer.

Hutcheson, Archibald, Esq., –1740. *A Member of the House of Commons.* An English politician, and writer on finance.

Hutchinson, E. *A Native American.* An American writer.

Hutchinson, Francis. *F. H.* An English clergyman; Bishop of Doun and Connor.

Hutchinson, Henry, 1800–31. *H.* An English architect, of Birmingham; d. at Leamington.

Hutchinson, Henry Howe, 1812–. *Henry Howe.* An English actor; b. at Norwich; made his *début* in London in 1834; and has remained there since.

Hutchinson, John, Esq., 1674–1737. *J. H.* An English writer; b. at Spennythorn, Yorkshire; was opposed to Sir Isaac Newton's system.

Hutchinson, William. *John Sands.* An American journalist.

Hutchisson, W. H. Florio. *George Trigger.* An Anglo-Indian sportsman and writer on sports; for 18 years resident in Bengal.

Hutton, Rev. **John,** B.D. *J. H.* An English clergyman.

Hutton, R. N. *An Old Rugbæan.* An English writer.

Hutton, Rev. **Wyndham Madden.** *W. M. H.; A Member of the Univ. of Oxford.* An English clergyman; St. Edmund Hall, Oxford, 1854; Vicar of Twyford *w.* Hungarton V., etc., 1877–80 *et seq.*

Huyn, Luise, 1843–. *M. Ludolff.* A German author; b. at Koblenz, where she passed her early life; commenced her literary career in 1876.

Hyde, Rev. **John.** *A Bible Student.* An English Swedenborgian minister.

Hyer, Rev. **G. W.** *A Clergyman of the P. E. Church.* An American writer.

I.

Iago, Rev. **William**, B.A., 1836–. *W. I.* An English clergyman; b. in London; Chaplain of the Cornwall Co. Asylum, 1862–83 *et seq.*

Ide, Simeon. *Their Wellwisher.* An American writer.

Iliff, Rev. **George.** *G. I.* An English educator; Head Master of Grange School, Sunderland; Bishop-Wearmouth.

Inchbald, Mrs. **Elizabeth (Simpson)**, 1756–1821. *Elfrida.* A celebrated English actress, dramatist, and novelist; b. in Stanningfield, Suffolk; from 1781 devoted to literary pursuits at Kensington.

Ingelow, Jean, 1830–. *Don John.* An English poet and prose writer; b. in Boston, Lincolnshire; resided for many years at Kensington, London.

Ingersleben, Emilie von. *Emmy von Rothenfels.* A German writer.

Ingersoll, Charles, A.M., 1805–. *A Citizen of Pennsylvania.* An American political writer; b. in Philadelphia; Univ. of Penn., 1822.

Ingersoll, Charles Jared, 1782–1862. *Inchiquin.* An American statesman; b. in Philadelphia; M.C., 1813–15 and 1841–47; lived and. d. in his native city.

Ingersoll, Joseph Reed, LL.D., 1786–1868. *A Northern Man.* An American lawyer and statesman; b. in Philadelphia; N.J. Coll., 1804; M.C., 1835–37 and 1841–49; Minister to England, 1849–53; d. in his native city.

Ingham, Rev. **Harvey A.** *A· Lover of the Word.* An American clergyman.

Ingham, Mrs. **W. A.** *Anne Hathaway.* An American writer.

Ingleby, Clement Mansfield, LL.D., 1823–. *Jabez.* An English critic and metaphysician; b. at Egbaston, Birmingham; Trin. Coll., Oxford, 1847; Vice-Pres. of the Royal Society of Literature.

Inglis, Charles, D.D., 1734–1816. *An American; Candidus; Papinian; A Son of Truth and Decency.* An American clergyman; of Trinity Church, New York City, 1777–83, then Bishop of Nova Scotia.

Inglis, Henry David, 1795–1835. *H. Derwent Conway.* A Scottish journalist; b. in Edinburgh; for a long time editor of the "Derbyshire Courier"; travelled extensively; published accounts of his travels, and d. in London.

Inglis, James. *Maori.* An East Indian planter and sportsman.

Inglis, John, D.D., –1850. *One of the Alumni.* A British colonial writer; Bishop of Nova Scotia, 1834–50.

Inglis, John, D.D., 1763–1834. *One of the Ministers of Edinburgh.* A Scottish clergyman; one of the ministers of Greyfriars Church, Edinburgh; b. in Perthshire; d. in Edinburgh.

Inglis, W. *J. B.* An English writer of educational works.

Ingraham, Rev. **Joseph Holt**, 1809–61. *Adina; Kate Conynghame; A Yankee.* An American novelist; b. in Portland, Me.; Rector of a parish, and of St. Thomas's Hall, an academy for boys, at Holly Springs, Miss.

Ingram, James, D.D., 1774–1850. *J. I.* An English clergyman; b. at East Codford; Trin. Coll., Oxford, 1796; President of Trin. Coll., Oxford, and Rector of Garsington, 1824–50; d. in Oxford.

Ingram, Rev. **Robert**, 1727–1804. *A Country Clergyman.* An English clergyman; b. at Beverly; Fellow of Corpus Christi Coll., Cambridge; Vicar of Wormington and Boxted, Essex; d. at Segrave, near Loughborough.

Innes, Cosmo. *C. I.* A Scottish advocate, of Edinburgh.

Innes, Duncan. *D. I.; A Layman.* A Scottish writer, of Edinburgh (?).

Innes, William. *A West India Merchant.* A British colonial writer.

Inshtatheamba. *Bright Eyes.* An Indian woman.

Ireland, Alexander. *Philobiblos.* An English bibliographer of the day.

Ireland, Joseph N. *A Play-goer.* An American writer.

Ireland, (Samuel) William Henry, 1777–1835. *Anser Pen-Dragon, Esq.; Charles Clifford; H. C., Esq.; Henry Fielding; Satiricus Sculptor, Esq.* An English literary forger; b. and d. in London; educ. in France; passed his life in literary pursuits.

Ireland, William W., M.D. *An Officer who served there.*

Iron, Mrs. **N. C.** *Stella.* An American writer.

Irons, William Josiah, D.D., 1812–83. *A Bachelor of Divinity.* An English clergyman; b. at Hoddesden, Herts.; Queen's Coll., Oxford, 1833; Prebendary in St. Paul's Cathedral, 1860; Rector of St. Mary Woolnoth *w.* St. Mary Woolchurch, London, 1872–83.

Irvine, Rev. **Alexander.** *W. P. &*

A. I.; A Minister of the Church of Scotland. A Scottish minister, of Rannoch.

Irvine, Mary Catherine. *Aura.* An English poet and novelist.

Irving, John Henry Brodribb, 1838–. *Henry Irving.* An English actor; b. at Keinton, near Glastonbury; first appeared on the stage in 1856, at Sunderland, in the character of " Richelieu."

Irving, John Treat, Jr., 1810–. *His Nephew; John Quod.* An American lawyer, of New York City; nephew of Washington Irving.

Irving, Peter, 1771–1838. *Percival G——.* An American journalist; b. and d. in New York City; brother of Washington Irving; resided in Europe, 1809–36.

Irving, Theodore, LL.D., D.D., 1809–. *A Layman.* An American clergyman; nephew of Washington Irving; b. in New York City; Columbia Coll., 1837; in 1875 Rector of St. John's School for young ladies, in New York City.

Irving, Thomas J. *Gerald Hart.* An American novelist.

Irving, Washington, LL.D., 1783–1859. *Fray Antonio Agapida; Geoffrey Crayon; Diedrich Knickerbocker; Jonathan Oldstyle; A Sentimental Philosopher.* A distinguished American miscellaneous writer.

Other pseudonyms ascribed to him are, " Anthony Evergreen, Gent." and " Launcelot Langstaff." The latter was rather the pseudonym for the whole staff of writers of " Salmagundi."

Irving, William, 1766–1821. *Pindar Cockloft, Esq.; A Gentleman of New York.* An American merchant and humorist; brother of Washington Irving; b., lived, and d. in New York City.

Isaacson, Rev. Stuteville, M.A. *A Barrow Knight.* An English clergyman; Rector of Bradfield St. Clare, Suffolk, 1836–60 *et seq.*

Ivers, Rev. Hardinge Furenzo. *Alethinos; A Roman Catholic.* An English clergyman.

J.

Jabet, George S. *Eden Warwick.* An English humorist.

Jackman, Rev. John. *A Clergyman.* An English divine of the first part of the 18th century.

Jackson, Andrew, LL.D., 1767–1845. *Old Hickory.* An eminent American soldier and politician; President of the United States, 1829–37.

Jackson, E. A. *E. A. J.* An American religious writer of the day.

Jackson, Hall, 1739–97. *A Gentleman of the Faculty.* An American physician; Hon. M.D., Harv. Univ., 1793; practised his profession at Portsmouth, N.H.

Jackson, Mrs. Helen Maria (Fiske Hunt), 1831–85. *H. H.; Saxe Holm (?).* An American poet and prose writer; b. in Amherst, Mass.; was first married to Major Hunt, U.S.A., who was killed in 1863; and then to Mr. Jackson; has resided at Newport, R.I., and at Denver, Col.; d. in San Francisco.

Jackson, Rev. J. L., M.A. *Clericus Dorcestriensis.* An English clergyman; Rector of Swanage, Dorset.

Jackson, Rev. John, 1686–1763. *A Clergyman; A Clergyman in the Country; Philalethes Cantabrigiensis; A Presbyter of the Church of England.* An English Arian divine; b. in Yorkshire; Master of Wigton's Hospital, 1729–63.

Jackson, Hon. Jonathan, 1743–1810. *A Native of Boston.* An American merchant and statesman, of Newburyport, Mass.; b. and d. in Boston; Harv. Univ., 1761; Member of Provincial Congress, 1775–77; M.C., 1782.

Jackson, M. E. *A Lady.* An English writer on botany.

Jackson, Rev. T., 1810–. *Pieter Maritzburg.* An English writer.

Jackson, Thomas W. *Hickory.* An American journalist, of New York City.

Jackson, Dr. William, –1797. *Curtius.* A London journalist; b. in Ireland; took part in the Irish rebellion of 1797; was arrested and sentenced to death, but committed suicide in prison.

Jackson, William, 1730–1803. *H. Nettle.* An English musician and landscape painter; b. in Exeter, where for many years he gave his time to music, painting, and literature.

Jackson, William, D.D., 1750–1815. *The Bishop of Oxford.* An English clergyman; b. at Stamford; Christ Church, Oxford, 1772; Regius Prof. of Greek at Oxford, and Bishop of Oxford, 1811–15; d. at Cuddesden, Co. Oxford.

Jacob, Alexandre André, 1826–78. *Alexandre Erdan.* A French journalist, of Paris; b. at Angles (Vienne); d. at Frascati, near Rome.

Jacob, C. *C. J.* An English (?) author.

Jacob, Giles, 1686–1744. *G. J.* An English poet, dramatist, and law-compiler; b. at Romsey, Co. of Southampton.

Jacob, Hildebrand, Esq., –1739. *H—d J—s, Esq.* An English poet and dramatist; son of Sir John Jacob; resided in Clarges Street, Piccadilly, London.

Jacob, Thomas Greer, 1797–1837. *A Member.* An Irish Friend, of Belfast; b. in Waterford.

Jacobs, Mrs. Harriet. *Linda Brent.* An American autobiographer; a slave girl.

Jacox, Rev. Francis. *Nicias Foxcar; A Recluse; Parson Frank.* An English clergyman; B.A., Cambridge, 1847; in 1880 *et seq.* resident at Prestwood, Charlwood, Crawley, Sussex.

Jacquot, Charles Jean Baptiste, de Mirecourt, 1812–80. *Eugène de Mirecourt.* A French author; b. at Mirecourt; commenced his literary career at Paris, with novels for the smaller journals. At the close of his 60th year he entered a cloister; assumed the priesthood; and retired to Hayti, where he died.

James, Edward. *Guy Fawkes.* An English writer.

James, Mrs. Edwin. *A Beauty.* An American (?) writer.

James, George Payne Rainsford, 1801–60. *G. P. R. Jacobus.* An English novelist; b. in London; resided at Stockbridge, Mass., 1850–52; British Consul at Norfolk, Va., 1852–58; and at Venice, from 1858, and d. there.

James, James Henry. *Aliquis.* An English poet and barrister, of the Middle Temple, London.

James, Thomas Chalkley, M.D., 1766–1835. *P. D.* An American physician; b. in Philadelphia; Univ. of Penn., 1787; professor there, 1811–35; d. in his native city.

Jameson, Mrs. Anna (Murphy), 1797–1860. *An Ennuyée; A Lady.* An Irish miscellaneous writer; b. in Dublin; d. at Ealing, Co. Middlesex.

Jamieson, John, D.D., 1759–1836. *Dr. Jehan, of the Hall Ryal.* A Scottish clergyman; b. in Glasgow; educ. at the Univ. of that city; minister at Edinburgh, 1797–1836, where he died.

Jamieson, William. *A Member of the Honourable Society of Writers to the Signet.* A Scottish lawyer of the 19th century.

Janin, Jules Gabriel, 1804–74. *Le critique marie; The Married Critic; Le prince de la critique.* A French journalist; b. at Saint-Etienne (Loire); lived and d. in Paris.

Janson, Charles William. *The Stranger.* An English writer; "late of the State of Rhode Island;" resided in America, 1793–1806.

Janvier, Margaret. *Margaret Vandergrift.*

Janvier, Thomas A. *Ivory Black.* An American novelist; author of "Chiquita," and contributor to the "Century."

Japp, Alexander Hay. *J. H. Alexander, B.A.; H. A. Page.* A British author and publisher, of London.

Jardine, Alexander. *An English Officer; An Officer.* An English officer; entered the army, 1826; Maj.-Gen., 1859; served with distinction during the Indian campaign of 1858.

Jarke, Franziska Julie (Schlesius), 1815–. *E. Rudorff.* A German author; b. at Königsberg; in 1850 married the rich nobleman Jarke; and in 1864 commenced her literary career.

Jarmain, E. *E. J–M–N.* An English writer.

Jarnac de Rohan-Chabot, Le Comte de. *Sir Charles Rockingham.* A French novelist; published chiefly at London.

Jarves, James Jackson, 1818–. *An American Amateur in Europe; An Inquirer.* An American art critic; b. in Boston; has resided in the Sandwich Islands, and much at Paris and Florence.

Jarvis, Edward, –1884. *E. J.* An American physiologist; b. in Concord, Mass.; Harv. Univ.; 1826; resided in Dorchester, Mass., and d. there.

Jarvis, Russell. *An Anti-Abolitionist; A Citizen of New York.* An American writer.

Jasmin, Jacques, 1798–1864. *The Barber Poet.* A French poet, of the south of France.

Jay, John, LL.D., 1745–1829. *Publius.* An American jurist and statesman; b. in New York City; Columbia Coll., 1764; Chief Justice of the U.S. Supreme Court, 1789–94; resided on his estate at Bedford, Westchester Co., N.Y., 1800–27, and d. there.

Jay, John, 1817–. *A Churchman; A Citizen of New York; The President.* An American lawyer; grandson of the preceding; b. in New York City; Columbia Coll., 1836; admitted to the bar in 1839; Minister to Austria, 1869–75.

Jay, William, LL.D., 1789–1858. *A Churchman; A Churchman of the Diocese of New York.* An American jurist, son of

Chief Justice Jay, and father of the preceding; b. in New York City; Yale Coll., 1807; first judge of Westchester Co., N.Y., 1820–43; d. at Bedford, N.Y.

Jeacocke, Caleb, 1706–86. *The Literary Baker.* An English man of letters; a baker of London.

Jebb, Ann. *W. Bull.* An English writer.

Jebb, Frederick. *Guatimozin.* An English (?) writer.

Jebb, John, M.D., F.R.S., 1736–86. *An Englishman; Paulinus.* An English physician; b. in London; Rector of Ovington, Norfolk, 1764–75.

Jebb, Mrs. —— (Torkington), 1736–86. *Priscilla.* A learned English lady; widow of Dr. John Jebb.

Jefferies, Richard. *R. J.* An English sporting writer of the day.

Jefferson, Rev. Joseph. *J. J.; Erastus; Iota.* An English Dissenting minister, of Basingbroke, Hants.

Jefferson, Thomas, LL.D., 1743–1826. *M. J***; Oliver Fairplay; Mary V. V.; A Native and Member of the House of Burgesses.* An American statesman; b. at Shadwell, Va.; President of the United States, 1809–13; d. at Monticello, Va.

Jeffrey, Mrs. Rosa Vertner (Griffith Johnson). *Rosa.* An American "Southland" writer; b. near Natchez; passed her early life at "Burlington," near Fort Gibson, Miss.; at an early age married Claude M. Johnson; after his death married Alexander Jeffrey, Esq.; in 1870 resided in Lexington, Ky.

Jeffreys, Mrs. Arnold. *Alton Clyde.*

Jeffries, Thomas Fayette. *Crippled Fayette.* An American writer, of Rockingham. Va.

Jeitteles, Isaak [or Itzig], 1814–75. *Julius Seidlitz.* A Bohemian author; b. at Prague; driven by the Austrian censorship away from home; he lived first in Saxony, then in Hungary, and later in Vienna, where he died.

Jekyll, Joseph, Esq., F.R.S., F.A.S. *J—ll.* An English lawyer and author; a friend of Charles Lamb; King's Counsel, Solicitor General to the Prince Regent, and M.P. for Calne, in Wiltshire.

Jenings, Mrs. Edmond. *Wyckliffe Lane.* An English novelist, of Hawkshurst, Kent.

Jenkins, Edward, 1838–. *A Guest.* An English satirist; b. in Mysore, India; educ. at Montreal and Philadelphia; called to the bar at Lincoln's Inn, 1864; Agent in London for Canada from 1874; M.P. for Dundee from 1874.

Jenkins, H. T., 1850–. *Tiny Tim.* An English writer, of Southsea.

Jenkins, Joseph, 1808–. *J. J., Philomath.* An English poet and prose writer; b. at Tresider, in St. Buryan, Cornwall.

Jenkins, Mary. *M. J.* An English writer.

Jenkinson, Charles, 1st Earl of Liverpool, 1727–1808. *Charles, Lord Hawkesbury.* An English statesman; b. in Oxfordshire; in political life, 1761–86; d. in London.

Jenks, William, LL.D., D.D., 1778–1866. *The Late Rev. Williamson Jahnsenykes.* An American clergyman; b. at Newton, Mass.; Harv. Univ., 1797; Pastor of Green Street Church, Boston, 1826–45.

Jennens, Charles, –1773. *The Editor of "King Lear."* An English gentleman, called "Solyman the Magnificent," from the splendor in which he lived.

Jenner, Rev. Charles, 1737–74. *C. J.; Altamont.* An English clergyman; Vicar of Claybrook, Leicestershire; author of novels, poems, etc.

Jenner, Rev. Stephen, M.A. *Theophilus Secundus.* An English clergyman; St. John's Coll., Cambridge, 1834; in 1874 resident at Clare House, Horn Park, Lee.

Jennings, Miss Clotilda. *Maude.* An American Nova Scotian writer.

Jennings, Henry Constantine, 1731–1819. *An Unfeigned Admirer of Genuine British Jurisprudence.* An English antiquary; b. at Shiplake, Oxfordshire; passed some years on the Continent; d. within the rules of the King's Bench, London.

Jennings, John J. *Magoogin.* An American journalist.

Jennings, Louis J. *L. J. J.; H. Dropper.* An American writer, formerly editor of the New York "Times."

Jennings, Paul. *A Colored Man.* An American writer.

Jennings, Samuel K., M.D. *A Layman.* An American writer, of Baltimore (?).

Jennison, Miss Lucy W. *Owen Innsley.* An American (?) poet of the day.

Jephson, John; Courtenay, John; Burroughs, etc. *Jeffrey Wagstaffe, Esq.* Irish essayists.

Jephson, Ralph. *R–ph J–ph—n.* An English lawyer of the 18th century.

Jerdan, William, F.S.A., 1782–1854. *W. J. André; Bushey Heath; Teutha; Viator.* A Scottish journalist; at London, 1801–54.

Jeremy, Henry, M.A. *A Barrister.* An English lawyer; A.B. of Trin. Coll., Cambridge, 1809.

Jerningham, Edward, 1727–1812. *The Bard; The Old Bard.* An English poet and dramatist; b. in Norfolk; educ. at Douay and Paris; lived and d. in London.

Jerram, Rev. **Charles,** M.S., 1770–1853. *Scrutator.* An English clergyman; Magdalen Coll., Cambridge, 1797; Rector of Witney, Oxfordshire, 1834–53, where he died.

Jerrold, Douglas William, 1803–57. *D. W. J.; Henry Brownrigg; Mrs. Margaret Caudle; Paul Prendergast; Punch; The Late Captain Barabbas Whitefeather.* An English humorist; b. at Sheerness, in Kent; devoted himself to literary pursuits in London; and d. there.

Jerrold, William Blanchard, 1826–84. *Fin-Bec.* An English writer; son of the preceding; b., lived, and d. in London.

Jervis, John B., 1796–1885. *Hampden.* An American civil engineer; b. at Huntington, L.I.; resided at Rome, N.Y., 86 years; and d. there.

Jewell, Joseph, 1763–1846. *A Layman.* An English Friend, of Stratford, Essex; last of Farringdon, Berkshire; b. at Stratford-in-the-Vale, Berkshire; d. at Farringdon.

Jewsbury, Miss **Maria Jane.** *M. J. J.* — See "Fletcher, Mrs. M. J. (J.)."

Johann Nepomuk Maria Joseph, King of Saxony. *Philalethes.* A German editor and poet.

John, Henriette Friederike Christiane Eugenie, 1825–. *E. Marlitt.* A German novelist; b. at Arnstadt, Thuringia.

Johnes, Col. **Thomas,** 1748–1816. *A Cardiganshire Landlord.* An English *littérateur* and bibliomaniac; b. in Shropshire; resident at Hafod, Co. Cardigan; M.P. and Lord-Lieutenant for that county; d. at Dolcothy, Co. Carmarthen, Wales.

Johns, Rev. **Charles Alexander,** F.L.S. *A Schoolmaster of Twenty Years' Standing.* An English clergyman; Trin. Coll., Dublin, 1841; in 1874 resident at Winton House, Winchester.

Johns, Rev. **William Stabback,** and Another, M.A., 1838–. *B. B.* An English clergyman; b. at Helston, Cornwall; Exeter Coll., Oxford, 1861; Vicar of St. Thomas-by-Launceston, 1875–83 *et seq.*

Johnson, Miss **Anna C.** — See "Miller, Mrs. A. C. (J.)."

Johnson, Miss **Evelyn Kimball.** *Flora McFlimsey.* An American author and journalist, of New York City.

Johnson, Elizabeth. *A Lady of Boston.*

Johnson, Mrs. **Emeline H. (Brown),** 1826–50. *Lillie Layton.* An American poet; b. at Haverhill, N.H.; educ. at Wooster, O.; in 1845 married Perry Johnson, of that town, where he died in 1845, and she soon afterwards.

Johnson, Miss **Esther,** –1726. *Stella.* A friend of Dean Swift; supposed to have married him in 1716.

Johnson, J. *An Old Author.* An English writer.

Johnson, James, M.D., 1777–1845. *Frederick Fag.* An Irish physician, of London.

Johnson, Mrs. **Jennie A. (Abbott),** 1808–72. *Margaret Bourne.* An American writer; wife of Oliver Johnson, of New York City.

Johnson, John G. *A Member of the Philadelphia Bar.* An American lawyer.

Johnson, Llewelyn H. *Ixion.* An American bicycle racer; Swarthmore Coll., Pa., about 1879–80; resident (1885) of Orange, N.J.

Johnson, Lorenzo D. *One of his Descendants.* An American writer; b. in Braintree; son of Mrs. Thomazin Johnson, of Braintree, Mass., who was a descendant of John Alden.

Johnson, Reverdy, LL.D., 1796–1876. *Lawrence Langston; A Marylander; A Southern Citizen.* An American statesman; b. at Annapolis, Md.; educ. at St. John's Coll.; called to the bar; settled in Baltimore; U.S. Senator, 1845–49 and 1863–69; Minister to England, 1868–69; d. in his native city.

Johnson, Mrs. **S. O.** *Daisy Eyebright.* An American writer of the day.

Johnson, Samuel, D.D., 1696–1772. *Aristocles.* An American writer; President of King's Coll. (now Columbia), 1755–63; Missionary at Stratford, Conn., 1723–55 and 1763–72.

Johnson, Samuel, LL.D., 1709–84. *S. J.; T.; An Impartial Hand; Probus Britannicus; The Great Cham of Literature; The Leviathan of Literature.* An English poet, critic, essayist and lexicographer; b. at Lichfield; in 1737 went to London and spent his life there, and d. there.

Johnson, Thomas, 1675–1750. *Mr. Chubb.* An English classical scholar and editor; b. at Stadhampton, in Oxfordshire.

Johnson, Virginia Wales. *Cousin Virginia.* An American novelist; b. in Brooklyn, N.Y.

Johnson, W. B. *Boswell.* An American writer, of Virginia.

Johnson, William, Esq. *A Barrister.* An English lawyer, of nearly 100 years ago.

Johnston, Mrs. Alma Calder. *Alma Calder.* An American novelist of the day.

Johnston, Andrew. *An Essex Justice.* An English writer of the day.

Johnston, Charles, –1800. *The Editor of "Chrysal"; The Editor of "The Adventures of a Guinea"; An Adept; Oneiropolos.* An Irish novelist; called to the bar; went to England, and engaged in chamber practice and literary work; in 1782 went to Bengal and became journalist, and d. there.

Johnston, D. B. S. *Lenial Seab.* An American writer.

Johnston, James. *A Gentleman of Middlesex.* An English writer, of the earlier part of the 18th century.

Johnston, Miss Keith. *Leslie Keith.* An English writer of the day.

Johnston, Mrs. Marianne C. (Howe). *His Mother.* An American writer of the day.

Johnston, Richard Malcolm, 1822–. *An Old Man; Mr. Philemon Perch.* An eminent American educator; b. in Hancock Co., Ga.; Mercer Univ., 1841; kept a classical school at Rockby, Ga., 1861–67, and at Chestnut Hill, near Baltimore, 1867–75 *et seq.*

Johnston, W. F. *Malakoff.* An American journalist.

Johnston, William, 1829–. *Wayne Hovey.* An Irish novelist; b. in Downpatrick; B.A., Dublin, 1852; M.P. for Belfast from 1868.

Johnstone, Mrs. Christina Jane. *Mistress Margaret Dods, of Cleikum Inn, St. Ronan's.* A Scottish writer.

Johnstone, George. *Philorthos.* An English religious writer of the earlier part of the 18th century.

Joinville, François Ferdinand Philippe Louis Marie d'Orleans, Prince de, 1818–. *A. Trognon.* A French writer.

Jolly, Miss Emily. *E. J.; Lady who prefers to be anonymous.* An English writer of the day.

Jones, Absalom. *A. J.* An American writer, of Philadelphia.

Jones, C., –1792. *The Crediton Poet.* An English poet, of Devonshire; d. at Keynsham, near Bristol.

Jones, Charles A., about 1815–51. *Dick Tinto.* An American poet and lawyer, of Cincinnati.

Jones, Rev. Charles Alfred, M.A *C. A. J.* An English teacher; St. John's Coll., Cambridge, 1857; Sen. Math. Master in Weston School, 1862–83 *et seq.*

Jones, Cornelia. *Jane R. Sommers.* An American religious writer.

Jones, David. *D. J.* An English writer of the first part of the 18th century.

Jones, Rev. David. *Welch Freeholder.* A Unitarian minister; colleague of Dr. Priestley.

Jones, George. *Leigh Cliffe.* An English writer.

Jones, George, 1810–79. *The Count Joannes.* An American actor and lawyer; b. in Boston; in 1870 a lawyer of New York City.

Jones, Giles. *Tom Trip.* An English (?) writer of books for the young.

Jones, Griffith Robert, –1867. *Gutto Lleyon.* A Welsh *littérateur;* an apt quoter of ancient Welsh Mss.; d. in London.

Jones, Henry. *Cavendish.* An English writer, of London, on whist.

Jones, Rev. J. P. *Devoniensis.* An English clergyman.

Jones, James Athearn, 1791–1854. *An Officer in the Army of Wolfe.* An American writer; b. at Martha's Vineyard; d. in Brooklyn, N.Y.

Jones, John, 1774–. *An Upper Servant.* An English uneducated poet; b. at Clearwell, Gloucestershire; patronized by Southey.

Jones, Rev. John Andrew. *Andrew, of Mitchell Street.* An English Baptist, of London.

Jones, John, LL.D., 1765–1827. *Ben David; Essenus; Philalethes.* A Welsh Unitarian clergyman, of London, about 1800–27.

Jones, John B., 1810–. *A Rebel War Clerk; A Roving Printer; A Squatter.* An American journalist, of Philadelphia, 1857; b. in Baltimore.

Jones, John Matthew, Esq. *The Naturalist.* An English writer.

Jones, Joseph Stevens, M.D., 1809–77. *Jefferson Scattering Batkins.* An American actor and dramatist; wrote about 200 plays; afterwards city physician of Boston for several years, and d. there.

Jones, Justin. *Harry Hazel.* An American (?) novelist of the day.

Jones, Leslie Grove, 1779–1839. *Radical.* An English officer and political writer; b. at Bearfield, near Bradford, Co. of Wilts.; d. in London.

Jones, Margaret Elizabeth Mary. *M. E. M. J.* An English poet.

Jones, Rev. Norris M. *A Presbyter of the Diocese of Maryland.* An American clergyman.

Jones, Owen. *Devonshire Poet.* An English uneducated wool-comber.

Jones, Richard. *R. J.*

Jones, Robert Baker. *R. B. J.* An English poet.

Jones, Sarah L. *S. L. J.; A Blockaded British Subject.* An English writer.

Jones, Stephen, 1763–1827. *S. J.; A Friend to Candour and Truth.* An English author, editor, and journalist, of London; b. and d. in that city.

Jones, Rev. Thomas. *Alun Glan.* A Welsh poet.

Jones, Rev. Thomas. *A Person who travelled, etc.* A Welsh clergyman; Rector of Great Creaton.

Jones, Rev. William, D.D., 1726–1800. *Thomas Bull; Trinity Jones; A Tutor; An Old Friend and Servant of the Church; A Presbyter of the Church of England.* A learned English clergyman; P.C. of Nayland, 1775, and Rector of Paston and of Hollingbourne, the latter till his death.

Jordan, G. W., Esq. *G. W. J.; The Agent for Barbadoes.* A British colonial writer.

Jordan, W. *W. J.* An American traveller.

Jordan, W. S. *W. S. J.; Visto.* An American journalist, of San Francisco.

Jourdan, Mrs. **Mary J.,** –1865.

M. J. J—n; A Lady. An Anglo-Indian poet; wife of Col. Jourdan, of the Madras Army; d. in London.

Joy, George. *A Calm Observer.* An English political writer.

Joy, Henry H. *A Barrister.* An English lawyer.

Joyce, Robert Dwyer, –1883. *Feardana Merulan.* An Irish poet; b. in the Co. of Limerick; sailed for this country in 1866, and settled in Boston; d. in Dublin.

Judah, Samuel B. H. *Terentius Phlogobombus.* An American satirical writer, of New York City.

Judson, Edward Z. C. *Ned Buntline.* An American novelist of the day.

Judson, Mrs. **Emily Chubbuck,** –1851. *Fanny Forrester.* An American writer; b. in Eaton, Madison Co., N.Y.; in 1846 married Dr. Judson; d. at Hamilton, N.Y.

Juel, Frau **Tekla (Svensson),** 1835–. *Carl Krone.* A Danish novelist; b. in Copenhagen; in 1866 married A. Juel, assistant in the Latin School at Aalborg, in Jutland.

Jurin, James, M.D., 1684–1750. *Philalethes Cantabrigiensis.* A learned English physician and mathematician, of London.

Justamond, John Obadiah, F.R.S., –1786. *A Professor of Surgery.* An English surgeon, of the 2d Regt. of Dragoon Guards.

Justice, Alexander. *A. J.; A Well-Wisher to Trade.* An English financial writer of the first part of the 18th century.

K.

Kaler, James Otis, 1846–. *James Otis; Abigail Perkins.* An American journalist, of New York City.

Kane, John Kintzing, A.M., 1795–1858. *A Pennsylvanian.* An American jurist; b. in Albany, N.Y.; Yale Coll., 1814; admitted to the Philadelphia bar, 1817; U.S. District Judge, 1846–58; d. at Philadelphia.

Kane, Paul. *An Artist.* "An American artist, who has studied in Europe, and apparently unites the refinement of the Old World with the Indian energy of the New."

Kauffman, C. H. *A Merchant.* An English commercial compiler, of London.

Kaufmann, Mathilde (Binder). 1835–. *Amara George.* A German writer; b. at Nürnberg; since 1857 has resided with her husband in Wertheim.

Kay, A. J. *An Upholsterer.* An English poet.

Kay, Robert. *An Odd-Fellow.* A Scottish writer, of Dumbarton.

Kaye, Sir **John William,** F.R.S., 1814–76. *An Optimist.* An English officer and historian; served some years in the East India Company's service; returned home in 1845, and devoted himself to literary pursuits; but entered the Indian Home Service, and was Secretary of the Secret Dept., India Office, 1859–74.

Keary, Miss **Annie**, 1825–79. *A. K.* An English novelist; the last year of her life she spent in sickness at Eastbourne, writing her last novel.

Keate, **John**. *J. K.* An English writer; the "*plagosus Orbilius*" of Eton. — See "R. S."

Keble, Rev. **John**, M.A., 1792–1866. *A; γ; A Contributor to Tracts for the Times.* An English lyric poet; b. at Fairford, Gloucestershire; Corpus Christi Coll., Oxford, 1810; Professor of Poetry at Oxford, 1831; Vicar of Hursley, near Winchester, 1835–66; d. at Bournemouth.

Keble, Rev. **Thomas**, B.D., –1873. *E.; Contributor to Tracts for the Times.* An English clergyman; Vicar of Bisley, etc., 1827–73. .

Keck, **Karl Heinrich Ch.**, 1824–. *Karl Heinrich.* A German writer; b. in Schleswig; studied philosophy at Kiel and Bonn; since 1870 Director of the Gymnasium at Husum.

Keddie, Miss **Henrietta**. *Sarah Tytler.* An English novelist of the day.

Keene, **Edmund**, D.D., 1713–81. *The Right Rev. Bishop Edmund.* An English prelate; Bishop of Chester, 1752–70; of Ely, 1770–81.

Keep, Rev. **John**, A.M., 1781–1870. *Her Husband.* An American Cong. minister; b. in Longmeadow, Mass.; Yale Coll., 1802; pastor at Ohio City from 1834; d. at Oberlin, O.

Keightley, **Thomas**, 1789–1872. *T. K.* An Irish historian; b. in Dublin; Univ. of Dublin, 1808; went to London to devote himself to literary pursuits; d. at Erith, in Kent.

Kelley, **A. M.** *A Rifleman, Esq., Gent.; A Virginia Confederate.* An American soldier in the late civil war.

Keir, **James**, Esq. *J. K., F.R.S., and S. A. Sc.* An English chemist.

Keir, Mrs. **James**. *A Lady.* An English writer; widow of the preceding.

Keith, Rev. **Alexander**. *Rev. A— K—, A.M.* An English clergyman; the famous Parson Keith of May-Fair Chapel.

Keith, Charles. *A Student of Marischal College.* A Scottish poet, of Montrose.

Keith, **George Skene**, D.D. *A Moderate Clergyman of the Synod of Aberdeen.* A Scottish divine, of Keith Hall, Aberdeenshire; and Presbyt. minister of Kinkell, in that county.

Kelley, **Albert W.**, 1838–84. *Parmenas Mix.* An American humorist and journalist, of Franklin, Ky.

Kellogg, **Edward**, 1790–1858. *Whitehook.* An American economist, of Brooklyn, N.Y., where he died.

Kellogg, **Ensign Hosmer**, 1812–82. *Pontoosuc.* An American lawyer and politician, of Pittsfield, Mass.; b. in Sheffield, Mass.; Amherst Coll., 1836; d. at Pittsfield.

Kelly, Miss **Caroline E.** *C. E. K.* — See "Davis, Mrs. Caroline E. (K.)."

Kelly, **Dennis Burrowes**. *A Member of the Irish Bar.* An Irish novelist.

Kelley, Miss **Frances Maria**, 1790–1882. *Barbara S.* An English actress; in 1882 the only living friend of Charles Lamb; first appeared on the stage in 1799.

Kelly, **Hugh**, 1739–77. *The Babbler.* An Irish author; b. on the banks of Killarney; "a staymaker by trade, an attorney's scribe by necessity, and a dramatic writer by choice."

Kelly, **John**. *Timothy Scrub, Esq., of Rag Fair; A Gentleman of the Temple.* An English lawyer, of the first part of the 18th century.

Kelly, **Jonathan F.** *Falconbridge; Jack Humphries; Stampede.* An American humorist.

Kelly, **William**. *W. K.* An English religious writer of the day.

Kelsall, **Charles**, Esq. *Junius Secundus; Mela Britannicus.* An English miscellaneous writer.

Kelsey, Mrs. **Charles E.** *Theodelinda.* An American writer of religious fiction.

Kelty, Mrs. **Mary Anne**. *M. A. K.; A Recluse.* An English author, of Cambridge; afterwards of Peckham, a suburb of London.

Kemble, **Ann**. *Ann of Swansea.* —See "Hatton, Mrs. Ann Kemble."

Kempe, **Alfred John**, Esq., F.S.A, 1785–1846. *A. J. K.* An English antiquary; brother of Mrs. Anna Eliza (Kempe Stothard) Bray, the novelist; b. in London; and d. at Stamford-villas, Fulham-road.

Kempe, **Anne**. *K. Parameny.*

Kempshall, **Julia A.** *Julia A. Willis.* An American writer of the day.

Kendall, **B. F.** *Timothy Tickle, Esq.* An American writer, of Vermont.

Kendall, **E. D.** *E. D. K.* An American writer.

Kendall, **Edward P.** *Galoot.*

Kenealy, **Edward Vaughan Hyde**, LL.D., D.C.L., 1819–79. *Y.* An Irish lawyer; b. in Cork; Trin Coll., Dublin; called to the Irish bar, 1840, and the English bar, 1847; devoted himself at London to literary work; M.P. for Stoke-on-Trent, 1875.

Kennedy, **A. K.** *A. K.; A Writer to the Signet.* A Scottish writer, of Edinburgh, on political economy.

Kennedy, Benjamin Hall, D.D., 1804-. *A Member of the Univ. of Cambridge.* An English clergyman; b. at Summer Hill, near Birmingham; Univ. of Cambridge, 1827; Regius Professor of Greek in the Univ. of Cambridge, and Can. Res. of Ely Cathl., 1867-83 et seq.; resident at "The Elms," Cambridge.

Kennedy, John Pendleton, LL.D., 1795-1870. *Clerke of Oxenforde; A Man of the Times; Mark Littleton; A Member of the 27th Congr.; Mephistopheles; Solomon Secondthoughts, Schoolmaster; A Southern Man.* An American lawyer and writer, of Baltimore; b. in that city; Baltimore Coll., 1812; admitted to the bar, 1816, and continued in successful practice for 20 years; M.C., 1839-45; Secretary of the Navy, 1852-53; Provost of the Univ. of Maryland, 1849-70; d. at Newport, R.I.

Kennedy, Patrick. *Harry Whitney.* An Irish writer on the legends of Ireland.

Kenner, S. A. *Essay Caigh.* An American journalist.

Kennet, White, D.D., 1660-1728. *W. K.; A Member of Convocation; A Member of the Said Society.* An English prelate; b. at Dover; Bishop of Peterborough, 1718-28.

Kenney, James, Esq., about 1770-1849. *K.* An Irish dramatist; at an early age was a clerk in a banking-house; d. at Brompton.

Kenrick, Francis Patrick, D.D., 1797-1863. *Omikron.* An Irish-American clergyman; b. in Dublin; came to the United States in 1821; Archbishop of Baltimore, 1851-63, where he died.

Kenrick, William, LL.D., -1779. *W. K., Esq.; W. Avon; A Friend; A Lady; Archimagirus Metaphoricus; Ontologos.* An English "critic of equal ability, impudence, and literary ferocity; was the terror of the new scribes, and the object of disgust to the old authors of his own day."

Kent, Anne. *Adrian.* An English novelist.

Kent, Benjamin. 1707-88. *Amicus.* An American loyalist; Harv. Univ., 1727; minister at Marlboro', Mass., for a time; but studied law and settled in Boston; d. at Halifax, Nova Scotia.

Kent, Charles. *C. K.* — See "Kent, William Charles Mark."

Kent, John. *Lycurgus.* An English journalist of the 18th century.

Kent, John. *Alan Fairford; Sir Minimus Pigmy.* A Canadian writer; for a time chief secretary to Sir Geo. Arthur, and then private tutor and secretary to the Earl of Carnarvon.

Kent, William Charles Mark, 1823-. *C. K.; Mark Rochester; An Oscotian; A Templar.* An English journalist; b. in London; called to the bar at the Middle Temple, 1859; but adopted literature as a profession.

Kenward, Philip. *Flaneur.* An American journalist, of Brooklyn.

Kenworthy, Dr. Charles J. *Al Fresco.* An American writer, of Jacksonville, Florida,

Keplinger, Mrs. E. M. (Patterson). *Queen of Hearts.* An American "Southland" writer; b. in Baltimore, Md.; for many years a teacher in the public schools of New Orleans.

Keppel, William Coutts, K.C.M.G., P.C., 1832-. *Viscount Bury.* An English gentleman; educ. at Eton; M.P. for Wick, etc., for Norwich, and later for Berwick; Treasurer for H. M.'s Household.

Ker, David. *D. K.* An American journalist; correspondent of the New York "Times."

Kerfoot, John Barrett, D.D. *The Bishop.* An American P. E. clergyman; President and Professor at Hobart Coll., 1864-66; Bishop of P. E. Church, Pittsburg, 1866-80 et seq.

Kernigan, ——. *The Khan.* A Canadian journalist.

Kerr, Charles. *A Student in the University of Edinburgh.* A Scottish poet, of Abbotrule.

Kerr, James. *An Officer in the E. I. Co.'s Service.* An English civilian and translator, of Patna, India.

Kerr, Robert Malcolm, LL.D. *R. M. K.* An English advocate and barrister.

Kersey, John. *J. K.* An English writer on algebra, in the time of Charles II.

Kershaw, Philip G., B.A. *Marcullus.* A Canadian writer, of Montreal; McGill Coll., 1867; d. some years since.

Kesson, John. *The Translator.* An English writer.

Kettell, Samuel, 1800-55. *Peeping Tom; Sampson, Short and Fat; Timothy Titterwell.* An American humorist; b. at Newburyport, Mass.; editor of the "Boston Courier," 1848-55; d. at Malden, Mass.

Kettle, Mary Rosa Stuart. *Rosa Mackenzie Kettle.* An English writer; b. at Overseale, near Ashby-de-la-Zouch, in Leicestershire; in 1880 resident at Heathside, Parkstone, Dorset.

Kewley, John, M.D., D.D. *An Episcopalian of * * Maryland.* An American clergyman; b. in England; Rector of the Parish of St. George's, New York City, 1813-16.

Kidd, Rev. **Samuel,** M.A., 1801–43. *Alfred.* An English Orientalist; b. in Hull; Prof. of Chinese in the Univ. of London; d. at Camden Town.

Kidder, Frederic. *Orient; Sagada-hoc.* An American bibliographer; for a time librarian of the New York Astor Library; now, 1885, librarian of the New Jersey College Library.

Kidder, Joseph. *Reddik.* An American newspaper contributor.

Kilvert, Adelaide Sophia. *A Mother and the Mistress of a Family.* An English writer.

Kimball, Edmund, 1793–1873. *A Citizen.* An American lawyer; b. in Newburyport; Harv. Univ., 1814; a lawyer in Boston for some years, and afterwards at Wenham, Mass., where he died.

Kimball, George. *Frank Hudson.* An American writer.

Kimber, Rev. **Isaac,** 1692–1758. *An Impartial Hand.* An English Dissenter; b. at Wantage, Berkshire.

Kimber, S., Jr. *Dr. Syntax, Jr.* An American political writer.

King, Counsellor ——. *A Gentleman of the Middle Temple.* An Irish poet and lawyer; son of Sir Anthony King, Knt.; Alderman of Dublin.

King, Edward, 1735–1807. *E. K***, of M*** S***; A Plain, Honest Layman.* An English antiquary; b. in Norfolk; of Clare Hall, Cambridge, and of Lincoln's Inn, London; devoted himself chiefly to literary pursuits in that city, and d. there.

King, Edward, 1795–1837. *Lord Kingsborough.* An English antiquary; son of the Earl of Kingston; d. in the Sheriff's prison at Dublin.

King, John, D.D., 1652–1732. *A Divine of the Church of England.* An English clergyman; b. at St. Coulomb, Cornwall; Rector of Chelsea, 1694–1732, where he died.

King, Peter, Lord King, 1669–1734. *An Impartial Hand.* An English jurist; b. at Exeter, Devonshire; Lord Chancellor of England, 1725–33.

King, Rev. **Richard,** 1749–1810. *Brother Abraham.* An English clergyman; Vicar of Steeple Morden, Cambridgeshire; and Rector of Worthin, Salop; d. at Steeple Morden.

King, Richard John, 1820–. *R. J. K.* An English antiquary; wrote for John Murray his series of Handbooks to the Cathedrals of England.

King, Rufus, LL.D., 1755–1827. *Camillus.* An American statesman; b. at Scarborough, Me.; Harv. Univ., 1777;

admitted to the bar, 1780; removed to New York City, 1788; U.S. Senator, 1789–96 and 1813–25; Minister to England, 1796–1804 and 1825–26; d. at Jamaica, L.I.

King, Mrs. **Sue (Petigru).** *A Heartless Woman; An Idle Woman.* An American "Southland" writer; b. at Charleston, S.C.; married Henry C. King; in 1872 resided at Washington, D.C.

King, William, LL.D., 1663–1712. *A Master of Arts; Tom Boggy; Mons. Samuel de Sorbiere.* An ingenious and humorous English writer; b. in London; resided in that city from 1708, and d. there.

King, William, LL.D., 1685–1763. *Frederick Scheffer; Peregrine O'Donald; Florio; Amias Riddinge, B.D.; Peregrine Smyth, Esq.* An English poet; b. at Stepney, Oxford; Principal of St. Mary's Hall, Oxford, 1718–22.

Kingdon, Rev. **Samuel Nicholson,** B.D., 1805–72. *A Clergyman in the West.* An English clergyman; b. at Bridgerule; Vicar of Bridgerule, near Holsworthy, 1844–72.

Kingman, Eugene. *Ion.* An American journalist.

Kingsbury, Rev. **O. A.** *Quercus.* An American writer.

Kingsford, William. *W. K.* A Canadian author and journalist; afterwards moved to England.

Kingsley, Dr. ——. *The Doctor.* — See "Earl, The."

Kingsley, Rev. **Charles,** 1819–75. *C. K; Chartist Parson; Parson Lot; Lord Dundreary; A Minute Philosopher.* An English clergyman, novelist, and social reformer; b. at Holne, Devon.; Magdalen Coll., Cambridge, 1842; Rector of Eversley, Hamps., 1844–75; lectured in the United States, 1873–74; d. at Eversley.

Kingsley, Mrs. **Fanny E. (Grenfell).** *His Wife.* An English lady; wife of Charles Kingsley.

Kingsley, Henry, 1830–76. *Granby Dixon; The Doctor.* An English journalist, reviewer, and novelist; brother of Charles; b. at Holne, Devon.; Worcester Coll., Oxford; editor of the Edinburgh "Daily Review," 1870–72.

Kingsley, Vine Wright. *Americus; A Member of the New York Bar.* An American political writer; a lawyer in New York City.

Kingsley, Z. *An Inhabitant of Florida.* An American writer on slavery.

Kingsman, William. *A Country Gentleman.* An English writer, of Petworth.

Kingston, William Henry Giles, 1814–80. *Barrington Beaver, Esq.; Bar-*

naby Brine, Esq. An English writer of books for boys; b. in London.

Kinney, Mrs. Elizabeth C. (Dodge). *Stedman.* An American poet and prose writer, of Newark, N.J.

Kinsella, Thomas. *Brooklyn.* An American journalist, of Brooklyn, N.Y.

Kip, Leonard. *A Member of the Bar.* An American lawyer and novelist.

Kip, William Ingraham, D.D., 1811-. *A Member of the N.Y. Geneal. and Biog. Society.* An American clergyman; b. in New York City; has been minister successively in Morristown, N.J., New York City, Albany, N.Y.; and missionary bishop; resident at San Francisco since 1853.

Kippis, Andrew, D.D., 1725-95. *A. K.* An English Unit. divine; minister of a congregation at Boston, Lincolnshire, 1746; of another, at Dorking, 1750; and of another, at Westminster, 1753; editor of the "Library," etc.

Kirk, Eleanor. *Mrs. Nelly Ames.* An American writer of the day.

Kirke, Charles D. *Se De Kay.* An American writer of the day.

Kirkland, Mrs. Caroline Matilda (Stansbury), 1801-64. *Mary Clavers.* An American writer; b. in New York City; about 1830 married William Kirkland, of Hamilton Coll.; editor of the "Union Magazine," N.Y., 1847-48.

Kirkland, Charles Pinckney, LL.D. *An Officer in the Field.* An American lawyer, of New York City; Hamilton Coll., 1816.

Kirkwood, Robert. *Roby Awl.* A Scottish writing master, of Edinburgh.

Kirschner, Miss L. *Ossip Schubin.* An American writer of the day.

Kirwan, Thomas. *One of the Seventeenth.* An American soldier of the 17th Massachusetts, in the late civil war.

Kister, W. H. *Richard Raleigh.* An American journalist.

Kitching, Mrs. **H. St. A.** *H. St. A. K.; A Lady.* An English writer.

Klencke, Hermann, 1813-81. *Hermann von Maltitz.* A German physician; b. at Hanover; studied medicine; practised in his native State; in 1837 removed to Leipsic; in 1839 to Brunswick, where he gave natural history lectures; and from 1855 again resided in Hanover.

Klopstock, Friedrich Gottlieb, 1724-1803. *The German Milton.* A celebrated German poet; resided at Hamburg, 1771-1803, as councillor of the Danish legation.

Knapp, Rev. **Henry Ryder,** M.A., -1817. *Peeping Tom.* An English clergyman, wit, and genius; Rector of Woodford, and Vicar of Rounds, Northamptonshire.

Knapp, John Leonard, Esq., F.S.A., F.L.S., 1767-1845. *A Naturalist.* An English naturalist; b. at Shenley, Bucks.; d. at Alveston, Gloucestershire.

Knapp, Martin. *Broadaxe.* An American writer.

Knapp, Samuel Lorenzo, LL.D., 1784-1838. *Ali Bey; Ignatius Loyola Robertson, LL.D.; Shahcolen, a Hindu Philosopher residing in Philadelphia.* An American lawyer and journalist; b. at Newburyport, Mass.; Dartmouth Coll., 1804; was an editor at Boston; in 1827 began to practise law in New York City; d. at Hopkinton, Mass.

Knatchbull, Misses ——. *Kingcups.* English authors.

Kneeland, Abner, 1774-1844. *A. K.* An American journalist, in New York City and Boston; d. at Salubria, Ind.

Kneppelhout, Jan, 1814-. *Klikspaan.* A Dutch author; b. at Leyden; studied there; and distinguished himself by his original pictures of the student-life.

Knevels, Mrs. D. C. *Frances Eastwood.* An American (?) novelist of the day.

Knight, ——. *Solomon Grildrig.*

Knight, Ashton. *Signor Sarti.*

Knight, Charles, 1791-1873. *S. T.; Grandfather Smith; Patterson Aymar; Vander von Bluggen.* An English editor and publisher; b. at Windsor; settled in London in 1820; d. at Addlestone, Surrey.

Knight, Frederick, Esq., 1791-1849. *A Student at Law.* An American poet; brother of the following; b. at Hampton, N.H.; d. at Rowley, Mass.

Knight, Rev. **Henry Cogswell,** Esq., 1788-1835. *Arthur Singleton, Esq.* An American poet; b. at Newburyport, Mass.; Brown Univ., 1812; ordained as an Epis. clergyman, but never settled.

Knight, Mrs. Henry Gally. *Grandmother Hope.* An English writer for the young; wife of H. G. Knight, M.P., 1786-1846.

Knight, John Collyer. *K.* An English writer, of the British Museum.

Knight, Oliver. *Pontiac.* An American writer.

Knight, T. *T. K.* An English writer, of Papcastle.

Knighton, William, LL.D. *An Indian Journalist.* An English colonist; for many years a planter in Ceylon.

Knott, Rev. **Robert Rowe.** *A Cambridge M.A.* An English clergyman; St. John's Coll., Cambridge, 1819; Chaplain of the W. London Union.

Knowles, Mrs. Mary, 1727–1807. *A Child of Candour.* An English Quaker lady; b. in Staffordshire; widow of Dr. Knowles, London; distinguished by various works in the polite arts of poetry, painting, needlework; d. in Ely-place, Holborn, London.

Knox, D. B. *Dalriada.* An Irish writer of the day.

Knox, Mrs. Isa Craig, 1831–. *Isa.* A Scottish writer; b. in Edinburgh; removed to London in 1857, and married her cousin, Mr. John Knox.

Knox, Rev. Spenser. *An Irish Clergyman.* An Irish divine; Rector of Maghera, Diocese of Derry.

Knox, Thomas. *Walneerg.* An English poet.

Knox, Vicesimus, 1752–1821. *Antipolemus; A Calm Observer.* An English clergyman; Master of Tunbridge School for 33 years, 1779–1812; after his retirement he lived in London, engaged in literary pursuits; d. at Tunbridge.

Knox, William, 1732–1810. *A Gentleman in London; A Late Under Secretary of State; A Layman of the Church of England.* An Irish statesman; Under Secretary of State at London, 1770–82; Agent of the Georgia Loyalists, 1784; d. at Great Ealing.

Koch, Ernst. *Edouard Helmar.*

König, Ewald August, 1833–. *Ernst Kaiser.* A German author; b. at Barmen; gave himself exclusively to a literary career; in 1871 he settled in Neuwied.

Kohlman, Rev. Anthony, 1771–1836. *Rev. John Beschter: A Countryman of Martin Luther.* A French R. C. priest; b. at Kaversberg, near Colmar (Haut-Rhin); officiated in the United States, 1807–25: Prof. of Theol. in the Rom. Coll., 1825–36; d. in Rome.

Kolzow-Massalski, Princess Helene Ghika, 1828–. *Dora D'Istria.* A Wallachian writer; in 1849 married Prince Alexander Kolzow-Massalski; since 1855 has resided in Western Europe; 1882 had a villa in Florence.

Korn, W. Feist. *Hilarius.*

Kortright, Miss Fanny Aikin, 1821– *Berkeley Aikin.* An English writer; b. in London; a daughter of the late commander, N. Berkeley Kortright, an American by birth, but for 50 years an officer in the British navy. She began her literary career at the age of 17.

Koster, John Theodore, Esq. *A Merchant.* An English writer; Member of the Royal Academy of Sciences at Lisbon.

Kotzebue, Wilhelm von, 1813–. *W. Augustsohn.* A German poet and diplomatist; b. at Reval; since 1870, Minister at Dresden.

Krackowizer, E. W. *T. S.; Theophrastus Schopenhauer.* An American writer, of Normal Park, Ill.

Krasinski, Count Valerian. *A Naturalist.* A Polish miscellaneous writer, of London.

Krause, Ernst Ludwig, 1839–. *Carus Sterne.* A German writer; b. at Zielenzig, in West Prussia; with Darwin and Häckel he founded the monthly "Kosmos" in 1877.

Kühne, August, 1829–. *Johannes van Dewall.* A German novelist; b. at Herford in Westphalia; served for many years in the army; and retired in 1875 with the rank of Lieut.-Colonel.

Kynaston, Herbert, D.D., 1809–78. *H. K.* An eminent English clergyman and hymn-writer; Prebendary of St. Paul's, 1853–78.

Kynaston, Thomas. *A Layman.* An English writer.

L.

Labarre, Louis, 1810–. *Jacques Bienaise.* A Belgian journalist; b. at Dinant (Namur); has been connected with advanced Republican sheets in Paris, Liege, and Brussels.

Labouchere, Henry Du Pré, 1831–. *Besieged Resident; Our Member for Paris; Scrutator.* An English politician; b. in London; educ. at Eton, and Trin. Coll., Cambridge; was in the diplomatic service, 1854–64; M.P. for Windsor, 1865–

66; for Middlesex, 1867–68; Northampton, 1880–82 *et seq.*

Laboulaye, Édouard, 1811–83. *Dr. Réné Lefebvre.* A French jurist and statesman; b. in Paris.

Lachlan, Major Robert. *L.* An English officer; retired from the army; for many years served in Canada; in 1867 resided in the United States.

La Corte, ——. *A Resident there.* A Spanish writer.

Lacoste, Mlle Mathilde, –1881. *Louise Gérald.* A French novelist.

Lacroix, Mme Louise. *Mme d'Aghonne.* A French writer of the day.

Lacroix, Paul, 1806–84. *Le bibliophile Jacob; P. L. Jacob, bibliophile; Antony Dubourg; Pierre Dufour.* An eminent French editor and literary antiquary; b. in Paris.

Lacunza, Emanuel, 1731–1801. *Juan Josafat Ben-Ezra.* A South American writer; Bishop of St. Jago of Chili.

Lacy, Willoughby. *One formerly possessed of the Place.* An English poet; son of James Lacy, Esq.

Ladd, Mrs. Catharine (Stratton), 1810–. *Alida; Arcturus; Minnie Mayflower; Morna.* An American "Southland" writer, of Winnsboro', S.C.; b. in Virginia.

Ladd, Joseph Brown, 1764–86. *Arouet.* An American poet and prosewriter; b. in Newport, R.I.; killed in a duel at Charleston, S.C.

Ladd, William, 1778–1841. *Philanthropos.* An eminent American peace reformer; b. in Exeter, N.H.; Harv. Univ., 1797; for many years editor of the "Friend of Peace," etc.; d. at Portsmouth, N.H.

Lafuente, Modesto, 1806–66. *Fray Gerundio; Tirabecque.* A Spanish historian; b. at Rabanel de los Caballeros, Province Palencia; was at first professor at Astorga; then in 1838 settled at Madrid as a journalist and satirist.

Lahee, M. R. *B. T.; M. R. L.* An English writer.

Laing, Alexander, 1787–1857. *The Brechin Poet.* A Scottish poet; b. at Brechin; was a flax-dresser for about 20 years.

Laing, David, LL.D. *D. L.; An Eminent Collector in Edinburgh.* A Scottish editor and literary antiquary; Librarian of the Signet Library, Edinburgh.

Laird, Lieut. Francis Charles, R.N. *George Howard, Esq.* An English seaman and writer.

Lake, Rev. ——. *An Episcopalian.* An English clergyman.

Lamb, Charles, 1775–1834. *Burton, Junior; Crito; Edax; Elia; An Eye-witness; Hospita; A Londoner; Moriturus.* An English essayist; b. in London; clerk in the office of the East India Company, 1792–1825; retired on a pension of £450; d. at Edmonton.

Lamb, Rev. J. *A Manchester Man.* An English writer.

Lamb, Sir James Bland Burges, Bart., D.C.L., 1752–1824. *Alfred; Serjeant Bradshaw; Verus.* An English statesman and man of letters; b. at Gibraltar; in 1795 he retired from politics and devoted himself to literature.

Lamb, John. *J. E.; James Elia; Lovel.* An English servant and friend of the benchers of the Inner Temple; father of Charles Lamb.

Lamb, Mrs. Joseph. *Ruth Buck.* An English writer for the young.

Lamb, Miss Mary Anne, 1765–1847. *Bridget Elia; Mrs. Leicester.* An English writer; sister of Charles Lamb; b. in London; d. at St. John's Wood.

Lambert, C. E. *C. E. L.* An English novelist.

Lambert, Henry. *An Ex-M.P.* An Irish writer; M.P. from Wexford Co., Ireland.

Lamboll, William, Jun. *W. L., Junior.* An English Friend, of Reading.

Lamothe-Langon, Étienne Léon, Baron de, 1786–. *Alfred Nettement; J. Pouchet; Mme la C*** D'Adhemar.* A French littérateur.

Lamotte-Fouqué, Friedrich Heinrich Karl, Baron von, 1777–1843. *Pellegrin.* An eminent German poet and novelist; b. in Brandenburgh; the latter part of his life resided in Paris, Halle, and on his estate of Nennhausen.

Lancaster, A. E. *A. E. L.* An American writer.

Lancaster, Joseph, 1778–1838. *Amicus.* An eminent English Friend and educator; b. in London; came to this country in 1818; and d. in New York City.

Lancaster, Thomas. *Philalethes Candaliensis.* An English Friend, of Sedbergh.

Landesmann, Heinrich. *Hieronymus Lorm.* A German writer of the day.

Landon, Letitia Elizabeth, 1802–38. *L. E. L.* An English poet; b. at Brompton, London; in 1838 married Mr. George Maclean, Governor of Cape Coast Castle, and sailed for her new home; but d. there in a few months.

Landon, Melville D. *Eli Perkins.* An American humorist.

Landor, Mrs. S. W. *S. W. L.* An American writer.

Landor, Walter Savage, 1775–1864. *W. S. L.; Boythorn; An Octogenarian.* An English poet, soldier, philosopher, essayist, and critic; resided in Italy for more than 30 years from 1815.

Lane, James Woods, D.D. *Cameroy.* An American clergyman.

Lane, Richard J. *A. E.; R. J. L.* An English writer.

Lang, John. *Mofussilite.* An English (?) humorist.

Lange, Ernst Philipp Karl, 1813–. *Philipp Galen.* A German novelist; b. at Potsdam; studied medicine at Berlin; entered the Prussian army as a surgeon; afterwards travelled extensively; and in 1878 retired from service on a pension.

Langhorne, Rev. **John,** 1735–79. *One of H. M.'s Justices of the Peace.* An English poet and translator; b. in Kirby Stephen; best known as the translator (with his brother William) of "Plutarch's Lives."

Langley, ——. *Pavo.* An English journalist, of London.

Langton, Joseph. *Thomas Bullion.* An English financial writer.

Langworthy, Asahel, A.M., –1835. *A Kentuckian.* An American writer; Univ. of Vermont, 1805.

Lanigan, George F., 1846–. *Allid; Toxopholite.* A Canadian journalist and sporting writer; b. at St. Charles, River Richelieu, Upper Canada; in 1867 joined the staff of the Montreal "Gazette."

Lanman, Charles, 1819–. *An Angler; A Landscape Painter; A Tourist.* An American journalist; b. at Monroe, Mich.; for some years private secretary to Daniel Webster; afterwards librarian to the U.S. House of Representatives; in 1871 became American Secretary of the Japanese Legation at Washington.

Lansing, Abraham. *One of the People.* An American political writer; a broker of Boston.

Larcombe, Miss **Jane Elizabeth.** *Kate Campbell.* — See "Lincoln, Mrs. Heman."

Lardner, Nathaniel, D.D., 1684–1768. *Philalethes.* An English Dissenter; b. at Hawkhurst, Kent; Asst. Minister at Crutched Friars, London, 1729–68.

Larking, Rev. **Lambert Blackwell,** M.A., –1868. *L. B. A.* An English clergyman; b. at Maidstone; Brasenose Coll., Oxford, 1820; Chaplain to Viscountess Falmouth, Baroness Despencer; d. at Ryarsh Vicarage, Maidstone.

La Rochefoucauld-Liancourt, François Alexandre Frédéric, duc de, 1747–1827. *Un Européen.* A French peer and philanthropist; travelled in the United States, 1792–99.

Laroue, Mlle **Léonie.** *René.* A French dramatist, of Mâcon, actuellement à Paris.

Larra, Mariano José de, 1809–37. *Ramon de Arriala; Figaro.* A witty and popular Spanish writer and journalist; b. and d. in Madrid.

La Rue, F. A. H., M.D. *Isidore de Méplats.* A Canadian journalist, of Quebec.

Larwood, Rev. **Joshua,** –1808. *A Sailor.* An English clergyman; Rector of Swanton Morley, Norfolk; and many years chaplain on board the "Britannia."

Lascelles, Robert. *Piscator.* An English angler.

Lascelles, Rowley, Esq., 1771–1841. *A Member of it; Numa; Publicola; Yorick.* An English lawyer; b. in the parish of St. James, Westminster; educ. at Harrow School; and called to the bar at the Middle Temple in 1797; afterwards resided in Dublin; and practised at the Irish bar about 20 years.

Lasselle, Mrs. **E. L.** *E. L. L.* An American writer.

Lasson, Adolf, 1832–. *L. Adolf.* A German poet and philosopher; b. at Altstrelitz in Mechlinburg; from 1877 teacher of Philosophy in the University of Berlin.

La Terrière, Pierre De Salles, M.D., –1834. *A Canadian.* A French Canadian physician; d. at Les Eboulements, Lower Canada.

Latey, John Lash. *A Working Man.* An English writer.

Latham, Rev. **Henry,** M.A. *Presbyter Cicestrensis.* An English clergyman; Vicar of Fittleworth, Petworth, Sussex, 1827–60 *et seq.*

Latham, Henry Jepson. *Ring Jepson.* An American writer of the day.

Lathbury, Miss **Mary A.** *Aunt Mary.* An American writer for the young.

Lathrop, John, Jr., A.M., 1772–1820. *Moral Censor.* A famous American wit, poet, and orator; son of the Rev. Dr. John Lathrop, of Boston; b. in Boston; Harv. Univ., 1789.

Lathrop, John Hiram, LL.D., 1799–1866. *A Citizen of New York.* An American educator; b. at Sherburne, N.Y.; Yale Coll., 1819; President of the Univ. of Columbia, Missouri, 1865–66; and d. there.

Lathrop, Mrs. **Mary (Torrans).** *Lena.* An American writer; b. in Central Michigan; in 1864 married Garnett C. Lathrop; began to write at the early age of 14 years.

Lathy, Thomas Pike, Esq., 1771–. *Piscator.* An English poet; b. in Exeter; bred to trade, but devoted himself chiefly to letters.

Latouche, J. D. *The Cheshire Weaver.* An English writer of the first part of the 18th century.

Latrobe, Charles Joseph. *The Rambler in Mexico.* An English traveller;

accompanied Irving in his "Tour on the Prairies."

Latrobe, John Hazelhurst Boneval, 1803-. ——. An American lawyer; b. in Philadelphia; admitted to the Baltimore bar in 1825; is a member of the Maryland Historical Society, and has given much time to historical and other literary work.

Latto, Thomas C. *Aiken Dunn.* An American journalist, of Brooklyn, N.Y.

Laughan, Dr. ——. *A Farmer.* An American writer.

Laujon, Pierre, 1727-1811. *The French Anacreon.* A French poet; b. in Paris; president of the "Caveau Moderne," a Paris club, noted for its good dinners, but every member must be a poet.

Laurence, Richard, D.L.C., 1760-1839. *R. C.; Enoch.* An English orientalist; b. in Bath; Corpus Christi Coll., Oxford, 1782; Arabic Professor at Oxford, 1814-22; Archbishop of Cashel, 1822-39; d. in Dublin.

Laurent, Émile, 1819-. *Émile Colombey; Un ancien enfant de chœur.* A French bibliographer; attached to the Royal Library, 1845-47; afterwards sub-librarian to the *Corps législatif.*

Laurie, Rev. Thomas, 1821-. *A Returned Missionary.* A Scottish-American missionary to Syria, 1841-57; and pastor at West Roxbury, Mass., from 1857.

Lausanne, Laurent Jean de, -1877. *Laurent-Jan.* A French humorist; friend of Balzac.

Law, Hon. Elizabeth Susan, 1799-. *E. S. L.; E. S. Z.* An English lady; afterwards Lady Colchester; wife of Charles Abbot, 2d Lord; 3d daughter of 1st Lord Ellenborough.

Law, Thomas, 1756-1834. *Justinian.* An English-American financier; a brother of Lord Ellenborough; d. at Washington, D.C.

Lawler, Peter. *Peter Pindar.* An English writer.

Lawrence, Bessie. *Agatha.* An American poet of the day.

Lawrence, Frederick, 1821-67. *A Barrister.* An English lawyer and biographer; b. at Bisham, Berks.; called to the bar at the Middle Temple, 1849; d. in London.

Lawrence, James, Esq., 1773-1840. *St. Ives.* An English writer; a Knight of Malta, who styled himself Sir James Lawrence, and on the Continent the Chevalier de Lawrence; d. in London.

Lawrence, John, 1756-about 1836. *Wm. Henry Scott.* An English sporting writer; a literary farmer; b. at Colchester; became a merchant in London.

Lawrence, Mrs. Margarette (Woods). *Meta Lander.* An American writer, of Lawrence, Mass.; wife of Dr. E. A. Lawrence, and daughter of Dr. Leonard Woods, of Andover.

Lawrence, Mrs. Mary (Hall), 1749-1815. *Una; Fidelia.* A celebrated beauty; b. in Jamaica; wife of Richard James Lawrence, Esq., of Fairfield, Jamaica; d. in London.

Lawrence, Roger. *A Lay Hand; A Known Friend of Mr. Leslie.* An English religious writer of the first part of the 18th century.

Lawrence, Mrs. Rose. *A Lady.* An English writer, of Wavertree Hall, Liverpool.

Lawrence, William Beach, LL.D., 1800-80. *An American Citizen.* An American jurist; b. in New York City; Columbia Coll., 1818; called to the Bar, 1823; Lieut.-Gov. of Rhode Island; passed the last years of his life in Washington, and d. there.

Lawrence, William Richards, M.D. *One of the Board of Managers.* An American physician; b., 1812, at Longwood, Mass.; Harv. Med. School, 1845; resident at Brookline, Mass.

Lawrie, W. F. B. *W. F. B. L.* An English writer.

Lawry, Rev. John. *L.* An English clergyman; Prebendary of Rochester.

Lawson, Miss Charlotte Eliza. — See "Riddell, Mrs. C. E. (L.)."

Lawson, E. M. *E. M. L.* An English writer of the day.

Lawson, James, 1799-. *A Cosmopolite.* A Scottish-American poet and prose writer; b. at Glasgow; of New York City from 1815.

Lawson, Rt. Hon. James Anthony, LL.D., 1817-. *John Bradley.* An eminent Irish lawyer; b. at Waterford; Trin. Coll., Dublin; called to the Irish bar, 1840; Judge of the Irish Court of Common Pleas from 1868.

Lawson, John, D.D., -1760. *A Late Eminent Divine of the Church of England.* An English clergyman; Trin. Coll., Dublin; Rector of Swanscombe, in Kent, where he died.

Lawton, Charlwood. *N. N.* An English writer of the first part of the 18th century.

Lay, E. Elizabeth. *E. E. L.* An American (?) writer of the day.

Lea, Mrs. Floride (Clemson). *C. de Flori.* An American "Southland" writer; a granddaughter of John C. Calhoun; b.

in Pendleton Village, S.C.; in 1870 resided in New York City.

Lea, Henry Charles, 1825-. *Mizpah.* An American author and publisher, of Philadelphia; and b. in that city; grandson of Mathew Carey.

Leach, Harry Harwood. *A Sentimental Idler.*

Leadbetter, J. *J. L.* An English writer of the day.

Leask, William, D.D. *A Dissenting Minister.* An English clergyman, of Kennington.

Leathes, Mrs. Stanley. *M. G.* An English novelist of the day; wife of a London clergyman.

Lebeau, Eugène. *Eugène Ruy-Blas.* A French poet; a ballad-maker, of Lice.

Le Breton, Mrs. Anna Letitia (Aikin). *One of a Literary Family.* An English lady; autobiographer of the day.

Lebrun, Pauline (Guyot), 1805-. *De Camille; Camille Lebrun.* A French woman of letters, of Paris; wrote also under the pseudonyms "Laure Dartigue" and "Fabien de Saint Leger."

Lechanteur, M. E. *De Pontaumont.* A French writer; Inspector of the Marine, Cherbourg.

Lechmere, E. *Edmund Stratford.*

Le Clerc, Miss Clara. *Harry Holt; Polly Holt.* An American "Southland" writer; b. in Alabama; in 1869 teacher at "College Temple," Newnan, Ga.

Leclerc, Louis, 1799-1854. *Ludovic Celler.* A French economist, of Paris.

Lecomte, Jules, 1814-64. *Jules Du Camp; Van Engelyom.* A French journalist and man of letters, of Paris; b. at Boulogne; d. at Paris.

Led'huy, Jean Baptiste Alphonse. *Chrysostôme Dagobert.* A French teacher at London.

Lee, Miss A. E. *A. E. L.* An English writer.

Lee, Miss Abby. *A. L.* An American writer.

Lee, Arthur, M.D., LL.D., 1740-92. *An American; An American Wanderer; Junius Americanus; Monitor; An Old Member of Parliament.* An American statesman, of Virginia; b. in Westmoreland Co.; educ. at Edinburgh and London; U.S. secret agent in Paris, 1776-79; M.C., 1782-89; d. in Middlesex Co., Va.

Lee, Charles, 1731-82. *Junius Americanus.* An English-American soldier; a Major-General in the American army; b. at Dernhall, Cheshire, England.

Lee, Mrs. Eleanor Percy (Ware), and Another, 1820-50. *Two Sisters of the West.* An American poet; sister of Mrs. C. A. Warfield; b. near Natchez; resided in Philadelphia and Cincinnati, and married H. W. Lee, of Vicksburg, Miss.

Lee, Dr. Francis. *A Lay Gentleman.* An English writer of 200 years ago.

Lee, Frederick George, D.D. *F. G. L.* An English clergyman and poet; St. Edmund Hall, Oxford, 1854; Vicar of All-Saints, Lambeth, 1867-83 et seq.

Lee, John, D.D., 1780-1859. *Alumni of the University of Edinburgh.* A Scottish divine and scholar; b. in a village on Gala Water; Univ. of Edinburgh; Principal of the Univ. of Edinburgh, 1840-59; d. at his residence in the college.

Lee, Miss Mary Elizabeth, 1813-49. *M. E. L.; A Friend.* An American writer in prose and verse, of Charleston, S.C.; b. and d. in that city.

Lee, Mrs. Rachel Frances Antonina Dashwood, about 1770-1829. *R. F. A.; Philopatria.* An English writer, calling herself Baroness Despencer.

Lee, Richard Henry, 1732-94. *The Federal Farmer.* An eminent American statesman, of Virginia; b. at Stratford, Westmoreland Co.; educ. in England; M.C., 1778, and its President, 1784; U.S. Senator, 1789-92; d. at Chantilly, Westmoreland Co., Va.

Lee, Mrs. Sarah (Wallis Bowdich), 1791-1856. *A Traveller.* An English lady; b. in Colchester; d. at Erith, Co. Kent.

Lee, William, -1840. *Un Américain Citoyen; The High Constable.* An American writer; consul at Bordeaux.

Leech, H. E. S. *H. E. S. L.* An English botanical writer.

Leeds, William Henry. *W. H. L.* An English architect.

Lees, James Cameron, D.D. *A. R. A.; Rev. Rory M'Rory; Rag, Tag, and Bobtail.* An eminent Scottish minister, of the High Kirk, Edinburgh.

Lefevre, Mrs. ——. *Mrs. L***.* An Irish writer.

Lefevre, Sir George William, Knt., M.D., 1797-1846. *A Travelling Physician.* An English physician, of the British Embassy at St. Petersburgh; d. in London.

Legge, Alfred Owen. *Augustus Stawell; One of her Sons.* An English writer, of Manchester.

Leggett, William, 1802-39. *A Country Schoolmaster; A Midshipman of the U.S. Navy; Several American Authors.* An American journalist; b. in New York City; d. at New Rochelle, N.Y.

Legh, Gerard. *A Christian; Gilbert Dalrymple, D.D.* A Scottish writer, of 200 years ago.

Le Grice, Rev. Charles Valentine, M.A., 1773–1858. *C. V. Le G.; Civis; Gronovius; Vigilans.* An English clergyman; friend of Lamb and Coleridge; b. at Bury St. Edmunds; in 1796 he visited Cornwall, which thenceforward became his home; d. at his seat, Tereife, near Penzance, in Cornwall.

Leidesdorf, Franz. *Franz Wallner.* A German writer.

Leigh, Mrs. ——. *Sator.* An English writer of the day.

Leigh, Benjamin Watkins, LL.D., 1781–1849. *Algernon Sydney; An Eminent Citizen of Virginia.* An eminent American lawyer and statesman; b. in Chesterfield Co., Va.; in 1813 removed to Richmond; U.S. Senator, 1835–37, when he retired into private life; d. at Richmond.

Leigh, Chandos, Baron Leigh, 1791–1850. *A Gloucestershire County Gentleman.* An English poet; b. at Stoneleigh, Co. Warwick; Christ Church, Oxford; a friend of Lord Byron and of Dr. Samuel Parr; d. at Bonn, on the Rhine.

Leigh, P. Brady. *A Member of Gray's Inn.* An English lawyer and law-writer.

Leigh, Percival. *Mr. Pips; Professor.* An English humorist and journalist, of London.

Leighton, John, F.S.A.,1822–. *Luke Limner.* An eminent English artist, of London; b. in Westminster; published ·his first work in 1844.

Leland, Aaron Whitney, D.D., 1787–1871. *Expositor.* An American clergyman, of Charleston, S.C., 1812–34; and from 1834 professor in the Theol. Sem. at Columbia, S.C.; b. in Peru, Mass.; Wms. Coll., 1808.

Leland, Charles Godfrey, 1824–. *Hans Breitmann; Meister Karl; Mace Sloper.* An American humorist; b. in Philadelphia; educ. at New Jersey Coll., and spent three years in European universities.

Le Mesurier, Rev. Thomas, B.D. *A Clergyman of the Diocese of Durham; ******, M.A., Fellow of New College.* An English clergyman; b. in Guernsey; New Coll., Oxford; Rector of Haughton, near Darlington.

Lemoine, Adolphe, 1805–80. *Lemoine Montigny.* A French dramatist; b. in Paris; in 1839 he renounced literature to devote himself to the direction of the "Gymnase" theatre; d. in Paris.

Lemon, Mark, 1809–70. *Uncle Mark.* An English humorist, dramatist, and journalist; b. in London; for many years one of the editors, or sole editor, of "Punch," and literary editor of the "Illustrated London News."

Lenny, Christian, D.D. *A Clergyman of the Church of England.* An English divine; St. John's Coll., Cambridge; B.D., 1842; in 1873 *et seq.* resident at Fern Lodge, Pinkneygreen, Maidenhead.

Lenox, James. *L.* An American bibliographer, of New York City.

Leonard, Miss Agnes. *Mollie Myrtle.* An American "Southland" poet and prose writer; b. in Louisville, Ky.; in 1868 was married to Dr. S. E. Scanland, formerly of Kentucky.

Leonard, Charles C. *Crocus.* An American Western writer of the day.

Leonard, Rev. Charles Hall. *C. H. L.* An American Univ. minister; Professor of Homiletics and Pastoral Theology at Tuft's Coll., 1869–84 *et seq.*

Leonard, Daniel, A.M., 1740–1829. *Massachusettensis; A Native of New England; A Person of Honor.* An American loyalist; b. in Norton, Mass.; Chief Justice of Bermuda; he was the *Beau Trumps* in Mrs. Warren's "Group."

Leonard, Rev. Henry Charles. *The Minister of the Church.* An American Univ. minister; at one time pastor at Orono, and afterwards at Waterville, Me.

Leonowens, Mrs. Anna Harriette (Crawford), 1834–. *The English Governess.* An English writer; governess in the family of the king of Siam, 1863–67; b. at Caernarvon, Wales; settled in the U.S. in 1867.

Leopold, Alexander. *A Rational Christian.* A German writer; Prince of Hohenhole and Bishop of Sardica.

L'Epine, Ernest Louis Victor Jules, 1826–. *Ernest Manuel; Quatrelles.* A French dramatist and novelist; b. in Paris; has held several positions, but was in 1865 appointed Counsellor at the Court of Accounts.

Le Reboullet, Adolphe Louis Auguste, 1845–. *Prosper Chazel.* A French *littérateur;* b. at Strasbourg; in 1872, entered the staff of "le Temps."

Lermont, L. *Cousin Cicely.* An American writer of the day.

Le Sieur, W. D. *Laon.* A Canadian writer.

Leslie, Charles, 1650–1722. *A Member of the Church of England; Philalethes; A Student of the Temple; A Gentleman in Scotland; A Gentleman in the City.* An

Irish religious and political writer; d. at Glaslough, County Monaghan.

Leslie, Sir **John,** Knt., 1766–1832. *A Gentleman.* A Scottish poet and scholar; b. at Largo, Fifeshire; educ. at St. Andrew's and at Edinburgh; then proceeded to London, where he engaged in literary work; Prof. of Nat. Hist. in the Univ. of Edinb., 1819–32; d. at his seat, at Coates, Fifeshire.

Leslie, Mrs. **Madeline.** *A Physician's Wife.* A Scottish writer of the day.

Lespès, Antoine Joseph Napoléon (called **Léo**), 1815–75. *Timothée Trimm.* A French author; b. at Bouchain (Nord); began his literary career in the minor Paris journals; founded in 1862 the "Petit Journal," which soon had a circulation of 200,000 copies; d. in Paris.

Lessing, Gotthold Ephraim, 1729–81. *The Father of German Literature.* An eminent German poet.

Lester, Rev. **Charles Edwards,** 1815–. *Helen Dhu; Berkeley Men.* An American journalist; b. at Griswold, Conn.; came to the Bar in Mississippi; afterwards ordained to the Presbyt. ministry; from 1847 resided at New York City.

Letchworth, Thomas, about 1736–84. *T. L.; Philaretus.* An English Friend, of Southwark, London; a minister about 26 years; d. at Newbury.

Letellier, Charles de Saint Malo. *Maximilien Raoul.* A French dramatist and miscellaneous writer, of Paris.

Letts, J. M. *A Returned Californian.* An American writer.

Lever, Charles James, M.D., LL.D., 1806–72. *Cornelius O'Dowd; Paul Gosebet; Harry Lorrequer.* An Irish novelist; b. in Dublin; Trin. Coll., Dublin; for a time, after 1845, he resided with his family at Florence; Vice-Consul at Spezia, 1858–67; d. at Trieste.

Leveson, Major **Henry A.** *H. A. L.,* the Old Shekarry; The Old Shekarry. An Irish sporting writer.

Levy, Julius, 1831–. *Julius von Rodenberg.* A German poet and dramatist; b. at Rodenberg in Hessen; since 1859 has resided at Berlin.

Lewes, George Henry, 1817–78. *Frank Churchill; Slingsby Lawrence; Vivian; The Author of "The Life of Goethe."* An English writer; b. in London; from 1839, devoted himself at London to literature and science.

Lewin, Ross. *A Field Officer.* An English soldier.

Lewis, Albert Henry. *Lewis Henry.* An American writer of the day.

Lewis, Alonzo, 1794–1861. *The Lynn Bard.* An American poet and local historian; b. and lived in Lynn, Mass., all his life, acting as a teacher, an editor, a map-maker, a civil engineer, and for many years a justice of the peace.

Lewis, Charles B. *M. Quad; The Detroit Free Press Man.* An American journalist and humorist.

Lewis, Emma. *E. L.* An American lady, of Philadelphia, "who, during years of weary confinement" by sickness, gave utterance to her consolations in poetry, for the support and consolation of others.

Lewis, Mrs. **Estella Anna Blanche (Robinson).** *Stella.* An American "Southland" poet; b. in Baltimore; educ. at the Troy Female Seminary; married S. D. Lewis, a lawyer; resided in Europe, 1858–70 *et seq.*

Lewis, Rev. **John,** M.A., 1675–1746. ****; *A Friend to Liberty and Property.* An English clergyman and antiquary; b. in Bristol; Vicar of Mynstre, 1708–46.

Lewis, John Delaware, M.A. *John Smith of Smith Hall, Gent.; An Undergraduate.* An English writer; Trin. Coll., Cambridge, 1850.

Lewis, Julius Warren. *F. Clinton Barrington.*

Lewis, Mrs. **L. P.** *L. P. L.* A German writer of the day.

Lewis, Mrs. **Mary.** *Meta.* An American poet of the day.

Lewis, Matthew Gregory, 1773–1818. *"Monk" Lewis; A West India Proprietor.* An English novelist and dramatist; b. in London; M.P., 1794; in 1797, commenced his literary career; the latter years of his life were passed in travelling; d. on board ship, returning to England from the West Indies.

Lewis, Richard. *Peter Pounce, Esq.* An English satirist, of the 18th century.

Lewis, Rev. **Thomas.** *A Clergyman; Anonymous Londinensis; T. L – – –; A Lay-Hand.* An English clergyman, of London, of the first part of the 18th century.

Lewis, Waller, M.D., 1711–81. *Cam.* An English writer on whist.

Lewison, William H., 1822–57. *Julius Cæsar Hannibal.* An American journalist, of New Orleans; editor and proprietor of the "Picayune"; d. in New York City.

Leypoldt, Friedrich, 1837–84. *F. Pylodet.* A German-American publisher; came to this country in 1854; in 1865, settled in New York City; d. there.

Liddell, The Hon. and Rev. **Robert,** M.A., 1808–. *A Sexagenarian.* An English clergyman and poet; Christ Church, Oxford, 1829; in 1883, resided at Wilton-place, London.

Lieber, Francis, LL.D., 1800–72. *Americus; Arnold Franz; The Stranger.* A German American historical and political writer; b. at Berlin; came to this country in 1827; Prof. at Columbia Coll., N.Y., 1857–72; d. in New York City.

Lieber, Oscar Montgomery. *Americus.* An American journalist.

Liebich, Augusta. *Marjorie March.* An American writer.

Lillie, L. C. *L. C. White.* An American writer of the day.

Lilly, William, 1602–81. *Zadkiel.* A famous English astrologer; b. in Leicestershire; d. at Hersham.

Lincoln, Mrs. Jane Elizabeth (Larcombe), 1829–. *Kate Campbell.* An American writer; b. at Colebrook, Conn.; in 1851 married Rev. Heman Lincoln, a Baptist clergyman.

Lincoln, Levi, A.M., 1749–1820. *A Farmer.* An eminent American lawyer and statesman, of Worcester, Mass.; Lieut.-Gov. of Mass., 1807–8, and Acting Gov., 1808–9.

Lind, John, Esq., –1780. *A Member of Lincoln's Inn.* An English lawyer and political writer; son of Charles Lind; Vicar of West Mersey, Essex, 1738–48.

Lindesay, H. H. *Her Sister.* An English lady; a writer of the day; sister of Charlotte Williams Wynn.

Lindo, Mark Prager, –1877. *Mr. Oude Neer Smitts.* An Englishman by birth, but long resident at the Hague, where he died.

Lindsay, Colin, –1722. *The Right Honourable the Earl of B——.* A Scottish nobleman; 3d Earl of Balcarres; succeeded, 1662.

Lindsey, Rev. Theophilus, M.A., 1723–1808. *A Late Member of the University.* An English Unit.; b. at Middlewich, Cheshire; St. John's Coll.; occupied a chapel in London, 1774–93, where he died.

Lindsley, John Berrien, M.D. *A Poor-Rich Man.* An American physician; b., 1822, at Princeton, N.J.; Secretary to the State Board of Education of Tennessee; 1875 resident at Nashville.

Ling, Nicholas. *V. S.*—See "R. J." Richard Jones.

Lingard, John, D.D., LL.D., 1771–1851. *A Catholic; Elias.* An English Roman Catholic clergyman; b. in Winchester; educ. at Douay, France; for 40

years held a small preferment at Hornsby, Lancashire, where he died.

Linn, Rev. John Blair, D.D., 1777–1804. *A Young Gentleman of New York.* An American Presbyt. minister; b. in Shippensburg, Penn.; Columbia Coll., 1795; asst. minister of the First Presbyt. Church, Philadelphia; was brother-in-law of Charles Brockden Brown.

Linning, Thomas. *A Friend.* An English writer of the first part of the 18th century.

Linskill, Miss——. *Stephen Yorke.* An English writer of the day, of Yorkshire.

Linton, Mrs. Eliza (Lynn), 1828–. *Girl of the Period.* An English writer; b. at Crosthwaite, Cumberland Co.; one of the twelve daughters of James Lynn, D.D., vicar of that place; in 1881 was very ill at Florence, threatened with total blindness; married the following.

Linton, William James, 1812–. *Spartacus.* An English-American author and engraver; b. in London; for many years of London; then of New York City; and finally of New Haven, Conn.

Linz, Amélie (Speyer), 1824–. *Amélie Godin.* A German novelist; b. at Bamberg; married, in 1845, the Prussian engineer, Lieut. Franz Linz (who died in 1870); and since 1873 has lived in Munich.

Lippincott, Esther J. T. *Esther J. Trimble.* An American writer of the day, of Philadelphia.

Lippincott, Mrs. Sara Jane (Clarke), 1823–. *Grace Greenwood.* An American writer, of Philadelphia; b. at Pompey; educ. at Rochester, N.Y.; in 1853 married Leander K. Lippincott, the publisher, of Philadelphia.

Lipscomb, George, M.D., 1773–1847. *Viator.* An English *littérateur;* b. at Quainton, Buckingham Co.; studied medicine in London, but seems to have chiefly devoted his life to literary pursuits; d. in London.

Lipsius, Marie, 1837–. *La Mara.* A German writer on music and musicians; b. at Leipsic; passed some time at Weimar in the study of music under Liszt; and now lives in Leipsic.

Lister, John. *A. F. G.* A Scottish advocate; a writer of the day.

Lister, Thomas, Esq., LL.D., –1828. *Hampden.* An English writer; a graduate of Oxford; resident at Armitage Park, Staffs., and for many years a magistrate for that county.

Littell, John Stockton. *J. S. L.* An American editor and compiler, of Germantown, Penn.; b. at Burlington,

N.J.; brother of Eliakim Littell, the eminent publisher.

Little, Harvey D., 1803–33. *Velasques.* An American poet, journalist, and lawyer, of Columbus, O.

Littlehales, Richard (?). *Cœmeterius.* An English scholar; a contributor to the "Microcosm," of Eton Coll, 1787.

Livandais, Augustus, M.D. *A. P. Knutt.*

Livermore, George, A.M., 1809–65. *The Antiquary.* An American merchant of Boston; b., lived, and d. in Cambridge, Mass.

Livingston, Brockholst, LL.D., 1757–1823. *Aquiline Nimblechops, Democrat.* An American jurist; b. in New York City; New Jersey Coll., 1774; justice of the U.S. Supreme Court, 1806–23; d. in Washington.

Livingston, Philip, A.M., 1716–78. *A Citizen.* An American politician; b. in Albany, N.Y.; Yale Coll., 1737; M.C., 1774 and 1776.

Livingston, Robert R., LL.D., 1747–1813. *Cato.* An American jurist and statesman; b. in New York City; Columbia Coll., 1765; Chancellor of New York, 1777–1801; and Minister to France, 1801–4.

Livingston, William, LL.D., 1723–90. *Un Cultivateur de New Jersey; A Farmer of New Jersey; A Gentleman Educated at Yale College; Hortensius; Tyro-Philolegis.* An American statesman; b. in New York; Yale Coll., 1741; Governor of New Jersey, 1776–90.

Lizardi, Don Joaquin Fernandez de, 1771–1827. *J. F. de L.* A Mexican writer.

Llorente, Juan Antonio, 1756–1823. *Don Juan Nellerto.* A learned Spanish historian, of Madrid; in 1809 promoted suppression of the Inquisition.

Lloyd, Charles. *An Old Man of Business; An Honest Man.* An English writer; private Secretary to Richard Grenville Temple, 1st Earl Temple.

Lloyd, Rev. Charles, LL.D. *A Dissenting Minister.* An English Dissenter; a good scholar and an able schoolmaster, of Palgrave, Suffolk.

Lloyd, Miss Emma F. *E. F. L.; A Clergyman's Daughter.* An English writer.

Lloyd, H. *A Member of the Revision Committee of the Church of Ireland.* An Irish writer of the day.

Locke, David Ross, 1833–. *Petroleum V. Nasby.* An American humorist; b. at Vestal, Broome Co., N.Y.; became a printer; and, after having charge of

several other sheets, is the editor of the Toledo (O.) "Blade."

Locke, Mrs. Jane Ermina (Stockweather). *A Lady of Massachusetts.* An American poet; b. at Worthington, Mass.; married, 1829, Mr. John Goodwin Locke, of Ashby, Mass.; from 1849 lived in Boston; d. in Ashburnham, Mass.

Lockerby, Miss Elizabeth N. *E. N. L.; An Untaught Minstrel.* A poet, of Prince Edward's Island, chiefly on religious topics.

Lockhart, John Gibson, 1792–1854. *Dr. Peter Morris, the Odontist; William Wastle; Z.* A Scottish writer; b. in Lanarkshire; educ. at Glasgow and Oxford; called to the bar in 1816; but preferred a literary life; about 1825 removed to London; d. at Abbotsford.

Lockhart, John Hugh. *Hugh Littlejohn.* A child of the preceding and grandchild of Sir Walter Scott.

Lockhart, Laurence, D.D. *A Parish Minister; A Minister of the Establishment.* A Scottish clergyman.

Lofft, Capel, 1751–1824. *A Fellow of a College; R. E. Storer.* An English lawyer; author of legal, theological, political, poetical, and other works; b. at Bury St. Edmunds; the latter part of his life he resided on the Continent till his death.

Lofland, Dr. John. *The Milford Bard.* An American poet.

Loftin, J. C. *Ace Clubs.* An American poet of the day.

Logan, Rev. George, 1674–1755. *A Minister of the Church of Scotland.* A Scottish clergyman; minister of Edinburgh.

Logan, M. C. *Ellerton Vincent.*

Logan, Miss Olive. — See "Sikes, Mrs. Olive (Logan)."

Logan, Thomas A. *Gloan.* An American writer of the day.

Logan, W. H. *H. M.; A Gentleman in Town.* A Scottish writer, of Edinburgh.

Lomax, E. Victoria. *Byrd Lyttle.* An American writer of the day, of Baltimore.

Lombard, Israel. *L.* An American merchant, of Boston, Mass.

Loménie, Louis Leonard de, 1815–78. *L'Homme de Rien.* A French author; b. at St. Yriex (Haute-Vienne); devoted himself at Paris to literary labor, especially for the "Revue des Deux Mondes" and the "Patrie"; d. in Mentone.

Long, Charles Edward, Esq., M.A., 1796–1861. *A.; λ.; L.; Blanche Croix; A Jamaica Proprietor.* An English gentleman; b. at Benham-park, Berks.; educ. at Harrow School and Trin. Coll., Cambridge, B.A., 1819; d. in Dover.

Long, Edward, -1809. *Cleon.* An English boy; a youthful friend of Lord Byron, at Harrow School.

Long, Edward, 1734-1813. *Nicholas Babble, Esq.; A Planter.* An English writer; b. at Rosilian, St. Blaize, Cornwall; Judge of the Vice-Admiralty Court at the island of Jamaica, 1757-97; d. at Arundel Park, Sussex.

Long, George, 1800-. *A Member of the University of Cambridge.* An English scholar; b. at Poulton, Lancashire; educ. at Camb. Univ.; Prof. of the Ancient Languages in the Univ. of Virginia, 1824-26; of Greek in the London Univ., 1826-31; of Latin in the Univ. of London, 1846-49; and of Class. Lit. at Brighton, 1849-71.

Long, Roger, S.T.D., 1680-1770. *Dicæophilus Cantabrigiensis.* An English divine and astronomer; Master of Pembroke Hall, Cambridge, 1733-70.

Longfellow, Henry Wadsworth, LL.D., 1807-82. *An American; Professor Strongfellow.* An American poet; b. at Portland, Me.; Bowdoin College, 1825; d. at Cambridge, Mass.

Longley, John. *An Eminent English Counsel.* An English lawyer, of Rochester.

Longstreet, Rev. Augustus Baldwin, LL.D., 1790-1870. *A Native Georgian; Bob Short.* An eminent American jurist, divine, and educator; b. at Augusta, Ga.; Yale Coll., 1813; Pres. of the Univ. of Mississippi, 1860-70; d. at Oxford, Miss.

Lord, E., 1788-1871. *E. L.* An English writer on education.

Lord, Miss Grace Virginia, -1885. *Virginia Champlin.* An American lady, of Boston, where she died.

Lord, John Keast. *The Wanderer.* An English writer of the day.

Lord, Nathan, D.D., LL.D., 1793-1870. *A Northern Presbyter.* An American minister; b. at South Berwick, Me.; Bowdoin Coll., 1809; Andover Theological Sem., 1815; President of Dartmouth Coll., 1828-63; d. at Hanover, N.H.

Lord, W. B., R.A. *W. B. L.* An English artist of the day.

Lorimer, Rev. John Gordon. *A Churchman.* A Scottish clergyman, of Free St. David's Church, Glasgow.

Lothian, Maurice. *A Sincere Friend of the People.* A Scottish lawyer.

Lothrop, Mrs. Harriet Mulford

(Stone). *Margaret Sidney.* An American writer of the day, of Boston.

Loudon, John Claudius, 1783-1843. *A Scottish Farmer and Land Agent.* An eminent Scottish writer on gardening and agriculture; b. at Cambuslang, in Lanarkshire; passed the latter part of his life in London, where he died.

Louis XV., 1710-74. *Zeokinizul.* The French king.

Lourdoneix, Paul de. *Pierre et Paul.* A French miscellaneous writer.

Love, James, -1774. *Scriblerus Maximus.* An English actor and dramatist, whose real name was James Dance; d. about 1774.

Love, John, Jr. *J. L.* An English writer of the first part of the 18th century.

Loveday, John, D.C.L., 1742-1809. *Academicus; Antiquarius; Scrutator; Vindex.* An English advocate and antiquary; b. at Caversham, near Reading; and d. at Williamson, near Banbury.

Lovejoy, Cornelia. *Paul Everett.*

Lovel, Robert. *Moschus.* An English poet; a friend of Southey.

Lovell, John. 1835-. *Zeta.* An English journalist, of London; manager of the Press Association, 1869-80 et seq.

Lover, Samuel, 1797-1868. *Ben Trovata.* An Irish poet, painter, singer, and novelist; b. in Dublin; removed to London in 1837; visited the United States before 1840, when he returned to England.

Lovering, John, 1788-. *Nehemiah Notional.* An American writer, of Boston.

Lovett, John, 1765-1818. *A Washingtonian.* An American poet; b. in Norwich, Conn.; Yale Coll., 1782; M.C., 1813-17; d. at Fort Meigs, O.

Low, Miss Mary. *Aunt Mary.* An English writer.

Low, Samuel, 1765-. *An American.* An American poet and dramatist.

Lowe, Bennett. *Justitia.* An English photograph artist.

Lowe, Mrs. Martha A. (Perry). *His Wife.* An American poet; b. in Keene, N.H.; wife of the Rev. Charles Lowe; for many years resident in Somerville, Mass.

Lowe, Solomon. *A Layman.* An English writer of the first part of the 18th century.

Lowell, James Russell, D.C.L., LL.D., 1819-. *J. R. L.; Hosea Biglow; Elmwood; Columbus Nye; Homer Wilbur; A Wonderful Quiz.* A distinguished American poet; U.S. Minister to Spain, 1878-80; to England, 1880-85.

Lowell, John, LL.D., 1769-1841.

Boston Rebel; A Bostonian; An Alumnus of that College; A Citizen of Massachusetts; A Layman; His Intimate Friend; A New England Farmer; A Massachusetts Lawyer; No Bel Esprit; An Old Farmer; A Yankee Farmer. An eminent American lawyer and political writer, of Boston; b. at Newburyport, Mass.; Harv. Univ., 1786; lived and d. in Boston.

Lower, Richard, 1782–1865. *Uncle Tim; Tim Cladpole; An Octogenarian.* An English schoolmaster, land-surveyor, and for nearly half a century factotum in most of the parochial offices; b. in Alfristin, Sussex; resided near Chiddingly; and d. in Tunbridge.

Lowrie, Rev. **Randolph W.** *R. W. L.* An American Epis. clergyman; in 1882, of Washington, D.C.

Lowrie, Hon. **Walter,** 1784–1868. *His Father.* An American statesman; b. in Edinburgh, Scotland; U.S. Senator for Pennsylvania; Secretary U.S. Senate, 1825–36; Secretary Presbyt. Board of Missions, 1836–68; d. in New York City.

Lowth, Robert, D.D., 1710–87. *The Lord Bishop of Oxford; A Young Gentleman of Winchester School.* An English writer; b. at Winchester; Professor of Poetry at Oxford, 1741–66; Bishop of London, 1777–87.

Lowth, Thomas Henry. *T. H. L.* An English writer of the 18th century.

Loyd, Samuel Jones, 1st Baron Overstone, 1796–. *Mercator.* An English writer; educ. at Eton, and Trin. Coll., Cambridge, 1815; is a Magistrate for Berkshire and Co. Carmarthen, etc.; formerly a banker in London; M.P. for Hythe, 1819–20; seat at Overstone Park, Northampton.

Loyson, Charles Jean Marie, 1827–. *Le Père Hyacinthe.* A French prelate; b. in Orleans; in 1870 he became a secular priest; in 1872 married an American lady in London.

Lubliner, Hugo, 1846–. *Hugo Bürger.* A German dramatist; b. at Breslau; since 1857, the time of the death of his father, has been actively engaged as a manufacturer at Berlin.

Lucas, Rev. **Charles.** —s —s, *M.A., of the University of Oxford.* An English clergyman; Exeter Coll., Oxford, 1791; Curate of Avebury, Wiltshire.

Lucas, Robert (?). *A Gentleman of the Middle Temple.* An Irish lawyer of Dublin, who was obliged to leave his country on account of his political writings.— See the "Monthly Review," vol. 2, p. 178.

Lucas, William. *A. Z.* An English barrister-at-law, of the Middle Temple.

Luçay, Henri Rochefort de. *H. de Luçay.* A French writer.

Luckey, Rev. **John.** *A Chaplain.* An American biographer, and chaplain of Sing Sing Prison, N.Y.

Lucy, Henry W., 1845–. *The Member for Chiltern Hundreds; Toby, M.P.* An English journalist, of London; b. at Crosby, near Liverpool.

Luders, Catharine. *Emily Hermann.* An American poet of the West, in Indiana.

Ludlam, George. *G. L.* An English dramatist.

Ludlow, Fitz-Hugh, 1837–70. *A Pythagorean.* An American author; b. in Poughkeepsie, N.Y.; Union Coll., 1856; a voluminous contributor of prose and poetry to the magazines, and his books were mainly made up of these contributions; d. in Geneva, Switzerland.

Lüders, Charles Henry, 1858–. *C. H. L.; Henry Karlsten. L. H. C.* An American journalist.

Lukens, Henry Clay, 1838–. *Erratic Enrique; Heinrich Yale Snekul.* An American journalist, of New York City.

Lukens, Mrs. **Mary C. (Painter),** 1842–. *Dolly Dawdle.* An American writer; wife of the preceding.

Lukin, Rev. **James.** *J. L.* An English clergyman; Brasenose Coll., Oxford, 1849; Rector of Wickford, Chelmsford, 1881–83 *et seq.*

Lum, Dyer Daniel. *A Gentile.* An English writer of the day.

Lumb, E. *E. L.* An English poet.

Lumley, Benjamin, 1812–75. *Hermes.* An English lawyer and opera manager, of London.

Lumley, H. R. *Lyulph.* An English journalist; in 1872, editor of the London "Court Journal"; author of dramas, works of fiction, etc.

Lumsden, James. *A Mercantile Man.* A Scottish writer; principal of the Free Church Coll., Aberdeen.

Lundy, Benjamin, 1789–1839. *A Citizen of the United States.* An American abolitionist; b. in Hardwich, Sussex Co., N.Y.; in 1808, removed to Wheeling, Va.; published the "Genius of Universal Emancipation" in several Southern towns, but about 1829 removed it to Washington; d. in Lowell, La Salle Co., Ill.

Lundy, John Patterson, D.D., 1823–. *A Presbyter of the Church in Phila.* An American clergyman; b. at Danville, Penn.; N. J. Coll., 1846; Princeton

Theol. Sem., 1846; in 1881, resident at Idlewild, Penn.

Lunn, Arthur Wallbridge. *Arthur Wallbridge.* An English writer.

Lunt, George, A.M., 1803–85. *Wesley Brooke.* An American lawyer, poet, novelist, and journalist, of Boston; b. at Newburyport, Mass.; U.S. District Attorney for Mass., 1849–53; d. in Boston.

Lupton, Rev. **James,** M.A. *J. L.* An English clergyman; Ch. Ch., Oxford, 1823; Rector of St. Michael Queenhithe w. Holy Trinity, London, 1832–74 *et seq.*

Lyman, Darius, Jr., 1826–. *A Former Resident of the South.* An American writer; b. at Ravenna (?), Portage Co., O.

Lyman, Joseph, D.D., 1750–1828. *An Old Republican.* An American Cong. minister; Yale Coll., 1767; pastor at Hatfield, Mass.

Lyman, Mrs. **Laura Elizabeth (Baker),** 1831–. *Kate Hunnibee.* An American writer; b. at Kent's Hill; wife of Joseph Bardwell Lyman, of Richmond Hill, L.I.

Lyman, Theodore, 1792–1849. *An American.* An eminent American lawyer and politician, of Boston; b. and d. in that city; Harv. Univ., 1810.

Lynch, Rev. **Thomas Toke.** *A Dissenting Minister; Silent Long.* An English Cong. minister; in London from 1848; afterwards at Mornington, Hampstead Road.

Lyne, Rev. **Charles,** M.A., 1802–73. *A Clergyman.* An English clergyman; b. at Castle Hill, Liskeard; Prebendary of Exeter, 1842–73; d. at Colby Villa, Dawlish.

Lyne, Rev. **Joseph Leycester.** *Ignatius, Deacon, etc.; Ignatius, O.S.B.; Brother Ignatius.* An English clergyman, once Curate of Claydon, Suffolk.

Lyon, Miss **H. F. D.** *Fredrika.*

Lyon, Isaac F., –1881. *An Old Cartman.* An American journalist, of Newark, N.J. (?).

Lyon, James T. *A Staff Officer.* An American soldier.

Lyon, Lemuel. *Two Private Soldiers.* An American soldier, 1758–75.

Lyon, Robert. *Anti-Tindalian.* An English controversial writer, of the 18th century.

Lyttelton, Lord **George,** 1708 or 9–73. *A Persian; A Young Nobleman.* An English poet and statesman; b. at Hagley, Worcestershire; Lord of the Treasury, 1744; Chancellor of the Exchequer, 1756; then retired to private life.

Lytton, Rt. Hon. Sir **Edward George Earle Lytton-Bulwer,** 1st Baron, D.C.L., 1803–73. *Pisistratus Caxton.* A celebrated English novelist and dramatist; b. in Norfolk; Univ. of Cambridge, 1826; d. in London.

Lytton, Rt. Hon. **Edward Robert Bulwer-Lytton,** 2d Baron, 1831–. *His Son; Edward Trevor; Owen Meredith.* An English poet and diplomatist; son of the preceding.

Lytton, Rosina Doyle (Wheeler) Lytton-Bulwer, Lady. *Chevely.* An Irish novelist; wife of 1st Baron Lytton.

M.

McAfee, Mrs. **Nelly (Marshall),** 1847–. *Sans Souci.* An American "Southland" writer; b. in Louisville, Ky.; in 1871, married Mr. McAfee at Frankfort, Ky.

Macallan, David. *Scrutator.* An English writer.

McAlpine, Robert W., 1838–. *R. W. M.; Oliver Ancient; Gath Brittle; Dhu; George Gregory Gregg; Uncle Jake; Sonica.* An American journalist, of New York City.

MacAndrew, Mrs. **Barbara (Miller).** *B. M.* A Scottish writer of the day.

Macartney, Sir **George** (afterwards Earl), 1737–1806. *A Late Chief Secretary of that Kingdom.* An Irish statesman; b. at Lissanore, near Belfast; Trin. Coll., Dublin, 1757; from 1798 lived in retirement; d. at Chiswick, Surrey.

Macartney, William H. *Major Muldoon.* An American journalist.

Macaulay, Rev. **Aulay,** about 1758–1819. *Academicus; Clericus Leicestriensis.* A Scottish clergyman; b. in Cardross, Dunbartonshire; educ. at the Univ. of Glasgow; was the uncle of Thomas Babington Macaulay. He was Vicar of Rothley, 1796–1819.

Macaulay, Patrick (?), M.D. *An American Physician.* An American writer, of Baltimore (?).

Macaulay, Rt. Hon. **Thomas Babington,** Baron Macaulay of Rothley, 1800–59. *Cid Hamet Benengeli; A Gentleman of the Middle Temple; Tristram*

Merton; Richard Quongti. An English historian; b. at Rothley Temple, Leicestershire; B.A., Cambridge, 1822; called to the bar at Lincoln's Inn, 1826, but never practised; d. at Holly Lodge, Kensington.

McBride, James, 1789–1859. *A Citizen of the United States.* An American author, of Hamilton, O.; one of the oldest and best-known pioneers of Southern Ohio.

McBurney, M. *Carroll Malone.* An American journalist.

McCabe, James D., about 1840–. *Edward Winslow Martin.* An American writer; b. at Richmond, Va.; resided in that city during the civil war, devoting his pen to the service of the Confederate cause; has since resided in Brooklyn, N.Y., engaged in literary work.

Maccall, William, M.A., 1812–. *Atticus.* A Scottish miscellaneous writer. of London; b. at Largs, Ayrshire; educ. at Glasgow and Geneva.

McCance, James Law. *J. L. McC——; McC——; Mac.* An English gentleman, of Inglewood, St. James's Road, Sutton, Surrey.

McCann, P. *The Man about Town.* An American writer.

McCarroll, James, 1815–. *Terry Finnegan.* A Canadian poet, humorist, and miscellaneous writer, of Upper Canada.

MacCarthy, Mrs. Charlotte. *A Lady.* An English writer.

McCarthy, Denis Florence, about 1820–82. *J. H.* An Irish poet, descended from the ancient royal Irish sept of MacCauras; from 1871, he received a pension of £100; d. in London.

McCaul, John, D.D., LL.D., 1807–. *A Graduate.* An eminent Irish-Canadian scholar; b. in Dublin; Trin. Coll., Dublin; Vice Chancellor of the Univ. of Toronto from 1859.

MacClean, Edward, 1847–. *Mac.* An American journalist and bibliographer.

McClellan, Mrs. Harriet (Hare). *Harford Flemming.* An American novelist, at one time of Philadelphia.

M'Clellan, Kate. *K. M.* An American writer.

McClenthen, Charles S. *A Private Soldier.* An American writer.

McClure, David, D.D., 1748–1820. *A Native of Philadelphia.* An American Presbyt. clergyman; b. at Newport, R.I.; Yale Coll., 1769; pastor at East Windsor (now South Windsor), Conn., 1786–1820, where he died.

McCluskey, Henry, 1827–70. *Paddy.*

An American journalist, of Philadelphia (?).

McCobb, Mrs. Mary Selden. *Mary Densel.* An American writer of the day.

McColl, Evan, 1808–. *The Mountain Minstrel.* A Scottish-Canadian lyric poet, of Kingston; b. at Kenmore; removed to Canada in 1850.

McColl, Rev. Malcolm, M.A., F.R.S.L., 1838–. *Expertus; Scrutator.* A Scottish clergyman of the English Church; b. at Glenfinan in Ross-shire; educ. at Edinburgh and in Germany; Rector of St. George, London, 1871–83 *et seq.*

McConnell, William. *Mac(Artist).* An English poet of the day.

McCord, Mrs. Adelaide, 1835–68. *Indigina.* An American writer.

McCord, Mrs. Louisa S. (Cheves), 1810–. *A Lady of South Carolina.* An American " Southland " writer; b. at Columbia, S.C.; in 1840 married David J. McCord; during the civil war resided in her native city.

MacCormick, Charles, LL.B., 1752–1807. *A Member of his Privy Council.* An Irish writer; studied law in London; but chiefly devoted himself to literary pursuits; d. in London.

McCormick, M. R. *The Forest Warbler.* An American writer of the day.

McCosh, John, M.D. *Nomentino.* An English writer of the day.

McCracken, J. L. H., about 1813–53. *An Emeritus Professor.* An American merchant and humorist; b. in New York City; d. in Sierra Leone, Africa.

McCrie, Thomas, D.D., 1772–1835. *Scoto-Britannicus.* An eminent Scottish critic, biographer, and historian; b. at Dunse; pastor at Edinburgh from 1795, where he died.

M'Crugar, Thomas. *Zeno.* A Scottish writer, of Edinburgh.

McCrum, Myra Daisy. *Daisy Howard.*

M'Culloch, David. *Oleander.* A Scottish writer, of Glasgow, of the day.

McCulloch, John Ramsay, 1789–1864. *J. R. M.* An eminent Scottish economist; b. at Whitborn; professor in the Univ. of London, 1828–32; d. at Westminster.

M'Culloh, James H., Jr., M.D. *An Officer of the U.S. Army.* An American physician, of Baltimore, Md.; b. in Maryland; Garrison Surgeon, 1814; disbanded, 1816.

McCullough, Joseph B. An American journalist of the day, of St. Louis, Mo.

McDaniel, Samuel Walton, LL.B.,

1833–. *Parsonus Rusticus.* An American lawyer; b. in Philadelphia; Harv. Law School, 1878; has practised in Boston, 1878–84 *et seq.*; resides in Cambridge, Mass.

McDermott, Hugh F., 1833–. *Pax.* An American journalist, of Boston.

Macdiarmid, John, about 1789–1852. *Atticus Secundus.* A Scottish journalist; b. in Edinburgh; and educ. at the Univ. of that city; in 1817 he became editor of the "Dumfries Courier."

MacDonald, Rev. Andrew, 1757–90. *Matthew Bramble.* A clever Scottish writer; b. and educ. in Leith; was a journalist, first at Glasgow, then in London.

Macdonald, Angus W. *A Virginian.* An American writer of the day.

MacDonald, Rev. George, 1825–. *Dalmocand.* A Scottish novelist; b. at Huntly; educ. at the Univ. of Aberdeen; settled in London, devoting himself to literature; lectured in this country, 1872–73.

Macdonald, John Hay Atholl. *Jean Jambon.* A Scottish humorist; Solicitor-General of Scotland.

MacDonald, Wilson. *Homo; Spiral Groove.* An American sculptor, of New York City.

McDonnell, John W., 1856–. *Patrick Fitzgibbons.* An American journalist and reporter, of New York City.

McDonough, C. J. *Warwick.*

M'Donough, Capt. Felix, –1836. *The Hermit.* An English writer, of London; wrote for the "Literary Gazette," but latterly, steeped in poverty, he dragged on existence as a "bookseller's hack."

McDowell, Mrs. Katherine, 1853–83. *Sherwood Bonner.* An American writer; wrote for "Harper's Weekly," etc.; d. at Holly Springs, Miss.

McElroy, William E. *Myron Hubbell.*

McFarlan, W. L. *A Special Correspondent.* A Scottish traveller; correspondent of the "Glasgow Herald."

Macfarlane, Robert, 1815–83. *Rutherglen.* A Scottish antiquary.

Macfarlane, William. *A Layman.* A Scottish writer.

M'Gaffey, Mrs. Louisa Amelia (Pratt), 1833–. *Ruth Crayne.* An American poet; b. at Darby Plains, Madison Co., O.; in 1855 married to John M'Gaffey, a lawyer of Springfield, O., where she afterwards resided.

MacGavock, Randal W., 1828–. *A Tennessean.* An American traveller; b. at Nashville, Tenn.

MacGeachy, Charles E. A. *Mac,* (*The Danburian*).

M'Gee, Thomas D'Arcy, 1823–68. *Philo-Veritas; A Backwoodsman.* An Irish-American journalist; b. in Carlingford; in 1848 came to America for a permanency; and was the editor of journals in the United States and Canada; d. at Ottawa, Canada.

Macgeorge, Andrew. *A Layman; Veritas.* A Scottish writer, of Glasgow.

MacGeorge, Rev. Robert Jackson, about 1811–. *Culpepper Crabtree, Esq.; Solomon of Streetsville.* A Scottish clergyman of the English Church; Incumbent of Streetsville, Upper Canada, 1841–58, when he returned to Scotland.

McGhee, Rev. Robert James, M.A., 1789–. *A Minister of the Church of Ireland.* An Irish Epis. divine; Trin. Coll., Dublin, 1811; Rector of Holywell-cum-Needingworth, Hants., from 1846.

M'Gibbon, Alexander. *A Lounger, an Old Maid, and Lady Honora.* A Scottish poet.

M'Gilchrist, John, M.D. *J. M'G.* A Scottish poet.

M'Gill, Rev. John. *A Chapel Minister.* A Scottish minister.

Macgowan, Rev. John, 1726(?)–80. *The Listener; The Shaver.* An English minister among the Particular Baptists.

M'Gregor, John, 1797–1857. *A Barrister; Simeon South.* A Scottish statistician; b. at Stornaway, Ross-shire; appointed one of the two Joint Secretaries of the English Board of Trade at London in 1840; d. at Boulogne.

MacGregor, John, 1825–. *Rob Roy.* An English traveller; b. at Gravesend; lives in Greenwich, near London.

McGrew, Alexander, 1826–. *Brandywine; Sandy Osborne.* An American journalist, of Memphis, Tenn.

McGuire, Mrs. J. W. (Brockenborough). *A Lady of Virginia.* An American "Southland" writer; b. at Richmond, Va.; wife of Rev. John P. McGuire, an Epis. clergyman; teacher of a school at Tappahannock, Va., 1865–70 *et seq.*

McHale, Frank. *Geraint.*

McHale, John, D.D., 1791–1881. *Hierophilus; John, Archbishop of Tuam.* An eminent Irish prelate; b. at Tubbernavine, Mayo; was a student at Maynooth, and then lecturer and professor there; on the death of Dr. Kelley, he was made Archbishop of Tuam.

Machar, Miss A. M. *Fidelis.* An American writer of the day.

McHenry, George. *An Old Acquaintance; A Native of Pennsylvania.* An American political writer.

McHenry, James, M.D. *Solomon*

Second-Sight. An American poet, novelist, and miscellaneous writer, of Philadelphia.

McIlvaine, Eliza Rodman. — See "Church, Mrs. Eliza Rodman (McIlvaine)."

Macintosh, ——. *M.* An American journalist, of Buffalo, N.Y.

McIntosh, Maria Jane, 1803–. *Aunt Kitty.* An American novelist; b. at Sunbury, Ga.; removed to New York City in 1835, and devoted herself to literary work.

Macintosh, William. *A Lover of his Country.* A Scottish writer of the 18th century, of Borlum.

McIntyre, Hugh D. *Aberdeen.*

Mackarness, Rt. Rev. John Fielder, D.D. *One of themselves.* An English clergyman; Merton Coll., Oxford, 1844; Bishop of Oxford, 1870–83 *et seq.*

Mackarness, Matilda Anne (Planché). *Susie Sunbeam.* An English writer for the young.

Mackay, Miss ——. *Jeannie Dods.* An English (?) journalist.

Mackay, Aberigh, 1849–81. *Ali Baba.* An Indian official; Principal of the Presidency Coll., at Indore, Ind.

Mackay, Andrew, LL.D., F.R.S.E., 1759–1809. *James Andrew, A.M.* A Scottish mathematician; Mathematical Examiner to the Hon. E. I. Co.; d. in George Street, Trinity Square, Minories.

Mackay, Charles, LL.D., 1814–. *Herman Grimbosh; John Wagstaffe, Esq., of Wilbye Grange; Launcelot Wagstaffe.* A Scottish poet and journalist; b. in Perth; educ. in London; of London from 1847; United States correspondent of the "London Times," 1862–65.

Mackay, Francis Alexander. *Francis Fitzhugh.* A Scottish poet of the day.

Mackay, Rev. James. *A Chaplain in H. M. Indian Service.* An English clergyman, at Fort George.

MacKellar, Thomas, 1812–. *Tam.* An American poet; b. in New York City; a type-founder of Philadelphia from 1833.

Macken, John. *Ismail Fitzadam.* An Irish sailor and poet; b. at Brookenborough; in 1820, wrote for the London "Literary Gazette."

MacKenna, Theobald, Esq., –1809. *A Catholic and a Burkist.* An Irish barrister-at-law.

McKenny, Thomas Lorraine, 1784–1858. *Aristides.* An American writer; Indian Agent, in the employ of the United States Indian Department; d. in New York City.

Mackenzie, Alexander Slidell, 1803–48. *The American in England; A Young American.* An American naval officer; b. in New York City; d. at Tarrytown, N.Y.

Mackenzie, Mrs. Anne Maria. *Ellen of Exeter.* An English novelist, of Exeter.

Mackenzie, C. F. *Il Musannif.* An English writer of the day.

McKenzie, G. A. *Ellis Dale.* A Canadian journalist.

Mackenzie, George, 1630 or 31–1714. *E. C.* An eminent Scottish statesman; Viscount Tarbat and Earl of Cromarty.

Mackenzie, Sir George Steuart, 7th Baronet, F.R.SS. L. and E., –1848. *M.* A Scottish baronet, of Coul, Co. Ross.

Mackenzie, Rev. H. M. *H. M'K.*

Mackenzie, Henry, Esq., 1745–1831. *Brutus.* A Scottish lawyer and man of letters; attorney in the Court of Exchequer at Edinburgh, 1766; later, Comptroller-General of taxes for Scotland; d. at Edinburgh.

Mackenzie, James, M.D., –1761. *A Physician.* A Scottish physician, of Worcester.

Mackenzie, Kenneth Robert H. *Cryptonymus.* An English (?) writer of the day.

Mackenzie, Mary Jane. *A Lady.* An English religious writer.

Mackenzie, Peter. *The Odd Fellow; A Ten-Pounder.* A Scottish writer, of Glasgow.

Mackenzie, Robert Shelton, LL.D., 1809–188–. *R. S. M.; Sholto; Littlejohn.* An Irish author and journalist; b. in Limerick Co.; of Philadelphia, from 1852.

Mackenzie, Rev. William. *W. M.* A Scottish minister, of North Leith.

Mackenzie, William Lyon, 1795–1861. *Patrick Swift.* A Canadian journalist; b. at Springfield, Forfar, Scotland; came to Toronto, 1824; was for a long time connected with the New York "Tribune"; d. at Toronto.

McKinney, H. D. *Mambrino.* An American journalist, of Janesville, O.

Mackinnon, Campbell. *C. M.* An English poet of the day.

Mackintosh, Rt. Hon. Sir James, Knt., M.D., LL.D., 1765–1832. *A Barrister; The Ghost of Vandegrab.* An eminent Scottish philosopher; b. at Aldourie House, near Inverness; educ. at King's Coll., Aberdeen; removed to Edinburgh and studied medicine; in 1787, removed to London; called to the bar at Lincoln's Inn in 1795; an M.P.,

1813–31; Lord Rector of the Univ. of Glasgow in 1822 and 1823; Commissioner for Indian Affairs, 1830.

Mackittrick, Richard Kendall. *R. K. M.*

McKoy, William. *Lang Syne.* An American writer, of Philadelphia.

Mackworth, Sir Digby, Bart., 1789–1852. *A Field Officer of Cavalry.* An English (?) soldier; b. at Oxford; entered the army in 1807; became colonel in 1851; d. at Glan Usk, County Monmouth.

Mackworth, Sir Humphrey. *Sir H. M.; A Member of Parliament.* An English political writer, of the first part of the 18th century.

Macky, John. *A Gentleman Here.* An English traveller, of the earlier part of the 18th century.

M'Laggan, Rev. Alexander. *A Gentleman in the North.* A Scottish minister, of Little Dunkeld.

McLane, Mary Jane. *Mary Jane Windle.* An American writer.

Maclaren, John. *A Fellow Labourer.* A Scottish writer.

M'Lauchlan, Thomas, D.D. *An Eye-Witness.* A Scottish writer.

McLaughlin, J. Fairfax. *Pasquino.* An American writer.

McLean, ——, D.D. *Minister of the Church of Scotland.*

Maclean, Lachlan, M.D. *Seneachie.* A Scottish writer.

Maclehose, Mrs. Agnes (Craig), 1759–1841. *Clarinda.* A Scottish lady; widow of Mr. A. Maclehose, writer, of Glasgow; well known to a large circle as the Clarinda of Burns; d. at Caltonhill, Edinburgh.

M'Lelland, George. *A Friend to the Peace of the Church of Scotland.* A Scottish writer.

McLeod, Daniel. *A Native of Virginia.* An American writer.

McLeod, Mrs. Georgie A. (Hulse). *Flora Neale.* An American "Southland" writer; b. in Florida; in 1853, married Dr. A. W. McLeod, of Halifax, N.S.; Principal of the "Southern Literary Institute" of Baltimore, in 1870.

Macleod, Malcolm. *A Lancashire Artisan.* An English writer.

Macleod, Xavier Donald, 1821–65. *Pynnshurst.* An American R. C. priest and miscellaneous writer; b. in New York City; professor at Mount St. Mary's College, near Cincinnati; d. near that city.

Maclise, Daniel, R.A., 1811–70. *Alfred Croquis.* An eminent Irish artist;

b. in Cork; went to London in 1828, and passed the rest of his life chiefly in that city, and d. there.

McMahon, Mrs. Margaret (Hale). *Pauline Markham.*

MacMullen, John. *A Late Staff Sergeant of the 13th Light Infantry.* An English soldier.

McMullen, Miss Mary A. *Una.* An American poet, of the West.

MacNally, Leonard, 1752–1820. *A Barrister of the Inner Temple.* An Irish lawyer and dramatist; b. in Dublin; called to the Irish bar in 1776; resided for a time in London, but returned to Ireland; d. in his native city.

McNaughton, James. *An Observer.* An American physician.

McNaughton, John H. *Babble Brook* An American poet, of Caledonia, N.Y.

M'Neill, Alexander. *The Odd Fellow.* A Scottish lawyer, of Glasgow.

M'Neill, Archibald. *A Member of the Society of Antiquaries of Scotland.* A Scottish writer of the day; writer to the Signet.

Macneill, Hector, Esq., 1746–1818. *An Eminent Editor.* A Scottish poet; b. at Rosebank, on the Esk; after residing in Glasgow, Bristol, and the West Indies, he spent his last years in Edinburgh, and d. there.

MacNeven, William James, M.D., 1763–1841. *An Irish Catholic.* An Irish physician; b. at Ballynahowne, Co. Galway; in 1805 came to New York City and practised physic till his death.

Macnish, Robert, M.D., LL.D., 1802–37. *The Modern Pythagorean.* A Scottish writer; b. and d. in Glasgow; studied his profession at Glasgow and Paris; wrote for "Blackwood."

Macomb, Robert. *A Whig of '76.* An American writer, of New York.

Macpherson, Mrs. Brewster. *X. H.* A Scottish religious writer of the day.

Macpherson, John. *A Pennsylvania Sailor.* An American political writer.

McPherson, Malcom. *M. McGuire.* An American (?) amateur journalist.

M'Quin, Abbé Angél Denis, 1756–1823. *Gleaner.* A French refugee in London; returned to France in 1814; but again went back to London, and d. there.

Macsparran, James, D.D., –1757. *A Divine of the Church of England.* An American clergyman; b. in Ireland; a missionary to South Kingston, Narragansett, from 1721.

Macsweeny, Joseph, M.D. *J. M'S.* An Irish writer.

M'Taggart, Mrs. ——, 1753-1834. *A Lady.* An English writer; d. at Bath.

McVickar, John, D.D., 1787-1868. *A New Yorker.* An American clergyman; b. in New York City; Columbia Coll., 1804; professor in Columbia Coll., N.Y., 1817-64.

McVickar, William Augustus, D.D., 1827-77. *His Son.* An American clergyman; son of the preceding; rector of the American chapel at Nice, France, for some time till 1876; rector of Christ Church, New York City, 1876-77, and d. there.

McVicker, Brock. *Wild Edgerton.*

McWatters, George S. *A Patrolman; Veritas.* An American writer, of New York City.

Madan, Cristobal. *Un Hacendado.* A Spanish writer, of Cuba.

Madden, Daniel Owen, 1815-52. *Danby North.* An Irish writer.

Madden, Sir Frederick, F.R.S., 1801-73. *F. M.* An English literary antiquary; b. at Portsmouth; employed in the British Museum, 1826-66; d. at London.

Madden, Mrs. H. *An Old Parishioner.* An Irish writer.

Maddock, Lady Emily Annie (Addis). *E. A. M.* An English religious writer; first married Sir Thomas Herbert Maddock, M.P., Deputy Governor of Bengal; second, George Jeremiah Mayhew.

Madison, James, LL.D., 1751-1836. *Helvidius; Publius.* An American statesman, of Virginia; President of the United States, 1809-17.

Madox, Isaac, D.D., 1697-1759. *Isaac, Lord Bishop of Worcester.* An English clergyman; b. in London; Bishop of Worcester, 1743-59.

Maginn, William, LL.D., 1794-1842. ******; *Augustinus; Rev. J. Barrett, D.D.; S.F.T.C.D.; Bob Buller; C. O. C(rossman); P. J. Crossman; P. P. Crossman; Jacobus Dapiferus, Corcagiensis; Richard Dowder; Dionysius Duggan; Blaise Fitztravesty, Esq.; Philip Forager; Rev. E. Hincks, F.T.C.D.; Wm. Holt; An Irish Gentleman lately deceased; Thomas Jennings, Soda Water Manufacturer; Giles Middlestitch; Morty Macnamara Mulligan; Sir Morgan O'Doherty, Bart.; O. P.; Olinthus Petre, D.D.: P. P. P.; R. F. P.; Thomas Pipes; The Modern Rabelais; R. T. S.; Ralph Tuckett Scott; W. Seward; Captain Shandon; P. T. T.; J—— T—n.* A learned and witty Irish writer and journalist; for many years

at or near London; b. at Cork; Trin. Coll., Dublin; d. at Walton-on-Thames.

Maglagan, Douglas, M.D. *The Poet Laureate of the New Town Dispensary.* A Scottish poet, of Edinburgh.

Magrath, E. *E. M.* A Canadian writer.

Magruder, Miss Julia. *Sherill Kerr.* An American writer of the day.

Maguire, Francis, 1839-. *Frank Mayo.* An Irish-American actor; b. in Boston; made his *début* at San Francisco, 1856; in 1869 first appeared in New York City.

Maguire, Very Rev. Thomas, -1854. *Vindex.* A Nova Scotian R. C. priest; b. at Halifax; Vicar General of the Diocese of Quebec, where he died.

Mahon, Capt. **Maurice Hartland (?).** *A Cavalry Officer; Magenta.* An English officer; in 1860 paymaster in the 9th Regt. of Light Dragoons.

Mahony, Miss ——. *Christabel.* An Irish poet, of Kenmare.

Mahony, Francis Sylvester, about 1805-66. *Father Prout; Don Jeremy Savonarola; Oliver Yorke, Esq.* An Irish humorist; b. in Cork; studied at Paris and Rome; a journalist of London, and for many years Paris correspondent of the London "Globe"; d. in Paris.

Mahony, Martin Francis. *Mr. Catlyne, Q.C.; Matthew Stradling.* A British author; nephew of Francis Sylvester Mahony ("Father Prout"); a young man of much promise, but died early; contributed to "Fraser's Magazine," etc.

Maidment, James. *J. M.* A Scottish editor, of Edinburgh, of the day.

Maistre, Comte **Xavier de**, 1764-1852. *Le Chev. X*****, O.A.S.D.M.S.* A French writer; b. at Chambéry, Savoy; and d. at St. Petersburg, where he had resided, engaged in literary and scientific pursuits.

Maitland, Agnes C. *A. C. M.* An English writer of the day.

Maitland, Edward. *Herbert Ainslie, B.A.* An English novelist of the day.

Maitland, Mrs. Julia Charlotte. *A Lady.* An English traveller.

Maitland, Samuel Roffey, D.D., 1795-1866. *A Churchman.* An English clergyman; b. in London; educ. at Cambridge; Keeper of the Mss. at Lambeth, and Librarian to the Archbishop of Canterbury, 1838-66.

Major, John, 1782-1849. *J. M.; One under a Hood.* An English bookseller and publisher, of London; d. in the Charter House.

Makemie, Francis. *A Well-Wisher*

to both Governments. An English political writer of the first part of the 18th century.

Malcolm, Sir **John**, G.C.B., 1769–1833. *A Traveller.* An eminent Scottish statesman and diplomatist; b. on the farm of Burnfoot, near Langholm; went to India in 1782; rose to be major general in the service of the East India Company, and returned to England in 1831; d. in London.

Malcome, Rev. **David.** *D.* A Scottish writer.

Malcome, Rev. **John.** *A True Lover of Presbyterian Principles.* An Irish minister, of Dunmuny, Co. of Antrim.

Malden, Henry, M.A., 1800–76. *Hamilton Murray.* An English poet, classical scholar, and philologist; b. at Putney; B.A., Cambridge, 1822; professor in the Univ. of London from 1831.

Male, Rev. **Christopher Parr**, M.A. *C. P. M.* An English clergyman; Christ Coll., Cambridge, 1843; Vicar of Cotes-Heath, Stone, Staffs., 1863–83 *et seq.*

Mallison, **William M.** *O'Pake.* An American journalist, of Brooklyn, N.Y.

Mallock, **William Hurrell.** *A Newdigate Prizeman.* An English writer; b. in Devonshire; educ. at Balliol Coll., Oxford; resides in Exeter.

Mallory, **John.** *A Gentleman of the Inner Temple.* An English barrister, of London, of the 18th century.

Malone, **Edmond**, 1741–1812. *Stultifex; Academicus.* A celebrated Irish Shakespearian; b. in Dublin; lived a literary life in London; and d. in that city.

Malone, **Richard**, 1797–1862. *Malone Raymond.* An Irish actor.

Man, **Thomas.** *Sui generis.* An American writer; mechanic, of Rhode Island.

Mandeville, **Bernard de**, 1670(?)–1733. An English writer; b. at Dort, Holland; settled in London.

Manfield, **Charles.** *A Gentleman formerly of Brazennose College, Oxford.* An English writer of the 18th century.

Mangin, Rev. **Edward**, A.M., 1772–1852. *An Absentee residing in Bath.* An Irish clergyman; Balliol Coll., Oxford, 1795; settled in Bath, and d. there.

Maning, Judge ——. *A Pakeha Maori.* A British colonial official, of New Zealand.

Mankin, **H.** *A Citizen of Maryland.* An American writer.

Manley, **James R.**, M.D., –1851. *Graviora manent.* An American physician; professor in the Med. Coll. of New York City.

Manley de la Riviere, Mrs. **N.**, –1724.

Sir Charles Lovemore. An English writer; b. in Guernsey.

Mann, **Herman**, –1833. *A Citizen of Massachusetts.* An American writer, of Dedham, Mass.

Mann, Mrs. **Mary Peabody.** *His Wife.* An American lady; wife of Horace; for many years resident in Cambridge.

Manne, **Edmond de**, 1801–77. *Alexis Barteville; Dupré; Armand Duplessis; Fernand de Lisle; Edmond Nouel; A. D. S.* An eminent French bibliographer; in the "Bibliotèque Nationale," 1820–66.

Manning, Miss **Anne.** — See "Rathbone, Mrs. A. (M.)."

Manning, Rev. **Charles Robertson**, M.A. *C. R. M.* An English clergyman; Christ Coll., Cambridge, 1847; Rector of Diss, 1857–83 *et seq.*

Manning, Most Rev. **Henry Edward**, D.D., 1808–. *H. E. M.* An English R. C. prelate; b. at Totteridge, Herts.; Baliol Coll., Oxford, 1830; Cardinal, 1875–85 *et seq.*

Manning, **Joseph Bolles**, A.M., 1787–1854. *Atticus Secundus.* An American lawyer; b. at Gloucester (now Rockport), Mass.; Harv. Univ., 1808; was for several years a lawyer in Ipswich, and afterwards in Gloucester; d. in Ipswich.

Manning, Rev. **Owen**, 1721–1801. *A. G. O. T. U. O. C.; A Consistent Protestant; A Gentleman of the University of Cambridge.* An English antiquary; b. in Northampton; Vicar of Godalming, 1763; and Rector of Pepperharrow, 1769.

Manning, **Robert**, –1730. *R. M.* An English writer; educ. at Douay Coll., where he was, for a time, Professor of Humanity and Philosophy; d. in Essex.

Manning, **Thomas**, 1774–1840. *M.; Trismegistus.* An English linguist and mathematical scholar; b. at Diss, Norfolk; educ. at Cambridge; travelled extensively in the East; d. at Bath.

Mannington, **A.** *A. M.* An English translator.

Mansfield, **Edward Deering**, LL.D., 1801–80. *A Veteran Observer.* An eminent American lawyer and journalist; b. at New Haven, Conn.; educ. at West Point, 1819, and New Jersey Coll., 1822; removed to Cincinnati; was a journalist, 1836–72; and Commissioner of Statistics for the State of Ohio, 1857–67.

Mansfield, **Lewis William.** *A Journalist; Z. P. (Zachary Pundison).* An American writer, of Waterford, N.Y.; graduated at Union Coll., 1835.

Mansfield, **Robert Blackford.** *An*

Oxford Man and Wykehamist. An English writer; Univ. of Oxford, 1846.

Manson, James Bolivar. *Ernest Warmley, M.A.; Euphranor.* A Scottish writer, of Bannockburn.

Mant, Rev. **Richard,** D.D., 1776–1848. *One who is also an Elder.* An English clergyman; b. at Southampton; educ. at Trin. Coll., Oxford; Bishop of Down, Connor, and Dromore; d. at Ballymony, Co. Antrim.

Mant, Walter Bishop. *A Brother of the Apollo Lodge,* 711, *Oxford.* An Irish clergyman and poet; Oriel Coll., Oxford, 1827; Archdeacon of Down.

Manville, Helen A. *Nellie A. Mann.* An American writer of the day.

Mapleton, Mrs. **S. E.** *A Clergyman's Wife.* An English writer.

Marana, Giovanni Paolo, about 1642–93. *Mahmut the Spy; The Turkish Spy.* An Italian writer; about 1682 removed to Paris, where he published his "Turkish Spy."

Marcet, Mrs. **Jane (Haldiman),** 1785–1858. *John Hopkins.* A popular English writer on science; b. in Geneva; d. in London.

March, Charles, 1815–64. *Pequot.* An American journalist; for some time Vice-Consul at Cairo; b. in Portsmouth, N.H.; Harv. Univ., 1837; d. at Alexandria, Egypt.

Maréchal, Pierre Sylvain, 1750–1803. *Sylvain M******l.* A French scholar; b. in Paris; d. at Montrouge, near Paris.

Margoliouth, Rev. **Moses,** Ph.D., LL.D., 1820–81. *A Clergyman of the Church of England.* An English clergyman; b. in London; educ. in Dublin; editor of the "Hebrew Christian Witness," London, where he died.

Markham, Gervase, 1570–1655. *G. M.* An English writer on horses, horsemanship, etc., who flourished in the reigns of James I. and Charles I.

Markham, Most Rev. **William,** D.D., –1807. *William, Lord Archbishop of York.* An English prelate; Bishop of Chester, 1771–76; Archbishop of York, 1776–1807; d. in London.

Markoe, Peter, –1792. *A Native of Algiers.* An American poet, of Philadelphia; d. there.

Marks, Harry H. *Grinder.* An American journalist, of New York City.

Marks, Rev. **Richard,** 1780–1848. *Aliquis; One who loves the Souls of the Lambs of Christ's Flock.* An English clergyman; Vicar of Great Missenden, Bucks., 1820–48, where he died.

Marlborough, Sarah Jennings, Duchess of, 1660–1774. *Zarah.* An

English lady; b. in Holywell, a suburb of St. Albans; for many years a favorite of her royal mistress.

Marmier, Xavier, 1809–. *Un Voyageur.* A French scholar and traveller, poet and journalist; from 1847 keeper of the Bibliothèque de Sainte-Geneviève.

Marrack, Richard, 1831–. *One of Ourselves.* An English solicitor; b. at the manor-house, Tregonebris, Sancreed; lawyer at Truro in 1880.

Marriott, George Wharton, Esq., B.C.L., 1778–1833. *G. W. M.* An English lawyer; b. at Cotesbach, in Leicestershire; Chancellor of the Diocese of St. David's, 1824–33; d. at Sydenham, Kent.

Marriott, Sir **James,** Knt., LL.D., 1731–1803. *The Advocate General.* An English jurist; b. in London; at one time Master of Trin. Hall, Cambridge; Advocate-General to H.M., 1764; appointed Judge of the Court of Admiralty in the room of Sir George Hay; twice M.C. for Sudbury; d. at Twinsted-Hall, near Sudbury.

Marryat, Miss **Florence.** — See "Ross-Church, Mrs. F. (M.)."

Marryat, Frederick, 1792–1848. *Monsieur Violet.* An English novelist; b. in London; served in the English navy from 1812; d. at Langham, Norfolk.

Marsden, Rev. **John Howard,** B.D. *Philomorus.* An English clergyman; Rector of Great Oakley, Harwich, 1840–80 *et seq.*

Marsden, Peter. *A Gentleman lately Resident on a Plantation.* An English colonial writer.

Marsh, Miss **C.** *His Daughter.* An American lady; daughter of the Rev. William Marsh.

Marsh, Charles, –1782. *A Bookseller.* An English poet and dramatist; once a clerk to the chapel in Duke Street, Westminster; afterwards a bookseller in Round Court, Strand, and at Charing Cross; and finally a justice of the peace for the liberty of Westminster; d. at Knightsbridge.

Marsh, Charles. *Vetus.* An English barrister, of Lincoln's Inn; b. at Norwich, and spent some time at St. John's Coll., Cambridge; from 1792, resided for some years, as a lawyer, at Madras; on his return to England was an M.P. for East Retford.

Marsh, Mrs. **Constance (Crane)** 1816–. *Virginia Gabriel.* An American writer; wife of George Perkins Marsh, b. at Berkeley, Mass.

Marsh, Rev. **Dwight Whitney,** 1823–.

Tennessean. An American missionary; b. at Dalton, Mass.; Williams Coll., 1842; Andover Theol. Sem., 1845; missionary, 1849–60; in 1882 residing at Amherst, Mass.

Marsh, Miss **F.** *Nellie.* An English novelist.

Marsh, James, D.D., 1794–1842. *Philopis.* An American philosopher, theologian, and educator; b. at Hartford, Vt.; Dartmouth Coll., 1817; President of the Univ. of Vermont, 1826–33; Professor of Philosophy, 1833–42.

Marshall, A. J. P. *A Bachelor of Arts.* An English writer of the day.

Marshall, Charles. *Harkaway; Heraclitus Grey.* An English sporting writer of the day.

Marshall, Rev. **Charles.** *C. M., Vicar of Brixworth.* An English clergyman.

Marshall, Rev. **Edmund,** 1724–97. *Cantianus.* An English clergyman; Curate of Egerton, 1773–97.

Marshall, George W. *G. W. M.* An English writer of the day.

Marshall, Oliver P. *Revilo.*

Marshall, Rev. **Thomas William.** *Archdeacon Chasuble, D.D.* An English R. C. clergyman; once Curate of Swallowcliffe.

Marston, Edward. *A Publisher.* An English publisher, of London, of the day.

Marteau, Amédée. *Marcellus.*

Martin, Alfred Tobias John, 1802–50. *A Cosmopolite.* An English poet; b. in Helston, Cornwall; d. at Adelaide, South Australia.

Martin, Mrs. **Bell,** –1850. *Mrs. Martin Bell.* An Irish lady; born to an inheritance which extended over a territory exceeding the domains of many a German prince, she was known as "the Irish heiress"; but within two years (about 1847) found herself at the head of her estates without a shilling she could call her own; d. in New York City.

Martin, Bon Louis Henri, 1810–83. *Felix.* A French historian, of Paris; professor at the Sorbonne from 1848; d. at Paris.

Martin, Mrs. **Clara (Barnes).** *C. B. M.* An American writer of the day.

Martin, Mrs. **E. Throop.** *A Lady.* An American compiler.

Martin, Edward Sanford, 1856–. *E. S. M.* An American poet; b. at "Willowbrook," near Auburn, N.Y.; studied law till Oct., 1879, when he became a clerk at Washington, in the Dept. of State; has since studied again at Cambridge, Mass.

Martin, Rev. **Frederick,** M.A., –1864.

F. M. An English clergyman, of Trin. Coll., Cambridge; B.A., 1828; Rector of South Somercotes, etc., where he died.

Martin, Sir **Henry,** 3d Bart., 1801–63. *A Lay Baronet; Phœnix.* An English antiquary; b. in London; d. at Tunbridge Wells.

Martin, J. F. *Hydrant Chuck.* An American writer.

Martin, J. L., –1848. *J. L. M.* An American satirical poet; chargé d'affaires of the United States to the Pontifical States; d. at Rome (?).

Martin, James Sullivan. *A Revolutionary Soldier.* An American writer.

Martin, John, Esq., F.S.A., 1791–1855. *J. M.* An English bookseller, of London; b. in that city; in 1836 became librarian to the Duke of Bedford at Woburn Abbey; d. at Froxfield, near Woburn.

Martin, Josiah. *J. M.* An English writer of the earlier part of the 18th century.

Martin, Michael. *Lightfoot.* An English highwayman.

Martin, Mrs. **Sallie M. (Davis).** *Sibyl.* An American "Southland" writer; b. in South Carolina; in 1863 married Mr. George W. Martin, of Atlanta, Ga.

Martin, Miss **Selina.** *S. M.* An English writer.

Martin, Sir **Theodore,** D.C.C., 1816–. *Bon Gaultier.* A Scottish poet; b. and educ. in Edinburgh; at first wrote for "Fraser's and Tait's Magazines"; edited, for Queen Victoria, "Life of H.R.H. the Prince Consort."

Martin, Thomas. *An Irish Land Owner.* An Irish lawyer, of Dublin; Trin. Coll., 1853.

Martin, William, –1867. *Old Chatty Cheerful; Peter Parley.* An English writer and publisher for the young; carried on "Peter Parley's Annual" for 26 years; d. at Holly Lodge, Woodbridge.

Martineau, Harriet, 1802–76. *H. M.; An Invalid.* An English miscellaneous writer; b. at Norwich; entered upon her literary life in 1823; visited the United States in 1834; d. at Ambleside.

Martyn, John, M.D., 1699–1768. *Bavius.* A learned English writer; b. in London; Professor of Botany in the Univ. of Cambridge.

Maseres, Francis, 1731–1824. *A Friend to the Church of England.* An English lawyer; b. in London; Attorney-General for Canada till 1773; and afterwards Cursitor Baron of the Exchequer; d. at Reigate, Surrey.

Maskell, Rev. **William,** 1814–. *W.*

M., A Beneficed Priest. An English clergyman; b. at Bath; removed to Bude-Haven in 1844; J. P., 1865; and Dep.-Lieut. for Cornwall, 1876.

Mason, Mrs. Caroline Atherton (Briggs), 1823-. *Caro; Thekla.* An American poet; b. at Marblehead, Mass.; wife of Charles Mason, Esq., of Fitchburg, Mass.

Mason, George, Esq., 1735–1806. *A British Freeholder.* An English writer; son of Mr. Mason, a distiller at Deptford Bridge; step-son of Dr. Jebb, of Oxford; d. at Aldenham Lodge, Herts.

Mason, George Champlin, 1820-. *Champlin; Robert O. Lincoln; The Editor of the "Newport Mercury."* An American artist and journalist; b. in Newport, R.I.; editor of the "Newport Mercury," a paper established by James Franklin, brother of Benjamin.

Mason, John. *An Ex-Orderly Sergeant.* An American soldier; a veteran of the New York National Guard.

Mason, Richard Sharp, D.D., 1795–1874. *The Chairman of the Committee on the State of the Church.* An American P. E. clergyman; b. in Barbadoes, W.I.; Univ. of Penn., 1812; President Delaware Coll., 1835–37; President Hobart Coll., 1837–74; d. at Raleigh, N.C.

Mason, Robert. *Ebenezer Lazarus.* A Scottish writer of the 18th century.

Mason, Thomas. *I. X. Peck.*

Mason, Thomas. *An Assistant Librarian.* A Scottish bibliographer, of Glasgow, of the day.

Mason, Thomson, 1730–85. *A British American.* An American jurist and statesman, of Virginia; studied law in London; was a strong friend of his country.

Mason, William, D.D., 1725–97. *A Gentleman of Cambridge; Malcolm Macgregor.* An English poet, painter, and musician; b. at Hull; Canon of York; d. in London.

Mason, William Shaw, Esq. *W. S. M.* An Irish bibliographer and statistical writer; Member of the Royal Irish Academy; Secretary of the Board of Public Records in Ireland.

Massary, Isabel. *A Resident.* An English writer, of Australia.

Massena, Mrs. A. M. C., 1845-. *Creole.* An American "Southland" writer; b. in New Orleans; commenced her literary career in 1864; in 1871, resided in the parish of Plaquemine.

Massett, Stephen C. *Jeemes Pipes, of Pipesville.* An English-American comic singer; in 1870, of New York City.

Massey, E. C. *Whatshisname.* An English novelist.

Massie, Joseph. *J. M.* An English writer on political economy, of the 18th century.

Masson, Mme Clémence (Harding). *Dixon.* A French lady; wife of Michel Masson.

Masson, Jean, 1680–1750. ——. A learned French critic and chronologist; after visiting England, became an evangelical minister, and held several pastorships in France; d. in England.

Masters, Rev. Robert, F.R.S., 1713–98. *A Late Vicar.* An English clergyman; Fellow and Tutor of Corpus Christi Coll., Cambridge.

Mather, Cotton, D.D., 1663–1728. *C. M.; A Fellow of the Royal Society; A Minister in Boston; One of the Ministers in Boston; One of their Number; Philalethes.* An American divine; son of the following; b. in Boston; Harv. Coll., 1678; minister of the North Church, Boston, 1684–1728; d. in Boston.

Mather, Increase, D.D., 1639–1723. *A Friend to the Churches.* An American divine; b. in Dorchester, Mass.; Harv. Coll., 1656; pastor of the North Church, Boston, 1664–1723; President of Harv. Coll., 1685–1701; d. in Boston.

Mather, Samuel, D.D., 1706–85. *An American Englishman; Aurelius Prudentius, Americanus.* An American divine; son of Cotton Mather; b. in Boston; Harv. Coll., 1723; was a pastor in his native city.

Mathew, Rev. Theobald, D.D., 1790–1856. *The Apostle of Temperance.* An Irish R. C. priest; b. at Thomastown, Tipperary; educ. at Maynooth; visited the United States, 1849–51; d. at Cork.

Mathews, Albert, 1820-. *Paul Siegvolk.* An American lawyer and *littérateur*; b. in New York City; Yale Coll., 1842; admitted to the New York bar in 1845; co-editor of the "Yale Literary Magazine," 1841–42; practises law in his native city.

Mathews, Charles Elkin. *Ch. El. Ma.* An English writer, of Exeter, of the day.

Mathews, Cornelius, 1817-. *The Late Ben Smith.* An American journalist; b. at Port Chester, N.Y.; educ. at the Univ. of New York; began his literary career in 1836; has edited various journals, and contributed largely to periodicals, etc.

Mathews, G. H. *Porte.* An American writer of the day.

Mathias, Thomas James, about

1757–1835. *Thomas James M*th**s; A Country Gentleman, formerly of the Univ. of Camb.; A Layman.* An English poet; educ. at Cambridge; resided for many years at Naples, where he died.

Matson, Henrietta. *Eric Arnold.* An English (?) writer of the day.

Matthews, Arthur Bache. *A. B. M.* An English editor.

Matthews, Henry, 1789–1828. *An Invalid.* An English writer; b. at Belmont, in Herefordshire; Advocate-Fiscal of Ceylon, 1821–27; and promoted to the Bench in 1827; d. at Ceylon.

Matthews, James Brander, 1852–. *Arthur Penn.* An American writer, of New York City; b. in Louisiana.

Matthews, John. *An Officer of the Royal Navy.* An English naval lieutenant.

Matthews, John, Esq. *A Lounger.* An English gentleman, of Belmont, Herefordshire.

Matthews, Nathan. *One of the Directors.* An American merchant and capitalist of Boston; gave "Matthews Hall" to Harv. Univ., Cambridge, Mass.

Matthews, William, –1816. *A Lover of Christian Liberty; Catholicus; Theophilus Freeman.* An English Friend, of Bath; at one time secretary to the West of England Agricultural Society, originally established in that city; d. at Bath.

Maturin, Rev. Robert Charles, 1782–1824. *Dennis Jasper Murphy.* An Irish clergyman, poet, novelist, and dramatist; Curate of St. Peter's, Dublin; b. and d. there.

Maude, Mrs. Mary Fawler. *M. F. M.* An English hymn-writer; wife of Rev. Joseph Maude, Vicar of Chirk, near Ruabon.

Maudet de Penhouët, le comte Armand Bon Louis, 1764–1839. *A Pedestrian Traveller.* A French antiquary; b. at the Chateau de Penhouët (Loire, Inferieure); was engaged in the American war; d. at Rennes.

Mauduit, Jasper. *J. M., of the Inner Temple.* An English political writer, of London.

Maunde, ——. *M.* An English boy; referred to in Lamb's "Elia," "Christ's Hospital."

Maurice, Rev. John Frederick Denison, M.A., 1805–72. *A Clergyman of the Church of England.* An eminent English divine; son of an Unit. minister; Professor of Moral Philosophy in the Univ. of Cambridge, 1866–72.

Maurice, J. F. *The "Daily News"*

Special Correspondent. An English journalist.

Maury, Matthew Fontaine, LL.D., 1806–73. *Harry Bluff.* An eminent American astronomer and meteorologist; b. in Virginia; professor in the Virginia Military Institute, 1868–73; d. at Lexington, Va.

Maury, Sarah (Mytton), –1848. *An English Woman.* An English writer; b. in Liverpool; d. in Virginia.

Maverick, Augustus. *Paul Peebles.* An American writer.

Mavor, Rev. William, LL.D., 1758–1837. *William Fredrick Martyn.* A Scottish clergyman and voluminous author; b. in the parish of New Deer, Aberdeenshire; Rector of Bladon w. Woodstock; Vicar of Hurley, Berks.; and a magistrate for Oxfordshire; d. at the rectory house, Woodstock.

Maw, Mary. *A Well-wisher.* An English writer; a Friend, of Woodbridge, in Suffolk.

Mawbrey, Rev. Thomas. *A Suffering Presbyter of the Church of Scotland.* A Scottish minister of the first part of the 18th century.

Mawer, John, D.D. *A Free Thinker and a Christian.* An English clergyman of the earlier part of the 18th century.

Mawson, Matthias, D.D., 1682–1770. *Matthias, Lord Bishop of Chichester.* An English prelate; b. at Chiswick, in Middlesex; Benet Coll., Cambridge; Bishop of Ely, 1754–70; d. at his house in Kensington Square.

Maxcy, Virgil, about 1785–1844. *A Citizen of Maryland.* An American statesman, of Baltimore; b. at Attleboro, Mass.; was killed on board the U.S. steamer "Princeton," on the Potomac River.

Maxwell, Lady Caroline Elizabeth Sarah (Sheridan Norton), 1808–77. *Aunt Carry; Pearce Stevenson, Esq.* An English poet; b. in London; first married the Hon. G. C. Norton; in 1876, Sir William Sterling Maxwell.

Maxwell, Mrs. Mary Elizabeth (Braddon), 1837–. *Babington White; Lady Caroline Lascelles.* A popular English novelist; b. in London; from an early age has been much devoted to literary pursuits; also edits annually the "Mistletoe Bough."

Maxwell, William H. *Max.* An English writer and publisher of the day.

Maxwell, William Hamilton, 1795–1851. *A Soldier of Fortune.* An Irish novelist; Trin. Coll., Dublin; in 1820 was collated to the prebend and rectory of Ballagh, a wild place in Connaught, destitute of any congregation or cure of souls, though it afforded what he was admirably capable of dealing with,— plenty of game; d. at Musselburgh, near Edinburgh.

May, Frederick. *Erasmus.* An English (?) Radical.

Maybrick, Mr. M. *Stephen Adams.* An English singer and writer of music; the author of "Nancy Lee," the most popular ballad ever written.

Mayer, Brantz, 1809–79. *John Smith, Jr.* An American lawyer and historical writer; b. in Baltimore; Secretary of Legation at Mexico; from 1843 resided in Baltimore.

Mayer, Franz Xaver, 1757–. *Gottlieb Ackermann.* A German writer.

Mayhew, Horace, 1819–72. *Susan Crick; Ponny.* An English author and journalist; one of the brothers Mayhew; b. and d. in London; for some time on the staff of "Punch."

Mayhew, Horace, Henry Mayhew, and **Robert B. Brough.** *Rigdum Funnidos.*

Maynard, Col. ——. *The Kentucky Colonel.* An American writer.

Maynard, Mrs. Sarah Elizabeth (Hillyer Ballard), 1841–. *Kaloolah; Mrs. Literary.* An American "Southland" writer; b. at Eatonton, Putnam Co., Ga.; in 1856 married Mr. J. J. Ballard, of Halletsville, Texas, and about 1870, Mr. Maynard; they reside near Bastrop, Texas.

Mayne, Miss Sarah Jane. *A Friend of the People.* An English novelist.

Mayo, Herbert, M.D., –1852. *Mac Davus.* An English author; Professor of Anatomy in King's Coll., London, till 1836; when he settled at Bad-Weilbach, near Mainz, on the Rhine, where he died.

Mayo, Mrs. Isabella (Fyvie), 1843–. *Edward and Ruth Garrett.* An English poet and novelist; b. in London; in 1870 married Mr. John R. Mayo, an English solicitor.

Mayo, William Starbuck, M.D., 1812–. *Jonathan Romer.* A popular American novelist, of New York City; b. at Ogdensburg, N.Y.; studied medicine, and practised for several years.

Mayow, Rev. Robert Wynell, B.A., 1777–1817. *Daniel Merdant.* An English clergyman; b. at Saltash; curate at Ardwick, near Manchester, and d. there.

Mead, Richard, M.D., 1673–1754. *Dr. M—d.* An eminent English physician, of London; one of the most learned men of his age.

Meadley, George Wilson, 1774–. *G.*

W. M.; A Lay Seceder. An English biographer; b. at Sunderland; in early life visited Italy, and resided in Germany for a time.

Meads, Orlando, A.M. *A Layman.* An American lawyer, of Albany; Union Coll., 1826.

Meagher, Thomas Francis, 1823–67. *Cornelius O'Keefe.* An Irish patriot; b. at Waterford; sentenced to death for sedition; he was transported to Tasmania, whence in 1842 he escaped to this country; was drowned at Fort Benton, while Secretary of Montana.

Meaney, Mary L. M. L. M. An American writer for the young of the day.

Meason, Gilbert Laing. G. L. M. A Scottish artist, of Lindertis, Forfarshire.

Measor, Charles Pennell. *Scrutator.* An English writer; Sub-Inspector of Factories.

Mecklenburg, Alfhilda (Svenson), 1830–. *Ivar Ring.* A Danish novelist; b. at Copenhagen; in 1864 married Captain Karl Mecklenburg, in the Norwegian service, and lives now (1882), since 1868, a widow in Copenhagen.

Mecom, Benjamin. *Urbanus Filter.* An American journalist, of Boston; a nephew of Benjamin Franklin.

Mecutchen, Samuel, and Sayre, George M. *S. M. and G. M. S.* American teachers, of Philadelphia.

Meding, Oskar, 1829–. *Benno Reden; Gregor Samarow.* A German novelist; b. at Königsberg; studied law in his native town, in Heidelburg, and Berlin; in 1873 he settled in Berlin, and devoted himself to literary work.

Medley, or Daily Tatler. Supposed editor *Jeremy Quick.*

Mee, Mr. William, 1788–1862. *Richard Sparkle.* An English poet and journalist; b. at Kegworth, County of Leicester; resided in London several years; about the year 1820 returned to Kegworth, but engaged in no steady occupation. He was the author of the song, "Alice Gray," which became so great a favorite with the public. He suggested for his epitaph, "Weep not for Mee" (me). D. at the Shardlow Union-house.

Meen, Rev. Henry, B.D., 1745–1817. *C. or Coadjutor.* An English poet and clergyman; rector of the united parishes of St. Nicholas Coleabbey and St. Nicholas Olave, London, 1792–1817; and prebendary in the Cathedral Church of St. Paul, where he was lecturer; d. in London.

Meighan, Thaddeus W. *Asmodeus.* An American writer.

Meigs, Return Jonathan, 1740–1823. *A Resident of Twelve Years at Marietta, in that State.* An eminent American soldier; b. in Middletown, Conn.; settled in Marietta, in 1788; d. at the Cherokee agency.

Meikleham, Robert. *Robert Stuart.* An English artist (?).

Mein, John. *Sagittarius.* An American political writer; a printer and bookseller of Boston; a strong Tory; kept a circulating library; was editor of the "Boston Chronicle," but becoming obnoxious to the patriots, in 1769 fled to England, and the "Chronicle" was discontinued in 1770.

Mein, Robert. *A Merchant Citizen.* A Scottish writer, of Edinburgh.

Meldrum, Rev. George, –1709. *A Friend in the City.* A Scottish minister at Edinburgh.

Meli, Giovanni, about 1740–1815. *Sicilian Anacreon.* An eminent Sicilian poet.

Meline, Miss Mary Miller. *Florence McCoomb.* An American (?) novelist of the day.

Mellen, Grenville, 1799–1841. *Reginald Reverie.* An American poet; b. in Biddeford, Me.; Harv. Univ., 1818; resided about five years in Boston, but removed to New York City in 1839.

Mellish, J. C. *J. C. M., Esq.* An English translator.

Mellish, Joseph. *M.* An English scholar, of Eton Coll.; a contributor to the "Microcosm," 1787.

Melmoth, William, Esq., 1710–99. *Sir Thomas Fitzosborne.* An elegant English writer; b. in London; was a lawyer; resided many years at Shrewsbury, and then at Bath, where he died.

Melnikow, Pawel Iwanowitsch, 1819–. *Andrei Petscherstij.* A Russian author; b. at Nishnij, Nowgorob; studied at Kasan, and entered the service of the State.

Memes, Mrs. Ann (Ritchie). *A Lady.* A Scottish writer; wife of Dr. John Smythe Memes, of Edinburgh.

Memminger, Charles Gustavus, 1803–. *A Spectator of the Past.* An American lawyer and politician; b. in Würtemberg; came to Charleston, S.C., when a child; Secretary of the Treasury in the Confederate States Cabinet, 1861–64.

Méndes, Judith (Gautier), 1850–. *Judith Walter; Judith Méndes.* A French writer; b. at Paris; daughter of Théophile Gautier; is at once a poet, musician, novelist, sculptor, and painter.

Mendham, Rev. Joseph. *Catholicus; Eupator.* An English clergyman, of Sutton Coldfield, near Birmingham.

Mennis, Sir John, 1598–1671. *Sr. J. M.* An English poet; vice-admiral, R.N.; Chief Comptroller of the Navy, and Governor of Dover Castle.

Mercer, Charles Fenton, LL.D., 1778–1858. *A Late American Statesman.* An American soldier and statesman; b. at Fredericksburg, Va.; New Jersey Coll., 1797; studied law; M.C., 1817–40; d. at Howard, near Alexandria, Va.

Mercer, Edward Smyth. *An Irish Sennachy.* An Irish poet of the day.

Mercer, William. *A Person Abroad.* A Scottish writer.

Mercier, Alfred. *M***, louisianais.* An American novelist, of New Orleans.

Mercier de Compiegne, Claude François Xavier, 1763–1800. *C. M. D. C.* A French editor, compiler, and writer, of Paris.

Meredith, Sir William. *A Member of Parliament.* An English political writer of the 18th century.

Mereweather, Rev. Francis, LL.B. *A Country Vicar.* An English clergyman; Rector of Cole Orton, Ashby-de-la-Zouche, 1815–60 *et seq.*

Merimée, Prosper, 1803–70. *Clara Gazul.* A French writer; b. in Paris; studied law, but did not practise; inspector of the monuments of Paris from 1834.

Merivale, John Herman, Esq., F.S.A., 1779–1844. *J. H. M.* An English lawyer; b. in Exeter; St. John's Coll., Cambridge; called to the Bar at Lincoln's Inn, but devoted his life chiefly to literary pursuits; d. at his house in Bedford Square, London.

Merrill, H. R. *Old Scout.*

Merrill, Royal W. *The Lounger in the Lobby.* An American journalist.

Merriman, Samuel, M.D., 1771–1853. *L. N.; S. M.; Correspondent;* 'Ιλαρανθρώπος. An English physician; b. at Marlborough, Wilts.; practised his profession in London, where he died.

Merry, Robert, 1755–98. *Della Crusca; Tom Thorne.* An English poet and dramatist, of London; b. in that city; came to the United States in 1796; and d. in Baltimore.

Merry, Robert, Roscoe, etc. *A Society called the Oziosi.*

Merryweather, Mrs. J. A. *J. A. M.* An English poet.

Mesonero y Romanos, Ramon de, 1803–. *Il Parlante Curioso.* A Spanish writer and journalist; b. in Madrid;

from 1833 devoted himself to literary pursuits.

Messenger, Mrs. Lilian T. (Rozell), 1844–. *Zena Clifton.* An American "Southland" poet; b. in Kentucky; in 1861 married Mr. Messenger of Tuscumbia, Ala., who d. in 1865; in 1869 her home was still in Tuscumbia.

Metcalfe, Rev. Frederick, M.A., about 1817–. *The Oxonian.* An English clergyman; St. John's Coll., Cambridge, 1838; Vicar of St. Michael, Oxford, 1849–83; Fellow of Lincoln Coll., Oxford, 1844–83 *et seq.*

Meteyard, Miss Eliza, 1816–79. *Silverpen.* An English poet; b. at Liverpool; received her *nom de plume* from Mr. Jerrold; d. in London.

Meusnier, Georges. *Karl Robert.*

Meyer, August Friedrich, 1811–. *Friedrich Brunold.* A German poet; b. at Pyritz, in Pomerania; successively at Berlin, Stettin, and Joachimsthal,—where he is still to-day, free from every office,—devoted to literary labor.

Meyer, Siegbert, 1841–. *Siegmey.* A German author; b. in Berlin; attended the French lyceum in that city; was engaged for some time in the silk-goods manufacture; but after the death of his father, devoted himself to literary pursuits.

Michel, F. Fernand. *Anthony Réal.* A French writer.

Michelborne, John. *A Gentleman who was in the Town.* An Irish historian, of the earlier part of the 18th century.

Michell, Mrs. Grace (Angove), 1839–. *Grace Angove.* An English writer; b. at Redruth, Cornwall.

Michell, Nicholas, 1807–80. *An Essayist on the Passions.* An English poet, novelist, and essayist; b. at Truro; d. at Falmouth.

Michie, Archibald. *Jack Robinson.* An English literary critic, of Melbourne, Australia.

Mickle, Charles Julius. *Mr. C. J. M.* An English writer.

Middlemass, Miss Hume. *Mignionette.* An English writer.

Middlemass, R. Hume. *Thistle.* An English writer.

Middleton, Conyers, D.D., 1683–1750. *The D—st D—r.* An eminent English scholar and writer; b. at York; about 1722 became principal librarian of the Public Library at Cambridge, and towards the close of his life was presented to the living of Hascomb, in Surrey.

Middleton, Henry, 1771–1846. *A South-Carolinian.* An American statesman, of South Carolina; U.S. Minister to Russia, 1820–31; b. and d. at Charleston, S.C.

Middleton, Rev. Patrick. *P. M* An English clergyman of the earlier part of the 18th century.

Milbourne, Rev. Luke, B.A., –1720. *Tom of Bedlam.* An English miscellaneous writer; was instituted to the living of St. Ethelburga, within Bishopsgate, London, in 1704–20.

Milburn, Rev. William Henry, 1823–. *The Blind Preacher.* An American M. E. minister; b. in Philadelphia; in 1860 was ordained in the Prot. Epis. Church; but in 1872 returned to Methodism.

Miles, Alfred, 1796–1851. *A. M.* An English author; b. at Woodbridge, Suffolk; d. at Lympston, Devon.

Miles, Henry, Jr. *Hermes.* An American writer.

Miles, Pliny, 1818–65. *Communipaw.* An American writer; b. at Watertown, N.Y.; devoted the later years of his life to postal reform; d. at Malta, N.Y.

Miles, Mrs. Sibella (Hatfield), 1800–. *S. E. Hatfield.* An English poet; born in Falmouth; wife of Alfred Miles; in 1874 resident in London.

Mill, John Stuart, 1806–73. *Wickliffe.* An English philosopher; b. in London; studied law; in the service of the East India Company 33 years, 1823–56; M.P., 1865; spent the last years of his life chiefly in the south of Europe, near Avignon.

Millar, John, 1735–1801. *Crito.* A Scottish jurist; b. in Lanarkshire; educ. at Glasgow; was Professor of Civil Law there, 1761–1801.

Millard, E. E. *E. E. M.; E. M. E.* An American sporting writer of the day.

Millard, John. *Henry Coxe, Esq.* An English author; ass't-librarian at the Surrey Literary Institution, in Black Friars' Road, London.

Millen, Gen. F. F. *Ardboe; Trefoil; Verdad.* An American journalist.

Miller, Mrs. Anna C. (Johnson), 1832–83. *Minnie Myrtle.* An American poet; wife of Joaquin Miller.

This is also given: Mrs. Minnie Theresa (Dyer); married in 1863, and divorced in 1870.

Miller, Cincinnatus Hiner, 1841–. *Joaquin Miller.* An American poet; b. in the Wabash district, Ind.; settled in Oregon; was a county judge, 1866–70; in 1870 went to England.

Miller, Mrs. Emily (Huntington). *Purdy.* An American novelist.

Miller, Mme **Eugenie Marie Gaude**, –1865. *Max Valrey*. A French novelist.

Miller, **George**. *A Country Bookseller*. A Scottish writer, of Dunbar, in East Lothian.

Miller, **Hugh**, 1802–56. *One of the Scotch People; The Stonemason of Cromartie; A Geologist; A Journeyman Mason*. An eminent Scottish geologist; b. at Cromarty; in 1840 went to Edinburgh as editor of "The Witness"; d. at Portobello, near that city.

Miller, Rev. **James**, 1703–44. *A Gentleman of Wadham College*. An English dramatist; b. in Dorsetshire; educ. at Oxford; d. in Cheyne Walk, Chelsea.

Miller, **James W**. *Four of Us*. An American writer, of Boston.

Miller, Mrs. **John A**. *Faith Latimer*. An American writer of the day.

Miller, **John Cale**, D.D. *A Birmingham Clergyman; Eight Clergymen*. An English clergyman; Lincoln Coll., Oxford, 1835; Rector of St. Martin, Birmingham, 1846–66; Vicar of Greenwith w. St. Mary, 1866–83 *et seq*.

Miller, Mrs. **Lydia Falconer**, –1876. *L. F. M.; Mrs. Harriet Myrtle*. An English writer; widow of Hugh Miller.

Miller, Lady M., 1741–81. *An Englishwoman*. An English lady, of Batheaston villa; d. at Bristol Hot Wells.

Miller, Mrs. **Mary (Ayer)**. *Luola*. An American "Southland" writer; b. in Fayetteville, N.C.; early married Mr. Willis M. Miller, a lawyer, and afterwards a Presbyt. minister; in 1868 resided in Charlotte, N.C.

Miller, Mrs. **Mary (Gillies)**. *Harriet Myrtle*. An English writer of the day.

Miller, Rev. **Tobias H**. *Uncle Toby*.

Mills, **Charles**, Esq., 1788–1826. *Theodore Ducas*. An English historian; b. at Greenwich; left the law for literature; d. at Southampton.

Mills, **John**. *A Man of Fashion*. An English sportsman and sporting writer.

Milner, **John**, 1752–1826. *Rev. J. M.*, D.D., F.S.A. An English R. C. divine; b. in London; educ. at Douay; Bishop of Castabala, and Vicar Apostolic of England, 1803–23; d. at Wolverhampton.

Milnor, **William**. *A Member*. An American statistical writer.

Miner, **Charles**, 1780–1865. *John Harwood; Poor Robert the Scribe*. An American journalist and humorous essayist; b. at Norwich, Conn.; latest of Philadelphia; d. at Wilkesbarre, Penn.

Miorcec de Kerdanet, **Daniel Louis Mathurin**, 1793–. *le R. P. Cyrille Pen-*

nec. A French lawyer; librarian of the town of Rennes.

Mitchel, **William**. *The Tinklarian Doctor*. An English writer of the first part of the 18th century.

Mitchell, **Agnes W**. *A. W. M*. An American writer.

Mitchell, **Donald Grant**, 1822–. *D. G. M.; A Bachelor; Ik. Marvel; An Opera Goer; John Timon*. An American author; b. at Norwich, Conn.; Yale Coll., 1841; resides at Edgewood, near New Haven, Conn.

Mitchell, **G**. *One from the Plough*. An English journalist, of London.

Mitchell, **John**, M.D., –1772. *An Impartial Hand*. An English-American physician; emigrated to America about 1700; and resided chiefly at Urbana, on the Rappahannock, about 73 miles from Richmond, for the remainder of his life.

Mitchell, **John**. *A Practical Printer*. An English writer, of Manchester.

Mitchell, Rev. **John**, 1794–1870. *Graduate of Yale of the Class of 1821; John Chester*. An American Cong. minister; b. at Chester, Conn.; Yale Coll., 1821; engaged in literary pursuits, 1843–70.

Mitchell, **John Kearsley**, M.D., 1796–1858. *A Yankee*. An American writer; b. at Shepherdstown, Va.; Univ. of Penn., 1819; professor in Jefferson Coll., at Philadelphia, 1841–58, where he died.

Mitchell, **R**. *Vigilant*. An English sporting writer.

Mitchell, **Thomas Peter**. *Twinrock Elmlicht, Esq*. An English theological writer.

Mitchell, **William**. *A Free Church Elder*. A Scottish writer.

Mitchill, **Samuel Latham**, M.D., LL.D., 1764–1831. *A Gentleman residing in this City*. An American scientist; b. at North Hampstead, N.Y.; professor in Columbia Coll., 1792–1801; M.C., 1801–3 and 1810–12; U.S. Senator, 1804–10; d. in New York City.

Mitford, **John**, R.N., –1831. *Alfred Burton*. An English journalist and poet, of London.

Moberley, **A**. *A Wanderer*. An English poet.

Moffat, **A. S**. *A. S. M*. An American writer for the young.

Moffatt, **J. O**. An English writer on botany.

Moggridge, **J. H.**, Esq. *A Monmouthshire Magistrate*. An English writer.

Mogridge, **George**, 1787–1854. *Ephraim Holding; Uncle Adam; Jeremy Jaunt; Peter Parley; My Uncle Newberry; Old*

Humphrey. An English writer for the young; b. at Ashted, near Birmingham; after being in business for a time in that city he removed to London; in 1828 he began to prepare works for the Religious Tract Society, of which millions of copies were distributed; d. at Hastings.

Moir, Rev. **Andrew.** *A Gentleman of the Law.* A Scottish clergyman; Secession minister, Selkirk.

Moir, David Macbeth, M.D., 1798–1851. Δ; *Delta; Mansie Waugh.* A Scottish poet and prose writer; b. at Musselburgh, near Edinburgh; d. at Dumfries.

Moithey, P. D. *M. de Vouziers.* A French writer, of Vouziers (Ardennes).

Molènes, Mme la Comtesse **Paul de.** *Ange Bénigne.*

Molesworth, Mrs. **Mary Louisa,** 1842–. *Ennis Graham.* An English writer of Scotch descent; has lived much in the manufacturing districts of the North of England; but of late years in France, and at present in Paris.

Molesworth, Robert, Viscount Molesworth, 1656–1725. *A Member of the House of Commons.* An Irish statesman; b. in Dublin; ambassador of William III. to the Danish court, 1692–95.

Molitor, Wilhelm, 1819–80. *Benno Bronner; Ulrich Riesler.* A German writer; b. at Zweibrücken, in Rhenish Bavaria; d. at Speier.

Molloy, J. Fitzgerald. *Ernest Wilding.*

Molyneux, Rev. **John William Henry,** B.A. *J. W. H. M.* An English clergyman; B.A., Cambridge, 1841; Vicar of St. Gregory's *w.* St. Peter's P. C., Sudbury, Suffolk, 1855–75 *et seq.*

Monckton, Rose C. *Rose C. M.* An English writer.

Moncrief, Major ——. *An Engineer upon that Expedition.* A British officer at the siege of Quebec in 1759.

Moncrieff, John. *J. M., of T.* A Scottish physician; "famous for his extraordinary skill and knowledge in the art of physick."

Moncrieff, Robert Hope. *Ascott R. Hope.* A Scottish writer of the day.

Mondelet, Hon. **Dominique,** –1863. *Un Avocat.* A Canadian judge, of Montreal; held office and sat in Parliament before the Union.

Money, Robert Colton. *R. C. M.* An English traveller.

Monk, James Henry, D.D., 1784–1856. *J. H. M.* An English scholar and clergyman; Bishop of Gloucester from 1830, and Bishop of Gloucester and Bristol, 1836–56.

Monmouth, Mrs. **Elizabeth H.** *Sophia Homespun.* An American writer of religious fiction, of the day.

Monro, Rev. **Thomas,** M.A., –1815. *Oxoniensis.* An English *littérateur,* of Magdalen Coll., Oxford; M.A., 1774; Rector of Little Easton, Essex.

Monroe, George H. *Templeton.* An American journalist; in 1884 retired from the charge of the Boston "Saturday Evening Post"; previously editor of the Hartford, Conn., "Courant"; in 1885 wrote for the Boston "Herald."

Monsell, John Samuel Bewley, LL.D. *The Old Vicar.* An English poet; Trin. Coll., Dublin, 1832; Rector of St. Nicholas, Guildford, 1870–74 *et seq.*

Monson, Frederick John, 5th Baron Monson, D.C.L., 1809–41. *A Layman.* An English nobleman, author, artist, and traveller; d. at Brighton.

Montagu, Basil, Esq., 1770–1851. *A Water Drinker.* An English lawyer; educ. at the Charterhouse, and at Cambridge; for ten years Accountant-General in Bankruptcy; d. at Boulogne.

Montagu, Mrs. **Basil.** *Mrs. M.* An English lady; wife of the preceding.

Montagu, Mrs. **Elizabeth,** 1720–1800. *Mrs. M.* An English lady of letters; daughter of Matthew Robinson, Esq., of West Layton, Yorkshire; was married in 1742 to Edward Montagu, Esq., of Denton Hall; resided for many years in London; a splendid leader in society and literature; called the "Queen of the Blues."

Montagu, M., Esq. *A Near Observer.* An English political writer.

Montagu, Capt., **Matthew,** R.N. *A Layman.* An English writer.

Montagu, Matthew Robinson. *Matt. Robinson M.* An English writer.

Montague, Right Hon. Lady **Mary Wortley,** 1690(?)–1762. *Right Hon. Lady M—y W—y M—e.* An English lady; by birth Lady Mary Pierrepont, the eldest daughter of Evelyn, Earl of Kingston; in 1712 married Edward Wortley Montague, Esq., grandson of the first Earl of Sandwich.

Montague, William Edward. *An Officer.* An English officer; entered the army in 1860 as ensign in the 2nd (the Queen's Royal) Regiment of Foot; in 1870 made captain of the 94th Regiment of Foot; and in 1877 was brigade major at the Mauritius.

Montefiore, Mrs. **Charlotte,** –1854. *One of themselves.* A Jewish writer of London.

Montépin, Xavier Aymon de,

1824–. *Georges de Rieux.* A French novelist; wrote, 1847–57, 169 volumes of romance.

Montgomerie, Hugh E. *Edmond Hugomont.* A Scottish Canadian writer, of Montreal; returned to Scotland in 1849.

Montgomery, ——. *A Popular Author.* An English writer and compiler.

Montgomery, James, 1771–1854. *Alcæus; Paul Positive; A Poet; Gabriel Silvertongue, Gent.* A Scottish religious poet; b. at Irvine, Ayrshire; d. at his residence, the Mount, Sheffield, England.

Montgomery, Rev. John. *A Minister of the Free Church of Scotland.*

Montgomery, Miss M. M. *M. M. M.* An American writer.

Monti, Luigi, 1830–. *A Consul Abroad; Samuel Sampleton, Esq.* An Italian writer; instructor at Harv. Univ., Cambridge, 1854–59; and afterwards U. S. Consul at Palermo.

Mooar, George, D.D., 1830–. *G. M.* An American clergyman; b. at Andover, Mass.; Williams Coll., 1851; And. Theol. Sem., 1855; professor at the Pacific Theol. Sem., Oakland, Cal. (also acting pastor of the Plymouth Avenue Church, Oakland, 1874–77), 1870–83 *et seq.*

Moody, C. L., LL.D., F.A.S. *A Lady.* An English traveller and writer.

Mooney, A., and **George Henry.** *Two Brothers.* English writers.

Moore, Mrs. Clara (Jessup). *Clara Moreton; Mrs. Harriette Oxnard Ward.* An American poet and prose writer; b. in Westfield, Mass.; since 1855, of Philadelphia.

Moore, Clement Clarke, LL.D., 1779–1863. *A Citizen of New York; Columella; A Landholder.* An American scholar and linguist; b. in New York City; Columbia Coll., 1798; professor in the Epis. Theol. Sem., New York City, 1821–50; and Emeritus Professor, 1850–63.

Moore, Cornelius, A.M., 1806–. *One of the Craft.* An American journalist; b. in Hunterden County, New Jersey; editor of the New York "Masonic Magazine."

Moore, Edward, ,etc. *Adam Fitz Adam.* English political writers, of London.

Moore, Emily H. *Mignonette.* An American writer of the day.

Moore, Frederick A. *Eugene Sinclair.* An American book-editor, of Manchester, N.H.; now (1885) residing in Washington, D.C.

Moore, Mrs. H. J. *A Lady.* An American writer.

Moore, Jacob Bailey, 1797–1853. *A Freeman.* An American journalist at Concord, N.H.; b. in Andover, N.H.; postmaster at San Francisco, 1848–52; d. at Bellows Falls, Vt.

Moore, John, 1730–1802. *John Mordaunt.* A Scottish writer; b. at Stirling; practised till 1770 in Glasgow; afterwards travelled on the Continent, and resided in Paris and London; d. in London.

Moore, John C. *Peter Snooks.* An American journalist, of Boston.

Moore, Joseph S. *Adersey Curiosibhoy; The Parsee Merchant.* An American writer, of New York City.

Moore, Morris. *Verax.* An English writer on the fine arts.

Moore, Thomas, 1779–1852. *T***y M***e; Amacreon Moore; Thomas Brown, the Younger; Tom Crib; Thomas Little, Esq.; Mr. Minus; Captain Rock; Trismagistus Rustifustius; An Irishman; An Irish Gentleman; One of the Fancy.* A popular Irish poet; d. at Sloperton, near Devizes, where he had lived several years.

Moorhead, Mrs. ——. *A Female Friend.* An American poet of the 18th century.

Moosmüller, Oswald. *O. M.* An American writer, of Pennsylvania, of the day.

Moquin-Tandon, Christian Horace Benedict Alfred, 1804–64. *Fredol.* A French physician and dialect writer, of Toulouse; b. at Montpellier.

Moran, Carlo, 1845–. *Harry Bloodgood.* An American minstrel singer.

Moran, Dominick. *Dominick Murray.* An Irish actor.

Morandi, Felicita, 1830–. *Una Lombarda.* An Italian poet; b. at Varese; at the present time is inspector of the female schools of Northern Italy.

Morant, Rev. Philip, 1700–78. *A Clergyman.* An English clergyman; Rector of St. Mary's, Colchester; afterwards of Aldham, Essex.

Mordaunt, Charles, Earl of Peterborough, 1658–1735. *Matthew Smith.* An English statesman and military commander.

Mordecai, Samuel. *An Old Citizen.* An American writer, of Richmond, Va.

More, Hannah, 1744–1833. *H—— M——; Z.; One of the Laity.* An excellent English author; b. at Stapleton; with four sisters kept a private school at Bristol; d. in Windsor-terrace, Clifton.

More, John J. *Thomas Doyle.* An American writer.

Morehead, Robert, D.D., -1840. *Martinus Scriblerus.* A —— clergyman, of St. Paul's, Edinburgh; afterwards Rector of Easington, Yorkshire.

Morell, Sir Charles. *A Neighbour.* An English author and diplomatist of the 18th century; at one time ambassador from the British Settlements in India to the Great Mogul.

Morey, Charles. *John Cogitans.* An American writer.

Morford, Henry, 1823–81. *An Ex-Pension Agent; The Governor; A Live American.* An American novelist; b. in New Jersey.

Morgan, ——. *Nagrom.* An American journalist, of Boston.

Morgan, Dr. ——. *Philanthropus Oxoniensis.* An English controversial writer, of the first part of the 18th century.

Morgan, A. de. *A. B.* An English editor.

Morgan, Mrs. Ann Jane. *Ann Jane.* An English novelist.

Morgan, James, D.D. *J. M.* An English poet and clergyman.

Morgan, John. *Presbyter.* An American writer, of New York City (?).

Morgan, Lewis Henry, 1818–. *Skenandoah.* An American author; b. at Aurora, N.Y.; Union Coll., 1840; from 1844, a lawyer at Rochester, N.Y.

Morgan, Maurice, Esq., LL.D. *Malcolm McGregor.* An English poet of the 18th century.

Morgan, Lady Sydney Owenson, about 1783–1859. *Miss Owenson.* An Irish authoress; b. in Dublin; in 1812 was married to Sir Charles Morgan, whom she accompanied to France and Italy; d. in London.

Morgan, Thomas, -1743. *A Country Minister; Philalethes; A Protestant Dissenter; A Society of Gentlemen.* An English writer, of the first part of the 18th century; his views seem to have been those of the Radicals of the present day.

Morgan, Sir Thomas Charles, Bart., M.D., about 1783–1843. *T. C. M., M. B., F.S.L.* An English physician; b. in London; resided chiefly in Ireland, France, and Italy; d. in London.

Morgan, W. J. *Spokes.* An American bicycler.

Morgan, William, 1775–1826. *One of the Fraternity.* An American Freemason, who betrayed the secrets of the fraternity, and was probably murdered by members of that society in 1826.

Moriarty, Miss Ellen A. *Evangeline;*

Lucy Ellice. An American "Southland" poet; b. in England; in 1868, lived near Baton Rouge, La.

Moriarty, Rev. Patrick Eugene, 1804–75. *Ermite; Hierophilus.* An American writer.

Morier, James, 1780–1849. *Hadji Baba; Peregrine Persic.* A popular English novelist; spent about six years in Persia as secretary of legation and minister-plenipotentiary; d. at Brighton.

Morison, James, Esq., 1770–1840. *The Hygeist.* A Scottish patent medicine inventor; b. at Bognie, County Aberdeen; in 1828 he formed an establishment in London, to which he gave the title of "The British College of Health." The latter part of his life he resided at Paris. From the year 1830–40 he paid to the British Government $300,000 for medicine stamps. D. in Paris.

Morison, Rev. John. *A Clergyman thirteen years resident in the Interior of New South Wales.* An English writer of the day.

Morley, Frances (Talbot), Dowager Countess of, 1781–1857. *Richard Sucklethumkin Spruggins.* An English novelist; celebrated as a woman of wit and the "first of talkers."

Morley, John, 1838–. *A Young English Positivist.* An English author and editor; b. at Blackburn, Lancashire; from 1867 editor of the "Fortnightly Review"; M.P., 1869.

Morren, Nathaniel. *N. M.* A Scottish writer, of Edinburgh, on ecclesiastical history.

Morres, Hervey Redmond, 2d Viscount Mountmorres. *A Member of the Irish Parliament.* An Irish law writer.

Morris, Bezaleel. *B. M.* An English poet, of London, early in the 18th century.

Morris, Corbyn, Esq., F.R.S. *A Bystander; A Gentleman of Cambridge.* An English writer of the 18th century.

Morris, Rev. Edward Dafydd, D.D. *The Pastor.* An American Presbyt. clergyman, of Columbus, O., in 1861; Yale Coll., 1849; Professor of Ecclesiastical History in Lane Theol. School, 1874.

Morris, Rev. Francis Orpen, B.A. *A Yorkshire Clergyman.* An English divine; Worcester Coll., Oxford, 1833; Rector of Nunburnholme, Hayton, York., 1854–83 *et seq.*

Morris, James W. *Jacques Maurice; K. N. Pepper.* An American humorist and journalist, of New York City.

Morris, Rev. Joseph, M.A., F.S.A., 1791–1833. *J. M.* An English clergy-

MO

505

MO

man; Vicar of Feltham, Middlesex, 1818–33, where he died.

Morris, Patrick. *A Member of the H. of A. of Newfoundland.* A Newfoundland politician; for some time leader of the Liberal Party; and colonial treasurer in that island.

Morris, Richard, 1708–92. *Dick Spot, the Conjuror.* An English astrologer; d. at Oswestry, in Shropshire.

Morris, Samuel V., 1835–. *Hoosier.* An American lawyer and poet, in 1860, of Indianapolis, Indiana.

Morrison, John, D.D., 1749–98. *Musæus.* A Scottish poet and minister, at Canisbay, Caithness-shire.

Morrison, Rev. John. *A Clergyman.* An English writer.

Morrison, Lieut. Richard James. *Zadkiel; Zadkiel the Seer; Zadkiel Tao Sze.* An English astrologer.

Morse, F. L. *F. L. M.* An American writer of the day.

Morse, Freeman H., 1807–. *The American Consul at London.* An American statesman; b. at Bath, Me.; M.C., 1843–45; American Consul in London, 1861–.

Morse, Rev. Jason, 1821–61. *The Pastor.* An American Cong. clergyman; b. in Southbridge, Mass.; Amherst Coll., 1845; pastor at Brimfield, Mass., 1849–61, and d. there.

Morse, Jedidiah, D.D., 1761–1826. *An Inhabitant of New England.* An eminent American clergyman; b. in Woodstock, Conn.; Yale Coll., 1783; at Charlestown, Mass., 1789–1820; d. at New Haven.

Morse, Samuel Finley Breese, LL.D., 1791–1872. *B.; An American; Brutus.* An eminent American artist; b. in Charlestown, Mass.; Yale Coll., 1810; inventor of the electric telegraph; d. in New York City.

Morse, Sidney Edwards, A.M., 1794–1871. *An American.* An American journalist; b. in Charlestown, Mass.; Yale Coll., 1811; editor of the Boston "Recorder," about 1815–23; founder and editor of the "New York Observer," 1823–71; d. in New York City.

Mortier, Arnold, –1885. *Un Monsieur de l'Orchestre.* A French dramatic critic, of Paris.

Mortimer, J. *J. M.* An American (?) writer, at Paris.

Mortimer, John. *J. M., Esq., F.R.S.* An English writer, of the first part of the 18th century.

Mortimer, Mrs. N. E. *Rose Rayland.* An American writer.

Mortimer, Thomas, Esq., 1730–1810. *Philanthropos.* An English writer; at one time British Consul at Ostend; d. in Clarendon-square, Somers-town.

Morton, Mrs. Sarah Wentworth (Apthorp), 1759–1846. *Philenia.* An American poet; b. in Braintree, Mass.; wife of Perez Morton; d. at Quincy, Mass.

Moser, Joseph, Esq., 1748–1819. *A Barber; Timothy Twig, Esq.* An English civilian and *littérateur*, of London; a leading correspondent of the "European Magazine" and other periodicals, and a miscellaneous writer; b. and d. in London.

Moses, W. S. *A. M., Oxon.* An English writer of the day.

Mosher, L. E. *Hank Wagoner.* An American writer of the day.

Motherwell, William, 1797–1835. *Isaac Brown.* A popular Scottish poet and journalist; b. and d. in Glasgow; connected with the "Glasgow Courier," 1830–35.

Mott, Mrs. Abigail. *A Mother.* An American Friend, of New York.

Mott, Albert Julius. *A. J. Barrowcliffe.* An English novelist, of Liverpool.

Mott, Jordan L. *A Member of the Executive Committee.* An American inventor.

Mottley, John, 1692–1750. *A Gentleman; Robert Seymour, of the Inner Temple; Joe Miller.* An old English writer; the real author of "Joe Miller's Jests"; for some years held a public office under the British Government.

Moule, Rev. Henry, M.A., 1801–. *A Country Parson.* An English clergyman; b. at Melksham, Wilts.; B.A., Cambridge, 1821; for some years chaplain to the troops in Dorchester barracks.

Moule, Rev. Joseph. *A Member of the Congregation.* A Scottish minister.

Moulton, Mrs. Ellen Louise (Chandler), 1835–. *Ellen Louise; L. C. M.* An American writer; b. in Pomfret, Conn.; in 1855 married William U. Moulton, a Boston journalist.

Moultrie, Rev. Gerard, M.A. *M.; D. P.; Desiderius Pastor.* An English clergyman and hymn-writer; son of Rev. John Moultrie; Exeter Coll., Oxford, 1851; Vicar of Southleigh, Witney, 1869–83 *et seq.*

Moultrie, Rev. John, 1800–74. *Gerard Montgomery.* An English poet and journalist; b. in London; educ. at Eton and Cambridge, 1823; d. at Rugby.

Mounsey, Thomas. *T. M.* An English Friend, of Sunderland.

Mountain, George Jehoshaphat, D.D., 1789–1863. *The Bishop of Montreal.* An American Prot. prelate; b. at Quebec, Canada; Bishop of Montreal, 1836; and of Quebec, 1850; d. near Quebec.

Mountain, Jacob, D.D., 1750–1825. *Jacob, Lord Bishop of Quebec.* An American prelate; b. at Thwaite Hall, Norfolk, Eng.; Bishop of Quebec, 1793–1825; d. near Quebec.

Mountain, Jacob Henry Brooke, D.D. *J. H. B. M.* An English clergyman; Rector of Blunham, 1831–70 *et seq.;* prebendary in Lincoln Cathedral, 1812.

Mowatt, Mrs. **Anna Cora (Ogden).** — See "Ritchie, Mrs. A. C. (O. M.)."

Mountenay, Barclay de. *B. A.* An English political writer.

Mountmorres, Harvey Redmond Morres, 2d Lord Viscount, 1743–97. *Themistocles.* An Irish peer, of Castle Morres, Co. Kilkenny; d. in York-street, St. James Square, London. — See "Morres, H. R."

Mowbray, Rev. **Thomas.** *T. M.* A Scottish minister; a suffering presbyter of the Church of Scotland.

Moxon, Edward, Esq., 1801–58. *E. M.* An English poet and publisher, of London; d. at Putney Heath, Surrey.

Mudford, William, 1782–1848. *Attalus; Martin Gribaldus Swammerdam.* An English journalist; b. in London; for many years editor of the "London Courier"; translator and author.

Mudge, Henry, 1806–74. *A Foe to Ignorance; One of Themselves; A Surgeon, M. R. C. S.; L. A. C.* An English temperance advocate; b. and d. at Bodmin; educ. at St. Bartholomew's Hospital, London.

Mudie, Robert, 1777–1842. *Laurence Langshank, Gent.; A Modern Greek.* A Scottish naturalist; b. in Forfarshire; from 1820, of London, where he died.

Mueller, Friedrich Max, LL.D., 1823–. *An Alien; Philindus.* An eminent German orientalist; b. at Dessau; Professor at Oxford Univ., 1850–75; has, since that time, resided alternately in England and Germany.

Müller, Karl, 1819–. *Otfried Mylius.* A German author; b. at Stuttgart; in 1840 entered the Univ. of Tübingen, where he completed his education; for 26 years from 1842 conducted the "Erheiterungen" of his time; and became in 1868 co-editor and co-writer of the "Allgemeine Familienzeitung," etc.

Münch-Bellinghausen, Eligius Franz Josef, Freiherr von, 1806–72. *Friedrich Halm.* A German poet; b. at Krakau; went early to Vienna, where he chiefly spent his life and where he died.

Muhlenberg, William Augustus, D.D., 1796–1877. *One of the Memorialists;* An American clergyman; b. in Pennsylvania; Superintendent and Rector of St. Luke's Hospital, 1858–77.

Muir, John, D.C.L., 1810–. *J. M.; A Layman.* A Scottish orientalist; b. at Glasgow; in 1828 entered the East India Civil Service; in 1862 endowed a chair of Sanscrit, etc., at the Univ. of Edinburgh, with £5000.

Muir, Thomas S. *T. S. M.; Unda.* A Scottish writer of the day.

Muir, William. *An Attorney.* A Scottish writer.

Muldoon, William H. *Mul; The Man about Town.* An American journalist, of New York City.

Mullany, Patrick F., 1847. *B. A. M.; Brother Azarias.* An American R. C. clergyman; Professor of English in the Rock Hill Coll., Ellicott City, Md.

Mumford, Miss **Angelina S.** *Picciola.* An American poet, of New York City; sister of Mrs. Mary L. Seward.

Mundt, Klara Müller, 1814–73. *Luise Mühlbach.* A German novelist; b. at Neubrandenburg; wife of Theodor Mundt, of Berlin, where she died.

Munsell, Joel, 1809–80. *Arthur Prynne.* An American author, printer, and publisher, of Albany; b. at North-field, Mass.; d. in Albany.

Murat, Paul Hyppolite de. *Paul Hyppolite de M***.* A French writer.

Murden, Mrs. **Eliza.** *A Lady of Charleston, S.C.* An American poet.

Murfree, Miss **Mary Noailles.** *Charles Egbert Craddock.* An American novelist; b. in Nashville, Tenn., where she lived till after the war, when the family removed to Murfreesborough, and three or four years ago to the vicinity of St. Louis, Mo.

Murphy, Arthur, Esq., 1727–1805. *Charles Ranger, Esq.* An Irish journalist and dramatist; "disliking his occupation as a merchant, unsuccessful as a player, an almost briefless barrister, a political writer of little depth (although more successful as a dramatist and biographer), and a commissioner of bankrupts, died in 1805 in the enjoyment of a pension of £200 a year." B. in Clooniquin, near Elphin, Co. Roscommon; lived and d. in London.

Murphy, George Mollett. *An Un-*

known. An English satirist of the 19th century.

Murphy, Henry Crude, 1810–82. *The Translator*. An American lawyer and *littérateur;* b. in Brooklyn, N.Y.; practised his profession in that city; M.C., 1843–49; d. in Brooklyn.

Murphy, James Cavanah, about 1760–1816. *Dominick Vandelli, LL.D.* An Irish traveller, author, and architectural artist.

Murphy, Jeremiah Daniel, Esq., 1805–24. *Jacobus Dapiferus, Corcagiensis.* An Irish poet and linguist; b. in Cork. He spoke or wrote the Greek, Latin, French, Spanish, Portuguese, German, and Irish languages with the utmost fluency and precision, and was profoundly versed in their respective literatures. D. in Cork.

Murray, Alexander. *A. M., a Layman*. A Scottish theological writer.

Murray, Daniel. *A Pious Lawyer.* An American writer; once a lieutenant in the American navy.

Murray, Rev. David. *Clericus*. A Scottish minister, of Dysart.

Murray, Mrs. Elizabeth. *An Artist.* An English writer on the fine arts.

Murray, Eustace Clare Grenville, –1881. *Trois-Étoiles; The Roving Englishman; Duke of Scampington.* An English journalist and miscellaneous writer; d. at Passy.

Murray, Mrs. Hannah L. *H. L. M.* An American writer.

Murray, James. *James B. Manson, of Bannockburn.* A Scottish writer.

Murray, Rev. James, –1782. *J. M.; A Clergyman; An Impartial Hand; Ahab Salem.* An English Dissenter, of Newcastle.

Murray, John, 1778–1843. ✱✱✱✱ ✱✱✱✱✱✱. An English gentleman.

Murray, John, F.S.A., F.L.S., F.G.R.S. *A Fellow of the Linnæar Society.* An English author.

Murray, Sir John Archibald, Lord Murray. *A Member of the Court; J. A. M.* A Scottish writer.

Murray, Mrs. Judith (Sargent), 1751–1820. *Constantia*. An American writer; wife of Rev. John Murray, of Boston.

Murray, Nicholas, D.D., 1802–62.

Kirwan. An American **Presbyt.** clergyman; b. in Ireland; Williams Coll., 1826; Princeton Theol. Sem., 1829; pastor of the First Presbyt. Church in Elizabethtown, N.J., 1834–62.

Murray, Patrick, 5th Lord Elibank. *A Peer of Scotland; A Peer of the Realm; A Person of Distinction.* A Scottish nobleman.

Murray, William Vans. *A Citizen of the United States.* An American political writer.

Mursell, Rev. Arthur. *John Search.* An English writer.

Musgrave, Rev. George, M.A. *Viator Verax*. An English clergyman; B.N.C., Oxford, 1819; Vicar of Borden, Kent, 1838–54; resident at Borden Hall, Kent, 1883 *et seq.*

Musset, Louis Charles Alfred de, 1810–57. *A. D. M.* A French poet; b. and d. in Paris; became a leader in the Romantic school of literature; librarian of the Ministry of the Interior under Louis Philippe.

Mussey, Benjamin Bussey, 1805–57. *A Proprietor of said Church.* An American publisher and bookseller, of Boston; b. in Bradford, Vt.; d. in Boston.

Musson, Eugène. *Un Créole de la Louisiane*. An American Southern writer.

Muybridge, E. J. *Helios*. An American writer.

Muzaková, Johanna, 1830–. *Caroline Světlá*. A Bohemian writer; b. in Prague; in 1871 she founded in her native city a society for the education of Bohemian girls.

Muzzey, Rev. Artemas Bowers. *A. B. M.* An American clergyman; **Harv.** Univ., 1824; resident at Newburyport and Cambridge, Mass., from 1830.

Myer, Albert J., 1828–80. *Old Prob.* An American meteorologist, of the Signal Office, Washington, D.C.; d. at Buffalo, N.Y.

Myers, Allen O. *Pickaway*. An American journalist.

Myers, P. N. *Norb*. An American bicycler, of Covington, Ky.

Myers, Peter Hamilton, 1812–. *First of the Knickerbockers.* An American lawyer and novelist; b. at Herkimer, N.Y.; in 1861, of Brooklyn, N.Y.

N.

Naghten, Frederick, Esq., B.A., 1822–45. *A Late Graduate of Oxford.* An English poet; Corpus Christi, Oxford; d. at Crofton House.

Nagle, J. E., M.D. *Cousin Nourma.*

Nairn, Lady **Carolina Oliphant,** 1766–1845. *B. B.; Flower of Strathearn.* A Scottish poet; b. at Gask, Perthshire; became a poet by attempting to write for the popular tunes of the peasantry better words than the loose and ribald lines which accompanied so many of them; in 1806 she married William Murray Nairn, who became 5th Lord Nairn; d. in her native place. — See Notes and Queries, 3d Ser. XII. 1867.

Naish, William. *W. N.* An English biographer.

Napier, Adm. Sir **Charles,** K.C.B., 1786–1860. *A Flag Officer of Her Majesty's Fleet.* A British seaman; b. at Merchistoun-castle, Co. Sterling; entered the navy in 1799; M.P. for Southwark, 1855–60; d. at Merchistoun-Hall, Horndean, Hants.

Napier, Sir **Charles James,** G.C.B., 1782–1853. *The Bayard of India.* An eminent British general; in India, 1841–47 and 1849–50; b. at Whitehall, Westminster; d. at his seat at Oatlands, near Portsmouth.

Napollon, Margarita Ernesta, 1840–. *E.; D'Inc.* A French-Italian writer; b. in Paris; writes for the Italian journals.

Nares, Edward, D.D., D.C.L., 1762–1841. *It matters not who; Thinks I to Myself, Who?* An English clergyman; b. in London; Fellow of Merton Coll., Oxford, 1788; Professor of Modern History and Modern Languages in the Univ. of Oxford, 1814–41; d. at Biddenden, in Kent.

Naron, L. N. *Chickasaw, the Scout.* An American writer.

Nary, Cornelius, 1660–1738. *C. N., C.F.C.D.* An Irish R. C. divine of great learning; b. in the Co. of Kildare.

Nash, Thomas, 1845–85. *A First Class Man of Balliol College, Oxford; Tom Palatine.* An English writer, well known in the political and literary circles of Manchester; b. and educ. in that city; grad. at Balliol Coll., Oxford; d. in his native city.

Nash, Willard G. *Dusty.* An American writer.

Nason, Daniel. *A Citizen of Cambridgeport.* An American writer; a carpenter by trade.

Nason, Rev. **Elias,** A.M., 1811–. *W. Waybridge.* An American minister; b. at Wrentham, Mass.; Brown Univ., 1835; has given much time to literary pursuits.

Navarro, Joachim. *J. N.* A Spanish writer.

Neal, Mrs. **Alice (Bradley).** — See "Haven, Mrs. A. (B. N.)."

Neal, Rev. **Daniel,** 1678–1743. *A Dissenter.* An English minister; b. in London; pastor in Jewin Street, in that city.

Neal, John, 1793–1876. *Will Adams; Paul Allen; Logan; Jehu O'Cataract; A New Englander over the Sea.* An American editor, lecturer, lawyer, poet, novelist, and teacher of gymnastics, of Portland, Me.; b. and d. in that city.

Neal, Nathaniel. *A Layman.* An English writer, of the first half of the 18th century; an attorney; and Secretary to the Million Bank.

Neal, Sir **Paul.** *Sidrophel.*

Neale, Rev. **Erskine,** M.A., about 1805–. *A Working Clergyman; A Coroner's Clerk; A Country Curate; A Gaol Chaplain.* An English writer of religious fiction; B.A., Cambridge, 1828; Vicar of Exning (w. Lanwade), Newmarket, 1854–83 et seq.

Neale, John Mason, D.D., 1818–66. *Aurelius Gratianus; Two Priests of the Church of England.* An English poet and theologian; b. in London; Trin. Coll., Cambridge, 1840; warden of Sackville Coll., East Grimstead, 1846–66, where he died.

Neale, W. Johnson. *Cavendish.* An English novelist.

Needham, Mrs. **Elizabeth Allen (Annable).** *E. A. A.* An American religious writer of the day.

Neild, James Edward. *John Brown.* An English colonial Shaksperian critic, of Melbourne.

Neill, Rev. **Edward Duffield,** 1823–. *E. D. N.* An American clergyman; b. in Philadelphia; Amherst Coll., 1842; Andover Theol. Sem., 1846; private secretary to President Johnson, 1867–68; and then consul at Dublin.

Neilson, Mrs. **Andrew.** *A Lady Resident near the Alma.* An English writer.

Nelson, Charles Alexander, A.M., 1839–. *C. A. N.; N. A. B.; Chelsea; Manhattan.* An American bibliographer;

b. at Calais, Me.; is now (1885) employed in the Astor Library, New York City.

Nelson, D. *A Delaware Waggoner.* An American writer.

Nelson, John. *Johannes Senilis.* An English writer of the day, on botany.

Nelson, William Nelson, D.D., 1st Earl, 1757–1835. *Earl N.* An English nobleman; brother and successor of Horatio Nelson; d. in London.

Nesmith, John, 1793–1869. *An Old Merchant.* An American manufacturer; b. in Londonderry, N.H.; removed in 1831 to Lowell, Mass.; Lieutenant-Governor of Massachusetts, 1862.

Ness, Richard Derby, 1796–1867. *P. H.* An English writer; son of the Rev. Dr. Richard Ness, Rector of West Parley, Dorset.

Netherlands. *Nicholas Frog.*

Nettle, G. *A Seven Years' Resident, etc.* An English writer.

Newbery, John. *Mrs. Mary Midnight.* An English printer and publisher, of London, early in the 19th century.

Newbould, Mrs. Susanna, 1821–188–. *Aunt Sue.* An American writer for the young; b. near London; for 40 years a resident of Brooklyn, N.Y.

Newell, Andrew. *An Inhabitant of Boston.* An American writer; at one time a printer in Boston; later, a teacher of navigation.

Newell, Charles M. *Capt. B. Barnacle.* An American writer of the day.

Newell, Mrs. Dolores A. (Fuertos Menken Heenan), 1835–68. *Indigina.*

Newell, E. J. *Vindex.* An American writer.

Newell, Robert Henry, 1836–. *Orpheus C. Kerr.* An American humorist; b. in New York City; editor of the New York "Hearth and Home" since 1874.

Newenham, Thomas. *T*****s N******m; One of the Laity of the Church of England.* An English writer of the 19th century; at one time an M.P.

Newhall, C. S. *Carl.* An American writer of the day.

Newhall, James Robinson. *Obadiah Oldpath.* An American lawyer; b. in Lynn, Mass.; entered upon the practice of his profession in that city in 1847; judge of the Lynn police court, 1866–76 et seq.

Newington, Samuel, M.D. *Sigma.* An English writer of the 19th century.

Newman, Mrs. E. E. *Evangeline.* An American writer of the day.

Newman, Edward, 1801–76. *Rusticus.* An English naturalist, who for many years made pedestrian tours through England, Wales, Scotland, and Ireland; b. at Hampstead, Middlesex.

Newman, John Henry, D.D., 1801–. *δ; D.; J. H. N.; Catholicus; Contributor to Tracts for the Times.* An eminent English theologian; b. in London; educ. at Oxford; became a Roman Catholic in 1845; head of the R. C. school at Egbaston.

Newman, Mrs. May Wentworth. *May Wentworth.* An Irish (?) novelist of the day.

Newman, Rev. M. W. *Exile of Erin.* An Irish-American journalist, of New York City.

Newton, Rev. John, 1725–1807. *A Minister of the Church of England.* An English clergyman; b. in London; Curate of Olney, Bucks., 1764–80; held a living in London, 1780–1807, where he died.

Niboyet, Jean Alexander Paulin, 1828–. *Paulin M. Fortunio.* A French novelist; b. at Mâcon; was for a time consul at Chicago from 1870; afterwards at Newcastle; and at Mannheim, 1879–80 et seq.

Nichol, John, 1833–. *J. N.* A Scottish poet and man of letters; b. in Montrose; towards the close of the civil war visited the United States; since 1861 Professor of English Literature and Language at Glasgow.

Nicholas, John. *Decius.* An American politician.

Nicholas, Samuel Smith, 1796–1869. *A Kentuckian.* An American jurist; b. at Lexington, Ky.; at first a merchant in New Orleans; afterwards practised law in Louisville, Ky.; Judge of the Court of Appeals from 1831; d. in Louisville.

Nichols, John, Esq., F.S.A., 1745–1826. *J. N.; Alphonso; The Cobbler of Alsatia; Eugenio; M. Green; A London Antiquary.* An eminent English man of letters; b. at Islington; editor of the "Gentleman's Magazine," 1778–1826; d. in London.

Nichols, John Bowyer, Esq., F.S.A., 1779–1863. *J. B. N.; N. R. S.* An English publisher and literary antiquary; b. in London; d. at his residence, Hanger Vale, Ealing, Middlesex.

Nichols, Mrs. Mary (Neal Sergeant Gove), 1810–. *Mary Orme.* An American lecturer and writer; b. at Goffstown, N.H.; wife of Dr. Thos. L. Nichols, of New York City.

Nichols, Philip. *A Proprietor of that Work.* An English author.

Nichols, Mrs. Rebecca S. (Reed),

about 1818–. *Ellen; Kate Cleaveland.* An American poet and journalist, of Cincinnati; b. at Greenwich, N.J.; in 1838 married Willard Nichols at Louisville, Ky.

Nichols, Thomas. *Asmodeus.* An American (?) writer of the day.

Nichols, Thomas. *T. Nickle Nichols.* An English writer.

Nicholson, Mrs. **Eliza Jane (Poitevent).** *Eliza; Pearl Rivers.* An American writer of the day.

Nicholson, Henry Joseph Boone, D.D. *H. J. B. N.* An English clergyman; Rector of St. Alban's, Herts., 1835–60 *et seq.*

Nicholson, William, 1782–1849. *The Galloway Poet.* A Scottish poet; d. at Kildarroch, Borgue.

Nickerson, Miss **Susan D.** *A Lady of Boston.*

Nicklin, Philip Houlbrooke, A.M., 1786–1842. *Peregrine Prolix.* An American lawyer, bookseller, and miscellaneous writer, of Philadelphia; b. in Philadelphia; New Jersey Coll., 1804; studied law, but did not practise.

Nickolls, Rev. **Robert Boucher,** LL.D., 1743–1814. *Eusebius.* An English clergyman; b. in the West Indies; Rector of Stoney Staunton, Leicestershire, from 1779; and Dean of Middleham in Yorkshire; had been chaplain of the 5th Regiment Foot in the war in America; d. at Stoney Staunton.

Nicol, Martha. *A Lady.* An English writer.

Nicolaïe, Louis François, 1811–79. *Clairville.* A French actor and dramatist, of Paris.

Nicolas, Sir **Nicholas Harris,** Knt., 1799–1848. *Clionas.* An eminent English antiquary and historian; b. at East Looe, in Cornwall; joint editor of the "Retrospective Review" from 1826; d. at Capé Cure, near Boulogne.

Nicolas, Lady **Sarah (Davison).** *A Soldier's Daughter.* An English lady: b. at Loughton-in-Essex; married Sir Nicholas Harris Nicolas in 1822.

Nightingale, Mrs. **A. E. (Parry).** *A Daughter of the Late Author of the "Cambrian Plutarch."* An English lady; daughter of John Humphreys, a barrister of London.

Nightingale, Rev. **Joseph,** 1775–1824. *A Committee Man; J. Elagnitin.* An English humorous poet; b. at Chowbert, Lancashire; settled in London, where he supported himself by literary labor; d. in London.

Nind, Rev. **William,** 1810–56. *W. N.* An English poet and clergyman;

Vicar of Cherryhinton; Fellow of St. Peter's Coll., Cambridge; d. in Paris.

Nisbet, Richard. *A West Indian.* A British colonial writer of the last century, of the Island of Nevis.

Nixon, Rev. **Edward John,** B.A. *A Member of the Univ. of Camb.* An English clergyman; chaplain to the London Hospital, 1852–60 *et seq.*

Noah, Mordecai Manuel, 1785–1851. *Howard; Muly Malack.* An American journalist; b. in Philadelphia; became a lawyer in Charleston, S.C.; in 1815 removed to New York City, where he died.

Noé, Comte **Amédée de,** 1819–79. *Cham.* A French caricaturist, of Paris, where he died.

Nogaret, François Félix, 1740–1830. *Aristénète.* A French man of letters, of Paris.

Nokes, William. *A Catholick.* An English religious writer, of the first part of the 18th century.

Nolan, Rev. **Frederick,** LL.D., F.R.S., 1784–1864. *A Reformer; Sarah Search; N. A. Vigors, Jun.* An Irish clergyman; b. at Old Rathmines Castle, County Dublin; Vicar of Prittlewell, Essex, 1822–64; d. at Geraldstoun House, Navan.

Nolan, Louis Edward. *Kenner Garrard.* A brave English officer; killed in the famous charge at the battle of Balaklava.

Noland, Charles Fenton Mercer, 1812–58. *N. of Arkansas; Pete Whetstone.* An American humorist; once governor of Arkansas; d. at Little Rock, Ark.

Nordhoff, Charles, 1830–. *A Boy; A Sailor; A Sailor Boy; Charles Holmes.* A German-American journalist; b. at Erwittle, Westphalia; came to the United States when a child; is now resident in New York City, attached to the N.Y. "Herald."

Norris, Henry, –1731. *H. N.* An English actor; performed for many years in the theatres of London and Dublin; but, later in life, retired to York, where he died.

Norris, Randal. *R. N.* An English lawyer; Sub-Treasurer Inner Temple, London.

North, ——. *An Embryo M.P.* An English novelist.

North, Edward, 1820–. *Dix Quævidi.* An eminent American scholar; b. at Berlin, Conn.; Hamilton Coll., 1841; Professor of Ancient Languages there, 1843–85 *et seq.*

North, Elisha, M.D. *Uncle Toby.* An American physician, of Connecticut.

North, Frederic, 2d Earl of Guilford (more familiarly known as Lord North), 1732–92. *Northelia.* An eminent English statesman; in 1783 he and Mr. Fox became Secretaries (the famous "Coalition") in the ministry formed by the Duke of Portland.

North, John, Esq., –1819. *Palermo.* An eminent English bibliomaniac; possessed a very valuable collection of missals and printed books; d. at East Acton.

North, Hon. **Roger,** 1650–1733. *A Person of Honour.* An English lawyer; Attorney-General to James II.; and Steward of the Courts of Archbishop Sheldon.

Northcote, Sir **Stafford Henry,** 8th Bart., 1818–. *Sir Warwick West End.* An English statesman; President of the Board of Trade, 1866–67; Secretary for India, 1867–68; Chancellor of the Exchequer from 1874.

Northend, William Dummer, 1823–. *W. D. N.* An American lawyer; b. in Newbury, Mass.; Bowdoin Coll., 1843; admitted to the Bar in 1845; has practised his profession in Salem, Mass., since 1847.

Northmore, Thomas, Esq., F.A.S. *Phileleutherus Devoniensis.* An English poet and miscellaneous writer; b. near Exeter; educ. at Jesus Coll., Cambridge; resided all his life on his estate, devoting much time to mechanics, literature, and politics.

Northrup, C. B. *N.; A Gentleman of South Carolina; The Outcast.* An American poet and politician.

Norton, Hon. Mrs. **Caroline Elizabeth Sarah (Sheridan),** 1808–77. *Libertas.* An eminent English poet and novelist; afterwards Mrs. Stirling-Maxwell, which see.

Norton, Charles Eliot, A.M., 1827–. *C. E. N.* An American man of letters; b. at Cambridge, Mass.; Harv. Univ., 1846; professor at Harv. Univ., Cambridge, 1875–85 *et seq.*

Norton, Edward. *Honestus.* An English writer, chiefly on finance.

Norton, James. *A Layman.* An English colonial writer, of New South Wales.

Norweb, Mrs. **Janetta (Scott),** –1817. *Janetta.* An unfortunate English widow; daughter of John Scott, Esq., a wealthy merchant of Madeira; d. in the poorhouse at Brigg.

Norwood, Abraham. *Abraham.* An American humorist (?).

Notley, Mrs. **Frances Eliza (Millett).** *Frances Derrick.* An English writer of the day.

Nott, Charles C. *An Officer in the Field.* An American soldier.

Nott, Henry Junius, 1797–1837. *Thomas Singularity; A Journeyman Printer.* An American lawyer and man of letters; b. in South Carolina; South Carolina Coll., 1812; professor in the South Carolina Coll., 1821–34. On his return from Europe, with his wife, on the steamer "Home," they were wrecked on the coast of North Carolina.

Nott, Dr. **John,** 1751–1826. *Mons. Vestris, Sen.* An English poet, scholar, and physician; b. at Worcester; in 1793 settled at Bristol Hot Wells, and d. there.

Novice, George William. *An Artist.* A Scottish writer of the day.

Novikoff, Olga de Kiréef, 1842–. *O. K.; A Russian Lady.* A Russian writer; b. at Moscow; made her first appearance in letters in 1876; has written for English papers, and an article in "Fraser's Magazine," in March, 1880.

Nowell, Mrs. **Harriett P. (Hardy).** *May Mannering.* An American writer of the day.

Noy, William, 1842–. *W. N.; W. Pendrea.* An English literary antiquary; b. in Penzance; contributor to "Notes and Queries," etc., 1865–71 *et seq.* (?).

Noyce, Elisha. *Uncle John.* An American (?) writer.

Noyes, Charles Henry, 1849–. *Charles Quiet.* An American lawyer and poet, of Warren, Penn.

Noyes, E. Herbert. *Norval; Saxon.* An American writer.

Noyes, James Oscar, M.D., 1829–. *Our Own Correspondent.* An American journalist; b. at Owasco, N.Y.; became a surgeon in the Turkish army, and a contributor to New York and London papers, and editor of the New York "Knickerbocker."

Noyes, Mrs. **Jane (McElhinney).** *Ada Clare.* An American actress and writer for periodical literature; in 1868, married Mr. J. F. Noyes, of Houston, Tex.

Nugent, George Nugent Grenville, Baron, 1788–1850. *John Hampden.* An English writer; b. at Buckingham Castle; educ. at Oxford; entered Parliament in 1812, and was again returned in 1847; d. at his seat, Lillies, Bucks.

Nugent, Lord and Lady. *The Lord and Lady there.*

Nunes, Joseph Q. *A Diplomat.* An American lawyer; once of Philadelphia, afterwards of California.

Nutt, Frederic, Esq. *A Person Late*

Apprentice, etc. An English confectioner, of the 18th century.

Nutting, H. *Cypher.* An English arithmetician.

Nutting, Mary O. *Mary Barrett.* An American writer.

Nye, E. W. *Bill Nye.* An American journalist, of Detroit (?).

O.

Oakes, Miss Elizabeth. — See "Smith, Mrs. E. (O)."

Oakes, James, 1807–78. *Acorn.* An American merchant, of Boston; for 50 years an intimate friend of Edwin Forrest.

Oakley, Frederick. *Joshua Short.*

O'Beirne, Rt. Rev. Thomas Lewis, D.D., Bishop of Meath, about 1748–1822. *A Consistent Whig; A Country Gentleman; An Irish Dignitary.* An Irish clergyman; chaplain in the fleet under Lord Howe; d. in Ireland.

Obolenski, Yevgenii. *Un Exilé.* A Russian exile.

O'Brien, Mrs. H. *Zell.* An American writer for the young, of the day.

O'Brien, J. W. *Le correspondant du "Canadien."* A Canadian traveller.

O'Brien, John, 1836–. *John T. Raymond.* An American actor; b. in Buffalo, N.Y.; first appeared at Rochester, N.Y., in 1853; in London, 1867.

O'Brien, Miss Mary. *Julia Scott.* An American writer, of St. Josephs, Mo.

Observator. *Humphrey Medlecott.* Supposed editor.

O'Connor, Eva M. *E. M. O'C.* An American bibliographer of the day.

O'Connor, John. *John Morris.* An American writer of the day.

O'Connor, Roger. *Captain Rock.* An Irish writer. — See "O'Sullivan, Mortimer."

O'Connor, Thomas. *An Impartial Reviewer.* An American political writer.

O'Conor, Charles, D.D., 1760–1828. *Columbanus.* An Irish R. C. divine; editor and translator of the "Irish Chronicles," and librarian to the Duke of Buckingham; acquired the *soubriquet* of Columbanus O'Conor; d. at Belanagare, the seat of his brother, O'Conor Don.

O'Conor, Charles P. *Corporal John; The Irish Peasant Poet.* An Irish poet.

O'Conor, E. *E. O'C.* An Irish philologist.

Odell, Jonathan, A.M. *Camillo Querno, Poet-Laureate to the Congress.* An English poet; a schoolmaster at Epsom.

Odling, Mrs. Elizabeth Mary (Smee). *His Daughter.* An English writer; daughter of Alfred Smee, the artist.

Oertel, Philipp Friedrich Wilhelm, 1798–1867. *W. O. von Horn.* A German man of letters, of Wiesbaden, 1863–67.

Oertzen, Georg, Baron von, 1829–. *Ludwig Robert.* A German poet; b. at the paternal country seat, Brunn, in Mecklenburg-Strelitz; educ. at home, at Wittenberg and at Bonn, at Göttingen and Berlin. In 1879, he was German consul-general at New York, and in 1880 at Constantinople.

O'Ferrall, Simon Ansley, Esq., 1780–1844. *S. A. Ferrall.* An Irish lawyer and traveller; b. at Dublin; spent two years in travel in the United States, 1828–30; in 1835 was called to the English Bar, at Gray's Inn, and practised his profession in London, where he died.

Offord, Cecil. *Harold Thornton.* An English writer.

O'Flaherty, Barney, 1823–76. *Barney Williams.* An Irish actor; b. in Cork; appeared in New York City in 1836; in London in 1855.

O'Francis, Mrs. Mary. *Margaret Blount.* An American writer of the day.

Ogden, Miss Anna Cora. — See "Ritchie, Mrs. A. C. (O. M.)."

Ogden, George W. *Notus Nimini.* An American writer, of New Bedford, Mass. (?).

Ogden, James de Peyster. *Publius.* An American writer on currency, etc.

Ogden, John Cosens, D.D., –1800. *A Citizen of the United States.* An American clergyman; b. in New Jersey; New Jersey Coll., 1770; rector at Portsmouth, N.H., 1786–93; d. at Chestertown, Md.

Ogden, R. L. *Podgers.* An American sporting writer.

Ogilvie, Jane. *A Labourer for Peace.* A Scottish religious writer.

Ogle, Annie. *Ashford Owen.* An English novelist of the day.

Ogle, George, –1746. *The Late Colonel Henry Mordaunt.* An English poetical translator.

O'Hanlon, Rev. John, M.R.I.A. *Lageniensis.* An Irish editor and writer of the day.

O'Harris, Lee. *Larry O'Hannegan.*

O'Kelly, Col. Charles. *A Herald Correspondent.* An Irish writer of the day.

Olcott, E. M. *Katherine Prevorst.* An American writer of the day.

Oldisworth, William, –1734. *A Layman; Walter Wagstaffe, Esq.* An English writer in the reigns of Queen Anne and George I.

Oldmixon, John, 1673–1742. *J. O.; A Friend; Mr. Omicron, "the Unborn Poet"; One very near akin to the Author of "the Tale of a Tub."* An early English writer for the stage; b. near Bridgewater, Somersetshire; was the author of poems and historical works; d. in London.

Oldys, William, 1696–1761. *W. O.; Mr. Thomas Betterton; Henry Stonecastle.* An English literary antiquary; librarian to Robert Harley, Earl of Oxford, and Norrey King-at-Arms; noted for his love of "old books" and "old wine."

Oliphant, ——. *Timothy Touchstone.* An English scholar; one of the editors, under this pseud., of the "Trifler"; at Westminster School in 1788; afterwards a student of Trin. Coll., Cambridge.

Oliphant, Caroline. — See "Nairn, the Baroness."

Oliphant, Laurence, 1829–. *Irene Macgillicuddy; Sionara, a Japanese Traveller.* An English miscellaneous writer; manager of the American interests of the Direct Cable Company, 1873–75.

Oliphant, Mrs. Margaret O. (Wilson), 1818–. *Margaret Maitland, of Sunnyside.* A popular English novelist; b. in Liverpool.

Oliver, Rev. Daniel, A.M., 1753–1840. *An Alumnus.* An American Cong. minister; b. at Boston; Dart. Coll., 1785; pastor at Beverly, Mass., 1787–97; then a missionary in Boston; d. at Roxbury, Mass.

Oliver, Daniel, M.D., LL.D., 1787–1852. *Investigator.* An American scholar; b. at Marblehead, Mass.; Harv. Univ., 1806; professor at Dartmouth Coll., 1820–37; at Cincinnati, 1840–42; d. at Cambridge, Mass.

Oliver, George, D.D., 1781–1861. *Curiosus.* An English clergyman; b. at Newington Butts, London; for more than 53 years a resident of Exeter; d. at St. Nicholas Priory, Exeter.

Oliver, Mrs. Harriet (Downing), 1778–1845. *A Monthly Nurse.* An English writer, in "Fraser's Magazine," etc.; d. at Chipping Norton.

Oliver, John Cardell, 1844–. *J. C. O.*

An English writer; b. at Newquay, Cornwall.

Oliver, Peter, 1821–55. *William Pynchon Oliver.* An American lawyer and historian; b. at Hanover, N.H.; Harv. Univ., 1842; d. while on a voyage for his health.

Olmsted, Frederick Law, 1822–. *An American Farmer.* An American architect and landscape gardener; b. in Hartford, Conn.; a resident of New York City since 1848; and in 1858 appointed superintendent of the Central Park in that city.

O'Mahony, Thaddeus. *A. M.* An English writer.

O'Meara, Miss Kathleen. *Grace Ramsay.* An Irish writer; a relative of Dr. O'Meara, Napoleon's physician at St. Helena.

Onderdonk, Henry Ustick, D.D., 1789–1858. *H. U. O.* An eminent American P. E. clergyman; b. in New York City; Columbia Coll., 1805; Bishop of Pennsylvania, 1827–58; d. in Philadelphia.

O'Neil, Miss Elizabeth. *Betty.* An —— lady; afterwards became Lady E. O'N. Beecher.

O'Neill, Daniel. *D. O'N.* An American journalist, of Pittsburg, Penn.

Ongley, Robert Henley Ongley, 1st Baron. *A Member of Parliament.* An English nobleman, originally Robert Henley, who represented Bedfordshire in Parliament, and upon inheriting the estates of his grand-uncle, Sir Samuel Ongley, Knt., assumed the name of Ongley, in addition to his patronymic.

Onis, Don Luis. *Verus.* A Spanish diplomatist; Minister to the United States.

Onwhyn, Thomas. *Peter Palette.* An English engraver.

Opie, Mrs. Amelia (Alderson), 1769–1853. *Mrs. ****.* An English writer; b. in Norwich; wife of John Opie, the painter; lived in Norwich, 1807–53; and d. at her residence, Castle Meadow, Norwich.

Oppermann, Heinrich Albert, 1812–70. *Hermann Forsch.* A German publicist; b. at Göttingen, where he pursued the study of jurisprudence and philosophy, 1831–35, and was afterwards employed as an attorney from 1842, at Hoya, and from 1852 at Nienberg, where he died.

O'Reilly, Rt. Rev. Bernard, D.D., 1824–. *Laval.* An Irish R. C. prelate; b. at Ballybeg, County Meath; educ. at St. Cuthbert's Coll., near Durham; Bishop of Liverpool from 1873.

Orford, Horace Walpole, Earl of
— See "Walpole, Horace, Earl of Orford."

Orme, Rev. William, 1787–1830. *Criticus.* A Scottish Cong. minister; b. at Falkirk; foreign secretary of the London Missionary Society; d. in London.

Ormsby, Waterman L., Jr., 1834–. *O., Jr.* An American writer, of the day, on bank-note engraving.

O'Rourke, Edmund. *Edmond Falconer.* An English poet and dramatist.

Orr, Hector, M.D., 1769–1855. *A Looker On.* An American physician; b. in East Bridgewater, Mass.; Harv. Univ., 1801; practised his profession in his native place, and d. there.

Orr, Isaac, 1793–1844. *Hamden; Timoleon.* An American mathematician and philanthropist; b. at Bedford, N.H.; Yale Coll., 1818; missionary to the colored people of Washington and the Southern States; d. at Amherst, Mass.

Orton, James. *Alastor.* An English poet.

Orton, Rev. Job, 1717–83. *A Parishioner of St. Chad's.* An English Dissenter; b. in Shrewsbury; assistant of Dr. Doddridge in his academy at Northampton, 1738 or 39 to 41; pastor at Shrewsbury, 1741–65; engaged in literary labors at Kidderminster, 1765–83, where he died.

Orvis, Rev. William B. *A Congregational Minister.* An American writer; a teacher in Philadelphia.

Osborn, Laughton, 1806–78. *Alethitheras; An American Artist; Arthur Caryl; Charles Erskine White, D.D.* An American poet; b. in New York City; Columbia Coll., 1827.

Osborne, John Dunlap, –1883. *Gamma; Leone Leoni; Spiridion.* An American journalist; b. in Petersburg, Va.; studied law in the Harvard Law School, Cambridge, Mass.; d. in Paris, where he had resided for 50 years.

Osborne, Rev. Lord Sidney Godolphin, 1808–73. *S. G. O.* An English philanthropist; Univ. of Oxford, 1830; Rector of Durweston, Dorset., 1841–73.

Osgood, Mrs. Frances Sargent (Locke), 1811–50. *Florence.* An American poet; b. in Boston; in 1835 married Mr. S. S. Osgood, an artist, with whom she visited London; in 1840 returned to Boston, and afterwards removed to New York City, where she lived and died.

Osmun, Thomas Embly, M.D. *Alfred Ayres.* An American orthoepist, of Ohio.

Osten, Mary. *Nellie Eyler.* A German writer.

O'Sullivan, Dennis, 1838–. *Corporal Morgan Rattler.* An American writer.

O'Sullivan, Farrar. *A Munster Farmer.* An Irish writer.

O'Sullivan, Mortimer, D.D. *Capt. Rock.* An Irish clergyman; Prebendary of Ballymore.

Oswald, John. *Sylvester Otway.* A Scottish poet and political writer; b. in Edinburgh; served for some time as a soldier; resided chiefly in London from 1783, supporting himself by his pen; went to Paris early in the French Revolution, and for a time entered the French service.

Otis, Mrs. Eliza Henderson (Boardman). *One of the Barclays.* An American novelist, of Boston; widow of Harrison Gray Otis, Jr.

Otis, F. N. *Oran.* An American writer.

Otis, George Edmund. *G. E. O.* An American poet of the day; Harv. Univ. Law School, 1869.

Otis, Harrison Gray, LL.D., 1765–1848. *A Member of the Suffolk Bar; One of the Convention.* An American lawyer and statesman; b. in Boston; Harv. Univ., 1783; practised law in Boston; M.C., 1797–1801; U.S. Senator, 1817–22; Mayor of Boston, 1829–32; d. in Boston.

Otis, James, A.M., 1725–83. *A. F.; Bluster.* An American lawyer and patriot; b. at Great Marshes (now West Barnstable); Harv. Univ., 1743; killed by a flash of lightning in Andover, Mass.

Ottarson, Frank B. *Warwick.* An American writer.

Ottarson, Franklin A., 1816–84. *Bayard.* An American journalist, of New York City.

Otway, Rev. Cæsar, –1842. *C. O.* An Irish clergyman, of English descent; "a large contributor to the 'Dublin Christian Examiner' and the 'Dublin University Magazine'; the former, indeed, principally owed its fame to the articles signed 'C. O.'"

Overs, John, 1808–44. *A Working Man.* An English mechanic; b. at Birmingham; d. in London; was assisted by Mr. Charles Dickens.

Owen, ——. *A British Officer of Hussars.*

Owen, C. B. *A Nova Scotian.* A Nova Scotia member of the Legislature.

Owen, David. *Brutus.*

Owen, Francis Browning. *Francis Browning.* An American poet of the day.

Owen, Rev. James, 1654–1706. *Eu-*

genius, junior. A Welsh Dissenter; b. at Carmarthen; minister at Swiney, Shropshire.

Owen, Rev. John, 1765–1822. *A Suburban Clergyman; Theophilus Christian, Esq.* An English clergyman; Incumbent of Paglesham, Essex; one of the earliest members of the Brit. and For. Bible Society, and its principal secretary till his death.

Owen, Robert, 1771–1858. *Celatus; One of H. M.'s Justices of the Peace.* A British reformer; b. at Newtown, Wales; the latter part of his life was spent in London, where he edited the "Millennial Gazette"; d. in his native town.

Owen, Robert Dale, LL.D., 1801–77. *A Citizen of the West.* A Scottish-American reformer; son of the preceding; b. in Glasgow, Scotland; Minister to Naples from the United States, 1855–58; d. at Lake George, U.S.A.

Owen, William, Esq., F.S.A. *W——O——, Esq.; Meirion.* A Welsh philologist.

Oxenford, John, 1812–77. *An English Play-goer.* An English dramatist; b. at Camberwell, near London; called to the Bar in 1833; for many years theatrical critic for the London press; visited the United States about 1872, and wrote a series of interesting letters on the theatres of New York City.

P.

Pace, Rev. William. *A Clergyman of the Church of England.* An English poet; chaplain to the Philanthropic Society, London.

Paching, Resta. *A Gentleman in London.* An English innkeeper, of Grace-church Street, London.

Packard, Frederick Adolphus, LL.D., 1794–1867. *A Citizen of Pennsylvania.* An American lawyer; b. in Marlborough, Mass.; Harv. Univ., 1814; removed to Philadelphia; and editor of the publications of the American Sunday School Union, 1829–67.

Pae, David. *Memoriter; One who has stood behind the Counter.* A Scottish writer.

Paez, Ramon. *R. P., de Venezuela.* An American artist and writer; for many years resident in New York City; son of Gen. José A. Ramon, of Venezuela, South America.

Page, John. *Felix Folio.* An English poet of the day.

Page, R. Channing M. *One of the Family.* An American genealogist.

Page, Richard, Esq., –1841. *Daniel Hardcastle.* An English writer on finance, of London, where he died.

Page, William Reynolds, 1850–. *Eleven Sophomores.* An American business-man, of Rutland, Vt.; Harv. Univ., 1876.

Paget, Rev. Francis Edward, M.A., 1806–. *F. E. P.; William Churne, of Staffordshire.* An English clergyman; Christ Church, Oxford, 1832; Rector of Elford, Tamworth, 1835–80 *et seq.*

Paget, Violet. *Vernon Lee.* An English writer; in 1884 of Florence, Italy.

Paige, Elbridge Gerry, 1816–59. *Dow, Jr.* An American humorist and journalist, first of New York City, then of California; b. at Hardwick, Mass.

Paige, Rhoda Ann. *R. A. P.*— See "Falkner, Mrs. R. A. (P.)."

Paine, Robert Treat, Jr., A.M., 1773–1811. *Menander.* An American lawyer, poet, and journalist, of Boston, 1803–11; b. at Taunton, Mass.; Harv. Univ., 1792; d. in Boston.

Paine, Rev. Thomas, A.M., about 1697–1757. *Philopatria.* An American Cong. minister; Harv. Univ., 1717; grandfather of the preceding; for several years a minister of Weymouth; afterwards a merchant of Boston.

Paine, Thomas, 1736–1809. *An Englishman.* An English Radical and politician; b. at Thetford, Co. of Norfolk; from 1802 resided in New York City and on his estate at New Rochelle, N.Y.; d. in New York City.

Pakenham, F. J. *F. J. P.* An English religious writer.

Palacio, ——. *A South American.*

Paley, William, D.D., 1743–1805. *A Friend of Religious Liberty.* An English moralist; b. near Peterborough; grad. at the Univ. of Cambridge in 1763; Archdeacon of Carlisle, 1782; Prebend. of St. Paul's, 1793; and a little later Sub-Dean of Lincoln; d. at Sunderland.

Palfray, Warwick, 1787–1838. *Another Layman.* An American journalist;

b. and d. at Salem, Mass.; editor of the "Salem Register," 1805–38.

Palfrey, John Gorham, D.D., LL.D., 1796–1881. *J. G. P.; An Alumnus; A Free Soiler from the Start; An Old Conservative.* An American scholar, divine, historian, and politician; b. in Boston; Harv. Univ., 1815; M.C., 1847–49; d. in Cambridge, Mass.

Palfrey, Miss Sarah Hammond. *E. Foxton.* An American poet and prose writer; b. in Boston; daughter of the preceding, of Cambridge, Mass.

Palgrave, Francis Turner, Jr., LL.D., 1824–. *Henry J. Thurston.* An English poet and educator, of London; educ. at the Charterhouse and Baliol Coll., Oxford; for some years private secretary to Earl Granville.

Palliser, Sir Hugh, Bart., 1721–96. *Hugh Paleface.* An English admiral; tried for misconduct whilst third in command of the great fleet, 1778, but acquitted.

Palmer, Mrs. James F. (Reynolds). *Raphael; A Lady.* An English dialect writer; a sister of Sir Joshua Reynolds.

Palmer, Rev. John, 1729–90. *A Friend to Religious Liberty.* An English clergyman; a Presbyt. minister in London; originally a Calvinist, afterwards a Unitarian.

Palmer, W. F. *W. F. P.* An American writer of the day.

Palmer, Rev. Sir William, Bart., M.A., about 1803–. *A Member of the Church of England; A Member of the Church of God at Oxford; A Member of the Church at Oxford; Umbra Oxoniensis.* An English clergyman; Magdalen Hall, Oxford, 1828; Vicar of Whit-Church-Canonicorum *w.* Chidcock, Marshwood, and Stanton, St. Gabriel, 1846–83 *et seq.*

Palmer, William. *Warhawk; English Correspondent.*

Paltock, Robert. *R. P.; Peter Wilkins; R. S., a Passenger.* An English writer, of Clement's Inn, London.

Pamplin, W. *W. P.* An English botanist.

Panam, Pauline Adelaide Alexandre. *A Young Greek Lady.*

Pantenius, Theodor Hermann, 1843–. *Theodor Hermann.* A German author; b. at Mitau; studied at Mitau, Berlin, and Erlangen; took in 1873 the position of editor of the "Baltische Monatsschrift" at Riga, which in 1876 he united with the "Daheim" at Leipsic.

Papworth, John Buonarotti, Esq., –1847. *J. P.* An English architect, of London; after 50 years' practice of his art in London, he retired to St. Neot's, where he died.

Pardon, George Frederick, 1825–84. *G. F. P.; Quiet George; Uncle George; Capt. Crawley; Capt. Rawdon Crawley; Pastel; Redgap.* An English writer on games.

Parent-Desbarres, Pierre François, 1798–. *P. D. de Saint Sylvestre.* A French author and bookseller, of Paris.

Parfect, Rev. Ca. *A Clergyman.* An English divine of the last century; Minister of Stroud.

Paris, John Ayrton, M.D., F.R.S., 1785–1856. *A Physician.* An English physician; b. at Cambridge; president of the London Coll. of Phys., 1844–56; lived chiefly in London; d. there.

Paris, Louis Albert Philippe d'Orleans, Comte de, 1838–. *Laugel.* A French nobleman; b. in Paris; educ. in England and Germany; in 1861, came with his brother to the United States, and served in the civil war on the personal staff of Gen. McClellan; has resided in or near Paris.

Parish, Henry Headly. *An Old Diplomatic Servant.* An English diplomatist; was at Washington, D.C., 1820–24.

Park, Andrew, 1808–63. *James Wilson.* A Scottish poet; b. at Renfrew.

Park, Sir James Allan, D.C.L., 1763–1838. *A Layman.* An English lawyer; b. at Newington, Surrey; called to the Bar in 1784; one of the justices of the Court of Common Pleas, 1816–38; d. in London.

Park, John, 1775–1852. *A Fellow Sufferer.* An American teacher and journalist; b. at Windham, N.H.; Dart. Coll., 1791; editor at Boston, 1803–11; for 20 years teacher at Worcester, Mass., where he died.

Park, John James, Esq., LL.D., 1795–1833. *Eunomus.* An English lawyer, of Lincoln's Inn; Professor of English Law and Jurisprudence at King's Coll., London, from 1831; d. at Brighton.

Parke, F. *The London Hermit.* An English poet and essayist.

Parke, James, 1782–1868. *J. P.* An English writer; b. near Liverpool; baron of the Court of Exchequer, 1832–56; in 1856 raised to the peerage, as Baron Wensleydale; d. at Ampthill Park, Beds. — See "S., R."

Parke, John, about 1750. *A Native of America.* An American poet; b. in Delaware; served in the Revolutionary War; after the peace was for some time in Philadelphia; and then in Arundel Co., Va.

Parker, Frederick. *Herman Hein-*

fetter. An English biblical scholar and writer, of Tunbridge Wells.

Parker, Mrs. Helen F. *H. F. P.* An American writer of biography.

Parker, Henry Webster, 1825–. *H. W. P.* An American poet; professor at the Agricultural Coll., Amherst, Mass.

Parker, John Henry, C.B., F.S.A., 1806–. *J. H. P.; The Editor of the "Glossary of Architecture."* An English bookseller, of Oxford; succeeded his uncle, Joseph Parker, in 1832; and succeeded by his son; in 1863 became keeper of the Ashmolean Museum, Oxford.

Parker, Richard. *Philoglottus.* An English writer of the 18th century.

Parker, Richard E. *Galen.* An American essayist, of Baltimore.

Parker, Richard Green, 1798–1869. *One who knew him well.* An American teacher and writer of school-books, of Boston, and later of New York City; b. in Boston; Harv. Univ., 1817; d. in New York City (?).

Parker, Rosa Abbott. *Rosa Abbott.* An American writer of the day, for the young.

Parker, Samuel, Yeoman Beadle. *S. P. Y. B.*

Parker, Theodore, 1810–60. *Levi Blodgett; One not of the Association.* An American clergyman and social reformer, of Boston, 1846–59; at Lexington, Mass.; Harv. Univ. Divinity School, 1836; d. at Florence, Italy.

Parker, William Harwar. *A Naval Officer.* An American writer; entered the U.S. Navy as a midshipman in 1841; served in the Confederate Navy, 1861–65; in 1883 resided at Norfolk, Va.

Parkes, Mrs. Fanny. — See "Parlby, Mrs. F. (P.)."

Parkinson, Anthony. *A. P.* An English literary antiquary, of the first part of the 18th century.

Parkinson, Mary. *Raven Witherne.* An English writer.

Parlby, Mrs. Fanny (Parkes). *A Pilgrim.* An English traveller.

Parliament, The English. *The Senate of Lilliput.*

Parnell, Edward Andrew. *An Experienced Dyer.* An English chemist, of the Univ. of London.

Parnell, William. *An Irish Country Gentleman.* An Irish statesman and Member of Parliament; Knight of the Shire for Wicklow, and brother of Rt. Hon. Henry Brooke Parnell, Lord Congleton.

Parr, Miss Harriet, 1837–. *Holme Lee.* An English novelist, of Yorkshire.

Parr, John. *A Gentleman of Halifax; A Consistent Loyalist.* An American loyalist, of Morris County, N.J. (?).

The tract by "A Consistent Loyalist" appears to be an answer to the other, and not to have been written by Parr.

Parr, John Hamilton. *N. Aaron Philomirth.* An English humorist.

Parr, Samuel, LL.D., 1747–1825. *Lucius; One of H. M.'s Justices of the Peace; A Member of the Established Church; Philopatris Varvicensis; Phileleutherus Norfolciensis.* An eminent English classical scholar and clergyman; b. at Harrow-on-the-Hill; d. at the Parsonage House, Hatton, Warwickshire.

Parrot. Supposed editor, *Mrs. Prattle.*

Parry, Charles Henry, M.D. *C. H. P.; A Descendant in the Fourth Generation.* An English physician; son of Dr. Caleb Hillier Parry, of St. Edmund Hall, Oxford.

Parry, John Humphreys, 1787–1825. *Anthony Griffinhoof, Gent.; W. Griffinhoof.* An English barrister and Welsh scholar, of London; b. at Mold, Flintshire; d. in London.

Parsons, Daniel, M.A. *D. P.* An English author; son of Rev. John Parsons, Vicar of Ma.den, Wilts. Mr. D. Parsons is M.A. of Oriel Coll., Oxford, and was married in 1845, at the R. C. Church, Exeter, to Miss Gertrude Hext.

Parsons, Mrs. Gertrude (Hext). *G. P.* An English writer for the young; b. at Restormel; in 1878, resident at Stuart Lodge, Malvern Wells.

Parsons, John Usher, A.M., 1761–1838. *An Analytical Teacher.* An American educator; b. and d. at Parsonsfield, Me.; Dartmouth Coll., 1791; studied law, but is supposed to have been a merchant in his native town most of his life.

Parsons, Theodore, A.M., A.A.S., –1779. *Two Candidates for the Bachelor's Degree.* An American scholar; Harv. Univ., 1773.

Parsons, Theophilus, LL.D., 1750–1813. *Peter Coffin.* An American jurist; b. at Byfield, Mass.; Harv. Univ., 1769; practised law at Newburyport, Mass., 1777–1800; at Boston, 1800–6; Chief Justice, 1806–13; d. at Boston.

Parsons, Theophilus, LL.D., 1797–1882. *T. P.* An American jurist; son of the preceding; b. in Newburyport, Mass.; Harv. Univ., 1815; professor at Harv. Univ., 1848–70; d. in Cambridge, Mass.

Parsons, Thomas. *T. P.* An English writer early in the 19th century.

Parsons, Tyler. *A Friend to Truth.* An English writer early in the 19th century.

Partee, W. B. *Nomistake.* An American writer on money.

Parton, James, 1822–. *An Old Smoker.* An American author; b. at Canterbury, England, and brought to the United States in 1827; has for many years devoted his life to literary labor, chiefly in New York City.

Parton, Mrs. Sara Payson (Willis Farrington Eldredge), 1811–72. *Fanny Fern.* An American writer; b. at Portland, Me.; lived chiefly in New York City, and d. there.

Partridge, J. Arthur. *A Birmingham Liberal.* An English writer of the day.

Partridge, S. W. *S. W. P.* An English religious poet and writer.

Paschall, Ann S. *A. S. P.* An American writer.

Pascoe, Mrs. Charlotte Champion (Willyams), 1781–1874. *Barzillai Baragweneth.* An English dialect writer, of Cornwall; d. at Nanskeval, Mawgan in Pydar.

Pascoe, Rev. Samuel, 1845–. *Allen Kenwyn.* An English poet and prose writer; b. at Truro; Curate of St. Paul's, Truro, 1878–83 *et seq.*

Pascual, Antonio Diodoro de, 1822–74. *Adadus Calpe.* A Spanish writer.

Paskco, ——. *Seneca.* An American journalist.

Pasquin, Antoine Claude. *Valery.* A French writer.

Patch, John, 1807–. *A Boston Amateur Poet.* An American lawyer; b. in Ipswich, Mass.; Bowdoin Coll., 1831; was a lawyer in Boston, Beverly, and Nantucket, all in Mass.; spent some years in California; but has now for many years resided at his Ipswich farm and home.

Paterson, Nathaniel, D.D. *A Clergyman.* A Scottish (?) minister.

Paterson, Samuel, 1728–1802. *Coriat, Junior.* An English bibliographer, of London; b. and d. in that city.

Paton, Andrew Archibald, F.R.G.S., 1809–74. *An Oriental Student.* An English traveller in the East; Consul at Ragusa and the Bocca di Cattaro from 1862.

Paton, Mme Émilie Euphémie Thérèse (Pacini). *Jacques Rozier.* A French writer; wife of Jules Paton.

Paton, James, D.D. *A Father.* A Scottish (?) minister of 100 years ago.

Paton, Sir Joseph Noel, R.S.A., LL.D., 1823–. *A Painter; Spindrift.* An eminent Scottish painter and poet; b. at Dunfermline, Fifeshire.

Patterson, Virginia S. *Garry Gaines.*

Pattison, Dorothy W. *Sister Dora.*

Paul, Sir John Dean, 2d Bart., D.C.L., 1802–68. *A Delinquent Banker.* An English banker; b. in London; succeeded his father in 1852 as partner in the banking firm of Snow, Strahan, Paul & Co., which failed in 1855, and Strahan, Bates, and Paul were tried for fraud, and sentenced to 14 years' penal servitude, but they were liberated before the expiration of the term, and Sir J. D. Paul took up his residence at Lancing, near Shoreham, and afterwards at St. Alban's, where he died.

Paul, Ven. Robert Bateman, M.A., 1798–1877. *R. B. P.; The Late James Hamley Tregenna.* An English clergyman; Prebendary of Lincoln, 1867–74; Confrater of Browne's Hospital, Stamford, and resident at Barn Hill, Stamford, 1874–77; d. at Stamford.

Paulding, James Kirke, 1779–1860. *An Amateur; An Amateur of Fashion; Hector Bull-us; Dominie Nicholas Ægidius Oudenarde; A Doubtful Gentleman; A New England Man; A Northern Man; An Obsolete Author; A Retired Common Councilman; Lancelot Langstaffe, Esq.; Several American Authors; W—— S——, Esq.; Sir W. Scott.* An American essayist, humorist, and miscellaneous writer, of New York City; d. at Hyde Park.

Paulding, William Irving. *David T. Valentine.* An American writer; son of James K. Paulding.

Pavier, Thomas. *T. P.* — See "R. J." (Richard Jones).

Paxton, Joseph Rupert, 1827–. *Hipponax Roset.* An American author, translator, and contributor to periodicals, of Philadelphia; was engaged in the military service of the United States, 1861–65.

Payne, Miss ——. *Flora.* An American Western writer.

Payne, A. R. Middletoun. *One who has seen them.* An American traveller.

Payne, Col. Alban S., 1822–. *Nicholas Spicer.* An American journalist.

Payne, Buckner H., 1799–1883. *Ariel.* An American writer, of Tennessee; at one time considered the greatest logician of the South; once in affluent circumstances, but died blind.

Payne, Lieut. J. Bertrand, 1833–. *J. B. P.* An English officer of the Royal Jersey Artillery; biographer and literary antiquary; b. in London.

Payson, Edward, 1813–. *A Citizen*

of Maine. An American writer; son of Rev. Dr. Payson; b. in Portland, Me.; Bowdoin Coll., 1832; is a farmer at Deering (formerly Westbrook), Me.

Payson, George, 1824–. *Francis Fogie, Sen., Esq.; Ralph Raven; Robert Dexter Romaine.* An American novelist; son of the Rev. Dr. Edward Payson, of Portland, Me.; Bowdoin Coll., 1843; spent two years, 1849–51, at the gold mines in California; on his return, studied law, and in 1856 settled in Chicago, Ill.

Peabody, Miss Elizabeth Palmer, 1804–. *A Teacher.* An American educator; b. at Billerica, Mass.; sister of Mrs. Horace Mann and of Mrs. Nathaniel Hawthorne.

Peabody, Nathaniel, M.D., 1774–1855. *A Teacher in Boston.* An American physician; b. in Lancaster, Mass.; Dartmouth Coll., 1800; practised his profession in Salem, Boston, and West Newton, Mass.; and finally at Perth Amboy, N.J., where he died.

Peabody, Oliver William Bourne, LL.B., 1799–1848. *His Twin Brother.* An American lawyer; b. in Exeter, N.H.; Harv. Univ., 1816; practised law in Exeter for 11 years; removed to Boston in 1830; was the minister of the Unit. society at Burlington, Vt., 1845–48, and d. in that town.

Peace, John, 1785–1861. *X. A. P.* An English bibliographer; b. in Bristol; for many years librarian of the city library in Bristol; d. at Durdham Green.

Peacock, James. *Jose Mac Packe, a bricklayer's labourer.* An English architect and cottage-building humorist.

Peacock, Thomas Love, 1785–1866. *Peter Peppercorn, M.D.* An English writer, of London; friend of Shelley and Charles Lamb; b. and d. in London.

Pearce, Miss Alice. *Amica.* An English poet, of Falmouth.

Pearce, Miss Ellen J., 1843–. *A Cornishwoman.* An English writer; b. and lived at St. Keverne, Cornwall.

Pearce, Henry, about 1779–1809. *The Game Chicken.* An English pugilist, once the champion of England; was a native of Bristol; d. in London.

Pearce, Rev. Thomas, M.A. *Idstone.* An English clergyman; Lincoln Coll., Oxford, 1843; Rector of Charborough, 1871–83 *et seq.*, and Vicar of Morden, 1853–83 *et seq.*

Pearce, Zachary, D.D., 1690–1774. *A.; R.; A Clergyman of the Church of England; A Gentleman of Christ Church College, Oxon.; Ned Mum.* An English

prelate; b. in London; educ. at Westminster School and Trin. Coll., Cambridge; Bishop of Rochester, 1756–74.

Peard, Frances Mary. *F. M. P.; Thorpe Regis.* An English novelist of the day.

Pearl, Rev. Cyril. *A Citizen of New England.* An American minister; a missionary in Boston (?).

Pearson, C. *The Late President of a Select Chess Club.* An English writer.

Pearson, Mrs. Charles H. *Pocahontas.* An American writer for the young.

Pearson, Edward, D.D., 1756–1811. *E. P.* An English divine; b. at Ipswich; educ. at Cambridge; Vice-Chancellor of Sidney Sussex Coll., Cambridge, 1808–11; d. at Rempstone, Notts.

Pearson, Eliphalet, LL.D., 1752–1826. *Two Candidates for the Bachelor's Degree.* An American scholar; b. in Byfield, Mass.; Harv. Univ., 1773; Professor of Hebrew, etc., at Harv. Univ., 1786–1806; first professor of Sacred Literature at the Theol. Sem., Andover, 1808–9; resided at Harvard, Mass., 1820–26.

Pearson, Mrs. Emily C. *Ervie.* An American writer of the day.

Peart, Emily. *One of them.* An English governess; a writer of the day.

Peat, J. B. *J. B. P.* An American writer of the day.

Peccatier, A. *M. Rit Toujours.* A French humorist.

Pech, Henriette, 1847–. *Eliska Krásnohorská.* A Bohemian poet; b. at Prague; her lyrics are much admired; she is also a successful æsthetic critic; and has written the text for the three operas, "Lejla," "Der Kuss," and "Das Geheimniss."

Peck, Ellen. *Cuyler Pine.* An American novelist of the day.

Peck, George Washington, 1817–59. *Cantell A. Bigly.* An American writer, of Michigan; b. at Rehoboth, Mass.; Brown Univ., 1837; d. at Boston.

Peck, John Mason, D.D., 1789–1858. *An Old Pioneer.* An American Baptist clergyman; was a pastor in various churches of Missouri, Illinois, and Kentucky, 1845–58; d. at Rock Spring, Ill.

Peck, Lillie, –1878. *Ruth Elliott.* An English writer; daughter of the Rev. James B. Peck, of Chelmsford.

Peck, William. *W. P.* An English topographer.

Peck, William R. *A Theophilanthropist.* An English writer.

Peckwell, Henry, D.D., 1748–87. *A Friend to Civil and Religious Liberty.* An English clergyman; Rector of Bloxam.

Pedder, James, 1775–1859. *J. P.* An English agriculturist; b. at Newport, Isle of Wight; came to this country about 1832; edited the "Boston Cultivator," 1844–59; d. at Roxbury, Mass.

Peebles, Mrs. Mary L., 1839–. *Lynde Palmer.* An American writer for the young; b. in Lansingburg, N.Y.

Peebles, William, D.D. *A Clergyman of the Church of Scotland.* A Scottish minister and poet, at Newton-upon-Ayr.

Peel, Sir Robert, 2d Bart., D.C.L., 1788–1850. *The Minister.* An English statesman; b. near Bury, Lancashire; educ. at Harrow and Oxford; English Premier, 1834–35 and 1841–46; d. in London.

Pegge, Samuel, LL.D., 1704–96. *S. P.; P.S.; G.; P.; P.E.; L.E.; P.G.; An Antiquary; L. Echard; Paul Gemsege; A Ploughist; Portius; T. Row; Senex; Vicarius Cantianus; A Late Learned and Reverend Divine.* An eminent English antiquary; b. in Chesterfield; Prebendary of Lincoln, 1772–96.

He published, besides his other works, several hundred articles on antiquities in "Archæologia," "Bibl. Top. Brit.," and "Gentleman's Magazine." See "Gent. Mag." LXVI., pp. 891, 892, 979, 1081, 1084.

Peignot, Étienne Gabriel, 1767–1849. *Jacques Rambler.* A learned French bibliographer.

Peirce, Augustus, M.D., 1802–49. *Poeta, Enginæ Societatis.* An American physician; b. at New Salem, Mass.; Harv. Univ., 1820; practised his profession at Tyngsborough, Mass., and d. there.

Peirce, Benjamin, LL.D., F.R.S., 1809–81. *Ben Yamen; Benjamin the Florentine.* An eminent American mathematician; b. at Salem, Mass.; Harv. Univ., 1831; professor at Harv. Univ., 1832–81; d. at Cambridge.

Peirce, Benjamin Osgood, Jun., Ph.D., 1854–. *Eleven Sophomores.* An American mathematician; b. at Beverly; Harv. Univ., 1876; instructor in his alma mater, 1876–77, 1881–84; and assistant professor, 1884–85.

Peirce, Bradford Kinney, D.D., 1819–. *B. K. P.; The Chaplain.* An American clergyman; b. in Royalton, Vt.; Wesleyan Univ., 1841; chaplain of the House of Refuge, Randall's Island, N.Y., 1863–72; editor of "Zion's Herald," Boston, from 1872.

Peirce, I. *A Wanderer.* An American writer.

Peirce, Rev. James, 1673–1726. *A Dissenter in the Country.* An eminent English Nonconformist divine, of Exon; b. in London.

Peirson, Mrs. Eliza O. *Aliqua.* An American writer for the press, of the day.

Pelham, the Right Hon. Henry, 1695–1754. *Mr. P****m.* An English statesman; Chancellor of the Exchequer, 1743–54.

Pell, Ferris. *Publicola.* An American writer on money and banking; a lawyer; Columbia Coll., 1806.

Pell, Robert Conger, 1835–68. *Chetwood Evelyn, Esq.* An American miscellaneous writer; b. in New York City; d. at Interlachen, Switzerland.

This is also given: *Robert Cruger Pell.* "Clement Evelyn, Esq."

Pelligrini, ——. *Spy.* An American journalist, of New York City.

Pelz, Edward, 1800–76. *Treumund Welp.* A German writer; b. at Penig, Saxony; was a publisher and bookseller in several European cities, 1815–50; spent in the United States 1850–66; was devoted to literary work at Gotha, 1869–76, where he died.

Pember, Arthur. *A. P.* An American writer, of New York City.

Pemberton, Lieut. Col. ——. *Leo.* An English officer; a writer of the day.

Pemberton, Charles Reece, 1790–1840. *A Sailor.* An English actor, elocutionist, and poet; in 1832–34 he contributed a series of papers to the "Monthly Repository," entitled "Autobiography of Pal Verjuice," which was believed to shadow forth some of the vicissitudes of his own early life; d. at Birmingham.

Pemberton, Edgar. *P. M. Berton.* An English novelist.

Pembroke, George Robert Charles Herbert, 13th Earl, 1850–. *The Earl.* An English nobleman; educ. at Eton; Under-Secretary of War, 1874–75.

Penfield, A. *A. P.* An American financier of the day.

Pengelly, William, F.R.S., F.G.S., 1812–. *Y. M.; A Geologist.* An English geologist, etc.; b. at Castle Street, East Looe; in 1878, resident at Lamorna, Torquay.

Penn, William, Esq., 1776–1845. *The Rajah of Vaneplysia; An Undergraduate.* An English gentleman; a descendant of Admiral Sir William Penn, father of the founder of Pennsylvania; passed most of his life within certain confines of Southwark; d. in Nelson-square, Southwark.

Penneck, Rev. Henry, M.A., 1800–62. *Mr. Bayle.* An English clergyman, of Penzance, Cornwall; b. at Market-Jew Street, Penzance; d. at Penzance.

Pennecuik, Alexander, M.D., 1652–

1722. *A. P., M.D.* A Scottish poet and botanist; b. at Newhall, County of Edinburgh.

Pennell, Mrs. Elizabeth (Robins). An American writer of the day, of Philadelphia; a niece of Charles Godfrey Leland.

Penney, William, Lord Kinloch, 1801–72. *A Layman.* A Scottish writer; senator of the College of Justice.

Pennie, John Fitzgerald, 1782–1848. *A Modern Genius; Sylvaticus.* An English writer; b. at East Lulworth, Dorsetshire; was an actor, schoolmaster, poet, etc.; d. at Rogvald Cottage, Wareham, Dorsetshire.

Pennington, Mrs. S. *S. P.* An English writer of the 18th century.

Penny, Mrs. Anne (Christian), 1731–84. ***** *****.* An English poet; her first husband was Capt. Hugh Christian, who commanded the batteries at Rhode Island when Count D'Estaing was repulsed; her second husband was in the navy; she was highly esteemed by Dr. Johnson; d. in London.

Pennyman, John. *Phil Ang.* An English anti-Quaker writer.

Penrose, Vice-Admiral Sir **Charles Vinicombe,** 1759–1830. *A Flag Officer.* An English seaman; b. at St. Gluvias; entered the Royal Navy in 1775; Rear-Admiral of the Blue in 1813; d. at Ethy, St. Winnow.

Penrose, Mrs. Elizabeth Cartwright, 1781–1837. *Mrs. Markham.* An English writer; wife of Rev. John Penrose, Vicar of Bracebridge; d. at Lincoln.

Penrose, Rev. John, M.A., 1778–1859. *A Senior; A Trinitarian.* An English clergyman; Corpus Christi Coll., Oxford, 1799; Vicar of Langton, near Wragby, Lincs., 1802–59, and P. C. of North Hykeham, 1838–59; d. at Langton.

Pentz, Jacob. *Gopher.*

Perceval, Hon. and Rev. **Arthur Philip,** B.C.L., 1800–53. *A Churchman; A Late Fellow, etc.; A Minister of the Church of Ireland; One of His Majesty's Chaplains; One of His Majesty's Servants; A Presbyter in the Diocese of Canterbury.* An English clergyman; All Soul's Coll., Oxford, 1820; Rector of E. Horsley, 1824; d. at Little Bookham, Surrey.

Perceval, Hon. and Rev. **Charles George,** 1796–. *The Rector of Calverton, Bucks.; A Country Clergyman.* An English clergyman; b. at the Admiralty, Whitehall; Rector of Calverton, Bucks., from 1822.

Perceval, Sir **John,** 1st Earl of Eg-

mont, 1685–1748. *A Nobleman of the other Kingdom.* An English lord; b. at Barton, in the County of York.

Pereira, Jonathan, M.D., F.R.S., 1804–53. *J. P.* An eminent English physician and pharmacologist; b. and d. in London; physician at the London Hospital, 1851–53.

Perkins, Miss Eliza. *A Lady.* An English writer on botany.

Perkins, Ellen M. *Christie Pearl.* An American writer for the young.

Perkins, Frederic Beecher. *Pharaoh Budlong.* An American bibliographer; Yale Coll., 1850; librarian at San Francisco.

Perkins, Henry. *An Experienced Clerk.* An English accountant.

Perrier, Miss Anna. *An Irishwoman.* An Irish writer of the day.

Perry, Capt. **David.** *An Old Soldier.* An American soldier, of Chelsea, Vt.

Perry, Mrs. E. C. *Elfin Hall.*

Perry, Rev. **Henry G.** *Regryph.* An An American journalist, of Chicago.

Perry, W. A. *Silalicum.* An American journalist, of Seattle, Wash. Ter.

Perry, William Stevens, D.D., 1832–. *W. S. P.* An eminent American clergyman; b. in Providence, R.I.; Harv. Univ., 1854; Bishop of Iowa, 1876–85; and resides at Davenport, Ia.

Pery, Edmund Sexton. *An Armenian in Ireland.*

Peter, William, 1788–1853. *A Layman.* An English poet and politician; b. at Harlyn, St. Merryn; H. M. Consul for Pennsylvania and New Jersey, 1840–53; d. in Philadelphia.

Peterkin, Alexander, 1781–1846. *Alumnus Edinensis; Anti-Harmonicus; Civis.* A Scottish poet, lawyer, and antiquary.

Peters, Bernard. *Pestalozzi.* An American journalist, of Brooklyn, N.Y.

Peters, Samuel Andrew, LL.D., 1735–1826. *A Gentleman of the Province; Parson Peter; John Viator, Esq.* An American loyalist; b. in Hebron, Conn.; Yale Coll., 1757; d. in New York City.

Peters, W. A., 1841–. *Doctor Bronson; Joel Sloper.* An American journalist, of New York City.

Peterson, Charles J., 1818–. *J. Thornton Randolph.* An American publisher and journalist, of Philadelphia; proprietor and co-editor of "Peterson's Ladies' National Magazine."

Petit-méré, Frédéric du. *Monkey.* A French writer.

Pettes, George William. *X, Y, Z, Club; G. W. P.* An American poet.

Pettigrew, Thomas Lettsom, 1813–37. *A Cornet in the E. I. Co.'s Service.* An English writer; son of Thomas Joseph Pettigrew; a literary antiquary, of London; d. at Bangalore.

Pettingell, Rev. **John Hancock**, A.M., 1815–. *Clericus.* An American bibliographer; b. at Waterbury, Conn.; Yale Coll., 1837; pastor at South Dennis, Mass., 1843–47; settled at Essex, Conn., 1848; in 1882 was at Philadelphia.

Pettitt, Charles. *Resurgam.*

Pettman, William, Esq. *One of the Barbarous Blockheads of the Lowest Mob; Philopolites.* An English writer; at one time a schoolmaster at Sandwich, and afterwards of Ham, in the county of Kent.

Petzel, Rosa. *Martin Claudius.* A German writer of the day.

Phelan, Charlotte Elizabeth. — See "Tonna, Mrs. C. E. (Tonna)."

Phelan, William, D.D., 1789–1830. *Declan.* An Irish clergyman; b. at Clonmel; Trin. Coll., Dublin; Rector of Killyman, Co. Tyrone, 1824–30, and of Artray, Co. Derry, 1825–30.

Phelps, Charles, A.B., –1854. *A Citizen of the United States.* An American political writer, of Vermont; Hon. A.B. at the Univ. of Vermont, 1812.

Phelps, Mrs. Elizabeth (Stuart), 1815–52. *H. Trusta.* An American novelist; daughter of Prof. Moses Stuart, and wife of Prof. Austin Phelps.

Phelps, Miss Elizabeth Stuart, 1844–. *Onyx.* An American novelist; daughter of the preceding; b. at Andover, Mass.

Phelps, Miss **L. L.** *Alpha.* An American writer of the day.

Phelps, W. D. *Webfoot.* An American novelist of the day.

Philes, George P., A.M., 1828–. *Paulus Silentiarius.* An American publisher of New York City, 1854–70; b. at Ithaca, N.Y.; Hon. A.M. at Dartmouth Coll., 1868.

Philip, Robert, D.D., 1791–1858, and Another. *A Minister and a Layman.* An English Dissenter, of Maberley Chapel.

Philippe, Adolphe, 1811–. *Dennery.* A French dramatist; b. in Paris; since 1831 has produced, either alone or with others, about 200 dramas.

Philips, Mrs. Katherine (Fowler), 1631–64. *Orinda.* An English lady of wit and accomplishments; b. in London; when young she married James Philips, Esq., of Cardigan; and afterwards went with the Viscountess of Dungannon into Ireland; d. in London.

Phillimore, Harriet Eleanor. *H.*

E. P. An English novelist of the day.

Phillipps, Miss ——. *Old Maid.* An English writer; daughter of Rev. Edward Thomas March Phillipps, of Hathern Rectory, Loughborough, Leicester.

Phillips, Mrs. ——. — See "Pontes, Madame de."

Phillips, Miss **Anna H.** *Helen W. Irving.* An American poet, of Lynn, Mass.

Phillips, Charles, 1787–1859. *A Man of the World.* An Irish barrister, poet, and novelist; b. at Sligo; educ. at Dublin; Commissioner of the Court of Insolvent Debtors, 1846–59; d. in London.

Phillips, Mrs. Constantia. *Mrs. C—— P——.* An English writer of the 18th century.

Phillips, Capt. **Edwin D.**, 1827–64. *An Officer of the Army.* An American officer; b. in New York; appointed from Michigan; U.S. Military Acad., 1852; Asst. Instructor of Infantry Tactics, 1861–62; d. at New Orleans, La.

Phillips, George Searle, 1818–. *January Searle.* An English-American journalist and novelist; b. at Peterborough, Northants.; educ. at Cambridge; has edited several journals both in the United States and in England.

Phillips, Gus. *Oofty Gooft.*

Phillips, Henry, Jr. *Antiquarian; A Member of the Numismatic Society of Phila.* An American lawyer and numismatist, of Philadelphia.

Phillips, John. *J. P., a Student of Astrology.* An English writer of the 17th and 18th centuries; nephew of John Milton.

Phillips, Melville. *Snap.* An American writer, of Philadelphia.

Phillips, Sir **Richard**, Knt., 1768–1840. *James Adair; Rev. S. Barrow; Rev. David Blair; M. l'abbé Bossut; Rev. C. C. Clarke; Rev. J. Goldsmith; M. Pelham; Common Sense.* An English publisher, of London, where he was b.; established, in 1790, the "Leicester Herald"; the "Monthly Magazine," London, 1796; the "Antiquary's Magazine," 1807; and re-purchased the "Monthly Magazine" about 1809, and continued to publish it for 25 years; d. at Brighton.

Phillips, Walter P. *John Oakum.*

Phillips, Watts, Esq., 1829–74. *Felix Balfour.* An English dramatist and journalist; b. in London; d. at West Brompton.

Phillips, Willard, LL.D., 1784–1873. *A Citizen of Massachusetts.* An American lawyer; b. at Bridgewater, Mass.; Harv.

Univ., 1810; Judge of Probate for Suffolk Co., 1839–47; lived and d. in Cambridge, Mass.

Phillips, Willard P. *W. P. P.* An American civil engineer, of Salem, Mass.

Phillips, William. *Paul Potion.* An English poet, of the Middle Temple. This is also ascribed to *William Shearsmith*.

Phillips, William Wirt, D.D., 1796–1865. *The Pastor.* An American Presbyt. clergyman; b. in Montgomery Co., N.Y.; Columbia Coll., 1826; pastor in New York City, 1818–65; and d. there.

Phillpotts, Henry, D.D., 1777–1869. *A Clergyman of the Diocese of Durham.* An English prelate; b. at Gloucester; educ. at Corpus Christi Coll., Oxford; Bishop of Exeter, 1831–69.

Phipps, Constantine John, Lord Mulgrave, 1746–92. *A Member of Parliament.* An English and Irish nobleman; entered very young the naval service; post-captain, R. N., 1765; M.P. for Lincoln, 1768; created an English peer, 1790; d. at Liege, Germany.

Piatt, John James, and Another, 1835–. *Two Friends.* An American poet, of Cincinnati; b. at Milton, Ind.; educ. at the Columbus (O.) High School and Kenyon Coll.

Piatt, Mrs. Louisa (Kirby), 1812–64. *Belle Smith.* An American author, of Cincinnati, where she died.

Piatt, Mrs. Sarah Morgan (Bryan), 1836–. *Minnie Myrtle; A Woman.* An American poet; wife of John James Piatt; b. at Lexington, Ky.; educ. at Newcastle, Ky.; in 1868 *et seq.* lived at Cincinnati.

Piazzi, Mme **Adrienne.** *Leila Hanoum.* A Hungarian novelist.

Pichon, Thomas. *An Impartial Frenchman.*

Pichot, Amédée, 1796–1877. *Sir J. Perriwig.* A French journalist; b. at Arles; studied medicine, and in 1819 settled in Paris, but soon devoted himself to literary pursuits; d. in Paris.

Pickard, Hannah Maynard, 1812–44. *A Lady.* An English writer.

Pickens, John. *Horatio.* An American humorist, of Boston; connected with several banking institutions.

Pickering, Henry, 1781–1838. *An American.* An American poet; b. at Newburg, N.Y.; was a merchant at Salem, Mass., 1801–25; in 1825 removed to New York City, but soon settled at Rondout-on-the-Hudson, and devoted himself to literary pursuits; d. in New York City.

Pickering, John, LL.D., 1777–1846.

A Member of the Massachusetts Bar. An American philologist; brother of the preceding; b. at Salem, Mass.; Harv. Univ., 1796; was a lawyer in Salem, 1801–27; City Solicitor of Boston, 1829–46; d. at Salem.

Pickering, Timothy, LL.D., 1745–1829. *The Secretary of State; Verus.* An American statesman; father of the preceding; b. in Salem, Mass.; Harv. Univ., 1763; was a lawyer in his native town; U.S. Secretary of State, 1795–1800; U.S. Senator, 1803–11; d. at Salem.

Pickersgill, Lieut. **Richard.** *A Sea Officer.* An English naval officer; after sailing three times round the world, and once in search of a north-west passage, he was drowned in the Thames by the upsetting of a boat in a gust of wind.

Pickford, Rev. **John,** M.A. *Oxoniensis.* An English clergyman; Queen's Coll., Oxford, 1851; Rector of Newbourne, Woodbridge, 1872–83 *et seq.*

Picton, Col. **Thomas,** 1822–. *An Ex-Editor; Gothamite; Paul Preston.* An American journalist, of New York City.

Pierpont, Rev. **John,** A.M., 1785–1866. *The Pastor of Hollis Street Society; Theron.* An American clergyman and poet; b. at Litchfield, Conn.; Yale Coll., 1804; pastor in Boston, 1819–45. at Troy, N.Y., 1845–49; at Medford, Mass., 1849–56; employed in the Treasury Department at Washington, 1861–64; d. at Medford.

Pierrepont, Henry Evelyn. *A Director.* An American writer, of Brooklyn, N.Y.; son of Hezekiah Beers Pierrepont, of that city.

Pierson, Miss **Susan.** *Miss Susan P——.* An English lady; friend of Charles Lamb.

Pietrowski, Rufin. *A Siberian Exile.*

Pigott, Richard. *An Irish National Journalist.* An Irish journalist of the day.

Pike, Albert, A.M., 1809–. *The Fine Arkansas Gentleman.* An American lawyer, politician, soldier, and journalist; b. in Boston; was in the Confederate service, 1861–65; editor of the "Memphis Appeal," 1867–.

Pike, Mrs. **Frances West (Atherton),** 1819–. *Anna Ahern; Katherine Morris.* An American novelist; b. at Prospect, Me.; widow of Rev. Richard Pike, of Dorchester, Mass.

Pike, Mrs. **Mary H. Greene,** 1827–. *Mary Langdon; Sydney A. Story, Jr.* An American novelist; b. at Eastport,

Me.; wife of Fred. A. Pike, M.C., of Calais, Me.

Pike, Noah W. *Gordox.* An American writer, of New York City.

Pilgrim, Thomas, –1882. *Arthur Morecamp; Eugene Owl.* An American writer, of Gonzales, Tex.

Pillet, Raymond François Léon, 1803–67. *Ernest Renaud.* A French journalist, theatrical manager, and dramatic author; b. in Paris; d. at Venice.

Pilon, Martin Regul. *Yanko-Sequor.* An American writer and publisher, of New York City.

Pim, Jonathan. *A Member of the Society of Friends.* An Irish Friend, of Dublin.

Pinchard, Mrs. ——. *A Lady.* An English writer; the wife of an attorney at Taunton, in Somersetshire.

Pinckney, Charles, LL.D., 1758–1824. *A Republican; A South Carolinian; A South Carolina Planter.* An American statesman; b. at Charleston, S.C.; was a lawyer; M.C., 1784–87; U.S. Senator, 1798–1801; Minister to Spain, 1802–5; again M.C., 1819–21; d. in his native city.

Pinckney, Thomas. *Achates.*

Pine, Rev. **George Stevenson,** 1853–. *Eleven Sophomores.* An American clergyman; b. in Philadelphia; Harv. Univ., 1876; rector of St. Mark's Church, New Canaan, Conn., 1881–85.

Pinkerton, John, F.S.A., 1758–1826. *H. Bennet, M.A.; Robert Heron, Esq.* A Scottish writer; b. in Edinburgh; settled in London in 1781; but resided in Paris the latter part of his life, and d. there.

Pinney, G. W. *Columella.* An American writer, of San Francisco.

Piozzi, Mrs. Hester Lynch (Thrale Salusbury), 1740–1821. *Anna Matilda.* A British authoress, of London; friend of Dr. Johnson; b. in Wales; d. at Clifton.

Piper, Mrs. ——. *Estelle.* An American writer of the day.

Pitcairne, Archibald, M.D., 1652–1713. *A Scots Gentleman.* A Scottish physician; b. in Edinburgh; studied at Montpelier and Paris; Prof. of Physic in the Univ. of Leyden, 1692–93; and the chief physician in Edinburgh, 1693–1713.

Pitcairns, The. *The P—s.* Pitcairn, Dr. David, was a minister of the Church of Scotland, and for more than 50 years pastor of the church of Dysart; Pitcairn, Major, lost his life, at the age of 52, at the battle of Bunker's Hill; Pitcairn, Dr. W., was very high in the profession of physic; Pitcairn, Dr. David, 2d, was the eldest son of Major Pitcairn.

Pitman, Ambrose, Esq. *Ephraim Epigram, Esq.; A Young Gentleman of Seventeen.* An English poet, composer, editor, and contributor to periodical literature; resided in London from about 1795.

Pitman, John, LL.D., 1784–1864. *One of the Rhode Island People.* An American jurist; b. in Rhode Island; Brown Univ., 1799; Judge of the U.S. District Court for 40 years; d. in Providence, R.I.

Pitman, Mrs. Marie J. (Davis). *Margery Deane.* An American writer of the day, of Newport, R.I.

Pitt, Right Hon. **William,** Earl of Chatham, 1708–78. *William the Fourth; The Celebrated Commoner; The Great Man.* An eminent English statesman; b. at St. James', Westminster; entered Parliament as M.P. for Old Sarum, 1734; created Earl of Chatham, 1766; Lord Privy Seal and Premier, 1766–68; d. at Hayes, Kent.

Pitt, Rt. Hon. **William,** 1759–1806. *Deep Will; Julius Florus; A Right Honourable Person.* An English statesman; son of the preceding; b. at Hayes, Kent; educ. at Pembroke Coll., Cambridge; called to the Bar at Lincoln's Inn; English Premier, 1784–1801 and 1804–6; d. at Putney.

Pitter, J. *Mercury.* An English poet.

Pittis, Rev. **John.** *A Presbyter of the Church of England.* An English clergyman of the first part of the 18th century.

Pitts, Rev. **Joseph.** *A Presbyter of the Church of England.* An English clergyman of the first part of the 18th century.

Pixley, Frank M., 1826–. *Olla Podrida.* An American author and editor, of San Francisco; b. in Leroy, N.Y.

Place, Francis. *Gamaliel Smith.* An English writer; a tailor at Charing Cross, London, who wrote for the "Westminster Review."

Planché, James Robinson, 1796–1880. *The Somerset Herald.* An English miscellaneous writer; b. in London; author of nearly 200 dramatic pieces, etc.; d. at St. Leonard's Terrace, Chelsea.

Platel, Félix. *Ignotus; Étienne Pall.* A French writer, of Paris, of the day.

Player, John. *Thomas Elbridge Rooke, Esq.* An English merchant at Fockington, near Bristol.

Playfair, William, 1759–1823. *Joshua Montefiore and J. Jephson Oddy.* A Scottish writer on politics and political economy; b. near Dundee; left Scotland for England, and, proceeding to Birmingham, was engaged in 1780 as a draughts-man at Soho, in the employment of Mr. James Watt. After various other em-ployments, he became an author in Lon-don, where he died.

Plinth, Octavius. *The Rain-Water Doctor.* An American quack, an imitator of Sylvan, enemy of human diseases.

Ploug, Parmo Karl, 1813–. *Poul Rytter.* A Danish poet; studied philol-ogy at Copenhagen from 1829, and after-wards devoted himself entirely to literary work.

Plumer, William, 1759–1850. *Cin-cinnatus.* An American lawyer and statesman; b. at Newbury, Mass.; in 1768, removed to Epping, N.H.; U.S. Senator, 1802–7; Governor of N.H., 1812–13 and 1816–19; afterwards en-gaged in literary pursuits; d. at Ep-ping.

Plummer, John, 1831–. *The North-amptonshire Poet.* An English poet and prose writer; b. near Tower Hill, Lon-don; settled at Kettering, Northants., in 1853.

Plumptre, Annabella. *A Lady.* An English writer; third daughter of the Rev. Dr. Robert Plumptre, who was for 28 years president of Queen's Coll., Cam-bridge.

Plumptre, Miss Anne. *Miss P*******.* An English writer; sister of the preced-ing; second daughter of Dr. Plumptre.

Plumptre, John, D.D. *A Clergyman of the Church of England.* An English divine; Dean of Gloucester, Canon of Worcester, and sometime Fellow of King's Coll., Cambridge.

Poe, Edgar Allan, 1809–49. *A Bostonian; Arthur Gordon Pym; Hans Pfaal; Quarles.* An eccentric American poet and prose writer; b. in Boston; educ. in London, in Virginia, and at West Point; was a journalist at Rich-mond, Va., in New York City, and in Philadelphia; d. in Baltimore.

Poilow de Saint-Mars, Gabrielle Anne (de Cisternes de Coutiras), Marquise de, 1805–. *Jacques Reynaud; la comtesse Dash.* A French writer; b. in Paris; was driven by her misfortunes to devote herself to literary labor.

Poinsett, Joel Roberts, LL.D., 1779–1851. *A Citizen of the United States.* An American statesman; b. at Charleston, S.C.; educ. in Connecticut, at Edinburgh, and at Woolwich; travelled in Europe and Asia, 1801–9; M.C., 1821–25; U.S. Secretary of War, 1837–41; d. at States-burg, S.C.

Poinsot, Antoine Edmond, 1834–.

Georges d'Heilly. A French bibliogra-pher, of Paris, of the day.

Pole, Thomas, M.D., 1753–1829. *A Friend to Education, etc.* An English Friend, of Bristol; a minister 56 years.

Pole, Prof. William, Mus. D., F.R.S., F.R.S.E., 1814–. *Prof. P.* An English civil engineer; b. at Birmingham; pro-fessor at the Univ. Coll., London, 1859–67; the author of a scientific work on whist, and a contributor to the "Quar-terly Review"; in 1875 resident in West-minster.

Polglase, Ann Eaton, 1803–65. *A. E. P.* An English Friend, of Bristol; b. at Helston; in 1842 married William Moon; d. at Bristol.

Polidori, Dr. Louis Eustache, –1830. *Lord Byron.* An Italian physi-cian; b. at Bientina, near Pisa; Profes-sor of Physiology at Florence, 1825–30.

Political Tatler. Supposed editor, *Joshua Standfast.*

Polk, Josiah F. *Akroates.* An Amer-ican writer.

Pollard, Edward Alfred, 1838–72. *A Distinguished Southern Journalist; The Southern Spy.* An American journalist and miscellaneous writer, of Richmond, Va.; b. in Nelson Co., Va.; educ. at the Univ. of Va., and at William and Mary Coll.; editor of the "Richmond Exam-iner," 1861–65, and of the "Southern Opinion," 1867–69.

Pollock, Rev. John. *A Well-wisher of the Good-old-way.* A Scottish minister of the first part of the 18th century.

Pollock, Rev. **John.** *A Member of the Church of Scotland.* A Scottish minister of the last part of the 18th century.

Polwhele, Rev. **Richard,** 1760–1838. *P.; R. P.; Eusebius Exoniensis; A Country Gentleman; An Undergraduate; A Young Gentleman of Truro School.* An English poet and clergyman; b. and d. at Truro; Vicar of Newlyn East, 1821–38.

Pomeroy, Mark M., 1833–. *Brick Pomeroy.* An American journalist, of New York City; late editor of the "La Crosse (Wisconsin) Democrat."

Pomfret, John, about 1667–1703. *A Person of Quality.* An English poet.

Pond, Frederick Eugene, 1856–. *Red Wing; Will Wildwood.* An Ameri-can journalist.

Pond, George E. *Philip Quillibet.*

Poniatowski, Jozef Anton, Prince, 1762–1813. *The Polish Bayard.* A Pol-ish general and marshal, of France.

Ponsonby, Miss ——. *Zara.* — See "Butler, Lady Eleanor."

Ponsonby, Hon. Frederick George

Brabazon, 1815–. *Richard Roe.* An English lawyer and dramatist; b. in London; Trin. Coll., Cambridge, M.A., 1837; called to the Bar, 1840; and given the Midland Circuit.

Ponsonby, Hon. **Spencer Cecil Brabazon**, 1824–. *Bolton Row.* An English writer; son of the 4th Earl of Besborough; private secretary to Lord Palmerston, and in 1853, to Lord Clarendon.

Pontes, Mme de —— **(Phillips).** *The Translator of the Niebelungen Treasure.* An English poet and dramatist; previously Miss Phillips.

Pool, Maria L. *Catharine Earnshaw.* An American writer of the day.

Poole, Richard, M.D. *An Aged Layman.* A Scottish physician of the 19th century.

Poole, Mrs. **Sophia (Lane).** *A Consul's Daughter and Wife; The Englishwoman; His Sister.* An English writer; sister of Edward William Lane; and wife of Stanley Poole.

Poole, William Frederick, A.M., 1821–. *P.; Philorthos.* An eminent American bibliographer; b. in Salem, Mass.; Yale Coll., 1849; librarian of the Chicago Public Library from 1873.

Pooley, ——. *A Gentleman of the Middle Temple.* An English barrister, of great eminence in his time.

Poore, Benjamin Perley, 1820–. *Perley; The Major; Raconteur.* An American editor and journalist; b. in Newbury, Mass.; chiefly at Washington from 1854.

Pope, Alexander, 1688–1744. *A.; Esdras Barnivelt, Apoth.; Dick Distich; An Eminent Hand; An Eye-Witness; Mr. Joseph Gay; Gnatho; M.; Martinus Scriblerus; Bob Short.* A celebrated English poet; b. in London; d. at Chiswick.

Popham, Rev. **Vyvyan Wallis,** M.A., 1833–. *V. W. P.* An English clergyman and composer; b. at Antron, near Helston; Exeter Coll., 1853; Curate of Illogan, 1863–79; afterwards resident at Windsor-terrace, Bedford.

Popplewell, Thomas, –1790. *Old Pop.* An English singer, of London.

Porson, Richard, D.D., 1759–1808. *Cantabrigiensis; J. N. Dawes; Sundry Whereof.* An English Greek scholar and critic; b. at East Ruston, in Norfolk, Regius Professor of Greek in the Univ. of Cambridge, 1790; Head Librarian of the London Institution, 1806–8; d. at his rooms in the Old Jewry.

Porteous, Rev. ——. *A Minister of the Church of Scotland.* A Scottish minister of the last part of the 18th century.

Porter, Mrs. **Anne Emerson,** 1816–.

Uncle Jerry. An American writer; b. at Newburyport, Mass.; wife of Charles E. Porter, Springfield, Vt.

Porter, David, 1780–1843. *An American long Resident at Constantinople.* An American naval officer; b. in Boston; served in the navy with great distinction from 1798 to 1826; Chargé d'Affaires to Turkey, 1830; and afterwards Minister till his death at Pera, near Constantinople.

Porter, Miss **Jane,** 1776–1850. *J. P.; An Englishwoman.* An English writer; b. at Durham; resided some years in London; then in Esher, and still later with her brother, Dr. W. O. Porter, at Bristol, where she died.

Porter, Sir **Robert Ker,** Knt., K.C.H., 1780–1842. *An Officer.* An English artist and traveller; brother of Anna Maria and Jane Porter; b. at Durham; d. at St. Petersburg.

Porter, Mrs. **Robert P.** *Cress; A Detective's Daughter.* An American writer of the day.

Porter, William Trotter, 1806–58. *York's Tall Son.* An American sporting journalist, of New York City; b. at Newbury, Vt.; founded "Porter's Spirit of the Times," and conducted it till his death in New York City.

Portland, William Henry Cavendish Bentinck, Duke of, 1738–1809. *A Late Prime Minister.* An English statesman.

Portsmouth, Henry, 1703–80. *Catholicus; Philalethes.* An English Friend, of Basingstoke, Hants., where he died.

Post, Mrs. **Lydia (Minturn).** *Sydney Barclay.* An American writer of the day.

Post, Sarah L. *Rosa Graham.* An American writer of the day.

Postel, Karl, 1793–1864. *Charles Sealsfield.* A German novelist; resided many years in the United States, and associate editor of the "Courrier des États-Unis."

Postlethwayt, James, Esq., F.R.S., 1688–1758. *J. P., Esq., F.R.S.* An English statistical and financial writer.

Postlethwayt, Malachy, about 1707–67. *A British Merchant.* An English writer on trade and commerce.

Potocki, Count **Léon.** *L. P.* A Polish writer.

Pott, Rev. **Joseph Holden,** M.A., 1759–1847. *Valentine.* An English clergyman; b. in London; Archdeacon of London, 1814–42; Chancellor of the Cathedral Church of Exeter, 1826–47; d. at his house in Woburn-place, London.

Potter, Albert Knight, D.D. *Six.*

An American Bapt. clergyman; b. in Coventry, R.I.; Brown Univ., 1859; pastor at Springfield, Mass., 1864–81 et seq.

Potter, Elisha Reynolds, 1811–82. *A Landholder.* An American writer; b. in S. Kingston, R.I.; Harv. Univ., 1830; M.C., 1843–45; d. in his native town.

Potter, Rev. **Robert,** 1721–1804. *Mr. P.* An eminent English classical scholar; educ. at Emmanuel Coll., Cambridge; Prebendary of Norwich, 1788; and Vicar of Lowestoft and Kensingland, 1789–1804.

Potter, Woodbourne. *A Late Staff Officer.* An American soldier; b. in Pennsylvania; appointed from that State; second lieutenant 7th Infantry, 1837; resigned, 1839.

Pottinger, J. *An American.*

Potts, Laurence Holkar, M.D., 1789–1850. *Æsculapius.* An English physician; b. and d. in London; inventor of the hydraulic pile-driver patent, etc.

Potts, Stacy Gardner, 1800–65. *Oliver Oakwood.* An American lawyer; b. at Harrisburg, Penn.; admitted to the Bar, 1827; Judge of the New Jersey Supreme Court, 1852–59; d. at Trenton, N.J.

Potvin, Charles, 1818–. *Dom Jacobus; Dom Liber.* A Belgian poet and literary historian; b. at Mons; studied at Löwen, and then became Professor of the National Literature at the public lectures of the City of Brussels; in 1869, he founded the " Revue de Belgique."

Potwin, Mrs. **H. K.** *H. K. P.* An American writer of the day, for the young.

Pouchkine, Alexandre Sergeié-vitch, 1799–1837. *Ivan Belkine.* A celebrated Russian poet, of Moscow, after the accession of Nicholas.

Poulet-Malassis, Auguste Paul, –1878. *Paul Rouillon.* A French political writer.

Poutré, Félix. *Un prisonnier d'État.* A Canadian writer.

Powell, Thomas, 1809–. *Pierce Pungent; Grandfather Whitehead.* An English-American journalist; b. in London; came to New York City in 1849, and has been engaged there since in editing several journals.

Powell, Thomas. *T. de Monmouth.* An English writer of the last century.

Power, Dr. ——, D.D. *Fidelis.* An Irish clergyman; Bishop of Waterford.

Power, Miss **Marguerite A.** *Honoria; Honoria N.* An English novelist; niece of the Countess of Blessington.

Power, Richard. *A Barrister.* An Irish lawyer; Baron of Exchequer.

Power, Samuel Browning. *S. B. P.* An English writer for the young.

Power, Mrs. **Susan C. (Dunning).** *Shirley Dare.* An American writer of the day.

Powers, Miss **S. Rugeley.** *S. R. P.* An English writer of the day; secretary to the Ladies' National Association for the Diffusion of Sanitary Knowledge, London.

Pownall, Henry. *H. P. ; An Inhabitant.* An English author, of Epsom, in 1829.

Pownall, Thomas, 1722–1805. *A King's Friend.* An English statesman; b. in Lincoln; Governor of Massachusetts, 1757–60; from 1780 spent his life in retirement and in antiquarian studies; d. at Bath.

Poyas, Mrs. **E. A.** *The Octogenarian Lady of Charleston, S.C.*

Poynder, John, Esq., 1779–1849. *A Layman.* An English writer; for many years one of the proprietors of the East India House; d. at South Lambeth.

Poyser, Thomas, Esq., F.R.C.S., 1790–1860. *T. P.* An English physician; for nearly 50 years the leading practitioner in Wirksworth and its district; gave Miss Nightingale her first hints in nursing and medicine; d. at Wirksworth, County Derby.

Praed, Winthrop Mackworth, 1802–39. *Peregrine Courtenay; Vyvian Joyeuse.* A brilliant English poet and classical scholar; b. and d. in London; educ. at Eton and Trin. Coll., Cambridge; called to the Bar, 1829; M.P., 1830–31 and 1835.

Prantner, Ferdinand, 1817–71. *Leo Wolfram.* A German author; b. at Vienna and d. there.

Pratt, Anna A. *Say Putnam.* An American writer of the day, for the young.

Pratt, Mrs. **Ella (Farnam).** *Dorothea Alice Shepherd.* An American writer of the day; b. in New York.

Pratt, L. Maria. *L. L.; Laura Loring.* An American writer of the day, for the young.

Pratt, Samuel Jackson, 1749–1814. *Courtney Melmoth.* An English writer; b. at St. Ives, in Huntingdonshire; d. at Birmingham; he was for a time an actor and then a bookseller at Bath.

Preble, George Henry, 1816–85. *Elberp.* An eminent American naval officer, 1835–78; b. in Portland, Me.; d. at his home at Cottage Farm, Brookline, Mass.

Prentice, George Denison, 1802–70.

Il Penseroso. An American journalist; b. at Preston, Conn.; Brown Univ., 1823; admitted to the Bar, 1829; editor of the "Louisville (Ky.) Journal," 1830–70; d. at Louisville.

Prentiss, Mrs. **Elizabeth (Payson),** 1823–78. *Aunt Susan.* An American writer for children; daughter of the Rev. Dr. Ed. Payson, of Portland, Me., and wife of the Rev. Dr. G. L. Prentiss, of Union Theol. Sem.; d. at Dorset, Vt.

Prescott, Rev. **Benjamin,** 1687–1777. *Philopolities.* An American Cong. minister, of Danvers, Mass., 1713–56; Harv. Univ., 1709.

Prescott, Kenrick. *K. P.* An English scholar of the 18th century.

Prest, Thomas Prescott. *Angelina.* An English (?) dramatist.

Prevost, Ven. Sir **George,** 2d Bart., 1804–. *F.; Contributor to the Tracts for the Times.* An eminent English clergyman; Archdeacon of Gloucester, 1865–81; Vicar of Stinchcombe, Dursley, 1834–83 *et seq.*

Price, Chace. *A Welch Member of Parliament.*

Price, Emanuel. *Peter Peppercorn.* An American poet of the day.

Price, James F. *An American.* An American writer.

Price, James H. *A Virginian.* An American poet.

Price, Joseph. *Recos Jepphi.* An English writer.

Price, Capt. **Joseph.** *A Free Merchant in Bengal.*

Price, Rev. **Thomas,** 1787–1849. *Carnhuanawc.* A Welsh minister; b. in Brecknockshire; Vicar of Cwmdu, 1825–49; d. at the vicarage house of that parish, near Crickhowell, Co. of Brecon.

Prichard, J. V. *J. V. P.* An —— Shakespearian scholar.

Priestley, Joseph, LL.D., F.R.S., 1733–1804. *A Lover of the Gospel; A Lover of Peace and Truth; A Patriot.* An English chemist, philosopher, and theologian; b. at Fieldhead, Birstall, Yorks.; resided in the United States from 1794.

Prime, Benjamin Young, M.D., 1733–91. *An American; An American Gentleman.* An American poet; b. in Huntingdon, Long Island; New Jersey Coll., 1751; wrote many Revolutionary songs and ballads, which circulated widely during the war.

Prime, Rev. **Edward Dorr Griffin,** 1814–. *Eusebius.* An American clergyman, journalist, and traveller; b. at Cambridge, N.Y.; Union Coll., 1832; journalist in New York City.

Prime, Samuel Irenæus, LL.D., D.D., 1812–85. *Irenæus.* An eminent American clergyman and journalist; b. at Ballston, N.Y.; Union Coll., 1829; of New York City from 1840; d. at Manchester, Vt.

Prime, William Cowper, 1825–. *W.* An American lawyer and journalist; b. at Cambridge, N.Y.; New Jersey Coll., 1843; editor and one of the proprietors of the New York "Journal of Commerce" from 1861.

Pring, Rev. **John,** B.A., 1777–1855. *A Supernumerary.* An English clergyman.

Pringle, Edward J. *E. J. P.; A Carolinian.*

Prinsep, John, Esq. *Gurreb Doos; A Planter and Distiller in Bengal.*

Proby, John. *King Porus.* An English reporter of a very eccentric character; was always in a perspiration (which earned him the name of "King Porus" from George Colman); he reported the Parliamentary debates entirely from memory, and without making a single note. He d. in the Lambeth workhouse.

Procter, Miss **Adelaide Anne,** 1835–64. *Miss Mary Berwick.* An English poet; "the golden tressed Adelaide," daughter of the following; b. and d. in London.

Procter, Bryan Waller, 1787–1874. *B.; Barry Cornwall; James Jessamine; X. X. X.; X. Y. Z.* An eminent English poet; b. and d. in London; educ. at Harrow; was called to the Bar at Gray's Inn in 1831; and from that time steadily practised his profession.

Proctor, Col. **George.** *Humphrey Ravelin, Esq.* An English officer of the Royal Military Coll., Sandhurst.

Proctor, John. *Puck.* An English caricaturist of the day.

Proctor, John J., 1833–. *A Ragged Philosopher.* A Canadian poet and prose writer; for some time a teacher at Lennoxville, L.C.

Prosser, Col. **G. W.** *Z.* An English writer.

Proud, Rev. **Joseph.** *Philo.* An English minister, of York Street Chapel, St. James's Square, London; he was at first a mechanic, but became a Swedenborgian minister, and gathered a congregation at Bristol, but afterwards removed to London.

Proudfit, David L. *Peleg Arkwright.* An American poet and journalist.

Prouting, Frederic J., 1859–. *Argus; Vandyke Brown; Verité sans Peur.* An English writer.

Prower, ——. *Emeritus.* An English writer.

Prudhomme, Louis Marie, 1752–1830. *L. M. B., Armateur.* A French revolutionist; b. at Lyons; issued an ultra republican journal in Paris, in 1789.

Pudsey, William. *W. P—y.* An English writer, of the first part of the 18th century.

Pückler-Muskau, Fürst Hermann Ludwig Heinrich von, 1785–1875. *A German Prince; Semilasso.* A German author; b. at Muskau, in Silesian Prussia; studied law at Leipsic; travelled extensively, and d. at Kranitz, near Kottbus.

Pugh, Edward, –1814. *A Native Artist.* An English miniature painter; practised in London; exhibited at the Royal Academy, 1793–1806; d. at Ruthin, North Wales.

Pugh, Edward. *David Hughson, LL.D.* An English writer, early in the 19th century.

Pugh, Mrs. Eliza Lofton (Phillips). *Arria.* An American "Southland" writer, of Louisiana.

Pullen, Charles Henry. *Cosmopolitan.* An English writer of the day.

Pullen, Rev. Henry William, M.A. *Canon.* An English clergyman; Clare Coll., Cambridge, 1859; chaplain of H. M. S. "Alert" in the Arctic expedition, 1875–76.

Pulman, George P. R. *John Trotandot; Piscator.* An English sporting writer of the day.

Pulsifer, David. *R. L. Midgeley.* An American antiquary, of Boston; b. in Ipswich, Mass.

Pulteney, William, Earl of Bath, 1682–1764. *A Freeholder; A Member of Parliament; Will Worthy.* An English peer; was at first a Whig and personal friend of Walpole, but from 1725 to 1742, one of his most bitter opponents; assisted Bolingbroke in the "Craftsman."

Purdy, Alderman. *The War-Horse.*

Purnell, Thomas. *Q.* An English antiquary and journalist, of London; on

the staff of the "Globe"; secretary to the Archæological Institute, London.

Purple, Edwin R., 1831–79. *Neafie.*

Purton, Rev. William, M.A. *X. Y. Z.* An English clergyman; Trin. Coll., Oxford, 1855; Vicar of St. Clement, Bournemouth, 1880–83 *et seq.*

Puseley, Daniel, –1882. *D. P.; Frank Foster.* An English traveller and writer.

Pusey, Edward Bouverie, D.D., 1800–. *C.; Contributors to the Tracts for the Times.* An eminent English clergyman and theologian; Christ Church, Oxford, 1822; Regius Professor of Hebrew, at Oxford, 1828–80 *et seq.,* with Canonry of Christ Church annexed.

Pusey, Pennock. *The Assistant Secretary of State.* An American writer, of Minnesota.

Putnam, Mrs. Ellen T. H. *Thrace Talmon.* An American writer of the day.

Putnam, Mrs. Mary (Lowell), 1810–. *Edward Colvil.* An American writer of distinction; b. in Boston; sister of James Russell Lowell, and wife of Samuel R. Putnam, a merchant of Boston.

Putnam, Mrs. Sallie A. (Brock). *A Lady; Virginia Madison; A Richmond Lady.* An American poet and novelist; from 1870, of New York City; b. at Madison Court House, Va.; in 1858 removed to Richmond.

Putney, Henry M. *Snoggins.* An American journalist, of Manchester, N.H.; 1860–70, correspondent of the Manchester "Mirror"; and now (1885) on the editorial staff of that paper.

Pycroft, Rev. James, 1813–. *J. P.; **** *** ***.* An English clergyman and miscellaneous writer; B.A., Oxford, 1836; in 1880 resident at Gloucester Gardens, Hyde Park, London.

Pyle, Rev. Philip, –1799. *Philip.* An English clergyman; Rector of Castle Rising and Lynn St. Edmund, Norfolk, Norfolk.

Pyne, William Henry, Esq., 1770–1843. *Ephraim Hardcastle.* An English painter and miscellaneous writer; b., lived, and d. in London.

Q.

Quanten, Emil von, 1827–. *Särkilax.* A Finnish poet; b. at Björneborg; settled in Sweden; and was librarian of King Charles XV., 1864–72.

Quanten, Frau Emil von. *Turdus;*

Merula. A Finnish translator; wife of the preceding.

Quarll, Philip. *An Englishman.* An old English writer.

Quérard, Joseph Marie, 1795–1865.

Marie Jozon d'Erquar. A French bibliographer, of Paris; b. in Rennes; d. in Paris.

Quevedo, Walter C. *Odds and Ends.* An American journalist, of New York City.

Quincey, Thomas. *T—— Q——.* An English writer; father of Thomas de Quincey.

Quincy, Edmund, A.M., 1808–77. *Byles.* An American scholar and writer; b. in Boston; Harv. Univ., 1827; lived and d. in Dedham, Mass.

Quincy, Josiah, Jr., 1744–75. *Edward Sexby; Calisthenes; Marchmont Needham; An Old Man.* An eminent

American lawyer and patriot, of Boston.

Quincy, Samuel Miller, 1833–. *A High Private.* An American lawyer and journalist; b. in Boston; Harv. Univ., 1852; served in the civil war, 1861–65; for several years one of the editors of the "Monthly Law Reporter," Boston.

Quivogne-Chartrouse, Marie Émilie, 1850–. *Marc de Montifaud.* A French author; b. at Paris; married at an early age the Spanish Count Quivogne, who became a bookseller, and his business was devoted almost entirely to the sale of the works of his wife, whose first book was published when she was 13 years old.

R.

Raabe, Wilhelm, 1831–. *Jakob Corvinus.* A German humorous writer; b. at Eschershausen in Brunswick; has taught philosophy at the University of Berlin for a time from 1855; since 1870 has resided in Brunswick.

Rack, Edmund, 1735–87. *Eusebius; A Friend to True Liberty.* An English Friend; b. in Attleborough, Norfolk; became a linen-draper at Bardfield, Essex; about 1775 removed to Bath, where he died.

Radcliffe, Alida G. *A. G. R.* An American (?) hymn writer.

Rae, William. *A Probationer of the Church of Scotland.*

Raffles, Thomas, D.D., LL.D., 1788–1863. *A Doctor of Divinity, but not of Oxford; Three Friends.* An English Dissenter; b. in Spitalfields; pastor of the Cong. Church at Hammersmith, 1808–11; and of the Great George Street Chapel, Liverpool, 1811–61; d. at Edge-Hill, Liverpool.

Raine, Rev. Matthew, 1760–1810. ****. An English clergyman; Fellow of Trin. Coll., Cambridge, 1783; schoolmaster of the Charter House, 1791; Preacher of Gray's Inn, 1809; Rector of Little Hallingbury, Essex, 1810.

Raisson, Horace Napoléon, 1798–1854. *A. B. Périgord.* A French man of letters; b. in Paris; was in the office of the ministry of finance, 1818–22; then devoted himself to literature.

Raithby, John, Esq. *A Member of Lincoln's Inn.* An English law writer; originally a law-stationer of Chancery Lane, London.

Raleigh, Walter S. *W. S. R.* An American (?) writer of the day.

Ralph, James, –1762. *A Gentleman of the Middle Temple; An Impartial Inquirer; Lilburne; A Lover of Truth and Liberty; A Primcock; A Woman of Quality.* An English political journalist and pamphleteer, dramatist, poet, and historian; probably b. in Philadelphia; in 1724 went to London with Benjamin Franklin; d. at Chiswick.

Ralph, Julian E. *The German Barber.* An American journalist, of New York City.

Ralphs, ——. *Issachar Barebone.* An English journalist, of London, of the 18th century. Probably James Ralph.

Ralston, Thomas N., D.D. *Eureka.* An American clergyman.

Ram, Rev. Stopford James, M.A. *Ruth Vernon.* An English clergyman; St. John's Coll., Cambridge, 1849; Vicar of Christ Church, Battersea, 1877–80 et seq.

Ramsay, ——. *R.* An English librarian, of London Library, Ludgate Street, long since extinct.

Ramsay, Allan, 1685–1758. *Quod Ar. Scot.* A Scottish poet; b. at Leadhills, Lanarkshire; was first a wig-maker; then a bookseller at Edinburgh.

Ramsay, Allan, Jr., 1713–84. *Britannicus; Marcellus; Steady; Zero.* A Scottish portrait painter; b. at Edinburgh; son of the poet; settled first in Edinburgh, then in London; "the son of the poet was a man of literature as well as genius"; d. at Dover.

Ramsay, D. *Hortensius.*

Ramsay, James. *A Gentleman.* **A**

Scottish writer, of Eyemouth, Co. of Berwick; of the first part of the 18th century.

Ramsay, Rev. James. *A Member of the Duddingston Curling Society.* A Scottish minister.

Ramsden, F. E. *Kalula.* An American journalist.

Rand, C. H. *Mabel Hazelton.* An American (?) novelist of the day.

Rand, Olive. *O. R.* An American author and journalist; now (1885) on the editorial staff of the Manchester (N.H.) "Mirror."

Randall, J. R. *J. R. R.* An American poet, of Maryland.

Randles, E., 1760–1820. *The Lyrist.* An English organist; a pupil of the celebrated Parry, harper to Sir W. W. Wynn; d. at Wrexham.

Randolph, Paschal Beverley, M.D., 1825–. *Griffin Lee; A Rosicrucian.* An American editor and novelist, of Boston and New York City; b. in the latter.

Rands, William Brighty, 1827–82. *Henry Holbeach; Matthew Browne; Timon Fieldmouse.* An English miscellaneous writer, of London.

Ranken, Major George, 1838–55. *A Soldier; X., Author of Nothing, and properly represented by the above Unknown Quantity.* An English officer of the Royal Engineers; killed at Sebastopol, while leading an assault party on the Redan.

Rankin, Fannie W. *F. W. R.* An American (?) novelist of the day.

Ranking, B. Montgomerie. *M. R.* An English poet of the day.

Ranyard, Mrs. Ellen, –1880. *L. N. R.* An English writer, of London; editor of the "Missing Link Magazine."

Rapallo, Mrs. S. F. Ludomilla (Schetky). *His Daughter.* An English author; daughter of J. C. Schetky, marine painter to the Queen.

Rarey, John S., 1828–66. *Scrutator.* An American horse-tamer; b. at Madison, Franklin Co., O.

Rashleigh, Sir John Colman, Bart., 1772–1847. *One of the 80,000 Incorrigible Jacobins.* An English politician; b. at Penquite; d. at Prideaux.

Rathbone, Mrs. Mary Anne (Manning), 1812–. *Beatrice; An English Girl; Margareta More; Edward Osborne.* An English writer of fiction.

Rathbone, William, 1819–. *A Man of Business.* An English merchant, of Liverpool; President of Queen's Coll., Liverpool, from 1874; M.P. from 1868.

Ratisbonne, Louis Gustave For-

tuné, 1827–. *Trim.* A French author and journalist; b. at Strasburg; studied at Paris, and was on the staff of the "Journal des Débats," 1853–76.

Rattazzi, Princesse Marie Studolmine (Bonaparte, dame de Solms). *Le vicomte d'Albens; Camille Bernard; Le baron Stock.* A French writer; b. at Waterford, Ireland; the daughter of Princesse Letitia Bonaparte; in 1850, married Frédéric de Solms, a rich Alsacian; in 1863, Urbain Rattazzi.

Rattenbury, John. *A Smuggler.*

Rawlinson, Richard, LL.D., F.R.S., F.A.S., –1755. *An Impartial Hand.* An English antiquary; son of the following; educ. at St. John's Coll., Oxford; labored zealously in the cause of letters while he lived, and left his lands, books, Mss., and medals to his university, when he died.

Rawlinson, Thomas, 1681–1725. *Tom Folio.* An English literary antiquary and great collector of books. While he lived in Gray's Inn, he had four chambers so completely filled with books that his bed was removed out into the passage. He afterwards removed to London-house, in Aldersgate Street, where he died.

Rawson, ——. *A Cambridge Gentleman.* An English writer early in the 18th century.

Rawson, George. *A Leeds Layman.* An English hymn-writer, of Leeds.

Rawson, Mrs. Harry. *A Lady.* An English traveller, of Manchester.

Rawston, George. *An Ex-Dissenter.* An English writer.

Ray, Dewitt Grinnell. *Widett Gray.*

Raybaud, Maxime. *Gustave d'Alaux.* A French writer; Consul-General at Hayti.

Raymond, Henry S. *Billy Bowline.*

Raymond, Rossiter Worthington, 1840–. *Robertson Gray.* An American mining engineer; b. at Cincinnati; educ. at Brooklyn, N.Y., and in Germany; in 1881 *et seq.* of New York City.

Rea, George James, 1820–64. *George Raynor.* An American minstrel; d. at Brooklyn, N.Y.

Read, H. Y. *An Actual Settler.* A Canadian writer, of Hopefield, U.C.

Reade, Alfred Arthur. *A Special Correspondent.* An English traveller, of Manchester; a writer of the day.

Reade, Rev. John, 1838–. *J. R.; R. J. C.; J. F. Home.* A Canadian Epis. clergyman, poet, and journalist, of Potton, L.C.

Reade, William Winwood, 1839–

75. *Francesco Abati.* An English novelist and traveller; nephew of Charles Reade; b. at Ipsden; correspondent of the London "Times" on the Ashantee expedition, 1873-74; d. at Wimbledon.

Reay, Henry Utrick, Esq. *A Gentleman Farmer.* An English gentleman, of Killingworth, near Newcastle; a great landowner, and one of the largest coalowners; was at one time high sheriff for the county of Northumberland.

Reay, Prof. **Stephen,** B.D., 1782-1861. *Pileus Quadratus.* A Scottish orientalist; b. at Montrose, N.B.; educ. at St. Alban's Hall, Oxford, and Laudian Prof. of Arabic there, 1840-61; sublibrarian of the Bodleian Library; d. at his residence, St. Giles, Oxford.

Reboul, Jean, 1796-1864. *The Baker Poet.* A French poet; a baker of Nismes.

Redcliffe, Viscount **Stratford de,** 1788-1880. *Sir Hector Stubble.* An English diplomatist; better known as Sir Stratford Canning; b. in London; raised to the peerage in 1852; d. at Tunbridge Wells.

Redden, Miss **Laura C.** — See "Searing, Mrs. L. C. (R.)."

Redding, Cyrus, 1785-1870. *U. U.; J. W. Hengiston, Esq.; Peter Wilkins.* An English poet and miscellaneous writer; b. at Penryn; removed to London in 1806; resided in Paris, 1815-18; d. in London.

Redfoord, A. *An Independent Observer.* An Irish writer, of one hundred years ago.

Redford, Albion H. *Tim Trimmer.* An American novelist of the day.

Redpath, James, 1833-. *Berwick; The Roving Editor.* A Scottish-American reformer and journalist; b. at Berwick-on-the-Tweed; came to this country in 1848; has occupied various positions here; in 1880, was lecturing in Massachusetts.

Reed, Emeline. *Emie Roseau.*

Reed, Isaac, F.A.S., 1742-1807. *The Editor of "Dodsley's Collection of Old Plays."* An English editor, critic, and biographer; b. and d. in London. It took 39 days to sell his library after his death, and it brought more than £4000.

Reed, Joseph, 1723-90. *J. R.; Benedict; A Halter-maker; Dr. Humbug.* An English dramatic and miscellaneous writer; b. at Stockton, County Durham; in 1757 removed to Sun Tavern Fields, at Stepney, near London, where he pursued his trade of rope-maker till his death.

Reed, Mary J., 1830-. *Marie Roseau.* An American writer; b. in Philadelphia.

Reed, Peter Fishe, 1819-. *Viva Mona.* An American poet and prose writer; b. in South Boston, Mass.; in 1860, of Indianapolis, Ind.; he commenced life a farmer, and became successively a shoemaker, a house and sign painter, an editor, a doctor, a photographer, a music-teacher, and finally an artist.

Reed, William Bradford, LL.D., 1806-76. *W. B. R.; A Citizen of Pennsylvania; A Northern Man.* An American statesman; b. in Philadelphia; Univ. of Penn., 1822; U.S. Minister to China, 1857-58; d. in New York City.

Rees, James, 1802-85. *Colley Cibber.* An American author and journalist, of Philadelphia; b. at Morristown, Penn.; in 1876, held a position in the Philadelphia post-office; d. in that city.

Reeve, Miss **Clara,** 1725-1807. *C. R.* An English poet and novelist; oldest daughter of the Rev. William Reeve, of St. Nicholas, in Ipswich; and d. there.

Reeve, Henry, F.S.A., C.B., D.C.L., 1813-. *H. R.* An English editor and essayist; b. at Norwich; Registrar of the Privy Council, 1837-76 *et seq.;* editor of the "Edinburgh Review," 1855.

Reeve, Robert, -1840. *Juvenis Suffolciensis.* An English antiquary; b. and d. at Lowestoft.

Reeve, Thomas, M.D., 1700-80. *T. R., M.D.* An English physician; b. in Middlesex; educ. at Emmanuel Coll., Cambridge; physician to St. Thomas's Hospital, London, 1740-60; d. in London.

Reeves, Miss **Marian C. Legaré.** — See "Rodney, Mrs. M. C. L. (R.)."

Regnier, Maria Sidonia (Serrur), 1840-. *Daniel Darc; Daniel Darcey.* A French writer; b. in Paris; in 1861 was married in that city to Dr. Regnier, of Mantes, where she devoted herself to a literary career.

Reid, Christopher. *Cosmo Caustic, Gent.; Tyro Trimstave, M.D.* A Scottish writer.

Reid, E. *E. R.* An American (?) writer of the day.

Reid, J. J. *J. J. R.* A Scottish author of the day.

Reid, T. Wemys. *An Extinguished Exile.* An English writer of the day.

Reilly, Edwin J. *Clio.*

Reitzenstein, Franziska, Baronin **von,** 1837-. *Franz von Nemmersdorf.* A German novelist; in 1852, married the Freiherrn von Reitzenstein, and after the early death of her husband, spent some time in travels; now, 1882, she lives at Munich.

Relly, James, 1720–78. *J. R.* An English Univ. minister, of the congregation, Coachmakers' Hall, London.

Renard, Mme **Céline**, 1834–. *Jenny Maria.* A French writer of the day; b. at Bourboune-les-Bains.

Rengade, le docteur **Jules**. *Aristide Roger.* A French writer.

Rennell, Major **James**, 1742–1830. *Major R.* An English traveller; b. near Chudleigh, Devonshire; travelled in Asia and Africa; d. in London.

Rennell, Thomas, B.D., F.R.S., 1787–1824. *A Student in Divinity.* An eminent English clergyman; b. and d. at Winchester; educ. at Eton and King's Coll., Cambridge; Prebendary of Salisbury, 1823–24.

Rennell, Dr. Thomas, Mr. Knight, George Canning, etc. *Solomon Grildrig.*

Renny, J. H. *A British Merchant.* An English economist.

Renouf, Peter Le Page, 1824–. *A Late Member of the University.* An English orientalist; b. at the Isle of Guernsey; Pemb. Coll., Oxford; professor at the Catholic Univ. of Ireland; has written for several journals.

Repton, John Adey, Esq., F.S.A., 1775–1860. *W. Wiar; Repandunum.* An English architect; b. at Norwich, where he studied and practised his profession; was for more than 50 years a welcome correspondent of the "Gentleman's Magazine"; d. at Springfield, near Chelmsford.

Revoil, Louise, 1810–76. *Madame Colet.* A French poet, novelist, and traveller; b. at Marseilles, and d. in Paris.

Reybaud, Marie Roch Louis, 1799–1879. *Léon Durocher.* A French traveller; b. at Marseilles; travelled much in India and other Eastern countries; in 1829, settled in Paris and devoted himself to literary labor; d. in Paris.

Reynolds, ——. *A Well-wisher to the Country.* An English writer, of the first part of the 18th century.

Reynolds, Edward, B.A. *A Barrister.* An English lawyer.

Reynolds, Frederick Mansell, Esq., –1850. *F. M. R.* An English novelist, of Wilton House, Jersey; eldest son of Frederick Reynolds, the dramatist; he was the first editor of Heath's "Keepsake"; d. at Fontainebleau, on his way to Italy.

Reynolds, George W. M. *Bos; Master Timothy; A Minor.* An English journalist, of London; editor of the "Weekly Messenger."

Reynolds, Henry Revell, Jr. *A*

Young Man. An English barrister-at-law.

Reynolds, Rev. Herbert Edward, M.A. *H. E. R.* An English clergyman; Trin. Coll., Cambridge, 1870; Priest-Vicar of Exeter, 1873; cathedral library, 1877; chaplain of the Exeter City Union, 1881–83 *et seq.*

Reynolds, James. *E. L. A. Berwick.* An English or Scottish surgeon.

Reynolds, John Hamilton, 1794–1852. *Curl-Pated; Nimrod; Edward Herbert; John Hamilton.* An English poet; brother-in-law to Thomas Hood; Clerk of the County Court of the Isle of Wight.

Rham, Rev. William Lewis, 1778–1843. *M.* An eminent English writer on agriculture; b. at Utrecht; educ. at Edinburgh and Cambridge; Rector of Fersfield, Norfolk, from 1803, and Vicar of Winkfield from 1808, and d. there.

Rhodes, John. *A Lover of his Memory.* An English writer, early in the 18th century.

Rhodes, William Barnes, Esq., 1772–1826. *Cornelius Crambo.* An English banker and humorist, of London; b. in Leeds; clerk in the Bank of England from 1799, and chief teller, 1823–26; d. in London.

Rhodes, William Henry, LL.B. *Caxton.* An American lawyer and poet.

Rhys, Rev. J. Bradley. *A Clergyman of the Church of England.*

Rialle, J. Girard de. *Dmitri Stephanowitch.*

Ribbans, F. Bolingbroke, LL.D., F.S.A. *A Layman.* An English poet and moralist.

Rice, George Edward, A.M., LL.B., 1822–61. *G. E. R.* An American lawyer; b. in Boston; Harv. Univ., 1842; practised his profession in his native city; d. in Roxbury, Mass.

Rice, Isaac L., 1850–. *Ecir.* An American journalist, of Philadelphia.

Rice, James, 1844–82. *J. R.* An English novelist; b. at Northampton; educ. at Queen's Coll., Cambridge; called to the Bar at Lincoln's Inn, 1871, but his work was wholly literary; d. at Redhill, Surrey.

Rice, Miss Rosella, about 1830–. *Chatty Brooks; Pipsey Potts.* An American writer of the day; b. at Perrysville, Ashland Co., O., and (1860) had always resided there.

Rice, Thomas D., 1808–60. *Jim Crow.* An American comic vocalist, of New York City.

Richards, ——. *A Federal Republi-*

can. An American political writer, of Connecticut.

Richards, Mrs. A. M. *A Lady of Massachusetts.* An American writer.

Richards, Mrs. Cornelia H. (Bradley), 1822-. *Mrs. Manners.* An American novelist; b. in Hudson, N.Y.; wife of Rev. William C. Richards, of New York City; sister of Mrs. Alize B. Haven.

Richards, George. *A Citizen of Boston.* An American poet and Freemason.

Richards, Rev. William Upton, M.A. *W. U. R.* An English clergyman; Vicar of All Saints, London, 1849-70 *et seq.*

Richardson, Albert Deane, 1833-69. *Junius Henri Browne.* An American journalist; b. at Franklin, Mass.; d. in New York City.

Richardson, Alexander. *Free Lance.* A Scottish writer, of Edinburgh.

Richardson, Edward, Jr. *An Ex-Member of the Society of Friends.* An English Friend, of Newcastle-upon-Tyne.

Richardson, J. S. *Jefferson.* An American political writer.

Richardson, James. *Adam Stevin.* An American (?) novelist.

Richardson, Hon. John, 1755-1831. *Veritas.* A Canadian merchant, of Montreal.

Richardson, Leander. *L. R.; The Town Listener.* An American journalist, of New York City.

Richardson, Robert. *A Gentleman of the Inner Temple.* An English lawyer of the 18th century.

Richardson, Rev. William Esdaile, B.A. *W. E. R.* An English clergyman; Trin. Coll., Cambridge, 1850; Rector of St. John, Southover, Lewes, 1869-83 *et seq.*

Richings, Rev. Benjamin, M.A. *A Clergyman.* An English clergyman; Vicar of Mancetter, Atherstone, Warwickshire, 1816-70 *et seq.*

Richmond, Rev. James Cook, 1808-66. *Admonish Crime; Nobody; Oliver Martext.* An American clergyman; b. at Providence, R.I.; Harv. Univ., 1828; murdered at Poughkeepsie, N.Y.

Richmond, Rev. Legh, D.D., 1772-1827. *A Clergyman of the Church of England.* An English clergyman; b. at Liverpool; Trin. Coll., Cambridge, 1794; Rector of Turvey, Beds., 1805-27, where he died.

Richter, Jean Paul Friedrich, 1763-1825. *Jean Paul.* An eminent German author; b. at Wunssedel, near Baireuth; resided in that town, 1804-25, and d. there.

Richter, Karl Thomas, 1838-78. *Karl Thomas.* A Bohemian poet and political economist; b. at Leitmeritz; studied at Prague and Vienna; Professor of Political Economy at Prague, 1872-78; and d. there.

Rickman, Edwin S. *A Solitaire.* An English Friend.

Rickman, John, 1771-1841. *J. R.; X. Y.* An English author and editor; b. at Newbern, Northumberland; 2d Clerk-Assistant, 1814-20; and Clerk-Assistant in the House of Commons, 1820-41; d. in Westminster.

Rickman, Thomas Clio. *A Gentleman resident there.* An English bookseller, of London; avowed himself the complete disciple of Thomas Paine, both in his religious principles and in his politics, and kept the table where that personage was accustomed to write his papers.

Riddel, James. *A Son of Bon Accord in North America.* A Scottish writer, of Aberdeen.

Riddell, Mrs. Charlotte Eliza Lawson (Cowan). *F. G. Trafford.* A popular Irish novelist, youngest daughter of James Cowan, of Carrickfergus, Co. Antrim; in 1857 married J. H. Riddell, Esq., of Winson Green House, Staffs.

Riddell, Maria. *Maria R******.* A Scottish traveller.

Riddle, Rev. Joseph Esmond, 1804-59. *An Absent Godfather.* An English clergyman; Incumbent of St. Philip and St. James, Leckhampton, Gloucestershire; d. at his residence,Tudor-lodge,Cheltenham.

Rider, Rev. William, -1785. *Philargyrus.* An English poet, historian, and clergyman; sub-master of St. Paul's School for many years; lecturer of St. Vedast, Foster Lane, and Curate of St. Paul's, London.

Ridley, Rev. James, -1765. *Horam, the Son of Asmar; Sir Charles Morell; Helter Van Scelter.* An English orientalist; chaplain to the East India Company.

Ridpath, Rev. George. *A Lover of his Country.* A Scottish clergyman; minister at Stitchel, County of Roxburghe, in the middle of the 18th century.

Rigby, Rt. Hon. Richard. *Drunken Rigdum.* An English statesman; about 1779, Paymaster-General.

Riggs, George Washington. *G. W. R., Jr.* An American banker, of Washington.

Riley, James Whitcomb. *Benj. F. Johnson.* An American dialect poet, of Boone, Ind.

Rimbault, Edward Francis, LL.D.,

1816–76. *Franz Nava.* An English
composer; a very popular arranger of
musical pieces, chiefly for the pianoforte; d. in London.

Ripley, George, LL.D., 1802–80.
G. R. An American scholar and journalist; b. at Greenfield, Mass.; Harv.
Univ., 1823; pastor in Boston, 1823–31;
literary editor of the N.Y. "Tribune,"
1849–80; d. in New York City.

Ritchie, Ann. *A Lady.* A Scottish
writer; afterwards Mrs. Dr. John Smythe
Memes.

**Ritchie, Mrs. Anna Cora (Ogden
Mowatt),** 1819–70. *An Actress; Mrs.
Helen Berkley; Isabel; A Lady.* An
American actress and author; b. in Bordeaux, France; made her *debut* as an
actress in New York City in 1845; retired from the stage in 1854; d. in England.

Ritchie, James Ewing. *Christopher
Crayon.* An American journalist of the
day.

Ritson, Joseph, 1752–1803. *J. R.*
An English critic and literary antiquary;
b. at Stockton-upon-Tees; was a lawyer
and conveyancer of London, but devoted
himself chiefly to literary pursuits; d. at
Hoxton.

Rivail, Hippolyte Léon Denizard,
1803–69. *Allan Kardec.* A French spiritualist, of Paris; b. at Lyons; d. in
Paris.

Rives, Mrs. William (Cabell), 1802–.
An American writer; b. at Castle Hill,
Albemarle Co., Va.

Rivington, ——, and Another. *Two
Englishmen.*

Rivington, Charles. *Scrutator.* An
English Shakespearian writer.

Rivington, William. *A Lay-member
of the Committee; A Layman.* An English writer, of London.

Roane, Spencer, 1788–1822. *Algernon
Sydney.* An American jurist; judge of
the Court of Errors in Virginia.

Robb, John S. *Solitaire; A Tyke.*
An American editor and humorist; b. in
Philadelphia; from 1851, of St. Louis,
Mo., connected with the "St. Louis Re-
veillé."

Robbins, Alfred Farthing, 1856–.
Dunheved; Nemesis; Tom Clifton.

Roberthin, Robert, 1600–48. *Berintho.* An English writer.

Roberts, Caroline Alice. *C. A. R.*
An English poet of the day.

Roberts, Daniel, –1811. *Philotesis.*
An English Friend, of Painswick,
Gloucestershire, where he died.

Roberts, J. P. *John Happy.*

Roberts, John. *Anti-Scriblerus Histrionicus; A Stroling Player.* An English
Shakespearian writer.

Roberts, Lester A. *An Artist.* An
American writer, of New York City.

Roberts, Maggie. *Eiggam Strebor*
An American writer of the day.

Roberts, Mary, 1789–1864. *Mary De
Gleva.* An English Friend, of Brompton, London, where she died.

Roberts, S. *A Llanbrynmair Farmer.*
An English writer.

Roberts, William, 1767–1849. *Rev.
Simon Olive Branch.* An English lawyer,
of Manchester; b. at Newton Butts, Surrey; educ. at Eton and Oxford; d. at St.
Alban's, Herts.

Robertson, Alexander. *R. Alister.*
A Scottish writer, of Dundonnochie.

Robertson, H. *A Scotch Episcopalian.*

Robertson, Henry D. *A Gentleman
in the Service of the East India Company.*

Robertson, John, D.D. *Godfrey Topping.* A Scottish clergyman; minister
of Glasgow Cathedral, 1824–65.

Robertson, Joseph, LL.D., 1811–66.
James Brown. A Scottish antiquary, of
Edinburgh, 1853–66; b. in Aberdeen; d.
at Edinburgh.

Robertson, Joseph Clinton, 1788–
1852. *Sholto Percy.* An English author
and journalist; d. at Brompton.

Robertson, Patrick, Lord Robertson,
1794–1855. *P. R.* A Scottish poet and
jurist; b. and d. in Edinburgh; Lord of
the Court of Sessions, 1843–55; Lord Rector of Marischall Coll., Aberdeen, 1848.

Robertson, William, D.D., 1721–93.
A Presbyter of the Church of England. A
Scottish clergyman; b. in Borthwick,
Co. of Mid-Lothian; educ. at the Univ.
of Edinburgh; and principal of that
Univ., 1762–93; d. at his seat near Edin-
burgh.

Robins, George. *An Auctioneer.* An
English writer, of London.

Robins, James, –1836. *Robert Scott.*
An English publisher and bookseller, in
Ivy-lane, Paternoster-row, London; d. at
Lewisham.

Robinson, ——. *A Gentleman.* An
English writer, of Kendal, of the 18th
century.

Robinson, Dr. ——. *B. G.* An English writer of the 18th century.

Robinson, A. *An American.* An
American writer, of California.

Robinson, Mrs. Annie D. (Greene).
Marion Douglas. An American(?) writer
of the day.

Robinson, Clara I. N. *Mrs. Glubbins.*
An English writer of the day.

Robinson, E. P. *Jasper.* An English writer.

Robinson, Miss Emma, 1794–1863. *Owanda.* An English novelist.

Robinson, Miss Esther. *Esther Warren.* An American journalist of the day.

Robinson, F. K. *An Inhabitant.* An English philologist, of Yorkshire.

Robinson, James, 1713–95. *Nobody.* An English poet and actor; connected with the theatre at York, where he died.

Robinson, John, 1782–1833. *Piomingo.* An American writer.

Robinson, Mrs. Lelia J. *Ida Clare.* An American writer of the day; afterwards Mrs. Chute.

Robinson, Mrs. Mary (Darby), 1758–1800. *Anna Maria; Laura Maria; Oberon; Perdita; Mrs. Anne Frances Randall; The English Sappho.* An English actress and poetess; b. in Bristol.

Robinson, Nugent. *Nym Rugby; Sam Clover.* An American dramatist and journalist of the day, of New York City.

Robinson, S. *A Layman.* An English theological writer.

Robinson, Samuel. *S. R.* An English scholar of Dukinfield, who had been educated at the Manchester Coll., at York, under Rev. Charles Wellbeloved.

Robinson, Solon, 1803–188–. *Blythe White, Jr.* An American journalist; b. near Tolland, Conn.; for many years agricultural editor of the New York "Tribune"; about 1870 settled on a farm at Jacksonville, Fla., where he died.

Robinson, Mrs. Thérèse Albertine Louise (von Jacob), 1797–1869. *Talvi; Ernst Berthold.* A German-American; b. in Halle; in 1820 she married Rev. Dr. Edward Robinson, and in 1830 came with him to this country; d. at Hamburg, Germany.

Robinson, William Erigena, 1814–. *Richelieu.* An Irish-American lawyer, journalist, and miscellaneous writer; b. near Cookstown, Co. Tyrone; came to this country in 1836; M.C., 1867–69.

Robinson, William L. *A Samaritan; A Member of the Howard Association of New Orleans.* An American writer.

Robinson, William Stevens, 1818–76. *Warrington; Kremlin; Boython; Gilbert; Middlesex; Bailey, Junior.* An eminent American journalist; b. in Concord, Mass.; d. in Malden, Mass., where he lived several years.

Robison, John, LL.D., 1739–1805. *Cornelius.* A Scottish natural philosopher; b. in Sterlingshire; M.A. at the Univ. of Glasgow, 1756; Professor of Natural Philosophy in his *alma mater,* 1773–1805; d. in Glasgow.

Robson, Henry. *H. R.* An English poet; a journeyman printer at Newcastle.

Robson, William James. *W. J. R.* An English poet. His youthful aspirations sadly failed. His frauds upon the Crystal Palace, to the amount of about £28,000, led, in 1856, to his transportation for 20 years.

Roby, John, Esq., 1793–1850. *An Admirer of Walter Scott; An Amateur of Fashion; Byro.* An English writer; b. at Rochdale, Lancashire; a lecturer on literature and botany, and an author; lost his life in the wreck of the "Orion" on its trip from Liverpool to Glasgow.

Roche, ——. *Mr. R.* An American merchant; resided for a time in London; afterwards had an establishment at Dunkirk, and another at l'Orient.

Roche, James, 1770–1853. *J. R.; An Octogenarian.* An Irish banker and writer, "the Roscoe of Cork"; b. in Limerick; d. in Cork.

Rochefoucauld - Liancourt, François Alexandre Frédéric, Duc de la, 1747–1827. *A European; Un Européen.* A French peer and philanthropist; travelled in the United States after 1792; returned to Paris in 1799.

Rochester, John Wilmot, Earl of, 1647 or 48–80. *Lord R—r.* An English nobleman; educ. at Wadham Coll., Oxford; was noted for drunkenness, buffoonery, and poetry, but was converted by Bishop Burnet, and died a sincere penitent.

Rodd, Thomas, Sr., 1763–1822. *The Father of the Late Thomas Rodd; Philobiblos; A Young Gentleman.* An eminent English bookseller, of London; d. at Clothall End, near Baldock, Co. Herts.

Rodd, William Henry, 1816–. *A Local Preacher.* An English writer; b. at Falmouth; Mayor of Penzance, 1874–75.

Rodda, Joseph Tonkin, 1834–. *Ralph Goldsworthy.* An English writer; b. at Tolcarne, near Penzance; in 1876, with Messrs. Harvey & Co., Hayle Foundry Wharf, Nine Elms, London.

Rodney, Mrs. Marian C. Legaré (Reeves). *Fadette.* An American novelist; in 1869 resided at New Castle, Del. The Library of Congress Cat. has the name *Mrs. Minne Reeves Rodney.*

Rodwell, James. *Uncle James.* An English writer for the young.

Roe, Miss Mary A. *C. M. Cornwall.*

An American writer; sister of Edward P. Roe, of Chicago.

Rösler, E. Robert, 1840–81. *Julius Mühlfeld.* A German author; b. at Köthen; became a bookseller; then a publisher; in 1861 lived at Leipsic; in 1872 became chief editor of the "Hartungschen Zeitung" in Königsberg; in 1877, editor of the "Deutschen" in Sondershausen; d. in Königsberg.

Roger, Aristide. *J. Rengade.* A French author of the day.

Rogers, Edward Coit, B.A. *O. S. Freeman.* An American anti-slavery writer.

Rogers, George. *Elder Triptolemus Tub.* An American writer.

Rogers, Henry, 1806–77. *Vindex; R. E. H. Greyson.* An eminent English critic and essayist; from 1858 President of the Lancashire Independent College, Manchester.

Rogers, J. *Tom Treddlehoyle.* An English dialect writer.

Rogers, Rev. John, M.A., 1778–1856. *J. R.* An English clergyman; b. at Plymouth; Rector of Penrose, Cornwall, 1832–56, and d. there.

Rogers, Mrs. Loula (Kendall). *Leola.* An American "Southland" poet; in 1868, of Thomaston, Upson Co., Ga.

Rogers, Nathaniel Peabody, 1794–1846. *Old Man of the Mountain.* An eminent American anti-slavery journalist, of Concord, N.H.; b. at Plymouth, N.H.; Dartmouth Coll., 1816; d. at Concord.

Rogers, Samuel, 1763–1855. *The Bard of Memory; S****** R*****.* An eminent English banker and poet, of London; b. at Newington Green, London; d. in the same city.

Rogers, Miss Sarah.— See "Haight, Mrs. S. (R.)."

Rogerson, Thomas. *A Private Person.* An English writer, of the first part of the 18th century.

Rokeby, Morris Robinson, 3d Lord of Armagh, and 5th Bart. of Rokeby, in Yorkshire, 1755–1829. *A Briton.* An English writer; M.P. for Boroughbridge, 1796; succeeded his uncle Matthew in 1800; d. at Thoralby, near Leyburn, Yorkshire.

Rollins, Rev. Edward B., 1793–. *The White Mountain Pilgrim.* An American minister and journalist; b. in New Britain (now Andover), N.H.; entered the ministry in 1815, and in 1870 had preached in 23 of the States of the Union, also in New Brunswick, Nova Scotia, and Canada, and had delivered

more than 14,000 public addresses, and had been a journalist in Massachusetts and Vermont.

Rollins, Mrs. Ellen Chapman (Hobbs), 1831–81. *E. H. Arr.* An American writer, of Philadelphia; b. in New Hampshire; daughter of Josiah H. Hobbs, of Wakefield; in 1855, married Hon. Edward Ashton Rollins; of Philadelphia, from 1869.

Rolls, Mrs. M. M. *His Mother.* An English writer; mother of Bernard Glanville Lyndon Rolls.

Rolt, Elizabeth. *A Lady.* An English poet, of the 18th century.

Romanes, George John. *Physicus.* An English philosopher.

Romilly, Hon. Henry, M.A., 1845–. *An Elector.* An English politician; son of the 1st Baron.

Ronalds, Alfred. *Piscator.* An English sporting writer.

Ronaldson, Richard. *A Friend of the People.* An English writer on the currency.

Ronger, Florimond, 1825–. *Hervé.* A French composer of operettas.

Rooke, Rev. George Henry. *R.* An English writer of the 18th century, of Christ Coll., Cambridge.

Rooney, M. W. *M. W. R.* An Irish publisher and bookseller, of Dublin.

Rooper, George. *A Fisherman; Salmo Salar, Esq.* An English sporting writer of the day.

Roosevelt, Robert Barnwell, 1829–. *Barnwell; Ira Zell.* An American journalist and miscellaneous writer; b. in New York City; studied law, and practised for several years, but finally devoted himself to literature, rural sports, and politics; M.C., 1871.

Ropes, Mrs. Hannah Anderson (Chandler). *A Lady.* An American writer; sister of Peleg W. and Theophilus Parsons Chandler, of Boston.

Rosales, Henry. *Pick and Pen.* An English colonial writer, of Melbourne (?).

Roscoe, Henry, 1800–36. *A Member of the Inner Temple.* An English lawyer; son of William Roscoe; assessor of the Mayor's Court at Liverpool, and one of the Municipal Corporation Commissioners; d. at his residence at Gateacre, near Liverpool.

Roscoe, Thomas, Jr. *Lee Gibbons, student of law.* An English novelist.

Rose, Rev. ——. *A Pioneer of the Wilderness.* An English writer.

Rose, Edward Hampden, –1810. *A Foremast Man.* An Irish sailor; b. in Dublin; in a youthful frolic entered the navy, and thus became estranged from his friends; d. in the Royal Naval Hospital, Stonehouse.

Rose, Rev. George, 1817–82. *Arthur Sketchley.* An English humorist; educ. at Oxford; entered holy orders, but resigned his position in the English Church, and was for five years tutor to the present Duke of Norfolk.

Rose, J. *A Caledonian Fisher.* A Scottish sporting writer.

Rose, William Stewart, 1775–1843. *W. S. R.* A Scottish poet and scholar; friend of Sir Walter Scott.

Ross, Charles H. *C. H. R.; Ally Sloper; Roswell Butt.* An English humorist of the day.

Ross, Rev. Duncan, –1834. *Solomon Wisewood.* A Scottish Nova-Scotian Presbyt. minister; came to Nova Scotia as a missionary in 1795; was soon settled at West River, Pictou, where he remained till his death.

Ross, Mrs. Ellen Church. *Nelsie Brook.* An English writer for the young.

Ross, Rev. Hugh. *H. R., A Minister of the Church of England.* An English clergyman early in the 18th century.

Ross, William Tait. *Herbert Martyne.* A Scottish poet.

Ross-Church, Mrs. Florence (Marryat), 1837–. *Florence Marryat.* An English writer; daughter of Capt. F. Marryat; b. at Brighton; editor of the "London Society" from 1872.

Rossetti, Christina Georgina, 1830–. *Ellen Allyn.* An English poet; sister of Dante Gabriel Rossetti; b. in London, and educ. at home.

Rossi, Rev. Gaudentius. *Pellegrino.* A R. C. priest, of Boston.

Rossiter, Anna M. S. *Lilla N. Cushman.*

Round, William Marshall Fitz, 1845–. *Rev. Peter Pennot.* An American writer of the day.

Rousseau, Jean Jacques, 1712–78. *Jean Jacques.* A French philosopher.

Rousseau, Léon. *L. Russelli.* A French journalist of the day.

Roussel, Pierre Joseph Alexis. *M. de Proussinalle.* A French historian, of Épinal.

Rovel, Joseph Jules. *J. J. R****.* A French author and officer; Chef d'escadron d'artillerie.

Row, Rev. Charles Adolphus, M.A. *A Member of the Oxford Convocation.* An English clergyman; Pemberton Coll., Oxford, 1838; Prebendary of Harleston, in St. Paul's Cathedral, 1874–83 et seq.

Rowan, Arthur Blennarhassett,

DD., –1861. *A. B. R.; Ignotus; A Minister.* An eminent Irish clergyman; Archdeacon of Ardfort, 1856–61; d. at Belmont, near Tralee, Co. Kerry.

Rowbotham, Samuel Birley. *Parallax.* An English author and lecturer.

Rowcroft, Charles. *An Etonian; Alfred Seedy.* An English novelist.

Rowe, Mrs. Elizabeth (Singer), 1674–1737. *Clerimont.* An English poet; b. at Ilchester, Somersetshire; in 1710 married Mr. Thomas Rowe; after his death, in 1715, she left London, and spent the rest of her life at Frome.

Rowe, Mrs. George F. *Kate Girard.*

Rowe, Dr. Nicholas. *Mohawk.* An American journalist, of Chicago.

Rowe, Nicholas, 1674–1718. *N. R.* An English poet; b. at Little Barford, Beds.; educ. at Westminster School, and at the Middle Temple; Under-Secretary of State, 1708–11; Poet-Laureate, 1714–18.

Rowe, Richard. *Peter 'Possum.* An English provincial dramatist of the day, of Australia.

Rowe, Rev. William, 1843–. *A Missioner.* An English clergyman; b. at Peter Tavy, Devon.; Vicar of St. Teath, Camelford, Cornwall, 1877–83 et seq.

Rowland, David. *A Layman.* An English writer, of London.

Rowland, Edward. *Senex.* An English translator of the Psalms of David.

Rowlands, Richard. *An Impartial Hand.* An Irish historian early in the 18th century.

Rowley, Charles, Jr. *Roland Gilderoy.* An English writer of the day, of Manchester.

Rowson, Mrs. Susanna (Haswell), 1762–1824. *S. R.* An English actress, teacher, and novelist; b. at Portsmouth; came to Massachusetts in 1767; in 1776 went back to England; but returned to this country in 1795; taught school at Medford, Newton, and Boston, and d. at the last place.

Roxby, Robert. *The Reedwater Minstrel; A Son of Reed.* An English sporting writer, of Newcastle.

Roy, Just Jean Étienne, 1791–. *Just Girard; Stéphanie Ory; Théophile Ménard.* A French author.

Royall, Mrs. Anne, 1769–1854. *A Traveller.* An American writer; b. in Virginia; editor of the Washington "Paul Pry" and the "Huntress"; d. in Washington, D.C.

Royston, W. H. *W. H. R.* An English sporting writer of the day.

Rud, T. *T. R.* An English writer in the first half of the 18th century.

Rudd, Margaret Caroline. *Margaret Caroline Stewart.* An English lady of the 18th century.

Ruding, Walter, Esq., 1744–1818. *Cato; Anglo-Saxon; Millions; &c.* An English politician, of Westcotes, near Leicester; and d. there.

Rückert, Friedrich, 1789–1866. *Freimund Reinmar.* A celebrated German lyric poet; of Berlin, 1840–49; b. at Schweinfurt; studied law, philology, and literature; d. at Neuses, his estate, near Coburg.

Ruelens, Madame **Estelle Marie Louise (Crèvecœur),** 1821–78. *Caroline Gravière.* A Belgian novelist, of Brussels; wife of Charles Ruelens.

Ruelle, Charles. *Claudius.* A French writer; Professor of Rhetoric at the Royal College of Lille.

Ruffini, Giovanni Domenico, 1807–81. *Lorenzo Benoni; A Friend.* An Italian novelist and politician; resided at Taggia, near San Remo, from 1875; b. and d. there.

Ruge, Arnold, 1802–80. *R. Durangelo.* A German writer; b. at Bergen, on the island of Rügen; studied at Jena and Halle, 1821–24; was compelled to leave Germany on account of his revolutionary activity, and for a time resided in London; from 1850, he resided in Brighton, and d. there.

Ruggles, C. Lorain. *General Bunker.* An American writer of the day.

Rule, William Harris, D.D. *W. H. R.* An English Wesleyan minister and hymn-writer.

Rumball, Charles. *Charles Delorme, Esq.* An English writer.

Rumsey, John. *Plinius Secundus.* A Canadian lawyer.

Rundell, Mrs. ——. *A Lady.* An English writer; wife of the senior partner of the eminent jewellers of London, Rundell & Bridges.

Rupp, Isaac Daniel, 1803–. *A Gentleman of the Bar.* An American author, of Lancaster, Penn.; b. near Harrisburg; a historian, a translator, and an agricultural writer.

Ruschenberger, William S. W., M.D., 1807–. *W. S. W. R.; Chloroform; An Officer of the U.S. Navy; A Surgeon.* An American naturalist and surgeon in the U.S. Navy; b. in Cumberland Co., N.J.; educ. in New York City and Philadelphia; retired from active service in 1869.

Rush, Benjamin, M.D., LL.D., 1745–

1813. *A Pennsylvanian.* An American physician; b. at Byberry, near Philadelphia; New Jersey Coll., 1760; studied medicine in Philadelphia, Edinburgh, London, and Paris; practised in Philadelphia, 1769–99; Treasurer of the U.S. Mint, 1799–1813; d. in Philadelphia.

Rush, Benjamin, 1811–. *A Citizen of Philadelphia.* An American lawyer; son of Richard Rush, and grandson of Benjamin Rush; b. in Philadelphia; since 1873 resides with his family in that city.

Rush, Miss **Rebecca.** *A Lady of Pennsylvania.* An American novelist; daughter of Judge Jacob Rush, of Philadelphia, and niece of Dr. Benjamin.

Rush, Richard, LL.D., 1780–1859. *Julius.* An eminent American lawyer and statesman; son of Dr. Benj. Rush; b. in Philadelphia; resided at Sydenham, near Philadelphia, 1849–59, where he died.

Ruskin, John, LL.D., 1818–. *J. R.; J. R., Christ Church, Oxon.; Author of "Modern Painters"; A Graduate of Oxford; Kata Phusin; The Younger Lady of the Thwaite, Coniston.* A celebrated English art-critic; b. in London; educ. at Christ Church, Oxford.

Russ, W. L. *Macswell; Persimmons.* An American journalist.

Russel, W. P. *W. P. R., a Political Observer; W. P. R., Verbotomist; A Briton; Patrioticus; A Philanthropist; A Political Apothecary; A Real Lover of Freedom.* An English political writer.

Russell, ——. *A Graduate of a University.* An English writer.

Russell, Clark. *A Seafarer.* An English journalist; son of Mr. Henry Russell.

Russell, Francis, the 5th Duke of Bedford, F.R.S., F.A.S., 1765–1802. *A Young Peer, etc.* An English nobleman; d. at his seat at Woburn Abbey.

Russell, Francis, Esq., F.R.S., F.A.S., –1795. *F. R.* An English writer; Extra-Secretary of the Board of Control for the Affairs of India.

Russell, Sir **Henry,** 2d Bart., 1783–1852. *Civis.* An English colonial civilian; admitted a writer on the Bengal establishment in 1792; resident at Hyderabad, 1810–20; d. at Swallowfield, Berks.

Russell, John, R.A., 1744–1806. *A Young Painter.* An English artist in crayons; b. at Guildford; portrait-painter to George III. and to the Prince of Wales; d. at Hull.

Russell, John, 1st Earl, LL.D., G.C.M.G., P.C., K.G., 1792–1878. *Joseph Skillet; A Gentleman who has left his*

Lodgings. An English statesman; son of the 6th Duke of Bedford; English Premier, 1846–52, 1854–55, and 1865–66; raised to the peerage, 1861.

Russell, Jonathan, LL.D., 1771–1832. *A Republican.* An American merchant and statesman; b. in Providence, R.I.; Brown Univ., 1791; U.S. Minister to Sweden for several years; one of the five commissioners who signed the Treaty of Ghent, 1814; M.C., 1821–23; d. at Milton, Mass.

Russell, R. *A Middle-Aged Citizen.* An English writer; in the employ of Messrs. Cassell, the publishers.

Russell, Richard, M.D. *Mœvius.* An English physician, of Leeds, Sussex.

Russell, Rev. Thomas. *A. S.* An English writer.

Russell, W. M. *W. M. R.* An English writer.

Russell, William. *A Law Clerk; A Custom-House Officer; A Detective; A Detective Police Officer; An English Detective; A French Detective; "Waters"; C. Waters; Thomas Waters.* An English novelist, of London.

Russell, William. *Lieut. Warneford.* An English novelist.

One might suppose that this writer was the same with the preceding; but the Edinburgh Advocates' Library Catalogue makes them different.

Ruter, P. S., M.D. *A Virginia Physician.* An American writer.

Rutlidge, Sir **John James.** *An Observer.* An English writer of the 18th century.

Rutter, John, 1796–1851. *A Constitu-*

tional Reformer. An English Friend; b. in Shaftesbury, Dorsetshire; for some years a printer and bookseller; afterwards a lawyer; and d. in his native town.

Rutty, John, M.D., 1698–1775. *Johannes Catholicus; Bernardus Utopiensis; An Unworthy Member of that Community.* An Irish physician, whose parents were Friends; practised his profession at Dublin, 1724–75.

Ryan, Rev. Father **Abram J.,** 184 – 188–. *Moïna.* An American R. C. priest and poet; b. in Norfolk, Va.; it is said of him: "Father Ryan, the Mobile poet-priest, is the most popular rhymester in the South."

Ryan, Carroll, 1840–. *A Wanderer.* A Canadian poet and journalist; b. at Toronto; in 1867 became editor of the "Volunteer Review" of Ottawa.

Ryder, W. J. D. *W. J. D. R.; A Carthusian.* An English writer.

Rye, Francis. *F. R., of Barrie.* A Canadian Shakespeare scholar, of Barrie, Ontario, Canada.

Ryland, John, D.D., 1753–1825. *J. R., Jun.* An English Bapt. divine; son of the following; b. at Warwick; president of the Baptist Coll., Bristol, and pastor of the Broadmead Chapel, 1794–1825; d. in Bristol.

Ryland, Rev. **John Collett,** 1723–92. *A Lover of Christ.* An English Bapt. minister; teacher at Enfield, 1786–92; b. at Lower Ditchford, Gloucestershire; d. at Enfield.

Rymer, Malcolm J. *Malcolm J. Errym.* An English writer.

S.

Sabin, Rev. **Elijah Robinson,** 1776–1818. *Charles Observator.* An American Meth. minister; b. at Tolland, Conn.; father of Lorenzo Sabine.

Sabine, Lorenzo, A.M., 1803–77. *Vindex.* An American historical writer; b. in Lisbon, N.H.; M.C., 1851–53; spent his last years in Boston, and d. there.

Sacher-Masoch, Aurora von. *Wanda von Dunajew.* A German writer; b. at Rümelin; married Ritter Leopold von Sacher-Masoch in 1873; and now lives in Budapest.

Sacheverell, Henry, D.D., 1672(?)–1724. *Don Sacheverellio, Knight of the Firebrand.* An English clergyman; roommate of Addison at Magdalen Coll., Ox-

ford; preacher at St. Saviour's, Southwark, Co. Surrey.

Sachsen, Amalie Frederike Auguste, Herzogin von, 1794–1870. *Amalie Heister.* A German dramatist, whose plays have been translated into English by Mrs. Jameson.

Sackett, Grenville Alfred. *Alfred.* An American lawyer.

Sackville, Charles, 2d Duke of Dorset, 1711–69. *C. S.* An English nobleman; author of prose and poetical compositions.

Sackville-West, Rev. and Hon. **Reginald Windsor,** 7th Earl of De-la-Warr, 1817–. *R. W. S.-W.* An English nobleman; Balliol Coll., Oxford, 1838; a magistrate for Kent, a J. P. and D. L. for Sussex and County Cambridge, and High-Steward of Stratford-upon-Avon.

Sadler, L. R. *Jacob Larwood.* An English author of the day.

Safford, Mary J. *M. S.* An American journalist of the day.

Sage, Bernard J. *P. C. Centz, barrister.* An American lawyer and political writer, of New Orleans.

St. Albans, the Most Noble **Harriet (Mellon) Coutts,** Duchess of, about 1774–1837. *Miss Harriet Pumpkin.* An English actress; original name, Harriet Mellon; married Mr. Coutts, the banker, in 1815. He died in 1822, aged 87, leaving her £600,000. In 1827 she married William, Duke of St. Albans, then in the 27th year of his age. At her death she left the bulk of her property, £1,800,000, to Miss Angela Burdett, youngest daughter of Sir Francis Burdett, and grand-daughter of Mr. Coutts, who in consequence took the name of Coutts.

Saint-Aubin, Karl, about 1800–65. *Bernhard.* An eminent Danish novelist and chronicler; acquired a great literary reputation through all Europe by his novels, his little romances, full of grace, of freshness, of sentiment, and imagination.

St. Aubyn, Rev. John Humphrey, 1790–1857. *Lionel Bouverie.* An English clergyman; b. in Cornwall; Jesus Coll., Cambridge, 1814; d. at Fontainebleau.

St. Barbe, Charles, Esq., F.S.A., 1776–1849. *S. B.; C. S. B.* An English literary antiquary; b. and d. at Lymington, Hampshire.

St. Clair, Rosalind. *A Lady.* An English novelist.

Saint-Cricq, Lorenzo de. *Paul Marcoy.* A French traveller of the day, in South America.

Saint Felix, Felix d'Amoreux, dit **Jules de,** 1806–74. *Trimalcion.* A French journalist and novelist, of Paris; b. at Uzès (Gard); d. in Paris.

Saint-George, Mrs. A. *An English Lady.* An English writer.

Saint-Hilaire, Émile Marco de, 1793–. *Un Page de la Cour Impériale.* A French writer, of Paris; b. at Versailles.

Saint John, Charles William George, 1809–56. *A Sportsman and Naturalist.* An English writer; son of Gen. St. John, of Chailey, Sussex; formerly of the South Coll., Elgin, N.B.; d. at Hazeleigh, Woolston.

Saint-John, Hector. —See "Crevecœur, H. S.-J."

Saint-John, Henry, Viscount Bolingbroke, 1678–1751. *Caleb D'Anvers, Esq.; Humphrey Oldcastle, Esq.; A Noble Duke; John Trott, Yeoman.* An English statesman; b. at Battersea, Surrey; educ. at Eton and Christ Church, Oxford; Secretary of State for War, 1704–8; for Foreign Affairs, 1710; fled to France charged with treason, 1714; returned to England, 1724: It is said of him that "he lived a worse than useless life."

St. John, James Augustus, 1801–75. *A Layman.* A Scottish *littérateur;* b. in Carmarthenshire; in 1817 went to London; in 1829 removed to Normandy, but later resided in London again.

Saint-John, Percy Bolingbroke, 1821–. *Paul Periwinkle.* An English writer, of London; b. in Plymouth; travelled in the United States about 1840.

Saint-John, Sergius. *A Grandfather.*

Saint-Mars, Gabrielle Anne Cisterne de Courtiras, Vicomtesse de, 1804–72. *La comtesse Dash; Jacques Reynaud.* A French novelist; b. at Poictiers; married early, and devoted herself after the loss of her fortune to literary work.

St. Maur, Harry. *Almaviva.* An American journalist.

Sainte-Beuve, Charles Augustin, 1804–69. *B. S.; Joseph Delorme.* A French poet and critic; b. at Boulogne-sur-Mer; early went to Paris, and lived and d. there.

Sainte-Lorette, Isnard de. *Ludwig de Sabaroth.* A French novelist of fifty years ago.

Sala, George Augustus Henry, 1828–. *G. A. S.; Benedict Cruiser, M.M.* An English writer and journalist; b. in London; educ. for an artist, but early devoted himself to literature; founder and editor of the "Temple Bar" magazine.

Saley, M. L. *Dick Ditson.* An American journalist.

Salisbury, Stephen, LL.D., 1798–1884. *S. S.* An American lawyer; b. in Worcester, Mass.; Harv. Univ., 1817; resided and d. in his native city.

Salisbury, Rev. W. *A Country Parson.* An English minister.

Salkeld, Joseph. *A Candidate for Orders in the Church.* An American writer.

Salmon, Mrs. ——. *A Lady.* An English poet; niece of Archdeacon Pott.

Salmon, Leon N., 1845–. *Ixion; Prince.* An American writer.

Salmon, Thomas, -about 1745. *A Gentleman.* An old English writer.

Salomons, Alfred. *A. Arnold.* An English translator of the day.

Salt, Henry, 1780–1827. *A Traveller.* An English artist, traveller, and diplomatist; b. at Lichfield; Consul-General in Egypt, 1815–27; d. at a village between Cairo and Alexandria.

Salter, Samuel, D.D., –1778. *S.* A learned English divine; Prebendary of Gloucester; Master of the Charter-House, 1761–78.

Salter, Thomas Frederick. *T. F. S., an Old Piscator.* An English tradesman in the Strand, London; a sporting writer; in 1816 resided at Hackney.

Saltikoff, Nicolai. *Nikolai Stchedrin.* A popular Russian writer.

Saltus, Frank S. *Cupid Jones.* An American journalist.

Salverte, Anne Joseph Eusèbe Baconniere de, 1771–1839. *Louis Randol.* A French man of letters, of Paris, 1820–39; b. and d. in that city.

Samber, Robert. *Boniface Oinophilus de Monte Frasconi, A. B. C.* An English translator, of the first part of the 18th century.

Sampson, Henry. *Pendragon.* An English sporting writer of the day.

Sampson, Henry J. M. *Augspur.* An English writer.

Is this the same as the preceding?

Samson, Rev. George Whitefield, D.D., 1819–. *Traverse Oldfield.* An eminent American Bapt. minister; b. at Harvard, Mass.; Brown Univ., 1839; Newton Theol. Institute, 1843; President of the Rutgers Female Coll., New York City, from 1771.

Samson, W. *Tertius Quartus Quintus.* An English poet and surgeon, at Sherborne, Dorsetshire, in the 18th century.

Sandeau, Léonard Sylvain Jules, 1811–83. *Jules Sand.* A French novelist and dramatist, of Paris; a keeper in the Mazarine Library from 1853; b. at Aubusson; d. in Paris.

Sanden, Thomas, M.D. *A Layman; An Old Unitarian; The President.* An English physician, of Chichester.

Sanders, Charles W., 1805–. *A Teacher.* An American educator and writer of school-books; b. in Herkimer Co., N.Y.; more than fifteen millions of them have been sold, and it is said that he receives $30,000 a year from his publishers.

Sanders, Mrs. Elizabeth (Elkins), 1762–1851. *A Lady.* An American writer, of Salem, Mass.; the mother of Charles Sanders, formerly steward of Harv. Univ.

Sanders, Robert, 1727–83. *Burlington; Gaffer Greybeard; Henry Southwell, LL.D.; Nath. Spencer; Murray; Llewellyn; A Nobleman.* A Scottish man of letters; b. at Breadalbane; a combmaker by trade, but left it to work for the booksellers.

Sanderson, John, 1783–1854. *An American in Paris; An American Gentleman; Robertjeot.* An American classical scholar and miscellaneous writer; b. near Carlisle, Penn.; lived and d. in Philadelphia.

Sanderson, Thomas, about 1759–1829. *Crito; An Aged Native.* An English provincial poet; b. in Sebergham, Co. Cumberland; for many years resided at Shieldgreen, Kirklington, on the romantic banks of the river Lyne, and d. there.

Sandham, Rev. James Munro, M.A. *A Parish Priest in the Diocese of Chichester.* An English clergyman; St. John's Coll., Oxford, 1840; Vicar of Cold-Waltham, Petworth, 1846–83 *et seq.;* Rector of Hardham, 1846–83 *et seq.*

Sandré, Gustave. *Adolphe Ricard.* A French novelist; a bookseller, of Paris.

Sands, Alexander Hamilton, 1828–. *A Southern Barrister.* An American lawyer; b. at Williamsburg, Va.; educ. at William and Mary Coll.; counsellor-at-law in Richmond, Va.

Sands, Robert Charles, 1799–1832. *Francis Herbert, Esq.; Several American Authors.* An American man of letters and journalist, of New York City; editor of the " Commercial Advertiser," 1827–32; b. at Flatbush, Long Island; Columbia Coll., 1815; d. at Hoboken, N.J.

Sandwich, John George Montagu, 4th Earl of, 1718–92. *Jemmy Twitcher.* An English statesman; First Lord of the Admiralty, 1763.

Sandwith, Humphry, M.D., D.C.L., 1822–81. *Giuseppe Antonelli.* An English physician; b. at Bridlington; Colonial Secretary at Mauritius, 1857–60; d. in Paris.

Sandys, Charles. *A Coontrie Atturney.* An English lawyer, of Canterbury.

Sandys, Miss Kate. *Kate Syndas.* An English poet and musician.

Sandys, Sampson, 1797–1880. *John.* An English author; b. in London; Clerk in the Court of Chancery, 1819–42; d. in London.

Sandys, William, F.S.A., 1792–1874. *Uncle Jan Treenoodle; W. S.* An English author and lawyer; b. and d. in London; a member of the law-firm of Sandys & Knott; Gray's Inn Square, W.C., 1861–73.

Sanford, Edward, 1805–54. *Pot-Pie Palmer.* An American poet and journalist, of Brooklyn, New York City, and Washington; b. in New York City; Union Coll., 1824.

Sanford, Mrs. Laura M., 1835–. *Fanchon.* An American historical writer of the day.

Sangston, Lawrence. *A Member of the Maryland Legislature.* An American political writer.

Sankey, Rev. Richard, M.A., 1802–63. *An English Churchman.* An English clergyman; Rector of Witney, Oxon.; d. at Crowshot-lodge, East-Woodhay, Hants.

Sansom, Joseph. *A Native of Pennsylvania.* An American writer, of Philadelphia.

Sarcey, Francisque, 1828–. *Satané Binet.* A French critic and journalist; b. at Dourdan (Seine-et-Oise); first wrote for the "Figaro" and the "Revue européene"; became in 1859 theatrical critic to the "Opinion nationale," and in 1867 to the "Temps."

Sardou, Victorien, 1831–. *Carle.* A French dramatist; b. in Paris.

Saredo, Luisa (Emmanuel). *Ludovico De Rosa.* An Italian writer; b. at Turin; married Giuseppe Saredo; is a constant contributor to the "Nuova Antologia," of Florence.

Sargant, Mrs. J. A. *A Mother.* An English lady.

Sargent, Mrs. Ella S. *Elinor Elliott.*

Sargent, Epes, 1812–82. *E. S.* An American poet, dramatist, and journalist, of Boston; b. at Gloucester, Mass.; educ. in Boston and Cambridge; lived and d. in Boston.

Sargent, Henry Jackson, 1809–. *Residuary Legatee of the Late Walter Anonym.* An American poet of the day.

Sargent, J. S. *J. S. S.* An American journalist of the day.

Sargent, John Osborne, 1810–. *A Berkshire Farmer; Ex-Surveyor General; Mr. Francis Hock; A Layman; Charles Sherry.* An American lawyer and journalist, of New York City; brother of Epes Sargent; b. at Gloucester, Mass.; Harv. Univ., 1830; resident in New York City since 1840.

Sargent, Miss Judith, 1760–1820. *Honoria Martesia.* — See "Murray, Mrs. Judith (S.)."

Sargent, Lucius Manlius, A.M., 1786–1867. *A Sexton of the Old School;*

Sigma; Van Tromp. An American author and ardent temperance reformer; b. in Boston; educ. at Harv. Univ., but did not graduate; studied law, but never practised; d. in West Roxbury, Mass.

Sargent, Moses H. *A Wayfarer.* An American bookseller, formerly of Boston, now of Newburyport, Mass.

Sargent, Nathan, 1794–1875. *Oliver Oldschool.* An American lawyer and journalist; b. at Putney, Vt.; for many years of Washington, where he died.

Sarjeant, Sargeant, or **Sergeant,** sometimes called **Smith,** sometimes **Holland,** about 1621–1707. *J. S.* An English metaphysician; b. at Barrow, Leicestershire; published about forty controversial books or pamphlets, some under the signature of "J. S."

Sass, Charles. *Centaur.* An American writer.

Sass, George Herbert, 1845–. *Barton Grey.* An American lawyer and hymn-writer; b., and has lived, in Charleston, S.C.

Satterlee, M. L. R., and **W. M. L. R. S.** and *W. S.* American (?) poets of the day.

Saumarez, R. B. N. *A Churchman.* An English writer.

Saunders, Frederic, 1807–. *F. S.; An Epicure; O. Hum & Co.* An American bibliographer; b. in London; librarian of the Astor Library, New York City, 1876–83 *et seq.*

Saunders, James. *Guinead Charfy, Esq.* An English writer, early in the 18th century, on angling.

Saunders, Samuel. *A Layman.* An English writer early in the 18th century.

Sautier, Heinrich, 1746–1810. *Erich Servati.* A German writer.

Savage, John, 1828–. *Ezek Richards.* An Irish-American poet and journalist, of New York City, Washington, and New Orleans; b. in Dublin; was engaged in the "Irish Movement" of 1848, and compelled to escape to this country.

Savage, Rev. Minot Judson, 1841–. *A Lunar Wray.* An American clergyman; b. in Maine; pastor of the Church of the Unity, Boston, 1874–85 *et seq.*

Savage, Thomas. *An Eye Witness.* An English Friend, of Clifton Moor, Cumberland; a writer of the 17th century.

Savary, Henry. *Quintus Servington.* An English colonial writer; the once celebrated Bristol baker; committed forgery, was transported to Tasmania;

was again a forger; transported to Port Arthur, and died there in 1842.

Sawtelle, Mrs. E. W. *Tracy Towne.* An American (?) miscellaneous writer.

Sawyer, Frederick William, 1810–. *Carl; Cauty Carl.* An American lawyer and humorist; b. at Saco, Me.; removed to Boston in 1838, and began to practise law there in 1840; was the originator and president of the Pawner's Bank.

Saxe, John Godfrey, LL.D., and two Others, 1816–. *X. Y. Z. Club.* An eminent American poet, lawyer, and journalist; b. at Highgate, Vt.; Middlebury Coll., 1839; admitted to the Bar, 1843; has resided of late years in Brooklyn, N.Y.

Saxon, Mrs. E. Lydell (or Annot Lyle), 1832–. *E. L. S.; Annot Lyle.* An American "Southland" poet and prose writer; b. in Tennessee; in 1848, married Mr. E. L. Saxon; in 1870, resided in New Orleans.

Saxony, Johann Nepomuk Maria Joseph, King of, 1801–. *Philalethes.* A German scholar and translator.

Scargill, William Pitt, 1787–1836. *A Contributor to "Blackwood's Magazine"; A Briefless Barrister.* An English novelist; had been a Unit. preacher, but joined the Church of England; d. at Bury.

Scarth, Rev. John. *A British Resident.* An English clergyman; King's Coll., London, 1865; Vicar of Holy Trinity, Milton-next-Gravesend, 1871–83 *et seq.;* Honorary Canon of Rochester Cathedral, 1877.

Scharling, Carl Henrik, 1836–. *Nicolai.* A Danish poet and philosopher; b. at Copenhagen; studied theology, then made a scientific tour in foreign lands, in which he visited the East, especially the Holy Land. In 1870, he became Professor of Theology in the Univ. of Copenhagen.

Schenck, Leopold. *Capt. Schreier.* A German-American journalist, of New York City.

Scherer, Edmund Henri Adolphe (?), 1815–. *The French Politician.* A French journalist and miscellaneous writer, of Paris.

Schiller, Henry Carl. *Grey Anthony.* An English poet, song-writer, and artist; in 1836 residing at Hull.

Schindler, Julius, 1818–. *Julius von der Traun.* A German poet and prose writer; b. at Vienna; studied philosophy and medicine there. After holding various positions, he now, 1882, as a great land-proprietor, lives sometimes at his castle Leopoldstron, in Salzburg, and sometimes in Vienna.

Schleiden, Matthias Jakob, 1804–81. *Ernst.* A German poet and botanist; b. at Hamburg; from 1866 was devoted to private teaching in Dresden and Wiesbaden; d. in Wiesbaden.

Schmid, Ferdinand von, 1823–. *Dranmor.* A Swiss poet; b. at Muri, in the Canton of Bern. Since 1875 he has resided at Rio Janerio, Brazil.

Schneider, Lina Weller, 1831–. *Wilhelm Berg.* A German writer; b. at Weimar; principal of the Victoria Lyceum, at Cologne.

Schöjen, Elisabeth. *Paul Agathon.* A Norwegian novelist; b. at Christiana; studied in Copenhagen, Rome, and Paris, where she has chiefly resided since 1875.

Scholander, Fredrik Vilhelm, 1816–81. *Acharius.* A Swedish poet and architect; b. at Stockholm, and d. in the same city.

Schomberg, Rev. Alexander Crowcher, 1756–92. *Cornelius Scriblerus Nothus; Scriblerus Secundus.* An English divine; Fellow of Magdalen Coll., Oxford, where he became tutor; d. at Bath.

Schoolcraft, Henry Rowe, LL.D., 1793–1864. *Henry Rowe Colcraft.* A celebrated American genealogist, mineralogist, antiquary, and ethnologist, of Washington, 1847–64; b. at Watervliet (now Guilderland), Albany Co., N.Y.; d. at Washington, D.C.

Schoolcraft, Oliver Johnson. *Sx.* An American poet of the day.

Schornstein, David, 1826–79. *Georges Stenne.* A French-Jewish journalist, translator, and novelist.

Schrader, F. F. *Royal Keen.* An American journalist of the day.

Schulz, Albert, 1802–. *San-Marte.* A German literary antiquary; b. at Schwedt; since 1843, principal of the college at Magdeburg; has made himself favorably known by his labors upon Literature and Sagas of the Middle Ages.

Schulze, Friedrich August, 1770–1849. *Friedrich Laun.* A German poet and novelist; b. at Dresden.

Schuster, Miss Lizzie F. *Polly Chromo.* An American writer of the day.

Schwab, Moise. *Le Marquis de M.* A French bibliographer of the day.

Schwartz, Marie Sophie Birarth, 1819–. *M. S. S.* A Swedish novelist; b. at Boras; in 1840, married Prof. Gustavus Magnus Schwartz, of Stockholm.

Schwarz, Marie Esperance

(Brandt) von, 1821–. *Elpis Melena.* A German author; the daughter of a Hamburg banker; b. at Southgate, near London; educ. at Geneva and Rome; was twice married, both times unhappily; took with her second husband, von Schwarz, a Hamburg banker, a long journey to the East, and in 1849 settled in Rome; later, she spent some time in Crete, but at the present time she lives again in Rome.

Sclater, Philip Lutley, M.A., Ph.D., F.R.S., 1829–. *A Naturalist.* An English naturalist and journalist; educ. at Oxford; called to the Bar at Lincoln's Inn, 1855; Secretary of the London Zoölogical Society, 1862; editor of the "Ibis."

Sclater, William, D.D., –1626. *A Presbyter of the Church of England.* An English clergyman; Fellow of King's Coll., Cambridge; Vicar of Pitminster, Somersetshire, where he died.

Scopoli-Biasi, Isabella, 1810–. *Mario S.* An Italian writer; b. at Milan; in 1871 was appointed inspector of the female schools in the provinces of Verona, Vicenza, and Mantua.

Scoresby, William, 1760–1829. *A Voyager.* An eminent English navigator; b. at Cropton, Yorks.; in 1785 he began a career of unprecedented success in the Greenland whale fishery; in 1823 he retired with a competency, having held command in thirty voyages.

Scott, ——. *S.*

Scott, Rev. ——. *A Divine of the Church of England.* An English clergyman of the first part of the 18th century.

Scott, Sir Claude Edward, 3d Bart., 1804–74. *Sir C. E. S.* An English artist; b. at Bromley, Kent; succeeded his father in 1849.

Scott, Clement. *Almaviva; Saville and Bolton Rowe.* An English musical critic and dramatist, of London; editor of the "Theatre" and on the staff of the "Telegraph."

Scott, David Dundas. *A Member of the Convention of Royal Burghs of Scotland.* A Scottish writer of the day.

Scott, Rev. George. *A Friend of Truth.* A Scottish religious writer of fifty years ago.

Scott, James, D.D., 1733–1814. *Anti-Sejanus; Old Slyboots; Philanglia.* An English clergyman; b. at Leeds; educ. at Cambridge; Rector of Simonbourn, Northumberland, till 1771; from 1771 of London, and d. there.

Scott, John. *Barbarossa.* An American politician; served in the C. S. Army.

Scott, John, 1730–83. *R. S.* An English Friend, of Amwell, Herts.; b. in Grange Walk, Bermondsey, and d. at Ratcliffe, — both in London.

Scott, Major (?) John. *T. Q. Z., Esq.* An English poet.

Is this John Scott Waring? Was he a poet? Or is this John Scott of Amwell?

Scott, Major John. *J. S., &c.* — See " Waring, Major John Scott."

Scott, John, 1784–1821. *Edgeworth Benson.* An English journalist, of London; was killed in a duel with Mr. Christie, a young barrister of Gray's Inn, the editor of "Blackwood's Magazine."

Scott, John F. *Brudder Bones.* An American humorist of the day.

Scott, John Robert, D.D. *Falkland.* An English writer, early in the 19th century.

Scott, Miss Margaret. — See " Gatty, Mrs. Margaret (Scott)."

Scott, Michael, 1789–1835. *Tom Cringle.* A Scottish novelist; b. at Glasgow, and educ. there; resided in Jamaica, W.I., 1806–22, engaged in agriculture and commerce.

Scott, Robert Bissett, Esq., 1774–1841. *R. B. S.* An English writer on military jurisprudence, and a military advocate; was a pensioner of the Charter House, 1836–41, where he died.

Scott, Mrs. Sarah, –1795. *A Gentleman on his Travels; A Person of Quality; Henry Augustus Raymond.* An English writer; sister of Mrs. Elizabeth Montagu, and wife of George Lewis Scott; separated from her husband, and took up her abode with Lady Bab Montagu.

Scott, Thomas J. *Prog.* An American journalist of the day.

Scott, Sir Walter, 1771–1832. *The Visionary; The Ariosto of the North; The Caledonian Comet; The Great Magician; The Great Unknown; A Layman; Minstrel of the Border; Paul; Somnambulus; Capt. Clutterbuck; Jedediah Cleishbotham; Chrystal Croftangry; The Rev. Dr. Dryasdust; Laurence Templeton; Malachi Malagrowther; Peter Pattieson.* A celebrated Scottish poet and novelist; b. in Edinburgh; d. at Abbotsford.

Scott, Sir William, Lord Stowell, D.C.L., 1745–1836. *Chrysal; Civis.* An English jurist; b. at Heworth, Co. Durham; educ. at Oxford; Judge of the High Court of Admiralty, 1798–1828; d. at Early Court, near Reading, Berks.

Scott, William B. *Diversity.* An American broker (?), of New York City.

Scoville, Joseph A., 1811–64. *Manhattan; Walter Barrett, Clerk.* An American writer; b. in Connecticut; was a States Rights Democrat, and for some years the private secretary of John C. Calhoun. During the civil war, he was violently opposed to Mr. Lincoln and the Republican party; d. in New York City.

Scribner, B. F. *A Volunteer; "One who was thar"; One who has seen the Elephant.* An American soldier, in the Mexican war, from New Albany, Ind.

Scribner, J. P. *An Old Mountaineer.* An American writer.

Scrymgeour, James. *Norval.* A Scottish writer of the day.

Scudamore, Miss Lily. *Ruhamah.* An American journalist, of Washington.

Scudder, Horace Elisha, 1838-. *S. T. James.* An American author, editor, and bibliographer, of Cambridge, Mass.; b. in Boston; Williams Coll., 1858.

Scudder, Vida D. *Davida Coit.* An American (?) author of the day.

Seabrook, Ephraim Baynard. *E. B. S.* An American writer of the day, of South Carolina.

Seabury, Samuel, D.D., 1729-96. *A Farmer; A. W. Farmer; A Westchester Farmer.* An American clergyman and loyalist; b. at Groton, Conn.; Yale Coll.; 1748; d. in New London, Conn.

Seager, Charles, M.A. *Academicus.* An English novelist and miscellaneous writer.

Seale, John Barlow, D.D., F.R.S. *A Friend of the Author.* An English scholar, of Christ Coll., Cambridge. "Who reads false quantities in Sele." — See Byron in his "Hours of Idleness."

Seaman, Augustus. *Titus Brick.* An American writer.

Searing, Mrs. Laura C. (Redden), about 1840-. *Howard Glyndon.* An American poet and journalist; b. in Somerset Co., Va.; at St. Louis, 1860; afterwards wife of Edward W. Searing, Professor of Latin in Milton Coll., Wisconsin.

Sears, George W. *Nessmuk.* An American *littérateur* of the day.

Seawell, Miss Molly Elliott. *Foxhall; Sydney.* An American writer of the day.

Seccombe, Rev. Joseph, A.M., 1706-60. *Fluviatulis Piscator.* An American Cong. minister, at Kingston, N.H., 1737-60; Harv. Univ., 1731.

Seckendorf, Gustav Anton, Baron von, 1775-1823. *Patrick Peale.* A German dramatist; b. near Altenburg; d. in America.

Seddon, John P. *His Brother.* An

English architect; secretary to the Royal Institute of British Architecture.

Sedgwick, Miss Catherine Maria, and Others, 1789-1867. *Several American Authors.* An American popular writer; b. at Stockbridge, Mass.; taught a private school for young ladies, for 50 years; d. near Roxbury, Mass.

Sedgwick, Miss C. M., J. K. Paulding, W. C. Bryant, W. Leggett, and **R. C. Sands.** *Several American Authors.*

Sedgwick, James, Esq., 1775-1851. *A Barrister.* An English lawyer and journalist, of Oxford, Edinburgh, and London; of Pembroke Coll., Oxford, and called to the Bar of the Middle Temple, 1801; d. in London.

Sedgwick, Theodore, 1781-1839. *An American.* An American lawyer; b. at Stockbridge, Mass.; practised law in Albany, N.Y., for about 20 years, when he removed, in 1822, to his native place, and resided there till his death.

Sedgwick, Theodore, 1811-59. *Veto.* An eminent American lawyer, of New York City; b. at Albany; U.S. District Attorney, N.Y., 1858-59.

Sedley, Sir Charles, 1639-1701. *Sir C. S.* An English dramatist; b. at Aylesford; at the Restoration removed to London, and "became a debauchee, set up for a satirical wit, a comedian, poet, and courter of ladies"; M.P. for New Romney, Kent; d. in London.

Seeley, John Robert, 1834-. *Pupils of the City of London School.* An English classical scholar; b. in London; Christ Coll., Cambridge, 1857; succeeded Charles Kingsley as Professor of Modern History at Cambridge in 1869.

Seeley, John Robert, William Young, and **Ernest Abraham Hart.** *Pupils of the City of London School.*

Seeley, Robert Benton. *A Layman; James White.* An English theological writer.

Seilhamer, George O. *G. O. S.* An American journalist of the day, of New York City.

Selby, Charles, 1801-63. *William Muggins; Tabitha Tickletooth.* A popular London comedian and dramatist; d. in London.

Selden, Richard Ely, Jr., A.M., 1797-1868. *Mon Droit.* An American farmer and bibliographer; Yale Coll., 1818; b., lived, and d. at Hadlyme, Conn.

Selous, H. C. *Kay Spen.* An English novelist of the day.

Selwyn, Major ——. *Major S**** W***** N.* An English officer and writer of the 18th century.

Sendall, E. *Caractacus.* An English journalist, of London.

Senior, William. *Uncle Hardy; Redspinner.* An English sporting writer, of London, of the day.

Sergeant, Mrs. E. F. A. *Adeline.* An English poet.

Serres, Olivia Wilmot, 1772–1834. *Olivia.* An English writer; the self-styled Princess Olive of Cumberland; d. in London, within the rules of the King's Bench, where she passed the latter years of her life in obscurity and poverty.

Seton, A. *A. S.* A Swedish writer.

Settle, Elkanah, 1648–1723 or 24. *E. S.* An English dramatist; b. at Dunstable, Beds.; entered Trin. Coll., Oxford; but left without a degree and went to London, where he spent the rest of his life, and d. at the Charterhouse.

Sewall, Jonathan Mitchell, 1748–1808. *A Gentleman of Portsmouth, N.H.; Vernon H. Quincey, Esq.* An American poet; b. in Salem, Mass.; Register of Probate for Grafton Co., N.H., 1774–1808; d. at Portsmouth, N.H.

Sewall, Samuel Edmund, LL.B. *Z.* An American lawyer, of Boston; Harv. Univ., 1817; has been a strong anti-slavery advocate.

Seward, Miss Anna, 1747–1809. *The Swan of Lichfield.* An English poetess, of Lichfield, where she was born, lived, and died.

Seward, William, 1747–99. *The Compiler of " Anecdotes of Distinguished Persons."* An English biographer; b. and d. in London; after travelling on the Continent, devoted his life to literary pursuits.

Sewell, ——. *Colonist.* A Canadian writer.

Sewell, Miss Elizabeth Missing, 1815–. *A Lady.* An English writer of High Church fiction; sister of Rev. William Sewell; b. in the Isle of Wight.

Sewell, George, M.D., –1726. *G. S.* An English physician; b. at Windsor; educ. at Peter House, Cambridge; practised his profession in London; spent his last days in Hampstead, where he d. in great poverty.

Sewell, Richard Clarke, Esq., D.C.L., 1804–64. *A Hampshire Fisherman.* A British colonial lawyer; Fellow of Magdalen Coll., Oxford; called to the Bar at the Middle Temple, 1830; d. at Melbourne, Victoria.

Sewell, Rev. William, 1805–74. *A Clergyman.* An English clergyman; b. in the Isle of Wight; brother of Miss E. M. Sewell; Curate of St. Nicholas-in-the

Castle, Newport, Isle of Wight, 1831–74.

Seymour, Caroline. *Edward Spencer.* An American writer of the day.

Seymour, Edward, 1835–77. An American journalist; b. in Bloomfield, N.J.; Yale Coll., 1858; in 1869 became a member of the publishing house of Scribner & Co., of New York City; d. at Bloomfield.

Seymour, Ernest R. *E. R. S.* An English writer.

Seymour, Hon. Mary Alice (Ives). *Octavia Hensel.* An English writer of the day.

Seymour, Mrs. Mary H. *M. H. S.* An American writer of the day.

Seymour, Richard Arthur. *A Settler.* An English writer of the day.

Shackleford, Miss Anna P. — See " Dinnies, Mrs. A. P. (S.)."

Shackleton, Abraham. *A. S.* An Irish poet of the 18th century.

Shade, Ellen. *Ella Ellwood.*

Shadwell, Charles, –1726. *C. S.* An English dramatist; nephew of Thomas Shadwell; he had served in Portugal, and held a post in the revenue in Dublin, where he died.

Shand, Alexander. *An Observer of the Times.* A Scottish lawyer, of Aberdeen.

Shanks, John. *The Old Cicerone of Elgin Cathedral.* An English writer of the day.

Shanks, William F. G. *Mary Gore.* An American printer and writer, of New York City.

Shannon, Mrs. Mary Eulalie (Fee), 1824–55. *Eulalie.* An American poet, of Auburn, Cal.

Sharp, ——. *A Presbyter of the Church of England.* An English writer early in the 18th century.

Sharp, Abraham, 1651–1742. *A. S., Philomath.* An eminent English mathematician; b. at Little Horton, Yorkshire; in 1668 was engaged by Flamsteed as his assistant in the Royal Observatory, and after his retirement to his native town continued to assist him and others.

Sharp, Granville, 1735–1813. *Granville S——.* An eminent English philanthropist, of London, devoted to the overthrow of slavery and the slave-trade; b. in Durham; d. in London.

Sharp, Richard, about 1759–1835. *"Conversation" Sharp; A Lay Dissenter.* An English critic and miscellaneous writer, of London; friend of Mr. Hallam and Sir James Mackintosh; d. at Dorchester.

Sharp, Thomas, Esq., 1771–1841. *Z;*

Philarchaismos; S. An eminent English antiquary; b. in Coventry (?), and educ. in the Free School of that town, where he resided till about 1831, he removed to Leamington, and d. there.

Sharp, William, Jr. *Englishman.* An English poet and prose writer of the 18th century.

Sharpe, C., Esq. *Him who should best understand it.* An English gentleman, of Woodbridge.

Sharpe, Charles Kirkpatrick, Esq., M.A., 1781–1851. *An Amateur.* A Scottish artist and author, of Edinburgh; for nearly half a century a distinguished member of the literary circles of that city, where he d., at his house in Drummond-place.

Sharpe, Miss **Emily.** *E. S.* An English editor of the day.

Sharples, Alfred. *John Plowshare.* An American author, of West Chester, Pa.; a writer on agricultural subjects.

Shaw, Cuthbert, 1738–71. *An Afflicted Husband; W. Seymour; Mercurius Spur, Esq.* An English actor and author; b. at Ravensworth, Yorkshire; was an usher at Scorton and Richmond; then removed to London; was dissipated and extravagant; a contributor to the "Freeholder's Magazine" and other papers.

Shaw, Donald. *Glenmore.* A Scottish poet.

Shaw, Henry W., 1818–. *Josh Billings.* An American humorist; b. at Lanesborough, Mass.; resided 25 years in the West, being successively a farmer and an auctioneer; about 1858 settled in Poughkeepsie, N.Y.; and in 1863 began to write for the newspapers; now living in Brooklyn, N.Y.

Shaw, Miss **L. J.** *His Daughter.* An American writer, daughter of Elder Elijah Shaw.

Shaw, Peter, M.D., –1763. *Fellow of a College.* An English physician-in-ordinary to George III.

Shaw, T. H. *An English Churchman.* An English religious writer; of St. Columb Minor, Cornwall, in 1868.

Shaw, William. *A Gold-Seeker.* An English (?) writer; a Californian miner.

Shaw, William, D.D., F.A.S. *Rev. Sir Archibald Mac Sarcasm, Bart.* An English clergyman; Rector of Chelvy, Somersetshire.

Shaw, Rev. **William.** *W. G. S.* A Scottish minister, of Forfar.

Sheahan, Dennis B., 1843–. *Critique.* An American sculptor and writer, of New York City.

Shears, Rev. **Alonzo Groesbeck,** A.M., M.D., 1811–. *Clement; Forfex; S. G. Alphonso.* An American journalist; b. in Washington, Duchess Co., N.Y.; educ. at the Wesleyan Univ., but did not graduate; founder and rector of the New Haven Suburban Home School for 17 years; editor of the New Haven "Musical and Masonic Magazine."

Shebbeare, John, M.D., 1709–88. *Battista Angeloni; Ferret.* An English political writer; b. in Bideford, Devonshire; lived for many years in London; and published 34 books and pamphlets.

Shedd, Rev. **William,** A.M., 1797–1830. *Canonicus.* An American Cong. minister; b. at Mt. Vernon, N.H.; Dartmouth Coll., 1819; Andover Theol. Sem., 1823; minister of the First Church in Abington, Mass., where he died.

Shee, Sir **Martin Archer,** Knt., D.C.L., 1770–1850. *A Painter.* An eminent Irish artist; b. in Dublin; President of the Royal Academy, 1830; d. at Brighton.

Sheehan, John, 1831–. *The Irish Whiskey Drinker; The Knight of Innishowen.* An Irish barrister and poet, and a member of the English Bar (Home Circuit); for some years he settled down in his native country, — in the romantic county of Wicklow, — and lived in literary ease, but has since resumed his pen. See "Notes and Queries," May, 1868, p. 514.

Shelburne, William Petty, Earl of, 1737–1805. *L—d Sh—lb—ne.* An English statesman; a political friend of the Earl of Chatham; Prime Minister of England, 1782–83; a liberal patron of learned men, and had one of the finest libraries in the kingdom.

Shelley, Percy Bysshe, 1792–1822. *S.; John Fitzvictor; A Gentleman of Oxford; The Hermit of Marlow; My Aunt Margaret Nicholson; The Poet of Poets; Victor.* An eminent English poet; b. at Field Place, Sussex; educ. at Eton and Oxford, but did not graduate; resided in Italy, near Leghorn; he was drowned in the Gulf of Lerici.

Shellman, Harry J., 1843–. *Puffo Smoko.* An American journalist, of Indianapolis, Ind.

Shelton, Rev. **Frederick William,** LL.D., 1814–81. *Nil Admirari, Esq.* An American P. E. clergyman; b. at Jamaica, L.I.; New Jersey Coll., 1834; from 1854, at Montpelier, Vt.; in 1874 *et seq.,* at Carthage Landing, N.Y.

Shelton, Mrs. **Julia (Finley).** *Laura Lorrimer.* An American "Southland" poet; b. on the Cumberland River, Tenn.; in 1855, married Mr. J. A. Shelton, of Bellefonte, Ala.

Shepard, Mrs. Hannah (McLaren), 1830-. *Scotch Granite.* An American writer of the day.

Shepard, Nathan. *Key-Note.* An American journalist, of New York City.

Shepherd, Jacob R. *Richmond.*

Shepherd, Richard Herne. *R. H. S.* An English poet; minister of Ranelagh Chapel, Chelsea.

Shepherd, Mrs. Sophy Winthrop (Weitzel). *Sophy Winthrop.* An American writer of the day.

Sheppard, Elizabeth Sara, 1830-62. *Elizabeth Berger; Mme Kinkel; Beatrice Reynolds.* An English novelist; daughter of a clergyman, of Blackheath; d. at Brixton.

Sheppard, George, about 1820-. *Caleb Wilkins.* An English and Canadian journalist; in 1867, resided in New York.

Sheppard, Sarah. *S. S.* An English writer.

Sherer, J. *A Gold-Digger.* An English writer.

Sheridan, Miss Caroline.—See "Maxwell, Mrs. C. (S.)."

Sheridan, Richard Brinsley Butler, 1751-1816. *The Most Artful Man Alive.* An eminent Irish orator, statesman, and dramatic poet; b. in Dublin; d. in London.

Sheridan, Thomas. *Tom Sparkle.* An English civilian; son of Richard Brinsley Sheridan; d. in 1817, at the Cape of Good Hope, where he was colonial paymaster.

Sherlock, Martin. *An English Traveller; Un Voyageur Anglois.* An Irish divine; chaplain to the Earl of Bristol.

Sherlock, W. *Photius, junior.* An Irish lawyer, of Dublin.

Sherwood, Hon. Henry. *A Citizen.* A Canadian legislator; M.P., 1843-54, and successively, solicitor, and Attorney-General.

Sherwood, John D., 1818-. *Harry Scratchley.* An American lawyer; b. at Fishkill, N.Y.; Yale Coll., 1839; admitted to the Bar, 1845; and has practised his profession in New York City.

Sherwood, Mrs. Mary Elizabeth (Wilson). *M. E. W. S.* An American novelist and writer of the day for "Appleton's Journal" and other magazines.

Sherwood, Mrs. Mary (Neal). *John Stirling.* An American (?) writer of the day.

Sherwood, Reuben, D.D., -1856.

Philalethes. An American clergyman, of the P. E. Church; Yale Coll., 1813.

Shewell, John Talwin, 1782-1866. *I. T. S.* An English Friend, of Ipswich; b. in London; was a minister; d. at his residence, Rushmere, near Ipswich.

Shields, G. O. *Coquina.* An American sporting writer.

Shields, Mrs. S. A. *S. Annie Frost.*

Shillaber, Benjamin Penhallow, 1814-. *Mrs. Partington; Ruth Partington; She P. Billaber.* An eminent American humorist and journalist, of Boston; b. at Portsmouth, N.H., and learned the trade of a printer in Dover, N.H.

Shillitoe, Thomas, about 1754-1836. *T. S.* An English Friend, of London; last of Tottenham; a minister for more than 50 years.

Shinn, Earl. *Edward Strahan.* An American (?) writer of the day.

Shipley, William Davies. *A Member of the Society for Constitutional Information.* An English writer; Dean of St. Asaphs.

Shippen, William, 1672-1743. An English statesman; successively M.P for Bramber, Saltash, and Newton.

Shipton, Anna. *A. S.* An English writer of the day, of hymns and devotional books.

Shirra, James. *A Member of the Guildry.* A Scottish writer of the day.

Shirra, Robert, 1724-1803. *A Protestant.* A Scottish clergyman; minister of Linktown, Kirkcaldy.

Shittler, Rev. Robert. *A Clergyman of the Church of England.* An English divine; Vicar of Alton Pancras, Dorset, 1842-60 *et seq.*

Shore, A. and Louisa. *A. and L.* English poets.

Shore, Rt. Hon. John, 1st Lord, 1752-1834. *A Late Resident of Bengal.* A British colonial civilian; b. in Devonshire; went early to India; Governor-General of India, 1793-98; d. in London.

Short, Charles William. *C. W. S.* An English officer of the Coldstream Guards.

Short, Miss Mary Asenath, 1833-. *Fanny True; Cultivator Mary.* An American poet; b. at Haverhill, Mass.; in 1860 of Plymouth, Richland Co., O.

Shorter, Thomas. *Thomas Brevior.* An English poet; secretary of the Working-Men's College, London (?).

Shorthouse, J. Henry. *Geoffrey Monk, M.A.* An English writer of the day.

Shortrede, Andrew. *Lieut. Abel Knockdunder, H.P.* A Scottish writer

Shuckburgh, Charles. *A Gentleman of Gloucestershire.* An English writer of the 18th century.

Shurtleff, Nathaniel Bradstreet, M.D., –1874. *N. B. S.* An American literary antiquary; b. in Boston; Harv. Univ., 1831; Harv. Med. School, 1834; practised in Boston; Mayor of Boston, 1868–70; d. in that city.

Shute, Rev. **Hardwick,** M.A. *One who Knows it.* An English clergyman; Pembroke Coll., Oxford, 1836; in 1883 resident at Lilian Villa, Queen's Road, Teddington, Middlesex.

Sibbald, Sir **Robert,** M.D., –about 1712. *Sir R—— S——.* An English naturalist and antiquary; educ. at Edinburgh and at Leyden; resided chiefly in Edinburgh, and d. there.

Sibley, Henry Hastings, 1811–. *Hal a Dacotah; The Walker in the Pines.* An American officer; major 1st Dragoons, May 13, 1861; resigned, May 13, 1861, and entered the Confederate service.

Sidney, James A. *F. Crucelli.* A Scottish (?) humorist of the day.

Sidmouth, Henry Addington, Viscount, 1757–1844. *Lord S.* An English nobleman; b. in London, and d. at the White Lodge, Richmond Park.

Sidney, L. *Densyli.* An English Unit. writer.

Sidney, Samuel. *Emigrant.* An English writer; for some time a resident in Australia.

Sigerson, George, M.D. *An Ulsterman.* An Irish writer of the day, on Ireland.

Sikes, Mrs. **Olive (Logan),** 1841–. *Olive Logan; Chroniqueuse.* An American actress and writer of great merit; b. in New York State; wife of W. W. Sikes, journalist, of New York City.

Sikes, Rev. **Thomas,** M.A. *A Country Clergyman.* An English divine; Vicar of Gilsborough, Northants.; M.A. at Pembroke Coll., Oxford, 1792.

Sill, Richard. *Charles Dirrill.* An English Shakespearian scholar of one hundred years ago.

Siller, Miss **Hulda.** *Hilda.* An American writer, of Milwaukee, Wis.

Silliman, George Joseph L. W. *Hannibal.*

Simcox, George Augustus, M.A. *A Rambler.* An English dramatist; Fellow of Queen's Coll., Oxford.

Simmel, August, 1815–78. *August Schrader.* A German novelist; b. at Wegeleben, near Halberstadt, where he was educated; about 1842 settled at Leipsic, where his first work was published, and where he died.

Simmonds, ——. *Sir Ferdinando Fungus, Gent.* An English writer, of Blandford, Dorsetshire.

Simmons, George W., 1815–82. *A Friend to American Enterprise.* An American merchant tailor, of Boston; senior proprietor of Oak Hall.

Simmons, William Hammatt, A.M., 1812–41. *C. Domal; Lockfast.* An American; Harv. Univ., 1831; a brilliant reader and rhetorician.

Simms, Jeptha Root, 1807–. An American writer; b. in Canterbury, Conn. — See "American Spy, The."

Simms, William Gilmore, LL.D., 1806–70. *A Collegian; Frank Cooper; Isabel; A Southron.* An American writer; b. and d. at Charleston, S.C.; admitted to the Bar, 1827, but did not practise; about 1833 settled at Woodlands, near Medway.

Simon, Emma (Couvely), 1848–. *Emma Vely.* A German author; b. at Braunfels, near Wetzler; in 1871 she married the bookseller Simon, in Stuttgart, and made their house the literary saloon for all distinguished persons who came to Stuttgart.

Simond, Louis, 1767–1831. *A French Traveller.* Resided and travelled many years in England and the United States.

Simonds, William, 1822–59. *Walter Aimwell.* An American journalist and writer of books for the young; b. at Charlestown, Mass.; editor and proprietor of the "Boston Saturday Rambler," 1846; and connected with the "New England Farmer."

Simons, Mrs. **Lydia Lillybridge.** *E. L.* An English poet; wife of Mr. Thomas Simons, of Maulmain (?), East Indies.

Simpson, Archibald. *Gillespie MacShinie.* A Scottish biographer of one hundred years ago.

Simpson, Mrs. **Jane Cross (Bell),** 1811–. *Gertrude.* A Scottish poet and hymn-writer, of Edinburgh; sister of Henry Glassford Bell; b. in Glasgow; author of the hymn, "Go when the morning shineth."

Simpson, S. S. *S. S. S.* An American writer for the young.

Simpson, Stephen, 1789–1854. *Brutus.* An American journalist; b. and d. at Philadelphia.

Simpson, Thomas, 1710–61. *Hurlothrumbo, etc.* An eminent English mathematician; b. at Market-Bosworth, Leicestershire; Professor of Mathematics in the Royal Academy at Woolwich, 1743–60; d. at Bosworth.

Sims, George Robert, 1847–. *Dagonet.* An English dramatist, ballad-writer, and journalist, of London; a principal contributor to the "Referee," a sporting and dramatic journal, of London; has recently produced a highly successful melodrama, "The Romany Rye."

Sinclair, Miss **Carrie Bell,** 1839–. *Clara.* An American "Southland" poet; b. in Milledgeville, Ga.; in 1871, residing in Philadelphia.

Sinclair, James. *Sigma.* A Scottish writer of the day.

Sinclair, Sir **John,** 1st Bart., LL.D., 1754–1835. *The President; —— ——, Esq., Member of Parliament for the County of ——.* A Scottish agricultural reformer; b. at Thurso Castle, Caithness; educ. at Glasgow and Oxford; admitted to the Scottish and English Bars, but never practised; M.P., 1780–1811; shared in the publication of 367 books and pamphlets; d. in Edinburgh.

Singleton, Mrs. **Mary (Montgomerie Lamb).** *Violet Fane.* An English poet; is the wife of Mr. Henry Singleton, an extensive Irish landowner.

Singleton, William. *A Late Teacher; A True Quaker.* An English Friend, of Owlerton, near Sheffield.

Sjöberg, Erik, 1794–1828. *Vitalis.* A Swedish poet; b. in Ljungo, Sudermania; educ. at the Univ. of Upsal; lived and d. in Stockholm.

Skeffington, Sir **Lumley St. George,** Bart., 1771–1851. *Sk—ff—ingt—n, Esq.* An English dramatist; b. in the parish of St. Pancras, Middlesex; educ. at Hackney; d. in London.— See "Gent. Mag.," February, 1851, p. 200.

Skelton, John. *Shirley.* A Scottish advocate.

Skelton, Rev. **Philip,** 1707–87. *An Old Man; An Old Officer.* An Irish clergyman; b. near Lisburn; Vicar of Fintona, 1766–80; d. in Dublin.

Skene, Felicia M. F. *F. M. F. S.* An English poet of the day.

Skene, James Henry. *A British Resident of Twenty Years in the East.* An English writer.

Skidmore, Harriet M. *Marie; Ruhamah.* An American poet of the day.

Skidmore, Joseph, Senior. *A. B.* An English Friend, of Rickmansworth, of the first part of the 18th century.

Skillman, Isaac, D.D., 1740–99. *A British Bostonian.* An American Baptist clergyman; b. in New Jersey; N.J. Coll., 1766; pastor at Boston, Mass., 1773–90; at Salem, N.J., 1790–99, where he died.

Skinner, Miss **Abby.** *Aunt Abbie.* An American writer for the young.

Skinner, Charles M., 1852–. *Tramp.* An American journalist, of Brooklyn, N.Y.

Skinner, Rev. **George.** *H. H. Bernard, Ph.D.* An English clergyman; Jesus Coll., Cambridge, 1818; Chaplain of King's Coll., Cambridge.

Skinner, Rev. **John,** 1744–1816. *A Layman.* A Scottish Epis. clergyman; Bishop of Aberdeen, 1788–1816.

Skinner, Dr. **Salmon,** 1818–81. *Amigo.* An American journalist, of New York City.

Slade, Daniel Denison, M.D., 1823–. *Medicus.* An American physician; b. in Boston, Mass.; Harv. Univ., 1844; Prof. of Practical Zoölogy, 1871–82; resides at Chestnut Hill.

Slater, George. *G. S.* An American journalist, of New York City.

Slaughter, Mrs. **M.** *Pleasant Riderhood.*

Sleech, Ven. **John,** –1788. *J. S., A. C.* An English clergyman; King's Coll., Cambridge, 1733; Archdeacon of Cornwall, 1741–88; d. at Exeter.

Sleeman, Major-General Sir **William Henry,** 1788–1856. *An Indian Official: An Officer in the Mil. and Civ. Service of the Hon. E. I. Co.* An eminent English officer; b. at Stratton; Brit. resident at Lucknow, Oude, 1849–56; d. at sea, returning from India.

Sleeper, John Sherburne, 1794–1878. *Hawser Martingale.* An American seaman and journalist, of Roxbury, Mass.; b. at Tyngsboro; d. at Roxbury.

Sleeper, Walter T. *Uncle Walter.* An American writer for the young.

Slidell, Mrs. **Edward.** *C. C. Fraser Tytler.* An English writer.

Sliver, W. A. *Frederick Marsden.* An American dramatist.

Sloan, James. *An American.* An American writer; N.J. Coll., 1805.

Slocum, Mary S. F. *Willa West.* An American writer of the day.

Slosson, Annie T. *The Youngest Member.* An American writer of the day, on the fine arts.

Slote, Daniel, 1830–83. *Dan.* An American blank-book manufacturer, of New York City.

Slous, F. L. *An Awkward Man.* An English writer.

Small, George G. *Bricktop.* An American humorist and journalist, of New York City.

Small, Rev. **John.** *J. S., A Presbyter of the Episcopal Church of Scotland.*

A Scottish writer of the first part of the 18th century.

Small, Samuel W., 1851–. *Old Si.* An American journalist, of Atlanta, Ga.

Smalley, George W. *G. W. S.* An American journalist; London correspondent New York "Tribune."

Smart, Mrs. Anna Maria, 1732–1809. *The Lass with the Golden Locks.* An English lady, of Reading, Berks.; for more than 40 years principal proprietor of the "Reading Mercury and Oxford Gazette."

Smart, Benjamin, 1756–1833. *T. Ramsneb; B. S****; A Lombard.* An English poet and prose writer, of the parish of St. James's, Westminster; bullion merchant and refiner; d. in London.

Smart, Benjamin Humphrey, about 1785–. *Francis Drake, Esq.; A Follower of Locke.* An English elocutionist; taught elocution more than 50 years in London, from 1815, and wrote much upon grammar, logic, rhetoric, and metaphysics.

Smart, Charles, M.D. *Polywarp Oldfellow, M.D.* An American novelist; b. in Scotland; asst.-surgeon in the late civil war, 1862–64; capt.-asst.-surg., 1866.

Smart, Christopher, 1722–70. *Ebenezer Pentweazle.* An English poet and translator, of London; b. at Shipbourne, Kent.; Fellow of Pemberton Hall, Cambridge; d. in London.

Smedley, Rev. Edward, 1789–1836. *A Churchman; A Protestant.* An English clergyman; b. in Westminster; Prebendary of Lincoln, 1829–36; d. at Dulwich.

Smedley, Francis Edward, 1819–64. *Frank Farleigh; Francis Phiz; Two Merry Men.* An English novelist and journalist, of Beechwood, Great Marlow; d. at Regent's Park, London.

Smedley, Miss Menella Bute. *M. S.* An English poet and prose writer; sister of the preceding.

Smeeton, George. *Guiniad Charfy.* An English sporting writer. — See "Saunders, James."

Smellie, William, 1740–95. *A Juryman.* A learned and ingenious Scottish printer and eminent naturalist; b. in the Pleasance of Edinburgh; resided in that city during his life, and d. there.

Smiles, R. W. *R. W. S.; One of their Own Order.* An English writer.

Smiles, Samuel, Jr. *A Boy.* An English writer.

Smith, ——. *An Eminent Lawyer.* An English lawyer; Fellow of King's Coll., Cambridge.

Smith, ——. *Publicola.* An English journalist, of London.

Smith, A. W. *A. W. S.* An English angler.

Smith, Mrs. Adolphe (Jerrold), –1882. *Corisande.* An English writer; daughter of Blanchard Jerrold.

Smith, Albert, 1816–60. *Jasper Buddle.* An English humorist; b. at Chertsey; settled in London, 1841; wrote for several journals; gave public entertainments; d. at Fulham, near London.

Smith, Rev. Alexander Mackay. *A. M. S.* An American poet; Trin. Coll., Hartford, Conn., 1872.

Smith, Mrs. Caroline L. *Aunt Carrie.* An American writer for the young.

Smith, Mrs. Castle. *Brenda.* An English writer for the young.

Smith, Rev. Charles. *Ebenezer Tom-Tit.* An English clergyman; Minor Canon of Norwich.

Smith, Charles H. *Bill Arp; Dr. Helle Bore.* An American humorist and Confederate States soldier.

" I'm a good Union man so-called, but I'll bet on Dixie as long as I've got a dollar." BILL ARP.

Smith, Charles J. *The Call-Boy.* An American journalist, of New York City.

Smith, Charles Manby. *A Journeyman Printer.* An English writer.

Smith, Charles William. *C. W. S.; One who is really an Englishman.* An English professor of elocution, of London.

Smith, Charlotte. *Kenner Deene.* An English novelist; later than the following.

Smith, Mrs. Charlotte (Turner), 1749–1806. *A Solitary Wanderer.* An English poet and novelist; before she was sixteen, married Mr. Benj. Smith, a West India merchant, by whom she was involved in difficulties, with her twelve children, which it required the diligent use of her pen to relieve; d. at Tetford, near Farnham, Surrey.

Smith, Rev. Clement Ogle, M.A. *A Priest of the English Church.* An English clergyman; Corpus Christi Coll., Cambridge, 1858; Rector of Shelfanger, Diss., 1863–83 *et seq.* He changed his name to Rev. C. O. Blakelock.

Smith, D. E., M.D. *A Physician.* An American physician.

Smith, Edward, M.D. *A London Physician.* An English writer; assistant physician to the Hospital for Consumptives, Brompton.

Smith, Elbert H. *A Western Tourist.* An American poet.

Smith, Eleanor. *Heatherbell.* An English writer of the day, of London.

Smith, Eli, D.D., 1801–57. *Palestinensis.* An eminent American missionary and orientalist; b. at Northford, Conn.; Yale Coll., 1821; Andover Theol. Sem., 1826; d. at Beyrout.

Smith, Rev. **Elisha,** –1739. *A Country Clergyman; A Corresponding Member of the Society, etc.* An English divine; Lecturer of Wisbech, and Rector of Tid St. Giles's, in the Isle of Ely, and Castle Rising, Norfolk.

Smith, Miss **Eliza.** *A Clergyman's Daughter.* An English or Scottish writer.

Smith, Mrs. **Eliza A. E.** *Honey Bee.* An American writer; wife of John Gregory Smith, formerly Governor of Vermont.

Smith, Miss **Elizabeth,** 1776–1806. *A Young Lady lately deceased.* An English lady, distinguished for her learning; b. at Burnhall, near Durham; taught herself ten different languages.

Smith, Mrs. **Elizabeth Oakes (Prince),** 1806–. *Ernest Helfenstein.* An American writer; b. at Cumberland, near Yarmouth, Me.; wife of Seba Smith, of Portland, Me.; in 1840 removed to New York City; in 1876 resident at Holywood, Carteret Co., N.C.

Smith, Elizabeth S. *Elizabeth S. Chester.* An American writer.

Smith, Fannie N. *Christabel Goldsmith.*

Thus the Library of Congress has it; others, *Julie P.,* which see.

Smith, Fanny. *Fanny Manetti.* An American writer.

Smith, Mrs. **Frances Elizabeth,** 1832–. *Fanny Fales.* An American poet.

Smith, Mrs. **Frances Irene (Burge),** 1826–. *Fan-Fan.* An American journalist; daughter of the Rev. L. Burge, of Wickford, R.I.; and b. there.

Smith, Francis Shubael, 1819–. *Tenpin Boy.* An American poet and journalist; b. in New York City; once coeditor of the New York "Dispatch"; afterwards, of the New York "Weekly."

Smith, George, D.D., 1693–1756. *G. S.; A Divine of the Univ. of Cambridge; A Lover of that Innocent and Healthful Diversion.* An English clergyman; son of John Smith, titular Bishop of Durham.

Smith, George, D.D. *Clericus.* An eminent English Cong. minister; of London from 1842.

Smith, Rev. **George,** M.A. *L. L.; Leonard Lovechurch.* An English clergyman; late of Trin. Coll., Cambridge; curate of the Parish Church, Sheffield.

Smith, Rev. **George Charles,** 1782–1863. *Capsicum.* An English minister; b. in London; pastor of the Baptist Chapel, Penzance, 1807–25 and 1848–63, and preacher to the sailors at Penzance, etc.; opened the First Mariners' Church, in London, in 1825; visited New York City, 1861; d. at Penzance.

Smith, Mrs. **George Clinton.** *The Widow in Blue.* An American writer of the day.

Smith, Goldwin, LL.D., 1823–. *A Layman.* An eminent English historian and journalist; b. at Reading; educ. at Eton and Oxford; of Toronto, Canada, from 1871.

Smith, Miss **Hannah,** 1841–. *Hesba Stretton.* An English novelist, of Wellington, Shropshire.

Smith, Helen C. *An American Woman.* An American writer of the day.

Smith, Helen E. *Ethel Gale.* An American writer of the day.

Smith, Rev. **Hely Hutchinson Augustus.** *H. H. A. S.* An English clergyman; B.A., Oxford, 1852; Rector of Tansley, Matlock, 1867–83 *et seq.*

Smith, Rev. **Henry.** *An Old Itinerant.* An American Meth.(?) minister.

Smith, Horace, 1779–1849. *The Late Paul Chatfield, M.D.; Jefferson Saunders, Esq.; One of the Authors of "Rejected Addresses."* An English poet and novelist; brother of James; b. in London; d. at Tunbridge Wells.

Smith, Mrs. **Horace Wemys.** *H. W. S.* An American writer; wife of the son of Richard Penn Smith, of Philadelphia.

Smith, Dr. **James.** *Sir J. M. and J. S.*—See "Mennis, Sir John."

Smith, James. *J. S.* A British colonial editorial writer on the "Argus"; a resident of Melbourne, Australia.

Smith, James and **Horace.** *An Amateur of Fashion.*

Smith, James, 1775–1839. *Momus Medlar.* An English poet and novelist; b. in London; brother of Horace; d. in London.

Smith, James Alexander. *J. A. S.* An English(?) theological writer.

Smith, James Moore, –1734. *Philomauri.* An English dramatist; b. and d. in London; finds a place in Pope's immortal satire, "The Dunciad."

Smith, John. *A.* An English scholar, of Eton Coll., and of King's Coll., Cambridge; was one of the editors of the "Microcosm, at Eton, in 1787."

Smith, John. *Ædituus.* An English poet, early in the 19th century.

Smith, Mrs. John. *A Housekeeper.* An American (?) author.

Smith, Mrs. John A. *Aunt Esther.* An American writer of the day.

Smith, John Gordon, M.D., F.R.S., about 1788–1833. *An Officer.* A Scottish surgeon; b. at Aberdeen; served in the Peninsula War; afterwards librarian to the Duke of Sutherland; professor in the Univ. of London, 1828; d. in Fleet prison, London, where he was confined for debt.

Smith, John Russell, 1810–. *J. R. S.* An English bookseller, of London; b. at Sevenoaks, Kent; co-editor of the "Library of Old Authors."

Smith, John Stores. *John Ackerlos.* An English translator and writer.

Smith, Joseph, D.D., 1670–1756. *An Orthodox Divine.* An English clergyman; b. at Lowther in Westmoreland; Provost of Queen's Coll., Oxford.

Smith, Joseph Edward Adams. *Godfrey Greylock.* An American writer, of the day, of Pittsfield, Mass.

Smith, Joshua. *A.* An English poet and hymn writer.

Smith, Mrs. Julie P., –1883. *Christabel Goldsmith.* An American novelist; resided at Esperanza, a large and beautiful estate at Hartford, Conn.; she was thrown from her carriage at her own door, and killed almost instantly.

Smith, Lister. *L. S.* An English Friend, of Halstead, in Essex.

Smith, Mrs. Marion C. *Marion Couthouy.* An American writer.

Smith, Mary Ann. *Rusco.* An American poet of the day.

Smith, Mrs. Mary Prudence (Wells), 1840–. *P. Thorne.* An American writer; b. in Attica, N.Y. In 1875 she married Lafayette Smith, Esq., of the Cincinnati Bar, in which city she now (1878) resides.

Smith, Matthew Hale, 1810–79. *Burleigh.* An American preacher, author, and journalist; b. in Connecticut; lived chiefly in New York City, and d. there.

Smith, R. C. *Raphael.* An English writer.

Smith, Robert. *C.* An English scholar, of Eton Coll.; one of the editors of the "Microcosm," 1787.

Smith, Robert Pearsall. *R. P. S.* An American theologian.

Smith, Robert Percy, 1770–1845. *R. S.* An English barrister; Advocate-General of Bengal; M.P. for Grantham, and afterwards for Lincoln; and younger brother of the Rev. Sydney Smith.

Smith, Robert Vernon, 1804–73.

R. V. S. An English statesman; son of the preceding; educ. at Christ Church, Oxford; M.P. for Northampton from 1831; held important public offices from 1830; assumed the name of Vernon instead of Vernon-Smith; became 1st Baron Lyveden, 1859.

Smith, Seba, 1792–1868. *Major Jack Downing; John Smith, Esq.* An eminent American journalist; b. at Buckfield, Me.; Bowdoin Coll., 1818; resided at Portland, 1820–42, and in New York City, 1848–68; d. at Patchogue, L.I.

Smith, Rev. Sydney, A.M., 1771–1845. *Mr. Dyson; Peter Plymley.* A celebrated English clergyman, wit, and philosopher; b. at Woodford, near London; educ. at Westminster School and New Coll., Oxford; Canon of St. Paul's, 1831–45; d. in London.

Smith, Thomas Assheton, 1777–1858. *A Huntsman.* An English sportsman; master of the Tedworth Hunt; d. at his seat at Vaenol, near Bangor, North Wales.

Smith, Col. W. *Coriolanus.* An American political writer, early in the 19th century.

Smith, W. Anderson. *Gowrie.* An English (?) writer of the day.

Smith, W. B. *Kelsic Etheridge.* An American writer of the day.

Smith, Rev. Walter Chalmers. *Hermann Kunst, Philol. Professor; Orwell.* A Scottish minister, of the Free High Church, Edinburgh.

Smith, William, D.D., 1727 or 28–1803. *A Gentleman in London; A Gentleman who has resided in Penn.; A Lover of his Country; An Officer employed on the Expedition.* A Scottish-American scholar; b. at Aberdeen; Provost of the College of Philadelphia, 1754–79 and 1789–91; d. at Philadelphia.

Smith, William, LL.D., 1762–1840. *A Citizen of South Carolina.* An American statesman; b. in North Carolina; admitted to the bar at Charleston, S.C.; M.C., 1797–99; U.S. Senator, 1817–23; spent his last years at Huntsville, Ala., and d. there.

Smith, William, LL.D., F.G.S., 1769–1839. *The Father of English Geology.* An English geologist; b. at Churchill, Oxon.; d. at Northampton.

Smith, William. *Akestes.* An English surgeon.

Smith, Sir William Cusack, LL.D., F.R.S., etc., 1766–1836. *A Yeoman; Warner Christian Search, LL.D., F.R.S., and M.R.I.A.* An eminent Irish jurist; 2d Baron of the Exchequer in Ireland,

1802–36; d. at his seat at Newtown, near Tullamore, King's Co.

Smith, William Loughton, LL.D., about 1745–1812. *Phocion.* An eminent American statesman, of South Carolina; M.C., 1789–97; Minister to Portugal, 1797–1800; to Spain, 1800–1; d. in South Carolina.

Smollett, Tobias George, 1721–71. *Drawcansir Alexander, etc.; Jonathan Dustwich.* An eminent British novelist; engaged in literary pursuits chiefly in or near London, 1746–71; d. near Leghorn, Italy.

Smyth, Charles John, M.A. *Quid-pro-quo.* An English writer; New Coll., Oxford, 1781.

Smyth, Frank. *Max Werter.* An American journalist, of the day, of Richmond, Va.

Smythe, Emily Anne Beaufort. *Viscountess Strangford.* An English lady; youngest daughter of Admiral Sir Francis Beaufort; in 1862 married the 8th Viscount Strangford, who d. in 1869.

Smythe, James M. *A Southerner.* An American author, of the South.

Smythies, T. B. *The Editor of the "British Workman."* An English journalist of the day.

Snart, Charles. *A Gentleman resident in the Neighborhood.* An English attorney, of Newark, and writer on angling.

Snead, Mrs. Fayette. *Fay.* An American journalist, of the day, of the South.

Sneed, Miss M. A. *Miss Grundy.* An American journalist of the day.

Snelling, William Joseph, 1804–48. *A Free Man; Solomon Bell; A Resident beyond the Frontier.* An American journalist; b. in Boston; educ. at West Point; for several years editor of the Boston "Herald"; d. at Chelsea, Mass.

Snow, Rev. Theodore William, A.M., –1802. *Geoffry La Touche.* An American clergyman; Harv. Univ., 1830.

Snow, William. *Mailliw Wons.* An English song writer.

Soler, Frederic. *Serafi Pitarra.* A Catalan author.

Solly, Samuel, F.R.S., F.S.A., Esq., 1781–1847. *Ylloss.* An English writer; at one time of Merton Woodland, Lincolnshire, but later of Heathside, Parkstone, near Poole; d. at his residence, Upper Gower-street, London.

Somerby, Frederick Thomas, 1814–. *Cymon.* An American sporting writer; b. at Newburyport, Mass.

Somerset, Frances Thynne, Countess of Hertford, 1699–1754. *Eusebia.* An English poet.

Somerset, Wellington. *May Fly.* An English diplomatist and writer of the day.

Somerville, Alexander, 1811–. *One who has whistled at the Plough; The Whistler; A Working Man.* A Scottish politician; b. near Douglass, Berwicks.; was for a time a paid writer in the Reform cause and that of the Anti-Corn-Law League.

Sommer, H. B. *Arry O'Pagus.* An American humorist of the day.

Sorel, W. J. *Captain Sock Buskin, Christian Le Ros.* An English writer.

Soromenho, Augusto Pereira, –1878. *Abdallah.* A Portuguese historian; librarian of the Royal Academy of Lisbon from 1869, where he died.

Soteldo, A. M. *Sol.* An American journalist, of Albany, N.Y.

Sotheran, Charles, 1847–. *Colmolyn; Southernwood.* An American writer of the day.

Sotheran, Henry, 1819–. *Savile.* An English writer, of York (?).

Souligné, Mons. de. *A Person of Quality, a Native of France.* An English writer, early in the 18th century.

Soust de Borkenfeldt, Adolphe van, 1824–77. *Paul Jane.* A Belgian poet and historian; b. at Brussels, and d. in the same city; Chief of the Bureau of Fine Arts in the Belgian Ministry of the Interior.

Souter, Joseph. *The Odd Fellow.* A Scottish dramatist.

South, Thomas. Θνος Μαθος. An English writer.

Southey, Mrs. Caroline Anne (Bowles), 1787–1854. *A.; C.* An English poet; b. at Buckland, Hants; married Robert Southey in 1839. Excepting the four years she lived with Mr. Southey before his death in 1843, she always lived in her native place.

Southey, Robert, Esq., 1774–1843. *S—y; R—— S——, Esq.; Bion; The Doctor; Don Manuel Alvarez Espriella; Inchiquin; Abel Shufflebottom.* A celebrated English poet and prose writer; b. at Bristol; educ. at Westminster School and Baliol Coll., Oxford; d. at Keswick.

Southwick, Solomon, 1773–1839. *Sherlock.* An American journalist; b. in Rhode Island; lived and d. in Albany, N.Y.

Southworth, Mrs. Emma Dorothy Eliza (Neville), 1818–. *E. D. E. N.* An American novelist; b. in Washington, D.C.; in 1841 was married to Mr. Southworth; since 1843 has been a teacher; and since 1849 a prolific and popular novelist.

Southworth, Sylvester S. *John Smith, Jr., of Arkansas.* An American writer.

Sowden, Thomas. *A Lancashire Lad.* An English writer.

Spach, Louis Adolphe, –1880. *Louis Levater.* A French historian; archivist of the Dept. of the Bas-Rhin.

Spain. *Lord Strutt.*

Spalding, William, 1809–59. *W. S.* A Scottish man of letters; professor in the Univ. of St. Andrews, 1845–59, where he died.

Sparkes, Joseph. *A Member.* An English Friend, of Exeter.

Sparks, Mrs. Mary (Crowninshield). *M. C. S.* An American lady; widow of Jared Sparks; long resident in Cambridge, Mass.

Spear, W. *U. S. E.* An English writer.

Speed, John, M.D. *An Impartial Bystander; Statutophilus.* An English physician.

Spence, Elizabeth Isabella, 1768–1832. *A Lady.* An English author; b. at Durham; resided in London, and d. in Chelsea.

Spence, George, Esq., Q.C., 1788–1851. *A Barrister of the Inner Temple.* An English lawyer; a Bencher of the Inner Temple; called to the Bar in 1811; d. in Hyde Park Square.

Spence, James Mudie, F.R.G.S. *Don T. B. Leevit, of Chickomango, Ohio, U.S.* An English humorist.

Spence, Joseph, 1698–1768. *J—— S——, Esq., Poetry Professor for the Univ. of Oxford; Sir Harry Beaumont; Phesoi Ecneps.* An English clergyman and polite scholar; Professor of Poetry, Oxford, 1728, and of Modern History, 1742; Rector of Great Horwood, in Buckinghamshire, 1742, but resident at Byfleet, in Surrey, where he died.

Spence, Thomas, 1752–1814. *Mr. Wishit.* An English schoolmaster; on the Quay Side, Newcastle, and b. in that city; he went to London, and d. there.

Spencer, Mrs. ——. *Enylla Allyne.*

Spencer, Miss Eliza. *Elise Beverly.* An American "Southland" writer, of Shipton, Md.; in 1869, of Newcastle, Del.

Spencer, Hon. and Rev. George, M.A., 1799–1864. *Father Ignatius, Passionist.* An English R. C. priest; educ. at Eton, and at Trin. Coll., Cambridge;

from 1862, superior of a House of the Passionists, at Highgate, near London; d. at Carstairs.

Spencer, Lord H. *Ironculus.* An English scholar; contributor of a letter and poem to the "Microcosm," of Eton Coll., 1787.

Spencer, Ichabod Smith, D.D., 1798–1854. *A Pastor.* An American Cong. minister; b. at Rupert, Vt.; Union Coll., 1822; pastor at Brooklyn, N.Y., 1832–54, where he died.

Spens, J. *A Retired Officer.*

Spenser, Mrs. Avis S. *Emma Carra.* An American writer of the day.

Spicer, Rev. John, 1713–85. *C—o.* An English clergyman; b. in Reading; St. John's Coll., Oxford, 1735; Rector of Tidmarsh and Pulham, Berks.; from 1750, master of the Reading school till some years before his death in that town.

Spilsbury, Francis. *F. Yrubslips.* An English writer of the 18th century.

Spinckes, Rev. Nathaniel, 1653 or 4–1727. *A Non-juror.* An English clergyman; b. at Castor, Northants.; Prebendary of Salisbury, 1687; deprived for refusing the oaths, 1690; consecrated a bishop among the Nonjurors, 1713.

Spink, William, S.S.C. *A Member of the College of Justice.* An English lawyer, of London.

Spinks, Mrs. ——. *Mrs. S.*

Spitteler, Karl. *K. Felix Tandem.* A German author; professor at Neuveville, in the canton of Berne, Switzerland.

Spooner, Alden Jeremiah, 1810–. *Tim Testy.* An American journalist; b. at Sag Harbor, L.I.; editor of the "Long Island Star," Brooklyn, N.Y.

Spooner, Very Rev. Edward, M.A. *A Clergyman.* An English clergyman; Exeter Coll., Oxford, 1843; Rector of Hadleigh, Ipswich, 1875–83 *et seq.*; Co-Dean of Brocking, 1875; Rural Dean of Sudbury, 1877.

Spotswood, John Boswel, D.D., 1808–. *The Pastor.* An American Presbyt. clergyman; b. in Exeter Mills, Va.; graduated at Amherst Coll., 1828; pastor at Newcastle, Del., 1842–83 *et seq.*

Sprague, Charles, A.M., 1791–1875. *The Banker Poet.* An American poet; b. and d. in Boston; educ. at the Franklin School; cashier of the Globe Bank, Boston, 1825–65.

Spring, Mrs. Elizabeth (Thompson). *Her Daughter.* An American biographer.

Spring, Samuel, D.D., 1746–1819. *Philalethes; Theophilus.* An eminent American Cong. minister; b. at Northbridge, Mass.; New Jersey Coll., 1771; at Newburyport, 1777–1819, where he died.

Springer, Robert, 1816–. *Adam Stein.* A German author; b. at Berlin; after passing some years in Paris, in 1853 he settled in Berlin, where he devoted himself to literary work.

Spurgeon, Rev. Charles Haddon, 1834–. *The Boy-Preacher; John Ploughman.* An eloquent English Baptist minister; b. at Kelveden, Essex; officiates in London.

Spurgin, John, M.D. *Medicus Cantabrigiensis.* An English physician; senior physician to the Foundling Hospital, London.

Squier, Ephraim George, 1821–. *Samuel A. Bard.* An American traveller and antiquary; b. at Bethlehem, N.Y.; U.S. Commissioner to Peru, 1863–65; afterwards resident in New York City.

Squire, Rev. Samuel, D.D., 1714–63. *Theophanes Cantabrigiensis; Duncan MacCarte, a Highlander.* An English clergyman; b. at Warminster, Wilts.; Bishop of St. David's, 1761–66.

Staats, Cuyler. *A Citizen of Albany.* An American biographer.

Staats, William. *Staats.* An American journalist; of the Chicago "Telegraph"; a writer of the day.

Stabler, Jennie Latham. *Jennie Woodville.* An American writer of the day.

Stacey, Mary, Jr. *A Member of the Society of Friends.* An English Friend, of Tottenham; seceded at the time of the "Beacon Controversy."

Stackhouse, Rev. Thomas, 1680–1752. *Philalethes; A Clergyman of the Church of England.* An English clergyman; was for some time minister of the English church at Amsterdam; afterwards curate successively at Richmond, Ealing, and Finchley, and in 1733 became Vicar of Beenham, Berks., where he died.

Stafford, Mrs. ——. *A Member of "The Victoria Discussion Society."* An English writer of the day.

Stahr, Mme Fanny (Lewald), 1811–. *Fanny Lewald.* A German writer; b. at Königsberg; in 1845 married Adolph Stahr.

Standish, George. *A Baltimore Trader.* An American writer of the day.

Stanford, Rev. Charles Stuart. *Anthony Poplar.* An Irish scholar and clergyman; Trin. Coll., Dublin; Preb. of St. Michael's and rector of St. Thomas's Church, Dublin.

Stanhope, Charles Stanhope, 3d Earl, 1753–1816. *St****pe.* An English nobleman; b. in London; educ. at Eton and Geneva; invented the "Stanhope press" and two calculating machines; d. at Chevening, Kent.

Stanhope, Leicester Fitzgerald Charles, C.B., 1784–1862. *The Earl of Harrington.* An English nobleman; b. in Dublin Barracks; entered the army, 1799; colonel, 1837; co-operated with Lord Byron in assisting the Greeks; d. at Harrington-house, Kensington Palace-gardens.

Stanley, Arthur Penrhyn, D.D., LL.D., 1815–81. *L. T. Anglicanus.* An eminent English scholar and clergyman; b. at Alderley, Cheshire; educ. at Rugby School, and at Univ. Coll., Oxford; Dean of Westminster, 1864–81, where he died.

Stanley, Charles. *C. S.* An English writer.

Stanley, Rt. Hon. Edward Henry Smith, Lord, 1826–. *E. H. S.* An English statesman; b. at Knowsley Park; educ. at Rugby, and Trin. Coll., Cambridge; Foreign Secretary, 1866–68.

Stanley, Mary. *Sketcher from Nature.* An English writer of the day.

Stannard, Eaton, Esq. *E–t–n St–n–n–d.* An Irish lawyer; Recorder of city of Dublin.

Stannus, Rev. Beauchamp Walter, M.A. *A Clergyman.* An Irish clergyman; Trin. Coll., Dublin, 1843; Rector of Arrow-Alcester, Warwickshire, 1863–80 et seq.

Stansbury, Miss Caroline M. — See "Kirkland, Mrs. C. M. (Stansbury)."

Stansfield, A. *A. S., K.* An English poet, of Kersal.

Stanton, John, 1826–71. *Corry O'Lanus.* An American journalist, of Brooklyn, N.Y.

Staples, Mrs. Mary Ellen (Edwards), 1839–. *M. E. E.* An English artist; b. at Kingston-on-Thames; has supplied many illustrations for "London Society," "Cornhill," "Belgravia," the "Illustrated London News," the "Graphic," etc.

Stapleton, Augustus Granville, 1800–. *Sulpicius; Lex Publica.* An English civilian and miscellaneous writer; educ. at Rugby, and St. John's Coll., Cambridge; private secretary to Mr. Canning, 1822.

Starbuck, Lucy Coffin. *L. C. S.* An American poet, of Nantucket, Mass.

Starey, Alfred B. *Sherwood Ryse.* An American writer of the day.

Stark, James. *A Member of the Fac-*

ulty of Advocates. A Scottish lawyer, of Edinburgh.

Starkey, Digby Pilot, LL.D., 1806–. *Advena.* An Irish lawyer and poet; b., educ., and resided in Dublin; called to the Irish Bar in 1831.

Starnes, Daniel. *Frank Mayfield.*

Starr, Frank. *A Traveller.* An English traveller, of Norwich.

Starr, Rev. **Frederick,** Jr., A.M., 1826–67. *Lynceus.* An American Presbyt. minister; b. in Rochester, N.Y.; Yale Coll., 1846; Auburn Theol. Sem., 1849; pastor in St. Louis, Mo., 1865–67, and d. there.

Starr, Mrs. **Laura Brady.** *Fanchon; Annie Laurie.* An American writer of the day.

Starr, N. W. *A Teacher of 30 Years' Experience.* An American author of the day.

Start, Miss **Sarah.** *One of the Bible Readers; S. S., your Bible Reader.* An American lady, formerly of Newton Corner, Mass.

Statham, F. Reginald. *Francis Reynolds.* An English poet of the day.

Staunton, C. *C. S.* An English biographer and critic.

Stearns, Edward Josiah, D.D., 1810–. *Austro-Borealis.* An American clergyman; son of Rev. Samuel Stearns, of Bedford, Mass.; Harv. Univ., 1833; professor in St. John's Coll., Annapolis, Md., 1849–53; Rector of St. Mary's, Whitechapel Parish, Denton, Md., 1871–78; in 1882 residing at Faulkland, Del.

Stearns, George Osborne. *Junius Americanus.* An American politician of the day.

Stebbing, Henry, D.D., 1716–87. *A Clergyman.* An English divine; b. at Rickinghall, Suffolk; preacher at Gray's Inn, 1750–87.

Stebbins, George Stanford, M.D. *Ikabod Izak.* An American humorist, of Springfield, Mass.; Bowdoin Med. School, 1864.

Stebbins, Mrs. **Mary Elizabeth (Moore Hewitt).** *Ione.* An American poet; b. at Malden, Mass.; in 1829 removed to New York City.

Stebbins, Mrs. **Sarah (Bridges).** *Sallie Bridges.* An American writer, of Philadelphia, of the day.

Steel, John W. *An Old Boy.* An American writer of the day.

Steele, Miss **Anne,** 1716–78. *Theodosia.* An English hymn writer; daughter of Rev. William Steele, a Bapt. minister of Broughton, Hampshire.

Steele, Sir **Richard,** 1671–1729.

Isaac Bickerstaff, Esq., Astrologer; English Tory; Sir John Edgar; The Venerable Nestor Ironside; An Impartial Hand; John Brightland; Marmaduke Myrtle, Gent.; Sir R—d S—le. An eminent British essayist; b. in Dublin; resided in London; and d. in Wales.

Steevens, George, 1736–1800. *Amner.* An English literary critic; a Shakespearian scholar and editor, of London; b. at Stepney; educ. at Eton, and King's Coll., Cambridge; spent the latter part of his life in obscurity at Hampstead, where he died.

Steimer, Francis Alfred. *Prometheus.* An American journalist of the day.

Steiner, Lewis Henry, M.D., 1827–. *L. H. S.* An American physician; b. at Frederick City, Md.; Professor of Chemistry in Columbian Univ., Washington; in 1877 resident of Frederick City, Md.

Steinhauer, Miss **H. A.** *Marie Cezinski.*

Stenhouse, Mrs. **Fanny.** *An Englishwoman in Utah.* An English writer; wife of T. B. H. Stenhouse.

Stephen, Miss **Caroline Emilia.** *Sarah Brook.* An English writer; daughter of Sir James Fitzjames Stephen.

Stephen, Sir **George,** 1794–1879. *G. S.; Caveat Emptor, Gent.; A Gentleman.* An English lawyer; called to the Bar at Gray's Inn, 1849; from 1855, of Australia; d. at Melbourne, Victoria.

Stephen, Sir **James Fitzjames,** M.A., 1829–. *A Barrister.* An eminent English lawyer; Trin. Coll., Cambridge, 1852; called to the Bar, 1854; member of the council of the governor-general of India, 1869–72.

Stephen, James, 1759–1832. *Truth.* An English lawyer; b. at Poole, Dorset.; educ. at Winchester; Under-Secretary for the Colonies, and for 20 years Master in Chancery, 1811–31; d. at Bath.

Stephen, Leslie, about 1835–. *L. S.* An English *littérateur;* educ. at Trin. Coll., Cambridge; Fellow and Tutor there; took holy orders; editor of the "Cornhill Magazine."

Stephens, Mrs. **Harriet Marion (Ward),** 1823–58. *Marion Ward; Miss Rosalie Somers.* An American actress till 1851, and a writer afterwards; d. at E. Hampton, Me.

Stephens, J. *J. S.* A Cornwall mine captain, at Wadebridge.

Stephens, John Lloyd, 1805–52. *George Stephens.* An American traveller; b. at Shrewsbury, N.J.; New Jersey Coll., 1822; studied law, and practised eight years in New York City; travelled all over Europe, in Egypt and Palestine, Central America, and all parts of this country; d. in New York City.

Stephens, William W. *A Civilian.* An English lawyer of the day.

Stephenson, B. C. *Bolton Rowe.*

Stephenson, Benjamin, 1768–. *Ebn Osn.* An English poet, of Pentonville.

Stephenson, J. W. *Juvenis.* An English novelist.

Sterling, Sir Anthony Coningham, K.C.B. *A Staff Officer who was there.* An English officer; captain 73d Regiment Royal Artillery; military secretary to Lord Clyde, in the suppression of the Indian mutiny, 1858–59.

Sterling, Edward, 1773–1847. *Captain Whirlwind; Vetus.* An Irish journalist; b. at Waterford; in early life, a captain in the army; about 1812 began to write for the London "Times," of which he became editor; d. at Knightsbridge, a suburb of London.

Sterling, John, 1806–44. *Archæus.* An English author; son of Edward; b. at Kaimes Castle, Island of Bute, Scotland; spent his literary life chiefly in London; d. at Ventnor, Isle of Wight.

Stern, Rev. Henry A., and Others. *The Captive Missionaries.* An English missionary to the East.

Sterne, Rev. Laurence, 1713–68. *A. B., Philologer; Tristram Shandy, Gent.; Yorick.* An English clergyman and miscellaneous writer; resided chiefly in France, 1762–67.

Sterne, Richard, D.D., 1596–1683. *J. Fell.* An eminent English divine; great-grandfather of the preceding; Archbishop of York, 1664–83.

Stevens, Abel, D.D., LL.D., 1815–. *Pastor; An Itinerant.* An eminent Meth. divine; b. in Philadelphia; is the author of many valuable works, and an extensive contributor to periodical literature.

Stevens, Charles Asbury. *Kit; Wade; Wash.* An American writer for the young.

Stevens, George Alexander, –1784. *Sir Henry Humm; A Lady; Peter; Wade Whipple; Zaphaniel.* An English strolling player, dramatic author, vocalist, and lecturer; b. in London; he visited America with his lecture on heads, and was well received in all the capital towns; at Boston his reception was far beyond what he expected, for there he had crowded audiences for the space of six weeks. This lecture, in the course of a few years, produced him nearly £10,000; d. at Biggleswade, Beds.

Stevens, H. S. *H. S. S.* An American journalist of the day.

Stevens, Henry, A.M., 1819–. *B. B. M. A. C., Son of Vermont.* An eminent American-English bibliographer; b. at Barnet, Vt.; Middlebury Coll., 1838–39; Yale Coll., 1843; Cambridge Law School, 1844; since 1845 has resided in London.

Stevens, John Austin, Jr., 1827–. *Knickerbocker.* An accomplished American antiquary and historian; b. in New York City; Harv. Univ., 1846; a merchant in his native city; prominent in the civil war.

Stevens, William, Esq., 1732–1807. *Ain; A Layman; Nobody.* An English merchant and author; b. in Southwark, London, and d. in London.

Stevenson, ——. *A Lay Member of the Church of Scotland.* A Scottish writer of the day.

Stevenson, Miss ——. *A Rustic Maiden.* A Scottish writer of the day.

Stevenson, Andrew. *A – – – – w S – – – – – – – n; A Lover of the Publick Welfare.* A Scottish writer to the Signet, of Edinburgh.

Stevenson, John. *A Lay Dissenter; A Seaman.* An English writer of the 18th century.

Stevenson, John Hall, 1718–85. *Cosmo, mythogelastic professor; Eugenius; Rt. Hon. R. B. Sheridan.* An English humorous and satirical poet; a friend of Sterne, and the "Eugenius" of Tristram Shandy. — See "Hall-Stevenson, J."

Stevenson, T. M. *A Layman.* An English writer of the day.

Stevenson, W. F. *A Fellow of the Royal Society.* An English chemist.

Stevenson, William G., M.D., 1843–. *An Impressed New Yorker.* An American journalist; b. at Troy, N.Y.; army correspondent, at the South, of the Memphis "Avalanche," 1861.

Stewart, Alexander P., M.D. *A Presbyterian Scot.*

Stewart, Andrew. *A Working Man.* A Scottish writer.

Stewart, Charles Edward, M.A. *The Author; A Suffolk Freeholder.* An English clergyman and poet; Magdalen Coll., Oxford; Rector of Reed, Suffolk.

Stewart, Douglas, 1830–80. *Edward Askew Sothern.* An American writer, of New York City.

Stewart, James. *A Lover of Peace and Good Government.*

Stewart, Sir James Denham, 1713–80. *Robert Frame.* A Scottish lawyer; b. at Edinburgh; d. at his family seat, Caithness, Co. of Lanark.

Stewart, Miss **Jessie**. *J. S.* A Scottish poet, of Edinburgh.

Stewart, Sir **James**. *A Lawyer*. An English (?) barrister.

Stewart, **John Allan**, 1838–. *Taswert*. An American journalist of the day.

Stewart, **Maria Stewart**. *A Chip of the Young Block*. A Scottish writer of the day.

Stewart, Mrs. **W**. *E. S.* An English writer.

Stewart, Rev. **William**. *W. S., M.P.* A Scottish writer, of Perth.

Stewarton, ——. —— *S.* An English writer.

Sthalberg, **George**. *A Gentleman who was a Swede*.

Stibbes, Mrs. **Agnes Jean**. *Emma Carra ; Ruth Fairfax*. An American "Southland" writer ; in 1872, of Savannah, Ga.

Stickney, **Caroline**. *Charles Landor*. An American writer of the day.

Stiles, **Sumner Burritt**, LL.B., 1851–. *Eleven Sophomores*. An American lawyer; b. at Middleton, Mass.; Harv. Univ., 1876 ; practised his profession (1882) in New York City.

Stillingfleet, **Benjamin**, 1702–71. *A Farmer in Cheshire*. An English writer; Trin. Coll., Cambridge; spent many years in a small cottage, occupied with natural history, on the grounds of Mr. Price, of Hertfordshire; d. in London.

Stillman, **W. O.**, M.D. *W. O. S.* An American writer of the day.

Stimson, **Frederic Jesup**, 1855–. *J. S., of Dale ; Two Gentlemen of Harvard; Eleven Sophomores*. An American lawyer, of Boston; Harv. Univ., 1876.

Stinde, **Julius**, 1841–. *Alfred de Valmy*. A Danish author; b. at Kirch-Rüchel, in Holstein; was in Hamburg for several years, as a practical chemist, but finally became an editor there, and devoted himself entirely to authorship.

Stith, Miss **Zoda**. *Elloie*. An American poet of the day, of the South.

Stock, **John**, LL.D. *An Old Smoker*. An English Cong. theological writer of the day.

Stock, **John Edmonds**, M.D., 1774–1835. *A Layman*. An English writer; physician at Bristol ; d. at Tewkesbury.

Stock, **Joseph**. *An Eye-Witness*. An Irish clergyman; Bishop of Killala, and brother-in-law to Archbishop Newcome.

Stockdale, Rev. **Percival**, 1736–1811. *Agricola*. A Scottish miscellaneous writer ; b. in the village of Branxton; Curate of Hincworth, Herts., and Vicar of Lesbury and of Long-Houghton, in Northumberland, where he died.

Stockton, Mrs. **Frank R.** *Deborah Dunn*. An American writer of the day.

Stockwell, **George A.** *Archer*. An American writer of the day.

Stocqueler, **Joachim Hayward**. *James H. Siddons*. An English officer ; served in Europe and in India.

Stoddard, **Richard Henry**, 1825–. *R. H. S.; S. Lang; Henry Richards*. A favorite American poet ; b. in Hingham, Mass.; has resided in New York City since 1835, and since 1870 has devoted himself to literature ; editor of the "Aldine" (N.Y.), 1870 *et seq.*

Stoddart, Sir **John**, LL.D., 1773–1856. *J. S.; Dr. Slop*. An English political, historical, and philosophical writer; b. at Westminster ; Christ Church, Oxford, 1794; Chief Justice at Malta, 1826–39 ; d. in London.

Stoddart, **Thomas Tod**. *An Angler*. A Scottish sporting writer, poet, etc.

Stokes, **C. W.** *A London Merchant*. An English writer of the day.

Stokes, **George**, Esq., 1789–1847. *Lay Member of the British and Foreign Bible Society*. An English writer; at one time, of Colchester; d. at Tyndale House, Cheltenham.

Stokes, **Henry Sewell**, 1808–. *H. S. S.* An English poet; b. in Gibraltar; became an advocate at Truro, Cornwall; was mayor of that city in 1856; in 1876 *et seq.* resided at Parkhill, Bodmin.

Stokes, Ven. **John Whitley**, M.A. *A Pastor*. An Irish clergyman; Trin. Coll., Dublin, 1821 ; Archdeacon of Armagh, 1842–83 *et seq.*

Stokes, Miss **Margaret Mac Nair**. *M. S.* An Irish literary antiquary of the day.

Stokes, **Whitley**, LL.D., 1830–. *W. S.* An Irish lawyer, historian, and philologist; b. and educ. at Dublin ; legal adviser to the vice-royal government of India, at Calcutta.

Stona, Rev. **Thomas**, M.M., –1792. *A Dumpling-Eater*. An English clergyman ; Rector of Warboys, Co. Huntingdon; and J. P. for that county.

Stone, **C. J.** *Edwarda Gibbon*. An English writer.

Stone, **Cecil Percival**. *Enos*. An English officer; in 1860 ensign of the 77th (the East Middlesex) Regiment of Foot.

Stone, Mrs. **Elizabeth**. *Sutherland Menzies*. An English writer of the day.

Stone, Miss **H. M.** — See "Lothrop, Mrs. H. M. (S.)."

Stone, J. L. *The Hebrew Wood Chopper.* An American writer of the West.

Stone, John. *A Society of Gentlemen.* An English writer.

Stone, John Saville. *Johann Saville Stein.* An English musician.

Stone, Miss Martha.— See "Hubbell, Mrs. Martha (Stone)."

Stone, Mrs. S. C. *Fleta Forester.* An American writer of the day.

Stone, Rev. William, M.A. *The Pastor of St. Paul's, Haggerstone.* An English clergyman; Wadham Coll., Oxford, 1833; Vicar of St. Paul's, Haggerstone, 1858–74 *et seq.*

Stonehouse, Rev. William Brocklehurst, D.C.L., –1862. *Fidelis.* An English clergyman; Brasenose Coll., Oxford, 1816; Vicar of Ewston, 1821–62; Archdeacon of Stowe, 1844–62; d. at Ewston Ferry.

Stonestreet, G. G. *Sussexiensis.* An English writer.

Stonhouse, Rev. Sir James, 10th Bart., M.D., 1716–95. *A Minister.* An English clergyman; educ. at St. John's Coll., Oxford; originally a physician at Northampton; and afterwards Rector of Great and Little Cheverel, Wilts.; and for many years Lecturer of All Saints, Bristol.

Storer, David. *Phillatins.* An American writer of the day.

Storer, Harriet G. *R. L. B.; Mrs. T. Narcisse Doutney.* An American author.

Story, Adeline E. *Helen Dixon.* An American writer of the day.

Story, Isaac, 1774–1803. *Peter Quince; The Traveller.* An American poet and journalist; b. and d. at Marblehead, Mass.

Story, Thomas, about 1662–1742. *T. S.* An English Friend, of Cumberland; afterwards of Pennsylvania; a minister about 50 years; d. at Carlisle, Penn.

Story, William Wetmore, LL.B., 1819–. *W. W. S.* An eminent American poet and sculptor; son of Joseph Story; b. in Salem, Mass.; Harv. Univ., 1838; since 1848 has resided chiefly in Italy.

Stothert, James Augustine. *A Member of the Gild.* A Scottish antiquary and poet.

Stothert, Rev. William, B.A. *Philalethes.* An English clergyman; St. John's Coll., Cambridge, 1832; Vicar of Thorpe-Hesley, Rotherham, 1865–81.

Stott, Robert. *Hafiz.* An Irish poet, of Dromore; contributor of odes to the London "Morning Post."

Stouder, O. C. *Lancer.* An American Shakespeare scholar, of Ohio.

Stow, John. *A Lay Member of the Church of England.* An English writer.

Stowe, Mrs. Harriet Elizabeth (Beecher), 1812–. *The American Novelist; Harry Henderson; Christopher Crowfield.* An eminent American writer; b. in Litchfield, Conn.; daughter of Lyman Beecher; in 1833 married Calvin E. Stowe.

Stowell, Rev. Hugh, D.D., 1799–1865. *A Clergyman; Eight Clergymen.* An English clergyman; b. at Douglas, Isle of Man; Hon. Canon in the Cathedral Church of Chester from 1845; and later Rural Dean of Salford, where he died.

Stowell, Sir William Scott, Baron, 1745–1836. *Civis.* An eminent English jurist; b. at Heworth, Durham; Corpus Christi Coll., Oxford, 1764; Judge of the High Court of Admiralty from 1798 for nearly 30 years; d. at Early Court, near Reading.

Strachan, Rt. Rev. John, D.D., LL.D., 1778–1867. *N. N.; Reckoner.* A Scottish Canadian clergyman; Bishop of Toronto, 1839–67.

Strahorn, Robert E. *Aletor, Esq.; Alter Ego.* An American journalist, of Cheyenne, Wyoming.

Straight, Douglas. *Sidney Daryl; An Old Harrovian.* An English writer.

Strandberg, Karl Wilhelm August, 1818–77. *Talis Qualis.* A Swedish poet; b. at Stigtamta, in Södermannland. He resided at Stockholm from 1840, and d. there.

Strang, John, Esq., LL.D., 1795–1863. *An Invalid.* A Scottish littérateur; b. at Downhill; the son of a Glasgow merchant; City Chamberlain of Glasgow, 1834–63, where he died.

Strange, Sir John, 1696–1754. *A Barrister at Law.* An English lawyer; b. in London; Master of the Rolls, 1750–54.

Strangford, Rt. Hon. Percy Clinton Sydney Smythe, Lord Viscount of Strangford, Co. Down, D.C.L., 1780–1855. *P. C. S. S.* An Irish noble author; educ. at Trin. Coll., Dublin; was a British diplomatist; d. at his residence in Harley-street, London.

Stratton, Charles Herwood, 1838–83. *General Tom Thumb.* An American dwarf; b. in Bridgeport, Conn.; d. at Middleboro, Mass.

Stratton, Thomas. *T. S.* An English compiler, of Ponder's End, a hamlet in the Co. of Essex.

Strickland, Lt.-Col. **Samuel**, 1809–67. *An Early Settler*. An English emigrant to Canada in 1825; brother of Agnes Strickland; d. at Lakefield, U.C.

Stringer, Mrs. ——. *A Lady*. An English (?) lady.

Stronach. George. *G. S.* A Scottish Shakespeare scholar of the day; connected (?) with the Advocate's Library, Edinburgh.

Strong, Rev. **George A.** *Marc Antony Henderson*. An American humorous poet; professor in Kenyon Coll., Gambier, Ohio.

Strong, George C., 1833–63. *An Officer of the U.S. Army*. An American soldier; b. at Stockbridge, Vt.; West Point, 1857; served with distinction in the civil war, 1861–63; was mortally wounded at Fort Wagner, near Charleston, and d. in New York City.

Strong, Miss **Helen P.** *H. P. S.* An American writer of the day.

Strong, Latham Cornell, 1845–. *Montague Shatt*. An American poet and journalist; b. in Troy, N.Y.; has devoted his life to literary work.

Strong, Rev. **Nehemiah**, A.M., 1728–1807. *N. S.* An American mathematician; b. in Northampton, Mass.; Yale Coll., 1755; professor in his *alma mater*, 1770–81.

Strong, Peter Remsen. *P. R. S.* An American poet of the day.

Strother, David Hunter, 1816–. *Porte Crayon*. An American soldier, artist, and man of letters; b. at Martinsburg, Va.; in New York City, 1845–49; now resides at Berkeley Springs, West Virginia.

Strubberg, Friedrich August, 1808–. *Armand*. A prolific German novelist; b. at Cassel; lives since 1854 at Heimat as an author.

Struensee, Gustav Otto von, 1803–75. *Gustav vom See*. A German novelist; b. at Greifenberg in Pomerania; studied law at Bonn and Berlin; was in 1834 Government Counsellor at Coblenz, and in 1847 Superior Government Counsellor at Berlin; d. in Breslau.

Stuart, George. *A Managing Clerk*. An English book-keeper.

Stuart, Ven. **George O'Kill**, D.D., LL.D. *Mentor*. A Canadian clergyman; Dean of Ontario, Upper Canada, for some years; now dead.

Stuart, Hector A. *Caliban; The South Sea Bard*. An American writer, of California.

Stuart, Hon. and Rev. **Henry Windsor Villiers**, M.A. *The Vicar of Napton*.

An English clergyman; Univ. Coll., Durham, 1849; Vicar of Napton-on-the-Hill, 1855–70 *et seq*.

Stuart, Isaac William, 1809–61. *Scæva*. An American scholar and miscellaneous writer; son of Prof. Moses Stuart; b. at New Haven; Yale Coll., 1828; resided the latter part of his life at Hartford, Conn.; and d. there.

Stuart, James Francis Edward, 1688–1765. *Æneas*. An English gentleman; son of James II. (termed the Chevalier de St. George and the Old Pretender); was styled James III. at his father's death, 1701; rebellions in his favor defeated, 1715 and 1746.

Stuart, Miss **M. B.** *Grace Mortimer*. An American (?) novelist of the day.

Stuart, Will. *Walsingham*. An American writer.

Sturgis, Robert S. *A Foreigner*. An English writer.

Styles, Rev. **John**, D.D., 1770–1860. *Jeremiah Ringletub*. An English Meth. preacher, of Brighton.

Suddorth, Mrs. **M. A. B.** *Lumina Silvervale*. An American novelist of the day.

Sue, Marie Joseph Eugène, 1808–57. *Eugène Sue; Eugène S....* A popular French novelist, of Paris; b. and d. in that city.

Sulivan, Sir **Richard Joseph**, –1806. *R. J. S.* An Irish writer; spent his early life in India; M.P., 1790–1806; made a baronet, 1804.

Sullivan, Mrs. **Arabella**, –1849. *A. B.; A Chaperon*. An English writer; daughter of Barbarina Brand, Lady Dacre, and wife of the Rev. Frederick Sullivan, Vicar of Kimpton, Herts.

Sullivan, James, 1744–1808. *J. S.; A Layman; A Citizen of Massachusetts*. An American statesman; b. at Berwick, Me.; studied law; in 1785 removed to Boston; Governor of Massachusetts, 1807–8; d. in Boston.

Sullivan, James Frank. *J. F. Sunavill*. An English humorist.

Sullivan, Hon. **Robert Baldwin**, –1853. *Legion; Cinna*. A Canadian statesman; judge in Upper Canada, 1848–53; b. and d. at Toronto.

Summers, Thomas Osmund, D.D., 1812–. *A Member of the Red River Conference*. An English-American Methodist clergyman; b. near Corfe Castle, Isle of Purbeck, Dorset.; came to this country and prepared for the ministry; Prof. of Theology in Vanderbilt Univ.; Dean of the Theological Department, and *ex officio* Pastor of the Institution in 1876 *et seq.*

Suplée, Thomas D. *Hugh Mility; Vernon Harcourt.* An American journalist, of Gambier, Ohio.

Surr, Thomas Skinner. *A Gentleman; A Hermit.* An English writer; a clerk in the Bank of England.

Surtees, Miss Fanny. *Cherith.* An English writer of the day.

Surtees, Robert Smith, Esq., 1804–64. *Mr. John Jorrocks; T. Scott, Esq.; Mr. Sponge.* An English sporting writer, of Hamsterley-hall, Co. Durham; high sheriff for that county in 1856; d. at Brighton.

Sutcliffe, Thomas. *The Retired Governor of the Island of Juan Fernandez.* An English civilian.

Sutherland, Rev. **J. M.** *Senator Bob Hart.* An American revival preacher; left the stage for the pulpit; has returned to the stage.

Sutherland, Mrs. —— **(Redding).** *Isabelle Saxon.* An English writer; daughter of Cyrus Redding; resident in California from 1861.

Sutherland, Thomas Jefferson. *A Late Patriot Prisoner.* An American lawyer; in 1837 of Buffalo; afterwards of New York City; in 1837 engaged in an expedition to Upper Canada to effect a political revolution there.

Sutton, Sir **John,** 3d Bart., 1820–73. *Sutton.* An English gentleman; b. at Sudbrooke Holme, Lincolnshire; Fellow-Commoner of Jesus Coll., Cambridge.

Sutton, Joseph. *J. S.* An English Friend, of Manchester.

Swaby, John. *Scricci.* An English writer.

Swain, Charles, 1803–74. *The Manchester Poet.* An English poet and engraver; "one of the most natural and sweetest of English bards."

Swain, Charles F. *R. O. Sault.* An American humorist.

Swan, Eliza B. *E. B. S.* An American writer of the day.

Swanwick, Miss Anna, 1813–. *A. S.* An English editor of Shakespeare.

Swanwick, Catherine. *L.* An English poet and dramatist.

Swett, Josiah, D.D., 1814–. *J. S.* An American P. E. clergyman; b. in Claremont, N.H.; Norwich Univ., 1837; ordained, 1847; professor in his *alma mater*, 1839–40 and 1844–45; in 1861 was of Bethel, Vt.

Swett, Rev. **William Gray,** A.M., –1843. *Quicksilver Smalltalk.* An American Unit. minister; Harv. Univ., 1828.

Swiedack, Karl, 1815–. *Karl Elmar.* A German dramatist; b. at Vienna; became an actor, and a writer of plays; later he retired from the stage, and became a humorous-satirical journalist.

Swift, Edmund Lenthal. *Basilicus.* An Irish writer.

Swift, Jonathan, D.D., 1667–1745. *J. S.; Dr. J. S.; Rev. Mr. J. S.; Dean S.; Dr. S.; Doctor Sw–ft; Doctor S—t; Doctor S – – – – t; Rev. Dr. S—t; D—n S—t; Rev. D—n S—t; A. B., Esqre.; C. B.; J. S. D. D. D. S. P.; J. S. D. S. P. D. D.; P. P.; S. P. A. M.; T. R. D. J. S. D. O. P. I. I.; Lord W *****n; Tom Ashe; Esquire Bickerstaff; Isaac Bickerstaff, Esq.,* Student in Astrology; James Blackwell; Cadenus; A Church of England Man; A Clergyman; The Copper-Farthing Dean; The Drapier; M. B. Draper; M. B. Drapier; Sieur Du Baudrier; An Enemy to Peace; An Eye Witness; Jack Frenchman; T. Fribble; A Friend of the Author; A Friend of Mr. St – – – le; Lemuel Gulliver; Hibernia; Thomas Hope, Esq.; Mary Howe; The Injured Lady; A Member of the House of Commons in Ireland; Gregory Miso-Sarum; A Modern Lady; A Modus; Dr. Robert Norris; M. Flor O'Squarr; A Person of Honour; A Person of Quality; T. N. Philomath; Sir Humphrey Polesworth; Presto; Publicola; The Rt. Hon. William Pulteney; Tom Pun-Sibi; Abel Roper; Martinus Scriblerus; Tristram Shandy; A Shoeboy; A Small Courtier; T. Tinker; Toby, Abel's Kinsman; Dr. Andrew Tripe; An Upper Servant; Simon Wagstaff, Esq.; William Wood.* An Irish clergyman, of English descent; Dean of Saint Patrick's, Dublin, 1713–45.

"But I'll detain you no longer from the entertainment of Master Toby, *alias* Gulliver, *alias* Sw–t, *alias* Examiner, *alias* D—n of St. P–'s, *alias* Draper, *alias* Bickerstaff, *alias* Remarker, *alias* Journalist, *alias* Sonnetteer, *alias* Scriblerus."—SWIFT, in "Gulliveriana."

Swinburne, Algernon Charles, 1837–. *An English Republican; Mrs. Horace Manners.* An English poet; b. in London; entered at Balliol Coll., Oxford, in 1857, but did not take a degree; afterwards visited Florence, and spent some time with Walter Savage Landor; has been devoted to literary labor from 1861.

Swinburne, Henry, Esq., 1743–1803. *Porcustus.* A celebrated English traveller; b. at Capheaton, Northumberland; d. at Trinidad.

Swiney, Admiral **William,** 1747–1829. *An Old Seaman.* An English writer; Admiral of the Red, 1808; d. at

Sydney Place, near Exeter, having served in the Royal Navy 70 years.

Swinton, Rev. **John**, F.R.S., 1703–77. *A Gentleman of Wadham Coll., Oxf.; Lord No Zoo.* An English clergyman and antiquary; b. at Bexton, Cheshire; chaplain to the county gaol at Oxford, and keeper of the archives of the University.

Swisshelm, Mrs. **Jane Gray**, 1816–84. *Jennie Deans.* An American journalist; b. at Wilkinsburg, Penn.; editor at Pittsburg from 1845; d. at Swissvale, a suburb of that city.

Sydenham, Rev. **Humphrey**, –1650. *Alexis, or the Worthy Unfortunate.* An English clergyman; Fellow of Wadham Coll., Oxford; Rector of Ash Brittle, of Pocklington, and of Oldcombe, all in Somersetshire, and was deprived of all during the Rebellion; called for his eloquence the "Silver-tongued Sydenham."

Sykes, **Arthur Ashley**, D.D., about 1684–1756. *A. V.; T. P. A. P. O. A. B. I. T. C. O. S.; A Clergyman; A Clergyman in the Country; A Clergyman of the Church of England; A Curate of London; A Lover of his Country; A Lover of Truth and Peace; Cornelius Paets; Philalethes; Eugenius Philalethes.* An English clergyman; b. in London; Prebendary of Winchester, 1740–56.

Sykes, **Joseph**. *J. S.; Julio.* An English poet.

Sym, **Robert**. *Timothy Tickler.* A Scottish lawyer, of Edinburgh; writer of the "Signet"; uncle to Prof. Wilson (Christ. North); the "Timothy Tickler" of the "Noctes Ambrosianæ," and a contributor under the same name to "Blackwood's Magazine."

Symes, Major **Michael**, –1809. *Major S——.* A distinguished British author, officer, and diplomatist; d. on board the "Mary" transport, on the passage from Corunna, in consequence of fatigue and exhaustion incurred in the Spanish campaign.

Symington, **Caroline**. *Caller Herrin'.* An English poet.

Symington, Miss **Charlotte**. *Maggie Symington.* An English writer of the day.

Symonds, ——. *A Gentleman of Suffolk.* An English "Sportsman of Suffolk."

Symonds, **Arthur**. *A Parliamentary Secretary.* An English civilian, of London.

Symonds, **John Addington**, the Younger. *His Son.* An English poet, etc.

Symonds, Rear-Admiral Sir **William**, Knt., 1782–1856. *Sir W. S.* An English naval officer; rear-admiral on the retired list, 1854.

Symonds, Rev. **William Samuel**, B.A., F.G.S. *W. S. S.* An English clergyman and geologist; Christ Coll., Cambridge, 1840; Rector of Pendock, Tewksbury, 1845–83 et seq.

Symons, Rev. **Benjamin Parsons**. *A Senior Member of Convocation.* An English clergyman; Wadham Coll., Oxford, 1805; in 1874 et seq. resident at Burnham House, Walton Manor, St. Giles', Oxford.

Symons, **Jelinger Cookson**, 1809–60. *His Son.* An English lawyer; Corpus Christi Coll., 1831; called to the Bar, 1843; inspector of schools, 1847; d. at Great Malvern.

Sympson, **John**. *J. S.* An English writer, early in the 18th century.

Symson, **Matthias**. *John What-You-Call-Him.* An English clergyman; Canon of Lincoln, 1718.

Synge, ——. *An Irish Traveller.* An Irish writer, of the 19th century.

Synge, Rev. **Edward**, D.D., 1659–1741. *A Private Gentleman; A Church of England Divine.* An Irish clergyman; b. at Inishonane; Christ Church, Oxford, and Trin. Coll., Dublin; Archbishop of Tuam, 1826–41.

T.

Tabor, Miss **Eliza**. *Cousin Alice; A Novelist.* An English writer of the day.

Taché, Sir **Etienne Paschal**, Knt., M.D., 1795–1865. *Un Vétéran de 1812.* A Canadian officer, physician, and author; b. and d. at St. Thomas, Quebec; colonel and aide-de-camp to the Queen, 1860.

Taché, **Jean Charles**, M.D., 1821–. *Gaspard Lemage; Isidore Méplats.* A Canadian miscellaneous writer; brother of the preceding; b. at Kamouraska, Lower Canada.

Taggard, **E. T.**, 1839–. *Paul Pryor.* An American writer of the day.

Taine, **Hippolyte Adolphe**, 1828–. *F. T. G.; Frédéric Thomas Graindorge.* An eminent French critic, of Paris; b. at

Vouziers (Ardennes); educ. at Paris; a frequent writer for the "Journal des Débats" and the "Revue des Deux Mondes."

Tait, Archibald Campbell, D.D., D.C.L, 1811-. *The Bishop of London.* A Scottish clergyman; b. in Edinburgh; educ. at Glasgow and Oxford; Bishop of London, 1856; Archbishop of Canterbury, 1868-83 *et seq.*

Talbot, Mrs. Catherine, 1720-70. *Sunday; T.* An accomplished English writer; only child of Edward Talbot; of her "Reflections on the Seven Days of the Week" (1770) 25,000 copies were sold.

Talbot, Charles Remington. *John Brownjohn; Magnus Merriweather.* An American novelist of the day; a bookkeeper of Boston.

Talbot, George Foster, 1819-. *A Layman.* An American lawyer; b. in East Machias, Me.; Bowdoin Coll., 1834; resident at Portland, 1864-85.

Talcott, Mrs. Hersey Bradford (Goodwin). *H. B. G.* An American writer of the day.

Taliaferro, H. E. *Skitt.* An American writer, of North Carolina.

Tangermann, Friedrich Wilhelm, 1815-. *Victor Granella.* A German author; b. at Essen on the Ruhr; studied theology; in 1872 assumed the pastorship of the new Old Catholic Congregation in Cologne.

Tanner, Henry. *An Eye-Witness.* An American writer, of the West, of the day.

Tappan, David, D.D., 1753-1803. *Toletus.* An eminent American theologian; b. at Manchester, Mass.; Harv. Univ., 1771; professor at Harv. Univ., 1792-1803.

Tappan, Lewis, 1788-1873. *A Gentleman in Boston.* An American merchant and philanthropist, of Boston and of New York City; b. at Northampton, Mass.; helped found the New York "Journal of Commerce" in 1827; d. at Brooklyn, N.Y.

Tappan, Mrs. Sarah (Jackson Davis). *S. J.* An American religious writer; daughter of the Hon. William Jackson, of Newton, Mass.; first married Thomas A. Davis, Mayor of Boston; afterwards, Lewis Tappan, of New York City.

Tarbox, Increase Niles, D.D., 1815-. *Uncle George.* An American Cong. minister and writer for the young; b. at East Windsor, Conn.; Yale Coll., 1839; Secretary of the American Educational Society at Boston from 1851; residing at West Newton, Mass.

Tardieu, Jules Romain, 1805-68. *J. T. de Saint-Germain.* A French poet and prose writer, of Paris; b. at Rouen; d. at Paris,

Tardy, Mrs. Mary T. *Ida Raymond.* An American biographer.

Tasker, E. *E. T.* An American bibliophile and bibliographer, of Greenwood, Wakefield, Middlesex Co., Mass.

Tatham, Rev. Arthur, M.A., 1809-74. *A Rural Dean.* An English clergyman; b. at Greenwich Hospital; Rector of Boconnock *w.* Broadoak, 1832-74; Prebendary of Exeter Cathedral, 1860-74; d. at Broadoak-rectory.

Tatler. *Isaac Bickerstaff.* Supposed editor.

Tattersall, George. *Wildrake.* An English sporting writer, of London.

Tattersall, Rev. John Cecil, B.A., 1788-1812. *Davus.* An English clergyman; youthful friend of Lord Byron, at Harrow School.

Taunton, William Elias. *Timothy Touchstone.* An English scholar; one of the editors of the "Trifler," at Westminster School in 1788; afterwards a student of Christ Church, Oxford, 1793.

Tautphœus, Jemima (Montgomery), Baroness. *Cyrilla.* An English novelist; wife of the chamberlain to the king of Bavaria; b. in Wales.

Taveau, A. L. *Alton.* An American poet, of Charleston, S.C.

Tayler, Rev. Charles Benjamin, M.A. *A Country Curate; Rev. Allan Temple.* An English clergyman; Trin. Coll., Cambridge, 1819; Rector of Otley, Ipswich, 1846-74 *et seq.*

Tayler, E. D. *S. Joshua Jenkins.* An American writer.

Tayler, Rev. John James, D.D., 1798-1869. *J. J. T.* An English Unit. minister; b. at Nottingham; Univ. of Glasgow, 1818; Principal of Manchester New College, London, 1853-69; d. at Hampstead, near London.

Taylor, Dr. ——. *A Member of the Literary and Scientific Assoc. of Elgin.* A Scottish writer.

Taylor, Dr. ——. *Cantabrigiensis.* An English writer, early in the 18th century.

Taylor, Ann, -1866. *A.* An English poetess; widow of the Rev. Joseph Gilbert.

Taylor, Benjamin Ogle. *Neptune.*

Taylor, Edgar, Esq., 1793-1839. *H. B. Denton.* An eminent English lawyer; b. at Banham Haugh, in Norfolk; having studied law, in 1814 he removed to London, and in 1816 established himself there as a solicitor, but afterwards devoted much time to literary pursuits; d. in London.

Taylor, F. *One of the Party.* An — writer.

Taylor, Frederick. *Ballinasloe; A Horse-Dealer.* An English sporting writer; once of the 8th Royal Irish Hussars.

Taylor, George Watson. *G. W. T.; George Watson.* An English poet, of Earlstoke, M.P.; added his last name on succeeding to the property of Sir Simon Taylor.

Taylor, Rev. Henry, about 1710–85. *Benjamin Ben Mordecai; Indignatio.* An English clergyman; Rector of Crawley, and Vicar of Portsmouth, Hampshire.

Taylor, Isaac, LL.D., 1787–1865. *I. T.* An English writer; b. at Lavenham, Suffolk; lived in studious retirement at Stanford Rivers, Essex, devoting himself to the education of his children and to literary work, where he died.

Taylor, Miss Jane, 1783–1824. *Q. Q.; Several Young Persons.* An English poet and writer for the young; b. in London; resided at Marazion, Cornwall, from 1814; d. at Ongar.

Taylor, John, 1580–1654. *The Water Poet; Thorny Ailo; John Alexander, a Joyner; Edward Allde (?); Mercvrivs Aqvaticvs; George Eld (?); My-heele Mendsoale; Misostratus; Sir Gregory Nonsence; Philanar; The Sculler; Henry Walker (?).* An eccentric English poet; b. in Gloucester; was a waterman, collector of wine-fees for the Lieutenant of the Tower, and keeper of a public house both at Oxford and Westminster.

Taylor, John. *A Layman.* An English writer on Puseyism.

Taylor, John, 1750–1824. *A Citizen of Virginia; Curtius.* An American agricultural and political writer; b. in Orange Co., Va.; William and Mary Coll., 1770; U.S. Senator, 1792–94, 1803, and 1822–24; d. in Caroline Co., Va.

Taylor, John, 1767–1832. *Monsieur Tonson.* An English writer; in early life oculist to George III., and subsequently for many years connected with the theatre as author of poetical sketches, prologues, etc.

Taylor, John, 1781–1864. *Verus.* An English publisher, of London, and a prominent "Junius" controversialist; b. at East Retford, Nottinghamshire; d. at Kensington.

Taylor, John A. *Paul Fairchild.* An American lawyer, of New York City; a writer of the day.

Taylor, Rev. Manton Robert. *A Clergyman.*

Taylor, Mr. "Sun." *A Macaroni.*

Taylor, Thomas, 1758–1835. *The Platonist.* An eminent English classical scholar and translator; b. in London; resided at Walworth, and d. there.

Taylor, Tom, 1817–81. *John Noakes; Claude Mellot; Roumany Rei.* An eminent English critic and dramatist; b. in Sunderland; educ. at Glasgow and Cambridge; was 10 years Prof. of English Literature in the Univ. Coll., London; studied law, and admitted to the Bar in 1845; wrote, either alone or with others, more than 100 dramas, besides doing much other literary work; d. in London.

Taylor, W. F. *W. F. T.* An English writer.

Taylor, W. H. *A Doctor of Physic.* An English writer of the day.

Taylor, Watson. *Sir Joseph Cheakill, K. F., K. S.* An English author.

Tegg, Thomas. *An Amateur of Fashion; Peter Parley.* An English publisher, of London.

Telfair, ——. *A Resident who has never possessed either Land or Slaves in the Colony.* An English resident at the Mauritius.

Telford, Thomas, 1757–1834. *Eskdale Tam.* An eminent Scottish civil engineer; b. at Westerkirk, Dumfriesshire; his most beautiful work is the suspension railway bridge over the Menai Strait; d. at Westminster.

Temple, Miss Laura Sophia, 1786–. *L. S. T.* An English poet; daughter of Lieutenant-Colonel Richard Temple; b. at Chester. When she was about ten years old, her parents removed to a gloomy mansion on the borders of the Lincolnshire fens, where she met with some of the works of Milton and Pope, and those ascribed to Ossian, which allured her to the pursuit of poesy.

Temple, William. *J—— B——,* M.D. An English writer on political economy, etc.

Tennant, William, LL.D., 1784–1848. *W. Crookleg.* A Scottish poet and eminent modern linguist; b. in Anstruther-Easter, County of Fife; studied at the Univ. of St. Andrew's, 1799–1801; Professor of Oriental Languages at St. Andrew's, 1834–48; d. at Ham Court, Upton-on-Severn.

Tennent, Sir James Emerson, K.C.S., LL.D., 1804–69. *Sir James Emerson.* An Irish writer; b. at Belfast; educ. at Dublin; one of the secretaries of the board of trade, 1852–67; d. in London.

Tenney, Rev. **Edward Tenney,** D.D. *Spriggs.* An American Cong. minister; Bangor Theol. Sem., 1858; President of the Colorado Coll., 1880 *et seq.*

Tennyson, Alfred, D.C.L., F.R.S., 1809–. *T.; Alcibiades; Merlin.* An eminent English poet; b. at Somersby, Lincs.; Univ. of Cambridge, 1831; poet laureate from 1850.

Tennyson, Alfred and Charles. *Two Brothers.* Rev. Charles T. assumed the name of Charles Tennyson Turner; Vicar of Grassby, Lincs.; Univ. of Cambridge, 1831.

Terhune, Mrs. **Mary Virginia (Hawes),** about 1835–. *Marion Harland.* An American novelist; b. in Amelia County, Va.; married Rev. E. P. Terhune, who in 1881 was pastor of the First Cong. Church, at Springfield, Mass.

Ternaux-Campans, Charles Henri, about 1810–64. *Charles Navarin.* A French diplomatist and bil: liographer, of Paris; collected a library peculiarly rich in Mss. and early printed books on America.

Terry, John Orville. *J. O. T.* An American poet, of Orient, Suffolk County, L.I.

Texier, Edmond, 1816–. *Sylvius.* A French author and journalist; b. at Rambouillet; studied in Paris, and in his 19th year, with Ménard, published a collection of poems, under the title of " En avant ! " After contributing largely to the popular daily journals, he was on the staff of the "Siècle," and in 1860 took charge of the " Illustration."

Teza, Emilio. *E. T.* An Italian author and editor of the day.

Thacher, Rev. **Samuel Cooper,** A.M., 1785–1813. *S. C. T.* An American clergyman; b. in Boston; Harv. Univ., 1804; pastor of the New South Church, Boston, 1811–13; d. at Moulins, France.

Thackeray, William Makepeace, 1811–63. ⊖.; *W. M. T.; Mr. Brown; Fitzroy Clarence; Henry Esmond, Esq.; The F. C.; The Fat Contributor; The Contributor at Paris; George Fitzboodle; George Savage Fitzboodle, Esq.; A Gentleman of the Force; Frederick Haltamont de Montmorency; Jacob Omnium's Hoss; Jeames; Jeames of Buckley Square; G. P. R. Jeames, Esq.; Barry Lyndon, Esq.; Theresa MacWhorter; Mulligan of Kilballymulligan; An Old Paris Man; One of themselves; Our Own Bashi-Bazouk; Arthur Pendennis; Je-mes Pl-sh, Esq.; Punch's Commissioner; Harry Rollicker;* *Ikey Solomons, Jr.; Mr. M. A. Titmarsh; Michael Angelo Titmarsh; Lancelot Wagstaff, Esq.; Theophile Wagstaff; Policeman X.; Charles Yellowplush, Esq.; Ch–s Y–ll–wpl–sh, Esq.* A celebrated English novelist and miscellaneous writer, of London; b. at Calcutta, India; educ. at the Charterhouse and the Univ. of Cambridge; was left an orphan with £10,000; having lost most of his fortune, he devoted himself to literary work; d. at Kensington Palace Gardens, London.

Tharin, Miss **C. G.** *Kate Clyde.* An American journalist of the day.

Thatcher, Benjamin Bussey, 1809–40. *A Bostonian.* An American lawyer and miscellaneous writer; b. at Warren, Me.; Bowdoin Coll., 1826; settled in Boston, and d. there.

Thaxter, Thomas. *An Inhabitant.* An American writer; a citizen of Hingham, Mass.

Thayer, Alexander Wheelock, 1817–. *The Late J. Brown; A Quiet Man; A Diarist.* An American lawyer, musical critic and biographer, and diplomatist; b. in Natick, Mass.; Harv. Univ., 1843; U.S. Consul at Trieste, Austria, 1859–82; has since devoted his time to the completion of his life of Beethoven; still (1884) residing at Trieste.

Theatre. *Sir John Edgar.* Supposed editor.

Thelwall, Rev. **Algernon Sydney,** 1795–1863. *Two Clergymen.* An English divine; son of the following; educ. at Cambridge; Lecturer on Elocution at King's Coll., London, 1850–63; d. in London.

Thelwall, John, 1764–1834. *John Beaufort, LL.D.; Sylvanus Theophrastus.* An English political agitator, lecturer, and miscellaneous writer; b. in London; was tried with Thomas Hardy and John Horne Tooke for high treason, but acquitted; d. at Bath.

Theobald, Lewis, –1744. *L. T.* An English literary attorney-at-law; b. at Sittingbourne, Kent; was an editor of Shakespeare and a hero of the " Dunciad."

Thicknesse, Philip, Esq., 1719–92. *P. T., Esq.; Thomas London; One of the Jurymen; A Piece of an Antiquary; Polyexena; A Wanderer.* An English traveller and miscellaneous writer; served in the West Indies and Georgia; afterwards Lieut.-Gov. of Landguard Fort; d. at Boulogne.

Thieblin, Nicolas Léon. *Azamat Batuk; Rigolo.* An English journalist; the mysterious "Turk" of the London "Pall Mall Gazette."

Thirlby, Dr. J. Ω. An English writer, early in the 18th century.

Thirlwall, Rev. Thomas, –1827. *An Independent Freeholder.* An English clergyman and author; b. at Cottingham, near Hull; Brazenose Coll., Oxford, M.A., 1786; Rector of Bower's Gifford, Essex, 1814–27, where he died.

Thisted, Valdemar Adolf, 1815–. *Emanuel Saint-Hermidad; M. Koran.* A Danish author; b. at Aarhus; studied theology in Copenhagen; was pastor in Goirup in 1858, and in Tommerup in 1862–70.

Thom, Adam, LL.D. *An Anti-Bureaucrat.* A Scottish-Canadian journalist, of Montreal, 1832–37; Recorder of Rupert's Land, 1837–55; resident in England from 1855.

Thom, Robert. *Sloth.* An English orientalist, at Canton, China.

Thom, Rev. William. *The R–v–d D—— T——.* A Scottish minister, of Govan, Cos. Lanark and Renfrew.

Thom, William, 1799–1850. *The Weaver Poet; A Handloom Weaver.* A Scottish poet; b. in Aberdeen; at ten years of age was bound to a weaver; afterwards carried on his trade in Aberdeen and Inverary.

Thomas, ——. *Mr. Aptommas.* An American harpist.

Thomas, Rev. Abel Charles, 1807–. *Iron Gray.* An American Univ. clergyman, of Lowell (Mass.), Brooklyn (N.Y.), and Cincinnati (O.); b. in Exeter township, Penn.; and educ. at Lancaster, Penn.

Thomas, Mrs. Ann (Mallett), 1808–. *A. T.; Ann.* An English author; b. at Plymouth; married Ralph Thomas, a London barrister-at-law, the father of Ralph Thomas ("Olphar Hamst").

Thomas, Benjamin. *A Petitioner.* An English writer of the 18th century.

Thomas, Ebenezer Smith, 1775–1845. *Junius; Hampden.* An eminent American journalist; b. in Lancaster, Mass.; removed to Charleston, S.C., in 1795; and to Cincinnati, O., in 1827.

Thomas, Mrs. Elizabeth, Jr., 1675–1730. *A Lady; Corinna.* An English poet; called "Corinna" by Dryden; impaled in the "Dunciad" by Pope; she was to have married Richard Gwinnett, Esq., but his death "prevented the marriage."

Thomas, Rev. Josiah, M.A., –1820. *Christopher Climax, Esq.* An English

divine, of St. James's Coll., Cambridge; Archdeacon of Bath.

Thomas, Ralph. *R. T.; H. S.* An English writer; a sergeant-at-law; a contributor to "Cobbett's," "Monthly," "Court," "Town and Country," Magazines.

Thomas, Ralph, Jr., 1843–. *Ralph Harrington; Olphar Hamst.* An eminent English bibliographer; son of the preceding.

Thomas, Samuel E. *S. E. T.* An English writer of the day.

Thomas, William. *William Thomas Moncrieff.* An English writer.

Thomayer, Joseph, 1852–. *R. E. Jamot.* A Bohemian author; b. at Txhanov, near Tauss; an M.D. at Prague.

Thomes, William H. *A Returned Australian; A Yankee.* An American writer, of Boston.

Thompson, Mrs. ——. *A Lady.* An English writer.

Thompson, Daniel Pierce, 1795–1868. *A Member of the Vermont Bar; Timothy Peacock, Esq.* An American lawyer, popular novelist, and journalist; b. in Charlestown, Mass.; Middlebury Coll., 1820; resided in Montpelier, Vt., from 1824, and d. there.

Thompson, D'Arcy Wentworth, about 1830–. *A Schoolmaster.* A Scottish (?) classical scholar; for several years master in the Edinburgh Academy, and afterwards Prof. of Greek in Queen's Coll., Galway, Ireland.

Thompson, Edward, 1738–86. *N. O.; Sailor.* An English naval officer, poet, and dramatist; b. in Hull; d. on board his ship, the "Grampus," on the coast of Africa. He wrote some greatly admired sea-songs.

Thompson, John, 1777–99. *Casca; Curtius; Gracchus.* An American political writer, of Virginia; b. and d. at Petersburg.

Thompson, Joseph Parrish, D.D., LL.D., 1819–79. *Berliner; Egyptus.* An eminent American clergyman and miscellaneous writer; b. in Philadelphia; Yale Coll., 1838; studied theology at Andover and at Yale; passed the last years of his life in Berlin, and d. there.

Thompson, Marmaduke. *Marmaduke T.* An English friend of Charles Lamb.

Thompson, Mortimer M., 1828–75. *Q. K. Philander Doesticks, P.B.; Knight Russ Ockside; No Author.* An eminent American humorist; b. at Riga, N.Y.; studied at the Univ. of Michigan, but did not graduate; was for some time a travelling actor; about 1852 became a clerk in a jewelry store of New York City; then employed on the New York press; d. in that city.

Thompson, Philip, 1785–1848. *A Member of the Society of Friends.* An English Friend, of Woodbridge, Suffolk; educ. in the Church of England, and for some years a jeweller and silversmith.

Thompson, Thomas Perronet, F.R.S., 1783–1869. *Audi Alteram Partem; A Member of the Univ. of Cambridge.* An eminent English soldier, political reformer, and author; b. at Hull; Queen's Coll., Cambridge, 1798; served in the British navy, 1803–6, and in the army from 1806, rising to be lieutenant-general; was M.P. for Hull, 1835, and for Bradford, 1847 and 1857–59.

Thompson, Thomas Phillips. *Jimuel Briggs.* A Canadian lawyer; b. in England; for a time editor of the "Post," St. Catharine's.

Thompson, William, –1833. *One of the Idle Classes.* An Irish writer on political economy; resided with Jeremy Bentham.

Thompson, William R. *Mata.* An American writer of the day.

Thompson, William Theodore. *Major Joseph Jones.* An American humorous writer and journalist, at Baltimore, Md., Augusta and Savannah, Ga.

Thoms, William John, 1803–85. *The Editor of " Notes and Queries"; Ambrose Merton; An Old Bookworm.* An eminent English literary antiquary; b. in Westminster; Secretary of the Camden Society, 1838–73; Dep. Librarian to the House of Lords from 1863 to near the end of his life; founder and editor of "Notes and Queries," 1849–78; d. in London.

Thomson, Adam. *A Young Scots Gentleman.* A Scottish dramatist, early in the 18th century.

Thomson, Adam, D.D., 1779–1861. *A Voluntary Advocate.* A Scottish minister for 54 years, of Coldstream, Co. Berwick, and d. there.

Thomson, Andrew, D.D., 1779–1831. *A Minister of the Church of Scotland.* A Scottish clergyman; b. at Sanquhar, Dumfriesshire; studied theology at Edinburgh; minister in that city, 1810–31; editor of the "Edinburgh Christian Instructor"; d. in Edinburgh.

Thomson, Arthur Dyot. *An M.A. of Balliol College, Oxford.* An English writer of the day.

Thomson, George, about 1759–1853.

Civis. A Scottish collector and editor of music; b. at Limekilns, Co. Fife; was the friend of Burns; a clerk in the Trustees' office at Edinburgh, 1800–33; d. in that city.

Thomson, John Cockburn, about 1825–60. *Philip Wharton; Megathym Splene, B.A., Oxon.* An English miscellaneous writer; son of the following; d. at Tenby, Wales.

Thomson, Mrs. Katharine (Byerley), 1800–62. *Grace Wharton; A Middle-Aged Man.* A popular miscellaneous writer; b. at Etruria, Staffs.; wife of Dr. Anthony Todd Thomson; wrote for "Fraser's" and "Bentley's" Magazines; d. at Dover.

Thomson, Richard, 1794–1865. *An Antiquary; Geoffrey Barbican.* An eminent English literary antiquary; librarian of the London Institution, 1834–65; d. in London.

Thomson, Sophia Edna. *Rosamond.* An American writer of the day.

Thomson, William, LL.D., 1746–1817. *The Man of the People; An Officer of Colonel Baillie's Detachment; Charles Stedman; Thomas Newte.* A Scottish writer; b. at Burnside, Perthshire; after some experience as a minister at Moniviard, went to London and engaged in literary work; d. at Kensington Gravel Pits, London.

Thomson, William, M.D., 1820–83. *W. T.; Cerimon.* A British colonial physician, of Melbourne, Australia.

Thomson, William Aird, D.D. *Amicus Secundus.* A Scottish writer, of Perth.

Thorburn, Rev. David, M.A. *A Clergyman of the Church of Scotland.* A Scottish minister, of the Free Church, South Leith; Univ. of Edinburgh, 1833.

Thorburn, Grant, 1773–1863. *Laurie Todd.* A Scottish-American gardener and author, of New York City, of Astoria, L.I., and of Winsted, Conn.; b. near Dalkeith, Scotland; came to this country in 1794; d. at New Haven.

Thorburn, Walter Millar. *A British Subject.* A British writer of the day.

Thoré, Théophile Étienne Joseph, 1807–69. *W. Bürger.* A French journalist and art writer, of Paris.

Thoreau, Henry David, 1817–62. *A Yankee.* An American eccentric student of nature and philosopher, of Concord, Mass.; b. and d. in that town; Harv. Univ., 1837.

Thorn, Rev. William, 1794–1870. *Biblicus; Theta.* An English Independent minister; b. at St. Neot, Cornwall; pastor at Penrith, 1817, at Redditch,

1824, and at Winchester, 1826–62; built and endowed a Congregational chapel at Liskeard, 1865; d. in Winchester.

Thorne, Sheldon B. *Saxifrage.* An American writer of the day.

Thornthwaite, J. A. *A Member of the Church of England.* An English clergyman.

Thornton, ——. *Th.* A pupil in Christ's Hospital with Charles Lamb.

Thornton, Bonnell, 1724–68. *Rev. Bushby Birch, LL.D., etc.; Critic and Censor General; A Deputy; Madame Roxana Termagant; Mr. Town.* An English poet and journalist; is said to have written the papers in the "Adventurer" signed "A."

Thornton, William, M.D. *W. T.* An American writer.

Thorpe, Charles. *Champagne Charlie.* An American writer of the day.

Thorpe, Henry, 1841–. *Walton.* An American writer.

Thorpe, Thomas Bangs, 1815–78. *Tom Owen, the Bee-hunter; Logan; Lynde Weiss.* An American miscellaneous writer; b. at Westfield, Mass.; Wesleyan Univ., 1842; for a time editor of the New York "Spirit of the Times"; clerk in the New York Custom House, 1869–78.

Threepland, Moncrieff, –1838. *Timothy Plain.* A Scottish advocate.

Thring, Rev. **Edward,** M.A. *Benjamin Place.* An English clergyman and educator; B.A., Cambridge, 1844; head master and warden of Uppingham School, 1853–83 *et seq.*

Thunderer, The. For the London "Times"; so-called for its "bold and fearless attacks upon national abuses, its defence of the Right, and its defiance of all obstructions which the Wrong might plant in its way."

Thurber, Charles, A.M. *His Father.* An American writer; Brown Univ., 1827; curator of the same from 1853.

Thurlow, Edward, 1st Baron Thurlow, 1732–1806. *L**d T**r**w; R—t H—e E—d L—d Churllow.* An eminent English lawyer; b. at Little Ashfield, Suffolk; Lord Chancellor, 1778–92; d. at Brighthelmstone.

Thwing, Rev. **Charles Franklin,** 1853–. *Eleven Sophomores.* An American clergyman; b. at New Sharon, Me.; Harv. Univ., 1876; pastor of North Avenue Cong. Church, Cambridge, Mass., from 1879.

Tichborne, Thomas. *A Phrenologist.* An English writer, of London.

Tickell, Thomas, 1686–1740. *A Lady in England.* An English poet; b.

at Bridekirk, Cumberland; M.A. at Oxford, 1708; Secretary to the Lord Justices of Ireland, 1724–40.

Tidmarsh, James. *S. H.* An English writer.

Tierney, George, 1761–1830. *Citizen T**rn*y.* An English politician; leader of the Whig party in the House of Commons; b. at Gibraltar; d. in London.

Tighe, William, Esq. *A Father.* An Irish author, of Woodstock Mistioge, Co. Kilkenny.

Tilden, Samuel Jones, 1814–. *Crino.* An American politician; b. at New Lebanon, N.Y.; studied law; has been prominent in city, state, and national politics.

Tileston, Mrs. **Mary Wilder (Foote).** *M. W. T.* An American writer, of Concord, N.H.; daughter of Caleb Foote of Salem, Mass.

Tillet, Auguste. *J. C. F. Maury.* A French dentist.

Tilloch, Alexander, LL.D., 1759–1825. *Biblicus.* A Scottish inventor and philosopher; b. at Glasgow; a journalist of London, 1789–1825, where he died.

Tillotson, John. *The Odd Boy.* An English writer for boys.

Tilt, Miss **Julia.** *May Hamilton.* An English novelist.

Tilton, Stephen Willis. *Uncle Willis.* An American poet and publisher, of Boston.

Tilton, Theodore, 1835–. *Sir Marmaduke.* An American miscellaneous writer and journalist; b. in New York City; educ. at the New York Free Academy; established and conducted the "Golden Age," 1872–74.

Tilton, Warren. *Trifle.* An American miscellaneous writer.

Timbs, John, F.S.A., 1801–75. *Horace Welby.* An English journalist, publisher, and miscellaneous writer; b. at Clerkenwell, London.

Timbury, Jane. *Hon. Edward Astell.* An English novelist of the 18th century.

Timmins, Samuel. *S. T.* An English bibliographer of the day.

Timrod, Henry, 1829–67. *Agläus.* An American poet and journalist, of Columbia and of Charleston, S.C.; b. at Charleston; and d. at Columbia.

Tincker, Mary Agnes. *M. A. T.* An American (?) R. C. writer; resident at Rome (?).

Tindal, Henrietta Euphemia (Harrison). *Diana Butler.* An English novelist and poet; daughter of Rev. John Harrison, of Ramsey, Essex; in 1846 was married to Acton Tindal, Esq., of the

Manor House, Aylesbury, Clerk of the Peace for Bucks.

Tissington, Anthony. *A Derbyshire Working Miner.* An English writer.

Titterington, Mrs. S. B. *Grace Graham.* An American (?) novelist of the day.

Tobin, James. *A Friend to the West India Colonies, etc.* A Scottish writer of the 18th century.

Tobin, John H. *John of York.* An American journalist of the day.

Tod, ——. *A Merchant.* A Scottish writer, of Kirtlands, of the 18th century.

Tod, Rev. George. *A Friend of the People.* A Scottish minister.

Tod, John. *John Strathesk.* A Scottish writer of the day.

Todd, H. C. *A Traveller.* A Canadian (?) writer.

Todd, Rev. Herbert, M.A. *T. Herbert.* An English poet and clergyman; b. in London; of Trin. Coll., Cambridge, 1858; Vicar of Kildwick, Leeds, 1875.

Todd, W. *A Sunday Scholar.* An English boy.

Tofte, Robert. *R. T., Gent., of London.* An English *littérateur*, of London.

Toland, John, 1669–1722. *Britto-Batavius; Hierophilus; Janus Junius Eoganesius.* An Irish pantheist; b. in the most northern peninsula of Ireland (in Inis-Eogan), the isthmus in which stands Londonderry; about 1697 he settled in London, where he afterwards chiefly resided; d. at Putney.

Tolderlund, Hother, –1880. *Viggo Lan.* A Danish poet, of Copenhagen.

Toll, Rev. Frederick, M.A. *A Friend to the Established Church.* An English clergyman; Rector of Dogmersfield, Hampshire.

Tolman, Mrs. Harriet (Smith). *H. S. T.* An American writer; widow of the late James Tolman, of Boston.

Tomlins, Frederic Guest, 1804–67. *Littlejohn.* An English publisher, then a dealer in second-hand books, in London. He was sub-editor of "Douglas Jerrold's Weekly Paper." D. at his residence, Painter-Stainer's Hall, Little Trinity Lane, London.

Tomlins, Thomas Edlyne. *A Barrister of the Inner Temple.* An English attorney and solicitor, of London.

Tomlinson, B. W. *Picket.* An American writer of the day.

Tomlinson, Miss Caroline. *Aunt Carrie.* An American writer; daughter of John Tomlinson, Esq., of Plymouth, Mass.

Tongue, Cornelius. *Cecil.* An English sporting writer.

Tonna, Mrs. Charlotte Elizabeth (Browne Phelan), 1792–1846. *C. E.; Charlotte Elizabeth.* An English writer; b. at Norwich; editor of the "Christian Lady's Magazine," 1834–46; d. at Ramsgate.

Tooke, John Horne, 1736–1812. *Citizen T**ke; An Englishman; A Freeholder of Surrey; Philosopher of Wimbledon; Strike but Hear.* An English philosopher, who was tried before Lord Mansfield, fined £200, and imprisoned 12 months because he raised money by subscription to relieve the widows and orphans of the Americans killed at Concord and Lexington in April, 1775; b. at Westminster; M.P. for Old Sarum, 1801; d. at Wimbledon.

Tooke, William, Esq., F.R.S., 1777–1863. *M. M. M.* An English lawyer and literary antiquary; b. at St. Petersburg; practised his profession in London, at the same time devoting much attention to literature; d. at his residence, Russell-Square, London.

Tootell, Hugh. *Charles Dodd.* An English R. C. priest, of the 18th century.

Töpffer, Rodolphe, 1799–1846. *Obadiah Oldbuck.* A Swiss humorous artist and author, of Geneva, where he died.
In French the pseudonym is "M. Vieux-Bois."

Toplady, Rev. Augustus Montague, 1740–78. *An Hanoverian; Philaretus; A Presbyter of the Church of England.* An English clergyman; b. at Farnham, Surrey; preached in a chapel near Leicester Fields, London, 1775–78.

Torelli, Giuseppe, 1721–81. *Ciu d'Arco.* An eminent Italian scholar and mathematician.

Tories and **Whigs.** *High-Heels and Low-Heels.*

Torrens, Robert, F.R.S., 1780–1864. *A Member of the Political Economy Club.* An Irish economist; entered the naval service in 1797; rose to be colonel of marines in 1837; afterwards major-general in India; M.P. for Ashburton, 1831; d. at Craven-hill.

Toulotte, E. L. J. *Civique de Gastine.* A French historian.

Toup, Jonathan, M.A., 1713–85. *Joannes Toupius.* An English scholar and literary critic; Prebendary of Exeter Cathedral from 1774.

Tour, M. Maitre De La. *M. M. D. L. T.* A French general; commander "of 10,000 men in the Army of the Mogul Empire, and before Commander in Chief of the Artillery of Hyder Ally, and of a Body of Europeans in the service of that Nabob."

Tourgee, Albion Winegar, 1838–. *One of the Fools; Henry Churton.* An American lawyer, soldier, and author; b. at Williamsfield, O.; Univ. of Rochester, N.Y., 1862; judge of the N.C. Superior Court from 1868–73; has lately resided in Philadelphia.

Tournachon, Gustave Félix, 1820–. *Nadar.* A French author, caricaturist, and photographer, of Paris.

Towgood, Rev. Micaiah, 1700–92. *A Dissenter; The Dissenting Gentleman.* An English minister; teacher in a Dissenters' academy at Exeter, 1761–92; pastor there, and d. there.

Towne, Rev. Edward Cornelius, 1834–. *E. C. T.; A Puritan.* An American clergyman; b. at Goshen, Mass.; graduated at Yale Coll. in 1856, and at Yale Theol. Div. School in 1860; s. p. of the Church of the Fraternity, New Haven, Conn., from 1872; resides in Westboro, Mass.

Towne, Rev. John, –1791. *An Impartial Hand.* An English clergyman; Archdeacon of Stowe, 1765; Rector of Little Paunton, County Lincoln, where he died.

Townley, Adam, D.D. *An Anglo-Canadian.* A Church of England clergyman, of Paris, U.C.

Townley, Daniel O'Connell, 1824–73. *Alderman Rooney.* An American journalist; b. in Newry, Ireland; came to this country in 1860, and was a journalist in New York City, where he died.

Townsend, ——. *A Graduate of the University of Oxford.* An English political writer, of the 19th century.

Townsend, Alice. *Florio Orsin.*

Townsend, Frederic. *An Invalid; A Whimsical Man.* An American writer and lawyer.

Townsend, George Alfred, 1841–. *A Broadway Lounger; Gath; Johnny Boquet; Laertes; A Non-Combatant.* An eminent American journalist; b. at Georgetown, Del.; educ. at the Philadelphia High School, 1859; has resided chiefly in New York City.

Townsend, Rev. George Henry, 1835–68. *John Green; Paddy Green.* An English writer.

Townsend, Rev. George Herbert. *A Tractarian British Critic.* An English clergyman.

This is different from the following, and it is doubtful whether the name is Herbert.

Townsend, George Herbert, about 1635–69. *An English Critic.* An English journalist, of London; prominent in the interest of the Conservative Party; d. at Kennington.

Townsend, James. *James T., of B. Castle.* An English gentleman, of London.

Townsend, Rev. Joseph, –1816. *A Well-wisher to Mankind.* An English clergyman; eminent as a scholar, a mineralogist, a fossilist, and conchologist; Rector of Pewsey, Wilts., where he died. He was the subject of Rev. R. Graves' "The Spiritual Quixote."

Townsend, Mrs. Mary Ashly (Van Voorhis). *Xariffa.* An American "Southland" poet and prose writer; b. at Lyons, Duchess Co., N.Y.; married Mr. Gideon Townsend; in 1872 was of New Orleans.

Townsend, Richard H. *A Citizen of Baltimore.* An American poet; a clerk in Baltimore.

Townsend, S. O. *A Patriot.* An American writer of the day.

Townshend, Lord Charles, 1725–67. *A Landowner.* An English statesman, called "Weathercock"; Secretary at War, 1761; Colonial Secretary, 1763; Paymaster-General, 1765; Chancellor of the Exchequer, 1766.

Townshend, Rev. Chauncy Hare, M.A., 1800–68. *C. H. T.; T. H. C.* An English clergyman; b. at Busbridge Hall, near Godalming, Surrey; Trin. Hall, Cambridge, 1821; during his last years he lived chiefly at Lausanne, Switzerland, though he possessed one of the finest houses in London; d. at Park Lane, London.

Townshend, S. Nugent. *St. Kames.* An English journalist, of London.

Toynbee, Joseph, 1815–66. *The Treasurer of the Wimbledon Local Museum.* An English aural surgeon; Vice-President of the London Pathological Association and Surgeon to St. Mary's Hospital; d. at Saville Row, London.

Tracy, Mrs. Ann Bromfield. *His Sister.* An American biographer; sister of John Bromfield, of Salem, Mass.

Tracy, Uriah, A.M., 1755–1807. *Scipio.* An American statesman; b. at Franklin, Conn.; Yale Coll., 1778; U.S. Senator from Connecticut, 1797–1807.

Trafton, Adeline, 1845–. *An American Girl Abroad.* An American author; b. at Saccarappa, Me.; in 1869 she spent some time in Europe. Her residence (1878) is divided between Springfield and Wollaston, Mass.

Trafton, Edwin H. *Noah Count.* An American journalist, of New York City; editor of the "Art Review," 1870–71.

Traill, Mrs. **Catharine Parr (Strickland),** about 1805–. *The Wife of an Emigrant Officer.* A Canadian writer; sister of Agnes Strickland; is a widow, residing at Lakefield, North Douro, Canada.

Trapp, Joseph, D.D., 1679–1747. *J. T., D.D.* An English clergyman; b. at Cherrington, Gloucs.; educ. at Wadham Coll., Oxford; first Professor of Poetry at Oxford, 1708–18; held charges in London, 1721–47, where he died.

Trask, Rev. **George,** 1798–1875. *Uncle Simeon Toby; Ziba Sproule.* An American Cong. minister and tobacco reformer; b. in Beverly, Mass.; Bowdoin Coll., 1826; Andover Theol. Sem., 1829; was a temperance agent at Fitchburg, Mass., many years, and d. there.

Trask, Mrs. **S.** *Clara Augusta.* An American writer, of Framingham, Mass.

Treby, Paul Ourry, Esq., 1786–1862. *The Foxhunter Rough and Ready.* An English gentleman, of Goodamoor, and Plympton, Devon.; d. at Goodamoor.

Treffry, Rev. **Richard,** 1771–1842. *Testis Oculatus.* An English Wesleyan Meth. minister; b. at Newton, near Tregony; governor of Wesleyan Theological Institute, Hoxton, 1838–41; d. at Cookham, Berks.

Trelawny, Edward John, 1792–1881. *A Younger Son.* An English writer; b. in London; was the friend of Byron and Shelley, meeting them at Pisa in 1822; went to Greece with the former in 1823, and was known as "The Greek"; was on his return a "lion" of London society, but gradually dropped out of it, and next became an amateur farmer in Monmouthshire; d. at Sompting, near Shoreham, in Sussex; his body was cremated, and the ashes carried to Rome to be placed beside those of Shelley and Keats.

Tremellier, Rev. ——. *A Presbyter of the Church of England.* An English clergyman, of the first part of the 18th century.

Trenchard, John, M.P., 1662–1723. *Cato.* An English political writer; a Somersetshire man; bred to the law, but became commissioner of forfeited estates in Ireland, and for a time was an M.P. for Taunton.

Trenhaile, John, 1792–1867. *A Cornubian.* An English popular poet, of Cornwall; b. in Truro; d. at Devonport.

Trenwith, William Henry. *T.* An American religious writer of the day.

Trevelyan, Sir **Charles Edward,** 1st Bart., K.C.B., 1807–. *Sir Gregory Hardlines; Indophilus.* An English financier; b. at Taunton; educ. at the Charterhouse and at Haileybury; East Indian Finance Minister, 1863–64.

Trevelyan, George Otto, K.C.B., 1838–. *A Competition Wallah.* An English statesman, son of the preceding; Lord of the Admiralty, 1869–70; wrote for "Macmillan's Mag.," 1864.

Trevenen, Miss **Emily,** 1785–1856. *A Lady.* An English poet; d. in Helston, Cornwall.

Treves, Mme **Virginia.** *Cordelia.*

Trimnell, Charles, D.D., 1663–1723. *A Member of the Lower House.* An English clergyman; Bishop of Winchester, 1721–23.

Trimmer, Mrs. **Sarah (Kirby),** 1741–1810. *Mrs. T——.* An English writer; b. at Ipswich; wrote many educational works, chiefly religious; d. at Brentford.

Tripp, Alonzo. *A Traveller and Teacher; Willie Triton.* An American teacher; b. in Harwich, Mass.; principal of the Highland Institute, Roxbury.

Trollope, Anthony, 1815–82. *One of the Firm.* An English novelist; a son of Mr. T. A. Trollope, an English barrister, and Frances (Milton) Trollope, an authoress of considerable reputation; educ. at Winchester and at Harrow, and from 1834–67 connected with the British postal service. He became known as an author some thirty-five years ago, and since that time has been a voluminous writer, employing his pen on works of travel as well as on novels. At one time he was editor of "St. Paul's Magazine." Among the countries visited by Mr. Trollope, the United States and Canada are included. D. in London.

Trollope, Mrs. **Frances E. (Ternan).** *A New Writer.* An English novelist; daughter of Thomas L. Ternan; in 1866, married Thomas Augustus Trollope.

Trollope, Mrs. **Frances (Milton),** 1778–1863. *F. T.* An English novelist; b. in Heckfield, Hants, and in 1809 was married to T. A. Trollope, a barrister-at-law. In 1829, she came to this country, and tried to establish herself in business at Cincinnati, but failed. She passed the last years of her life at Florence, Italy, and d. there.

Trollope, William, D.D. *Dr. T—e.* An English philologist; of Pembroke Coll.; once a master of Christ's Hospital.

Trotter, John. *Don José Balscopo.* An English writer.

Trotter, William. *W. T.* An English religious writer.

Trowbridge, John Townsend, 1827–. *Paul Creyton.* An American popular writer; b. at Ogden, N.Y.; in 1846, settled in New York City as a writer for periodicals; removed in 1847 to Boston, where he has since chiefly resided.

Trueblood, N. A. *Frank Winter.* An American writer of the day.

Truinet, Charles Louis Étienne, 1828–. *C. L. É. Nuitter.* A French stage-poet; b. at Paris; studied law, and then devoted himself to literature, and sometimes alone, sometimes with others, produced a large number of vaudevilles and operettas, as well as lyric poetry.

Trumble, Alfred, 1846–. *Antonio Aquaverde; Babbler; Jack Manley; Matt. Marling.* An American writer.

Trumbull, Henry (?). *A Citizen of Connecticut.* An American author.

Trumbull, J. H. *Vertaur.* An English writer; contributor to "Notes and Queries," etc.

Trumbull, James Hammond, LL.D., 1821–. *Loammi N. Hurlbut, M.D.* An eminent American philologist; b. at Stonington, Conn.; Yale Coll., 1842; since 1847, resident at Hartford, Conn.; Asst.-Secretary of State, 1847–52 and 1858–61; Secretary, 1861–65; librarian of the Watkinson Library, Hartford, since 1863; lecturer at Yale Coll., 1873.

Tucker, Abraham, 1705–74. *Cuthbert Comment, Esq.; Edward Search; The Country Gentleman.* An eminent English *littérateur*; b. in London; studied at Merton Coll., Oxford, and in the Inner Temple; purchased Betchworth Castle, Dorking, in 1727, and then devoted himself chiefly to literary pursuits.

Tucker, Miss Blanche. *Rosavella.* Afterwards Madame Marocho.

Tucker, Miss Charlotte. *A. L. O. E.* An English writer for the young.

Tucker, George, 1775–1861. *A Citizen of Virginia; Enquirer; A Virginian.* An American lawyer; b. in Bermuda; came to Virginia about 1787; M.C., 1819–25; lived in retirement, chiefly in Philadelphia, till his death at Sherwood, Albemarle Co., Va.

Tucker, Rev. **John,** 1795–1870. *Scrutator.* An English clergyman; b. at Newport, Cornwall; Vicar of Lannarth, Gwennap, 1845–70, and d. there.

Tucker, Rev. **John Kinsman.** *A Country Clergyman.* An English clergyman; Rector of Pettaugh, Stonham, Suffolk.

Tucker, Josiah, D.D., 1711–99. *J. T., of Bristol; A Merchant in London.* An English clergyman; b. at Langhorne, Carmarthen; St. John's Coll., Oxford; Dean of Gloucester, 1858–99. Owes his reputation chiefly to his tracts on politics and political economy.

Tucker, Nathaniel Beverley, 1784–1851. *Edward William Sydney.* An American jurist and man of letters; resided in the West, where, in Missouri, he was raised to the Bench, 1815–30; professor in William and Mary Coll., 1834–51.

Tucker, Saint George, 1752–1827. *Melmoth; Jonathan Pindar.* An American poet and jurist; Judge of the Court of Appeals from 1803, and Prof. of Law in William and Mary Coll. from 1813 till his death.

Tucker, Miss **Sarah.** *S. T.* An English writer of religious works.

Tuckerman, Edward, 1817–. *Notitia Literaria.* An American botanist; b. in Boston, Mass.; Harv. Univ., 1847; Prof. at Amherst Coll., 1854–85 *et seq.*

Tuckerman, Henry Theodore, 1813–71. *A Dreamer.* A popular American miscellaneous writer; b. in Boston; from 1845 resided chiefly in New York City.

Tuckett, Miss **E.** *One of the Party.* An English lady.

Tuel, J. E. *J. E. T.* An American poet.

Tuke, Esther, 1727–94. *A Lover of Peace and Order.* An English Friend; wife of William Tuke, of York.

Tulloch, Maj.-Gen. Sir **Alexander Murray,** K.C.B., 1804–60. *Dugald Dalgetty.* A distinguished Irish soldier; b. at Newry, Ireland; obtained an ensign's commission in the 45th Reg't in 1826, and sailed for India in 1827; rose to be major-general in 1859; d. at Winchester.

Tupper, Miss **Ellin Isabella, Margaret Elenore,** and **Mary Frances.** *Three Sisters.* English poets; daughters of the following.

Tupper, Martin Farquhar, D.C.L., F.R.S., 1810–. *T.; Peter Query; The Late Mr. Æsop Smith.* A popular English poet; b. in London; educ. at Charterhouse, and Christ Church, Oxford, 1831; lives at Albury, Surrey.

Tupy, Karl Eugen, 1813–. *Boleslaw Jablonsky.* A Bohemian poet; b. at Kardasch-Rzetschitz; is one of the favorite lyric poets of Bohemia and Moravia.

Turnbull, Lieut. **Gordon.** *An Eye Witness; An Old Planter.* A British colonial writer.

Turnbull, Robert James, M.D., 1775–1833. *Brutus.* An American physician, planter, and politician; b. at North Smyrna, Fla.; prominent at the S.C. Nullification Convention, 1832; d. at Charleston, S.C.

Turnbull, William Barclay David Donald, 1811–63. *A Delver into Antiquity.* An eminent Scottish antiquary; b. in Edinburgh; became a lawyer; calenderer of the foreign correspondence of the State Paper Office, London, 1859–61.

Turner, Rev. **Daniel**, M.A., 1710–98. *An Impartial Hand.* An English writer; minister of the Bapt. church at Abingdon, Berks.; b. in Hertfordshire.

Turner, George. *Philalethes.* An English writer.

Turner, J. Fox. *Pyngle Layne.* An English writer.

Turner, James. *Aristobulus.* An English religious writer.

Turner, John M. *Archibald Head.* An American writer of the day.

Turner, Samuel, 1759–1801. *The Ambassador.* An English diplomatist; distinguished himself in the East India Service under Warren Hastings.

Turner, Samuel Hulbeart, D.D., 1790–1861. *Presbyter.* An eminent American Prot. Epis. clergyman; b. in Philadelphia; professor in the Gen. Theol. Sem., New York City, 1821–61, and in Columbia Coll., 1831–61.

Turner, Sharon, Esq., 1768–1847. *A Layman.* An eminent English historian; b. in London; studied law, but devoted his life chiefly to literary pursuits; d. at the house of his son, in Red-Lion-square, London.

Turton, Thomas, D.D., 1780–1864. *Crito Cantabrigiensis; Clemens Anglicanus; Philalethes Cantabrigiensis.* An eminent English prelate; b. at Hatfield, Yorkshire; Bishop of Ely, 1845–64; d. at Ely House, Dover-street, London.

Turton, Sir **Thomas**, 1st Bart., 1764–1844. *A Country Gentleman.* An English baronet; son of William Turton, Esq., of Soundes, Co. Oxford; a military officer who served at the battles of Minden and Warbourg; was created a baronet in 1796.

Tuthall, Hon. **William H.**, 1808–1880. *Anti-Quary.* An American lawyer; b. in New York City; practised law in that city till 1840, when he removed to Tipton, Ia., where he resided till his death.

Tuttle, E. C. *Judge Vernon.* An English journalist of the day.

Tuttle, Rev. **Joseph Farrand.** *J.*

F. T. An American clergyman and educator; President of Wabash Coll., Crawfordsville, Ind.

Twining, Miss Louisa. *L. T.* An English religious writer, of London; a leading member of "The Woman's Dress Association."

Twining, Rev. **Thomas.** *Philalethes.* An English Baptist minister, of Trowbridge, Wilts.

Twiss, Horace, Esq., Q.C., 1787–1849. *Horatius.* An English lawyer; the senior Queen's Counsel; Vice-Chancellor of the Duchy of Lancaster; and a Bencher of the Inner Temple; d. in London.

Twiss, Richard, 1747–1821. *An Irish Traveller.* A lover of literature, music, and chess; d. in Somers Town.

Twiss, Sir **Travers**, D.C.L., 1819–. *Corvinus.* An English lawyer; b. at Trevallyn, Denbighshire; educ. at Oxford; called to the Bar at Lincoln's Inn, 1840; Queen's Advocate-General, 1867–72.

Twombly, Rev. **Alexander Stevenson**, 1832–. *Abner Perk.* An American Cong. minister; b. in Boston; Yale Coll., 1854; pastor at Winthrop Church, Boston, 1872–85 *et seq.*

Twort, Charles William. *A Protestant.* An English writer.

Tyas, Rev. **Robert**, M.A. *R. T.* An English clergyman; Queen's Coll., Cambridge, 1848; Vicar of East Tilbury, Essex, 1871–80 *et seq.*

Tyers, Thomas, 1726–87. *Tim Restless.* An English miscellaneous writer; d. at Ashted.

Tyler, Bennet, D.D., 1783–1858. *A New England Minister.* An American theologian; b. at Middlebury, Conn.; Yale Coll., 1804; Pres. and Prof. at East Windsor, 1834–58; d. at East Windsor Hill.

Tyler, Major **John.** *Python.* An American writer.

Tyler, Robert. *A Virginian.* An American poet; son of President John Tyler.

Tyler, Royall, A.M., 1757–1826. *S.; Trash; Colon and Spondee; Dr. Updike Underhill.* An eminent American jurist and humorous writer; b. in Boston; Harv. Univ., 1776; Judge of the Supreme Court of Vermont, 1794–1800; Chief-Justice, 1800–6; d. at Brattleborough, Vt.

Tyng, Miss Florence. *Florence.* An American writer of the day.

Tyrwhitt, Rev. **Richard.** *A Clergyman.* An English clergyman.

Tyson, John S. *A Citizen of Balti-*

more. An American writer; son of Elisha Tyson.

Tyssen, Amhurst Daniel, D.C.L., 1843–. *A. D. T.* An English barrister of the Inner Temple, 1869, and antiquary.

Tytler, Alexander Fraser, Lord Woodhouselee, 1747–1813. *Paul Pas-*

quin. An eminent Scottish scholar and writer; b. in Edinburgh; educ. at Kensington and at Edinburgh; Lord of Session, 1802–11; Lord of Justiciary, 1811–13; d. in Edinburgh.

Tytler, Miss **Anne Fraser.** *A. F. T.* A Scottish novelist; eldest daughter of the preceding.

U.

Ulbach, Louis, 1822–. *Ferragus; Jacques Souffrant, ouvrier.* A French poet and political writer, of Paris; b. at Troyes (Aube); in 1868 he started "La Cloche," which he left in 1872, and became co-editor of "l'Indépendance belge" and of the "Revue politique et littéraire."

Underhill, Cave. *Elephant Smith.* A British dramatist of the last part of the 17th century.

Underhill, Edward Bean, LL.D. *Eli Fant.* An English writer; secretary of the Baptist Missionary Society.

Underwood, T. *T. U—d.* An English poet, of St. Peter's Coll., Cambridge; a writer of the 18th century.

Uniacke, Mary. *M. U.* An English writer of the day, for children.

"Universal Spectator." Supposed editor *Henry Stonecastle, of Northumberland, Esq.*

Updike, Wilkins, A.M., 1786–1867. *A Landholder.* An American lawyer; b. and d. in North Kingston, R.I.; a member of the Rhode Island Bar; Hon. A.M. at Brown Univ., 1846.

Upham, Edward, Esq., F.S.A.,–1834. *E. U.* An English bookseller; first of Exeter, then of Dawlish, and last of Bath, where he died.

Upshur, Miss **Mary J. S.** *Fanny Fielding.* An American "Southland" poet and prose writer; b. in Accomac Co., Va.; about 1869 she married a Mr. Sturges, of New York City.

Upton, George P. *Peregrine Pickle.* An American journalist; for many years the literary editor and dramatic and musical critic of the Chicago "Tribune."

Upton, John, –1760. *J. U.* An English clergyman; Prebendary of Rochester, 1736–37, and Rector of Great Rissington.

Urbino, Mrs. **Levina Buoncuore.** *L. Boncœur; Lavinia Buon Cuore.* An American writer, of Boston; wife of Samson R. Urbino.

Ure, G. P., –1860. *A Member of the Press.* A Scottish-Canadian journalist, of Toronto, and of Montreal, where he died.

Urner, Nathan D. *Burke Brentford; Mentor.* An American writer of the day, of New York City.

Urquhart, C. K., 1855–. *Scotty.* An American journalist, of Chicago.

Urquhart, David, 1805–77. *An Old Diplomatic Servant.* A Scottish statesman; b. at Brackanwell, County Cromarty; educ. at St. John's Coll., Oxford, and became Secretary of the British Embassy at Constantinople; M.P. for Stafford, 1847–52; d. at Naples, Italy.

Urquhart, Rev. **David Henry**, M.A. *Querulous Moody.* An English poet and clergyman; Prebendary of Lincoln, 1792.

Urquhart, William Pollard, 1815–. *An M.P.* An Irish statesman; b. at Castle Pollard, Westmeath County, and educ. at Trin. Coll., Cambridge; M.P. for Westmeath, 1852–57 and 1859.

Uschner, Karl Richard Waldemar, 1834–. *Julian; Chr. Klausner.* A German lawyer; b. at Wittenberg; since 1875, established in Oppeln; has succeeded as a dramatic poet.

Usher, Charles. *C. U.* An early English writer, of the Univ. of Cambridge.

Usher, James, about 1720–72. *J. U.* An Irish writer; b. in the county of Dublin; was successively a farmer, a linen-draper, a R. C. priest, and a schoolteacher, of Shaftesbury.

Utterson, Edward Vernon. *E. V. U.* An English literary antiquary, and editor of rare books.

V.

Vachette, Eugène, 1827-. *Eugène Chavette.* A French novelist; b. at Paris; wrote first for "Figaro." "Événement," etc., and made himself remarkable for his sharp and minute observations.

Vail, Floyd. *Flambeau; Floyd Valentine.* An American writer of the day.

Vail, John Cooper. *Zekel Allspice.* An American humorous writer of the day.

Valbezene, A. de. *Le Major Fridolin.* A French writer of the day.

Valentia, George Annesley, Viscount, 1770-1844. *The Last Traveller.* An English nobleman; b. at Arley Hall, Staffs.; educ. at Rugby and at Oxford, but did not graduate; spent some years in the army; in the West Indies, 1802-6; M.P. for Yarmouth, Isle of Wight, from 1808; d. at his birthplace.

Valentine, Mrs. Laura (Jewry). *L. V.* An English editor of the day.

Valentine, Mrs. Richard. *Aunt Louisa.* An American (?) writer of the day, for children.

Vallancey, Charles, (originally Vallance), LL.D., 1722-1812. *C. V.* An Irish antiquary; general in the Engineer Department of the Royal Army, 1803-12; resided chiefly in Dublin, and d. there.

Vallentine, B. B. *John Iredale; Francis Fitznoodle.* An American humorist of the day.

Valpy, Abraham John, 1777-1854. *A. J. V.* An English scholar, publisher, and bookseller, of London; b. at Reading; educ. at Oxford; d. in St. John's Wood Road, London.

Valpy, Rev. Edward, B.D., 1764-1832. *A Member of the University of Cambridge.* An English clergyman; b. in the island of Jersey; of Trin. Coll., Camb.; brother of Richard Valpy, D.D., and for many years his assistant in Reading School; d. at Yarmouth.

Valpy, Rev. Francis Edward Jackson, M.A. *F. E. J. V.* An English scholar, of Trin. Coll., Camb.; youngest son of Richard Valpy, D.D., and his successor as head master of the Reading Grammar School, etc.; Rector of Garveston, Attleborough, Norfolk, 1845-73.

Valpy, Henrietta F. *H. F. V.* An English writer of fifty years ago.

Valpy, Richard, D.D., F.A.S., 1754-1836. *R. V.; A Young Gentleman; A Clergyman.* An English clergyman and educator; b. in the island of Jersey;

educ. at Pembroke Coll., Oxford; Rector of Stradishall, Suffolk, 1787-1836; head master of Reading School, 1781-1830; d. at Earl's Terrace, Kensington.

Van Arden, J. Howard, 1856-. *Paul Braddon.* An American writer of the day.

Van Ness, Judge William P. *Aristides; Lysander; Marcus.* An American lawyer and politician; b. in New York City; Columbia Coll., 1797; U.S. Judge for the Southern District of New York from 1812.

Vandenburgh, Theodore H. *Jack Bunsby.* An American writer of the day.

Vanderbuilt, Mrs. G. L. *G. L. V.* An American writer of the day, for the young.

Vandenbussche, Mme ——. *Marie Ennery.* A French writer for children.

Vane, the Hon. Anne. *Vanella.* An English lady of the 18th century.

Vane, Lady Frances, Viscountess. *Lady V—ss V——.* An English lady of the 18th century.

Vanhomrigh, Miss Esther. *Vanessa.* An Irish lady; a friend of Dean Swift.

Vardill, Miss Anna Jane. *A Lady.* An English poet.

Varela, Héctor F. *Orion.*

Varnum, Joseph Bradley, Jr., A.M., 1818-74. *Viator.* An American lawyer; b. in Washington; Yale Coll., 1838; admitted to the Bar in Baltimore, and practised there for a few years, but removed to New York City, where he remained till his death; d. at Astoria, L.I.

Vasey, George. *A Beefeater.* An English writer of the day, of schoolbooks, etc.

Vaudoncourt, Guillaume G. de. *G. G. d. V.*

Vaughan, C. M. *C. M. V.* An English compiler of educational works.

Vaughan, Rev. David James, M.A. *A Private Tutor.* An English clergyman; Trin. Coll., Cambridge, 1848; Vicar of St. Martin, Leicester, 1860-83 *et seq.*; Hon. Can. of Pet. Cathedral, 1872; R.D. of Leicester, 1875.

Vaughan, Herbert. *H. V.* An English novelist of the day.

Vaughan, Rev. Thomas. *A Member of Convocation.* An English clergyman; Vicar of Yarnton.

Vaulabelle, Eléonore Tenaille de, 1801-59. *Jules Cordier; Ernest Desprez.* A French dramatist, of Paris.

Veazie, Joseph. *J. V. Z.* An American (?) writer of the day.

Veasey, T. *T. V.* An English poet.

Venables, Gilbert. *G. V.* An English writer of the day.

Vergy, Treysac de. *A Member of Parliament.* An English writer of the 18th century.

Vernon, ——. *Carmichael.* An English writer.

Vernon, Admiral Edward, 1684–1757. *An Honest Sailor.* An English naval officer; b. at Westminster; d. at his seat at Nanton, Suffolk.

Vernon, Francis V. *A Sea-Officer.* A British seaman.

Verplanck, Gulian Crommelin, LL.D., 1786–1870. *Scriblerus Busby, LL.D.; Abimelech Coody; ¬Francis Herbert; Brevet Major Pindar Puff.* An American scholar and writer; b. in New York City; Columbia Coll., 1801; Vice-Chancellor of the State University, 1829–70; d. in his native city.

Verrall, Miss Georgiana. *Elfin.* An English lady; b. at Worthing; mistress of the Endowed School, at Crowan; governess to the family of the Rev. Vernon Page, Rector of St. Tudy.

Viardot, Louis, 1800–. *L. V.* A French writer; b. at Dijon; removed to Paris in 1817, and devoted himself ultimately to literature.

Viaud, Julien. *Pierre Loti.* A French writer of the day.

Vicary, Rev. Michael, B.A. *A Protestant Clergyman.* An Irish (?) clergyman; Trin. Coll., Dublin, 1838; in 1883 resident at Wexford, Co. Wexford.

Victor, Mrs. Frances (Fuller). *Florence Fane.* An American writer of the day.

Victor, Henry, 1837–. *A Novice.* An English dramatist; b. at Gulval; is a linen-draper at Penzance, Cornwall.

Victor, Mrs. Metta Victoria (Fuller), 1831–. *Mrs. Mark Peabody; Seeley Register; Singing Sybil.* An American miscellaneous writer and journalist; b. at Erie, Penn.; wife of Orville J. Victor; of New York City from 1857.

Victor, Orville James, 1827–. *An American Citizen.* An American writer; b. at Sandusky, O.; has acted as journalist in his native city and in New York City; editor of Beadle's dime publications, 1860–64 *et seq.*

Victor, Thomas, 1828–80. *A Traveller.* An English poet, etc.; b. at The Parade, Mousehole, near Penzance; was a farmer, miller, and general merchant in Australia, 1849–67; in 1877 was a resident at Lynwood, Paul, where he died.

Viger, Jacques, 1787–1858. *Le Bon Vieux Temps.* A Canadian antiquary; b., lived, and d. in Montreal; was the first mayor of that city.

Vigor, Mrs. —— (Ward Rondeau). *A Lady.* An English writer, of one hundred years ago.

Villari, Linda White, 1836–. *M. Dalin.* An English writer; b. at Brighton; in 1876 married the Italian historian, Prof. Pasquale Villari.

Vincent, William, D.D., 1739–1815. *The Reverend Dean.* An English clergyman; b. and d. in London; educ. at Westminster and Cambridge; Dean of Westminster, 1802–15.

Vining, Pamela S. *Xenette.* An American poet; in 1860 a teacher in the Seminary for Young Women at Alton, Mich.

Virtue, Peter, the Younger. *A Layman.* A British colonial writer and lecturer, of Maryborough, Australia.

Vischer, Friedrich Theodor, 1807–. *Schartenmeyer.* A German humorist; b. at Ludwigsburg, Wurtemburg; studied theology at Tübingen; Prof. of Æsthetics at Tübingen, 1844; at Zurich, 1855; again at Tübingen, 1866.

Visscher, William L. *Vissch.* An American writer of the day.

Vitelleschi, Marchese **Francesco Nobili.** *Pomponio Leto.*

Vivian, George, –1873. *G. V.* An English architect.

Vivian, Mrs. Isabella Jane (Houlton). *I. V.* An English poet and musical composer; third daughter of John Houlton, of Farley Castle, Somerset; in 1834 married Major Quintus Vivian, F.R.G.S.; resident, in 1880, at 17 Chesham Street, London, S.W.

Viviana, Emilia. *Emilia V.* An unfortunate Italian lady.

Vizard, John. *J. V.* An English writer of the day.

Vizettelly, Henry. *H. V.* An English compiler.

Vogel, Elisa, 1823–. *Elise Polko.* A German writer of the day.

Voïart, Anne Elisabeth Élise (Petit-Pain), 1786–1866. *Eliza.* A French novelist; b. and d. at Nancy.

Voigtel, Valeska, –1877. *Arthur Stahl.* A German novelist; passed her early life in Westphalia; married the jurist Voigtel at Magdeburg; from 1868 a widow; she lived chiefly at her villa on Lake Maggiore, employed with the translation of her works into the Italian language; d. at Milan.

Volk, Wilhelm Ludwig, 1804–188–. *Clarus.* A German mystical writer; b. in Berlin; educ. at Göttingen; in 1855 he abjured the Protestant faith.

Volkmann, Richard, 1830–. *Richard Leander.* A German poet and prose writer; b. at Leipsic; is Director of Surgical Clinics and Prof. of Medicine in the Univ. of Halle, and consulting surgeon of the army.

Volleau, Adolphe. *Revel.* A French writer.

Voltaire, François Marie Arouët de, 1694–1778. *A . . . . t de V***; M. Abouzit; L'Abbé Bazin; L'Abbé Big . . . .; M. L'Abbé Caille; M. L'Abbé d'Arty; L'Abbé de Tilladet; L'Abbé Mauduit; L'Abbé Tamponet; Un Académicien de Lyon; L'Admiral Sheremetof; Alexis, Archevêque de Novgorod-la-Grande; Amabed; Un Amateur de Belles-Lettres; Les Amateurs; Anne Dubourg; Antoine Vadé; Frère de Guillaume; L'Archevêque de Cantorbéry; Un Auteur célèbre, etc.; Un Avocat de Besançon; Un Avocat de Province; Un Bachelier en Théologie; M. Baudinet; Une Belle Dame; McBelleguier; Un Bénédictin; Un Bénédictin de Franche-Comté; Bigex; Caïus Memmius Gemellus; Cassen, Avocat au Conseil du Roi; Catherine Vadé; M. Chambon; Charles Gouju; Un Chrétièn; Les Cinquante; Un Citoyen de Genève; M. Clair; M. Clocpitre; Le Comte Da . . . .; Comte de Corbera; Comte de Passeran; M. le Comte de Tournay; Corps des Pasteurs; M. Cubstorf; Curé de Frêne; Curé Meslier; Damilaville; M. Demad; Desjardins; Docteur Akakia; Le Docteur Goodheart; Docteur Good Natur'd Wellwisher; Le Docteur Obern; Docteur Ralph; Dom Calmet; Dumarsais; Dumoulin; Un Ecclésiastique; M. de L'Ecluse, etc.; M. Eratou; M. d'Etallonde; Evhémère; M. Fatéma; M. Formey; Gabriel Gras-*
set; Gardien des Capucins; Genest Ramponeau; Gérofle; Guillaume Vadé; Un Homme de Lettres; M. Hude; M. Huet; L'Humble Évêque d'Aletopolis; M. Imhof; Irenée Alethès; M. Ivan Alethof; Jacq. Aimon; Jean Meslier; Jean Plokof; Jérome Carre; Jos. Bourdillon; M. Joseph Laffichard; Josias Rosette; Joussouf-Cherebi; La Roupillière; M. de La Visclède, etc.; M. Lantin; M. D*** M***; M. L.; M. Mairet; Le Major Kaiserling; Malicourt; M. Mamaki; Marquis de Ximenez; M. de Mauléon; Maxime Madeure; Un Membre du Conseil de Zurich; Un Membre d'un Corps; Milord Bolingbrocke; M. Montmolin; M. de Morza; M. Needham; Le P. Fouquet; P. Quesnel; Papa Nicolas Charisteski; Pasteur Bourn; Plusieurs Aumônieres, etc.; Un Prêtre de la Doctrine Chrétienne; M. le Proposant Thero, etc.; Un Quaker; R. P. L'Escarbotier; Le R. P. Polycarpe; Rabbin Akib; M. Robert Covelle; M. de Saint-Didier, etc.; M. Saint-Hyacinthe; Scarmentado; Le Secrétaire de M. de Voltaire; M. Sherloc; Le Sieur Aveline lui-même; Le Sieur Tamponet; Une Société de Bacheliers en Théologie; Soranus; M. Thomson; Trois Avocats d'un Parlement; M. V***; M. de V . . . . .; Verzenot; La Veuve Denis; La Vieillard du Mont Caucasse; Zapata. A French philosopher; b. at Châtenay, near Sceaux; visited England, 1724; resided in Prussia, 1750–53; d. in Paris.

This list, prepared by Mr. Frey, is so remarkable that it is inserted here, though very few of the pseudonyms will be found in the first part.

Von Valkenburg, Miss Julia. *Gladys Wayne.* An American writer of the day.

Vosburgh, F. W. *Vigilant.* An American writer of the day.

Vose, Reuben. *Invisible Sam.* An American political writer.

W.

Wace, Henry T. *A Wanderer in Egypt.* An English traveller.

Wadd, William, Esq., F.L.S., 1777–1829. *A Member of the Royal College of Surgeons; Unus quorum.* An English surgeon to George IV.; b. in London; killed by an accident on the road from Killarney to Mitchelstoun.

Waddell, Rev. **Peter Hately,** LL.D. *A Preacher of the Gospel.* An English clergyman.

Waddilove, Rev. **William James Darley.** *W. J. D. W.* An English clergyman, of Canada.

Waddington, Charles, 1819–. *Kastus.* A French philosopher; nephew of the statesman; b. at Mailand, of an English Protestant family; was educ. at the Lyceum of Versailles and at the Normal School in Paris; since 1864, has been Professor of Philosophy, and a lecturer upon it, at Paris.

Waddington, Samuel Ferrand, M.D. *Algernon Sidney.* An English physician, of London.

Wade, John, about 1800-. *J. W.; The Original Editor.* An English lawyer, of London; Vice-President of the Historical Section of the "Institut d'Afrique," of Paris.

Wadman, Elmer E. *Ellsworth.* An American writer of the day.

Wager, Miss **Mary A. E.** *Mintwood.* An American writer of the day.

Waggamon, Mrs. **Mary T.** *Fannie Fairie; Queerquill.* An American writer.

Wagstaffe, William, M.D., 1685-1725. *Crispin; Dr. Andrew Tripe.* An English physician, of St. Bartholomew's Hospital, London; b. at Cublington, Bucks.; d. at Bath.

Wahab, Charles James. *One who knows.* An English sanitary writer of the day, of London.

Wainewright, Jeremiah, M.D. *A Member of the College of Physicians.* An English physician of the first part of the 18th century.

Wainewright, Thomas Griffiths. *Janus Weathercock; Varney.* An English author; a friend of Lamb; "the gentlemanly murderer"; a contributor to the "London Magazine" (see his sketch of Hood — paper styled "Janus Weathercock," etc., in the No. for January, 1822), of whose criminal career a full account will be found in Talfourd's "Final Memorials of Charles Lamb."

Wainwright, Rev. **Latham,** M.A., F. S. A., -1833. *F. S. A.* An English clergyman; Rector of Great Brickhill, Buckinghamshire, 1803-33; resided in his parish a few years, but afterwards in London, where he died.

Wainwright, Reader. *Another Barrister.* An English lawyer; a Unit. writer.

Wake, Rev. **William,** D.D., 1657-1736-37. *A Country Clergyman.* An English divine; b. at Blandford, Dorsetshire; Archbishop of Canterbury, 1715-16; d. and was buried at Croydon.

Wakefield, Edward Gibbon, 1796-1862. *A Member.* An English writer; accompanied the Earl of Durham to Canada as his private secretary in 1839; resided some years in the South of France, but removed to New Zealand, and d. there.

Wakefield, Priscilla (Bell), 1750-1832. *Priscilla ****; A Gentleman.* An English Friend, of Tottenham; afterwards of Ipswich, Suffolk. She is said to have been the original promoter of those institutions called "Frugality Banks," for the benefit of the industrious poor.

Wakefield, Thomas, 1752-1806. *Philanthropos.* An English clergyman; brother of Gilbert Wakefield; minister at Richmond, Surrey, for 30 years, and d. there.

Walcott, Eliza. *The Two Sisters.* An American poet; sister of Sarah G. Walcott.

Walcott, Josephine. *Cordelia Havens.* An American writer of the day.

Walcott, Rev. **Mackenzie Edward Clarke,** B.D., 1822-. *M. E. C. W.* An English clergyman and poet; Exeter Coll., Oxford, 1844; Precentor and Prebendary of Oving in Chichester Cathedral, 1863-83 *et seq.*

Walcott, Sarah G. *The Two Sisters.* An American poet; sister to Eliza Walcott.

Waldie, Miss **Charlotte Ann.** *An Englishwoman.* An English writer; sister of John Waldie, of Hendersyde Park, near Newcastle, afterwards Mrs. Eaton, of Stamford.

Waldie, Walter S. *Retlaw.* An American writer of the day.

Waldo, ——. *Tim Linkenwater.* An American writer of the day.

Waldo, Leonard, 1853-. *L. W.* An American astronomer; b. at Cincinnati; educ. at Woodward Coll.; assistant at the Harv. Univ. Observatory, Cambridge, 1875-80 *et seq.;* is now connected with the observatory at Yale Coll.

Waldo, Peter. *A Layman.* An English religious writer for the Society for Promoting Christian Knowledge.

Waldron, Francis Godolphin. *F. G. W.* An English actor, editor, and dramatist; editor of the "Literary Museum," London, 1792; the "Shakespearian Miscellany," 1802; and editor or author of the "Biographical Mirror," 1793.

Walford, Bessie G. *Flora Walford.* An English writer.

Walford, Edward, v. **Elliott Stock.** *Editor v. Publisher.* **Walford,** Rev. **Edward,** M.A., 1823-. An English author; b. at Hatfield; M.A. of Balliol Coll., Oxford; editor of the "Gentleman's Magazine," 1865-68; and of the "Register," 1869 *et seq.*

Walford, Thomas. *An Irish Gentleman.*

Walker, ——. *Comet.* An American writer of the day.

Walker, Mrs. **——.** *A Lady.* An English writer of the 18th century.

Walker, Miss **——.** *Anna Freduir.* An American "Southland" writer; in 1872, of Tuscaloosa, Ala.

Walker, Benjamin. *Rewk Albin.* An English writer of the day.

Walker, Miss C. *Lottie.* An English author.

Walker, Rev. Charles, M.A. *C. W.* An English clergyman; Trin. Coll., Cambridge, 1861; Asst.-Curate of St. Michael's, Brighton, 1863–83 *et seq.*

Walker, Mrs. D. M. (F.). *Helen Mar.* An English author.

Walker, E. C. *Veritas.* An American writer of the day.

Walker, G. R. *An Amateur.* An English writer.

Walker, George, M.D. *Alpha.* An English colonial writer, of Sydney, New South Wales.

Walker, J. ⚶.

Walker, Rev. James, B.C.L., 1712–93(?). *Jonas Salvage.* An English clergyman; Vicar of Lanlivery, 1752–93; d. at Lostwithiel.

Walker, James Barr, D.D., 1805–. *An American Citizen.* An American clergyman; b. in Philadelphia; from 1841 a resident of Mansfield, O., where he established an asylum for orphans.

Walker, John, 1732–1807. *Elocution Walker.* An English lexicographer, of London; was honored with the friendship of Dr. Johnson, Edmund Burke, etc.; d. in London.

Walker, Joseph Cooper, 1762–1810. *A Member of the Arcadian Academy of Rome.* An Irish literary critic, biographer, and historian; b. in Dublin; travelled in Italy; d. at St. Valeri, near Bray, Ireland.

Walker, Katherine C. *K. K. Kind.* An American writer of the day.

Walker, Rev. Richard, B.D. *Philomath: Oxoniensis.* An English botanist; Fellow of Magdalen Coll., Oxford.

Walker, Richard. *W.; Basil.* An English author.

Walker, Robert. *R. W.* An English author of the day.

Walker, Robert. *Tim Bobbin the Second.* An English dialect writer, of Littlemoss, Lancashire.

Walker, Rev. Samuel. *S. W.; S. W., A.B.; A Presbyter of the Church of England.* An English clergyman of the first part of the 18th century.

Walker, Rev. Samuel Abraham, M.A. *S. A. W.* An English clergyman; Trin. Coll., Dublin, 1832; Rector of St. Mary-le-Port, Bristol, 1857–70 *et seq.*

Walker, W. E. *W. E. W.* An English writer on tailoring; a London tailor (?).

Walker, William Sidney, 1795–

1846. *Edward Haselfoot.* An English man of letters; friend of Praed and others; b. at Pembroke; educ. at Eton and Trin. Coll., Cambridge; d. after a life of embarrassments.

Wall, G. *G. W.* An English botanist of the day.

Wallace, Lady Eglantine. *Lady —— ——; E. W.* A Scottish writer; daughter of Sir William Maxwell, Bart.; and married Sir James Wallace, Knt., a captain in the navy, from whom she was soon divorced.

Wallace, James. *An Odd Fellow.* A Scottish writer, of Glasgow.

Wallace, James, M.D. *J. W., M.D.* A Scottish physician; a son of James Wallace; minister of Kirkwall, Orkney; a writer of the first part of the 18th century.

Wallace, Robert Grenville. *An Officer in H. M.'s Service.* An English soldier in the East India service.

Wallace, William A. *W. A. W.* An English writer.

Waller, John Francis, LL.D., 1810–. *Iota; Jonathan Freke Slingsby.* An Irish lawyer and journalist; for many years editor of the "Dublin University Magazine"; b. at Limerick; Trin. Coll., Dublin, 1831; admitted to the Irish Bar, 1833.

Waller, Sir William, 1597–1668. *Sir W***m.* An English writer; a Parliamentary general; an "active man against the papists."

Walley, Samuel Hurd, 1805–77. *W.* An American lawyer, statesman, and banker, of Boston; b. in that city; Harv. Univ., 1826; M.C., 1853–55.

Wallington, Charles. *Πιλόμουσος.* An English editor.

Wallis, Mrs. Mary Davis (Cook). *A Lady.* An American author.

Wallis, Rev. Stamford. *A Clergyman living in the Neighborhood, etc.* An English writer of the earlier part of the 18th century.

Walmesley, Charles, D.D., F.R.S., 1721–97. *Signor Pastorini.* An English mathematician and astronomer; in 1756 was made Bishop and Apostolical Vicar of the Western District of England; d. at Bath.

Waln, Robert, Jr., 1797–1825. *The Hermit; Peter Atall.* An American poet; b. and d. in Philadelphia; received a liberal education, and devoted himself to literature.

Walpole, Rt. Hon. Horace, 4th Earl of Orford, 1717–97. *H. W.; The Hon. Mr. H——ce W——le; H***** W******; A Man; William Marshall, Gent.; Onu-

phrio Muralto; Xo-Ho. An English man of letters; b. and d. in London; educ. at Eton and Cambridge; succeeded to the peerage in 1791, but never took his seat in the House of Lords.

Walpole, Sir **Robert,** Earl of Orford, 1676–1745. *S:r R—t W—lp—le; R—— W—p—le, Esq.; R. W*****le; R***** E—l of O*****; Sir ***; Or—d; Sir Bob; Bob Booty; Bob Hush; Bob of Lyn; Mr. R. Lyn; Flimnap, the Lilliputian Premier; Iago; The Knight; A Member of the Lower House; A Member of Parliament; Punch; Robin.* An English statesman; Prime Minister, 1715–17 and 1721–42; created Earl of Orford in 1742.

Walrée, Mme **E. C. W. (Goble) van,** *Christine Müller.*

Walsh, John Henry, F.R.C.S. *Stonehenge.* An English sporting writer.

Walsh, Marie A. *Sandette.* An American novelist, of San Francisco.

Walsh, Robert, LL.D., 1784–1859. *An American recently returned from Europe.* An eminent American journalist and miscellaneous writer; b. and educ. in Baltimore; resided in Paris, 1837–59, and d. there.

Walsh, William W. *Harry Fenwood.* An American writer of the day.

Walter, Rev. **Henry,** B.D. *A Clergyman of the Church of England.* An English historian; Fellow of St. John's Coll., Cambridge; professor in the E. I. Coll., Hertford.

Walters, Robert. *George Roberts.* An English writer.

Walters, Thomas, 1757–1825. *T. W.* An English writer; b. in Portsmouth; lived in London, and d. at Portchester, Hants.

Walther, David. *D. W.* An English religious writer of the day.

Walton, W. H. *Walworth Mansfield.* An English (?) writer.

Walton, William, Esq., 1784–1857. *An English Civilian; An Eye Witness; A Friend of Truth and Peace.* An English writer; British agent at Hayti and San Domingo; d. at Oxford.

Walworth, Mansfield Tracy, 1830–73. *Hotspur.* An American; son of Chancellor Walworth; b. at Albany; Union Coll., 1849; practised law in his native city; was killed by his son at the Sturtevant House, New York City.

Wanley, Humphrey, 1671 or 2–1762. *A Good Hand.* A learned English antiquary; b. at Coventry; librarian to the Earls of Oxford.

Wanostrocht, Nicholas, Jr. *N.*

Felix. An English sporting writer; son of N. Wanostrocht, author of educational works.

Warburton, Rowland Eyles Egerton. *R. E. E. W.* An English poet and song writer.

Warburton, William, D.D., 1698–1779. *Mr. W—'s; W—m W—n; An Author; A Late Eminent Prelate; The Most Impudent Man Living; Paulus Purgantius Pedasculus.* An English divine; b. at Newark; Bishop of Gloucester, 1759–79, where he died.

Ward, ——. *A Citizen of Boston.*

Ward, ——. *A Master Mason.* An American writer.

Ward, C. A. *Feltham Burghley.* An English writer.

Ward, Crosbie, Esq. *A Member of the Dramatic Lunatic Asylum.* An Australian dramatist; M. L. C. of Christchurch, Canterbury, New Zealand.

Ward, Edward, about 1667–1731. *E. W.* An English dramatist familiarly called *Ned Ward;* b. in Oxfordshire; was almost destitute of education; an imitator of the famous "Hudibras" Butler, and wrote several burlesque poems; kept a public house in Moorfield in a genteel way, then in Clerkenwells, and lastly a punch-house in Fulwood's Rents, near Gray's Inn, where he died.

Ward, Rev. **Edward,** M.A. *An Old Friend of the Society for Promoting Christian Knowledge.* An English clergyman, of Wadham Coll., Oxford; M.A., 1799; minister of Iver, Bucks.

Ward, Miss Ellen. *Nella.* An English writer for the young.

Ward, F. O. *Fow.* An English journalist; leader-writer on the London "Times."

Ward, Rev. **Henry Dana,** A.M., –1884. *Senior Harvard.* An American writer; Harv. Univ., 1816; a renouncing Freemason, of New York.

Ward, Rev. **James Charles.** *Outis.* An English clergyman.

Ward, James Warren, 1818– *Yorick.* An American poet and prose writer; b. at Newark, N.J.; was partly educ. at the Boston High School; has resided in Cincinnati and New York City, largely engaged in literary work.

Ward, John. *Zion.* An English religious author.

Ward, Mabella Ann. *Kate Dashaway.* An American writer of the day.

Ward, Mrs. **Maria.** *The Wife of a Mormon Elder.*

Ward, Nathaniel Bagshaw, about

1790–1864. *N. B. W.* An English surgeon; for 40 years vaccinator to the National Vaccine Establishment.

Ward, Paul. *An Old Cheltonian.* An English writer of the day.

Ward, Mrs. R. *A Lady.* An English writer.

Ward, Robert Plumer, 1765–1846. *R. P. W.* An English lawyer and statesman; b. in London and d. in Chelsea.

Ward, Thomas, M.D., 1807–73. *Flaccus.* An American poet; b. at Newark, N.J.; educ. at New Jersey Coll. and Rutgers Med. Coll., N.Y.

Ward, Thomas Humphrey. *Ol. Socius.* An English editor of the day.

Ward, Townsend. *Logan.* An American writer, of Philadelphia.

Ward, William George, 1812–. *W. G. W.* An English clergyman; was for some time Math. Tutor at Christ Church, Oxford; afterwards joined the Roman Catholic Church, and became Professor of Dogmatic Theology in the R. C. Coll. of St. Edmund's, near Ware, Herts.

Wardrop, James, M.D., –1869. *A Layman.* A Scottish physician, of Edinburgh; afterwards of London; surgeon to George IV.; a strenuous Unitarian.

Ware, C. N. Cumberlege. *A Layman.* An English writer of the day.

Ware, Henry, Jr., D.D., 1794–1843. *An Unitarian Clergyman.* An eminent American minister and pulpit orator; b. at Hingham, Mass.; Harv. Univ., 1812; professor at Harv. Univ. Divinity School, 1830–42; d. at Framingham, Mass.

Ware, Rev. John Fothergill Waterhouse, 1818–81. *J. F. W. W.* An eminent Unitarian clergyman; b. in Cambridge, Mass.; d. in Milton, Mass.; minister of the Arlington Street Church, Boston, 1872–81.

Ware, Mrs. Mary Clementina. *Mary Clementina Stewart.* An English writer of the day; wife of Mr. Hibbert Ware.

Ware, Mrs. Mary (Harris). *Gertrude Glenn.* An American "Southland" poet and prose writer; b. in Tennessee; resided afterward in Alabama; in 1864 married Mr. Horace Ware; and in 1871 lived in Columbiana, Ala.

Ware, N. A. *A Southern Planter.* An American writer of the South.

Ware, William. *X.* An Irish writer.

Ware, Rev. William, A.M., 1797–1852. *Lucius M. Piso.* An American clergyman and novelist; b. at Hingham, Mass.; Harv. Univ., 1816; editor of the "Christian Examiner," 1838–44; d. at Cambridge.

Warfield, Mrs. Catharine Ann (Ware), about 1814–. *A Southern Lady;*

Two Sisters of the West. A popular American poet and novelist; b. at Natchez, Miss.; in 1868 residing on a farm in Pewee Valley, near Louisville, Ky.

Waring, Miss Anna Lætitia. *A. L. W.* An English hymn writer; b. at Neath, South Wales; "is better known through her beautiful spiritual hymns than many others whose life story has long been written."

Waring, Elijah. *Crito.* An English Friend, of Alton; but left there to reside at Neath, and afterwards became a Wesleyan minister.

Waring, John Burley. *An Architect; Hon. Botibol Bareacres.* An English artist and poet, of London.

Waring, John Scott. *J. S.; Asiaticus; Bengalensis; A Whig.* An English soldier and M.P.; engaged in the East India Service; the friend and agent of Warren Hastings.

Waring, Miss S. *S. W.* An English poet; sister of Samuel Miller Waring (1792–1827).

Waring, S. D. *S. D. W.* An American translator of the day.

Warne, Jonathan. *A Lover of the Truth.* An English anti-Quaker writer, of London, early in the 18th century.

Warner, Miss Anna B. *Amy Lothrop.* An American novelist; sister of Susan Warner; b. in New York City; daughter of Henry W. Warner, also an American author.

Warner, Rev. Beverly Ellison. *Pascarel.* An American Epis. clergyman and journalist of the day; in 1882 Rector at South Manchester, Conn.

Warner, Mrs. H. P. *H. P. W.* An American poet of the day.

Warner, Rev. Richard, 1763–1857. *An Aged Parson; A Retired Country Parson; Peter Paul Pallet.* An English clergyman and voluminous writer; b. in the parish of Marylebone, London; Curate of St. James's Parish, Bath, for 23 years; Rector of Chelwood, Somerset *w.* Great Chalfield (1809), 1827–57; d. at Chelwood.

Warner, Miss Susan, 1818–85. *E. W.; S. W.; Elizabeth Wetherell.* An American novelist; b. in New York City; for some years resided with her family on Constitution Island, in the Hudson, opposite West Point; d. at Highland Falls, N.Y.

Warner, William. *W. W.* — See "J., R." (Richard Jones).

Warren, Arthur. *Timothy Quill.* An American writer of the day.

Warren, Ira, M.D., 1806–64. *Laicus.* An American physician and journalist; b. in Hawkesburg, Canada; educ. at Brown Univ., and Kenyon Coll.; editor in Boston.

Warren, Hon. John Byrne Leicester, 1835–. *W. P. Lancaster.* An English author; M.A., Oxon.; called to the Bar at Lincoln's Inn, 1860; a magistrate for Cheshire.

Warren, S. M. *S. M. W.* An English compiler; a Swedenborgian of the day.

Warren, Samuel, D.C.L., 1807–77. *S. W.; An Attorney; Gustavus Sharp, etc.; Warren Warner, etc.* An English lawyer; b. at Racre, Denbighshire, Wales; educ. at Edinburgh; studied medicine, then law; called to the Bar at the Inner Temple, 1830; M.P., 1856–59; wrote exclusively for "Blackwood."

Warriner, Rev. **Edward A.** *A Broad Churchman.* An American poet and novelist; b. at Agawam, Mass.; Union Coll., N.Y., 1855; in 1877 Epis. Rector at Montrose, Pa.

Warter, John Wood, B.D., 1806–78. *Cedric Oldacre, of Sax-Normanbury; An Old Vicar.* An English clergyman; B.A., Oxford, 1827; Vicar of West Tarring, Worthing, Sussex; son-in-law of Robert Southey.

Warton, Joseph, D.D., 1722–1800. *Z.* An English poet and critic; b. at Dunsford, Surrey; educ. at Winchester School, and Oriel Coll., Oxford; head master of the school, 1766–93; d. in Wickham.

Warton, Thomas, 1728–90. *T. W.; Brother Tom.* An eminent English poet; younger brother of the preceding; b. at Basingstoke; Prof. of Poetry at Oxford, 1757–67; Camden Prof. of Anc. Hist. there, and Poet-Laureate, 1785–90; d. in Oxford.

Warwick, J. H. *Broadbrim.* An American Shakespeare scholar of the day.

Warwick, William Atkinson. *A. W.* An English author.

Warying, Miss Jane. *Varina.* An Irish (?) lady; a friend of Dean Swift.

Wasborough, ——. *The King.* An English writer.

Wash, Henry. *H. W.* An English compiler of school books; an educator of the day.

Washburn, Henry Stevenson. *H. S. W.* An American poet, etc., of Boston; in 1871–72, Member of the Massachusetts House of Representatives; in 1873–74, of the Massachusetts Senate.

Washburne, Miss Mary B. *Mary Morrison.* An American (?) writer of the day.

Washington, John. *J. W.* An English hydrographer to the British Admiralty; entered the navy in 1812, and was made captain in 1842.

Wasse, Rev. **Joseph,** 1672–1738. п. An English clergyman; b. in Yorkshire; educ. at Queen's Coll., Cambridge; Rector of Aynhoe, Northants., 1711–38.

Wästberg, Anna (Andersson), 1832–. *Anna Andersson.* A Swedish poet; b. at Bidtsköfle; married in 1857, and since that time has resided in Wenersborg.

Waterfield, Charles. *The Registrar of the Birmingham County Court.* An English lawyer.

Waterhouse, Benjamin, M.D., 1754–1846. *A Young Man of Massachusetts.* An eminent American physician; b. at Newport, R.I.; studied medicine in Edinburgh and Leyden, and began practice at Newport; Professor of Physics at Harv. Univ., 1783–1812; d. at Cambridge, Mass.

Waters, E. S. *E. S. W.* An American compiler, of Chicago.

Waters, Frank. *Our Bard.* An American poet, of Philadelphia; b. in that city; since his twelfth year, resident alternately in New York and Philadelphia.

Waters, John. *Flaccus.* An English poet.

Waterston, Mrs. Anna C. (Quincy). *A. C. Q. W.* An American lady; daughter of Josiah Quincy, and wife of Rev. R. C. Waterston, of Boston.

Waterston, Rev. **Robert Cassie,** A.M. *R. C. W.* An American clergyman, poet, and miscellaneous writer; b. in Kennebunk, Me., but has always lived in Boston.

Watkins, Tobias, M.D., 1780–1855. *Paul Allen.* An American author and journalist; for many years Auditor of Accounts at Washington, where he died.

Watson, Miss A. *A. de Yonge.* An English poet.

Watson, Alexander. *A Layman.* A Scottish poet and essayist; town clerk of Port Glasgow.

Watson, Alfred E. T. *R.* An English sporting writer of the day; London correspondent of the New York "Spirit of the Times."

Watson, E. H. *E. H. W.* An American (?) author of the day.

Watson, Rev. **Edward John,** M.A. *An Ex-Curate.* An English clergyman;

Christ Coll., Cambridge, 1869; Curate of Frome-Selwood, 1872–74 *et seq.*

Watson, Forbes, –1871. *A Medical Man.* An English botanist.

Watson, George Bott Churchill. *Medicus.* An English physician.

Watson, James. *A Member of the College of Justice.* A Scottish advocate.

Watson, Jean L. *J. L. W.* A Scottish writer of the day.

Watson, John. *A Layman of the Church of England.* An English writer.

Watson, Richard, D.D., 1737–1816. *A Christian Whig; A Consistent Protestant.* An English clergyman; b. at Heversham, Westmoreland; Bishop of Llandaff, 1782–1816.

Watson, Walker, –1854. *The Poet of Kirkintillock.* A Scottish poet; author of "Jockie's Far Awa'."

Watson, William Robinson, A.M., 1799–1864. *Hamilton.* An American political writer; b. in South Kingstown, R.I.; Brown Univ., 1823; lived and d. at Providence, R.I.; for nearly 40 years was devoted almost exclusively to politics.

Watterson, Henry, 1832–. *Asa Trenchard.* An American journalist; b. at Washington; but from 1868 has been at Louisville most of the time, part owner and editor-in-chief of the "Courier-Journal."

Watterston, George. *A Foreigner; The Wanderer.* An American miscellaneous writer; librarian of Congress, 1825–29.

Watts, Phillips. *Felix Balfour.* An English dramatist and journalist.

Watts, S. *S. W.* An English writer.

Watts, Thomas, 1811–69. *P. P. C. R.* An eminent English linguist; b. and d. in London; assistant in the British Museum, 1837–69.

Watts, Walter Henry. *W. H. W.; An Old Reporter.* An English journalist; wrote the "Annual Biography and Obituary" from 1817 to 1831.

Wauchope, John. *J. W.* A Scottish writer, of Edmondstone; Lieut.-Col. of the Mid Lothian Militia.

Waugh, Rev. John, A.M. *Chor-Episcopus.* An American clergyman; Hon. A.M. at Hamilton Coll., N.Y., 1852.

Way, Arthur S. *Avia.* An English scholar and translator of the day.

Way, B. *Musidorus.* An English scholar; contributor to the "Microcosm" of Eton Coll., 1787.

Way, Rev. Lewis. *Basilicus.* An English clergyman, of Stanstead, Sussex.

Wayland, Rev. Heman Lincoln, D.D., 1830–. *Rev. Philetus Dobbs, D.D.* An American Bapt. clergyman; son of Dr. Francis Wayland; b. at Providence; Brown Univ., 1849; Pastor of the Third Bapt. Church, at Worcester, Mass., 1854–61; editor at Philadelphia, 1872–84 *et seq.*

Weale, William Henry James. *W. H. J. W.* An English publisher, of London.

Weamys, Mrs. Anna. *Mrs. A. W.; A Young Gentlewoman, Mrs. A. W.* An English poet of the 17th century.

Weatherly, Rev. Frederick Edward, M.A. *A Resident M.A.* An English clergyman, poet, and prose writer of the day; Brasenose Coll., Oxford, 1871.

Weaver, Lieut. ——. *A Seaman.*

Weaver, Rev. Robert. *A Quadragenarian.* An English Cong. minister.

Weaver, Thomas. *Job Shuttle.*

Webb, Charles Henry, 1831–. *John Paul.* An American journalist; b. at Rouse's Point, N.Y.; became a well-known humorous correspondent of the New York "Tribune," and travelled in Europe in that capacity in 1876.

Webb, Charles Hull, 1843–. *Caqueteur; Jack Manley; Matt Marling; Pierce Cutting.* An American writer of the day for the young.

Webb, Col. F. *Philalethes.* An English writer; a Shakespearian scholar.

Webb, Foster. *Telarius; Vedastus.* An English poet; a clerk to a merchant of London; amused himself with translating from the Latin classics for the "Gent. Mag.," 1740 *et seq.* He d. in his 22d year.

Webb, Francis, Esq., 1735–1815. *Verus.* An English writer; b. at Taunton; was settled in the ministry, and afterwards in London, but left it after about ten years' service, and distinguished himself in the literary world by many elegant publications on various subjects. About the year 1810 he went to reside in Somersetshire.

Webb, James Watson, 1802–84. *An Amateur Traveller.* An American journalist and politician; b. at Claverack, N.Y.; was an officer in the U.S. army, 1819–27; editor of the "New York Courier," 1827–29, and of the New York "Courier and Inquirer," 1829–61; U.S. Minister to Brazil, 1861–69; d. in New York City.

Webb, Joseph, 1735–87. *Josephus Tela.* An American writer; Grand Master of Freemasons in America; d. in Boston.

Webb, Mrs. Laura S. *Stannie Lee.* An American poet and teacher; wife of Dr. W. T. Webb; in 1868 a teacher in the St. Joseph's Institute, Mobile.

Webb, Philip Carteret, 1700-70. *P. C. W.; A Gentleman of Lincoln's Inn; A Member of the House of Commons.* An English antiquary; Joint-Solicitor of the Treasury, 1756-65.

Webb, Rev. William. *The Protestant Rector of Tixall, Stafford.* An English clergyman.

Webb, William H. *Magpie.* An American writer.

Webb, William Locock. *W. L. W.* An English writer of the day.

Webbe, Cornelius. *A Person lately about Town.* An English *littérateur;* for many years proof-reader of the "Quarterly Review," and a contributor to several periodicals.

Webber, Charles Edmund. *C. E. W.; An Officer of the Royal Engineers.* An English soldier; 1st Lieut. of the R.E. in 1855; served throughout the campaigns of 1858 and 1859 in Central India.

Webber, Charles Wilkins, 1819-56. *C. W. Eimi.* An American adventurer and journalist; b. at Russellville, Ky.; went to Central America in 1855; joined Walker in Nicaragua, and was there killed.

Webber, Samuel, M.D., 1797-1880. *S.* An American physician; b. in Cambridge, Mass.; Harv. Univ., 1815; practised his profession at Charlestown, N.Y., 1822-80, and d. there.

Webster, Alexander, D.D., 1707-84. *A. W—b—r, M.A.* An eminent Scottish minister, of the Tolbooth Church, Edinburgh, 1737-84.

Webster, Mrs. Augusta (Davies). *Cecil Home.* An English poet and scholar, of London; daughter of Admiral George Davies; married Thomas Webster, Fellow of Trin. Coll., Cambridge; she commenced her literary career in 1860; resident, 1877, in Victoria Street, London.

Webster, Ezekiel, A.M., 1780-1829. *Cato.* An American lawyer; b. in Salisbury, N.H.; Dart. Coll., 1804; studied law, and practised his profession at Boscawen, N.H.; d. at Concord, N.H.

Webster, Rev. George Edis, M.A. *A Minister of the Church of England.* An English clergyman; Rector of Grundisburgh, Woodbridge, Suffolk, 1832-70 *et seq.*

Webster, Rev. James. *One of the Country Party; A Sincere Lover of the Church and State.* A Scottish clergyman, of the first part of the 18th century; minister of the Tolbooth Church, Edinburgh.

Webster, Noah, LL.D., 1758-1843. *An American; Aristides; Aurelius; B.; Candor; Curtius; A Federalist; Hampden; Honorius; Lover of Stability; Marcellus; Peace and Justice; Seneca; Sidney; Trumbull.* An eminent American lexicographer; b. in Hartford, Conn.; grad. at Yale Coll. in 1778; resided at New Haven, Conn., 1798-1812; at Amherst, Mass., 1812-22; again at New Haven, 1822-43; and d. there.

Webster, Pelatiah, A.M., 1725-95. *A Citizen of the United States.* An American patriot; b. at Lebanon, Conn.; Yale Coll., 1746; preached at Greenwich, Mass., 1748-49; a merchant of Philadelphia, about 1755-95, and d. there.

Webster, Rev. Thomas, B.D., 1780-1840. *W.; T. W.* An English clergyman; Rector of St. Botolph, Cambridge, and Vicar of Oakington.

Webster, William, D.D., 1689-1758. *The Draper; A Draper of London; A Friend to the Government; Richard Hooker, Esq., of the Inner Temple.* An English clergyman; Vicar of Ware and of Thundridge, Herts., 1741-58.

Weed, Thurlow, 1797-1884. *T. W.* An American journalist and politician; for many years proprietor and editor of the "Albany Evening Argus."

Weekes, John Ernest. *J. E. W.* An English writer of the day.

Weeks, Mrs. Helen Campbell. *Campbell Wheaton.* An American writer of the day for the young.

Wehlen, Feodor zu, 1821-. *Feodor Wehl.* A German author; b. at Kunzendorf in Silesia; was general intendant of theatres, 1874-82 *et seq.,* at Stuttgart.

Weidemeyer, John William, 1819-. *John W. Montclair.* An American broker and poet; b. at Fredericksburg, Va.; from 1875 has resided in New York City.

Weitzel, Miss Sophy Winthrop. *Sophy Winthrop.* An American novelist of the day.

Welby, Mrs. Amelia B. (Coppuck), 1821-52. *Amelia.* An American poet; b. at St. Michaels, Md.; in 1838 married George B. Welby, a merchant of Louisville, Ky.; afterwards lived and d. there.

Welchman, Rev. Edward, about 1665-1739. *A Minister in the Country.* Magdalen Coll., Oxford, 1684; Archdeacon of Cardigan, 1727-39.

Weld, Theodore Dwight, 1803-. *T. D. W.; Wythe.* An American anti-slavery reformer; b. at Hampton, Conn.; educ. at Hamilton Coll.; studied theol. at the Lane Sem.; in 1854 established a high school at Eagleswood, N.J.; in 1864 removed to Hyde Park, Mass.

Welfitt, William. *Civis.* An English compiler.

Wellbeloved, Rev. Charles, 1769–1858. *The Curator of the Antiquities.* An English clergyman; a Unitarian divine, of York from 1792 to the time of his death in that city in 1858; was for 37 years (1803–39) at the head of the Manchester College.

Wellman, Mary W. *Prairie Bird.* An American poet.

Wells, Charles Jeremiah, about 1798–. *H. L. Howard.* An eminent English poet; an early and intimate friend of Keats.

Wells, David, Esq. *Observator.* An English writer.

Wells, Edward, D.D., –1727. *A Minister of the Church of England.* An English clergyman; A.M., Oxford, 1693; Rector of Cottesbuch, Leicestershire, 1717–27.

Wells, J. C. *An Attorney-at-Law.* An American writer of the day.

Wells, John G. *Gracchus Americanus.* An American writer of the day.

Wells, Samuel A. *An Underwriter.* An American business man of Boston(?); President of the Atlas Insurance Co.

Wells, Prof. William, 1820–. *Uncle Will.* An American scholar; b. in New York City; Hon. A.M., Williams Coll., 1856; Professor at Genesee Coll., N.Y., 1852–65; and at Union Coll, N.Y., from 1865.

Wells, William Benjamin, 1809–. *Cinna.* A Canadian journalist; in 1867 judge of the Co. Kent, U.C.

Wells, William Charles, M.D., F.R.S., 1757–1817. *Marcus.* An eminent physician; b. in Charleston, S.C.; studied medicine in Edinburgh, 1775–78; resided in the United States, 1780–84; and in London, 1785–1817, and d. there.

Welsh, James Jacob. *J. J. W.* An English biographer.

Welsted, Leonard, 1689–1747. *L. W.; A Gentleman; Palemon.* An English poet and miscellaneous writer; b. at Abington, Northants.; held a position in the Tower of London, where he died.

Welton, Richard, D.D. Ευσεβεῖς. An English clergyman; Rector of St. Mary's, Whitechapel, London, the first part of the 18th century.

Wentworth, Dorothea. *An Impartial Hand.* An Irish (?) writer, of the 18th century.

Wentworth, John, LL.D., 1736–1820. *The Governor.* An American statesman; Governor of New Hampshire, 1767–75;

was a loyalist, and removed to Nova Scotia, where he was Lieut.-Governor, 1792–1808; and d. at Halifax.

Wentworth-Fitzwilliam, Charles William, 4th Earl, 1748–1833. *A Venerated Nobleman; Viscount Milton.* An English nobleman; educ. at Eton, and King's Coll., Cambridge; Lord-Lieut. of Ireland, 1794–95; d. at Milton House, near Peterborough.

Werner, Franz von, 1836–81. *Murad Efendi.* A German writer; b. at Vienna; entered the Turkish service, and in 1877 was Minister Resident at Court of Stockholm, and after that at the Hague, where he died.

Wesley, Rev. Charles, 1708–88. *Bard of Epworth.* An English clergyman; b. in Epworth; preached among the Methodists till his death in London.

Wesley, Rev. John, 1703–91. *Anglicanæ Presbyter; The Greatest Hypocrite in England; A Lover of Free Grace; A Lover of Mankind and Common Sense; A Methodist; Philalethes.* An eminent English Meth. preacher and reformer; b. at Epworth, Lincolnshire; labored diligently in the ministry, 1739–91.

Wesley, Mehetabel, afterwards **Wright.** *Bard of Epworth.* An English poet; b. in Epworth; sister of Charles and John Wesley.

Wesley, Rev. Samuel, Sr., 1660 or 68–1735. *Bard of Epworth; A Country Divine; Mr. D–nt–n; A Schollar.* An English clergyman; Rector of Epworth.

Wesley, Rev. Samuel, Jr., about 1691–1739. *Bard of Epworth.* An English clergyman; b. in Epworth; Head Master of Tiverton School, 1732–39.

West, Aaron. *A. W.* An English author.

West, Sir Edward, 1783–1828. *A Fellow of the University College, Oxford.* An English jurist; Recorder of Bombay, 1823, and on the establishment of the Supreme Court, Chief Justice; d. at Poonah.

West, Edward. *E. W.* An English poet and prose writer.

West, F. H. *One of his Sons.* An English writer; son of Francis Athon West.

West, Gilbert, LL.D., 1706–56. *Edmund Spenser, the Poet.* An English poet; educ. at Eton and Oxford; Clerk of the Privy Council, 1752; and afterwards Under-Treasurer of Chelsea Hospital.

West, James B. *A Naval Officer.* An English writer of the day.

West, Rev. John Otho, M.A., 1829–.

Omicron. An English clergyman; b. at St. Agnes; Rector of St. Pinnock, Liskeard, 1870–83 *et seq.*

West, Rev. **John Rowland,** M.A. *J. R. W.* An English clergyman; Trin. Coll., Cambridge, 1832; Vicar of Wrawby, Glandford Bridge, 1847–83 *et seq.*

West, Joshua. *Harry Helicon, Esq.* An English satirical poet.

West, Richard, –1726. *The New Lord Chancellor.* An eminent Irish jurist; Lord Chancellor of Ireland, 1725–26.

West, Samuel, D.D., 1738–1808. *The Old Man.* An eminent American clergyman; b. at Martha's Vineyard; Harv. Univ., 1761; pastor of Hollis Street Church, Boston, 1789–1808, where he died.

West, William, 1770–1854. *An Old Bookseller; One of the Old School; W. W.* An English bookseller; b. at Whaddon, Croyden, Surrey; was in business at Cork and at London; d. in the Charter-House, London.

West, Rev. **William,** B.A. *The Editor of that Edition; Incumbent of the English Church, Nairn.* An English clergyman; Trin. Coll., Dublin, 1856; Rector of Puttenham, Guildford, 1882–83 *et seq.*

Westcott, Thompson, 1820–. *Joe Miller, Jr.* An American lawyer and journalist; b. in Philadelphia; admitted to the Bar of that city, 1841, and editor of the "Sunday Dispatch," Philadelphia, 1848–70 *et seq.*

Westerton, Charles. *One of the Churchwardens.* An English miscellaneous writer.

Westlake, William Colson. *A Merchant.* An English Friend, of Southampton.

Westley, F. C. *F. C. W.* An English writer, of Cheltenham.

Westmacott, Charles Molloy, 1787–1868. *Bernard Blackmantle.* An English journalist; proprietor and editor of the "Age," London; d. at Paris.

Westmoreland, John Fane, 11th Earl of, D.C.L., 1784–1859. *An Officer employed in his Army.* An eminent English soldier and diplomatist; d. at Althorpe House, London.

Westmoreland, Mrs. **Maria Elizabeth (Jourdan),** 1815–. *Mystery.* An American "Southland" writer; b. in Georgia; in 1832 married Dr. W. F. Westmoreland, of Atlanta, where in 1869 she still resided.

Weston, Ambrose. *A. W.* An English financial writer.

Weston, Rt. Hon. **Edward.** *A Country Gentleman.* An English civilian; Privy Counsellor of Ireland, 1746.

Weston, Edward Payson, 1819–. *The Pedestrian.* An American teacher; Bowdoin Coll., 1839; in 1876 opened a school for young ladies at Highland Park, near Chicago, Ill.

Weston, H. H. *Three Friends.* An American writer of the day.

Weston, Rev. **Stephen,** B.D., 1747–1830. *S. W., F.R.S., F.S.A.; The Englishman Abroad; An Admirer of a Great Genius; An Oxonian; P. A. R.; Philoxenus Secundus; A Trimester; Terræ Filius.* An English classical and oriental scholar; b. in Exeter; d. in London.

Wetham, R. *R. W., D.P.* A Roman Catholic; President of the College of Douay.

Wetherby, ——. *A British American.* A Canadian political writer.

Wetherspoon, George, Jr. *Spectator.* An American journalist of the day.

Wetmore, Henry Carmer, 1823–. *A Penciler.* An American poet and prose writer; b. in New York City; son of Apollos Russell Wetmore (?).

Wetmore, John P. *Jonah.* An American bicycler; secretary of the Elizabeth (N.J.) Wheelmen.

Wetterbergh, Carl Anton, 1804–. *Onkel Adam.* A Swedish novelist; b. at Jönköping; a physician in the regiment of Jutland; since 1850 has devoted himself to literature at Stockholm.

Weyland, John, Esq. *One of H. M.'s Justices of the Peace for the Three Inland Counties.* An English Justice for Oxford, Berks., and Surrey; helped establish the "British Review," of which he was for some time the reputed editor.

Whalley, Thomas Sedgwick, D.D., 1746–1828. *A Beautiful and Unfortunate Young Lady.* An English clergyman, poet, and novelist; more than 50 years Rector of Hagworthingham in the Fens.

Wharton, Charles Henry, D.D., 1748–1833. *C. H. W.; The Chaplain of that Society; Dr. Gauden; An Inhabitant of the State of Maryland.* An American Epis. clergyman; b. in St. Mary's Co., Md.; was a Roman Catholic priest, but became a Protestant; Rector of St. Mary's Church, Burlington, N.J., 1798–1833.

Wharton, Francis, D.D., LL.D., 1820–. *F. W.* An eminent American clergyman; b. in Philadelphia; Yale Coll., 1839; practised law in his native city till 1855; professor at the Epis. Divinity School at Cambridge, Mass., 186 –1885 *et seq.*

Wharton, George F. *Orleanian.* An American novelist, of New Orleans.

Wharton, Richard, Esq., M.P., F.R.S. *R. W.* An English barrister-at-law; Joint Secretary of the Treasury; a poet and prose writer.

Wharton, Thomas, Marquis of Wharton, about 1640–1715. *Lord W****n; M—s W—n.* An eminent English Whig statesman; Lord Lieutenant of Ireland, 1708; Lord Privy Seal, 1714; said to be the author of the famous ballad of "Lilli-Burlero."

Whately, Miss E. Jane. *E. J. W.* An English lady; daughter to Richard Whately.

Whately, H. *H. W.* An English writer of the day.

Whately, Richard, D.D., 1787–1863. *The Same Author; An Episcopalian; Rev. Aristarchus Newlight; A Country Pastor; John Search; Konx Ompax.* An English divine; b. in London; Oriel Coll., Oxford, 1809; Archbishop of Dublin, 1831–63, where he died.

Whatley, Robert. *R. W.* An English clergyman; Prebendary of York; a writer early in the 18th century.

Wheeler, A. O. *A. O. W.* An American writer of the day, of North Carolina.

Wheeler, Alfred Allison, 1855–. *Eleven Sophomores.* An American correspondent and *littérateur;* b. at San Francisco; Harv. Univ., 1876; spent in Europe, 1876–79; has, since 1879, been busily occupied at the West.

Wheeler, Andrew C., 1825–. *Nym Crinkle; Trinculo.* An American journalist; art critic of the N.Y. "World."

Wheeler, C. A. *C. A. W.* An English sporting writer of the day.

Wheeler, Major C. C. *Crispus.* An American journalist, of Brooklyn, N.Y.

Wheeler, Charles Stearns, about 1818–43. *C. S. W.* An American scholar; Harv. Univ., 1837; tutor there, 1838–42; d. at Leipsic.

Wheeler, David Hilton. *David Hilton.* An English writer.

Wheeler, Edmund. *An Englishman.* An English writer.

Wheeler, Miss Fanny. — See "Hart, Mrs. F. (W.)."

Wheeler, J. Talboys. *J. T. W.; A Tourist.* An English civilian; Assistant-Secretary to the Government of India in the Foreign Dept., and Secretary to the Indian Record Commission.

Wheeler, Samuel. *Investigator.* An American writer.

Wheelright, John Tyler, and Anoth-

er, 1856–. *Two Gentlemen of Harvard.* An American lawyer, of Boston; b. at Roxbury, Mass.; Harv. Univ., 1876; admitted to the Bar, 1879.

Wheelwright, Horace William, –1867. *An Old Bushman.* An English traveller, naturalist, and sporting writer.

Wheler, Charles S. *Stern Wheeler.* An American poet and journalist, of Pontiac, Mich.

Wheler, C. T. *C. T. W.* An English writer.

Whellier, Alexander. *John Gifford, Esq.* An English lawyer and law-writer.

Whelpley, Rev. Samuel, 1766–1817. *Philadelphus.* An American minister; was ordained a Bapt. preacher, 1792, and a Presbyt. preacher, 1806; Brown Univ., 1790.

Whewell, William, 1795–1866. *W. W.* An eminent English scholar; b. in Lancaster; Master of Trin. Coll., Cambridge, 1841–66, where he died.

Whicher, Mrs. Frank. *Maud Hilton.* An American author.

Whipple, Charles K. *C. K. W.* An American anti-slavery and radical writer, of Boston.

Whitaker, Rev. Charles, B.A. *Agricola.* An English clergyman; in 1880 resident at West Parade, Rhyl.

Whitaker, John, 1735–1808. *The Historian of Manchester.* An English clergyman; b. in Manchester; Rector of Ruan Langhome, Cornwall, 1778–1808, where he died.

Whitcher, Rev. B. W. *A Convert.* An American clergyman.

Whitcher, Mrs. Frances Miriam (Berry), 1812–52. *Aunt Maguire; Widow Bedott.* An American humorous writer; in 1847 married Rev. B. W. Whitcher, of the P. E. Church.

Whitcomb, James. *An Indianian.* An American economist.

Whitcomb, Otis, 1795–1882. *Uncle Josh.* An American citizen, of Swanzey, N.H.

Whitcomb, Rev. William Chalmers, 1820–64. *W. C. W.* An American Cong. minister; b. in Marlborough, N.H.; Gilmanton Theol. Sem., 1847; d. at Morehead City, N.C.

White, Adam. *Arachnophilus.* A Scottish naturalist, of Duddington, Co. of Edinburgh; assistant in the Zoölogical Dept. of the British Museum.

White, Mrs. Alexina B. *Alba.* An American writer of the day.

White, Charles, D.D., 1795–1861. *Martingale.* An American clergyman and educator; b. at Randolph, Vt.;

Dart. Coll., 1821; Andover Theol. Sem., 1824; Pres. of Wabash Coll., Crawfordsville, Ind., 1841–61, where he died.

White, Charles Albert. *Harry Birch.* An American musical composer, of Boston.

White, Charlotte. *C. W.* An English poet.

White, Eliza A. *Alex.* An American writer of the day.

White, Miss **Harriet.** *Harriet.* An Irish poet, of Cashel.

White, Rev. **James,** 1804–62. *J. W.; A Country Curate.* A Scottish clergyman and author; b. near Edinburgh; for many years lived at Bonchurch, devoted to literary pursuits; d. at Bonchurch, Isle of Wight.

White, James. *A Gentleman, a Descendant of Dame Quickly.* An English writer; a newspaper agent of London; the "Jim White" of Charles Lamb, who instituted an annual feast for chimneysweepers, "at which it was his pleasure to officiate as host and head waiter." — See Lamb's "Elia."

White, Rev. **John,** – about 1760. *A Gentleman.* An English clergyman; Fellow of St. John's Coll., Cambridge; Vicar of Nayland, Suffolk.

White, John, 1846–. *A. C. I. G., i.e., A Cornishman in Gloucestershire.* An English music printer, bookseller, and stationer at Stroud, from 1871.

White, Joseph Blanco, 1775–1841. *Don Leucadio Doblado.* A Spanish priest; first joined the Church of England, then became an avowed Unitarian, and settled in Liverpool, where he died.

White, Joseph M., about 1790–1839. *An Old Man.* An American lawyer and politician; b. in Franklin Co., Ky.; delegate to Congress from Fla., 1823–37; d. at St. Louis, Mo., in 1839.

White, Mrs. **M. E. (Harding).** *One of his Children.* An American editor; daughter of Chester Harding.

White, Mrs. **Rhoda E. (Waterman).** *Uncle Ben.* An American author.

White, Richard Grant, 1821–85. *R. G. W.; A Learned Gorilla; Saint Benjamin; U. Donough Outis: A Yankee.* An eminent American miscellaneous writer; b. in New York City; Univ. of the City of New York, 1837; studied both medicine and law, but devoted his life to literary work; d. in his native city.

White, Robert. *R. W.* An English poet, of Newcastle-upon-Tyne.

White, Mrs. **Rose C. (King).** *Roselinda.* An American poet of the day.

White, Thomas. *T. H. W.* An English writer.

White, Mrs. **W. H.** *One of them.* An American writer of the day.

White, Walter. *A Londoner.* An English author; b. at Reading; Assist.-Secretary of the Royal Society, 1844–61; from 1861 Secretary.

White, Zebulon L. *Z. L. W.* An American writer of the day.

Whitefield, Rev. **George,** 1714–70. *Rev. Mr. G—— W—te—d; Wh*********d; The Mock Preacher.* An eminent English Meth. preacher; b. in Gloucester; came to the U.S. in 1737, and again in 1738, and spent the rest of his life here, often preaching in the open air. D. at Newburyport, Mass. During his life he preached 18,000 sermons, crossed the Atlantic seven times, and travelled many thousand miles.

Whitefoord, Caleb, 1734–1810. *Emendator; Junia; Papirius Cursor.* A Scottish man of letters; b. in Edinburgh; became a wine merchant of London, where he died.

Whitehead, Mrs. **C. B.** *Josephine Jackson.* An American writer of the day.

Whitehead, Rev. **Henry,** M.A. *The Senior Curate of St Luke's, Berwick Street.* An English clergyman; Lincoln Coll., Oxford, 1850; Vicar of Brampton, Cumberland, 1874–83 *et seq.*

Whitehead, Mrs. **S. R.** *A Scotch Minister's Daughter.*

Whitehead, Hon. **William Adee,** 1810–84. An American writer; b. in Newark, N.J.; Collector of Customs at Key West, Fla., 1830–38; afterwards connected with different R. R. Co.'s; resident at Newark, 1843–84; d. at Perth Amboy, N.J.

Whitehouse, W. F. *Agricola.* An English colonial writer; a sugar farmer, of Jamaica.

Whiteing, Richard, 1840–. *Mr. Sprout.* An English journalist; correspondent, at Paris, of two journals of London and New York, 1875–79 *et seq.;* b. in London; lives in Paris.

Whitelaw, Rev. **John M.** *M—— W——.* A Scottish minister, of Athelstaneford.

Whiteway, Miss ——. *Winter Daisy.* An English writer of the day.

Whiting, Henry, 1790–1851. *An Officer of the Army at Detroit.* An American soldier; b. at Lancaster, Mass.; entered the U.S. army in 1808; became brigadier-general in 1847; d. at St. Louis, Mo.

Whiting, Sydney. *A Minister of*

the Interior. An English writer of the day, of London.

Whitling, Henry John. *Nil.* An English traveller.

Whitley, Jonas E., 1849–. *J. E. W.; Nick.* An American writer of the day.

Whitman, Mrs. Sarah Helen (Power), 1803–78. *Helen.* An American poet; widow of John Winslow Whitman, a lawyer, of Boston; b., resided chiefly, and d. at Providence, R.I.

Whitman, Walter, 1819–. *Walt; The Good Gray Poet.* An American poet; b. at West Hills, L.I.; since 1874 of Camden, N.J.

Whitmarsh, Caroline Snowdon. *Hetty Holyoke.* — See "Guild, Mrs. C. S. (W.)."

Whitmarsh, William Burt. *W. B. W.* An English poet of the day.

Whitmore, Rev. John. *A Suffolk Clergyman.* An English writer.

Whitmore, William Henry, 1836–. *W. H. W.* An American genealogist and politician; b. and lives in Boston.

Whitney, Mrs. Adeline Dutton (Train), 1824–. *A. D. T. W.* A popular American novelist; b. in Boston; wife of Seth D. Whitney, of Milton, Mass.

Whitney, Henry Austin, A.M. *H. A. W.* An American biographer; b. in Boston; Harv. Univ., 1846; in 1880 *et seq.* president of the Boston & Providence R. R. Company, residing in Boston.

Whitney, Mrs. Louisa (Goddard), 1819–83. *L. W.* An American lady; wife of Prof. James Dwight Whitney, of Harv. Univ., Cambridge; was one of the pupils at the Ursuline Convent, in Charlestown, Mass., at the time of its burning; d. at Cambridge.

Whitney, Moses, Jr. *Four of Us; Trismegistus.* An American writer, of Boston, engaged in mercantile pursuits.

Whiton, Rev. James Morris, Ph.D., 1833–. *An Orthodox Minister of the Gospel.* An American educator; b. in Boston; Yale Coll., 1853; Yale Divinity School, 1857; pastor at Newark, N.J., 1865–85 *et seq.*

Whittaker, Frederick, 1838–. *Launce Poyntz.* An American writer of the day.

Whittier, John Greenleaf, 1808–. *Margaret Smith.* An eminent American poet; b. near Haverhill, Mass.; from 1876, of Peabody, Mass.; spent his first 20 years on his father's farm; has since resided in Boston, Hartford (Conn.), Philadelphia, Amesbury, and finally at Peabody.

Whittier, Matthew Francis, 1812–82. *Ethan Spike.* An American writer; brother of the preceding; in the Boston Custom House, 1868–81; d. in Boston.

Whittlesey, Oscar C. *Ben Bloomer.* An American writer of the day.

Whitty, Edward Michael, 1827–60. *The Stranger in Parliament.* An English journalist, of London and of Belfast; b. in Liverpool; educ. there and in Germany; removed to Melbourne, and d. there.

Whitty, J. M. *Captain Rock in London.* An English journalist, of Liverpool, Dublin, and London; father of the preceding.

Whitworth, Richard. *Veridicus.* An English politician; M.P. for Stafford, 1769.

Whytehead, Rev. Thomas, M.A., 1815–43. *An Undergraduate.* An English clergyman and hymn writer; b. at Thormanby, Yorks.; St. John's Coll., Cambridge, 1837; principal of the Bishops' Coll. in New Zealand, where he died.

Wickenden, Rev. William, B.A., about 1801–. *The Bard of the Forest.* An English poet; at the age of 24 became a sizar of St. John's Coll., Cambridge, and afterwards held two curacies in Gloucestershire.

Wickins, Stephen B. *S. B. W.* An English biographer.

Wickliffe, Robert, Jr., –1850. *R. W., Jr.; William Pitt.* An American political writer, of Louisville, Ky.; Chargé d'Affaires to Sardinia, 1843–48; d. in his native city.

Wickstead, John. *A Fellow-Townsman.* An English attorney, of Shrewsbury.

Widdemer, Irene. *Ireland Ward.* An American novelist.

Wieland, Christoph Martin, 1733–1813. *The German Voltaire.* A celebrated German poet; from 1792 passed his life near Weimar.

Wierzbicki, Felix Paul, M.D., –1861. *Philokalist.* A Polish-American, of California, 1848–61.

Wiffen, Jeremiah Holmes, 1792–1836. *Three Friends.* An English Friend; b. at Woburn, Beds.; librarian of the Duke of Bedford, at Woburn Abbey, 1821–36; resided in Froxfield, 1828–36, and d. there.

Wight, Rev. J. Ambrose. *Ambrose.* An American clergyman, of Bay City, Mich.

Wightman, Mrs. **Julia** (**Bainbrigge**). *Mrs. C. W.* An English religious writer; wife of Charles Wightman.

Wightwick, George, 1802-72. *Henry Vernon.* An English architect; a poet and dramatist; b. at Albrighton; practised his profession at Plymouth, 1829-50; d. at Portishead.

Wigram, Herbert. *H. W.* A British colonial lawyer of the day, of Madras.

Wigram, S. R. *Hookanit Bee, Esquire.* An English poet.

Wikoff, Henry. *An Idler; A Rising Diplomatist; A New Yorker.* An American lawyer; b. in Philadelphia, where he studied law and was admitted to the Bar; in 1834 Hon. A.B. at Yale Coll.; removed to New York City, and became a journalist; resided in London, 1874-84, where he died.

Wilberforce, Rev. **Henry William**, 1809-73. z; *A Clerical Member of the Convocation.* An English clergyman; b. at Clapham; Oriel Coll., Oxford, 1830; became a Roman Catholic in 1850.

Wilberforce, Samuel, D.D., 1805-73. *A Country Clergyman; The Cowkeeper.* An English clergyman; son of William Wilberforce. "In my own recollections of the "John Bull" about that period [1827], there survive three topics, repeated till they were stale enough. The first was *The Cowkeeper*, that is, Mr. Wilberforce's eldest [third (?)] son, who had been persuaded by the religious secretary of a Milk Company to take its stock, and who had been ruined by an unexampled drought." — T. MOZLEY'S "Reminiscences," Vol. I., p. 123.

Wilbur, Asa. *A Layman.* An American theologian; b. in Sidney, Me.; early removed to Boston, and for 35 years pursued a mechanical profession in that city.

Wilburn, George T. *Sam Simple.* An American writer of the day.

Wilcox, Orlando Bolivar, 1822-. *Walter March.* An American soldier and lawyer; b. at Detroit, Mich.; West Point, 1847; U.S. regular army from 1866.

Wilcox, Phineas Bacon, 1706-1863. *A Member of the Bar.* An American lawyer; b. in Middletown, Conn.; Yale Coll., 1821; studied law, and practised at Columbus, O., 1823-63, and d. there.

Wilde, Lady **Jane Francesca Speranza**, 1830-. *Speranza.* An Irish poet; the youngest daughter of James Elgee, Esq.; in 1851 married Sir William Robert Wills Wilde, Knt., of Moyteura, Cong., Co. Mayo, Ireland.

Wildegoose, Charles. *C. W.; An Old Resident in the Parish of Slaverton.* An English writer.

Wilder, Alexander, M.D., F.A.S., F.A.A., 1823-. *A. W.; Merlin; Plautus.* An American editor and *littérateur;* b. in Verona, N.Y.; from 1858 till 1871 on the staff of the New York "Evening Post"; author of several philosophical, medical, etc., works; assist.-editor of "The Platonist"; now (1885) resident at Newark (Roseville), N.J.

Wilding, Rev. **Charles James**, M.A. *C. J. W.* An English clergyman; Trin. Coll., Cambridge, 1848; Vicar of Upper Arley, Bewdley, 1862-83 *et seq.*

Wildman, Albert Charles, 1831-. *The Cornish Chough; Our Boy Jack; Whachum.* An English journalist, of Penzance, 1851-77 *et seq.*

Wildman, Thomas. *Its Present Owner.* An English gentleman; owner of Newstead Abbey.

Wileman, W. *W. W.* An English religious writer of the day.

Wiley, Mrs. **Mary** (**Evans**). *Margaret Stilling.* An American "Southland" writer; a native and resident of Amelia Co., Va.; since the war married Mr. William Wiley.

Wilkes, John, 1727-97. *J——— W———, Esq.; W****s.* An English politician; b. at Clerkenwell; educ. at Leyden; M.P. from 1757; commenced the "North Briton" in 1762; Chamberlain of London, 1779-97; and d. in that city.

Wilkie, Frank B., 1830-. *Poliuto.* An American writer of the day.

Wilkins, Edward G. P., 1830-61. *Personne.* An American journalist; writer of dramatic articles for the New York "Herald," the New York "Leader," and the "Saturday Express."

Wilkins, Mrs. **Harriet Annie.** *Harriet Annie.* A Canadian poet, of Hamilton.

Wilkins, Rev. **Isaac**, 1741-1830. *A. W., Farmer; A Farmer.* An American loyalist; for about 30 years Rector at West Chester, N.Y.

Wilkins, Rev. **Thomas.** *T. W.* An English poet of the 18th century.

Wilkins, William A. *Hiram Greene.* An American writer of the day.

Wilkins, William Walker. *W. W.* An English literary antiquary.

Wilkinson, A. *A. W.* An English author, of Greenwich.

Wilkinson, M. J. *M. J. W.* An English writer; a member of the family of Michael Wilkinson, a missionary to India.

Wilkinson, James John Garth, 1812-. *J. J. G. W.* An eminent English Swedenborgian; b. in London; translated many of the works of Swedenborg.

Wilkinson, John. *A Blockade Runner.* An American captain in the Confederate States Navy; a writer of the day.

Wilkinson, Rebecca. *A Lady.* An English religious writer.

Wilkinson, Tate, 1739-1803. *The Wandering Patentee.* An English actor and theatrical manager, of York and Hull.

Wilkinson, W. C. T. *W. C. T. W.* An English writer of the day.

Wilkinson, Rev. William Francis. *A Churchman; W. F. W.* An English clergyman; Vicar of St. Werburgh's, Derby; previously Theological Tutor in Cheltenham College.

Wilks, Rev. Samuel Charles, A.B. *A Clerical Member of the Society for promoting Christian Knowledge.* An English clergyman; St. Edmund Hall, Oxford; Rector of Nursling, near Southampton; and editor of the "Christian Observer."

Willard, Joseph, D.D., LL.D., 1738-1804. *Sympathes.* An eminent American clergyman; b. at Biddeford, Me.; Harv. Coll., 1765; president of that institution, 1781-1804; d. at New Bedford, Mass.

Willard, Samuel, D.D., 1775-1859. *A Friend of Youth.* An American Cong. clergyman; b. at Petersham, Mass.; Harv. Univ., 1803; Pastor at Deerfield, Mass., 1807-59; d. in that town.

Willcocks and Dawson. *W*****cks and D****n.* Irish bankers, of the city of Dublin.

Willes, Irwin, -1871. *Argus.* An English sporting writer.

Williams, ——. *Sir Ferdinando Fungus, Gent.* An English writer, of Wadham College.

Williams, Mrs. Bessie W. (Johnson). *Constance.* An American "Southland" writer; b. at Beaufort, S.C.; in 1868, of Marietta, Ga.

Williams, Mrs. Catherine R., 1790-. *C. R. W.; A Rhode Islander.* An American author; b. in Providence, R.I.

Williams, David, 1738-1816. *Philander; An Old Statesman.* An English literary and religious projector; b. near Cardigan; preached as a dissenting minister for some years; but in 1776 opened a chapel in London, on the avowed principles of deism, which was, however, soon deserted and closed; he is best known as the founder of the "Literary Fund," by which he was himself supported near the close of his life; d. in London.

Williams, Edward, 1745-1826. *Iolo Morganwg.* A Welsh bard and editor; b. at Llancarvan, Glamorganshire; d. at Flemingstone, near his birthplace.

Williams, Edward, 1774-1854. *Iolo Fardd Glas.* A Welsh bard and writer of prose and verse; d. at the workhouse of Peny-bont, Glamorganshire.

Williams, Edward (1797-1854), and Another. *Berkeley Men.* An American statistician and journalist, of New York City.

Williams, Miss Eva. *Viva.* An American writer of the day.

Williams, Miss Helen Maria, 1762-1827. *H—— M—— W.; A Young Lady.* An English poet; b. in London; resided in Paris, 1788-1827, and d. there.

Williams, Henry Llewellyn, Jr. *H. L. W.; An Old Traveller.* An American novelist of the day.

Williams, Sir Hugh, 1802-76. *Cadvan.* An elegant Welsh writer; b. at Bodelwyddan; translator of "Uncle Tom's Cabin" into Welsh.

Williams, Rev. Isaac, B.D., 1802-65. *E; I. W.; Contributor to Tracts for the Times; The Writer of these Tracts.* An English poet and mystic; b. in Wales; Trin. Coll., 1826; d. at Stinchcombe, Gloucs.

Williams, Jackson Muspratt. *A Member of the Univ. of Cambridge.* An English writer.

Williams, John, -1818. *Anthony Pasquin.* An English poet and dramatist; came to the United States, and was the editor of a Democratic paper; d. at Brooklyn, N.Y., in great poverty.

Williams, John A. B. *A Trooper.* An American soldier in the civil war.

Williams, John Dingwall. *A Peninsula Officer.* An English writer.

Williams, John H. *B. Dadd.* An American writer of the day.

Williams, Rev. Joseph Stone. *J. S. W.* An English clergyman; in 1870 Vicar of Hendon, Middlesex Co., London.

Williams, Mary. *M. W.* An English poet and religious writer.

Williams, Rev. Morris, M.A. *Nicander.* A Welsh clergyman, of Llanrhyddhad Rectory, Holyhead, 1858-70 *et seq.*

Williams, Moses. *Neighbor Smith.* An American merchant, of Boston; resident in Roxbury.

Williams, R. *A Merchant.* An English writer, early in the 18th century.

Williams, R. D. *Shamrock.* An American poet of the day.

Williams, Robert Folkstone, about 1805–. *A Prime Minister.* An eminent English scholar and miscellaneous writer; editor of Colburn's "New Monthly Magazine."

Williams, Rowland, D.D., 1817–70. *Goronva Camlan.* An eminent Welsh clergyman; b. at Halkym, Flintshire; educ. at Eton and Cambridge, 1841; Vicar of Broad Chalke, Wilts., 1859–70, where he died.

Williams, Sarah, –1868. *Sadie.* An English poet; a pupil of Queen's Coll., Harley Street, London.

Williams, T. H. *An Arbitrator.* An English financier, of Manchester.

Williams, Rev. Theodore Chickering, 1855–. *Eleven Sophomores.* An American clergyman; b. at Brookline, Mass.; Harv. Univ., 1876; pastor at Winchester, Mass., 1882–; now of New York City.

Williams, Thomas. *T. W.; A Layman.* An English bookseller in Stationer's Court, London; a Calvinistic preacher, and from its commencement editor of the "Evangelical Magazine."

Williams, Thomas, 1844–. *Thornton Wells.* An English poet; b. at Pendeen, St. Just, in Penwith; educ. at Penzance, 1853; Clerk in the Trinity House, London, 1863–80 *et seq.*

Williams, W. F. *Blondel.* An American journalist of the day.

Williams, William. *A Philadelphian.* An American map engraver.

Williams, Rev. William, M.A. *Gwilym Caledfryn.* A Welsh poet, of Menaifron, near Caernarvon; for 40 years one of "the poetical choir," 1820–60.

Williams, William Francis, 1836–. *Trovator.* An American correspondent, in Europe, of "Dwight's Journal of Music."

Williamson, Mrs. J. *Mrs. J. W.* An English hymn writer and composer, of Bath.

Willis, Cecil, D.D. *The Vicar of Holbeach.* An English clergyman.

Willis, Duke. *Demetrius Wyseman, Gent.* An English writer; a son of one of the Willises of St. James's Street, London; was placed as an articled clerk with some eminent solicitors in Lincoln's Inn, but was more fond of literature than law, and is supposed to have never practised, but to have come to America and d. here.

Willis, J. H. *A Literary Lounger.* A Canadian writer.

Willis, Nathaniel Parker, 1807–67. *Roy; Philip Slingsby.* An eminent American poet and journalist, of New York City; b. at Portland, Me.; Yale Coll., 1827; d. at Idlewild.

Willis, Robert, M.D., 1810–. *R. W., M.D.* An English physician to the Royal Infirmary for Children, London; a writer of the day.

Willison, Rev. John, 1680–1750. *A Parochial Bishop; A Minister of the Church of Scotland.* A Scottish divine; minister at Brechin, and afterwards at Dundee.

Wills, ——. *Simon Stukeley.* An English writer.

Willyams, Edward William Brydges, 1834–. *Tressilian.* An English banker; b. at Carnanton; M.P. for Truro, 1857–59; East Cornwall, 1868–74; partner in the firm of Willyams & Co., Miners Bank, Truro, Camborne, and St. Columb.

Willyams, James Brydges. *J. B. W********.* An English poet and artist.

Willyams, Miss Jane Louisa, 1786–1878. *J. L. W.; An Old Friend.* An English poet; b. at Carnanton; resident at Budleigh Salterton, where she died.

Wilmer, William H., D.D., 1782–1827. *Quæro.* An American Epis. clergyman; b. in Kent Co., Md.; Rector of St. Paul's Church, Alexandria, Va., 1812–26; Prof. in the Theol. Sem. there, 1823–26; Pres. of William and Mary Coll., and Rector of the Church at Williamsburg, 1826–27.

Wilmot, Rev. George. *Olim Oxoniensis.* An English minister, of the 18th century.

Wilmot, Sir John Eardley Eardley, 2d Bart., 1810–. *A Barrister at Law.* An English lawyer; b. at Wootton, Warwicks.; educ. at Rugby, Winchester, and Balliol Coll., Oxford; called to the Bar at Lincoln's Inn, 1842; Judge of the Court of the Marylebone District, London, 1863–71; M.P. for South Warwickshire from 1874.

Wilshere, W. *One of H. M.'s Justices of the Peace.* An English writer.

Wilson, ——. *Mountaineer.* An East Indian traveller, of Mussoorie.

Wilson, Mrs. A. G. *N. J. N.* A Scottish writer of the day.

Wilson, A. J. *Axis; Faed; Mem O'Randum; An Old File; Waverley.* An English tricycler and journalist.

Wilson, Andrew, M.D. *A Gentleman; A Layman; A Physician; A. W.* A Scottish physician; son of Rev. Gabriel Wilson, of Maxton, Scotland; practised at Newcastle and London.

Wilson, Miss Anne. *A Lady; A*

Daughter of the Late Serjeant Wilson. A Scottish writer, of Glasgow.

Wilson, Anthony. *Henry Bromley.* An English writer.

Wilson, Mrs. Caroline (Fry), 1787–1846. *The Listener.* An English Friend; b. and d. at Tunbridge Wells; editor for several years, from 1823, of an educational publication, from which she issued separately "The Listener," 1832; in 1831 she married Mr. Wilson.

Wilson, Daniel, D.D., 1778–1858. *D. W.; The Bishop; An Absent Brother; Daniel, Bp. of Calcutta.* An eminent English clergyman; b. at Spitalfields; Bishop of Calcutta, 1832–58; d. in that city.

Wilson, Daniel, LL.D., 1816–. *Wil. D'Leina, Esq., of the Outer Temple.* A Scottish antiquary; b. at Edinburgh; Prof. of History at Toronto, Canada, from 1853; editor, for several years, of the "Canadian Journal."

Wilson, Rev. David. *A Lover of Truth; A Protestant.* An English Cong. minister, of the Associate Congregation, Bow Lane, London.

Wilson, Mrs. E. V. *May Farmer.* An American writer of the day.

Wilson, Erasmus, F.R.S., 1809–. *W. J. Erasmus.* An English surgeon, of London; Prof. in the Coll. of Surgeons, 1869.

Wilson, F. T. *Saul Wright.* An English writer of the day.

Wilson, Francis. *F. W.* An English poet of the day.

Wilson, Frederick. *The Wandering Minstrel.* An American writer of the day.

Wilson, Frederick J. *A Comprehensionist.* An English journalist, of London; editor of the "Comprehensionist," 1872.

Wilson, George, M.D., 1818–59. *Alumni of the University of Edinburgh.* An eminent Scottish physician; b. in Edinburgh; Regius Prof. of Technology in the Univ. of Edinburgh, 1856–59.

Wilson, G. L. *Frank Falkland.* An American writer of the day.

Wilson, James. *Daft Jamie.* A Scotchman.

Wilson, James, 1795–1856. *An Animal Painter; Claudero, Son of Nimrod.* A Scottish naturalist and scientific writer; brother of Prof. John Wilson; b. at Paisley; resided at a beautiful cottage at Woodville, near Edinburgh, and d. there.

Wilson, James Edwin. *Chancery Lane, Esq.; Serjeant Zinn.* An English political writer.

Wilson, James Grant, 1832–. *Allan Grant.* A Scottish-American author and bookseller; b. in Edinburgh; was brought to this country when a child; served in the late civil war; before 1861 was engaged in the book business at Chicago; in 1861 removed to New York City.

Wilson, Miss Jessie Aitken. *His Sister.* A Scottish lady; sister of Prof. George Wilson, M.D., of Edinburgh.

Wilson, John, 1750–1826. *J. W.; J. W., deceased, in usum Amicorum.* An English poet, deceased.

Wilson, Prof. John, 1785–1854. *Aquilius; The Late Arthur Austin; Eremus; Kit; Mathetes; Mordecai Mullion; C. N.; Christopher North; Polyanthus; Siluriensis.* A Scottish writer, critic, poet, and philosopher; b. at Paisley; professor at Edinburgh, 1820–54, where he died.

Wilson, John Alfred. *Alf Wilson.* An American writer of the day.

Wilson, John Iliffe, 1791–1861. *J. I. W.* An English author; a bookseller and afterwards a reader in Messrs. Clowes' office; d. in Prince's-street, Lambeth.

Wilson, Rev. Joseph. *A Minister of the Gospel.* An American Presbyt. clergyman.

Wilson, Mrs. Mamie. *May Clayton.* An American writer of the day.

Wilson, Mrs. Mary. *Francis Palliser.* A Scottish novelist.

Wilson, Rev. Plumpton, LL.B. *A Country Clergyman.* An English divine; Rector of Ilchester, afterwards of Newmarket and of Ruaptoft, Leicestershire.

Wilson, Richard, D.D. *D. D., Cantab.* An English clergyman; St. John's Coll., Cambridge, 1824; Curate of St. Saviour's, Upper Chelsea, London, 1872–74 *et seq.*

Wilson, Robert. *Pedestrian.* An English traveller.

Wilson, Robert A. *Barney Maglone.* An American writer of the day.

Wilson, Rev. Robert Francis, M.A. *G.; Contributor, etc.* An English clergyman; Oriel Coll., Oxford, 1831; Vicar of Rownhams, Southampton, 1863–83 *et seq.*

Wilson, Thomas. *An Amateur; T. W.* An English fine-art amateur and Shakespearian scholar; agent to Lord Portman (?).

Wilson, Thomas, D.D., 1703–84. *A Sufferer.* An eminent English clergyman; b. at Kirk-Michael, Isle of Man; was for 46 years Rector of St. Stephen's, Walbrook; d. in Bath.

Wilson, Major Thomas Fourness. *A Staff Officer.* An English officer.

Wilson, Thomas L. V. *One who knows them.* An American publisher, of Boston, 1848.

Wilson, William, 1801–60. *Alpin; Allan Grant.* An eminent Scottish-American *littérateur;* b. in Perthshire; a bookseller at Poughkeepsie, N.Y., 1833–60, where he died.

Wilson, Rev. William, –1741. *A Minister of the Church of Scotland.* A Scottish minister at Perth.

Wilson, Rev. William Carus, B.A. *The Editors of the Children's Friend.* An English clergyman; Wadham Coll., Oxford, 1867; Vicar of Maryland, Maldon, 1874–83 *et seq.*

Wilson, William Rae, LL.D., 1774–1849. *A Veteran Traveller.* A Scottish lawyer; b. in Paisley; the son of Mr. Rae; added Wilson to his name in 1806, on succeeding to the estate of his uncle, John Wilson, of Glasgow; d. in London.

Wilton, J. H. *A Soldier.* An English officer; 23d Royal Welsh Fusiliers; served in the East, 1839–43.

Wilton, Mary Margaret Egerton, the Countess of, –1858. *A Lady of Rank.* An English lady; daughter of Edward, twelfth Earl of Derby; wife of Thomas Egerton, second Earl of Wilton.

Winchelsea, ——, the Earl of, 1752–1826. *Caius Claudius Nero.* An English nobleman; M.A., Christ Church, Oxford, 1771; Groom of the Stole, 1804–20; d. in London.

Winchelsea, Lady ——. — See "Finch, Anne."

Winchester, Rev. Samuel Gover, 1805–41. *Wickliffe.* An American Presbyt. clergyman; b. at Rock Run, Maryland; pastor at Philadelphia, 1830–37; and at Natchez, Miss., 1837–41.

Windham, Colonel William, –1761. *An English Gentleman.* An English writer, of Felbrigg, Norfolk.

Windham, Sir William. *An Absented Member.* An English nobleman; a writer of the early part of the 18th century.

Wingate, Charles Frederick, 1847–. *Carlfried.* An American journalist, of New York City.

Wingate, W. H. *Spectator.* An English poet of the day.

Wingfield, John, 1792–1811. *Alonzo.* An English officer of the Coldstream Guards; an early friend of Lord Byron, at Harrow School; d. at Coimbra, Portugal.

Winkler, Karl Gottfried Theodor, 1775–1856. *Thedor Hell.* A German poet and musical composer; director of the opera at Dresden from 1825.

Winn, Alice. *Alice W—n.* An English lady; afterwards Mrs. Bartram, wife of Mr. Bartram, pawnbroker of Princes street, Coventry street, London.

Winner, Septimus, 1827–. *Alice Hawthorne.* An American song composer, of Philadelphia.

Winnington, Rt. Hon. Thomas, –1746. *Mr. W—n.* An English statesman.

Winslow, Forbes Benignus, M.D., D.C.L., 1810–74. *F. W.; Medicus.* An eminent English physician; b. in London; studied medicine in New York City and London; devoted himself from 1847 to the care of the insane at the Sussex House Asylum, Hammersmith.

Winstanley, William. *W. W.* An English author in the reigns of Charles I., Charles II., and James II.; originally a barber, afterwards a poet, a biographer, etc.

Winston, Charles, Esq., F.S.A., 1814–64. *C. W.; An Amateur.* An English artist and lawyer; entered at the Inner Temple, 1834 or 35; called to the Bar, 1845; d. at his chambers in London.

Winston, Thomas B. *A Southern Pre-Emptor.* An American writer.

Winter, George. *Benjamin Bramble.* An English farmer; author of "New System of Husbandry," Bristol, 1788.

Winter, Sally. *Sally W—r.* An Englishwoman; an acquaintance of Charles Lamb.

Winter, William, 1836–. *Mercutio.* An American poet and journalist; b. in Gloucester, Mass.; LL.B., Harv. Univ., 1857; removed to New York City, 1859; dramatic critic there, 1861–85 *et seq.*

Winthrop, Robert Charles, Sr., LL.D. *Blank Etcetera, Sen.* An eminent American statesman; b. in Boston; Harv. Univ., 1828; M.C., 1841–50; U.S. Senator, 1850–51; devotes his leisure to historical researches at his residence in Brookline, near Boston.

Wintringham, Clifton, M.D., –1748. *C. W., M.D.* An English physician; practised at York, England, and d. there.

Wirt, Mrs. Elizabeth Washington (Gamble), 1784–1857. *A Lady.* An American writer; wife of the following; b. in Richmond, Va.; d. at Annapolis, Md.

Wirt, William, LL.D., 1772–1834. *The Old Bachelor; A Young Englishman.*

An eminent American lawyer; b. in Bladensburg, Md.; admitted to the Bar in 1794; in 1806 settled in Richmond, Va.; in 1829 removed to Baltimore, and d. there.

Wise, Daniel, D.D., 1813–. *Cousin Clara; Francis Forrester, Esq.; Lawrence Lancewood, Esq.* An English-American Meth. minister, journalist, and writer for the young; b. at Portsmouth, England; came to this country in 1833; has been editor of various religious papers and journals in Boston.

Wise, Francis, 1695–1767. *F. W., R.L.; A Member of the Society of Antiquaries, London.* An English literary antiquary; b. at Oxford; Radcliffe Librarian, 1748–67; d. at Ellesfield.

Wise, Lieut. **Henry Augustus,** 1819–69. *Harry Gringo.* An American naval officer, and writer of sea-stories; b. at Brooklyn, N.Y.; entered the U.S. navy, 1834; Ass't.-Chief of the Bureau of Ordnance, etc., 1862–68; d. at Naples.

Wise, John S. *Plover.* An American journalist of the day.

Wise, Rev. Richard Farquhar, B.A., 1815–. *One of Our Club.* An English clergyman; b. at Camborne; Rector of Ladock, 1846–83 *et seq.; R. D.* of Powder, and Hon. Canon in Truro Cathedral, 1879–83.

Wiseman, Mrs. Mary. *A Lady.* An English religious writer, of the 18th century.

Wiseman, Nicholas Patrick Stephen, 1802–65. *H. E. C. W.; His Eminence; N. C. W.* An eminent R.C. ecclesiastic; b. at Seville; Archbishop of Westminster, and Cardinal Priest, 1850–65; d. in London.

Wishart, Rev. **John.** *A Minister of the Church of Scotland.* A Scottish minister, early in the 18th century.

Wisniewski, Michael Pius de, 1794–. *James William Whitecross.* A Polish author; partly educ. at the Univ. of Edinburgh; Prof. at the Univ. of Cracow, 1830–63 *et seq.*

Witherby, William, 1758–1840. *A Layman.* An English merchant, of Islington; the senior member of the Court of Assistants of the Company of Stationers, and Master in 1821–22; d. at Islington.

Withers, Philip, D.D., –1790. *Alfred; A Page of the Presence.* An English clergyman; Chaplain to Lady Dowager Hereford; for a libel on Mrs. Fitzherbert was sentenced, Nov. 21, 1789, to a fine of £50 and a year's imprisonment at Newgate, where he d., July 24, 1790.

Witherspoon, John, D.D., LL.D., 1722–94. *A Blacksmith.* A Scottish-American clergyman; b. at Yester, Scotland; Pres. of the Coll. of New Jersey, 1768–94.

Withington, Leonard, D.D., 1789–1885. *John Oldbug, Esq.; The Thirty-One.* An eminent American clergyman; b. in Dorchester, Mass.; Yale Coll., 1814; Andover Theol. Sem., 1816; pastor of the First Church in Newburyport, Mass., 1816–85; d. in Newbury.

Withy, Nathan. *The Wandering Bard.* An English poet, of the last part of the 18th century.

Witt, Henriette (Guizot) de, 1829–. *His Daughter; W.* A French writer; daughter of M. Guizot; b. in Paris; in 1850 married M. Conrad de Witt.

Wix, Ven. **Edward,** M.A., 1802–66. *A Newfoundland Missionary.* An English clergyman; Trin. Coll., Oxford, 1824; for some time Archdeacon of Newfoundland, and a frequent contributor to the "Gent. Mag."; d. at St. Michael's Parsonage, Swanmore, Ryde, Isle of Wight.

Wix, Henry. *H. W.* An English writer on angling.

Wolcot, John, M.D., 1738–1819. *Brother Peter; P. Hamlin, Tinman; Peter Pindar.* An English satirical poet; b. at Dodbrooke, Devon.; d. at Somers Town.

Wolcott, Oliver, LL.D., 1760–1833. *Marcus.* An American statesman; b. at Litchfield, Conn.; Yale Coll., 1778; Governor of New York, 1818–27; d. in New York City.

Wollaston, Rev. Francis, LL.D., 1731–1815. *A Private Man.* An English clergyman; Rector of Chislehurst, Kent, 1769–79; at London, 1779–1815; d. at Chislehurst.

Wollaston, George, Esq. *G——W——.* An Irish writer, of the 18th century.

Wolley, Rev. Charles, A.M. *C. W.* An English clergyman, who came to New York with Governor Andros in 1678 in the capacity of chaplain to the garrison at Fort James; afterwards settled at Alford, Lincolnshire.

Wollstonecraft, Miss Mary. — See "Godwin, Mrs. M. (W.)."

Wood, Mrs. Ann (Michell). *A. M. W.* An English poet; daughter of Admiral Sampson Michell; in 1815 married Benjamin Wood, M.P. for Southwark, London, 1840, who d. in 1845 at Eltham Lodge, Kent.

Wood, Mrs. Anne T. (Wilbur), 1817–. *Florence Leigh.* An American editor and novelist; b. at Wendell, Mass.; resident at Newburyport, Mass.

Wood, Charles W. *C. W. W.* An English writer of to-day.

Wood, Mrs. Ellen (Price), about 1820–. *Johnny Ludlow.* An English editor and novelist, of London; b. at Worcester; better known as Mrs. Henry Wood.

Wood, Lady Emma Caroline (Michell), 1802–. *C. Sylvester.* An English novelist, of London; daughter of Admiral Sampson Michell, sister of Mrs. Ann (Michell) Wood, and wife of Rev. Sir John Page Wood, 2d Bart.

Wood, George, 1799–1870. *Peter Schlemihl.* An American writer; b. at Newburyport, Mass.; studied law; settled in Alexandria, Va., 1816; offices at Washington, D.C., 1819–45 and 1847–70; d. at Saratoga Springs.

Wood, Henry. *An American Lady.* An American writer.

Wood, Rev. J. A. *A Clergyman of the Established Church.* An English clergyman.

Wood, Rev. John George, M.A., F.L.S., 1827–. *George Forrest, Esq., M.A.* An English naturalist; b. in London; Merton Coll., Oxford, 1845; Precentor of the Canterbury Diocesan Choral Union, 1868–76; in 1855 *et seq.* resident at Selwyn-terrace, Jasper-road, Upper Norwood.

Wood, John Philip, –1839. *J. P. W.* A Scottish writer; for many years Auditor of Excise, Scotland; was deaf and dumb from infancy; d. in Edinburgh at an advanced age.

Wood, Rev. John Ryle, M.A. *J. R. W.* An English clergyman; Christ Church Coll., Oxford, 1827; Canon Res. of Worcester Cathedral, 1841–83 *et seq.*

Wood, Mrs. Julia Amanda (Sargent). *Minnie Mary Lee.* An American editor, poet, and prose writer, of Sauk Rapids, Minn.; one of the editors of the "New Era."

Wood, L. A. *A West-Yankee-elf.* An American humorist, of the West.

Wood, Silas, 1769–1847. *A Citizen of the United States.* An American writer; b. in Suffolk Co., N.Y.; New Jersey Coll., 1789; M.C. from New York, 1819–29; d. at Huntington, Suffolk Co., Long Island.

Wood, Simon. *A Prisoner on the Common-side.* An English writer; a prisoner in Fleet Prison, London.

Wood, T. *Aristocratic Tout.* An English sporting writer.

Wood, W. S. *Mat Merchant.* An American writer of the day.

Wood, William, B.D., 1770–1841. *Dr. John Warton.* An English divine; Rector of Coulsdon, Surrey, 1830–41; and Prebendary of Canterbury, 1834–41; d. at Coulsdon.

Wood, Rev. William, F.L.S. *A Protestant Dissenter.* An English Unitarian minister, of Mill Hill Chapel, Leeds.

Wood, William McDonald. *Nichol Jarvie.* An American journalist of the day.

Wood, Lady William Page. *Helen Carr.* An English poet; wife of W. Page, Baron Hatherley.

Woodard, Col. J. H. *Jayhawker.* An American journalist of the day.

Woodburn, H. N. F. *H. N. F. W.* An English author.

Woodd, Rev. Basil, 1760–1831. *B. W.* An English clergyman; b. at Richmond, Surrey; Rector of Drayton Beauchamp, Bucks.; 1808–31; d. at Paddington Green, a suburb of London.

Woodfin, Mrs. ——. *A Lady.* An English novelist, of the 18th century.

Woodhead, Joshua T. *Medicus & Co.* An English writer of the day.

Woodhull, Maxwell. *M. W.* An American naval writer.

Woodley, Charles. *C. W., A.M.* An American poet of the day.

Woodley, George. *G. W.* An English poet, early in the 19th century.

Woodman, M. S. *M. S. W.* An American (?) writer of the day.

Woodruff, Julia Louisa Matilda. *W. L. M. Jay.* An American writer of the day.

Woods, Mrs. Anne (Hindley). *A Young Pilgrim.* An English traveller.

Woods, Caroline H. *Belle Otis.* An American writer of the day.

Woods, Miss Harriet Newell. — See "Baker, Mrs. H. N. (W.)."

Woods, Mrs. Helen Jane. *Helen Hawthorne; Saxe Horne.* A Canadian writer of the day, of Montreal.

Woods, Joseph, Esq., F.S.A., etc., 1776–1864. *An Architect.* An English architect; b. at Stoke Newington; spent some years abroad, and was a resident of Lewes for 34 years, and d. there.

Woods, Miss Margarette. — See "Lawrence, Mrs. M. (W.)."

Woodward, Miss Annie Aubertine. *Auber Forestier.* An American poet and translator; b. in Montgomery Co., Pa.; formerly of Philadelphia; in 1881, of Madison, Wis.

Woodward, Augustus B. *Epaminondas.* An American jurist; b. in Virginia; emigrated to Michigan, 1805;

judge of Michigan Terr., 1805–24; and of Florida Terr., 1824–27.

Woodward, Rev. Charles, LL.B. *C. W.* An English clergyman; Rector of Exbourne, Exeter.

Woodward, George M. *The Ghost of Willy Shakspeare.* An English artist, caricaturist, and poet, of the first part of the 19th century.

Woodward, George W., 1809–75. *A Man who wishes to be Governor of Pennsylvania.* An American jurist; b. in Bethany, Penn.; Chief-Justice of the Supreme Court of Pennsylvania until 1867; then an M.C. to the 40th and 41st Congresses; d. at Rome, Italy.

Woodward, Henry, 1717–77. *Hal W—dw—d; Simon Partridge.* An English comedian and dramatist; b. in the borough of Southwark, and educ. at Merchant Taylors' School; had great success as a comic actor in London, where he died.

Woodward, Henry Lovett. *H. L. W.* An English writer of religious poetry.

Woodward, John, M.D., 1665–1728. *Don Bilioso de L'Estomac; J. Freind, M.D.; T. Byfield, M.D.; Timothy Vanbustle, M.D.* An eminent English geologist; Prof. of Physic in Gresham Coll., 1692–1728.

Woodward, Josiah, D.D. *A Member of the Church of England; A Minister of the Church of England.* An English clergyman, of Poplar, and afterwards of Maidstone, Kent.

Woodward, Richard, LL.D. *Richard, Lord Bishop of Cloyne.* An Irish clergyman; Dean of Clogher; in 1781 became Bishop of Cloyne.

Woodward, Sarah. *Onyx Titian.* An English writer of the day.

Woodward, W. Elliot. *W.* An American apothecary, of Roxbury, Mass.

Woodworth, Francis Channing, 1812–59. *Uncle Frank; Theodore Thinker.* An American writer for the young; b. at Colchester, Conn.; was for eight years a printer, then three years a minister; afterwards devoted himself to juvenile literature; d. on a voyage from Savannah to New York City.

Woodworth, Samuel, 1785–1842. *Sampfilius Philocrin.* An American poet and journalist; b. at Scituate, Mass.; editor at New Haven, Conn., and at New York City, where he died.

Wooler, Thomas Jonathan, 1791–1859. *The Black Dwarf.* An English journalist and political writer, at London.

Wooley, Rev. Charles, M.A. *C. W.; C. W., A.M.*

Woolfrey, Mrs. Mary Anne. *Alethphilos.* An English writer.

Woolgar, J. W. *J. W. W.* An English bibliographer.

Woolrych, Humphry Fitzroy. *Aleph.* An English writer of the day.

Woolsey, Sarah Chauncey. *Susan Coolidge.* An American authoress; b. in Cleveland, O.; is a niece of Pres. Woolsey, of New Haven, Conn.; published her first book in 1871.

Woolson, Constance Fenimore. *Anne March.* An American novelist of the day.

Woolston, Rev. Thomas, 1669–1732 or 3. *Aristobulus.* An English divine; b. at Northampton; sentenced to King's Bench Prison for his discourses on the miracles of our Saviour, and fined £100; d. in prison.

Worcester, Noah, D.D., 1757–1837. *Philo Pacificus.* An American clergyman and eminent peace reformer; b. at Hollis, N.H.; resided at Brighton, Mass., 1813–37, where he died.

Worcester, Samuel Melanchton, 1801–66. *Vigornius.* An American clergyman; b. at Fitchburg, Mass.; Harv. Univ., 1822; Andover Theol. Sem., 1823; pastor at Salem, Mass., 1834–60, and d. there.

Worcester, Rev. Thomas, 1768–1831. *Timothy.* An American minister; brother of Noah; b. at Hollis, N.H.; pastor at Salisbury, N.H., 1791–1823.

Wordsworth, Charles, D.C.L., 1806–. *C. W.* An eminent English clergyman; Christ Church, Oxford, 1830; Bishop of St. Andrews, from 1853–83 *et seq.*

Wordsworth, Christopher, D.D., 1774–1846. *C. W.* An eminent English divine; a younger brother of the poet; b. at Cockermouth, in Cumberland; Master of Trin. Coll., Cambridge, 1820–41; Rector of Buxted-with-Uckfield, 1820–46; d. at Buxted parsonage, Sussex.

Wordsworth, William, D.C.L., 1770–1850. *Bard of Rydal Mount; The Cumberland Poet.* An eminent English poet; b. at Cockermouth, Cumberland; lived at Rydal Mount, 1813–50, and d. there.

Workman, William. *A Merchant.* A Canadian writer.

Wormeley, Katharine Prescott, and two Others. *His Three Daughters.* American ladies, if not by birth, in spirit; daughters of Rear-Admiral Ralph Randolph Wormeley, R.N., of England.

Wormeley, Miss Mary Elizabeth,

1822–. *His Three Daughters.* An English lady; b. in London; resided many years at Newport, R.I.

Wornum, Ralph Nicholson, 1812–77. *A Layman.* An English artist; b. at Thornton, Co. Durham; Univ. Coll., London; Keeper and Secretary of the National Gallery, 1855.

Worsley, Mrs. ——. *A Watcher.* An English religious writer of the day.

Worsley, Sir **Richard,** Bart., 1751–1805. *Sir Finical Whimsy.* An English literary antiquary; b. in the Isle of Wight; resided for some time in Italy; was M.P. for the borough of Newport, and governor of the Isle of Wight, where he died.

Wortley, Charles Stuart. *Captain the Honble. C. S. W.* An English officer of the R. A.

Wotton, William, D.D., 1666–1726. *M. N.; William W—tt—n.* An English scholar and clergyman; b. at Wrentham, Suffolk; Prebendary of Salisbury, 1705–26; d. at Buxted, Essex.

Woty, William, Gent., about 1731–91. *James Copywell.* An English poet, of Loughborough. — See "Notes and Queries," 1868, November, p. 498.

Wrangham, Rev. **Francis,** F.S.A., 1769–1843. *F. W.; Samuel Foote, Jr.; An Old Pen; W.* An English clergyman; b. at Raithorpe, Yorks.; Trin. Coll., Cambridge, 1790; Archdeacon of the East Riding of Yorks., 1828–43; d. in Chester.

Wraxall, Sir **Frederick Charles Lascelles,** 1828–65. *Lascelles Wraxall.* An English writer; b. at Boulogne-sur-Mer; d. at Vienna.

Wray, Mrs. **Mary.** *A Lady.* An English writer; granddaughter of Jeremy Taylor, and wife of Sir Cecil Wray.

Wrifford, Anson. *An Experienced Teacher.* An American chirographer.

Wright, Charles. *Mountaineer.* An American political writer.

Wright, E. M. *Verity Victor.* An American writer of the day.

Wright, Elizur. *One of the "Eighteen Millions of Bores"; A Friend of the Road.* An American author and journalist; b. in South Canaan, Conn.; Yale Coll., 1826; now (1885) resident at Medford, Mass.

Wright, Miss **Frances.** — See "Darusmont, Mrs. F. (W.)."

Wright, Frederick. *A Pilgrim.* An Irish-Canadian poet; in 1867 resided at Delta, U.C.

Wright, George. *An Old Colonist.* A British colonial writer, of Melbourne.

Wright, Ven. **Henry Press,** M.A. *A Crimean Chaplain.* An English clergyman; St. Peter's Coll., Cambridge, 1841; Canon of Christ Church, Victoria, British Columbia, 1876; Rector of Grantham, Petersfield, 1880–83 *et seq.*

Wright, Hezekiah Hartley, A.M., –1840. *An American.* An American traveller; Harv. Univ., 1831.

Wright, J. Hornsby. *A Charity-Organizationist.* An English writer of the day; a Sunday-school teacher, of London.

Wright, Rev. **James.** *Philander.* An English clergyman.

Wright, John. *J. W.* An English author, of Tysoe.

Wright, Joseph X. *Joe Tukesbury.* An American journalist, of St. Louis, Mo.

Wright, Mrs. **Julia McNair,** 1840–. *Aunt Sophronia.* An American writer; b. in Oswego, N.Y.

Wright, Miss **Lucy Pauline.** *L. P. W.* An English poet; afterwards Mrs. L. P. (W.) Hobart.

Wright, Mrs. **Mary (Booth),** 1831–. *Carrie Carleton.* An American writer for the young; wife of Washington Wright.

Wright, Rev. **Richard,** 1764–1836. *Beccaria Anglicus.* An English Unit. Bapt. minister, of Wisbeach, Cornwall; missionary of the Unitarian Fund.

Wright, Robert. *R. W.* An English writer, of Jesus Coll., Cambridge.

Wright, Robert W. *Quevedo Redivivus, Jr.* An American writer of the day.

Wright, Mrs. **Sarah Anna** (?). *Aunt Sue.* An American writer for the young; b. at Accomac, Va.

Wright, Thomas. *The Journeyman Engineer.* An English writer, of London.

Wright, Thomas, 1810–77. *A Trinity Man; An Antiquary.* An English antiquary; Trin. Coll., Cambridge, 1834; resided in London from 1835, and wrote for "Fraser's Mag.," the "Foreign Quarterly Review," etc.

Wright, Thomas, 1788–. *The Manchester Prison Philanthropist.* An Englishman, who devoted his life to the alleviation of human suffering.

Wright, W. W. *A Stroller in Europe.* An American writer of the day.

Wright, Rev. **William.** *A Lover of the Protestant Religion.* A Scottish minister, of Kilmarnock.

Wroe, Rev. **Caleb,** –1728. *A Country Minister.* An English Dissenting divine, of Cheshunt, Hertsfordshire.

Wulff, Sigismund. *M. W. Sieg.* A German dramatist.

Wurderman, Dr. ——. *A Physician.* An — physician.

Wurst, Richard Paul. *Richard Paul.* An American writer of the day.

Wyatt, Gertrude. *A Young Lady.* An English poet.

Wyche, Joseph. *J. W., M.O.S.B.* An English religious writer, early in the 18th century.

Wylde, Mrs. Flora Frances. *Her Granddaughter; Totty Testudo.* A Scottish (?) lady; granddaughter of Flora M'Donald.

Wylie, Rev. Robert. *A Gentleman in the City.* A Scottish writer, of Hamilton.

Wyman, Mrs. John C. *S. A. L. E. M.* An American writer, of Fall River, Mass.

Wyman, Oliver C. *Four of Us.* An American writer, of Boston.

Wyman, Rufus, M.D., -1842. *Omnivagant.* An American physician, of Chelmsford, Mass.; Harv. Univ., 1799; father of Jeffries and Morrill Wyman.

Wyman, William Henry. *W. H. W.* An American Shakespearian writer of the day.

Wyndham, Henry Penruddocke, 1736-1819. *A Gentleman.* An English author; b. in Wiltshire; became Knight of the shire of his native county; d. at Salisbury.

Wyndham, Sir William, 1687-1740. *Sir W—m W—m.* An eminent English statesman; Secretary at War, 1711; Chancellor of the Exchequer, 1713; committed to the Tower, 1715.

Wynkoop, Matthew Bennett. *An American.* An American poet and printer, of New York City.

Wynn, Miss Frances Williams, about 1780-1857. *A Lady of Quality.* An English lady; niece of the first Marquis of Rockingham.

Wynne, Edward, 1734-84. *E. W.* An eminent English lawyer; d. at Chelsea.

Wynne, Mrs. Emma (Moffett), 1844-. *Lola.* An American novelist, of Columbus, Ga.

Wynne, George Robert. *G. R. W.* An Irish (?) novelist.

Wynne, John Huddleston, 1743-88. *J. H. W.; George Osborn, Esq.* An English printer, journalist, naval officer, and author; he edited the "Lady's" and the "British" Magazines, and the "Gazetteer," and contributed many essays, poems, etc., to periodicals; d. in London.

Wynne, Justine, Countess of Rosenberg. *J. W., C—t—ss of R—s—g.* An English writer of the 18th century.

Wynne, Thomas H. *T. H. W.* An English editor of the day.

Wynter, Andrew, M.D. *Werdna Retnyw.* An English writer; editor of the "Assoc. Med. Journal" at London.

Wyse, Rt. Hon. Thomas, K.C.B., 1791-1862. *Dr. Abraham Eldon.* An Irish statesman and diplomatist; educ. at Stonehurst and Dublin; Minister to Athens, 1849-62, where he died.

Wyse, William Charles Bonaparte. *W. C. B.-W.; A Grand Nephew of Napoleon the Great.* An English poet of the day.

Y.

Yardley, Edward. *E. Y.* An English clergyman; Fellow of St. John's Coll., Cambridge; Archdeacon of Cardigan from 1743.

Yardley, John. *J. Y.* An English writer.

Yates, Edmund Hodgson, 1831-. *Q.; The Flaneur; The Lounger at the Clubs; The Merry Men; Mrs. Seaton.* An English author and journalist, of London; for many years clerk in the English Post-Office, till 1872, when he retired to devote himself to literature.

Yates, Frederic B. *Deane Roscoe.* An American novelist.

Yates, Thomas. *A Steward.* An English writer.

Yates, William, D.D. *W. Y.* An eminent Bapt. missionary and oriental scholar at Calcutta, for many years.

Yeardley, Mrs. Martha Savory, 1782-1851. *Mrs. Smith.* An English Friend, of London; educ. at Frenchay; wife of John Yeardley.

Yearsley, Mrs. Anne, about 1756-1806. *Lactilla.* An English poet; a milk-woman near Bristol; assisted by Hannah More.

Yeats, Grant David, M.D. *'Ιατρος.* A English physician.

Yeiser, Mrs. Sarah C. (Smith). *Azelée; Aunt Charity.* An American writer, of Alexandria, La.

Yeldham, Walter S. *Aliph Cheem.* An English East Indian poet of the day.

Yonge, Charlotte Mary, 1823-. *Aunt*

Charlotte. An English popular author; b. at Otterbourne, Hants. It is said she gave £2000, the profits of her "Daisy Chain," for the building of a Missionary College at Auckland, New Zealand, and devoted a great portion of the proceeds of "The Heir of Redclyffe" to fitting out the missionary schooner, "Southern Cross," for the use of Bishop Selwyn.

Yonge, Rev. **Duke John**, 1809–46. *Launcelot Pendennis.* An English clergyman and poet; minister at Alloa.

Yorke, Hon. **Charles**, 1722–70. *C.* An English lawyer; brother of the following; called to the Bar, 1747; M.P., 1747–70; Lord High Chancellor, 1770.

Yorke, Hon. **Philip**, 1st Earl of Hardwicke, 1690–1764. *P.* An English jurist; b. in Dover; educ. for the law; called to the Bar in 1715; M.P., from 1719; Lord Chief Justice of King's Bench, 1733; Lord Chancellor, 1737–56; d. in London.

Young, **Archibald**. *The Hon. Secretary of the Royal Eastern Yacht Club.* A Scottish advocate.

Young, **Arthur**, Esq., 1741–1820. *A. Y.; A. Y****, Esq.; The Secretary of the Board.* An English agriculturist; b. in Suffolk Co.; editor of the "Annals of Agriculture"; d. at Bradford.

Young, **Berd H.** *Simon Suggs.* An American journalist, of New York City.

Young, **Cuthbert G.** *A Wayfarer.* An English traveller.

Young, Mrs. **E. A. G.** *E. A. G. Y.* An English writer.

Young, **Edward**, D.C.L., 1684–1765. *John Lizard; Philalethes.* An English poet; b. at Upham, near Winchester; educ. at Winchester School and Oxford Univ.; in 1719 received the degree of D.C.L., but did not practise law; Rector of Welwyn, Herts., 1730–65.

Young, Rev. **Edward James.** *E. J. Y.* An American minister; professor at Harv. Univ., 1869–80; pastor at Waltham, Mass., from 1880.

Young, Rev. **James Alexander.** *Nobody, Nothing of Nowheres.* An American writer, of Laurell, Md.

Young, **John**, –1808. *Simplex.* A Scottish writer or solicitor in Edinburgh, and an elder in the Sandemanian or Glasite Church there.

Young, Hon. **John**, 1811–. *Agricola.* A Canadian merchant and statesman, of Montreal.

Young, **John Russell**, 1841–. *Bizarre.* An American journalist, of New York City.

Young, **Maria Julia.** *A Lady; A Young Lady.* An English writer; a relative of the celebrated author of the "Night Thoughts."

Young, Mrs. **Maud J. (Fuller).** *The Confederate Lady; The Soldier's Friend; J. M. Y.* An American "Southland" writer, of Houston, Texas; b. in South Carolina.

Young, **Robert.** *R. Y.* A Scottish bookseller and orientalist, of Edinburgh.

Young, **Samuel.** *Calvin Philanax; Trepidantium Malleus.* An English controversialist.

Young, **Samuel.** *T. Q.; A Wall Street Bear.* An American writer.

Young, **William.** *Pupils of the City of London School.* An English Shakespearian scholar and writer.

Young, Rev. **William**, –1757. *The Modern Parson Adams.* An English translator, etc. "Of Edward Young, an anecdote which wanders among readers is not true, that he was Fielding's 'Parson Adams.' The original of that famous painting was William Young, who was a clergyman."

Young, **William**, 1809–. *An Ex-Editor.* An English-American author and journalist; b. at Deptford, Kent; emigrated to the United States, and was editor of the "Albion," N.Y., 1848–67.

Young, **William H.** *One of the Party.* An American writer, of Troy N.Y. (?).

Z.

Zabriskie, Rev. **F. N.** *Old Colony.* An American theologian.

Zechmeister, **Alexander Viktor**, 1817–77. *A. V. Wilhelmi.* A Hungarian player and dramatist; b. at Ofen, and d. at Meran.

Zeigle, **Kate M.** *Catherine Stewart.*

Zeigler, **Carl**, 1812–77. *Carlopago.* A German poet; d. at Vienna.

Ziehen, **Eduard**, 1819–. *Eduard Ellersberg.* A German writer; b. at Tostedt, in Hanover; studied at Bonn and

Göttingen, 1840–43; has resided in his native place, and since 1855 has been on the staff of the "Oberpostamtszeitung."

Zimmerman, Mrs. Bettie (Meredith). *Mrs. B. M. Z——.* An American "Southland" writer; b. in North Carolina; in 1869 of Atlanta, Ga.

Zitz, Kathinka (Halein), 1801–. *Emmeline; Eugenie; Pauline; Rosalba; Stephanie; Theophile Christlieb; Tina Halein; Viola; K. Th.; Zianitzka.* A German author; b. at Mainz; educ. at Strassburg, and in 1824 published her first volume of poems. She was for a time a teacher, first in Darmstadt, then in Kaiserlautern. She has of late years lived in Mainz. Her writings have sometimes appeared under her maiden name, and sometimes under her pseudonyms.

Zorawski, V. S. *An Expatriated.* A Polish (?) poet.

Zornlin, Mrs. Elizabeth (Alsager), 1770–1851. *A Lady.* An English poet; in 1787 married John Jacob Zornlin, of London.

Zuccalmaglio, Florentin von, 1803–69. *Wilhelm von Waldbrühl.* A German author; b. at Waldbrühl, and d. on a journey to Nachod.

Zuccalmaglio, Vincenz von, 1806–76. *Montanus.* A German author; b. at Schlebusch, near Mülheim; studied law, 1826–28, at the Univ. of Heidelberg; also employed himself zealously with literature, music, and antiquities; held various appointments at various places, until he became counsellor-at-law at Grevenbroich, in the Rhine province, where he died.